13th Edition
2004 North American
Coins & Prices

A GUIDE TO U.S., CANADIAN AND MEXICAN COINS

Edited by David C. Harper, editor of *Numismatic News*,
World Coin News and *Bank Note Reporter*

Published by

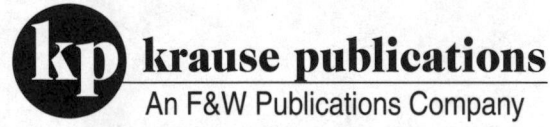

krause publications
An F&W Publications Company

700 East State Street • Iola, WI 54990-0001
715-445-2214 • 888-457-2873
www.krause.com

Please call or write us for our free catalog of numismatic publications.
To place an order or receive a free catalog call 800-258-0929.

ISBN: 0-87349-711-2
L C Number: 91-76402
Printed in the United States of America

Contents

Preface

Providing coin collectors with accurate, independently produced pricing information on collectible coins has become a trademark of Krause Publications in its 50 years of publishing. Visit our Web site at www.collect.com for more information about us. We employ a full-time staff of market analysts who monitor auction results, trading on the Internet and trading at major shows.

This information is compiled by our analysts and they determine what price most accurately reflects the trading that has occurred for each date and mintmark in each grade listed in *North American Coins & Prices*. By studying this information and referring back to it repeatedly, a collector can arm himself with the necessary knowledge to go out in the market and make wise purchasing decisions. It must be remembered that these prices are intended solely as a guide. They are neither offers to buy or sell. Because prices do fluctuate, those that appear in this book may be in some cases obsolete by the time of publication. By checking the more than 40 price charts in the U.S. section, you can get a feel as to how price swings have occurred since 1972.

U.S. coins are the most popularly collected issues in the world. This is attributable in part to the popularity of coin collecting in the United States, but collectors in many other countries also covet collectible U.S. coins. After collecting U.S. coins for a while, many collectors in the United States branch out into issues of Canada and Mexico. These coins also enjoy a popular following in their countries of origin.

Thus, *North American Coins & Prices* brings together pricing information on all three of these countries. But this book also takes the price-guide concept a step further by providing information on the nuts and bolts of collecting coins: acquiring coins, grading them, organizing them into a collection, storing them properly and much more. Novice collectors can gain the necessary knowledge to collect coins enjoyably; veterans can pick up some pointers to add to their knowledge.

1

'A small beginning'
The U.S. Mint grew from a modest start

By Robert R. Van Ryzin

It was a "small beginning" but a significant one. In July 1792, a site for the new U.S. Mint not yet having been secured, 1,500 silver half dismes were struck on a small screw press nestled in the cellar of a Philadelphia building owned by sawmaker John Harper. Though some have since categorized these early emissions of the fledgling U.S. Mint as patterns, it is clear that first President George Washington – who is said to have deposited the silver from which the coins were struck – considered this small batch of half dismes the first official U.S. coins.

It is true that this limited coinage, the first since passage of the act establishing the Mint on April 2, 1792, pales by comparison to modern U.S. Mint presses. Today's machines can churn out up to 750 coins a minute, striking as many as four coins at a time and boasting yearly mintages in the billions. But it is also true that these first small pieces – struck from silver and stamped with a plump Liberty on the obverse and a scrawny eagle in flight on the reverse – have tremendous historical importance.

For within what Washington would declare in his 1792 address to Congress as a "small beginning" were the seeds of a monetary system that has lasted more than 200 years and has become the study and admiration of many.

Before the U.S. Mint

Collectors today can trace much of the nation's development and learn of its struggles and growth through its coinage: from a cumbersome system first proposed by Robert Morris, a Revolutionary War financier and first superintendent of finance, to the refinements tendered by Thomas Jefferson and Alexander Hamilton, which firmly placed the nation on an easily understood decimal system of coinage.

At first there was little coinage in circulation, except for foreign coins that arrived through trade or in the purses of the first settlers. Despite a dire need for coinage in the Colonies, Great Britain considered it a royal right and granted franchises sparingly. Much of the Colonial economy, therefore, revolved around barter, with food staples, crops, and goods serving as currency. Indian waupum or bead money also was used, first in the fur trade and later as a form of money for Colonial use.

Copper pieces were produced around 1616 for the Sommer Islands (now Bermuda), but coinage within the American Colonies apparently didn't begin until 1652, when John Hull struck silver threepence, sixpence and shillings under authority of the General Court of Massachusetts. This coinage continued, with design changes (willow, oak and pine trees), through 1682. Most of the coins were dated 1652, apparently to avoid problems with England.

In 1658 Cecil Calvert, second Lord Baltimore, commissioned coins to be struck in England for use in Maryland. Other authorized and unauthorized coinages – including those of Mark Newby, John Holt, William Wood, and Dr. Samuel Higley – all became part of the landscape of circulating coins. In the 1780s this hodgepodge of coinage was augmented by influxes of counterfeit British halfpenny coins and various state coinages.

In terms of the latter, the Articles of Confederation had granted individual states the right to produce copper coins. Many states found this to be appealing, and merchants in the mid-1780s traded copper coins of Vermont, Connecticut, Massachusetts, New Jersey, and New York. Not all were legal issues; various entrepreneurs used this as an invitation to strike imitation state coppers and British halfpence. Mutilated and worn foreign coins also circulated in abundance. Included among these were coins of Portugal, Great Britain and France, with the large majority of the silver arriving from Spain.

The accounting system used by the states was derived from the British system of pounds, shillings and pence. Each state was allowed to set its own rates at which foreign gold and silver coins would trade in relation to the British pound.

In 1782 Robert Morris, newly named superintendent of finance, was appointed to head a committee to determine the values and weights of the gold and silver coins in circulation. Asked simply to draw up a table of values, Morris took the opportunity to propose the establishment of a federal mint. In his Jan. 15, 1782, report (largely prepared by his assistant, Gouverneur Morris), Morris noted that the exchange rates between the states were complicated.

He observed that a farmer in New Hampshire would be hard-pressed if asked to determine the value of a bushel of wheat in South Carolina. Morris recorded that an amount of wheat worth four shillings in his home state of New Hampshire would be worth 21 shillings and eightpence under the accounting system used in South Carolina.

Morris claimed these difficulties plagued not only farmers, but that "they are perplexing to most Men and troublesome to all." Morris further pressed for the adoption of an American coin to solve the problems of the need for small change and debased foreign coinages in circulation.

In essence, what he was advocating was a monometallic system based on silver. He said that gold and silver had fluctuated throughout history. Because these fluctuations resulted in the more valuable metal leaving the country, any nation that adopted a bimetallic coinage was doomed to have its gold or silver coins disappear from circulation.

Robert Morris devised a complicated plan for a national coinage based on a common denominator of 1,440.

Gouverneur Morris calculated the rate at which the Spanish dollar traded to the British pound in the various states. Leaving out South Carolina, because it threw off his calculations, Gouverneur Morris arrived at a common denominator of 1,440. Robert Morris, therefore, recommended a unit of value of 1/1,440, equivalent to a quarter grain of silver. He suggested the striking of a silver 100-unit coin, or cent; a silver 500-unit coin, or quint; a silver 1,000-unit coin, or mark; and two copper coins, one of eight units and the other of five units.

On Feb. 21, 1782, the Grand Committee of Congress approved the proposal and directed Morris to press forward and report with a plan to establish a mint. Morris had already done so. Apparently feeling confident that Congress would like his coinage ideas, Morris (as shown by his diary) began efforts at the physical establishment prior to his January 1782 report. He had already engaged Benjamin Dudley to acquire necessary equipment for the mint and hoped to have sample coins available to submit with his original report to Congress.

Things went awry, however.

By Dec. 12, 1782, 10 months after Congress had approved his plan, Morris still could not show any samples of his coins. He was forced, ironically, to suggest that Congress draw up a table of rates for foreign coins to be used until his report was ready. It was not until April 2, 1783, that Morris was able to note in his diary that the first of his pattern coins were being struck.

"I sent for Mr. Dudley who delivered me a piece of Silver Coin," he wrote, "being the first that has been struck as an American Coin."

He also recorded that he had urged Dudley to go ahead with production of the silver patterns.

It wasn't until April 23, 1783, that Morris was able to send his Nova Constellatio patterns to Congress and suggest that he was ready to report on establishing a mint. Apparently nothing came of Morris' efforts. Several committees looked into the matter, but nothing was accomplished. Dudley was eventually discharged as Morris' hopes dimmed.

Thomas Jefferson was the next to offer a major plan. Jefferson liked the idea of a decimal system of coinage, but disliked Morris' basic unit of value. As chairman of the Currency Committee, Jefferson reviewed Morris' plan and formulated his own ideas.

To test public reaction, Jefferson gave his "Notes on Coinage" to *The Providence Gazette*, and *Country Journal,* which published his plan in its July 24, 1784, issue. Jefferson disagreed with Morris' suggestion for a 1/1,440 unit of value and instead proposed a decimal coinage based on the dollar, with the lowest unit of account being the mil, or 1/1,000.

"The most easy ratio of multiplication and division is that by ten," Jefferson wrote. "Every one knows the facility of Decimal Arithmetic."

Jefferson argued that although Morris' unit would have eliminated the unwanted fraction that occurred when merchants converted British farthings to dollars, this was of little significance. After all, the original idea of establishing a mint was to get rid of foreign currencies.

Morris' unit, Jefferson said, was too cumbersome for use in normal business transactions. According to Jefferson, under Morris' plan a horse valued at 80 Spanish dollars would require a notation of six figures and would be shown as 115,200 units.

Jefferson' coinage plan suggested the striking of a dollar, or unit; half dollar, or five-tenths; a double tenth, or fifth of a dollar, equivalent to a pistereen; a tenth, equivalent to a Spanish bit; and a one-fifth copper coin, relating to the British farthing. He also wanted a gold coin of $10, corresponding to the British double guinea; and a copper one-hundredth coin, relating to the British halfpence.

In reference to his coinage denominations, Jefferson said, it was important that the coins "coincide in value with some of the known coins so nearly, that the people may by quick reference in the mind, estimate their value."

More than a year, however, passed without any further action on his plan or that proposed by Morris. In a letter to William Grayson, a member of the Continental Congress, Washington expressed concern for the establishment of a national coinage system, terming it "indispensably necessary." Washington also complained of the coinage in circulation: "A man must travel with a pair of scales in his pocket, or run the risk of receiving gold at one-fourth less than it counts."

A plan at last

On May 13, 1785, the 13-member Grand Committee, to whom Jefferson's plan had been submitted, filed its report, generally favoring Jefferson's coinage system. The committee did, however, make slight alterations, including the elimination of the gold $10 coin, the addition of a gold $5 coin, and the dropping of Jefferson's double

Thomas Jefferson proposed that the United States adopt a decimal system of coinage.

tenth, which it replaced with a quarter dollar. The committee also added a coin equal to 1/200th of a dollar (half cent). On July 6, 1785, Congress unanimously approved the Grand Committee's plan. It failed, however, to set a standard weight for the silver dollar or to order plans drawn up for a mint. These two factors led to new proposals.

On April 8, 1786, the Board of Treasury, which had been reinstated after Morris' resignation as superintendent of finance two years prior, tendered three distinct coinage proposals based on varying weights and bimetallic ratios for the silver dollar. The first of these three plans (the one passed by Congress on Aug. 8, 1786) required the silver dollar to contain 375.64 grains of pure silver. The board's proposal varied from earlier coinage plans in that it advocated a higher bimetallic ratio of 15.256-to-1 and differing charges to depositors for coining of gold and silver. It called for minting of gold $5 and $10 coins, and silver denominations of the dime, double dime, half dollar, and dollar. In copper were a cent and half cent. The proposal came during the peak of state coinages and influxes of debased coppers, which, as the board reported, were being "Imported into or manufactured in the Several States."

Concerned over the need to control state coinages and foreign coppers, the board suggested that, within nine months of passage of its proposal, the legal-tender status of all foreign coppers be repealed and that values be set at which the state coppers would circulate. The board obviously expected immediate action and ordered a supply of copper that was being stored in Boston to be brought to New York in the hope that it might soon be coined. Their hopes, however, rested on the positive and quick action of Congress, something that hadn't occurred with the other proposals and would not occur this time.

Opposition to the mint was beginning to surface. Several members of Congress expressed their belief that the supply of foreign gold and silver coins in circulation was sufficient to preclude any need for a mint. They also argued that the problem with debased coppers could be solved by contracting with private individuals to strike the nation's cents and half cents.

Several proposals were offered for a contract coinage. On April 21, 1787, the board accepted a proposal by James Jarvis to strike 300 tons of copper coin at the federal standard. Jarvis, however, delivered slightly less than 9,000 pounds of his contract. The contract was voided the following year for his failure to meet scheduled delivery times, but helped to delay further action on a mint. Concerted action on a coinage system and a mint would wait until the formation of the new government.

Alexander Hamilton, named in September 1789 to head the new Treasury, offered three different methods by which the new nation could achieve economic stability, including the funding of the national debt, establishment of the Bank of North America, and the founding of the U.S. Mint. On Jan. 21, 1791, Hamilton submitted to Congress a "Report on the Establishment of a Mint." It was compiled through his study of European economic theories and the earlier works of Morris and Jefferson, along with the 1786 report of the Board of Treasury.

Hamilton agreed with Jefferson that the dollar seemed to be best suited to serve as the basic unit, but believed it necessary to establish a proper weight and fineness for the new coin. To do so, Hamilton had several Spanish coins assayed to determine the fine weight of the Spanish dollar. He also watched the rate at which Spanish dollars traded for fine gold (24 3/4 grains per dollar) on the world market.

From his assays and observations he determined that the Spanish dollar contained 371 grains of silver. He then multiplied 24 3/4 by 15 (the gold value of silver times his suggested bimetallic ratio) and arrived at 371 1/4 as the proper fine silver weight for the new silver dollar.

In regard to his findings, Hamilton admitted that Morris had made similar assays and had arrived at a weight of 373 grains for the Spanish dollar. Hamilton attributed the discrepancy to the differing equipment used in making the assays. He failed, however, to observe that silver coins were traded in the world market at actual weight rather than the weight at time of issue. The Spanish dollar contained 376 grains of pure silver when new, 4 3/4 grains more than Hamilton's proposed silver dollar.

Hamilton also wanted a bimetallic ratio of 15-to-1, in contrast to the Board of Treasury's 15.6-to-1 ratio. Hamilton said his ratio was closer to Great Britain's, which would be important for trade, and Holland's, which would be important for repaying loans from that country.

His report suggested the striking of a gold $10; gold dollar; silver dollar; silver tenth, or disme; and copper one-hundredth and half-hundredth. Hamilton felt the last of these, the half cent, was necessary because it would enable merchants to lower their prices, which would help the poor.

Congress passed the act establishing the U.S. Mint in April 1792. It reinstated several coin denominations left out by Hamilton and dropped his gold dollar. In gold, the act authorized at $10 coin, or "eagle"; a $5 coin, or "half eagle"; and a $2.50 coin, or "quarter eagle." In silver were to be a dollar, half dollar, quarter dollar, disme, and half disme, and in copper a cent and half cent.

Though it established a sound system of U.S. coinage, the act failed to address the problem of foreign coins in circulation. It was amended in February 1793 to cancel their legal-tender status within three years of the Mint's opening.

Coinage begins

Coinage totals at the first mint were understandably low. Skilled coiners, assayers and others who could handle the mint's daily operations were in short supply in the United States. Also in want were adequate equipment and supplies of metal for coinage. Much of the former had to be built or imported. Much of the latter was also imported or salvaged from various domestic sources, including previously struck tokens and coins, and scrap metal.

Coinage began in earnest in 1793 with the striking of half cents and cents at the new mint located at Seventh Street between Market and Arch streets in Philadelphia. Silver coinage followed in 1794, with half dimes, half dollars and dollars. Gold coinage did not begin until 1795 with the minting of the first $5 and $10 coins. Silver dimes and quarters and gold $2.50 coins did not appear until 1796.

Under the bimetallic system of coinage by which gold and silver served as equal representations of the unit of value, much of the success and failure of the nation's coinage to enter and remain in circulation revolved around the supply and valuation of precious metals. One need only to gain a cursory knowledge of such movements to understand what role precious metals played in development of U.S. coinage. That role, to a large extent, determined why some coins today are rare and why some passed down from generation to generation are still plentiful and of lower value to collectors.

From the Mint's beginning, slight miscalculations in the proper weight for the silver dollar and a proper bimetallic ratio led gold and silver to disappear from circulation. The U.S. silver dollar traded at par with Spanish and Mexican dollars, but because the U.S. coin was lighter, it was doomed to export.

A depositor at the first mint could make a profit at the mint's expense by sending the coins to the West Indies. There they could be traded at par for the heavier Spanish or Mexican eight reales, which were then shipped back to the United States for recoinage. As a result, few early silver dollars entered domestic circulation; most failed to escape the melting pots.

Gold fared no better. Calculations of the bimetallic ratio by which silver traded for gold on the world market were also askew at first and were always subject to fluctuations. Gold coins either disappeared quickly after minting or never entered circulation, languishing in bank vaults. These problems led President Jefferson to halt coinage of the gold $10 and silver dollar.

Production at the first U.S. mint, in Philadelphia, was minuscule by today's standards.

The gold $10 reappeared in 1838 at a new, lower-weight standard. The silver dollar, not coined for circulation since 1803, returned in 1836 with a limited mintage. Full-scale coinage waited until 1840.

Nor was the coinage of copper an easy matter for the first mint. Severe shortages of the metal led the Mint to explore various avenues of obtaining sufficient supplies for striking cents and half cents.

Witness, for example, the half-cent issues of 1795 and 1797 struck over privately issued tokens of the New York firm of Talbot, Allum & Lee because of a shortage of copper for the federal issue. Rising copper prices and continued shortages forced the Mint to lower the cent's weight from 208 grains to 168 grains in 1795.

By that same year Congress had begun to investigate the Mint. Complaints about high costs and low production had been raised. Suggestions that a contract coinage might be more suitable for the new nation surfaced again, despite bad experiences with previous attempts.

The Mint survived this and another investigation, but the problems of fluctuating metal supplies continued to plague the nation. In 1798, because of the coinage shortage, the legal-tender status of foreign coins was restored. Several more extensions were given during the 1800s, ending with the withdrawal of legal-tender status for Spanish coins in 1857.

In the 1830s great influxes of silver from foreign mints raised the value of gold in relation to silver, which made it necessary for the Mint to lower the standard weight of all gold coins in 1834. It also led to the melting of great numbers of gold coins of the old specifications.

By the 1850s discovery of gold in California had again made silver the dearer metal. All silver quickly disappeared from circulation. Congress reacted in 1853 by lowering the weight of the silver half dime, dime, quarter, and half dollar, hoping to keep silver in circulation. A new gold coin of $20 value was introduced to absorb a great amount of the gold from Western mines.

Not long after, silver was discovered in Nevada. By the mid-1870s the various mines that made up what was known as the Comstock Lode (after its colorful early proprietor, Henry P. Comstock) had hit the mother lode. Large supplies of silver from the Comstock, combined with European demonetization, caused a severe drop in its value, which continued through the close of the 19th century.

It was believed that the introduction of a heavier, 420-grain silver dollar in 1873, known as the Trade dollar, would create a market for much of the Comstock silver, bolster its price, and at the same time wrest control from Great Britain of lucrative trade with the Orient. It didn't. Large numbers of Trade dollars eventually flooded back into the United States, where they were, ironically, accepted only at a discount to the lesser-weight Morgan dollars.

The latter had been introduced in 1878 as a panacea to the severe economic problems following the Civil War. Those who proudly carried the banner of free silver contended that by taking the rich output of the Comstock mines and turning it into silver dollars, a cheaper, more plentiful form of money would become available. In its wake, they believed, would be a much needed economic recovery.

The Free Silver Movement gained its greatest support during the late 19th century when William Jennings Bryan attempted to gain the White House on a plank largely based on restoration of the free and unlimited coinage of the standard 412.5-grain silver dollar. He failed. Silver failed. Shortly thereafter the United States officially adopted a gold standard.

Silver continued to be a primary coinage metal until 1964, when rising prices led the Mint to remove it from the dime and quarter. Mintage of the silver dollar had ended in 1935. The half dollar continued to be coined through 1970 with a 40-percent-silver composition. It, too, was then debased.

Gold coinage ended in 1933 and exists today only in commemorative issues and American Eagle bullion coins with fictive face values. A clad composition of copper and nickel is now the primary coinage metal. Even the cent is no longer all copper; a copper-coated zinc composition has been used since 1982.

Precious-metal supplies were also linked to the opening of additional mints, which served the parent facility in Philadelphia. The impact of gold discoveries in the 1820s in the southern Appalachian Mountains was directly tied to the construction of branch mints in Dahlonega, Ga., and Charlotte, N.C., in 1838. These new mints struck only gold coins. New Orleans also became the site of a branch mint in the same year as Dahlonega and Charlotte. It took in some of the outflow of gold from Southern mines, but also struck silver coins.

Discovery of gold in California in the late 1840s created a gold rush, and from it sprang a great western migration. Private issues of gold coinage, often of debased quality, were prevalent, and the cost of shipping the metal eastward for coinage at Philadelphia was high. A call for an official branch mint was soon heard and heeded in 1852 with the authorization of the San Francisco Mint, which began taking deposits in 1854.

The discovery of silver in the Comstock Lode led to yet another mint. Located only a short distance via Virginia & Truckee Railroad from the fabulous Comstock Lode, the Carson City mint began receiving bullion in early 1870. It struck only silver coins during its tenure.

Denver, also located in a mineral-rich region, became the site of an assay office in 1863 when the government purchased the Clark, Gruber & Co. private mint. It became a U.S. branch mint in 1906. In addition to the Denver and Philadelphia mints, San Francisco and a facility in West Point, N.Y., continue to serve as U.S. mints, but the others have left behind a rich legacy.

The collector taking a more extended journey into the history of U.S. coinage can find plenty of interesting tales – some as tall as the day is long and others factually based – all of which are part of the rich and ever-changing panoply of U.S. coinage history. There are stories of denominations that failed, great discoveries, great rarities, great collectors, and, for those with an artistic bent, a rich field of pattern coins to be explored and a wealth of much-heralded designs by famous sculptors such as Augustus Saint-Gaudens, Adolph Weinman, James Earle Fraser, and others.

For those who are drawn to the hobby by the allure of age-old relics of days gone by, or by coins handed down through the family, or even by dreams of great wealth, coin collecting has much to offer. The history of the U.S. Mint, with its small but ever so important beginning, is the starting point.

2

Making money
How coins are manufactured

By Alan Herbert

Just as printing is the process by which paper money is made, so is minting the method of manufacturing coins. The two are often confused by the public, but they are completely different.

The history of minting goes back several centuries before the birth of Christ. The Lydians are credited with making the first crude coins in the Middle East about 700 B.C., although the Chinese and Koreans trace their coinage back even further.

Some early coins were cast. That process continued in China into the 1900s, but only for low-value pieces. Here again the average person often assumes that all coins are cast, but as you will see, only a tiny fraction of a percent are – or were – actually made that way.

The methods developed by the Greeks and Romans centered on making dies that could be hammered by hand into the surface of a lump of metal, flattening it and impressing a design. Hammered coinage continued until after the end of the Middle Ages, about 1500. After that the first machines that could strike coins were invented. Today their successors can pound out 750 or more coins a minute.

From the early days when the fixed die was driven into a stump or a hole drilled in a rock, through fixing it in an anvil (the fixed die is still called the anvil die), to today's modern coin presses, the process is much the same. Force is applied to devices that impress or apply a design to a piece of material, which is transformed into a coin.

Early dies were made of wood. Then came copper, bronze, and finally iron as technology advanced. Today dies are made from exotic steels with special qualities that make them ideal for striking coins.

The history of coinage is fascinating. Interwoven into it are several familiar names: Leonardo da Vinci is credited with inventing one of the first coin presses. James Watt, English inventor of the steam engine, was the first to incorporate steam power to drive the coin presses that earlier had depended on horses or human arms.

Whether the power comes from a hand holding a hammer or a mechanical ram, and whether it comes from above, below, or the side, the process is called "striking" a coin. Modern coin presses use a variety of methods in applying brute force to a piece of metal to turn it into a coin.

Another fable that traces to casting coins is the common belief that coins are made from liquid metal or at the least are red hot when they are struck. Neither is true. A coin's design is formed by the pressure that causes the metal to cold-flow into the pattern that you see on the coins in your pocket.

There are three basic parts of the minting process: (1) the making of the planchet, which is divided into the selection and processing of the metal and the preparation of the planchets, (2) the making of the dies, and (3) the use of the dies to strike the planchets. To help you remember these three parts, think of "P," "D" and "S" for planchet, die and striking.

Choosing a metal

Many different metals have and are being used for coins. The most popular coinage metals are those commonly found and relatively cheap, so they can be used for striking low-value coins. Precious metals – like silver, gold and platinum – are still used for commemorative coins.

A good coinage metal requires certain properties. The metal must be soft enough to be easily worked yet hard enough to withstand the wear and tear of a thousand pockets, a hundred thousand transactions. Few metals have all the right properties, so coin metals usually are an alloy, or mixture of two or more metals.

Copper is a favorite coin metal, either by itself or in an alloy. Zinc, nickel, iron, and aluminum are also found in coins struck by the United States and other countries. Silver and gold have to be alloyed with some metal, usually copper, to be hard enough to withstand commercial life. The so-called "pure" coins of silver or gold are known as "bullion coins," bought and sold primarily for their precious-metal content.

The metals chosen for a coin are melted and mixed together, and either poured into ingots or blocks, or extruded from furnaces that continuously cast a long strip of the metal. The ingots are passed several times between the big rolls in a rolling mill to reduce the ingot to the thickness of the blanks needed.

Once the strip is rolled to the correct thickness, it is sent to a blanking press. A gang of blunt-end punches are driven through the sheet, producing a dozen or more blanks with each stroke. The rough blanks are then ready to be processed.

Making the 'blanks'

The piece of metal (occasionally some other material, so it isn't always metal) that becomes a coin is known as a "blank." This is a usually round, flat piece that usually has been punched or cut from a sheet or strip of coin metal.

Strips of coin metal stand ready to be cut into "blanks."

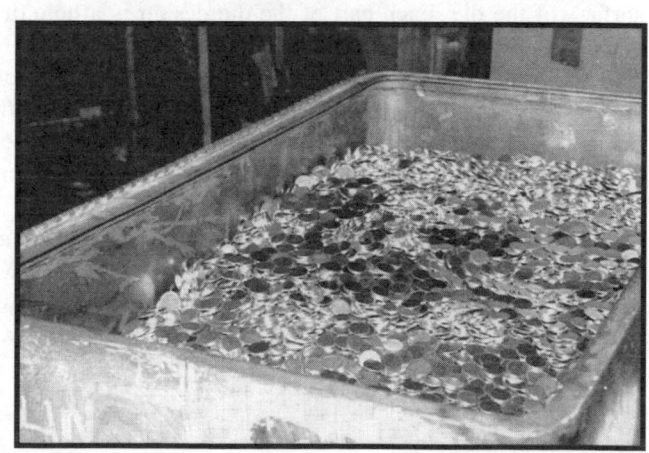

A binful of blanks are ready for the coin press.

Before a blank can become a coin it has to be processed, cleaned, softened, and given what is known as an "upset edge" – a raised ridge or rim around both sides. The blank then becomes a "planchet" and is ready to be struck into a coin by the dies.

First they go through what looks like a monstrous cement mixer. A huge cylinder revolves slowly as the planchets are fed in at one end and spiral their way through. This is an annealing oven, which heats the planchets to soften them. When they come out the end, they fall into a bath where they are cleaned with a diluted acid or soap solution.

As the final step, they go through the upsetting mill, the machine that puts the raised rim on the blank and turns it into a planchet, ready to be struck. In a different department the process of making the dies used to strike the coins has already begun.

Preparing the dies

For those who haven't studied metallurgy, the concept of hard metal flowing about is pretty hard to swallow, but this is actually what happens. It is basically the same process as the one used in an auto plant to turn a flat sheet of steel into a fender with multiple curves and sharp bends. The cold metal is moved about by the pressure applied.

To make the metal move into the desired design, there has to be a die. Actually there has to be two dies, because one of the laws of physics is that for every action there has to be an equal and opposite reaction. You cannot hold a piece of metal in midair and strike one side of it. Instead you make two dies, fix one, and drive the other one against it – with a piece of metal in between to accept the design from each die.

A die is a piece of hard metal, like steel, with a design on its face that helps to form a mirror image on the struck coin. Early dies were made by hand. Engravers used hand tools to laboriously cut each letter, each digit, and each owl or eagle or whatever design was being used into the face of the die. Notice that this is "into" the surface of the die. Each part of the die design is a hole or cavity of varying shape and depth.

This is because we want a mirror image on the coin, but we want it raised, or in "relief." To make a relief image on a coin, the image on the die has to be into the face of the die, or "incuse." Of course, if we want an incuse image on the coin, such as the gold $2.50 and $5 coins of 1908-1929, the design on the die face would have to be in relief.

To fully understand this, take a coin from your pocket and a piece of aluminum foil. Press the foil down over the coin design and rub it with an eraser. When you take the foil off and look at the side that was in contact with the coin, you have a perfect copy of a die. Everywhere there is a relief design on the coin there is an incuse design on your foil "die."

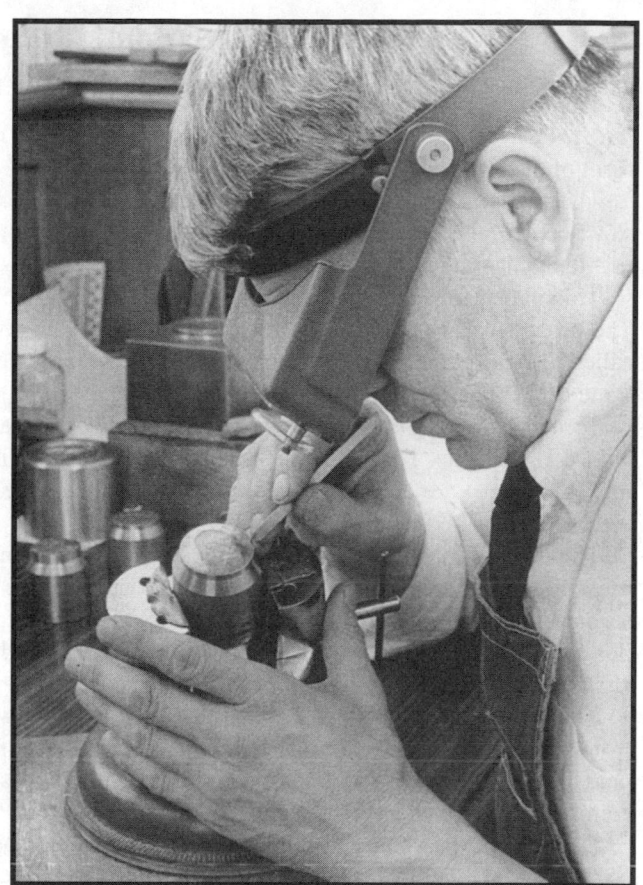

An engraver at the
U.S. Mint puts the
finishing touches on
a die.

A galvano goes on the
reducing lathe.

From sketchbook to coin

The design process begins with an artist's sketch. This is translated into a three-dimensional relief design that is hand-carved from plaster or, in recent years, from a form of plastic.

The plaster or plastic design is then transformed into a "galvano," which is an exact copy of the design that has been plated with a thin layer of copper. This is used as a template or pattern in a reducing lathe, which cuts the design into a die blank.

This die becomes the master die, from which all of the following steps descend. The process can be reversed so that the designs will be cut in relief, forming a tool called a "hub," which is simply a piece of steel with the design in relief, exactly the same as the relief design on the intended coin.

To make working dies, pieces of special steel are prepared, with one end shaped with a slight cone. The die blank is softened by heating it. Then the hub is forced into the face of the die, forming the incuse, mirror-image design in the face of the die.

The process usually has to be repeated because the die metal will harden from the pressure. The die is removed, softened, and returned to the hubbing press for a second impression from the hub. As you can imagine, it takes several hundred tons per square inch to force the hub into the die. Logically, this process is called "hubbing" a die.

The advantage of hubbing a die is that thousands of working dies can be made from a single hub, each one for all practical purposes as identical as the proverbial peas in a pod. This enables, for example, U.S. mints to strike billions of one-cent coins each year, each with the identical design.

Die making has come a long way from the early days when it took a skilled engraver a full day to carve a single letter into a die. The use of punches with the digits, letters or even parts of the design on the end reduced the amount of time required for the process. Today, thanks to the use of hubs, a complete die can be finished in a matter of hours.

Striking the coin

Yesterday's die might strike only a few hundred coins. Today it is not unusual for a die to strike well over a million coins.

The coin press used to strike modern coins is a complicated piece of equipment that consists basically of a feed system to place the planchets in position for the stroke of the hammer die to form a coin. This process takes only a fraction of a second, so the press has to operate precisely to spew out the hundreds of coins that are struck every minute.

The end of the early hammered coinage came with the introduction of the collar, which often is called the "third" die. The collar is nothing more than a steel plate with a hole in it. This hole is the exact diameter of the intended coin and often is lined with carbide to prolong its life. It surrounds the lower, or fixed, die. Its sole

Rows of modern coin presses at the Philadelphia Mint turn out billions of coins a year.

A hopper is full of shiny new one-cent coins ready for shipment.

purpose is to contain the coin metal to keep it from spreading sideways under the force of the strike.

If the intended coin has serrations, or "reeds," on the edge, then the collar has the matching design. The strike forces the coin metal against the serrations in the collar, forming the reeded edge at the same time that the two dies form the front and back, or obverse and reverse, of the coin.

Lettered-edge coins are produced usually by running the planchets through an edge-lettering die, or by using a segmented collar that is forced against the edge of the planchet during the strike by hydraulic pressure.

Several hundred tons were required to drive a hub into a die. Not as much but still significant amounts of force are needed to strike coins. A cent, for example, requires about 30 tons per square inch. One of the silver dollars took 150 tons. The other denominations fall in between.

Modern coin presses apply pressure in a variety of ways. A ram, carrying the moving or "hammer" die, is forced against the planchet. Most commonly this is with the mechanical advantage of a "knuckle" or connected pieces to which pressure is applied from the side. When the joint straightens – like straightening your finger – the ram at the end of the piece is driven into the planchet.

Once the strike is complete, at the final impact of the die pair, the coin has been produced. It is officially a coin now, and it's complete and ready to be spent.

The making of proof coins

While the high-speed coining presses are turning out billions of coins for commerce, there are other presses working at much slower speeds to produce collector coins, such as "proof" coins.

Proof coins started out as special presentation pieces. They were and still are struck on specially prepared planchets with specially prepared dies. Today the definition of a proof coin also requires that it be struck two or more times.

To make a proof coin, the planchets go through much the same process, but with some special care and some extra steps. Currently all proof versions of circulating U.S. coins are struck at the San Francisco Mint, but some of the proof commemorative coins have been struck at the other mints, including West Point.

After the proof blanks are punched from the strip, they go through the annealing oven, but on a conveyor belt rather than being tumbled in the revolving drum. After cleaning and upsetting they go into a huge vibrating machine where they are mixed with steel pellets that look like tiny footballs. The movement of the steel pellets against the planchets burnishes, or smooths, the surface so any scratches and gouges the planchets pick up during processing are smoothed over.

Proof dies get an extra polishing before the hubbing process. Like all other dies, they are made at Philadelphia and shipped to the branch mints.

When the proof dies arrive at San Francisco, they are worked on by a team of specialists who use diamond dust and other polishing agents to turn the fields of the proof dies into mirrorlike surfaces. The incuse design is sandblasted to make the surface rough, producing what is known as a "frosted" design.

Because collectors like the frosted proofs, the design is periodically swabbed with acid to keep the surface rough and increase the number of frosted proofs from each die. This is a relatively recent improvement, so frosted examples of earlier proofs are considerably scarcer.

The presses that strike proof coins usually are hand-operated rather than automatic. Some of the newer presses use equipment such as vacuum suction devices to pick up the planchets, place them in the coining chamber, and then remove the struck coins. This avoids handling the pieces any more than necessary.

On a hand-operated press, the operator takes a freshly washed and dried planchet and, using tongs, places it in the collar. The ram with the die descends two or more times before the finished coin is removed from the collar and carefully stored in a box for transport to storage or the packaging line. After each strike the operator wipes the dies to make sure that lint or other particles don't stick to the dies and damage the coins as they are struck.

Proof dies are used for only a short time before being discarded. Maximum die life is usually less than 10,000 coins, varying with the size of the coin and the alloy being struck.

Keeping up with demand

The minting process has come a long way from the first metal pellets that are barely recognizable as coins. Companies that manufacture equipment used in the world's mints are constantly researching to develop new methods of producing coins.

The purpose is to strike coins at as low a cost as possible and still retain the desired beauty in the design. Modern machines and new methods help the mints keep up with demand for coins.

The important point to remember is that the coins in your pocket are made no differently from the coins in the pocket of an English schoolchild or a Spanish police officer or an Italian opera singer. Mints around the world use the same methods, same equipment, and same common coin metals, with few if any variations from the basic methods. The minting process was shrouded in secrecy for centuries, but now has become common knowledge.

For the collector, knowing exactly how coins are minted can be some of the most valuable knowledge that can be learned. It often will make the difference between accepting a coin as a valuable addition to a collection or spotting it as a fake, counterfeit, or altered coin.

Because of the improvements in the making of coins, collecting the rare misstrikes and defective coins that escape quality control has become an important segment of the numismatic hobby. For a detailed description of over 400 categories of minting varieties, see the "U.S. Minting Varieties and Errors" section in this book.

3

The thrill of the hunt

How to acquire coins for your collection

By Al Doyle

Among the many pleasures coin collecting offers is the satisfaction of acquiring that long-sought piece that fills an important hole in a set or completes a collection. Many collectors say half the fun of pursuing the hobby is the thrill of the hunt — trying to find that needed coin in the condition desired and for a good price. Following are the main sources from which collectors acquire coins.

Circulation finds

Once the most popular method of building a collection, hunting through pocket change has declined substantially since 1965, when silver dimes and quarters were replaced by clad (base-metal) coinage.

Most collectors from 1935 into the 1960s got started in numismatics by searching through circulating coinage. It was worth the effort, as scarce and interesting coins such as the 1909-S VDB and 1914-D Lincoln cents, Liberty and Buffalo nickels, 1916-D and 1921 Mercury dimes, and Barber and Standing Liberty quarters were often found. Hobbyists who searched bank rolls and bags obtained at face value had no downside risk, and entire date collections of Lincoln cents were obtained in this manner.

Other denominations were also pursued in the treasure hunt. One Midwestern dealer found dozens of 1939-D Jefferson nickels (worth $1 to $30 each at the time, depending on condition) by searching through change obtained from parking meters of a nearby city. Another well-known numismatist put together a complete date and mintmark set of Walking Liberty half dollars in one afternoon by searching through coins obtained at his bank. Needless to say, those days are gone forever.

What is available to pocket-change searchers today? Even the pre-1959 cents, with the Wheat-Ears reverse, are rare sights, but some interesting coins remain undiscovered.

It's still possible to find collectible coins by searching large quantities of change, such as rolls.

Jefferson nickels can provide plenty of collecting enjoyment for virtually no financial commitment. A recent sampling of five rolls (200 coins, or $10) turned up 58 different date and mintmark combinations. Some of the highlights were a 1938-S (mintage 4.1 million) in grade fine, a 1947 in very fine, and a 1953-S. Looking through Jeffersons on a regular basis should lead to building the better part of a date and mintmark set.

Washington quarters experienced a circulation finds rebirth of sorts when the 50-state commemorative program began in 1999. Millions of Americans who had never collected coins before joined the hunt to acquire each of the new state designs as they were released at the rate of five per year.

Half dollars in your area may be another relatively untapped area in modern coinage. The 40-percent-silver pieces of 1965 to 1969 can sometimes be found in bank rolls. Half dollars seldom circulate, which means that older coins may be gathering dust in your local bank vault at this very moment.

Collecting Lincoln cents with the Memorial reverse, from 1959 to date, makes an excellent starter set. Many of the dates can be found in circulation.

What else might turn up in pocket change? Modern proofs enter circulation from time to time, and foreign coins are found occasionally. Canadian and U.S. coins frequently cross their respective borders.

Collectors of error coins sometimes find unusual pieces in circulation. What may be scorned as a reject by the average person is a valuable item to the error and variety specialist.

Start examining your pocket change. It's an inexpensive and pleasant way to get involved in the coin hobby.

Coin shops

Most medium-sized or larger cities and suburbs have at least one coin shop within driving distance, and a surprising number of small towns also boast of having a store that caters to local numismatists. Living in or near a metropolitan area is an advantage for the coin-shop enthusiast. For example, more than 15 dealers live in or near

Cincinnati, and southern California and the New York area are home to hundreds of numismatic firms.

In some ways, a coin shop is similar to a small museum. All kinds of items from early coppers to gold coinage and other collectibles such as paper currency, stock certificates, and historic curiosities can be seen. A visit to a well-stocked shop is a visual treat.

It is likely that some of those coins in the display cases will appeal to you, and that means some comparison shopping and determining the value of your favorite coin are desirable. Prices do fluctuate, although collector-oriented coins tend to maintain steadier values than coins sought by investors.

If you are a casual collector, consider a subscription to *Coins* magazine. A monthly publication, *Coins* offers articles on a wide range of topics as well as a Coin Value Guide of retail prices for U.S. coins in most grades.

Serious collectors and others who want more frequent information will find *Numismatic News* to be a timely source of knowledge. Published weekly, the *News* includes coverage of recent market trends and reports from major coin conventions. *World Coin News* is published monthly and covers non-U.S. issues. All three publications also carry display advertisements from dozens of coin dealers.

Prices are determined by supply and demand as well as the grade, or state of preservation. Grading is often described as a subjective art rather than an exact science, and it does take some study and experience to become a competent grader (see Chapter 4).

Numismatic education is a never-ending process. Getting to know an experienced dealer who is enthusiastic about his product will certainly increase your knowledge of coins. Most shops carry a wide assortment of items, but dealers (like anyone else) have their personal favorites. If you find a dealer who is especially knowledgeable about a certain series, it could be to your advantage to do business with him or her if that also happens to be your favorite area too.

Strangely enough, doing business with a dealer who does not share your particular interest could work in your favor. Learning about collectible coins is a massive undertaking, and no one knows everything. Collectors of large cents and Bust half dollars are willing to pay substantial premiums for coins that have minor differences from other specimens struck during the same year, and specialists in those areas frequently "cherrypick" rare varieties that are offered at common-date prices.

Never be embarrassed to ask questions about coins or the dealer's experience in the hobby. As the old saying goes, "There is no such thing as a dumb question." A question asked at the right time could save you plenty of grief and money.

Mail order

This is one area that generates a fair amount of emotion among collectors. Many hobbyists swear by the convenience of shopping at home; others swear at mail-order firms that send overgraded and overpriced coins. Common sense and the same guidelines that apply to shopping for any other item should be used in selecting a mail-order coin dealer.

Look for someone who has a fair amount of experience in coins as well as enthu-

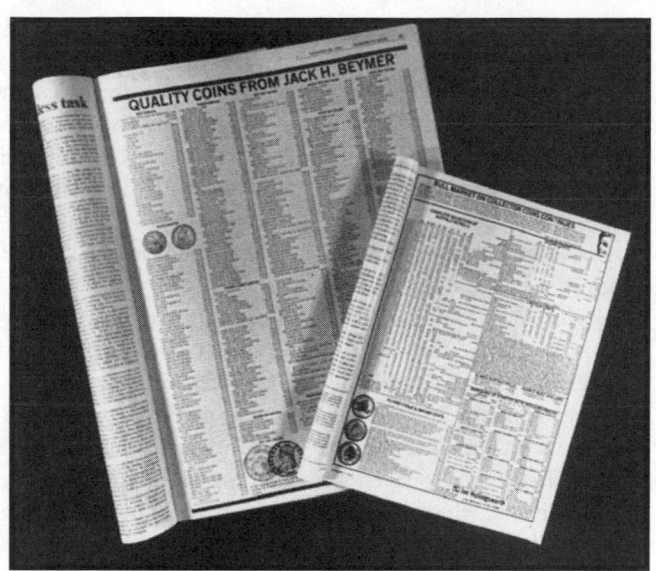

Advertisements in numismatic publications provide the convenience of shopping at home.

siasm for the hobby. Reputable dealers are willing to answer questions about their numismatic backgrounds and business practices. Word of mouth is often said to be one of the most effective forms of advertising, and it pays to ask other collectors about their favorite mail-order companies.

If several people agree that a firm provides accurately graded coins at fair prices, chances are excellent that you will also be a satisfied customer. How do you avoid being cheated? Collectors can be their own worst enemies and are often victimized by their own greed.

Take a coin that has a retail value in the $100 range in a particular grade. If that same coin is advertised at the same grade for $49.95, the savvy collector should immediately become suspicious. When a coin is offered at a price far under the going rate, remember these two sayings: "If it sounds too good to be true, it usually is," and "there is no Santa Claus in numismatics."

A dealer will generally pay $70 to $80 to acquire a popular coin with a retail value of $100. With that in mind, how can someone offer the same coin in the same grade at far less than wholesale cost? Wouldn't it be much easier to sell those coins to other dealers at a higher price and save on advertising expenses?

Obviously, the "underpriced" coins are not the same quality as their properly graded counterparts. It pays to keep up with current prices and grading standards. It is possible to find good deals at less than full retail cost, but don't expect to purchase decent coins for half price.

Does that mean all coins sold at real market prices are properly graded? Don't get complacent; overgraded coins are sometimes sold at full retail. But not everyone who sells an overgraded coin is intentionally fraudulent.

Grading standards are not carved in stone, which means that one person's MS-63 can be someone else's MS-64. Even though most dealers are extremely knowledgeable about coins, they can be fooled at times. The altered coin that a dealer bought as problem-free may be passed on to a collector in good faith, with no intention of deceit.

There is one important means of protection for consumers who buy through the mail: the return policy. Reputable firms allow buyers to return any unsatisfactory item for a full refund. The time allowed for returns varies widely from three working days to a month, but seven to ten days seems to be the most popular policy among mail-order dealers.

Look for "terms of sale" in dealer ads. Always read them before placing your order.

If you don't like coins received through the mail for any reason, send them back within the alloted time for a full refund. Companies might extend the deadline by a day or two if you call and ask for extra time.

What happens if you don't receive a refund or cannot satisfactorily resolve a problem with a mail-order dealer? There are several options:

The first step is to file a written complaint with the advertising department of any publication in which the dealer advertises. Include copies of invoices and other documentation. The publication cannot act on verbal complaints.

Written complaints can also be filed with a local or state chapter of the Better Business Bureau as well as any hobby-related organizations (the American Numismatic Association, Professional Numismatists Guild, and so on) in which the dealer holds membership. If you do business with a reputable dealer, it is unlikely that you will ever have to endure such a drawn-out complaint process, but be ready to take the proper steps if necessary.

For those who live in rural areas or prefer to shop at home, buying coins through the mail can be a rewarding experience and a convenient way to build a collection.

Coin shows

Dozens of shows are held every weekend across the nation. These events range from simple one-day shows with 10 to 20 tables to nationally known events such as the annual American Numismatic Association convention, Florida United Numismatists convention, the three-times-a-year shows held in Long Beach, Calif., and the Central States Numismatic Society convention.

Admission to club-sponsored shows is usually free. Commercially sponsored shows oftentimes charge a small admission fee.

Somewhere between the show at the local VFW hall and Long Beach are state and regional conventions. Often sponsored by a club, these shows will have 40 to 150 dealer tables as compared to the 400 to 600 tables at a major convention. Tables at local and some regional conventions are often manned by part-time, or "vest pocket," dealers. Smaller shows tend to feature less expensive items; the larger shows will have a greater variety of scarce and expensive coins in addition to the more affordable pieces.

Major conventions will have a stunning array of merchandise ranging from coins of ancient Greece to major U.S. rarities. Even if you can't afford the expensive items, it doesn't cost anything to stroll the aisles and see some historic coins.

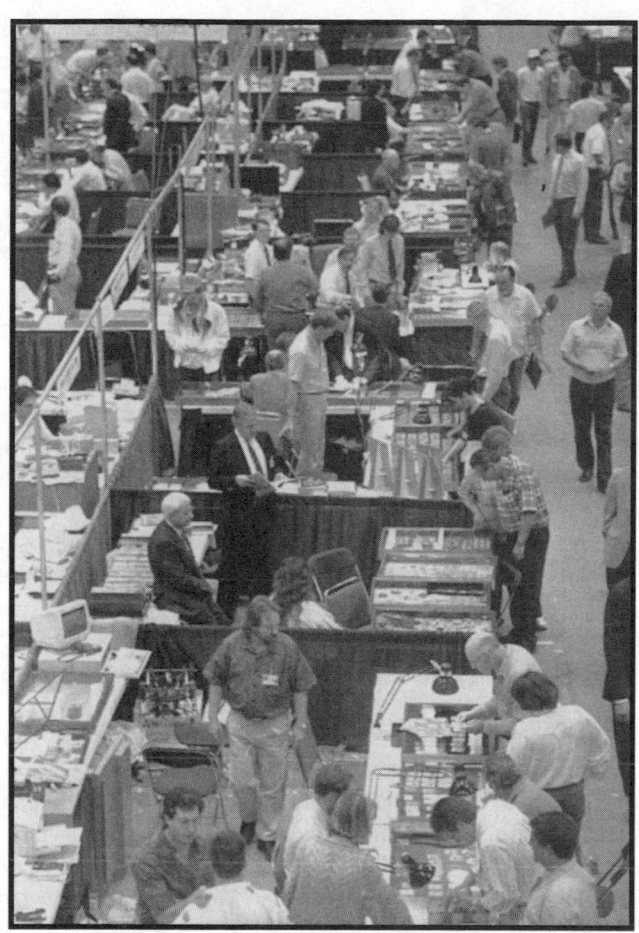

Shows big and small are held across the nation every weekend.

The big-ticket items are just part of the action at regional and major shows. A large assortment of affordable coins are available, and prices are often lower than at coin shops.

Dealers buy and sell thousands of coins among themselves at shows, and new purchases can often be had for a small markup. Good buys can sometimes be found later in the show when dealers are preparing to return home. A reasonable offer will often result in a new addition to your collection.

Speaking of offers, negotiating and dickering are as much a part of coin shows as silver dollars, but be reasonable. Tossing out an offer of $50 on a $200 coin is not shrewd; it's insulting.

If you make an offer on a coin and it is accepted, the coin is yours. Backing out of a deal is considered bad form. The coin business tends to be informal, and verbal offers carry serious weight. Your word is your bond on the bourse floor.

Purchases at a coin show do not carry a return policy. Unlike a mail-order transaction, you have ample opportunity to carefully examine the coin firsthand before making a financial commitment.

Why attend a show when you can acquire coins through the mail or from a local shop? There are many reasons to give the show circuit a try:

Conventions are an educational experience. Touring the bourse floor and talking to dealers and other collectors will increase your knowledge of numismatics, but there are other learning opportunities as well.

Many shows offer educational forums featuring speakers and presentations on various topics. These seminars cover everything from little-known specialties to advice on obtaining the best buys in a particular area of numismatics.

Exhibits will also add to your knowledge. Most medium-sized and major shows reserve a section of the bourse for collectors to display some of their holdings and compete for awards based on the educational value of their exhibit. The exhibit section offers an excellent opportunity to view something new and different.

You might be motivated to put together an exhibit yourself after a visit to a show. Keep in mind that it does not require a major collection to create a decent exhibit. Some of the most interesting displays incorporate low-priced coins and other collectibles.

Shows are excellent places to search for key-date coins and other material that may not be in stock at your local shop. Dealers do much of their shopping at shows, which should tell you something about the opportunities at a good-sized convention.

Want to introduce a friend or relative to coin collecting? Take them to a show and let them look around. Chances are excellent that the newcomer will become a fellow collector.

Looking for something different to collect? Paper money, world coins, tokens, medals, and medieval coins are often found at shows. You could find a new area of interest, and shows provide collectors with a chance to meet dealers and well-known hobbyists from across the country.

Have a game plan when you attend a show. Decide beforehand what you want to buy and how much money you plan to spend. Buying whatever looks nice will soon deplete your funds.

Coin shows offer something for everyone, so consider bringing the family. Jewelry (usually for much less than jewelry-store prices), baseball cards, antiques, and arts and crafts are also sometimes found at bourse tables.

One final note on coin-show etiquette: If you don't agree with a dealer's prices or grading, do not tell him that you can buy the same coin for less at another table or call him a crook. Just move on to the next table, and enjoy the rest of the show.

Information on upcoming shows in your area can be found in *Coins* and *Numismatic News*. Shows that feature a significant number of world coins are also listed in *World Coin News*. Coin-show advertising sometimes appears in local newspapers during the week prior to a show or in the paper's free listings of community events.

Auctions

Public auctions play an important role in the coin business. Prices realized at major auctions can indicate where the coin market is headed, as price fluctuations are a fact of life in numismatics. Important collections with major rarities are usually

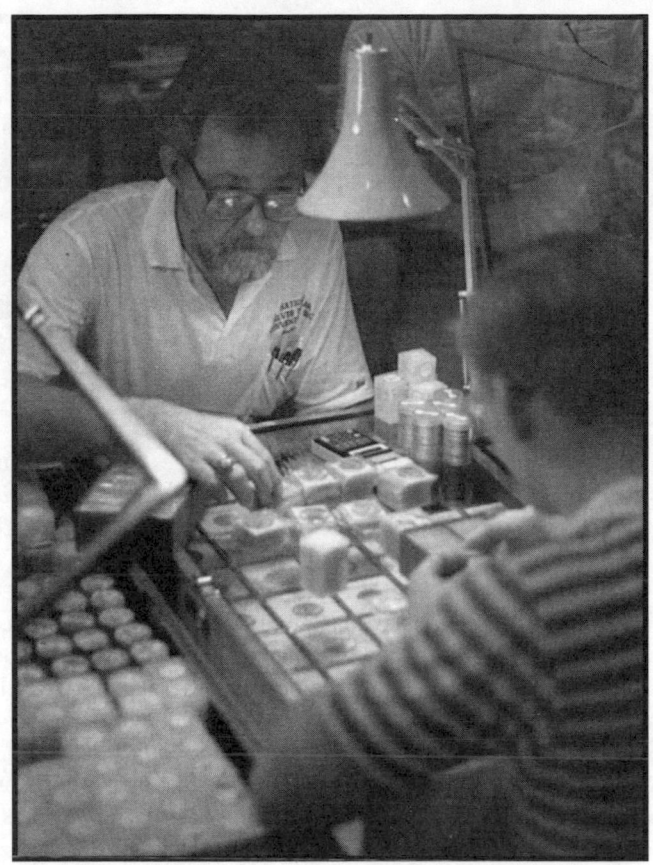

It's OK to bargain with a dealer at a show or shop, but collectors should be reasonable with their offers.

sold at a public auction. These sales are often held in conjunction with major shows.

However, affordable coins are often sold along with the rarities. A typical sale for a major auction firm will contain 1,000 to 6,000 lots, and most of those coins are not of the headline-grabbing variety. The larger the sale, the greater the likelihood that it will be broken into sessions conducted over a number of days.

The vast number of coins offered at a typical coin auction can work in favor of the collector who has a limited budget. Typical low- to medium-priced coins are often overlooked, as dealers and collectors focus on the trophy items. That may allow you to pick up some coins at reasonable prices. Internet auctions are another venue for lower priced items (See Chapter 13 for Web addresses and information.)

How can you participate in a public auction that is being held thousands of miles from your home? Catalogs are produced by auction companies for each sale, and mail, telephone and Internet bids are encouraged.

A typical auction catalog is illustrated with black and white as well as color photos of hundreds of coins. Descriptions of each lot give you an idea of the appearance of any coins that might be of interest. Many major firms post their catalogs on their Internet Web site.

If you are located near an auction site, it pays to examine your potential purchases

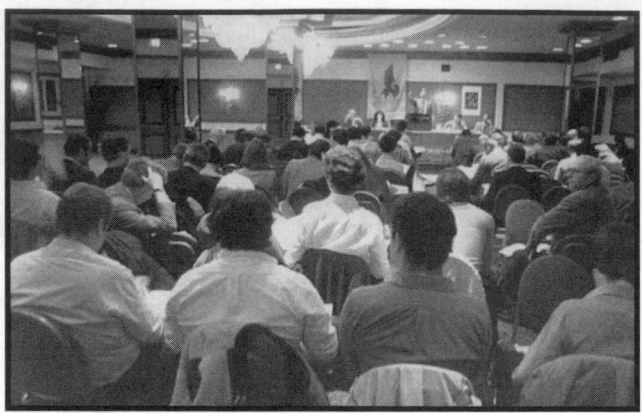

A collector doesn't have to actually attend an auction to participate in it.

at the pre-auction viewing session. The process is simple: Just visit the auction location (usually a major hotel or convention center) prior to the sale. The auction company sets up a room where the lots can be viewed. Long rows of tables with good lighting are provided. All you have to do is tell one of the attendants the lot numbers of the coins you want to view.

You can place written bids before you leave the premises, but it might pay to hang around for the auction and bid on coins in person. The action can be fast and furious at a major auction. Bidding increments of thousands of dollars are the rule when an expensive coin is being sold. It's an unforgettable sight to watch five or six serious competitors run up the price on a truly rare coin.

Keep several things in mind before you get involved in buying through auctions:

■ You are legally responsible to honor all winning bids placed, so plan accordingly. It is unlikely that you will win every coin on which you bid, but placing too many bids could be hazardous to your financial health.

■ Return policies vary among the major firms. Generally, floor bidders (those who personally attend the sale) do not have return privileges, as it is assumed that an adequate opportunity was provided to examine coins during the pre-auction viewing session.

One auction house does not allow any returns by mail bidders on certified coins, which are independently graded and encapsulated in a protective holder by an outside grading service. However, return privileges are the rule for all coins graded by the auction company's staff.

■ Winning bids are generally subject to a 15 percent premium, or buyer's fee. If you successfully bid $300 on a coin, your final cost will be $345 plus postage and handling. Consider the buyer's fee when deciding on bids.

Getting started in buying through auctions requires a catalog of an upcoming sale. Typically priced at $10 to $25, auction catalogs can be excellent buys even if you don't participate in the sale, as they provide a wealth of numismatic information.

Following are six major U.S. auction houses:

■ American Numismatic Rarities, LLC, P.O. Box 1804, Wolfeboro, NH 03894.

■ Bowers and Merena Galleries, No. 1 Sanctuary Blvd., Suite 201, Mandeville, LA 70471-3307.

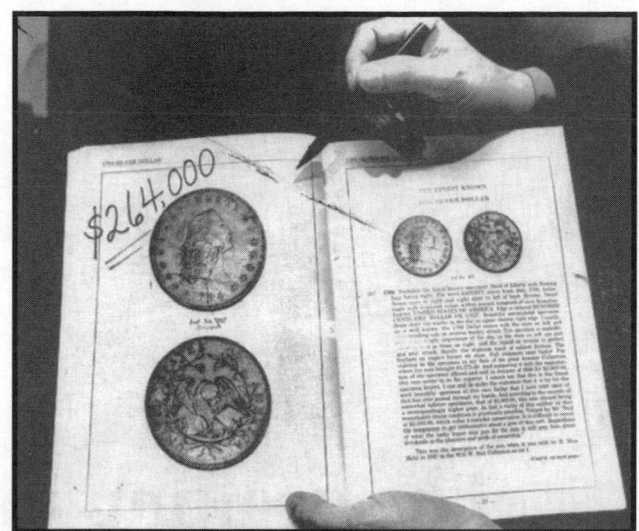

An auction catalog describes each lot offered.

■ Ira and Larry Goldberg Coins and Collectibles, Inc., 350 S. Beverly Drive, Suite 350, Beverly Hills, CA 90212.

■ Heritage Numismatic Auctions, Heritage Plaza, 100 Highland Park Village, Second Floor, Dallas, TX 75205-2788.

■ Stack's, 123 W. 57th St., New York, NY 10019.

■ Superior Galleries, 9478 W Olympic Blvd., Beverly Hills, CA 90212-4246.

Smaller auctions will allow you to test the bidding process before you compete at a major sale. Local firms concentrate on less expensive coins, and a typical sale for these companies ranges from 250 to 1,000 lots. Catalogs are less elaborate, but they are also inexpensive. Prices range from free to $3, and mail bids are accepted.

Among the dozens of local companies that conduct coin auctions are the following:

■ Michael Aron, P.O. Box 4388, San Clemente, CA 92674.

■ Sonny Henry's Auction Service, 1510 Illinois Ave., Mendota, IL 61342.

Where to write for more information

Coins Magazine: 700 E. State St, Iola, WI 54990.
Numismatic News: 700 E. State St., Iola, WI 54990.
World Coin News: 700 E. State St., Iola, WI 54990.
American Numismatic Association: 818 N. Cascade Ave., Colorado Springs, CO 80903-3279. Web address is http://www.money.org

Visit the Krause Publications Web site
http://www.collect.com

4

The grading factor
How to classify a coin's condition

By Arlyn G. Sieber

Grading is one of the most important factors in buying and selling coins as collectibles. Unfortunately, it's also one of the most controversial. Since the early days of coin collecting in the United States, buying through the mail has been a convenient way for collectors to acquire coins. As a result, there has always been a need in numismatics for a concise way to classify the amount of wear on a coin and its condition in general.

A look back

In September 1888, Dr. George Heath, a physician in Monroe, Mich., published a four-page pamphlet titled *The American Numismatist*. Publication of subsequent issues led to the founding of the American Numismatic Association, and *The Numismatist*, as it's known today, is the association's official journal. Heath's first issues were largely devoted to selling world coins from his collection. There were no formal grades listed with the coins and their prices, but the following statement by Heath indicates that condition was a consideration for early collectors:

"The coins are in above average condition," Heath wrote, "and so confident am I that they will give satisfaction, that I agree to refund the money in any unsatisfactory sales on the return of the coins."

As coin collecting became more popular and *The Numismatist* started accepting paid advertising from others, grading became more formal. The February 1892 issue listed seven "classes" for the condition of coins (from worst to best): mutilated, poor, fair, good, fine, uncirculated, and proof. Through the years, the hobby has struggled with developing a grading system that would be accepted by all and could apply to all coins. The hobby's growth was accompanied by a desire for more grades, or classifications, to more precisely define a coin's condition. The desire for more precision, however, was at odds with the basic concept of grading: to provide a concise method for classifying a coin's condition.

For example, even the conservatively few classifications of 1892 included fudge factors.

"To give flexibility to this classification," *The Numismatist* said, "such modification of fine, good and fair, as 'extremely,' 'very,' 'almost,' etc., are used to express slight variations from the general condition."

The debate over grading continued for decades in *The Numismatist*. A number of articles and letters prodded the ANA to write grading guidelines and endorse them as the association's official standards. Some submitted specific suggestions for terminology and accompanying standards for each grade. But grading remained a process of "instinct" gained through years of collecting or dealing experience.

A formal grading guide in book form finally appeared in 1958, but it was the work of two individuals rather than the ANA, *A Guide to the Grading of United States Coins* by Martin R. Brown and John W. Dunn was a break-through in the great grading debate. Now collectors had a reference that gave them specific guidelines for specific coins and could be studied and restudied at home.

The first editions of Brown and Dunn carried text only, no illustrations. For the fourth edition, in 1964, publication was assumed by Whitman Publishing Co. of Racine, Wis., and line drawings were added to illustrate the text.

The fourth edition listed six principal categories for circulated coins (from worst to best): good, very good, fine, very fine, extremely fine, and about uncirculated. But again, the desire for more precise categories were evidenced. In the book's introduction, Brown and Dunn wrote, "Dealers will sometimes advertise coins that are graded G-VG, VG-F, F-VF, VF-XF. Or the description may be ABT. G. or VG plus, etc. This means that the coin in question more than meets minimum standards for the lower grade but is not quite good enough for the higher grade."

When the fifth edition appeared, in 1969, the "New B & D Grading System" was introduced. The six principal categories for circulated coins were still intact, but variances within those categories were now designated by up to four letters: "A," "B," "C" or "D." For example, an EF-A coin was "almost about uncirculated." An EF-B was "normal extra fine" within the B & D standards. EF-C had a "normal extra fine" obverse, but the reverse was "obviously not as nice as obverse due to poor strike or excessive wear." EF-D had a "normal extra fine" reverse but a problem obverse.

But that wasn't the end. Brown and Dunn further listed 29 problem points that could appear on a coin – from No. 1 for an "edge bump" to No. 29 for "attempted re-engraving outside of the Mint." The number could be followed by the letter "O" or "R" to designate whether the problem appeared on the obverse or reverse and a Roman numeral corresponding to a clock face to designate where the problem appears on the obverse or reverse. For example, a coin described as "VG-B-9-O-X" would grade "VG-B"; the "9" designated a "single rim nick"; the "O" indicated the nick was on the obverse; and the "X" indicated it appeared at the 10 o'clock position, or upper left, of the obverse.

The author's goal was noble – to create the perfect grading system. They again, however, fell victim to the age-old grading-system problem: Precision comes at the expense of brevity. Dealer Kurt Krueger wrote in the January 1976 issue of *The Numismatist*, "Under the new B & D system, the numismatist must contend with a minimum of 43,152 different grading combinations! Accuracy is apparent, but simplicity has been lost." As a result, the "New B & D Grading System" never caught on in the marketplace.

The 1970s saw two important grading guides make their debut. The first was *Photograde* by James F. Ruddy. As the title implies, Ruddy uses photographs instead of line drawings to show how coins look in the various circulated grades. Simplicity is also a virtue of Ruddy's book. Only seven circulated grades are listed (about good, good, very good, fine, very fine, extremely fine, and about uncirculated), and the designations stop there.

In 1977 the longtime call for the ANA to issue grading standards was met with the release of *Official A.N.A. Grading Standards for United States Coins*. Like Brown and Dunn, the first edition of the ANA guide used line drawings to illustrate coins in various states of wear. But instead of using adjectival descriptions, the ANA guide adopted a numerical system for designating grades.

The numerical designations were based on a system used by Dr. William H. Sheldon in his book *Early American Cents*, first published in 1949. He used a scale of 1 to 70 to designate the grades of large cents.

"On this scale," Sheldon wrote, "1 means that the coin is identifiable and not mutilated – no more than that. A 70-coin is one in flawless Mint State, exactly as it left the dies, with perfect mint color and without a blemish or nick."

(Sheldon's scale also had its pragmatic side. At the time, a No. 2 large cent was worth about twice a No. 1 coin; a No. 4 was worth about twice a No. 2, and so on up the scale.)

With the first edition of its grading guide, the ANA adopted the 70-point scale for grading all U.S. coins. It designated 10 categories of circulated grades: AG-3, G-4, VG-8, F-12, VF-20, VF-30, EF-40, EF-45, AU-50, and AU-55. The third edition, released in 1987, replaced the line drawings with photographs, and another circulated grade was added: AU-58. A fourth edition was released in 1991.

Grading circulated U.S. coins

Dealers today generally use either the ANA guide or Photograde when grading circulated coins for their inventories. (Brown and Dunn is now out of print.) Many local coin shops sell both books. Advertisers in *Numismatic News*, *Coins* Magazine, and *Coin Prices* must indicate which standards they are using in grading their coins. If the standards are not listed, they must conform to ANA standards.

Following are some general guidelines, accompanied by photos, for grading circulated U.S. coins. Grading even circulated pieces can be subjective, particularly when attempting to draw the fine line between, for example, AU-55 and AU-58. Two longtime collectors or dealers can disagree in such a case.

But by studying some combination of the following guidelines, the ANA guide, and *Photograde*, and by looking at a lot of coins at shops and shows, collectors can gain enough grading knowledge to buy circulated coins confidently from dealers and other collectors. The more you study, the more knowledge and confidence you will gain. When you decide which series of coins you want to collect, focus on the guidelines for that particular series. Read them, reread them, and then refer back to them again and again.

AU-50

Indian cent

Lincoln cent

Buffalo nickel

Jefferson nickel

Mercury dime

Standing Liberty quarter

Washington quarter

Walking Liberty half dollar

Morgan dollar

Barber coins

AU-50 (about uncirculated): Just a slight trace of wear, result of brief exposure to circulation or light rubbing from mishandling, may be evident on elevated design areas. These imperfections may appear as scratches or dull spots, along with bag marks or edge nicks. At least half of the original mint luster generally is still evident.

XF-40

Indian cent

Lincoln cent

Buffalo nickel

Jefferson nickel

Mercury dime

Standing Liberty quarter

Washington quarter

Walking Liberty half dollar

Morgan dollar

Barber coins

XF-40 (extremely fine): The coin must show only slight evidence of wear on the highest points of the design, particularly in the hair lines of the portrait on the obverse. The same may be said for the eagle's feathers and wreath leaves on the reverse of most U.S. coins. A trace of mint luster may still show in protected areas of the coin's surface.

VF-20

Indian cent

Lincoln cent

Buffalo nickel

Jefferson nickel

Mercury dime

Standing Liberty quarter

Washington quarter

Walking Liberty half dollar

Morgan dollar

Barber coins

VF-20 (very fine): The coin will show light wear at the fine points in the design, though they may remain sharp overall. Although the details may be slightly smoothed, all lettering and major features must remain sharp.

Indian cent: All letters in "Liberty" are complete but worn. Headdress shows considerable flatness, with flat spots on the tips of the feathers.

Lincoln cent: Hair, cheek, jaw, and bow-tie details will be worn but clearly separated, and wheat stalks on the reverse will be full with no weak spots.

Buffalo nickel: High spots on hair braid and cheek will be flat but show some detail, and a full horn will remain on the buffalo.

Jefferson nickel: Well over half of the major hair detail will remain, and the pillars on Monticello will remain well defined, with the triangular roof partially visible.

Mercury dime: Hair braid will show some detail, and three-quarters of the detail will remain in the feathers. The two diagonal bands on the fasces will show completely but will be worn smooth at the middle, with the vertical lines sharp.

Standing Liberty quarter: Rounded contour of Liberty's right leg will be flattened, as will the high point of the shield.

Washington quarter: There will be considerable wear on the hair curls, with feathers on the right and left of the eagle's breast showing clearly.

Walking Liberty half dollar: All lines of the skirt will show but will be worn on the high points. Over half the feathers on the eagle will show.

Morgan dollar: Two-thirds of the hair lines from the forehead to the ear must show. Ear should be well defined. Feathers on the eagle's breast may be worn smooth.

Barber coins: All seven letters of "Liberty" on the headband must stand out sharply. Head wreath will be well outlined from top to bottom.

F-12

Indian cent

Lincoln cent

Buffalo nickel

Jefferson nickel

Mercury dime

Standing Liberty quarter

Washington quarter

Walking Liberty half dollar

Morgan dollar

Barber coins

F-12 (fine): Coins show evidence of moderate to considerable but generally even wear on all high points, though all elements of the design and lettering remain bold. Where the word "Liberty" appears in a headband, it must be fully visible. On 20th century coins, the rim must be fully raised and sharp.

VG-8

Indian cent

Lincoln cent

Buffalo nickel

Jefferson nickel

Mercury dime

Standing Liberty quarter

Washington quarter

Walking Liberty half dollar

Morgan dollar

Barber coins

VG-8 (very good): The coin will show considerable wear, with most detail points worn nearly smooth. Where the word "Liberty" appears in a headband, at least three letters must show. On 20th century coins, the rim will start to merge with the lettering.

G-4

Indian cent

Lincoln cent

Buffalo nickel

Jefferson nickel

Mercury dime

Standing Liberty quarter

Washington quarter

Walking Liberty half dollar

Morgan dollar

Barber coins

G-4 (good): Only the basic design remains distinguishable in outline form, will all points of detail worn smooth. The word "Liberty" has disappeared, and the rims are almost merging with the lettering.

About good or fair: The coin will be identifiable by date and mint but otherwise badly worn, with only parts of the lettering showing. Such coins are of value only as fillers in a collection until a better example of the date and mintmark can be obtained. The only exceptions would be rare coins

Grading uncirculated U.S. coins

The subjectivity of grading and the trend toward more classifications becomes more acute when venturing into uncirculated, or mint-state, coins. A minute differ-

Collectors have a variety of grading services to choose from. This set of Arkansas half dollars that appeared in an Early American History Auctions sale used two of the services.

ence between one or two grade points can mean a difference in value of hundreds or even thousands of dollars. In addition, the standards are more difficult to articulate in writing and illustrate through drawings or photographs. Thus, the possibilities for differences of opinion on one or two grade points increase in uncirculated coins.

Back in Dr. George Heath's day and continuing through the 1960s, a coin was either uncirculated or it wasn't. Little distinction was made between uncirculated coins of varying condition, largely because there was little if any difference in value. When *Numismatic News* introduced its value guide in 1962 (the forerunner of today's Coin Market section in the *News*), it listed only one grade of uncirculated for Morgan dollars.

But as collectible coins increased in value and buyers of uncirculated coins became more picky, distinctions within uncirculated grade started to surface. In 1975 *Numismatic News* still listed only one uncirculated grade in Coin Market, but added this note: "Uncirculated and proof specimens in especially choice condition will also command proportionately higher premiums than these listed."

The first edition of the ANA guide listed two grades of uncirculated, MS-60 and MS-65, in addition to the theoretical but non-existent MS-70 (a flawless coin). MS-60 was described as "typical uncirculated" and MS-65 as "choice uncirculated." *Numismatic News* adopted both designations for Coin Market. In 1981, when the second edition of the ANA grading guide was released, MS-67 and MS-63 were added. In 1985 *Numismatic News* started listing six grades of uncirculated for Morgan dollars: MS-60, MS-63, MS-65, MS-65+, and MS-63 prooflike.

Then in 1986, a new entity appeared that changed the nature of grading and trading uncirculated coins ever since. A group of dealers led by David Hall of Newport Beach, Calif., formed the Professional Coin Grading Service. For a fee, collectors could submit a coin through an authorized PCGS dealer and receive back a professional opinion of its grade.

The concept was not new; the ANA had operated an authentication service since 1972 and a grading service since 1979. A collector or dealer could submit a coin directly to the service and receive a certificate giving the service's opinion on authenticity and grade. The grading service was the source of near constant debate among dealers and ANA officials. Dealers charged that ANA graders were too young and inexperienced, and that their grading was inconsistent.

Grading stability was a problem throughout the coin business in the early 1980s, not just with the ANA service. Standards among uncirculated grades would tighten during a bear market and loosen during a bull market. As a result, a coin graded MS-65 in a bull market may have commanded only MS-63 during a bear market.

PCGS created several innovations in the grading business in response to these problems:

1. Coins could be submitted through PCGS-authorized dealers only.

2. Each coin would be graded by at least three members of a panel of "top graders," all prominent dealers in the business. (Since then, however, PCGS does not allow its graders to also deal in coins.)

3. After grading, the coin would be encapsulated in an inert, hard-plastic holder with a serial number and the grade indicated on the holder.

4. PCGS-member dealers pledged to make a market in PCGS-graded coins and honor the grades assigned.

5. In one of the most far-reaching moves, PCGS said it would use all 11 increments of uncirculated on the 70-point numerical scale: MS-60, MS-61, MS-62, MS-63, MS-64, MS-65, MS-66, MS-67, MS-68, MS-69, and MS-70.

The evolution of more uncirculated grades had reached another milestone.

Purists bemoaned the entombment of classic coins in the plastic holders and denounced the 11 uncirculated grades as implausible. Nevertheless, PCGS was an immediate commercial success. The plastic holders were nicknamed "slabs," and dealers couldn't get coins through the system fast enough.

In subsequent years, a number of similar services have appeared. Among them, one of the original PCGS "top graders," John Albanese, left PCGS to found the Numismatic Guaranty Corp. The ANA grading service succumbed to "slab mania" and introduced its own encapsulated product.

There now are numerous other reputable private third-party grading services. PCGS and NGC are the oldest and remain the leaders. In 1990 the ANA sold its grading service to a private company. It operates under the ANACS acronym.

How should a collector approach the buying and grading of uncirculated coins? Collecting uncirculated coins worth thousands of dollars implies a higher level of numismatic expertise by the buyer. Those buyers without that level of expertise should cut their teeth on more inexpensive coins, just as today's experienced collectors did. Inexperienced collectors can start toward that level by studying the guidelines for mint-state coins in the ANA grading guide and looking at lots of coins at shows and shops.

Study the condition and eye appeal of a coin and compare it to other coins of the same series. Then compare prices. Do the more expensive coins look better? If so, why? Start to make your own judgments concerning relationships between condition and value.

According to numismatic legend, a collector walked up to a crusty old dealer at a show one time and asked the dealer to grade a coin the collector had with him. The dealer looked at the coin and said, "I grade it a hundred dollars." Such is the bottom line to coin grading.

Grading U.S. proof coins

Because proof coins are struck by a special process using polished blanks, they receive their own grading designation. A coin does not start out being a proof and then become mint state if it becomes worn. Once a proof coin, always a proof coin.

In the ANA system, proof grades use the same numbers as circulated and uncirculated grades, and the amount of wear on the coin corresponds to those grades. But the number is preceded by the word "proof." For example, Proof-65, Proof-55, Proof-45, and so on. In addition, the ANA says a proof coin with many marks, scratches or other defects should be called an "impaired proof."

Grading world coins

The state of grading non-U.S. issues is similar to U.S. coin grading before Brown and Dunn. There is no detailed, illustrated guide that covers the enormous scope and variety of world coins; collectors and dealers rely on their experience in the field and knowledge of the marketplace.

The *Standard Catalog of World Coins* gives the following guidelines for grading world coins, which apply to the Canadian and Mexican value listings in this book:

In grading world coins, there are two elements to look for: (1) overall wear and (2) loss of design details, such as strands of hair, feathers on eagles, designs on coats of arms, and so on. Grade each coin by the weaker of the two sides. Age, rarity or type of coin should not be considered in grading.

Grade by the amount of overall wear and loss of detail evident in the main design on each side. On coins with a moderately small design element that is prone to early wear, grade by that design alone.

In the marketplace, adjectival grades are still used for Mexican coins. The numerical system for Canadian coins is now commonplace:

Uncirculated, MS-60: No visible signs of wear or handling, even under a 30X microscope. Bag marks may be present.

Almost uncirculated, AU-50: All detail will be visible. There will be wear on only the highest points of the coin. There will often be half or more of the original mint luster present.

Extremely fine, XF-40: About 95 percent of the original detail will be visible. Or, on a coin with a design that has no inner detail to wear down, there will be light wear over nearly the entire coin. If a small design is used as the grading area, about 90 percent of the original detail will be visible. This latter rule stems from the logic that a smaller amount of detail needs to be present because a small area is being used to grade the whole coin.

Very fine, VF-20: About 75 percent of the original detail will be visible. Or, on a coin with no inner detail, there will be moderate wear over the entire coin. Corners of letters and numbers may be weak. A small grading area will have about 60 percent of the original detail.

Fine, F-12: About 50 percent of the original detail will be visible. Or, on a coin with no inner detail, there will be fairly heavy wear over the entire coin. Sides of letters will be weak. A typically uncleaned coin will often appear dirty or dull. A small grading area will have just under 50 percent of the original detail.

Very good, VG-8: About 25 percent of the original detail will be visible. There will be heavy wear on the entire coin.

Good, G-4: Design will be clearly outlined but with substantial wear. Some of the larger detail may be visible. The rim may have a few weak spots of wear.

About good, AG-3: Typically only a silhouette of a large design will be visible. The rim will be worn down into the letters, if any.

Where to write for more information

American Numismatic Association: 818 N. Cascade Ave., Colorado Springs, CO 80903-3279.

Independent Coin Grading Co.: 7901 E. Belleview Ave., Suite 50, Englewood, CO 80111.

Numismatic Guaranty Corp: P.O. Box 4776, Sarasota, FL 34230.

Numistrust Corp., 9045 La Fontana Blvd., #C13, Boca Raton, FL 33434.

Photo Certified Coin Institute, Inc.: P.O. Box 8609, Chattanooga, TN 37414.

Photograde: Bowers and Merena Galleries, Inc., Books Dept., Box 1224, Wolfeboro, NH 03894.

Professional Coin Grading Service: P.O. Box 9458, Newport Beach, CA 92658.

Sovereign Entities Grading Service: 401 Chestnut St., Suite 103, Chattanooga, TN 37402-4924.

Visit the Krause Publications Web site
http://www.collect.com

5

Get a map
How to organize a collection

By David C. Harper

Do you have a jar full of old coins? Did a favorite relative give you a few silver dollars over the years? Or did you just come across something unusual that you set aside?

All three circumstances make good beginnings for collecting coins. It may surprise you, but this is how just about everybody starts in the hobby. It is a rare collector who decides to start down the hobby road without first having come into a few coins one way or another.

What these random groupings lack is organization. It is organization that makes a collection. But think about it another way: Organization is the map that tells you where you can go in coin collecting and how you can get there.

Have you ever been at a large fair or a huge office building and seen the maps that say "you are here"? Did you ever consider that, over time, thousands of other people have stood on the same spot? This is true in numismatics also. Figuratively, you are standing on the same spot on which the writers of this book stood at some point in their lives.

At a fair, the map helps you consider various ways of seeing all the sights. In coin collecting, too, there are different ways to organize a collection. The method you choose helps you see the hobby sights you want to see.

It should be something that suits you. Remember, do what you want to do. See what you want to see. But don't be afraid to make a mistake; there aren't any. Just as one can easily retrace steps at a fair, one can turn around and head in another direction in the coin-collecting hobby. Besides, when you start off for any given point, often you see something along the way that was unplanned but more interesting. That's numismatics.

There are two major ways to organize a collection: by type, and by date and mint-mark. These approaches work in basically the same fashion for coins of the United States, Canada and Mexico. Naturally, there are differences. But to establish the concepts, let's focus first on U.S. coins.

United States

Let's take collecting by type first. Look at your jar of coins, or take the change out of your pocket. You find Abraham Lincoln and the Lincoln Memorial on current cents. You find Thomas Jefferson and his home, Monticello, on the nickel. Franklin D. Roosevelt and a torch share the dime. George Washington and an eagle (or since 1999, designs honoring states) appear on the quarter. John F. Kennedy and the presidential seal are featured on the half dollar. Sacagawea and an eagle are on the dollar.

Each design is called a "type." If you took one of each and put the five coins in a holder, you would have a type set of the coins that are currently being produced for circulation by the U.S. Mint.

With just these six coins, you can study various metallic compositions. You can evaluate their states of preservation and assign a grade to each. You can learn about the artists who designed the coins, and you can learn of the times in which these designs were created.

As you might have guessed, many different coin types have been used in the United States over the years. You may remember seeing some of them circulating. These designs reflect the hopes and aspirations of people over time. Putting all of them together forms a wonderful numismatic mosaic of American history.

George Washington did not mandate that his image appear on the quarter. Quite the contrary. He would have been horrified. When he was president, he headed off those individuals in Congress who thought the leader of the country should have his image on its coins. Washington said it smacked of monarchy and would have nothing of it.

Almost a century and a half later, during the bicentennial of Washington's birth in 1932, a nation searching for its roots during troubled economic times decided that it needed his portrait on its coins as a reminder of his great accomplishments and as reassurance that this nation was the same place it had been in more prosperous days.

In its broadest definition, collecting coins by type requires that you obtain an example of every design that was struck by the U.S. Mint since it was founded in 1792. That's a tall order. You would be looking for denominations like the half cent, two-cent piece, three-cent piece, and 20-cent piece, which have not been produced in over a century. You would be looking for gold coins ranging in face value from $1 to $50.

But even more important than odd-sounding denominations or high face values is the question of rarity. Some of the pieces in this multi-century type set are rare and expensive. That's why type collectors often divide the challenge into more digestible units.

Type collecting can be divided into 18th, 19th, 20th and 21st century units. Obviously, a 21st century set is a short one. Just pull the change out of your pocket and ask the local bank for the half and dollar. Starting type collectors can focus on 20th century coin designs, which are easily obtainable. The fun and satisfaction of putting the 20th century set together then creates the momentum to continue backward in time.

In the process of putting a 20th century type set together, one is also learning how to grade, learning hobby jargon, and discovering how to obtain coins from dealers, the U.S. Mint, and other collectors. All of this knowledge is then refined as the collector increases the challenge to himself.

This book is designed to help. How many dollar types were struck in the 20th century? Turn to the U.S. price-guide section and check it out. We see the Morgan dollar, Peace dollar, Eisenhower dollar, and Anthony dollar. Hobbyists could also add the Ike dollar with the Bicentennial design of 1976 and the silver American Eagle bullion coin struck since 1986. One can also find out their approximate retail prices from the listings.

The beauty of type collecting is that one can choose the most inexpensive example of each type. There is no need to select a 1903-O Morgan when the 1921 will do just as well. With the 20th century type set, hobbyists can dodge some truly big-league prices.

As a collector's hobby confidence grows, he can tailor goals to fit his desires. He can take the road less traveled if that is what suits him. Type sets can be divided by denomination. You can choose over two centuries of one-cent coins. You can take just obsolete denominations or copper, silver or gold denominations.

You can even collect by size. Perhaps you would like to collect all coin types larger than 30 millimeters or all coins smaller than 20 millimeters. Many find this freedom of choice stimulating.

Type collecting has proven itself to be enduringly popular over the years. It provides a maximum amount of design variety while allowing collectors to set their own level of challenge.

The second popular method of collecting is by date and mintmark. What this means, quite simply, is that a collector picks a given type – Jefferson nickels, for example – and then goes after an example of every year, every mintmark, and every type of manufacture that was used with the Jefferson design.

Looking at this method of collecting brings up the subject of mintmarks. The "U.S. Mint" is about as specific as most non-collectors get in describing the government agency that provides everyday coins. Behind that label are the various production facilities that actually do the work.

In the more than two centuries of U.S. coinage, there have been eight such facilities. Four are still in operation. Those eight in alphabetical order are Carson City, Nev., which used a "CC" mintmark to identify its work; Charlotte, N.C. ("C"); Dahlonega, Ga. ("D"); Denver (also uses a "D," but it opened long after the Dahlonega Mint closed, so there was never any confusion); New Orleans ("O"); Philadelphia (because it was the primary mint, it used no mintmark for much of its history, but currently uses a "P"); San Francisco ("S"); and West Point, N.Y. ("W").

A person contemplating the collecting of Jefferson nickels by date and mintmark will find that three mints produced them: San Francisco, Denver and Philadelphia. Because of first two are branch mints serving smaller populations, their output has tended over time to be smaller than that of Philadelphia. This fact, repeated in other series, has helped give mintmarks quite an allure to collectors. It provides one of the major attractions in collecting coins by date and mintmark.

The key date for Jeffersons is the 1950-D when using mintages as a guide. In that year, production was just 2.6 million pieces. Because collectors of the time were aware of the coin's low mintage, many examples were saved. As a result, prices are

A basic type set of 20th century dollar coins would consist of (from top) a Morgan type, Peace type, Eisenhower type and Anthony type.

reasonable.

The Depression-era 1939-D comes in as the most valuable regular-issue Jefferson nickel despite a mintage of 3.5 million – almost 1 million more than the 1950-D. The reason: Fewer were saved for later generations of coin collectors.

Date and mintmark collecting teaches hobbyists to use mintage figures as a guide but to take them with a grain of salt. Rarity, after all, is determined by the number of surviving coins, not the number initially created.

The Jefferson series is a good one to collect by date and mintmark, because the mintmarks have moved around, grown in size, and expanded in number.

When the series was first introduced, the Jefferson nickel was produced at the three mints previously mentioned. In 1942, because of a diversion of certain metals to wartime use, the coin's alloy of 75 percent copper and 25 percent nickel was

Jefferson nickels have been produced at the (from top) Philadelphia, Denver and San Francisco Mints. Note the Denver and San Francisco mintmarks to the right of Monticello.

The wartime nickels of 1942-1945 marked the first time a "P" mintmark, for Philadelphia, was used.

changed. The new alloy was 35 percent silver, 56 percent copper, and 9 percent manganese.

To denote the change, the mintmarks were moved and greatly enlarged. The pre-1942 mintmarks were small and located to the right of Monticello; the wartime mintmarks were enlarged and placed over the dome. What's more, for the first time in American history, the Philadelphia Mint used a mintmark ("P").

The war's end restored the alloy and mintmarks to their previous status. The "P" disappeared. This lasted until the 1960s, when a national coin shortage saw all mintmarks removed for three years (1965-1967) and then returned, but in a different location. Mintmarks were placed on the obverse, to the right of Jefferson's portrait near the date in 1968. In 1980 the "P" came back in a smaller form and is still used.

Another consideration arises with date and mintmark collecting: Should the hobbyist include proof coins in the set? This can be argued both ways. Suffice to say that anyone who has the desire to add proof coins to the set will have a larger one. It is not necessary nor is it discouraged.

Some of the first proof coins to carry mintmarks were Jefferson nickels. When proof coins were made in 1968 after lapsing from 1965 to 1967, production occurred at San Francisco instead of Philadelphia. The "S" mintmark was placed on the proof coins of that year, including the Jefferson nickel, to denote the change. Since that time, mintmarks used on proof examples of various denominations have included the "P", "D", "S", and "W".

For all of the mintmark history that is embodied in the Jefferson series, prices are reasonable. For a first attempt at collecting coins by date and mintmark, it provides excellent background for going on to the more expensive and difficult types. After all, if you are ever going to get used to the proper handling of a coin, it is far better to experiment on a low-cost coin than a high-value rarity.

As one progresses in date and mintmark collecting and type collecting, it is important to remember that all of the coins should be of similar states of preservation. Sets look slapdash if one coin is VG and another is MS-65 and still another is VF. Take a look at the prices of all the coins in the series before you get too far, figure out what you can afford, and then stick to that grade or range of grades.

Sure, there is a time-honored practice of filling a spot with any old example until a better one comes along. That is how we got the term "filler." But if you get a few placeholders, don't stop there. By assembling a set of uniform quality, you end up

In 1968 the mintmarks reappeared on U.S. coins and production of proof coins resumed, this time at the San Francisco Mint. On the nickels, the mintmark moved from the reverse to the obverse below the date.

with a more aesthetically pleasing collection.

The date and mintmark method used to be the overwhelmingly dominant form of collecting. It still has many adherents. Give it a try if you think it sounds right for you.

Before we leave the discussion of collecting U.S. coins, it should be pointed out that the two major methods of organizing a collection are simply guidelines. They are not hard-and-fast rules that must be followed without questions. Collecting should be satisfying to the hobbyist. It should never be just one more item in the daily grind. Take the elements of these collecting approaches that you like or invent your own.

It should also be pointed out that U.S. coinage history does not start with 1792 nor do all of the coins struck since that time conform precisely to the two major organizational approaches. But these two areas are good places to start.

There are coins and tokens from the American Colonial period (1607-1776) that are just as fascinating and collectible as regular U.S. Mint issues. There are federal issues struck before the Mint was actually established. See the Colonial price-guide section in this book.

There are special coins called commemoratives, which have been struck by the U.S. Mint since 1892 to celebrate some aspect of American history or a contemporary event. They are not intended for circulation. There was a long interruption between 1954 and 1982, but currently annual commemoratives are being offered for sale directly to collectors by the Mint.

Collecting commemoratives has always been considered something separate from collecting regular U.S. coinage. It is, however, organized the same way. Commemoratives can be collected by date and mintmark or by type.

Current commemoratives can be purchased from the U.S. Mint. To get on its mailing list, write U.S. Mint, Customer Care Center, 801 Ninth St., N.W., Washington, D.C. 20220. Check the U.S. Mint Web site at www.usmint.gov. Once on the list, hobbyists will get the various solicitations for not only commemoratives, but regular proof sets and mint sets and proof American Eagle bullion coins. Hobbyists who order from the U.S. Mint's Web site receive notices of product availability by e-mail.

Buying coins from the Mint can be considered a hobby pursuit in its own right. Some collectors let the Mint organize their holdings for them. They buy complete sets and put them away. They never buy anything from anywhere else.

Admittedly, this is a passive form of collecting, but there are individuals around the world who enjoy collecting at this level without ever really going any deeper. They like acquiring every new issue as it comes off the Mint's presses.

Once done, there is a certain knowledge that one has all the examples of the current year. Obviously, too, collectors by date and mintmark of the current types would have to buy the new coins each year, but, of course, they do not stop there.

Varieties and errors make up another area. Under this heading come the coins the Mint did not intend to make. There are all kinds of errors. Many of them are inexpensive. Check out the U.S. Minting Varieties and Errors section in the price guide. If you want to pursue it further, there are specialty books that deal with the topic in more detail.

Canada

Starting point for the national coinage of Canada is popularly fixed at 1858. In that year a large cent was first produced for use in Upper and Lower Canada (Ontario and Quebec). These prices were intended to supplant local copper coinage, which in turn had been attempts to give various regions a medium of exchange.

What was circulating in Canada at the time was a hodgepodge of world issues. The large cent predates a unified national government by nine years, but it is considered the beginning of national issues nevertheless.

There are many similarities between the United States and Canada and their respective monetary systems. Both continent-sized nations thought in terms of taming the frontier, new settlements, and growth. Both came to use the dollar as the unit of account because of the pervasiveness of the Spanish milled dollar in trade. For each, the dollar divides into 100 cents.

However, Canada had a far longer colonial history. Many of its residents resisted the tide that carried the United States to independence and worked to preserve their loyalties to the British crown. As a result, Canada was firmly a part of the British Empire. So even today with its constitution (the British North America Act transferred from Westminster to Ottawa in 1982), parliamentary democracy, and a national consciousness perhaps best symbolized by the maple leaf, Canada retains a loyalty to the crown in the person of Queen Elizabeth II of the United Kingdom. Canada is a member of the British Commonwealth of Nations.

The effect of this on coins is obvious. Current issues carry the queen's effigy. How Canada got its coins in the past was also influenced. The fledgling U.S. government set about creating its own mint as one of its earliest goals, despite that better-quality pieces could be purchased abroad at lower cost. Canada found that ties to mints located in England were logical and comfortable.

The Royal Canadian Mint was not established until 1908, when it was called the Ottawa branch of the British Royal Mint, and it was not given its present name until 1931. Both events are within living memory. Canadian coins, therefore, have a unique mixture of qualities. They are tantalizingly familiar to U.S. citizens yet distinctly different.

The coinage of a monarchy brings its own logic to the organization of a collec-

Canadian coins have depicted (from top) Queen Victoria, King Edward VII, King George V, King George VI and Queen Elizabeth II.

tion. Type collecting is delineated by the monarch. United Canada has had six. The first was Queen Victoria, whose image appeared on those large cents of 1858. Her reign began in 1837 and lasted until 1901.

She was followed by Edward VII, 1901-1910; George V, 1910-1936; Edward VII, 1936; George VI, 1936-1952; and Queen Elizabeth II, 1952-present. All but Edward VIII had coins struck for circulation in Canada. The collectible monarchs, therefore, number five, but the longer reigns inspired changes of portraits over time to show the aging process at work. Legends also changed. When George VI ceased being emperor of India, Canada's coins were modified to recognize the change.

Like U.S. coins, sizes and alloys were altered to meet new demands placed on the coinage. However, the separateness of each nation might best be summed up this way: Though the United States abolished its large cent in 1857, Canada's was just getting under way in 1858. The United States put an end to the silver dollar in 1935, the very year Canada finally got its series going.

And Canada, the nickel-mining giant, used a small-sized silver five-cent coin until 1921, almost 50 years after the half dime was abolished in the United States. But whereas the Civil War was the major cause of the emergence of modern U.S. coinage as specified by the Coinage Act of 1873, World War I influenced the alterations that made Canada's coins what they are today.

It might be assumed that change in the monarch also signaled a change in the reverse designs of the various denominations. A check of the Canadian price guide section shows this is not necessarily the case. Current designs paired with Queen Elizabeth II basically date back to the beginning of her father's reign. The familiar maple-leaf cent, beaver five-cent piece, schooner 10-cent, caribou 25-cent, and coat-of-arms 50-cent have been running for over 50 years. Significant changes were made to the 50-cent coin in 1959, but the reverse design remains the coat of arms.

So where does that leave type collectors? It puts them in a situation similar to categorizing the various eagles on U.S. coins. They can be universalists and accept the broadest definitions of type, or they can narrow the bands to whatever degree suits them best.

By checking the price-guide section, date and mintmark collectors will quickly note that their method of organization more or less turns into collecting by date. Though currently there are three mints in Canada – Hull, Quebec; Ottawa, Ontario; and Winnipeg, Manitoba – they don't use mintmarks. Historically, few mintmarks were employed.

Ottawa used a "C" on gold sovereigns of 1908-1919 and on some exported colonial issues. The private Heaton Mint in Birmingham, England, used an "H" on coins it supplied to Canada from 1871 to 1907.

But the coins supplied to Canada by the British Royal Mint and later by its Ottawa branch did not carry any identifying mark. Collectors who confine their activities to the more recent issues need never think about a mintmark.

It would be easy to slant a presentation on Canadian issues to stress similarities or differences to U.S. issues. One should remember that the monetary structures of each evolved independently, but each was always having an impact on the other.

Common events, such as World War II, had a similar impact. For example, the Canadian five-cent coin changed in much the same way as the U.S. nickel. In

Canada, nickel was removed and replaced first by a tombac (brass) alloy and then by chromium-plated steel. Peace brought with it a return to the prewar composition.

To see an example of differences between the United States and Canada, take the Canadian approach to the worldwide trend of removing silver from coinage. Canada made its move in 1968, three years after the United States. Instead of choosing a copper-nickel alloy as a substitute for silver, Canada looked to its own vast natural resources and employed pure nickel.

Canada also seems more comfortable with its coinage than the United States. Whereas the United States often feared confusion and counterfeiting from making the least little changes in its coins, Canada has long embraced coinage to communicate national events, celebrations and culture. Its silver-dollar series actually began as a celebration of George V's 25 years on the throne.

Succeeding years saw additional commemorative $1 designs interspersed with the regular Voyageur design. When the centennial of national confederation was observed in 1967, all of the denominations were altered for one year. The United States only reluctantly tried out the idea on three of its denominations for the nation's Bicentennial.

Ultimately, Canada began an annual commemorative dollar series in 1971. It issued coins for the 1976 Montreal Olympic Games and again in 1988 for the Calgary Olympic Games. Bullion coins were created to market its gold, silver and platinum output. A commemorative series of gold $100 coins was also undertaken. Canada, too, issues special proof, prooflike and specimen sets, similar to the United States.

Hobbyists who would like to be informed of new issues should write Royal Canadian Mint, P.O. Box 457, Station A, Ontario K1A 8V5, Canada. The mint also maintains special toll-free lines. In the United States, hobbyists may telephone the Royal Canadian Mint at 1-800-268-6468. In Canada, the number is 1-800-267-1871. You can get on the mailing list by using these numbers and you can buy currently available coins. (See Chapter 6 for Web information.)

When collecting Canada, another thing to remember is the importance varieties play in the nation's various series. Certainly, a type collector has no need to dwell on this information, but the date and mintmark collector may puzzle over the many extra identifying abbreviations in the price guide for certain coins. These varieties should not be confused with the U.S. variety-and-error category.

Here the varieties are not mistakes; they are deliberately created and issued variations of the standard design. We see Voyageur dollars on which the number of water lines changes. Other dollars count the number of beads.

These differences are minor. Though they were deliberately done to meet varying mint needs, they were not intended to be set apart in the public mind. The hobby, however, likes to look at things under a microscope.

Some varieties were indeed intended to be deliberately and noticeably different. An example of this occurs with 1947-dated issues. A maple leaf was placed on the 1947-dated cent through 50-cent issues. This indicated the coin was struck after George VI lost his title of emperor of India, as proclaimed in the Latin legend, but that the design had not yet been altered to reflect this. All of these varieties are considered integral parts of the Canadian series, and they are listed as such.

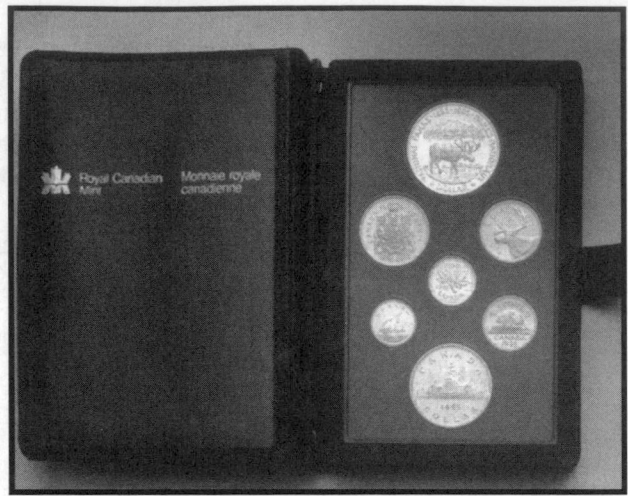

Like the U.S. Mint, the Royal Canadian Mint offers sets of coins in a variety of finishes to the collector market.

Do not construe any of this to mean there is no collecting of varieties and errors of the type common in the United States. There is. Collecting Royal Canadian Mint mistakes is just as active, just as interesting, and just as rewarding. After all, mint errors are universal. The methods of manufacture are the same. So the mistakes can be classified in the same manner.

Canada's numismatic listings also include items from various provinces issued before they were part of the confederation. The largest portion of this section is devoted to Newfoundland, because it retained a separate status far longer than the other provinces – until 1949 in fact.

Advice given to collectors of U.S. coins also applies to collectors of Canadian coins: Do what interests you. Do what you can afford. Create sets of uniform grade.

The rules of rarity transcend national boundaries. The only thing to keep in mind is the relative size of the collecting population. Because Canada has only a tenth of the U.S. population, it stands to reason that the number of collectors in that nation is but a fraction of the U.S. number. A mintage that seems to indicate scarcity for U.S. coin, therefore, could indicate something quite common in Canada. Don't forget that mintage is just a guide. The same factors that caused loss of available specimens or preserved unusually large quantities were at work in Canada, too.

Mexico

Coinage produced in Mexico dates to the establishment of a mint in Mexico City in 1536, over 250 years before a federal mint was set up in the United States and more than 300 years before Canada circulated its own coins. The output of those extra centuries alone would make organizing a Mexican coin collection more challenging than a collection of U.S. or Canadian coins. But there are numerous other factors involved.

You say you like the kings and queens on Canada's coins? Mexico has kings, too

– nearly 300 years' worth, plus a couple of emperors. You say the ideals of liberty embodied by the great men and women on U.S. coins is more your cup of tea? Mexico's coins also feature men and women committed to liberty.

In addition, Mexico is the crossroads of civilizations and empires. The great pyramid-building society of southern Mexico and Central America met its end at the hands of the Spanish conquistadors led initially by Hernando Cortez. The great Aztec empire was looted and overturned in 1519-1521 in the name of Spain.

The great natural resources of the area then supported successive Spanish kings in their grand dreams of dominating Europe. Through the doors of the Mexico City Mint and later facilities scattered about the country passed legendary quantities of silver. Even today the country ranks at the top of the list of silver producers.

But while Spain could dominate Mexico for a long time, the basic ideals of liberty and human dignity eventually motivated the people to throw off the foreign yoke. Unfortunately, victory was often neither complete nor wisely led. And in more recent years, the scourge of inflation had exacted a high toll on the currency itself. The numismatic consequences of a long history punctuated by periods of turmoil are an abundance of denominations, metals and types.

It is tempting for a would-be collector of Mexican coins to forget about anything that happened in the country prior to its monetary reform of 1905. By starting at that point, a hobbyist can happily overlook anything other than a decimal monetary system in which 100 centavos equal 1 peso. That system is as modern as any. The coins' striking quality is high. Legends are easy to read and understand, and the variety of issues is wide but not overwhelming.

There always is a certain logic to begin the collecting of any country with recent issues. The costs of learning are minimized, and as one becomes comfortable, a level of confidence can be built up sufficient to prompt diving further into the past.

The issues of 1905 to date also more easily fit into the mold of type collecting and collecting by date and mintmark. To take type collecting, for example, let's look at the peso. In 1905 it was a silver-dollar-sized coin with a silver-dollar-sized quantity of bullion in it, 0.786 ounces. In 1918 it was reduced to 0.4663 ounces; in 1920, 0.3856 ounces; in 1947, 0.2250 ounces; 1950, 0.1285 ounces; 1957, 0.0514 ounces; and in 1970 silver was eliminated completely in favor of a copper-nickel alloy.

At almost every one of those steps, the design changed, too. After sinking to 3,300 to the U.S. dollar, monetary reform dropped three zeroes in 1993. The new peso, equal to 1,000 old ones, is now 10 to the U.S. dollar.

By beginning with 1905, a date and mintmark collector misses out on issues of the various branch mints that were located around the country. Regular issues were all struck in Mexico City. Yearly output was reasonably regular for the various denominations, so date sets are extensive.

There have been rumblings since the early 1980s that Mexico would abandon the peso because of its greatly reduced value. The government, however, has been working hard to retain it since the monetary reform. So far it has succeeded.

One thing the government cannot do, however, is turn the clock back to a time when the fractional denominations of 1, 2, 5, 10, 20, 25, and 50 centavos were relatively high face values. However, it is stimulating to assemble sets because they offer a range of rarities. They are neither so expensive that it would prevent a collector

One thousand of these equaled one new peso as 1993 began.

from acquiring them at some point, but neither are they so common that you can walk into a shop, write a check, and come away with all of the 20th century sets complete. Check out the price guide section and see.

Gold in the post-1905 era is basically so much bullion. There are some scarcer pieces and some strikingly beautiful designs, such as the Centenario, a gold 50-peso coin containing 1.2 ounces of bullion. It was first struck in 1921 to mark 100 years of independence. Because Mexico actively restruck its gold coins, however, it is virtually impossible to tell an original issue from the newer version.

The result is a retail price structure based on metallic content. Gold, however, does not conjure up the images that silver does. Silver is the magic word for Mexico. That, of course, means the peso.

The modern Mexico City Mint also strikes commemoratives and collector sets from time to time. These are generally marketed to collectors through private firms, details of which are published in hobby newspapers like *World Coin News*. Mexico, like the United States and Canada, also issues gold and silver bullion coins.

These also are marketed through arrangements with private firms. Interestingly, Mexico's many gold-coin restrikes were the bullion coins of their day. They had the advantage of ready identification, and they were legally tradable according to gold-coin regulations that existed in the United States from 1933 through 1974.

It is appropriate that we conclude discussion of the modern period on the concept of bullion, because bullion is at the root of Mexico's numismatic history. That is a period to which we now turn.

When Cortez toppled the Aztec Empire, for a time the wealth returning to Spain was merely that taken by the victors from the vanquished. But the business of permanently administering a vast area in the name of the Spanish king, exploiting its natural resources, and funneling the proceeds to Spain quite soon involved the establishment of a mint in Mexico City. This was undertaken in 1536, just 15 years after the end of Aztec dominion.

At first, the authorized coins were low denominations: silver quarter, half, 1, 2, 3, and 4 reales, and copper 2 and 4 maravedis. To understand their face values and how they related to each other, let's take the common reference point of a silver dollar. The silver dollar is 8 reales, and you might recognize the nickname for the denomination of "piece of eight" from pirate lore. The eighth part, the silver real, was divided into 34 copper maravedis. That means the 8 reales was worth 272 copper maravedis.

Mexico also strikes commemorative coins for the collector market. They are available through private firms in the United States.

The copper coinage was hated and soon abolished, not to reappear until 1814. The silver coins were fine as far as they went. When the mines of Mexico began producing undreamed of quantities of metal, however, it was the 8 reales that took center stage. This occurred after 1572. The piece of eight became the standard form for shipping silver back to Spain.

Mexico City's output was prodigious. Minting standards were crude. All denominations produced are called "cobs," because they are basically little more than irregular-looking lumps of metal on which bits and pieces of design can be seen. The only constant was weight, fineness, and the appearance of assayer's initials (which guaranteed the weight and fineness). Not showing those initials was cause for severe punishment.

Designs showed the arms of the monarch on one side, a cross on the other, appropriate legends, and an indication of denomination. The period of cob issues lasted until 1732. Rulers of the period start with Charles and Johanna, 1516-1556; Philip II, 1556-1598; Philip III, 1598-1621; Philip IV, 1621-1665; Charles II, 1665-1700; Philip V, 1700-1724 and 1724-1746; and Luis I, 1724.

Modern mint machinery began turning out coins in 1732. Quality was similar to today. The arms design was continued. It was not until 1772 that the monarch's portrait began appearing. The honor of this numismatic debut belongs to Charles III. Kings of this period are Ferdinand VI, 1746-1759; Charles III, 1760-1788; Charles IV, 1788-1808; and Ferdinand VII, 1808-1821. *The Standard Catalog of Mexican Coins* by Colin R. Bruce II and Dr. George W. Vogt is recommended to those who want to study this period in greater depth.

The revolutionary period begins in 1810, when a parish priest, Miguel Hidalgo y Costilla, issued the call for independence. The first attempts to achieve this were violently suppressed. Hidalgo was executed, but independence did come in 1821.

With revolt against central authority came a dispersal of the right to strike coins. Mexico City continued as the major facility, but other operations began. The list of these over the next century is lengthy. Mintmarks and assayer initials proliferated.

The old colonial coinage standard survived the period. The 8 reales and its parts carried on. A slight reduction in bullion content had been ordered by the king in 1760, but otherwise things continued as they were. Gold was coined during the colonial period beginning in 1679 based on an 8-escudo piece, which divided into eighths just like the 8 reales. Gold, however, was not as important as silver.

Mexico's first emperor came shortly after independence. He was a leader in the struggle that set Mexico free from Spain. Augustin de Iturbide, originally an officer in the service of Spain, was proclaimed emperor in 1822. He abdicated in 1823 and was executed in 1824.

The second emperor had a reign almost as short as the first. Maximilian I, emperor only because he had a French army to secure the throne, reigned from 1863 to 1867. He was shot by a firing squad when the French left.

He is remembered numismatically because he decided to decimalize the coinage. The centavo and peso were born. Soon afterward, the republic was re-established. Further monetary changes were minor thereafter until 1905.

Collectors focusing on Mexico can devote much time to the study of the quasi-official issues of rebels during the periods of instability. They can look at hacienda tokens, which were issued by large farms or ranches that employed hundreds or thousands of people. Or they can pick whichever period in Mexico's history that fascinates them most. Whatever collectors of Mexico eventually settle on, they will find it rewarding.

Where to write for more information

World Coin News: 700 E. State St., Iola, WI 54990.

Better than map

Three mints have Web sites

By David C. Kranz

Here's a handy electronic means of finding North American coinage.

The U.S. Mint's Web site, www.usmint.gov, has been most active, making several limited, exclusively online offers. These have involved small bags of the nation's 50 states quarter issues as well as numismatic-philatelic covers and Sacagawea dollars. The U.S. Mint also sells its traditional annual products such as mint sets and proof sets on the Web, along with commemorative coins and other Mint sales catalog items.

Online orders can be more convenient for many hobbyists. Shipping charges are currently the same between sets ordered online or by mail.

Canadian gold and silver, annual sets and commemoratives are available for purchase on the Royal Canadian Mint's site, www.mint.ca. Both French and English language versions of the RCM site are available. The site is set up for online orders (placed from Canada and the United States only), and the mint accepts Visa, Mastercard and American Express.

At the site of the Mexican Mint, www.cmonedam.com.mx/cmm, you can learn that it was the first mint in America, and that it has served without interruption since its inception by Spanish decree. The Mexican Mint site has Spanish and English language versions, with coinage history, current news, sales and promotions Web pages as well as technical information about the circulating coinage of Mexico. Telephone, fax, mail and e-mail information is provided for placing orders.

The fourth component of the North American continent, Greenland, has no mint within its borders and uses coins of Denmark in commerce. For more on these coins, see the *Standard Catalog of World Coins*, published by Krause Publications (www.collect.com).

For a quick introduction to these countries' latest coinage, their Web sites can't be beat.

7

Caring for coins
How to store and preserve your collection

By Alan Herbert

From the day you acquire your first collectible coin, you have to consider where and how to store your collection. Often a shoebox or a small cardboard or plastic box of some kind will be the principal storage point as you start to gather coins, even before they can be considered a collection. Sooner or later you will outgrow that first box and need to think seriously about what to do with your coins to protect and preserve them.

All too often security takes precedence over preservation. We're more worried that the kids will dip into the coins for candy or ice cream or that burglars will somehow learn about your "valuable" collection and pay a visit. It often isn't until years later when you suddenly notice that your once beautiful coins are now dingy and dull, with spots and fingerprints all over them, that preservation becomes a primary consideration.

Learning good storage habits should be one of the first things to do right along with acquiring those first coins. There are a multitude of storage products on the market that are intended for more or less specific situations, so learning which to use and how to use them is vital to the health of your collection. Most if not all of the products mentioned here should be available at your nearest coin shop or hobby store.

Safe storage methods

The common impulse is to use what's available around the house; never allow that impulse to control your collecting. Plastic wrap, aluminum foil, cardboard, stationery envelopes, and other common household products are not designed for coin storage and never should be used for your collection. The same goes for soaps and cleansers found around the home.

There are specific products that have been designed, tested and found safe to use for coins. These are the media your collection deserves. The slight added expense

Two-by-two cardboard holders are a common form of short-term, inexpensive coin storage.

Many dealers sell coins in 2-by-2 plastic "flips," but these should not be used for long-term storage.

will pay a thousand dividends years from now when you sell you collection or pass it on to your heirs.

The most common storage media are 2-inch by 2-inch cardboard holders with Mylar windows, 2-by-2 plastic "flips," coin tubes, hard-plastic holders, coin boards, and coin albums.

The 2-by-2 cardboard holders are the cheapest and most commonly used storage method. They are usually folded and stapled around the coin. They are intended for short-term general storage. They are not airtight or watertight, and staples driven too close to the coin can ruin it.

The 2-by-2 plastic flips come in good and bad varieties. The old, usually soft flips are made of plastics that contain polyvinyl chloride, a chemical found in many plastics. Over time it breaks down into substances that put a green slime on your coins, which attacks the surface and ruins them.

The good flips are made of Mylar, but they are brittle and prone to splitting. So they should not be used to mail coins or when the coins are moved about frequently. Mylar flips, too, are for short-term general storage.

Often you will find coins in PVC holders when you buy them from a dealer. Remove them immediately and put them in some better storage medium.

Coin tubes come in clear and cloudy, or translucent, plastic. These are made of an inert plastic that will not harm your coins. Tubes are intended for bulk, medium- to long-term storage, with one caution: Use care when inserting the coins. Merely

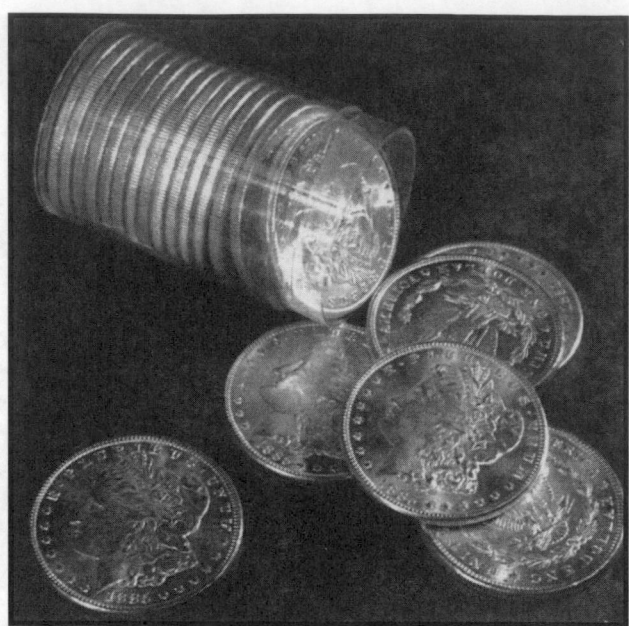

Coin tubes are often used for bulk storage, but there is a proper technique to placing the coins in the tube.

dropping one coin onto another in a tube can damage both coins. The best technique is to make a stack or pile of the coins, then slide the pile carefully into the tube while holding it at an angle.

Hard-plastic holders are the elite items for storing your collection. There are a number of varieties, some of which come in three parts that are screwed together. Some come in two pieces that fit together. Some of these are airtight and watertight. They are more expensive, but they deserve to be used for any really valuable coins in your collection.

Coins processed by the third-party grading services come in hard-plastic holders, most of which are at least semi-airtight. The hard-plastic holders used by the U.S. Mint for proof sets since 1968 are not airtight, so coins should be watched carefully for signs of problems. In recent years these holders have been improved, but you should check your proof sets periodically.

Any stored coins should be checked regularly, at least twice a year. Check coins for signs of spotting or discoloration. Check the storage media for any signs of deterioration, rust, mildew, or other problems.

The older mint sets and proof sets – issued from 1955 to 1964 – come in soft-plastic envelopes that are not intended for long-term storage. Coins in these envelopes should be put in better storage media for the long term. In recent years the Mint has switched to an inert, stiffer plastic for the mint sets. This plastic is safe.

A coin folder is frequently the first piece of equipment the beginning collector buys. It is simply a piece of cardboard with holes to hold the coins. The holder folds up for storage. It is intended for inexpensive circulated coins only.

They give no protection from contamination or fingerprints. Worn coins will often fall out of the holes, which leads some novice collectors to tape the coins in the

Hard-plastic holders are the top of the line in coin storage.

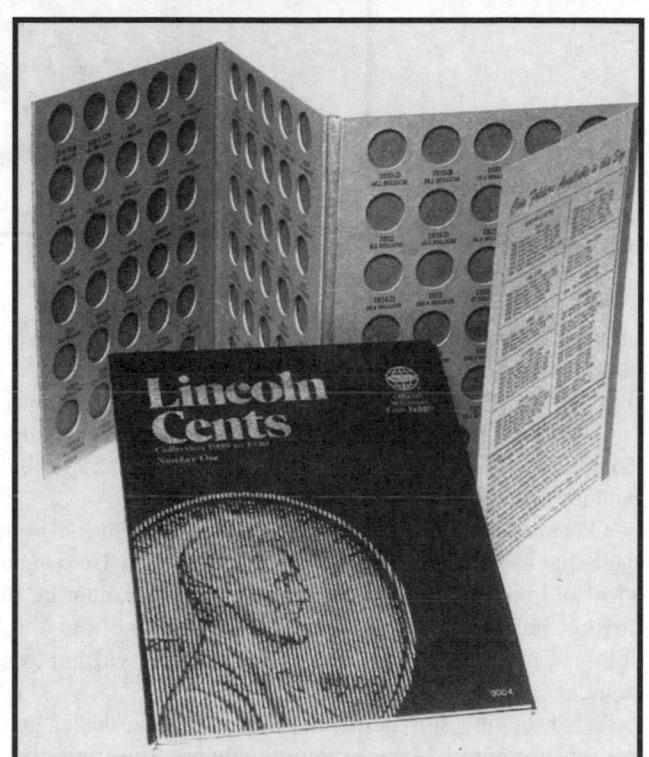

Coin folders are a low-cost and attractive way to store inexpensive circulated coins.

album. This is another example of misuse of a household product; tape can permanently damage a coin's surface.

Pride of ownership and the desire to show off a collection are the moving forces behind the sale of thousands of coin albums. They should also be used for inexpensive circulated coins only, with a couple of exceptions.

Some albums are merely coin boards mounted between covers. Others have pages with sliding plastic strips on both sides of the page so both sides of the coin can be seen.

The open-face albums are subject to fingerprints and contamination. Sneezing on your coins can do as much damage as gouging them with a knife. The slides will rub

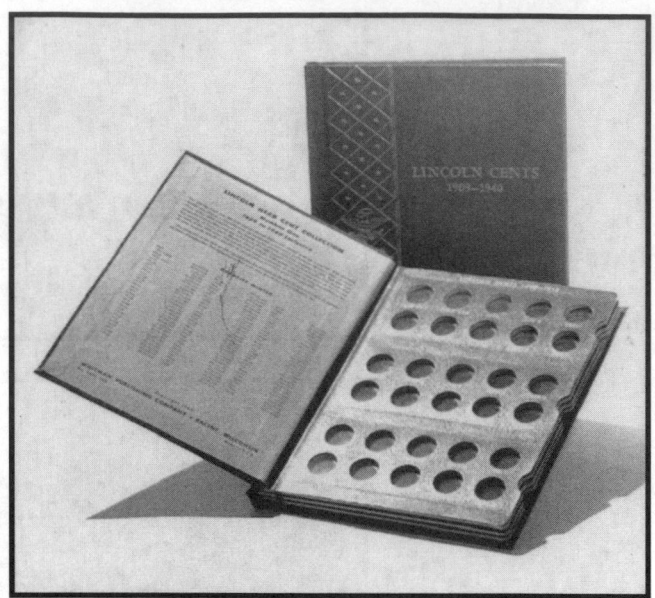

Coin albums also provide attractive storage for inexpensive circulated coins.

on your coins, damaging the high points of the design over time. These two types of albums should never be used for expensive uncirculated or proof coins, although they are fine for circulated coins that you want to display.

Fairly new on the market are albums designed for coins in inert, airtight holders. This allows you to display your coins and still keep them safe from handling and contact with the atmosphere.

One more storage medium that deserves mention is the clear-plastic notebook page that has pockets for 2-by-2 holders or flips. Here again there are good and bad. Most old pocket sheets contain PVC, so they cannot be used to hold coins in non-airtight holders because the gases will migrate into the holders and damage the coins. The newer Mylar pages are brittle but will not generate damaging gases or liquids.

When buying storage media, make sure the dealer guarantees that his products are safe for coins. Many of the old albums, flips and pocket pages are still around, especially at flea markets. If you are in doubt, don't buy.

There are also thin, two-piece, inert plastic holders that many collectors use to protect coins put in flips or 2-by-2 cardboard holders, especially to protect them from moving about against the holder and getting scratched. They are virtually airtight, so they do offer some protection.

Coins need to be protected from burglars. A box under the bed or in the closet offers no protection. If you must keep coins at home, a good, fireproof safe is a must. Otherwise, rent a safe-deposit box at a bank, but read the fine print on your box contract to make sure a coin collection is covered.

Most homeowner's insurance policies will not cover a coin collection or will cover only a fraction of its value. Special riders are expensive, but if you keep most of your coins at the bank, this will cut costs. For details, consult your insurance agent. The American Numismatic Association also offers collection insurance.

Where to store coins is often a problem. The commonest solution is to put them in the attic or basement. Those are the two worst places for your collection. Attics are notoriously hot. Heat can damage almost any storage media, and if there is the slightest hint of PVC, you've got trouble.

Basements are equally bad. They can flood, and humidity is high. Mildew can attack holders and other material stored with your coins.

So what's left? Ideally coins should be treated like a family member. They should be stored in some part of the house where temperature and humidity are relatively constant year round. If it's comfortable for you, it's probably much more comfortable for your coins than the basement or attic.

Protecting coins from humidity is always a good idea, even in areas where it is not a major health problem. For your coins, too much dampness can become a serious problem, often before you realize it. A good solution is to get several good-sized packets of silica gel and store them with your coins in your safe or a container of some kind that will isolate them from the general climate in the home.

To clean or not to clean

Before you store your coins, you should be aware that coins are like dishes: They should never be put away dirty. Ah, but you've probably already heard or read that you should never clean a coin. If you haven't, I'll say it now: Never clean a coin.

OK, so there are exceptions, but be careful of those exceptions and for good reason. Ignoring the exception can be excruciatingly and embarrassingly expensive.

Coins get dirty, just like anything else. The impulse is to shine them up – polish them to a brilliance that will dazzle the viewer. If you've already succumbed to the temptation to clean even a single coin, stand up, kick yourself, then sit back down and read on. The one exception is loose dirt, grease, oil, or something similar, and there are even exceptions to that rule.

Use a neutral solvent to dissolve the grease and oils that usually coat uncirculated coins as they come from the mint. Follow the instructions on the container exactly, and if the directions say to use the product outdoors, they mean it.

For circulated coins, lighter fluid will often dissolve the accumulated "gunk" that sticks to them, but I don't recommend it for uncirculated coins, especially copper alloy coins. Air dry the coins; don't rub or wipe them. Even the softest cloth or paper towel can pick up sharp-edged particles that will ruin a coin's surface. Proof coins are clean when they are packaged, so this should not be necessary and should be done only as a last resort if they have somehow picked up oil in handling.

Using dips, household cleansers, metal polish, and even soap can permanently damage a coin. Avoid acid-based cleaners at all costs. They work by eating away the coin's surface to remove the embedded dirt or discoloration. Cleaning a coin with any of these products will sharply reduce its collectible value. To put it simply, collectors do not want cleaned coins, so they are heavily discounted.

One of the reasons for this is that once a coin has been cleaned, it will discolor much more quickly, requiring fresh cleaning. Each time it is cleaned, the surface is further dulled, reducing the coin's appeal and reducing its value.

Obviously this advice applies especially to uncirculated and proof coins, but it applies to any coin that is or has the potential to become valuable. But if you clean it, its career ends right there.

There are products specifically designed for removing the green PVC slime from coins. They do not contain acid, so they are safe. They will stop but cannot reverse the damage that the PVC has already done to the coin. Read the label, and use exactly as directed.

I frequently am asked about ultrasonic cleaners. They fall under the same heading as the various cleaning products I've described. In other words, the apparatus should not be used for uncirculated, proof, or other valuable coins. If you do use one, do one coin at a time so there is no chance for the vibration to rub two coins together. Change or filter the cleaning solution frequently to keep abrasive particles from coming in contact with the vibrating coin.

Like anything else, cleaning can be carried to an extreme, so I'll give you one horror story and just such a mistake: Years ago I had a collector fly several hundred miles to bring his collection for me to sell for him. When he laid out the coins on the table, I was shocked to discover that the hundreds of coins had all been harshly cleaned.

When I questioned him he calmly recounted that he had decided that the coins needed cleaning, so he dumped them all into a rock tumbler and left it on for several hours. It ruined all his coins, reducing them to face value. With his passion for cleanliness he had destroyed several thousand dollars worth of collectible value, plus air fare, a rental car, and a motel bill.

The key to a long-term collection that might appreciate in value is to learn what not to do to your coins and what care they need to survive years of waiting in the wings. Learning to protect your coins with the best available storage methods and media is a key first step toward enjoying your collection for years to come.

A private firm, Numismatic Conservation Services, LLC, will clean coins that need it for a fee. The firm's Web site address is www.ncscoin.com.

Where to write for more information

American Numismatic Association: 818 N. Cascade Ave., Colorado Springs, CO 80903-3279. Web address is http://www.money.org.

8

Join the club
Coin collecting has lots of organizations

By David C. Harper

More than 160 years ago, Alexis de Tocqueville noted in his *Democracy in America* the penchant of people in the United States to create and voluntarily join public groups for a multitude of purposes. This urge to join carries over into coin collecting.

Whether it be a national organization or local coin club, groups have been organized in the United States, Canada and Mexico to help collectors enhance their hobby knowledge and enjoyment. They serve as clearinghouses for new information, maintain libraries, and bring collectors together in meetings to share their hobby experiences with each other. Clubs are so well defined that collectors can find one to serve any activity level and any degree of personal interaction with other collectors.

At the extreme, you can join a national organization by mail, spend a hobby lifetime utilizing its services, and yet never leave the privacy and comfort of home. At the other end, some areas offer such a multitude of clubs that you can find a meeting to attend on many nights of the week.

There are many ways to find a club. Some hobbyists inquire at the local coin shop to identify the organization nearest them. *Numismatic News* publishes news about clubs. Also, watch your local newspaper for listings of community events.

How does a collector match his needs with an appropriate club? The closest thing to a one-stop shopping place for an answer is the American Numismatic Association.

It is the United States' national coin-collecting organization and was granted a perpetual charter by Congress with a mission of education. It can be reached at 818 N. Cascade Ave., Colorado Springs, CO 80903-3279. Its Web address is www.money.org. It offers a wide array of personal hobby services, and its benefits cross national boundaries. In fact, when it was founded in 1891, it was expected that Canadians and Mexicans would be just as likely to join as U.S. citizens.

The most obvious benefit to an ANA member is a subscription to *The Numismatist*, the association's monthly magazine. In it you find news, historical features, membership information, and advertisements placed by dealers who are ready to fill every collector's want list.

More than 30,000 titles are available in the ANA library, and you don't have to walk into the ANA building to check them out. Any member anywhere can do that by mail. The ANA has called upon renowned numismatic authorities to create a correspondence course, which distills into 29 separate readings information that has taken many people a lifetime to learn. There are ANA educational seminars held in Colorado Springs and other sites across the United States.

The ANA sponsors two conventions annually. The early spring convention is usually held in March at locations across the country, selected and announced well in advance. The summer convention, which is so huge that it's billed as the "World's Fair of Money," is a tradition that dates back almost to the organization's founding.

Members also are offered a variety of optional services, ranging from coin-collection insurance to credit cards and car rental discounts. And if you do go to Colorado Springs, the ANA maintains its Money Museum at its headquarters. In it are some of the rarest and most famous coins in history.

Joining the ANA is easy. The membership fee is $39 the first year and $33 thereafter. Members over 65 years old get a $4 discount, and junior members (those under 18) are charged $15.

Beyond simply belonging to the ANA, though, are the doors that open to members. If you want to find a regional, state or local club, you can get help from the ANA. The important thing to remember is that you set your own level of involvement. If your profession is so hectic that you don't need another meeting to go to, the ANA is the place for you. If your hours are so regular that joining in the fun and camaraderie of a local club is just what you are looking for, the ANA can help you find that, too.

And just because the American Numismatic Association has "American" in its name, it doesn't mean that members are focused only on U.S. coins. Far from it. It is more accurate to say that if a coin was struck at any time anywhere in the world in the last 2,600 years, there are ANA members who collect it.

The ANA, if it connotes any exclusivity at all, is basically a regional designation based on where its members live. The farther one gets from the United States, the longer correspondence takes and the greater the possibility of a language barrier between the ANA staff and a potential member. It is therefore not surprising to find that 29,000 members are predominantly located in the United States.

The Canadian Numismatic Association dates to 1950. It publishes *The Canadian Numismatic Journal*, published 11 times a year, and it also sponsors an annual convention. Membership is considerably smaller than the ANA's, in line with the population difference between the United States and Canada. Membership fee is $33 a year. The mailing address is Executive Secretary, Canadian Numismatic Association, P.O. Box 226, Barrie, Ontario L4M 4T2, Canada.

The Sociedad Numismatica de Mexico A.C. was established in 1952. Basically, it oversees an annual convention in Mexico City. It may be contacted through its U.S. representative, Don Bailey, at PMB #139, 250 "D" South Lyon Ave., Hemet, CA 92543. A related group at the same address is the U.S. Mexican Numismatic Society.

That covers the national hobby umbrella groups. There are many more organizations of a national character that have somewhat narrower poses. Among these is the American Numismatic Society in New York City. It is older than the ANA, having been established in 1858. It also maintains a superb museum of U.S. and world coins, and a world-class library. Emphasis in the ANS is on scholarly research.

Numismatics would be nothing if it were not for its research pioneers. If that is what appeals to you, you can write the ANS at Broadway and 155th St., New York, NY 10032, for information regarding its structure and various classes of membership.

Other national organizations focus on specific collectible areas, such as Seated Liberty coinage or tokens and medals. These are popular and active. Many are member organizations of the ANA and hold meetings in conjunction with the ANA's conventions.

Coin dealers have organizations of their own. The Professional Numismatists Guild Inc. maintains high standards of membership qualification and conduct. Members are a who's who of the commercial sector of the hobby. All are ready to serve you in furthering your collecting goals. For a membership roster, contact Robert Brueggeman, Executive Director, 3950 Concordia Lane, Fallbrook, CA 92028.

This brief review merely puts you on the threshold of the organized numismatic world. It is up to you to open that door or walk away. Over the years, many collectors have found membership to be the most rewarding aspect of the hobby. They have benefited from working with others with a common interest to further their own knowledge and advance their collecting goals in an environment of mutual support and friendship.

9

American Eagle
Bullion investment or collectible?

By Todd Haefer

The United States entered the bullion coin market in 1986 to compete with the South African gold Krugerrand, which had become a favorite with investors of the 1970s looking to diversify their portfolios and then a pariah in the 1980s. Since then, American Eagle gold bullion coins have become the preferred gold investment coin.

Other countries offering their own bullion coin versions include Canada (Maple Leaf), Great Britain (Britannia), Austria (Philharmonic) and China (Panda).

Gold American Eagles come in 1/10- ($5), 1/4- ($10), 1/2- ($25) and 1-ounce ($50) gold weight sizes. There are also the one-ounce $1 silver American Eagle and the platinum 1/10- ($10), 1/4- ($25), 1/2- ($50) and 1-ounce ($100). The silver and gold were introduced in 1986; the platinum in 1997.

The value of American Eagle bullion coins is based, in part, on the fluctuating prices of their metal on the current market, plus an added premium. The $1 silver is 0.9993 fine silver, and contains exactly one troy ounce of silver – 31.103 grams – which is also very close to the total weight of the coin because of the purity content of the silver. The $50 gold has one troy ounce of gold, with a fineness of 0.9167 – less than silver because other metals are needed with the softer-metal gold to make the coin more durable, making the total weight of the coin 33.931 grams. All the gold coins adhere to the 22-karat gold standard. The platinum American Eagles are much more pure at .9995 fine.

The bullion coins come in two main types: brilliant uncirculated and proofs. The proofs are struck for collectors and are more expensive to purchase because their dies are specially polished to produce a mirror-like surface and frosted devices and the blanks are struck from two to 10 times to bring up the fine detail.

But the Eagles straddle two worlds: while they can be an investment floating in the financial waters with the ebb and flow of the precious metals market, they can also be a numismatic collectible.

Like all coins, the American Eagle's future value can rise through the years slowly or quickly, especially in light of a low mintage. For instance, a proof 1989-S silver

The silver American Eagle will have legs as a collectible in the future because of its wildly differing mintages in the years since its 1986 introduction.
Eagle minted in San Francisco, with a mintage of 617,694, is valued at $30, while a 1995-W, with a mintage of only 30,125, is valued at $2,250.

The gold Eagles, since they are expensive to collect and fairly new (less than 20 years old), have not risen in numismatic value, but have risen in price due to the higher price of gold on the market.

But the numismatic value will kick in. In the first year of issue in 1986, there were nearly 1.4 million brilliant uncirculated $50 gold Eagles produced at the Philadelphia Mint. In 1996, only 189,148 uncirculateds were produced. At some point in time, the 1996 Eagles will be worth more numismatically than the 1986s. The same goes for proofs – West Point produced 446,290 $50 coins in 1986, but only 34,389 in 1993.

The general public can purchase proof bullion coins directly from the U.S. Mint, either individually or in sets. The price in June 2003 for the four-piece gold proof bullion set was $1,098 – obviously not a purchase for the casual collector.

The Mint distributes brilliant uncirculated Eagles through a network of wholesalers, brokerage companies, precious metal firms and coin dealers. The coins are sold based on the current market price of platinum, gold, or silver, plus a premium to cover minting and distribution.

The Mint generally sells out all of its bullion coins by the end of the year of issue. This doesn't mean they're hard to find after that – many are still available from coin dealers.

Buying bullion coins from a precious-metal standpoint has the same perils as buying stock or designating percentages of investment types to your 401(k) plan. For instance, an ounce of gold was worth $252.80 on July 20, 1999. If you sold it on May 29, 2003, its $365-an-ounce price would have resulted in a 44-percent return – which makes even the best years of a 401(k) plan pale in comparison. However, if you bought an ounce of gold on Feb. 5, 1996, for its $414.80 price, you would still be waiting to see a return on your investment.

Ditto for silver. If you bought an ounce in September 1993 at its low price of $3.92 an ounce and sold it on Feb. 6, 1998, for its $7.81 an ounce, you would have

The gold Eagle continues Augustus Saint-Gaudens' obverse design (left) of Lady Liberty that the sculptor created in 1907.

realized a 99 percent return on your investment! However, its price in May 1993 is virtually the same as May 2003, so if you bought it then and hung onto it that long, you would have nothing extra to show for it.

Joel Edler, market analyst for Krause Publications' numismatic division, said he looks at silver Eagles as numismatic items more than a bullion investment. "It's such a great design and the mintages are low compared to most other coins from the Mint," he said. "As far as gold proofs, he said, "Proofs are never traded at bullion value – they're already priced so high over the bullion price. They'd be much harder to sell in a down market."

As an example, on May 30, 2003, while gold was selling for $369.60 per ounce, the U.S. Mint was selling 2003 gold Eagle proofs for $630 apiece. Brilliant uncirculated 2003 gold Eagles were selling for around $404. The difference is the lesser mintage (more cost to produce per coin) and the extra work needed to properly prepare and strike a proof coin. Also, proofs are made specifically for collectors, so they are sold at a premium. Uncirculated pieces are made for metal investors.

As far as numismatic value, gold Eagle proofs were something of a dead end in June 2003, with pieces valued at $570, no matter the year or mintage, except for the $520 the 1987 West Point was valued at. Brilliant uncirculated gold Eagles don't show much variation in current prices between the various dates of issue. Future prices will depend on the future price of gold bullion and the future level of collector demand for each date.

Silver Eagles are more interesting. Some dates are valued much more highly by the secondary market in both proof and brilliant uncirculated versions. Collectors are eagerly making distinctions and varying the prices they are willing to pay accordingly.

American Eagle bullion proof coins and sets can be ordered from the U.S. Mint online at www.usmint.gov. Its toll-free phone number for within the 50 U.S. states is (800) 872-6468. Its mailing address is: United States Mint, Customer Care Center, 801 Ninth St. NW, Washington, DC 20220. Brilliant uncirculated bullion coins can be found at most coin dealer shops. They are not sold by the Mint to collectors.

10

More ways to collect
State quarter program brings variety

By Ray Sidman

Now that the U.S. Mint's 10-year 50-state quarter program is passing its midpoint, consider where it has gone in five years. Better yet, take a look at the many options spawned during the program for the millions of collectors that joined the bandwagon attracted by the multitude of commemorative quarters. No matter the collector preference – world coins, philatelics and more – the Mint has accommodated with a cornucopia of products to attract state quarter collectors' tastes.

According to the Mint, more than 130 million U.S. citizens collect the state quarters, a number that rapidly built within the first two years after the 50-state program began. To keep up with such a large number and the accompanying variety of collecting interests found within such a microcosm, the Mint has offered several atypical merchandise options either involving or revolving around the state quarter program.

An earlier quarter-related product from the Mint was the Formation of the Union Set. Released in June 2001, its 50,000 mintage sold out.

Collectors hoping to build up value on their state quarters have perked up in the last couple of years. Mint production of these coins has decreased notably since 2001, making long-term investments a more intriguing prospect. Accompanying this – or perhaps because of it – are the quarter-oriented products the Mint has issued in recent years.

After evolving during its first couple years, the bag and roll sale opening with the release of each quarter now has 100-coin and 1,000-coin bag options, along with the two-roll set that debuted in 2000, making the coins more appealing to those who prefer storing coins in rolls.

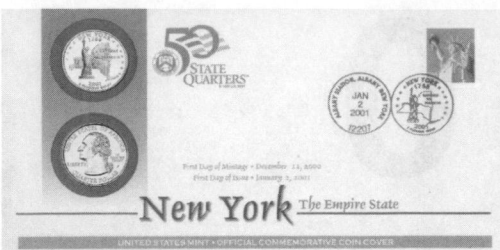

One constant in the state quarter program has been the releases of first-day coin covers, which have been issued within a few weeks after the particular quarter hits circulation. As of summer 2003, only five achieved sellout status.

These optional items have met with mixed success. At one end is the ill-fated Combined Proof Sets issued in May 2002, meant to help rookie collectors that missed earlier proof sets from the state-quarter era. The Combined Proof Set contained three proof sets, one each from 1999, 2000 and 2001. However, after reports surfaced that the sets had decayed in storage, the Mint pulled the product after selling only approximately 15,300 of its planned maximum 150,000 mintage.

A year earlier, the Mint teamed with the National Archives and Records Administration to release the Formation of the Union Set, containing 26 quarters – Philadelphia and Denver mintmarks of each of the original 13 colonies. It included an added bonus: the first Mint product to include a message from the U.S. President, as President George W. Bush discussed the Latin phrase "E Pluribus Unum."

The issue price of $49.95 and mintage of 50,000 worked: the product became popular among collectors and eventually sold out.

One program boasting both sellouts as well as non-sellouts is the first-day coin covers. After each quarter release, the coin cover usually follows within a few weeks. Maxi-

Mintages of state quarters have declined rapidly since 2001. Where will values of these rarer coins be in 5 years? 10 years?

State quarter production figures	
Delaware-P:	373,400,000
Delaware-D:	401,424,000
Pennsylvania-P:	349,000,000
Pennsylvania-D:	358,332,000
New Jersey-P:	363,200,000
New Jersey-D:	299,028,000
Georgia-P:	451,188,000
Georgia-D:	488,744,000
Connecticut-P:	688,744,000
Connecticut-D:	657,880,000
Massachusetts-P:	628,600,000
Massachusetts-D:	535,184,000
Maryland-P:	678,200,000
Maryland-D:	556,532,000
South Carolina-P:	742,576,000
South Carolina-D:	566,208,000
New Hampshire-P:	673,040,000
New Hampshire-D:	495,976,000
Virginia-P:	943,000,000
Virginia-D:	651,616,000
New York-P:	655,400,000
New York-D:	619,640,000
North Carolina-P:	627,600,000
North Carolina-D:	427,876,000
Rhode Island-P:	423,000,000
Rhode Island-D:	447,100,000
Vermont-P:	423,400,000
Vermont-D:	459,404,000
Kentucky-P:	353,000,000
Kentucky-D:	370,564,000
Tennessee-P:	361,600,000
Tennessee-D:	286,468,000
Ohio-P:	217,200,000
Ohio-D:	414,832,000
Louisiana-P:	362,000,000
Louisiana-D:	402,204,000
Indiana-P:	362,600,000
Indiana-D:	327,200,000
Mississippi-P:	290,000,000
Mississippi-D:	289,600,000
Illinois-P:	225,800,000
Illinois-D:	237,400,000
Alabama-P:	225,000,000
Alabama-D:	232,400,000

mum mintages began optimistically, it seems, as the 1999 covers had ceilings of 100,000. Since then, the Mint has assigned a 75,000 limit on all except for New York (2001).

For the most part, the first-day covers have sold at a steady if quiet pace. In early 2002, though, the secondary market heated up amid sellouts and near sellouts among the 1999-2000 covers. Prices skyrocketed for the sold-out ones. As of summer 2003, five have sold out: Delaware (1999), Pennsylvania (1999), New Jersey (1999), Massachusetts (2000) and Maryland (2000). (Note that the first three had a 100,000 mintage.)

On Jan. 1, 2002, the European Union officially launched its new currency, the euro. That year the Mint launched the 50 State Quarters **The Greetings from America series arrived in 2003.**

and Euro Coin Collection. The tri-fold item had a one-euro coin from each euro nation (12 of them at the time) along with one of each of the five state quarters in uncirculated condition. Its maximum mintage of 100,000 had not sold out before this book went to press, though it approached the 65,000 mark.

On a new-product roll, the Mint went into April 2002 touting the Mixed Quarters Bag. Like the Combined Proof Sets (unreleased at that point), the Mint said this item would help collectors that missed the early years of the quarter program to find pieces to complete their collection. The bag contained 100 quarters: 20 dated 1999 and 80 dated 2000 and a guarantee that each 1999 and 2000 state and mintmark would have at least one coin in every bag.

The Mint didn't set a maximum production on the Mixed Quarters Bags. As of mid-2003 it had amassed nearly 39,000 in sales.

More recently, the Mint partnered with the U.S. Postal Service to introduce the Greetings from America series. Its options included a state card set of five and a more elaborate portfolio. The card set had one baseball card-size for every state that year containing a quarter and a Greetings from America postage stamp.

The 2002 quarters (and correlating stamps) came in January 2003, with plans to stagger releases of the previous three years' quarters throughout 2003. The Mint issued the 1999s in May that year. Despite its five-month head start, the 2002s almost immediately fell behind 1999 set sales: in one week the 1999 card set surpassed its 2002 counterpart, and the 1999 portfolio was a small percentage behind the 2002 of the option. It appears this program is picking up speed.

In turn, it seems probable that more state-quarter products will be created for collectors. With more than 130 million of them, the audience is there.

11

Ultra-grade jackpot
Old grades get new uses

By David C. Harper

When the numerical grading system was adapted for use with all U.S. coins and given the official American Numismatic Association seal of approval in 1977, critics noted with alarm that there were 11 grades for uncirculated. This was being introduced to a hobby that essentially used the grades of uncirculated, brilliant uncirculated, gem BU and perhaps choice gem BU. They said that the creation of MS-60 to MS-70 opened the door to a system of dizzying complexity. Defenders of the new system pointed out, quite rightly for the time, that virtually the whole of the market fit into using MS-60, MS-63 and MS-65, while the other grades had the same significance as unused channels from your local cable TV company.

Time has proved both sides partly right, but time also has turned the critics of a generation ago into prophets. There are now 11 fully used grades in the uncirculated range. The grades MS-69 and MS-70 and Proof-69 and Proof-70 have now been staked out with all the vigor of the Oklahoma Land Rush. While the Sooners were looking for rich farm and ranch lands in 1889, the users of what have been called the ultra-grades of -69 and -70 have staked out rich territories of another type in the 21st century coin market

Take an uncirculated Statue of Liberty half dollar that many of us purchased from the U.S. Mint in 1986 to help pay for the restoration of that patriotic landmark in New York harbor. Traded in the original polyester film packet, the coin retails for $6.50 to $8.50 depending on the seller and the season. Put this very same coin in a plastic slab from a major third-party grading service with an MS-69 grade on it and the retail price rockets to $41.95. A 1992 Olympic half dollar that retails for $8 to $10 in the original holder slabbed and graded MS-70 has a retail price of $299.

This phenomenon is occurring in all recent series made especially for collectors. Modern commemoratives are joined by gold, silver and platinum American Eagles and recent proof sets and proof state quarter sets. Anything designated -69 or -70 rockets the price higher.

At first this widespread use of grades that used to stand for nearly perfect (69)

Ultra-grades give common coins higher prices.

and virtually perfect (70) was rationalized by the explanation that coins made especially for collectors should rank very high on the grading scale. They were made that way. However, the ultra-grade phenomenon is extending down into other series where this was not the case. Take a 1930 Lincoln cent. It was struck for circulation at the Philadelphia Mint. This coin has always been considered rather common. In MS-60 it retails for around $4, in MS-63 it is $9 and in MS-65 it is $35. Call it MS-66 red and put it into a slab and its value is up to $79.95. Another Lincoln cent caught the hobby totally by surprise in early 2003 by its incredible leap in price as an ultra-grade. A Deep Cameo Proof-70 1963 Lincoln cent sold for $39,100 in a Heritage auction at the Florida United Numismatists convention in Orlando. This compares to a $1 retail price for a Proof-65. That kind of price differential sent many collectors scrambling to look at the cent in their 1963 proof set.

How the ultra-grade phenomenon will play out is an open question. Certainly more coins will be examined to see if they meet the standards of a -69 or -70. More coins will be submitted to the third-party grading services to get their official endorsements and market forces will then be turned loose on them. In the early stages of anything new, there is a scarcity factor simply because of the novelty. Everyone seems to focus on it at once. As the novelty wears off and a more formal market for coins at the top end of the grading scale develops, prices tend to settle down into longer term value. The $39,100 price for the proof 1963 cent may turn out to be the high water mark for this particular date.

As a collector at this early stage of the development of this market, it will be up to you to check your collection and see if you might have any coins that will measure up to Proof-69, MS-69 or Proof-70 and MS-70 grades. If you think you have one or more, you might have hit the jackpot. But the only way to know for sure is to have your coin or coins examined by a third-party grading service. Collectors can't just walk into a neighborhood coin shop with a proof 1963 cent and walk out with thousands of dollars. Getting a coin graded costs money. What do you do with coins that don't measure up? The grading service might grade your proof 1963 cent a Proof-65 worth just $1. Then you are out the cost of the grading fee. But just like trying to win a jackpot at a casino, you push the button or pull the handle on a slot machine and then wait to see what happens.

12

Hot buys for 2004
They might just be your favorite coins

By David C. Kranz

It is said that in every collector is an investor, and that the profit motive doesn't conflict or impair the fun of numismatics. It probably enhances it. Moreover, the desire to make money helps to make the coin hobby unique for each person and add thrill to the hunt. If the two motives could be isolated, though, there are times when the collector and investor in you could point in quite different directions.

Imagine you have about $600 to spend on coins. You could get several coins in top condition for that amount – a good number of nice Buffalo nickels, probably the entire Roosevelt dime series excepting the 1982 no mintmark piece, two or three type gold dollars or a group of very pretty silver dollars – the options are many. Or, you could put your money on a single date in top condition. What do you choose?

The pure collector aspect would prefer two, four or 40 coins over a single acquisition: more pieces to look over, more to show to fellow collectors, more holes filled. The prime value would be found in the coins themselves and the organization they bring to a set.

Meanwhile, the investor aspect would seek the best bet for the most price appreciation. Market movements affect harder-to-find pieces first and most, so buying a single tough coin should maximize the profit potential – if it's the right coin.

The individual coins in the following list are examples of interesting coins that would have been great investments if you'd bought in December 2002 at prices listed in the Coin Market monthly value guide in *Numismatic News* and sold at Coin Market's June 2003 prices (an admittedly short period, many people hold coins much longer):

1909-S Indian Head cent, from the final year of the Indian Head cent series and a desirable "S" mintmark, with only four other dates in the series valued higher in MS-63 in December 2002. It moved from $535 to $700 as of June 2003, an increase of 31 percent.

1909-S VDB Lincoln cent, one of the best-known collector coins, admittedly outside the price area we're targeting but valuable as an example of a coin in constant demand, moved in MS-60 from $850 to $1,100, up 29 percent – it went up in lower grades, too.

1921-D Mercury dime, second-lowest mintage of this series, priced at $500 in XF-40, moved to $550 in six months, up 10 percent.

1928 Peace dollar, by far the lowest mintage of the series, moved from $630 to $725 in MS-64, up about 15 percent.

2001 Capitol Visitors Center unc. gold $5, with only one other $5 commem ahead of it in price in MS-65, went from $500 to $635, up 27 percent.

An uncirculated roll of 1948 Franklin half dollars, first year of issue for this design, increased from $300 to $385, about 28 percent.

But, at the same time, some of the toughest Walking Liberty half dollars went down, in VF-20 the 1921 from $600 to $575, the 1921-D $700 to $675, the 1921-S $630 to $600. Thousands of other coin values had changed little in the period.

How does the investor select the best date for the money? That's the challenge, and the risk. The truism is that collector coins historically in demand will likely continue to be in demand, and prices for these coins have generally gone up over longer periods. It's a matter of determining what may be undervalued, what will probably see continued or increased consumer interest in the future, when that increase is likely to come and what price levels are appropriate. Experience in the hobby helps to refine a sense for these things.

Luckily, we don't have to be pure investor or pure collector. We blend the two aspects to suit our hobby pursuits, taking risks we find appropriate to our budgets and personalities. Here's what I like for 2004:

Lincoln cents. Demand is traditionally strong, especially for upper grades, and could increase due to the attention the cent will be getting as its centennial in 2009 approaches – design changes to honor the milestone 2007-2009 have been mentioned. Whether you get the 1909-S VDB now or save it for a crowning achievement, there are nearly 100 years of other dates worth pursuing. As of this writing, prices of second-tier keys hadn't moved in a while. You might beat a rush if you get started soon.

Large cents, in the VF-XF-AU grade range. These are the most collectible of the early coins of the United States, and current prices are within reach of most serious collectors. Taken on as a long-term challenge, large cents should prove rewarding even if you don't get them all. I think now is a good time to start.

Roosevelt dimes 1946-1964. No one can say for sure why Roosevelt dimes aren't more popular – is it size, mintages, design? Regardless, these Roosevelts are silver coins of the mid-20th century that I find attractive at today's prices. The lowest-mintage date, 1949-S, is $60 in MS-65 and most others are $10-$25 or less – do you see them going lower? I can't say they will be top rarities, but it's a great set for a beginner willing to see if time might be kind as far as value.

Seated Liberty half dollars. This is a set that will take time but has great variety and to some degree you can choose your price level by condition. Prices haven't moved much for these lately, so perhaps they are at a plateau. Added interest should take them higher.

Define your budget, your timeline and your interests. Watch prices for a while. What do you see for the future? Make sure that, if your selections don't increase in value, you'll still have fun collecting them along the way!

13

Join online community
Internet an active hobby hub

By Ray Sidman

The "dot-com" boom may be over, but that hasn't stopped people from flocking to the World Wide Web. Each day the online community grows: collectors, dealers, buyers and sellers all look to the Internet to find what they want, and in a much faster manner than ever before.

Beyond a place to buy and sell wares, the Internet has become known as the primary source for doing or finding anything fast. Chat with friends across the country, ask questions of dealers or hobbyists and get immediate responses – it's all possible online.

Grading Services
ANACS
www.anacs.com
Currency Grading & Certification
*www.currencygradingcertification.co
  m*
Digital Coin Grading Service
www.digitalcoingrading.com
Global Certification Services
www.globalcertified.com
Independent Coin Grading Company
www.icgcoin.com
Numismatic Guaranty Corporation of
  America
www.ngccoin.com
Numistrust
www.numistrust.com
PCI Coin Grading Services
www.chattanooga.net/pci
Professional Coin Grading Service
www.pcgs.com

Sovereign Entities Grading Service
www.segsgrading.com

Auction Firms
America West Archives
www.americawestarchives.com
American Numismatic Rarities
www.anrcoins.com
Best Collectors
www.bestcollectors.com
BidXS.com
www.bidxs.com
Bowers & Merena Galleries
www.bowersandmerena.com
Centennial Auctions
www.centennialauctions.com
Certified Coin Auction
www.cce-auction.com
CoinsWanted.com
www.coinswanted.com

Collector Online
www.collectoronline.com
Currency Auctions of America
www.currencyauction.com
Gary Duskie Rare Coins
www.coinmall.com/duskie
eBay
www.ebay.com
E-Bid
www.ebid.com.au
Early American History Auctions
www.earlyamerican.com
El Mundo de la Moneda
www.elmundodelamoneda.com
Jean Elsen s.a.
www.elsen.be
eWanted
www.ewanted.com
Ira & Larry Goldberg Coins &
    Collectibles
www.goldbergcoins.com
Heritage Numismatic Auctions
www.heritagecoin.com
Jeffrey Hoare Auctions
www.jeffreyhoare.on.ca
Fred Holabird Americana
www.holabird.org
Jackson's
www.jacksonsauction.com
Lyn Knight Currency Auctions
www.lynknight.com

Lone Star Auctioneers
www.lonestarauctioneers.com
Malter Galleries
www.maltergalleries.com
Greg Manning Auctions
www.gregmanning.com
MastroNet
www.mastronet.com
Ponterio & Associates
www.ponterio.com
Roxbury's Auction House
www.roxburys.com
R.M. Smythe & Company
www.smytheonline.com
Sotheby's
www.sothebys.com
Spink & Son Ltd
www.spink-online.com
Stack's
www.stacks.com
Superior Galleries
www.sgbh.com
Surpluzz.com
www.surpluzz.com
Tangible Asset Galleries
www.tagz.com
Teletrade Auctions
www.teletrade.com
Whyte's
www.whytes.ie

Please Note

Web sites often incorporate capital letters as part or all of their addresses. This is not always necessary. Please note that capital letters found in the addresses shown in this directory are ones necessary in order to arrive at the correct Web site.

Also, the prefix "www." is not always needed, and often it is necessary to leave it off. Please note that when a Web address listed here does not start with "www." that address will only work without this prefix.

Numismatic Dealers

A-Mark Precious Metals
www.amark.com
Abbott's Corporation
www.abbottscorp.com
Alaska Mint
www.akmint.com
Albanese Rare Coins
www.coinace.com
All American Coin Company
www.aacoinco.com
American Gold Exchange
www.amergold.com
American Heritage Mint
www.mtnhighcoin.com
American Rare Coin Supply
www.rarecoinsupply.com
American Rarities
www.americanrarities.com
Amphora Coins
www.amphoracoins.com

Joel Anderson
www.joelscoins.com
Antique Carta
www.antiquecarta.com
Aspen Coins
www.aspencoins.com
Aspen Park Rare Coins
www.aprci.com
ATSnotes.com
www.atsnotes.com
Austin Rare Coins & Bullion
www.austincoins.com
Lois & Don Bailey Numismatic
    Services
www.donbailey-mexico.com
BankNote1 Currency
www.banknote1.com
Ken Barr Numismatics
www.kenbarr.com
Alexander Basok
www.rustypennies.com
Tim Bauer Rare Coins
www.timbauer.com
Harlan J. Berk, Ltd.
www.harlanjberk.com
Allen G. Berman
www.bermania.com
Blanchard and Company
www.blanchardonline.com
Bob's Coins & Collectibles
www.bobscoins.com

Want the eNewsletter?

Subscribe to the FREE
Numismatic eNewsletter.
Enjoy the latest news and
information about the coin and
paper money hobby delivered
electronically.
Simply complete and
submit the form at our Web site
www.collect.com/coinemail to
become a registered user of the
Collect.com site and begin
receiving the biweekly *Numismatic eNewsletter*!

Bob's Coins, Collectibles and More
biblecom.tripod.com/aa-index.html
Bonavita Ltd.
www.eligi.ca/bonavita
Brooklyn Gallery Coins & Stamps
www.brooklyngallery.com
Byers Numismatic Corporation
www.byersnc.com
C & D Gale
www.cdgale.com/default.htm
Calgary Coin & Antique
www.calgarycoin.com
California Numismatic Investments
www.golddealer.com
Camco
www.camcocoin.com
Cameo CC
www.cameocc.com
Canadian Coinoisseur
www.coinoisseur.com
Cape Mint
www.exinet.co.za/pagliari/index.htm
Capital Collectors Plastics
www.capitalplastics.com/nnn
Carat-Coin-Collectibles
www.caratcoin.com
Carolina Gold & Silver
www.carolinacoin.com
CDA Bullion Precious Metals
www.cdabullion.com
Tom Cederlind Numismatics & Antiq-
    uities
www.tomcederlind.com
Centerville Coin & Jewelry
www.centercoin.com
CH Coins
www.chcoins.com
Robert Charles Coin Company
www.robertcharlescoins.com
Cheap Slab Store
www.cheapslabs.com
Chicago Coin Company
www.chicagocoin.com
David F. Cieniewicz
www.banknotestore.com
Civil War Tokens
www.civilwartokens.com
Cline's Rare Coins
www.slqs.com
Coast to Coast Coins
www.coastcoin.com
Cochran's Coins
www.cochran14k.com

The Coin and Currency Institute
www.coin-currency.com
Coincraft
www.coincraft.com
CoinCrazy.com
www.coincrazy.com
Coin Dealer Newsletter
www.greysheet.com
CoinFacts.com
www.coinfacts.com
Coin Gallery Online
www.coin-gallery.com
TheCoinGuy.com
www.thecoinguy.com
CoinIndex.com
www.coinindex.com
Coin Restoration Service
www.crs-stockton.com
CoinScape
www.coinscape.com
Coin Shop
www.coin-shop.com
Coins International
www.coinsinternational.com
Coins, Jewelry & Collectibles
www.monexclub.com
CoinsOfTheUSA.com
www.coinsoftheusa.com
Coin Webstore
www.coinwebstore.com
Coinwire.com
www.coinwire.com
CoinZone.com
www.coinzone.com
Collectors Universe
www.collectors.com
Colonial Acres Coins
www.colonialacres.com
Compu-Quote
www.compu-quote.net
Continental Coin Investors
www.internet4coins.com
Corrosion Free Coin Supply, LLC
www.coinshield.com
Cybercoins
www.cybercoins.net
D & M Coins
www.dmcoins.com
Chuck D'Ambra Coins
www.telesphere.com/ts/coins
Dallas Gold & Silver Exchange
www.dgse.com

David Hall Rare Coins
www.davidhall.com
Denly's of Boston
www.denlys.com
Dibit.com
www.dibit.com
Distinctive Coins
www.distinctivecoins.com
DistinctiveGiftware.com
www.distinctivegiftware.com
Michael Dixon Rare Coins
www.michaeldixonrarecoins.com
Dolphin Coins and Medals Ltd.
www.dolphincoins.com
Downie's Ltd.
www.downies.com
Eagle Coin Supplies
www.eaglecoinholders.com
Eagle Eye Rare Coins
www.indiancent.com
Eagle Numismatics
www.coinmaven.com
Eureka Trading System
www.eurekatrading.com
Educational Coin Company
www.educationalcoin.com
Eligi Consultants
www.eligi.ca
Ellesmere Numismatics
www.ellesmerecoin.com
Elusive Spondulix
www.rarecoin.com
Estate Wholesalers
www.estatewholesaler.com
Steve Estes, P.N.
www.steveestes.com
Euro Collections International
www.eurocollections.com
Steve Eyer
www.eyersworld.com
Florida Coin & Jewelry
www.floridacoin.com
The Franklin Mint
www.franklinmint.com
Gaithersburg Coin Exchange
www.gaithersburgcoin.com
Gallery Mint Museum
www.coin-gallery.com/gmm
Gatewest Coin Ltd.
www.gatewestcoin.com
Ronald J. Gillio
www.gillio.com

Goldline International
www.goldline.com
Gold Rarities Gallery
www.goldrarities.com
Graded Currency
www.gradedcurrency.com
Orville J. Grady
www.gradybooks.com
Great Lakes Coin Company
www.greatlakescoin.com
Hallenbeck Coin Gallery
www.hallenbeck-coins.com
Hancock & Harwell
www.raregold.com
H.E. Harris & Co.
www.heharris.com
Hans W. Hercher Muenzen GmbH
www.herchercoins.com
Wayne Herndon Rare Coins
www.wayneherndon.com
Hobby Coin Exchange
www.hobbycoinexchange.com
Hoffman Mint
www.hoffmanmint.com
Richard Hokanson Rare Coin Invest-
    ments
www.hokanson-coins.com
Randall P. Holder Rare Coins
www.rpholdercoins.bigstep.com
Horwedel's Currency
www.horwedelscurrency.com
House of Coins
www.houseofcoins.com
Hudson Rare Coins
www.hudsonrarecoins.com
International Coins & Currency
www.iccoin.com
J & J Coins
www.jjcoins.com
J & M Coin
www.jandm.com
Eric Jackson
www.ericjackson.com
Jake's Marketplace
www.jakesmp.net
Jamestown Stamp Company
www.jamestownstamp.com
Jefferson Coin & Bullion
www.jeffinc.com
Jencius Coins
www.vaticancoins.com

J.G.M. Numismatics
www.jgmnumismatics.com
Jim's Stamp & Coin Shop
www.thepilot.com/busdir/jimsstamp
Glen Johnson Rare U.S. Currency
www.uspapermoney.com
Kagin's
www.kagins.com
The Kanawha Coin Shop
www.kanawhacoin.com
Kelgory Coin and Currency Supply
www.kelgory.com
Don C. Kelly
www.donckelly.com
Jonathan Kern Company
www.jkerncoins.com
Keshequa Coins
www.keshequacoins.com
Jeff Kierstead Rare Coins
www.jkrarecoin.com
King of Carson City
www.carsoncityking.com
Kitco
www.kitco.com
Knight Coin
www.knightcoin.com
George Frederick Kolbe
www.numislit.com
Bill Kracov
www.choiceworldbanknotes.com
Krause Publications
www.collect.com
www.krause.com
www.coincollecting.net
Tim Kyzivat
www.kyzivatcurrency.com
George H. LaBarre Galleries
www.glabarre.com
Harry Laibstain Rare Coins
www.hlrc.com
David Lawrence Rare Coins
www.davidlawrence.com
Legend Numismatics
www.legendcoin.com
Julian M. Leidman
www.juliancoin.com
Bret Leifer Numismatics
www.coinguy.com
Liberty Coin Service
www.libertycoinservice.com
Liberty Mint Ltd.
www.libertymint.com

Libnick's Coins and Currency
www.webbtexas.com/libnick
Limited Editions
www.limitededitionsinc.org
Littleton Coin Company
www.littletoncoin.com
Lone Star Coins & Collectibles
www.lonestarcoins.com
Lone Star Mint
www.lsmint.com
Louisiana Gold & Gems
www.louisianagold.com
L.S.C.O.A. Barry Ciociola
www.iwannagetitnow.com
Luck 'E' Penny
www.wcmassey.com/lep/index.htm
Marc One Numismatics
www.marconenumismatics.com
Mark Johnson Coins & Supplies
www.mjcoins.com
Mayer Mint GmbH Germany
www.mayermint.com
McKinn's Coins
www.mckinn.com
McQueeney Coins
www.mcqueeneycoins.com
Mexican Coin Company
www.mexicancoincompany.com
Midwest Estate Buyers
www.midwest-estate-buyers.com
Mietens & Partner
www.mietens.de
Miller's Mint Ltd.
www.millersmint.com
Minneapolis Gold, Silver and Numismatic Services
www.coindeals.com
Mintmark Numismatics
www.mintmark.com
Money-Changers
*www.home.earthlink.net/~money-
changer/index.html*
Mountain High Coins & Collectibles
www.mtnhighcoin.com
Mount Vernon Coin Company
www.mtvcoins.com
The Naples Bank Note Company
www.banknotables.com
Colin Narbeth & Son
www.colin-narbeth.com
National Collectors Mint
www.ncmint.com

National Gold Exchange
www.ngegold.com
New World Rarities Ltd.
www.nwrarities.com
North American Certified Trading
www.natcoin.com
Northeast Numismatics
www.northeastcoin.com
www.foreigncoin.com
Nostomania
www.nostomania.com
NumisAd
www.numisgroup.com
Numismatic Assets
www.numismaticassets.com
NumisMedia
www.numismedia.com
Numis-Phil Pte. Ltd.
www.worldcurrency.com
Old Coin Shop
www.oldcoinshop.com
Olde Towne Coin Company
www.oldetownecoin.com
Old Pueblo Coin
www.oldpueblocoin.com
Original Weather Coin Company
www.weathercoin.com
Pacific Atlantic Coin Company
www.pacoin.com
PandaAmerica
www.pandaamerica.com
PaperMoneyFacts.com
www.papermoneyfacts.com
Paradise Coin & Gift
www.paradisecoin.com
Park Avenue Numismatics
www.parkavenumis.com
Jay Parrino's The Mint LLC
www.jp-themint.com
Penny Farmer
www.pennyfarmer.com
Perth Numismatics
www.perthmoney.com
Pinnacle Rarities
www.pinnaclerarities.com
Tony Pisciotta
www.banknotesoftheworld.com
Ken Potter
koinpro.tripod.com
Premier Precious Metals
www.premierpreciousmetals.com

Tim Prusmack
www.money-art.com
Puro's Coins and Jewelry
www.vtcoins.com
R & I Coins
www.ricoins.com
Rare Coin Company of America
www.coinsthatmatter.com
RareCurrency.com
www.rarecurrency.com
Hans & Beate Rauch
www.apcpapercollect.com
Richard J. Reed World Paper Money
www.misterbanknote.com
James J. Reeves
www.jamesjreeves.com
Regency Coins
www.rgncycoin.com
Bob Reis' Anything Anywhere
www.anythinganywhere.com
Joel D. Rettew
www.fastcoin.com
Roy Reynolds Coins
*www.geocities.com/rodeodrive/7533/r
    oyhomepage.html*
River City Coins & Jewelry
www.rivercitycoins.com
Rob's Coins and Currency
www.robscurrency.com
Frank S. Robinson
www.albany.net/~fr/index.html
RR Rare Coins and Currency
www.rrcoins.net
Sahara Coins LLC
www.saharacoins.com
San Joaquin Valley Rare Coins
goldcoin.dds-tech.net
Wayne G. Sayles
www.ancientcoins.ac
Jim Sazama
www.jimsazama.com
Rich Schemmer
www.richerrors.com
Reinhard Schimmer GmbH
www.schimmer.de
Scotsman Coin and Currency
www.scoins.com
Daniel Frank Sedwick
www.sedwickcoins.com
David Seelye
www.thempcman.net
Shawnee Coin Company
www.shawneecoin.com

Showcase Coins
www.showcasecoins.com
Showgard
www.showgard.com
Sigma Ancient Coins
www.sigmacoins.com
Silver State Coin & Bullion
www.silverstatecoin.com
SilverTowne
www.silvertowne.com
Slater Numismatics
www.slatercoins.com
Sam Sloat Coins
sloat.coinnet.com
Southern Coin Investments
www.southerncoin.com
Southern Coins and Precious Metals
www.scpm.com
Spectrum Numismatics
www.spectrumnumismatics.com
Stanton Books & Supplies
www.stantonbooks.com
Steinberg's
www.steinbergs.com
Sunshine Rarities
www.sunshinerarities.com
Anthony J. Swiatek Numismatics
www.anthonyjswiatek.com
Swiss America Trading Corporation
www.swissamerica.com
M. Louis Teller Numismatic Company
www.tellercoins.com
G.R. Tiso Numismatics
www.grtiso.com
Tiitus Syngraphics
www.syngraphics.net/imbl
Token Publishing
www.medal-news.com
Scott Travers Rare Coin Galleries
www.inch.com/~travers/travers3.htm
Trove Software
www.trovesoftware.com
The Tulving Company
www.tulving.com
UBS Gold & Numismatics
*www.ubs.com/e/pb/solutions/numis-
    matics.html*
USA Rare
www.usarare.com
USCents.com
www.uscents.com

U.S. Currency Online
www.uscurrencyonline.com
USMintQuarters.com
www.usmintquarters.com
U.S. State Quarters.com
www.usstatequarters.com
Valley View Coins & Collectibles
www.valleyviewcoins.com
Edward J. Waddell, Ltd.
www.coin.com
Wall Street Rarities
www.wsrarities.com
Washington Mint
www.washingtonmint.com
Washington Square Coin Exchange
www.wscoin.com
Fred Weinberg & Co.
www.fredweinberg.com
West Bay Trading Company
www.westbaytrading.com
Pam West British Bank Notes
www.west-banknotes.co.uk
Scott J. Winslow Associates
www.scottwinslow.com
Douglas Winter Numismatics
www.raregoldcoins.com
Charles Woodruff Rare Coins &
    Currency
www.cwwoodruff.com
The Working Man's Rare Coins
www.www.workingmancoins.com
World Exonumia
www.exonumia.com
WorldWide Coins
www.wwc.coins.ru
WVW Classics
www.wvwclassics.com
William Youngerman
www.williamyoungerman.com
Jeffrey S. Zarit
www.klippes.com

Numismatic Organizations

Albuquerque Coin Club
www.albuquerquecoinclub.org
Alexandria Coin Club
*www.members.cox.net/alexandriaco-
    inclub*
American Israel Numismatic Associa-
    tion
www.amerisrael.com

American Medallic Sculpture Associ-
    ation
www.amsamedals.org
American Numismatic Association
www.money.org
American Numismatic Society
www.amnumsoc.org
American Play Money Society
*www.members.tripod.com/playmoney-
    too/apms/home.html*
American Society of Check Collectors
members.aol.com/asccinfo
Americans for Common Cents
www.pennies.org
APL Coin Club
www.money.org/clubs/apl_index.html
Atlantic Provinces Numismatic Asso-
    ciation
www.nunetcan.net/apna.htm
Baltimore Coin Club
www.money.org/club_bcc.html
Bexley Coin Club
www.bexleycoinclub.org.uk
Big Island Coin Club
www.collectibleshawaii.com
Blue Ridge Numismatic Association
www.brna.org
British Association of Numismatic
    Societies
www.coinclubs.freeserve.co.uk
Calgary Numismatic Society
www.ucalgary.ca/~cns
California State Numismatic Associa-
    tion
www.coinmall.com/CSNA
Canadian Association of Numismatic
    Dealers
www.nunetcan.net/cand.htm
Canadian Association of Token
    Collectors
www.nunetcan.net/catc.htm
Canadian Association of Wooden
    Money Collectors
www.nunetcan.net/cawmc.htm
Canadian Numismatic Association
www.canadian-numismatic.org
Canadian Numismatic Research Soci-
    ety
www.nunetcan.net/cnrs.htm
Canadian Paper Money Society
www.nunetcan.net/cpms.htm

Casino Chips and Gaming Tokens
    Collectors Club
www.ccgtcc.com
Central Florida Coin Club
www.centralfloridacoinclub.com
Central States Numismatic Society
www.centralstates.info
Chicago Coin Club
www.chicagocoinclub.org
Chippewa Valley Coin Club
www.54701.com/clubs/cvcc/index.htm
Civil War Token Society
www.cwtsociety.com
Classical & Medieval Numismatic
    Society
www.nunetcan.net/cmns.htm
Clements High School Coin Club
*www.fortbendisd.com/campuses/chs/A
    ctivityDetail.cfm?activityIn-
    dex=10067*
Coin Master's Online Coin Club
www.coinmasters.org
Columbus Numismatic Society/
    Central Ohio International Numis-
    matic Society
www.cnscoins.com
Combined Organization of Numis-
    matic Error Collectors of America
www.conecaonline.org
CopperCoins.com
www.coppercoins.com
Crescent City Coin Club
www.money.org/clubs/cccc_index.html
Croatian Philatelic Society
www.croatianmall.com/cps/index.htm
CSA Collectors Page
www.csacurrency.com
Denver Coin Club
www.telesphere.com/ts/dcc
Early American Coppers
www.eacs.org
Edmonton Numismatic Society
www.edmontoncoinclub.com
Elgin Coin Club
www.prairienet.com/coins/ecc
The Elongated Collectors
www.tecnews.org
Erie County Coin & Stamp Club
www.coinlink.com/sites/eccsc.html
Florida Token Society
www.mratliff.com/fts/index.htm
Florida United Numismatists
www.funtopics.com

Fort Worth Coin Club
pweb.netcom.com/~ropertex/fwcc.html
Fox Valley Coin Club
www.prairienet.com/coins/fvcc
Fractional Currency Collectors Board
www.fractionalcurrency.org
Full Horn Buffalo Nickel Club
*www.geocities.com/Rodeo-
    Drive/4044/fullhorn.html*
Garden State Numismatic Association
www.money.org/clubs/gsna.html
Glendale Coin Club
www.glencoin.com
Greater Houston Coin Club
www.money.org/sum-ross.html
Greater Jacksonville Coin Club
www.angelfire.com/fl/gjccweb
Hawaii State Numismatic Association
www.hawaiicollectibles.org
Ike Coin Club
ike.coinmonger.com
Illinois Numismatic Association
www.ilnaclub.org
International Association of Profes-
    sional Numismatists
www.iapn.ch/iapn
International Bank Note Society
www.ibns.it
International Bond & Share Society
www.scripophily.org
International Numismatic Commis-
    sion
www.amnumsoc.org/inc
Islamic Coins Group
www.islamiccoinsgroup.50g.com
Jackson Area Coin Clubs
jcoinclub.tripod.com
John Reich Collectors Society
www.jrcs.org
Johnson County Numismatic Society
www.money.org/club_jcns.html
Liberty Seated Collectors Club
www.numismalink.com/lscc.html
Lincoln Coin Club
*www.geocities.com/jb91437/Lincol-
    nCoinClub.html*
Lower Cape Fear Coin Club
www.money.org/clubs/lcfcc.html
Marion Coin Club
*www.members.tripod.com/marionco-
    inclub*

Maryland State Numismatic Association
www.money.org/club_msna.html
Maryland Token and Medal Society
*www.money.org/clubs/mdtams/mdtams
.html*
Metropolitan Coin Club of Atlanta
*www.money.org/clubs/mcca_index.ht
m*
Michigan State Numismatic Society
www.workingnet.com/msns
Model City Coin Club
home.tricon.net/alanphil/mccc.html
Montgomery County Coin Club
www.money.org/club_mccc.html
Mount Vernon Numismatic Society
www.money.org/clubs/mvns_main.htm
National Collectors Association of Die
Doubling
*www.geocities.com/ResearchTrian-
gle/Facility/4968/NCADD.html*
National Token Collectors Association
home.pacbell.net/tokenbob
North Carolina Numismatic Association
www.ncnaonline.org
Numismatic Association of Southern
California
www.nasc.net
Numismatic Bibliomania Society
www.coinbooks.org
Numismatic Literary Guild
www.numismaticliteraryguild.org
Numismatic Network Canada
www.nunetcan.net
Oak Park Coin Club
www.oakparkcoinclub.com
Ontario Numismatic Society
www.nunetcan.net/ona.htm
Oriental Numismatic Society
www.onsnumis.org
Original Hobo Nickel Society
www.hobonickels.org
Oslo Numismatic Society
www.mynter.org/onf
Pacific Coast Numismatic Society
www.pcns.org
Pacific County Friends of Lewis and
Clark
www.lewisandclarkingot.com
Pacific Northwest Numismatic Association
www.pnna.org

Peninsula Coin Club
www.stanford.edu/~clint/pcc
Pennsylvania Association of Numismatists
www.money.org/club_pan.html
Pensacola Numismatic Association
coinclub.freeyellow.com
Pierre Coin and Stamp Club
members.aol.com/byronreed/pcsc.htm
Prince Edward Island Numismatic
Association
www.angelfire.com/art/peina
Professional Numismatists Guild
www.pngdealers.com
Raleigh Coin Club
www.raleighcoinclub.org
Rockford Area Coin Club
www.exonumia.com/racc.htm
Roxbury Coin Club
www.ledgewood.net/rcc
Royal Numismatic Society
www.rns.dircon.co.uk
Royal Numismatic Society of New
Zealand
www.geocities.com/rnsnz
San Jose Coin Club
www.sanjosecoinclub.org
Society for U.S. Commemorative
Coins
www.money.org/clubs/suscc.html
Society of Paper Money Collectors
www.spmc.org
Society of Philatelists and Numismatists
span.atsecure.net
Society of U.S. Pattern Collectors
www.uspatterns.com
Stanislaus County Coin Club
www.stancocoinclub.com
Swedish Numismatic Society
www.users.wineasy.se/snf
Tasmanian Numismatic Society
www.vision.net.au/~pwood/tns.html
Tennessee State Numismatic Society
www.tsns.org
Texas Numismatic Association
www.tna.org
Token and Medal Society
www.money.org/clubs/tams/index.html
U.S. Mexican Numismatic Association
*www.grasshoppernet.com/walrafen/us
mexna.html*

Verdugo Hills Coin Club
*www.coinshows.com/vannuys_vhcc.ht
ml*
Victoria Numismatic Society
www.victoria.tc.ca/Recreation/VNS
Washington Historical Autograph and
Certificate Organization
www.whaco.com
Washington Numismatic Society
*www.money.org/clubs/wns/wns_index.
html*
Waterloo Coin Society
www.angelfire.com/tx/wcshomepage
Willamette Coin Club
www.pdxcoinclub.org
Wilmington Coin Club
www.money.org/clubs/wcc.html
Women In Numismatics
www.money.org/sum-baber.html
Wooden Nickel Collector's Organization
www.wooden-nickel.org
Worldwide Bi-Metallic Collectors
Club
www.wbcc-online.com
Young Numismatists of America
www.ynaclub.org

Miscellaneous Related Sites
American Bankers Association
www.abacoins.com
Art in the Hand Gallery
www.artinthehand.com
Asset Strategies International
www.assetstrategies.com
Bank for International Settlements –
Central Bank Web sites
www.bis.org/cbanks1.htm
The Harry Bass Research Foundation
www.hbrf.org
Bick International
www.bick.net
The British Museum
www.thebritishmuseum.ac.uk
Bureau of Engraving and Printing
www.moneyfactory.com
www.bep.treas.gov
California Gold Marketing Group
www.sscentralamerica.com
Canadian Coin Reference Site
www.canadiancoin.com

Canadian Numismatic Bibliography
Project
www.julaine.ca/canbiblio
Carlisle Development Corporation
www.carlisledevelopment.com
CCE and FACTS
www.certifiedcoinexchange.com
www.cce-auction.com
CNN Financial Network
cnnfn.cnn.com
CoinClubs.com
www.coinclubs.com
Coin Coalition
www.coincoalition.org
CoinGrading.com
www.coingrading.com
CoinLink
www.coinlink.com
Coin Optics
www.coinoptics.com
CoinResource.com
www.coinresource.com
Coinsheet Numismatic Directory
www.coinsheetlinks.com
Coinstar
www.coinstar.com
Coin Today
*www.goldinvestornews.com/cointo-
day.htm*
Collectify
www.collectify.com
Collectorama Show
*www.hometown.aol.com/collectora-
mashow/index.html*
Collectors Software
www.vpackrat.com
Congressional Medal of Honor Society
www.cmohs.org
Enroute.ca
www.enroute.ca
Federal Reserve Bank of Richmond
Money Museum
*www.rich.frb.org/econed/museum/inde
x.html*
Forrest's Token Page
*users.pullman.com/fjstevens/tokens/in
dex.html*
Gallery Mint Museum
*www.coin-gallery.com/gmm/
gmm.htm*
Gold Fields Mineral Service
www.gfms.co.uk

Gold Institute
www.goldinstitute.org
Gold Rush Gallery
www.goldrushgallery.com
Goldsheet Numismatic Web Page
www.goldsheetlinks.com/index.htm
Industry Council for Tangible Assets
www.ictaonline.org
International Collectible Expo
www.collectibleshow.com
Jewish-American Hall of Fame
www.amuseum.org/jahf
Johnson Matthey
www.johnsonmatthey.com
Krause Publications
www.collect.com
www.krause.com
www.coincollecting.net
Londoh.com
www.londoh.com
London Banknote and Monetary
    Research Centre Ltd.
www.lbmrc.co.uk
Long Beach Coin & Collectibles Expo
www.longbeachshow.com
MonsterCoin.com
www.monstercoin.com
Museum of American Financial
    History
www.financialhistory.org
National Numismatic Collection
*www.americanhistory.si.edu/csr/cadn
    nc.htm*
National Trust for Historic Preserva-
    tion
www.nationaltrust.org
Norfed
www.norfed.org
Numismatica
www.limunltd.com/numismatica
Numismaticards
www.cointradingcards.com
Platinum Guild International
www.platinumguild.org
Saint-Gaudens National Historic Site
www.sgnhs.org
Silver Institute
www.silverinstitute.org
Smithsonian Institute
www.si.edu
Southeast Asian Treasury
www.seasiantreasury.com

Stonewalls Civil War Currency
www.home.earthlink.net/~icepick119
Trade Token Tales
*members.fortunecity.com/tokenguy/tok
    entales*
U.S. Treasury
www.ustreas.gov
U.S. Treasury – Office of the Inspec-
    tor General
www.ustreas.gov/oig
U.S. Secret Service
www.treas.gov/usss
Universal Currency Converter
www.xe.net/ucc
University of Notre Dame – Coin and
    Currency Collections
www.coins.nd.edu
Vendio
www.vendio.com
Where's George?
www.wheresgeorge.com
Where's Willy?
www.whereswilly.com
World Gold Council
www.gold.org

World Mint Sites

Austrian Mint
www.austrian-mint.com
    Austria's North American rep.
        www.eurocollections.com
Bermuda Monetary Authority
www.bma.bm
British Royal Mint
www.royalmint.com
Czech Mint
www.bcm.cz
The French Mint
www.monnaiedeparis.com
Israel Government Coins and Medals
    Corp. Ltd.
www.coins.co.il
Mexican Mint
www.cmonedam.com.mx
The Mint Bureau (Japan)
www.mint.go.jp
Mint of Finland
www.mint.fi
Perth Mint
www.perthmint.com.au
Pobjoy Mint Ltd.
www.pobjoy.com

Polish State Mint
www.mennica.com.pl
Royal Australian Mint
www.ramint.gov.au
Royal Canadian Mint
www.mint.ca
www.monnaie.ca
Royal Norwegian Mint
www.dkm.no
San Marino Mint
www.aasfn.sm
Singapore Mint
www.singaporemint.com.sg
South African Mint
www.samint.co.za
Spanish Mint
www.fnmt.es
State Mint of Romania
www.kappa.ro/yoursite/monetaria
Turkish State Mint
www.mint.gov.tr/english.htm
U.S. Mint
www.usmint.gov

U.S. Federal Reserve Banks
Atlanta, Ga.
www.atl.frb.org
Board of Governors of the Federal
    Reserve System
www.federalreserve.gov
Boston, Mass.
www.bos.frb.org
Chicago, Ill.
www.chicagofed.org
Cleveland, Ohio
www.clev.frb.org
Dallas, Texas
www.dallasfed.org
Kansas City, Kan.
www.kc.frb.org
Minneapolis, Minn.
www.minneapolisfed.org
New York, N.Y.
www.ny.frb.org
Philadelphia, Pa.
www.phil.frb.org
Richmond, Va.
www.rich.frb.org
San Francisco, Calif.
www.sf.frb.org
St. Louis, Mo.
www.stls.frb.org

Theft Reporting Sites
CoinFacts.com
www.coinfacts.com/Administrative/sto
    len_coin_reports.htm
World Exonumia
www.exonumia.com/stolen.htm

Euro Sites
Euro Bill Tracker
www.eurobilltracker.com
Euro Issues
home.hetnet.nl/~asliesem
European Union
www.europa.eu.int/euro
Euro-sceptic Web Resource
www.euro-sceptic.org
Microsoft Windows – Euro Support
www.microsoft.com/windows/euro.asp

Newsgroups

For those who wish to communicate with other collectors more directly, there are newsgroups.

    search.mailgate.org/rec/rec.colle cting.coins
    search.mailgate.org/rec/rec.colle cting.paper-money
    groups.google.com

Missing?

If your group or organization's Internet address has never appeared in our Web directory, let us know and we'll put it in a future edition.

Just contact us by writing to *North American Coins & Prices*, Krause Publications, 700 E. State St., Iola, WI 54990 or send e-mail to sidmanr@krause.com.

Glossary of coin terms

Adjustment marks: Marks made by use of a file to correct the weight of over-weight coinage planchets prior to striking. Adjusting the weight of planchets was a common practice at the first U.S. Mint in Philadelphia and was often carried out by women hired to weigh planchets and do any necessary filing of the metal.

Altered coin: A coin that has been changed after it left the mint. Such changes are often to the date or mintmark of a common coin in an attempt to increase its value by passing to an unsuspecting buyer as a rare date or mint.

Alloy: A metal or mixture of metals added to the primary metal in the coinage composition, often as a means of facilitating hardness during striking. For example, most U.S. silver coins contain an alloy of 10 percent copper.

Anneal: To heat in order to soften. In the minting process planchets are annealed prior to striking.

Authentication: The act of determining whether a coin, medal, token or other related item is a genuine product of the issuing authority.

Bag marks: Scrapes and impairments to a coin's surface obtained after minting by contact with other coins. The term originates from the storage of coins in bags, but such marks can occur as coins leave the presses and enter hoppers. A larger coin is more susceptible to marks, which affect its grade and, therefore, its value.

Base metal: A metal with low intrinsic value.

Beading: A form of design around the edge of a coin. Beading once served a functional purpose of deterring clipping or shaving parts of the metal by those looking to make a profit and then return the debased coin to circulation.

Blank: Often used in reference to the coinage planchet or disc of metal from which the actual coin is struck. Planchets or blanks are punched out of a sheet of metal by what is known as a blanking press.

Business strike: A coin produced for circulation.

Beading

Cast copy: A copy of a coin or medal made by a casting process in which molds are used to produce the finished product. Casting imparts a different surface texture to the finished product than striking and often leaves traces of a seam where the molds came together.

Center dot: A raised dot at the center of a coin caused by use of a compass to aid the engraver in the circular positioning of die devices, such as stars, letters, and dates. Center dots are prevalent on early U.S. coinage.

Chop mark

Chop mark: A mark used by Oriental merchants as a means of guaranteeing the silver content of coins paid out. The merchants' chop marks, or stamped insignia, often obliterated the original design of the host coin. U.S. Trade dollars, struck from 1873 through 1878 and intended for use in trade with China, are sometimes found bearing multiple marks.

Clash marks: Marks impressed in the coinage dies when they come together without a planchet between them. Such marks will affect coins struck subsequently by causing portions of the obverse design to appear in raised form on the reverse, and vice versa.

Clipping: The practice of shaving or cutting small pieces of metal from a coin in circulation. Clipping was prevalent in Colonial times as a means of surreptitiously extracting precious metal from a coin before placing it back into circulation. The introduction of beading and a raised border helped to alleviate the problem.

Coin alignment: U.S. coins are normally struck with an alignment by which, when a coin is held by the top and bottom edge and rotated from side-to-side, the reverse will appear upside down.

Collar: A ring-shaped die between which the obverse and reverse coinage dies are held during striking. The collar contains the outward flow during striking and can be used to produce edge reeding.

Commemorative: A coin issued to honor a special event or person. United States commemorative coins have historically been produced for sale to collectors and not placed in circulation, though the 50-states quarters are circulating commemoratives.

Copy: A replica of an original issue. Copies often vary in quality and metallic composition from the original. Since passage of the Hobby Protection Act (Public Law 93-167) of Nov. 29, 1973, it has been illegal to produce or import copies of coins or other numismatic items that are not clearly and permanently marked with the word "Copy."

Counterfeit: A coin or medal or other numismatic item made fraudulently, either for entry into circulation or sale to collectors.

Denticles: The toothlike pattern found around a coin's obverse or reverse border.

Die: A cylindrical piece of metal containing an incuse image that imparts a raised image when stamped into a planchet.

Die crack: A crack that develops in a coinage die after extensive usage, or if the die is defective or is used to strike harder metals. Die cracks, which often run through border lettering, appear as raised lines on the finished coin.

Device: The principal design element.

Double eagle: Name adopted by the Act of March 3, 1849, for the gold coin valued at 20 units or $20.

Rim

Field

Mintmark

Exergue

Obverse

Legend

Reverse

Eagle: Name adopted by the Coinage Act of 1792 for a gold coin valued at 10 units or $10. Also a name used to refer to gold, silver, and platinum coins of the American Eagle bullion coinage program begun in 1986.

Edge: The cylindrical surface of a coin between the two sides. The edge can be plain, reeded, ornamented, or lettered.

Electrotype: A copy of a coin, medal, or token made by electroplating.

Exergue: The lower segment of a coin, below the main design, generally separated by a line and often containing the date, designer initials, and mintmark.

Face value: The nominal legal-tender value assigned to a given coin by the governing authority.

Fasces: A Roman symbol of authority consisting of a bound bundle of rods and an axe.

Field: The flat area of a coin's obverse or reverse, devoid of devices or inscriptions.

Galvano: A reproduction of a proposed design from an artist's original model produced in plaster or other substance and then electroplated with metal. The galvano is then used in a reducing lathe to make a die or hub.

Glory: A heraldic term for stars, rays or other devices placed as if in the sky or luminous.

Grading: The largely subjective practice of providing a numerical or adjectival ranking of the condition of a coin, token, or medal. The grade is often a major determinant of value.

Gresham's law: The name for the observation made by Sir Thomas Gresham, 16th century English financier, that when two coins with the same face value but different intrinsic values are in circulation at the same time, the one with the lesser intrinsic value will remain in circulation while the other is hoarded.

Half eagle: Name adopted by the Coinage Act of 1792 for a gold coin valued at five units or $5.

Hub: A piece of die steel showing the coinage devices in relief. The hub is used to produce a die that, in contrast, has the relief details incuse. The die is then used to produce the final coin, which looks much the same as the hub. Hubs may be reused to make new dies.

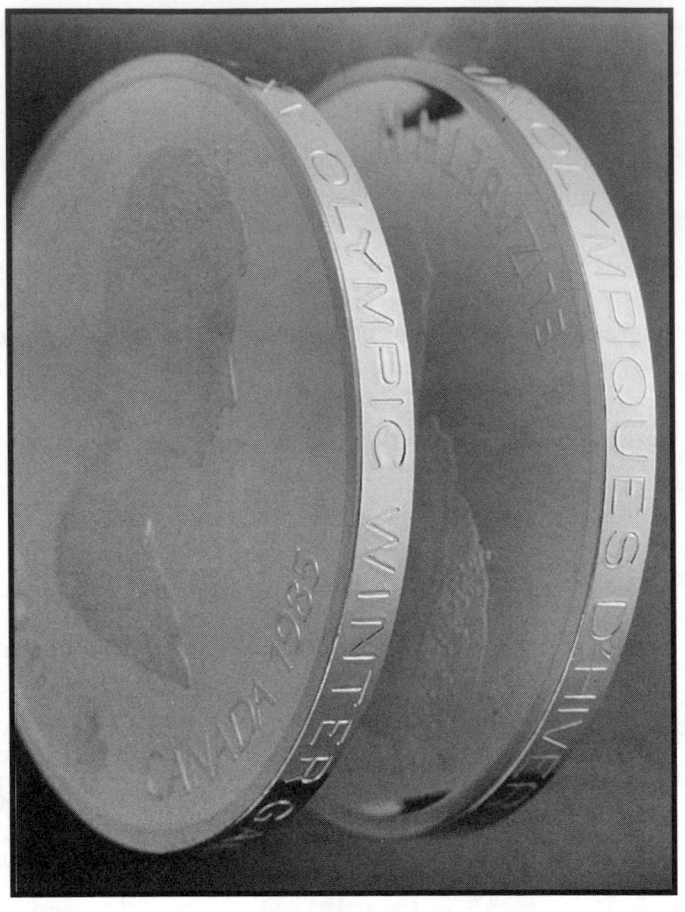

These Canadian Olympic commemoratives have lettered edges.

Legend: A coin's principal lettering, generally shown along its outer perimeter.

Lettered edge: Incuse or raised lettering on a coin's edge.

Matte proof: A proof coin on which the surface is granular or dull. On U.S. coins this type of surface was used on proofs of the early 20th century. The process has since been abandoned.

Magician's coin: A term sometimes used to describe a coin with two heads or two tails. Such a coin is considered impossible in normal production due to physical differences in obverse and reverse die mountings, though as of 2001 two have been certified as genuine by professional coin authenticators. The vast majority are products made outside the Mint as novelty pieces.

Medal: Made to commemorate an event or person. Medals differ from coins in that a medal is not legal tender and, in general, is not produced with the intent of circulating as money.

A medal usually commemorates an event but has no monetary value. It can be issued by a private entity or a government.

Medal alignment: Medals are generally struck with the coinage dies facing the same direction during striking. When held by the top and bottom edge and rotated from side-to-side, a piece struck in this manner will show both the obverse and reverse right side up.

Mintage: The total number of coins struck during a given time frame, generally one year.

Mintmark: A letter or other marking on a coin's surface to identify the mint at which the coin was struck.

Mule: The combination of two coinage dies not intended for use together.

Numismatics: The science, study or collecting of coins, tokens, medals, paper money, and related items.

Obverse: The front or "heads" side of a coin, medal, or token.

Overdate: Variety produced when one or more digits of the date are repunched over an old date on a die at the Mint, generally to save on dies or correct an error. Portions of the old date can still be seen under the new one.

Overmintmark: Variety created at the Mint when a different mintmark is punched over an already existing mintmark, generally done to make a coinage die already punched for one mint usable at another. Portions of the old mintmark can still be seen under the new one.

Overstrike: A coin, token or medal struck over another coin, token, or medal.

Pattern: A trial strike of a proposed coin design, issued by the Mint or authorized agent of a governing authority. Patterns can be in a variety of metals, thicknesses, and sizes.

This U.S. Trade dollar has a reeded edge.

Phrygian cap: A close-fitting, egg-shell-shaped hat placed on the head of a freed slave when Rome was in its ascendancy. Hung from a pole, it was a popular symbol of freedom during the French Revolution and in 18th century United States.

Planchet: A disc of metal or other material on which the image of the dies are impressed, resulting in a finished coin. Also sometimes called a blank.

Proof: A coin struck twice or more from specially polished dies and polished planchets. Modern proofs are prepared with a mirror finish. Early 20th century proofs were prepared with a matte surface.

Prooflike: A prooflike coin exhibits some of the characteristics of a proof despite having been struck by regular production processes. Many Morgan dollars are found with prooflike surfaces. The field will have a mirror background similar to that of a proof, and design details are frosted like some proofs.

Quarter eagle: Name adopted by the Coinage Act of 1792 for a gold coin valued at 2.5 units or $2.50.

Reeding: Serrated (toothlike) ornamentation applied to the coin's edge during striking.

Relief: The portion of a design raised above the surface of a coin, medal, or token.

A token is issued by a private entity and can be redeemed for its face value in trade or service.

Restrike: A coin, medal or token produced from original dies at a later date, often with the purpose of sale to collectors.

Reverse: The backside or "tails" side of a coin, medal or token, opposite from the principal figure of the design or obverse.

Rim: The raised area bordering the edge and surrounding the field.

Series: The complete group of coins of the same denomination and design and representing all issuing mints.

Token: A privately issued piece, generally in metal, with a represented value in trade or offer of service. Tokens are also produced for advertising purposes.

Type coin: A coin from a given series representing the basic design. A type coin is collected as an example of a particular design rather than for its date and mint-mark.

Variety: Any coin noticeably different in dies from another of the same design, date and mint. Overdate and overmintmarks are examples of varieties.

Wire edge: Created when coinage metal flows between the coinage die and collar, producing a thin flange of coin metal at the outside edge or edges of a coin.

Introduction to pricing

The following value guide is divided into six sections:
1. U.S. minting varieties and errors.
2. Colonial coins, issued prior to the establishment of the United States
3. U.S. issues of 1792.
4. U.S. issues of 1793-present.
5. Canadian coins.
6. Mexican coins.

Value listings

Values listed in the following price guide are average retail prices. These are the approximate prices collectors can expect to pay when purchasing coins from dealers. They are not offers to buy or sell. The pricing section should be considered a guide only; actual selling prices will vary.

The values were compiled by Krause Publications' independent staff of market analysts. They derived the values listed by monitoring auction results, business on electronic dealer trading networks, and business at major shows, and in consultation with a panel of dealers. For rare coins, when only a few specimens of a particular date and mintmark are known, a confirmed transaction may occur only once every several years. In those instances, the most recent auction result is listed.

Grading

Values are listed for coins in various states of preservation, or grades. Standards used in determining grades for U.S. coins are those set by the American Numismatic Association. See Chapter 4 for more on grading.

Dates and mintmarks

The dates listed are the individual dates that appear on each coin. The letter that follows the date is the mintmark and indicates where the coin was struck: "C" — Charlotte, N.C. (1838-1861); "CC" — Carson City, Nev. (1870-1893); "D" — Dahlonega, Ga. (1838-1861), and Denver (1906-present); "O" New Orleans (1838-1909); "P" — Philadelphia (1793-present); "S" San Francisco (1854-present); and "W" — West Point, N.Y. (1984-present). Coins without mintmarks were struck at Philadelphia.

A slash mark in a date indicates an overdate. This means a new date was engraved on a die over an old date. For example, if the date is listed as "1899/8," an 1898 die had a 9 engraved over the last 8 in the date. Portions of the old numeral are still visible on the coin.

A slash mark in a mintmark listing indicates an overmintmark (example: "1922-P/D"). The same process as above occurred, but this time a new mintmark was engraved over an old.

See the "U.S. Minting Varieties and Errors" section for more information on overdates and overmintmarks.

Price charts

Pricing data for the selected charts in the U.S. section were taken from the January issues of "Coin Prices" for the years indicated.

Mexican coin mintages

Quantities minted of each date are indicated when that information is available, generally stated in millions and rounded off to the nearest 10,000 pieces. The following mintage conversion formulas are used:

10,000,000 —10.000.
1,000,000 — 1,000.
100,000 — 100.
10,000 — .010.
9,999 — 9,999.
1,000 — 1,000.
842 — 842 pcs. (pieces).
27 — 27 pcs.

Precious-metal content

Throughout this book precious-metal content is indicated in troy ounces. One troy ounce equals 480 grains, or 31.103 grams.

Abbreviations

AGW. Actual gold weight.

APW. Actual platinum weight.

ASW. Actual silver weight.

BV. Bullion value. This indicates the coin's current value is based on the amount of its precious-metal content and the current price for that metal.

Est. Indicates the exact mintage is not known and the figure listed is an estimate.

G. Grams.

Inc. Abv. Indicates the mintage for the date and mintmark listed is included in the previous listing.

KM#. In the Canadian and Mexican price sections, indicates "Krause-Mishler number." This sequential cataloging numbering system originated with the *Standard Catalog of World Coins* by Chester L. Krause and Clifford Mishler, and provides collectors with a means for identifying world issues.

Leg. Legend.

Mkt value. Market value.

MM. Millimeters.

Obv. Obverse.

P/L. Indicates "prooflike," a type of finish used on some Canadian coins.

Rev. Reverse.

Spec. Indicates "specimen," a type of finish used on some Canadian coins.

PRICING SECTION

U.S. Minting Varieties and Errors

Introduction

By Alan Herbert

The P.D.S. cataloging system used here to list minting varieties was originally compiled by Alan Herbert in 1971. PDS stands for the three main divisions of the minting process, "planchet," "die" and "striking." Two more divisions cover collectible modifications after the strike, as well as non-collectible alterations, counterfeits and damaged coins.

This listing includes 445 classes, each a distinct part of the minting process or from a specific non-mint change in the coin. Classes from like causes are grouped together. The PDS system applies to coins of the world, but is based on U.S. coinage with added classes for certain foreign minting practices.

Price ranges are based on a U.S. coin in MS-60 grade (uncirculated.) The ranges may be applied in general to foreign coins of similar size or value although collector values are not usually as high as for U.S. coins. Prices are only a guide as the ultimate price is determined by a willing buyer and seller.

To define minting varieties, "A coin which exhibits a variation of any kind from the normal, as a result of any portion of the minting process, whether at the planchet stage, as a result of a change or modification of the die, or during the striking process. It includes those classes considered to be intentional changes, as well as those caused by normal wear and tear on the dies or other minting equipment and classes deemed to be "errors."

The three causes are represented as follows:
1. (I) = Intentional Changes
2. (W) = Wear and Tear
3. (E) = Errors
Note: A class may show more than one cause and could be listed as (IWE).

Rarity level

The rarity ratings are based on the following scale:
1 - Very Common. Ranges from every coin struck down to 1,000,000.
2 - Common. From 1,000,000 down to 100,000.
3 - Scarce. From 100,000 down to 10,000.

4 - Very Scarce. From 10,000 down to 1,000.
5 - Rare. From 1,000 down to 100.
6 - Very Rare. From 100 down to 10.
7 - Extremely Rare. From 10 down to 1.
Unknown: If there is no confirmed report of a piece fitting a particular class, it is listed as Unknown. Reports of finds by readers would be appreciated in order to update future presentations.

An Unknown does not mean that your piece automatically is very valuable. Even a Rarity 7 piece, extremely rare, even unique, may have a very low collector value because of a lack of demand or interest in that particular class.

Classes, definitions and price ranges are based on material previously offered in Alan Herbert's book, *The Official Price Guide to Minting Varieties and Errors* and in *Coin Prices* Magazine.

Pricing information has also been provided by John A. Wexler and Ken Potter, with special pricing and technical advice from Del Romines.

Also recommended is the *Cherrypicker's Guide to Rare Die Varieties* by Bill Fivaz and J.T. Stanton. Check your favorite coin shop, numismatic library or book seller for availability of the latest edition.

For help with your coin questions, to report significant new finds and for authentication of your minting varieties, include a loose first class stamp and write to Alan Herbert, 700 E. State St., Iola, WI 54990-0001. Don't include any numismatic material until you have received specific mailing instructions from me.

Quick check index

If you have a coin and are not sure where to look for the possible variety:
If your coin shows doubling, first check V-B-I.
Then try II-A, II-B, II-C, II-I (4 & 5), III-J, III-L, or IV-C.
If part of the coin is missing, check III-B, III-C, or III-D.
If there is a raised line of coin metal, check II-D, II-G.
If there is a raised area of coin metal, check II-E, II-F, or III-F.
If the coin is out of round, and too thin, check III-G.
If coin appears to be the wrong metal, check III-A, III-E, III-F-3 and III-G.
If the die appears to have been damaged, check II-E, II-G. (Damage to the coin itself usually is not a minting variety.)
If the coin shows incomplete or missing design, check II-A, II-E, III-B-3, III-B-5 or III-D.
If only part of the planchet was struck, check III-M.
If something was struck into the coin, check III-J and III-K.
If something has happened to the edge of the coin, check II-D-6, II-E-10, III-I, III-M and III-O.
If your coin shows other than the normal design, check II-A or II-C.
If a layer of the coin metal is missing, or a clad layer is missing, check III-B and III-D.
If you have an unstruck blank, or planchet, check I-G.
If your coin may be a restrike, check IV-C.
If your coin has a counterstamp, countermark, additional engraving or apparent official modifications, check IV-B and V-A-8.
Do not depend on the naked eye to examine your coins. Use a magnifying lens whenever possible, as circulation damage, wear and alterations frequently can be mistaken for legitimate minting varieties.

Division I: planchet varieties

The first division of the PDS System includes those minting varieties that occur in the manufacture of the planchet upon which the coins will ultimately be struck and includes classes resulting from faulty metallurgy, mechanical damage, faulty processing, or equipment or human malfunction prior to the actual coin striking.

Planchet alloy mix (I-A)

This section includes those classes pertaining to mixing and processing the various metals which will be used to make a coin alloy.
I-A-1 Improper Alloy Mix (WE), Rarity Level: 3-4, Values: $5 to $10.
I-A-2 Slag Inclusion Planchet (WE), Rarity Level: 5-6, Values: $25 up.

Damaged and defective planchets (I-B)

To be a class in this section the blank, or planchet, must for some reason not meet the normal standards or must have been damaged in processing. The classes cover the areas of defects in the melting, rolling, punching and processing of the planchets up to the point where they are sent to the coin presses to be struck.

I-B-1 Defective Planchet (WE), Rarity Level: 6, Values: $25 up.

I-B-2 Mechanically Damaged Planchet (WE), Rarity Level: –, Values: No Value. (See values for the coin struck on a mechanically damaged planchet.)

I-B-3 Rolled Thin Planchet (WE), Rarity Level: 6 - (Less rare on half cents of 1795, 1797 and restrikes of 1831-52.) Values: $10 up.

I-B-4 Rolled Thick Planchet (WE), Rarity Level: 7 - (Less rare in Colonial copper coins. Notable examples occur on the restrike half cents of 1840-52.) Values: $125 up.

I-B-5 Tapered Planchet (WE), Rarity Level: 7, Values: $25 up.

I-B-6 Partially Unplated Planchet (WE), Rarity Level: 6, Values: $15 up.

I-B-7 Unplated Planchet (WE), Rarity Level: 6-7, Values: $50 up.

I-B-8 Bubbled Plating Planchet (WE), Rarity Level: 1, Values: No Value.

I-B-9 Included Gas Bubble Planchet (WE), Rarity Level: 6-7, Values: $50 up.

I-B-10 Partially Unclad Planchet (WE), Rarity Level: 6, Values: $20 up.

I-B-11 Unclad Planchet (WE), Rarity Level: 6-7, Values: $50 up.

I-B-12 Undersize Planchet (WE), Rarity Level: 7, Values: $250 up.

I-B-13 Oversize Planchet (WE), Rarity Level: 7, Values: $250 up.

I-B-14 Improperly Prepared Proof Planchet (WE), Rarity Level: 7, Values: $100 up.

I-B-15 Improperly Annealed Planchet (WE), Rarity Level: - , Values: No Value.

I-B-16 Faulty Upset Edge Planchet (WE), Rarity Level: 5-6, Values: $10 up.

I-B-17 Rolled-In Metal Planchet (WE), Rarity Level: 6-7, Values: $50 up.

I-B-18 Weld Area Planchet (WE), Rarity Level: Unknown, Values: No Value Established. (See values for the coins struck on weld area planchets.)

I-B-19 Strike Clip Planchet (WE), Rarity Level: 7, Values: $150 up.

I-B-20 Unpunched Center-Hole Planchet (WE), Rarity Level: 5-7, Values: $5 and up.

I-B-21 Incompletely Punched Center-Hole Planchet (WE), Rarity Level: 6-7, Values: $15 up.

I-B-22 Uncentered Center-Hole Planchet (WE), Rarity Level: 6-7, Values: $10 up.

I-B-23 Multiple Punched Center-Hole Planchet (WE), Rarity Level: 7, Values: $35 up.

I-B-24 Unintended Center-Hole Planchet (WE), Rarity Level: Unknown, Values: -.

I-B-25 Wrong Size or Shape Center-Hole Planchet (IWE), Rarity Level: 5-7, Values: $10 up.

Clipped planchets (I-C)

Clipped blanks, or planchets, occur when the strip of coin metal fails to move forward between successive strokes of the gang punch to clear the previously punched holes, in the same manner as a cookie cutter overlapping a previously cut hole in the dough. The size of the clip is a function of the amount of overlap of the next punch.

The overlapping round punches produce a missing arc with curve matching the outside circumference of the blanking punch. Straight clips occur when the punch overlaps the beginning or end of a strip which has had the end sheared or sawed off. Ragged clips occur in the same manner when the ends of the strip have been left as they were rolled out.

The term "clip" as used here should not be confused with the practice of clipping or shaving small pieces of metal from a bullion coin after it is in circulation.

I-C-1 Disc Clip Planchet (WE), Rarity Level: 3-5, Values: $5 up.

I-C-2 Curved Clip Planchet - (To 5%) (WE), Rarity Level: 5-6, Values: $5 up.

I-C-3 Curved Clip Planchet - (6 to 10%) (WE), Rarity Level: 6, Values: $10 up.

I-C-4 Curved Clip Planchet - (11 to 25%) (WE), Rarity Level: 5-6, Values: $15 up.

I-C-5 Curved Clip Planchet - (26 to 60%) (WE), Rarity Level: 6-7, Values: $25 up.

I-C-6 Double Curved Clip Planchet (WE), Rarity Level: 6, Values: $10 up.

I-C-7 Triple Curved Clip Planchet (WE), Rarity Level: 5-6, Values: $25 up.

I-C-8 Multiple Curved Clip Planchet (WE), Rarity Level: 6-7, Values: $35 up.

I-C-9 Overlapping Curved Clipped Planchet (WE), Rarity Level: 6-7, Values: $50 up.

I-C-10 Incompletely Punched Curved Clip Planchet (WE), Rarity Level: 6, Values: $35 up.

I-C-11 Oval Curved Clip Planchet (WE), Rarity Level: 6-7, Values: $50 up.

I-C-12 Crescent Clip Planchet - (61% or more) (WE), Rarity Level: 7, Values: $200 up.

I-C-13 Straight Clip Planchet (WE), Rarity Level: 6, Values: $30 up.

I-C-14 Incompletely Sheared Straight Clip Planchet (WE), Rarity Level: 6, Values: $50 up.

I-C-15 Ragged Clip Planchet (WE), Rarity Level: 6-7, Values: $35 up.

I-C-16 Outside Corner Clip Planchet (E), Rarity Level: -, Values: No Value.

I-C-17 Inside Corner Clip Planchet (E), Rarity Level: -, Values: No Value.

I-C-18 Irregularly Clipped Planchet (E) Rarity Level: -, Values: Value not established.
I-C-19 Incompletely Punched Scalloped or Multi-Sided Planchet (E), Rarity Level: 7, Values: $25 up.

Laminated, split, or broken planchet (I-D)

For a variety of reasons the coin metal may split into thin layers (delaminate) and either split completely off the coin, or be retained. Common causes are included gas or alloy mix problems. Lamination cracks usually enter the surface of the planchet at a very shallow angle or are at right angles to the edge. The resulting layers differ from slag in that they appear as normal metal.

Lamination cracks and missing metal of any size below a split planchet are too common in the 35 percent silver 1942-1945 nickels to be collectible or have any significant value.

I-D-1 Small Lamination Crack Planchet (W), Rarity Level: 4-5, Values: $1 up.
I-D-2 Large Lamination Crack Planchet (W), Rarity Level: 3-4, Values: $5 up.
I-D-3 Split Planchet (W), Rarity Level: 5-6, Values: $15 up.
I-D-4 Hinged Split Planchet (W), Rarity Level: 6-7, Values: $75 up.
I-D-5 Clad Planchet With a Clad Layer Missing (W), Rarity Level: 5-6, Values: $35 up.
I-D-6 Clad Planchet With Both Clad Layers Missing (W), Rarity Level: 6-7, Values: $75 up.
I-D-7 Separated Clad Layer (W), Rarity Level: 5, Values: $25 up.
I-D-8 Broken Planchet (WE), Rarity Level: 3-4, Values: $5 up.

Wrong stock planchet (I-E)

The following classes cover those cases where the wrong coin metal stock was run through the blanking press, making blanks of the correct diameter, but of the wrong thickness, alloy or metal or a combination of the wrong thickness and the wrong metal.

I-E-1 Half Cent Stock Planchet (IE), Rarity Level: Unknown, Values: No Value Established.
I-E-2 Cent Stock Planchet (IE), Rarity Level: Unknown, Values: No Value Established.
I-E-3 Two Cent Stock Planchet (E), Rarity Level: Unknown, Values: No Value Established.
I-E-4 Three Cent Silver Stock Planchet (E), Rarity Level: Unknown, Values: No Value Established.
I-E-5 Three Cent Nickel Stock Planchet (E), Rarity Level: Unknown, Values: No Value Established.
I-E-6 Half Dime Stock Planchet (E), Rarity Level: Unknown, Values: No Value Established.
I-E-7 Dime Stock Planchet (E), Rarity Level: 7, Values: $200 up.
I-E-8 Twenty Cent Stock Planchet (E), Rarity Level: Unknown, Values: No Value Established.
I-E-9 Quarter Stock Planchet (E), Rarity Level: Unknown, Values: No Value Established.
I-E-10 Half Dollar Stock Planchet (E), Rarity Level: Unknown, Values: No Value Established.
I-E-11 Dollar Stock Planchet (E), Rarity Level: 7, Values: $300 up.
I-E-12 Token or Medal Stock Planchet (E), Rarity Level: Unknown, Values: No Value Established.
I-E-13 Wrong Thickness Spoiled Planchet (IWE), Rarity Level: Unknown, Values: No Value Established.
I-E-14 Correct Thickness Spoiled Planchet (IWE), Rarity Level: Unknown, Values: No Value Established.
I-E-15 Cut Down Struck Token Planchet (IWE), Rarity Level: Unknown, Values: No Value Established.
I-E-16 Experimental or Pattern Stock Planchet (IE), Rarity Level: Unknown, Values: No Value Established.
I-E-17 Proof Stock Planchet (IE), Rarity Level: Unknown, Values: No Value Established.
I-E-18 Adjusted Specification Stock Planchet (IE), Rarity Level: 7, Values: $25 up.
I-E-19 Trial Strike Stock Planchet (IE), Rarity Level: Unknown, Values: No Value Established.
I-E-20 U.S. Punched Foreign Stock Planchet (E), Rarity Level: 7, Values: $75 up.
I-E-21 Foreign Punched Foreign Stock Planchet (E), Rarity Level: 7, Values: $75 up.
I-E-22 Non-Standard Coin Alloy Planchet (IE), Rarity Level: 7, Values: Unknown.

Extra metal on a blank, or planchet (I-F)

True extra metal is only added to the blank during the blanking operation. This occurs as metal is scraped off the sides of the blanks as they are driven down through the thimble, or lower die in the blanking press. The metal is eventually picked up by a blank passing through, welded to it by the heat of friction.

A second form of extra metal has been moved to this section, the sintered coating planchet, the metal deposited on the planchet in the form of dust during the annealing operation.

I-F-1 Extra Metal on a Type 1 Blank (W), Rarity Level: 7, Values: $50 up.
I-F-2 Extra Metal on a Type 2 Planchet (W), Rarity Level: 6-7, Values: $75 up.
I-F-3 Sintered Coating Planchet (W), Rarity Level: 7, Values: $75 up.

Normal or abnormal planchets (I-G)

This section consists of the two principal forms – the blank as it comes from the blanking press – and in the form of a planchet after it has passed through the upsetting mill. It also includes a class for purchased planchets and one for planchets produced by the mint.

I-G-1 Type I Blank (IWE), Rarity Level: 3-5, Values: $2 up.
I-G-2 Type II Planchet (IWE), Rarity Level: 3-4, Values: 50 up.
I-G-3 Purchased Planchet (I), Rarity Level: 1, Values: No Value.
I-G-4 Mint Made Planchet (I), Rarity Level: 1, Values: No Value.
I-G-5 Adjustment-Marked Planchet (I), Rarity Level: Unknown, Values: No Value.
I-G-6 Hardness Test-Marked Planchet (I), Rarity Level: -, Values: No Value Established.
Note: There are no classes between I-G-6 and I-G-23
I-G-23 Proof Planchet (IE), Rarity Level: 6-7, Values: $1 up.

Coin metal strip (I-H)

When the coin metal strip passes through the blanking press it goes directly to a chopper. This cuts the remaining web into small pieces to be sent back to the melting furnace. Pieces of the web or the chopped up web may escape into the hands of collectors.

I-H-1 Punched Coin Metal Strip (IWE), Rarity Level: 4-6, Values: $5 up, depending on size, denomination and number of holes showing.
I-H-2 Chopped Coin Metal Strip (IE), Rarity Level: 3-5, Values: $5 up.

The die varieties
Division II

Die varieties may be unique to a given die, but will repeat for the full life of the die unless a further change occurs. Anything that happens to the die will affect the appearance of the struck coin. This includes all the steps of the die making:

● Cutting a die blank from a tool steel bar.
● Making the design.
● Transferring it to a model.
● Transferring it to the master die or hub.
● The hubbing process of making the die.
● Punching in the mintmark.
● Heat treating of the die.

The completed dies are also subject to damage in numerous forms, plus wear and tear during the striking process and repair work done with abrasives. All of these factors can affect how the struck coin looks.

Engraving varieties (II-A)

In all cases in this section where a master die, or master hub is affected by the class, the class will affect all the working hubs and all working dies descending from it.

Identification as being on a master die or hub depends on it being traced to two or more of the working hubs descended from the same master tools.

II-A-1 Overdate (IE), Rarity Level: 1-7, Values: $1 up.
II-A-2 Doubled Date (IE), Rarity Level: 1-7, Values: $1 up.
II-A-3 Small Date (IE), Rarity Level: 2-5, Values: $1 up.
II-A-4 Large Date (IE), Rarity Level: 2-5, Values: $1 up.
II-A-5 Small Over Large Date (IE), Rarity Level: 4-6, Values: $15 up.
II-A-6 Large Over Small Date (IE), Rarity Level: 3-5, Values: $10 up.
II-A-7 Blundered Date (E), Rarity Level: 6-7, Values: $50 up.
II-A-8 Corrected Blundered Date (IE), Rarity Level: 3-5, Values: $5 up.
II-A-9 Wrong Font Date Digit (IE), Rarity Level: 5-6, Values: Minimal.
II-A-10 Worn, Broken or Damaged Punch (IWE), Rarity Level: 5-6, Values: $5 up.
II-A-11 Expedient Punch (IWE), Rarity Level: 5-6, Values: $10 up.
II-A-12 Blundered Digit (E), Rarity Level: 4-5, Values: $50 up.
II-A-13 Corrected Blundered Digit (IE), Rarity Level: 3-6, Values: $10 up.

II-A-14 Doubled Digit (IWE), Rarity Level: 2-6, Values: $2 up.

II-A-15 Wrong Style or Font Letter or Digit (IE), Rarity Level: 3-5, Values: Minimal.

II-A-16 One Style or Font Over Another (IE), Rarity Level: 4-6, Values: $10 up.

II-A-17 Letter Over Digit (E), Rarity Level: 6-7, Values: $25 up.

II-A-18 Digit Over Letter (E), Rarity Level: 6-7, Values: $25 up.

II-A-19 Omitted Letter or Digit (IWE), Rarity Level: 4-6, Values: $5 up.

II-A-20 Blundered Letter (E), Rarity Level: 6-7, Values: $50 up.

II-A-21 Corrected Blundered Letter (IE), Rarity Level: 1-3, Values: $10 up.

II-A-22 Doubled Letter (IWE), Rarity Level: 2-6, Values: $2 up.

II-A-23 Blundered Design Element (IE), Rarity Level: 6-7, Values: $50 up.

II-A-24 Corrected Blundered Design Element (IE), Rarity Level: 3-5, Values: $10 up.

II-A-25 Large Over Small Design Element (IE), Rarity Level: 4-6, Values: $2 up.

II-A-26 Omitted Design Element (IWE), Rarity Level: 5-7, Values: $10 up.

II-A-27 Doubled Design Element (IWE), Rarity Level: 2-6, Values: $2 up.

II-A-28 One Design Element Over Another (IE), Rarity Level: 3-6, Values: $5 up.

II-A-29 Reducing Lathe Doubling (WE), Rarity Level: 6-7, Values: $50 up.

II-A-30 Extra Design Element (IE), Rarity Level: 3-5, Values: $10 up.

II-A-31 Modified Design (IWE), Rarity Level: 1-5, Values: No Value up.

II-A-32 Normal Design (I), Rarity Level: 1, Values: No Extra Value.

II-A-33 Design Mistake (IE), Rarity Level: 2-6, Values: $1 up.

II-A-34 Defective Die Design (IWE), Rarity Level: 1, Values: No Value.

II-A-35 Pattern (I), Rarity Level: 6-7, Values: $100 up.

II-A-36 Trial Design (I), Rarity Level: 5-7, Values: $100 up.

II-A-37 Omitted Designer's Initial (IWE), Rarity Level: 3-7, Values: $1 up.

II-A-38 Layout Mark (IE), Rarity Level: 5-7, Values: Minimal.

II-A-39 Abnormal Reeding (IWE), Rarity Level: 2-5, Values: $1 up.

II-A-40 Modified Die or Hub (IWE), Rarity Level: 1-5, Values: No Value up.

II-A-41 Numbered Die (I), Rarity Level: 3-5, Values: $5 up.

II-A-42 Plugged Die (IW), Rarity Level: 5-6, Values: Minimal.

II-A-43 Cancelled Die (IE), Rarity Level: 3-6, Values: No Value up.

II-A-44 Hardness Test Marked Die (IE), Rarity Level: 7, Values: $100 up.

II-A-45 Coin Simulation (IE), Rarity Level: 6-7, Values: $100 up, but may be illegal to own.

II-A-46 Punching Mistake (IE), Rarity Level: 2-6, Values: $1 up.

II-A-47 Small Over Large Design (IE), Rarity Level: 4-6, Values: $5 up.

II-A-48 Doubled Punch (IE), Rarity Level: 5-7, Values: $5 up.

II-A-49 Mint Display Sample (I) Rarity Level: 7, Values not established.

II-A-50 Center Dot, Stud or Circle (IE) Rarity Level: 7, much more common on early cents, Values not established

Hub doubling varieties (II-B)

Rotated hub doubling

Hub break

This section includes eight classes of hub doubling. Each class is from a different cause, described by the title of the class. At the latest count over 2,500 doubled dies have been reported in the U.S. coinage, the most famous being examples of the 1955, 1969-S and 1972 cent dies.

II-B-I Rotated Hub Doubling (WE), Rarity Level: 3-6, Values: $1 up

II-B-II Distorted Hub Doubling (WE), Rarity Level: 3-6, Values: $1 up.

II-B-III Design Hub Doubling (IWE), Rarity Level: 3-6, Values: $1 up to five figure amounts.

II-B-IV Offset Hub Doubling (WE), Rarity Level: 4-6, Values: $15 up.
II-B-V Pivoted Hub Doubling (WE), Rarity Level: 3-6, Values: $10 up.
II-B-VI Distended Hub Doubling (WE), Rarity Level: 2-5, Values: $1 up.
II-B-VII Modified Hub Doubling (IWE), Rarity Level: 2-5, Values: $1 up.
II-B-VIII Tilted Hub Doubling (WE), Rarity Level: 4-6, Values: $5 up.

Mintmark varieties (II-C)

Double   **Triple**

Mintmarks are punched into U.S. coin dies by hand (Up to 1985 for proof coins, to 1990 for cents and nickels and 1991 for other denominations). Variations resulting from mistakes in the punching are listed in this section. Unless exceptionally mispunched, values are usually estimated at 150 percent of numismatic value. Slightly tilted or displaced mintmarks have no value.

II-C-1 Doubled Mintmark (IE), Rarity Level: 2-6, Values: 50 cents up.
II-C-2 Separated Doubled Mintmark (IE), Rarity Level: 5-6, Values: $15 up.
II-C-3 Over Mintmark (IE), Rarity Level: 3-6, Values: $2 up.
II-C-4 Tripled Mintmark (IE), Rarity Level: 3-5, Values: 50 up.
II-C-5 Quadrupled Mintmark (IE), Rarity Level: 4-6, Values: $1 up.
II-C-6 Small Mintmark (IE), Rarity Level: 2-5, Values: No Extra Value up.
II-C-7 Large Mintmark (IE), Rarity Level: 2-5, Values: No Extra Value up.
II-C-8 Large Over Small Mintmark (IE), Rarity Level: 2-5, Values: $2 up.
II-C-9 Small Over Large Mintmark (IE), Rarity Level: 3-6, Values: $5 up.
II-C-10 Broken Mintmark Punch (W), Rarity Level: 5-6, Values: $5 up.
II-C-11 Omitted Mintmark (IWE), Rarity Level: 4-7, Values: $125 up.
II-C-12 Tilted Mintmark (IE), Rarity Level: 5-7, Values: $5 up.
II-C-13 Blundered Mintmark (E), Rarity Level: 4-6, Values: $5 up.
II-C-14 Corrected Horizontal Mintmark (IE), Rarity Level: 4-6, Values: $5 up.
II-C-15 Corrected Upside Down Mintmark (IE), Rarity Level: 4-6, Values: $5 up.
II-C-16 Displaced Mintmark (IE), Rarity Level: 4-6, Values: $5 to $10.
II-C-17 Modified Mintmark (IWE), Rarity Level: 1-4, Values: No Extra Value up.
II-C-18 Normal Mintmark (I), Rarity Level: 1, Values: No Extra Value.
II-C-19 Doubled Mintmark Punch (I), Rarity Level: 6-7, Values: No Extra Value up.
II-C-20 Upside Down Mintmark (E) Rarity Level 6-7, Values: $5 up.
II-C-21 Horizontal Mintmark (E) Rarity Level 6-7, Values: $5 up.
II-C-22 Wrong Mintmark (E) Rarity Level 6-7, Values $15 up. (Example has a D mintmark in the date, but was used at Philadelphia.)

Die, collar and hub cracks (II-D)

Die cracks

Cracks in the surface of the die allow coin metal to be forced into the crack during the strike, resulting in raised irregular lines of coin metal above the normal surface of the coin. These are one of the commonest forms of die damage and wear, making them easily collectible.

Collar cracks and hub cracks are added to this section because the causes and effects are similar or closely associated.

Die cracks, collar cracks and hub cracks are the result of wear and tear on the tools, with intentional use assumed for all classes.

II-D-1 Die Crack (W), Rarity Level: 1-3, Values: 10 to $1, $25 up on a proof coin with a rarity level of 6-7.

II-D-2 Multiple Die Cracks (W), Rarity Level: 1-3, Values: 25 cents to $2.

II-D-3 Head-To-Rim Die Crack (Lincoln Cent) (W), Rarity Level: 2-6, Values: 25 to $10 for multiple die cracks.

II-D-4 Split Die (W), Rarity Level: 5-6, Values: $10 up.

II-D-5 Rim-To-Rim Die Crack (W), Rarity Level: 2-5, Values: $1 up.

II-D-6 Collar Crack (W), Rarity Level: 4-6, Values: $10 up.

II-D-7 Hub Crack (W), Rarity Level: 3-5, Values: $1-$2.

Small die break II-E-2

Clogged letter II-E-1

Major die break, date missing, II-E-5

Rim die break II-E-4

Die breaks (II-E)

Breaks in the surface of the die allow coin metal to squeeze into the resulting holes, causing raised irregular areas above the normal surface of the coin. Die chips and small die breaks are nearly as common as the die cracks, but major die breaks, which extend in from the edge of the coin, are quite rare on the larger coins.

If the broken piece of the die is retained, the resulting design will be above or below the level of the rest of the surface.

II-E-1 Die Chip (W), Rarity Level: 1-2, Values: 10 to $1.

II-E-2 Small Die Break (W), Rarity Level: 1-3, Values: 10 to $2.

II-E-3 Large Die Break (W), Rarity Level: 3-5, Values: $1 to $50 and up.

II-E-4 Rim Die Break (W), Rarity Level: 2-3, Values: 25 cents to $5.

II-E-5 Major Die Break (WE), Rarity Level: 3-6, Values: $5 to $100 and up.

II-E-6 Retained Broken Die (W), Rarity Level: 3-5, Values: $1 to $10 and up.

II-E-7 Retained Broken Center of the Die (W), Rarity Level: 6-7, Values: $100 up.

II-E-8 Laminated Die (W), Rarity Level: 3-5, Values: 10 cents to $5.

II-E-9 Chipped Chrome Plating (W), Rarity Level: 4-5, Values: $10 to $25 on proofs.

II-E-10 Collar Break (W), Rarity Level: 4-6, Values: $5 to $25 and up.

II-E-11 Broken Letter or Digit on an Edge Die (W), Rarity Level: 4-6, Values: Minimal.

II-E-12 "Bar" Die Break (W), Rarity Level: 3-5, Values: 25 to $20.

II-E-13 Hub Break (W), Rarity Level: 4-6, Values: 50 to $10 and up.

"BIE" varieties (II-F)

A series of small die breaks or die chips in the letters of "LIBERTY" mostly on the wheat-reverse Lincoln cent are actively collected. The name results from the resemblance to an "I" between the "B" and "E" on many of the dies, but they are found between all of the letters in different cases. Well over 1,500 dies are known and cataloged. Numerous more recent examples are known.

II-F-1 ILI Die Variety (W), Rarity Level: 4-5, Values: 25 cents to $10.

II-F-2 LII Die Variety (W), Rarity Level: 3-5, Values: 50 cents to $15.

II-F-3 IIB Die Variety (W), Rarity Level: 3-5, Values: 50 cents to $15.

BIE variety II-F-4

II-F-4 BIE Die Variety (W), Rarity Level: 3-5, Values: $1 to $20.
II-F-5 EIR Die Variety (W), Rarity Level: 3-5, Values: 50 to $15.
II-F-6 RIT Die Variety (W), Rarity Level: 4-5, Values: $2 to $25.
II-F-7 TIY Die Variety (W), Rarity Level: 4-5, Values: $5 to $30.
II-F-8 TYI Die Variety (W), Rarity Level: 4-5, Values: $2 to $25.

Worn and damaged dies, collars and hubs (II-G)

Die clashes and design transfer

Many dies are continued deliberately in service after they have been damaged, dented, clashed or show design transfer, since none of these classes actually affect anything but the appearance of the coin. The root cause is wear, but intent or mistakes may enter the picture.

II-G-1 Dented Die, Collar or Hub (IWE), Rarity Level: 3-5, Values: 25 to $5.
II-G-2 Damaged Die, Collar or Hub (IWE), Rarity Level: 3-5, Values: 25 to $5.
II-G-3 Worn Die, Collar or Hub (IWE), Rarity Level: 2-3, Values: No Extra Value to Minimal Value.
II-G-4 Pitted or Rusted Die, Collar or Hub (IWE), Rarity Level: 3-4, Values:No Extra Value, marker only.
II-G-5 Heavy Die Clash (IWE), Rarity Level: 4-5, Values: $1 to $10 and up.
II-G-6 Heavy Collar Clash (IWE), Rarity Level: 3-4, Values: $1 to $5 and up.
II-G-7 Heavy Design Transfer (IWE), Rarity Level: 3-4, Values: 10 cents to $1.

Die progressions (II-H)

The progression section consists of three classes. These are useful as cataloging tools for many different die varieties, but especially the die cracks and die breaks which may enlarge, lengthen or increase in number.

II-H-1 Progression (W), Rarity Level: 3-5, Values: $1 up.
II-H-2 Die Substitution (IW), Rarity Level: 2-4, Values: No Extra Value to Minimal Value.
II-H-3 Die Repeat (I), Rarity Level: 2-4, Values: No Extra Value to Minimal Value.

Die scratches, polished and abraded dies (II-I)

Die scratches II-I-1

This section consists of those classes having to do with the use of an abrasive in some form to intentionally polish proof dies, or repair the circulating die surface. Several classes which previously were referred to as "polished" now are listed as "abraded."

II-I-1 Die Scratch (IW), Rarity Level: 1-2, Values: No Extra Value to 10 cents to 25 cents, as a marker.
II-I-2 Polished (proof) Die (IW), Rarity Level: 1, Values: No Extra Value.
II-I-3 Abraded (Circulation) Die (IW), Rarity Level: 1-2, Values: No Extra Value up to $10.

II-I-4 Inside Abraded Die Doubling (IW), Rarity Level: 1-3, Values: No Extra Value to $1.
II-I-5 Outside Abraded Die Doubling (IW), Rarity Level: 1-3, Values: No Extra Value to $1.
II-I-6 Lathe Marks (IW), Rarity Level: 5-7, Values: No Extra Value, marker only.

Striking varieties
Division III

Once the dies are made and the planchets have been prepared, they are struck by a pair of dies and become a coin. In this division, we list the misstrikes resulting from human or mechanical malfunction in the striking process. These are one-of-a-kind varieties, but there may be many similar coins that fall in a given class.

Multiples and combinations of classes must be considered on a case by case basis. The first several sections match the planchet sections indicated in the title.

Struck on defective alloy mix planchets (III-A)

This section includes those classes of coins struck on planchets that were made from a defective alloy.
III-A-1 Struck on an Improper Alloy Mix Planchet (IE), Rarity Level: 2-3, Values: 10 cents to $2.
III-A-2 Struck on a Planchet With Slag Inclusions(IE), Rarity Level: 5-6, Values: $10 up.

Struck on damaged, defective or abnormal planchet (III-B)

Struck on a defective planchet III-B-1   **Struck on a tapered planchet III-B-5**

Coins get struck on many strange objects. The more common of course are planchets which have been damaged in some way in the production process. In most of the classes in this section intent is at least presumed, if not specifically listed as a cause.

III-B-1 Struck on a Defective Planchet (IWE), Rarity Level: 4-6, Values: $5 to $10 and up.
III-B-2 Struck on a Mechanically Damaged Planchet (IWE), Rarity Level: 5-6, Values: $10 to $20 and up.
III-B-3 Struck on a Rolled Thin Planchet (IWE), Rarity Level: 5-6, Values: $2 to $5 and up.
III-B-4 Struck on a Rolled Thick Planchet (IWE), Rarity Level: 5-6, Values: $35 to $50 and up.
III-B-5 Struck on a Tapered Planchet (WE), Rarity Level: 4-6, Values: $2 to $5 and up.
III-B-6 Struck on a Partially Unplated Planchet (WE), Rarity Level: 5, Values: $10 up.
III-B-7 Struck on an Unplated Planchet (WE), Rarity Level: 6-7, Values: $100 up.
III-B-8 Struck on a Bubbled Plating Planchet (IWE), Rarity Level: 1, Values: No Value.
III-B-9 Struck on an Included Gas Bubble Planchet (WE), Rarity Level: 5-6, Values: $5 up.
III-B-10 Struck on a Partially Unclad Planchet (WE), Rarity Level: 5-6, Values: $5 up.
III-B-11 Struck on an Unclad Planchet (WE), Rarity Level: 4-5, Values: $5 and up.
III-B-12 Struck on an Undersize Planchet (WE), Rarity Level: 4-6, Values: Minimal.
III-B-13 Struck on an Oversize Planchet (WE), Rarity Level: 6-7, Values: Minimal.
III-B-14 Struck on an Improperly Prepared Proof Planchet (IWE), Rarity Level: 3-5, Values: $5 up.
III-B-15 Struck on an Improperly Annealed Planchet (IWE), Rarity Level: 4-5, Values: $5 up.
III-B-16 Struck on a Faulty Upset Edge Planchet (IWE), Rarity Level: 4-5, Values: $1 to $2.
III-B-17 Struck on a Rolled In Metal Planchet (WE), Rarity Level: 4-6, Values: $2 up.
III-B-18 Struck on a Weld Area Planchet (WE), Rarity Level: 6, Values: $25 to $50.
III-B-19 Struck on a Strike Clip Planchet (W), Rarity Level: 6-7, Values: $25 up.
III-B-20 Struck on an Unpunched Center Hole Planchet (WE), Rarity Level: 4-6, Values: $1 and up.
III-B-21 Struck on an Incompletely Punched Center Hole Planchet (WE), Rarity Level: 6-7, Values: $5 up.

III-B-22 Struck on an Uncentered Center Hole Planchet (WE), Rarity Level: 6-7, Values: $10 up.

III-B-23 Struck on a Multiple Punched Center Hole Planchet (WE), Rarity Level: 7, Values: $25 up.

III-B-24 Struck on an Unintended Center Hole Planchet (WE), Rarity Level: 6-7, Values: $25 and up.

III-B-25 Struck on a Wrong Size or Shape Center Hole Planchet (WE), Rarity Level: 5-7, Values: $5 up.

III-B-26 Struck on Scrap Coin Metal (E), Rarity Level: 4-6, Values: $10 up.

III-B-27 Struck on Junk Non Coin Metal (E), Rarity Level: 4-6, Values: $15 up.

III-B-28 Struck on a False Planchet (E), Rarity Level: 3-5, Values: $35 up.

III-B-29 Struck on Bonded Planchets (E), Rarity Level: 6-7, Values: $50 up.

Struck on a clipped planchet (III-C)

Ragged edge clip III-C-15

Multiple clip III-C-8   **Incomplete curved clip III-C-10**

Coins struck on clipped blanks, or planchets, exhibit the same missing areas as they did before striking, modified by the metal flow from the strike which rounds the edges and tends to move metal into the missing areas. Values for blanks will run higher than planchets with similar clips.

III-C-1 Struck on a Disc Clip Planchet (WE), Rarity Level: 4-5, Values: $1 on regular coins, $20 and up for clad coins.

III-C-2 Struck on a Curved Clip Planchet - to 5% (WE), Rarity Level: 3-5, Values: 50 cents up.

III-C-3 Struck on a Curved Clip Planchet - (6 to 10%) (WE), Rarity Level: 4-5, Values: $1 up.

III-C-4 Struck on a Curved Clip Planchet - (11 to 25%) (WE), Rarity Level: 4-5, Values: $2 up.

III-C-5 Struck on a Curved Clip Planchet - (26 to 60%) (WE), Rarity Level: 4-6, Values: $10 up.

III-C-6 Struck on a Double Curved Clip Planchet (WE), Rarity Level: 3-4, Values: $2 up.

III-C-7 Struck on a Triple Curved Clip Planchet (WE), Rarity Level: 4-5, Values: $5 up.

III-C-8 Struck on a Multiple Curved Clip Planchet (WE), Rarity Level: 4-6, Values: $5 up.

III-C-9 Struck on an Overlapping Curved Clipped Planchet (WE), Rarity Level: 5-6, Values: $15 up.

III-C-10 Struck on an Incomplete Curved Clip Planchet (WE), Rarity Level: 4-5, Values: $10 up.

III-C-11 Struck on an Oval Clip Planchet (WE), Rarity Level: 5-6, Values: $20 up.

III-C-12 Struck on a Crescent Clip Planchet - (61% or more) (WE), Rarity Level: 6-7, Values: $100 up.

III-C-13 Struck on a Straight Clip Planchet (E), Rarity Level: 4-6, Values: $10 up.

III-C-14 Struck on an Incomplete Straight Clip Planchet (WE), Rarity Level: 5-6, Values: $20 up.

III-C-15 Struck on a Ragged Clip Planchet (E), Rarity Level: 4-6, Values: $15 up.

III-C-16 Struck on an Outside Corner Clip Planchet (E), Rarity Level: 7, Values: $100 up.

III-C-17 Struck on an Inside Corner Clip Planchet (E), Rarity Level: Unknown outside mint., Values: -.

III-C-18 Struck on an Irregularly Clipped Planchet (E), Rarity Level: 6-7, Values: $20 up.

III-C-19 Struck on an Incompletely Punched Scalloped or Multi-Sided Planchet (E), Rarity Level: 7, Values: $20 up.

Struck on a laminated, split or broken planchet (III-D)

This section has to do with the splitting, cracking or breaking of a coin parallel to the faces of the coin, or at least very nearly parallel, or breaks at right angles to the faces of the coin.

| Lamination crack III-D-1 | Layer peeled off III-D-2 | Split planchet III-D-3 |

Lamination cracks and missing metal of any size below a split planchet are too common in the 35-percent silver 1942-1945 nickels to be collectible or have any significant value.

III-D-1 Struck on a Small Lamination Crack Planchet (W), Rarity Level: 3-4, Values: 10 up.

III-D-2 Struck on a Large Lamination Crack Planchet (W), Rarity Level: 3-6, Values: $1 up.

III-D-3 Struck on a Split Planchet (W), Rarity Level: 4-6, Values: $5 up.

III-D-4 Struck on a Hinged Split Planchet (W), Rarity Level: 5-6, Values: $35 up.

III-D-5 Struck on a Planchet With a Clad Layer Missing (W), Rarity Level: 4-5, Values: $15 up.

III-D-6 Struck on a Planchet With Both Clad Layers Missing (W), Rarity Level: 4-5, Values: $25 up.

III-D-7 Struck on a Separated Clad Layer or Lamination (W), Rarity Level: 6-7, Values: $75 up.

III-D-8 Struck on a Broken Planchet Before the Strike (W), Rarity Level: 3-5, Values: $10 up.

III-D-9 Broken Coin During or After the Strike (W), Rarity Level: 4-6, Values: $20 up.

III-D-10 Struck Coin Fragment Split or Broken During or After the Strike (W), Rarity Level: 3-5, Values: $5 up.

III-D-11 Reedless Coin Broken During or After the Strike (W), Rarity Level: Unknown, Values: -.

Struck on wrong stock planchets (III-E)

| Quarter on dime stock III-E-7 (lower coin edge) | |

These classes cover those cases where the wrong stock was run through the blanking press, making planchets of the correct diameter, but of the wrong thickness, alloy or metal or a combination of incorrect thickness and metal.

III-E-1 Struck on a Half Cent-Stock Planchet (IE), Rarity Level: Unknown, Values: No Value Established.

III-E-2 Struck on a Cent-Stock Planchet (IE), Rarity Level: Unknown, Values: No Value Established.

III-E-3 Struck on a Two-Cent-Stock Planchet (E), Rarity Level: Unknown, Values: -.

III-E-4 Struck on a Three-Cent-Silver Stock Planchet (E), Rarity Level: Unknown, Values: -.

III-E-5 Struck on a Three-Cent-Nickel Stock Planchet (E), Rarity Level: Unknown, Values: -.

III-E-6 Struck on a Half Dime-Stock Planchet (E), Rarity Level: Unknown, Values: -.

III-E-7 Struck on a Dime-Stock Planchet (E), Rarity Level: 5-6, Values: $20 up.

III-E-8 Struck on a Twenty-Cent-Stock Planchet (E), Rarity Level: Unknown, Values: -.

III-E-9 Struck on a Quarter-Stock Planchet (E), Rarity Level: 6, Values: $50 up.

III-E-10 Struck on a Half Dollar-Stock Planchet (E), Rarity Level: 6-7, Values: $100 up.

III-E-11 Struck on a Dollar-Stock Planchet (E), Rarity Level: 6-7, Values: $300 up.

III-E-12 Struck on a Token/Medal-Stock Planchet (E), Rarity Level: 7, Values: No Value Established.

III-E-13 Struck on a Wrong Thickness Spoiled Planchet (IWE), Rarity Level: 7, Values: $50 up.

III-E-14 Struck on a Correct Thickness Spoiled Planchet (IWE), Rarity Level: Unknown, Values: No Value Established.

III-E-15 Struck on a Cut Down Struck Token (IWE), Rarity Level: 6-7, Values: $50 up.

III-E-16 Struck on an Experimental or Pattern-Stock Planchet (IE), Rarity Level: 7, Values: $50 up.

III-E-17 Struck on a Proof-Stock Planchet (IE), Rarity Level: 7, Values: $100 up.

III-E-18 Struck on an Adjusted Specification-Stock Planchet (IE), Rarity Level: 3-7, Values: No Value to $5 and up.

III-E-19 Struck on a Trial Strike-Stock Planchet (IE), Rarity Level: Unknown, Values: No Value Established.

III-E-20 U.S. Coin Struck on a Foreign-Stock Planchet. (E), Rarity Level: 5, Values: $35 up.

III-E-21 Foreign Coin Struck on a Foreign-Stock Planchet (E), Rarity Level: 5-6, Values: $25 up.

III-E-22 Struck on a Non-Standard Coin Alloy (IE), Rarity Level: 4-7, Values: $20 up.

Extra metal (III-F)

Extra metal on a struck coin (III-F-2)

Sintered coating III-F-3

The term "extra metal" for the purpose of this section includes both extra metal added to the blank during the blanking operation and metal powder added to the planchet during the annealing operation.

III-F-1 Struck on a Type 1 Blank With Extra Metal (W), Rarity Level: Unknown, Values: -.

III-F-2 Struck on a Type 2 Planchet With Extra Metal (W), Rarity Level: 4-5, Values: $10 up.

III-F-3 Struck on a Sintered Coating Planchet (W), Rarity Level: 6-7, Values: $35 up.

Struck on normal or abnormal blanks, or planchets (III-G)

Cent on dime planchet III-G-10

Half on dime planchet III-G-10

Half on quarter planchet III-G-11

This section includes coins struck on either a blank, as it comes from the blanking press, or as a planchet that has passed through the upsetting mill. Added to this section are those planchets which are normal until they are struck by the wrong dies. These differ from the wrong stock planchets because the wrong stock planchets are already a variety before they are struck.

III-G-1 Struck on a Type 1 Blank (IWE), Rarity Level: 4-6, Values: $10 up.

III-G-2 Struck on a Type 2 Planchet (I), Rarity Level: 1, Values: No Extra Value.

III-G-3 Struck on a Purchased Planchet (I), Rarity Level: 1, Values: No Extra Value.

III-G-4 Struck on a Mint-Made Planchet (I), Rarity Level: 1, Values: No Extra Value.

III-G-5 Struck on an Adjustment-Marked Planchet (I), Rarity Level: 4-7, Values: Minimal, and may reduce value of coin in some cases.

III-G-6 Struck on a Hardness Test-Marked Planchet (I), Rarity Level: 6-7, Values: $10 up.

III-G-7 Wrong Planchet or Metal on a Half Cent Planchet (IE), Rarity Level: 5-7, Values: $100 up.

III-G-8 Wrong Planchet or Metal on a Cent Planchet (IE), Rarity Level: 3-6, Values: $25 up.

III-G-9 Wrong Planchet or Metal on a Nickel Planchet (E), Rarity Level: 4-6, Values: $35 up

III-G-10 Wrong Planchet or Metal on a Dime Planchet (E), Rarity Level: 4-6, Values: $50 up.

III-G-11 Wrong Planchet or Metal on a Quarter Planchet (E), Rarity Level: 4-6. Values: $100 up.

III-G-12 Wrong Planchet or Metal on a Half Dollar Planchet (E), Rarity Level: 6-7, Values: $500 up.

III-G-13 Wrong Planchet or Metal on a Dollar Planchet (E), Rarity Level: 7, Values: $500 up.

III-G-14 Wrong Planchet or Metal on a Gold Planchet (E), Rarity Level: 7, Values: $1000 up.

III-G-15 Struck on a Wrong Series Planchet (IE), Rarity Level: 6-7, Values: $1500 up.

III-G-16 U.S. Coin Struck on a Foreign Planchet (E), Rarity Level: 5-7, Values: $35 up.

III-G-17 Foreign Coin Struck on a U.S. Planchet (E), Rarity Level: 6-7, Values: $50 up.

III-G-18 Foreign Coin Struck on a Wrong Foreign Planchet (E), Rarity Level: 6-7, Values: $50 up.

III-G-19 Struck on a Medal Planchet (E), Rarity Level: 6-7, Values: $100 up.

III-G-20 Medal Struck on a Coin Planchet (IE), Rarity Level: 3-5, Values: $10 up.

III-G-21 Struck on an Official Sample Planchet (IE), Rarity Level: Unknown, Values: No Value Established.

III-G-22 Struck Intentionally on a Wrong Planchet (I), Rarity Level: 6-7, Values: Mainly struck as Presentation Pieces, full numismatic value.

III-G-23 Non-Proof Struck on a Proof Planchet (IE), Rarity Level: 6-7, Values: $500 up.

Struck on coin metal strip (III-H)

Pieces of the coin metal strip do manage at times to escape into the coin press.

III-H-1 (See I-H-1 Punched Coin Metal Strip), Rarity Level: Impossible, Values: -.

III-H-2 Struck on Chopped Coin Metal Strip (E), Rarity Level: 6-7, Values: $25 up.

Die adjustment strikes (III-I)

As the dies are set up and adjusted in the coin press, variations in the strike occur until the dies are properly set. Test strikes are normally scrapped, but on occasion reach circulation.

III-I-1 Die Adjustment Strike (IE), Rarity Level: 5-6, Values: $35 up.

III-I-2 Edge Strike (E), Rarity Level: 5-6, Values: $10 to $20 and up.

III-I-3 Weak Strike (W), Rarity Level: 1, Values: No Extra Value.

III-I-4 Strong Strike (IWE), Rarity Level: 1, Values: No value except for the premium that might be paid for a well struck coin.

III-I-5 Jam Strike (IE), Rarity Level: 7, Values: $50 up.

III-I-6 Trial Piece Strike (I), Rarity Level: 6-7, Values: $100 up.

III-I-7 Edge-Die Adjustment Strike (I), Rarity Level: 5-7, Values: $5 up.

III-I-8 Uniface Strike (I), Rarity Level 7, Values: $50 up.

Indented, brockage and counter-brockage strikes (III-J)

Indented strike III-J-1   **Counter-brockage strike III-J-11**   **Capped die strike III-J-15**

Indented and uniface strikes involve an extra unstruck planchet between one of the dies and the planchet being struck. Brockage strikes involve a struck coin between one of the dies and the planchet and a counter-brockage requires a brockage coin between one of the dies and the planchet.

A cap, or capped die strike results when a coin sticks to the die and is squeezed around it in the shape of a bottle cap.

III-J-1 Indented Strike (W), Rarity Level: 3-6, Values: $5 up.

III-J-2 Uniface Strike (W), Rarity Level: 3-5, Values: $15 up.

III-J-3 Indented Strike By a Smaller Planchet (WE), Rarity Level: 5-7, Values: $100 up.

III-J-4 Indented Second Strike (W), Rarity Level: 3-5, Values: $10 up, about the same as a regular double strike of comparable size.

III-J-5 Partial Brockage Strike (W), Rarity Level: 3-6, Values: $15 up.

III-J-6 Full Brockage Strike (W), Rarity Level: 3-6, Values: $5 up.

III-J-7 Brockage Strike of a Smaller Coin (WE), Rarity Level: 6-7, Values: $200 up.

III-J-8 Brockage Strike of a Struck Coin Fragment (WE), Rarity Level: 4-6, Values: $5 up.

III-J-9 Brockage Second Strike (WE), Rarity Level: 3-5, Values: $5 up.

III-J-10 Partial Counter-Brockage Strike (WE), Rarity Level: 3-5, Values: $10 up.

III-J-11 Full Counter-Brockage Strike (WE), Rarity Level: 5-7, Values: $100 up.

III-J-12 Counter-Brockage Second Strike (WE), Rarity Level: 4-6, Values: $10 up.
III-J-13 Full Brockage-Counter-Brockage Strike (WE), Rarity Level: 6-7, Values: $150 up.
III-J-14 Multiple Brockage or Counter-Brockage Strike (WE), Rarity Level: 5-7, Values: $100 up.
III-J-15 Capped Die Strike (WE), Rarity Level: 6-7, Values: $500 up.
III-J-16 Reversed Capped Die Strike (WE), Rarity Level: 7, Values: $1,000 up.

Struck through abnormal objects (III-K)

Struck through cloth III-K-1   **Struck through a**   **Struck through a**
                                    filled die III-K-4   **dropped filling III-K-5**

This section covers most of the objects or materials which might come between the planchet and the die and be struck into the surface of the coin. Unless noted, the materials - even the soft ones - are driven into the surface of the coin.

III-K-1 Struck Through Cloth (IWE), Rarity Level: 3-6, Values: $35 up.
III-K-2 Struck Through Wire (IWE), Rarity Level: 3-6, Values: $5 up.
III-K-3 Struck Through Thread (IWE), Rarity Level: 3-6, Values: $5 up.
III-K-4 Struck Through Dirt-and-Grease-Filled Die (IWE), Rarity Level: 1-4, Values: 10 cents to 25 cents up, but no value on a worn or circulated coin.
III-K-5 Struck Through a Dropped Filling (IWE), Rarity Level: 5-6, Values: $10 up.
III-K-6 Struck Through Wrong Metal Fragments (IWE), Rarity Level: 4-6, Values: $1 up.
III-K-7 Struck Through an Unstruck Planchet Fragment (IWE), Rarity Level: 3-5, Values: $1 up.
III-K-8 Struck Through a Rim Burr (IWE), Rarity Level: 3-5, Values: $1 to $2 and up.
III-K-9 Struck Through plit-Off Reeding (IWE), Rarity Level: 5-6, Values: $25 up.
III-K-10 Struck Through a Feed Finger (IWE), Rarity Level: 5-7, Values: $25 to $50 and up.
III-K-11 Struck Through Miscellaneous Objects (IWE), Rarity Level: 4-6, Values: $1 up.
III-K-12 Struck Through Progression (IWE), Rarity Level: 4-6, Values: $1 up.

Note: Some 1987 through 1994 quarters are found without mintmarks, classed as III-K-4, a Filled Die. Values depend on market conditions. Filled dies have value ONLY on current, uncirculated grade coins.

Double strikes (III-L)

Only coins which receive two or more strikes by the die pair fall in this section and are identified by the fact that both sides of the coin are affected. Unless some object interferes, an equal area of both sides of the coin will be equally doubled.

The exception is the second strike with a loose die, which will double only one side of a coin, but is a rare form usually occurring only on proofs. A similar effect is flat field doubling from die chatter.

III-L-1 Close Centered Double Strike (WE), Rarity Level: 4-6, Values: $15 up.
III-L-2 Rotated Second Strike Over a Centered First Strike (WE), Rarity Level: 4-6, Values: $15 up.
III-L-3 Off-Center Second Strike Over a Centered First Strike (WE), Rarity Level: 4-6, Values: $15 up.
III-L-4 Off-Center Second Strike Over an Off-Center First Strike (WE), Rarity Level: 4-6, Values: $10 up.
III-L-5 Off-Center Second Strike Over a Broadstrike (WE), Rarity Level: 5-6, Values: $20 up.
III-L-6 Centered Second Strike Over an Off-Center First Strike (WE), Rarity Level: 5-6, Values: $50 up.
III-L-7 Obverse Struck Over Reverse (WE), Rarity Level: 5-6, Values: $25 up.
III-L-8 Nonoverlapping Double Strike (WE), Rarity Level: 5-6 Values: $20 up.
III-L-9 Struck Over a Different Denomination or Series (WE), Rarity Level: 6, Values: $300 and up.
III-L-10 Chain Strike (WE), Rarity Level: 6, Values: $300 up for the pair of coins that were struck together.

Off-center second strike over centered first strike III-L-3

Non-overlapping double strike III-L-8

Multiple strike III-L-16

Chain strike III-L-10

III-L-11 Second-Strike Doubling From a Loose Die (W), Rarity Level: 6-7, Values: $200 up.

III-L-12 Second-Strike Doubling From a Loose Screw Press Die (W), Rarity Level: 5-6, Values: $100 up.

III-L-13 Second Strike on an Edge Strike (WE), Rarity Level: 5-6, Values: $20 up.

III-L-14 Folded Planchet Strike (WE), Rarity Level: 5-7, Values: $100 up.

III-L-15 Triple Strike (WE), Rarity Level: 6-7, Values: $100 up.

III-L-16 Multiple Strike (WE), Rarity Level: 6-7, Values: $200 up.

III-L-17 U.S. Coin Struck Over a Struck Foreign Coin (WE), Rarity Level: 6-7, Values: $300 up.

III-L-18 Foreign Coin Struck Over a Struck U.S. Coin (WE), Rarity Level: 6-7, Values: $400 up.

III-L-19 Foreign Coin Struck Over a Struck Foreign Coin (WE), Rarity Level: 7, Values: $500 up.

III-L-20 Double Strike on Scrap or Junk (E), Rarity Level: 6, Values: $50 up.

III-L-21 Struck on a Struck Token or Medal (E), Rarity Level: 5-6, Values: $100 up.

III-L-22 Double-Struck Edge Motto or Design (E), Rarity Level: 6-7, Values: $200 up.

III-L-23 One Edge Motto or Design Struck Over Another (E), Rarity Level: 7, Values: $300 up.

III-L-24 Flat Field Doubling (W), Rarity Level: 2-3, Values: $1 to $5.

III-L-25 Territorial Struck over Struck U.S. Coin: (I) Rarity Level: 6-7, Values: $200 up.

III-L-26 Pattern Struck over Struck U.S. Coin: (I) Rarity Level: 6-7, Values: $200 up.

III-L-27 Pattern Struck over Struck Pattern:(I) Rarity Level 6-7, Values: $200 up.

III-L-28 Pattern Struck Over Foreign Coin:(I) Rarity Level 6-7, Values - $200 up.

Collar striking varieties (III-M)

The collar is often referred to as the "Third Die," and is involved in a number of forms of misstrikes. The collar normally rises around the planchet, preventing it from squeezing sideways between the dies and at the same time forming the reeding on reeded coins.

If the collar is out of position or tilted, a partial collar strike results; if completely missing, it causes a broadstrike; if the planchet is not entirely between the dies, an off-center strike.

III-M-1 Flanged Partial Collar Strike (WE), Rarity Level: 5-6, Values: $20 up.

III-M-2 Reversed Flanged Partial Collar Strike (WE), Rarity Level: 6-7, Values: $35 up.

III-M-3 Tilted Partial Collar Strike (WE), Rarity Level: 5-6, Values: $20 up.

III-M-4 Centered Broadstrike (WE), Rarity Level: 5-6, Values: $5 up.

III-M-5 Uncentered Broadstrike (WE), Rarity Level: 5, Values: $3 up.

III-M-6 Reversed Broadstrike (WE), Rarity Level: 6, Values: $10 up.

III-M-7 Struck Off-Center 10-30% (W), Rarity Level: 3-6, Values: $3 up.

Flanged partial collar III-M-1

Struck off center
10 to 30 percent III-M-7

Struck off center
31 to 70 percent III-M-8

Struck off center
71 percent or more
III-M-9

III-M-8 Struck Off-Center 31-70% (W), Rarity Level: 4-6, Values: $5 up.
III-M-9 Struck Off-Center 71% or More (W), Rarity Level: 3-5, Values: $2 up.
III-M-10 Rotated Multi-sided Planchet Strike (W), Rarity Level: 5-6, Values: $10 up.
III-M-11 Wire Edge Strike (IWE), Rarity Level: 1-2, Values: No Extra Value.
III-M-12 Struck With the Collar Too High (WE), Rarity Level: 6-7, Values: $20 up.
III-M-13 Off-Center Slide Strike (W), Rarity Level:3-6 $4 up.

Misaligned and rotated (die) strike varieties (III-N)

Misaligned die III-N-1

Normal rotation

90 degrees

180 degrees

One (rarely both) of the dies may be Offset Misaligned, off to one side, or may be tilted (Vertically Misaligned). One die may either have been installed so that it is turned in relation to the other die, or may turn in the holder, or the shank may break allowing the die face to rotate in relation to the opposing die.

Vertical misaligned dies are rarely found, and like rotated dies, find only limited collector interest. Ninety and 180 degree rotations are the most popular. Rotations of 14 degrees or less have no value. The 1989-D Congress dollar is found with a nearly 180 degree rotated reverse, currently retailing for around $2,000. Only about 30 have been reported to date.

III-N-1 Offset Die Misalignment Strike (WE), Rarity Level: 3-5, Values: $2 up.
III-N-2 Vertical Die Misalignment Strike (WE), Rarity Level: 4-6, Values: $1 up.
III-N-3 Rotated Die Strike - 15 to 45 Degrees (IWE), Rarity Level: 4-6, Values: $2 up.
III-N-4 Rotated Die Strike - 46 to 135 Degrees (IWE), Rarity Level: 5-6, Values: $10 up.
III-N-5 Rotated Die Strike - 136 to 180 Degrees (IWE), Rarity Level: 5-6, Values: $25 up.

Lettered and design edge strike varieties (III-O)

Early U.S. coins and a number of foreign coins have either lettered edges, or designs on the edge of the coin. Malfunctions of the application of the motto or design to the edge fall in this section.

Overlapping edge letters III-O-1

III-O-1 Overlapping Edge Motto or Design (WE), Rarity Level: 3-4, Values: $5 to $10 and up.
III-O-2 Wrong Edge Motto or Design (WE), Rarity Level: 5-6-7, Values: $50 up.
III-O-3 Missing Edge Motto, Design or Security Edge (IWE), Rarity Level: 5-6-7, Values: $50 up.
III-O-4 Jammed Edge Die Strike (W), Rarity Level: 6, Values: $10 up.
III-O-5 Misplaced Segment of an Edge Die (E), Rarity Level: 4-7, Values: $25 up.
III-O-6 Reeded Edge Struck Over a Lettered Edge (IE), Rarity Level: 3-6, Values: No Extra Value up.

Defective strikes and mismatched dies (III-P)

The final section of the Striking Division covers coins which are not properly struck for reasons other than those in previous classes, such as coins struck with mismatched (muled) dies. The mismatched die varieties must be taken on a case by case basis, while the otherclasses presently have little collector demand or premium.

III-P-1 Defective Strike (WE), Rarity Level: 1, Values: No Extra Value.
III-P-2 Mismatched Die Strike (E), Rarity Level: 4-7, Values: $25 up.
III-P-3 Single-Strike Proof (WE), Rarity Level: 4-5, Values: Minimal.
III-P-4 Single Die-Proof Strike (IE), Rarity Level: 5-6, Values: $100 up.
III-P-5 Reversed Die Strike (I), Rarity Level: 4-5, Values: No Extra Value to Minimal.

Official Mint modifications
Division IV

Several mint produced varieties occur after the coin has been struck, resulting in the addition of the fourth division to my PDS System. Since most of these coins are either unique or are special varieties, each one must be taken on a case by case basis. All classes listed here are by definition intentional.

I have not listed values as the coins falling in these classes which are sold through regular numismatic channels, are cataloged with the regular issues or are covered in specialized catalogs in their particular area.

Matte proofs (IV-A)

**Matte proofs
IV-A-1**

Matte proofs as a section include several of the forms of proof coins which have the striking characteristics of a mirror proof but have been treated AFTER striking to give them a grainy, non-reflective surface.

IV-A-1 Matte Proof (I), Rarity Level: 3-5, Values: Normal Numismatic Value.
IV-A-2 Matte Proof on One Side (I), Rarity Level: 7, Values: Normal Numismatic Value.
IV-A-3 Sandblast Proof (I), Rarity Level: 4-6, Values: Normal Numismatic Value.

Additional engraving (IV-B)

Counterstamp IV-B-3

This section includes any added markings which are placed on the struck coin and struck coins which later were cut into pieces for various purposes. The warning is repeated: Anything done to a coin after the strike is extremely difficult to authenticate and is much easier to fake than a die struck coin.

IV-B-1 Counterstamp and Countermark (I), Rarity Level: 3-6, Values: Normal Numismatic Value.
IV-B-2 Perforated and Cut Coins (I), Rarity Level: 4-6, Values: Normal Numismatic Value.

Restrikes (IV-C)

Restrike with new dies IV-C-7

Restrikes cover a complicated mixture of official use of dies from a variety of sources. Whether or not some were officially sanctioned is always a problem for the collector.

IV-C-1) Restrike on the Same Denomination Planchet (I), Rarity Level: 4-6, Values: Normal Numismatic Value.

IV-C-2 Restrike on a Different Denomination or Series Planchet (I), Rarity Level: 4-6, Values: Normal Numismatic Value.

IV-C-3 Restrike on a Foreign Coin (I), Rarity Level: 6-7, Values: Normal Numismatic Value.
IV-C-4 Restrike on a Token or Medal (I), Rarity Level: 5-6, Values: Normal Numismatic Value.
IV-C-5 Restruck With the Original Dies (I), Rarity Level: 4-6, Values: Normal Numismatic Value.
IV-C-6 Restruck With Mismatched Dies (I), Rarity Level: 4-6, Values: Normal Numismatic Value.
IV-C-7 Copy Strike With New Dies (I), Rarity Level: 3-5, Values: Normal Numismatic Value.
IV-C-8 Fantasy Strike (I), Rarity Level: 4-6, Values: Normal Numismatic Value.

After strike modifications
Division V

This division includes both modifications that have value to collectors – and those that don't. I needed a couple of divisions to cover other things that happen to coins to aid in cataloging them. This avoids the false conclusion that an unlisted coin is quite rare, when the exact opposite is more likely to be the case.

Collectible modifications after strike (V-A)

Mint modification V-A-8

This section includes those classes having to do with deliberate modifications of the coin done with a specific purpose or intent which makes them of some value to collectors. Quite often these pieces were made specifically to sell to collectors, or at least to the public under the guise of being collectible.

V-A-1 Screw Thaler, Rarity Level: 5-6, Values: Normal Numismatic Value.
V-A-2 Love Token, Rarity Level: 3-6, Values: $10 up.
V-A-3 Satirical or Primitive Engraving, Rarity Level: 6-7, Values: $5 up.
V-A-4 Elongated Coin, Rarity Level: 2-7, Values: 50 cents to $1 and up.
V-A-5 Coin Jewelry, Rarity Level: 2-5, Values: $1 up.
V-A-6 Novelty Coin, Rarity Level: 1-3, Values: No Value up to $5 to $10.
V-A-7 Toning, Rarity Level: 3-6, Values: No value up, depending on coloration. Easily faked.
V-A-8 Mint Modification, Rarity Level: 4-7, Values: $5 up. Easily faked.
V-A-9 Mint Packaging Mistake, Rarity Level: 5-7, Values: Nominal $1. Very easily faked.

Alterations and damage after the strike (V-B)

Machine doubling damage V-B-1

This section includes those changes in a coin which have no collector value. In most cases their effect on the coin is to reduce or entirely eliminate any collector value - and in the case of counterfeits they are actually illegal to even own.

V-B-1 Machine Doubling Damage: NOTE: Machine doubling damage is defined as: "Damage to a coin after the strike, due to die bounce or chatter or die displacement, showing on the struck coin as scrapes on the sides of the design elements, with portions of the coin metal in the relief elements either displaced sideways or downward, depending on the direction of movement of the loose die." Machine doubling damage, or MDD, is by far the most common form of doubling found on almost any coin in the world. Rarity Level: 0, Values: Reduces the coin's value.

V-B-2 Accidental or Deliberate Damage, Rarity Level: 0, Values: Reduces the coin's value.

V-B-3 Test Cut or Mark, Rarity Level: 0, Values: Reduces value of coin to face or bullion value.

V-B-4 Alteration, Rarity Level: 0, Values: Reduces value to face or bullion value.

V-B-5 Whizzing, Rarity Level: 0, Values: Reduces value sharply and may reduce it to face or bullion value.

V-B-6 Counterfeit, Copy, Facsimile, Forgery or Fake, Rarity Level: 0, Values: No Value and may be illegal to own.

V-B-7 Planchet Deterioration. Very common on copper-plated zinc cents. Rarity level: 0, Values: No Value.

COLONIAL AMERICA
COLONIAL COINAGE
MARYLAND

LORD BALTIMORE

PENNY (DENARIUM)

KM#1   Composition: Copper

Date	AG	Good	VG	Fine	VF	XF	Unc
(1659) 4 known	—	—	—	—	—	—	—

4 PENCE (GROAT)

KM#2   Composition: Silver **Obverse:** Large bust **Reverse:** Large shield

Date	AG	Good	VG	Fine	VF	XF	Unc
(1659)	750	1,250	2,500	4,500	8,500	15,000	—

KM#3   Composition: Silver **Obverse:** Small bust **Reverse:** Small shield

Date	AG	Good	VG	Fine	VF	XF	Unc
(1659) unique	—	—	—	—	—	—	—

Note: Norweb $26,400

6 PENCE

KM#4   Composition: Silver **Obverse:** Small bust **Note:** Known in two other rare small-bust varieties and two rare large-bust varieties.

Date	AG	Good	VG	Fine	VF	XF	Unc
(1659)	450	950	1,750	3,500	6,750	12,500	—

SHILLING

KM#6   Composition: Silver **Note:** Varieties exist; one is very rare.

Date	AG	Good	VG	Fine	VF	XF	Unc
(1659)	500	1,000	2,000	4,000	8,000	14,500	—

MASSACHUSETTS

NEW ENGLAND

3 PENCE

KM#1   Composition: Silver **Obverse:** NE **Reverse:** III

Date	AG	Good	VG	Fine	VF	XF	Unc
(1652) 2 known	—	—	—	—	—	—	—

6 PENCE

KM#2   Composition: Silver **Obverse:** NE **Reverse:** VI

Date	AG	Good	VG	Fine	VF	XF	Unc
(1652) 8 known	—	—	—	—	—	—	—

Note: Garrett $75,000

SHILLING

KM#3   Composition: Silver **Obverse:** NE **Reverse:** XII

Date	AG	Good	VG	Fine	VF	XF	Unc
(1652)	2,000	4,500	7,500	15,000	35,000	—	—

OAK TREE

2 PENCE

KM#7

Date	AG	Good	VG	Fine	VF	XF	Unc
1662	150	300	550	850	2,150	—	—

3 PENCE

KM#8   Note: Two types of legends.

Date	AG	Good	VG	Fine	VF	XF	Unc
1652	200	400	650	1,000	2,600	—	—

6 PENCE

KM#9   **Note:** Three types of legends.

Date	AG	Good	VG	Fine	VF	XF	Unc
1652	250	450	750	1,250	3,000	—	—

SHILLING

KM#10   **Note:** Two types of legends.

Date	AG	Good	VG	Fine	VF	XF	Unc
1652	175	300	650	1,150	2,850	—	—

PINE TREE

3 PENCE

KM#11   **Obverse:** Tree without berries

Date	AG	Good	VG	Fine	VF	XF	Unc
1652	150	300	450	750	1,600	—	—

KM#12   **Obverse:** Tree with berries

Date	AG	Good	VG	Fine	VF	XF	Unc
1652	165	325	500	850	1,850	—	—

6 PENCE

KM#13   **Obverse:** Tree without berries; "spiney tree"

Date	AG	Good	VG	Fine	VF	XF	Unc
1652	525	950	1,650	2,000	3,000	—	—

KM#14   **Obverse:** Tree with berries

Date	AG	Good	VG	Fine	VF	XF	Unc
1652	150	300	575	1,150	2,100	—	—

SHILLING

KM#15   **Note:** Large planchet. Many varieties exist; some are very rare.

Date	AG	Good	VG	Fine	VF	XF	Unc
1652	200	425	775	1,350	2,650	—	—

KM#16   **Note:** Small planchet; large dies. All examples are thought to be contemporary fabrications.

Date	AG	Good	VG	Fine	VF	XF	Unc
1652	—	—	—	—	—	—	—

KM#17   **Note:** Small planchet; small dies. Many varieties exist; some are very rare.

Date	AG	Good	VG	Fine	VF	XF	Unc
1652	150	300	575	1,250	2,300	—	—

WILLOW TREE

3 PENCE

KM#4

Date	AG	Good	VG	Fine	VF	XF	Unc
1652 3 known	—	—	—	—	—	—	—

6 PENCE

KM#5

Date	AG	Good	VG	Fine	VF	XF	Unc
1652	3,500	7,500	10,000	18,000	35,000	—	—

SHILLING

KM#6

Date	AG	Good	VG	Fine	VF	XF	Unc
1652	4,000	10,000	12,500	20,000	36,500	—	—

NEW JERSEY

ST. PATRICK OR MARK NEWBY

FARTHING

KM#1

Date	AG	Good	VG	Fine	VF	XF	Unc
(1682)	20.00	40.00	80.00	200	425	—	—

KM#1a   **Composition:** Silver

Date	AG	Good	VG	Fine	VF	XF	Unc
(1682)	350	550	1,150	1,650	2,750	—	—

HALFPENNY

KM#2

Date	AG	Good	VG	Fine	VF	XF	Unc
(1682)	50.00	100.00	200	400	900	—	—

EARLY AMERICAN TOKENS

AMERICAN PLANTATIONS

1/24 REAL

KM#Tn5.1   **Composition:** Tin **Obverse Legend:** ET HIB REX

Date	AG	Good	VG	Fine	VF	XF	Unc
(1688)	65.00	125	165	210	285	450	—

KM#Tn5.3   **Composition:** Tin **Reverse:** Horizontal 4

Date	AG	Good	VG	Fine	VF	XF	Unc
(1688)	175	300	400	500	650	1,350	—

KM#Tn5.4   **Composition:** Tin **Obverse Legend:** ET HIB REX

Date	AG	Good	VG	Fine	VF	XF	Unc
(1688)	—	—	—	—	—	—	6,000

KM#Tn6   **Composition:** Tin **Reverse:** Arms of Scotland left, Ireland right

Date	AG	Good	VG	Fine	VF	XF	Unc
(1688)	450	750	1,250	2,000	2,500	—	—

KM#Tn5.2   **Obverse:** Rider's head left of "B" in legend **Note:** Restrikes made in 1828 from two obverse dies.

Date	AG	Good	VG	Fine	VF	XF	Unc
(1828)	35.00	65.00	100.00	150	225	325	—

ELEPHANT

KM#Tn1.1   **Note:** Thick planchet.

Date	AG	Good	VG	Fine	VF	XF	Unc
(1664)	60.00	100.00	150	250	450	850	—

KM#Tn1.2   **Note:** Thin planchet.

Date	AG	Good	VG	Fine	VF	XF	Unc
(1664)	80.00	150	200	350	600	1,250	—

KM#Tn2   **Reverse:** Diagnols tie shield

Date	AG	Good	VG	Fine	VF	XF	Unc
(1664)	120	185	225	400	700	1,450	—

KM#Tn3   **Reverse:** Sword right side of shield

Date	AG	Good	VG	Fine	VF	XF	Unc
(1664) 3 known	—	—	—	—	—	—	—

Note: Norweb $1,320

KM#Tn4   **Obverse Legend:** LON DON.

Date	AG	Good	VG	Fine	VF	XF	Unc
(1684)	175	300	500	1,000	1,850	3,750	—

KM#Tn7   **Obverse Legend:** NEW ENGLAND.

Date	AG	Good	VG	Fine	VF	XF	Unc
1694 2 known	—	—	—	—	—	—	—

Note: Norweb $25,300

KM#Tn8.1   **Obverse Legend:** CAROLINA (PROPRIETORS)

Date	AG	Good	VG	Fine	VF	XF	Unc
1694 5 known	—	—	—	—	—	—	—

Note: Norweb $35,200

KM#Tn8.2   **Obverse Legend:** CAROLINA (PROPRIETORS, O over E)

Date	AG	Good	VG	Fine	VF	XF	Unc
1694	700	1,100	1,700	2,750	5,750	11,000	—
Note: Norweb $17,600							

GLOUCESTER

KM#Tn15

Date	AG	Good	VG	Fine	VF	XF	Unc
(1714) 2 known	—	—	—	—	—	—	—
Note: Garrett $36,000							

HIBERNIA-VOCE POPULI

FARTHING

KM#Tn21.1   **Note:** Large letters

Date	AG	Good	VG	Fine	VF	XF	Unc
1760	90.00	150	275	450	750	1,550	—

KM#Tn21.2   **Note:** Small letters

Date	AG	Good	VG	Fine	VF	XF	Unc
1760 extremely rare	—	—	—	—	—	—	—
Note: Norweb $5,940							

HALFPENNY

KM#Tn22

Date	AG	Good	VG	Fine	VF	XF	Unc
1700 date is error, extremely rare	—	—	—	—	—	—	—
Note: ex-Roper $575. Norweb $577.50. Stack's Americana, VF, $2,900							
1760 varieties	10.00	30.00	50.00	100.00	185	350	—
1760 legend VOOE POPULI	20.00	35.00	60.00	110	200	400	—

HIGLEY OR GRANBY

KM#Tn20   **Obverse Legend:** THE WHEELE GOES ROUND **Reverse:** J CUT MY WAY THROUGH

Date	AG	Good	VG	Fine	VF	XF	Unc
(1737) unique	—	—	—	—	—	—	—

Note: Roper $60,500

KM#Tn16 Composition: Copper **Obverse Legend:** CONNECTICVT. **Note:** THE VALVE OF THREE PENCE.

Date	AG	Good	VG	Fine	VF	XF	Unc
1737	—	—	—	—	—	—	—

Note: Garrett $16,000

KM#Tn17 Composition: Copper **Obverse Legend:** THE VALVE OF THREE PENCE **Reverse Legend:** I AM GOOD COPPER

Date	AG	Good	VG	Fine	VF	XF	Unc
1737 2 known	—	—	—	—	—	—	—

Note: ex-Norweb $6,875

KM#Tn18.1 Composition: Copper **Obverse Legend:** VALUE ME AS YOU PLEASE **Reverse:** I AM GOOD COPPER

Date	AG	Good	VG	Fine	VF	XF	Unc
1737	6,500	8,500	10,500	14,500	25,000	—	—

KM#Tn19 Composition: Copper **Reverse:** Broad axe

Date	AG	Good	VG	Fine	VF	XF	Unc
(1737)	—	—	—	—	—	—	—

Note: Garrett $45,000

1739 5 known	—	—	—	—	—	—	—

Note: Eliasberg $12,650. Oechsner $9,900. Steinberg (holed) $4,400

KM#Tn18.2 Composition: Copper **Obverse Legend:** VALVE ME AS YOU PLEASE **Reverse Legend:** I AM GOOD COPPER

Date	AG	Good	VG	Fine	VF	XF	Unc
1737 2 known	—	—	—	—	—	—	—

NEW YORKE

KM#Tn9 Composition: Brass **Note:** The 1700 date is circa.

Date	AG	Good	VG	Fine	VF	XF	Unc
1700	650	1,250	2,850	4,500	7,500	—	—

KM#Tn9a Composition: White Metal

Date	AG	Good	VG	Fine	VF	XF	Unc
1700 4 known	—	—	—	—	—	—	—

PITT

FARTHING

KM#Tn23

Date	AG	Good	VG	Fine	VF	XF	Unc
1766	—	—	—	1,350	2,850	6,000	—

HALFPENNY

KM#Tn24

Date	AG	Good	VG	Fine	VF	XF	Unc
1766	45.00	85.00	175	350	700	1,500	—

ROYAL PATENT COINAGE

HIBERNIA

FARTHING

KM#20   **Note:** Pattern.

Date	AG	Good	VG	Fine	VF	XF	Unc
1722	25.00	50.00	125	220	325	700	—

KM#24   **Obverse:** 1722 obverse **Obverse Legend:** ...D:G:REX.

Date	AG	Good	VG	Fine	VF	XF	Unc
1723	20.00	40.00	60.00	90.00	150	350	—

KM#25   **Obverse Legend:** DEI • GRATIA • REX •

Date	AG	Good	VG	Fine	VF	XF	Unc
1723	10.00	20.00	40.00	65.00	90.00	200	—

KM#25a   **Composition:** Silver

Date	(Proof)Good	VG	Fine	VF	XF	Unc	
1723	—	—	—	800	1,600	—	2,700
1724	45.00	75.00	125	250	485	—	—

HALFPENNY

KM#21   **Reverse:** Harp left, head right

Date	AG	Good	VG	Fine	VF	XF	Unc
1722	—	15.00	35.00	65.00	135	350	—

KM#22   Obverse: Harp left, head right **Note:** Pattern.

Date	AG	Good	VG	Fine	VF	XF	Unc
1722	7.00	—	—	1,150	1,750	3,000	—

KM#23.1   Reverse: Harp right

Date	AG	Good	VG	Fine	VF	XF	Unc
1722	2.00	15.00	35.00	60.00	125	250	—
1723	7.00	15.00	25.00	40.00	80.00	175	—
1723/22	10.00	20.00	45.00	90.00	185	375	—
1724	7.00	15.00	35.00	60.00	125	265	—

KM#23.2   Obverse: DEII error in legend

Date	AG	Good	VG	Fine	VF	XF	Unc
1722	40.00	90.00	180	300	500	750	—

KM#26   Reverse: Large head **Note:** Rare. Generally mint state only. Probably a pattern.

Date	AG	Good	VG	Fine	VF	XF	Unc
1723	—	—	—	—	—	—	—

KM#27   Reverse: Continuous legend over head

Date	AG	Good	VG	Fine	VF	XF	Unc
1724	30.00	65.00	150	300	475	750	—

ROSA AMERICANA

HALFPENNY

KM#1   Obverse Legend: D • G • REX •

Date	AG	Good	VG	Fine	VF	XF	Unc
1722	20.00	40.00	60.00	100.00	220	475	—

KM#2   Obverse: Uncrowned rose **Obverse Legend:** DEI GRATIA REX. **Note:** Several varieties exist.

Date	AG	Good	VG	Fine	VF	XF	Unc
1722	18.00	35.00	55.00	100.00	200	475	—
1723	285	525	750	1,350	2,250	—	—

KM#3   Reverse Legend: VTILE DVLCI

Date	AG	Good	VG	Fine	VF	XF	Unc
1722	250	450	650	1,100	—	—	—

KM#9   Reverse: Crowned rose

Date	AG	Good	VG	Fine	VF	XF	Unc
1723	18.00	35.00	55.00	100.00	200	450	—

PENNY

KM#4   Reverse Legend: UTILE DULCI **Note:** Several varieties exist.

Date	AG	Good	VG	Fine	VF	XF	Unc
1722	18.00	35.00	55.00	100.00	175	385	—

KM#5   Note: Several varieties exist. Also known in two rare pattern types with long hair ribbons, one with V's for U's on the obverse.

Date	AG	Good	VG	Fine	VF	XF	Unc
1722	18.00	35.00	55.00	100.00	220	475	—

KM#10   Note: Several varieties exist.

Date	AG	Good	VG	Fine	VF	XF	Unc
1723	18.00	35.00	55.00	100.00	200	420	—

KM#12   Note: Pattern.

Date	AG	Good	VG	Fine	VF	XF	Unc
1724 2 known	—	—	—	—	—	—	—

KM#13

Date	AG	Good	VG	Fine	VF	XF	Unc
(1724) 5 known	—	—	—	—	—	—	—

Note: Norweb $2,035

KM#14 Obverse: George II **Note:** Pattern.

Date	AG	Good	VG	Fine	VF	XF	Unc
1727 2 known	—	—	—	—	—	—	—

2 PENCE

KM#6 Reverse: Motto with scroll

Date	AG	Good	VG	Fine	VF	XF	Unc
(1722)	35.00	60.00	110	200	350	700	—

KM#7 Reverse: Motto without scroll

Date	AG	Good	VG	Fine	VF	XF	Unc
(1722) 3 known	—	—	—	—	—	—	—

KM#8.1 Obverse: Period after REX **Reverse:** Dated

Date	AG	Good	VG	Fine	VF	XF	Unc
1722	25.00	40.00	70.00	125	265	500	—

KM#8.2 Obverse: Without period after REX

Date	AG	Good	VG	Fine	VF	XF	Unc
1722	22.00	40.00	70.00	125	275	525	—

KM#11 Note: Several varieties exist.

Date	AG	Good	VG	Fine	VF	XF	Unc
1723	25.00	45.00	75.00	140	285	550	—

KM#15   Note: Pattern. Two verieties exist; both extremely rare.

Date	AG	Good	VG	Fine	VF	XF	Unc
1724	—	—	—	—	—	—	—

Note: ex-Garrett $5,775. Stack's Americana, XF, $10,925

KM#16   Note: Pattern.

Date	AG	Good	VG	Fine	VF	XF	Unc
1733 4 known	—	—	—	—	—	—	—

Note: Norweb $19,800

VIRGINIA HALFPENNY

KM#Tn25.1   Composition: Copper **Reverse:** Small 7s in date **Note:** Struck on Irish halfpenny planchets.

Date	(Proof)Good	VG	Fine	VF	XF	Unc
1773	—	—	—	—	—	3,500

KM#Tn25.2   Composition: Copper **Obverse:** Period after GEORGIVS **Reverse:** Varieties with 7 or 8 strings in harp

Date	AG	Good	VG	Fine	VF	XF	Unc
1773	6.00	12.00	25.00	50.00	100.00	250	465

KM#Tn25.3   Composition: Copper **Obverse:** Without period after GEORGIVS **Reverse:** Varieties with 6, 7 or 8 strings in harp

Date	AG	Good	VG	Fine	VF	XF	Unc
1773	7.00	15.00	30.00	60.00	135	275	525

KM#Tn25.4   Composition: Copper **Obverse:** Without period after GEORGIVS **Reverse:** 8 harp strings, dot on cross

Date	AG	Good	VG	Fine	VF	XF	Unc
1773	—	—	—	—	—	—	—

Note: ex-Steinberg $2,600

KM#Tn26   Note: So-called "shilling" silver proofs.

Date	AG	Good	VG	Fine	VF	XF	Unc
1774 6 known	—	—	—	—	—	—	—

Note: Garrett, $23,000

UNITED STATES
REVOLUTIONARY COINAGE

CONTINENTAL "DOLLAR".

KM#EA1   Composition: Pewter **Obverse Legend:** CURRENCY.

Date	AG	Good	VG	Fine	VF	XF	Unc
1776	—	—	1,850	3,000	4,750	8,750	18,500

KM#EA2   Composition: Pewter **Obverse Legend:** CURRENCY, EG FECIT.

Date	AG	Good	VG	Fine	VF	XF	Unc
1776	—	—	1,750	2,850	4,250	7,750	16,000

KM#EA2a   Composition: Silver **Obverse Legend:** CURRENCY, EG FECIT.

Date	AG	Good	VG	Fine	VF	XF	Unc
1776 2 known	—	—	—	—	—	—	—

KM#EA3   Composition: Pewter **Obverse Legend:** CURRENCY.

Date	AG	Good	VG	Fine	VF	XF	Unc
1776 extremely rare	—	—	—	—	—	—	—

KM#EA4   Composition: Pewter **Obverse Legend:** CURRENCY **Reverse:** Floral cross

Date	AG	Good	VG	Fine	VF	XF	Unc
1776 3 recorded	—	—	—	—	—	—	—

Note: Norweb $50,600. Johnson $25,300

KM#EA5   Composition: Pewter **Obverse Legend:** CURENCY.

Date	AG	Good	VG	Fine	VF	XF	Unc
1776	—	—	1,650	2,750	4,000	8,000	16,000

KM#EA5a   Composition: Brass **Obverse Legend:** CURENCY. **Note:** Two varieties exist.

Date	AG	Good	VG	Fine	VF	XF	Unc
1776	—	—	—	—	13,500	17,500	—

KM#EA5b   Composition: Silver **Obverse Legend:** CURENCY.

Date	AG	Good	VG	Fine	VF	XF	Unc
1776 unique	—	—	—	—	—	—	—

Note: Romano $99,000

STATE COINAGE
CONNECTICUT

KM#1   **Obverse:** Bust facing right

Date	AG	Good	VG	Fine	VF	XF	Unc
1785	20.00	30.00	50.00	85.00	190	450	—

KM#2   **Obverse:** "African head"

Date	AG	Good	VG	Fine	VF	XF	Unc
1785	25.00	45.00	85.00	200	450	1,500	—

KM#3.1   **Obverse:** Bust facing left

Date	AG	Good	VG	Fine	VF	XF	Unc
1785	60.00	100.00	150	275	400	750	—
1786	20.00	30.00	50.00	90.00	185	465	—
1787	22.00	35.00	60.00	110	125	350	—
1788	20.00	30.00	50.00	100.00	220	500	—

KM#4   **Obverse:** Small mailed bust facing right **Reverse Legend:** ETLIB INDE.

Date	AG	Good	VG	Fine	VF	XF	Unc
1786	22.00	35.00	55.00	85.00	165	400	—

KM#5   **Obverse:** Small mailed bust facing right **Reverse Legend:** INDE ET LIB.

Date	AG	Good	VG	Fine	VF	XF	Unc
1786	30.00	55.00	75.00	115	225	475	—

KM#6   **Obverse:** Large mailed bust facing right

Date	AG	Good	VG	Fine	VF	XF	Unc
1786	30.00	50.00	90.00	165	350	850	—

KM#7   Obverse: "Hercules head."

Date		AG	Good	VG	Fine	VF	XF	Unc
1786		25.00	40.00	75.00	135	300	700	—

KM#8.1   Obverse: Draped bust

Date		AG	Good	VG	Fine	VF	XF	Unc
1786		22.00	35.00	65.00	120	275	600	—

KM#9   Obverse: Small head **Reverse Legend:** ETLIB INDE.

Date		AG	Good	VG	Fine	VF	XF	Unc
1787		25.00	40.00	90.00	150	350	800	—

KM#10   Obverse: Small head **Reverse Legend:** INDE ET LIB.

Date		AG	Good	VG	Fine	VF	XF	Unc
1787		75.00	135	175	275	450	950	—

KM#11   Obverse: Medium bust **Note:** Two reverse legend types exist.

Date		AG	Good	VG	Fine	VF	XF	Unc
1787		50.00	80.00	140	200	325	625	—

KM#12   Obverse: "Muttonhead" variety **Note:** Extremely rare with legend INDE ET LIB.

Date		AG	Good	VG	Fine	VF	XF	Unc
1787		30.00	50.00	120	250	650	1,500	—

KM#3.3   Obverse: Perfect date **Reverse Legend:** IN DE ET.

Date		AG	Good	VG	Fine	VF	XF	Unc
1787		35.00	65.00	85.00	135	250	600	—

KM#13   Obverse: "Laughing head"

Date	AG	Good	VG	Fine	VF	XF	Unc
1787	22.00	35.00	60.00	110	250	700	—

KM#14   Obverse: "Horned head"

Date	AG	Good	VG	Fine	VF	XF	Unc
1787	15.00	25.00	40.00	70.00	175	475	—

KM#15   Reverse Legend: IND ET LIB.

Date	AG	Good	VG	Fine	VF	XF	Unc
1787/8	25.00	40.00	75.00	130	250	650	—
1787/1887	20.00	30.00	50.00	90.00	200	520	—

KM#16   Obverse Legend: CONNECT. **Reverse Legend:** INDE ET LIB. **Note:** Two additional scarce reverse legend types exist.

Date	AG	Good	VG	Fine	VF	XF	Unc
1787	22.00	37.50	60.00	115	220	550	—

KM#8.2   Obverse: Draped bust **Note:** Many varieties exist.

Date	AG	Good	VG	Fine	VF	XF	Unc
1787	12.00	20.00	40.00	80.00	135	275	—

KM#8.3   Obverse Legend: AUCIORI.

Date	AG	Good	VG	Fine	VF	XF	Unc
1787	15.00	25.00	50.00	110	250	600	—

KM#8.4   Obverse Legend: AUCTOPI.

Date	AG	Good	VG	Fine	VF	XF	Unc
1787	20.00	30.00	60.00	125	265	650	—

KM#8.5   Obverse Legend: AUCTOBI.

Date	AG	Good	VG	Fine	VF	XF	Unc
1787	15.00	25.00	50.00	110	225	550	—

KM#8.6   Obverse Legend: CONNFC.

Date	AG	Good	VG	Fine	VF	XF	Unc
1787	12.00	20.00	40.00	85.00	200	525	—

KM#8.7   Obverse Legend: CONNLC.

Date	AG	Good	VG	Fine	VF	XF	Unc
1787	—	30.00	60.00	125	265	650	—

KM#8.8   Reverse Legend: FNDE.

Date	AG	Good	VG	Fine	VF	XF	Unc
1787	15.00	25.00	45.00	90.00	210	535	—

KM#8.9   Reverse Legend: ETLIR.

Date	AG	Good	VG	Fine	VF	XF	Unc
1787	15.00	25.00	45.00	90.00	210	535	—

KM#8.10   Reverse Legend: ETIIB.

Date	AG	Good	VG	Fine	VF	XF	Unc
1787	20.00	30.00	50.00	100.00	225	550	—

KM#20   Obverse: Mailed bust facing right

Date	AG	Good	VG	Fine	VF	XF	Unc
1788	15.00	25.00	45.00	90.00	200	425	—

KM#21   Obverse: Small mailed bust facing right

Date	AG	Good	VG	Fine	VF	XF	Unc
1788	75.00	150	285	550	1,100	2,500	—

KM#3.4   Obverse Legend: CONNLC.

Date	AG	Good	VG	Fine	VF	XF	Unc
1788	15.00	25.00	40.00	80.00	175	400	—

KM#22.1   Obverse: Draped bust facing left **Reverse Legend:** INDE ET LIB.

Date	AG	Good	VG	Fine	VF	XF	Unc
1788	12.00	20.00	35.00	55.00	135	375	—

KM#22.2   Reverse Legend: INDLET LIB.

Date	AG	Good	VG	Fine	VF	XF	Unc
1788	20.00	30.00	55.00	90.00	185	400	—

KM#22.3   Obverse Legend: CONNLC. **Reverse Legend:** INDE ET LIB.

Date	AG	Good	VG	Fine	VF	XF	Unc
1788	22.00	35.00	60.00	100.00	200	425	—

KM#22.4   Obverse Legend: CONNLC. **Reverse Legend:** INDL ET LIB.

Date	AG	Good	VG	Fine	VF	XF	Unc
1788	22.00	35.00	60.00	100.00	200	425	—

MASSACHUSETTS
HALF CENT

KM#19   Note: Varieties exist; some are rare.

Date	AG	Good	VG	Fine	VF	XF	Unc
1787	30.00	50.00	90.00	175	350	800	—
1788	35.00	55.00	100.00	185	375	850	—

HALFPENNY

KM#17

Date	AG	Good	VG	Fine	VF	XF	Unc
1776 unique	—	—	—	—	—	—	—

Note: Garrett $40,000

CENT

KM#20.1   Reverse: Arrows in right talon

Date	AG	Good	VG	Fine	VF	XF	Unc
1787 7 known	—	—	—	—	—	—	—

Note: Ex-Bushnell-Brand $8,800. Garrett $5,500

KM#20.2   Reverse: Arrows in left talon

Date	AG	Good	VG	Fine	VF	XF	Unc
1787	25.00	40.00	65.00	120	285	785	—

KM#20.3   Reverse: "Horned eagle" die break

Date	AG	Good	VG	Fine	VF	XF	Unc
1787	28.00	45.00	70.00	130	300	785	—

KM#20.4   Reverse: Without period after Massachusetts

Date	AG	Good	VG	Fine	VF	XF	Unc
1788	28.00	45.00	70.00	135	320	850	—

KM#20.5   Reverse: Period after Massachusetts, normal S's

Date	AG	Good	VG	Fine	VF	XF	Unc
1788	28.00	45.00	70.00	120	275	775	—

KM#20.6   Reverse: Period after Massachusetts, S's like 8's

Date	AG	Good	VG	Fine	VF	XF	Unc
1788	22.00	35.00	60.00	120	275	775	—

PENNY

KM#18

Date	AG	Good	VG	Fine	VF	XF	Unc
1776 unique	—	—	—	—	—	—	—

NEW HAMPSHIRE

KM#1

Date	AG	Good	VG	Fine	VF	XF	Unc
1776 extremely rare	—	—	—	—	—	—	—

Note: Garrett $13,000

NEW JERSEY

KM#8   Obverse: Date below draw bar

Date	AG	Good	VG	Fine	VF	XF	Unc
1786 extremely rare	—	—	—	—	—	—	—

Note: Garrett $52,000

KM#9   Obverse: Large horse head, date below plow, no coulter on plow

Date	AG	Good	VG	Fine	VF	XF	Unc
1786	75.00	150	285	550	1,450	5,500	—

KM#10   Reverse: Narrow shield, straight beam

Date	AG	Good	VG	Fine	VF	XF	Unc
1786	25.00	40.00	65.00	150	350	975	—

KM#11.1   Reverse: Wide shield, curved beam **Note:** Varieties exist.

Date	AG	Good	VG	Fine	VF	XF	Unc
1786	28.00	45.00	85.00	180	425	1,000	—

KM#11.2   Obverse: Bridle variety (die break) **Note:** Reverse varieties exist.

Date	AG	Good	VG	Fine	VF	XF	Unc
1786	30.00	50.00	90.00	185	425	1,000	—

KM#12.1   Reverse: Plain shield **Note:** Small planchet. Varieties exist.

Date	AG	Good	VG	Fine	VF	XF	Unc
1787	20.00	30.00	60.00	100.00	200	675	—

KM#12.2   Reverse: Shield heavily outlined **Note:** Small planchet.

Date	AG	Good	VG	Fine	VF	XF	Unc
1787	22.00	35.00	75.00	125	285	800	—

KM#13   Obverse: "Serpent head."

Date	AG	Good	VG	Fine	VF	XF	Unc
1787	40.00	60.00	120	285	700	1,275	—

KM#14   Reverse: Plain shield **Note:** Large planchet. Varieties exist.

Date	AG	Good	VG	Fine	VF	XF	Unc
1787	22.00	35.00	75.00	135	300	850	—

KM#15   Reverse Legend: PLURIBS.

Date	AG	Good	VG	Fine	VF	XF	Unc
1787	30.00	50.00	100.00	225	600	1,100	—

KM#16   Obverse: Horse's head facing right **Note:** Varieties exist.

Date	AG	Good	VG	Fine	VF	XF	Unc
1788	20.00	30.00	65.00	125	375	750	—

KM#17   Reverse: Fox before legend **Note:** Varieties exist.

Date	AG	Good	VG	Fine	VF	XF	Unc
1788	—	55.00	110	275	725	1,550	—

KM#18   Obverse: Horse's head facing left **Note:** Varieties exist.

Date	AG	Good	VG	Fine	VF	XF	Unc
1788	65.00	125	285	575	1,150	3,000	—

NEW YORK

KM#1   Composition: Copper **Obverse Legend:** NON VI VIRTUTE VICI.

Date	AG	Good	VG	Fine	VF	XF	Unc
1786	1,200	2,200	3,750	6,000	11,500	—	—

KM#2   Composition: Copper **Obverse:** Eagle on globe facing right

Date	AG	Good	VG	Fine	VF	XF	Unc
1787	175	750	1,250	3,500	6,500	12,750	—

KM#3   Composition: Copper **Obverse:** Eagle on globe facing left

Date	AG	Good	VG	Fine	VF	XF	Unc
1787	350	700	1,200	3,250	6,000	12,000	—

KM#4   Composition: Copper **Reverse:** Large eagle, arrows in right talon

Date	AG	Good	VG	Fine	VF	XF	Unc
1787 2 known	—	—	—	—	—	—	—

Note: Norweb $18,700

KM#5   Obverse: George Clinton

Date	AG	Good	VG	Fine	VF	XF	Unc
1787	2,250	4,000	5,500	9,500	20,000	—	—

KM#6   Obverse: Indian **Reverse:** New York arms

Date	AG	Good	VG	Fine	VF	XF	Unc
1787	1,000	2,000	4,000	6,500	10,500	25,000	—

KM#7   Obverse: Indian **Reverse:** Eagle on globe

Date	AG	Good	VG	Fine	VF	XF	Unc
1787	1,650	3,000	6,500	11,500	23,500	35,000	—

KM#8   Obverse: Indian **Reverse:** George III

Date	AG	Good	VG	Fine	VF	XF	Unc
1787	125	200	350	650	1,350	4,200	—

MACHIN MILL

KM#13   Composition: Copper **Note:** British halfpenny imitation.

Date	AG	Good	VG	Fine	VF	XF	Unc
1776	25.00	45.00	75.00	150	300	875	—

NOVA EBORACS

KM#9   Obverse Legend: NOVA EBORAC. **Reverse:** Figure seated right

Date	AG	Good	VG	Fine	VF	XF	Unc
1787	40.00	75.00	125	260	525	1,100	—

KM#10   Reverse: Figure seated left

Date	AG	Good	VG	Fine	VF	XF	Unc
1787	35.00	55.00	110	225	500	1,000	—

KM#11   Obverse: Small head, star above **Obverse Legend:** NOVA EBORAC.

Date	AG	Good	VG	Fine	VF	XF	Unc
1787	300	600	1,750	3,000	4,500	6,500	—

KM#12   Obverse: Large head, two quatrefoils left **Obverse Legend:** NOVA EBORAC.

Date	AG	Good	VG	Fine	VF	XF	Unc
1787	200	300	400	650	1,150	2,500	—

VERMONT

KM#1   Reverse Legend: IMMUNE COLUMBIA

Date	AG	Good	VG	Fine	VF	XF	Unc
(1785)	1,250	2,000	3,000	5,000	9,000	—	—

KM#2   Obverse Legend: VEMONTIS

Date	AG	Good	VG	Fine	VF	XF	Unc
1785	120	200	300	600	1,150	—	—

KM#3   Obverse Legend: VERMONTS

Date	AG	Good	VG	Fine	VF	XF	Unc
1785	85.00	150	225	450	900	3,200	—

KM#9.1   Reverse Legend: INDE ET LIB. **Note:** Varieties exist.

Date	AG	Good	VG	Fine	VF	XF	Unc
1788	40.00	65.00	120	220	550	1,850	—

KM#4   Obverse Legend: VERMONTENSIUM

Date	AG	Good	VG	Fine	VF	XF	Unc
1786	75.00	125	200	450	950	3,250	—

KM#5   Obverse: "Baby head." **Obverse Legend:** AUCTORI: VERMON:

Date	AG	Good	VG	Fine	VF	XF	Unc
1786	120	200	300	550	1,150	4,500	—

KM#6   Obverse: Bust facing left **Obverse Legend:** VERMON: AUCTORI:

Date	AG	Good	VG	Fine	VF	XF	Unc
1786	60.00	100.00	185	300	750	2,250	—
1787 extremely rare	—	—	—	—	—	—	—

KM#7   Obverse: Bust facing right **Note:** Varieties exist.

Date	AG	Good	VG	Fine	VF	XF	Unc
1787	30.00	50.00	100.00	200	425	1,250	—

KM#8   Note: Brittania mule.

Date	AG	Good	VG	Fine	VF	XF	Unc
1787	25.00	40.00	65.00	140	285	950	—

KM#9.2   **Obverse:** "C" backward in AUCTORI

Date	AG	Good	VG	Fine	VF	XF	Unc
1788 extremely rare	—	—	—	—	—	—	—

Note: Stack's Americana, Fine, $9,775

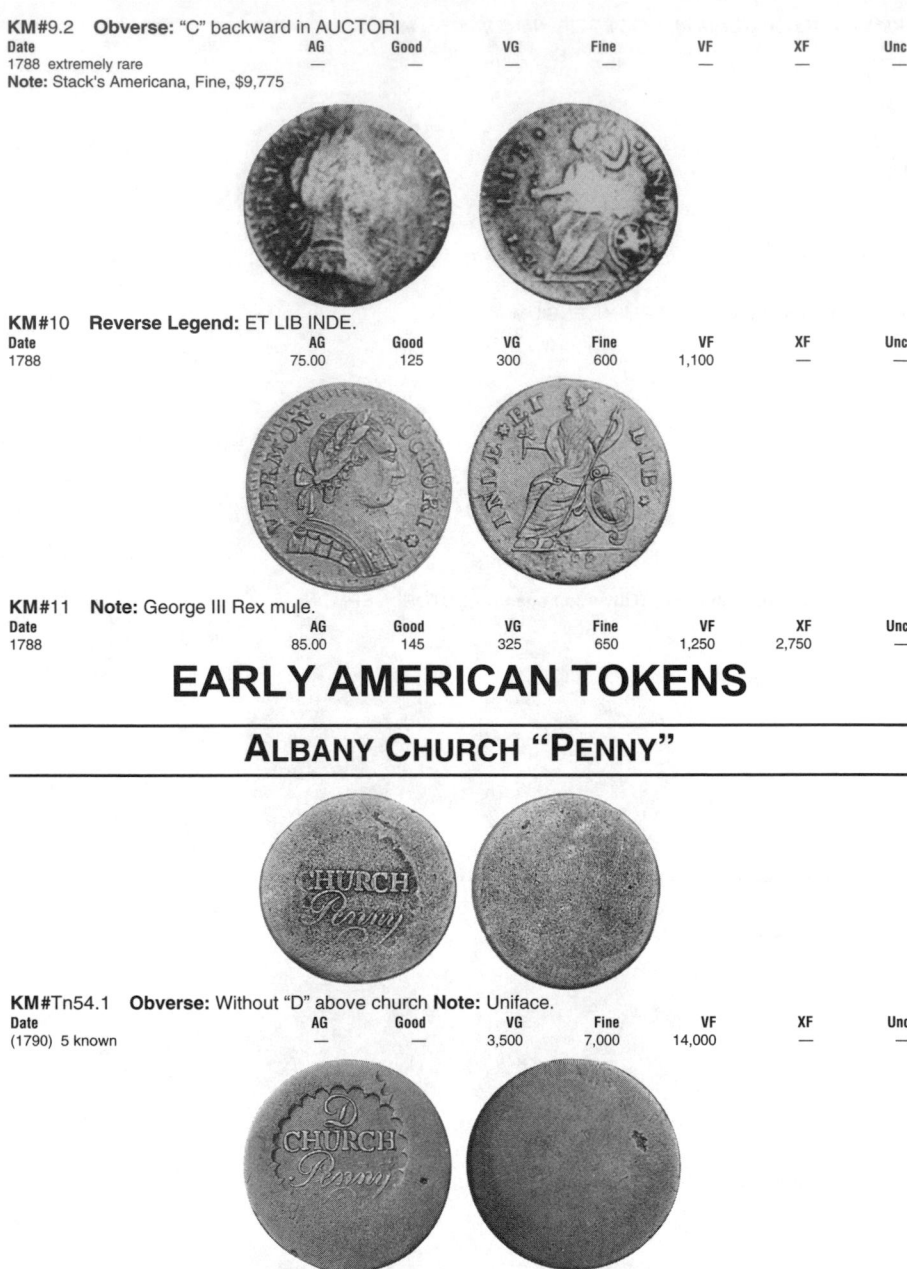

KM#10   **Reverse Legend:** ET LIB INDE.

Date	AG	Good	VG	Fine	VF	XF	Unc
1788	75.00	125	300	600	1,100	—	—

KM#11   **Note:** George III Rex mule.

Date	AG	Good	VG	Fine	VF	XF	Unc
1788	85.00	145	325	650	1,250	2,750	—

EARLY AMERICAN TOKENS

ALBANY CHURCH "PENNY"

KM#Tn54.1   **Obverse:** Without "D" above church **Note:** Uniface.

Date	AG	Good	VG	Fine	VF	XF	Unc
(1790) 5 known	—	—	3,500	7,000	14,000	—	—

KM#Tn54.2   **Obverse:** With "D" above church **Note:** Uniface.

Date	AG	Good	VG	Fine	VF	XF	Unc
(1790) rare	—	—	3,000	5,000	10,000	—	—

AUCTORI PLEBIS

KM#Tn50

Date	AG	Good	VG	Fine	VF	XF	Unc
1787	20.00	45.00	90.00	150	300	600	—

BAR "CENT"

KM#Tn49

Date	AG	Good	VG	Fine	VF	XF	Unc
(1785)	85.00	150	275	675	1,200	2,500	—

BRASHER DOUBLOON

KM#Tn51.1 Composition: Gold **Reverse:** EB on wing

Date	AG	Good	VG	Fine	VF	XF	Unc
1787 6 known	—	—	—	—	—	—	—

Note: Garrett $725,000

KM#Tn51.2 Composition: Gold **Reverse:** EG on breast

Date	AG	Good	VG	Fine	VF	XF	Unc
1787 unique	—	—	—	—	—	—	—

Note: Garrett $625,000

CASTORLAND "HALF DOLLAR"

KM#Tn87.1   **Edge:** Reeded. **Composition:** Silver

Date	AG	Good	VG	Fine	VF	XF	Unc
1796	—	—	—	—	—	3,550	—

KM#Tn87.1a   **Edge:** Reeded. **Composition:** Copper

Date	AG	Good	VG	Fine	VF	XF	Unc
1796 3 known	—	—	—	—	—	1,650	—

KM#Tn87.1b   **Edge:** Reeded. **Composition:** Brass

Date	AG	Good	VG	Fine	VF	XF	Unc
1796 unique	—	—	—	—	—	—	—

KM#Tn87.2   **Edge:** Plain. **Composition:** Copper **Note:** Thin planchet.

Date	AG	Good	VG	Fine	VF	XF	Unc
1796 unique	—	—	—	—	—	—	—

Note: Norweb $467.50

KM#Tn87.3   **Edge:** Reeded. **Composition:** Silver **Note:** Thin planchet. Restrike.

Date	Good	VG	Fine	VF	XF	Unc	Proof
1796	—	—	—	—	—	—	325

KM#Tn87.4   **Edge:** Lettered. **Composition:** Silver **Note:** Thin planchet. Restrike.

Date	Good	VG	Fine	VF	XF	Unc	Proof
1796	—	—	—	—	—	—	60.00

KM#Tn87.3a   **Edge:** Reeded. **Composition:** Copper **Note:** Thin planchet. Restrike.

Date	Good	VG	Fine	VF	XF	Unc	Proof
1796	—	—	—	—	—	—	285

KM#Tn87.5   **Edge:** Lettered. **Composition:** Copper **Note:** Thin planchet. Restrike.

Date	Good	VG	Fine	VF	XF	Unc	Proof
1796	—	—	—	—	—	—	40.00

CHALMERS

3 PENCE

KM#Tn45   **Composition:** Silver

Date	AG	Good	VG	Fine	VF	XF	Unc
1783	250	500	1,000	1,500	2,650	5,500	—

6 PENCE

KM#Tn46.1   **Composition:** Silver **Reverse:** Small date

Date	AG	Good	VG	Fine	VF	XF	Unc
1783	350	700	1,500	2,250	5,500	12,000	—

KM#Tn46.2   **Composition:** Silver **Reverse:** Large date

Date	AG	Good	VG	Fine	VF	XF	Unc
1783	300	600	1,300	2,000	4,000	10,000	—

SHILLING

KM#Tn47.1   Composition: Silver **Reverse:** Birds with long worm

Date	AG	Good	VG	Fine	VF	XF	Unc
1783	180	300	500	1,000	2,000	4,500	—

KM#Tn47.2   Composition: Silver **Reverse:** Birds with short worm

Date	AG	Good	VG	Fine	VF	XF	Unc
1783	150	250	475	900	1,850	4,500	—

KM#Tn48   Composition: Silver **Reverse:** Rings and stars

Date	AG	Good	VG	Fine	VF	XF	Unc
1783 4 known	—	—	—	—	—	—	—

Note: Garrett $75,000

COPPER COMPANY OF UPPER CANADA

HALFPENNY

KM#Tn86   Composition: Copper

Date	Good	VG	Fine	VF	XF	Unc	Proof
1796	—	—	—	—	—	—	3,750

FRANKLIN PRESS

KM#Tn73   Edge: Plain.

Date	AG	Good	VG	Fine	VF	XF	Unc
1794	18.00	35.00	55.00	85.00	175	300	600

KENTUCKY TOKEN

KM#Tn70.1   **Edge:** Plain. **Note:** 1793 date is circa.

Date	AG	Good	VG	Fine	VF	XF	Unc
(1793)	12.00	25.00	40.00	60.00	100.00	265	575

KM#Tn70.2   **Edge:** Engrailed.

Date	AG	Good	VG	Fine	VF	XF	Unc
(1793)	35.00	75.00	125	200	350	950	1,850

KM#Tn70.3   **Edge:** Lettered.

Date	AG	Good	VG	Fine	VF	XF	Unc
(1793) unique	—	—	—	—	—	1,980	—

KM#Tn70.4   **Edge:** Lettered.

Date	AG	Good	VG	Fine	VF	XF	Unc
(1793)	14.00	28.00	45.00	65.00	110	285	725

KM#Tn70.5   **Edge:** Lettered.

Date	AG	Good	VG	Fine	VF	XF	Unc
(1793) unique	—	—	—	—	—	—	—

KM#Tn70.6   **Edge:** Lettered.

Date	AG	Good	VG	Fine	VF	XF	Unc
(1793) unique	—	—	—	—	1,800	—	—

KM#Tn70.7   **Edge:** Ornamented branch with two leaves

Date	AG	Good	VG	Fine	VF	XF	Unc
(1793) unique	—	—	—	—	—	—	—

MOTT TOKEN

KM#Tn52.1   **Note:** Thin planchet.

Date	AG	Good	VG	Fine	VF	XF	Unc
1789	30.00	60.00	120	220	350	825	—

KM#Tn52.2   **Note:** Thick planchet. Weight generally about 170 grams.

Date	AG	Good	VG	Fine	VF	XF	Unc
1789	25.00	50.00	100.00	175	300	700	—

KM#Tn52.3   **Edge:** Fully engrailed. **Note:** Specimens struck with perfect dies are scarcer and generally command higher prices.

Date	AG	Good	VG	Fine	VF	XF	Unc
1789	40.00	85.00	175	350	600	1,250	—

MYDDELTON TOKEN

KM#Tn85   **Composition:** Copper

Date	Good	VG	Fine	VF	XF	Unc	Proof
1796	—	—	—	—	—	—	6,500

KM#Tn85a Composition: Silver

Date	Good	VG	Fine	VF	XF	Unc	Proof
1796	—	—	—	—	—	—	5,500

NEW YORK THEATRE

KM#Tn90 Note: 1796 date is circa.

Date	AG	Good	VG	Fine	VF	XF	Unc
1796	—	—	300	900	2,000	3,250	8,000

NORTH AMERICAN

HALFPENNY

KM#Tn30

Date	AG	Good	VG	Fine	VF	XF	Unc
1781	6.50	12.50	25.00	75.00	135	365	750

RHODE ISLAND SHIP

KM#Tn27a Composition: Brass **Obverse:** Without wreath below ship

Date	AG	Good	VG	Fine	VF	XF	Unc
1779	50.00	100.00	175	275	500	1,000	2,000

KM#Tn27b Composition: Pewter **Obverse:** Without wreath below ship

Date	AG	Good	VG	Fine	VF	XF	Unc
1779	—	—	—	—	1,250	2,500	5,500

KM#Tn28a Composition: Brass **Obverse:** Wreath below ship

Date	AG	Good	VG	Fine	VF	XF	Unc
1779	60.00	120	200	325	600	1,150	2,200

KM#Tn28b Composition: Pewter **Obverse:** Wreath below ship

Date	AG	Good	VG	Fine	VF	XF	Unc
1779	—	—	—	—	1,500	3,000	6,500

KM#Tn29   Composition: Brass **Obverse:** VLUGTENDE below ship

Date	AG	Good	VG	Fine	VF	XF	Unc
1779 unique	—	—	—	—	—	—	—

Note: Garrett $16,000

STANDISH BARRY

3 PENCE

KM#Tn55   Composition: Silver

Date	AG	Good	VG	Fine	VF	XF	Unc
1790	850	1,350	2,000	3,000	6,500	12,000	—

TALBOT, ALLUM & LEE

CENT

KM#Tn71.1   Edge: Lettered. **Composition:** Copper **Reverse:** NEW YORK above ship

Date	AG	Good	VG	Fine	VF	XF	Unc
1794	12.00	25.00	45.00	90.00	175	300	925

KM#Tn71.2   Edge: Plain. **Composition:** Copper **Reverse:** NEW YORK above ship **Note:** Size of ampersand varies on obverse and reverse dies.

Date	AG	Good	VG	Fine	VF	XF	Unc
1794 4 known	—	—	—	—	2,350	3,000	—

KM#Tn72.1   Edge: Lettered. **Composition:** Copper **Reverse:** Without NEW YORK above ship

Date	AG	Good	VG	Fine	VF	XF	Unc
1794	100.00	200	350	650	1,000	2,250	4,550

KM#Tn72.2   Edge: Lettered. **Composition:** Copper

Date	AG	Good	VG	Fine	VF	XF	Unc
1795	10.00	20.00	40.00	75.00	160	300	725

KM#Tn72.3   Edge: Lettered. **Composition:** Copper

Date	AG	Good	VG	Fine	VF	XF	Unc
1795 unique	—	—	—	—	—	—	—

KM#Tn72.4   Edge: Olive leaf. **Composition:** Copper

Date	AG	Good	VG	Fine	VF	XF	Unc
1795 unique	—	—	—	—	—	—	—

Note: Norweb $4,400

KM#Tn72.5   Edge: Plain. **Composition:** Copper

Date	AG	Good	VG	Fine	VF	XF	Unc
1795 plain edge, 2 known	—	—	—	—	—	—	—
1795 edge: Cambridge Bedford Huntington.X.X., unique	—	—	—	—	—	—	—

Note: Norweb, $3,960

WASHINGTON PIECES

KM#Tn35 **Obverse Legend:** GEORGIVS TRIUMPHO

Date	AG	Good	VG	Fine	VF	XF	Unc
1783	25.00	40.00	65.00	150	325	750	—

KM#Tn36 **Obverse:** Large military bust **Note:** Varieties exist.

Date	AG	Good	VG	Fine	VF	XF	Unc
1783	8.00	15.00	25.00	50.00	110	280	—

KM#Tn37.1 **Edge:** Plain. **Obverse:** Small military bust

Date	AG	Good	VG	Fine	VF	XF	Unc
1783	10.00	20.00	35.00	65.00	125	300	—

Note: One proof example is known. Value: 12,500

KM#Tn37.2 **Edge:** Engrailed. **Obverse:** Small military bust

Date	AG	Good	VG	Fine	VF	XF	Unc
1783	18.00	35.00	50.00	80.00	175	345	—

KM#Tn38.1 **Obverse:** Draped bust, no button on drapery, small letter

Date	AG	Good	VG	Fine	VF	XF	Unc
1783	10.00	20.00	35.00	65.00	125	285	—

KM#Tn38.2 **Obverse:** Draped bust, button on drapery, large letter

Date	AG	Good	VG	Fine	VF	XF	Unc
1783	25.00	40.00	60.00	100.00	200	350	—

KM#Tn38.4 **Edge:** Engrailed. **Note:** Restrike.

Date	Good	VG	Fine	VF	XF	Unc	Proof
1783	—	—	—	—	—	—	400

KM#Tn38.4a **Note:** Bronzed. Restrike.

Date	Good	VG	Fine	VF	XF	Unc	Proof
1783	—	—	—	—	—	—	300

KM#Tn38.3 **Edge:** Plain. **Composition:** Copper **Obverse:** Large modern lettering **Note:** Restrike.

Date	Good	VG	Fine	VF	XF	Unc	Proof
1783	—	—	—	—	—	—	500

KM#Tn38.4b **Composition:** Silver **Note:** Restrike.

Date	Good	VG	Fine	VF	XF	Unc	Proof
1783	—	—	—	—	—	—	1,000

KM#Tn38.4c **Composition:** Gold **Note:** Restrike.

Date	AG	Good	VG	Fine	VF	XF	Unc
1783 2 known	—	—	—	—	—	—	—

KM#Tn60.1 **Edge:** Plain. **Composition:** Copper **Obverse Legend:** WASHINGTON PRESIDENT

Date	AG	Good	VG	Fine	VF	XF	Unc
1792	850	1,450	3,250	5,000	7,500	—	—

Note: Steinberg $12,650. Garrett $15,500

KM#Tn60.2   **Edge:** Lettered. **Composition:** Copper **Obverse Legend:** WASHINGTON PRESIDENT

Date	AG	Good	VG	Fine	VF	XF	Unc
1792	1,350	2,250	4,500	7,500	12,500	—	—

KM#Tn61.1   **Composition:** Copper **Obverse Legend:** BORN VIRGINIA **Note:** Varieties exist.

Date	AG	Good	VG	Fine	VF	XF	Unc
(1792)	250	500	1,000	2,200	3,750	7,500	—

KM#Tn61.2   **Edge:** Lettered. **Composition:** Silver

Date	AG	Good	VG	Fine	VF	XF	Unc
(1792) 2 known	—	—	—	—	—	—	—

KM#Tn61.1a   **Edge:** Plain. **Composition:** Silver

Date	AG	Good	VG	Fine	VF	XF	Unc
(1792) 4 known	—	—	—	—	—	—	—

Note: Roper $16,500

KM#Tn62   **Reverse:** Heraldic eagle. 1792 half dollar **Note:** Mule.

Date	AG	Good	VG	Fine	VF	XF	Unc
(1792) 3 known	—	—	—	—	—	—	—

KM#Tn77.1   **Edge:** Lettered. **Obverse Legend:** LIBERTY AND SECURITY. **Note:** "Penny."

Date	AG	Good	VG	Fine	VF	XF	Unc
(1795)	25.00	40.00	75.00	135	275	625	2,000

KM#Tn77.2   **Edge:** Plain. **Note:** "Penny."

Date	AG	Good	VG	Fine	VF	XF	Unc
(1795) extremely rare	—	—	—	—	—	—	—

KM#Tn77.3   **Note:** "Penny." Engine-turned borders.

Date	AG	Good	VG	Fine	VF	XF	Unc
(1795) 12 known	—	—	—	—	—	—	3,750

KM#Tn78   **Note:** Similar to "halfpenny" with date on reverse.

Date	AG	Good	VG	Fine	VF	XF	Unc
1795 very rare	—	—	—	—	—	—	—

Note: Roper $6,600

KM#Tn81.2   **Edge:** Lettered. **Obverse Legend:** NORTH WALES.

Date	AG	Good	VG	Fine	VF	XF	Unc
(1795)	120	250	400	600	950	2,000	4,500

CENT

KM#Tn39   **Obverse Legend:** UNITY STATES

Date	AG	Good	VG	Fine	VF	XF	Unc
1783	12.00	22.00	40.00	70.00	160	325	—

KM#Tn40   **Note:** Double head.

Date	AG	Good	VG	Fine	VF	XF	Unc
(1783)	10.00	20.00	35.00	65.00	135	300	—

KM#Tn41   **Obverse:** "Ugly head." **Note:** 3 known in copper, 1 in white metal.

Date	AG	Good	VG	Fine	VF	XF	Unc
1784	—	—	—	—	—	—	—

Note: Roper $14,850

KM#Tn57   **Reverse:** Small eagle

Date	AG	Good	VG	Fine	VF	XF	Unc
1791	30.00	60.00	125	250	335	675	—

KM#Tn58   **Reverse:** Large eagle

Date	AG	Good	VG	Fine	VF	XF	Unc
1791	35.00	65.00	145	275	375	725	—

KM#Tn65   **Obverse:** "Roman" head

Date	Good	VG	Fine	VF	XF	Unc	Proof
1792	—	—	—	—	—	—	17,600

HALF DOLLAR

KM#Tn63.1   **Edge:** Plain. **Reverse:** Small eagle

Date	AG	Good	VG	Fine	VF	XF	Unc
1792	4,500	7,000	9,000	12,500	20,000	37,500	—

KM#Tn63.2   **Edge:** Ornamented, circles and squares.

Date	AG	Good	VG	Fine	VF	XF	Unc
1792 5 known	—	—	—	—	—	—	—

KM#Tn59.1   **Edge:** Lettered. **Composition:** Copper

Date	AG	Good	VG	Fine	VF	XF	Unc
1792 2 known	—	—	—	—	—	—	—

Note: Roper $2,860. Benson, EF, $48,300

KM#Tn59.2   **Edge:** Plain. **Composition:** Copper

Date	AG	Good	VG	Fine	VF	XF	Unc
1792 3 known	—	—	—	—	—	—	—

KM#Tn59.1a   **Edge:** Lettered. **Composition:** Silver

Date	AG	Good	VG	Fine	VF	XF	Unc
1792 rare	—	—	—	—	—	—	—

Note: Roper $35,200

KM#Tn59.2a   **Edge:** Plain. **Composition:** Silver

Date	AG	Good	VG	Fine	VF	XF	Unc
1792 rare	—	—	—	—	—	—	—

KM#Tn59.1b   **Edge:** Lettered. **Composition:** Gold

Date	AG	Good	VG	Fine	VF	XF	Unc
1792 unique	—	—	—	—	—	—	—

KM#Tn63.1a   **Edge:** Plain. **Composition:** Copper

Date	AG	Good	VG	Fine	VF	XF	Unc
1792	750	1,500	3,500	5,750	8,500	—	—

Note: Garrett $32,000

KM#Tn63.3   **Edge:** Two olive leaves. **Composition:** Silver

Date	AG	Good	VG	Fine	VF	XF	Unc
1792 unique	—	—	—	—	—	—	—

KM#Tn64   **Composition:** Silver **Reverse:** Large heraldic eagle

Date	AG	Good	VG	Fine	VF	XF	Unc
1792 unique	—	—	—	—	—	—	—

Note: Garrett $16,500

HALFPENNY

KM#Tn56   **Obverse Legend:** LIVERPOOL HALFPENNY

Date		AG	Good	VG	Fine	VF	XF	Unc
1791		300	450	550	850	1,650	2,350	—

KM#Tn66.1   **Edge:** Lettered. **Reverse:** Ship

Date		AG	Good	VG	Fine	VF	XF	Unc
1793		20.00	30.00	60.00	110	235	500	—

KM#Tn66.2   **Edge:** Plain. **Reverse:** Ship

Date		AG	Good	VG	Fine	VF	XF	Unc
1793 5 known		—	—	—	—	2,000	—	—

KM#Tn75.1   **Edge:** Reeded. **Obverse:** Large coat buttons **Reverse:** Grate

Date		AG	Good	VG	Fine	VF	XF	Unc
1795		12.00	20.00	30.00	60.00	120	265	575

KM#Tn75.2   **Edge:** Lettered. **Reverse:** Grate

Date		AG	Good	VG	Fine	VF	XF	Unc
1795		45.00	85.00	165	225	300	625	1,200

KM#Tn75.3   **Edge:** Reeded. **Obverse:** Small coat buttons **Reverse:** Grate

Date		AG	Good	VG	Fine	VF	XF	Unc
1795		10.00	35.00	60.00	100.00	175	375	850

KM#Tn76.1   **Edge:** Plain. **Obverse Legend:** LIBERTY AND SECURITY.

Date		AG	Good	VG	Fine	VF	XF	Unc
1795		18.00	35.00	60.00	100.00	175	435	975

KM#Tn76.2   **Edge:** Lettered.

Date		AG	Good	VG	Fine	VF	XF	Unc
1795		12.00	20.00	30.00	60.00	125	375	800

KM#Tn76.3   **Edge:** Lettered.

Date		AG	Good	VG	Fine	VF	XF	Unc
1795		14.00	22.00	35.00	70.00	150	425	950

KM#Tn76.4   **Edge:** Lettered.

Date		AG	Good	VG	Fine	VF	XF	Unc
1795		18.00	35.00	60.00	100.00	225	450	1,000

KM#Tn76.5   **Edge:** Lettered.

Date		AG	Good	VG	Fine	VF	XF	Unc
1795 unique		—	—	—	—	—	—	—

KM#Tn76.6   **Edge:** Lettered.

Date		AG	Good	VG	Fine	VF	XF	Unc
1795 unique		—	—	—	—	—	—	—

KM#Tn81.1   Edge: Plain. **Obverse Legend:** NORTH WALES.

Date	AG	Good	VG	Fine	VF	XF	Unc
(1795)	25.00	45.00	85.00	145	250	550	1,450

KM#Tn82   Obverse Legend: NORTH WALES. **Reverse:** Four stars at bottom

Date	AG	Good	VG	Fine	VF	XF	Unc
(1795)	200	400	700	1,500	2,850	5,500	—

EARLY AMERICAN PATTERNS

CONFEDERATIO

KM#EA22   Reverse: Small circle of stars

Date	AG	Good	VG	Fine	VF	XF	Unc
1785	—	—	—	—	8,800	16,500	—

KM#EA23   Composition: Copper **Reverse:** Large circle of stars **Note:** The Confederatio dies were struck in combination with 13 other dies of the period. All surviving examples of these combinations are extremely rare.

Date	AG	Good	VG	Fine	VF	XF	Unc
1785 extremely rare	—	—	—	—	—	—	—

IMMUNE COLUMBIA

KM#EA20   Obverse: George III

Date	AG	Good	VG	Fine	VF	XF	Unc
1785	750	1,250	1,850	2,250	5,000	9,000	—

KM#EA21   Obverse: Vermon

Date	AG	Good	VG	Fine	VF	XF	Unc
1785	600	1,000	1,650	2,000	4,750	8,500	—

KM#EA17a   Composition: Silver **Reverse Legend:** CONSTELLATIO.

Date	AG	Good	VG	Fine	VF	XF	Unc
1785	—	—	—	—	—	20,700	—

KM#EA19a   Composition: Gold **Reverse Legend:** CONSTELATIO.

Date	AG	Good	VG	Fine	VF	XF	Unc
1785 unique	—	—	—	—	—	—	—

KM#EA17   Composition: Copper **Reverse Legend:** CONSTELLATIO

Date	AG	Good	VG	Fine	VF	XF	Unc
1785	—	—	—	—	—	14,375	—

KM#EA18   Composition: Copper **Obverse Legend:** Extra star in border **Reverse Legend:** CONSTELLATIO

Date	AG	Good	VG	Fine	VF	XF	Unc
1785	—	—	—	—	—	—	—

Note: Caldwell $4,675

KM#EA19   Rev. Designer: CONSTELATIO **Composition:** Copper **Reverse:** Blunt rays

Date	AG	Good	VG	Fine	VF	XF	Unc
1785 2 known	—	—	—	—	—	—	—

Note: Norweb $22,000

KM#EA24   Obverse: Washington

Date	AG	Good	VG	Fine	VF	XF	Unc
(1786) 3 known	—	—	—	—	—	—	—

Note: Garrett $50,000. Steinberg $12,650

KM#EA25   Obverse: Eagle

Date	AG	Good	VG	Fine	VF	XF	Unc
1786 unique	—	—	—	—	—	—	—

Note: Garrett $37,500

KM#EA26   Obverse: Washington **Reverse:** Eagle

Date	AG	Good	VG	Fine	VF	XF	Unc
1786 2 known	—	—	—	—	—	—	—

KM#EA27   Obverse Legend: IMMUNIS COLUMBIA

Date	AG	Good	VG	Fine	VF	XF	Unc
1786 extremely rare	—	—	—	—	—	—	—

Note: Rescigno, AU, $33,000. Steinberg, VF, $11,000

KM#EA28   Obverse Legend: IMMUNIS COLUMBIA. **Reverse:** Eagle

Date	AG	Good	VG	Fine	VF	XF	Unc
1786 3 known	—	—	—	—	—	—	—

NOVA CONSTELLATIO

5

KM#EA12   Composition: Copper

Date	AG	Good	VG	Fine	VF	XF	Unc
1783 unique	—	—	—	—	—	—	—

100 (BIT)

KM#EA13.1   Edge: Leaf. **Composition:** Silver

Date	AG	Good	VG	Fine	VF	XF	Unc
1783 2 known	—	—	—	—	—	—	—

Note: Garrett $97,500. Stack's auction, May 1991, $72,500

KM#EA13.2   Edge: Plain. **Composition:** Silver

Date	AG	Good	VG	Fine	VF	XF	Unc
1783 unique	—	—	—	—	—	—	—

500 (QUINT)

KM#EA15   Obverse: Without legend

Date	AG	Good	VG	Fine	VF	XF	Unc
1783 unique	—	—	—	—	—	—	—

Note: Garrett $55,000

KM#EA14   Composition: Silver **Obverse Legend:** NOVA CONSTELLATIO

Date	AG	Good	VG	Fine	VF	XF	Unc
1783 unique	—	—	—	—	—	—	—

Note: Garrett $165,000

1000 (MARK)

KM#EA16   Composition: Silver

Date	AG	Good	VG	Fine	VF	XF	Unc
1783 unique	—	—	—	—	—	—	—

Note: Garrett $190,000

EARLY FEDERAL COINAGE

FUGIO "CENT"

KM#EA30.1   Composition: Copper **Obverse:** Club rays, round ends

Date	AG	Good	VG	Fine	VF	XF	Unc
1787	40.00	75.00	150	375	850	1,600	—

KM#EA30.2   Composition: Copper **Obverse:** Club rays, concave ends

Date	AG	Good	VG	Fine	VF	XF	Unc
1787	250	700	1,800	2,750	5,000	—	—

KM#EA30.3   Composition: Copper **Obverse Legend:** FUCIO.

Date	AG	Good	VG	Fine	VF	XF	Unc
1787	—	750	1,850	2,850	5,500	—	—

KM#EA31.1   Composition: Copper **Obverse:** Pointed rays **Reverse:** UNITED above, STATES below

Date	AG	Good	VG	Fine	VF	XF	Unc
1787	100.00	250	550	1,000	1,500	3,500	—

KM#EA31.2   Composition: Copper **Reverse:** UNITED STATES at sides of ring

Date	AG	Good	VG	Fine	VF	XF	Unc
1787	20.00	45.00	90.00	175	300	650	—

KM#EA31.3   Composition: Copper **Reverse:** STATES UNITED at sides of ring

Date	AG	Good	VG	Fine	VF	XF	Unc
1787	25.00	55.00	110	220	350	700	—

KM#EA31.4   Composition: Copper **Reverse:** Eight-pointed stars on ring

Date	AG	Good	VG	Fine	VF	XF	Unc
1787	30.00	65.00	120	250	400	800	—

KM#EA31.5   Composition: Copper **Reverse:** Raised rims on ring, large lettering in center

Date	AG	Good	VG	Fine	VF	XF	Unc
1787	35.00	75.00	135	275	450	950	—

KM#EA32.1   Composition: Copper **Obverse:** No cinquefoils, cross after date **Obverse Legend:** UNITED STATES.

Date	AG	Good	VG	Fine	VF	XF	Unc
1787	50.00	110	250	425	650	1,250	—

KM#EA32.2   Composition: Copper **Obverse:** No cinquefoils, cross after date **Obverse Legend:** STATES UNITED.

Date	AG	Good	VG	Fine	VF	XF	Unc
1787	60.00	135	285	475	750	1,500	—

KM#EA32.3   Composition: Copper **Obverse:** No cinquefoils, cross after date **Reverse:** Raised rims on ring

Date	AG	Good	VG	Fine	VF	XF	Unc
1787	—	—	—	—	2,600	—	—

KM#EA33   Composition: Copper **Obverse:** No cinquefoils, cross after date **Reverse:** With rays **Reverse Legend:** AMERICAN CONGRESS.

Date	AG	Good	VG	Fine	VF	XF	Unc
1787 extremely rare	—	—	—	—	—	—	—

Note: Norweb $63,800

KM#EA34   Composition: Brass **Note:** New Haven restrike.

Date	AG	Good	VG	Fine	VF	XF	Unc
(1858)	—	—	—	—	—	—	500

KM#EA34a   Composition: Copper **Note:** New Haven restrike.

Date	AG	Good	VG	Fine	VF	XF	Unc
(1858)	—	—	—	—	—	500	—

KM#EA34b   Composition: Silver **Note:** New Haven restrike.

Date	AG	Good	VG	Fine	VF	XF	Unc
(1858)	—	—	—	—	—	—	1,850

KM#EA34c   Composition: Gold **Note:** New Haven restrike.

Date	AG	Good	VG	Fine	VF	XF	Unc
(1858) 2 known	—	—	—	—	—	—	—

Note: Norweb (holed) $1,430

NOVA CONSTELLATIO

KM#EA6.1   Composition: Copper **Obverse:** Pointed rays **Obverse Legend:** CONSTELLATIO. **Reverse:** Small "US"

Date	AG	Good	VG	Fine	VF	XF	Unc
1783	20.00	35.00	65.00	125	255	585	—

KM#EA6.2 **Composition:** Copper **Obverse:** Pointed rays **Obverse Legend:** CONSTELLATIO. **Reverse:** Large "US"

Date	AG	Good	VG	Fine	VF	XF	Unc
1783	20.00	35.00	70.00	140	285	650	—

KM#EA7 **Composition:** Copper **Obverse:** Blunt rays **Obverse Legend:** CONSTELATIO.

Date	AG	Good	VG	Fine	VF	XF	Unc
1783	22.00	40.00	80.00	150	350	750	—

KM#EA8 **Composition:** Copper **Obverse:** Blunt rays **Obverse Legend:** CONSTELLATIO.

Date	AG	Good	VG	Fine	VF	XF	Unc
1785	22.00	40.00	80.00	160	375	775	—

KM#EA9 **Composition:** Copper **Obverse:** Pointed rays **Obverse Legend:** CONSTELLATIO.

Date	AG	Good	VG	Fine	VF	XF	Unc
1785	20.00	35.00	70.00	140	285	650	—

KM#EA10 **Composition:** Copper **Note:** Contemporary circulating countefeit. Similar to previously listed coin.

Date	AG	Good	VG	Fine	VF	XF	Unc
1786 extremely rare	—	—	—	—	—	—	—

ISSUES OF 1792

CENT

KM#PnH1 **Obverse:** One star in edge legend **Note:** Commonly called "Birch cent."

Date	AG	Good	VG	Fine	VF	XF	Unc
1792 2 known	—	—	—	—	—	—	—

Note: Norweb, EF-40, $59,400

KM#Pnl1 **Obverse:** Two stars in edge legend **Note:** Commonly called "Birch cent."

Date	AG	Good	VG	Fine	VF	XF	Unc
1792 6 known	—	—	—	—	—	—	—

Note: Hawn, strong VF, $57,750

KM#PnE1   Composition: SILVER.

Date	AG	Good	VG	Fine	VF	XF	Unc
1792 12 known	—	—	—	—	—	—	—

Note: Norweb, MS-60, $143,000

KM#PnF1   Composition: COPPER. **Note:** No silver center.

Date	AG	Good	VG	Fine	VF	XF	Unc
1792 8 known	—	—	—	—	—	—	—

Note: Norweb, EF-40, $35,200; Benson, VG-10, $57,500

KM#PnG1   Edge: Plain. **Composition:** COPPER. **Note:** Commonly called "Birch cent."

Date	AG	Good	VG	Fine	VF	XF	Unc
1792 unique	—	—	—	—	—	—	—

KM#PnJ1   Composition: WHITE METAL. **Reverse:** "G.W.Pt." below wreath tie **Note:** Commonly called "Birch cent."

Date	AG	Good	VG	Fine	VF	XF	Unc
1792 unique	—	—	—	—	—	—	—

Note: Garrett, $90,000

HALF DISME

KM#5   Composition: SILVER.

Date	AG	Good	VG	Fine	VF	XF	Unc
1792	1,250	—	3,500	6,500	8,500	16,500	—

KM#PnA1   Composition: COPPER.

Date	AG	Good	VG	Fine	VF	XF	Unc
1792 unique	—	—	—	—	—	—	—

DISME

KM#PnB1 **Composition:** SILVER.

Date	AG	Good	VG	Fine	VF	XF	Unc
1792 3 known	—	—	—	—	—	—	—

Note: Norweb, EF-40, $28,600

KM#PnC1 **Edge:** Reeded. **Composition:** COPPER.

Date	AG	Good	VG	Fine	VF	XF	Unc
1792 14 known	—	—	—	—	—	—	—

Note: Hawn, VF, $30,800; Benson, EF-45, $109,250

KM#PnD1 **Edge:** Plain. **Composition:** COPPER.

Date	AG	Good	VG	Fine	VF	XF	Unc
1792 2 known	—	—	—	—	—	—	—

Note: Garrett, $45,000

QUARTER

KM#PnK1 **Edge:** Reeded. **Composition:** COPPER. **Note:** Commonly called "Wright quarter."

Date	AG	Good	VG	Fine	VF	XF	Unc
1792 2 known	—	—	—	—	—	—	—

KM#PnL1 **Edge:** Plain. **Composition:** WHITE METAL. **Note:** Commonly called "Wright quarter."

Date	AG	Good	VG	Fine	VF	XF	Unc
1792 2 known	—	—	—	—	—	—	—

Note: Norweb, VF-30 to EF-40, $28,600

KM#PnM1 **Composition:** WHITE METAL. **Note:** Commonly called "Wright quarter."

Date	AG	Good	VG	Fine	VF	XF	Unc
1792 die trial	—	—	—	—	—	—	—

Note: Garrett, $12,000

CIRCULATION COINAGE

HALF CENT

Liberty Cap. Head facing left.

KM# 10 Designer: Adam Eckfeldt **Obverse:** Head facing left **Weight:** 6.7400 g. **Composition:** Copper **Size:** 22 mm.

Date	Mintage	G-4	VG-8	F-12	VF-20	XF-40	MS-60
1793	35,334	2,000	2,750	3,800	5,850	11,500	35,000

Liberty Cap. Head facing right.

KM# 14   Designer: Robert Scot (1794) and John Smith Gardner (1795) **Obverse:** Head facing right **Composition:** Copper **Size:** 23.5 mm. **Note:** The "lettered edge" varieties have "Two Hundred for a Dollar" inscribed around the edge. The "pole" varieties have a pole upon which the cap is hanging, resting on Liberty's shoulder. The "punctuated date" varieties have a comma after the 1 in the date. The 1797 "1 above 1" variety has a second 1 above the 1 in the date.

Date	Mintage	G-4	VG-8	F-12	VF-20	XF-40	MS-60
1794	81,600	315	500	750	1,500	3,250	18,000
1795 lettered edge, pole	25,600	300	450	700	1,250	3,500	15,000
1795 plain edge, no pole	109,000	325	400	685	1,200	3,000	15,000
1795 lettered edge, punctuated date	Inc. above	350	500	750	1,200	3,500	18,500
1795 plain edge, punctuated date	Inc. above	300	400	670	1,100	2,500	25,000
1796 pole	5,090	8,000	12,000	17,500	20,000	27,500	—
1796 no pole	1,390	22,500	30,000	45,000	85,000	—	—
1797 plain edge	119,215	315	440	800	1,700	4,500	25,000
1797 lettered edge	Inc. above	1,100	1,900	3,400	7,350	21,000	—
1797 1 above 1	Inc. above	290	390	800	1,450	3,000	15,000
1797 gripped edge	Inc. above	15,000	37,500	48,000	60,000	70,000	—

Draped Bust.

Stemless   Stems

KM# 33 Designer: Robert Scot **Weight:** 5.4400 g. **Composition:** Copper **Size:** 23.5 mm. **Note:** The wreath on the reverse was redesigned slightly in 1802, resulting in "reverse of 1800" and "reverse of 1802" varieties. The "stems" varieties have stems extending from the wreath above and on both sides of the fraction on the reverse. On the 1804 "crosslet 4" variety, a serif appears at the far right of the crossbar on the 4 in the date. The "spiked chin" variety appears to have a spike extending from Liberty's chin, the result of a damaged die. Varieties of the 1805 strikes are distinguished by the size of the 5 in the date. Varieties of the 1806 strikes are distinguished by the size of the 6 in the date.

Date	Mintage	G-4	VG-8	F-12	VF-20	XF-40	MS-60
1800	211,530	45.00	60.00	85.00	170	450	1,800
1802/0 rev. 1800	14,366	12,000	19,500	27,500	—	—	—
1802/0 rev. 1802	Inc. above	600	975	2,400	5,800	15,000	—
1803	97,900	45.00	60.00	90.00	220	800	6,500
1804 plain 4, stemless wreath	1,055,312	44.00	58.00	75.00	115	220	1,200
1804 plain 4, stems	Inc. above	45.00	75.00	125	250	1,500	12,000
1804 crosslet 4, stemless	Inc. above	44.00	58.00	75.00	110	220	1,250
1804 crosslet 4, stems	Inc. above	44.00	58.00	75.00	110	220	1,100

Date	Mintage	G-4	VG-8	F-12	VF-20	XF-40	MS-60
1804 spiked chin	Inc. above	50.00	65.00	90.00	150	300	1,050
1805 small 5, stemless	814,464	44.00	58.00	80.00	125	350	2,750
1805 small 5, stems	Inc. above	550	1,000	2,000	4,000	7,500	—
1805 large 5, stems	Inc. above	44.00	58.00	75.00	110	350	2,500
1806 small 6, stems	356,000	165	300	500	900	2,500	—
1806 small 6, stemless	Inc. above	44.00	58.00	75.00	110	215	1,250
1806 large 6, stems	Inc. above	44.00	58.00	80.00	115	225	1,050
1807	476,000	44.00	58.00	80.00	115	400	3,000
1808/7	400,000	175	275	550	1,000	5,000	25,000
1808	Inc. above	44.00	58.00	80.00	120	300	4,500

Classic Head.

KM# 41 Designer: John Reich **Weight:** 5.4400 g. **Composition:** Copper **Size:** 23.5 mm. **Note:** Restrikes listed were produced privately in the mid-1800s. The 1831 restrikes have two varieties with different-size berries in the wreath on the reverse. The 1828 strikes have either 12 or 13 stars on the obverse.

Date	Mintage	G-4	VG-8	F-12	VF-20	XF-40	MS-60
1809/6	1,154,572	34.00	70.00	80.00	110	140	850
1809	Inc. above	32.00	38.00	52.50	75.00	200	750
1809 circle in 0	—	32.00	39.00	55.00	95.00	225	2,000
1810	215,000	32.00	50.00	100.00	160	575	3,000
1811	63,140	135	200	500	1,250	3,500	—
1825	63,000	30.00	37.50	52.50	75.00	150	850
1826	234,000	30.00	37.50	52.50	65.00	125	600
1828 13 stars	606,000	30.00	37.50	52.50	60.00	75.00	300
1828 12 stars	Inc. above	30.00	38.50	52.50	75.00	180	600
1829	487,000	30.00	37.50	52.50	62.50	125	475
1831 original	2,200	3,500	4,200	4,900	6,700	9,500	—
1832	154,000	32.00	40.00	54.00	60.00	75.00	300
1833	120,000	30.00	37.50	52.50	60.00	75.00	250
1834	141,000	30.00	37.50	52.50	60.00	75.00	250
1835	398,000	30.00	37.50	52.50	60.00	75.00	250
1836 original, proof	—	—	—	—	—	—	5,000

1825 Half Cent
Grade F-12

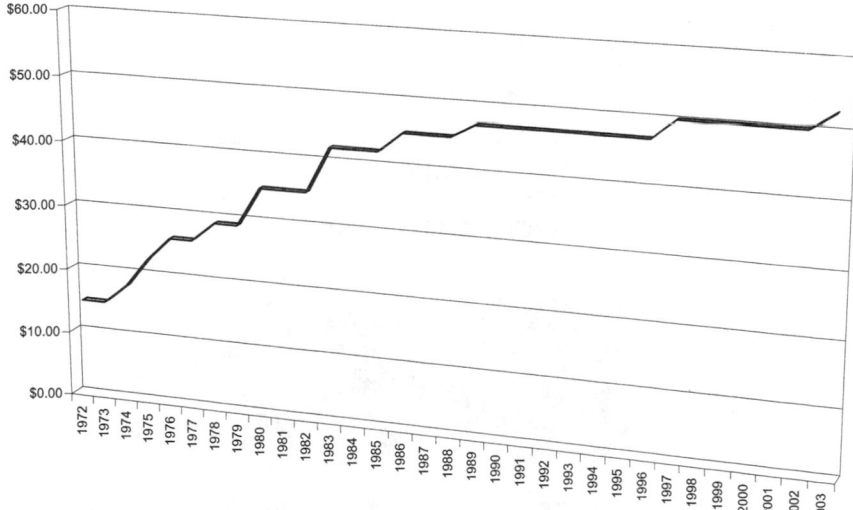

Retail Price

Braided Hair.

KM# 70 **Designer:** Christian Gobrecht **Weight:** 5.4400 g. **Composition:** Copper **Size:** 23 mm. **Note:** 1840-1849 and 1852 strikes, both originals and restrikes, are known in proof only; mintages are unknown. The small-date varieties of 1849, both originals and restrikes, are known in proof only. The Restrikes were produced clandestinely by Philadelphia Mint personnel in the mid-1800s.

Date	Mintage	G-4	VG-8	F-12	VF-20	XF-40	MS-60	Prf-60
1840 original	—	—	—	—	—	—	—	3,800
1840 1st restrike	—	—	—	—	—	—	—	3,500
1840 2nd restrike	—	—	—	—	—	—	—	3,200
1841 original	—	—	—	—	—	—	—	3,800
1841 1st restrike	—	—	—	—	—	—	—	3,500
1841 2nd restrike	—	—	—	—	—	—	—	3,000
1842 original	—	—	—	—	—	—	—	3,800
1842 1st restrike	—	—	—	—	—	—	—	3,500
1842 2nd restrike	—	—	—	—	—	—	—	3,200
1843 original	—	—	—	—	—	—	—	3,800
1843 1st restrike	—	—	—	—	—	—	—	3,500
1843 2nd restrike	—	—	—	—	—	—	—	3,200
1844 original	—	—	—	—	—	—	—	3,800
1844 1st restrike	—	—	—	—	—	—	—	3,500
1844 2nd restrike	—	—	—	—	—	—	—	3,200
1845 original	—	—	—	—	—	—	—	3,800
1845 1st restrike	—	—	—	—	—	—	—	3,500
1845 2nd restrike	—	—	—	—	—	—	—	3,200
1846 original	—	—	—	—	—	—	—	3,800
1846 1st restrike	—	—	—	—	—	—	—	3,500
1846 2nd restrike	—	—	—	—	—	—	—	3,200
1847 original	—	—	—	—	—	—	—	3,800
1847 1st restrike	—	—	—	—	—	—	—	10,000
1847 2nd restrike	—	—	—	—	—	—	—	3,200
1848 original	—	—	—	—	—	—	—	3,800
1848 1st restrike	—	—	—	—	—	—	—	3,500
1848 2nd restrike	—	—	—	—	—	—	—	3,200
1849 original, small date	—	—	—	—	—	—	—	3,800
1849 1st restrike small date	—	—	—	—	—	—	—	3,200
1849 large date	39,864	38.00	43.00	60.00	75.00	125	250	—
1850	39,812	34.00	42.00	60.00	75.00	110	300	—
1851	147,672	28.00	38.00	52.00	60.00	72.00	165	—
1852 original	—	—	—	—	—	—	—	35,000
1852 1st restrike	—	—	—	—	—	—	—	3,500
1852 2nd restrike	—	—	—	—	—	—	—	5,000
1853	129,694	28.00	38.00	52.00	60.00	72.00	165	—
1854	55,358	28.00	38.00	52.00	60.00	72.00	165	—
1855	56,500	29.00	39.00	54.00	60.00	72.00	165	—
1856	40,430	32.00	42.00	53.00	66.00	90.00	240	—
1857	35,180	60.00	75.00	90.00	85.00	145	275	—

CENT

Flowing Hair. Chain.

KM# 11 **Designer:** Henry Voigt **Reverse:** Chain **Weight:** 13.4800 g. **Composition:** Copper **Size:** 26-27 mm.

Date	Mintage	G-4	VG-8	F-12	VF-20	XF-40	MS-60
1793	36,103	4,500	7,500	9,000	14,000	21,000	75,000

Flowing Hair. Wreath.

KM# 12 Designer: Adam Eckfeldt **Reverse:** Wreath **Weight:** 13.4800 g. **Composition:** Copper
Size: 26-28 mm.

Date	Mintage	G-4	VG-8	F-12	VF-20	XF-40	MS-60
1793	63,353	1,300	2,000	3,200	6,000	9,000	26,500

Liberty Cap.

KM# 13 Designer: Joseph Wright (1793-1795) and John Smith Gardner (1795-1796) **Composition:** Copper
Size: 29 mm. **Note:** The heavier pieces were struck on a thicker planchet. The Liberty design on the obverse
was revised slightly in 1794, but the 1793 design was used on some 1794 strikes. A 1795 "lettered edge" variety
has "One Hundred for a Dollar" and a leaf inscribed on the edge.

Date	Mintage	G-4	VG-8	F-12	VF-20	XF-40	MS-60
1793 cap	11,056	3,000	5,000	7,000	15,000	22,500	—
1794	918,521	165	250	500	1,100	3,000	—
1794 head '93	Inc. above	1,100	2,100	3,300	6,500	10,000	—
1795	501,500	165	275	375	630	1,750	3,500

Liberty Cap.

KM# 13a Designer: Joseph Wright (1793-1795) and John Smith Gardner (1795-1796) **Weight:** 10.8900 g.
Composition: Copper **Size:** 29 mm.

Date	Mintage	G-4	VG-8	F-12	VF-20	XF-40	MS-60
1795 lettered edge, "One Cent" high in wreath	37,000	300	400	600	1,750	3,300	11,000
1796	109,825	145	260	600	1,500	3,100	6,100

Draped Bust.

Stemless   Stems

KM# 22 Designer: Robert Scot **Weight:** 10.9800 g. **Composition:** Copper **Size:** 29 mm. **Note:** The "stemless"
variety does not have stems extending from the wreath above and on both sides of the fraction on the reverse.
The 1801 "3 errors" variety has the fraction on the reverse reading "1/000," has only one stem extending from
the wreath above and on both sides of the fraction on the reverse, and "United" in "United States of America"
appears as "Iinited."

1804 Cent
Grade F-12

☐ Retail Price

Date	Mintage	G-4	VG-8	F-12	VF-20	XF-40	MS-60
1796	363,375	225	350	700	1,800	3,400	—
1797	897,510	49.00	100.00	160	335	1,150	3,300
1797 stemless	Inc. above	300	495	600	910	3,200	—
1798	1,841,745	48.00	85.00	130	385	975	3,100
1798/7	Inc. above	100.00	180	310	1,050	3,900	—
1799	42,540	3,000	4,000	5,500	15,000	27,500	—
1800	2,822,175	40.00	65.00	130	350	1,250	—
1801	1,362,837	36.00	65.00	125	280	1,000	—
1801 3 errors	Inc. above	85.00	275	900	1,750	5,500	—
1802	3,435,100	34.00	55.00	110	225	775	2,250
1803	2,471,353	34.00	55.00	110	225	775	2,250
1804	96,500	950	1,400	2,000	2,550	7,000	—
1805	941,116	37.00	60.00	125	300	875	2,450
1806	348,000	39.00	75.00	125	350	1,100	4,700
1807	727,221	31.00	53.00	110	225	775	2,250
1807/6 large 7/6	—	34.00	55.00	125	250	1,275	—
1807/6 small 7/6	—	600	1,200	2,500	—	—	—

Classic Head.

KM# 39 Designer: John Reich **Weight:** 10.8900 g. **Composition:** Copper **Size:** 29 mm.

Date	Mintage	G-4	VG-8	F-12	VF-20	XF-40	MS-60
1808	1,109,000	45.00	80.00	220	575	1,200	3,600
1809	222,867	90.00	175	420	1,300	2,650	6,300
1810	1,458,500	36.00	70.00	200	550	1,100	3,850
1811	218,025	90.00	150	400	1,000	1,500	7,000
1811/10	Inc. above	90.00	175	440	1,200	2,200	—
1812	1,075,500	36.00	65.00	180	525	975	2,800
1813	418,000	60.00	95.00	375	600	1,200	—
1814	357,830	36.00	65.00	180	530	975	2,800

Coronet.

KM# 45 Designer: Robert Scot **Weight:** 10.8900 g. **Composition:** Copper **Size:** 28-29 mm. **Note:** The 1817 strikes have either 13 or 15 stars on the obverse.

Date	Mintage	G-4	VG-8	F-12	VF-20	XF-40	MS-60
1816	2,820,982	14.00	25.00	50.00	100.00	175	420
1817 13 stars	3,948,400	12.50	16.00	24.00	56.00	120	275
1817 15 stars	Inc. above	16.00	25.00	45.00	125	350	1,550
1818	3,167,000	12.50	16.00	24.00	56.00	125	250
1819	2,671,000	12.50	16.00	23.00	63.00	120	275
1820	4,407,550	12.50	16.00	23.00	63.00	120	275
1821	389,000	25.00	38.00	250	400	1,500	6,000
1822	2,072,339	12.50	16.00	32.00	84.00	195	575
1823 Included in 1824 mintage	—	90.00	120	310	690	2,750	—
1823/22 Included in 1824 mintage	—	80.00	110	300	675	2,450	—
1823 Restrike	—	300	400	450	500	550	700
1824	1,262,000	14.00	23.00	38.00	145	350	625
1824/22	Inc. above	17.00	30.00	56.00	225	975	—
1825	1,461,100	13.00	16.00	35.00	110	300	840
1826	1,517,425	12.50	16.00	26.00	84.00	175	700
1826/25	Inc. above	16.00	24.00	60.00	175	600	1,800
1827	2,357,732	12.50	16.00	23.00	75.00	135	385
1828	2,260,624	12.50	16.00	26.00	84.00	175	425
1829	1,414,500	12.50	16.00	22.00	100.00	140	425
1830	1,711,500	12.50	16.00	22.00	70.00	135	385
1831	3,359,260	12.50	16.00	22.00	63.00	125	315
1832	2,362,000	12.50	16.00	22.00	63.00	125	315
1833	2,739,000	12.50	16.00	22.00	56.00	120	265
1834	1,855,100	12.50	16.00	22.00	56.00	140	250
1835	3,878,400	12.50	16.00	22.00	56.00	91.00	225
1836	2,111,000	13.00	16.00	24.00	60.00	105	250
1837	5,558,300	12.50	16.00	22.00	51.00	91.00	300
1838	6,370,200	12.50	16.00	22.00	51.00	91.00	225
1839	3,128,661	12.50	16.00	22.00	51.00	105	350
1839/36	Inc. above	400	500	700	1,500	3,900	—

Braided Hair.

KM# 67 Designer: Christian Gobrecht **Weight:** 10.8900 g. **Composition:** Copper **Size:** 27.5 mm. **Note:** 1840 and 1842 strikes are known with both small and large dates, with little difference in value. 1855 and 1856 strikes are known with both slanting and upright 5s in the date, with little difference in value. A slightly larger Liberty head and larger reverse lettering were used beginning in 1843. One 1843 variety uses the old obverse with the new reverse.

Date	Mintage	G-4	VG-8	F-12	VF-20	XF-40	MS-60
1840	2,462,700	11.00	14.00	17.00	38.00	70.00	475
1841	1,597,367	14.00	18.00	22.00	44.00	80.00	440
1842	2,383,390	11.00	15.00	17.00	38.00	70.00	425
1843	2,425,342	11.00	15.00	17.00	38.00	75.00	445
1843 obverse 1842 with reverse of 1844	Inc. above	12.00	15.00	21.00	38.00	80.00	350
1844	2,398,752	11.00	15.00	16.00	22.00	54.00	215
1844/81	Inc. above	20.00	50.00	75.00	100.00	200	600
1845	3,894,804	11.00	15.00	16.00	20.00	44.00	225
1846	4,120,800	11.00	15.00	16.00	20.00	44.00	225
1847	6,183,669	11.00	15.00	16.00	20.00	44.00	160
1848	6,415,799	11.00	15.00	16.00	20.00	44.00	160
1849	4,178,500	11.00	15.00	16.00	28.00	60.00	275
1850	4,426,844	11.00	15.00	16.00	20.00	44.00	160
1851	9,889,707	11.00	15.00	16.00	20.00	41.00	160
1851/81	Inc. above	15.00	15.00	35.00	80.00	150	500
1852	5,063,094	11.00	15.00	16.00	20.00	41.00	160
1853	6,641,131	11.00	15.00	16.00	20.00	41.00	160

1857 Cent
Grade XF-40

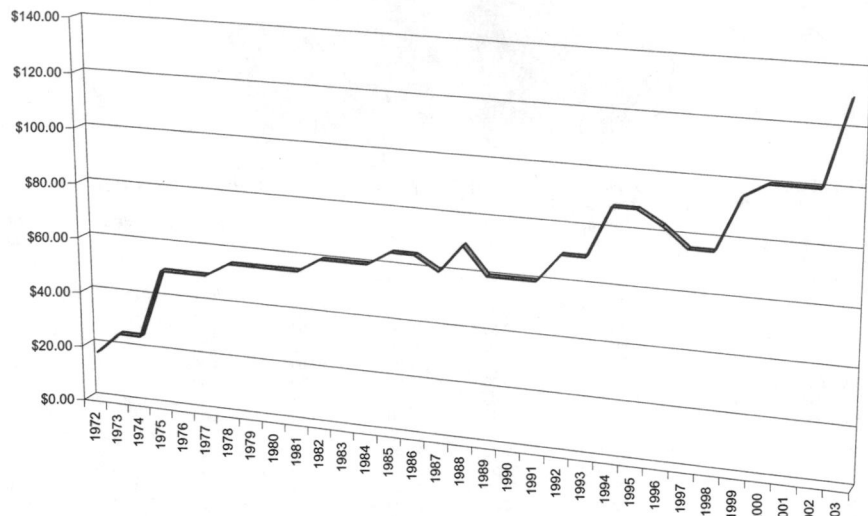

Retail Price

Date	Mintage	G-4	VG-8	F-12	VF-20	XF-40	MS-60
1854	4,236,156	11.00	15.00	16.00	20.00	41.00	160
1855	1,574,829	14.00	18.00	20.00	26.00	50.00	170
1856	2,690,463	12.00	15.00	17.00	22.00	42.00	160
1857	333,456	50.00	60.00	75.00	100.00	150	250

Flying Eagle.

Large Letters   **Small Letters**

KM# 85 Designer: James B. Longacre **Weight:** 4.6700 g. **Composition:** Copper-Nickel **Size:** 19 mm. **Note:** On the large-letter variety of 1858, the "A" and "M" in "America" are connected at their bases; on the small-letter variety, the two letters are separated.

Date	Mintage	G-4	VG-8	F-12	VF-20	XF-40	AU-50	MS-60	MS-65	Prf-65
1856	Est. 2,500	5,850	6,700	7,300	7,800	8,500	9,500	9,800	57,000	24,500
1857	17,450,000	18.50	21.50	27.50	38.50	115	160	280	3,750	29,000
1858/7	—	65.00	90.00	175	390	750	1,500	2,500	75,000	—
1858 large letters	24,600,000	18.50	21.50	27.50	38.50	120	175	290	3,750	23,500
1858 small letters	Inc. above	18.50	21.50	27.50	38.50	120	175	290	3,750	30,000

Indian Head.

KM# 87 Designer: James B. Longacre **Weight:** 4.6700 g. **Composition:** Copper-Nickel **Size:** 19 mm.

Date	Mintage	G-4	VG-8	F-12	VF-20	XF-40	AU-50	MS-60	MS-65	Prf-65
1859	36,400,000	11.50	13.00	16.00	40.00	100.00	175	200	2,750	5,000

Indian Head. Shield added at top of wreath.

KM# 90 **Designer:** James B. Longacre **Reverse:** Shield added at top of wreath **Weight:** 4.6700 g.
Composition: Copper-Nickel **Size:** 19 mm.

Date	Mintage	G-4	VG-8	F-12	VF-20	XF-40	AU-50	MS-60	MS-65	Prf-65
1860	20,566,0001,000	8.00	10.00	13.00	16.00	50.00	80.00	130	1,000	3,900
1861	10,100,000	19.50	29.00	38.00	44.00	90.00	160	175	900	7,150
1862	28,075,000	7.00	8.50	10.00	14.50	26.50	55.00	80.00	900	2,100
1863	49,840,000	7.00	8.50	9.00	12.00	24.00	54.00	65.00	900	3,200
1864	13,740,000	14.50	19.50	29.00	40.00	64.00	80.00	140	1,200	3,200

Indian Head.

1864 "L"

KM# 90a **Designer:** James B. Longacre **Weight:** 3.1100 g. **Composition:** Bronze **Size:** 19 mm. **Note:** The 1864 "L" variety has the designer's initial in Liberty's hair to the right of her neck.

Date	Mintage	G-4	VG-8	F-12	VF-20	XF-40	AU-50	MS-60	MS-65	Prf-65
1864	39,233,714	5.50	12.00	17.50	30.00	54.00	60.00	80.00	325	4,300
1864 L	Inc. above	50.00	60.00	95.00	120	200	225	300	1,500	110,000
1865	35,429,286	5.50	10.00	17.50	20.00	32.50	50.00	80.00	450	1,550
1866	9,826,500	38.50	45.00	60.00	85.00	165	210	240	1,250	950
1867	9,821,000	37.50	50.00	67.50	100.00	165	210	240	1,250	1,050
1868	10,266,500	35.00	40.00	50.00	80.00	145	180	220	950	985
1869/9	6,420,000	115	140	230	335	465	550	640	1,800	—
1869	Inc. above	55.00	80.00	180	240	290	365	400	1,450	950
1870	5,275,000	40.00	65.00	175	230	320	370	415	1,400	1,075
1871	3,929,500	55.00	70.00	225	275	325	385	425	2,400	1,100
1872	4,042,000	65.00	80.00	275	300	335	385	500	4,200	1,100
1073	11,676,500	18.50	27.00	44.00	55.00	145	170	200	1,300	850
1874	14,187,500	14.00	17.50	27.50	42.50	90.00	120	165	700	800
1875	13,528,000	14.00	25.00	42.50	50.00	90.00	120	160	800	1,500

1864-L Indian Cent
Grade F-12

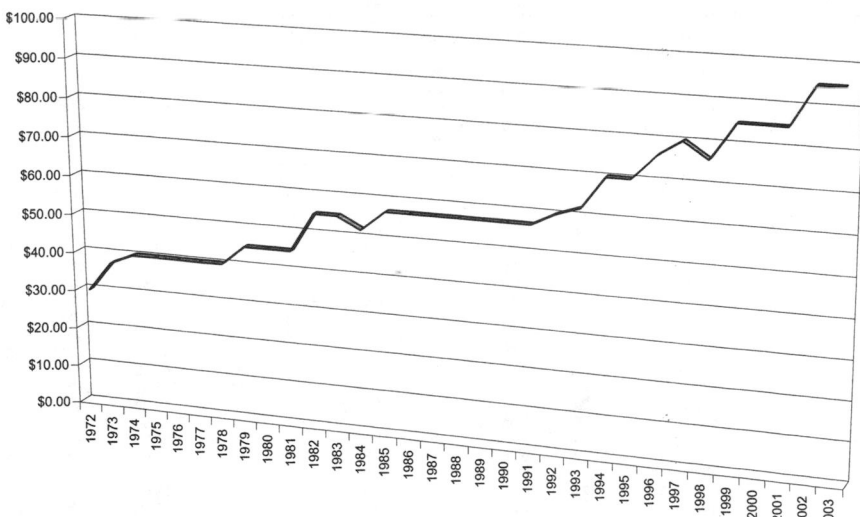

Retail Price

Date	Mintage	G-4	VG-8	F-12	VF-20	XF-40	AU-50	MS-60	MS-65	Prf-65
1876	7,944,000	27.00	32.00	45.00	67.00	160	195	230	1,100	925
1877	852,500	525	670	975	1,200	1,450	1,900	2,300	8,400	4,900
1878	5,799,850	26.00	34.00	50.00	80.00	175	215	250	900	490
1879	16,231,200	5.50	9.00	14.00	30.00	60.00	65.00	75.00	350	450
1880	38,964,955	3.00	5.00	5.50	8.00	22.00	37.50	60.00	350	435
1881	39,211,575	3.00	3.75	5.50	6.50	16.00	24.00	40.00	330	425
1882	38,581,100	3.00	3.75	4.50	8.00	15.00	24.00	37.50	330	425
1883	45,589,109	2.75	3.50	4.00	6.00	15.00	24.00	38.50	330	425
1884	23,261,742	3.00	3.75	6.50	10.00	24.00	32.50	60.00	500	425
1885	11,765,384	5.50	7.00	12.00	25.00	52.50	65.00	95.00	750	425
1886	17,654,290	3.25	6.00	15.00	37.50	105	120	135	1,150	460
1887	45,226,483	1.75	2.20	3.00	4.50	15.00	24.00	50.00	395	475
1888	37,494,414	2.00	2.40	4.00	6.00	20.00	24.00	42.00	950	525
1889	48,869,361	1.75	2.20	2.50	4.00	10.00	22.00	35.00	395	450
1890	57,182,854	1.50	1.80	2.50	3.50	9.00	18.00	35.00	395	500
1891	47,072,350	1.70	2.25	3.00	4.50	9.00	18.00	35.00	400	520
1892	37,649,832	2.00	2.25	3.00	4.25	11.50	18.00	34.00	395	525
1893	46,642,195	1.70	2.25	3.00	4.35	9.00	18.00	30.00	340	540
1894	16,752,132	3.25	4.00	8.25	10.00	40.00	45.00	60.00	375	525
1895	38,343,636	1.75	2.00	3.00	3.50	11.00	18.00	32.00	200	475
1896	39,057,293	1.50	2.00	2.75	3.30	8.50	21.00	33.00	230	425
1897	50,466,330	1.50	1.80	2.10	3.00	8.50	20.00	30.00	200	425
1898	49,823,079	1.50	2.00	2.25	3.20	8.50	18.00	30.00	200	425
1899	53,600,031	1.50	1.80	2.00	3.00	10.00	18.00	27.50	140	415
1900	66,833,764	1.25	1.65	2.00	2.75	11.00	18.00	25.00	175	425
1901	79,611,143	1.20	1.60	1.80	2.50	7.50	17.00	25.00	140	425
1902	87,376,722	1.20	1.60	1.80	2.50	7.25	17.00	25.00	140	425
1903	85,094,493	1.20	1.60	1.80	2.50	7.25	17.00	25.00	140	425
1904	61,328,015	1.20	1.60	1.80	2.50	8.00	17.00	25.00	140	475
1905	80,719,163	1.20	1.60	1.80	2.50	7.25	17.00	25.00	140	475
1906	96,022,255	1.20	1.60	1.80	2.50	7.25	17.00	25.00	140	395
1907	108,138,618	1.20	1.60	1.80	2.50	7.25	17.00	25.00	145	485
1908	32,327,987	1.25	2.00	2.25	2.50	7.50	18.00	26.00	145	395
1908S	1,115,000	61.00	65.00	75.00	88.00	135	135	210	650	—
1909	14,370,645	2.75	3.00	3.25	4.00	15.00	21.00	30.00	150	400
1909S	309,000	300	320	390	415	470	485	610	1,400	—

Lincoln. Wheat.

KM# 132 **Designer:** Victor D. Brenner **Reverse:** Wheat **Weight:** 3.1100 g. **Composition:** Bronze **Size:** 19 mm. **Note:** The 1909 "VDB" varieties have the designer's initials inscribed at the 6 o'clock position on the reverse. The initials were removed until 1918, when they were restored on the obverse.

Date	Mintage	G-4	VG-8	F-12	VF-20	XF-40	AU-50	MS-60	MS-65	Prf-65
1909	72,702,618	1.35	1.60	1.90	2.10	2.75	9.00	13.50	80.00	520
1909 VDB	27,995,000	4.00	425	4.40	4.50	5.25	5.75	9.50	72.50	6,000
1909S	1,825,000	63.50	73.00	90.00	135	180	220	230	670	—
1909S VDB	484,000	500	610	670	720	850	950	1,100	5,150	—
1910	146,801,218	0.25	0.30	0.40	0.50	2.00	5.50	14.50	100.00	700
1910S	6,045,000	7.00	8.00	8.50	10.50	23.00	56.00	60.00	375	—
1911	101,177,787	0.25	0.45	1.00	1.35	3.50	7.50	16.00	180	600
1911D	12,672,000	5.00	5.75	8.50	12.50	40.00	62.50	80.00	990	—
1911S	4,026,000	16.00	18.00	20.00	24.00	43.00	85.00	145	1,450	—
1912	68,153,060	1.25	1.50	1.75	4.50	9.00	17.00	30.00	295	950
1912D	10,411,000	6.00	6.50	7.00	18.00	43.00	70.00	135	1,100	—
1912S	4,431,000	11.00	14.00	18.00	26.00	45.00	72.50	115	1,750	—
1913	76,532,352	0.65	0.75	1.40	3.00	12.50	16.00	27.50	265	550
1913D	15,804,000	2.75	3.00	3.50	7.50	25.00	55.00	90.00	1,300	—
1913S	6,101,000	6.25	7.00	7.50	12.00	32.50	70.00	135	2,800	—
1914	75,238,432	0.45	0.70	1.25	3.50	10.00	27.50	38.00	350	600
1914D	1,193,000	110	160	200	275	500	900	1,150	12,000	—
1914S	4,137,000	10.00	13.00	17.00	25.00	50.00	125	240	10,000	—
1915	29,092,120	1.35	1.75	3.50	8.00	40.00	64.00	70.00	575	600
1915D	22,050,000	1.50	1.75	2.00	2.75	11.50	27.00	60.00	700	—
1915S	4,833,000	8.00	10.00	12.00	16.00	40.00	62.50	135	3,300	—
1916	131,833,677	0.20	0.25	0.30	1.25	3.00	7.00	11.00	120	1,650
1916D	35,956,000	0.35	0.40	1.15	2.00	8.50	17.50	52.00	1,800	—
1916S	22,510,000	1.00	1.35	1.50	2.25	9.50	20.00	65.00	4,500	—
1917	196,429,785	0.20	0.25	0.30	1.15	3.00	7.00	11.00	140	—
1917D	55,120,000	0.25	0.35	0.70	1.65	8.50	20.00	54.00	1,450	—
1917S	32,620,000	0.50	0.55	0.75	1.50	7.00	17.00	54.00	4,500	—
1918	288,104,634	0.20	0.25	0.30	0.70	3.50	6.50	11.00	200	—
1918D	47,830,000	0.30	0.50	0.75	1.35	7.00	17.00	54.00	1,800	—
1918S	34,680,000	0.30	0.55	0.70	1.50	7.00	30.00	55.00	5,000	—
1919	392,021,000	0.20	0.25	0.30	0.50	1.35	4.00	8.00	100.00	—
1919D	57,154,000	0.30	0.35	0.45	1.15	4.50	26.50	45.00	1,250	—
1919S	139,760,000	0.20	0.25	1.00	1.20	2.75	12.00	33.50	3,000	—
1920	310,165,000	0.20	0.25	0.30	0.50	1.50	3.50	9.25	110	—

1914-D Cent
Grade F-12

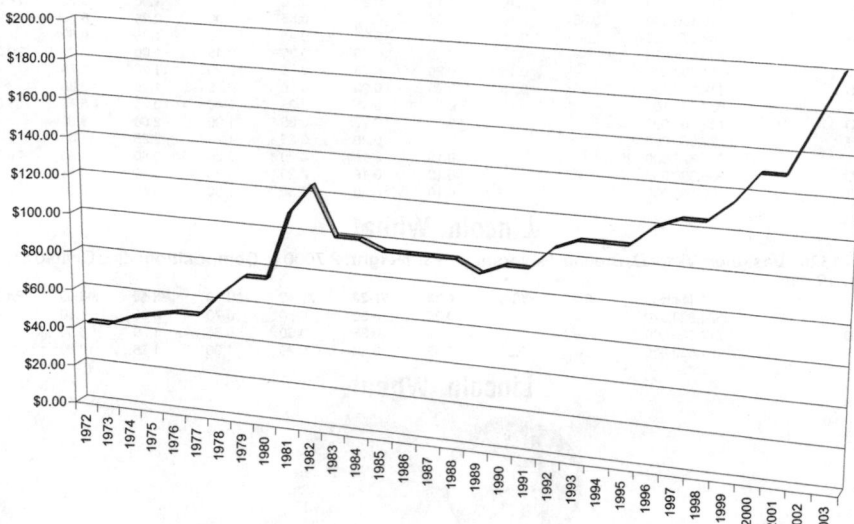

☐ Retail Price

Date	Mintage	G-4	VG-8	F-12	VF-20	XF-40	AU-50	MS-60	MS-65	Prf-65
1920D	49,280,000	0.30	0.45	0.95	2.50	8.50	20.00	52.50	950	—
1920S	46,220,000	0.25	0.35	1.10	1.75	6.50	28.00	80.00	4,900	—
1921	39,157,000	0.25	0.30	0.50	1.00	4.50	16.00	35.00	195	—
1921S	15,274,000	1.25	1.35	1.65	3.00	16.50	65.00	85.00	4,500	—
1922D	7,160,000	8.00	9.50	11.00	14.50	23.00	42.00	75.00	930	—
1922 No D-T.2	Inc. above	395	490	610	730	1,525	3,000	5,000	175,000	—
1923	74,723,000	0.20	0.25	0.30	0.60	2.50	7.00	11.00	210	—
1923S	8,700,000	1.40	1.65	2.50	4.00	22.50	70.00	185	4,500	—
1924	75,178,000	0.20	0.30	0.40	0.60	3.00	8.00	20.00	150	—
1924D	2,520,000	14.00	16.00	19.00	30.00	83.00	150	235	5,000	—
1924S	11,696,000	0.80	1.00	1.50	2.50	11.00	55.00	95.00	7,800	—
1925	139,949,000	0.20	0.25	0.30	0.50	2.50	6.00	8.50	95.00	—
1925D	22,580,000	0.30	0.60	0.75	1.50	7.50	20.00	45.00	1,800	—
1925S	26,380,000	0.25	0.40	0.70	1.00	6.00	18.00	60.00	6,850	—
1926	157,088,000	0.15	0.20	0.25	0.50	1.35	4.00	7.00	64.00	—
1926D	28,020,000	0.25	0.30	0.50	1.25	6.00	22.50	55.00	1,800	—
1926S	4,550,000	3.00	4.00	6.00	8.00	13.50	55.00	100.00	60,000	—
1927	144,440,000	0.15	0.20	0.25	0.50	1.35	3.25	7.00	95.00	—
1927D	27,170,000	0.20	0.25	0.50	1.25	3.00	13.50	55.00	1,250	—
1927S	14,276,000	0.80	1.00	1.40	3.00	9.00	25.00	60.00	4,100	—
1928	134,116,000	0.15	0.25	0.25	0.50	1.25	3.00	7.50	90.00	—
1928D	31,170,000	0.20	0.25	0.50	0.75	3.00	8.50	26.50	550	—
1928S	17,266,000	0.60	0.75	1.00	1.25	4.00	11.00	60.00	1,800	—
1929	185,262,000	0.15	0.20	0.25	0.40	0.75	4.00	6.00	85.00	—
1929D	41,730,000	0.15	0.20	0.40	0.60	3.00	7.00	16.00	240	—
1929S	50,148,000	0.15	0.20	0.30	0.50	2.75	4.50	11.00	130	—
1930	157,415,000	0.15	0.20	0.30	0.50	1.10	2.25	3.65	35.00	—
1930D	40,100,000	0.20	0.25	0.40	0.60	2.00	5.00	11.00	95.00	—
1930S	24,286,000	0.20	0.25	0.35	0.50	1.10	6.50	10.00	49.00	—
1931	19,396,000	0.50	0.60	1.00	1.20	1.50	6.00	17.50	100.00	—
1931D	4,480,000	3.00	3.25	3.50	4.00	8.00	37.50	52.00	590	—
1931S	866,000	42.50	45.00	55.00	57.50	60.00	76.00	82.50	485	—
1932	9,062,000	1.00	1.25	2.00	2.50	3.00	8.00	18.50	75.00	—
1932D	10,500,000	0.75	1.25	1.35	1.50	2.00	7.00	14.50	80.00	—
1933	14,360,000	0.75	1.00	1.25	1.50	3.00	8.00	16.50	70.00	—
1933D	6,200,000	1.60	2.00	2.50	3.00	6.00	11.00	16.50	66.00	—
1934	219,080,000	—	0.15	0.20	0.25	0.75	1.50	4.00	27.00	—
1934D	28,446,000	0.15	0.20	0.25	0.45	1.50	5.00	16.50	52.00	—
1935	245,338,000	—	0.10	0.15	0.25	0.75	1.00	2.50	13.00	—
1935D	47,000,000	—	0.15	0.20	0.30	0.95	2.50	5.50	9.50	—
1935S	38,702,000	0.10	0.20	0.30	0.40	1.00	3.00	12.00	46.00	—
1936	309,637,569	—	0.10	0.15	0.25	0.75	1.00	2.00	6.00	1,200
1936D	40,620,000	—	0.10	0.15	0.25	0.75	1.50	2.75	8.50	—
1936S	29,130,000	0.10	0.15	0.25	0.35	0.85	1.75	2.75	8.50	—
1937	309,179,320	—	0.10	0.15	0.20	0.70	0.90	1.75	7.00	125
1937D	50,430,000	—	0.10	0.15	0.25	0.70	1.00	2.50	9.50	—
1937S	34,500,000	—	0.10	0.15	0.25	0.60	1.25	3.00	8.50	—

Date	Mintage	G-4	VG-8	F-12	VF-20	XF-40	AU-50	MS-60	MS-65	Prf-65
1938	156,696,734	—	0.10	0.15	0.20	0.50	1.00	2.00	5.75	85.00
1938D	20,010,000	0.20	0.25	0.35	0.45	0.75	1.50	3.50	8.50	—
1938S	15,180,000	0.30	0.40	0.50	0.70	1.00	2.00	2.80	8.50	—
1939	316,479,520	—	0.10	0.15	0.20	0.30	0.50	1.00	5.75	78.00
1939D	15,160,000	0.35	0.40	0.35	0.60	0.85	1.90	2.25	8.50	—
1939S	52,070,000	—	0.15	0.20	0.25	0.45	0.90	1.35	9.50	—
1940	586,825,872	—	0.15	0.20	0.25	0.30	0.45	1.00	5.75	70.00
1940D	81,390,000	—	0.15	0.20	0.25	0.35	0.50	1.20	5.75	—
1940S	112,940,000	—	0.15	0.20	0.25	0.30	0.75	1.25	5.85	—
1941	887,039,100	—	—	0.10	0.15	0.25	0.40	0.85	5.75	65.00
1941D	128,700,000	—	—	0.15	0.20	0.25	1.00	2.00	8.50	—
1941S	92,360,000	—	—	0.15	0.20	0.25	1.25	2.25	11.00	—
1942	657,828,600	—	—	0.10	0.15	0.20	0.25	0.50	4.60	78.00
1942D	206,698,000	—	—	0.10	0.15	0.20	0.30	0.50	5.75	—
1942S	85,590,000	—	—	0.10	0.20	0.30	1.50	3.50	16.00	—

Lincoln. Wheat.

KM# 132a Designer: Victor D. Brenner **Reverse:** Wheat **Weight:** 2.7000 g. **Composition:** Zinc Coated Steel **Size:** 19 mm.

Date	Mintage	G-4	VG-8	F-12	VF-20	XF-40	AU-50	MS-60	MS-65	Prf-65
1943	684,628,670	—	—	0.25	0.30	0.50	0.70	0.85	4.60	—
1943D	217,660,000	—	—	0.25	0.35	0.60	0.65	1.00	6.50	—
1943S	191,550,000	—	0.30	0.35	0.40	0.70	1.00	1.75	12.50	—

Lincoln. Wheat.

KM# A132 Designer: Victor D. Brenner **Reverse:** Wheat **Weight:** 3.1100 g. **Composition:** Copper-Zinc **Size:** 19 mm. **Note:** KM#132 design and composition resumed.

Date	Mintage	XF-40	MS-65	Prf-65	Date	Mintage	XF-40	MS-65	Prf-65
1944	1,435,400,000	0.20	2.00	—	1951D	625,355,000	0.10	1.65	—
1944D	430,578,000	0.20	2.00	—	1951S	136,010,000	0.15	3.00	—
1944D/S	—	175	1,600	—	1952	186,856,980	0.15	2.75	34.00
1944S	282,760,000	0.20	5.50	—	1952D	746,130,000	0.10	1.60	—
1945	1,040,515,000	0.20	2.00	—	1952S	137,800,004	0.15	3.00	—
1945D	226,268,000	0.20	2.00	—	1953	256,883,800	0.10	1.25	28.00
1945S	181,770,000	0.20	5.50	—	1953D	700,515,000	0.10	1.25	—
1946	991,655,000	0.20	2.00	—	1953S	181,835,000	0.15	1.75	—
1946D	315,690,000	0.20	4.50	—	1954	71,873,350	0.15	1.25	9.00
1946S	198,100,000	0.20	4.60	—	1954D	251,552,500	0.10	0.50	—
1947	190,555,000	0.20	2.25	—	1954S	96,190,000	0.15	0.75	—
1947D	194,750,000	0.20	2.00	—	1955	330,958,000	0.10	0.75	13.00
1947S	99,000,000	0.20	5.50	—	1955 doubled die	—	850	33,500	—
1948	317,570,000	0.20	2.00	—	**Note:** The 1955 "doubled die" has distinct doubling of the				
1948D	172,637,000	0.20	2.25	—	date and lettering on the obverse.				
1948S	81,735,000	0.20	5.50	—	1955D	563,257,500	0.10	0.75	—
1949	217,775,000	0.20	3.50	—	1955S	44,610,000	0.25	1.00	—
1949D	153,132,000	0.20	3.50	—	1956	421,414,384	—	0.50	3.00
1949S	64,290,000	0.25	6.00	—	1956D	1,098,201,100	—	0.50	—
1950	272,686,386	0.20	1.75	40.00	1957	283,787,952	—	0.50	2.00
1950D	334,950,000	0.20	1.50	—	1957D	1,051,342,000	—	0.50	—
1950S	118,505,000	0.20	2.50	—	1958	253,400,652	—	0.50	3.00
1951	295,633,500	0.20	2.00	40.00	1958D	800,953,300	—	0.50	—

Lincoln. Lincoln Memorial.

KM# 201 Rev. Designer: Frank Gasparro **Reverse:** Lincoln Memorial **Weight:** 3.1100 g. **Composition:** Copper-Zinc **Note:** The dates were modified in 1960, 1970 and 1982, resulting in large-date and small-date varieties for those years. The 1972 "doubled die" shows doubling of "In God We Trust." The 1979-S and 1981-S Type II proofs have a clearer mint mark than the Type I proofs of those years. Some 1982 cents have the predominantly copper composition; others have the predominantly zinc composition. They can be distinguished by weight.

Date	Mintage	XF-40	MS-65	Prf-65	Date	Mintage	XF-40	MS-65	Prf-65
1959	610,864,291	—	0.50	1.50	1960D small date	1,580,884,000	—	0.30	—
1959D	1,279,760,000	—	0.50	—	1960D large date	Inc. above	—	0.30	—
1960 small date	588,096,602	2.10	5.00	16.00	1961	756,373,244	—	0.30	1.00
1960 large date	Inc. above	—	0.30	1.25	1961D	1,753,266,700	—	0.30	—

Date	Mintage	XF-40	MS-65	Prf-65	Date	Mintage	XF-40	MS-65	Prf-65
1962	609,263,019	—	0.30	1.00	1974	4,232,140,523	—	0.25	—
1962D	1,793,148,400	—	0.30	—	1974D	4,235,098,000	—	0.25	—
1963	757,185,645	—	0.30	1.00	1974S	412,039,228	—	0.25	0.75
1963D	1,774,020,400	—	0.30	—	1975	5,451,476,142	—	0.25	—
1964	2,652,525,762	—	0.30	1.00	1975D	4,505,245,300	—	0.25	—
1964D	3,799,071,500	—	0.30	—	1975S	2,845,450	—	—	5.50
1965	1,497,224,900	—	0.30	—	1976	4,674,292,426	—	0.25	—
1966	2,188,147,783	—	0.30	—	1976D	4,221,592,455	—	0.25	—
1967	3,048,667,100	—	0.30	—	1976S	4,149,730	—	—	5.00
1968	1,707,880,970	—	0.30	—	1977	4,469,930,000	—	0.25	—
1968D	2,886,269,600	—	0.40	—	1977D	4,149,062,300	—	0.25	—
1968S	261,311,510	—	0.40	1.00	1977S	3,251,152	—	—	3.00
1969	1,136,910,000	—	0.60	—	1978	5,558,605,000	—	0.25	—
1969D	4,002,832,200	—	0.40	—	1978D	4,280,233,400	—	0.25	—
1969S	547,309,631	—	0.40	1.10	1978S	3,127,781	—	—	3.50
1970	1,898,315,000	—	0.40	—	1979	6,018,515,000	—	0.25	—
1970D	2,891,438,900	—	0.40	—	1979D	4,139,357,254	—	0.25	—
1970S	693,192,814	—	0.40	1.20	1979S type I, proof	3,677,175	—	—	4.00
1970S small date	—	—	55.00	60.00	1979S type II, proof	Inc. above	—	—	4.25
1971	1,919,490,000	—	0.35	—	1980	7,414,705,000	—	0.25	—
1971D	2,911,045,600	—	0.40	—	1980D	5,140,098,660	—	0.25	—
1971S	528,354,192	—	0.25	1.20	1980S	3,554,806	—	—	2.25
1972	2,933,255,000	—	0.25	—	1981	7,491,750,000	—	0.25	—
1972 doubled die	—	210	550	—	1981S type II, proof	Inc. above	—	—	60.00
1972D	2,665,071,400	—	0.25	—	1981D	5,373,235,677	—	0.25	—
1972S	380,200,104	—	0.25	1.15	1981S type I, proof	4,063,083	—	—	3.50
1973	3,728,245,000	—	0.25	—	1982 large date	10,712,525,000	—	0.25	—
1973D	3,549,576,588	—	0.25	—	1982D large date	6,012,979,368	—	0.25	—
1973S	319,937,634	—	0.25	0.80					

Lincoln. Lincoln Memorial.

KM# 201a Reverse: Lincoln Memorial **Weight:** 2.5000 g. **Composition:** Copper Plated Zinc **Size:** 19 mm.

Date	Mintage	XF-40	MS-65	Prf-65	Date	Mintage	XF-40	MS-65	Prf-65
1982 large date	—	—	0.50	—	1982D large date	—	—	0.30	
1982 small date	—	—	2.00	—	1982D small date	—	—	0.25	—

Lincoln. Lincoln Memorial.

KM# 201b Reverse: Lincoln Memorial **Composition:** Copper Plated Zinc **Size:** 19 mm. **Note:** The 1983 "doubled die reverse" shows doubling of "United States of America." The 1984 "doubled die" shows doubling of Lincoln's ear on the obverse.

Date	Mintage	XF-40	MS-65	Prf-65	Date	Mintage	XF-40	MS-65	Prf-65
1982S	3,857,479	—	—	3.00	1993D	6,426,650,571	—	0.25	—
1983	7,752,355,000	—	0.25	—	1993S	3,394,792	—	—	9.50
1983D	6,467,199,428	—	0.25	—	1994	6,500,850,000	—	0.25	—
1983S	3,279,126	—	—	4.00	1994D	7,131,765,000	—	0.25	—
1984	8,151,079,000	—	0.25	—	1994S	3,269,923	—	—	8.50
1984 doubled die	—	—	275	—	1995	6,411,440,000	—	0.25	—
1984D	5,569,238,906	—	0.75	—	1995 doubled die	—	—	27.00	—
1984S	3,065,110	—	—	4.50	1995D	7,128,560,000	—	0.25	—
1985	5,648,489,887	—	0.25	—	1995S	2,707,481	—	—	9.50
1985D	5,287,399,926	—	0.25	—	1996	6,612,465,000	—	0.25	—
1985S	3,362,821	—	—	6.00	1996D	6,510,795,000	—	0.25	—
1986	4,491,395,493	—	1.50	—	1996S	2,915,212	—	—	6.50
1986D	4,442,866,698	—	0.75	—	1997	4,622,800,000	—	0.25	—
1986S	3,010,497	—	—	7.50	1997D	4,576,555,000	—	0.25	—
1987	4,682,466,931	—	0.25	—	1997S	2,796,678	—	—	11.50
1987D	4,879,389,514	—	0.25	—	1998	5,032,155,000	—	0.25	—
1987S	4,227,728	—	—	5.00	1998D	5,255,353,500	—	0.25	—
1988	6,092,810,000	—	0.25	—	1998S	2,957,286	—	—	9.50
1988D	5,253,740,443	—	0.25	—	1999	5,237,600,000	—	0.25	—
1988S	3,262,948	—	—	12.50	1999D	6,360,065,000	—	0.25	—
1989	7,261,535,000	—	0.25	—	1999S	3,362,462	—	—	5.00
1989D	5,345,467,111	—	0.25	—	2000	5,503,200,000	—	0.25	—
1989S	3,220,194	—	—	12.50	2000D	8,774,220,000	—	0.25	—
1990	6,851,765,000	—	0.25	—	2000S	4,063,361	—	—	4.00
1990D	4,922,894,533	—	0.25	—	2001P	4,959,600,000	—	0.25	—
1990S	3,299,559	—	—	5.75	2001D	5,374,990,000	—	0.25	—
1990 no S	—	—	—	2,750	2001S	3,099,096	—	—	4.00
1991	5,165,940,000	—	0.25	—	2002P	3,260,800,000	—	0.25	—
1991D	4,158,442,076	—	0.25	—	2002D	4,028,055,000	—	0.25	—
1991S	2,867,787	—	—	30.00	2002S	—	—	—	4.00
1992	4,648,905,000	—	0.25	—	2003P	—	—	0.25	—
1992D	4,448,673,300	—	0.25	—	2003S	—	—	—	4.00
1992S	4,176,560	—	—	5.50	2003D	—	—	0.25	—
1993	5,684,705,000	—	0.25	—					

2 CENTS

Small Motto   Large motto

KM# 94 Designer: James B. Longacre **Weight:** 6.2200 g. **Composition:** Copper-Tin-Zinc **Size:** 23 mm.
Note: The motto "In God We Trust" was modified in 1864, resulting in small-motto and large-motto varieties
for that year.

Date	Mintage	G-4	VG-8	F-12	VF-20	XF-40	AU-50	MS-60	MS-65	Prf-65
1864 small motto	19,847,500	100.00	125	160	290	475	515	725	1,800	45,000
1864 large motto	Inc. above	13.00	14.00	18.50	25.00	34.00	65.00	70.00	500	1,400
1865	13,640,000	13.00	14.00	18.50	25.00	34.00	65.00	70.00	500	850
1866	3,177,000	14.00	17.00	20.00	28.00	34.00	65.00	70.00	630	850
1867	2,938,750	14.00	17.00	20.00	28.00	34.00	70.00	95.00	550	850
1868	2,803,750	14.00	17.00	20.00	28.00	37.50	75.00	120	600	850
1869	1,546,000	16.00	19.00	23.00	32.00	42.00	82.50	120	625	850
1870	861,250	17.00	21.00	25.00	35.00	66.00	100.00	200	750	850
1871	721,250	20.00	23.00	29.00	40.00	82.50	125	200	725	850
1872	65,000	160	260	300	400	590	610	850	2,800	900
1873 proof	Est. 1,100	—	—	1,000	1,050	1,100	1,150	—	—	2,100

SILVER 3 CENTS

Type 1. No outlines in star.

KM# 75 Designer: James B. Longacre **Obverse:** No outlines in star **Weight:** 0.8000 g. **Composition:** 0.7500
Silver 0.0193 oz. ASW **Size:** 14 mm.

Date	Mintage	G-4	VG-8	F-12	VF-20	XF-40	AU-50	MS-60	MS-65	Prf-65
1851	5,447,400	22.50	25.00	27.50	33.50	60.00	135	160	900	—
1851O	720,000	30.00	35.00	40.00	77.00	125	220	310	2,400	—
1852	18,663,500	22.50	25.00	27.50	33.50	60.00	135	160	900	—
1853	11,400,000	22.50	25.00	27.50	33.50	60.00	135	160	900	—

Type 2. Three outlines in star.

KM# 80 Designer: James B. Longacre **Obverse:** Three outlines in star **Weight:** 0.7500 g. **Composition:**
0.9000 Silver 0.0218 oz. ASW **Size:** 14 mm.

Date	Mintage	G-4	VG-8	F-12	VF-20	XF-40	AU-50	MS-60	MS-65	Prf-65
1854	671,000	22.50	25.00	27.50	40.00	95.00	220	345	3,200	33,500
1855	139,000	30.00	40.00	52.00	95.00	150	280	500	9,500	15,000
1856	1,458,000	22.50	25.00	27.50	50.00	88.00	170	265	4,300	15,500
1857	1,042,000	22.50	25.00	27.50	45.00	88.00	235	295	3,200	13,500
1858	1,604,000	22.50	25.00	27.50	40.00	88.00	170	235	3,200	6,400

Type 3. Two outlines in star.

KM# 88 Designer: James B. Longacre **Obverse:** Two outlines in star **Weight:** 0.7500 g. **Composition:**
0.9000 Silver 0.0218 oz. ASW **Size:** 14 mm.

Date	Mintage	G-4	VG-8	F-12	VF-20	XF-40	AU-50	MS-60	MS-65	Prf-65
1859	365,000	21.00	25.00	27.50	39.00	60.00	135	160	850	2,150

1851-O Silver Three-Cent Piece
Grade XF-40

☐ Retail Price

Date	Mintage	G-4	VG-8	F-12	VF-20	XF-40	AU-50	MS-60	MS-65	Prf-65
1860	287,000	21.00	25.00	27.50	40.00	66.00	135	160	850	4,000
1861	498,000	21.00	25.00	27.50	37.50	60.00	135	165	850	1,800
1862	343,550	21.00	25.00	27.50	45.00	60.00	135	135	850	1,400
1863	21,460	300	330	340	350	385	480	660	2,150	1,350
1863/62 proof only; Rare	Inc. above	—	—	—	—	—	—	—	—	—
1864	12,470	300	330	340	350	385	480	590	1,650	1,350
1865	8,500	360	390	420	440	450	480	660	1,650	1,350
1866	22,725	300	3,355	340	350	385	420	600	1,850	1,325
1867	4,625	360	390	420	440	450	480	660	2,650	1,300
1868	4,100	360	390	420	440	450	480	660	5,500	1,400
1869	5,100	360	390	420	440	450	480	660	2,100	1,400
1869/68 proof only; Rare	Inc. above	—	—	—	—	—	—	—	—	—
1870	4,000	360	390	420	440	450	480	800	4,700	1,350
1871	4,360	360	390	420	440	450	480	660	1,625	1,450
1872	1,950	390	420	450	480	500	575	750	5,200	1,350
1873 proof only	600	630	660	690	700	725	800	—	—	1,575

NICKEL 3 CENTS

KM# 95 **Designer:** James B. Longacre **Weight:** 1.9400 g. **Composition:** Copper-Nickel **Size:** 17.9 mm.

Date	Mintage	G-4	VG-8	F-12	VF-20	XF-40	AU-50	MS-60	MS-65	Prf-65
1865	11,382,000	13.50	13.75	15.00	18.00	22.00	46.00	85.00	920	6,000
1866	4,801,000	13.50	13.75	15.00	18.00	22.00	46.00	85.00	640	1,550
1867	3,915,000	13.50	14.00	15.00	18.00	22.00	46.00	85.00	800	1,450
1868	3,252,000	13.50	13.75	15.00	18.00	22.00	46.00	85.00	640	1,400
1869	1,604,000	13.50	14.50	15.00	18.00	22.00	55.00	110	760	1,050
1870	1,335,000	13.50	14.00	15.00	19.00	24.50	55.00	115	760	1,500
1871	604,000	13.50	14.00	15.00	18.00	24.50	56.00	120	800	1,200
1872	862,000	13.50	14.00	15.00	18.00	22.00	55.00	120	1,100	1,050
1873	1,173,000	13.50	14.00	15.00	18.00	23.00	55.00	115	1,325	1,050
1874	790,000	13.50	14.00	15.00	18.00	22.00	56.00	120	1,000	950
1875	228,000	13.50	14.00	16.00	19.00	33.00	66.50	150	825	1,500
1876	162,000	14.00	15.50	17.00	26.00	36.00	85.00	170	1,700	1,000
1877 proof	Est. 900	950	975	1,000	1,025	1,050	1,100	—	—	2,300
1878 proof	2,350	465	475	480	485	490	500	—	—	700
1879	41,200	50.00	58.50	77.00	85.00	95.00	125	250	760	525
1880	24,955	77.00	88.00	100.00	115	135	160	280	780	525

Date	Mintage	G-4	VG-8	F-12	VF-20	XF-40	AU-50	MS-60	MS-65	Prf-65
1881	1,080,575	13.50	14.00	15.00	16.00	21.50	45.00	85.00	700	525
1882	25,300	75.00	80.00	92.50	100.00	115	145	260	1,025	565
1883	10,609	145	160	200	225	280	300	385	4,200	560
1884	5,642	300	330	475	485	490	500	780	5,600	550
1885	4,790	375	395	540	550	575	630	795	2,300	590
1886 proof	4,290	250	260	270	275	290	300	—	—	525
1887/6 proof	7,961	300	310	320	330	350	360	—	—	700
1887	Inc. above	225	265	275	290	325	400	485	1,200	1,050
1888	41,083	37.50	46.00	50.00	55.00	70.00	110	225	700	525
1889	21,561	65.00	80.00	100.00	105	115	120	265	775	525

HALF DIME

Flowing Hair.

KM# 15 Designer: Robert Scot **Weight:** 1.3500 g. **Composition:** 0.8920 Silver 0.0388 oz. ASW **Size:** 16.5 mm.

Date	Mintage	G-4	VG-8	F-12	VF-20	XF-40	MS-60
1794	86,416	850	1,000	1,350	2,150	4,000	9,500
1795	Inc. above	575	700	1,000	1,600	2,850	7,200

Draped Bust. Small eagle.

KM# 23 Designer: Robert Scot **Reverse:** Small eagle **Weight:** 1.3500 g. **Composition:** 0.8920 Silver 0.0388 oz. ASW **Size:** 16.5 mm. **Note:** Some 1796 strikes have "Liberty" spelled as "Likerty." The 1797 strikes have either 13, 15 or 16 stars on the obverse.

Date	Mintage	G-4	VG-8	F-12	VF-20	XF-40	MS-60
1796	10,230	800	950	1,400	2,500	4,750	9,600
1796 "Likerty"	Inc. above	825	950	1,450	2,500	4,850	12,000
1796/5	Inc. above	850	1,100	1,600	2,700	5,000	17,000

1802 Half Dime
Grade F-12

□ Retail Price

Date	Mintage	G-4	VG-8	F-12	VF-20	XF-40	MS-60
1797 13 stars	44,527	1,350	1,500	1,850	2,850	5,350	18,000
1797 15 stars	Inc. above	725	900	1,350	2,400	4,700	11,000
1797 16 stars	Inc. above	825	950	1,400	2,550	5,000	9,500

Draped Bust. Heraldic eagle.

KM# 34 Designer: Robert Scot **Reverse:** Heraldic eagle **Weight:** 1.3500 g. **Composition:** 0.8920 Silver 0.0388 oz. ASW **Size:** 16.5 mm. **Note:** Some 1800 strikes have "Liberty" spelled as "Libekty."

Date	Mintage	G-4	VG-8	F-12	VF-20	XF-40	MS-60
1800	24,000	425	550	885	1,250	3,000	7,000
1800 "Libekty"	Inc. above	440	575	975	1,350	3,250	7,500
1801	33,910	550	690	1,100	1,450	3,400	9,000
1802	13,010	9,000	1,500	25,000	40,000	55,000	—
1803 Large 8	37,850	600	700	950	1,350	3,250	7,200
1803 Small 8	Inc. above	725	850	1,125	2,000	4,000	9,000
1805	15,600	700	850	1,100	1,750	3,900	11,000

Liberty Cap.

KM# 47 Designer: William Kneass **Weight:** 1.3500 g. **Composition:** 0.8920 Silver 0.0388 oz. ASW **Size:** 15.5 mm. **Note:** Design modifications in 1835, 1836 and 1837 resulted in variety combinations with large and small dates, and large and small "5C." inscriptions on the reverse.

Date	Mintage	G-4	VG-8	F-12	VF-20	XF-40	AU-50	MS-60	MS-65
1829	1,230,000	24.00	28.00	32.00	60.00	125	210	270	2,650
1830	1,240,000	23.00	28.00	32.00	60.00	120	205	270	2,650
1831	1,242,700	22.00	27.00	30.00	60.00	115	205	270	2,600
1832	965,000	21.00	27.00	30.00	60.00	115	205	270	2,600
1833	1,370,000	21.00	27.00	30.00	60.00	115	205	290	2,650
1834	1,480,000	20.00	27.00	29.00	58.00	110	200	270	2,600
1835 lg. dt., lg. 5C.	2,760,000	20.00	27.00	30.00	58.00	110	200	270	2,600
1835 lg. dt., sm. 5C	Inc. above	20.00	27.00	30.00	58.00	110	200	270	2,600
1835 sm. dt., lg. 5C	Inc. above	20.00	30.00	30.00	58.00	110	200	270	2,600
1835 sm. dt., sm. 5C	Inc. above	20.00	28.00	30.00	58.00	110	200	270	2,600
1836 lg. 5C.	1,900,000	20.00	25.00	34.00	58.00	110	200	270	2,600
1836 sm. 5C.	Inc. above	20.00	25.00	34.00	58.00	110	200	270	2,600
1837 lg. 5C.	2,276,000	22.00	28.00	36.00	60.00	115	200	300	3,500
1837 sm. 5C.	Inc. above	26.00	32.00	42.00	88.00	145	350	950	8,750

Seated Liberty. No stars around rim.

KM# 60 Designer: Christian Gobrecht **Obverse:** No stars around rim **Weight:** 1.3400 g. **Composition:** 0.9000 Silver 0.0388 oz. ASW **Size:** 15.5 mm. **Note:** A design modification in 1837 resulted in small-date and large-date varieties for that year.

Date	Mintage	G-4	VG-8	F-12	VF-20	XF-40	AU-50	MS-60	MS-65
1837 small date	Inc. above	26.00	35.00	53.00	100.00	185	375	600	3,400
1837 large date	Inc. above	25.00	35.00	53.00	100.00	210	375	600	3,250
1838O	70,000	80.00	125	225	400	750	1,450	2,000	—

Seated Liberty. Stars around rim. No drapery.

KM# 62.1 Designer: Christian Gobrecht **Obverse:** Stars around rim. No drapery **Weight:** 1.3400 g. **Composition:** 0.9000 Silver 0.0388 oz. ASW **Size:** 15.5 mm. **Note:** The two varieties of 1838 are distinguished by the size of the stars on the obverse. The 1839-O with reverse of 1838-O was struck from rusted reverse dies. The result is a bumpy surface on this variety's reverse.

Date	Mintage	G-4	VG-8	F-12	VF-20	XF-40	AU-50	MS-60	MS-65
1838 large stars	2,255,000	12.00	13.50	16.00	25.00	60.00	150	240	2,250

Date	Mintage	G-4	VG-8	F-12	VF-20	XF-40	AU-50	MS-60	MS-65
1838 small stars	Inc. above	18.00	27.50	45.00	100.00	175	300	650	3,850
1839	1,069,150	13.50	15.00	18.00	29.00	65.00	160	250	2,500
1839O	1,034,039	14.00	16.00	19.00	31.00	70.00	170	550	5,500
1839O reverse 1838O	—	375	575	750	1,200	2,250	3,500	—	—
1840	1,344,085	14.00	16.00	19.00	25.00	60.00	140	240	2,100
1840O	935,000	15.00	17.00	27.00	30.00	75.00	210	700	—

Seated Liberty. Drapery added to Liberty's left elbow.

KM# 62.2 Designer: Christian Gobrecht **Obverse:** Drapery added to Liberty's left elbow **Weight:** 1.3400 g. **Composition:** 0.9000 Silver 0.0388 oz. ASW **Size:** 15.5 mm. **Note:** In 1840 drapery was added to Liberty's left elbow. Varieties for the 1848 Philadelphia strikes are distinguished by the size of the numerals in the date.

Date	Mintage	G-4	VG-8	F-12	VF-20	XF-40	AU-50	MS-60	MS-65
1840	Inc. above	22.00	35.00	60.00	115	200	325	450	300
1840O	Inc. above	33.00	55.00	100.00	165	400	950	6,500	—
1841	1,150,000	11.00	12.00	14.00	24.00	55.00	115	150	1,250
1841O	815,000	12.50	15.00	22.50	42.00	110	275	650	6,500
1842	815,000	11.00	12.00	14.00	24.00	55.00	115	150	1,750
1842O	350,000	28.00	40.00	60.00	150	425	850	1,150	—
1843	1,165,000	11.00	12.00	14.00	24.00	50.00	110	150	1,350
1844	430,000	11.00	12.00	14.00	24.00	50.00	110	150	1,150
1844O	220,000	75.00	105	175	450	950	1,900	5,400	—
1845	1,564,000	11.00	12.00	14.00	22.00	50.00	110	150	1,150
1845/1845	Inc. above	12.00	13.00	15.00	24.00	50.00	115	160	1,200
1846	27,000	300	350	500	750	1,550	3,600	7,500	—
1847	1,274,000	11.00	12.00	14.00	20.00	55.00	110	160	1,150
1848 medium date	668,000	12.00	13.00	15.00	25.00	60.00	115	210	2,600
1848 large date	Inc. above	15.00	20.00	30.00	50.00	110	250	450	4,000
1848O	600,000	13.00	17.50	25.00	45.00	95.00	240	400	1,950
1849/8	1,309,000	14.00	20.00	25.00	50.00	100.00	180	375	1,800
1849/6	Inc. above	12.00	13.00	15.00	40.00	85.00	175	375	1,500
1849	Inc. above	11.00	12.00	14.00	20.00	50.00	110	175	1,650
1849O	140,000	22.00	35.00	75.00	175	425	650	1,950	14,000
1850	955,000	11.00	12.00	14.00	20.00	50.00	110	150	1,400
1850O	690,000	13.00	16.00	22.50	50.00	100.00	275	675	4,000
1851	781,000	11.00	12.00	14.00	20.00	50.00	110	150	1,500
1851O	860,000	12.00	15.00	20.00	35.00	95.00	185	500	3,750
1852	1,000,500	11.00	12.00	14.00	20.00	50.00	110	150	1,150
1852O	260,000	23.00	32.00	55.00	115	250	475	750	10,000
1853	135,000	28.00	36.00	56.00	100.00	185	350	650	3,000
1853O	160,000	200	250	350	600	1,200	2,500	4,800	25,000

1846 Half Dime Grade XF-40

Seated Liberty. Arrows at date.

KM# 76 Designer: Christian Gobrecht **Obverse:** Arrows at date **Weight:** 1.2400 g. **Composition:** 0.9000 Silver 0.0362 oz. ASW

Date	Mintage	G-4	VG-8	F-12	VF-20	XF-40	AU-50	MS-60	MS-65	Prf-65
1853	13,210,020	11.00	12.00	14.00	17.00	50.00	120	190	1,850	35,000
1853O	2,200,000	12.00	14.00	16.00	25.00	65.00	135	275	3,500	—
1854	5,740,000	10.50	12.00	14.00	17.00	45.00	110	185	1,850	16,000
1854O	1,560,000	11.00	13.00	15.00	23.00	60.00	145	250	4,250	—
1855	1,750,000	11.00	13.00	15.00	18.00	47.00	115	190	1,950	18,000
1855O	600,000	15.00	20.00	28.00	55.00	125	210	600	4,000	—

Seated Liberty. Arrows at date removed.

KM# A62.2 Designer: Christian Gobrecht **Obverse:** Arrows at date removed **Weight:** 1.2400 g. **Composition:** 0.9000 Silver 0.0362 oz. ASW **Note:** On the 1858/inverted date variety, the date was engraved into the die upside down and then re-engraved right side up. Another 1858 variety has the date doubled.

Date	Mintage	G-4	VG-8	F-12	VF-20	XF-40	AU-50	MS-60	MS-65	Prf-65
1856	4,880,000	10.50	12.00	14.00	18.00	45.00	95.00	140	1,650	15,000
1856O	1,100,000	11.00	13.00	15.00	38.00	80.00	250	550	2,000	—
1857	7,280,000	10.00	12.00	14.00	18.00	45.00	95.00	150	1,550	5,500
1857O	1,380,000	11.00	13.00	18.00	33.00	55.00	180	325	1,800	—
1858	3,500,000	10.50	12.00	14.00	18.00	55.00	175	300	1,700	5,500
1858 inverted date	Inc. above	25.00	40.00	60.00	90.00	175	275	650	2,600	—
1858 double date	Inc. above	45.00	60.00	90.00	175	285	425	700	—	—
1858O	1,660,000	11.00	13.00	16.00	36.00	65.00	135	265	1,600	—
1859	340,000	11.00	13.00	20.00	34.00	70.00	135	225	1,550	4,000
1859O	560,000	12.00	14.00	23.00	38.00	110	200	240	1,700	—

Seated Liberty.

KM# PN242 Weight: 1.2400 g. **Composition:** 0.9000 Silver 0.0362 oz. ASW **Note:** These non-circulation pieces were struck as experiments in transferring the legend "United States of America" from the reverse to the obverse.

Date	Mintage	G-4	VG-8	F-12	VF-20	XF-40	AU-50	MS-60	MS-65	Prf-65
1859 obverse 1859, reverse 1860	—	—	—	—	—	—	—	—	8,500	17,500

Seated Liberty.

KM# PN277 Weight: 1.2400 g. **Composition:** 0.9000 Silver 0.0362 oz. ASW **Note:** These non-circulation pieces were struck as experiments in transferring the legend "United States of America" from the reverse to the obverse.

Date	Mintage	G-4	VG-8	F-12	VF-20	XF-40	AU-50	MS-60	MS-65	Prf-65
1860 obverse 1859, reverse 1860	—	—	—	—	—	—	—	3,250	6,500	—

Seated Liberty. "United States of America" replaced stars.

KM# 91 Designer: Christian Gobrecht **Obverse:** "United States of America" replaced stars **Weight:** 1.2400 g. **Composition:** 0.9000 Silver 0.0362 oz. ASW **Note:** In 1860 the legend "United States of America" replaced the stars on the obverse.

Date	Mintage	G-4	VG-8	F-12	VF-20	XF-40	AU-50	MS-60	MS-65	Prf-65
1860	799,000	11.00	13.00	15.00	17.00	30.00	65.00	125	1,150	1,850
1860O	1,060,000	12.00	14.00	16.00	18.00	36.00	75.00	175	1,450	—
1861	3,361,000	11.00	13.00	15.00	17.00	30.00	65.00	125	1,175	2,500
1861/0	Inc. above	20.00	30.00	55.00	125	260	360	500	4,000	—
1862	1,492,550	12.00	14.00	16.00	20.00	33.00	68.00	135	1,150	1,650
1863	18,460	150	175	220	270	400	500	650	1,650	1,700

Date	Mintage	G-4	VG-8	F-12	VF-20	XF-40	AU-50	MS-60	MS-65	Prf-65
1863S	100,000	20.00	28.00	35.00	40.00	110	260	700	2,500	—
1864	48,470	275	350	425	600	750	900	1,050	2,250	1,750
1864S	90,000	38.00	45.00	85.00	115	225	425	650	3,750	—
1865	13,500	275	300	375	450	550	625	750	1,950	1,750
1865S	120,000	22.00	28.00	37.00	55.00	135	375	800	—	—
1866	10,725	275	300	375	450	525	600	750	2,550	1,700
1866S	120,000	20.00	30.00	34.00	55.00	125	285	450	5,000	—
1867	8,625	400	425	500	575	675	800	975	2,250	1,750
1867S	120,000	20.00	27.00	32.00	60.00	120	265	550	3,850	—
1868	89,200	45.00	60.00	95.00	150	250	375	570	2,400	1,750
1868S	280,000	13.00	15.00	20.00	25.00	40.00	110	300	3,250	—
1869	208,600	13.00	15.00	22.00	30.00	45.00	125	235	1,500	1,750
1869S	230,000	13.00	15.00	20.00	25.00	40.00	115	325	4,000	—
1870	536,600	9.50	10.00	12.50	17.00	35.00	125	175	1,200	1,650
1870S unique	—	—	—	—	—	—	—	—	—	—

Note: 1870S, Superior Galleries, July 1986, brilliant uncirculated, $253,000.

Date	Mintage	G-4	VG-8	F-12	VF-20	XF-40	AU-50	MS-60	MS-65	Prf-65
1871	1,873,960	11.00	13.00	15.00	17.00	32.00	65.00	120	1,250	1,650
1871S	161,000	14.00	22.00	30.00	45.00	65.00	165	250	2,450	—
1872	2,947,950	11.00	13.00	15.00	18.00	32.00	65.00	120	1,200	1,650
1872S mint mark in wreath	837,000	11.00	13.00	15.00	18.00	32.00	65.00	120	1,200	—
1872S mint mark below wreath	Inc. above	11.00	13.00	15.00	18.00	32.00	65.00	120	1,200	—
1873	712,600	11.00	13.00	15.00	20.00	35.00	70.00	125	1,300	1,750
1873S	324,000	16.00	18.00	22.00	27.00	45.00	90.00	150	1,350	—

5 CENTS

Shield. Rays between stars.

KM# 96 Designer: James B. Longacre **Reverse:** Rays between stars **Weight:** 5.0000 g. **Composition:** Copper-Nickel **Size:** 20.5 mm.

Date	Mintage	G-4	VG-8	F-12	VF-20	XF-40	AU-50	MS-60	MS-65	Prf-65
1866	14,742,500	18.50	25.00	28.00	41.00	110	160	240	2,500	3,400
1867	2,019,000	19.50	25.00	29.00	42.50	145	210	330	3,650	75,000

Shield. No rays between stars.

KM# 97 Reverse: No rays between stars **Weight:** 5.0000 g. **Composition:** Copper-Nickel

Date	Mintage	G-4	VG-8	F-12	VF-20	XF-40	AU-50	MS-60	MS-65	Prf-65
1867	28,890,500	14.00	16.00	18.00	20.00	34.00	60.00	90.00	780	2,750
1868	28,817,000	14.00	16.00	18.00	20.00	34.00	60.00	90.00	785	1,400
1869	16,395,000	14.00	16.00	18.00	20.00	38.50	60.00	90.00	740	1,025
1870	4,806,000	14.00	16.00	21.50	24.00	38.50	65.00	110	1,250	1,275
1871	561,000	45.00	60.00	70.00	95.00	145	175	250	1,440	1,075
1872	6,036,000	14.00	16.00	18.00	21.50	37.50	65.00	110	950	750
1873	4,550,000	14.00	17.00	21.50	30.00	43.50	70.00	135	1,250	800
1874	3,538,000	15.00	20.00	29.00	36.50	57.00	75.00	135	1,100	850
1875	2,097,000	15.00	23.00	35.00	50.00	65.00	95.00	170	1,750	1,750
1876	2,530,000	15.00	17.00	26.50	38.50	62.50	80.00	135	975	950
1877 proof	Est. 900	1,100	1,200	1,250	1,450	1,500	1,550	—	—	2,900
1878 proof	2,350	525	550	565	670	690	695	—	—	850
1879	29,100	275	365	440	475	495	505	660	1,650	790
1880	19,995	335	425	475	550	900	1,200	1,600	7,300	650
1881	72,375	175	220	280	310	430	510	660	1,300	630
1882	11,476,600	14.00	16.00	18.00	20.00	33.50	60.00	90.00	600	600
1883	1,456,919	15.00	17.00	19.00	22.00	35.00	65.00	90.00	575	570
1883/2	—	75.00	100.00	145	190	265	300	445	3,600	—

Liberty. Without "Cents" below "V".

KM# 111 Designer: Charles E. Barber **Reverse:** Without "Cents" below "V" **Weight:** 5.0000 g. **Composition:** Copper-Nickel **Size:** 21.2 mm.

Date	Mintage	G-4	VG-8	F-12	VF-20	XF-40	AU-50	MS-60	MS-65	Prf-65
1883	5,479,519	4.50	5.00	5.50	6.25	8.00	11.50	24.00	275	1,200

Liberty. "Cents" below "V".

KM# 112 Reverse: "Cents" below "V" **Weight:** 5.0000 g. **Composition:** Copper Nickel

Date	Mintage	G-4	VG-8	F-12	VF-20	XF-40	AU-50	MS-60	MS-65	Prf-65
1883	16,032,983	9.00	11.00	17.00	22.50	48.00	72.00	95.00	575	500
1884	11,273,942	14.00	17.50	20.00	25.00	55.00	88.00	140	1,725	550
1885	1,476,490	335	375	465	575	630	875	1,100	4,300	950
1886	3,330,290	150	195	250	350	490	555	670	4,250	525
1887	15,263,652	8.00	10.00	22.50	25.00	50.00	70.00	100.00	1,125	520
1888	10,720,483	16.00	19.50	25.00	60.00	72.50	195	200	1,400	520
1889	15,881,361	5.25	8.50	18.00	20.00	40.00	72.50	100.00	885	520
1890	16,259,272	5.25	12.50	18.00	21.50	40.00	80.00	135	1,650	600
1891	16,834,350	5.25	6.50	12.50	19.00	38.00	72.00	135	1,035	520
1892	11,699,642	5.25	8.00	16.00	20.00	44.00	85.00	120	1,350	520
1893	13,370,195	4.00	5.25	14.00	19.00	38.00	72.00	100.00	1,125	520
1894	5,413,132	9.00	19.00	65.00	95.00	170	200	225	1,275	500
1895	9,979,884	3.00	4.00	18.00	26.50	55.00	85.00	115	1,925	600
1896	8,842,920	5.25	10.00	21.50	30.00	50.00	85.00	120	1,825	600
1897	20,428,735	2.50	3.00	8.50	12.50	27.50	52.50	87.50	1,050	600
1898	12,532,087	2.00	3.50	8.50	12.00	30.00	65.00	135	1,150	500
1899	26,029,031	1.30	1.75	4.50	9.25	25.00	45.00	88.00	570	500
1900	27,255,995	1.60	2.00	5.00	9.50	25.00	52.50	75.00	570	500

1884 Nickel Five-Cent
Grade F-12

Retail Price

Date	Mintage	G-4	VG-8	F-12	VF-20	XF-40	AU-50	MS-60	MS-65	Prf-65
1901	26,480,213	1.25	2.50	5.50	8.50	25.00	45.00	60.00	570	500
1902	31,480,579	1.25	2.50	4.00	7.00	25.00	45.00	65.00	570	500
1903	28,006,725	1.25	2.50	4.00	8.50	25.00	45.00	60.00	565	500
1904	21,404,984	1.25	2.50	4.25	8.50	26.50	45.00	60.00	565	675
1905	29,827,276	1.25	1.75	3.25	7.50	25.00	45.00	60.00	570	520
1906	38,613,725	1.25	1.75	2.75	7.00	25.00	45.00	60.00	570	500
1907	39,214,800	1.25	1.75	2.75	6.50	25.00	45.00	60.00	1,150	590
1908	22,686,177	1.25	1.75	2.75	6.50	25.00	45.00	60.00	1,100	500
1909	11,590,526	2.25	2.75	3.50	7.50	27.50	45.00	75.00	900	500
1910	30,169,353	1.25	1.75	2.75	6.50	21.50	40.00	60.00	660	490
1911	39,559,372	1.25	1.75	2.75	6.50	21.50	40.00	60.00	565	490
1912	26,236,714	1.25	1.75	2.75	7.50	21.50	40.00	60.00	565	535
1912D	8,474,000	2.00	2.50	7.00	24.00	65.00	120	225	1,200	—
1912S	238,000	110	125	180	335	640	1,100	1,125	4,600	—
1913 5 known	—	—	—	—	—	—	—	—	—	—

Note: 1913, Superior Sale, March 2001, Proof, $1,840,000.

Buffalo. Buffalo standing on a mound.

KM# 133   Designer: James Earle Fraser **Reverse:** Buffalo standing on a mound **Weight:** 5.0000 g. **Composition:** Copper-Nickel **Size:** 21.2 mm.

Date	Mintage	G-4	VG-8	F-12	VF-20	XF-40	AU-50	MS-60	MS-65	Prf-65
1913	30,993,520	7.00	8.00	9.00	9.50	16.00	23.00	32.00	125	2,350
1913D	5,337,000	10.00	12.00	13.50	16.00	22.00	42.00	50.00	315	—
1913S	2,105,000	22.00	25.00	28.00	36.00	54.00	60.00	80.00	670	—

Buffalo. Buffalo standing on a line.

1918/17D

1937 D 3-legged

KM# 134   Designer: James Earle Fraser **Reverse:** Buffalo standing on a line **Weight:** 5.0000 g. **Composition:** Copper Nickel **Size:** 21.2 mm. **Note:** In 1913 the reverse design was modified so the ground under the buffalo was represented as a line rather than a mound. On the 1937D 3-legged variety, the buffalo's right front leg is missing, the result of a damaged die.

Date	Mintage	G-4	VG-8	F-12	VF-20	XF-40	AU-50	MS-60	MS-65	Prf-65
1913	29,858,700	7.50	8.50	9.50	10.00	17.00	24.00	30.00	340	1,675
1913D	4,156,000	55.00	72.50	95.00	98.00	105	125	160	1,400	—
1913S	1,209,000	160	250	280	290	300	340	395	3,750	—
1914	20,665,738	13.00	15.00	16.00	17.50	20.00	30.00	44.00	440	1,475
1914D	3,912,000	55.00	65.00	85.00	100.00	150	160	220	1,650	—
1914S	3,470,000	15.00	18.00	24.00	27.50	47.00	82.50	135	2,250	—
1915	20,987,270	4.50	5.00	6.00	10.50	17.50	35.00	45.00	290	1,400
1915D	7,569,500	12.50	15.00	24.00	40.00	80.00	110	200	2,300	—
1915S	1,505,000	28.00	40.00	60.00	110	325	320	480	2,950	—
1916	63,498,066	3.50	4.25	4.50	5.00	8.00	15.00	40.00	300	2,350
1916/16	Inc. above	2,000	3,800	6,600	9,150	12,500	23,500	41,000	340,000	—
1916D	13,333,000	9.00	13.50	16.50	25.00	70.00	95.00	140	2,300	—
1916S	11,860,000	4.50	6.50	12.50	21.50	50.00	95.00	160	2,250	—
1917	51,424,029	3.50	4.00	4.50	6.00	12.00	26.50	50.00	540	—
1917D	9,910,800	9.00	13.50	24.00	55.00	110	180	290	4,000	—
1917S	4,193,000	15.00	23.00	38.50	66.00	150	250	335	4,750	—
1918	32,086,314	3.25	365	4.85	10.00	25.00	40.00	85.00	1,525	—
1918/17D	8,362,314	800	1,250	2,400	4,900	8,200	9,400	20,000	280,000	—
1918D	Inc. above	7.50	15.00	25.00	92.50	180	290	350	4,750	—
1918S	4,882,000	8.00	18.00	30.00	72.00	150	260	400	31,000	—
1919	60,868,000	1.25	1.50	1.75	4.00	11.00	25.00	44.00	540	—
1919D	8,006,000	9.50	14.50	35.00	80.00	200	320	500	7,500	—
1919S	7,521,000	5.25	14.50	29.00	80.00	200	320	460	14,000	—
1920	63,093,000	0.75	1.25	1.50	4.00	8.50	23.00	45.00	685	—
1920D	9,418,000	5.50	11.00	23.00	85.00	250	300	450	7,250	—
1920S	9,689,000	3.00	5.25	16.00	80.00	175	250	435	27,500	—
1921	10,663,000	1.80	2.40	2.65	12.50	35.00	50.00	100.00	700	—
1921S	1,557,000	42.50	72.50	130	500	775	1,100	1,500	7,500	—
1923	35,715,000	1.25	1.35	1.50	3.00	8.00	29.00	44.00	580	—
1923S	6,142,000	3.90	5.00	9.00	115	240	300	400	9,600	—
1924	21,620,000	1.00	1.25	1.50	5.00	11.50	26.50	60.00	875	—

1921-S Nickel
Grade F-12

Retail Price

Date	Mintage	G-4	VG-8	F-12	VF-20	XF-40	AU-50	MS-60	MS-65	Prf-65
1924D	5,258,000	4.00	4.50	14.50	65.00	185	240	330	5,200	—
1924S	1,437,000	10.00	17.00	70.00	435	1,100	1,600	2,150	12,000	—
1925	35,565,100	2.00	2.10	2.25	4.00	9.00	23.00	38.50	525	—
1925D	4,450,000	6.00	13.50	30.00	72.00	145	220	350	6,100	—
1925S	6,256,000	3.90	8.50	14.00	66.00	150	230	380	4,400	—
1926	44,693,000	0.65	0.75	0.90	1.75	5.50	16.00	29.00	160	—
1926D	5,638,000	4.25	8.25	15.00	72.00	140	230	235	5,150	—
1926S	970,000	14.00	27.00	60.00	440	750	2,300	3,900	80,000	—
1927	37,981,000	0.65	0.75	0.90	1.50	7.50	16.00	26.50	280	—
1927D	5,730,000	1.75	4.00	5.00	21.00	70.00	110	145	8,800	—
1927S	3,430,000	1.75	3.00	6.00	27.50	75.00	150	480	20,000	—
1928	23,411,000	0.85	0.90	1.00	2.00	6.00	18.50	27.50	310	—
1928D	6,436,000	1.10	2.00	3.30	11.00	36.00	43.00	45.00	900	—
1928S	6,936,000	1.35	1.45	2.10	9.00	21.50	92.50	200	5,200	—
1929	36,446,000	0.65	0.75	0.90	1.50	5.75	14.50	29.00	310	—
1929D	8,370,000	0.85	1.10	1.75	5.50	30.00	40.00	53.00	1,900	—
1929S	7,754,000	0.75	0.85	1.00	1.50	11.50	25.00	45.00	450	—
1930	22,849,000	0.65	0.75	0.85	1.10	4.00	14.50	26.50	170	—
1930S	5,435,000	0.80	0.80	0.85	1.35	10.00	24.00	40.00	500	—
1931S	1,200,000	12.00	13.00	15.00	20.00	24.00	42.00	46.00	265	—
1934	20,213,003	0.60	0.75	0.85	1.75	3.75	12.00	46.00	370	—
1934D	7,480,000	0.75	0.95	1.35	3.75	13.50	40.00	67.00	810	—
1935	58,264,000	0.60	0.75	0.80	1.25	1.75	8.00	19.00	100.00	—
1935D	12,092,000	0.80	1.00	1.50	5.00	12.50	36.00	60.00	450	—
1935S	10,300,000	0.65	0.75	0.85	1.40	3.00	15.00	49.00	150	—
1936	119,001,420	0.60	0.70	0.85	1.00	1.75	6.50	14.50	90.00	1,100
1936D	24,814,000	0.60	0.75	0.85	1.00	3.00	11.50	34.00	95.00	—
1936S	14,930,000	0.60	0.75	0.85	1.00	1.75	9.50	34.00	105	—
1937	79,485,769	0.60	0.75	0.85	0.95	1.50	6.50	14.00	53.00	850
1937D	17,826,000	0.60	0.75	0.85	1.10	1.50	8.00	18.00	60.00	—
1937D 3-legged	Inc. above	200	370	415	450	510	800	1,450	24,000	—
1937S	5,635,000	0.75	0.80	0.90	1.25	2.20	8.00	24.00	65.00	—
1938D	7,020,000	1.50	1.60	2.00	2.50	3.00	8.00	17.00	40.00	—
1938D/D	—	2.50	4.50	6.00	8.00	10.00	17.00	20.00	60.00	—
1938D/S	Inc. above	4.50	6.50	9.00	10.00	12.50	27.50	45.00	180	—

Jefferson.

KM# 192 Designer: Felix Schlag **Weight:** 5.0000 g. **Composition:** Copper-Nickel **Size:** 21.2 mm. **Note:** Some 1939 strikes have doubling of the word "Monticello" on the reverse.

Date	Mintage	VG-8	F-12	VF-20	XF-40	MS-60	MS-65	-65FS	Prf-65
1938	19,515,365	0.25	0.40	0.80	1.25	4.00	8.00	125	70.00
1938D	5,376,000	0.90	1.00	1.25	1.75	3.50	8.00	95.00	—
1938S	4,105,000	1.60	1.75	2.00	2.25	4.25	8.50	165	—
1939 T I	—	—	—	—	—	—	—	300	70.00
1939 T II	120,627,535	—	0.20	0.25	0.30	1.75	3.50	40.00	300
1939D T I	—	—	—	—	—	—	—	275	—
1939D T II	3,514,000	3.00	3.50	5.00	10.00	42.00	85.00	250	—
1939S T I	—	—	—	—	—	—	—	250	—
1939S T II	6,630,000	0.45	0.60	1.50	2.75	15.00	40.00	275	—
1940	176,499,158	—	—	—	0.25	1.00	2.50	35.00	65.00
1940D	43,540,000	—	0.20	0.30	0.40	1.50	2.75	25.00	—
1940S	39,690,000	—	0.20	0.25	0.50	2.50	5.00	45.00	—
1941	203,283,720	—	—	—	0.20	0.75	2.00	40.00	60.00
1941D	53,432,000	—	0.20	0.30	0.50	2.50	5.00	25.00	—
1941S	43,445,000	—	0.20	0.30	0.50	3.75	6.75	60.00	—
1942	49,818,600	—	—	—	0.40	5.00	8.50	75.00	55.00
1942D	13,938,000	0.30	0.40	0.60	2.00	27.00	50.00	70.00	—

Note: Fully Struck Full Step nickels command higher prices. Bright, Fully Struck coins command even higher prices. 1938 thru 1989 - 5 Full Steps. 1990 to date - 6 Full Steps. Without bag marks or nicks on steps.

Jefferson. Mint mark above Monticello.

1943/2 P

KM# 192a **Designer:** Felix Schlag **Reverse:** Mint mark above Monticello **Composition:** 0.3500 Copper-Silver-Manganese 0.0563 oz. **Size:** 21.2 mm. **Note:** War-time composition nickels have a large mint mark above Monticello on the reverse.

Date	Mintage	VG-8	F-12	VF-20	XF-40	MS-60	MS-65	-65FS	Prf-65
1942P	57,900,600	0.65	0.85	1.00	1.75	6.00	22.50	70.00	140
1942S	32,900,000	0.70	1.00	1.10	1.75	6.00	20.00	125	—
1943P	271,165,000	0.50	0.85	1.00	1.50	2.75	15.00	35.00	—
1943/2P	Inc. above	15.00	20.00	30.00	40.00	125	450	1,000	—
1943D	15,294,000	0.90	1.20	1.50	1.75	4.00	13.00	30.00	—
1943S	104,060,000	0.55	0.70	1.00	1.50	3.00	13.00	55.00	—
1944P	119,150,000	0.50	0.70	1.00	1.50	4.00	17.00	100.00	—
1944D	32,309,000	0.60	0.80	1.00	1.75	6.50	13.00	30.00	—
1944S	21,640,000	0.70	1.00	1.25	2.00	3.50	13.00	185	—
1945P	119,408,100	0.50	0.70	1.00	1.50	3.50	12.00	125	—
1945D	37,158,000	0.55	0.75	1.00	1.50	3.50	7.00	40.00	—
1945S	58,939,000	0.50	0.70	0.80	0.90	3.00	6.50	250	—

Note: Fully Struck Full Step nickels command higher prices. Bright, Fully Struck coins command even higher prices. 1938 thru 1989 - 5 Full Steps. 1990 to date - 6 Full Steps. Without bag marks or nicks on steps.

Jefferson. Pre-war design resumed.

KM# A192 **Designer:** Felix Schlag **Reverse:** Pre-war design resumed **Weight:** 5.0000 g. **Composition:** Copper-Nickel **Size:** 21.2 mm. **Note:** KM#192 design and composition resumed. The 1979-S and 1981-S Type II proofs have clearer mint marks than the Type I proofs of those years.

Date	Mintage	VG-8	F-12	VF-20	XF-40	MS-60	MS-65	-65FS	Prf-65
1946	161,116,000	—	—	0.20	0.25	0.80	1.00	40.00	—
1946D	45,292,200	—	—	0.25	0.35	0.95	1.50	30.00	—
1946S	13,560,000	—	—	0.30	0.40	0.50	1.00	45.00	—
1947	95,000,000	—	—	0.20	0.25	0.75	2.00	30.00	—
1947D	37,822,000	—	—	0.20	0.30	0.90	2.00	30.00	—
1947S	24,720,000	—	—	0.20	0.25	1.00	2.25	55.00	—
1948	89,348,000	—	—	0.20	0.25	0.50	1.50	60.00	—
1948D	44,734,000	—	—	0.25	0.35	1.20	2.75	30.00	—
1948S	11,300,000	—	—	0.25	0.50	1.20	2.25	45.00	—
1949	60,652,000	—	—	0.25	0.30	2.25	4.50	200	—
1949D	36,498,000	—	—	0.30	0.40	1.25	3.00	75.00	—
1949D/S	Inc. above	—	35.00	40.00	65.00	170	325	1,750	—
1949S	9,716,000	0.25	0.35	0.45	0.90	1.50	3.50	145	—
1950	9,847,386	0.20	0.30	0.35	0.75	1.50	3.50	150	45.00

Date	Mintage	VG-8	F-12	VF-20	XF-40	MS-60	MS-65	-65FS	Prf-65
1950D	2,630,030	5.50	6.00	6.50	7.00	8.00	10.00	45.00	—
1951	28,609,500	—	—	0.40	0.50	1.50	2.75	90.00	30.00
1951D	20,460,000	0.25	0.30	0.40	0.50	3.00	6.00	45.00	—
1951S	7,776,000	0.30	0.40	0.50	1.10	1.75	4.00	150	—
1952	64,069,980	—	—	0.20	0.25	0.85	3.00	125	26.00
1952D	30,638,000	—	—	0.30	0.45	2.00	4.50	65.00	—
1952S	20,572,000	—	—	0.20	0.25	0.75	3.50	195	—
1953	46,772,800	—	—	0.20	0.25	0.40	1.50	200	28.00
1953D	59,878,600	—	—	0.20	0.25	0.40	1.50	100.00	—
1953S	19,210,900	—	—	0.20	0.25	0.60	2.50	1,750	—
1954	47,917,350	—	—	—	—	0.60	1.75	95.00	16.00
1954D	117,136,560	—	—	—	—	0.35	2.00	175	—
1954S	29,384,000	—	—	—	0.20	1.00	3.00	1,000	—
1954S/D	Inc. above	—	6.00	9.00	13.00	22.00	65.00	—	—
1955	8,266,200	0.25	0.35	0.40	0.45	0.75	2.00	85.00	16.00
1955D	74,464,100	—	—	—	—	0.40	1.00	150	—
1955D/S	Inc. above	—	5.00	8.50	13.00	33.00	75.00	—	—
1956	35,885,384	—	—	—	—	0.30	0.70	35.00	2.50
1956D	67,222,940	—	—	—	—	0.25	0.60	90.00	—
1957	39,655,952	—	—	—	—	0.25	0.60	40.00	1.50
1957D	136,828,900	—	—	—	—	0.25	0.60	55.00	—
1958	17,963,652	—	—	0.15	0.20	0.30	0.65	80.00	6.00
1958D	168,249,120	—	—	—	—	0.25	0.60	30.00	—

Note: Fully Struck Full Step nickels command higher prices. Bright, Fully Struck coins command even higher prices. 1938 thru 1989 - 5 Full Steps. 1990 to date - 6 Full Steps. Without bag marks or nicks on steps.

Date	Mintage	VG-8	F-12	VF-20	XF-40	MS-60	MS-65	-65FS	Prf-65
1959	28,397,291	—	—	—	—	0.30	0.65	30.00	1.25
1959D	160,738,240	—	—	—	—	0.25	0.55	45.00	—
1960	57,107,602	—	—	—	—	0.25	2.00	60.00	1.00
1960D	192,582,180	—	—	—	—	0.25	0.55	650	—
1961	76,668,244	—	—	—	—	0.25	0.55	100.00	1.00
1961D	229,342,760	—	—	—	—	0.25	0.55	800	—
1962	100,602,019	—	—	—	—	0.25	1.50	75.00	1.00
1962D	280,195,720	—	—	—	—	0.25	0.55	600	—
1963	178,851,645	—	—	—	—	0.25	0.55	45.00	1.00
1963D	276,829,460	—	—	—	—	0.25	0.55	650	—
1964	1,028,622,762	—	—	—	—	0.25	0.55	55.00	1.00
1964D	1,787,297,160	—	—	—	—	0.25	0.50	500	—
1965	136,131,380	—	—	—	—	0.25	0.50	225	—
1966	156,208,283	—	—	—	—	0.25	0.50	350	—
1967	107,325,800	—	—	—	—	0.25	0.50	275	—
1968 none minted	—	—	—	—	—	—	—	—	—
1968D	91,227,880	—	—	—	—	0.25	0.50	750	—
1968S	103,437,510	—	—	—	—	0.25	0.50	300	0.75
1969 none minted	—	—	—	—	—	—	—	—	—
1969D	202,807,500	—	—	—	—	0.25	0.50	—	—
1969S	123,099,631	—	—	—	—	0.25	0.50	450	0.75
1970 none minted	—	—	—	—	—	—	—	—	—
1970D	515,485,380	—	—	—	—	0.25	0.50	500	—
1970S	241,464,814	—	—	—	—	0.25	0.50	125	0.75
1971	106,884,000	—	—	—	—	0.75	2.00	35.00	—
1971D	316,144,800	—	—	—	—	0.25	0.50	25.00	—
1971S	3,220,733	—	—	—	—	—	—	—	2.00
1972	202,036,000	—	—	—	—	0.25	0.50	35.00	—
1972D	351,694,600	—	—	—	—	0.25	0.50	25.00	—
1972S	3,260,996	—	—	—	—	—	—	—	2.00
1973	384,396,000	—	—	—	—	—	0.50	20.00	—
1973D	261,405,000	—	—	—	—	—	0.50	20.00	—
1973S	2,760,339	—	—	—	—	—	—	—	1.75
1974	601,752,000	—	—	—	—	—	0.50	75.00	—
1974D	277,373,000	—	—	—	—	—	0.50	50.00	—
1974S	2,612,568	—	—	—	—	—	—	—	2.00
1975	181,772,000	—	—	—	—	—	0.75	65.00	—
1975D	401,875,300	—	—	—	—	—	0.50	60.00	—
1975S	2,845,450	—	—	—	—	—	—	—	2.25
1976	367,124,000	—	—	—	—	—	0.75	150	—
1976D	563,964,147	—	—	—	—	—	0.60	55.00	—
1976S	4,149,730	—	—	—	—	—	—	—	2.00
1977	585,376,000	—	—	—	—	—	0.40	65.00	—
1977D	297,313,460	—	—	—	—	—	0.55	35.00	—
1977S	3,251,152	—	—	—	—	—	—	—	1.75
1978	391,308,000	—	—	—	—	—	0.40	40.00	—
1978D	313,092,780	—	—	—	—	—	0.40	35.00	—
1978S	3,127,781	—	—	—	—	—	—	—	1.75
1979	463,188,000	—	—	—	—	—	0.40	95.00	—
1979D	325,867,672	—	—	—	—	—	0.40	35.00	—
1979S type I, proof	3,677,175	—	—	—	—	—	—	—	1.50
1979S type II, proof	Inc. above	—	—	—	—	—	—	—	1.75
1980P	593,004,000	—	—	—	—	—	0.40	30.00	—
1980D	502,323,448	—	—	—	—	0.25	0.40	25.00	—
1980S	3,554,806	—	—	—	—	—	—	—	1.50
1981P	657,504,000	—	—	—	—	0.25	0.40	70.00	—
1981D	364,801,843	—	—	—	—	0.25	0.40	40.00	—
1981S type I, proof	4,063,083	—	—	—	—	—	—	—	2.00
1981S type II, proof	Inc. above	—	—	—	—	—	—	—	2.50
1982P	292,355,000	—	—	—	—	2.00	4.50	80.00	—

Date	Mintage	VG-8	F-12	VF-20	XF-40	MS-60	MS-65	-65FS	Prf-65
1982D	373,726,544	—	—	—	—	1.50	3.50	45.00	—
1982S	3,857,479	—	—	—	—	—	—	—	3.50
1983P	561,615,000	—	—	—	—	1.50	4.00	45.00	—
1983D	536,726,276	—	—	—	—	1.00	2.50	35.00	—
1983S	3,279,126	—	—	—	—	—	—	—	4.00
1984P	746,769,000	—	—	—	—	1.25	3.00	65.00	—
1984D	517,675,146	—	—	—	—	0.30	0.85	30.00	—
1984S	3,065,110	—	—	—	—	—	—	—	5.00
1985P	647,114,962	—	—	—	—	0.35	0.75	60.00	—
1985D	459,747,446	—	—	—	—	0.35	0.75	35.00	—
1985S	3,362,821	—	—	—	—	—	—	—	4.00
1986P	536,883,483	—	—	—	—	0.40	1.00	70.00	—
1986D	361,819,140	—	—	—	—	1.00	2.00	60.00	—
1986S	3,010,497	—	—	—	—	—	—	—	7.00
1987P	371,499,481	—	—	—	—	0.25	0.75	30.00	—
1987D	410,590,604	—	—	—	—	0.25	0.75	25.00	—
1987S	4,227,728	—	—	—	—	—	—	—	3.50
1988P	771,360,000	—	—	—	—	0.25	0.75	30.00	—
1988D	663,771,652	—	—	—	—	—	—	25.00	—
1988S	3,262,948	—	—	—	—	—	—	—	6.50
1989P	898,812,000	—	—	—	—	0.25	0.75	75.00	—
1989D	570,842,474	—	—	—	—	0.25	0.75	25.00	—
1989S	3,220,194	—	—	—	—	—	—	—	5.50
1990P	661,636,000	—	—	—	—	0.25	0.75	25.00	—
1990D	663,938,503	—	—	—	—	0.25	0.75	25.00	—
1990S	3,299,559	—	—	—	—	—	—	—	5.50
1991P	614,104,000	—	—	—	—	0.25	0.75	25.00	—
1991D	436,496,678	—	—	—	—	0.25	0.75	25.00	—
1991S	2,867,787	—	—	—	—	—	—	—	5.00
1992P	399,552,000	—	—	—	—	0.65	2.00	25.00	—
1992D	450,565,113	—	—	—	—	0.25	0.75	25.00	—
1992S	4,176,560	—	—	—	—	—	—	—	4.00
1993P	412,076,000	—	—	—	—	0.25	0.75	25.00	—
1993D	406,084,135	—	—	—	—	0.25	0.75	25.00	—
1993S	3,394,792	—	—	—	—	—	—	—	4.50
1994P	722,160,000	—	—	—	—	0.25	0.75	25.00	—
1994P matte	167,703	—	—	—	—	—	75.00	—	—
1994D	715,762,110	—	—	—	—	0.25	0.75	25.00	—
1994S	3,269,923	—	—	—	—	—	—	—	4.00
1995P	774,156,000	—	—	—	—	0.25	0.75	25.00	—
1995D	888,112,000	—	—	—	—	0.35	0.85	25.00	—
1995S	2,707,481	—	—	—	—	—	—	—	7.50
1996P	829,332,000	—	—	—	—	0.25	0.75	25.00	—
1996D	817,736,000	—	—	—	—	0.25	0.75	25.00	—
1996S	2,915,212	—	—	—	—	—	—	—	3.00
1997P	470,972,000	—	—	—	—	0.25	0.75	25.00	—
1997P matte	25,000	—	—	—	—	—	250	—	—
1997D	466,640,000	—	—	—	—	0.30	0.80	25.00	—
1997S	1,975,000	—	—	—	—	—	—	—	5.00
1998P	688,272,000	—	—	—	—	0.25	0.80	25.00	—
1998D	635,360,000	—	—	—	—	0.25	0.80	25.00	—
1998S	2,957,286	—	—	—	—	—	—	—	4.50
1999P	1,212,000,000	—	—	—	—	0.25	0.80	20.00	—
1999D	1,066,720,000	—	—	—	—	0.25	0.80	20.00	—
1999S	3,362,462	—	—	—	—	—	—	—	3.50
2000P	846,240,000	—	—	—	—	0.25	0.80	20.00	—
2000D	1,509,520,000	—	—	—	—	0.25	0.80	20.00	—
2000S	4,063,361	—	—	—	—	—	—	—	2.00
2001P	675,704,000	—	—	—	—	0.25	0.50	20.00	—
2001D	627,680,000	—	—	—	—	0.25	0.50	20.00	—
2001S	3,099,096	—	—	—	—	—	—	—	2.00
2002P	539,280,000	—	—	—	—	0.25	0.50	—	—
2002D	691,200,000	—	—	—	—	0.25	0.50	—	—
2002S	—	—	—	—	—	—	—	—	2.00
2003P	—	—	—	—	—	0.25	0.50	—	—
2003D	—	—	—	—	—	0.25	0.50	—	—
2003S	—	—	—	—	—	—	—	—	2.00

DIME

Draped Bust. Small eagle.

KM# 24 **Designer:** Robert Scot **Reverse:** Small eagle **Weight:** 2.7000 g. **Composition:** 0.8920 Silver 0.0775 oz. ASW **Size:** 19 mm. **Note:** 1797 strikes have either 13 or 16 stars on the obverse.

Date	Mintage	G-4	VG-8	F-12	VF-20	XF-40	MS-60
1796	22,135	1,000	1,700	1,900	2,750	4,400	8,000
1797 13 stars	25,261	1,200	1,750	2,000	2,900	5,400	9,000
1797 16 stars	Inc. above	1,200	1,750	2,000	2,900	5,400	8,500

Draped Bust. Heraldic eagle.

KM# 31 **Designer:** Robert Scot **Reverse:** Heraldic eagle **Weight:** 2.7000 g. **Composition:** 0.8920 Silver 0.0775 oz. ASW **Size:** 19 mm. **Note:** The 1798 overdates have either 13 or 16 stars on the obverse. Varieties of the regular 1798 strikes are distinguished by the size of the 8 in the date. The 1805 strikes have either 4 or 5 berries on the olive branch held by the eagle.

Date	Mintage	G-4	VG-8	F-12	VF-20	XF-40	MS-60
1798	27,550	450	525	750	1,050	2,000	4,000
1798/97 13 stars	Inc. above	1,750	2,400	4,000	5,750	8,500	—
1798/97 16 stars	Inc. above	475	600	800	1,100	2,100	4,300
1798 small 8	Inc. above	600	850	1,350	1,950	3,000	7,500
1800	21,760	450	560	750	1,125	2,150	—
1801	34,640	450	560	950	1,600	3,200	—
1802	10,975	600	750	1,300	2,100	4,800	11,000
1803	33,040	450	550	800	1,100	2,900	—
1804 13 stars	8,265	1,200	1,600	2,300	4,400	10,000	—
1804 14 stars	Inc. above	1,400	1,800	2,750	5,000	11,000	—
1805 4 berries	120,780	375	525	725	950	1,800	4,100
1805 5 berries	Inc. above	650	800	1,000	1,500	2,500	4,500
1807	165,000	375	525	725	975	1,800	4,100

Liberty Cap.

1809 Dime
Grade F-12

Retail Price

KM# 42 Designer: John Reich **Weight:** 2.7000 g. **Composition:** 0.8920 Silver .0775 oz. ASW **Size:** 18.8 mm.
Note: Varieties of the 1814, 1821 and 1828 strikes are distinguished by the size of the numerals in the dates.
The 1820 varieties are distinguished by the size of the 0 in the date. The 1823 overdates have either large E's
or small E's in "United States of America" on the reverse.

Date	Mintage	G-4	VG-8	F-12	VF-20	XF-40	AU-50	MS-60	MS-65
1809	51,065	100.00	200	375	650	925	2,500	4,200	22,500
1811/9	65,180	90.00	165	240	425	750	1,500	4,000	22,500
1814 small date	421,500	40.00	60.00	90.00	210	500	700	800	8,000
1814 large date	Inc. above	17.50	26.00	44.00	115	350	625	800	8,000
1820 large O	942,587	17.00	24.00	38.00	105	330	625	800	8,000
1820 small O	Inc. above	22.00	40.00	55.00	175	425	725	975	8,000
1821 large date	1,186,512	16.00	23.00	38.00	105	330	625	800	8,000
1821 small date	Inc. above	18.50	25.00	45.00	125	370	625	800	8,000
1822	100,000	300	450	800	1,450	2,500	4,450	6,000	—
1823/22 large E's	440,000	15.00	22.00	40.00	110	300	625	800	8,000
1823/22 small E's	Inc. above	15.00	22.00	40.00	110	300	625	800	8,000
1824/22 mintage undetermined	—	30.00	48.00	90.00	325	525	1,275	2,500	—
1825	510,000	20.00	27.00	45.00	145	375	800	1,250	8,000
1827	1,215,000	15.00	22.00	35.00	95.00	300	775	1,000	8,000
1828 large date	125,000	80.00	110	150	265	650	900	2,600	—

Liberty Cap.

KM# 48 Designer: John Reich **Composition:** Silver **Size:** 18.5 mm. **Note:** The three varieties of 1829 strikes
and two varieties of 1830 strikes are distinguished by the size of "10C." on the reverse. On the 1833 "high 3"
variety, the last 3 in the date is higher than the first 3. The two varieties of the 1834 strikes are distinguished
by the size of the 4 in the date.

Date	Mintage	G-4	VG-8	F-12	VF-20	XF-40	AU-50	MS-60	MS-65
1828 small date	Inc. above	30.00	45.00	75.00	195	475	775	1,750	—
1829 very large 10C.	770,000	35.00	45.00	85.00	150	375	600	1,500	—
1829 medium 10C.	Inc. above	21.00	24.00	30.00	60.00	185	350	725	8,000
1829 small 10C.	Inc. above	21.00	24.00	30.00	60.00	185	350	725	8,000
1830 large 10C.	510,000	21.00	24.00	29.00	55.00	175	345	675	8,000
1830 small 10C.	Inc. above	21.00	24.00	29.00	55.00	175	345	675	8,000
1830/29	Inc. above	26.50	45.00	92.50	165	360	550	1,000	—
1831	771,350	21.00	24.00	29.00	55.00	175	330	675	6,000
1832	522,500	21.00	24.00	29.00	55.00	175	330	675	6,500
1833	485,000	21.00	24.00	29.00	55.00	175	330	675	6,700
1834	635,000	21.00	24.00	29.00	55.00	175	330	675	6,500
1835	1,410,000	21.00	24.00	29.00	55.00	175	330	675	6,500
1836	1,190,000	21.00	24.00	29.00	55.00	175	330	675	6,500
1837	1,042,000	21.00	24.00	29.00	55.00	175	330	675	6,600

Seated Liberty. No stars around rim.

KM# 61 Designer: Christian Gobrecht **Obverse:** No stars around rim **Weight:** 2.6700 g. **Composition:** 0.9000
Silver 0.0773 oz. ASW **Size:** 17.9 mm. **Note:** The two 1837 varieties are distinguished by the size of the
numerals in the date.

Date	Mintage	G-4	VG-8	F-12	VF-20	XF-40	AU-50	MS-60	MS-65
1837 small date	Inc. above	29.00	40.00	75.00	275	550	750	1,100	6,500
1837 large date	Inc. above	29.00	40.00	75.00	275	550	750	1,100	6,500
1838O	406,034	35.00	45.00	90.00	300	725	1,250	3,500	21,000

Seated Liberty. Stars around rim. No drapery.

KM# 63.1 Obv. Designer: Christian Gobrecht **Obverse:** Stars around rim. No drapery **Weight:** 2.6700 g.
Composition: 0.9000 Silver 0.0773 oz. ASW **Size:** 17.9 mm. **Note:** The two 1838 varieties are distinguished
by the size of the stars on the obverse. The 1838 "partial drapery" variety has drapery on Liberty's left elbow.
The 1839-O with reverse of 1838-O variety was struck from rusted dies. This variety has a bumpy surface on
the reverse.

Date	Mintage	G-4	VG-8	F-12	VF-20	XF-40	AU-50	MS-60	MS-65
1838 small stars	1,992,500	1,600	22.00	38.00	65.00	145	350	600	—
1838 large stars	Inc. above	12.50	1,300	1,700	25.00	63.50	195	275	8,500
1838 partial drapery	Inc. above	30.00	45.00	60.00	125	195	325	550	—
1839	1,053,115	12.50	13.00	17.50	35.00	70.00	170	265	2,500
1839O	1,323,000	12.50	13.00	20.00	45.00	85.00	300	1,250	—
1839O reverse 1838O	—	145	200	350	550	950	—	—	—
1840	1,358,580	12.50	13.00	20.00	30.00	60.00	170	300	2,500
1840O	1,175,000	13.00	14.50	40.00	70.00	125	295	975	—

Seated Liberty. Drapery added to Liberty's left elbow.

Drapery

KM# 63.2 Designer: Christian Gobrecht **Obverse:** Drapery added to Liberty's left elbow **Weight:** 2.6700 g. **Composition:** 0.9000 Silver 0.0773 oz. ASW **Size:** 17.9 mm.

Date	Mintage	G-4	VG-8	F-12	VF-20	XF-40	AU-50	MS-60	MS-65
1840	Inc. above	30.00	45.00	85.00	165	275	1,250	—	—
1841	1,622,500	10.00	13.00	16.00	23.00	50.00	175	260	2,550
1841O	2,007,500	9.00	11.00	15.00	28.00	60.00	250	1,500	—
1841O large O	Inc. above	600	900	1,200	2,500	—	—	—	—
1842	1,887,500	8.75	9.50	10.00	18.00	45.00	175	260	2,550
1842O	2,020,000	10.00	18.00	30.00	75.00	225	1,350	2,900	—
1843	1,370,000	8.75	9.25	10.00	18.00	45.00	175	260	2,550
1843/1843	—	9.00	12.00	18.00	30.00	75.00	200	295	—
1843O	150,000	35.00	65.00	125	250	700	2,000	—	—
1844	72,500	275	350	550	800	1,450	2,200	3,000	—
1845	1,755,000	8.75	9.25	10.00	19.00	45.00	120	260	2,550
1845/1845	Inc. above	12.00	15.00	35.00	55.00	100.00	175	—	—
1845O	230,000	19.00	35.00	60.00	165	475	1,200	—	—
1846	31,300	200	225	300	400	850	2,000	—	—
1847	245,000	17.50	25.00	35.00	60.00	125	350	950	—
1848	451,500	12.00	15.00	22.00	40.00	75.00	185	750	7,050
1849	839,000	10.00	13.00	18.00	28.00	60.00	140	500	7,050
1849O	300,000	15.00	22.00	35.00	90.00	190	750	—	—
1850	1,931,500	8.75	9.25	10.00	18.00	55.00	120	260	2,550
1850O	510,000	14.00	17.00	28.00	60.00	160	400	1,250	—
1851	1,026,500	8.75	9.25	12.00	19.00	60.00	120	325	—
1851O	400,000	14.00	17.00	30.00	75.00	175	450	1,500	—
1852	1,535,500	8.75	9.25	12.00	19.00	50.00	120	290	2,550
1852O	430,000	16.00	22.00	39.00	100.00	195	425	1,800	—
1853	95,000	70.00	100.00	130	180	300	450	800	—

Seated Liberty. Arrows at date.

KM# 77 Designer: Christian Gobrecht **Obverse:** Arrows at date **Weight:** 2.4900 g. **Composition:** 0.9000 Silver 0.0721 oz. ASW

Date	Mintage	G-4	VG-8	F-12	VF-20	XF-40	AU-50	MS-60	MS-65	Prf-65
1853	12,078,010	8.00	9.00	10.00	14.00	45.00	125	330	2,500	31,500
1853O	1,100,000	11.00	14.00	20.00	45.00	145	400	900	—	—
1854	4,470,000	8.75	9.25	10.00	15.00	45.00	125	330	2,500	31,500
1854O	1,770,000	10.00	11.00	14.00	25.00	75.00	175	600	—	—
1855	2,075,000	8.75	9.25	14.00	20.00	55.00	150	350	3,800	31,500

Seated Liberty. Arrows at date removed.

KM# A63.2 Designer: Christian Gobrecht **Obverse:** Arrows at date removed **Weight:** 2.4900 g. **Composition:** 0.9000 Silver 0.0721 oz. ASW **Note:** The two 1856 varieties are distinguished by the size of the numerals in the date.

Date	Mintage	G-4	VG-8	F-12	VF-20	XF-40	AU-50	MS-60	MS-65	Prf-65
1856 small date	5,780,000	8.75	9.25	10.00	12.50	32.00	115	250	7,050	38,000
1856 large date	Inc. above	10.00	12.00	15.00	25.00	65.00	175	475	—	—
1856O	1,180,000	9.00	15.00	20.00	35.00	85.00	200	500	—	—
1856S	70,000	145	200	275	425	900	1,750	—	—	—

Date	Mintage	G-4	VG-8	F-12	VF-20	XF-40	AU-50	MS-60	MS-65	Prf-65
1857	5,580,000	8.75	9.25	11.25	15.00	32.00	100.00	260	2,500	3,400
1857O	1,540,000	10.00	12.00	14.00	25.00	65.00	200	350	—	—
1858	1,540,000	10.00	14.00	20.00	35.00	55.00	145	260	2,500	3,400
1858O	290,000	15.00	19.00	35.00	70.00	125	275	800	—	—
1858S	60,000	110	150	200	325	675	1,400	—	—	—
1859	430,000	11.00	16.00	22.00	40.00	60.00	140	350	—	3,400
1859O	480,000	11.00	15.00	22.00	38.00	70.00	225	550	—	—
1859S	60,000	125	160	250	425	1,000	2,000	—	—	—
1860S	140,000	30.00	40.00	55.00	110	275	800	—	—	—

Seated Liberty.

KM# PN243 **Weight:** 2.4900 g. **Composition:** 0.9000 Silver 0.0724 oz. ASW **Note:** This non-circulation strike was an experiment in transferring the legend "United States of America" from the reverse to the obverse.

Date	Mintage	G-4	VG-8	F-12	VF-20	XF-40	AU-50	MS-60	MS-65	Prf-65
1859 obverse 1859, reverse 1860	—	—	—	—	—	—	—	—	—	25,000

Seated Liberty. "United States of America" replaced stars.

KM# 92 **Obv. Designer:** Christian Gobrecht **Obverse:** "United States of America" replaced stars **Weight:** 2.4900 g. **Composition:** 0.9000 Silver 0.0721 oz. ASW **Note:** The 1873 "closed-3" and "open-3" varieties are distinguished by the amount of space between the upper left and lower left serifs of the 3 in the date.

Date	Mintage	G-4	VG-8	F-12	VF-20	XF-40	AU-50	MS-60	MS-65	Prf-65
1860	607,000	15.00	22.00	29.00	31.00	55.00	125	275	—	1,400
1860O	40,000	300	425	600	1,150	2,500	4,200	6,000	—	—
1861	1,884,000	8.75	10.00	13.00	18.00	35.00	65.00	125	—	1,400
1861S	172,500	45.00	80.00	125	225	375	900	—	—	—
1862	847,550	10.00	13.00	19.00	25.00	45.00	65.00	150	—	1,400
1862S	180,750	40.00	60.00	95.00	175	300	775	—	—	—
1863	14,460	250	375	500	600	750	900	1,200	—	1,400
1863S	157,500	30.00	35.00	55.00	90.00	275	550	1,200	—	—
1864	11,470	250	325	400	500	600	775	1,200	—	1,400
1864S	230,000	24.00	30.00	40.00	80.00	225	425	1,200	—	—
1865	10,500	275	350	450	550	675	1,050	1,250	—	1,400
1865S	175,000	35.00	45.00	60.00	100.00	250	700	—	—	—
1866	8,725	300	375	575	675	800	1,200	1,800	—	1,750
1866S	135,000	35.00	45.00	75.00	145	325	675	1,900	—	—
1867	6,625	425	575	800	900	1,150	1,300	1,600	—	1,750
1867S	140,000	35.00	45.00	70.00	125	275	575	1,200	—	—

1866-S Dime
Grade F-12

Retail Price

Date	Mintage	G-4	VG-8	F-12	VF-20	XF-40	AU-50	MS-60	MS-65	Prf-65
1868	464,000	13.00	17.00	22.00	32.00	70.00	175	300	—	1,400
1868S	260,000	20.00	25.00	35.00	70.00	145	285	600	—	—
1869	256,600	20.00	26.00	40.00	60.00	115	220	600	—	1,400
1869S	450,000	12.00	17.00	30.00	38.00	65.00	150	400	—	—
1870	471,000	15.00	19.00	23.00	32.00	70.00	135	300	—	1,400
1870S	50,000	215		280	375	450	575	850	2,000	—	—
1871	907,710	11.00	15.00	20.00	28.00	45.00	130	300	—	1,400
1871CC	20,100	850	1,150	1,950	3,500	6,750	10,500	—	—	—
1871S	320,000	35.00	55.00	75.00	115	175	350	900	—	—
1872	2,396,450	8.75	9.50	11.00	18.00	31.00	95.00	175	—	1,400
1872CC	35,480	350	525	850	1,750	3,000	4,750	—	—	—
1872S	190,000	40.00	50.00	70.00	125	215	450	1,100	—	—
1873 closed 3	1,568,600	9.00	11.00	14.00	27.00	50.00	100.00	200	—	1,400
1873 open 3	Inc. above	15.00	18.00	30.00	55.00	100.00	225	650	—	—
1873CC	12,400	—	—	—	—	—	—	—	—	—

Note: 1873-CC, Heritage Sale, April 1999, MS-64, $632,500.

Seated Liberty. Arrows at date.

KM# 105 Designer: Christian Gobrecht **Obverse:** Arrows at date **Weight:** 2.5000 g. **Composition:** 0.9000 Silver 0.0724 oz. ASW

Date	Mintage	G-4	VG-8	F-12	VF-20	XF-40	AU-50	MS-60	MS-65	Prf-65
1873	2,378,500	8.75	13.00	25.00	50.00	150	350	500	4,500	4,500
1873CC	18,791	750	975	1,850	3,750	5,750	9,750	—	—	—
1873S	455,000	15.00	20.00	28.00	60.00	180	320	1,500	—	—
1874	2,940,700	8.75	13.00	17.50	50.00	150	315	500	4,500	4,500
1874CC	10,817	2,950	4,500	6,500	9,750	17,500	—	—	—	—
1874S	240,000	60.00	75.00	100.00	160	250	450	1,500	—	—

Seated Liberty. Arrows at date removed.

KM# A92 Designer: Christian Gobrecht **Obverse:** Arrows at date removed **Weight:** 2.5000 g. **Composition:** 0.9000 Silver 0.0724 oz. ASW **Note:** On the 1876-CC doubled-obverse variety, doubling appears in the words "of America" in the legend.

Date	Mintage	G-4	VG-8	F-12	VF-20	XF-40	AU-50	MS-60	MS-65	Prf-65
1875	10,350,700	8.75	9.25	10.00	14.00	22.00	60.00	125	2,250	4,600
1875CC mint mark in wreath	4,645,000	8.75	9.50	11.00	18.00	37.50	90.00	160	2,700	—
1875CC mint mark under wreath	Inc. above	10.00	15.00	22.50	37.50	65.00	165	235	3,000	—
1875S mint mark in wreath	9,070,000	12.00	17.50	28.00	43.00	65.00	125	225	3,100	—
1875S mint mark under wreath	Inc. above	10.00	14.00	17.50	25.00	35.00	70.00	125	1,100	—
1876	11,461,150	8.75	9.25	11.00	14.00	24.00	60.00	110	1,100	1,200
1876CC	8,270,000	8.75	9.25	11.00	18.00	30.00	60.00	175	—	—
1876CC doubled obverse	Inc. above	12.00	20.00	25.00	75.00	110	300	500	—	—
1876S	10,420,000	10.00	13.00	15.00	20.00	35.00	85.00	165	1,100	—
1877	7,310,510	8.75	9.25	9.75	14.00	23.00	60.00	110	1,100	1,200
1877CC	7,700,000	8.75	9.25	10.75	18.00	35.00	75.00	175	—	—
1877S	2,340,000	14.00	18.00	20.00	30.00	50.00	105	225	—	—
1878	1,678,800	9.00	9.50	10.00	18.00	30.00	60.00	110	1,100	1,200
1878CC	200,000	60.00	75.00	110	165	275	450	775	3,900	—
1879	15,100	165	200	250	285	350	475	675	1,750	1,500
1880	37,335	130	165	190	220	250	325	450	1,750	1,500
1881	24,975	145	175	215	260	325	425	650	2,500	1,600
1882	3,911,100	8.75	9.25	11.00	15.00	27.00	60.00	110	1,100	1,200
1883	7,675,712	8.75	9.25	11.00	14.00	24.00	60.00	110	1,100	1,200
1884	3,366,380	8.75	9.25	11.00	15.00	27.00	60.00	110	1,100	1,200
1884S	564,969	30.00	35.00	45.00	65.00	125	200	500	—	—
1885	2,533,427	8.75	9.25	10.75	15.00	27.00	60.00	110	—	1,200
1885S	43,690	350	475	725	1,450	2,200	2,950	3,750	—	—
1886	6,377,570	8.75	9.25	10.00	14.00	22.00	60.00	110	1,100	1,200
1886S	206,524	50.00	70.00	80.00	110	155	280	600	—	—
1887	11,283,939	8.75	9.25	10.00	14.00	22.00	60.00	110	1,100	1,200
1887S	4,454,450	9.00	12.00	16.00	22.00	38.00	80.00	110	1,100	—
1888	5,496,487	8.75	9.25	10.00	14.00	22.00	60.00	110	1,100	1,200
1888S	1,720,000	10.00	13.00	17.00	25.00	40.00	95.00	200	—	—
1889	7,380,711	8.75	9.25	10.00	14.00	22.00	60.00	110	1,100	1,200
1889S	972,678	14.00	18.00	25.00	45.00	70.00	150	475	4,500	—

Date	Mintage	G-4	VG-8	F-12	VF-20	XF-40	AU-50	MS-60	MS-65	Prf-65
1890	9,911,541	8.75	9.25	10.00	14.00	22.00	60.00	110	1,100	1,200
1890S	1,423,076	11.00	14.00	20.00	50.00	85.00	155	400	4,900	—
1891	15,310,600	8.75	9.25	10.00	14.00	22.00	60.00	110	1,100	1,200
1891O	4,540,000	9.00	9.75	11.00	14.00	24.00	70.00	175	1,750	—
1891O /horizontal O	Inc. above	65.00	95.00	125	175	225	400	—	—	—
1891S	3,196,116	10.00	11.00	13.00	15.00	24.00	75.00	225	1,650	—
1891S/S	Inc. above	25.00	30.00	40.00	85.00	135	250	—	—	—

Barber.

KM# 113 Designer: Charles E. Barber **Weight:** 2.5000 g. **Composition:** 0.9000 Silver 0.0724 oz. ASW **Size:** 17.9 mm. **Note:** Commonly called "Barber dime."

Date	Mintage	G-4	VG-8	F-12	VF-20	XF-40	AU-50	MS-60	MS-65	Prf-65
1892	12,121,245	3.90	5.75	16.00	21.50	24.00	68.00	95.00	700	1,450
1892O	3,841,700	7.50	11.50	25.00	42.50	50.00	72.00	145	1,200	—
1892S	990,710	55.00	95.00	175	195	245	260	395	3,600	—
1893	3,340,792	6.00	11.00	16.00	24.00	35.00	65.00	150	950	1,450
1893O	1,760,000	25.00	38.50	110	120	150	155	295	3,200	—
1893S	2,491,401	9.50	18.00	25.00	35.00	55.00	115	275	4,200	—
1894	1,330,972	15.50	29.00	100.00	120	145	160	250	1,200	1,450
1894O	720,000	50.00	85.00	185	235	325	630	1,200	10,500	—
1894S	24	—	—	—	—	—	—	—	—	—

Note: 1894S, Eliasberg Sale, May 1996, Prf-64, $451,000.

Date	Mintage	G-4	VG-8	F-12	VF-20	XF-40	AU-50	MS-60	MS-65	Prf-65
1895	690,880	66.00	120	300	400	480	525	675	2,700	2,000
1895O	440,000	275	400	660	950	1,900	2,900	4,000	16,000	—
1895S	1,120,000	36.00	42.50	120	160	190	230	465	7,500	—
1896	2,000,762	9.00	20.00	50.00	65.00	80.00	105	145	1,450	1,450
1896O	610,000	60.00	125	250	330	400	660	1,000	7,200	—
1896S	575,056	70.00	140	300	340	375	600	740	3,500	—
1897	10,869,264	2.25	3.30	6.30	12.00	24.00	65.00	120	650	1,450
1897O	666,000	60.00	100.00	250	310	385	540	925	4,500	—
1897S	1,342,844	20.00	30.00	90.00	95.00	120	200	400	4,000	—
1898	16,320,735	2.00	2.70	6.30	10.00	21.00	65.00	95.00	690	1,450
1898O	2,130,000	8.00	18.00	80.00	100.00	145	200	435	4,000	—
1898S	1,702,507	5.00	11.00	24.50	35.00	57.50	115	335	3,700	—
1899	19,580,846	2.10	2.70	6.30	9.50	20.00	65.00	95.00	670	1,450
1899O	2,650,000	5.75	14.50	65.00	90.00	125	210	360	4,700	—
1899S	1,867,493	6.00	12.00	19.00	24.00	38.50	85.00	300	490	—
1900	17,600,912	2.20	3.90	6.30	10.00	21.00	65.00	95.00	800	1,450

1901-S Dime
Grade F-12

□ Retail Price

Date	Mintage	G-4	VG-8	F-12	VF-20	XF-40	AU-50	MS-60	MS-65	Prf-65
1900O	2,010,000	14.00	34.00	95.00	125	200	340	570	5,800	—
1900S	5,168,270	3.90	4.50	10.00	12.50	23.00	72.00	150	1,750	—
1901	18,860,478	2.10	2.70	5.70	8.00	20.00	60.00	95.00	825	1,450
1901O	5,620,000	2.10	3.90	11.50	20.00	42.00	120	430	3,000	—
1901S	593,022	70.00	115	335	385	415	640	975	5,000	—
1902	21,380,777	2.50	3.00	4.50	6.75	20.00	60.00	95.00	575	1,450
1902O	4,500,000	2.70	4.50	12.00	23.00	42.00	110	370	4,500	—
1902S	2,070,000	5.00	14.00	49.00	65.00	95.00	145	370	3,300	—
1903	19,500,755	2.40	2.70	3.30	7.20	20.00	60.00	95.00	1,150	1,450
1903O	8,180,000	2.40	3.90	10.00	14.50	25.50	85.00	240	4,950	—
1903S	613,300	65.00	115	330	450	800	820	1,100	3,200	—
1904	14,601,027	2.75	3.00	6.00	8.00	20.00	60.00	105	2,250	1,450
1904S	800,000	34.00	58.50	140	190	265	450	720	4,300	—
1905	14,552,350	2.45	2.75	4.50	6.25	18.50	60.00	95.00	575	1,450
1905O	3,400,000	2.65	7.00	29.00	43.00	60.00	115	275	1,800	—
1905S	6,855,199	2.40	2.75	5.75	12.50	31.00	72.00	210	800	—
1906	19,958,406	1.75	2.10	3.25	5.50	20.00	60.00	95.00	575	1,450
1906D	4,060,000	2.40	2.75	5.75	12.50	28.50	72.00	165	1,550	—
1906O	2,610,000	4.25	11.00	43.00	62.50	85.00	130	200	1,250	—
1906S	3,136,640	2.10	4.25	10.00	16.00	38.00	90.00	230	1,250	—
1907	22,220,575	1.75	2.10	2.70	5.50	20.00	60.00	95.00	575	1,450
1907D	4,080,000	2.10	4.00	7.50	14.00	33.50	95.00	270	4,200	—
1907O	5,058,000	2.40	5.50	29.00	44.00	54.00	72.00	200	1,300	—
1907S	3,178,470	2.40	4.00	11.00	17.50	42.00	95.00	380	2,200	—
1908	10,600,545	2.10	2.40	3.30	5.50	20.00	60.00	95.00	575	1,450
1908D	7,490,000	2.10	2.40	4.50	9.00	27.50	60.00	125	950	—
1908O	1,789,000	4.50	11.00	42.00	53.00	72.00	135	290	1,850	—
1908S	3,220,000	2.10	3.70	9.00	15.00	35.00	150	300	2,000	—
1909	10,240,650	2.10	2.40	3.30	5.50	20.00	60.00	100.00	575	1,700
1909D	954,000	5.75	14.50	57.50	85.00	115	200	480	3,000	—
1909O	2,287,000	2.75	5.50	9.50	16.00	27.50	185	180	1,450	—
1909S	1,000,000	6.25	16.00	80.00	120	160	300	515	3,000	—
1910	11,520,551	1.70	2.10	3.30	8.50	20.00	60.00	95.00	575	1,450
1910D	3,490,000	2.00	3.90	7.50	15.00	36.00	90.00	210	1,500	—
1910S	1,240,000	5.00	8.00	47.00	68.50	90.00	155	420	2,200	—
1911	18,870,543	1.70	1.85	2.70	5.00	20.00	60.00	95.00	550	1,700
1911D	11,209,000	1.70	1.85	3.00	5.00	20.00	60.00	95.00	720	—
1911S	3,520,000	2.15	2.75	7.00	14.00	33.00	85.00	200	850	—
1912	19,350,700	1.70	1.85	2.75	5.00	20.00	60.00	95.00	550	1,700
1912D	11,760,000	1.70	1.85	3.20	5.50	20.00	60.00	95.00	550	—
1912S	3,420,000	1.70	2.10	5.00	10.00	28.00	87.50	160	850	—
1913	19,760,622	1.70	2.10	2.75	5.00	20.00	60.00	95.00	550	1,450
1913S	510,000	12.50	22.00	75.00	115	195	265	480	1,400	—
1914	17,360,655	1.70	1.85	2.75	5.50	20.00	60.00	95.00	550	1,700
1914D	11,908,000	1.70	1.85	3.50	5.50	20.00	60.00	95.00	550	—
1914S	2,100,000	2.10	2.70	7.20	14.50	35.00	72.00	145	1,000	—
1915	5,620,450	2.10	2.50	2.75	5.50	20.00	60.00	95.00	550	2,000
1915S	960,000	4.50	8.00	30.00	40.00	54.00	125	240	1,600	—
1916	18,490,000	1.70	2.25	3.00	7.00	20.00	60.00	95.00	540	—
1916S	5,820,000	1.70	2.25	4.00	6.50	20.00	60.00	95.00	850	—

Mercury.

Mint mark

1942/41

KM# 140 Designer: Adolph A. Weinman **Weight:** 2.5000 g. **Composition:** 0.9000 Silver 0.0724 oz. ASW **Size:** 17.9 mm. **Note:** All specimens listed as -65FSB are for fully struck MS-65 coins with fully split and rounded horizontal bands on the fasces.

Date	Mintage	G-4	VG-8	F-12	VF-20	XF-40	MS-60	MS-65	Prf-65	-65FSB
1916	22,180,080	3.50	4.50	6.00	6.25	9.00	30.00	90.00	—	120
1916D	264,000	670	990	1,525	2,200	3,350	5,500	19,000	—	38,500
1916S	10,450,000	3.90	4.20	7.75	8.50	18.00	35.00	155	—	600
1917	55,230,000	1.85	2.00	2.50	5.00	7.50	30.00	155	—	400
1917D	9,402,000	3.90	5.00	10.00	21.50	42.00	120	1,100	—	6,000
1917S	27,330,000	1.80	2.00	3.50	5.75	10.00	62.00	470	—	1,150
1918	26,680,000	2.50	2.75	5.50	10.00	25.00	70.00	420	—	1,150
1918D	22,674,800	2.65	3.00	4.50	10.00	21.50	105	600	—	33,500
1918S	19,300,000	2.40	2.75	3.50	8.50	16.00	90.00	660	—	6,600
1919	35,740,000	1.85	2.00	3.00	5.00	10.00	37.00	320	—	700
1919D	9,939,000	3.50	6.00	11.00	21.50	35.00	175	1,400	—	38,500
1919S	8,850,000	2.75	3.00	8.00	15.00	31.00	175	1,000	—	13,000
1920	59,030,000	1.35	1.45	2.00	3.50	6.50	27.50	235	—	515
1920D	19,171,000	2.40	2.75	4.00	7.00	18.00	105	750	—	4,000
1920S	13,820,000	2.40	2.75	4.00	7.50	15.00	110	1,300	—	8,000
1921	1,230,000	33.00	57.00	90.00	220	485	1,000	3,200	—	4,000
1921D	1,080,000	46.00	90.00	140	280	550	1,100	2,850	—	5,200
1923	50,130,000	1.20	1.60	2.00	3.50	6.00	27.50	110	—	295
1923S	6,440,000	2.40	2.75	7.00	12.50	65.00	160	1,150	—	6,900
1924	24,010,000	1.35	1.60	2.50	4.25	12.00	42.00	175	—	520

1916-D Dime
Grade F-12

Date	Mintage	G-4	VG-8	F-12	VF-20	XF-40	MS-60	MS-65	Prf-65	-65FSB
1924D	6,810,000	2.75	4.00	6.00	14.00	44.00	160	950	—	1,400
1924S	7,120,000	2.75	3.50	4.00	8.75	44.00	170	1,100	—	14,000
1925	25,610,000	1.15	1.45	2.00	3.75	7.50	27.00	195	—	1,000
1925D	5,117,000	4.00	4.25	11.50	38.00	110	350	1,750	—	3,500
1925S	5,850,000	2.40	2.75	7.00	12.50	65.00	175	1,400	—	4,400
1926	32,160,000	1.10	1.45	1.70	2.75	4.25	25.00	240	—	525
1926D	6,828,000	2.75	4.00	4.50	8.50	24.00	125	550	—	2,650
1926S	1,520,000	7.00	10.00	22.00	49.00	215	870	3,000	—	6,500
1927	28,080,000	1.10	1.45	1.75	3.50	4.50	26.00	125	—	400
1927D	4,812,000	2.75	5.00	7.25	18.50	65.00	175	1,200	—	8,500
1927S	4,770,000	2.10	3.50	4.75	8.00	23.00	280	1,400	—	7,700
1928	19,480,000	1.10	1.45	1.75	3.50	4.00	27.50	110	—	300
1928D	4,161,000	3.00	3.25	8.00	18.50	44.00	170	875	—	2,500
1928S	7,400,000	1.80	2.10	2.75	5.50	16.00	125	425	—	1,900
1929	25,970,000	1.35	1.60	1.95	2.75	4.00	20.00	60.00	—	265
1929D	5,034,000	1.80	3.00	3.50	6.25	14.50	25.00	70.00	—	225
1929S	4,730,000	1.35	1.60	2.00	4.00	7.00	32.50	120	—	525
1930	6,770,000	1.35	1.50	2.00	3.50	7.00	26.00	115	—	525
1930S	1,843,000	2.50	3.50	4.50	5.50	14.00	70.00	195	—	565
1931	3,150,000	2.10	2.50	2.75	4.25	8.75	35.00	135	—	725
1931D	1,260,000	6.00	7.00	12.00	15.00	28.00	85.00	210	—	350
1931S	1,800,000	2.40	2.75	4.00	6.25	11.50	85.00	210	—	2,100
1934	24,080,000	1.00	1.45	1.75	3.00	5.00	21.50	40.00	—	150
1934D	6,772,000	1.60	2.10	2.75	4.00	8.00	50.00	72.00	—	360
1935	58,830,000	0.80	1.00	1.50	2.15	4.25	8.00	30.00	—	70.00
1935D	10,477,000	1.25	1.75	2.50	3.75	7.50	34.00	72.00	—	600
1935S	15,840,000	1.00	1.50	1.75	3.00	5.50	24.00	31.50	—	500
1936	87,504,130	0.80	1.00	1.50	2.25	3.50	8.00	25.00	2,000	90.00
1936D	16,132,000	1.00	1.25	1.50	3.00	6.50	26.00	42.00	—	295
1936S	9,210,000	1.00	1.25	1.50	2.50	3.00	20.00	31.50	—	85.00
1937	56,865,756	0.80	1.00	1.50	2.00	3.25	8.00	23.00	800	42.00
1937D	14,146,000	1.00	1.25	1.50	3.00	5.50	21.00	43.00	—	100.00
1937S	9,740,000	1.00	1.25	1.50	3.00	5.50	24.00	34.00	—	195
1938	22,198,728	0.80	1.00	1.50	2.25	3.50	13.00	27.50	450	80.00
1938D	5,537,000	1.50	1.75	2.00	3.50	6.00	16.00	26.00	—	65.00
1938S	8,090,000	1.35	1.55	1.75	2.35	3.75	20.00	35.00	—	135
1939	67,749,321	0.80	1.00	1.50	2.00	3.25	8.50	25.00	425	170
1939D	24,394,000	1.00	1.25	1.50	2.00	3.50	7.50	26.00	—	45.00
1939S	10,540,000	1.25	1.50	2.00	2.50	4.25	21.00	35.00	—	750
1940	65,361,827	0.60	0.70	0.90	1.10	2.50	6.00	26.00	385	57.50
1940D	21,198,000	0.60	0.70	0.90	1.10	1.50	8.00	30.00	—	55.00
1940S	21,560,000	0.60	0.70	0.90	1.10	1.50	8.50	30.00	—	95.00
1941	175,106,557	0.60	0.70	0.90	1.10	1.50	5.00	30.00	385	42.00
1941D	45,634,000	0.60	0.70	0.90	1.10	1.50	8.00	23.00	—	40.00
1941S	43,090,000	0.60	0.70	0.90	1.10	1.50	7.00	30.00	—	50.00
1942	205,432,329	0.60	0.70	0.90	1.10	1.50	8.00	24.00	385	52.50
1942/41	Inc. above	465	485	530	600	725	1,850	12,500	—	37,000
1942D	60,740,000	0.60	0.70	0.90	1.10	1.50	8.00	27.50	—	40.00

Date	Mintage	G-4	VG-8	F-12	VF-20	XF-40	MS-60	MS-65	Prf-65	-65FSB
1942/41D	Inc. above	325	365	450	500	610	1,900	5,400	—	19,000
1942S	49,300,000	0.60	0.70	0.90	1.10	1.50	9.50	24.00	—	140
1943	191,710,000	0.60	0.70	0.90	1.10	1.50	5.50	30.00	—	50.00
1943D	71,949,000	0.60	0.70	0.90	1.10	1.50	7.50	27.50	—	40.00
1943S	60,400,000	0.60	0.70	0.90	1.10	1.50	8.25	25.00	—	66.00
1944	231,410,000	0.60	0.70	0.90	1.10	1.50	5.50	23.00	—	80.00
1944D	62,224,000	0.60	0.70	0.90	1.10	1.50	6.50	23.00	—	40.00
1944S	49,490,000	0.60	0.70	0.90	1.10	1.50	6.50	30.00	—	50.00
1945	159,130,000	0.60	0.70	0.90	1.10	1.50	5.50	23.00	—	8,000
1945D	40,245,000	0.60	0.70	0.90	1.10	1.50	6.00	24.00	—	40.00
1945S	41,920,000	0.60	0.70	0.90	1.10	1.50	6.50	24.00	—	135
1945S micro	Inc. above	1.00	1.25	1.50	3.00	4.25	26.00	85.00	—	650

Roosevelt.

Mint mark 1946-64

KM# 195 Designer: John R. Sinnock **Weight:** 2.5000 g. **Composition:** 0.9000 Silver 0.0724 oz. ASW
Size: 17.9 mm.

Date	Mintage	G-4	VG-8	F-12	VF-20	XF-40	AU-50	MS-60	MS-65	Prf-65
1946	225,250,000	—	—	—	0.50	0.65	0.95	2.30	4.50	—
1946D	61,043,500	—	—	—	0.50	0.65	1.10	2.00	8.00	—
1946S	27,900,000	—	—	—	0.50	0.65	0.90	2.70	11.00	—
1947	121,520,000	—	—	—	0.50	0.65	0.95	3.25	4.75	—
1947D	46,835,000	—	—	—	0.50	0.95	1.50	4.50	11.00	—
1947S	34,840,000	—	—	—	0.50	0.95	1.25	3.40	13.00	—
1948	74,950,000	—	—	—	0.50	0.95	1.50	3.00	14.00	—
1948D	52,841,000	—	—	—	0.50	1.20	2.00	3.00	10.00	—
1948S	35,520,000	—	—	—	0.50	0.95	1.10	3.00	11.00	—
1949	30,940,000	—	—	—	1.00	1.50	4.00	21.50	40.00	—
1949D	26,034,000	—	—	0.60	0.80	1.25	2.00	9.30	20.00	—
1949S	13,510,000	—	1.00	1.25	1.50	2.75	6.00	33.50	60.00	—
1950	50,181,500	—	—	—	0.50	0.95	1.35	6.40	12.00	37.00
1950D	46,803,000	—	—	—	0.50	0.65	1.60	3.65	8.00	—
1950S	20,440,000	—	0.85	1.00	1.10	1.25	6.00	34.50	50.00	—
1951	102,937,602	—	—	—	0.50	0.85	1.00	1.25	3.50	26.00
1951D	56,529,000	—	—	—	0.50	0.65	0.95	1.50	5.00	—
1951S	31,630,000	—	—	—	0.75	1.05	3.25	8.75	24.00	—
1952	99,122,073	—	—	—	0.50	0.90	1.10	1.35	5.00	29.00
1952D	122,100,000	—	—	—	0.50	0.65	0.95	1.35	5.00	—
1952S	44,419,500	—	—	—	0.75	1.05	1.50	4.25	11.00	—
1953	53,618,920	—	—	—	0.50	0.65	1.00	2.15	5.00	24.00
1953D	136,433,000	—	—	—	0.50	0.65	0.95	2.15	5.00	—
1953S	39,180,000	—	—	—	0.50	0.65	0.75	1.00	4.00	—
1954	114,243,503	—	—	—	0.50	0.65	0.75	1.00	4.00	11.00
1954D	106,397,000	—	—	—	0.50	0.65	0.75	1.00	3.25	—
1954S	22,860,000	—	—	—	0.50	0.65	0.80	0.90	3.15	—
1955	12,828,381	—	—	—	0.70	0.00	0.85	1.00	5.00	15.00
1955D	13,959,000	—	—	—	0.50	0.55	0.60	0.65	3.50	—
1955S	18,510,000	—	—	—	0.50	0.60	0.65	0.65	4.50	—
1956	109,309,384	—	—	—	0.50	0.50	0.60	0.70	2.50	2.50
1956D	108,015,100	—	—	—	0.50	0.50	0.60	0.65	2.75	—
1957	161,407,952	—	—	—	0.50	0.50	0.60	0.65	2.50	2.00
1957D	113,354,330	—	—	—	0.50	0.50	0.60	0.65	3.50	—
1958	32,785,652	—	—	—	0.50	0.50	0.60	0.65	3.80	2.00
1958D	136,564,600	—	—	—	0.50	0.50	0.60	0.65	3.50	—
1959	86,929,291	—	—	—	0.50	0.50	0.60	0.65	2.50	2.00
1959D	164,919,790	—	—	—	0.50	0.50	0.60	0.65	3.00	—
1960	72,081,602	—	—	—	0.50	0.50	0.60	0.65	2.50	2.00
1960D	200,160,400	—	—	—	0.50	0.50	0.60	0.65	2.50	—
1961	96,758,244	—	—	—	0.50	0.50	0.60	0.65	2.50	2.00
1961D	209,146,550	—	—	—	0.50	0.50	0.60	0.65	2.50	—
1962	75,668,019	—	—	—	0.50	0.50	0.60	0.65	2.50	2.00
1962D	334,948,380	—	—	—	0.50	0.50	0.60	0.65	2.50	—
1963	126,725,645	—	—	—	0.50	0.50	0.60	0.70	2.35	2.00
1963D	421,476,530	—	—	—	0.50	0.50	0.60	0.70	2.35	—
1964	933,310,762	—	—	—	0.50	0.50	0.60	0.65	2.50	2.00
1964D	1,357,517,180	—	—	—	0.50	0.50	0.60	0.65	2.50	—

Roosevelt.

Mint mark 1968 - Present   **1982 No mint mark**

KM# 195a Designer: John R. Sinnock **Weight:** 2.2700 g. **Composition:** Copper-Nickel Clad Copper **Size:** 17.9 mm. **Note:** The 1979-S and 1981-S Type II proofs have clearer mint marks than the Type I proofs of those years. On the 1982 no-mint-mark variety, the mint mark was inadvertently left off.

Date	Mintage	MS-65	Prf-65	Date	Mintage	MS-65	Prf-65
1965	1,652,140,570	1.00	—	1985D	587,979,970	0.80	—
1966	1,382,734,540	0.80	—	1985S	3,362,821	—	1.10
1967	2,244,007,320	0.80	—	1986P	682,649,693	1.70	—
1968	424,470,000	0.70	—	1986D	473,326,970	1.60	—
1968D	480,748,280	0.80	—	1986S	3,010,497	—	2.50
1968S	3,041,506	—	0.75	1987P	762,709,481	0.75	—
1969	145,790,000	2.00	—	1987D	653,203,402	0.75	—
1969D	563,323,870	1.00	—	1987S	4,227,728	—	1.50
1969S	2,934,631	—	0.65	1988P	1,030,550,000	0.80	—
1970	345,570,000	0.70	—	1988D	962,385,488	0.80	—
1970D	754,942,100	0.70	—	1988S	3,262,948	—	3.50
1970S	2,632,810	—	0.65	1989P	1,298,400,000	0.50	—
1971	162,690,000	1.00	—	1989D	896,535,597	0.50	—
1971D	377,914,240	0.80	—	1989S	3,220,194	—	4.00
1971S	3,220,733	—	0.60	1990P	1,034,340,000	1.00	—
1972	431,540,000	0.70	—	1990D	839,995,824	0.80	—
1972D	330,290,000	0.60	—	1990S	3,299,559	—	2.75
1972S	3,260,996	—	1.00	1991P	927,220,000	0.80	—
1973	315,670,000	0.70	—	1991D	601,241,114	1.00	—
1973D	455,032,426	0.75	—	1991S	2,867,787	—	3.25
1973S	2,760,339	—	1.00	1992P	593,500,000	0.75	—
1974	470,248,000	0.70	—	1992D	616,273,932	0.80	—
1974D	571,083,000	0.70	—	1992S	2,858,981	—	4.00
1974S	2,612,568	—	1.00	1993P	766,180,000	0.80	—
1975	585,673,900	0.70	—	1993D	750,110,166	0.80	—
1975D	313,705,300	0.75	—	1993S	2,633,439	—	6.00
1975S	2,845,450	—	1.25	1994P	1,189,000,000	0.80	—
1976	568,760,000	0.80	—	1994D	1,303,268,110	0.80	—
1976D	695,222,774	0.80	—	1994S	2,484,594	—	4.50
1976S	4,149,730	—	1.00	1995P	1,125,500,000	0.80	—
1977	796,930,000	0.70	—	1995D	1,274,890,000	1.20	—
1977D	376,607,228	0.70	—	1995S	2,010,384	—	20.00
1977S	3,251,152	—	1.00	1996P	1,421,163,000	0.75	—
1978	663,980,000	0.70	—	1996D	1,400,300,000	0.75	—
1978D	282,847,540	0.70	—	1996W	1,457,949	15.00	—
1978S	3,127,781	—	1.00	1996S	2,085,191	—	2.50
1979	315,440,000	0.70	—	1997P	991,640,000	0.75	—
1979D	390,921,184	0.70	—	1997D	979,810,000	0.75	—
1979S type I	3,677,175	—	1.00	1997S	1,975,000	—	6.50
1979S type II	Inc. above	—	1.25	1998P	1,163,000,000	0.80	—
1980P	735,170,000	0.70	—	1998D	1,172,250,000	0.80	—
1980D	719,354,321	0.70	—	1998S	2,078,494	—	3.50
1980S	3,554,806	—	1.00	1999P	2,164,000,000	0.80	—
1981P	676,650,000	0.70	—	1999D	1,397,750,000	0.80	—
1981D	712,284,143	0.70	—	1999S	2,557,897	—	3.00
1981S type I	—	—	1.00	2000P	1,842,500,000	0.80	—
1981S type II	—	—	4.00	2000D	1,818,700,000	0.75	—
1982P	519,475,000	5.00	—	2000S	3,097,440	—	2.00
1982D	542,713,584	3.00	—	2001P	1,369,590,000	0.80	—
1982S	3,857,479	—	1.20	2001D	1,412,800,000	0.75	—
1983P	647,025,000	6.00	—	2001S	2,249,496	—	3.00
1983D	730,129,224	2.00	—	2002P	1,187,500,000	0.50	—
1983S	3,279,126	—	1.10	2002D	1,379,500,000	0.50	—
1984P	856,669,000	0.80	—	2002S	—	—	2.00
1984D	704,803,976	0.90	—	2003P	—	0.50	—
1984S	3,065,110	—	1.60	2003D	—	0.50	—
1985P	705,200,962	0.80	—	2003S	—	—	2.00

Roosevelt.

KM# A195 Composition: Silver

Date	Mintage	Prf-65	Date	Mintage	Prf-65
1992S	1,317,579	5.00	1998S	878,792	8.00
1993S	761,353	9.00	1999S	804,565	6.00
1994S	785,329	8.00	2000S	965,921	4.00
1995S	838,953	25.00	2001S	849,600	5.00
1996S	830,021	8.00	2002S	—	5.00
1997S	821,678	26.00	2003S	—	—

20 CENTS

KM# 109 Designer: William Barber **Weight:** 5.0000 g. **Composition:** 0.9000 Silver 0.1447 oz. ASW
Size: 22 mm.

Date	Mintage	G-4	VG-8	F-12	VF-20	XF-40	AU-50	MS-60	MS-65	Prf-65
1875	39,700	70.00	80.00	90.00	130	225	320	575	5,500	9,500
1875S	1,155,000	62.50	65.00	70.00	100.00	150	280	465	4,900	—
1875CC	133,290	75.00	95.00	110	150	270	485	700	9,500	—
1876	15,900	95.00	110	175	220	300	450	650	5,200	9,500
1876CC	10,000	—	—	—	—	—	—	—	—	—

Note: 1876CC, Eliasberg Sale, April 1997, MS-65, $148,500. Heritage 1999 ANA, MS-63, $86,500.

| 1877 proof | 510 | — | — | 1,650 | 1,800 | 2,100 | 2,300 | — | — | 10,000 |
| 1878 proof | 600 | — | — | 1,450 | 1,600 | 1,450 | 1,650 | — | — | 9,500 |

1876 20-Cent
Grade F-12

Retail Price

QUARTER

Draped Bust. Small eagle.

KM# 25 Designer: Robert Scot **Reverse:** Small eagle **Weight:** 6.7400 g. **Composition:** 0.8920 Silver 0.1935 oz. ASW **Size:** 27.5 mm.

Date	Mintage	G-4	VG-8	F-12	VF-20	XF-40	AU-50	MS-60	MS-65
1796	6,146	4,600	6,000	10,000	12,500	18,500	23,000	32,500	125,000

Draped Bust. Heraldic eagle.

KM# 36 Designer: Robert Scot **Reverse:** Heraldic eagle **Weight:** 6.7400 g. **Composition:** 0.8920 Silver .1935 oz. ASW **Size:** 27.5 mm.

Date	Mintage	G-4	VG-8	F-12	VF-20	XF-40	AU-50	MS-60	MS-65
1804	6,738	2,000	2,400	3,200	3,650	8,500	16,500	40,000	—
1805	121,394	175	225	385	750	1,600	2,750	4,750	62,000
1806	206,124	180	250	375	725	1,450	2,400	4,650	46,500
1806/5	Inc. above	195	300	485	850	2,250	3,450	5,500	60,000
1807	220,643	175	225	365	675	1,500	2,600	4,650	48,500

1804 Quarter
Grade XF-40

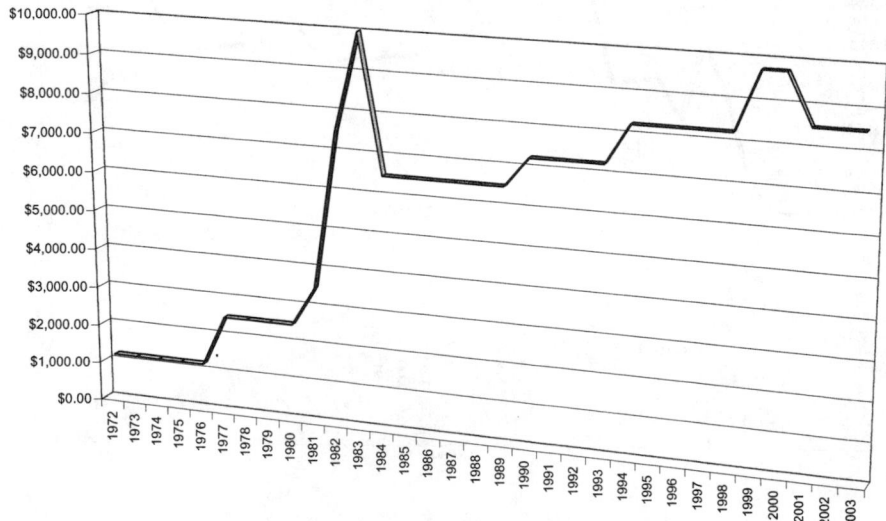

☐ Retail Price

Liberty Cap. "E Pluribus Unum" above eagle.

KM# 44 **Designer:** John Reich **Reverse:** "E Pluribus Unum" above eagle **Weight:** 6.7400 g. **Composition:** 0.8920 Silver 0.1935 oz. ASW **Size:** 27 mm. **Note:** Varieties of the 1819 strikes are distinguished by the size of the 9 in the date. Varieties of the 1820 strikes are distinguished by the size of the 0 in the date. One 1822 variety and one 1828 variety have "25" engraved over "50" in the denomination. The 1827 restrikes were produced privately using dies sold as scrap by the U.S. Mint.

Date	Mintage	G-4	VG-8	F-12	VF-20	XF-40	AU-50	MS-60	MS-65
1815	89,235	55.00	70.00	120	315	725	1,200	2,200	25,000
1818	361,174	50.00	65.00	110	285	675	1,200	2,000	16,000
1818/15	Inc. above	55.00	70.00	110	350	750	1,350	2,250	20,000
1819 small 9	144,000	55.00	65.00	110	265	650	1,200	2,000	22,000
1819 large 9	Inc. above	55.00	65.00	110	265	650	1,200	2,000	22,000
1820 small O	127,444	60.00	75.00	110	265	700	1,250	3,000	28,000
1820 large O	Inc. above	50.00	65.00	100.00	235	600	1,100	1,900	25,000
1821	216,851	50.00	60.00	100.00	275	675	1,250	1,850	16,500
1822	64,080	65.00	90.00	140	375	775	1,500	2,850	—
1822 25/50C.	Inc. above	1,250	2,750	4,250	5,750	8,900	17,500	—	—
1823/22	17,800	7,500	10,000	17,500	27,500	36,000	50,000	—	—

Note: 1823/22, Superior, Aug. 1990, Proof, $62,500.

Date	Mintage	G-4	VG-8	F-12	VF-20	XF-40	AU-50	MS-60	MS-65
1824/2 mintage unrecorded	—	80.00	130	200	550	1,550	2,150	5,500	—
1825/22	168,000	70.00	100.00	145	350	850	1,500	2,300	22,500
1825/23	Inc. above	50.00	65.00	100.00	265	650	1,200	1,850	16,500
1825/24	Inc. above	50.00	65.00	100.00	265	650	1,200	1,850	16,500
1827 original	4,000	—	—	—	—	—	—	—	—

Note: Eliasberg, April 1997, VF-20, $39,600.

Date	Mintage	G-4	VG-8	F-12	VF-20	XF-40	AU-50	MS-60	MS-65
1827 restrike	Inc. above	—	—	—	—	—	—	—	—

Note: 1827 restrike, Eliasberg, April 1997, Prf-65, $77,000.

Date	Mintage	G-4	VG-8	F-12	VF-20	XF-40	AU-50	MS-60	MS-65
1828	102,000	50.00	65.00	95.00	275	650	1,400	2,500	19,500
1828 25/50C.	Inc. above	110	265	385	825	1,350	2,750	6,500	—

Liberty Cap. "E Pluribus Unum" removed from above eagle.

KM# 55 **Designer:** William Kneass **Reverse:** "E Pluribus Unum" removed from above eagle **Composition:** 0.8920 Silver **Size:** 24.3 mm. **Note:** Varieties of the 1831 strikes are distinguished by the size of the lettering on the reverse.

Date	Mintage	G-4	VG-8	F-12	VF-20	XF-40	AU-50	MS-60	MS-65
1831 small letter	398,000	47.50	55.00	60.00	92.50	235	600	825	13,500
1831 large letter	Inc. above	47.50	55.00	60.00	92.50	235	600	825	18,500
1832	320,000	47.50	55.00	60.00	92.50	235	600	825	16,000
1833	156,000	50.00	57.50	62.50	100.00	260	650	1,000	13,500
1834	286,000	47.50	55.00	60.00	92.50	230	600	825	13,500
1835	1,952,000	47.50	55.00	60.00	90.00	230	600	825	13,500
1836	472,000	47.50	55.00	60.00	90.00	230	600	825	14,500
1837	252,400	60.00	65.00	75.00	110	260	625	850	13,500
1838	832,000	55.00	60.00	70.00	85.00	230	625	850	14,750

Seated Liberty. No drapery.

KM# 64.1 **Designer:** Christian Gobrecht **Obverse:** No drapery **Weight:** 6.6800 g. **Composition:** 0.9000 Silver 0.1934 oz. ASW **Size:** 24.3 mm.

Date	Mintage	G-4	VG-8	F-12	VF-20	XF-40	AU-50	MS-60	MS-65
1838	Inc. above	18.00	25.00	35.00	65.00	300	550	1,250	23,000
1839	491,146	20.00	28.00	35.00	65.00	275	550	1,250	25,000
1840O	425,200	14.00	25.00	45.00	110	375	575	1,350	30,000

Seated Liberty. Drapery added to Liberty's left elbow.

KM# 64.2 Designer: Christian Gobrecht **Obverse:** Drapery added to Liberty's left elbow **Weight:** 6.6800 g. **Composition:** 0.9000 Silver 0.1934 oz. ASW **Size:** 24.3 mm. **Note:** Two varieties for 1842 and 1842-O are distinguished by the size of the numerals in the date. 1852 obverse dies were used to strike the 1853 no-arrows variety, with the 2 being recut to form a 3.

Date	Mintage	G-4	VG-8	F-12	VF-20	XF-40	AU-50	MS-60	MS-65
1840	188,127	30.00	55.00	80.00	115	215	350	950	12,000
1840O	Inc. above	29.00	39.00	70.00	115	250	450	1,000	—
1841	120,000	75.00	90.00	120	185	300	385	750	11,000
1841O	452,000	16.00	27.00	50.00	85.00	165	350	700	10,000
1842 small date	88,000	—	—	—	—	—	—	—	—
Note: 1842 small date, Eliasberg, April 1997, Prf-63, $66,000.									
1842 large date	Inc. above	75.00	110	140	225	300	500	1,250	—
1842O small date	769,000	425	650	1,100	1,850	4,000	—	—	—
1842O large date	Inc. above	16.00	20.00	30.00	45.00	125	300	—	4,000
1843	645,600	16.00	20.00	27.00	37.00	55.00	150	400	3,500
1843O	968,000	20.00	28.00	42.00	100.00	275	750	2,000	11,000
1844	421,200	17.00	22.00	30.00	40.00	65.00	160	450	5,000
1844O	740,000	16.00	24.00	37.50	60.00	115	275	1,000	6,000
1845	922,000	16.00	20.00	27.00	37.00	50.00	150	450	5,000
1846	510,000	19.00	23.00	36.50	50.00	75.00	160	475	6,000
1847	734,000	16.00	20.00	27.00	37.00	50.00	150	425	5,000
1847O	368,000	22.00	35.00	50.00	110	235	600	1,900	—
1848	146,000	25.00	36.00	70.00	145	175	325	1,000	10,000
1849	340,000	18.00	22.00	36.00	65.00	125	275	750	9,000
1849O mintage unrecorded	—	390	595	975	1,500	2,750	5,000	7,500	—
1850	190,800	28.00	37.50	60.00	90.00	125	250	800	—
1850O	412,000	20.00	30.00	45.00	90.00	135	450	1,300	—
1851	160,000	35.00	50.00	80.00	125	185	300	850	8,500
1851O	88,000	135	265	375	575	1,000	2,250	4,000	—
1852	177,060	40.00	50.00	85.00	145	185	300	500	4,800
1852O	96,000	165	240	335	595	1,200	3,500	8,000	—
1853 recut date	44,200	225	425	600	750	1,100	1,600	2,600	9,000

Seated Liberty. Arrows at date. Rays around eagle.

KM# 78 Designer: Christian Gobrecht **Obverse:** Arrows at date **Reverse:** Rays around eagle **Weight:** 6.2200 g. **Composition:** 0.9000 Silver 0.1800 oz. ASW **Size:** 24.3 mm.

Date	Mintage	G-4	VG-8	F-12	VF-20	XF-40	AU-50	MS-60	MS-65	Prf-65
1853	15,210,020	15.00	20.00	27.50	45.00	150	275	950	19,000	90,000
1853/4	Inc. above	40.00	65.00	100.00	200	275	750	1,750	—	—
1853O	1,332,000	18.00	35.00	50.00	100.00	275	1,100	2,750	—	—

Seated Liberty. Rays around eagle removed.

KM# 81 Designer: Christian Gobrecht **Reverse:** Rays around eagle removed **Weight:** 6.6800 g. **Composition:** 0.9000 Silver .1934 oz. ASW **Size:** 24.3 mm. **Note:** The 1854-O "huge O" variety has an oversized mint mark.

Date	Mintage	G-4	VG-8	F-12	VF-20	XF-40	AU-50	MS-60	MS-65	Prf-65
1854	12,380,000	15.00	20.00	27.50	35.00	75.00	225	440	7,500	17,500
1854O	1,484,000	17.00	24.00	35.00	60.00	125	300	1,750	—	—
1854O huge O	Inc. above	230	260	300	425	750	—	—	—	—
1855	2,857,000	15.00	20.00	27.50	35.00	75.00	225	440	8,500	18,500
1855O	176,000	50.00	75.00	110	240	400	950	2,750	—	—
1855S	396,400	40.00	60.00	80.00	225	500	1,250	2,000	—	—

Seated Liberty. Arrows at date removed.

KM# A64.2 **Designer:** Christian Gobrecht **Obverse:** Arrows at date removed **Weight:** 6.2200 g.
Composition: 0.9000 Silver 0.1800 oz. ASW **Size:** 24.3 mm.

Date	Mintage	G-4	VG-8	F-12	VF-20	XF-40	AU-50	MS-60	MS-65	Prf-65
1856	7,264,000	15.00	20.00	27.50	35.00	60.00	145	290	4,250	15,000
1856O	968,000	17.00	24.00	30.00	50.00	90.00	250	1,000	8,500	—
1856S	286,000	45.00	65.00	110	250	375	900	2,200	—	—
1856S/S	Inc. above	60.00	80.00	175	350	550	1,250	—	—	—
1857	9,644,000	15.00	20.00	27.50	35.00	60.00	145	290	4,000	9,500
1857O	1,180,000	15.00	20.00	29.00	40.00	80.00	275	975	—	—
1857S	82,000	100.00	140	240	375	600	950	2,750	—	—
1858	7,368,000	15.00	20.00	27.50	35.00	60.00	160	300	4,000	6,500
1858O	520,000	18.00	25.00	35.00	55.00	110	360	1,350	—	—
1858S	121,000	50.00	85.00	150	250	500	1,250	—	—	—
1859	1,344,000	17.00	24.00	30.00	40.00	75.00	175	375	6,000	7,000
1859O	260,000	22.00	28.00	40.00	65.00	200	400	1,000	15,000	—
1859S	80,000	90.00	125	195	300	1,100	2,500	—	—	—
1860	805,400	18.00	22.00	28.00	33.00	60.00	160	500	—	5,250
1860O	388,000	18.00	22.00	33.00	50.00	80.00	275	1,200	—	—
1860S	56,000	165	285	425	750	2,250	6,000	—	—	—
1861	4,854,600	16.00	19.00	27.00	32.00	55.00	150	290	4,200	5,500
1861S	96,000	60.00	80.00	190	310	950	2,750	—	—	—
1862	932,550	18.00	22.00	33.00	40.00	65.00	165	300	4,350	5,350
1862S	67,000	80.00	125	165	275	500	1,600	2,750	—	—
1863	192,060	30.00	45.00	60.00	110	195	300	650	4,350	5,500
1864	94,070	65.00	75.00	115	150	250	400	650	5,000	5,500
1864S	20,000	275	450	600	1,100	2,200	3,750	7,000	—	—
1865	59,300	75.00	90.00	115	140	250	375	875	9,500	5,500

1856-S Quarter
Grade F-12

☐ Retail Price

Date	Mintage	G-4	VG-8	F-12	VF-20	XF-40	AU-50	MS-60	MS-65	Prf-65
1865S	41,000	85.00	125	175	325	600	1,250	2,350	11,500	—
1866 unique	—	—	—	—	—	—	—	—	—	—

Seated Liberty. "In God We Trust" above eagle.

KM# 98 Designer: Christian Gobrecht **Reverse:** "In God We Trust" above eagle **Weight:** 6.2200 g. **Composition:** 0.9000 Silver 0.1800 oz. ASW **Size:** 24.3 mm. **Note:** The 1873 closed-3 and open-3 varieties are distinguished by the amount of space between the upper left and lower left serifs in the 3.

Date	Mintage	G-4	VG-8	F-12	VF-20	XF-40	AU-50	MS-60	MS-65	Prf-65
1866	17,525	400	500	650	850	1,200	1,500	2,250	7,500	3,000
1866S	28,000	200	290	525	900	1,250	2,000	3,000	—	—
1867	20,625	195	260	425	500	675	875	1,100	—	2,450
1867S	48,000	165	250	390	525	600	1,250	2,350	—	—
1868	30,000	130	155	200	275	400	525	900	7,000	3,450
1868S	96,000	65.00	80.00	135	245	575	975	2,000	—	—
1869	16,600	235	300	425	550	675	950	1,275	—	2,500
1869S	76,000	75.00	125	180	325	625	1,400	2,400	16,000	—
1870	87,400	45.00	70.00	110	165	250	350	850	6,000	2,750
1870CC	8,340	2,000	3,250	6,000	11,000	16,000	25,000	35,000	—	—
1871	119,160	40.00	60.00	70.00	125	175	350	650	6,000	2,500
1871CC	10,890	1,700	2,750	4,000	8,500	14,500	25,000	40,000	—	—
1871S	30,900	275	400	460	750	1,100	1,850	3,000	10,000	—
1872	182,950	30.00	40.00	80.00	110	155	300	600	6,500	2,500
1872CC	22,850	500	675	1,150	2,400	4,000	7,500	14,000	—	—
1872S	83,000	900	1,250	1,650	2,000	2,750	4,250	6,750	—	—
1873 closed 3	212,600	125	210	325	525	600	1,000	2,000	—	2,600
1873 open 3	Inc. above	30.00	42.50	70.00	110	150	210	450	5,000	—
1873CC 6 known	4,000	—	75,000	—	—	—	—	—	—	—

Note: 1873CC, Heritage, April 1999, MS-62, $106,375.

Seated Liberty. Arrows at date.

KM# 106 Designer: Christian Gobrecht **Obverse:** Arrows at date **Weight:** 6.2500 g. **Composition:** 0.9000 Silver 0.1808 oz. ASW **Size:** 24.3 mm.

Date	Mintage	G-4	VG-8	F-12	VF-20	XF-40	AU-50	MS-60	MS-65	Prf-65
1873	1,271,700	16.00	23.00	30.00	60.00	200	400	775	4,250	8,000
1873CC	12,462	1,700	2,500	4,250	7,750	12,000	18,000	35,000	—	—
1873S	156,000	25.00	40.00	85.00	140	275	550	1,200	8,000	—
1874	471,900	20.00	26.00	40.00	70.00	220	420	850	4,000	6,750
1874S	392,000	23.00	30.00	50.00	110	240	425	900	4,500	—

Seated Liberty. Arrows at date removed.

KM# A98 Designer: Christian Gobrecht **Obverse:** Arrows at date removed **Weight:** 6.2500 g. **Composition:** 0.9000 Silver 0.1808 oz. ASW **Size:** 24.3 mm. **Note:** The 1876-CC fine-reeding variety has a more finely reeded edge.

Date	Mintage	G-4	VG-8	F-12	VF-20	XF-40	AU-50	MS-60	MS-65	Prf-65
1875	4,293,500	14.00	17.00	25.00	30.00	50.00	135	225	1,600	2,300
1875CC	140,000	60.00	90.00	160	250	500	775	1,600	15,000	—
1875S	680,000	25.00	36.00	67.00	110	175	275	575	3,200	—
1876	17,817,150	14.00	17.00	25.00	30.00	50.00	135	225	1,600	2,250
1876CC	4,944,000	17.00	20.00	30.00	40.00	70.00	150	325	3,600	—
1876CC fine reeding	Inc. above	18.00	28.00	33.00	42.00	72.00	150	325	3,600	—

Date	Mintage	G-4	VG-8	F-12	VF-20	XF-40	AU-50	MS-60	MS-65	Prf-65
1876S	8,596,000	16.00	19.00	25.00	30.00	50.00	135	225	2,000	—
1877	10,911,710	14.00	17.00	25.00	30.00	50.00	135	225	1,600	2,250
1877CC	4,192,000	18.00	28.00	33.00	42.00	72.00	150	325	2,000	—
1877S	8,996,000	14.00	17.00	25.00	30.00	50.00	135	225	1,600	—
1877S /horizontal S	Inc. above	32.00	48.00	75.00	125	225	375	650	—	—
1878	2,260,800	16.00	18.00	28.00	34.00	55.00	145	250	2,750	2,300
1878CC	996,000	19.00	29.00	45.00	85.00	110	150	450	3,500	—
1878S	140,000	125	160	260	300	550	750	1,450	—	—
1879	14,700	140	180	220	250	300	375	475	1,700	2,250
1880	14,955	140	180	220	250	300	375	500	1,600	2,250
1881	12,975	150	190	250	260	325	385	525	1,650	2,200
1882	16,300	155	190	225	275	340	425	550	1,850	2,200
1883	15,439	155	195	240	275	330	400	525	2,450	2,200
1884	8,875	250	285	375	400	475	550	650	1,900	2,200
1885	14,530	150	185	215	275	300	385	525	2,600	2,200
1886	5,886	500	600	700	800	900	1,000	1,250	2,600	2,400
1887	10,710	225	275	345	400	475	550	650	2,350	2,200
1888	10,833	185	240	290	380	450	500	600	2,000	2,350
1888S	1,216,000	15.00	20.00	27.50	30.00	60.00	160	245	2,450	—
1889	12,711	155	185	235	285	340	425	550	1,750	2,350
1890	80,590	50.00	75.00	85.00	110	185	275	400	—	2,350
1891	3,920,600	15.00	20.00	27.50	30.00	60.00	160	245	1,750	2,350
1891O	68,000	125	175	300	475	875	1,100	3,000	14,500	—
1891S	2,216,000	16.00	22.00	29.00	65.00	52.50	185	275	2,400	—

Barber.

KM# 114 **Designer:** Charles E. Barber **Weight:** 6.2500 g. **Composition:** 0.9000 Silver 0.1809 oz. ASW **Size:** 24.3 mm. **Note:** Commonly called "Barber quarter."

Date	Mintage	G-4	VG-8	F-12	VF-20	XF-40	AU-50	MS-60	MS-65	Prf-65
1892	8,237,245	5.00	7.50	21.50	32.50	65.00	115	180	1,100	2,000
1892O	2,640,000	5.75	11.00	30.00	38.00	72.00	135	290	1,600	—
1892S	964,079	16.00	32.00	60.00	80.00	115	265	450	4,700	—
1893	5,484,838	5.00	7.00	22.50	31.50	65.00	115	200	1,700	2,000
1893O	3,396,000	5.00	8.50	25.00	40.00	72.00	145	265	1,850	—
1893S	1,454,535	12.00	20.00	65.00	80.00	110	265	465	8,000	—
1894	3,432,972	5.00	7.50	27.50	40.00	77.00	135	240	1,550	2,000

1896-S Quarter
Grade F-12

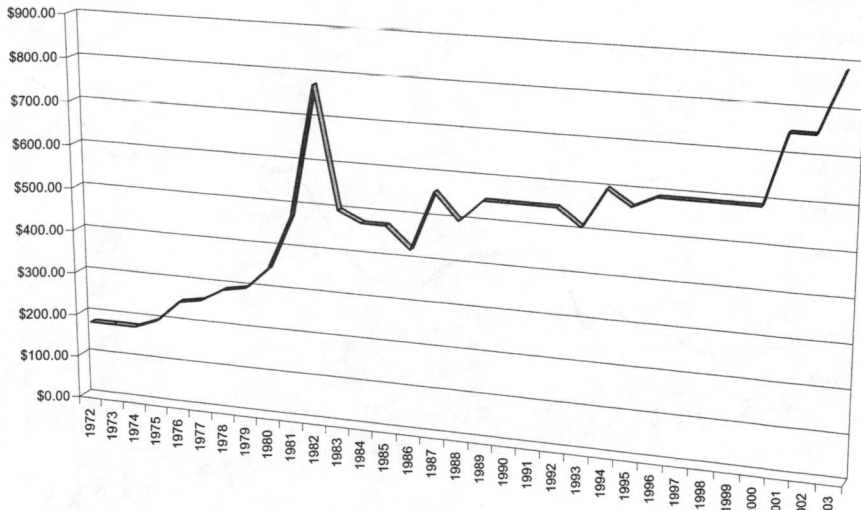

Retail Price

Date	Mintage	G-4	VG-8	F-12	VF-20	XF-40	AU-50	MS-60	MS-65	Prf-65
1894O	2,852,000	6.00	9.00	31.50	50.00	85.00	195	330	2,250	—
1894S	2,648,821	6.25	9.00	31.50	47.00	85.00	175	300	3,300	—
1895	4,440,880	5.00	6.25	24.00	31.50	65.00	135	220	1,850	2,000
1895O	2,816,000	6.00	10.00	35.00	50.00	85.00	200	390	2,650	—
1895S	1,764,681	9.00	15.00	43.00	72.00	95.00	210	360	3,850	—
1896	3,874,762	5.00	6.25	21.50	33.00	65.00	135	230	1,600	2,000
1896O	1,484,000	7.50	21.50	80.00	210	335	625	825	7,500	—
1896S	188,039	390	600	885	1,250	2,500	3,800	5,400	27,000	—
1897	8,140,731	5.00	6.00	20.00	31.50	65.00	115	180	1,100	2,000
1897O	1,414,800	8.00	21.50	75.00	180	335	600	800	3,600	—
1897S	542,229	60.00	85.00	200	275	360	700	950	6,700	—
1898	11,100,735	5.00	5.50	21.50	31.50	65.00	115	180	1,100	2,000
1898O	1,868,000	6.00	14.00	57.50	110	215	370	600	10,000	—
1898S	1,020,592	6.50	15.00	40.00	48.00	65.00	180	400	7,000	—
1899	12,624,846	5.00	5.50	19.00	32.00	65.00	115	180	1,100	2,000
1899O	2,644,000	5.00	11.50	26.50	43.00	85.00	250	380	3,500	—
1899S	708,000	15.00	30.00	60.00	75.00	100.00	225	400	3,650	—
1900	10,016,912	5.50	6.50	19.00	31.50	65.00	135	180	1,100	2,000
1900O	3,416,000	7.50	20.00	55.00	95.00	115	330	550	3,600	—
1900S	1,858,585	6.50	11.50	35.00	49.00	65.00	115	360	5,000	—
1901	8,892,813	5.50	9.50	19.00	31.50	65.00	110	180	2,200	2,200
1901O	1,612,000	27.50	40.00	95.00	185	335	625	800	5,750	—
1901S	72,664	2,600	4,700	6,400	8,200	10,700	14,500	27,500	47,000	—
1902	12,197,744	5.50	6.50	16.00	30.00	65.00	110	180	1,000	2,100
1902O	4,748,000	6.00	12.00	36.00	56.00	100.00	180	385	4,700	—
1902S	1,524,612	8.00	13.50	37.00	60.00	85.00	190	510	3,400	—
1903	9,670,064	5.50	6.50	16.00	30.00	65.00	110	180	2,500	2,000
1903O	3,500,000	5.50	8.50	32.00	48.00	85.00	230	400	5,500	—
1903S	1,036,000	12.00	20.00	40.00	65.00	100.00	260	425	2,800	—
1904	9,588,813	5.50	6.50	16.00	31.50	65.00	110	180	1,400	2,000
1904O	2,456,000	6.25	12.00	45.00	75.00	175	375	775	3,100	—
1905	4,968,250	5.50	6.50	21.50	32.00	65.00	110	180	1,650	2,000
1905O	1,230,000	10.00	20.00	72.00	125	195	340	465	6,500	—
1905S	1,884,000	6.25	11.50	34.00	50.00	90.00	200	325	3,600	—
1906	3,656,435	5.50	6.50	16.00	30.00	65.00	110	170	1,000	2,000
1906D	3,280,000	5.50	6.50	22.00	37.50	65.00	145	210	2,100	—
1906O	2,056,000	5.50	8.50	33.50	47.50	85.00	185	285	1,200	—
1907	7,192,575	5.00	6.00	16.00	30.00	65.00	110	180	1,100	2,000
1907D	2,484,000	5.00	7.50	25.00	44.00	80.00	175	240	2,650	—
1907O	4,560,000	5.00	8.50	16.00	31.50	65.00	135	195	2,400	—
1907S	1,360,000	6.00	9.50	37.00	56.00	100.00	250	440	3,450	—
1908	4,232,545	4.50	5.75	18.00	30.00	65.00	110	195	1,100	2,200
1908D	5,788,000	4.50	5.75	16.00	29.00	65.00	115	215	1,750	—
1908O	6,244,000	4.50	8.50	16.00	29.00	72.00	120	195	1,100	—
1908S	784,000	14.00	28.00	70.00	110	235	415	700	5,200	—
1909	9,268,650	4.50	5.75	16.00	29.00	65.00	110	180	1,100	2,000
1909D	5,114,000	4.50	5.50	17.00	30.00	65.00	145	195	2,300	—

1913-S Quarter
Grade XF-40

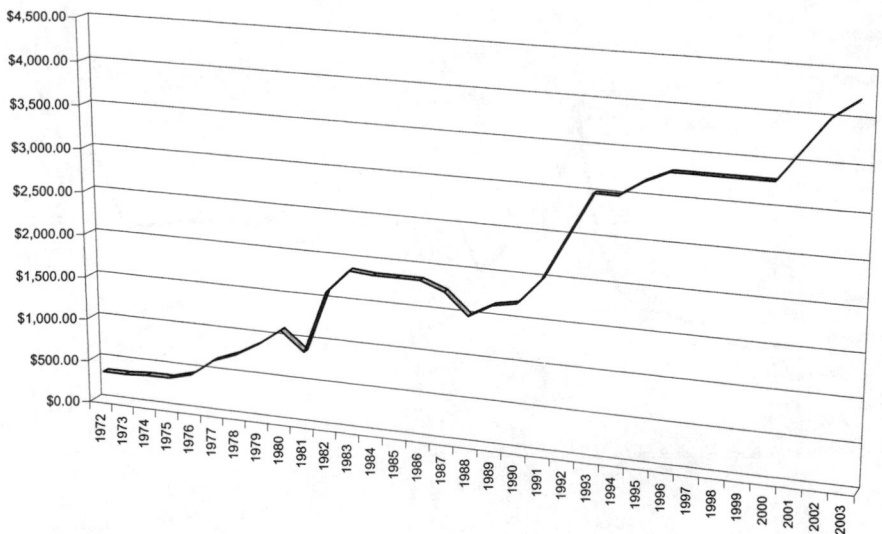

Retail Price

Date	Mintage	G-4	VG-8	F-12	VF-20	XF-40	AU-50	MS-60	MS-65	Prf-65
1909O	712,000	12.50	31.50	80.00	175	290	460	800	8,700	—
1909S	1,348,000	5.00	8.50	27.50	42.00	65.00	180	275	2,400	—
1910	2,244,551	5.00	6.50	23.00	33.50	65.00	140	190	1,175	2,000
1910D	1,500,000	5.75	7.00	37.00	56.00	98.00	235	335	2,200	—
1911	3,720,543	4.50	6.00	16.00	31.50	72.00	120	180	1,100	2,000
1911D	933,600	6.00	15.00	75.00	185	300	450	630	6,000	—
1911S	988,000	5.00	8.50	45.00	57.50	135	300	375	1,500	—
1912	4,400,700	5.00	6.00	16.00	32.00	65.00	110	180	1,100	2,000
1912S	708,000	6.00	8.50	40.00	57.50	95.00	220	375	2,700	—
1913	484,613	9.50	18.00	65.00	145	380	480	900	4,200	2,200
1913D	1,450,800	6.50	9.50	30.00	45.00	75.00	160	265	1,150	—
1913S	40,000	640	950	2,100	3,200	4,200	4,750	5,800	14,000	—
1914	6,244,610	4.50	5.75	16.00	26.50	55.00	110	180	1,100	2,200
1914D	3,046,000	4.50	5.75	16.00	26.50	56.00	110	180	1,100	—
1914S	264,000	58.00	80.00	150	190	390	585	850	3,500	—
1915	3,480,450	4.50	5.75	16.00	26.50	65.00	110	180	1,100	2,200
1915D	3,694,000	4.50	5.75	16.00	26.50	65.00	110	180	1,100	—
1915S	704,000	6.00	8.50	23.50	37.50	75.00	185	225	1,100	—
1916	1,788,000	4.50	5.75	16.00	26.50	54.00	110	180	1,100	—
1916D	6,540,800	4.50	5.75	16.00	26.50	54.00	110	180	1,100	—

Standing Liberty. Right breast exposed; Type 1.

KM# 141 Designer: Hermon A. MacNeil **Obverse:** Right breast exposed; Type 1 **Weight:** 6.2500 g. **Composition:** 0.9000 Silver 0.1809 oz. ASW **Size:** 24.3 mm.

Date	Mintage	G-4	VG-8	F-12	VF-20	XF-40	AU-50	MS-60	MS-65	-65FH
1916	52,000	1,750	2,400	3,500	4,900	6,100	6,700	8,000	14,500	24,000
1917	8,792,000	20.00	32.00	44.00	56.00	80.00	165	195	750	1,300
1917D	1,509,200	22.50	33.00	45.00	57.50	95.00	165	200	950	1,900
1917S	1,952,000	25.00	33.00	45.00	70.00	135	195	215	1,250	2,600

Standing Liberty. Right breast covered; Type 2. Three stars below eagle.

Mint mark

KM# 145 Designer: Hermon A. MacNeil **Obverse:** Right breast covered; Type 2 **Reverse:** Three stars below eagle **Weight:** 6.2500 g. **Composition:** 0.9000 Silver 0.1809 oz. ASW **Size:** 24.3 mm.

Date	Mintage	G-4	VG-8	F-12	VF-20	XF-40	AU-50	MS-60	MS-65	-65FH
1917	13,880,000	18.50	22.00	27.00	29.00	44.00	80.00	125	530	800
1917D	6,224,400	37.50	41.00	65.00	67.50	90.00	125	195	1,200	3,400
1917S	5,522,000	35.00	44.00	61.00	67.00	77.00	105	180	1,150	3,300
1918	14,240,000	15.00	17.50	27.50	30.00	45.00	80.00	125	485	1,700
1918D	7,380,000	22.00	30.00	45.00	62.50	80.00	130	200	1,200	4,500
1918S	11,072,000	16.00	21.00	30.00	35.00	46.50	80.00	175	1,200	9,000
1918/17S	Inc. above	1,100	1,350	2,150	2,800	4,700	8,800	12,500	90,000	300,000
1919	11,324,000	31.00	41.50	52.50	55.00	70.00	100.00	135	500	1,450
1919D	1,944,000	70.00	95.00	145	230	350	480	575	2,400	22,000
1919S	1,836,000	67.00	95.00	160	255	470	520	700	3,100	25,000
1920	27,860,000	12.50	15.00	24.00	27.50	38.00	70.00	120	480	1,950
1920D	3,586,400	42.00	49.00	75.00	90.00	110	165	235	2,000	6,250
1920S	6,380,000	16.00	22.00	28.00	36.00	55.00	100.00	220	2,400	18,500
1921	1,916,000	120	145	180	250	325	380	485	1,525	3,950
1923	9,716,000	13.50	15.00	27.00	30.00	39.00	63.50	125	560	4,000
1923S	1,360,000	230	340	420	520	560	640	750	1,750	4,000
1924	10,920,000	13.50	16.00	21.00	25.00	35.00	73.00	120	450	1,400
1924D	3,112,000	52.00	60.00	80.00	90.00	110	125	150	500	4,200
1924S	2,860,000	24.00	28.00	37.50	40.00	90.00	180	250	1,800	5,250
1925	12,280,000	2.50	3.00	4.25	12.50	32.00	68.00	110	450	800
1926	11,316,000	2.50	3.00	4.00	10.00	30.00	63.00	100.00	450	1,850
1926D	1,716,000	5.00	9.00	14.00	26.50	50.00	85.00	135	450	19,000
1926S	2,700,000	3.00	4.00	10.00	20.00	100.00	220	300	2,100	25,000
1927	11,912,000	2.50	3.00	4.00	10.00	30.00	65.00	100.00	450	950
1927D	976,400	6.50	9.00	12.50	35.00	82.50	140	160	2,400	2,500
1927S	396,000	11.00	12.50	50.00	165	1,000	2,750	4,000	9,500	175,000
1928	6,336,000	2.50	3.00	4.25	11.50	29.00	65.00	100.00	450	1,300

Date	Mintage	G-4	VG-8	F-12	VF-20	XF-40	AU-50	MS-60	MS-65	-65FH
1928D	1,627,600	3.25	4.00	8.00	18.00	37.50	75.00	125	450	5,000
1928S	2,644,000	3.00	4.00	6.00	14.00	32.00	72.00	125	450	900
1929	11,140,000	2.50	3.00	4.00	11.50	30.00	65.00	100.00	450	750
1929D	1,358,000	3.50	5.00	6.00	14.00	34.00	72.00	125	450	5,200
1929S	1,764,000	3.00	3.50	4.50	14.00	30.00	70.00	125	450	750
1930	5,632,000	2.50	3.00	4.00	10.00	30.00	65.00	100.00	450	725
1930S	1,556,000	3.50	4.50	5.00	11.00	30.00	70.00	110	450	750

Washington.

Mint mark 1932-64

KM# 164 Designer: John Flanagan **Weight:** 6.2500 g. **Composition:** 0.9000 Silver 0.1809 oz. ASW
Size: 24.3 mm.

Date	Mintage	G-4	VG-8	F-12	VF-20	XF-40	AU-50	MS-60	MS-65	Prf-65
1932	5,404,000	3.75	5.25	6.00	7.50	9.50	14.50	22.00	400	—
1932D	436,800	95.00	100.00	115	130	185	360	880	15,000	—
1932S	408,000	100.00	105	110	115	125	135	365	5,500	—
1934	31,912,052	2.00	2.25	2.50	3.00	4.00	9.00	25.00	80.00	—
1934D	3,527,200	3.75	5.50	6.50	10.00	15.00	80.00	210	1,450	—
1935	32,484,000	1.75	2.00	2.50	2.75	4.00	8.00	21.00	70.00	—
1935D	5,780,000	2.00	3.00	5.00	10.00	18.50	125	240	800	—
1935S	5,660,000	2.00	2.50	4.75	5.75	12.00	32.50	80.00	300	—
1936	41,303,837	1.75	2.00	2.25	2.75	3.50	8.50	21.00	70.00	1,050
1936D	5,374,000	2.50	3.25	4.75	15.00	44.00	220	420	950	—
1936S	3,828,000	2.00	2.50	4.00	7.00	12.00	45.00	90.00	350	—
1937	19,701,542	1.75	2.00	3.00	3.50	4.00	16.00	22.00	90.00	380
1937D	7,189,600	2.00	2.50	3.00	4.50	12.00	28.00	60.00	135	—
1937S	1,652,000	3.00	4.50	5.00	11.00	18.50	85.00	125	275	—
1938	9,480,045	3.00	4.50	5.00	6.00	13.50	35.00	70.00	180	225
1938S	2,832,000	3.50	5.00	5.50	7.00	14.00	38.00	72.00	175	—
1939	33,548,795	1.75	2.00	2.25	2.50	3.50	7.00	14.00	55.00	150
1939D	7,092,000	2.00	2.25	3.25	4.00	8.00	16.00	34.00	85.00	—
1939S	2,628,000	3.00	3.25	3.50	5.00	12.00	45.00	72.00	215	—
1940	35,715,246	1.75	2.00	2.25	2.50	3.00	6.50	15.00	65.00	150
1940D	2,797,600	2.00	2.50	6.00	8.50	18.00	55.00	95.00	230	—
1940S	8,244,000	1.75	2.25	4.75	5.00	6.50	14.00	24.00	55.00	—
1941	79,047,287	—	—	1.65	1.75	2.50	4.00	9.00	43.00	110

1932-D Quarter
Grade F-12

Date	Mintage	G-4	VG-8	F-12	VF-20	XF-40	AU-50	MS-60	MS-65	Prf-65
1941D	16,714,800	—	—	1.75	2.25	3.50	7.50	35.00	110	—
1941S	16,080,000	—	—	1.75	2.25	3.25	6.50	30.00	85.00	—
1942	102,117,123	—	—	1.65	1.75	2.50	3.00	6.00	37.50	110
1942D	17,487,200	—	—	1.75	2.50	3.75	7.00	22.50	65.00	—
1942S	19,384,000	—	—	2.00	3.00	5.50	16.00	75.00	240	—
1943	99,700,000	—	—	1.50	1.75	2.10	2.75	5.00	45.00	—
1943D	16,095,600	—	—	1.75	2.25	4.00	7.00	27.50	75.00	—
1943S	21,700,000	—	—	1.75	2.25	5.50	11.00	27.50	75.00	—
1944	104,956,000	—	—	1.50	1.75	2.10	2.85	5.00	44.00	—
1944D	14,600,800	—	—	1.75	2.50	3.75	8.00	13.00	45.00	—
1944S	12,560,000	—	—	1.85	2.75	4.00	9.00	14.00	45.00	—
1945	74,372,000	—	—	1.50	1.75	2.10	2.85	4.50	44.00	—
1945D	12,341,600	—	—	1.75	3.00	6.00	10.50	16.00	50.00	—
1945S	17,004,001	—	—	1.65	2.50	3.75	6.00	10.00	45.00	—
1946	53,436,000	—	—	1.50	1.85	2.25	2.75	5.00	42.00	—
1946D	9,072,800	—	—	1.50	1.85	2.25	2.75	5.00	42.00	—
1946S	4,204,000	—	—	1.65	2.00	3.00	4.00	7.00	42.00	—
1947	22,556,000	—	—	1.65	2.25	2.75	3.50	12.50	55.00	—
1947D	15,338,400	—	—	1.65	2.25	2.50	2.75	11.00	45.00	—
1947S	5,532,000	—	—	1.65	2.25	2.75	3.00	10.00	45.00	—
1948	35,196,000	—	—	1.65	1.85	2.25	2.75	3.50	40.00	—
1948D	16,766,800	—	—	1.65	1.85	2.25	2.75	10.00	54.00	—
1948S	15,960,000	—	—	1.75	1.95	2.50	3.00	6.00	50.00	—
1949	9,312,000	—	—	1.65	2.50	4.50	14.00	36.00	80.00	—
1949D	10,068,400	—	—	1.60	2.25	4.00	5.00	20.00	70.00	—
1950	24,971,512	—	—	1.50	1.65	1.75	2.10	4.50	28.00	55.00
1950D	21,075,600	—	—	1.65	1.85	2.10	2.40	3.50	30.00	—
1950D/S	Inc. above	25.00	28.00	40.00	60.00	150	225	275	650	—
1950S	10,284,004	—	—	1.65	1.85	2.40	4.50	7.50	30.00	—
1950S/D	Inc. above	25.00	28.00	40.00	60.00	185	315	400	750	—
1951	43,505,602	—	—	1.50	1.65	1.75	2.25	7.00	40.00	40.00
1951D	35,354,800	—	—	1.50	1.75	2.00	2.25	6.50	35.00	—
1951S	9,048,000	—	—	1.50	1.75	3.75	7.00	22.00	65.00	—
1952	38,862,073	—	—	1.50	1.65	1.75	2.25	6.50	35.00	37.00
1952D	49,795,200	—	—	1.50	1.65	1.75	2.25	5.00	28.00	—
1952S	13,707,800	—	—	1.50	1.75	3.25	7.00	17.50	45.00	—
1953	18,664,920	—	—	1.50	1.65	1.75	2.10	7.50	30.00	25.00
1953D	56,112,400	—	—	1.50	1.65	1.75	1.95	3.00	25.00	—
1953S	14,016,000	—	—	1.50	1.75	2.10	2.75	4.50	28.00	—
1954	54,645,503	—	—	—	1.50	1.65	1.75	6.50	30.00	13.00
1954D	42,305,500	—	—	—	1.50	1.65	1.75	4.50	28.00	—
1954S	11,834,722	—	—	—	1.50	1.75	2.00	4.00	25.00	—
1955	18,558,381	—	—	—	1.65	1.75	2.00	4.00	25.00	14.00
1955D	3,182,400	—	—	2.00	2.25	2.50	2.75	3.00	25.00	—
1956	44,813,384	—	—	—	1.65	1.85	2.00	3.50	22.00	4.00
1956D	32,334,500	—	—	—	1.75	1.85	2.10	3.00	24.00	—
1957	47,779,952	—	—	—	1.65	1.75	1.95	2.75	26.00	4.00
1957D	77,924,160	—	—	—	1.65	1.75	1.95	2.25	20.00	—
1958	7,235,652	—	—	—	1.65	1.75	2.00	2.00	20.00	6.00
1958D	78,124,900	—	—	—	1.65	1.75	1.95	2.25	20.00	—
1959	25,533,291	—	—	—	1.65	1.75	1.95	2.25	20.00	4.25
1959D	62,054,232	—	—	—	1.65	1.75	1.95	2.25	20.00	—
1960	30,855,602	—	—	—	1.65	1.75	1.95	2.25	17.00	3.75
1960D	63,000,324	—	—	—	1.65	1.75	1.95	2.25	17.00	—
1961	40,064,244	—	—	—	1.65	1.75	1.95	2.50	18.00	3.50
1961D	83,656,928	—	—	—	1.65	1.75	1.95	2.25	16.00	—
1962	39,374,019	—	—	—	1.65	1.75	1.95	2.50	18.00	3.50
1962D	127,554,756	—	—	—	1.65	1.75	1.95	2.25	16.00	—
1963	77,391,645	—	—	—	1.50	1.60	1.75	1.95	15.00	3.50
1963D	135,288,184	—	—	—	1.50	1.60	1.75	1.95	15.00	—
1964	564,341,347	—	—	—	1.50	1.60	1.75	1.95	15.00	3.50
1964D	704,135,528	—	—	—	1.50	1.60	1.75	1.95	15.00	—

Washington.

KM# 164a Designer: John Flanagan **Weight:** 5.6700 g. **Composition:** Copper-Nickel Clad Copper **Size:** 24.3 mm.

Date	Mintage	MS-65	Prf-65	Date	Mintage	MS-65	Prf-65
1965	1,819,717,540	2.75	—	1971S	3,220,733	—	1.05
1966	821,101,500	2.75	—	1972	215,048,000	2.00	—
1967	1,524,031,848	2.75	—	1972D	311,067,732	2.00	—
1968	220,731,500	2.75	—	1972S	3,260,996	—	1.10
1968D	101,534,000	3.00	—	1973	346,924,000	2.00	—
1968S	3,041,506	—	1.00	1973D	232,977,400	2.25	—
1969	176,212,000	4.50	—	1973S	2,760,339	—	1.00
1969D	114,372,000	3.00	—	1974	801,456,000	2.00	—
1969S	2,934,631	—	1.25	1974D	353,160,300	2.25	—
1970	136,420,000	2.50	—	1974S	2,612,568	—	1.25
1970D	417,341,364	2.25	—	1975 none minted	—	—	—
1970S	2,632,810	—	1.00	1975D none minted	—	—	—
1971	109,284,000	2.25	—	1975S none minted	—	—	—
1971D	258,634,428	2.25	—				

Washington. Bicentennial design, drummer boy.

Mint mark 1968 - Present

KM# 204 Rev. Designer: Jack L. Ahr **Reverse:** Bicentennial design, drummer boy **Weight:** 5.6700 g.
Composition: Copper-Nickel Clad Copper **Size:** 24.3 mm.

Date	Mintage	G-4	VG-8	F-12	VF-20	XF-40	MS-60	MS-65	Prf-65
1976	809,784,016	—	—	—	—	—	0.95	1.75	—
1976D	860,118,839	—	—	—	—	—	0.95	1.75	—
1976S	4,149,730	—	—	—	—	—	—	—	1.00

Washington. Bicentennial design, drummer boy.

KM# 204a Rev. Designer: Jack L. Ahr **Reverse:** Bicentennial design, drummer boy **Weight:** 5.7500 g.
Composition: Silver Clad 0.074 oz. ASW **Size:** 24.3 mm.

Date	Mintage	G-4	VG-8	F-12	VF-20	XF-40	MS-60	MS-65	Prf-65
1976S	4,908,319								
	3,998,621	—	—	—	—	—	1.25	1.75	2.00

Washington. Regular design resumed.

KM# A164a Reverse: Regular design resumed **Weight:** 5.6700 g. **Composition:** Copper-Nickel Clad Copper
Size: 24.3 mm. **Note:** KM#164 design and composition resumed. The 1979-S and 1981 Type II proofs have
clearer mint marks than the Type I proofs for those years.

Date	Mintage	MS-65	Prf-65	Date	Mintage	MS-65	Prf-65
1977	468,556,000	1.00	—	1987S	4,227,728	—	1.50
1977D	256,524,978	1.00	—	1988P	562,052,000	3.00	—
1977S	3,251,152	—	1.10	1988D	596,810,688	1.50	—
1978	521,452,000	1.00	—	1988S	3,262,948	—	2.10
1978D	287,373,152	1.00	—	1989P	512,868,000	1.50	—
1978S	3,127,781	—	1.20	1989D	896,535,597	1.50	—
1979	515,708,000	1.00	—	1989S	3,220,194	—	2.10
1979D	489,789,780	1.00	—	1990P	613,792,000	1.00	—
1979S T-I	—	—	1.00	1990D	927,638,181	1.00	—
1979S T-II	—	—	1.50	1990S	3,299,559	—	5.00
1980P	635,832,000	1.00	—	1991P	570,968,000	1.00	—
1980D	518,327,487	1.00	—	1991D	630,966,693	1.00	—
1980S	3,554,806	—	1.15	1991S	2,867,787	—	2.50
1981P	601,716,000	1.00	—	1992P	384,764,000	1.00	—
1981D	575,722,833	1.00	—	1992D	389,777,107	1.35	—
1981S T-I	—	—	1.10	1992S	2,858,981	—	3.00
1981S T-II	—	—	3.00	1993P	639,276,000	1.20	—
1982P	500,931,000	6.50	—	1993D	645,476,128	1.50	—
1982D	480,042,788	3.00	—	1993S	2,633,439	—	5.00
1982S	3,857,479	—	2.00	1994P	825,600,000	1.25	—
1983P	673,535,000	30.00	—	1994D	880,034,110	1.25	—
1983D	617,806,446	20.00	—	1994S	2,484,594	—	4.00
1983S	3,279,126	—	2.25	1995P	1,004,336,000	1.20	—
1984P	676,545,000	1.75	—	1995D	1,103,216,000	1.20	—
1984D	546,483,064	2.50	—	1995S	2,010,384	—	20.00
1984S	3,065,110	—	2.40	1996P	925,040,000	1.20	—
1985P	775,818,962	3.50	—	1996S	—	—	4.00
1985D	519,962,888	5.00	—	1996D	906,868,000	1.20	—
1985S	3,362,821	5.00	1.45	1997P	595,740,000	1.25	—
1986P	551,199,333	6.00	—	1997D	599,680,000	1.25	—
1986D	504,298,660	10.00	—	1997S	1,975,000	—	10.00
1986S	3,010,497	—	2.25	1998P	896,268,000	1.00	—
1987P	582,499,481	1.00	—	1998D	821,000,000	1.00	—
1987D	655,594,696	1.00	—	1998S	—	—	10.00

Washington.

KM# A164b Composition: Silver

Date	Mintage	Prf-65	Date	Mintage	Prf-65
1992S	1,317,579	7.00	1996S	—	18.00
1993S	761,353	6.00	1997S	—	7.00
1994S	785,329	9.50	1998S	—	9.00
1995S	838,953	18.00			

50 STATE QUARTERS
Delaware

KM# 290 Series: 50 State Quarters **Subject:** Delaware **Weight:** 5.6700 g. **Composition:** Copper-Nickel Clad Copper **Size:** 24.3 mm.

Date	Mintage	MS-63	MS-65	Prf-65
1999P	373,400,000	1.25	1.50	—
1999D	401,424,000	1.25	1.50	—
1999S	3,713,359	—	—	10.00

KM# 290a Series: 50 State Quarters **Subject:** Delaware **Composition:** 0.9000 Silver

Date	Mintage	MS-63	MS-65	Prf-65
1999S	804,565	—	—	40.00

Pennsylvania

KM# 291 Series: 50 State Quarters **Subject:** Pennsylvania **Weight:** 5.6700 g. **Composition:** Copper-Nickel Clad Copper **Size:** 24.3 mm.

Date	Mintage	MS-63	MS-65	Prf-65
1999P	349,000,000	1.50	2.00	—
1999D	358,332,000	1.25	1.50	—
1999S	3,713,359	—	—	10.00

KM# 291a Series: 50 State Quarters **Subject:** Pennsylvania **Composition:** 0.9000 Silver

Date	Mintage	MS-63	MS-65	Prf-65
1999S	804,565	—	—	40.00

New Jersey

KM# 292 Series: 50 State Quarters **Subject:** New Jersey **Composition:** Copper-Nickel Clad Copper

Date	Mintage	MS-63	MS-65	Prf-65
1999P	363,200,000	1.00	1.50	—
1999D	299,028,000	1.00	1.75	—
1999S	3,713,359	—	—	10.00

KM# 292a Series: 50 State Quarters **Subject:** New Jersey **Composition:** 0.9000 Silver

Date	Mintage	MS-63	MS-65	Prf-65
1999S	804,565	—	—	40.00

Georgia

KM# 293 Series: 50 State Quarters **Subject:** Georgia **Composition:** Copper-Nickel Clad Copper

Date	Mintage	MS-63	MS-65	Prf-65
1999P	451,188,000	0.75	1.00	—

Date	Mintage	MS-63	MS-65	Prf-65
1999D	488,744,000	0.75	1.00	—
1999S	3,713,359	—	—	10.00

KM# 293a Series: 50 State Quarters **Subject:** Georgia **Composition:** 0.9000 Silver

Date	Mintage	MS-63	MS-65	Prf-65
1999S	804,565	—	—	40.00

Connecticut

KM# 294 Series: 50 State Quarters **Subject:** Connecticut **Composition:** Copper-Nickel Clad Copper

Date	Mintage	MS-63	MS-65	Prf-65
1999P	688,744,000	0.75	1.00	—
1999D	657,480,000	0.75	1.00	—
1999S	3,713,359	—	—	10.00

KM# 294a Series: 50 State Quarters **Subject:** Connecticut **Composition:** 0.9000 Silver

Date	Mintage	MS-63	MS-65	Prf-65
1999S	804,565	—	—	40.00

Massachusetts

KM# 306 Series: 50 State Quarters **Subject:** Massachusetts **Composition:** Copper-Nickel Clad Copper

Date	Mintage	MS-63	MS-65	Prf-65
2000P	629,800,000	0.75	1.00	—
2000D	535,184,000	0.75	1.00	—
2000S	4,078,747	—	—	5.00

KM# 306a Series: 50 State Quarters **Subject:** Massachusetts **Composition:** 0.9000 Silver

Date	Mintage	MS-63	MS-65	Prf-65
2000S	965,921	—	—	7.50

Maryland

KM# 307 Series: 50 State Quarters **Subject:** Maryland **Composition:** Copper-Nickel Clad Copper

Date	Mintage	MS-63	MS-65	Prf-65
2000P	678,200,000	0.75	1.00	—
2000D	556,526,000	0.75	1.00	—
2000S	4,078,747	—	—	5.00

KM# 307a Series: 50 State Quarters **Subject:** Maryland **Composition:** 0.9000 Silver

Date	Mintage	MS-63	MS-65	Prf-65
2000S	965,921	—	—	7.50

South Carolina

KM# 308 Series: 50 State Quarters **Subject:** South Carolina **Composition:** Copper-Nickel Clad Copper

Date	Mintage	MS-63	MS-65	Prf-65
2000P	742,756,000	0.75	1.00	—

Date	Mintage	MS-63	MS-65	Prf-65
2000D	566,208,000	0.75	1.00	—
2000S	4,078,747	—	—	5.00

KM# 308a **Series:** 50 State Quarters **Subject:** South Carolina **Composition:** 0.9000 Silver

Date	Mintage	MS-63	MS-65	Prf-65
2000S	965,921	—	—	7.50

New Hampshire

KM# 309 **Series:** 50 State Quarters **Subject:** New Hampshire **Composition:** Copper-Nickel Clad Copper

Date	Mintage	MS-63	MS-65	Prf-65
2000P	673,040,000	0.75	1.00	—
2000D	495,976,000	0.75	1.00	—
2000S	4,078,747	—	—	5.00

KM# 309a **Series:** 50 State Quarters **Subject:** New Hampshire **Composition:** 0.9000 Silver

Date	Mintage	MS-63	MS-65	Prf-65
2000S	965,921	—	—	7.50

Virginia

KM# 310 **Series:** 50 State Quarters **Subject:** Virginia **Composition:** Copper-Nickel Clad Copper

Date	Mintage	MS-63	MS-65	Prf-65
2000P	943,000,000	0.75	1.00	—
2000D	651,616,000	0.75	1.00	—
2000S	4,078,747	—	—	5.00

KM# 310a **Series:** 50 State Quarters **Subject:** Virginia **Composition:** 0.9000 Silver

Date	Mintage	MS-63	MS-65	Prf-65
2000S	965,921	—	—	7.50

New York

KM# 319 **Series:** 50 State Quarters **Subject:** New York **Composition:** Copper-Nickel Clad Copper

Date	Mintage	MS-63	MS-65	Prf-65
2001P	655,400,000	0.75	1.00	—
2001D	619,640,000	0.75	1.00	—
2001S	3,009,800	—	—	6.50

KM# 319a **Series:** 50 State Quarters **Subject:** New York **Composition:** 0.9000 Silver

Date	Mintage	MS-63	MS-65	Prf-65
2001S	849,600	—	—	20.00

North Carolina

KM# 320 **Series:** 50 State Quarters **Subject:** North Carolina **Composition:** Copper-Nickel Clad Copper

Date	Mintage	MS-63	MS-65	Prf-65
2001P	627,600,000	0.75	1.00	—
2001D	427,876,000	0.75	1.00	—
2001S	3,009,800	—	—	6.50

KM# 320a Series: 50 State Quarters **Subject:** North Carolina **Composition:** 0.9000 Silver

Date	Mintage	MS-63	MS-65	Prf-65
2001S	849,600	—	—	20.00

Rhode Island

KM# 321 Series: 50 State Quarters **Subject:** Rhode Island **Composition:** Copper-Nickel Clad Copper

Date	Mintage	MS-63	MS-65	Prf-65
2001P	423,000,000	0.75	1.00	—
2001D	447,100,000	0.75	1.00	—
2001S	3,009,800	—	—	6.50

KM# 321a Series: 50 State Quarters **Subject:** Rhode Island **Composition:** 0.9000 Silver

Date	Mintage	MS-63	MS-65	Prf-65
2001S	849,600	—	—	20.00

Vermont

KM# 322 Series: 50 State Quarters **Subject:** Vermont **Composition:** Copper-Nickel Clad Copper

Date	Mintage	MS-63	MS-65	Prf-65
2001P	423,400,000	0.75	1.00	—
2001D	459,404,000	0.75	1.00	—
2001S	3,009,800	—	—	6.50

KM# 322a Series: 50 State Quarters **Subject:** Vermont **Composition:** 0.9000 Silver

Date	Mintage	MS-63	MS-65	Prf-65
2001S	849,600	—	—	20.00

Kentucky

KM# 323 Series: 50 State Quarters **Subject:** Kentucky **Composition:** Copper-Nickel Clad Copper

Date	Mintage	MS-63	MS-65	Prf-65
2001P	353,000,000	0.75	1.00	—
2001D	370,564,000	0.75	1.00	—
2001S	3,009,800	—	—	6.50

KM# 323a Series: 50 State Quarters **Subject:** Kentucky **Composition:** 0.9000 Silver

Date	Mintage	MS-63	MS-65	Prf-65
2001S	849,500	—	—	20.00

Tennessee

KM# 324 Series: 50 State Quarters **Subject:** Tennessee **Composition:** Copper-Nickel Clad Copper

Date	Mintage	MS-63	MS-65	Prf-65
2002P	361,600,000	0.75	1.00	—
2002S	2,956,721	—	—	7.50
2002D	286,468,000	0.75	1.00	—

KM# 324a Series: 50 State Quarters **Subject:** Tennessee **Composition:** 0.9000 Silver

Date	Mintage	MS-63	MS-65	Prf-65
2002S	878,542	—	—	7.50

Ohio

KM# 325 Series: 50 State Quarters **Subject:** Ohio **Composition:** Copper-Nickel Clad Copper

Date	Mintage	MS-63	MS-65	Prf-65
2002P	217,200,000	—	—	—
2002D	414,832,000	—	—	—
2002S	3,009,800	—	—	6.00

KM# 325a Series: 50 State Quarters **Subject:** Ohio **Composition:** 0.9000 Silver

Date	Mintage	MS-63	MS-65	Prf-65
2002S	—	—	—	—

Louisiana

KM# 326 Series: 50 State Quarters **Subject:** Louisiana **Composition:** Copper-Nickel Clad Copper

Date	Mintage	MS-63	MS-65	Prf-65
2002P	—	—	—	—
2002D	—	—	—	—
2002S	—	—	—	—

KM# 326a Series: 50 State Quarters **Subject:** Louisiana **Composition:** 0.9000 Silver

Date	Mintage	MS-63	MS-65	Prf-65
2002S	—	—	—	—

Indiana

KM# 327 Series: 50 State Quarters **Subject:** Indiana **Composition:** Copper-Nickel Clad Copper

Date	Mintage	MS-63	MS-65	Prf-65
2002P	—	—	—	—
2002D	—	—	—	—
2002S	—	—	—	—

KM# 327a **Series:** 50 State Quarters **Subject:** Indiana **Composition:** 0.9000 Silver

Date	Mintage	MS-63	MS-65	Prf-65
2002S	—			

Mississippi

KM# 328 **Series:** 50 State Quarters **Subject:** Mississippi **Composition:** Copper-Nickel Clad Copper

Date	Mintage	MS-63	MS-65	Prf-65
2002P	—	—	—	
2002D	—	—	—	
2002S	—	—	—	—

KM# 328a **Series:** 50 State Quarters **Subject:** Mississippi **Composition:** 0.9000 Silver

Date	Mintage	MS-63	MS-65	Prf-65
2002S	—			

Illinois

KM# 339 **Series:** 50 State Quarters **Subject:** Illinois **Composition:** Copper-Nickel Clad Copper

Date	Mintage	MS-63	MS-65	Prf-65
2003P	—	—	—	
2003D	—	—	—	
2003S	—	—	—	—

KM# 339a **Series:** 50 State Quarters **Subject:** Illinois **Composition:** 0.9000 Silver

Date	Mintage	MS-63	MS-65	Prf-65
2003S	—			

Alabama

KM# 340 **Series:** 50 State Quarters **Subject:** Alabama **Composition:** Copper-Nickel Clad Copper

Date	Mintage	MS-63	MS-65	Prf-65
2003P	—	—	—	
2003D	—	—	—	
2003S	—	—	—	—

KM# 340a **Series:** 50 State Quarters **Subject:** Alabama **Composition:** 0.9000 Silver

Date	Mintage	MS-63	MS-65	Prf-65
2003S	—			

Maine

KM# 341 **Series:** 50 State Quarters **Subject:** Maine **Composition:** Copper-Nickel Clad Copper

Date	Mintage	MS-63	MS-65	Prf-65
2003P	—	—	—	
2003D	—	—	—	
2003S	—	—	—	—

KM# 341a **Series:** 50 State Quarters **Subject:** Maine **Composition:** 0.9000 Silver

Date	Mintage	MS-63	MS-65	Prf-65
2003S	—			

Missouri

KM# 342 Series: 50 State Quarters **Subject:** Missouri **Composition:** Copper-Nickel Clad Copper

Date	Mintage	MS-63	MS-65	Prf-65
2003P	—	—	—	—
2003D	—	—	—	—
2003S	—	—	—	—

KM# 342a Series: 50 State Quarters **Subject:** Missouri **Composition:** 0.9000 Silver

Date	Mintage	MS-63	MS-65	Prf-65
2003S	—	—	—	—

Arkansas

KM# 343 Series: 50 State Quarters **Subject:** Arkansas **Composition:** Copper-Nickel Clad Copper

Date	Mintage	MS-63	MS-65	Prf-65
2003P	—	—	—	—
2003D	—	—	—	—
2003S	—	—	—	—

KM# 343a Series: 50 State Quarters **Subject:** Arkansas **Composition:** 0.9000 Silver

Date	Mintage	MS-63	MS-65	Prf-65
2003S	—	—	—	—

HALF DOLLAR

Flowing Hair.

KM# 16 Designer: Robert Scot **Weight:** 13.4800 g. **Composition:** 0.8920 Silver 0.3869 oz. ASW **Size:** 32.5 mm. **Note:** The 1795 "recut date" variety had the date cut into the dies twice, so both sets of numbers are visible on the coin. The 1795 "3 leaves" variety has three leaves under each of the eagle's wings on the reverse.

Date	Mintage	G-4	VG-8	F-12	VF-20	XF-40	MS-60
1794	23,464	1,600	2,700	3,900	7,500	13,500	80,000
1795	299,680	500	725	950	2,200	5,400	20,000
1795 recut date	Inc. above	550	750	1,000	2,500	5,750	22,500
1795 3 leaves	Inc. above	900	1,500	2,000	4,000	10,000	—

Draped Bust. Small eagle.

KM# 26 Designer: Robert Scot **Reverse:** Small eagle **Weight:** 13.4800 g. **Composition:** 0.8920 Silver 0.3869 oz. ASW **Size:** 32.5 mm. **Note:** The 1796 strikes have either 15 or 16 stars on the obverse.

Date	Mintage	G-4	VG-8	F-12	VF-20	XF-40	MS-60
1796 15 stars	3,918	14,500	17,500	23,000	31,500	51,500	100,000
1796 16 stars	Inc. above	15,000	18,000	25,000	35,000	60,000	120,000
1797	Inc. above	14,500	17,500	23,000	32,500	54,000	100,000

1797 Half Dollar
Grade F-12

□ Retail Price

Draped Bust. Heraldic eagle.

KM# 35 Designer: Robert Scot **Reverse:** Heraldic eagle **Weight:** 13.4800 g. **Composition:** 0.8920 Silver 0.3869 oz. ASW **Size:** 32.5 mm. **Note:** The two varieties of the 1803 strikes are distinguished by the size of the 3 in the date. The several varieties of the 1806 strikes are distinguished by the style of 6 in the date, size of the stars on the obverse, and whether the stem of the olive branch held by the reverse eagle extends through the claw.

Date	Mintage	G-4	VG-8	F-12	VF-20	XF-40	MS-60
1801	30,289	225	300	700	1,500	3,800	35,000
1802	29,890	225	300	700	1,500	3,500	40,000
1803 small 3	188,234	150	170	285	450	900	7,500
1803 large 3	Inc. above	125	150	200	350	800	9,000
1805	211,722	125	150	200	380	900	9,000
1805/4	Inc. above	190	250	400	750	1,900	20,000
1806 round-top 6, large stars	839,576	125	150	190	325	700	6,000
1806 round-top 6, small stars	Inc. above	125	140	180	320	700	6,250
1806 knobbed 6, stem not through claw	—	—	35,000	40,000	50,000	65,000	—
1806 pointed-top 6, stem not through claw	Inc. above	115	130	160	290	550	5,000
1806 pointed-top 6, stem through claw	Inc. above	120	150	190	290	600	5,750
1806/5	Inc. above	125	160	210	350	675	6,500
1806 /inverted 6	Inc. above	200	250	475	750	1,750	150,000
1807	301,076	120	150	190	290	600	5,750

Bust. "50 C." below eagle.

KM# 37 Designer: John Reich **Reverse:** "50 C." below eagle **Weight:** 13.4800 g. **Composition:** 0.8920 Silver 0.3869 oz. ASW **Size:** 32.5 mm. **Note:** There are three varieties of the 1807 strikes. Two are distinguished by the size of the stars on the obverse. The third was struck from a reverse die that had a 5 cut over a 2 in the "50C" denomination. Two varieties of the 1811 are distinguished by the size of the 8 in the date. A third has a period between the 8 and second 1 in the date. One variety of the 1817 has a period between the 1 and 7 in the date. Two varieties of the 1819/18 overdate are distinguished by the size of the 9 in the date. Two varieties of the 1820 are distinguished by the size of the date. On the 1823 varieties, the "broken 3" appears to be almost separated in the middle of the 3 in the date; the "patched 3" has the error repaired; the "ugly 3" has portions of its detail missing. The 1827 "curled-2" and "square-2" varieties are distinguished by the numeral's base -- either curled or square. Among the 1828 varieties, "knobbed 2" and "no knob" refers to whether the upper left serif of the digit is rounded. The 1830 varieties are distinguished by the size of the 0 in the date. The four 1834 varieties are distinguished by the sizes of the stars, date and letters in the inscriptions. The 1836 "50/00" variety was struck from a reverse die that had "50" recut over "00" in the denomination.

Date	Mintage	G-4	VG-8	F-12	VF-20	XF-40	AU-50	MS-60	MS-65
1807 small stars	750,500	65.00	90.00	180	475	800	3,500	5,900	35,000
1807 large stars	Inc. above	65.00	90.00	180	475	800	3,500	5,500	—
1807 50/20 C.	Inc. above	45.00	92.50	125	225	475	2,100	4,000	30,000
1807 bearded goddess	—	300	500	900	1,500	2,750	7,500	—	—
1808	1,368,600	41.00	52.50	58.00	95.00	235	600	1,800	15,000
1808/7	Inc. above	41.00	60.00	72.50	130	300	900	1,750	17,500
1809	1,405,810	44.00	52.00	60.00	90.00	190	525	1,600	15,000
1810	1,276,276	42.50	46.00	54.00	75.00	170	475	1,550	13,000
1811 small 8	1,203,644	41.00	50.00	60.00	88.00	135	375	800	7,500
1811 large 8	Inc. above	40.00	46.00	55.00	95.00	150	500	1,000	8,500
1811 dated 18.11	Inc. above	40.00	52.50	80.00	150	290	800	2,100	12,000
1812	1,628,059	40.00	45.00	51.50	65.00	125	330	775	7,500
1812/1 small 8	Inc. above	41.00	52.50	80.00	150	250	700	2,000	12,000
1812/1 large 8	Inc. above	1,000	1,700	2,500	4,250	7,500	15,000	—	—
1813	1,241,903	40.00	46.00	54.00	80.00	150	500	1,250	11,000
1813 50/UNI reverse	1,241,903	41.00	50.00	80.00	125	300	900	1,900	12,000
1814	1,039,075	42.00	50.00	54.00	75.00	165	500	1,350	9,000
1814/3	Inc. above	43.50	60.00	80.00	130	250	850	1,800	12,000
1815/2	47,150	750	1,000	1,475	1,750	3,000	4,750	11,000	50,000
1817	1,215,567	43.50	50.00	55.00	67.50	150	385	900	10,000
1817/3	Inc. above	70.00	115	150	350	800	1,800	3,750	25,000
1817 dated 181.7	Inc. above	43.50	47.00	65.00	100.00	175	650	1,500	10,000
1818	1,960,322	45.00	46.00	53.00	64.00	115	375	900	8,500
1818/7	Inc. above	45.00	50.00	55.00	75.00	150	675	1,500	11,000
1819	2,208,000	40.00	45.00	49.00	60.00	115	375	900	8,500
1819/8 small 9	Inc. above	45.00	50.00	62.00	85.00	185	550	1,300	9,500
1819/8 large 9	Inc. above	45.00	50.00	62.00	85.00	185	550	1,300	9,000
1820 small date	751,122	48.00	55.00	65.00	145	250	650	1,500	12,000
1820 large date	Inc. above	48.00	55.00	65.00	120	225	600	1,350	12,000
1820/19	Inc. above	50.00	58.00	75.00	130	265	900	2,000	15,000
1821	1,305,797	41.00	46.00	53.00	70.00	95.00	525	1,200	9,750
1822	1,559,573	41.00	46.00	50.00	72.50	100.00	300	750	8,000
1822/1	Inc. above	47.50	55.00	72.50	130	235	800	1,750	11,000
1823	1,694,200	41.00	46.00	49.00	58.00	105	300	825	7,500
1823 broken 3	Inc. above	43.50	63.00	90.00	150	300	900	1,750	12,000
1823 patched 3	Inc. above	42.00	53.00	80.00	125	200	750	1,300	10,000
1823 ugly 3	Inc. above	43.50	58.00	83.00	145	235	900	1,700	11,000
1824	3,504,954	40.00	46.00	47.50	57.00	100.00	250	650	7,500
1824/21	Inc. above	41.00	46.00	54.00	65.00	135	400	1,000	7,900
1824 1824/various dates	Inc. above	41.00	45.00	70.00	125	200	750	1,750	12,000
1825	2,943,166	40.00	45.00	49.00	55.00	95.00	240	550	7,000
1826	4,004,180	40.00	45.00	49.00	55.00	195	240	550	7,000
1827 curled 2	5,493,400	40.00	45.00	58.00	85.00	110	325	900	8,500
1827 square 2	Inc. above	40.00	45.00	49.00	55.00	95.00	240	650	7,500
1827/6	Inc. above	40.00	46.00	50.00	72.50	130	375	975	9,000
1828 curled-base 2, no knob	3,075,200	40.00	42.00	49.00	55.00	90.00	240	650	7,000
1828 curled-base 2, knobbed 2	Inc. above	40.00	42.00	49.00	65.00	100.00	250	700	7,250
1828 small 8s, square-base 2, large letters	Inc. above	40.00	42.00	49.00	55.00	90.00	240	550	6,250
1828 small 8s, square-base 2, small letters	Inc. above	45.00	60.00	80.00	125	200	700	1,200	9,500
1828 large 8s, square-base 2	Inc. above	41.00	42.00	49.00	55.00	95.00	325	750	9,000

Date	Mintage	G-4	VG-8	F-12	VF-20	XF-40	AU-50	MS-60	MS-65
1829	3,712,156	40.00	45.00	49.00	55.00	90.00	240	600	9,000
1829/7	Inc. above	41.00	46.00	60.00	85.00	165	330	800	—
1830 small 0 in date	4,764,800	40.00	45.00	49.00	55.00	90.00	240	575	6,500
1830 large 0 in date	Inc. above	40.00	45.00	49.00	55.00	90.00	240	575	6,500
1831	5,873,660	40.00	45.00	49.00	55.00	90.00	240	575	6,500
1832 small letters	4,797,000	40.00	45.00	36.00	55.00	90.00	240	575	6,500
1832 large letters	Inc. above	40.00	45.00	49.00	85.00	145	300	700	7,500
1833	5,206,000	40.00	45.00	49.00	55.00	90.00	240	575	6,500
1834 small date, large stars, small letters	6,412,004	40.00	45.00	49.00	55.00	90.00	240	575	6,500
1834 small date, small stars, small letters	Inc. above	40.00	45.00	49.00	55.00	90.00	240	575	6,500
1834 large date, small letters	Inc. above	40.00	45.00	49.00	55.00	90.00	240	575	6,500
1834 large date, large letters	Inc. above	40.00	45.00	49.00	55.00	90.00	240	575	6,500
1835	5,352,006	40.00	45.00	49.00	55.00	90.00	275	600	9,000
1836	6,545,000	40.00	45.00	49.00	55.00	90.00	240	500	6,500
1836 50/00	Inc. above	55.00	80.00	100.00	185	300	800	1,750	10,000

Bust. "50 Cents" below eagle.

KM# 58 Designer: Christian Gobrecht **Reverse:** "50 Cents" below eagle **Edge:** Reeded. **Weight:** 13.3600 g. **Composition:** 0.9000 Silver 0.3867 oz. ASW **Size:** 30 mm.

Date	Mintage	G-4	VG-8	F-12	VF-20	XF-40	AU-50	MS-60	MS-65
1836	1,200	700	1,000	1,200	1,400	2,100	3,200	6,000	40,000
1837	3,629,820	40.00	45.00	50.00	80.00	135	335	750	12,500

Bust. "Half Dol." below eagle.

KM# 65 Designer: Christian Gobrecht **Reverse:** "Half Dol." below eagle **Weight:** 13.3600 g. **Composition:** 0.9000 Silver 0.3867 oz. ASW **Size:** 30 mm.

Date	Mintage	G-4	VG-8	F-12	VF-20	XF-40	AU-50	MS-60	MS-65
1838	3,546,000	40.00	45.00	50.00	80.00	140	475	825	17,000
1838O proof only	Est. 20	—	—	—	—	52,500	80,000	95,000	20,000
1839	1,392,976	40.00	45.00	54.00	80.00	140	365	990	30,000
1839O	178,976	130	165	1,230	280	640	1,200	2,500	45,000

Seated Liberty.

KM# 68 Designer: Christian Gobrecht **Weight:** 13.3600 g. **Composition:** 0.9000 Silver .3867 oz. ASW **Size:** 30.6 mm. **Note:** The 1839 varieties are distinguished by whether there's drapery extending from Liberty's left elbow. One variety of the 1840 strikes has smaller lettering; another used the old reverse of 1838. Varieties of 1842 and 1846 are distinguished by the size of the numerals in the date.

Date	Mintage	G-4	VG-8	F-12	VF-20	XF-40	AU-50	MS-60	MS-65
1839 no drapery from elbow	Inc. above	38.00	65.00	110	315	725	1,650	4,500	150,000
1839 drapery	Inc. above	20.00	30.00	50.00	75.00	145	265	450	—
1840 small letters	1,435,008	23.00	32.00	47.50	67.00	110	350	575	8,250
1840 reverse 1838	Inc. above	115	150	225	300	550	1,100	2,900	12,000
1840O	855,100	23.00	28.00	45.00	80.00	100.00	200	430	—
1841	310,000	39.00	49.00	80.00	130	200	280	1,100	5,700
1841O	401,000	19.00	28.00	44.00	75.00	110	200	550	5,900
1842 small date	2,012,764	35.00	42.00	60.00	95.00	165	325	1,300	12,000
1842 large date	Inc. above	18.00	28.00	43.00	52.00	85.00	160	1,250	12,000
1842O small date	957,000	600	800	1,400	2,250	4,000	—	—	—
1842O large date	Inc. above	22.00	29.00	48.00	115	225	750	1,750	—
1843	3,844,000	17.00	28.00	43.00	52.00	85.00	180	350	4,500
1843O	2,268,000	17.00	28.00	43.00	60.00	95.00	250	550	—
1844	1,766,000	17.00	28.00	43.00	52.00	85.00	180	350	4,500
1844O	2,005,000	18.00	28.00	43.00	52.00	80.00	195	525	—
1844/1844O	Inc. above	425	650	1,000	1,375	2,300	4,900	—	—
1845	589,000	30.00	40.00	50.00	90.00	170	340	900	—
1845O	2,094,000	18.00	28.00	43.00	52.00	110	240	550	—
1845O no drapery	Inc. above	25.00	35.00	65.00	115	185	375	750	—
1846 medium date	2,210,000	18.00	28.00	43.00	52.00	80.00	175	500	9,000
1846 tall date	Inc. above	22.00	30.00	60.00	85.00	145	250	650	12,000
1846 /horizontal 6	Inc. above	140	215	285	375	550	1,000	2,500	—
1846O medium date	2,304,000	18.00	28.00	43.00	52.00	100.00	225	550	12,000
1846O tall date	Inc. above	135	245	325	575	950	2,000	3,600	—
1847/1846	1,156,000	2,000	2,750	3,200	4,250	6,500	—	—	—
1847	Inc. above	20.00	30.00	45.00	60.00	95.00	190	480	9,000
1847O	2,584,000	18.00	28.00	43.00	52.00	95.00	250	640	7,000
1848	580,000	35.00	55.00	75.00	150	240	475	1,000	9,000
1848O	3,180,000	18.00	28.00	43.00	52.00	95.00	285	750	9,000
1849	1,252,000	26.00	40.00	55.00	90.00	150	365	1,250	9,000
1849O	2,310,000	17.00	28.00	43.00	60.00	115	250	650	9,000
1850	227,000	250	300	340	400	575	875	1,500	—
1850O	2,456,000	20.00	28.00	45.00	65.00	125	250	650	9,000
1851	200,750	500	600	750	900	1,000	1,350	1,950	—
1851O	402,000	37.00	45.00	75.00	105	175	300	675	9,000
1852	77,130	300	375	525	700	875	1,150	1,450	—
1852O	144,000	100.00	125	200	350	525	1,050	1,850	—
1853O mintage unrecorded	—	—	—	—	—	—	—	—	—

Note: 1853O, Eliasberg Sale, 1997, VG-8, $154,000.

Seated Liberty. Arrows at date. Rays around eagle.

KM# 79 Designer: Christian Gobrecht **Obverse:** Arrows at date **Reverse:** Rays around eagle **Weight:** 12.4400 g. **Composition:** 0.9000 Silver 0.3600 oz. ASW

Date	Mintage	G-4	VG-8	F-12	VF-20	XF-40	AU-50	MS-60	MS-65	Prf-65
1853	3,532,708	17.00	27.00	40.00	90.00	250	505	1,700	21,500	—
1853O	1,328,000	21.00	32.00	50.00	125	290	700	2,100	21,500	—

Seated Liberty. Rays around eagle removed.

KM# 82 Designer: Christian Gobrecht **Reverse:** Rays around eagle removed **Weight:** 12.4400 g. **Composition:** 0.9000 Silver 0.3600 oz. ASW

Date	Mintage	G-4	VG-8	F-12	VF-20	XF-40	AU-50	MS-60	MS-65	Prf-65
1854	2,982,000	17.00	28.00	43.00	55.00	100.00	270	675	8,000	—
1854O	5,240,000	17.00	28.00	43.00	55.00	100.00	270	600	8,000	—

1855-S Half Dollar
Grade XF-40

| Retail Price |

Date	Mintage	G-4	VG-8	F-12	VF-20	XF-40	AU-50	MS-60	MS-65	Prf-65
1855	759,500	23.00	33.00	45.00	65.00	150	325	1,200	8,000	22,500
1855/4	Inc. above	35.00	60.00	80.00	125	225	400	1,500	—	—
1855O	3,688,000	17.00	28.00	43.00	55.00	100.00	270	650	8,000	—
1855S	129,950	220	325	600	1,300	2,400	6,000	—	—	—

Seated Liberty. Arrows at date removed.

KM# A68   Designer: Christian Gobrecht **Obverse:** Arrows at date removed **Weight:** 12.4400 g. **Composition:** 0.9000 Silver 0.3600 oz. ASW

Date	Mintage	G-4	VG-8	F-12	VF-20	XF-40	AU-50	MS-60	MS-65	Prf-65
1856	938,000	19.00	31.00	43.00	55.00	90.00	195	425	6,500	12,500
1856O	2,658,000	17.00	28.00	43.00	52.00	90.00	190	385	12,500	—
1856S	211,000	85.00	120	160	260	475	1,250	3,500	19,000	—
1857	1,988,000	17.00	28.00	43.00	52.00	90.00	190	385	5,150	12,500
1857O	818,000	21.00	31.00	43.00	65.00	110	250	885	12,500	—
1857S	158,000	100.00	120	145	285	575	975	3,500	19,000	—
1858	4,226,000	17.00	28.00	43.00	52.00	90.00	190	385	6,500	12,500
1858O	7,294,000	17.00	28.00	43.00	52.00	90.00	190	385	12,500	—
1858S	476,000	20.00	30.00	48.00	90.00	175	400	950	12,500	—
1859	748,000	17.00	28.00	43.00	60.00	110	200	650	6,600	5,500
1859O	2,834,000	17.00	28.00	43.00	50.00	90.00	190	450	6,500	—
1859S	566,000	20.00	38.00	55.00	85.00	215	375	750	12,500	—
1860	303,700	25.00	35.00	47.50	75.00	90.00	350	1,000	6,500	5,500
1860O	1,290,000	17.00	28.00	43.00	52.00	90.00	190	450	5,150	—
1860S	472,000	20.00	30.00	50.00	75.00	130	245	850	12,500	—
1861	2,888,400	17.00	28.00	43.00	52.00	90.00	190	440	5,150	5,500
1861O	2,532,633	18.00	29.00	43.00	60.00	90.00	190	450	5,150	—
1861S	939,500	18.00	29.00	44.00	60.00	100.00	195	975	9,500	—
1862	253,550	28.00	40.00	55.00	95.00	175	285	750	5,150	5,500
1862S	1,352,000	18.00	29.00	43.00	60.00	90.00	195	460	9,000	—
1863	503,660	20.00	32.00	43.00	75.00	130	250	750	5,150	5,500
1863S	916,000	18.00	29.00	43.00	55.00	90.00	195	460	9,000	—
1864	379,570	29.00	35.00	55.00	85.00	160	250	750	5,150	5,500

Date	Mintage	G-4	VG-8	F-12	VF-20	XF-40	AU-50	MS-60	MS-65	Prf-65
1864S	658,000	18.00	28.00	45.00	60.00	115	215	675	9,000	—
1865	511,900	25.00	32.00	49.00	80.00	125	260	750	5,150	5,500
1865S	675,000	18.00	29.00	43.00	55.00	90.00	235	500	9,000	—
1866 proof, unique	—	—	—	—	—	—	—	—	—	—
1866S	60,000	80.00	120	170	325	795	1,500	5,000	—	—

Seated Liberty. "In God We Trust" above eagle.

KM# 99 Designer: Christian Gobrecht **Reverse:** "In God We Trust" above eagle **Weight:** 12.4400 g. **Composition:** 0.9000 Silver 0.3600 oz. ASW **Note:** In 1866 the motto "In God We Trust" was added to the reverse. The "closed-3" and "open-3" varieties are distinguished by the amount of space between the upper and lower left serifs of the 3.

Date	Mintage	G-4	VG-8	F-12	VF-20	XF-40	AU-50	MS-60	MS-65	Prf-65
1866	745,625	18.00	27.00	45.00	65.00	90.00	185	350	4,800	3,750
1866S	994,000	19.00	29.00	45.00	60.00	95.00	275	650	5,000	—
1867	449,925	25.00	35.00	55.00	90.00	145	240	350	4,800	3,750
1867S	1,196,000	19.00	29.00	40.00	55.00	75.00	235	350	7,000	—
1868	418,200	35.00	49.00	80.00	135	225	300	525	7,100	3,750
1868S	1,160,000	19.00	29.00	41.00	55.00	105	250	350	7,000	—
1869	795,900	19.00	29.00	41,055	45.00	185	160	385	4,600	3,750
1869S	656,000	20.00	29.00	41.00	55.00	100.00	265	600	7,000	—
1870	634,900	21.00	31.00	42.00	65.00	100.00	185	475	7,000	3,750
1870CC	54,617	500	800	1,450	2,750	10,000	—	—	—	—
1870S	1,004,000	19.00	31.00	45.00	70.00	110	275	575	7,000	—
1871	1,204,560	18.00	29.00	41.00	55.00	75.00	165	350	7,000	3,750
1871CC	153,950	200	325	600	1,150	1,800	10,000	15,000	—	—
1871S	2,178,000	18.00	29.00	41.00	55.00	165	155	400	7,000	—
1872	881,550	18.00	29.00	40.00	55.00	80.00	165	430	2,850	3,750
1872CC	272,000	100.00	175	300	600	1,500	4,000	8,000	50,000	—
1872S	580,000	24.00	31.00	55.00	90.00	170	375	975	7,000	—
1873 closed 3	801,800	23.00	30.00	50.00	90.00	125	250	500	4,500	3,750
1873 open 3	Inc. above	2,200	2,700	4,100	5,500	7,500	—	—	—	—
1873CC	122,500	150	230	350	625	1,500	2,500	4,100	9,000	3,750
1873S no arrows	5,000	—	—	—	—	—	—	—	—	—

Note: 1873S no arrows, no specimens known to survive.

Seated Liberty. Arrows at date.

KM# 107 Designer: Christian Gobrecht **Obverse:** Arrows at date **Weight:** 12.5000 g. **Composition:** 0.9000 Silver 0.3618 oz. ASW

Date	Mintage	G-4	VG-8	F-12	VF-20	XF-40	AU-50	MS-60	MS-65	Prf-65
1873	1,815,700	18.00	27.00	40.00	85.00	210	400	850	17,500	9,000
1873CC	214,560	115	220	335	725	1,700	2,400	5,700	42,000	—
1873S	233,000	42.50	62.50	100.00	200	375	675	2,200	40,000	—
1874	2,360,300	18.00	27.00	40.00	85.00	210	400	850	12,750	9,000
1874CC	59,000	350	450	750	1,250	2,000	4,000	8,000	—	—
1874S	394,000	30.00	40.00	70.00	160	315	600	1,600	—	—

Seated Liberty. Arrows at date removed.

KM# A99 **Designer:** Christian Gobrecht **Obverse:** Arrows at date removed **Weight:** 12.5000 g. **Composition:** 0.9000 Silver 0.3618 oz. ASW

Date	Mintage	G-4	VG-8	F-12	VF-20	XF-40	AU-50	MS-60	MS-65	Prf-65
1875	6,027,500	17.00	25.00	39.00	47.00	70.00	160	425	3,500	3,200
1875CC	1,008,000	20.00	34.00	53.00	95.00	185	300	540	5,450	—
1875S	3,200,000	17.00	26.00	40.00	47.00	80.00	165	340	2,700	—
1876	8,419,150	17.00	25.00	39.00	45.00	70.00	160	340	5,300	3,200
1876CC	1,956,000	18.00	30.00	48.00	85.00	175	275	560	4,200	—
1876S	4,528,000	17.00	25.00	39.00	45.00	70.00	160	340	2,700	—
1877	8,304,510	17.00	25.00	39.00	45.00	70.00	160	340	2,700	3,750
1877CC	1,420,000	18.00	33.00	43.00	75.00	145	275	630	3,250	—
1877S	5,356,000	17.00	25.00	39.00	45.00	70.00	160	340	2,700	—
1878	1,378,400	20.00	28.00	36.00	55.00	115	170	425	3,650	3,200
1878CC	62,000	320	450	625	1,250	2,750	4,400	6,750	42,500	—
1878S	12,000	15,000	17,500	22,000	27,500	33,000	40,000	52,500	125,000	—
1879	5,900	215	245	290	350	400	475	700	2,900	3,250
1880	9,755	190	210	240	310	375	475	700	2,900	3,250
1881	10,975	180	195	240	300	365	465	700	2,900	3,250
1882	5,500	275	300	330	400	470	550	850	3,600	3,250
1883	9,039	210	235	260	290	375	475	750	2,900	3,250
1884	5,275	275	300	365	425	475	550	800	2,900	3,250
1885	6,130	245	265	300	360	435	525	800	2,900	3,250
1886	5,886	300	345	410	450	495	600	850	4,800	3,250
1887	5,710	365	420	475	550	650	750	900	2,900	3,250
1888	12,833	200	215	260	300	390	450	700	2,900	3,250
1889	12,711	185	210	240	310	375	425	700	2,900	3,250
1890	12,590	190	210	245	310	385	450	700	3,250	3,250
1891	200,600	50.00	60.00	70.00	100.00	140	290	500	3,250	3,250

1878-S Half Dollar
Grade F-12

□ Retail Price

Barber.

Mint mark

KM# 116 Designer: Charles E. Barber **Weight:** 12.5000 g. **Composition:** 0.9000 Silver 0.3618 oz. ASW **Size:** 30.6 mm.

Date	Mintage	G-4	VG-8	F-12	VF-20	XF-40	AU-50	MS-60	MS-65	Prf-65
1892	935,245	25.00	34.00	50.00	90.00	175	280	400	2,750	3,300
1892O	390,000	215	275	335	375	425	450	850	4,200	—
1892 micro o	—	1,500	3,450	4,250	5,750	9,500	16,500	—	55,000	—
1892S	1,029,028	185	275	300	335	375	600	900	5,000	—
1893	1,826,792	14.50	21.50	54.00	85.00	160	310	510	4,000	3,300
1893O	1,389,000	23.00	42.00	75.00	120	275	370	540	8,500	—
1893S	740,000	110	135	200	330	420	540	1,200	26,500	—
1894	1,148,972	19.00	36.00	75.00	100.00	220	350	485	3,000	3,300
1894O	2,138,000	14.50	24.00	65.00	95.00	230	300	510	6,250	—
1894S	4,048,690	15.00	21.50	50.00	72.00	200	330	440	11,000	—
1895	1,835,218	11.50	16.00	52.00	80.00	180	310	570	3,300	3,300
1895O	1,766,000	14.00	23.00	57.50	95.00	230	360	560	7,000	—
1895S	1,108,086	30.00	45.00	80.00	130	275	360	550	7,700	—
1896	950,762	18.00	23.00	60.00	95.00	230	325	540	6,000	3,400
1896O	924,000	25.00	36.00	110	150	365	630	1,200	11,500	—
1896S	1,140,948	70.00	95.00	125	210	375	550	1,200	11,000	—
1897	2,480,731	10.00	12.00	33.50	77.00	135	310	440	3,800	3,300
1897O	632,000	70.00	145	350	680	900	1,200	1,600	6,500	—
1897S	933,900	125	150	270	420	700	1,000	1,350	9,300	—
1898	2,956,735	9.00	11.50	29.00	72.00	135	310	420	3,400	3,300
1898O	874,000	20.00	55.00	145	250	400	500	1,000	10,000	—
1898S	2,358,550	12.00	20.00	42.00	83.00	200	350	840	8,000	—
1899	5,538,846	9.00	11.50	29.00	72.00	135	300	420	4,250	3,900
1899O	1,724,000	10.00	14.50	50.00	92.50	230	360	630	6,900	—
1899S	1,686,411	14.00	23.00	50.00	85.00	190	340	635	6,000	—
1900	4,762,912	9.00	11.50	27.50	72.00	135	300	400	3,300	3,300
1900O	2,744,000	9.00	14.00	40.00	90.00	250	310	840	15,500	—
1900S	2,560,322	10.00	14.00	42.00	95.00	190	300	625	11,000	—
1901	4,268,813	9.00	11.00	27.50	65.00	135	285	400	4,250	3,500
1901O	1,124,000	11.00	18.00	54.00	115	285	450	1,300	12,000	—
1901S	847,044	19.00	36.00	115	240	550	920	1,500	18,500	—
1902	4,922,777	9.00	11.00	25.00	65.00	135	280	400	4,200	3,700
1902O	2,526,000	10.00	13.00	40.00	80.00	190	350	700	7,200	—
1902S	1,460,670	11.00	18.00	50.00	90.00	200	360	635	5,750	—
1903	2,278,755	9.00	13.00	40.00	78.00	185	325	450	8,400	3,825
1903O	2,100,000	9.00	12.50	42.00	80.00	200	330	650	9,500	—
1903S	1,920,772	9.00	12.50	42.00	78.00	215	365	590	4,800	—
1904	2,992,670	9.00	11.00	28.50	65.00	135	300	420	5,500	4,100
1904O	1,117,600	11.50	19.00	55.00	115	310	500	1,100	12,900	—
1904S	553,038	20.00	36.00	150	370	690	1,250	3,000	32,000	—
1905	662,727	12.50	18.00	57.50	84.00	220	330	550	6,700	3,900
1905O	505,000	18.00	30.00	85.00	150	260	420	730	5,200	—
1905S	2,494,000	9.00	11.00	40.00	78.00	190	345	620	9,500	—
1906	2,638,675	8.50	9.25	24.00	65.00	135	285	400	3,000	3,300
1906D	4,028,000	8.50	9.50	27.50	72.00	140	300	430	4,250	—
1906O	2,446,000	8.50	9.25	36.00	78.00	160	310	600	5,500	—
1906S	1,740,154	10.00	14.00	44.00	80.00	190	300	585	5,250	—
1907	2,598,575	8.50	9.25	24.00	65.00	135	300	400	3,000	4,000
1907D	3,856,000	8.50	9.50	26.00	65.00	135	300	400	3,000	—
1907O	3,946,000	8.50	9.50	27.50	72.00	150	310	570	3,300	—
1907S	1,250,000	10.00	14.00	62.50	105	310	625	1,250	13,000	—
1908	1,354,545	9.00	10.00	26.00	72.00	135	280	400	3,000	4,000
1908D	3,280,000	8.50	9.25	26.00	72.00	145	310	530	3,000	—
1908O	5,360,000	8.50	9.25	26.00	72.00	145	310	530	3,000	—
1908S	1,644,828	9.00	13.00	47.00	80.00	210	340	765	5,500	—
1909	2,368,650	8.50	9.25	24.00	65.00	135	280	400	3,000	4,000
1909O	925,400	10.00	13.00	42.00	84.00	260	480	750	4,500	—
1909S	1,764,000	8.50	10.00	30.00	78.00	180	340	570	3,800	—
1910	418,551	11.00	20.00	68.00	115	260	400	600	3,300	4,250
1910S	1,948,000	8.50	11.50	27.50	72.00	180	330	630	5,000	—
1911	1,406,543	8.50	9.25	26.00	65.00	135	300	410	3,000	3,300
1911D	695,080	10.00	13.00	35.00	72.00	190	280	545	3,000	—
1911S	1,272,000	9.00	10.00	32.50	78.00	160	320	560	5,600	—
1912	1,550,700	8.50	9.00	24.00	65.00	135	280	400	3,100	4,000
1912D	2,300,800	8.50	9.00	24.00	65.00	135	310	430	3,000	—
1912S	1,370,000	9.00	9.00	30.00	72.00	160	320	520	5,750	—
1913	188,627	23.00	34.00	115	185	360	670	925	4,100	3,800

Date	Mintage	G-4	VG-8	F-12	VF-20	XF-40	AU-50	MS-60	MS-65	Prf-65
1913D	534,000	10.00	13.00	32.00	72.00	190	295	450	5,200	—
1913S	604,000	12.00	15.00	42.00	85.00	190	350	600	4,200	—
1914	124,610	40.00	55.00	175	330	500	750	950	7,500	4,300
1914S	992,000	9.00	10.00	32.50	72.00	180	300	550	3,800	—
1915	138,450	30.00	35.00	95.00	200	375	660	1,000	5,350	4,250
1915D	1,170,400	8.50	9.25	24.00	65.00	135	280	400	3,000	—
1915S	1,604,000	8.75	9.25	26.00	65.00	135	280	400	3,000	—

Walking Liberty.

Obverse
mint mark

Reverse
mint mark

KM# 142 Designer: Adolph A. Weinman **Weight:** 12.5000 g. **Composition:** 0.9000 Silver 0.3618 oz. ASW **Size:** 30.6 mm. **Note:** The mint mark appears on the obverse below the word "Trust" on 1916 and some 1917 issues. Starting with some 1917 issues and continuing through the remainder of the series, the mint mark was changed to the reverse, at about the 8 o'clock position near the rim.

Date	Mintage	G-4	VG-8	F-12	VF-20	XF-40	AU-50	MS-60	MS-65	Prf-65
1916	608,000	32.50	37.00	57.00	115	145	215	270	1,425	—
1916D	1,014,400	25.00	29.00	44.00	80.00	135	200	275	1,750	—
1916S	508,000	110	120	145	330	485	670	950	4,400	—
1917D obv.	765,400	16.00	23.00	44.00	95.00	130	230	500	5,900	—
1917S obv.	952,000	19.00	31.00	57.00	265	655	1,125	2,100	16,000	—
1917	12,292,000	3.75	5.00	8.75	17.00	33.00	60.00	120	775	—
1917D rev.	1,940,000	10.00	16.00	16.00	90.00	200	485	750	15,000	—
1917S rev.	5,554,000	4.50	8.00	14.50	29.00	48.00	140	315	10,500	—
1918	6,634,000	4.50	6.25	16.00	50.00	125	245	525	3,250	—
1918D	3,853,040	5.75	8.50	20.00	58.00	145	350	900	21,000	—
1918S	10,282,000	4.50	5.75	14.50	28.00	55.00	150	470	15,500	—
1919	962,000	18.50	24.00	42.00	160	390	670	1,000	4,700	—
1919D	1,165,000	14.50	18.50	50.00	160	550	925	3,400	100,000	—
1919S	1,552,000	15.50	20.00	33.50	160	700	1,500	2,650	13,500	—
1920	6,372,000	4.50	5.00	11.00	27.50	60.00	95.00	300	5,000	—
1920D	1,551,000	10.00	12.00	30.00	135	350	750	1,200	10,000	—
1920S	4,624,000	5.00	8.00	15.00	55.00	210	400	750	11,500	—
1921	246,000	115	150	200	575	1,350	2,350	3,200	12,000	—
1921D	208,000	160	210	290	675	2,000	2,750	3,400	15,500	—
1921S	548,000	29.00	31.50	110	600	4,000	7,500	11,000	60,000	—
1923S	2,178,000	8.50	11.50	22.00	65.00	210	625	1,250	12,500	—
1927S	2,392,000	4.50	5.75	11.00	31.50	95.00	300	800	8,200	—
1928S	1,940,000	4.00	5.75	12.00	38.00	95.00	315	800	8,500	—
1929D	1,001,200	6.25	9.00	12.50	21.50	67.00	160	340	2,300	—
1929S	1,902,000	4.50	6.25	10.00	21.00	75.00	180	340	2,200	—
1933S	1,786,000	6.50	9.00	11.00	15.00	45.00	215	550	3,000	—
1934	6,964,000	3.25	3.50	3.75	4.00	8.00	25.00	65.00	390	—
1934D	2,361,400	4.58	5.50	6.00	7.50	25.00	85.00	180	850	—
1934S	3,652,000	3.75	4.00	4.25	5.00	25.00	105	350	3,400	—
1935	9,162,000	3.25	3.50	3.75	4.50	5.50	22.00	44.00	350	—
1935D	3,003,800	3.75	4.00	4.25	6.00	22.50	53.00	140	1,525	—
1935S	3,854,000	3.25	3.50	3.75	4.50	23.00	100.00	280	1,850	—
1936	12,617,901	3.25	3.50	3.75	4.00	5.50	22.00	40.00	145	5,000
1936D	4,252,400	3.25	3.50	4.00	4.50	16.00	42.00	80.00	360	—
1936S	3,884,000	3.25	3.50	4.00	5.00	19.00	60.00	130	540	—
1937	9,527,728	3.25	3.50	3.75	4.50	6.00	22.00	38.00	180	1,250
1937D	1,676,000	5.00	5.25	5.50	8.50	26.50	105	205	490	—
1937S	2,090,000	3.50	4.00	4.50	6.00	17.00	65.00	155	430	—
1938	4,118,152	4.00	4.25	4.50	5.50	9.00	37.00	70.00	340	925
1938D	491,600	30.00	32.50	38.50	40.00	95.00	240	400	950	—
1939	6,820,808	3.25	3.50	3.75	4.00	5.50	22.00	40.00	135	845
1939D	4,267,800	3.25	3.50	3.75	4.00	7.00	23.00	47.00	155	—
1939S	2,552,000	4.00	4.25	5.25	6.50	13.00	51.00	110	175	—
1940	9,167,279	3.25	3.50	3.75	4.00	4.75	11.00	27.00	145	725
1940S	4,550,000	3.30	3.60	3.85	4.00	5.25	16.50	39.00	390	—
1941	24,207,412	3.25	3.50	3.75	4.00	4.25	11.00	30.00	115	675
1941D	11,248,400	3.25	3.50	3.75	4.00	4.70	14.50	37.00	165	—
1941S	8,098,000	3.25	3.50	3.75	4.20	5.75	26.00	72.00	1,100	—
1942	47,839,120	3.25	3.50	3.75	4.00	4.25	11.00	32.50	115	675
1942D	10,973,800	3.25	3.50	3.75	4.00	4.70	16.00	37.00	265	—
1942S	12,708,000	3.25	3.50	3.75	4.00	5.00	16.00	37.00	625	—
1943	53,190,000	3.25	3.50	3.75	4.25	4.50	11.00	32.50	110	—
1943D	11,346,000	3.25	3.50	3.75	4.00	4.70	20.00	40.00	270	—
1943S	13,450,000	3.25	3.50	3.75	4.00	4.70	18.00	40.00	400	—
1944	28,206,000	3.25	3.50	3.75	4.00	4.25	11.00	32.50	160	—
1944D	9,769,000	3.25	3.50	3.75	4.00	4.70	16.00	34.00	135	—

1923-S Half Dollar
Grade XF-40

☐ Retail Price

Date	Mintage	G-4	VG-8	F-12	VF-20	XF-40	AU-50	MS-60	MS-65	Prf-65
1944S	8,904,000	3.25	3.50	3.75	4.10	4.75	16.00	38.50	600	—
1945	31,502,000	3.25	3.50	3.75	4.00	4.25	11.00	31.50	135	—
1945D	9,966,800	3.25	3.50	3.75	4.00	4.75	15.00	32.50	135	—
1945S	10,156,000	3.25	3.50	3.75	4.00	5.00	15.00	33.00	175	—
1946	12,118,000	3.25	3.50	3.75	4.00	4.75	11.00	31.00	220	—
1946D	2,151,000	3.75	4.50	5.50	6.50	9.50	19.00	38.00	95.00	—
1946S	3,724,000	3.25	3.50	3.75	4.00	5.50	16.00	32.50	135	—
1947	4,094,000	3.25	3.50	3.75	4.00	7.25	18.00	38.00	210	—
1947D	3,900,600	3.25	3.50	3.75	4.00	7.00	20.00	38.00	135	—

Franklin.

Mint mark

KM# 199 Designer: John R. Sinnock **Weight:** 12.5000 g. **Composition:** 0.9000 Silver 0.3618 oz. ASW **Size:** 30.6 mm.

Date	Mintage	G-4	VG-8	F-12	VF-20	XF-40	AU-50	MS-60	MS-65	-65FBL	-65CAM
1948	3,006,814	—	3.00	4.00	4.25	4.50	6.00	13.75	90.00	315	—
1948D	4,028,600	—	3.00	3.25	3.50	3.75	5.00	10.00	195	325	—
1949	5,614,000	—	3.00	3.25	3.50	4.00	10.00	28.00	150	290	—
1949D	4,120,600	—	3.00	3.50	3.75	4.00	13.00	29.00	1,050	2,350	—
1949S	3,744,000	—	3.50	4.00	6.25	8.00	21.00	48.00	210	775	—
1950	7,793,509	—	—	3.00	3.50	6.00	7.00	20.00	150	350	3,700
1950D	8,031,600	—	—	3.00	3.50	6.50	7.75	16.00	575	1,150	—
1951	16,859,602	—	—	3.00	3.50	4.00	4.50	9.00	95.00	375	2,200
1951D	9,475,200	—	—	3.00	4.25	5.00	11.50	15.00	300	550	—
1951S	13,696,000	—	—	2.75	3.00	3.50	10.00	18.00	125	775	—
1952	21,274,073	—	—	2.50	2.75	3.00	4.00	7.00	90.00	325	1,100
1952D	25,395,600	—	—	2.50	2.75	3.00	4.00	8.50	250	450	—
1952S	5,526,000	—	—	2.50	3.25	3.75	17.00	38.00	135	1,100	—
1953	2,796,920	3.00	3.00	3.25	3.50	5.00	10.00	14.00	275	1,100	475
1953D	20,900,400	—	—	2.25	3.50	4.00	4.25	7.00	250	400	—
1953S	4,148,000	—	—	2.60	4.25	4.75	8.50	17.00	70.00	9,000	—
1954	13,421,503	—	—	2.25	3.50	3.75	4.00	5.50	85.00	275	250
1954D	25,445,580	—	—	2.25	3.25	3.50	4.00	5.50	165	250	—

1953 Half Dollar
Grade MS-60

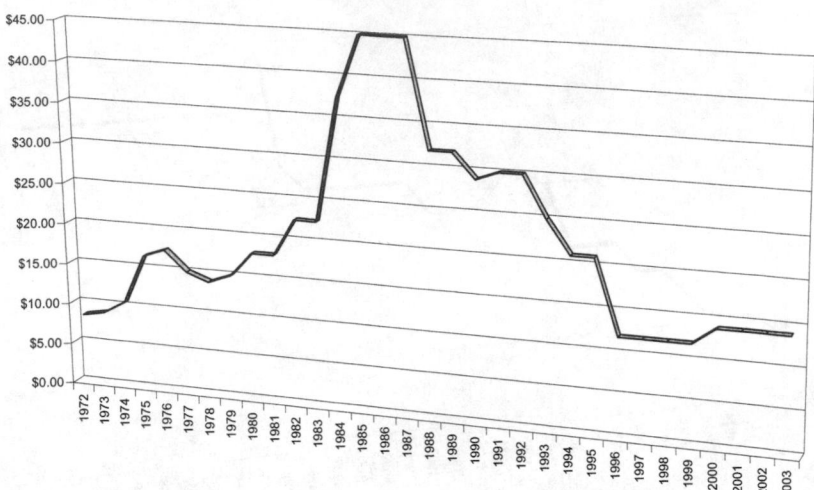

Date	Mintage	G-4	VG-8	F-12	VF-20	XF-40	AU-50	MS-60	MS-65	-65FBL	-65CAM
1954S	4,993,400	—	—	2.25	3.75	4.00	4.25	8.50	60.00	425	—
1955	2,876,381	5.00	5.00	5.25	5.50	5.75	6.00	8.00	75.00	160	195
1956	4,701,384	—	—	2.50	3.00	3.50	4.25	5.00	50.00	120	75.00
1957	6,361,952	—	—	2.50	2.75	3.00	3.75	6.00	50.00	120	135
1957D	19,966,850	—	—	—	2.10	2.25	2.50	5.00	50.00	105	—
1958	4,917,652	—	—	2.25	2.50	2.75	3.00	5.00	50.00	135	250
1958D	23,962,412	—	—	—	2.25	2.50	2.75	4.25	50.00	105	—
1959	7,349,291	—	—	—	2.25	2.50	2.75	4.50	150	295	475
1959D	13,053,750	—	—	—	2.25	2.50	2.75	5.00	150	275	—
1960	7,715,602	—	—	—	2.25	2.50	2.75	4.25	175	400	75.00
1960D	18,215,812	—	—	—	2.25	2.50	2.75	4.50	750	1,450	—
1961	11,318,244	—	—	—	2.25	2.50	2.75	4.25	275	1,900	75.00
1961D	20,276,442	—	—	—	2.25	2.50	2.75	4.50	450	1,050	—
1962	12,932,019	—	—	—	2.25	2.50	2.75	4.25	290	2,600	50.00
1962D	35,473,281	—	—	—	2.25	2.50	2.75	4.25	400	1,000	—
1963	25,239,645	—	—	—	—	2.50	2.75	4.00	90.00	975	50.00
1963D	67,069,292	—	—	—	—	2.50	2.75	4.00	90.00	250	—

Retail Price

Kennedy.

Mint mark 1964

KM# 202 Obv. Designer: Gilroy Roberts **Rev. Designer:** Frank Gasparro **Weight:** 12.5000 g. **Composition:** 0.9000 Silver 0.3618 oz. ASW **Size:** 30.6 mm.

Date	Mintage	G-4	VG-8	F-12	VF-20	XF-40	MS-60	MS-65	Prf-65
1964	277,254,766	—	—	—	—	—	3.00	9.00	10.00
1964D	156,205,446	—	—	—	—	—	3.50	12.00	—

Kennedy.

Mint mark
1968 - Present

KM# 202a Obv. Designer: Gilroy Roberts **Rev. Designer:** Frank Gasparro **Weight:** 11.5000 g. **Composition:** 0.4000 Silver 0.1480 oz. ASW **Size:** 30.6 mm.

Date	Mintage	G-4	VG-8	F-12	VF-20	XF-40	MS-60	MS-65	Prf-65
1965	65,879,366	—	—	—	—	—	1.25	9.50	—
1966	108,984,932	—	—	—	—	—	1.40	11.00	—
1967	295,046,978	—	—	—	—	—	1.50	9.50	—
1968D	246,951,930	—	—	—	—	—	1.25	9.00	—
1968S	3,041,506	—	—	—	—	—	—	—	5.00
1969D	129,881,800	—	—	—	—	—	1.25	7.50	—
1969S	2,934,631	—	—	—	—	—	—	—	5.00
1970D	2,150,000	—	—	—	—	—	16.00	32.00	—
1970S	2,632,810	—	—	—	—	—	—	—	10.00

Kennedy.

KM# 202b Obv. Designer: Gilroy Roberts **Rev. Designer:** Frank Gasparro **Weight:** 11.3400 g. **Composition:** Copper-Nickel Clad Copper **Size:** 30.6 mm.

Date	Mintage	G-4	VG-8	F-12	VF-20	XF-40	MS-60	MS-65	Prf-65
1971	155,640,000	—	—	—	—	—	1.50	12.00	—
1971D	302,097,424	—	—	—	—	—	1.00	5.00	—
1971S	3,244,183	—	—	—	—	—	—	—	3.00
1972	153,180,000	—	—	—	—	—	1.00	9.00	—
1972D	141,890,000	—	—	—	—	—	1.00	6.00	—
1972S	3,267,667	—	—	—	—	—	—	—	2.50
1973	64,964,000	—	—	—	—	—	1.00	6.00	—
1973D	83,171,400	—	—	—	—	—	—	5.50	—
1973S	2,769,624	—	—	—	—	—	—	—	2.50
1974	201,596,000	—	—	—	—	—	1.00	5.00	—
1974D	79,066,300	—	—	—	—	—	1.00	6.00	—
1974S	2,617,350	—	—	—	—	—	—	—	3.00
1975		—	—	—	—	—	—	—	—
1975D none minted		—	—	—	—	—	—	—	—
1975S none minted		—	—	—	—	—	—	—	—

Kennedy. Bicentennial design, Independence Hall.

KM# 205 Rev. Designer: Seth Huntington **Reverse:** Bicentennial design, Independence Hall **Composition:** Copper-Nickel Clad Copper

Date	Mintage	G-4	VG-8	F-12	VF-20	XF-40	MS-60	MS-65	Prf-65
1976	234,308,000	—	—	—	—	—	1.00	10.00	—
1976D	287,565,248	—	—	—	—	—	1.00	4.50	—
1976S	7,059,099	—	—	—	—	—	—	—	2.00

Kennedy. Bicentennial design, Independence Hall.

KM# 205a Rev. Designer: Seth Huntington **Reverse:** Bicentennial design, Independence Hall **Weight:** 11.5000 g. **Composition:** 0.4000 Silver 0.1480 oz. ASW

Date	Mintage	G-4	VG-8	F-12	VF-20	XF-40	MS-60	MS-65	Prf-65
1976S	4,908,319								
	3,998,621	—	—	—	—	—	—	6.50	5.00

Kennedy. Regular design resumed.

KM# A202b Reverse: Regular design resumed **Weight:** 11.3400 g. **Composition:** Copper-Nickel Clad Copper **Size:** 30.6 mm. **Note:** KM#202b design and composition resumed. The 1979-S and 1981-S Type II proofs have clearer mint marks than the Type I proofs of those years.

Date	Mintage	MS-65	Prf-65	Date	Mintage	MS-65	Prf-65
1977	43,598,000	6.50	—	1982P	10,819,000	5.00	—
1977D	31,449,106	6.00	—	1982D	13,140,102	5.00	—
1977S	3,251,152	—	2.00	1982S	38,957,479	—	3.50
1978	14,350,000	6.50	—	1983P	34,139,000	5.00	—
1978D	13,765,799	6.50	—	1983D	32,472,244	5.00	—
1978S	3,127,788	—	2.00	1983S	3,279,126	—	3.00
1979	68,312,000	5.50	—	1984P	26,029,000	5.00	—
1979D	15,815,422	6.00	—	1984D	26,262,158	5.00	—
1979S type I, proof	3,677,175	—	2.00	1984S	3,065,110	—	4.00
1979S type II, proof	Inc. above	—	18.00	1985P	18,706,962	5.00	—
1980P	44,134,000	5.00	—	1985D	19,814,034	5.00	—
1980D	33,456,449	4.50	—	1985S	3,962,138	—	4.50
1980S	3,547,030	—	2.00	1986P	13,107,633	16.00	—
1981P	29,544,000	4.50	—	1986D	15,336,145	12.00	—
1981D	27,839,533	4.50	—	1986S	2,411,180	—	7.50
1981S type I, proof	4,063,083	—	2.00	1987P	2,890,758	9.00	—
1981S type II, proof	Inc. above	—	14.50	1987D	2,890,758	9.00	—

Date	Mintage	MS-65	Prf-65	Date	Mintage	MS-65	Prf-65
1987S	4,407,728	—	3.50	1996P	24,442,000	6.00	—
1988P	13,626,000	10.00	—	1996D	24,744,000	6.00	—
1988D	12,000,096	6.00	—	1996S	2,085,191	—	10.00
1988S	3,262,948	—	7.00	1997P	20,882,000	7.00	—
1989P	24,542,000	8.00	—	1997D	19,876,000	6.00	—
1989D	23,000,216	8.00	—	1997S	1,975,000	—	25.00
1989S	3,220,194	—	7.00	1998P	15,646,000	9.00	—
1990P	22,780,000	15.00	—	1998D	15,064,000	8.00	—
1990D	20,096,242	15.00	—	1998S	2,078,494	—	14.00
1990S	3,299,559	—	5.00	1998S matte	62,350	—	400
1991P	14,874,000	8.00	—	1999P	8,900,000	6.00	—
1991D	15,054,678	12.00	—	1999D	10,682,000	6.00	—
1991S	2,867,787	—	11.50	1999S	2,557,897	—	10.00
1992P	17,628,000	7.00	—	2000P	22,600,000	4.00	—
1992D	17,000,106	7.00	—	2000D	19,466,000	4.00	—
1992S	2,858,981	—	10.00	2000S	3,082,944	—	4.50
1993P	15,510,000	1.50	—	2001P	21,200,000	3.00	—
1993D	15,000,006	7.00	—	2001D	19,504,000	3.00	—
1993S	2,633,439	—	14.00	2001S	2,235,000	—	10.00
1994P	23,718,000	6.00	—	2002P	3,100,000	15.00	—
1994D	23,828,110	6.00	—	2002D	2,500,000	10.00	—
1994S	2,484,594	—	8.00	2002S	—	—	7.00
1995P	26,496,000	6.00	—	2003P	—	—	—
1995D	26,288,000	6.00	—	2003D	—	—	—
1995S	2,010,384	—	47.50	2003S	—	—	—

Kennedy.

KM# B202b Composition: Silver

Date	Mintage	Prf-65	Date	Mintage	Prf-65
1992S	1,317,579	15.00	1998S	878,792	30.00
1993S	761,353	25.00	1999S	804,565	15.00
1994S	785,329	35.00	2000S	965,921	12.50
1995S	838,953	100.00	2001S	849,600	12.50
1996S	830,021	50.00	2002S	—	—
1997S	821,678	100.00	2003S	—	—

DOLLAR

Flowing Hair.

KM# 17   Designer: Robert Scot **Weight:** 26.9600 g. **Composition:** 0.8920 Silver 0.7737 oz. ASW **Size:** 39-40 mm. **Note:** The two 1795 varieties have either two or three leaves under each of the eagle's wings on the reverse.

Date	Mintage	G-4	VG-8	F-12	VF-20	XF-40	MS-60	MS-63
1794	1,758	1,600	23,000	30,000	60,000	100,000	—	—
1795 2 leaves	203,033	900	1,275	2,350	3,900	7,800	33,000	58,000
1795 3 leaves	Inc. above	850	1,200	2,150	3,600	7,350	29,000	55,000

1794 Silver Dollar
Grade XF-40

☑ Retail Price

Draped Bust. Small eagle.

KM# 18 Designer: Robert Scot **Reverse:** Small eagle **Weight:** 26.9600 g. **Composition:** 0.8920 Silver 0.7737 oz. ASW **Size:** 39-40 mm. **Note:** The 1796 varieties are distinguished by the size of the numerals in the date and letters in "United States of America." The 1797 varieties are distinguished by the number of stars to the left and right of the word "Liberty" and by the size of the letters in "United States of America." The 1798 varieties have either 13 or 15 stars on the obverse.

Date	Mintage	G-4	VG-8	F-12	VF-20	XF-40	MS-60	MS-63
1795	Inc. above	800	1,050	2,000	3,300	5,900	24,500	57,500
1796 small date, small letters	72,920	800	1,050	2,000	3,300	5,900	24,500	—
1796 small date, large letters	Inc. above	825	1,075	2,050	11,350	6,000	25,500	—
1796 large date, small letters	Inc. above	785	1,025	1,975	3,250	5,850	27,000	65,000
1797 9 stars left, 7 stars right, small letters	7,776	1,250	1,900	3,000	4,800	9,000	42,500	70,000
1797 9 stars left, 7 stars right, large letters	Inc. above	825	1,075	2,050	3,350	6,000	28,500	60,000
1797 10 stars left, 6 stars right	Inc. above	785	1,025	1,975	3,250	5,850	24,500	60,000
1798 13 stars	327,536	1,000	1,150	1,875	3,350	6,250	28,500	—
1798 15 stars	Inc. above	1,225	1,550	2,350	3,800	8,000	33,500	—

Draped Bust. Heraldic eagle.

KM# 32 Designer: Robert Scot **Reverse:** Heraldic eagle **Weight:** 26.9600 g. **Composition:** 0.8920 Silver 0.7737 oz. ASW **Size:** 39-40 mm. **Note:** The 1798 "knob 9" variety has a serif on the lower left of the 9 in the date. The 1798 varieties are distinguished by the number of arrows held by the eagle on the reverse and the number of berries on the olive branch. On the 1798 "high-8" variety, the 8 in the date is higher than the other numerals. The 1799 varieties are distinguished by the number and positioning of the stars on the obverse and by the size of the berries in the olive branch on the reverse. On the 1700 "irregular date" variety, the first 9 in the date is smaller than the other numerals. Some varieties of the 1800 strikes had letters in the legend cut twice into the dies; as the dies became worn, the letters were touched up. On the 1800 "very wide date, low 8" variety, the spacing between the numerals in the date are wider than other varieties and the 8 is lower than the other numerals. The 1800 "small berries" variety refers to the size of the berries in the olive branch on the reverse. The 1800 "12 arrows" and "10 arrows" varieties refer to the number of arrows held by the eagle. The 1800 "Americai" variety appears to have the faint outline of an "I" after "America" in the reverse legend. The "close" and "wide" varieties of 1802 refer to the amount of space between the numerals in the date. The 1800 large-3 and small-3 varieties are distinguished by the size of the 3 in the date.

Date	Mintage	G-4	VG-8	F-12	VF-20	XF-40	MS-60	MS-63
1798 knob 9	Inc. above	585	585	1,125	1,775	2,850	16,750	34,500
1798 10 arrows	Inc. above	585	585	1,125	1,775	2,850	16,750	34,500
1798 4 berries	Inc. above	585	585	1,125	1,775	2,850	16,750	34,500
1798 5 berries, 12 arrows	Inc. above	585	585	1,125	1,775	2,850	16,750	34,500
1798 high 8	Inc. above	585	585	1,125	1,775	2,850	16,750	34,500
1798 13 arrows	Inc. above	585	585	1,125	1,775	2,850	16,750	34,500
1799/98 13-star reverse	423,515	675	675	1,350	2,050	3,300	18,500	36,000
1799/98 15-star reverse	Inc. above	635	635	1,225	1,825	3,000	19,500	36,000
1799 irregular date, 13-star reverse	Inc. above	625	625	1,200	1,850	2,900	18,500	38,500
1799 irregular date, 15-star reverse	Inc. above	610	610	1,175	1,825	2,850	16,500	36,000
1799 perfect date, 7- and 6-star obverse, no berries	Inc. above	600	600	1,100	1,750	2,750	13,500	33,500
1799 perfect date, 7- and 6-star obverse, small berries	Inc. above	600	600	1,100	1,350	2,750	13,500	33,500
1799 perfect date, 7- and 6-star obverse, medium large berries	Inc. above	575	575	1,125	1,350	2,750	13,500	33,500
1799 perfect date, 7- and 6-star obverse, extra large berries	Inc. above	625	625	1,125	1,350	2,750	13,500	33,500
1799 8 stars left, 5 stars right on obverse	Inc. above	700	700	1,200	1,850	2,900	19,000	42,500
1800 "R" in "Liberty" double cut	220,920	610	610	1,175	1,825	2,850	16,500	36,000
1800 first "T" in "States" double cut	Inc. above	610	610	1,175	1,825	2,850	16,500	36,000
1800 both letters double cut	Inc. above	610	610	1,175	1,825	2,850	16,500	36,000
1800 "T" in "United" double cut	Inc. above	610	610	1,175	1,825	2,850	16,500	36,000
1800 very wide date, low 8	Inc. above	610	610	1,175	1,825	2,850	16,500	36,000
1800 small berries	Inc. above	625	625	1,200	1,850	2,900	17,000	
1800 dot date	Inc. above	675	675	1,350	2,050	3,300	16,500	39,500
1800 12 arrows	Inc. above	610	610	1,175	1,825	2,850	16,500	36,000
1800 10 arrows	Inc. above	610	610	1,175	1,825	2,850	16,500	36,000
1800 "Americai"	Inc. above	675	675	1,350	2,050	3,300	16,500	39,500
1801	54,454	610	610	1,175	1,825	2,850	20,000	40,000
1801 proof restrike	—	—	—	—	—	—	—	—
1802/1 close	Inc. above	675	675	1,350	2,050	3,300	15,500	—
1802/1 wide	Inc. above	675	675	1,350	2,050	3,300	15,500	—
1802 close, perfect date	Inc. above	625	625	1,200	1,850	2,900	15,500	—
1802 wide, perfect date	Inc. above	610	610	1,175	1,825	2,850	16,500	—
1802 proof restrike, mintage unrecorded	—	—	—	—	—	—	—	—
1803 large 3	85,634	635	635	1,225	1,925	3,000	15,500	37,500
1803 small 3	Inc. above	675	675	1,350	2,050	3,300	16,500	38,500
1803 proof restrike, mintage unrecorded	—	—	—	—	—	—	—	—
1804 15 known	—	—	—	—	—	—	—	—

Note: 1804, Childs Sale, Aug. 1999, Prf-68, $4,140,000.

Gobrecht. "C. Gobrecht F." below base. Eagle flying left amid stars.

KM# 59.1 **Obv. Designer:** Christian Gobrecht **Obverse:** "C. Gobrecht F." below base **Reverse:** Eagle flying left amid stars **Edge:** Plain. **Weight:** 26.7300 g. **Composition:** 0.9000 Silver 0.7736 oz. ASW **Size:** 38.1 mm.

Date	Mintage	VF-20	XF-40	AU-50	Prf-60
1836	1,000	3,750	4,750	—	12,500

Gobrecht. "C. Gobrecht F." below base. Eagle flying in plain field.

KM# 59.2 **Obv. Designer:** Christian Gobrecht. **Obverse:** "C. Gobrecht F." below base **Reverse:** Eagle flying in plain field **Edge:** Plain. **Weight:** 26.7300 g. **Composition:** 0.9000 Silver 0.7736 oz. ASW **Size:** 38.1 mm.

Date	Mintage	VF-20	XF-40	AU-50	Prf-60
1836 Restrike	—	—	—	—	—

Gobrecht. "C. Gobrecht F." on base.

KM# 59a.1 **Obverse:** "C. Gobrecht F." on base **Obv. Legend:** Eagle flying left amid stars. **Edge:** Plain. **Weight:** 26.7300 g. **Composition:** 0.9000 Silver 0.7736 oz. ASW **Size:** 38.1 mm.

Date	Mintage	VF-20	XF-40	AU-50	Prf-60
1836	600				

Gobrecht. "C. Gobrecht F." on base. Eagle flying left amid stars.

KM# 59a.2 **Obverse:** "C. Gobrecht F." on base **Reverse:** Eagle flying left amid stars **Edge:** Reeded. **Weight:** 26.7300 g. **Composition:** 0.9000 Silver 0.7736 oz. ASW **Size:** 38.1 mm.

Date	Mintage	VF-20	XF-40	AU-50	Prf-60
1836 Restrike					

Gobrecht. Similar to 1836 but designer's name omitted. Eagle in plain field.

KM# 59a.3 **Obverse:** Similar to 1836 but designer's name omitted **Reverse:** Eagle in plain field **Edge:** Reeded. **Weight:** 26.7300 g. **Composition:** 0.9000 Silver 0.7736 oz. ASW **Size:** 38.1 mm.

Date	Mintage	VF-20	XF-40	AU-50	Prf-60
1839	300	—	—	—	—

KM# 59a.4 **Weight:** 26.7300 g. **Composition:** 0.9000 Silver .7734 oz. ASW **Size:** 38.1 mm.

Date	Mintage	VF-20	XF-40	AU-50	Prf-60
1839 Restrike	—	—	—	—	—

Note: All other combinations are restrikes of the late 1850's.

Seated Liberty. No motto above eagle.

KM# 71 **Designer:** Christian Gobrecht **Reverse:** No motto above eagle **Weight:** 26.7300 g. **Composition:** 0.9000 Silver 0.7736 oz. ASW **Size:** 38.1 mm.

Date	Mintage	G-4	VG-8	F-12	VF-20	XF-40	AU-50	MS-60	MS-63	MS-65	Prf-65
1840	61,005	160	180	225	300	525	750	1,750	12,500	—	—
1841	173,000	145	165	210	250	360	625	1,500	4,200	42,500	—
1842	184,618	145	165	210	250	350	600	1,100	3,750	24,000	—
1843	165,100	145	165	210	250	350	625	1,400	4,350	24,000	—
1844	20,000	180	245	300	385	500	850	3,000	7,000	44,500	—
1845	24,500	200	260	285	350	550	800	4,850	17,000	—	—
1846	110,600	145	165	225	275	385	625	1,450	4,650	30,000	—
1846O	59,000	150	250	300	475	1,250	3,000	12,000	24,500	—	—

Date	Mintage	G-4	VG-8	F-12	VF-20	XF-40	AU-50	MS-60	MS-63	MS-65	Prf-65
1847	140,750	145	165	210	250	350	600	950	3,500	26,500	—
1848	15,000	220	300	425	550	750	1,500	3,000	7,500	40,000	—
1849	62,600	165	190	250	325	400	700	1,650	4,600	32,500	—
1850	7,500	400	635	750	900	1,000	2,000	4,500	13,000	47,500	—
1850O	40,000	255	300	375	650	1,275	2,850	6,250	15,500	55,000	—
1851	1,300	4,000	5,000	8,000	9,500	13,500	21,500	27,500	35,000	60,000	—
1852	1,100	3,800	4,800	7,500	8,500	11,500	21,500	26,500	33,500	55,000	—
1853	46,110	185	235	285	375	600	850	2,350	6,500	26,500	—
1854	33,140	1,000	1,200	1,600	2,350	3,650	4,850	7,000	9,800	24,500	—
1855	26,000	800	1,150	1,400	1,900	2,950	3,800	6,500	15,000	—	—
1856	63,500	400	500	600	750	975	1,650	3,450	6,500	—	—
1857	94,000	375	475	550	750	950	1,300	2,750	4,200	27,500	—
1858 proof	Est. 800	2,250	2,650	3,350	4,200	5,500	6,250	9,000	12,000	—	—

Note: Proof Only restruck in later years.

Date	Mintage	G-4	VG-8	F-12	VF-20	XF-40	AU-50	MS-60	MS-63	MS-65	Prf-65
1859	256,500	180	220	300	450	600	850	1,800	5,000	15,000	13,500
1859O	360,000	145	175	220	275	375	600	950	2,600	32,000	—
1859S	20,000	235	300	400	600	1,350	3,000	8,000	25,500	60,000	—
1860	218,930	165	200	275	350	475	600	1,100	2,600	26,000	13,500
1860O	515,000	145	165	210	250	350	550	900	2,500	15,000	—
1861	78,500	440	500	650	800	1,000	1,500	2,800	4,600	22,500	13,500
1862	12,090	450	525	675	850	950	1,600	2,750	5,000	34,500	13,500
1863	27,660	325	375	450	550	1,200	2,350	3,800	11,250	1,400	13,500
1864	31,170	240	265	315	425	600	1,200	2,300	4,600	20,000	13,500
1865	47,000	225	245	290	400	560	1,150	2,150	4,450	32,500	13,500
1866 2 known without motto	—	—	—	—	—	—	—	—	—	—	—

Seated Liberty. "In God We Trust" above eagle.

KM# 100 **Designer:** Christian Gobrecht **Reverse:** "In God We Trust" above eagle **Weight:** 26.7300 g. **Composition:** 0.9000 Silver 0.7736 oz. ASW **Size:** 38.1 mm. **Note:** In 1866 the motto "In God We Trust" was added to the reverse above the eagle.

Date	Mintage	G-4	VG-8	F-12	VF-20	XF-40	AU-50	MS-60	MS-63	MS-65	Prf-65
1866	49,625	175	220	285	400	550	900	1,650	2,900	23,500	7,000
1867	47,525	170	215	265	415	525	875	1,500	3,000	24,500	7,000
1868	162,700	165	205	245	375	475	850	1,600	6,000	33,500	7,000
1869	424,300	155	195	235	325	440	650	1,450	3,350	24,500	7,000
1870	416,000	165	185	225	320	440	600	1,400	2,750	24,500	7,000
1870CC	12,462	275	345	500	800	1,450	3,000	9,500	20,000	38,500	—
1870S 12-15 known	—	30,000	—	—	—	—	—	—	—	—	—

Note: 1870S, Eliasberg Sale, April 1997, EF-45 to AU-50, $264,000.

Date	Mintage	G-4	VG-8	F-12	VF-20	XF-40	AU-50	MS-60	MS-63	MS-65	Prf-65
1871	1,074,760	155	190	265	340	425	600	1,100	2,600	21,500	7,000
1871CC	1,376	1,650	2,500	3,750	5,750	8,950	18,500	41,000	96,000	150,000	—
1872	1,106,450	155	190	265	340	425	600	1,100	2,600	21,500	7,000
1872CC	3,150	900	1,250	1,750	2,850	4,250	8,500	18,500	35,000	—	—
1872S	9,000	220	285	400	575	1,100	2,750	8,500	23,500	—	—
1873	293,600	165	200	275	350	475	600	1,100	2,600	21,500	7,000
1873CC	2,300	3,250	4,750	6,500	9,000	16,000	30,000	63,500	110,000	—	—
1873S none known	700	—	—	—	—	—	—	—	—	—	—

Trade.

KM# 108 Designer: William Barber **Weight:** 27.2200 g. **Composition:** 0.9000 Silver 0.7878 oz. ASW
Size: 38.1 mm.

Date	Mintage	G-4	VG-8	F-12	VF-20	XF-40	AU-50	MS-60	MS-65	Prf-65
1873	397,500	100.00	110	125	165	250	325	1,000	12,000	12,000
1873CC	124,500	175	200	300	450	700	1,200	2,100	80,000	—
1873S	703,000	130	145	160	180	260	375	1,200	25,000	—
1874	987,800	120	130	150	185	240	340	700	15,000	12,000
1874CC	1,373,200	80.00	90.00	105	165	240	350	1,000	40,000	—
1874S	2,549,000	70.00	80.00	95.00	120	165	250	675	30,000	—
1875	218,900	260	350	425	525	675	800	1,850	13,000	6,500
1875CC	1,573,700	80.00	90.00	105	130	200	375	900	40,000	—
1875S	4,487,000	60.00	70.00	85.00	100.00	120	210	500	7,000	—
1875S/CC	Inc. above	275	325	400	525	695	1,100	1,900	—	—
1876	456,150	70.00	80.00	100.00	125	165	400	675	7,500	6,500
1876CC	509,000	150	175	220	250	375	500	2,100	75,000	—
1876S	5,227,000	60.00	70.00	85.00	100.00	120	210	475	10,000	—
1877	3,039,710	60.00	70.00	85.00	105	130	210	525	16,000	19,000
1877CC	534,000	150	175	210	260	370	600	1,275	70,000	—
1877S	9,519,000	60.00	70.00	85.00	100.00	120	210	475	8,000	—
1878 proof	900	—	—	—	1,100	1,300	1,500	—	—	22,000
1878CC	97,000	425	525	675	850	1,750	2,100	5,500	67,500	—
1878S	4,162,000	60.00	70.00	85.00	100.00	120	210	475	7,000	—
1879 proof	1,541	—	—	—	900	950	1,100	—	—	22,000
1880 proof	1,987	—	—	—	900	950	1,100	—	—	19,500
1881 proof	960	—	—	—	950	1,000	1,250	—	—	20,000
1882 proof	1,097	—	—	—	950	1,000	1,250	—	—	20,000
1883 proof	979	—	—	—	1,100	1,200	1,400	—	—	20,000
1884 proof	10	—	—	—	—	—	—	—	—	—

Note: 1884, Eliasberg Sale, April 1997, Prf-66, $396,000.

| 1885 proof | 5 | — | — | — | — | — | — | — | — | — |

Note: 1885, Eliasberg Sale, April 1997, Prf-65, $907,500.

1875 Trade Dollar
Grade F-12

Morgan.

7 tail feathers

8 tail feathers

7/8 tail feathers

KM# 110 Designer: George T. Morgan **Weight:** 26.7300 g. **Composition:** 0.9000 Silver 0.7736 oz. ASW **Size:** 38.1 mm. **Note:** "65DMPL" values are for coins grading MS-65 deep-mirror prooflike. The 1878 "8 tail feathers" and "7 tail feathers" varieties are distinguished by the number of feathers in the eagle's tail. On the "reverse of 1878" varieties, the top of the top feather in the arrows held by the eagle is straight across and the eagle's breast is concave. On the "reverse of 1879 varieties," the top feather in the arrows held by the eagle is slanted and the eagle's breast is convex. The 1890-CC "tail-bar variety has a bar extending from the arrow feathers to the wreath on the reverse, the result of a die gouge.

Date	Mintage	VG-8	F-12	VF-20	XF-40	AU-50	MS-60	MS-63	MS-64	MS-65	65DMPL	Prf-65
1878 8 tail feathers	750,000	19.00	20.00	21.00	25.00	42.00	125	150	300	1,300	6,300	6,250
1878 7 tail feathers, reverse of 1878	Inc. above	14.00	15.00	16.50	18.00	34.00	54.00	80.00	230	1,200	6,300	5,350
1878 7 tail feathers, reverse of 1879	Inc. above	15.50	16.50	17.00	18.00	34.00	63.50	135	350	2,800	8,800	55,000
1878 7 over 8 tail feathers	9,759,550	16.00	17.50	21.00	27.50	50.00	125	225	340	3,300	14,500	—
1878CC	2,212,000	80.00	85.00	88.00	90.00	100.00	220	255	400	1,250	3,450	—
1878S	9,744,000	15.00	16.00	17.00	18.00	32.50	45.00	58.50	90.00	260	2,250	—
1879	14,807,100	12.50	13.00	13.50	16.50	18.00	25.00	60.00	125	950	6,950	5,500
1879CC	756,000	80.00	85.00	145	550	1,000	1,750	3,800	5,600	18,500	65,000	—
1879O	2,887,000	12.50	14.50	15.00	17.00	20.00	72.00	150	420	3,300	16,500	—
1879S reverse of 1878	9,110,000	14.00	14.50	16.00	17.50	33.00	90.00	360	1,350	7,600	22,000	—
1879S reverse of 1879	9,110,000	14.00	14.50	16.00	17.00	21.00	39.00	42.00	48.00	96.00	450	—
1880	12,601,335	14.00	13.50	14.00	17.00	19.00	25.00	55.00	115	750	3,450	5,500
1880CC reverse of 1878	591,000	83.00	100.00	115	185	245	400	420	710	2,300	11,000	—
1880CC reverse of 1879	591,000	110	145	150	220	300	395	415	465	875	3,650	—
1880O	5,305,000	13.00	13.50	14.50	17.00	20.00	60.00	310	1,200	19,000	70,000	—
1880S	8,900,000	14.00	14.50	15.00	16.50	20.00	29.00	37.50	47.50	96.00	450	—
1881	9,163,975	14.00	14.50	15.00	17.00	20.00	30.00	55.00	110	850	13,750	5,500
1881CC	296,000	235	255	270	315	325	415	420	425	650	1,450	—
1881O	5,708,000	13.00	14.00	14.50	16.50	19.00	25.00	40.00	115	1,650	15,000	—
1881S	12,760,000	13.00	14.00	16.00	15.50	19.00	27.50	37.50	47.50	96.00	450	—
1882	11,101,100	13.50	13.75	14.00	16.00	19.00	25.00	42.00	54.00	450	4,100	5,500
1882CC	1,133,000	80.00	85.00	88.00	90.00	92.00	155	160	225	445	725	—
1882O	6,090,000	13.00	14.00	14.50	16.00	19.00	25.00	40.00	70.00	720	4,200	—
1882S	9,250,000	13.00	13.50	16.00	15.50	25.00	32.00	40.00	50.00	96.00	1,100	—
1883	12,291,039	12.00	13.00	14.00	16.00	19.00	26.50	40.00	52.00	150	760	5,500
1883CC	1,204,000	80.00	82.50	85.00	88.00	90.00	155	145	200	325	830	—
1883O	8,725,000	12.50	13.50	14.50	16.50	19.00	25.00	37.50	47.50	100.00	575	—
1883S	6,250,000	13.50	15.50	17.00	32.50	165	495	1,600	3,800	22,000	94,500	—
1884	14,070,875	13.00	13.50	14.00	16.50	20.00	25.00	40.00	55.00	270	2,200	5,500
1884CC	1,136,000	80.00	83.00	85.00	88.00	90.00	155	145	200	325	600	—
1884O	9,730,000	13.00	13.50	14.00	16.50	19.00	25.00	37.50	47.50	96.00	670	—
1884S	3,200,000	13.00	14.50	17.00	42.00	280	3,600	25,000	110,000	200,000	220,000	—
1885	17,787,767	12.00	13.00	14.00	16.00	19.00	25.00	37.50	47.50	100.00	570	5,500
1885CC	228,000	325	330	355	365	380	420	435	495	800	1,450	—
1885O	9,185,000	13.00	13.50	14.00	16.00	19.00	25.00	37.50	47.50	96.00	490	—
1885S	1,497,000	14.50	15.50	16.00	21.00	54.00	185	240	450	1,900	16,500	—
1886	19,963,886	13.50	14.00	14.50	16.00	19.00	25.00	37.50	47.50	96.00	575	5,500
1886O	10,710,000	13.00	14.00	14.50	18.00	80.00	420	2,500	7,500	210,000	283,500	—
1886S	750,000	21.00	26.00	46.00	53.00	80.00	240	330	520	3,200	16,500	—
1887	20,290,710	14.00	14.50	15.00	17.50	21.00	25.00	37.50	47.50	96.00	530	5,500

1889-O Silver Dollar
Grade F-12

Retail Price

1897-O Dollar
Grade MS-60

Retail Price

1903-O Dollar
Grade MS-60

☐ Retail Price

Date	Mintage	VG-8	F-12	VF-20	XF-40	AU-50	MS-60	MS-63	MS-64	MS-65	65DMPL	Prf-65
1887O	11,550,000	12.50	14.00	14.50	17.00	21.00	54.00	100.00	335	4,000	8,500	—
1887S	1,771,000	14.50	15.00	17.50	20.00	39.00	100.00	200	500	3,800	27,000	—
1888	19,183,833	12.50	13.50	14.00	15.50	19.00	25.00	39.00	55.00	210	2,350	5,500
1888O	12,150,000	12.50	14.50	15.50	16.50	19.00	28.00	41.00	55.00	400	1,600	—
1888S	657,000	40.00	60.00	72.50	94.00	100.00	235	350	550	3,500	10,500	—
1889	21,726,811	12.00	13.00	13.50	14.00	19.00	25.00	39.00	55.00	300	2,950	5,500
1889CC	350,000	380	485	835	1,850	4,750	9,800	19,500	49,000	300,000	285,000	—
1889O	11,875,000	12.50	13.00	13.50	17.50	30.00	135	325	565	5,550	14,500	—
1889S	700,000	27.00	32.00	33.00	37.00	65.00	190	315	375	1,900	7,550	—
1890	16,802,590	12.50	13.00	14.00	16.00	19.00	28.00	48.00	110	2,250	12,500	5,500
1890CC	2,309,041	80.00	85.00	88.00	90.00	125	335	525	975	5,500	9,750	—
1890CC tail bar	Inc. above	80.00	85.00	88.00	110	180	425	540	1,350	8,000	9,750	—
1890O	10,701,000	12.50	14.00	14.50	18.00	24.00	50.00	85.00	180	1,900	7,500	—
1890S	8,230,373	12.50	14.00	14.50	16.50	19.00	56.00	100.00	195	950	8,200	—
1891	8,694,206	12.50	14.00	14.50	16.50	22.50	53.00	135	510	7,250	25,000	5,500
1891CC	1,618,000	80.00	85.00	88.00	90.00	135	345	495	640	3,250	20,000	—
1891O	7,954,529	13.50	14.00	14.50	18.00	33.00	135	270	670	9,000	21,500	—
1891S	5,296,000	12.50	14.00	15.00	19.00	24.00	60.00	120	250	1,250	7,250	—
1892	1,037,245	16.00	17.50	18.00	30.00	72.50	150	325	600	4,150	15,750	5,500
1892CC	1,352,000	80.00	85.00	88.00	200	335	700	950	1,425	6,500	27,000	—
1892O	2,744,000	13.00	15.50	16.50	30.00	60.00	135	250	550	5,300	27,000	—
1892S	1,200,000	17.50	20.00	43.00	170	1,700	22,000	55,000	95,000	145,000	157,500	—
1893	378,792	90.00	98.00	105	175	225	475	885	1,250	7,500	38,000	5,500
1893CC	677,000	140	185	335	975	1,350	2,500	4,400	7,400	47,500	85,000	—
1893O	300,000	72.00	110	145	235	640	1,400	6,000	17,000	21,500	201,500	—
1893S	100,000	1,400	1,925	2,800	6,800	19,000	54,000	94,000	250,000	400,000	380,000	—
1894	110,972	460	580	610	650	800	1,300	4,000	6,500	23,000	44,000	5,500
1894O	1,723,000	21.00	26.50	32.50	53.00	165	520	3,000	6,600	49,000	56,500	—
1894S	1,260,000	30.00	40.00	60.00	110	300	500	830	1,400	5,500	19,000	—
1895 proof only	12,880	14,500	16,000	17,500	20,000	22,000	26,000	30,000	34,000	36,500	—	32,000
1895O	450,000	95.00	120	175	280	885	12,000	35,000	95,000	220	—	—
1895S	400,000	160	200	240	440	825	1,800	4,000	5,400	19,000	40,500	—
1896	9,967,762	13.00	14.00	14.50	15.50	19.00	29.00	38.00	72.50	170	975	5,500
1896O	4,900,000	13.50	14.50	16.50	18.00	190	885	6,400	46,000	185,000	170,000	—
1896S	5,000,000	17.50	26.00	47.00	145	460	850	1,600	2,650	15,000	25,000	—
1897	2,822,731	14.00	14.50	15.00	17.00	19.00	29.00	38.00	55.00	250	2,900	5,500
1897O	4,004,000	13.50	14.50	16.00	24.00	110	640	4,400	13,500	50,000	56,500	—
1897S	5,825,000	13.50	14.50	16.50	17.50	24.00	56.00	100.00	125	600	1,700	—
1898	5,884,735	14.50	15.50	16.00	17.50	19.00	27.50	38.00	55.00	210	1,075	5,500
1898O	4,440,000	14.00	15.00	15.50	17.00	20.00	29.00	38.00	50.00	115	510	—
1898S	4,102,000	14.00	15.50	16.50	28.00	68.00	250	335	530	2,500	11,250	—
1899	330,846	25.00	40.00	44.00	54.00	72.50	100.00	145	220	660	2,250	5,500
1899O	12,290,000	13.00	13.50	14.00	17.50	21.00	28.00	38.00	50.00	120	825	—
1899S	2,562,000	14.50	17.00	22.00	36.00	90.00	300	385	550	2,150	8,600	—
1900	8,880,938	13.00	15.00	16.00	18.00	19.00	30.00	38.00	55.00	195	11,000	5,500
1900O	12,590,000	13.00	15.00	16.00	20.00	24.00	32.00	42.00	52.00	135	3,000	—
1900O/CC	Inc. above	20.00	25.00	34.00	49.00	120	225	540	725	1,500	19,000	—
1900S	3,540,000	16.00	17.00	19.00	36.00	85.00	245	335	365	1,350	9,450	—
1901	6,962,813	18.50	20.00	30.00	60.00	350	1,675	17,500	55,000	215,000	220,000	8,100

1921 Silver Dollar
Grade MS-60

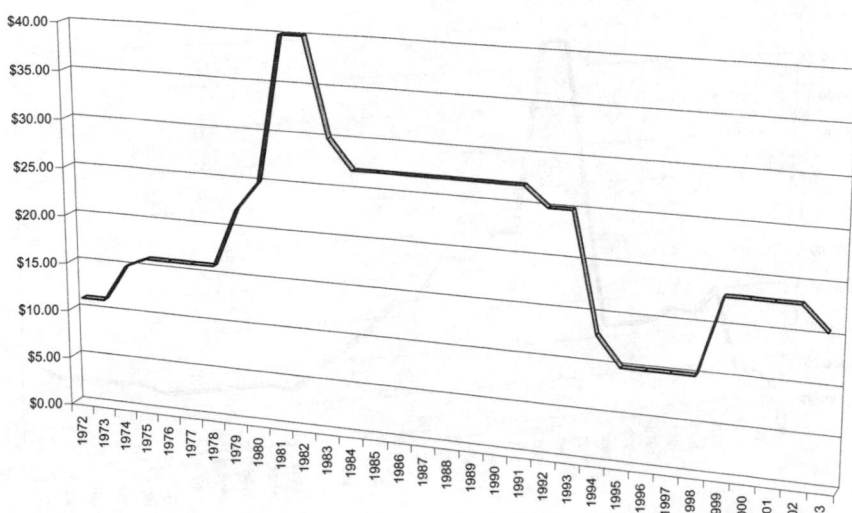

□ Retail Price

Date	Mintage	VG-8	F-12	VF-20	XF-40	AU-50	MS-60	MS-63	MS-64	MS-65	65DMPL	Prf-65
1901O	13,320,000	13.00	14.50	16.00	19.00	20.00	30.00	38.00	52.00	170	3,800	—
1901S	2,284,000	15.00	20.00	29.00	45.00	175	330	575	850	3,500	12,500	—
1902	7,994,777	15.50	16.00	18.00	19.00	23.00	42.00	90.00	130	465	15,750	5,750
1902O	8,636,000	13.50	15.50	16.50	20.00	21.00	29.00	38.00	47.50	140	3,600	—
1902S	1,530,000	27.00	42.00	90.00	105	135	285	365	580	2,700	15,000	—
1903	4,652,755	24.00	28.50	30.00	40.00	46.00	53.00	57.00	72.00	215	9,150	5,500
1903O	4,450,000	190	200	245	280	330	370	420	425	535	4,650	—
1903S	1,241,000	23.00	29.00	90.00	245	1,100	2,900	4,250	5,200	7,000	35,000	—
1904	2,788,650	15.50	16.00	16.50	18.00	30.00	80.00	230	560	4,700	38,000	5,500
1904O	3,720,000	14.50	15.50	16.00	18.00	20.00	30.00	38.00	47.50	105	550	—
1904S	2,304,000	17.00	25.00	46.00	190	540	1,000	2,100	1,750	6,500	19,000	—
1921	44,690,000	10.00	10.25	10.50	11.00	12.00	15.50	25.00	35.00	135	8,800	—
1921D	20,345,000	10.00	10.25	10.50	11.75	13.00	39.50	48.00	100.00	260	15,000	—
1921S	21,695,000	10.00	10.25	11.00	12.00	14.00	26.00	54.00	135	1,700	22,000	—

Peace.

Mint mark

KM# 150 Designer: Anthony DeFrancisci **Weight:** 26.7300 g. **Composition:** 0.9000 Silver 0.7736 oz. ASW **Size:** 38.1 mm. **Note:** Commonly called Peace dollars.

Date	Mintage	G-4	VG-8	F-12	VF-20	XF-40	AU-50	MS-60	MS-63	MS-64	MS-65
1921	1,006,473	29.00	48.00	49.00	50.00	56.00	100.00	170	290	485	2,400
1922	51,737,000	8.00	8.50	9.00	9.00	9.25	9.50	15.50	26.50	36.00	100.00
1922D	15,063,000	8.00	8.50	9.00	10.00	11.00	12.00	24.00	44.00	72.00	395
1922S	17,475,000	8.00	8.50	9.00	10.25	12.00	13.00	22.50	65.00	210	2,200
1923	30,800,000	8.00	8.50	9.00	9.00	9.25	9.50	15.50	26.50	36.00	88.00
1923D	6,811,000	8.00	8.50	10.00	10.50	11.00	18.00	53.00	120	215	1,000
1923S	19,020,000	8.00	8.50	10.00	10.50	11.00	13.00	26.00	65.00	200	8,400
1924	11,811,000	8.00	8.50	9.50	10.00	10.50	11.00	15.50	27.50	42.00	100.00
1924S	1,728,000	8.50	9.00	11.25	14.50	24.00	48.00	195	430	1,000	8,500
1925	10,198,000	8.00	8.50	9.00	9.25	10.00	12.50	15.50	27.50	42.00	95.00

1927-S Dollar
Grade MS-60

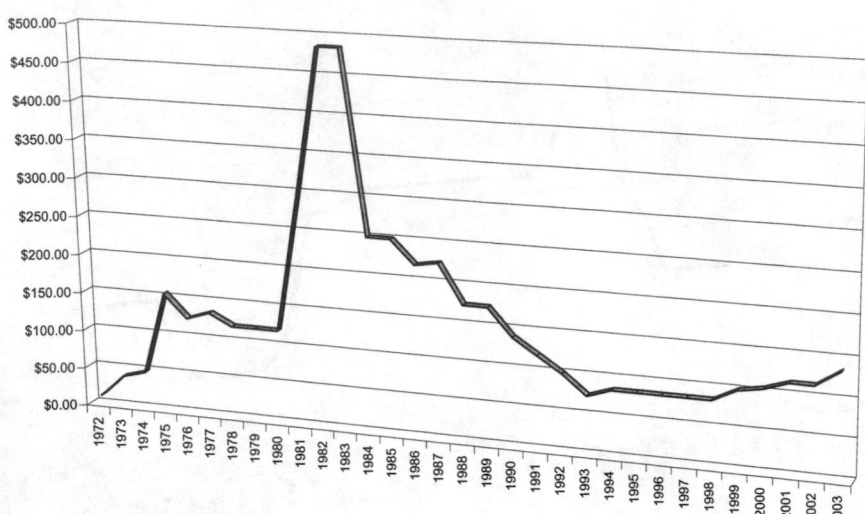

Retail Price

Date	Mintage	G-4	VG-8	F-12	VF-20	XF-40	AU-50	MS-60	MS-63	MS-64	MS-65
1925S	1,610,000	9.00	10.00	12.00	13.00	15.00	30.00	65.00	145	550	20,500
1926	1,939,000	8.00	11.50	12.50	13.50	14.00	16.00	32.00	60.00	95.00	360
1926D	2,348,700	8.00	11.00	11.50	12.50	16.00	25.00	58.50	135	260	620
1926S	6,980,000	8.00	10.00	11.00	11.50	12.00	15.00	35.00	77.00	235	850
1927	848,000	12.00	16.00	20.00	22.00	27.00	45.00	67.00	140	260	2,000
1927D	1,268,900	11.00	15.50	17.00	20.00	24.00	75.00	145	300	625	5,800
1927S	866,000	13.00	16.00	17.00	20.00	25.00	67.00	135	250	725	11,000
1928	360,649	135	165	200	225	245	250	260	360	725	3,700
1928S	1,632,000	11.00	17.00	18.50	18.50	24.00	42.00	140	330	1,000	24,000
1934	954,057	11.00	14.50	15.00	17.50	20.00	36.00	90.00	170	285	850
1934D	1,569,500	11.00	14.50	15.00	17.50	20.00	40.00	95.00	265	500	2,100
1934S	1,011,000	11.00	15.00	15.50	52.50	135	495	1,600	2,700	4,200	6,700
1935	1,576,000	11.00	15.00	15.50	15.50	16.00	30.00	60.00	100.00	160	640
1935S	1,964,000	11.00	14.50	15.00	15.50	24.00	72.00	180	335	485	1,150

Eisenhower.

KM# 203 **Designer:** Frank Gasparro **Weight:** 22.6800 g. **Composition:** Copper-Nickel Clad Copper **Size:** 38.1 mm.

Date	Mintage	Proof	MS-63	Prf-65
1971	47,799,000	—	3.75	—
1971D	68,587,424	—	2.00	—
1972	75,890,000	—	2.75	—
1972D	92,548,511	—	2.25	—
1973	2,000,056	—	11.00	—
1973D	2,000,000	—	11.00	—
1973S	2,769,624	—	—	11.00
1974	27,366,000	—	3.00	—
1974D	35,466,000	—	2.75	—
1974S	—	(2,617,350)	—	6.50

Eisenhower.

KM# 203a Designer: Frank Gasparro **Weight:** 24.5900 g. **Composition:** Silver **Size:** 38.1 mm.

Date	Mintage	Proof	MS-63	Prf-65
1971S	6,868,530	(4,265,234)	6.00	7.00
1972S	2,193,056	(1,811,631)	7.50	7.00
1973S	1,833,140	(1,005,617)	8.50	30.00
1974S	1,720,000	(1,306,579)	7.50	7.25

Eisenhower. Bicentennial design, moon behind Liberty Bell.

Type I

Type II

KM# 206 Rev. Designer: Dennis R. Williams **Reverse:** Bicentennial design, moon behind Liberty Bell **Weight:** 22.6800 g. **Composition:** Copper-Nickel Clad Copper **Size:** 38.1 mm. **Note:** In 1976 the lettering on the reverse on the reverse was changed to thinner letters, resulting in Type I and Type II varieties for that year.

Date	Mintage	Proof	MS-63	Prf-65
1976 type I	117,337,000	—	4.00	—
1976 type II	Inc. above	—	2.00	—
1976D type I	103,228,274	—	3.25	—
1976D type II	Inc. above	—	2.00	—
1976S type I	—	(2,909,369)	—	5.75
1976S type II	—	(4,149,730)	—	5.75

Eisenhower. Bicentennial design, moon behind Liberty Bell.

KM# 206a Rev. Designer: Dennis R. Williams **Reverse:** Bicentennial design, moon behind Liberty Bell **Weight:** 24.5900 g. **Composition:** 0.4000 Silver 0.3162 oz. ASW

Date	Mintage	Proof	MS-63	Prf-65
1976S	4,908,319	(3,998,621)	14.00	12.50

Eisenhower. Regular design resumed.

KM# A203 Reverse: Regular design resumed **Composition:** Copper-Nickel Clad Copper **Size:** 38.1 mm.

Date	Mintage	Proof	MS-63	Prf-65
1977	12,596,000	—	4.25	—
1977D	32,983,006	—	3.25	—
1977S	—	(3,251,152)	—	8.00
1978	25,702,000	—	2.75	—
1978D	33,012,890	—	3.00	—
1978S	—	(3,127,788)	—	10.00

Susan B. Anthony.

KM# 207 Designer: Frank Gasparro **Weight:** 8.1000 g. **Composition:** Copper-Nickel Clad Copper **Size:** 26.5 mm. **Note:** The 1979-S and 1981-S Type II coins have a clearer mint mark than the Type I varieties for those years.

Date	Mintage	MS-63	Prf-65	Date	Mintage	MS-63	Prf-65
1979P	360,222,000	2.00	—	1981P	3,000,000	5.75	—
1979P Near date	Inc. above	12.00	—	1981D	3,250,000	5.75	—
1979D	288,015,744	1.75	—	1981S	3,492,000	6.00	—
1979S	109,576,000	2.00	8.00	1981S Proof, Type I	4,063,083	—	8.00
1979S Proof, Type I	3,677,175	—	100	1981S Proof, Type II	Inc. above	—	220
1979S Proof, Type II	Inc. above	—	—	1999P	29,592,000	1.50	—
1980P	27,610,000	2.00	—	1999D	11,776,000	1.75	—
1980D	41,628,708	2.00	—	1999P Proof;			
1980S	20,422,000	2.00	—	*maximum mintage	750,000	—	9.50
1980S Proof	3,547,030	—	8.00				

Sacagawea.

KM# 311   Weight: 8.0700 g. **Composition:** Copper-Zinc-Manganese-Nickel Clad Copper **Size:** 26.4 mm.

Date	Mintage	MS-63	Prf-65	Date	Mintage	MS-63	Prf-65
2000P	767,140,000	1.50	—	2002P	3,865,610	1.75	—
2000D	518,916,000	1.50	—	2002D	3,732,000	1.75	—
2000S	4,048,865	—	9.50	2002S	2,321,848	—	9.50
2001P	62,468,000	2.50	—	2003P	—	1.50	—
2001D	70,909,500	2.75	—	2003D	—	1.50	—
2001S	3,084,600	—	9.50	2003S	—	—	9.50

Type 1.

KM# 73   Designer: James B. Longacre **Weight:** 1.6720 g. **Composition:** 0.9000 Gold 0.0484 oz. AGW **Size:** 13 mm. **Note:** On the "closed wreath" varieties of 1849, the wreath on the reverse extends closer to the numeral 1.

Date	Mintage	F-12	VF-20	XF-40	AU-50	MS-60
1849 open wreath	688,567	110	125	165	190	450
1849 closed wreath	Inc. above	110	125	165	180	365
1849C closed wreath	11,634	275	425	875	1,600	7,500
1849C open wreath	Inc. above	—	—	—	—	—
1849D open wreath	21,588	285	400	800	1,100	2,900
1849O open wreath	215,000	135	165	210	325	700
1850	481,953	120	135	170	190	380
1850C	6,966	390	585	950	2,200	6,000
1850D	8,382	350	575	1,200	2,000	6,100
1850O	14,000	195	260	370	650	2,750
1851	3,317,671	120	135	165	175	275
1851C	41,267	275	410	650	950	2,300
1851D	9,882	275	400	750	1,600	3,200
1851O	290,000	150	175	195	250	690
1852	2,045,351	100.00	120	165	190	255
1852C	9,434	275	450	750	1,200	3,400
1852D	6,360	315	600	1,150	1,600	4,600
1852O	140,000	125	160	225	330	1,300
1853	4,076,051	115	130	165	190	255
1853C	11,515	240	500	1,150	1,650	5,000
1853D	6,583	325	675	1,150	1,700	7,200
1853O	290,000	140	160	195	220	650
1854	736,709	115	150	170	195	265
1854D	2,935	530	840	1,900	4,800	12,500
1854S	14,632	260	300	460	650	2,100

Type 2.

KM# 83   Designer: James B. Longacre **Weight:** 1.6720 g. **Composition:** 0.9000 Gold 0.0484 oz. AGW **Size:** 15 mm.

Date	Mintage	F-12	VF-20	XF-40	AU-50	MS-60
1854	902,736	210	265	375	520	2,700
1855	758,269	210	265	375	520	2,700
1855C	9,803	625	985	2,700	5,750	18,000
1855D	1,811	1,300	2,100	5,400	9,500	27,500
1855O	55,000	315	425	595	975	5,200
1856S	24,600	390	650	1,100	1,700	6,900

Type 3.

KM# 86 Designer: James B. Longacre **Weight:** 1.6720 g. **Composition:** 0.9000 Gold 0.0484 oz. AGW **Size:** 15 mm. **Note:** The 1856 varieties are distinguished by whether the 5 in the date is slanted or upright. The 1873 varieties are distinguished by the amount of space between the upper left and lower left serifs in the 3.

Date	Mintage	F-12	VF-20	XF-40	AU-50	MS-60	Prf-65
1856 upright 5	1,762,936	130	155	195	315	475	—
1856 slanted 5	Inc. above	120	140	170	190	300	—
1856D	1,460	2,100	3,500	5,150	7,500	30,000	—
1857	774,789	120	140	170	190	300	—
1857C	13,280	350	500	1,300	3,500	11,000	—
1857D	3,533	275	825	1,650	3,800	11,000	—
1857S	10,000	260	500	600	1,000	5,650	—
1858	117,995	120	140	170	190	300	20,000
1858D	3,477	415	775	1,300	2,400	9,000	—
1858S	10,000	280	375	500	1,200	5,600	—
1859	168,244	120	140	160	190	300	13,000
1859C	5,235	300	500	1,500	3,600	15,000	—
1859D	4,952	475	700	1,300	2,200	9,000	—
1859S	15,000	225	250	480	1,000	5,500	—
1860	36,668	120	140	170	190	360	13,500
1860D	1,566	1,550	2,500	3,800	5,750	25,000	—
1860S	13,000	200	325	475	600	2,500	—
1861	527,499	120	140	160	190	250	15,000
1861D mintage unrecorded	—	4,300	6,000	8,500	15,000	32,500	—
1862	1,361,390	110	120	150	175	280	18,000
1863	6,250	360	450	875	1,900	4,000	16,500
1864	5,950	285	370	475	750	1,000	23,000
1865	3,725	285	370	585	750	1,600	16,500
1866	7,130	290	380	450	700	1,000	16,500
1867	5,250	345	440	550	750	1,200	18,000
1868	10,525	260	295	400	585	1,100	16,000
1869	5,925	325	360	520	800	1,100	14,000
1870	6,335	260	285	500	775	1,050	15,000
1870S	3,000	350	475	800	1,400	2,300	—
1871	3,930	260	285	440	480	700	—
1872	3,530	285	315	480	575	900	16,750
1873 closed 3	125,125	325	425	700	1,000	2,000	—
1873 open 3	Inc. above	110	120	150	190	280	—
1874	198,820	110	120	155	190	280	—
1875	420	1,800	2,200	3,300	4,000	5,400	38,000
1876	3,245	220	250	360	475	600	17,500
1877	3,920	150	175	335	480	525	18,500
1878	3,020	180	215	365	470	575	16,000
1879	3,030	165	190	300	330	600	12,500
1880	1,636	145	160	200	235	440	17,500
1881	7,707	145	160	200	235	425	13,500
1882	5,125	160	175	210	235	425	9,750
1883	11,007	145	165	200	235	425	9,750
1884	6,236	140	160	190	230	415	9,750
1885	12,261	145	160	200	235	400	9,750
1886	6,016	145	165	200	235	400	9,750
1887	8,543	145	165	200	235	400	9,750
1888	16,580	145	165	200	235	400	9,750
1889	30,729	145	165	200	235	400	9,750

$2.50 (QUARTER EAGLE)

Liberty Cap.

No stars   Stars

KM# 27 Designer: Robert Scot **Weight:** 4.3700 g. **Composition:** 0.9160 Gold 0.1289 oz. AGW **Size:** 20 mm. **Note:** The 1796 "no stars" variety does not have stars on the obverse. The 1804 varieties are distinguished by the number of stars on the obverse.

Date	Mintage	F-12	VF-20	XF-40	MS-60		Date	Mintage	F-12	VF-20	XF-40	MS-60
1796 no stars	963	11,000	20,000	36,000	125,000		1798	1,094	3,500	4,250	6,500	48,000
1796 stars	432	8,500	14,000	22,000	105,000		1802/1	3,035	3,000	4,100	5,400	22,000
1797	427	8,500	11,000	13,750	110,000							

Date	Mintage	F-12	VF-20	XF-40	MS-60	Date	Mintage	F-12	VF-20	XF-40	MS-60
1804						1806/4	1,616	3,000	4,200	5,500	20,000
13-star reverse	3,327	16,000	30,000	62,000	200,000	1806/5	Inc. above	5,750	13,000	11,500	65,000
1804						1807	6,812	3,000	4,000	5,000	17,500
14-star reverse	Inc. above	3,250	4,200	6,500	21,000						
1805	1,781	3,000	5,000	6,500	20,000						

Turban Head.

KM# 40 Designer: John Reich **Weight:** 4.3700 g. **Composition:** 0.9160 Gold 0.1289 oz. AGW **Size:** 20 mm.

Date	Mintage	F-12	VF-20	XF-40	MS-60
1808	2,710	9,000	14,000	20,000	52,500

Turban Head.

KM# 46 Designer: John Reich **Weight:** 4.3700 g. **Composition:** 0.9160 Gold 0.1289 oz. AGW **Size:** 18.5 mm.

Date	Mintage	F-12	VF-20	XF-40	MS-60	Date	Mintage	F-12	VF-20	XF-40	MS-60
1821	6,448	3,000	3,600	4,500	16,250	1826/25	760	3,450	4,250	5,000	30,000
1824/21	2,600	3,100	3,700	4,200	14,000	1827	2,800	3,600	4,500	5,800	15,500
1825	4,434	3,000	3,600	4,200	12,000						

Turban Head.

KM# 49 Designer: John Reich **Weight:** 4.3700 g. **Composition:** 0.9160 Gold 0.1289 oz. AGW **Size:** 18.2 mm.

Date	Mintage	F-12	VF-20	XF-40	MS-60	Date	Mintage	F-12	VF-20	XF-40	MS-60
1829	3,403	2,600	3,250	4,000	9,250	1832	4,400	2,800	3,250	4,000	10,000
1830	4,540	2,800	3,250	4,000	9,500	1833	4,160	3,000	3,500	4,150	11,000
1831	4,520	2,800	3,250	4,000	9,500	1834	4,000	6,750	9,800	15,000	31,000

Classic Head.

KM# 56 Designer: William Kneass **Weight:** 4.1800 g. **Composition:** 0.8990 Gold 0.1209 oz. AGW **Size:** 18.2 mm.

Date	Mintage	VF-20	XF-40	AU-50	MS-60	MS-65
1834	112,234	300	440	600	1,750	25,000
1835	131,402	265	420	600	1,900	25,000
1836	547,986	255	420	565	1,750	25,000
1837	45,080	265	420	700	2,450	25,000
1838	47,030	265	420	700	1,800	25,000
1838C	7,880	950	2,100	5,750	22,000	45,000
1839	27,021	300	600	1,600	3,800	—
1839C	18,140	800	1,800	3,500	19,500	—
1839D	13,674	940	2,500	5,750	21,000	—
1839O	17,781	455	875	1,300	5,150	—

Coronet Head.

1948 "Cal."

KM# 72 Designer: Christian Gobrecht **Weight:** 4.1800 g. **Composition:** 0.9000 Gold 0.121 oz. AGW **Size:** 18 mm. **Note:** Varieties for 1843 are distinguished by the size of the numerals in the date. One 1848 variety has "Cal." inscribed on the reverse, indicating it was made from California gold. The 1873 "closed-3" and "open-3" varieties are distinguished by the amount of space between the upper left and lower left serifs in the 3 in the date.

Date	Mintage	F-12	VF-20	XF-40	AU-50	MS-60	Prf-65
1840	18,859	180	240	800	2,950	6,000	—
1840C	12,822	325	600	1,150	4,700	13,000	—
1840D	3,532	800	2,400	7,250	15,500	35,000	—
1840O	33,580	225	270	700	1,700	9,000	—
1841	—	—	—	35,000	58,000	90,000	—
1841C	10,281	275	600	1,100	3,250	18,500	—
1841D	4,164	600	1,300	3,000	9,000	22,500	—
1842	2,823	350	800	2,900	6,500	20,000	—
1842C	6,729	525	1,050	2,800	7,500	27,000	—
1842D	4,643	660	1,375	2,700	11,750	33,000	—
1842O	19,800	220	400	1,100	2,400	13,000	—
1843	100,546	150	200	205	325	1,500	—
1843C small date	26,064	900	1,900	5,000	8,400	23,000	—
1843C large date	Inc. above	440	575	975	3,000	8,500	—
1843D small date	36,209	370	600	1,050	2,200	8,700	—
1843O small date	288,002	150	190	250	375	1,600	—
1843O large date	76,000	200	250	450	1,250	7,000	—
1844	6,784	225	400	825	1,950	6,400	—
1844C	11,622	365	750	1,600	6,250	19,000	—
1844D	17,332	330	590	1,150	2,200	7,800	—
1845	91,051	150	220	300	440	1,300	—
1845D	19,460	350	600	1,300	2,500	13,000	—
1845O	4,000	525	900	2,500	5,500	16,000	—
1846	21,598	200	275	500	975	5,500	—
1846C	4,808	485	975	3,500	8,400	18,750	—
1846D	19,303	345	700	1,250	2,300	10,500	—
1846O	66,000	170	270	525	1,000	5,000	—
1847	29,814	140	225	475	800	3,750	—
1847C	23,226	325	500	1,250	1,850	6,700	—
1847D	15,784	345	600	1,350	1,950	9,500	—
1847O	124,000	150	240	525	1,050	4,200	—
1848	7,497	315	490	1,100	1,675	6,200	—
1848 "Cal."	1,389	6,000	8,500	15,000	20,000	34,000	—
1848C	16,788	360	575	1,600	2,750	14,000	—
1848D	13,771	375	550	1,700	2,100	10,000	—
1849	23,294	140	250	525	900	2,700	—
1849C	10,220	375	675	2,200	4,500	20,500	—
1849D	10,945	390	750	1,500	3,100	18,000	—
1850	252,923	135	160	200	300	1,100	—
1850C	9,148	300	600	2,200	3,000	17,500	—
1850D	12,148	330	675	1,600	2,900	14,000	—
1850O	84,000	160	225	450	1,375	4,500	—
1851	1,372,748	120	150	170	190	325	—
1851C	14,923	330	600	1,600	4,400	13,500	—
1851D	11,264	315	700	1,650	3,100	12,250	—
1851O	148,000	140	160	365	900	5,000	—
1852	1,159,681	120	155	170	225	325	—
1852C	9,772	300	600	2,200	3,900	19,000	—
1852D	4,078	400	975	3,400	7,000	22,000	—
1852O	140,000	145	180	350	950	5,000	—
1853	1,404,668	115	150	250	225	350	—
1853D	3,178	500	1,400	2,500	4,700	18,500	—
1854	596,258	135	150	170	200	330	—
1854C	7,295	300	675	1,700	4,400	15,500	—
1854D	1,760	1,500	2,600	6,600	13,000	34,000	—
1854O	153,000	140	170	200	400	1,500	—
1854S	246	11,500	17,500	35,000	58,000	145,000	—
1855	235,480	135	150	180	215	330	—
1855C	3,677	500	1,150	2,850	5,500	29,000	—
1855D	1,123	1,500	3,500	7,500	18,500	36,000	—
1856	384,240	115	155	175	200	330	—
1856C	7,913	385	880	1,975	4,400	15,500	—
1856D	874	3,150	5,400	9,750	22,000	49,000	—
1856O	21,100	150	300	650	1,400	7,000	—
1856S	71,120	130	185	375	1,100	5,500	—
1857	214,130	135	150	175	215	360	—
1857D	2,364	450	900	2,000	3,500	16,000	—
1857O	34,000	140	165	335	1,100	5,100	—
1857S	69,200	140	165	350	950	7,500	—
1858	47,377	130	150	220	330	1,200	—

Date	Mintage	F-12	VF-20	XF-40	AU-50	MS-60	Prf-65
1858C	9,056	325	600	1,100	2,600	9,800	—
1859	39,444	130	190	250	400	1,150	—
1859D	2,244	550	1,250	2,400	4,400	24,000	—
1859S	15,200	180	425	850	2,500	7,750	—
1860	22,675	130	150	250	450	1,100	19,000
1860C	7,469	350	775	1,600	3,650	22,500	—
1860S	35,600	160	250	675	1,150	4,400	—
1861	1,283,878	120	150	180	205	325	20,000
1861S	24,000	150	375	950	3,100	7,000	—
1862	98,543	140	175	250	500	1,350	20,000
1862/1	Inc. above	450	900	2,000	3,300	11,000	—
1862S	8,000	400	825	2,100	4,500	17,000	—
1863	30	—	—	—	—	—	50,000
1863S	10,800	300	575	1,500	4,000	16,500	—
1864	2,874	2,400	5,400	13,000	24,000	37,500	22,500
1865	1,545	2,000	4,250	8,500	19,000	32,000	32,000
1865S	23,376	150	240	575	1,450	5,200	—
1866	3,110	550	1,200	3,500	7,500	16,000	24,000
1866S	38,960	170	300	800	1,700	9,000	—
1867	3,250	175	300	600	1,250	3,500	25,000
1867S	28,000	150	250	600	1,600	5,000	—
1868	3,625	150	200	350	600	2,450	28,000
1868S	34,000	125	190	400	1,150	5,200	—
1869	4,345	135	210	390	650	3,100	24,500
1869S	29,500	135	215	440	775	5,000	—
1870	4,555	140	190	385	700	3,400	30,000
1870S	16,000	135	200	355	900	4,800	—
1871	5,350	150	205	285	550	2,350	30,000
1871S	22,000	130	175	290	525	2,450	—
1872	3,030	200	400	675	1,100	5,250	28,000
1872S	18,000	120	190	450	1,050	4,300	—
1873 closed 3	178,025	110	160	190	240	575	24,000
1873 open 3	Inc. above	110	150	180	200	345	—
1873S	27,000	120	225	450	975	2,500	—
1874	3,940	140	235	390	700	2,400	28,000
1875	420	1,750	3,500	4,800	7,500	17,500	—
1875S	11,600	120	180	350	650	4,000	—
1876	4,221	160	300	500	1,000	3,300	25,000
1876S	5,000	140	220	500	950	3,700	—
1877	1,652	250	380	550	850	3,000	32,500
1877S	35,400	125	160	185	210	700	—
1878	286,260	125	150	175	190	300	34,000
1878S	178,000	125	150	175	210	330	—
1879	88,990	125	150	175	190	335	24,500
1879S	43,500	135	160	225	700	1,900	—
1880	2,996	160	200	300	500	1,300	26,000
1881	691	700	1,750	2,500	4,500	9,500	27,500
1882	4,067	150	210	260	360	675	15,000
1883	2,002	150	220	440	850	2,000	15,000
1884	2,023	150	210	400	575	1,500	17,000
1885	887	400	700	1,650	2,350	3,900	16,000
1886	4,088	150	190	260	425	1,150	17,000
1887	6,282	150	175	235	325	875	15,000
1888	16,098	150	175	195	230	500	6,250
1889	17,648	150	180	195	200	400	5,500
1890	8,813	150	175	195	210	515	7,750
1891	11,040	150	175	200	210	375	6,700
1892	2,545	155	240	285	400	700	8,000
1893	30,106	145	165	180	215	375	14,000
1894	4,122	155	170	260	375	650	14,000
1895	6,199	135	145	200	250	490	14,000
1896	19,202	135	140	170	185	340	14,000
1897	29,904	130	140	170	190	330	14,000
1898	24,165	130	140	170	185	330	14,000
1899	27,350	135	150	170	195	325	13,000
1900	67,205	135	160	250	315	400	13,000
1901	91,322	130	145	170	180	285	13,000
1902	133,733	130	145	170	180	285	13,000
1903	201,257	130	145	170	180	285	13,000
1904	160,960	130	145	170	180	285	13,000
1905	217,944	130	145	170	180	285	13,000
1906	176,490	130	145	170	180	285	13,000
1907	336,448	130	145	170	180	285	13,000

Indian Head.

KM# 128 Designer: Bela Lyon Pratt **Weight:** 4.1800 g. **Composition:** 0.9000 Gold 0.121 oz. AGW **Size:** 18 mm.

1911-D $2.50 Gold
Grade MS-60

☐ Retail Price

Date	Mintage	VF-20	XF-40	AU-50	MS-60	MS-63	MS-65	Prf-65
1908	565,057	135	175	185	250	800	2,500	15,000
1909	441,899	135	175	185	275	950	2,800	29,000
1910	492,682	135	175	185	265	900	4,900	16,000
1911	704,191	135	175	185	250	900	3,500	15,000
1911D	55,680	700	1,000	1,450	3,100	8,250	44,000	—
1912	616,197	135	175	185	285	1,000	5,500	15,500
1913	722,165	135	175	185	270	900	3,500	15,800
1914	240,117	135	175	200	450	2,750	10,000	16,500
1914D	448,000	135	175	185	300	1,300	12,000	—
1915	606,100	135	175	185	240	800	3,500	15,250
1925D	578,000	135	175	185	230	750	2,500	—
1926	446,000	135	175	185	230	725	2,500	—
1927	388,000	135	175	185	230	725	2,500	—
1928	416,000	135	175	185	230	725	2,500	—
1929	532,000	135	175	185	230	725	3,000	—

$3

KM# 84 Designer: James B. Longacre **Weight:** 5.0150 g. **Composition:** 0.9000 Gold 0.1452 oz. AGW **Size:** 20.5 mm. **Note:** The 1873 "closed-3" and "open-3" varieties are distinguished by the amount of space between the upper left and lower left serifs of the 3 in the date.

Date	Mintage	VF-20	XF-40	AU-50	MS-60	MS-65	Prf-65
1854	138,618	550	650	875	1,900	13,500	35,000
1854D	1,120	7,250	12,000	30,000	75,000	—	—
1854O	24,000	900	1,300	2,800	19,000	55,000	—
1855	50,555	550	675	900	2,200	17,000	—
1855S	6,600	950	1,700	4,750	20,000	—	—
1856	26,010	600	700	900	2,250	24,000	—
1856S	34,500	650	950	1,900	8,500	45,000	—
1857	20,891	600	650	900	2,700	27,500	40,000
1857S	14,000	975	1,700	4,000	15,000	—	—
1858	2,133	800	1,175	2,300	6,500	35,000	35,000
1859	15,638	600	675	880	2,200	20,000	35,000
1860	7,155	600	750	1,000	2,400	18,000	35,000
1860S	7,000	700	1,500	5,000	12,000	—	—
1861	6,072	670	800	1,350	2,700	22,500	35,000

Date	Mintage	VF-20	XF-40	AU-50	MS-60	MS-65	Prf-65
1862	5,785	670	800	1,400	2,700	25,000	34,000
1863	5,039	680	770	1,375	2,700	20,000	32,000
1864	2,680	700	900	1,375	2,500	24,000	33,000
1865	1,165	1,200	2,000	3,800	9,500	36,000	35,000
1866	4,030	700	825	1,350	2,500	23,500	35,000
1867	2,650	700	850	1,500	2,450	25,000	27,000
1868	4,875	700	850	1,275	2,500	22,500	31,000
1869	2,525	725	900	1,275	3,800	24,000	35,000
1870	3,535	650	850	1,350	3,750	34,500	35,000
1870S unique	—	—	—	—	—	—	—
Note: 1870S, private sale, 1992, XF-40, $1,500,000.							
1871	1,330	725	1,000	1,450	3,400	24,000	35,000
1872	2,030	700	850	1,300	3,300	26,000	35,000
1873 open 3, proof only	25	—	—	—	—	—	—
1873 closed 3, mintage unknown	—	3,500	4,500	7,750	20,000	—	—
1874	41,820	550	625	750	1,700	13,000	28,000
1875 proof only	20	—	—	32,000	—	—	195,000
1876	45	—	9,000	12,000	—	—	50,000
1877	1,488	1,100	2,450	5,400	14,000	58,000	37,000
1878	82,324	550	625	825	1,800	9,500	40,000
1879	3,030	600	725	1,250	2,250	13,000	27,000
1880	1,036	660	1,250	1,800	2,350	14,000	26,000
1881	554	1,100	1,850	3,600	5,950	35,000	30,000
1882	1,576	675	925	1,500	2,300	16,000	24,000
1883	989	675	1,100	1,750	3,250	16,500	24,000
1884	1,106	1,000	1,400	2,000	3,400	18,000	24,000
1885	910	950	1,500	2,000	3,400	18,000	25,000
1886	1,142	975	1,200	1,800	3,400	—	21,000
1887	6,160	625	700	1,300	2,100	14,000	24,000
1888	5,291	625	800	1,150	2,100	13,000	21,000
1889	2,429	625	800	1,100	2,100	12,500	24,000

$5 (HALF EAGLE)

Liberty Cap.

Small eagle   Large eagle

KM# 19 Designer: Robert Scot **Weight:** 8.7500 g. **Composition:** 0.9160 Gold 0.258 oz. AGW **Size:** 25 mm.
Note: From 1795 through 1798, varieties exist with either a "small eagle" or a "large (heraldic) eagle" on the reverse. After 1798, only the heraldic eagle was used. Two 1797 varieties are distinguished by the size of the 8 in the date. 1806 varieties are distinguished by whether the top of the 6 has a serif.

Date	Mintage	F-12	VF-20	XF-40	MS-60
1795 small eagle	8,707	5,250	7,250	10,000	37,500
1795 large eagle	Inc. above	7,000	10,000	16,500	85,000
1796/95 small eagle	6,196	6,100	8,500	14,000	—
1797/95 large eagle	3,609	5,000	10,000	17,500	130,000
1797 15 stars, small eagle	Inc. above	8,300	12,500	25,000	98,000
1797 16 stars, small eagle	Inc. above	7,250	10,000	23,000	99,000
1798 small eagle	—	75,000	125,000	230,000	—
1798 large eagle, small 8	24,867	1,500	2,400	4,500	18,500
1798 large eagle, large 8, 13-star reverse	Inc. above	1,400	2,200	3,600	17,500
1798 large eagle, large 8, 14-star reverse	Inc. above	1,750	2,750	6,500	25,000
1799	7,451	1,550	1,950	3,500	15,000
1800	37,628	1,300	1,600	2,300	6,700
1802/1	53,176	1,300	1,600	2,300	6,500
1803/2	33,506	1,300	1,600	2,300	6,500
1804 small 8	30,475	1,375	1,650	2,500	6,500
1804 large 8	Inc. above	1,375	1,600	2,300	6,600
1805	33,183	1,375	1,600	2,300	6,200
1806 pointed 6	64,093	1,375	1,625	2,350	9,000
1806 round 6	Inc. above	1,375	1,600	2,300	6,100
1807	32,488	1,400	1,650	2,450	6,600

Turban Head. Capped draped bust.

KM# 38 Designer: John Reich **Obverse:** Capped draped bust **Weight:** 8.7500 g. **Composition:** 0.9160 Gold 0.258 oz. AGW **Size:** 25 mm. **Note:** The 1810 varieties are distinguished by the size of the numerals in the date and the size of the 5 in the "5D." on the reverse. The 1811 varieties are distinguished by the size of the 5 in the "5D." on the reverse.

Date	Mintage	F-12	VF-20	XF-40	MS-60
1807	51,605	1,350	1,650	2,150	5,200
1808	55,578	1,350	1,650	2,150	5,200
1808/7	Inc. above	1,400	1,775	2,350	10,000
1809/8	33,875	1,250	1,650	2,150	5,400
1810 small date, small 5	100,287	8,250	18,500	31,000	84,000
1810 small date, large 5	Inc. above	1,300	1,650	2,250	5,750
1810 large date, small 5	Inc. above	12,000	24,000	35,000	100,000
1810 large date, large 5	Inc. above	1,350	1,600	2,100	5,250
1811 small 5	99,581	1,350	1,600	2,100	5,200
1811 large 5	Inc. above	1,350	1,500	2,000	5,400
1812	58,087	1,350	1,600	2,200	5,300

Turban Head. Capped head.

KM# 43 Designer: John Reich **Obverse:** Capped head **Weight:** 8.7500 g. **Composition:** 0.9160 Gold 0.258 oz. AGW **Size:** 25 mm. **Note:** 1820 varieties are distinguished by whether the 2 in the date has a curved base or square base and by the size of the letters in the reverse inscriptions. 1832 varieties are distinguished by whether the 2 in the date has a curved base or square base and by the number of stars on the reverse. 1834 varieties are distinguished by whether the 4 has a serif at its far right.

Date	Mintage	F-12	VF-20	XF-40	MS-60
1813	95,428	1,550	1,875	2,400	5,600
1814/13	15,454	1,650	2,200	2,800	8,000
1815	635	—	—	—	—
Note: 1815, private sale, Jan. 1994, MS-61, $150,000					
1818	48,588	1,700	2,100	2,800	7,250
1819	51,723	7,750	13,500	23,000	36,500
1820 curved-base 2, small letters	263,806	1,700	2,200	2,850	8,500
1820 curved-base 2, large letters	Inc. above	1,700	2,200	2,850	20,000
1820 square-base 2	Inc. above	1,750	2,200	2,850	8,500
1821	34,641	4,400	8,500	13,500	31,000
1822 3 known	—	—	750,000	—	—
Note: 1822, private sale, 1993, VF-30, $1,000,000.					
1823	14,485	1,750	2,750	3,700	14,500
1824	17,340	4,000	8,000	12,000	26,000
1825/21	29,060	4,100	6,750	9,000	26,500
1825/24	Inc. above	—	—	250,000	—
Note: 1825/4, Bowers & Merena, March 1989, XF, $148,500.					
1826	18,069	3,500	6,000	7,100	20,000
1827	24,913	4,500	6,750	9,000	27,000
1828/7	28,029	15,000	20,000	25,000	100,000
Note: 1828/7, Bowers & Merena, June 1989, XF, $20,900.					
1828	Inc. above	7,000	10,000	26,000	56,000
1829 large planchet	57,442	—	—	50,000	—
Note: 1829 large planchet, Superior, July 1985, MS-65, $104,500.					
1829 small planchet	Inc. above	—	—	60,000	—
Note: 1829 small planchet, private sale, 1992 (XF-45), $89,000.					
1830 small "5D."	126,351	3,500	5,000	5,850	15,000
1830 large "5D."	Inc. above	3,500	5,000	6,400	17,000
1831	140,594	3,500	5,400	7,000	26,000
1832 curved-base 2, 12 stars	157,487	45,000	65,000	125,000	—
1832 square-base 2, 13 stars	Inc. above	3,000	5,400	6,500	17,500
1833	193,630	3,300	5,300	5,800	14,000
1834 plain 4	50,141	3,600	5,000	6,000	19,500
1834 crosslet 4	Inc. above	3,800	5,500	7,500	27,000

Classic Head.

KM# 57   Designer: William Kneass **Weight:** 8.3600 g. **Composition:** 0.8990 Gold 0.2418 oz. AGW **Size:** 22.5 mm. **Note:** 1834 varieties are distinguished by whether the 4 has a serif at its far right.

Date	Mintage	VF-20	XF-40	AU-50	MS-60	MS-65
1834 plain 4	658,028	275	425	700	2,500	46,000
1834 crosslet 4	Inc. above	1,300	2,750	5,300	14,000	—
1835	371,534	265	425	675	2,650	55,000
1836	553,147	285	425	650	2,400	55,000
1837	207,121	285	440	800	3,300	57,000
1838	286,588	275	415	750	3,200	58,000
1838C	17,179	1,600	3,700	13,000	31,000	—
1838D	20,583	1,450	3,200	5,850	23,000	—

Coronet Head. No motto above eagle.

KM# 69   Designer: Christian Gobrecht **Reverse:** No motto above eagle **Weight:** 8.3590 g. **Composition:** 0.9000 Gold 0.242 oz. AGW **Size:** 21.6 mm. **Note:** Varieties for the 1842 Philadelphia strikes are distinguished by the size of the letters in the reverse inscriptions. Varieties for the 1842-C and -D strikes are distinguished by the size of the numerals in the date. Varieties for the 1843-O strikes are distinguished by the size of the letters in the reverse inscriptions.

Date	Mintage	F-12	VF-20	XF-40	MS-60	Prf-65
1839	118,143	220	250	400	3,300	—
1839/8 curved date	Inc. above	240	300	600	1,750	—
1839C	17,205	450	1,000	2,400	24,000	—
1839D	18,939	475	950	2,100	16,500	—
1840	137,382	180	255	340	3,500	—
1840C	18,992	400	775	2,400	24,000	—
1840D	22,896	400	700	1,400	15,000	—

1852-C $5 Gold
Grade MS-60

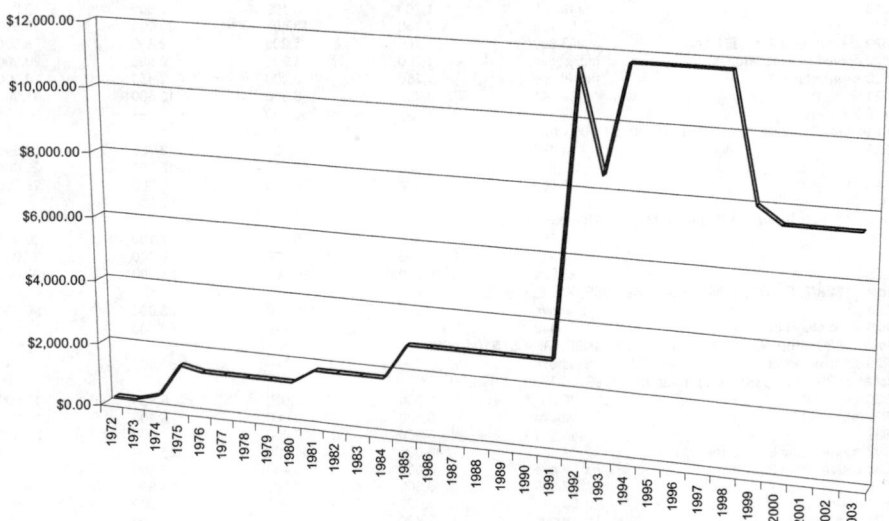

Date	Mintage	F-12	VF-20	XF-40	MS-60	Prf-65
1840O	40,120	200	350	800	6,500	—
1841	15,833	210	350	850	5,200	—
1841C	21,467	345	750	1,450	18,500	—
1841D	30,495	350	700	1,300	12,000	—
1841O 2 known	50	—	—	—	—	—
1842 small letters	27,578	150	325	1,000	12,000	—
1842 large letters	Inc. above	300	750	1,800	11,000	—
1842C small date	28,184	2,500	7,000	23,000	125,000	—
1842C large date	Inc. above	300	750	1,450	17,000	—
1842D small date	59,608	400	750	1,200	13,500	—
1842D large date	Inc. above	900	1,950	5,000	44,000	—
1842O	16,400	350	900	3,100	22,000	—
1843	611,205	150	200	200	1,500	—
1843C	44,201	330	625	1,250	16,000	—
1843D	98,452	300	550	1,000	9,500	—
1843O small letters	19,075	275	450	1,850	26,000	—
1843O large letters	82,000	175	225	1,000	11,000	—
1844	340,330	140	190	200	2,000	—
1844C	23,631	450	900	2,600	18,500	—
1844D	88,982	400	600	1,200	11,000	—
1844O	364,600	170	225	300	4,400	—
1845	417,099	150	200	225	1,850	—
1845D	90,629	400	650	1,150	11,750	—
1845O	41,000	190	350	800	13,000	—
1846	395,942	150	200	215	1,600	—
1846C	12,995	400	950	2,500	21,000	—
1846D	80,294	375	600	1,100	11,000	—
1846O	58,000	190	350	900	12,000	—
1847	915,981	150	190	200	1,250	—
1847C	84,151	375	575	1,150	12,800	—
1847D	64,405	385	550	1,200	7,500	—
1847O	12,000	500	2,200	6,000	22,000	—
1848	260,775	150	200	200	1,300	—
1848C	64,472	325	650	1,100	18,000	—
1848D	47,465	315	675	1,250	13,000	—
1849	133,070	150	190	235	2,500	—
1849C	64,823	350	550	1,100	12,000	—
1849D	39,036	365	675	1,200	14,000	—
1850	64,491	185	250	600	3,450	—
1850C	63,591	350	550	1,000	13,000	—
1850D	43,984	365	800	1,300	24,500	—
1851	377,505	150	200	215	1,700	—
1851C	49,176	375	600	1,100	15,000	—
1851D	62,710	360	625	1,400	13,500	—
1851O	41,000	265	550	1,200	12,750	—
1852	573,901	150	200	200	1,250	—
1852C	72,574	325	675	900	7,500	—
1852D	91,584	350	575	1,000	10,750	—
1853	305,770	150	190	200	1,500	—
1853C	65,571	350	600	900	8,000	—
1853D	89,678	365	600	900	6,500	—
1854	160,675	160	200	240	2,000	—
1854C	39,283	365	650	1,350	12,000	—
1854D	56,413	335	600	1,000	8,500	—
1854O	46,000	200	275	450	7,500	—
1854S	268	—	—	—	—	—

Note: 1854S, Bowers & Merena, Oct. 1982, AU-55, $170,000.

Date	Mintage	F-12	VF-20	XF-40	MS-60	Prf-65
1855	117,098	140	185	225	1,500	—
1855C	39,788	400	750	1,600	17,000	—
1855D	22,432	425	725	1,250	16,500	—
1855O	11,100	280	650	1,950	20,000	—
1855S	61,000	200	350	1,100	13,500	—
1856	197,990	160	200	200	1,700	—
1856C	28,457	385	700	1,400	19,500	—
1856D	19,786	375	725	1,250	12,000	—
1856O	10,000	335	600	1,425	15,750	—
1856S	105,100	185	275	660	5,900	—
1857	98,188	150	190	200	1,650	—
1857C	31,360	325	575	1,285	10,500	—
1857D	17,046	365	600	1,100	12,750	—
1857O	13,000	325	625	1,275	18,000	—
1857S	87,000	200	300	650	7,250	—
1858	15,136	180	235	500	3,600	70,000
1858C	38,856	350	650	1,150	13,500	—
1858D	15,362	360	700	1,350	12,000	—
1858S	18,600	400	800	2,350	20,000	—
1859	16,814	185	275	475	5,500	—
1859C	31,847	350	715	1,500	17,500	—
1859D	10,366	375	725	1,600	13,000	—
1859S	13,220	500	1,475	3,750	28,000	—
1860	19,825	175	265	400	3,400	—
1860C	14,813	375	900	1,850	15,000	—
1860D	14,635	400	875	2,000	16,000	—
1860S	21,200	400	1,100	1,950	26,000	—
1861	688,150	150	200	200	1,100	—

Date	Mintage	F-12	VF-20	XF-40	MS-60	Prf-65
1861C	6,879	675	1,850	3,900	33,000	—
1861D	1,597	2,200	4,000	7,000	45,000	—
1861S	18,000	425	1,000	3,850	30,000	—
1862	4,465	300	750	1,600	19,000	—
1862S	9,500	1,200	3,150	5,350	52,000	—
1863	2,472	400	1,150	3,450	22,000	—
1863S	17,000	450	1,200	3,900	32,000	—
1864	4,220	300	600	1,700	14,500	—
1864S	3,888	2,300	6,900	13,500	47,500	—
1865	1,295	500	1,250	3,500	22,000	—
1865S	27,612	450	1,325	2,400	20,000	—
1866S	9,000	675	1,600	4,000	34,000	—

Coronet Head. "In God We Trust" above eagle.

KM# 101 **Designer:** Christian Gobrecht **Reverse:** "In God We Trust" above eagle **Weight:** 8.3590 g. **Composition:** 0.9000 Gold 0.242 oz. AGW **Size:** 21.6 mm. **Note:** The 1873 "closed-3" and "open-3" varieties are known and are distinguished by the amount of space between the upper left and lower left serifs of the 3 in the date.

Date	Mintage	VF-20	XF-40	AU-50	MS-60	MS-65	Prf-65
1866	6,730	750	1,500	3,500	14,000	—	80,000
1866S	34,920	900	2,600	6,000	21,000	—	—
1867	6,920	440	1,650	3,500	8,000	—	70,000
1867S	29,000	1,300	2,700	12,000	23,000	—	—
1868	5,725	550	950	3,300	10,000	—	70,000
1868S	52,000	400	1,550	3,900	19,000	—	—
1869	1,785	850	1,800	3,800	19,500	—	70,000
1869S	31,000	500	1,700	5,000	23,500	—	—
1870	4,035	700	1,900	2,850	20,000	—	70,000
1870CC	7,675	4,400	12,500	25,000	90,000	—	—
1870S	17,000	950	2,300	8,250	25,000	—	—
1871	3,230	825	1,750	3,500	13,500	—	70,000
1871CC	20,770	1,050	3,200	13,500	54,500	—	—
1871S	25,000	400	1,000	3,700	14,500	—	—
1872	1,690	750	1,400	3,700	15,000	—	60,000
1872CC	16,980	1,100	4,500	20,000	55,000	—	—
1872S	36,400	425	850	3,300	12,000	—	—
1873 closed 3	49,305	180	225	375	1,150	—	70,000
1873 open 3	63,200	180	215	350	700	—	—
1873CC	7,416	2,200	10,000	26,000	48,000	—	—
1873S	31,000	500	1,250	3,600	19,500	—	—
1874	3,508	550	1,575	2,750	12,500	—	66,000
1874CC	21,198	750	1,700	9,500	33,000	—	—
1874S	16,000	600	2,200	4,000	20,000	—	—
1875	220	33,000	50,000	58,000	165,000	—	185,000
1875CC	11,828	1,400	4,500	10,500	42,500	—	—
1875S	9,000	675	2,800	4,800	17,500	—	—
1876	1,477	1,100	2,600	3,600	11,000	—	60,000
1876CC	6,887	1,250	4,500	14,000	42,000	—	—
1876S	4,000	1,700	3,750	9,500	28,000	—	—
1877	1,152	800	2,600	3,750	11,000	—	75,000
1877CC	8,680	1,000	3,300	10,000	47,000	—	—
1877S	26,700	340	625	1,700	8,300	—	—
1878	131,740	160	175	230	425	—	50,000
1878CC	9,054	3,200	7,000	18,000	52,000	—	—
1878S	144,700	165	190	285	575	—	—
1879	301,950	165	180	195	400	11,000	55,000
1879CC	17,281	475	1,375	3,000	19,000	—	—
1879S	426,200	165	175	260	800	—	—
1880	3,166,436	160	170	190	230	—	54,000
1880CC	51,017	350	700	1,550	9,000	—	—
1880S	1,348,900	160	170	185	240	—	—
1881	5,708,802	160	165	190	225	6,600	54,000
1881/80	Inc. above	275	600	750	1,400	—	—
1881CC	13,886	450	1,400	6,250	20,000	—	—
1881S	969,000	160	165	190	290	—	—
1882	2,514,568	150	160	185	225	5,850	54,000
1882CC	82,817	300	475	700	6,900	—	—
1882S	969,000	140	175	215	240	—	—
1883	233,461	140	175	225	350	—	40,000
1883CC	12,958	375	900	2,800	18,000	—	—
1883S	83,200	165	220	240	1,000	—	—
1884	191,078	165	175	210	600	—	35,000
1884CC	16,402	470	875	2,500	16,000	—	—
1884S	177,000	140	170	200	350	—	—

Date	Mintage	VF-20	XF-40	AU-50	MS-60	MS-65	Prf-65
1885	601,506	140	165	180	225	—	35,000
1885S	1,211,500	135	155	175	240	5,000	—
1886	388,432	135	160	175	260	—	44,000
1886S	3,268,000	135	155	170	240	—	—
1887	87	—	—	14,000	—	—	130,000
1887S	1,912,000	130	155	170	225	—	—
1888	18,296	150	185	275	575	—	28,000
1888S	293,900	145	170	300	1,200	—	—
1889	7,565	260	440	515	1,100	—	29,000
1890	4,328	385	425	515	2,100	—	27,000
1890CC	53,800	280	340	500	1,100	—	—
1891	61,413	150	180	200	450	5,400	28,000
1891CC	208,000	250	335	475	750	25,000	—
1892	753,572	150	165	185	235	—	30,000
1892CC	82,968	285	400	550	1,400	—	—
1892O	10,000	450	900	1,350	3,100	—	—
1892S	298,400	160	190	210	675	—	—
1893	1,528,197	160	170	185	235	3,100	34,000
1893CC	60,000	250	415	700	1,400	—	—
1893O	110,000	215	300	475	975	—	—
1893S	224,000	160	210	240	260	—	—
1894	957,955	150	175	190	250	2,000	35,000
1894O	16,600	180	375	450	1,300	—	—
1894S	55,900	230	325	600	2,800	—	—
1895	1,345,936	150	160	185	225	4,400	29,000
1895S	112,000	180	260	415	2,800	23,000	—
1896	59,063	155	160	225	285	—	30,000
1896S	155,400	190	235	330	1,300	—	—
1897	867,883	150	165	180	230	4,150	35,000
1897S	354,000	155	165	260	940	—	—
1898	633,495	150	160	175	250	5,500	30,000
1898S	1,397,400	155	165	185	230	—	—
1899	1,710,729	155	165	185	230	2,700	30,000
1899S	1,545,000	155	165	185	230	7,800	—
1900	1,405,730	155	165	185	235	2,600	30,000
1900S	329,000	170	180	275	250	11,500	—
1901	616,040	160	175	200	350	3,100	12,500
1901S	3,648,000	155	165	185	230	2,900	—
1902	172,562	165	170	190	240	4,400	22,000
1902S	939,000	160	165	180	230	2,650	—
1903	227,024	160	170	185	240	3,400	22,000
1903S	1,855,000	160	165	180	220	2,700	—
1904	392,136	160	165	180	225	2,700	25,000
1904S	97,000	165	180	265	850	9,000	—
1905	302,308	160	165	180	215	3,300	25,000
1905S	880,700	160	175	195	500	9,200	—
1906	348,820	160	165	185	220	2,950	22,000
1906D	320,000	160	165	185	220	3,500	—
1906S	598,000	160	165	185	250	4,500	—
1907	626,192	160	165	180	215	2,750	23,000
1907D	888,000	160	165	185	215	2,750	—
1908	421,874	160	165	185	215	2,750	—

Indian Head.

KM# 129 Designer: Bela Lyon Pratt **Weight:** 8.3590 g. **Composition:** 0.9000 Gold .2420 oz. AGW
Size: 21.6 mm.

Date	Mintage	VF-20	XF-40	AU-50	MS-60	MS-63	MS-65	Prf-65
1908	578,012	180	215	225	325	1,100	11,000	16,000
1908D	148,000	180	215	225	325	1,000	18,000	—
1908S	82,000	195	415	450	1,200	2,500	14,000	—
1909	627,138	180	215	225	325	1,200	11,500	29,000
1909D	3,423,560	175	200	220	310	1,150	11,500	—
1909O	34,200	650	1,350	1,600	6,000	40,000	190,000	—
1909S	297,200	185	240	285	1,300	6,800	39,000	—
1910	604,250	175	215	240	300	1,500	14,000	32,000
1910D	193,600	175	215	240	350	1,750	34,500	—
1910S	770,200	175	230	275	925	5,500	36,000	—
1911	915,139	175	215	240	300	1,200	12,750	26,000
1911D	72,500	350	450	500	2,900	16,500	115,000	—
1911S	1,416,000	180	230	270	550	2,700	31,000	—
1912	790,144	180	210	240	315	1,200	12,900	26,000
1912S	392,000	195	275	310	1,500	7,500	75,000	—
1913	916,099	180	210	230	310	1,150	11,500	26,000
1913S	408,000	200	250	290	1,300	9,800	100,000	—
1914	247,125	180	225	240	335	1,250	12,500	26,000

Date	Mintage	VF-20	XF-40	AU-50	MS-60	MS-63	MS-65	Prf-65
1914D	247,000	185	235	250	325	2,600	25,000	—
1914S	263,000	260	285	300	1,400	8,000	72,000	—
1915	588,075	190	225	250	335	1,200	14,000	33,000
1915S	164,000	270	350	385	1,900	8,000	85,000	—
1916S	240,000	260	280	295	530	2,800	18,500	—
1929	662,000	2,400	4,800	5,300	6,100	7,800	23,500	—

$10 (EAGLE)

Liberty Cap. Small eagle.

KM# 21 **Designer:** Robert Scot **Reverse:** Small eagle **Weight:** 17.5000 g. **Composition:** 0.9160 Gold 0.5159 oz. AGW **Size:** 33 mm.

Date	Mintage	F-12	VF-20	XF-40	MS-60
1795 13 leaves	5,583	6,000	8,500	16,000	47,000
1795 9 leaves	Inc. above	17,000	30,000	47,000	84,000
1796	4,146	6,700	9,500	16,500	57,500
1797 small eagle	3,615	8,000	12,500	22,500	85,000

Liberty Cap. Heraldic eagle.

KM# 30 **Designer:** Robert Scot **Reverse:** Heraldic eagle **Weight:** 17.5000 g. **Composition:** 0.9160 Gold 0.5159 oz. AGW **Size:** 33 mm. **Note:** The 1798/97 varieties are distinguished by the positioning of the stars on the obverse.

Date	Mintage	F-12	VF-20	XF-40	MS-60
1797 large eagle	10,940	2,500	3,500	5,500	20,000
1798/97 9 stars left, 4 right	900	5,500	11,000	20,000	70,000
1798/97 7 stars left, 6 right	842	15,000	30,000	52,000	—
1799	37,449	2,300	3,300	5,250	10,000
1800	5,999	2,400	3,600	5,500	17,000
1801	44,344	2,300	3,250	5,250	10,000
1803	15,017	2,300	3,500	5,400	12,500
1804	3,757	3,400	4,250	6,500	25,000

Coronet Head. Old-style head. No motto above eagle.

KM# 66.1 **Designer:** Christian Gobrecht **Obverse:** Old-style head **Reverse:** No motto above eagle **Weight:** 16.7180 g. **Composition:** 0.9000 Gold 0.4839 oz. AGW **Size:** 27 mm.

Date	Mintage	F-12	VF-20	XF-40	MS-60	Prf-65
1838	7,200	800	1,100	2,900	27,000	—
1839 large letters	38,248	700	1,000	1,800	23,000	—

1853 $10 Gold
Grade XF-40

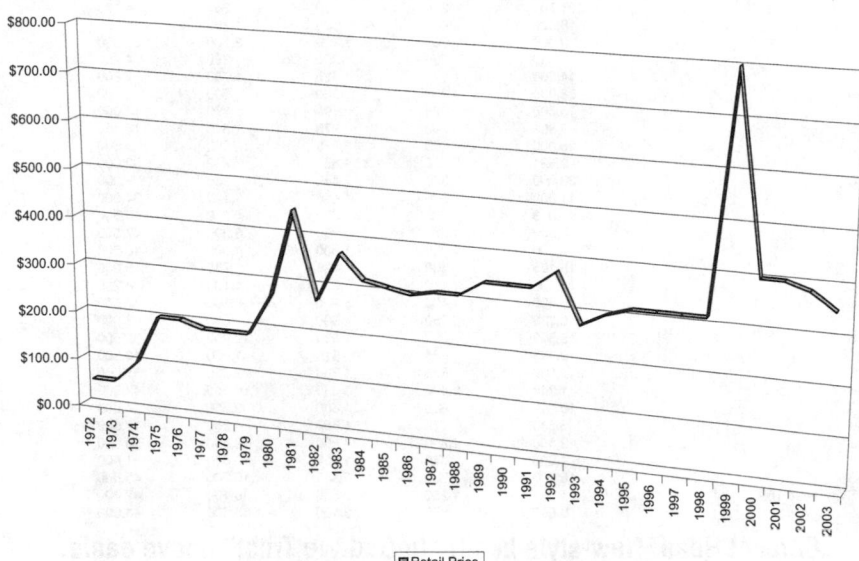

Coronet Head. New-style head. No motto above eagle.

KM# 66.2 Designer: Christian Gobrecht **Obverse:** New-style head **Reverse:** No motto above eagle **Weight:** 16.7180 g. **Composition:** 0.9000 Gold 0.4839 oz. AGW **Size:** 27 mm. **Note:** The 1842 varieties are distinguished by the size of the numerals in the date.

Date	Mintage	F-12	VF-20	XF-40	MS-60	Prf-65
1839 small letters	Inc. above	800	1,500	3,500	25,000	—
1840	47,338	300	360	600	9,250	—
1841	63,131	300	360	600	9,500	—
1841O	2,500	1,100	2,100	4,500	29,500	—
1842 small date	81,507	275	375	600	11,500	—
1842 large date	Inc. above	260	325	450	9,200	—
1842O	27,400	250	340	500	22,500	—
1843	75,462	250	325	400	15,000	—
1843O	175,162	250	315	400	11,500	—
1844	6,361	800	1,350	2,700	16,750	—
1844O	118,700	245	325	475	15,000	—
1845	26,153	290	600	775	14,000	—
1845O	47,500	250	380	650	16,500	—
1846	20,095	410	625	900	20,000	—
1846O	81,780	250	425	770	14,750	—
1847	862,258	240	300	350	3,000	—
1847O	571,500	250	325	375	4,850	—
1848	145,484	260	340	375	4,300	—
1848O	38,850	325	525	1,050	14,000	—
1849	653,618	240	300	350	3,400	—
1849O	23,900	375	710	2,100	21,000	—
1850	291,451	240	300	380	3,600	—
1850O	57,500	285	380	880	—	—
1851	176,328	275	325	475	5,150	—
1851O	263,000	250	315	440	5,750	—
1852	263,106	240	300	350	4,200	—
1852O	18,000	375	650	1,100	19,000	—
1853	201,253	240	300	350	3,500	—
1853O	51,000	285	325	485	12,500	—
1854	54,250	290	320	400	6,000	—

Date	Mintage	F-12	VF-20	XF-40	MS-60	Prf-65
1854O small date	52,500	290	375	675	10,500	—
1854O large date	Inc. above	375	475	875	—	—
1854S	123,826	275	325	410	5,500	—
1855	121,701	250	300	350	4,150	—
1855O	18,000	400	625	1,250	20,000	—
1855S	9,000	700	1,250	2,100	29,500	—
1856	60,490	250	300	350	4,200	—
1856O	14,500	375	725	1,250	9,800	—
1856S	68,000	250	320	500	8,500	—
1857	16,606	325	490	850	12,000	—
1857O	5,500	600	975	1,850	18,000	—
1857S	26,000	300	375	950	9,500	—
1858	2,521	2,600	4,650	7,250	32,000	—
1858O	20,000	300	440	750	9,000	—
1858S	11,800	825	1,450	3,100	34,000	—
1859	16,093	325	390	750	10,500	—
1859O	2,300	1,850	3,800	8,200	47,500	—
1859S	7,000	1,000	1,800	4,500	40,000	—
1860	15,105	300	420	775	8,000	—
1860O	11,100	410	575	1,100	8,250	—
1860S	5,000	1,400	3,250	6,100	40,500	—
1861	113,233	250	300	350	3,600	—
1861S	15,500	690	1,600	2,950	32,500	—
1862	10,995	265	515	1,000	13,500	—
1862S	12,500	675	1,750	2,950	37,000	—
1863	1,248	2,400	3,650	10,000	42,500	—
1863S	10,000	625	1,600	3,350	24,000	—
1864	3,580	775	1,600	4,200	17,500	—
1864S	2,500	2,300	4,900	12,500	50,000	—
1865	4,005	875	1,950	3,500	31,500	—
1865S	16,700	1,700	5,350	10,500	45,000	—
1865S /inverted 186	—	1,250	2,850	6,100	47,000	—
1866S	8,500	950	2,400	3,300	44,000	—

Coronet Head. New-style head. "In God We Trust" above eagle.

KM# 102 Designer: Christian Gobrecht **Obverse:** New-style head **Reverse:** "In God We Trust" above eagle **Weight:** 16.7180 g. **Composition:** 0.9000 Gold 0.4839 oz. AGW **Size:** 27 mm. **Note:** The 1873 "closed-3" and "open-3" varieties are distinguished by the amount of space between the upper left and lower left serifs of the 3 in the date.

Date	Mintage	VF-20	XF-40	AU-50	MS-60	MS-65	Prf-65
1866	3,780	775	1,650	3,500	15,500	—	75,000
1866S	11,500	1,550	3,400	6,400	23,000	—	—
1867	3,140	1,500	2,600	4,800	26,000	—	75,000
1867S	9,000	2,000	5,200	8,900	40,000	—	—
1868	10,655	500	750	1,700	15,000	—	60,000
1868S	13,500	1,250	2,100	3,800	24,000	—	—
1869	1,855	1,400	2,800	5,400	27,500	—	—
1869S	6,430	1,500	2,500	6,250	25,000	—	—
1870	4,025	800	1,175	2,350	17,000	—	60,000
1870CC	5,908	9,000	22,000	42,000	90,000	—	—
1870S	8,000	1,100	2,500	6,500	32,000	—	—
1871	1,820	1,450	2,400	4,000	19,500	—	75,000
1871CC	8,085	2,150	4,950	16,500	53,500	—	—
1871S	16,500	1,075	1,500	5,700	26,000	—	—
1872	1,650	2,200	3,600	9,500	16,500	—	60,000
1872CC	4,600	3,000	8,800	20,000	55,000	—	—
1872S	17,300	550	850	1,800	22,000	—	—
1873 closed 3	825	4,500	9,500	17,500	55,000	—	60,000
1873CC	4,543	5,000	12,000	26,000	57,500	—	—
1873S	12,000	950	1,950	4,750	24,500	—	—
1874	53,160	240	265	315	1,850	—	60,000
1874CC	16,767	850	2,500	8,000	40,000	—	—
1874S	10,000	1,150	3,250	6,800	39,500	—	—
1875	120	38,000	53,000	80,000	95,000	—	185,000

Note: 1875, Akers, Aug. 1990, Proof, $115,000.

1875CC	7,715	3,700	8,800	25,000	65,000	—	—
1876	732	3,500	4,750	15,000	55,000	—	60,000
1876CC	4,696	3,200	6,500	20,500	50,000	—	—
1876S	5,000	1,250	2,000	5,500	38,000	—	—
1877	817	2,100	3,800	8,500	—	—	—
1877CC	3,332	2,300	4,750	14,000	47,000	—	—

Date	Mintage	VF-20	XF-40	AU-50	MS-60	MS-65	Prf-65
1877S	17,000	500	700	2,200	22,500	—	—
1878	73,800	220	265	285	900	—	60,000
1878CC	3,244	3,600	7,500	14,000	47,000	—	—
1878S	26,100	450	550	1,650	15,000	—	—
1879	384,770	200	220	315	665	—	50,000
1879/78	Inc. above	300	400	700	800	—	—
1879CC	1,762	6,500	12,000	21,750	60,000	—	—
1879O	1,500	2,300	3,750	10,000	28,750	—	—
1879S	224,000	200	220	250	1,100	—	—
1880	1,644,876	210	225	250	280	—	45,000
1880CC	11,190	475	700	1,450	12,500	—	—
1880O	9,200	415	700	1,200	12,750	—	—
1880S	506,250	200	230	315	415	—	—
1881	3,877,260	200	225	240	275	—	45,000
1881CC	24,015	360	515	950	6,500	—	—
1881O	8,350	375	650	1,250	6,750	—	—
1881S	970,000	200	225	240	350	—	—
1882	2,324,480	200	225	240	270	—	41,500
1882CC	6,764	950	1,300	3,000	13,000	—	—
1882O	10,820	375	575	1,200	7,700	—	—
1882S	132,000	200	230	240	350	—	—
1883	208,740	200	225	240	300	—	41,500
1883CC	12,000	425	700	2,350	12,500	—	—
1883O	800	2,950	6,800	9,500	33,500	—	—
1883S	38,000	200	250	340	1,100	—	—
1884	76,905	190	225	250	750	—	46,000
1884CC	9,925	600	950	2,250	10,750	—	—
1884S	124,250	210	220	235	525	—	—
1885	253,527	210	220	230	375	—	43,000
1885S	228,000	210	225	250	375	6,500	—
1886	236,160	210	225	250	375	—	42,500
1886S	826,000	200	225	250	340	—	—
1887	53,680	200	225	295	800	—	37,000
1887S	817,000	200	225	240	315	—	—
1888	132,996	225	235	315	700	—	38,500
1888O	21,335	225	250	275	515	—	—
1888S	648,700	210	225	240	300	—	—
1889	4,485	575	700	1,100	2,700	—	43,000
1889S	425,400	210	220	240	350	4,200	—
1890	58,043	225	275	300	700	7,750	37,500
1890CC	17,500	385	450	650	2,000	—	—
1891	91,868	225	250	275	325	—	32,500
1891CC	103,732	350	400	515	750	—	—
1892	797,552	210	225	250	285	12,000	37,500
1892CC	40,000	350	450	625	3,100	—	—
1892O	28,688	250	275	300	400	—	—
1892S	115,500	210	220	250	360	—	—
1893	1,840,895	200	210	235	275	—	34,500
1893CC	14,000	425	625	1,450	6,200	—	—
1893O	17,000	260	315	350	625	—	—
1893S	141,350	220	230	250	440	—	—
1894	2,470,778	210	225	250	265	11,500	35,000
1894O	107,500	225	260	360	900	—	—
1894S	25,000	260	385	875	3,500	—	—
1895	567,826	200	210	240	280	8,800	33,000
1895O	98,000	220	230	280	480	—	—
1895S	49,000	225	300	600	2,250	—	—
1806	76,348	200	220	260	300	—	31,500
1896S	123,750	215	265	450	2,500	—	—
1897	1,000,159	200	215	250	285	6,500	35,000
1897O	42,500	225	265	335	700	—	—
1897S	234,750	200	250	335	870	—	—
1898	812,197	200	215	255	285	3,800	35,000
1898S	473,600	205	235	250	350	—	—
1899	1,262,305	200	220	245	285	2,800	31,000
1899O	37,047	230	275	325	550	—	—
1899S	841,000	200	235	265	320	—	—
1900	293,960	200	225	230	300	7,750	30,500
1900S	81,000	210	275	350	850	—	—
1901	1,718,825	200	215	240	285	2,800	30,500
1901O	72,041	225	250	285	400	—	—
1901S	2,812,750	200	215	240	285	2,500	—
1902	82,513	230	260	295	330	—	30,500
1902S	469,500	230	250	260	400	2,700	—
1903	125,926	215	260	290	315	—	30,000
1903O	112,771	225	250	295	375	—	—
1903S	538,000	200	225	250	290	2,650	—
1904	162,038	215	230	260	325	—	31,500
1904O	108,950	220	250	285	360	—	—
1905	201,078	200	220	250	285	4,800	30,000
1905S	369,250	210	230	300	1,100	—	—
1906	165,497	225	230	250	295	7,750	30,000
1906D	981,000	230	245	275	325	3,850	—
1906O	86,895	235	250	330	450	—	—
1906S	457,000	220	250	300	475	12,500	—

Date	Mintage	VF-20	XF-40	AU-50	MS-60	MS-65	Prf-65
1907	1,203,973	195	210	220	275	—	30,000
1907D	1,030,000	230	240	250	310	—	—
1907S	210,500	240	260	280	600	—	—

Indian Head. No motto next to eagle.

KM# 125 **Designer:** Augustus Saint-Gaudens **Reverse:** No motto next to eagle **Weight:** 16.7180 g. **Composition:** 0.9000 Gold 0.4839 oz. AGW **Size:** 27 mm. **Note:** 1907 varieties are distinguished by whether the edge is rolled or wired, and whether the legend "E Pluribus Unum" has periods between each word.

Date	Mintage	VF-20	XF-40	AU-50	MS-60	MS-63	MS-65	Prf-65
1907 wire edge, periods before and after legend	500	—	4,500	6,000	11,500	18,000	45,000	—
1907 rolled edge, periods	42	13,000	18,000	22,000	28,000	35,000	95,000	—
1907 without periods	239,406	350	375	400	550	2,000	6,100	—
1908 without motto	33,500	350	390	450	625	2,400	9,700	—
1908D without motto	210,000	335	390	425	740	4,800	40,000	—

Indian Head. "In God We Trust" left of eagle.

KM# 130 **Designer:** Augustus Saint-Gaudens **Reverse:** "In God We Trust" left of eagle **Weight:** 16.7180 g. **Composition:** 0.9000 Gold 0.4839 oz. AGW **Size:** 27 mm.

Date	Mintage	VF-20	XF-40	AU-50	MS-60	MS-63	MS-65	Prf-65
1908	341,486	315	370	385	475	1,400	5,000	29,500
1908D	836,500	320	375	390	650	3,700	18,000	—
1908S	59,850	360	390	400	1,675	5,800	20,000	—
1909	184,863	330	375	400	485	1,850	8,400	31,500
1909D	121,540	330	380	400	690	2,300	42,000	—
1909S	292,350	330	380	395	600	3,200	10,750	—
1910	318,704	335	375	400	480	900	5,600	37,000
1910D	2,356,640	330	365	390	465	900	5,500	—
1910S	811,000	330	370	390	700	3,250	45,000	—
1911	505,595	325	345	375	480	1,050	4,875	32,000
1911D	30,100	425	690	890	3,900	11,500	100,000	—
1911S	51,000	365	550	630	1,100	4,800	10,500	—
1912	405,083	330	350	385	450	900	6,800	32,000
1912S	300,000	345	375	390	800	2,750	47,500	—
1913	442,071	340	360	375	460	925	4,600	32,000
1913S	66,000	360	640	850	3,650	15,000	100,000	—
1914	151,050	345	360	350	525	1,525	6,750	32,000
1914D	343,500	330	360	360	535	1,550	10,000	—
1914S	208,000	340	365	415	700	4,200	38,000	—
1915	351,075	340	360	385	525	1,200	5,600	40,000
1915S	59,000	400	625	775	2,900	8,500	54,000	—
1916S	138,500	340	375	415	675	2,350	14,250	—
1920S	126,500	5,000	6,200	8,200	17,000	35,000	195,000	—
1926	1,014,000	290	325	380	430	615	3,650	—
1930S	96,000	4,000	5,250	6,500	9,300	11,000	26,750	—
1932	4,463,000	290	325	380	430	615	2,750	—
1933	312,500	10,000	30,000	37,500	60,000	100,000	360,000	—

1933 $10 Gold
Grade MS-60

☐ Retail Price

$20 (DOUBLE EAGLE)

Liberty. "Twenty D." below eagle. No motto above eagle.

KM# 74.1 Designer: James B. Longacre **Reverse:** "Twenty D." below eagle. No motto above eagle **Weight:** 33.4360 g. **Composition:** 0.9000 Gold 0.9677 oz. AGW **Size:** 34 mm.

Date	Mintage	VF-20	XF-40	AU-50	MS-60	MS-65	Prf-65
1849 unique, in Smithsonian collection	1	—	—	—	—	—	—
1850	1,170,261	625	850	2,100	5,400	—	—
1850O	141,000	725	1,250	5,200	28,000	—	—
1851	2,087,155	615	675	825	3,200	—	—
1851O	315,000	700	750	1,500	14,000	—	—
1852	2,053,026	600	675	800	3,100	—	—
1852O	190,000	675	740	1,800	13,000	—	—
1853	1,261,326	600	625	900	4,400	—	—
1853O	71,000	625	975	2,700	27,000	—	—
1854	757,899	585	650	875	5,400	—	—
1854O	3,250	24,000	50,000	82,500	225,000	—	—
1854S	141,468	650	850	1,400	4,000	35,000	—
1855	364,666	625	675	1,100	7,500	—	—
1855O	8,000	2,200	5,500	16,000	66,000	—	—
1855S	879,675	675	850	1,300	6,750	—	—
1856	329,878	675	700	950	8,000	—	—
1856O	2,250	33,000	55,000	97,500	185,000	—	—
1856S	1,189,750	600	675	1,100	5,250	—	—
1857	439,375	600	675	850	3,600	—	—
1857O	30,000	950	1,600	4,000	21,500	—	—
1857S	970,500	650	750	1,050	3,400	—	—
1858	211,714	685	850	1,450	4,200	—	—
1858O	35,250	1,200	1,850	4,500	23,000	—	—

Date	Mintage	VF-20	XF-40	AU-50	MS-60	MS-65	Prf-65
1858S	846,710	600	750	1,000	7,900	—	—
1859	43,597	875	2,000	4,400	32,000	—	—
1859O	9,100	3,150	6,500	14,500	70,000	—	—
1859S	636,445	600	700	1,000	4,350	—	—
1860	577,670	615	625	800	5,000	—	—
1860O	6,600	3,200	5,500	14,500	75,000	—	—
1860S	544,950	615	650	1,100	5,300	—	—
1861	2,976,453	575	600	800	2,600	—	—
1861O	17,741	1,600	3,000	7,500	40,000	—	—
1861S	768,000	600	625	1,100	12,000	—	—

Liberty. Paquet design.

KM# 93 Reverse: Paquet design **Weight:** 33.4360 g. **Composition:** 0.9000 Gold 0.9677 oz. AGW **Note:** In 1861 the reverse was redesigned by Anthony C. Paquet, but it was withdrawn soon after its release. The letters in the inscriptions on the Paquet-reverse variety are taller than on the regular reverse.

Date	Mintage	VF-20	XF-40	AU-50	MS-60	MS-65	Prf-65
1861S	Inc. above	5,950	14,500	23,000	60,000	—	—

Note: 1861S Paquet reverse, Bowers & Merena, Nov. 1988, MS-67, $660,000.

Liberty. Longacre design resumed.

KM# A74.1 Reverse: Longacre design resumed **Weight:** 33.4360 g. **Composition:** 0.9000 Gold 0.9677 oz. AGW

Date	Mintage	VF-20	XF-40	AU-50	MS-60	MS-65	Prf-65
1862	92,133	825	1,400	2,500	14,000	—	—
1862S	854,173	575	675	1,500	9,750	—	—
1863	142,790	575	675	1,800	16,000	—	—
1863S	966,570	575	660	1,750	16,000	—	—
1864	204,285	690	850	1,600	14,000	—	—
1864S	793,660	600	650	1,750	6,600	—	—
1865	351,200	615	665	975	6,100	—	—
1865S	1,042,500	545	630	1,250	3,850	18,500	—
1866S	1,600	2,700	9,750	26,000	—	—	

Liberty. "Twenty D." below eagle. "In God We Trust" above eagle.

KM# 74.2 Designer: James B. Longacre **Reverse:** "Twenty D." below eagle. "In God We Trust" above eagle **Weight:** 33.4360 g. **Composition:** 0.9000 Gold 0.9677 oz. AGW **Size:** 34 mm. **Note:** The 1873 "closed-3" and "open-3" varieties are known and are distinguished by the amount of space between the upper left and lower left serif in the 3 in the date.

Date	Mintage	VF-20	XF-40	AU-50	MS-60	MS-65	Prf-65
1866	698,775	600	700	1,050	5,200	—	—
1866S	842,250	540	650	1,350	15,000	—	—
1867	251,065	540	575	775	2,150	—	—
1867S	920,750	565	650	1,750	13,000	—	—
1868	98,600	750	1,100	1,800	7,850	—	—
1868S	837,500	525	635	1,200	7,800	—	—
1869	175,155	600	775	1,100	5,000	—	—
1869S	686,750	525	575	1,000	4,900	—	—
1870	155,185	600	800	2,000	7,500	—	—
1870CC	3,789	75,000	95,000	160,000	215,000	—	—
1870S	982,000	550	600	875	5,000	—	—
1871	80,150	675	950	1,500	4,000	—	—

Date	Mintage	VF-20	XF-40	AU-50	MS-60	MS-65	Prf-65
1871CC	17,387	3,200	5,400	13,750	4,250	—	—
1871S	928,000	525	570	750	3,850	—	—
1872	251,880	525	565	700	2,500	—	—
1872CC	26,900	1,500	2,000	4,750	21,500	—	—
1872S	780,000	500	525	600	3,600	—	—
1873 closed 3	Est. 208,925	525	575	625	2,800	—	—
1873 open 3	Est. 1,500,900	525	560	525	900	—	—
1873CC	22,410	1,100	2,150	4,600	22,500	—	—
1873S	1,040,600	500	525	560	1,650	—	—
1874	366,800	500	525	570	1,250	—	—
1874CC	115,085	900	1,200	2,600	7,800	—	—
1874S	1,214,000	525	550	565	1,650	—	—
1875	295,740	525	540	550	1,200	—	—
1875CC	111,151	985	1,100	1,275	2,400	—	—
1875S	1,230,000	490	510	535	1,100	—	—
1876	583,905	420	450	500	1,100	—	—
1876CC	138,441	1,000	1,200	1,475	3,750	—	—
1876S	1,597,000	465	485	525	950	—	—

Liberty. "Twenty Dollars" below eagle.

KM# 74.3 **Reverse:** "Twenty Dollars" below eagle **Weight:** 33.4360 g. **Composition:** 0.9000 Gold 0.9677 oz. AGW

Date	Mintage	VF-20	XF-40	AU-50	MS-60	MS-65	Prf-65
1877	397,670	425	475	500	600	—	—
1877CC	42,565	1,100	1,275	1,750	15,500	—	—
1877S	1,735,000	400	440	485	650	—	—
1878	543,645	425	460	490	625	—	—
1878CC	13,180	1,450	2,000	3,850	20,000	—	—
1878S	1,739,000	410	440	485	750	—	—
1879	207,630	440	450	485	1,100	—	—
1879CC	10,708	1,500	2,100	4,750	23,000	—	—
1879O	2,325	4,500	6,750	14,000	38,000	—	—
1879S	1,223,800	370	425	450	1,450	—	—
1880	51,456	440	460	500	3,300	—	—
1880S	836,000	405	450	500	1,000	—	—
1881	2,260	5,000	6,500	13,000	38,000	—	105,000
1881S	727,000	405	425	450	1,150	—	—
1882	630	6,800	13,750	24,000	60,000	—	—
1882CC	39,140	950	1,100	1,400	6,000	—	—
1882S	1,125,000	405	415	500	700	—	—
1883 proof only	92	—	—	10,000	—	—	—
1883CC	59,962	900	1,100	1,300	3,200	—	—
1883S	1,189,000	405	410	415	525	—	—
1884 proof only	71	—	—	10,000	—	—	150,000
1884CC	81,139	900	1,100	1,250	2,600	—	—
1884S	916,000	400	415	440	525	—	—
1885	828	6,250	7,750	10,500	29,000	—	—
1885CC	9,450	1,500	2,150	4,500	10,750	—	—
1885S	683,500	405	420	440	515	—	—
1886	1,106	8,000	10,500	19,500	38,000	—	67,000
1887	121	—	—	8,000	—	—	85,000
1887S	283,000	400	410	430	550	—	—
1888	226,266	400	410	430	500	—	—
1888S	859,600	400	415	430	550	—	—
1889	44,111	425	450	475	650	—	57,500
1889CC	30,945	1,100	1,250	1,650	3,200	—	—
1889S	774,700	390	400	415	525	—	—
1890	75,995	390	410	425	525	—	27,000
1890CC	91,209	1,100	1,300	1,450	2,600	—	—
1890S	802,750	390	410	425	600	—	—
1891	1,442	3,300	5,000	8,000	27,500	—	62,500
1891CC	5,000	2,500	4,150	5,900	13,000	—	—
1891S	1,288,125	390	400	425	475	—	—
1892	4,523	1,250	1,600	2,750	5,500	—	55,000
1892CC	27,265	950	1,150	1,600	3,100	—	—
1892S	930,150	390	400	410	440	—	—
1893	344,339	390	400	410	465	—	60,000
1893CC	18,402	1,200	1,400	1,650	2,450	—	—
1893S	996,175	390	400	410	460	—	—
1894	1,368,990	390	400	410	440	—	55,000

1907-S $20 Gold
Grade VF-20

☐ Retail Price

Date	Mintage	VF-20	XF-40	AU-50	MS-60	MS-65	Prf-65
1894S	1,048,550	390	400	410	430	—	—
1895	1,114,656	390	400	410	430	—	54,000
1895S	1,143,500	390	400	410	440	13,500	—
1896	792,663	390	400	410	450	—	49,000
1896S	1,403,925	390	400	410	450	—	—
1897	1,383,261	390	400	410	450	—	55,000
1897S	1,470,250	390	400	410	450	—	—
1898	170,470	410	420	450	525	—	49,000
1898S	2,575,175	390	400	410	425	9,000	—
1899	1,669,384	390	400	410	425	11,500	49,000
1899S	2,010,300	390	400	410	425	10,500	—
1900	1,874,584	390	400	410	425	4,250	49,000
1900S	2,459,500	390	400	410	425	—	—
1901	111,526	390	400	410	700	3,200	—
1901S	1,596,000	390	400	410	465	—	—
1902	31,254	400	450	475	875	—	—
1902S	1,753,625	400	450	475	525	—	—
1903	287,428	400	450	475	525	3,400	51,500
1903S	954,000	400	450	475	525	9,750	—
1904	6,256,797	400	450	475	525	3,300	50,000
1904S	5,134,175	400	450	475	525	4,700	—
1905	59,011	400	450	475	875	—	—
1905S	1,813,000	400	450	475	550	—	—
1906	69,690	400	450	475	525	13,500	52,500
1906D	620,250	400	450	475	550	—	—
1906S	2,065,750	400	450	475	550	—	—
1907	1,451,864	400	450	475	525	6,800	—
1907D	842,250	400	450	475	540	4,500	—
1907S	2,165,800	400	450	475	540	—	—

Saint-Gaudens. Roman numerals in date. No motto below eagle.

KM# Pn1874   Designer: Augustus Saint-Gaudens **Obverse:** Roman numerals in date **Reverse:** No motto below eagle **Edge:** Plain. **Weight:** 33.4360 g. **Composition:** 0.9000 Gold 0.9677 oz. AGW **Size:** 34 mm. **Note:** The "Roman numerals" varieties for 1907 use Roman numerals for the date instead of Arabic numerals. The lettered-edge varieties have "E Pluribus Unum" on the edge, with stars between the words.

Date	Mintage	VF-20	XF-40	AU-50	MS-60	MS-63	MS-65	Prf-65
1907 extremely high relief, lettered edge	—	—	—	—	—	—	—	—

Note: 1907 extremely high relief, lettered edge, Prf-68, private sale, 1990, $1,500,000.

Saint-Gaudens. Roman numerals in date. No motto below eagle.

KM# 126 **Designer:** Augustus Saint-Gaudens **Obverse:** Roman numerals in date **Reverse:** No motto below eagle **Edge:** Plain. **Weight:** 33.4360 g. **Composition:** 0.9000 Gold 0.9677 oz. AGW **Size:** 34 mm.

Date	Mintage	VF-20	XF-40	AU-50	MS-60	MS-63	MS-65	Prf-65
MCMVII (1907) high relief, wire rim	11,250	3,500	5,500	5,400	8,500	14,500	29,000	—
MCMVII (1907) high relief, flat rim	Inc. above	3,600	5,750	5,650	9,000	15,500	30,000	—

Saint-Gaudens. Arabic numerals in date. No motto below eagle.

KM# 127 **Designer:** Augustus Saint-Gaudens **Obverse:** Arabic numerals in date **Reverse:** No motto below eagle **Edge:** Lettered; large letters. **Weight:** 33.4360 g. **Composition:** 0.9000 Gold 0.9677 oz. AGW **Size:** 34 mm.

Date	Mintage	VF-20	XF-40	AU-50	MS-60	MS-63	MS-65	Prf-65
1907 small letters on edge	361,667	430	450	450	565	850	2,500	—
1908	4,271,551	415	435	440	465	550	1,200	—
1908D	663,750	425	440	450	550	900	10,500	—

Saint-Gaudens. "In God We Trust" below eagle.

KM# 131 **Designer:** Augustus Saint-Gaudens **Reverse:** "In God We Trust" below eagle **Weight:** 33.4360 g. **Composition:** 0.9000 Gold 0.9677 oz. AGW **Size:** 34 mm.

Date	Mintage	VF-20	XF-40	AU-50	MS-60	MS-63	MS-65	Prf-65
1908	156,359	400	420	430	460	750	1,250	38,000
1908D	349,500	400	400	420	460	800	5,300	—
1908S	22,000	650	1,200	1,250	4,400	11,000	37,000	—
1909/8	161,282	525	580	650	1,150	4,000	26,000	—
1909	Inc. above	450	560	625	700	2,950	48,000	49,000
1909D	52,500	500	690	775	1,200	3,800	36,000	—
1909S	2,774,925	360	415	450	485	675	5,750	—
1910	482,167	365	400	445	485	675	6,750	49,000
1910D	429,000	365	400	425	550	675	3,300	—
1910S	2,128,250	365	425	425	500	750	8,500	—
1911	197,350	365	410	425	515	1,850	11,000	39,500
1911D	846,500	365	410	425	485	650	1,275	—
1911S	775,750	365	400	425	480	750	5,700	—
1912	149,824	385	425	475	520	1,100	16,000	40,000
1913	168,838	365	400	430	500	1,850	26,000	40,000
1913D	393,500	380	415	430	525	900	5,500	—
1913S	34,000	550	800	840	1,250	3,100	43,000	—

Date	Mintage	VF-20	XF-40	AU-50	MS-60	MS-63	MS-65	Prf-65
1914	95,320	400	515	530	580	1,475	14,750	41,500
1914D	453,000	380	400	430	525	725	3,250	—
1914S	1,498,000	380	450	430	515	625	2,100	—
1915	152,050	390	450	520	625	1,675	14,500	47,500
1915S	567,500	380	400	425	500	725	2,000	—
1916S	796,000	380	400	430	585	750	2,150	—
1920	228,250	380	400	450	590	825	33,500	—
1920S	558,000	4,300	8,000	10,500	25,000	48,500	165,000	—
1921	528,500	8,000	14,000	20,000	35,000	90,000	225,000	—
1922	1,375,500	380	400	420	515	625	3,900	—
1922S	2,658,000	500	750	800	925	2,400	38,000	—
1923	566,000	380	400	440	525	625	1,050	—
1923D	1,702,250	380	410	450	540	740	1,375	—
1924	4,323,500	380	400	430	515	600	1,200	—
1924D	3,049,500	800	1,325	1,500	1,900	5,200	56,000	—
1924S	2,927,500	750	1,200	1,400	2,500	6,100	35,000	—
1925	2,831,750	380	400	425	485	585	1,150	—
1925D	2,938,500	1,000	1,750	2,300	3,400	7,600	52,500	—
1925S	3,776,500	900	1,350	1,550	5,800	16,750	80,000	—
1926	816,750	380	400	425	485	585	1,200	—
1926D	481,000	1,100	2,850	3,200	7,900	18,750	88,000	—
1926S	2,041,500	700	1,250	1,375	1,850	3,350	35,000	—
1927	2,946,750	380	400	425	475	575	1,100	—
1927D	180,000	—	—	225,000	260,000	425,000	750,000	—
1927S	3,107,000	2,500	4,400	4,550	12,500	27,000	100,000	—
1928	8,816,000	380	410	425	500	625	1,050	—
1929	1,779,750	4,750	7,000	8,000	13,000	12,500	35,000	—
1930S	74,000	6,000	8,500	9,300	18,000	35,000	80,000	—
1931	2,938,250	4,250	8,000	9,250	14,000	24,000	50,000	—
1931D	106,500	5,500	8,000	8,500	17,500	20,000	58,000	—
1932	1,101,750	7,000	10,000	11,500	19,000	25,000	36,000	—
1933 Sotheby/Stack Sale, July 2002	445,500	—	—	—	—	—	7,590,000	—

1908-D $20 Gold
Grade MS-60

MINT SETS

Mint, or uncirculated, sets contain one uncirculated coin of each denomination from each mint produced for circulation that year. Values listed here are only for those sets sold by the U.S. Mint. Sets were not offered in years not listed. In years when the Mint did not offer the sets, some private companies compiled and marketed uncirculated sets. Mint sets from 1947 through 1958 contained two examples of each coin mounted in cardboard holders, which caused the coins to tarnish. Beginning in 1959, the sets have been packaged in sealed Pliofilm packets and include only one specimen of each coin struck for that year. Listings for 1965, 1966 and 1967 are for "special mint sets," which were of higher quality than regular mint sets and were prooflike. They were packaged in plastic cases. The 1970 large-date and small-date varieties are distinguished by the size of the date on the coin. The 1976 three-piece set contains the quarter, half dollar and dollar with the Bicentennial design. The 1971 and 1972 sets do not include a dollar coin; the 1979 set does not include an S-mint-marked dollar.

Date	Sets Sold	Issue Price	Value	Date	Sets Sold	Issue Price	Value
1947 Est. 5,000	—	4.87	1,300	1975	1,921,488	6.00	12.00
1948 Est. 6,000	—	4.92	600	1976 3 coins	4,908,319	9.00	17.50
1949 Est. 5,200	—	5.45	900	1976	1,892,513	6.00	11.25
1950 None issued	—	—	—	1977	2,006,869	7.00	9.00
1951	8,654	6.75	850	1978	2,162,609	7.00	10.00
1952	11,499	6.14	750	1979	2,526,000	8.00	6.00
1953	15,538	6.14	575	1980	2,815,066	9.00	7.00
1954	25,599	6.19	330	1981	2,908,145	11.00	17.00
1955	49,656	3.57	180	1982 & 1983 None issued	—	—	—
1956	45,475	3.34	160	1984	1,832,857	7.00	6.00
1957	32,324	4.40	260	1985	1,710,571	7.00	7.50
1958	50,314	4.43	170	1986	1,153,536	7.00	24.00
1959	187,000	2.40	40.00	1987	2,890,758	7.00	9.00
1960	260,485	2.40	24.00	1988	1,646,204	7.00	8.25
1961	223,704	2.40	45.00	1989	1,987,915	7.00	7.25
1962	385,285	2.40	19.00	1990	1,809,184	7.00	6.75
1963	606,612	2.40	13.75	1991	1,352,101	7.00	12.50
1964	1,008,108	2.40	10.00	1992	1,500,143	7.00	6.75
1965 SMS*	2,360,000	4.00	10.50	1993	1,297,094	8.00	11.00
1966 SMS*	2,261,583	4.00	12.00	1994	1,234,813	8.00	12.00
1967 SMS*	1,863,344	4.00	17.00	1995	1,038,787	8.00	21.00
1968	2,105,128	2.50	5.25	1996	1,457,949	8.00	22.50
1969	1,817,392	2.50	7.25	1997	950,473	8.00	24.50
1970 large date	2,038,134	2.50	17.00	1998	1,187,325	8.00	19.00
1970 small date	Inc. above	2.50	52.50	1999	1,421,625	14.95	32.00
1971	2,193,396	3.50	4.50	2000	1,490,160	14.95	16.50
1972	2,750,000	3.50	4.50	2001	1,066,900	14.95	24.75
1973	1,767,691	6.00	24.00	2002	—	14.95	17.00
1974	1,975,981	6.00	8.00	2003	—	—	—

PROOF SETS

Proof coins are produced through a special process involving specially selected, highly polished planchets and dies. They usually receive two strikings from the coin press at increased pressure. The result is a coin with mirrorlike surfaces and, in recent years, a cameo effect on its raised design surfaces. Proof sets have been sold off and on by the U.S. Mint since 1858. Listings here are for sets from what is commonly called the modern era, since 1936. Values for earlier proofs are included in regular date listings. Sets were not offered in years not listed. Since 1968, proof coins have been produced at the San Francisco Mint; before that they were produced at the Philadelphia Mint. In 1942 the five-cent coin was struck in two compositions. Some proof sets for that year contain only one type (five-coin set); others contain both types. Two types of packaging were used in 1955 -- a box and a flat, plastic holder. The 1960 large-date and small-date sets are distinguished by the size of the date on the cent. Some 1968 sets are missing the mint mark on the dime, the result of an error in the preparation of an obverse die. The 1970 large-date and small-date sets are distinguished by the size of the date on the cent. Some 1970 sets are missing the mint mark on the dime, the result of an error in the preparation of an obverse die. Some 1971 sets are missing the mint mark on the five-cent piece, the result of an error in the preparation of an obverse die. The 1976 three-piece set contains the quarter, half dollar and dollar with the Bicentennial designs. The 1979 and 1981 Type II sets have clearer mint marks than the Type I sets for those years. Some 1983 sets are missing the mint mark on the dime, the result of an error in the preparation of an obverse die. Prestige sets contain the five regular-issue coins plus a commemorative silver dollar from that year.

Date	Sets Sold	Issue Price	Value	Date	Sets Sold	Issue Price	Value
1936	3,837	1.89	6,400	1953	128,800	2.10	300
1937	5,542	1.89	3,500	1954	233,300	2.10	170
1938	8,045	1.89	1,350	1955 box	378,200	2.10	135
1939	8,795	1.89	1,400	1955 flat pack	Inc. above	2.10	140
1940	11,246	1.89	1,150	1956	669,384	2.10	58.50
1941	15,287	1.89	1,000	1957	1,247,952	2.10	23.00
1942 6 coins	21,120	1.89	1,150	1958	875,652	2.10	55.00
1942 5 coins	Inc. above	1.89	1,000	1959	1,149,291	2.10	29.00
1950	51,386	2.10	585	1960 large date	1,691,602	2.10	20.00
1951	57,500	2.10	600	1960 small date	Inc. above	2.10	39.00
1952	81,980	2.10	300	1961	3,028,244	2.10	11.50

Date	Sets Sold	Issue Price	Value
1962	3,218,019	2.10	11.50
1963	3,075,645	2.10	14.50
1964	3,950,762	2.10	12.00
1968S	3,041,509	5.00	8.50
1968S no mint mark dime	Inc. above	5.00	10,000
1969S	2,934,631	5.00	8.50
1970S large date	2,632,810	5.00	14.50
1970S small date	Inc. above	5.00	95.00
1970S no mint mark dime	Inc. above	5.00	1,150
1971S	3,224,138	5.00	7.25
1971S no-mint mark nickel Est. 1,655	1,655	5.00	1,150
1972S	3,267,667	5.50	6.00
1973S	2,769,624	7.00	14.00
1974S	2,617,350	7.00	12.50
1975S	2,909,369	7.00	17.50
1975S no mint mark dime	Inc. above	7.00	47,000
1976S 3 coins	3,998,621	12.00	24.00
1976S	4,149,730	7.00	9.00
1977S	3,251,152	9.00	9.50
1978S	3,127,788	9.00	10.00
1979S Type I	3,677,175	9.00	11.00
1979S Type II	Inc. above	9.00	120
1980S	3,547,030	10.00	11.00
1981S Type I	4,063,083	11.00	9.50
1981S Type II	Inc. above	11.00	400
1982S	3,857,479	11.00	6.00
1983S	3,138,765	11.00	7.50
1983S Prestige Set	140,361	59.00	83.00
1983S no mint mark dime	Inc. above	11.00	1,050
1984S	2,748,430	11.00	13.00
1984S Prestige Set	316,680	59.00	22.00
1985S	3,362,821	11.00	7.50
1986S	2,411,180	11.00	22.00
1986S Prestige Set	599,317	48.50	37.50
1987S	3,972,233	11.00	6.00
1987S Prestige Set	435,495	45.00	23.00
1988S	3,031,287	11.00	12.00
1988S Prestige Set	231,661	45.00	30.00
1989S	3,009,107	11.00	10.50
1989S Prestige Set	211,087	45.00	36.50
1990S	2,793,433	11.00	15.00
1990S no S 1¢	3,555	11.00	3,400
1990S Prestige Set	506,126	45.00	31.50
1990S Prestige Set, no S 1¢	Inc. above	45.00	4,400

Date	Sets Sold	Issue Price	Value
1991S	2,610,833	11.00	21.00
1991S Prestige Set	256,954	59.00	70.00
1992S	2,675,618	12.00	11.00
1992S Prestige Set	183,285	59.00	43.00
1992S Silver	1,009,585	21.00	17.00
1992S Silver premier	308,055	37.00	19.00
1993S	2,337,819	12.50	16.50
1993S Prestige Set	224,045	57.00	52.00
1993S Silver	570,213	21.00	36.00
1993S Silver premier	191,140	37.00	42.50
1994S	2,308,701	13.00	24.00
1994S Prestige Set	175,893	57.00	57.00
1994S Silver	636,009	21.00	40.00
1994S Silver premier	149,320	37.50	50.00
1995S	2,010,384	12.50	67.00
1995S Prestige Set	17,112	57.00	140
1995S Silver	549,878	21.00	100.00
1995S Silver premier	130,107	37.50	110
1996S	2,085,191	16.00	16.00
1996S Prestige Set	55,000	57.00	300
1996S Silver	623,655	21.00	54.00
1996S Silver premier	151,366	37.50	56.00
1997S	1,975,000	12.50	62.00
1997S Prestige Set	80,000	57.00	175
1997S Silver	605,473	21.00	90.00
1997S Silver premier	136,205	37.50	96.00
1998S	2,078,494	12.50	36.50
1998S Silver	638,134	21.00	40.00
1998S Silver premier	240,658	37.50	38.00
1999S	2,543,401	19.95	85.00
1999S 5 quarter set	1,169,958	13.95	50.00
1999S Silver	804,565	—	185
2000S	3,082,944	19.95	20.00
2000S 5 quarter set	995,803	13.95	17.50
2000S Silver	965,921	31.95	36.50
2001S	2,235,000	19.95	66.00
2001S 5 quarter set	774,800	13.95	31.00
2001S Silver	849,600	31.95	95.00
2002S	2,321,848	19.95	24.00
2002S 5 quarter set	764,092	13.95	17.00
2002S Silver	—	31.95	70.00
2003S	—	—	—
2003S 5 quarter set	—	—	—
2003S Silver	—	—	—

1952 Proof Set

Retail Price

UNCIRCULATED ROLLS

Listings are for rolls containing uncirculated coins. Large date and small date varieties for 1960 and 1970 apply to the one cent coins.

Date	Cents	Nickels	Dimes	Quarters	Halves
1938	180	220	1,000	3,200	2,000
1938D	325	170	900	—	—
1938S	210	225	1,250	3,200	—
1939	54.00	70.00	600	1,000	1,200
1939D	185	2,600	540	1,800	2,000
1939S	100.00	1,000	1,250	3,200	2,400
1940	67.00	34.00	400	1,600	1,000
1940D	100.00	70.00	630	4,400	—
1940S	105	120	510	1,300	1,200
1941	67.00	45.00	385	720	765
1941D	145	120	635	2,900	1,200
1941S	195	150	400	2,200	3,200
1942	30.00	210	385	400	750
1942P	—	325	—	—	—
1942D	19.50	1,450	580	1,350	1,350
1942S	415	325	725	4,700	1,400
1943	65.00	210	340	410	750
1943D	115	250	475	2,000	1,800
1943S	340	145	575	2,000	1,400
1944	16.00	325	400	415	750
1944D	16.50	320	415	750	1,200
1944S	17.50	175	415	850	1,250
1945	28.00	175	380	350	700
1945D	27.00	170	380	1,100	1,000
1945S	20.00	160	380	650	950
1946	13.50	54.00	115	400	1,000
1946D	14.50	50.00	85.00	395	850
1946S	19.00	12.50	200	415	880
1947	56.00	32.00	160	825	950
1947D	13.00	33.00	230	740	850
1947S	26.00	34.00	165	670	—
1948	27.00	35.00	145	260	385
1948D	23.00	32.00	145	675	330
1948S	60.00	50.00	140	460	—
1949	67.00	115	1,100	2,200	1,350
1949D	29.00	64.00	465	1,600	1,300
1949S	80.00	60.00	1,700	—	1,900
1950	27.00	80.00	315	360	700
1950D	27.00	265	185	300	760
1950S	37.00	—	1,700	520	—
1951	32.00	110	60.00	450	325
1951D	11.00	160	72.00	440	640
1951S	29.00	60.00	435	1,200	575
1952	63.50	28.00	65.00	430	290
1952D	10.00	98.00	65.00	375	220
1952S	98.00	22.00	215	1,100	880
1953	16.00	8.00	110	465	320
1953D	11.00	10.00	110	240	135
1953S	21.50	20.00	50.00	350	500
1954	11.00	40.00	48.00	420	180
1954D	12.00	24.00	44.00	370	170
1954S	15.00	78.00	44.00	280	175
1955	16.00	20.00	40.00	200	320
1955D	14.00	6.00	30.00	125	—
1955S	20.00	—	30.00	—	—
1956	10.00	6.00	34.00	260	130
1956D	11.00	6.25	29.00	180	—
1957	10.00	8.50	34.00	160	125
1957D	9.00	5.00	48.00	100.00	110
1958	10.00	5.50	30.00	70.00	100.00
1958D	8.00	5.00	29.00	64.00	100.00
1959	1.50	3.80	29.00	60.00	120
1959D	1.50	3.80	29.00	60.00	125
1960 large date	1.50	3.40	29.00	60.00	100.00
1960 small date	105	—	—	—	—
1960D large date	1.50	3.80	29.00	60.00	100.00
1960D small date	2.00	—	—	—	—
1961	1.50	3.40	29.00	90.00	120
1961D	1.50	4.00	29.00	64.00	100.00
1962	1.50	25.00	29.00	90.00	100.00
1962D	1.50	6.00	29.00	55.00	95.00
1963	1.50	2.90	29.00	60.00	85.00
1963D	1.50	5.50	29.00	60.00	85.00
1964	1.50	2.90	29.00	60.00	60.00
1964D	1.50	4.40	29.00	55.00	60.00
1965	2.70	3.60	12.50	28.00	25.00

Date	Cents	Nickels	Dimes	Quarters	Halves
1966	4.50	3.50	10.00	20.00	24.00
1967	12.00	3.60	9.50	33.00	20.00
1968	4.00	—	8.00	33.00	—
1968D	2.50	4.00	9.50	33.00	20.00
1968S	1.75	4.00	—	—	—
1969	8.00	—	34.00	100.00	—
1969D	1.50	4.65	12.50	60.00	20.00
1969S	3.25	3.65	—	—	—
1970	4.50	—	9.50	16.50	—
1970D	3.25	3.40	8.80	16.00	300
1970S	3.25	2.80	—	—	—
1970S small date	1,200	—	—	—	—
1971	7.00	30.00	12.50	40.00	22.00
1971D	7.00	5.00	8.50	20.00	17.00
1971S	5.00	—	—	—	—
1972	2.75	5.00	8.50	22.00	24.00
1972D	2.75	3.20	11.00	20.00	24.00
1972S	2.75	—	—	—	—
1973	1.50	4.00	8.00	21.50	30.00
1973D	1.40	3.60	8.50	22.50	22.50
1973S	2.75	—	—	—	—
1974	1.20	2.80	8.00	21.50	21.50
1974D	1.20	5.80	7.50	21.50	22.50
1974S	3.00	—	—	—	—
1975	2.00	10.00	9.50	—	—
1975D	2.00	4.40	11.50	—	—
1976	1.80	13.50	13.50	16.00	20.00
1976D	4.25	11.50	13.50	16.50	20.00
1977	2.00	3.10	7.50	15.00	26.00
1977D	2.00	6.00	8.00	16.00	25.00
1978	2.00	3.20	7.50	16.00	30.00
1978D	2.00	4.00	7.50	16.50	64.00
1979	1.75	3.65	8.00	16.00	28.00
1979D	1.75	4.20	7.50	18.00	34.00
1980	1.75	3.80	8.25	16.00	20.00
1980D	1.75	3.30	7.50	15.00	22.00
1981	1.75	3.30	7.50	15.00	30.00
1981D	1.50	3.30	7.50	15.00	24.00
1982	1.75	78.00	165	190	50.00
1982D	1.75	45.00	52.50	68.00	40.00
1983	2.25	52.00	100.00	920	60.00
1983D	2.25	32.00	30.00	500	60.00
1984	3.50	25.00	8.50	20.00	36.00
1984D	20.00	5.00	14.50	31.00	45.00
1985	7.00	7.40	10.00	40.00	58.00
1985D	3.50	6.00	9.50	25.00	65.00
1986	27.50	7.60	27.00	120	125
1986D	22.00	28.00	26.00	270	85.00
1987	4.00	4.40	7.50	15.00	80.00
1987D	3.50	3.65	7.50	15.00	75.00
1988	7.00	5.20	10.00	38.00	85.00
1988D	7.00	6.50	9.50	21.00	54.00
1989	2.40	4.20	8.50	19.00	50.00
1989D	2.40	5.80	8.00	20.00	40.00
1990	2.40	8.00	12.00	25.00	50.00
1990D	2.40	6.00	10.00	29.00	68.00
1991	2.40	9.50	10.00	32.00	67.00
1991D	2.40	8.50	13.50	32.00	95.00
1992	2.60	46.00	7.00	24.00	22.50
1992D	2.60	6.00	9.00	33.00	52.00
1993	2.60	6.50	8.50	32.00	30.00
1993D	2.60	6.50	8.00	34.00	40.00
1994	2.25	4.00	8.00	30.00	15.00
1994D	2.25	4.60	7.50	27.00	23.00
1995	2.25	4.20	7.50	24.00	15.00
1995D	2.25	12.50	13.50	36.00	14.50
1996	2.00	4.20	7.50	22.00	15.50
1996D	2.00	4.20	7.50	27.00	15.00
1997	2.00	7.50	7.25	21.00	15.00
1997D	2.00	10.50	7.25	24.00	24.00
1998	2.00	8.00	9.00	27.00	15.00
1998D	2.00	8.00	9.00	27.00	15.00
1999P	1.75	4.30	9.00	—	15.00
1999D	1.75	5.00	7.50	—	15.00
2000P	1.75	4.70	9.00	—	15.00
2000D	1.75	3.30	7.00	—	15.00
2001P	1.75	4.00	9.00	—	70.00
2001D	1.75	3.65	7.00	—	17.00
2002P	1.50	4.00	9.00	—	60.00
2002D	1.50	3.50	7.00	—	60.00

COMMEMORATIVE COINAGE
1892-1954

All commemorative half dollars of 1892-1954 have the following specifications: diameter -- 24.3 millimeters; weight -- 6.2500 grams; composition -- 0.9000 silver, 0.1808 ounces actual silver weight. Values for "PDS sets" contain one example each from the Philadelphia, Denver and San Francisco mints. "Type coin" prices are the most inexpensive single coin available from the date and mint-mark combinations listed.

QUARTER

KM# 115 COLUMBIAN EXPOSITION Weight: 6.2500 g. **Composition:** 0.9000 Silver 0.1808 oz. ASW **Obverse:** Queen Isabella **Size:** 24.3 mm.

Date	Mintage	AU-50	MS-60	MS-63	MS-64	MS-65
1893	24,214	425	600	655	1,050	3,000

HALF DOLLAR

KM# 117 COLUMBIAN EXPO Obv. Designer: Charles E. Barber **Rev. Designer:** George T. Morgan **Size:** 30.6 mm.

Date	Mintage	AU-50	MS-60	MS-63	MS-64	MS-65
1892	950,000	16.50	27.00	85.00	200	700
1893	1,550,405	14.00	27.00	85.00	200	715

1892 Columbian Expo Half
Grade MS-60

Retail Price

KM# 135 PANAMA-PACIFIC EXPOSITION Designer: Charles E. Barber **Size:** 30.6 mm.

Date	Mintage	AU-50	MS-60	MS-63	MS-64	MS-65
1915S	27,134	285	340	625	1,150	2,400

KM# 143 LINCOLN-ILLINOIS Obv. Designer: George T. Morgan **Rev. Designer:** John R. Sinnock
Size: 30.6 mm.

Date	Mintage	AU-50	MS-60	MS-63	MS-64	MS-65
1918	100,058	80.00	105	115	140	400

KM# 146 MAINE CENTENNIAL Designer: Anthony de Francisci **Size:** 30.6 mm.

Date	Mintage	AU-50	MS-60	MS-63	MS-64	MS-65
1920	50,028	110	140	145	260	460

KM# 147.1 PILGRIM TERCENTENARY Designer: Cyrus E. Dallin **Size:** 30.6 mm.

Date	Mintage	AU-50	MS-60	MS-63	MS-64	MS-65
1920	152,112	59.00	70.00	85.00	145	475

KM# 147.2 PILGRIM TERCENTENARY Designer: Cyrus E. Dallin **Obverse:** 1921 date next to Pilgrim
Size: 30.6 mm.

Date	Mintage	AU-50	MS-60	MS-63	MS-64	MS-65
1921	20,053	105	120	155	260	575

KM# 149.1 MISSOURI CENTENNIAL Designer: Robert Aitken **Size:** 30.6 mm.

Date	Mintage	AU-50	MS-60	MS-63	MS-64	MS-65
1921	15,428	225	410	775	1,400	5,000

2☆4

KM# 149.2 MISSOURI CENTENNIAL Designer: Robert Aitken **Obverse:** 2 star 4 in field at left **Size:** 30.6 mm.

Date	Mintage	AU-50	MS-60	MS-63	MS-64	MS-65
1921	5,000	380	470	900	1,650	4,850

2 x 2

KM# 148.1 ALABAMA CENTENNIAL Designer: Laura G. Fraser **Obverse:** "2x2" at right above stars **Size:** 30.6 mm.

Date	Mintage	AU-50	MS-60	MS-63	MS-64	MS-65
1921	6,006	175	300	525	875	2,380

KM# 148.2 ALABAMA CENTENNIAL Obv. Designer: Laura G. Fraser **Size:** 30.6 mm.

Date	Mintage	AU-50	MS-60	MS-63	MS-64	MS-65
1921	59,038	125	210	450	750	2,275

KM# 151.1 GRANT MEMORIAL Designer: Laura G. Fraser **Size:** 30.6 mm.

Date	Mintage	AU-50	MS-60	MS-63	MS-64	MS-65
1922	67,405	80.00	85.00	160	295	925

KM# 151.2 GRANT MEMORIAL Designer: Laura G. Fraser Obverse: Star above the word "Grant" Size: 30.6 mm.

Date	Mintage	AU-50	MS-60	MS-63	MS-64	MS-65
1922	4,256	650	1,200	1,550	2,275	6,900

KM# 153 MONROE DOCTRINE CENTENNIAL Designer: Chester Beach Size: 30.6 mm.

Date	Mintage	AU-50	MS-60	MS-63	MS-64	MS-65
1923S	274,077	29.00	41.00	155	400	2,750

KM# 154 HUGUENOT-WALLOON TERCENTENARY Designer: George T. Morgan Size: 30.6 mm.

Date	Mintage	AU-50	MS-60	MS-63	MS-64	MS-65
1924	142,080	95.00	110	170	220	475

KM# 156 LEXINGTON-CONCORD SESQUICENTENNIAL Designer: Chester Beach Size: 30.6 mm.

Date	Mintage	AU-50	MS-60	MS-63	MS-64	MS-65
1925	162,013	65.00	70.00	105	185	425

KM# 155 CALIFORNIA DIAMOND JUBILEE Designer: Jo Mora Size: 30.6 mm.

Date	Mintage	AU-50	MS-60	MS-63	MS-64	MS-65
1925S	86,594	105	120	170	300	1,025

KM# 158 FORT VANCOUVER CENTENNIAL Designer: Laura G. Fraser **Size:** 30.6 mm.

Date	Mintage	AU-50	MS-60	MS-63	MS-64	MS-65
1925	14,994	230	295	375	575	1,325

KM# 157.1 STONE MOUNTAIN MEMORIAL Designer: Gutzon Borglum **Size:** 30.6 mm.

Date	Mintage	AU-50	MS-60	MS-63	MS-64	MS-65
1925	1,314,709	42.00	55.00	70.00	90.00	210

KM# 159 OREGON TRAIL MEMORIAL Designer: James E. and Laura G. Fraser **Size:** 30.6 mm.

1926 Oregon Trail Half
Grade MS-60

Retail Price

Date	Mintage	AU-50	MS-60	MS-63	MS-64	MS-65
1926	47,955	95.00	100.00	110	140	200
Type coin	—	95.00	100.00	110	140	260
1926S	83,055	95.00	100.00	110	140	205
1928	6,028	150	160	170	175	285
1933D	5,008	225	240	260	290	460
1934D	7,006	145	150	160	190	290
1936	10,006	105	115	125	145	200
1936S	5,006	125	135	160	200	285
1937D	12,008	125	140	150	180	225
1938 PDS set	6,005	490	490	600	620	660
1939 PDS set	3,004	1,050	1,200	1,350	1,450	1,750

KM# 160 U.S. SESQUICENTENNIAL Designer: John R. Sinnock **Size:** 30.6 mm.

Date	Mintage	AU-50	MS-60	MS-63	MS-64	MS-65
1926	141,120	60.00	78.00	155	565	5,100

KM# 162 VERMONT SESQUICENTENNIAL Obv. Designer: Charles Keck **Size:** 30.6 mm.

Date	Mintage	AU-50	MS-60	MS-63	MS-64	MS-65
1927	28,142	150	165	180	290	825

KM# 163 HAWAIIAN SESQUICENTENNIAL Designer: Juliette M. Fraser **Size:** 30.6 mm.

Date	Mintage	AU-50	MS-60	MS-63	MS-64	MS-65
1928	10,008	1,050	1,300	1,850	2,600	4,900

KM# 166 MARYLAND TERCENTENARY Designer: Hans Schuler **Size:** 30.6 mm.

Date	Mintage	AU-50	MS-60	MS-63	MS-64	MS-65
1934	25,015	110	125	160	190	330

KM# 165.2 DANIEL BOONE BICENTENNIAL Designer: Augustus Lukeman **Reverse:** "1934" added above the word "Pioneer." **Size:** 30.6 mm.

Date	Mintage	AU-50	MS-60	MS-63	MS-64	MS-65
1935 PDS set	5,005	550	625	820	1,075	1,850
1936 PDS set	5,005	210	225	295	325	550
1937 PDS set	2,506	525	675	660	800	1,050
1938 PDS set	2,100	725	775	975	1,150	1,500

KM# 167 TEXAS CENTENNIAL Designer: Pompeo Coppini **Size:** 30.6 mm.

Date	Mintage	AU-50	MS-60	MS-63	MS-64	MS-65
1934	61,463	90.00	100.00	110	120	170
1935 PDS set	9,994	270	300	320	340	490
1936 PDS set	8,911	270	290	300	320	480
1937 PDS set	6,571	280	300	310	330	510
1938 PDS set	3,775	525	625	740	775	1,150

KM# 165.1 DANIEL BOONE BICENTENNIAL Designer: Augustus Lukeman **Size:** 30.6 mm.

Date	Mintage	AU-50	MS-60	MS-63	MS-64	MS-65
1934	10,007	65.00	72.00	90.00	110	185
1935 PDS set	2,003	210	225	300	325	540

KM# 171 SAN DIEGO-CALIFORNIA-PACIFIC EXPOSITION Designer: Robert Aitken **Size:** 30.6 mm.

Date	Mintage	AU-50	MS-60	MS-63	MS-64	MS-65
1935S	70,132	58.00	85.00	92.00	100.00	120
1936D	30,092	59.00	92.00	100.00	110	140

KM# 172 OLD SPANISH TRAIL Designer: L.W. Hoffecker **Size:** 30.6 mm.

Date	Mintage	AU-50	MS-60	MS-63	MS-64	MS-65
1935	10,008	725	780	850	950	1,075

KM# 168 ARKANSAS CENTENNIAL Designer: Edward E. Burr Size: 30.6 mm.

Date	Mintage	AU-50	MS-60	MS-63	MS-64	MS-65
1935 PDS set	5,505	200	215	235	320	750
1936 PDS set	9,600	200	215	235	300	780
1937 PDS set	5,505	210	225	290	325	975
1938 PDS set	3,155	270	360	420	500	1,900
1939 PDS set	—	550	625	900	1,100	3,200

KM# 169 CONNECTICUT TERCENTENARY Designer: Henry Kreiss Size: 30.6 mm.

Date	Mintage	AU-50	MS-60	MS-63	MS-64	MS-65
1935	25,018	170	195	215	320	560

KM# 170 HUDSON, N.Y., SESQUICENTENNIAL Designer: Chester Beach Size: 30.6 mm.

Date	Mintage	AU-50	MS-60	MS-63	MS-64	MS-65
1935	10,008	405	465	510	710	1,275

KM# 182 LONG ISLAND TERCENTENARY Designer: Howard K. Weinman Size: 30.6 mm.

Date	Mintage	AU-50	MS-60	MS-63	MS-64	MS-65
1936	81,826	58.00	65.00	75.00	120	375

KM# 183 LYNCHBURG, VA., SESQUICENTENNIAL Designer: Charles Keck **Size:** 30.6 mm.

Date	Mintage	AU-50	MS-60	MS-63	MS-64	MS-65
1936	20,013	145	155	170	215	275

KM# 184 NORFOLK, VA., BICENTENNIAL Designer: William M. and Marjorie E. Simpson **Size:** 30.6 mm.

Date	Mintage	AU-50	MS-60	MS-63	MS-64	MS-65
1936	16,936	345	365	385	400	450

KM# 179 DELAWARE TERCENTENARY Designer: Carl L. Schmitz **Size:** 30.6 mm.

Date	Mintage	AU-50	MS-60	MS-63	MS-64	MS-65
1936	20,993	200	210	225	265	355

KM# 180 ELGIN, ILL., CENTENNIAL Designer: Trygve Rovelstad **Size:** 30.6 mm.

Date	Mintage	AU-50	MS-60	MS-63	MS-64	MS-65
1936	20,015	160	175	180	195	230

KM# 181 BATTLE OF GETTYSBURG 75TH ANNIVERSARY Designer: Frank Vittor **Size:** 30.6 mm.

Date	Mintage	AU-50	MS-60	MS-63	MS-64	MS-65
1936	26,928	250	285	320	385	600

KM# 176 CINCINNATI MUSIC CENTER Designer: Constance Ortmayer Size: 30.6 mm.

Date	Mintage	AU-50	MS-60	MS-63	MS-64	MS-65
1936 PDS set	5,005	625	720	765	880	2,475
Type coin	—	200	215	225	300	600

KM# 177 CLEVELAND-GREAT LAKES EXPOSITION Designer: Brenda Putnam Size: 30.6 mm.

Date	Mintage	AU-50	MS-60	MS-63	MS-64	MS-65
1936	50,030	62.00	68.00	75.00	95.00	220

KM# 178 COLUMBIA, S.C., SESQUICENTENNIAL Designer: A. Wolfe Davidson Size: 30.6 mm.

Date	Mintage	AU-50	MS-60	MS-63	MS-64	MS-65
1936 PDS set	9,007	490	525	555	600	720
Type coin	—	160	170	180	195	240

KM# 174 SAN FRANCISCO-OAKLAND BAY BRIDGE Designer: Jacques Schnier Size: 30.6 mm.

Date	Mintage	AU-50	MS-60	MS-63	MS-64	MS-65
1936	71,424	100.00	110	120	160	270

KM# 175 BRIDGEPORT, CONN., CENTENNIAL Designer: Henry Kreiss Size: 30.6 mm.

Date	Mintage	AU-50	MS-60	MS-63	MS-64	MS-65
1936	25,015	105	120	130	150	240

KM# 173 ALBANY, N.Y., CHARTER ANNIVERSARY Designer: Gertrude K. Lathrop **Size:** 30.6 mm.

Date	Mintage	AU-50	MS-60	MS-63	MS-64	MS-65
1936	17,671	190	205	215	235	325

KM# 187 ARKANSAS CENTENNIAL   Obverse: Sen. Joseph T. Robinson **Obv. Designer:** Henry Kreiss **Rev. Designer:** Edward E. Burr **Size:** 30.6 mm.

Date	Mintage	AU-50	MS-60	MS-63	MS-64	MS-65
1936	25,265	95.00	100.00	120	130	310

KM# 185 RHODE ISLAND TERCENTENARY Designer: Arthur G. Carey and John H. Benson **Size:** 30.6 mm.

Date	Mintage	AU-50	MS-60	MS-63	MS-64	MS-65
1936 PDS set	15,010	190	210	270	305	700
Type coin	—	65.00	70.00	85.00	115	215

KM# 188 WISCONSIN TERRITORIAL CENTENNIAL Designer: David Parsons **Size:** 30.6 mm.

Date	Mintage	AU-50	MS-60	MS-63	MS-64	MS-65
1936	25,015	140	150	165	210	240

KM# 189 YORK COUNTY, MAINE, TERCENTENARY Designer: Walter H. Rich **Size:** 30.6 mm.

Date	Mintage	AU-50	MS-60	MS-63	MS-64	MS-65
1936	25,015	135	145	158	168	190

KM# 186 ROANOKE ISLAND, N.C. Designer: William M. Simpson **Size:** 30.6 mm.

Date	Mintage	AU-50	MS-60	MS-63	MS-64	MS-65
1937	29,030	160	200	215	220	240

KM# 190 BATTLE OF ANTIETAM 75TH ANNIVERSARY Designer: William M. Simpson **Size:** 30.6 mm.

Date	Mintage	AU-50	MS-60	MS-63	MS-64	MS-65
1937	18,028	395	430	460	550	650

KM# 191 NEW ROCHELLE, N.Y. Designer: Gertrude K. Lathrop **Size:** 30.6 mm.

Date	Mintage	AU-50	MS-60	MS-63	MS-64	MS-65
1938	15,266	250	270	285	305	355

KM# 197 IOWA STATEHOOD CENTENNIAL Designer: Adam Pietz **Size:** 30.6 mm.

Date	Mintage	AU-50	MS-60	MS-63	MS-64	MS-65
1946	100,057	60.00	66.00	71.00	80.00	115

KM# 198 BOOKER T. WASHINGTON Designer: Isaac S. Hathaway **Size:** 30.6 mm.

Date	Mintage	AU-50	MS-60	MS-63	MS-64	MS-65
1946 PDS set	200,113	—	43.00	70.00	80.00	130

Date	Mintage	AU-50	MS-60	MS-63	MS-64	MS-65
1947 PDS set	100,017	—	72.00	80.00	110	280
1948 PDS set	8,005	—	135	140	160	210
1949 PDS set	6,004	—	215	225	240	325
1950 PDS set	6,004	—	120	135	140	200
1951 PDS set	7,004	—	110	140	145	200

KM# 200 BOOKER T. WASHINGTON AND GEORGE WASHINGTON CARVER Designer: Isaac S. Hathaway **Size:** 30.6 mm.

Date	Mintage	AU-50	MS-60	MS-63	MS-64	MS-65
1951 PDS set	10,004	—	80.00	105	120	550
1952 PDS set	8,006	—	80.00	110	125	370
1953 PDS set	8,003	—	80.00	110	130	540
1954 PDS set	12,006	—	82.00	90.00	110	385

DOLLAR

KM# 118 LAFAYETTE Weight: 26.7300 g. **Composition:** 0.9000 Silver 0.7736 oz. ASW **Designer:** Charles E. Barber **Size:** 38.1 mm.

Date	Mintage	AU-50	MS-60	MS-63	MS-64	MS-65
1900	36,026	325	565	1,400	2,850	8,000

KM# 119 LOUISIANA PURCHASE EXPOSITION Weight: 1.6720 g. **Composition:** 0.9000 Gold 0.0484 oz. AGW **Designer:** Charles E. Barber **Obverse:** Jefferson **Size:** 15 mm.

Date	Mintage	AU-50	MS-60	MS-63	MS-64	MS-65
1903	17,500	340	420	670	1,850	3,100

KM# 120 LOUISIANA PURCHASE EXPOSITION Weight: 1.6720 g. **Composition:** 0.9000 Gold 0.0484 oz. AGW **Obverse:** McKinley **Obv. Designer:** Charles E. Barber **Size:** 15 mm.

Date	Mintage	AU-50	MS-60	MS-63	MS-64	MS-65
1903	17,500	300	370	650	1,675	3,350

KM# 121 LEWIS AND CLARK EXPO Weight: 1.6720 g. **Composition:** 0.9000 Gold 0.7736 oz. AGW **Obv. Designer:** Charles E. Barber **Size:** 15 mm.

Date	Mintage	AU-50	MS-60	MS-63	MS-64	MS-65
1904	10,025	520	775	1,875	4,275	9,000
1905	10,041	495	860	2,200	6,100	17,500

KM# 136 PANAMA-PACIFIC EXPO Weight: 1.6720 g. **Composition:** 0.9000 Gold 0.0484 oz. AGW
Obv. Designer: Charles Keck **Size:** 15 mm.

Date	Mintage	AU-50	MS-60	MS-63	MS-64	MS-65
1915S	15,000	320	380	500	1,325	2,775

KM# 144 MCKINLEY MEMORIAL Weight: 1.6720 g. **Composition:** 0.9000 Gold 0.0484 oz. AGW
Obv. Designer: Charles E. Barber **Rev. Designer:** George T. Morgan **Size:** 15 mm.

Date	Mintage	AU-50	MS-60	MS-63	MS-64	MS-65
1916	9,977	270	360	550	1,175	2,700
1917	10,000	365	510	925	2,150	3,725

Star

KM# 152.3 GRANT MEMORIAL Weight: 1.6720 g. **Composition:** 0.9000 Gold 0.0484 oz. AGW **Obverse:**
With a star above the word "Grant" **Obv. Designer:** Laura G. Fraser **Size:** 15 mm.

Date	Mintage	AU-50	MS-60	MS-63	MS-64	MS-65
1922	5,000	1,100	1,300	1,775	2,975	3,650

KM# 152.1 GRANT MEMORIAL Weight: 1.6720 g. **Composition:** 0.9000 Gold 0.0484 oz. AGW **Obverse:**
Without a star above the word "Grant" **Obv. Designer:** Laura G. Fraser **Size:** 15 mm. **Note:** The Grant gold-
dollar varieties are distinguished by whether a star appears on the obverse above the word 'Grant.'

Date	Mintage	AU-50	MS-60	MS-63	MS-64	MS-65
1922	5,016	1,025	1,150	1,500	2,975	3,650

$2.50 (QUARTER EAGLE)

KM# 137 PANAMA PACIFIC EXPO Weight: 4.1800 g. **Composition:** 0.9000 Gold 0.121 oz. AGW
Obv. Designer: Charles E. Barber **Rev. Designer:** George T. Morgan **Size:** 18 mm.

Date	Mintage	AU-50	MS-60	MS-63	MS-64	MS-65
1915S	6,749	1,200	1,425	2,750	4,250	5,350

KM# 161 PHILADELPHIA SESQUICENTENNIAL Weight: 4.1800 g. **Composition:** 0.9000 Gold 0.121 oz.
AGW **Obv. Designer:** John R. Sinnock **Size:** 18 mm.

Date	Mintage	AU-50	MS-60	MS-63	MS-64	MS-65
1926	46,019	265	295	525	1,075	3,875

$50

KM# 138 PANAMA PACIFIC EXPO. Weight: 83.5900 g. **Composition:** 0.9000 Gold 2.419 oz. AGW
Obv. Designer: Robert Aitken **Shape:** Round **Size:** 44 mm.

Date	Mintage	AU-50	MS-60	MS-63	MS-64	MS-65
1915S	483	22,500	26,500	37,000	47,000	109,000

KM# 139 PANAMA PACIFIC EXPO. Weight: 83.5900 g. **Composition:** 0.9000 Gold 2.419 oz. AGW
Obv. Designer: Robert Aitken **Shape:** Octagon **Size:** 44 mm.

Date	Mintage	AU-50	MS-60	MS-63	MS-64	MS-65
1915S	645	20,000	23,500	34,000	46,500	94,500

Note: In 1982, after a hiatus of nearly 20 years, coinage of commemorative half dollars resumed. Those designated with a 'W' were struck at the West Point Mint. Some issues were struck in copper-nickel. Those struck in silver have the same size, weight and composition as the prior commemorative half-dollar series.

COMMEMORATIVE COINAGE
1982-PRESENT

All commemorative silver dollar coins of 1982-present have the following specifications: diameter -- 38.1 millimeters; weight -- 26.7300 grams; composition -- 0.9000 silver, 0.7736 ounces actual silver weight. All commemorative $5 coins of 1982-present have the following specificiations: diameter -- 21.6 millimeters; weight -- 8.3590 grams; composition: 0.9000 gold, 0.242 ounces actual gold weight.

HALF DOLLAR

KM# 208 250TH ANNIVERSARY OF GEORGE WASHINGTON'S BIRTH Weight: 12.5000 g. **Composition:** 0.9000 Silver 0.3618 oz. ASW **Obv. Designer:** Elizabeth Jones **Size:** 30.6 mm.

Date	Mintage	Proof	MS-65	Prf-65
1982D	2,210,458	—	6.50	—
1982S	—	(4,894,044)	—	6.50

KM# 212 STATUE OF LIBERTY CENTENNIAL **Weight:** 11.3400 g. **Composition:** Copper-Nickel Clad Copper

Date	Mintage	Proof	MS-65	Prf-65
1986D	928,008	—	6.50	—
1986S	—	(6,925,627)	—	7.00

KM# 224 BICENTENNIAL OF THE CONGRESS **Weight:** 11.3400 g. **Composition:** Copper-Nickel Clad Copper

Date	Mintage	Proof	MS-65	Prf-65
1989D	163,753	—	8.00	—
1989S	—	—	—	8.00

KM# 228 MOUNT RUSHMORE GOLDEN ANNIVERSARY **Weight:** 11.3400 g. **Composition:** Copper-Nickel Clad Copper

Date	Mintage	Proof	MS-65	Prf-65
1991D	172,754	—	13.50	—
1991S	—	—	—	13.50

KM# 233 OLYMPICS **Weight:** 11.3400 g. **Composition:** Copper-Nickel Clad Copper

Date	Mintage	Proof	MS-65	Prf-65
1992P	161,607	—	8.00	—
1992S	—	(519,645)	—	8.00

KM# 237 500TH ANNIVERSARY OF COLUMBUS DISCOVERY Weight: 11.3400 g. **Composition:** Copper-Nickel Clad Copper

Date	Mintage	Proof	MS-65	Prf-65
1992D	135,702	—	11.00	—
1992S	—	(390,154)	—	11.50

KM# 240 JAMES MADISON AND BILL OF RIGHTS   Weight: 12.5000 g. **Composition:** 0.9000 Silver 0.3618 oz. ASW

Date	Mintage	Proof	MS-65	Prf-65
1993W	173,224	—	16.50	—
1993S	—	(559,758)	—	16.50

KM# 243 WORLD WAR II 50TH ANNIVERSARY Weight: 11.3400 g. **Composition:** Copper-Nickel Clad Copper

Date	Mintage	Proof	MS-65	Prf-65
1993P	192,968	(290,343)	21.00	20.00

KM# 246 1994 WORLD CUP SOCCER Weight: 11.3400 g. **Composition:** Copper-Nickel Clad Copper

Date	Mintage	Proof	MS-65	Prf-65
1994D	168,208	—	10.00	—
1994P	122,412	(609,354)	—	10.00

KM# 254 CIVIL WAR Weight: 11.3400 g. **Composition:** Copper-Nickel Clad Copper

Date	Mintage	Proof	MS-65	Prf-65
1995S	119,510	(330,099)	30.00	30.00

KM# 257 ATLANTA OLYMPICS Weight: 11.3400 g. **Composition:** Copper-Nickel Clad Copper **Obverse:** Basketball

Date	Mintage	Proof	MS-65	Prf-65
1995S	171,001	(169,655)	22.00	22.50

KM# 262 ATLANTA OLYMPICS Weight: 11.3400 g. **Composition:** Copper-Nickel Clad Copper **Obverse:** Baseball

Date	Mintage	Proof	MS-65	Prf-65
1995S	164,605	(118,087)	22.00	16.50

KM# 271 ATLANTA OLYMPICS Weight: 11.3400 g. **Composition:** Copper-Nickel Clad Copper **Obverse:** Soccer

Date	Mintage	Proof	MS-65	Prf-65
1996S	52,836	(122,412)	45.00	83.00

KM# 267 ATLANTA OLYMPICS Weight: 11.3400 g. **Composition:** Copper-Nickel Clad Copper **Obverse:** Swimming

Date	Mintage	Proof	MS-65	Prf-65
1996S	49,533	(114,315)	98.00	25.50

KM# 332 CAPITOL VISITOR CENTER Weight: 11.3400 g. **Composition:** Copper-Nickel Clad Copper

Date	Mintage	Proof	MS-65	Prf-65
2001	99,157	(77,962)	12.00	17.50

DOLLAR

KM# 209 LOS ANGELES XXIII OLYMPIAD Obv. Designer: Elizabeth Jones **Size:** 38.1 mm.

Date	Mintage	Proof	MS-65	Prf-65
1983P	294,543	—	11.25	—
1983D	174,014	—	11.50	—
1983S	174,014	(1,577,025)	11.25	12.75

KM# 210 LOS ANGELES XXIII OLYMPIAD Obv. Designer: Robert Graham **Size:** 38.1 mm.

Date	Mintage	Proof	MS-65	Prf-65
1984P	217,954	—	13.50	—
1984D	116,675	—	21.00	—
1984S	116,675	(1,801,210)	22.00	12.75

KM# 214 STATUE OF LIBERTY CENTENNIAL Obv. Designer: John Mercanti **Size:** 38.1 mm.

Date	Mintage	Proof	MS-65	Prf-65
1986P	723,635	—	16.00	—
1986S	—	(6,414,638)	—	16.50

KM# 220 CONSTITUTION BICENTENNIAL Obv. Designer: Patricia Lewis Verani **Size:** 38.1 mm.

Date	Mintage	Proof	MS-65	Prf-65
1987P	451,629	—	12.75	—
1987S	—	(2,747,116)	—	13.00

KM# 222 OLYMPICS Obv. Designer: Patricia Lewis Verani **Rev. Designer:** Sherl Joseph Winter
Size: 38.1 mm.

Date	Mintage	Proof	MS-65	Prf-65
1988D	191,368	—	12.75	—
1988S	—	(1,359,366)	—	13.00

KM# 225 BICENTENNIAL OF THE CONGRESS Obv. Designer: William Woodward **Size:** 38.1 mm.

Date	Mintage	Proof	MS-65	Prf-65
1989D	135,203	—	16.00	—
1989S	—	(762,198)	—	17.50

KM# 227 EISENHOWER CENTENNIAL Obv. Designer: John Mercanti **Rev. Designer:** Marcel Jovine **Size:** 38.1 mm.

Date	Mintage	Proof	MS-65	Prf-65
1990W	241,669	—	17.00	—
1990P	—	(638,335)	—	21.00

KM# 229 MOUNT RUSHMORE GOLDEN ANNIVERSARY Obv. Designer: Marika Somogyi **Rev. Designer:** Frank Gasparro **Size:** 38.1 mm.

Date	Mintage	Proof	MS-65	Prf-65
1991P	133,139	—	29.00	—
1991S	—	(738,419)	—	39.00

KM# 231 KOREAN WAR Obv. Designer: John Mercanti **Rev. Designer:** James Ferrell **Size:** 38.1 mm.

Date	Mintage	Proof	MS-65	Prf-65
1991D	213,049	—	16.00	—
1991P	—	(618,488)	—	17.00

KM# 232 USO 50TH ANNIVERSARY Obv. Designer: Robert Lamb **Rev. Designer:** John Mercanti **Size:** 38.1 mm.

Date	Mintage	Proof	MS-65	Prf-65
1991D	124,958	—	16.00	—
1991S	—	(321,275)	—	17.00

KM# 234 OLYMPICS Obv. Designer: John R. Deecken **Rev. Designer:** Marcel Jovine **Size:** 38.1 mm.

Date	Mintage	Proof	MS-65	Prf-65
1992D	187,552	—	24.00	—
1992S	—	(504,505)	—	27.00

KM# 236 WHITE HOUSE BICENTENNIAL Size: 38.1 mm.

Date	Mintage	Proof	MS-65	Prf-65
1992D	123,803	—	38.00	—
1992W	—	(375,851)	—	39.00

KM# 238 COLUMBUS QUINCENTENARY Size: 38.1 mm.

Date	Mintage	Proof	MS-65	Prf-65
1992D	106,949	—	30.50	—
1992P	—	(385,241)	—	41.50

KM# 241 JAMES MADISON AND BILL OF RIGHTS Size: 38.1 mm.

Date	Mintage	Proof	MS-65	Prf-65
1993D	98,383	—	20.00	—
1993S	—	(534,001)	—	21.50

KM# 244 WORLD WAR II 50TH ANNIVERSARY Size: 38.1 mm.

Date	Mintage	Proof	MS-65	Prf-65
1993D	94,708	—	27.00	—
1993W	—	(322,422)	—	36.50

KM# 249 THOMAS JEFFERSON 250TH ANNIVERSARY OF BIRTH Size: 38.1 mm.

Date	Mintage	Proof	MS-65	Prf-65
1993P	266,927	—	27.00	—
1993S	—	(332,891)	—	30.50

KM# 247 WORLD CUP SOCCER Size: 38.1 mm.

Date	Mintage	Proof	MS-65	Prf-65
1994D	81,698	—	27.00	—
1994S	—	(576,978)	—	30.00

KM# 251 NATIONAL PRISONER OF WAR MUSEUM Size: 38.1 mm.

Date	Mintage	Proof	MS-65	Prf-65
1994W	54,790	—	67.00	—
1994P	—	(220,100)	—	45.00

KM# 250 VIETNAM VETERANS MEMORIAL Size: 38.1 mm.

Date	Mintage	Proof	MS-65	Prf-65
1994W	57,317	—	57.50	—
1994P	—	(226,262)	—	73.00

KM# 252 WOMEN IN MILITARY SERVICE MEMORIAL Size: 38.1 mm.

Date	Mintage	Proof	MS-65	Prf-65
1994W	53,054	—	33.00	—
1994P	—	(213,201)	—	28.00

KM# 253 U.S. CAPITOL BICENTENNIAL Size: 38.1 mm.

Date	Mintage	Proof	MS-65	Prf-65
1994D	68,352	—	22.50	—
1994S	—	(279,416)	—	25.50

KM# 255 CIVIL WAR Size: 38.1 mm.

Date	Mintage	Proof	MS-65	Prf-65
1995P	45,866	—	40.00	—
1995S	—	(55,246)	—	52.00

KM# 266 SPECIAL OLYMPICS WORLD GAMES Size: 38.1 mm.

Date	Mintage	Proof	MS-65	Prf-65
1995W	89,301	—	23.00	—
1995P	—	(351,764)	—	22.00

KM# 260 ATLANTA OLYMPICS Obverse: Gymnastics **Size:** 38.1 mm.

Date	Mintage	Proof	MS-65	Prf-65
1995D	42,497	—	61.00	—
1995P	—	(182,676)	—	30.50

KM# 259 ATLANTA OLYMPICS, PARALYMPICS Obverse: Blind runner **Size:** 38.1 mm.

Date		Mintage	Proof	MS-65	Prf-65
1995D		28,649	—	85.00	—
1995P		—	(138,337)	—	35.00

KM# 264 ATLANTA OLYMPICS Obverse: Track and field **Size:** 38.1 mm.

Date		Mintage	Proof	MS-65	Prf-65
1995D		24,796	—	62.00	—
1995P		—	(136,935)	—	29.00

KM# 263 ATLANTA OLYMPICS Obverse: Cycling **Size:** 38.1 mm.

Date		Mintage	Proof	MS-65	Prf-65
1995D		19,662	—	93.00	—
1995P		—	(118,795)	—	38.00

KM# 269 ATLANTA OLYMPICS Obverse: Tennis **Size:** 38.1 mm.

Date		Mintage	Proof	MS-65	Prf-65
1996D		15,983	—	185	—
1996P		—	(92,016)	—	57.50

KM# 268 ATLANTA OLYMPICS, PARALYMPICS Obverse: Wheelchair racer **Size:** 38.1 mm.

Date	Mintage	Proof	MS-65	Prf-65
1996D	14,497	—	265	—
1996P	—	(84,280)	—	57.50

KM# 272 ATLANTA OLYMPICS Obverse: Rowing **Size:** 38.1 mm.

Date	Mintage	Proof	MS-65	Prf-65
1996D	16,258	—	225	—
1996P	—	(151,890)	—	49.00

KM# 275 NATIONAL COMMUNITY SERVICE Size: 38.1 mm.

Date	Mintage	Proof	MS-65	Prf-65
1996S	23,500	—	220	—
1996S	—	(101,543)	—	67.00

KM# 276 SMITHSONIAN 150TH ANNIVERSARY Size: 38.1 mm.

Date	Mintage	Proof	MS-65	Prf-65
1996D	31,230	—	100.00	—
1996P	—	(129,152)	—	49.00

KM# 272A ATLANTA OLYMPICS Obverse: High jumper

Date	Mintage	Proof	MS-65	Prf-65
1996D	15,697	—	270	—
1996P	—	(124,502)	—	43.00

KM# 278 U.S. BOTANIC GARDENS 175TH ANNIVERSARY Size: 38.1 mm.

Date	Mintage	Proof	MS-65	Prf-65
1997P	57,272	(264,528)	36.50	40.00

KM# 279 JACKIE ROBINSON 50TH ANNIVERSARY Size: 38.1 mm.

Date	Mintage	Proof	MS-65	Prf-65
1997S	30,007	(110,495)	61.00	45.00

KM# 281 NATIONAL LAW ENFORCEMENT OFFICERS MEMORIAL Size: 38.1 mm.

Date	Mintage	Proof	MS-65	Prf-65
1997P	28,575	(110,428)	130	120

KM# 287 ROBERT F. KENNEDY **Size:** 38.1 mm.

Date	Mintage	Proof	MS-65	Prf-65
1998S	106,422	(99,020)	32.00	40.00

KM# 288 BLACK PATRIOTS **Obverse:** Crispus Attucks **Size:** 38.1 mm.

Date	Mintage	Proof	MS-65	Prf-65
1998S	37,210	(75,070)	95.00	80.00

KM# 299 DOLLEY MADISON **Size:** 38.1 mm.

Date	Mintage	Proof	MS-65	Prf-65
1999P	22,948	(158,247)	40.00	42.50

KM# 300 YELLOWSTONE **Size:** 38.1 mm.

Date	Mintage	Proof	MS-65	Prf-65
1999P	23,614	(128,646)	42.50	44.00

KM# 318 LEIF ERICSON

Date	Mintage	Proof	MS-65	Prf-65
2000P	28,150	(58,612)	61.00	49.00
2000 Iceland	—	(15,947)	—	—

KM# 316 LIBRARY OF CONGRESS

Date	Mintage	Proof	MS-65	Prf-65
2000P	52,771	(196,900)	36.50	40.00

KM# 334 AMERICAN BUFFALO

Date	Mintage	Proof	MS-65	Prf-65
2001	197,131	(272,869)	145	145

KM# 333 CAPITOL VISITOR CENTER

Date	Mintage	Proof	MS-65	Prf-65
2001	66,636	(143,793)	44.00	46.00

KM# 336 WINTER OLYMPICS - SALT LAKE CITY Size: 38.1 mm.

Date	Mintage	Proof	MS-65	Prf-65
2002	—	—	38.00	40.00

KM# 338 WEST POINT Size: 38.1 mm.

Date	Mintage	Proof	MS-65	Prf-65
2002	—	—	38.00	40.00

$5 (HALF EAGLE)

KM# 215 STATUE OF LIBERTY CENTENNIAL Size: 21.6 mm.

Date	Mintage	Proof	MS-65	Prf-65
1986W	95,248	(404,013)	120	115

KM# 221 CONSTITUTION BICENTENNIAL Obv. Designer: Marcel Jovine **Size:** 21.6 mm.

Date	Mintage	Proof	MS-65	Prf-65
1987W	214,225	(651,659)	118	118

KM# 223 OLYMPICS Obv. Designer: Elizabeth Jones **Rev. Designer:** Marcel Jovine **Size:** 21.6 mm.

Date	Mintage	Proof	MS-65	Prf-65
1988W	62,913	(281,456)	145	135

KM# 226 BICENTENNIAL OF THE CONGRESS Obv. Designer: John Mercanti **Size:** 21.6 mm.

Date	Mintage	Proof	MS-65	Prf-65
1989W	46,899	(164,690)	145	140

KM# 230 MOUNT RUSHMORE GOLDEN ANNIVERSARY Obv. Designer: John Mercanti **Rev. Designer:** Robert Lamb **Size:** 21.6 mm.

Date	Mintage	Proof	MS-65	Prf-65
1991W	31,959	(111,991)	175	155

KM# 235 OLYMPICS Obv. Designer: James C. Sharpe **Rev. Designer:** James M. Peed **Size:** 21.6 mm.

Date	Mintage	Proof	MS-65	Prf-65
1992W	27,732	(77,313)	165	150

KM# 239 COLUMBUS QUINCENTENARY Size: 21.6 mm.

Date	Mintage	Proof	MS-65	Prf-65
1992W	24,329	(79,730)	195	165

KM# 245 WORLD WAR II 50TH ANNIVERSARY Size: 21.6 mm.

Date	Mintage	Proof	MS-65	Prf-65
1993W	23,089	—	200	—
1993W	—	—	—	180

KM# 242 JAMES MADISON AND BILL OF RIGHTS Size: 21.6 mm.

Date	Mintage	Proof	MS-65	Prf-65
1993W	22,266	(70,051)	200	180

KM# 248 WORLD CUP SOCCER Size: 21.6 mm.

Date	Mintage	Proof	MS-65	Prf-65
1994W	22,464	(89,619)	190	155

KM# 261 OLYMPICS Obverse: Torch runner **Size:** 21.6 mm.

Date	Mintage	Proof	MS-65	Prf-65
1995W	14,675	(57,442)	280	200

KM# 265 OLYMPICS Obverse: Stadium **Size:** 21.6 mm.

Date	Mintage	Proof	MS-65	Prf-65
1995W	10,579	(43,124)	345	275

KM# 256 CIVIL WAR Size: 21.6 mm.

Date	Mintage	Proof	MS-65	Prf-65
1995W	12,735	(55,246)	430	345

KM# 274 OLYMPICS Obverse: Flag bearer **Size:** 21.6 mm.

Date	Mintage	Proof	MS-65	Prf-65
1996W	9,174	(32,886)	385	340

KM# 270 OLYMPICS Obverse: Cauldron **Size:** 21.6 mm.

Date	Mintage	Proof	MS-65	Prf-65
1996W	9,210	(38,555)	385	300

KM# 277 SMITHSONIAN 150TH ANNIVERSARY Size: 21.6 mm.

Date	Mintage	Proof	MS-65	Prf-65
1996W	9,068	(21,772)	500	330

KM# 280 JACKIE ROBINSON 50TH ANNIVERSARY Size: 21.6 mm.

Date	Mintage	Proof	MS-65	Prf-65
1997W	5,202	(24,546)	1,350	410

KM# 282 FRANKLIN DELANO ROOSEVELT Size: 21.6 mm.

Date	Mintage	Proof	MS-65	Prf-65
1997W	11,894	(29,474)	310	295

KM# 301 GEORGE WASHINGTON Size: 21.6 mm.

Date	Mintage	Proof	MS-65	Prf-65
1999W	—	—	300	300

KM# 325 CAPITOL VISITOR CENTER

Date	Mintage	Proof	MS-65	Prf-65
2001	38,017	(27,652)	635	285

KM# 337 WINTER OLYMPICS - SALT LAKE CITY Size: 21.6 mm.

Date	Mintage	Proof	MS-65	Prf-65
2002	—	—	285	235

$10 (EAGLE)

KM# 211 LOS ANGELES XXIII OLYMPIAD Weight: 16.7180 g. **Composition:** 0.9000 Gold 0.4839 oz. AGW **Size:** 27 mm.

Date	Mintage	Proof	MS-65	Prf-65
1984W	75,886	(381,085)	225	225
1984P	33,309	—	—	300
1984D	34,533	—	—	300
1984S	48,551	—	—	240

KM# 317 LIBRARY OF CONGRESS Weight: 16.2590 g. **Composition:** Platinum-Gold-Alloy
Note: Composition is 48 percent platinum, 48 percent gold, and 4 percent alloy.

Date	Mintage	Proof	MS-65	Prf-65
2000W	6,683	(27,167)	1,100	600

MODERN COMMEMORATIVE COIN SETS

Olympic, 1983-1984

Date	Price
1983 & 1984 6 coin set: One 1983 and one 1984 uncirculated and proof dollar, one uncirculated and one proof gold $10; KM209, 210, 211.	500
1983 & 1984 gold and silver uncirculated set: One 1983 and one 1984 uncirculated dollar and one 1984P uncirculated gold $10; KM209, 210, 211.	250
1983 & 1984S gold and silver proof set: One 1983 and one 1984 proof dollar and one 1984 proof gold $10; KM209, 210, 211.	250
1983 collectors set: 1983 PDS uncirculated dollars; KM209.	33.00
1984 collectors set: 1984 PDS uncirculated dollars; KM210.	41.50

Statue of Liberty

Date	Price
1986 2 coin set: proof silver dollar and clad half dollar; KM212, 214.	21.50
1986 2 coin set: uncirculated silver dollar and clad half dollar; KM212, 214.	21.50
1986 3 coin set: proof silver dollar, clad half dollar and gold $5; KM212, 214, 215.	135
1986 3 coin set: uncirculated silver dollar, clad half dollar and gold $5; KM212, 214, 215.	135
1986 6 coin set: 1 each of the proof and uncirculated issues; KM212, 214, 215.	270

Constitution

Date	Price
1987 2 coin set: proof silver dollar and gold $5; KM220, 221.	120
1987 2 coin set: uncirculated silver dollar and gold $5; KM220, 221.	125
1987 4 coin set: 1 each of the proof and uncirculated issues; KM220, 221.	250

Olympic, 1988

Date	Price
1988 2 coin set: Proof silver dollar and gold $5; KM222, 223.	120
1988 2 coin set: uncirculated silver dollar and gold $5; KM222, 223.	125
1988 4 coin set: 1 each of proof and uncirculated issues; KM222, 223.	250

Congress

Date	Price
1989 2 coin set: proof silver dollar and clad half dollar; KM224, 225.	21.50
1989 2 coin set: uncirculated silver dollar and clad half dollar; KM224, 225.	21.50
1989 3 coin set: proof silver dollar, clad half and gold $5; KM224, 225, 226.	135
1989 3 coin set: uncirculated silver dollar, clad half and gold $5; KM224, 225, 226.	140
1989 6 coin set: 1 each of the proof and uncirculated issues; KM224, 225, 226.	285

Mt. Rushmore

Date	Price
1991 2 coin set: proof half dollar and silver dollar; KM228, 229.	45.00
1991 2 coin set: uncirculated half dollar and silver dollar; KM228, 229.	36.00
1991 3 coin set: proof half dollar, silver dollar and gold $5; KM228, 229, 230.	180
1991 3 coin set: uncirculated half dollar, silver dollar and gold $5; KM228, 229, 230.	180
1991 6 coin set: 1 each of proof and uncirculated issues; KM228, 229, 230.	350

Columbus Quincentenary

Date	Price
1992 2 coin set: proof half dollar and silver dollar; KM237, 238.	46.00
1992 2 coin set: uncirculated half dollar and silver dollar; KM237, 238.	34.00
1992 3 coin set: proof half dollar, silver dollar and gold $5; KM237, 238, 239.	180
1992 3 coin set: uncirculated half dollar, silver dollar and gold $5; KM237, 238, 239.	200
1992 6 coin set: 1 each of proof and uncirculated issues; KM237, 238, 239.	390

Olympic, 1992

Date	Price
1992 2 coin set: proof half dollar and silver dollar; KM233, 234.	32.00
1992 2 coin set: uncirculated half dollar and silver dollar; KM233, 234.	28.00
1992 3 coin set: proof half dollar, silver dollar and gold $5; KM233, 234, 235.	153
1992 3 coin set: uncirculated half dollar, silver dollar and gold $5; KM233, 234, 235.	175
1992 6 coin set: 1 each of proof and uncirculated issues; KM233, 234, 235.	320

World War II

Date	Price
1993 2 coin set: proof half dollar and silver dollar; KM243, 244.	39.00
1993 2 coin set: uncirculated half dollar and silver dollar; KM243, 244.	35.00
1993 3 coin set: proof half dollar, silver dollar and gold $5; KM243, 244, 245.	205
1993 3 coin set: uncirculated half dollar, silver dollar and gold $5; KM243, 244, 245.	225
1993 6 coin set: 1 each of proof and uncirculated issues; KM243, 244, 245.	425

Madison / Bill of Rights

Date	Price
1993 2 coin set: proof half dollar and silver dollar; KM240, 241.	32.00
1993 2 coin set: uncirculated half dollar and silver dollar; KM240, 241.	29.00
1993 3 coin set: proof half dollar, silver dollar and gold $5; KM240, 241, 242.	195
1993 3 coin set: uncirculated half dollar, silver dollar and gold $5; KM240, 241, 242.	210
1993 6 coin set: 1 each of proof and uncirculated issues; KM240, 241, 242.	390

Jefferson

Date	Price
1993 Jefferson: dollar, nickel and $2 note; KM249, 192.	100.00

U.S. Veterans

Date	Price
1994 3 coin set: proof POW, Vietnam, Women dollars; KM250, 251, 252.	120
1994 3 coin set: uncirculated POW, Vietnam, Women dollars; KM250, 251, 252.	120

World Cup

Date	Price
1994 2 coin set: proof half dollar and silver dollar; KM246, 247.	34.00
1994 2 coin set: uncirculated half dollar and silver dollar; KM246, 247.	34.00
1994 3 coin set: proof half dollar, silver dollar and gold $5; KM246, 247, 248.	175
1994 3 coin set: uncirculated half dollar, silver dollar and gold $5; KM246, 247, 248.	185
1994 6 coin set: 1 each of proof and uncirculated issues; KM246, 247, 248.	375

Olympic, 1995-96

Date	Price
1995 4 coin set: proof basketball half, $1 gymnast & blind runner, $5 torch runner; KM257, 259, 260, 261.	270
1995 4 coin set: uncirculated basketball half, $1 gymnast & blind runner, $5 torch runner; KM257, 259, 260, 261.	465
1995-96 4 coin set: proof halves, basketball, baseball, swimming, soccer; KM257, 262, 267, 271.	100.00
1996P 2 coin set: proof $1 track & field, cycling; KM263, 264.	75.00
1996P 2 coin set: proof $1 wheelchair & tennis; KM268, 269.	83.00
1996P 2 coin set: proof $1 rowing & high jump; KM272, 272A.	72.00

Civil War

Date	Price
1995 2 coin set: proof half and dollar; KM254, 255.	75.00
1995 2 coin set: uncirculated half and dollar; KM254, 255.	61.00
1995 3 coin set: proof half, dollar and gold $5; KM254, 255, 256.	380
1995 3 coin set: uncirculated half, dollar and gold $5; KM254, 255, 256.	460
1995 6 coin set: 1 each of proof and uncirculated issues; KM254, 255, 256.	880

Smithsonian

Date	Price
1996 2 coin set: proof dollar and $5 gold; KM276, 277.	350
1996 4 coin set: proof and B.U. ; KM276, 277.	825

Botanic Garden

Date	Price
1997 2 coin set: dollar, Jefferson nickel and $1 note; KM278, 192.	225

Jackie Robinson

Date	Price
1997 2 coin set: proof dollar & $5 gold; KM279, 280.	450
1997 4 coin set: proof & BU; KM279, 280.	1,700

Franklin Delano Roosevelt

Date	Price
1997W 2 coin set: uncirculated and proof; KM282.	475

Kennedy

Date	Price
1998 2 coin collectors set: Robert Kennedy dollar and John Kennedy half dollar; KM287, 202b. Matte finished.	315
1998 2 coin set: proof; KM287.	67.00

Black Patriots

Date	Price
1998S 2 coin set: uncirculated and proof; KM288.	165

Dolley Madison

Date	Price
1999 2 coin set: proof and uncirculated silver dollars; KM299.	72.00

George Washington

Date	Price
1999 2 coin set: proof and uncirculated gold $5; KM301.	540

Yellowstone National Park

Date	Price
1999 2 coin set: proof and uncirculated silver dollars; KM300.	80.00

Leif Ericson

Date	Price
2000 2 coin set: proof and uncirculated silver dollars; KM318.	85.00

American Buffalo

Date	Price
2001 2 coin set: 90% Silver unc. & proof $1.; KM334.	260
2001 coin & currency set 90% unc. dollar & replicas of 1899 $5 silver cert.; KM334.	145

Capitol Visitor Center

Date	Price
2001 3 coin set: proof half, silver dollar, gold $5; KM332, 333, 335.	265

AMERICAN EAGLE BULLION COINS

SILVER DOLLAR

KM#273 **Obv. Designer:** Adolph A. Weinman. **Rev. Designer:** John Mercanti. **Diameter:** 40.6 **Weight:** 31.1010 g. **Composition:** 0.9993 SILVER, 1 oz. **Notes:** Prices based on $5.50 spot silver.

Date	Mintage	Unc	Prf.	Date	Mintage	Unc	Prf.
1986	5,393,005	16.50	—	1995P	395,400	—	105
1986S	1,446,778	—	26.00	1995W 10th Anniversary	30,125	—	2,250
1987	11,442,335	8.00	—	1996	3,603,386	26.00	—
1987S	904,732	—	26.00	1996P	473,021	—	50.00
1988	5,004,646	10.00	—	1997	4,295,004	12.50	—
1988S	557,370	—	90.00	1997P	429,682	—	90.00
1989	5,203,327	10.00	—	1998	4,847,549	8.00	—
1989S	617,694	—	30.00	1998P	452,319	—	40.00
1990	5,840,210	12.50	—	1999	7,408,640	9.50	—
1990S	695,510	—	30.00	1999P	549,769	—	70.00
1991	7,191,066	8.50	—	2000P	—	—	30.00
1991S	511,924	—	60.00	2000	9,239,132	8.50	—
1992	5,540,068	9.50	—	2001	9,001,711	7.50	—
1992S	498,552	—	35.00	2001W	—	—	30.00
1993	6,763,762	9.00	—	2002	10,539,026	7.50	—
1993P	403,625	—	120	2002W	—	—	29.00
1994	4,227,319	14.00	—	2003	—	8.00	—
1994P	372,168	—	110	2003W	—	—	—
1995	4,672,051	12.50	—				

GOLD $5

KM#216 **Obv. Designer:** Augustus Saint-Gaudens. **Rev. Designer:** Miley Busiek. **Diameter:** 16.5 **Weight:** 3.3930 g. **Composition:** 0.9167 GOLD, 0.1 oz.

Date	Mintage	Unc	Prf.	Date	Mintage	Unc	Prf.
MCMLXXXVI (1986)	912,609	50.00	—	1992	209,300	52.00	—
MCMLXXXVII (1987)	580,266	50.00	—	1992P	64,902	—	71.00
MCMLXXXVIII (1988)	159,500	190	—	1993	210,709	52.00	—
MCMLXXXVIIIP (1988)P	143,881	—	56.00	1993P	58,649	—	66.00
MCMLXXXIX (1989)	264,790	90.00	—	1994	206,380	52.00	—
MCMLXXXIXP (1989)P	82,924	—	56.00	1994W	—	—	60.00
MCMXC (1990)	210,210	70.00	—	1995	223,025	52.00	—
MCMXCP (1990)P	99,349	—	56.00	1995W	—	—	56.00
MCMXCI (1991)	165,200	115	—	1996	401,964	47.00	—
MCMXCIP (1991)P	70,344	—	58.00	1996W	—	—	74.00

Date	Mintage	Unc	Prf.	Date	Mintage	Unc	Prf.
1997	528,515	45.00	—	2000W	—	—	59.00
1997W	—	—	91.00	2001	269,147	50.00	70.00
1998	1,344,520	43.00	—	2001W	—	—	—
1998W	—	—	58.00	2002	230,027	47.00	—
1999	2,750,338	42.00	—	2002W	—	—	70.00
1999W	—	—	58.00	2003	—	50.00	—
2000	569,153	50.00	—	2003W	—	—	—

GOLD $10

KM#217 **Obv. Designer:** Augustus Saint-Gaudens. **Rev. Designer:** Miley Busiek. **Diameter:** 22 **Weight:** 8.4830 g. **Composition:** 0.9167 GOLD, 0.25 oz.

Date	Mintage	Unc	Prf.	Date	Mintage	Unc	Prf.
MCMLXXXVI (1986)	726,031	125	—	1995W	—	—	150
MCMLXXXVII (1987)	269,255	125	—	1996	60,318	130	—
MCMLXXXVIII (1988)	49,000	140	—	1996W	—	—	150
MCMLXXXVIIIP (1988)P	98,028	—	150	1997	108,805	120	—
MCMLXXXIX (1989)	81,789	130	—	1997W	—	—	150
MCMLXXXIX (1989)P	53,593	—	150	1998	309,829	115	—
MCMXC (1990)	41,000	145	—	1998W	—	—	150
MCMXCP (1990)P	62,674	—	150	1999	564,232	115	—
MCMXCI (1991)	36,100	255	—	1999W	—	—	150
MCMXCIP (1991)P	50,839	—	150	2000	128,964	125	—
1992	59,546	130	—	2000W	—	—	146
1992P	46,290	—	150	2001	71,280	120	—
1993	71,864	130	—	2001W	—	—	—
1993P	46,271	—	150	2002	62,027	115	—
1994	72,650	130	—	2002W	—	—	150
1994W	—	—	150	2003	—	125	—
1995	83,752	130	—	2003W	—	—	—

GOLD $25

KM#218 **Obv. Designer:** Augustus Saint-Gaudens. **Rev. Designer:** Miley Busiek. **Diameter:** 27 **Weight:** 16.9660 g. **Composition:** 0.9167 GOLD, 0.5 oz.

Date	Mintage	Unc	Prf.	Date	Mintage	Unc	Prf.
MCMLXXXVI (1986)	599,566	250	—	1996	39,287	290	—
MCMLXXXVII (1987)	131,255	250	—	1996W	—	—	280
MCMLXXXVIIP (1987)P	143,398	—	295	1997	79,605	225	—
MCMLXXXVIII (1988)	45,000	290	—	1997W	—	—	280
MCMLXXXVIIIP (1988)P	76,528	—	280	1998	169,029	220	—
MCMLXXXIX (1989)	44,829	385	—	1998W	—	—	280
MCMLXXXIXP (1989)P	44,264	—	280	1999	263,013	220	—
MCMXC (1990)	31,000	400	—	1999W	—	—	280
MCMXCP (1990)P	51,636	—	280	2000	79,287	230	—
MCMXCI (1991)	24,100	540	—	2000W	—	—	280
MCMXCIP (1991)P	53,125	—	280	2001	48,047	285	—
1992	54,404	280	—	2001W	—	—	—
1992P	40,982	—	280	2002	70,027	230	—
1993	73,324	240	—	2002W	—	—	285
1993P	43,319	—	280	2003	—	230	—
1994	62,400	240	—	2003W	—	—	—
1994W	—	—	280				
1995	53,474	250	—				
1995W	—	—	285				

GOLD $50

KM#219   Obv. Designer: Augustus Saint-Gaudens. **Rev. Designer:** Miley Busiek. **Diameter:** 32.7 **Weight:** 33.9310 g. **Composition:** 0.9167 GOLD, 1 oz.

Date	Mintage	Unc	Prf.	Date	Mintage	Unc	Prf.
MCMLXXXVI (1986)	1,362,650	440	—	1995	200,636	440	—
MCMLXXXVIW (1986)W	446,290	—	570	1995W	—	—	570
MCMLXXXVII (1987)	1,045,500	440	—	1996	189,148	440	—
MCMLXXXVIIW (1987)W	147,498	—	520	1996W	—	—	570
MCMLXXXVIII (1988)	465,000	440	—	1997	664,508	435	—
MCMLXXXVIIIW (1988)W	87,133	—	570	1997W	—	—	570
MCMLXXXIX (1989)	415,790	440	—	1998	1,468,530	435	—
MCMLXXXIXW (1989)W	53,960	—	570	1998W	—	—	570
MCMXC (1990)	373,210	440	—	1999	1,505,026	430	—
MCMXCW (1990)W	62,401	—	570	1999W	—	—	570
MCMXCI (1991)	243,100	450	—	2000	433,319	440	—
MCMXCIW (1991)W	50,411	—	570	2000W	—	—	570
1992	275,000	440	—	2001	143,605	440	—
1992W	44,835	—	570	2001W	—	—	—
1993	480,192	440	—	2002	222,029	430	—
1993W	34,389	—	570	2002W	—	—	570
1994	221,633	440	—	2003	—	440	—
1994W	—	—	570	2003W	—	—	—

PLATINUM $10

KM#283   Obv. Designer: John Mercanti. **Rev. Designer:** Thomas D. Rogers Sr.. **Composition:** 0.9990 PLATINUM, 0.1 oz.

Date	Mintage	Unc	Prf.	Date	Mintage	Unc	Prf.
1997	70,250	80.00	—	2000W	—	—	125
1997W	—	—	125	2001	52,017	—	—
1998	39,525	80.00	—	2001W	—	—	—
1998W	—	—	125	2002	23,005	—	—
1999	55,955	85.00	—	2002W	—	—	—
1999W	—	—	125	2003	—	—	—
2000	34,027	80.00	—	2003W	—	—	—

PLATINUM $25

KM#284   Obv. Designer: John Mercanti. **Rev. Designer:** Thomas D. Rogers Sr. **Composition:** 0.9995 PLATINUM, 0.25 oz.

Date	Mintage	Unc	Prf.	Date	Mintage	Unc	Prf.
1997	27,100	220	—	1999	39,734	195	—
1997W	—	—	210	1999W	—	—	225
1998	38,887	195	—	2000	20,054	195	—
1998W	—	—	225	2000W	—	—	225

Date	Mintage	Unc	Prf.	Date	Mintage	Unc	Prf.
2001	21,815	—	—	2002W	—	—	—
2001W	—	—	—	2003	—	—	—
2002	27,405	—	—	2003W	—	—	—

PLATINUM $50

KM#285 Obv. Designer: John Mercanti. **Rev. Designer:** Thomas D. Rogers Sr. **Composition:** 0.9995 PLATINUM, 0.5 oz.

Date	Mintage	Unc	Prf.	Date	Mintage	Unc	Prf.
1997	20,500	430	—	2000W	—	—	415
1997W	—	—	370	2001	12,815	550	—
1998	32,415	350	—	2001W	—	—	430
1998W	—	—	410	2002	24,005	—	—
1999	32,309	300	—	2002W	—	—	405
1999W	—	—	410	2003	—	—	—
2000	18,892	340	—	2003W	—	—	—

PLATINUM $100

KM#286 Composition: 0.9995 PLATINUM, 1 oz. **Notes:** Prices based on $374.00 spot platinum.

Date	Mintage	Unc	Prf.	Date	Mintage	Unc	Prf.
1997	56,000	700	—	2000W	—	—	750
1997W	—	—	775	2001	14,070	725	—
1998	133,002	700	—	2001W	—	—	750
1998W	—	—	750	2002	11,502	725	—
1999	56,707	700	—	2002W	—	—	750
1999W	—	—	750	2003	—	—	—
2000	18,892	700	—	2003W	—	—	—

CANADA
CIRCULATION COINAGE
CENT

KM# 1   Weight: 3.2400 g. **Composition:** Bronze

Date	Mintage	VG-8	F-12	VF-20	XF-40	MS-60	MS-63	Proof
1858	421,000	35.00	45.00	60.00	90.00	225	800	—
1859/8 wide 9	Inc. above	22.00	29.00	50.00	80.00	225	900	—
1859 narrow 9	9,579,000	2.25	3.00	4.00	5.00	25.00	140	—
1859 double punched narrow 9 type I	Inc. above	175	250	350	540	1,150	2,000	—
1859 double punched narrow 9 type II	Inc. above	35.00	60.00	85.00	100.00	250	1,000	—

KM# 7   Weight: 3.2400 g. **Composition:** Bronze

Date	Mintage	VG-8	F-12	VF-20	XF-40	MS-60	MS-63	Proof
1876H	4,000,000	1.60	2.75	4.00	7.00	40.00	180	—
1881H	2,000,000	2.50	3.50	5.00	10.00	50.00	200	—
1882H	4,000,000	1.60	2.75	4.00	6.00	30.00	140	—
1884	2,500,000	2.00	3.00	4.00	7.50	40.00	180	—
1886	1,500,000	3.50	4.50	9.00	15.00	75.00	250	—
1887	1,500,000	2.75	4.00	5.00	11.00	50.00	200	—
1888	4,000,000	1.50	2.50	3.00	5.00	30.00	100.00	—
1890H	1,000,000	4.00	7.00	12.00	20.00	80.00	300	—
1891 lg. date	1,452,000	4.50	7.00	11.00	20.00	90.00	300	—
1891 S.D.L.L.	Inc. above	40.00	60.00	85.00	135	500	1,500	—
1891 S.D.S.L.	Inc. above	30.00	45.00	60.00	90.00	200	550	—
1892	1,200,000	3.00	4.50	6.00	10.00	40.00	130	—
1893	2,000,000	2.00	2.50	4.00	6.00	30.00	100.00	—
1894	1,000,000	7.00	9.00	13.00	20.00	65.00	175	—
1895	1,200,000	3.00	5.00	7.00	10.00	45.00	160	—
1896	2,000,000	1.75	2.75	3.50	5.50	30.00	100.00	—
1897	1,500,000	2.00	2.75	4.00	6.00	30.00	110	—
1898H	1,000,000	4.00	6.00	8.00	11.00	55.00	200	—
1899	2,400,000	1.50	2.25	3.00	5.00	30.00	90.00	—
1900	1,000,000	3.00	6.00	10.00	15.00	60.00	250	—
1900H	2,600,000	2.00	2.50	4.00	5.00	22.00	60.00	—
1901	4,100,000	1.50	2.50	3.00	5.00	22.00	70.00	—

KM# 8   Weight: 3.2400 g. **Composition:** Bronze

Date	Mintage	VG-8	F-12	VF-20	XF-40	MS-60	MS-63	Proof
1902	3,000,000	1.25	1.50	2.00	5.00	13.00	45.00	—
1903	4,000,000	1.25	1.50	2.00	4.00	18.00	50.00	—
1904	2,500,000	1.50	2.00	3.25	5.00	25.00	75.00	—
1905	2,000,000	2.50	4.00	5.00	7.00	30.00	85.00	—

Date	Mintage	VG-8	F-12	VF-20	XF-40	MS-60	MS-63	Proof
1906	4,100,000	1.25	1.50	2.00	4.00	22.00	125	—
1907	2,400,000	1.25	2.00	3.00	5.00	25.00	90.00	—
1907H	800,000	8.00	11.00	16.00	30.00	80.00	350	—
1908	2,401,506	1.25	2.00	3.00	5.00	22.00	80.00	150
1909	3,973,339	1.25	1.50	2.00	4.00	18.00	65.00	—
1910	5,146,487	1.25	1.50	2.00	3.00	13.00	65.00	—

KM# 15 Weight: 3.2400 g. **Composition:** Bronze

Date	Mintage	VG-8	F-12	VF-20	XF-40	MS-60	MS-63	Proof
1911	4,663,486	0.80	1.30	1.75	3.50	15.00	50.00	250

KM# 21 Weight: 3.2400 g. **Composition:** Bronze

Date	Mintage	VG-8	F-12	VF-20	XF-40	MS-60	MS-63	Proof
1912	5,107,642	0.75	1.00	1.50	2.50	15.00	50.00	—
1913	5,735,405	0.75	1.00	1.50	2.50	15.00	75.00	—
1914	3,405,958	0.75	1.00	1.50	2.50	25.00	90.00	—
1915	4,932,134	0.75	1.00	1.50	2.50	18.00	65.00	—
1916	11,022,367	0.50	0.65	0.90	2.00	12.00	45.00	—
1917	11,899,254	0.50	0.65	0.90	1.50	8.00	40.00	—
1918	12,970,798	0.50	0.65	0.90	1.50	8.00	40.00	—
1919	11,279,634	0.50	0.65	0.90	1.50	8.00	40.00	—
1920	6,762,247	0.60	0.75	1.00	2.00	10.00	50.00	—

Dot

KM# 28 Weight: 3.2400 g. **Composition:** Bronze

Date	Mintage	VG-8	F-12	VF-20	XF-40	MS-60	MS-63	Proof
1920	15,483,923	0.25	0.50	1.00	2.00	7.00	30.00	—
1921	7,601,627	0.50	0.75	1.75	3.00	18.00	90.00	—
1922	1,243,635	8.75	10.00	14.50	22.00	130	600	—
1923	1,019,002	14.25	16.25	23.00	34.00	200	1,200	—
1924	1,593,195	3.00	4.00	5.00	10.00	70.00	350	—
1925	1,000,622	10.00	12.00	18.75	28.00	130	500	—
1926	2,143,372	2.25	3.00	4.50	8.75	65.00	250	—
1927	3,553,928	0.90	1.25	2.25	4.00	30.00	110	—
1928	9,144,860	0.15	0.30	0.65	1.50	10.00	50.00	—
1929	12,159,840	0.15	0.30	0.65	1.50	10.00	50.00	—
1930	2,538,613	1.35	1.80	3.00	5.00	30.00	110	—
1931	3,842,776	0.65	1.00	1.75	3.50	25.00	100.00	—
1932	21,316,190	0.15	0.20	0.50	1.50	9.00	40.00	—
1933	12,079,310	0.15	0.20	0.50	1.50	9.00	40.00	—
1934	7,042,358	0.20	0.30	0.75	1.50	9.00	40.00	—
1935	7,526,400	0.20	0.30	0.75	1.50	9.00	35.00	—
1936	8,768,769	0.15	0.20	0.75	1.50	9.00	30.00	—
1936 dot below date; Rare	678,823	—	—	—	—	—	—	—

Note: Only one possible business strike is known to exist. No other examples (or possible business strikes) have ever surfaced.
1936 dot below date, specimen, 3 known
Note: At the David Akers auction of the John Jay Pittman collection (Part 1, 10-97), a gem specimen realized $121,000. At the David Akers auction of the John Jay Pittman collection (Part 3, 10-99), a near choice specimen realized $115,000.

Maple Leaf

KM# 32 Weight: 3.2400 g. **Composition:** Bronze

Date	Mintage	VG-8	F-12	VF-20	XF-40	MS-60	MS-63	Proof
1937	10,040,231	0.60	0.90	1.50	2.00	3.00	9.00	—
1938	18,365,608	0.50	0.75	1.00	1.25	2.00	6.50	—
1939	21,600,319	0.20	0.35	0.50	0.75	1.75	5.00	—
1940	85,740,532	0.10	0.15	0.25	0.50	1.50	5.50	—
1941	56,336,011	0.10	0.15	0.25	0.50	4.00	50.00	—

Date	Mintage	VG-8	F-12	VF-20	XF-40	MS-60	MS-63	Proof
1942	76,113,708	0.10	0.15	0.25	0.50	4.00	40.00	—
1943	89,111,969	0.10	0.15	0.25	0.50	1.50	25.00	—
1944	44,131,216	0.20	0.25	0.30	0.60	5.50	70.00	—
1945	77,268,591	0.10	0.15	0.20	0.30	1.00	14.00	—
1946	56,662,071	0.10	0.15	0.20	0.30	1.00	5.00	—
1947	31,093,901	0.10	0.15	0.20	0.30	1.00	6.00	—
1947 maple leaf	47,855,448	0.10	0.15	0.20	0.30	1.00	5.00	—

KM# 41   Obverse: Modified legend **Weight:** 3.2400 g. **Composition:** Bronze

Date	Mintage	VG-8	F-12	VF-20	XF-40	MS-60	MS-63	Proof
1948	25,767,779	—	0.10	0.25	0.60	2.25	20.00	—
1949	33,128,933	—	0.10	0.15	0.25	1.25	6.00	—
1950	60,444,992	—	0.10	0.15	0.25	0.85	6.00	—
1951	80,430,379	—	0.10	0.15	0.20	0.85	8.00	—
1952	67,631,736	—	0.10	0.15	0.20	0.85	4.00	—

   Without Strap With Strap

KM# 49   Obv. Designer: Gillick **Obverse:** Elizabeth II effigy **Weight:** 3.2400 g. **Composition:** Bronze

Date	Mintage	VG-8	F-12	VF-20	XF-40	MS-60	MS-63	Proof
1953 without strap	67,806,016	0.15	0.20	0.25	0.30	0.65	1.50	—
1953 with strap	Inc. above	0.50	1.00	1.50	2.50	10.00	35.00	—
1954 with strap	22,181,760	0.10	0.15	0.30	0.40	1.00	4.00	—
1954 without strap, proof-like only	Inc. above	—	—	—	—	150	300	—
1955 with strap	56,403,193	—	0.10	0.15	0.20	0.35	1.00	—
1955 without strap	Inc. above	70.00	100.00	125	225	400	1,000	—
1956	78,658,535	—	—	—	0.10	0.50	0.90	—
1957	100,601,792	—	—	—	0.10	0.25	0.50	—
1958	59,385,679	—	—	—	0.10	0.25	0.50	—
1959	83,615,343	—	—	—	0.10	0.25	0.30	—
1960	75,772,775	—	—	—	0.10	0.25	0.30	—
1961	139,598,404	—	—	—	—	0.15	0.20	—
1962	227,244,069	—	—	—	—	0.10	0.20	—
1963	279,076,334	—	—	—	—	0.10	0.20	—
1964	484,655,322	—	—	—	—	0.10	0.20	—

KM# 59.1   Obv. Designer: Machin **Obverse:** Elizabeth II effigy **Weight:** 3.2400 g. **Composition:** Bronze

Date	Mintage	VG-8	F-12	VF-20	XF-40	MS-60	MS-63	Proof
1965 sm. beads, pointed 5	304,441,082	—	—	—	0.45	1.00	4.00	—
1965 sm. beads, blunt 5	Inc. above	—	—	—	—	0.20	0.30	—
1965 lg. beads, pointed 5	Inc. above	—	—	3.00	5.00	12.00	30.00	—
1965 lg. beads, blunt 5	Inc. above	—	—	—	0.10	0.15	0.30	—
1966	184,151,087	—	—	—	—	0.10	0.20	—
1968	329,695,772	—	—	—	—	0.10	0.20	—
1969	335,240,929	—	—	—	—	0.10	0.20	—
1970	311,145,010	—	—	—	—	0.10	0.20	—
1971	298,228,936	—	—	—	—	0.10	0.20	—
1972	451,304,591	—	—	—	—	0.10	0.20	—
1973	457,059,852	—	—	—	—	0.10	0.20	—
1974	692,058,489	—	—	—	—	0.10	0.20	—
1975	642,318,000	—	—	—	—	0.10	0.20	—
1976	701,122,890	—	—	—	—	0.10	0.20	—
1977	453,762,670	—	—	—	—	0.10	0.20	—
1978	911,170,647	—	—	—	—	0.10	0.20	—

KM# 59.2   Obv. Designer: Machin **Obverse:** Elizabeth II effigy. Smaller bust **Weight:** 3.2400 g. **Composition:** Bronze

Date	Mintage	VG-8	F-12	VF-20	XF-40	MS-60	MS-63	Proof
1979	754,394,064	—	—	—	—	0.10	0.20	—

KM# 127   Obv. Designer: Machin **Obverse:** Elizabeth II effigy **Weight:** 2.8000 g. **Composition:** Bronze
Note: Reduced weight.

Date	Mintage	VG-8	F-12	VF-20	XF-40	MS-60	MS-63	Proof
1980	912,052,318	—	—	—	—	0.10	0.15	—
1981	1,209,468,500	—	—	—	—	0.10	0.15	—
1981 Proof	199,000	—	—	—	—	—	—	1.50

KM# 132 Obv. Designer: Machin **Obverse:** Elizabeth II effigy **Edge:** Multisided. **Weight:** 2.5000 g.
Composition: Bronze **Note:** Reduced weight.

Date	Mintage	VG-8	F-12	VF-20	XF-40	MS-60	MS-63	Proof
1982	911,001,000	—	—	—	—	0.10	0.15	—
1982 Proof	180,908	—	—	—	—	—	—	1.50
1983	975,510,000	—	—	—	—	0.10	0.15	—
1983 Proof	168,000	—	—	—	—	—	—	1.50
1984	838,225,000	—	—	—	—	0.10	0.15	—
1984 Proof	161,602	—	—	—	—	—	—	1.50
1985 pointed 5	771,772,500	—	—	—	5.00	10.00	18.50	—
1985 blunt 5	Inc. above	—	—	—	—	0.10	0.15	—
1985 blunt 5, proof	157,037	—	—	—	—	—	—	1.50
1986	740,335,000	—	—	—	—	0.10	0.15	—
1986 Proof	175,745	—	—	—	—	—	—	1.50
1987	774,549,000	—	—	—	—	0.10	0.15	—
1987 Proof	179,004	—	—	—	—	—	—	1.50
1988	482,676,752	—	—	—	—	0.10	0.15	—
1988 Proof	175,259	—	—	—	—	—	—	1.50
1989	1,077,347,200	—	—	—	—	0.10	0.15	—
1989 Proof	170,928	—	—	—	—	—	—	1.50

KM# 181 Obv. Designer: dePedery-Hunt **Obverse:** Elizabeth II effigy **Weight:** 2.5000 g. **Composition:**
Bronze

Date	Mintage	VG-8	F-12	VF-20	XF-40	MS-60	MS-63	Proof
1990	218,035,000	—	—	—	—	0.10	0.15	—
1990 Proof	140,649	—	—	—	—	—	—	2.50
1991	831,001,000	—	—	—	—	0.10	0.15	—
1991 Proof	131,888	—	—	—	—	—	—	3.50
1993	752,034,000	—	—	—	—	0.10	0.15	—
1993 Proof	145,065	—	—	—	—	—	—	2.00
1994	639,516,000	—	—	—	—	0.10	0.15	—
1994 Proof	146,424	—	—	—	—	—	—	2.50
1995	624,983,000	—	—	—	—	0.10	0.15	—
1996	445,746,000	—	—	—	—	0.10	0.15	—
1996 Proof	—	—	—	—	—	—	—	2.50

Composition: Copper Plated Zinc

Date	Mintage	VG-8	F-12	VF-20	XF-40	MS-60	MS-63	Proof
1996	445,746,000	—	—	—	—	0.10	0.15	2.50
1996 Proof	—	—	—	—	—	—	—	—

KM# 289 Edge: Round and plain. **Composition:** Copper Plated Zinc

Date	Mintage	VG-8	F-12	VF-20	XF-40	MS-60	MS-63	Proof
1997	506,928,000	—	—	—	—	0.10	0.15	—
1997 Proof	—	—	—	—	—	—	—	2.75
1998	—	—	—	—	—	0.10	0.15	—
1998 Proof	—	—	—	—	—	—	—	3.00
1998W	—	—	—	—	—	—	1.75	—
1999P	—	—	—	—	—	—	6.00	—
Note: Plated, from test token set								
1999	—	—	—	—	—	0.10	0.15	—
1999W	—	—	—	—	—	—	—	—
1999 Proof	—	—	—	—	—	—	—	4.00
2000	—	—	—	—	—	0.10	0.15	—
2000W	—	—	—	—	—	—	1.75	—
2000 Proof	—	—	—	—	—	—	—	4.00
2001	—	—	—	—	—	—	0.10	—
2001 Proof	—	—	—	—	—	—	—	4.00
2003	—	—	—	—	—	—	0.10	—
2003 Proof	—	—	—	—	—	—	—	4.00

KM# 289a Composition: Bronze

Date	Mintage	VG-8	F-12	VF-20	XF-40	MS-60	MS-63	Proof
1998 In Specimen sets only	—	—	—	—	—	—	0.75	—

KM# 445 Subject: Elizabeth II Golden Jubilee **Composition:** Bronze-Plated Zinc **Note:** Double-dated 1952-2002.

Date	Mintage	VG-8	F-12	VF-20	XF-40	MS-60	MS-63	Proof
ND(2002)	—	—	—	—	—	—	0.75	—
ND(2002) In proof sets only	—	—	—	—	—	—	—	2.50

KM# 490 Obverse: New effigy by Susanna Blunt **Composition:** Bronze-Plated Zinc

Date	Mintage	VG-8	F-12	VF-20	XF-40	MS-60	MS-63	Proof
2003W	—	—	—	—	—	—	.25	—

5 CENTS

Oval O's   Round O's

KM# 2 Weight: 1.1620 g. **Composition:** 0.9250 Silver 0.0346 oz. ASW

Date	Mintage	VG-8	F-12	VF-20	XF-40	MS-60	MS-63	Proof
1858 small date	1,500,000	10.00	15.00	25.00	40.00	225	450	—
1858 large date over small date	Inc. above	90.00	150	250	375	1,000	2,350	—
1870 flat rim	2,800,000	9.00	15.00	25.00	45.00	225	500	—
1870 wire rim	Inc. above	9.00	15.00	25.00	45.00	200	450	—
1871	1,400,000	9.00	15.00	25.00	45.00	250	550	—
1872H	2,000,000	6.00	12.00	25.00	40.00	225	600	—
1874H plain 4	800,000	12.50	27.00	55.00	100.00	350	875	—
1874H crosslet 4	Inc. above	10.00	20.00	40.00	65.00	350	750	—
1875H large date	1,000,000	125	175	325	575	2,200	4,250	—
1875H small date	Inc. above	80.00	150	250	450	1,400	3,250	—
1880H	3,000,000	4.00	7.50	16.00	35.00	225	550	—
1881H	1,500,000	4.50	9.00	17.50	35.00	225	600	—
1882H	1,000,000	5.00	10.00	20.00	40.00	250	650	—
1883H	600,000	13.00	25.00	60.00	125	650	1,750	—
1884	200,000	75.00	125	225	475	2,200	6,000	—
1885 small 5	1,000,000	7.50	14.00	35.00	70.00	400	1,250	—
1885 large 5	Inc. above	8.25	15.50	35.00	80.00	425	1,350	—
1885 large 5 over small 5	Inc. above	35.00	75.00	150	400	1,950	2,750	—
1886 small 6	1,700,000	4.50	9.00	17.50	35.00	250	700	—
1886 large 6	Inc. above	7.00	10.00	20.00	45.00	300	750	—
1887	500,000	13.00	25.00	45.00	85.00	300	675	—
1888	1,000,000	3.50	6.00	14.00	25.00	140	350	—
1889	1,200,000	14.00	28.00	60.00	100.00	350	1,000	—
1890H	1,000,000	4.50	8.00	18.00	35.00	165	400	—
1891	1,800,000	3.00	5.00	10.00	16.00	125	285	—
1892	860,000	4.50	8.00	16.00	35.00	200	550	—
1893	1,700,000	3.00	5.00	10.00	18.00	150	350	—
1894	500,000	9.50	20.00	40.00	80.00	285	850	—
1896	1,500,000	3.50	7.00	12.00	25.00	150	325	—
1897	1,319,283	3.75	6.50	12.00	25.00	125	285	—
1898	580,717	8.00	15.00	30.00	50.00	180	500	—
1899	3,000,000	2.75	4.00	7.50	18.00	90.00	275	—
1900 oval O's	1,800,000	3.00	4.50	8.00	18.00	100.00	300	—
1900 round O's	Inc. above	13.00	25.00	45.00	90.00	250	750	—
1901	2,000,000	2.75	4.00	8.00	18.00	100.00	325	—

KM# 9 Weight: 1.1620 g. **Composition:** 0.9250 Silver 0.0346 oz. ASW

Date	Mintage	VG-8	F-12	VF-20	XF-40	MS-60	MS-63	Proof
1902	2,120,000	1.50	2.00	3.25	7.00	30.00	50.00	—
1902 lg. broad H	2,200,000	1.50	2.00	3.25	7.00	30.00	50.00	—
1902 sm. narrow H	Inc. above	5.00	9.00	20.00	35.00	80.00	150	—

KM# 13 Weight: 1.1620 g. **Composition:** 0.9250 Silver 0.0346 oz. ASW

Date	Mintage	VG-8	F-12	VF-20	XF-40	MS-60	MS-63	Proof
1903 22 leaves	1,000,000	4.00	7.00	14.00	30.00	120	280	—
1903H 21 leaves	2,640,000	1.75	3.00	7.00	13.00	90.00	200	—
1904	2,400,000	1.75	3.00	7.00	18.00	140	400	—
1905	2,600,000	1.75	3.00	6.00	12.00	85.00	200	—
1906	3,100,000	1.50	2.00	4.00	8.00	65.00	175	—
1907	5,200,000	1.50	2.00	4.00	7.00	45.00	125	—
1908	1,220,524	4.00	6.50	12.00	25.00	85.00	150	—
1909 round leaves	1,983,725	2.00	3.75	7.00	15.00	125	350	—
1909 pointed leaves	Inc. above	8.00	12.00	25.00	50.00	300	1,000	—
1910 pointed leaves	3,850,325	1.50	1.75	3.25	7.00	45.00	75.00	—
1910 round leaves	Inc. above	10.00	14.00	28.00	70.00	320	1,100	—

KM# 16   Weight: 1.1620 g. **Composition:** 0.9250 Silver 0.0346 oz. ASW

Date	Mintage	VG-8	F-12	VF-20	XF-40	MS-60	MS-63	Proof
1911	3,692,350	1.25	2.00	4.00	8.00	50.00	85.00	—

KM# 22   Weight: 1.1620 g. **Composition:** 0.9250 Silver 0.0346 oz. ASW

Date	Mintage	VG-8	F-12	VF-20	XF-40	MS-60	MS-63	Proof
1912	5,863,170	1.25	2.00	3.00	6.00	45.00	125	—
1913	5,488,048	1.25	1.75	2.50	5.00	20.00	40.00	—
1914	4,202,179	1.25	2.00	3.00	6.00	45.00	110	—
1915	1,172,258	5.50	10.50	20.00	40.00	175	400	—
1916	2,481,675	1.75	3.00	5.00	11.00	75.00	175	—
1917	5,521,373	1.25	1.75	2.00	4.00	25.00	60.00	—
1918	6,052,298	1.25	1.75	2.00	4.00	25.00	50.00	—
1919	7,835,400	1.25	1.75	2.00	4.00	25.00	50.00	—

KM# 22a   Weight: 1.1664 g. **Composition:** 0.8000 Silver .0300 oz. ASW

Date	Mintage	VG-8	F-12	VF-20	XF-40	MS-60	MS-63	Proof
1920	10,649,851	1.25	1.75	2.00	4.00	20.00	35.00	—
1921	2,582,495	1,600	2,000	2,700	3,500	6,000	13,500	—

Note: Approximately 460 known; balance remelted. Stack's A.G. Carter Jr. Sale (12-89) choice BU, finest known, realized $57,200.

Near 6   Far 6

KM# 29   Composition: Nickel

Date	Mintage	VG-8	F-12	VF-20	XF-40	MS-60	MS-63	Proof
1922	4,794,119	0.25	0.75	1.75	7.00	35.00	75.00	—
1923	2,502,279	0.40	1.25	3.50	12.00	75.00	200	—
1924	3,105,839	0.30	0.70	2.50	7.00	60.00	150	—
1925	201,921	30.00	40.00	75.00	155	800	2,500	—
1926 near 6	938,162	1.50	4.00	12.00	40.00	300	1,200	—
1926 far 6	Inc. above	60.00	85.00	150	275	1,000	3,000	—
1927	5,285,627	0.25	0.65	1.75	6.50	45.00	110	—
1928	4,577,712	0.25	0.65	1.75	6.50	40.00	90.00	—
1929	5,611,911	0.25	0.65	1.75	6.50	45.00	130	—
1930	3,704,673	0.25	0.65	1.75	6.50	70.00	150	—
1931	5,100,830	0.25	0.65	2.00	10.25	75.00	325	—
1932	3,198,566	0.25	0.65	2.25	10.50	75.00	200	—
1933	2,597,867	0.40	1.00	4.00	13.00	150	500	—
1934	3,827,304	0.25	0.65	3.00	10.75	80.00	275	—
1935	3,900,000	0.25	0.65	1.75	6.50	70.00	180	—
1936	4,400,450	0.25	0.65	1.75	6.50	40.00	85.00	—

KM# 33   Composition: Nickel

Date	Mintage	VG-8	F-12	VF-20	XF-40	MS-60	MS-63	Proof
1937 dot	4,593,263	0.20	0.30	1.25	2.50	9.00	22.00	—
1938	3,898,974	0.20	1.00	2.00	7.00	50.00	100.00	—
1939	5,661,123	0.20	0.30	1.25	3.00	30.00	55.00	—
1940	13,920,197	0.15	0.20	0.75	2.25	12.00	35.00	—
1941	8,681,785	0.10	0.20	0.75	2.25	15.00	42.00	—
1942 round	6,847,544	0.20	0.25	0.75	1.75	12.00	35.00	—

KM# 39 Composition: Tombac

Date	Mintage	VG-8	F-12	VF-20	XF-40	MS-60	MS-63	Proof
1942 - 12 sided	3,396,234	0.40	0.65	1.25	1.75	3.00	9.00	—

Dot   Maple Leaf

KM# 39a Composition: Nickel

Date	Mintage	VG-8	F-12	VF-20	XF-40	MS-60	MS-63	Proof
1946	6,952,684	0.15	0.25	0.50	2.00	8.00	18.00	—
1947	7,603,724	0.15	0.25	0.50	1.25	6.50	12.50	—
1947 dot	Inc. above	12.00	15.00	22.00	50.00	150	250	—
1947 maple leaf	9,595,124	0.15	0.25	0.50	1.25	6.00	12.00	—

KM# 42 Obverse: Modified legend Composition: Nickel

Date	Mintage	VG-8	F-12	VF-20	XF-40	MS-60	MS-63	Proof
1948	1,810,789	0.40	0.50	1.00	3.00	12.00	20.00	—
1949	13,037,090	0.15	0.20	0.35	0.75	4.00	7.00	—
1950	11,970,521	0.15	0.20	0.35	0.75	4.00	7.00	—

KM# 42a Composition: Chromium And Nickel-Plated Steel

Date	Mintage	VG-8	F-12	VF-20	XF-40	MS-60	MS-63	Proof
1951 Low relief	4,313,410	0.15	0.25	0.50	0.85	2.50	4.50	—
Note: "A" in GRATIA points between denticles								
1951 High relief	Inc. above	400	525	700	950	1,400	1,850	—
Note: "A" in GRATIA points to a denticle								
1952	10,891,148	0.15	0.25	0.50	0.85	3.00	5.00	—

KM# 50 Obv. Designer: Gillick Obverse: Elizabeth II effigy Composition: Chromium And Nickel-Plated Steel Shape: 12-sided

Date	Mintage	VG-8	F-12	VF-20	XF-40	MS-60	MS-63	Proof
1953 without strap	16,635,552	0.15	0.25	0.40	1.00	3.00	4.50	—
1953 without strap, near leaf	Inc. above	75.00	125	200	350	800	1,500	—
1953 with strap, far leaf	Inc. above	75.00	100.00	150	250	600	1,500	—
1953 with strap	Inc. above	0.15	0.25	0.45	1.00	3.50	7.00	—
1954	6,998,662	0.15	0.25	0.50	1.00	4.00	8.00	—

KM# 50a Composition: Nickel

Date	Mintage	VG-8	F-12	VF-20	XF-40	MS-60	MS-63	Proof
1955	5,355,028	0.15	0.25	0.40	0.75	2.50	4.50	—
1956	9,399,854	—	0.20	0.30	0.45	1.50	3.00	—
1957	7,387,703	—	—	0.25	0.30	1.25	3.00	—
1958	7,607,521	—	—	0.25	0.30	1.25	3.00	—
1959	11,552,523	—	—	—	0.20	0.40	1.00	—
1960	37,157,433	—	—	—	0.15	0.35	0.70	—
1961	47,889,051	—	—	—	—	0.20	0.40	—
1962	46,307,305	—	—	—	—	0.20	0.40	—

KM# 57   Composition: Nickel **Shape:** Round

Date	Mintage	VG-8	F-12	VF-20	XF-40	MS-60	MS-63	Proof
1963	43,970,320	—	—	—	—	0.20	0.35	—
1964	78,075,068	—	—	—	—	0.20	0.35	—
1964 extra water line	—	8.00	10.00	12.00	15.00	25.00	40.00	—

KM# 60.1   Obv. Designer: Machin **Obverse:** Elizabeth II effigy **Composition:** Nickel

Date	Mintage	VG-8	F-12	VF-20	XF-40	MS-60	MS-63	Proof
1965	84,876,018	—	—	—	—	0.20	0.30	—
1966	27,976,648	—	—	—	—	0.20	0.30	—
1968	101,930,379	—	—	—	—	0.20	0.30	—
1969	27,830,229	—	—	—	—	0.20	0.30	—
1970	5,726,010	—	—	—	0.20	0.35	0.75	—
1971	27,312,609	—	—	—	—	0.20	0.30	—
1972	62,417,387	—	—	—	—	0.20	0.30	—
1973	53,507,435	—	—	—	—	0.20	0.30	—
1974	94,704,645	—	—	—	—	0.20	0.30	—
1975	138,882,000	—	—	—	—	0.20	0.30	—
1976	55,140,213	—	—	—	—	0.20	0.30	—
1977	89,120,791	—	—	—	—	0.20	0.30	—
1978	137,079,273	—	—	—	—	0.20	0.30	—

KM# 60.2   Obverse: Smaller bust **Composition:** Nickel

Date	Mintage	VG-8	F-12	VF-20	XF-40	MS-60	MS-63	Proof
1979	186,295,825	—	—	—	—	0.20	0.30	—
1980	134,878,000	—	—	—	—	0.20	0.30	—
1981	99,107,900	—	—	—	—	0.20	0.30	—
1981 Proof	199,000	—	—	—	—	—	—	1.50
1982	—	—	—	—	—	—	—	—
1982 Proof	—	—	—	—	—	—	—	—

KM# 60.2a   Composition: Copper-Nickel

Date	Mintage	VG-8	F-12	VF-20	XF-40	MS-60	MS-63	Proof
1982	64,924,400	—	—	—	—	0.20	0.30	—
1982 Proof	180,908	—	—	—	—	—	—	1.50
1983	72,596,000	—	—	—	—	0.20	0.30	—
1983 Proof	168,000	—	—	—	—	—	—	1.50
1984	84,088,000	—	—	—	—	0.20	0.30	—
1984 Proof	161,602	—	—	—	—	—	—	1.50
1985	126,618,000	—	—	—	—	0.20	0.30	—
1985 Proof	157,037	—	—	—	—	—	—	1.50
1986	156,104,000	—	—	—	—	0.20	0.30	—
1986 Proof	175,745	—	—	—	—	—	—	1.50
1987	106,299,000	—	—	—	—	0.10	0.20	—
1987 Proof	179,004	—	—	—	—	—	—	1.50
1988	75,025,000	—	—	—	—	0.10	0.20	—
1988 Proof	175,259	—	—	—	—	—	—	1.50
1989	141,570,538	—	—	—	—	0.10	0.20	—
1989 Proof	170,928	—	—	—	—	—	—	1.50

KM# 182   Obv. Designer: dePedery-Hunt **Obverse:** Elizabeth II effigy **Composition:** Copper-Nickel

Date	Mintage	VG-8	F-12	VF-20	XF-40	MS-60	MS-63	Proof
1990	42,537,000	—	—	—	—	0.10	0.20	—
1990 Proof	140,649	—	—	—	—	—	—	2.50
1991	10,931,000	—	—	—	—	0.20	0.55	—
1991 Proof	131,888	—	—	—	—	—	—	7.00

Date	Mintage	VG-8	F-12	VF-20	XF-40	MS-60	MS-63	Proof
1993	86,877,000	—	—	—	—	0.10	0.20	—
1993 Proof	143,065	—	—	—	—	—	—	2.50
1994	99,352,000	—	—	—	—	0.10	0.20	—
1994 Proof	146,424	—	—	—	—	—	—	3.00
1995	78,528,000	—	—	—	—	0.10	0.20	—
1995 Proof	50,000	—	—	—	—	—	—	2.50
1996 far 6	36,686,000	—	—	—	—	0.75	1.50	—
1996 near 6	Inc. above	—	—	—	—	0.10	0.20	—
1996 Proof	—	—	—	—	—	—	—	6.00
1997 Proof	—	—	—	—	—	—	—	5.00
1997	27,354,000	—	—	—	—	0.10	0.20	—
1998	156,873,000	—	—	—	—	0.10	0.20	—
1998 Proof	—	—	—	—	—	—	—	5.00
1998W	—	—	—	—	—	—	1.50	—
1999	124,861,000	—	—	—	—	0.10	0.20	—
1999 Proof	—	—	—	—	—	—	—	5.00
1999W	—	—	—	—	—	—	—	—
2000 Proof	—	—	—	—	—	—	—	5.00
2000	108,514,000	—	—	—	—	0.10	0.20	—
2000W	—	—	—	—	—	—	1.50	—
2001 Proof	—	—	—	—	—	—	—	5.00
2001	20,036,000	—	—	—	—	0.10	0.20	—
2002	—	—	—	—	—	0.10	—	—
2003	—	—	—	—	—	0.10	0.20	—

KM# 182b Obverse: Queen's head right. **Reverse:** Beaver. **Edge:** Reeded. **Weight:** 3.9000 g. **Composition:** Nickel Plated Steel **Size:** 21.2 mm.

Date	Mintage	VG-8	F-12	VF-20	XF-40	MS-60	MS-63	Proof
1999 P	Est. 20,000	—	—	—	—	—	15.00	—
2000 P	Est. 2,300,000	—	—	—	—	1.50	2.25	—
2001 P	136,650	—	—	—	—	0.20	0.35	—
2002 P	—	—	—	—	—	—	0.10	—

KM# 182a Weight: 5.3500 g. **Composition:** 0.9250 Silver 0.1591 oz. ASW

Date	Mintage	VG-8	F-12	VF-20	XF-40	MS-60	MS-63	Proof
1999	—	—	—	—	—	—	—	5.00
2000	—	—	—	—	—	—	—	5.00
2001	—	—	—	—	—	—	—	5.00
2002 Proof	—	—	—	—	—	—	—	5.00
2003 Proof	—	—	—	—	—	—	—	5.00

KM# 446 Subject: Elizabeth II Golden Jubilee **Composition:** Copper-Nickel **Note:** Double-dated 1952-2002.

Date	Mintage	VG-8	F-12	VF-20	XF-40	MS-60	MS-63	Proof
ND(2002)	—	—	—	—	—	—	0.75	—

KM# 445a Subject: Elizabeth II Golden Jubilee **Composition:** 0.9250 Silver **Note:** Double-dated 1952-2002.

Date	Mintage	VG-8	F-12	VF-20	XF-40	MS-60	MS-63	Proof
ND(2002) In sets only	100,000	—	—	—	—	—	—	2.50

KM# 491 Obverse: New effigy by Susanna Blunt **Composition:** Copper-Nickel

Date	Mintage	VG-8	F-12	VF-20	XF-40	MS-60	MS-63	Proof
2003W	—	—	—	—	—	—	—	1.50

10 CENTS

KM# 3 Obverse: Victoria bust left **Weight:** 2.3240 g. **Composition:** 0.9250 Silver 0.0691 oz. ASW

Date	Mintage	VG-8	F-12	VF-20	XF-40	MS-60	MS-63	Proof
1858/5	400	600	900	1,450	3,250	—	—	
1858	1,250,000	15.00	25.00	45.00	80.00	275	850	—
1870 narrow 0	1,600,000	13.00	27.50	60.00	100.00	300	900	—
1870 wide 0	Inc. above	20.00	40.00	80.00	150	375	1,000	—
1871	800,000	20.00	35.00	80.00	160	400	1,550	—
1871H	1,870,000	20.00	35.00	85.00	175	450	1,000	—
1872H	1,000,000	80.00	125	250	425	1,400	2,850	—
1874H	600,000	10.00	20.00	40.00	80.00	275	750	—
1875H	1,000,000	175	325	575	1,150	4,050	7,500	—

Date	Mintage	VG-8	F-12	VF-20	XF-40	MS-60	MS-63	Proof
1880H	1,500,000	10.00	20.00	35.00	60.00	250	700	—
1881H	950,000	12.00	25.00	45.00	90.00	325	750	—
1882H	1,000,000	12.00	25.00	45.00	90.00	385	1,100	—
1883H	300,000	30.00	65.00	150	250	600	1,500	—
1884	150,000	140	300	575	1,300	5,150	10,000	—
1885	400,000	25.00	50.00	125	300	1,500	3,250	—
1886 small 6	800,000	15.00	30.00	75.00	150	600	1,550	—
1886 large 6	Inc. above	25.00	35.00	75.00	150	575	1,350	—
1887	350,000	25.00	55.00	125	300	900	2,750	—
1888	500,000	6.75	18.00	40.00	75.00	275	800	—
1889	600,000	400	725	1,450	2,900	8,750	14,000	—
1890H	450,000	11.50	25.00	50.00	125	325	750	—
1891 21 leaves	800,000	12.00	25.00	60.00	125	450	950	—
1891 22 leaves	Inc. above	12.00	25.00	65.00	125	375	825	—
1892/1	520,000	110	175	325	525	1,750	2,550	—
1892	Inc. above	12.00	25.00	40.00	90.00	350	800	—
1893 flat top 3	500,000	18.00	45.00	80.00	150	475	1,450	—
1893 round top 3	Inc. above	450	900	1,700	2,900	6,950	13,000	—
1894	500,000	20.00	30.00	70.00	130	350	1,000	—
1896	650,000	8.00	15.00	30.00	65.00	250	550	—
1898	720,000	8.00	20.00	35.00	65.00	275	600	—
1899 small 9's	1,200,000	6.75	12.00	30.00	65.00	210	575	—
1899 large 9's	Inc. above	12.00	20.00	40.00	100.00	325	850	—
1900	1,100,000	6.75	10.50	25.00	60.00	150	390	—
1901	1,200,000	6.75	10.50	25.00	60.00	150	390	—

KM# 10 Obverse: Edward VII bust right **Weight:** 2.3240 g. **Composition:** 0.9250 Silver 0.0691 oz. ASW

Date	Mintage	VG-8	F-12	VF-20	XF-40	MS-60	MS-63	Proof
1902	720,000	3.50	9.00	20.00	50.00	250	650	—
1902H	1,100,000	2.75	5.00	12.50	28.00	75.00	200	—
1903	500,000	8.00	20.00	50.00	150	800	1,900	—
1903H	1,320,000	4.50	7.00	20.00	42.00	200	450	—
1904	1,000,000	4.50	9.00	30.00	65.00	250	450	—
1905	1,000,000	4.00	10.00	30.00	80.00	350	800	—
1906	1,700,000	2.75	7.50	15.00	40.00	200	400	—
1907	2,620,000	2.75	7.50	15.00	30.00	180	350	—
1908	776,666	5.00	10.00	27.00	65.00	180	250	—
1909 Victorian leaves, similar to 1902-1908 coinage	1,697,200	3.50	9.00	25.00	60.00	285	800	—
1909 broad leaves, similar to 1910-1912 coinage	Inc. above	6.00	12.00	30.00	70.00	375	1,000	—
1910	4,468,331	2.75	5.00	12.50	28.00	100.00	250	—

KM# 17 Weight: 2.3240 g. **Composition:** 0.9250 Silver 0.0691 oz. ASW

Date	Mintage	VG-8	F-12	VF-20	XF-40	MS-60	MS-63	Proof
1911	2,737,584	3.00	7.00	12.00	30.00	80.00	180	—

Small Leaves

Broad Leaves

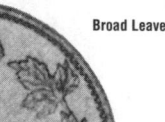

KM# 23 Weight: 2.3240 g. **Composition:** 0.9250 Silver 0.0691 oz. ASW

Date	Mintage	VG-8	F-12	VF-20	XF-40	MS-60	MS-63	Proof
1912	3,235,557	1.75	2.50	6.00	22.00	150	400	—
1913 sm. leaves	3,613,937	1.50	2.25	5.00	17.50	80.00	250	—
1913 lg. leaves	Inc. above	70.00	125	250	650	4,000	10,000	—
1914	2,549,811	1.50	2.50	5.50	18.50	80.00	350	—
1915	688,057	4.00	10.00	22.00	70.00	225	550	—
1916	4,218,114	1.25	1.50	4.00	11.00	60.00	200	—
1917	5,011,988	1.00	1.50	3.00	8.75	40.00	70.00	—
1918	5,133,602	1.00	1.50	3.00	6.00	35.00	65.00	—
1919	7,877,722	1.00	1.50	3.00	6.00	35.00	65.00	—

KM# 23a   Weight: 2.3328 g. Composition: 0.8000 Silver 0.0600 oz. ASW

Date	Mintage	VG-8	F-12	VF-20	XF-40	MS-60	MS-63	Proof
1920	6,305,345	1.00	1.50	3.00	8.00	40.00	75.00	—
1921	2,469,562	1.25	2.00	4.00	12.50	50.00	150	—
1928	2,458,602	1.00	1.75	4.00	8.00	40.00	100.00	—
1929	3,253,888	1.00	2.25	3.50	8.00	40.00	90.00	—
1930	1,831,043	1.00	2.50	4.50	9.00	40.00	90.00	—
1931	2,067,421	1.00	1.75	4.00	8.00	40.00	90.00	—
1932	1,154,317	1.50	2.50	6.00	15.00	60.00	120	—
1933	672,368	2.00	3.00	8.00	25.00	100.00	275	—
1934	409,067	3.00	6.00	16.00	40.00	200	400	—
1935	384,056	3.50	6.00	15.00	40.00	200	400	—
1936	2,460,871	0.60	1.25	3.00	6.00	30.00	65.00	—
1936 dot on rev. Specimen, 4 known	—	—	—	—	—	—	—	—

Note: At the David Akers sale of the John Jay Pittman collection, Part 1, 10-97, a gem specimen realized $120,000.

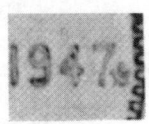

Maple Leaf

KM# 34   Weight: 2.3328 g. Composition: 0.8000 Silver 0.0600 oz. ASW

Date	Mintage	VG-8	F-12	VF-20	XF-40	MS-60	MS-63	Proof
1937	2,500,095	0.50	1.00	2.25	3.75	8.00	12.00	—
1938	4,197,323	1.00	2.00	3.25	6.50	40.00	55.00	—
1939	5,501,748	0.70	1.50	2.50	5.00	30.00	40.00	—
1940	16,526,470	BV	0.50	1.50	3.00	10.00	20.00	—
1941	8,716,386	BV	1.50	2.50	6.00	25.00	60.00	—
1942	10,214,011	BV	0.50	1.25	4.00	20.00	30.00	—
1943	21,143,229	BV	0.50	1.25	4.00	11.00	20.00	—
1944	9,383,582	BV	0.50	1.50	4.50	15.00	25.00	—
1945	10,979,570	BV	0.50	1.25	4.00	11.00	15.00	—
1946	6,300,066	BV	1.00	2.00	4.50	20.00	30.00	—
1947	4,431,926	BV	1.25	2.50	6.00	20.00	30.00	—
1947 maple leaf	9,638,793	BV	0.50	1.50	3.00	7.00	10.00	—

KM# 43   Obverse: Modified legend Weight: 2.3328 g. Composition: 0.8000 Silver 0.0600 oz. ASW

Date	Mintage	VG-8	F-12	VF-20	XF-40	MS-60	MS-63	Proof
1948	422,741	2.00	3.50	7.50	13.00	30.00	45.00	—
1949	11,336,172	—	BV	0.85	2.00	6.00	10.00	—
1950	17,823,075	—	BV	0.65	1.50	5.00	7.00	—
1951	15,079,265	—	BV	0.50	1.50	4.00	7.00	—
1951 Doubled die	—	—	1.50	2.50	7.00	22.00	—	—
1952	10,474,455	—	BV	0.50	1.50	3.00	5.00	—

KM# 51   Obv. Designer: Gllick Obverse: Elizabeth II effigy Weight: 2.3328 g. Composition: 0.8000 Silver 0.0600 oz. ASW

Date	Mintage	VG-8	F-12	VF-20	XF-40	MS-60	MS-63	Proof
1953 without straps	17,706,395	—	—	BV	1.25	2.00	4.00	—
1953 with straps	Inc. above	—	—	BV	1.25	3.00	5.00	—
1954	4,493,150	—	BV	1.00	2.25	5.00	8.00	—
1955	12,237,294	—	—	BV	0.75	2.00	4.00	—
1956	16,732,844	—	—	BV	0.75	2.00	3.50	—
1956 dot below date	Inc. above	—	1.50	2.00	3.00	8.00	15.00	—

Date	Mintage	VG-8	F-12	VF-20	XF-40	MS-60	MS-63	Proof
1957	16,110,229	—	—	—	0.70	1.00	1.50	—
1958	10,621,236	—	—	—	0.70	1.00	1.50	—
1959	19,691,433	—	—	—	0.70	0.75	1.25	—
1960	45,446,835	—	—	—	BV	0.50	1.00	—
1961	26,850,859	—	—	—	BV	0.50	1.00	—
1962	41,864,335	—	—	—	BV	0.50	1.00	—
1963	41,916,208	—	—	—	BV	0.50	1.00	—
1964	49,518,549	—	—	—	BV	0.50	1.00	—

KM# 61 Obv. Designer: Machin **Obverse:** Elizabeth II effigy **Weight:** 2.3328 g. **Composition:** 0.8000 Silver 0.0600 oz. ASW

Date	Mintage	VG-8	F-12	VF-20	XF-40	MS-60	MS-63	Proof
1965	56,965,392	—	—	—	BV	0.50	0.75	—
1966	34,567,898	—	—	—	BV	0.50	0.75	—

OTTAWA

KM# 72 Weight: 2.3328 g. **Composition:** 0.8000 Silver 0.0600 oz. ASW

Date	Mintage	VG-8	F-12	VF-20	XF-40	MS-60	MS-63	Proof
1968 Ottawa reeding	70,460,000	—	—	—	BV	0.50	0.75	—

KM# 72a Composition: Nickel

Date	Mintage	VG-8	F-12	VF-20	XF-40	MS-60	MS-63	Proof
1968 Ottawa reeding	87,412,930	—	—	—	0.15	0.25	0.35	—

Philadelphia
Reeding

KM# 73 Composition: Nickel

Date	Mintage	VG-8	F-12	VF-20	XF-40	MS-60	MS-63	Proof
1968 Philadelphia reeding	85,170,000	—	—	—	0.15	0.25	0.35	—
1969 lg. date, lg. ship, 10-20 known	—	—	4,750	6,600	10,000	14,150	—	—

KM# 77.1 Reverse: Redesigned smaller ship **Composition:** Nickel

Date	Mintage	VG-8	F-12	VF-20	XF-40	MS-60	MS-63	Proof
1969	55,833,929	—	—	—	0.15	0.25	0.35	—
1970	5,249,296	—	—	—	0.25	0.45	0.95	—
1971	41,016,968	—	—	—	0.15	0.25	0.35	—
1972	60,169,387	—	—	—	0.15	0.25	0.35	—
1973	167,715,435	—	—	—	0.15	0.25	0.35	—
1974	201,566,565	—	—	—	0.15	0.25	0.35	—
1975	207,680,000	—	—	—	0.15	0.25	0.35	—
1976	95,018,533	—	—	—	0.15	0.25	0.35	—
1977	128,452,206	—	—	—	0.15	0.25	0.35	—
1978	170,366,431	—	—	—	0.15	0.25	0.35	—

KM# 77.2 Obverse: Smaller bust **Composition:** Nickel

Date	Mintage	VG-8	F-12	VF-20	XF-40	MS-60	MS-63	Proof
1979	237,321,321	—	—	—	0.15	0.25	0.35	—
1980	170,111,533	—	—	—	0.15	0.25	0.35	—
1981	123,912,900	—	—	—	0.15	0.25	0.35	—
1981 Proof	199,000	—	—	—	—	—	—	1.50
1982	93,475,000	—	—	—	0.15	0.25	0.35	—
1982 Proof	180,908	—	—	—	—	—	—	1.50
1983	111,065,000	—	—	—	0.15	0.25	0.35	—
1983 Proof	168,000	—	—	—	—	—	—	1.50
1984	121,690,000	—	—	—	0.15	0.25	0.35	—
1984 Proof	161,602	—	—	—	—	—	—	1.50
1985	143,025,000	—	—	—	0.15	0.25	0.35	—
1985 Proof	157,037	—	—	—	—	—	—	1.50
1986	168,620,000	—	—	—	0.15	0.25	0.35	—
1986 Proof	175,745	—	—	—	—	—	—	1.50
1987	147,309,000	—	—	—	0.15	0.25	0.35	—
1987 Proof	179,004	—	—	—	—	—	—	1.50
1988	162,998,558	—	—	—	0.15	0.25	0.35	—
1988 Proof	175,259	—	—	—	—	—	—	1.50
1989	199,104,414	—	—	—	0.15	0.25	0.35	—
1989 Proof	170,528	—	—	—	—	—	—	1.50

KM# 183   Obv. Designer: dePedery-Hunt **Obverse:** Elizabeth II effigy **Composition:** Nickel

Date	Mintage	VG-8	F-12	VF-20	XF-40	MS-60	MS-63	Proof
1990	65,023,000	—	—	—	0.15	0.25	0.35	—
1990 Proof	140,649	—	—	—	—	—	—	2.50
1991	50,397,000	—	—	—	0.15	0.25	0.35	—
1991 Proof	131,888	—	—	—	—	—	—	4.00
1993	135,569,000	—	—	—	0.15	0.25	0.35	—
1993 Proof	143,065	—	—	—	—	—	—	2.00
1994	145,800,000	—	—	—	0.15	0.25	0.35	—
1994 Proof	146,424	—	—	—	—	—	—	2.50
1995	123,875,000	—	—	—	0.15	0.25	0.35	—
1995 Proof	50,000	—	—	—	—	—	—	2.50
1996 Proof	—	—	—	—	—	—	—	—
1996	51,814,000	—	—	—	—	—	—	—
1997	203,514,000	—	—	—	—	—	—	—
1997 Proof	—	—	—	—	—	—	—	—
1998 Proof	—	—	—	—	—	—	—	—
1998	203,514,000	—	—	—	0.15	0.25	0.35	—
1998W	—	—	—	—	—	—	1.50	—
1999	258,462,000	—	—	—	0.15	0.25	0.35	—
1999 Proof	—	—	—	—	—	—	—	—
2000 Proof	—	—	—	—	—	—	—	—
2000	159,125,000	—	—	—	0.15	0.25	0.35	—
2000W	—	—	—	—	—	—	1.50	—
2002	—	—	—	—	—	—	0.25	—
2003	—	—	—	—	—	—	0.25	—

KM# 183a   Weight: 2.4000 g. **Composition:** 0.9250 Silver 0.0713 oz. ASW

Date	Mintage	VG-8	F-12	VF-20	XF-40	MS-60	MS-63	Proof
1998 Proof	—	—	—	—	—	—	—	4.00
1998O Proof	—	—	—	—	—	—	—	4.00
1999 Proof	—	—	—	—	—	—	—	5.00
2000 Proof	—	—	—	—	—	—	—	5.00
2001 Proof	—	—	—	—	—	—	—	5.00
2002 Proof	—	—	—	—	—	—	—	5.00
2003 Proof	—	—	—	—	—	—	—	5.00

KM# 183b   Obverse: Queen's head right **Reverse:** Sailboat **Edge:** Reeded **Composition:** Nickel Plated Steel **Size:** 18 mm.

Date	Mintage	VG-8	F-12	VF-20	XF-40	MS-60	MS-63	Proof
1999 P	Est. 20,000	—	—	—	—	—	15.00	—
2000 P	Est. 200	—	—	—	—	400	600	—
2001 P	266,000	—	—	—	—	0.30	0.65	—
2002 P	—	—	—	—	—	—	0.20	—

KM# 447   Subject: Elizabeth II Golden Jubilee **Composition:** Nickel Plated Steel **Note:** Double-dated 1952-2002.

Date	Mintage	VG-8	F-12	VF-20	XF-40	MS-60	MS-63	Proof
ND(2002)	—	—	—	—	—	—	1.00	—

KM# 492   Obverse: New effigy by Susanna Blunt **Composition:** Nickel

Date	Mintage	VG-8	F-12	VF-20	XF-40	MS-60	MS-63	Proof
2003W	—	—	—	—	—	—	1.50	—

20 CENTS

KM# 4   Weight: 4.6480 g. **Composition:** 0.9250 Silver 0.1382 oz. ASW

Date	Mintage	VG-8	F-12	VF-20	XF-40	MS-60	MS-63	Proof
1858	750,000	40.00	60.00	90.00	170	725	1,950	—

25 CENTS

KM# 5   Weight: 5.8100 g. **Composition:** 0.9250 Silver 0.1728 oz. ASW

Date	Mintage	VG-8	F-12	VF-20	XF-40	MS-60	MS-63	Proof
1870	900,000	11.00	25.00	55.00	110	450	1,250	—
1871	400,000	14.00	30.00	75.00	180	600	1,800	—
1871H	748,000	16.00	30.00	85.00	175	500	1,500	—
1872H	2,240,000	7.00	15.00	35.00	75.00	365	1,000	—
1874H	1,600,000	7.00	12.00	35.00	80.00	300	800	—
1875H	1,000,000	225	450	1,200	2,250	8,750	14,750	—
1880H narrow 0	400,000	30.00	60.00	165	345	800	2,250	—
1880H wide 0	Inc. above	75.00	165	325	750	2,150	4,250	—
1880H wide/narrow 0	Inc. above	90.00	165	350	650	—	—	—
1881H	820,000	15.00	35.00	65.00	175	800	1,600	—
1882H	600,000	15.00	35.00	65.00	175	800	1,700	—
1883H	960,000	12.00	25.00	50.00	120	450	1,250	—
1885	192,000	75.00	150	325	825	3,000	6,000	—
1886/3	540,000	15.00	35.00	75.00	215	850	2,200	—
1886	Inc. above	12.00	25.00	65.00	200	800	2,000	—
1887	100,000	75.00	175	350	845	3,650	7,000	—
1888	400,000	12.00	25.00	55.00	150	550	1,400	—
1889	66,324	95.00	175	350	825	3,500	6,500	—
1890H	200,000	15.00	35.00	75.00	200	950	2,250	—
1891	120,000	50.00	90.00	210	410	1,200	2,500	—
1892	510,000	9.00	16.00	45.00	130	550	1,600	—
1893	100,000	75.00	145	275	540	1,450	3,000	—
1894	220,000	15.00	28.00	70.00	180	700	1,600	—
1899	415,580	6.00	9.75	27.00	80.00	450	1,000	—
1900	1,320,000	6.00	9.75	27.00	80.00	325	975	—
1901	640,000	6.00	9.75	27.00	80.00	350	975	—

KM# 11   Weight: 5.8100 g. **Composition:** 0.9250 Silver 0.1728 oz. ASW

Date	Mintage	VG-8	F-12	VF-20	XF-40	MS-60	MS-63	Proof
1902	464,000	7.00	12.00	35.00	110	500	1,450	—
1902H	800,000	4.00	7.25	32.00	60.00	200	400	—
1903	846,150	5.00	12.00	35.00	110	400	1,450	—
1904	400,000	10.00	28.00	80.00	250	1,250	4,000	—
1905	800,000	5.50	15.00	65.00	160	1,350	4,000	—
1906 large crown	1,237,843	5.00	7.25	27.00	70.00	350	1,200	—
1906 small crown; Rare	Inc. above	—	—	—	—	—	—	—
1907	2,088,000	4.00	7.25	27.00	70.00	325	1,000	—

Date	Mintage	VG-8	F-12	VF-20	XF-40	MS-60	MS-63	Proof
1908	495,016	6.00	12.00	45.00	125	300	700	—
1909	1,335,929	5.00	9.00	40.00	150	485	1,450	—

KM# 11a　Weight: 5.8319 g. **Composition:** 0.9250 Silver 0.1734 oz. ASW

Date	Mintage	VG-8	F-12	VF-20	XF-40	MS-60	MS-63	Proof
1910	3,577,569	3.00	7.25	26.00	60.00	200	500	—

KM# 18　Weight: 5.8319 g. **Composition:** 0.9250 Silver 0.1734 oz. ASW

Date	Mintage	VG-8	F-12	VF-20	XF-40	MS-60	MS-63	Proof
1911	1,721,341	4.00	12.00	25.00	60.00	200	350	—

KM# 24　Weight: 5.8319 g. **Composition:** 0.9250 Silver 0.1734 oz. ASW

Date	Mintage	VG-8	F-12	VF-20	XF-40	MS-60	MS-63	Proof
1912	2,544,199	2.25	3.50	10.00	30.00	250	1,000	—
1913	2,213,595	2.25	3.50	10.00	30.00	200	850	—
1914	1,215,397	2.50	4.00	15.00	40.00	400	1,500	—
1915	242,382	6.00	22.00	95.00	300	1,750	5,000	—
1916	1,462,566	1.75	3.25	10.00	25.00	150	500	—
1917	3,365,644	1.75	3.00	7.00	15.00	100.00	175	—
1918	4,175,649	1.75	3.00	6.00	15.00	75.00	150	—
1919	5,852,262	1.75	3.00	6.00	15.00	75.00	150	—

Dot

KM# 24a　Weight: 5.8319 g. **Composition:** 0.8000 Silver 0.1500 oz. ASW

Date	Mintage	VG-8	F-12	VF-20	XF-40	MS-60	MS-63	Proof
1920	1,975,278	1.75	3.00	8.00	22.00	125	375	—
1921	597,337	7.00	16.00	55.00	175	825	2,250	—
1927	468,096	15.00	28.00	65.00	175	550	1,200	—
1928	2,114,178	1.75	3.00	8.00	22.00	110	275	—
1929	2,690,562	1.75	2.75	8.00	22.00	110	275	—
1930	968,748	1.75	3.50	10.00	25.00	175	450	—
1931	537,815	1.75	3.50	12.00	27.50	175	450	—
1932	537,994	2.50	4.00	13.00	30.00	175	450	—
1933	421,282	3.00	4.50	15.00	30.00	150	250	—
1934	384,350	3.50	6.00	22.00	45.00	175	450	—
1935	537,772	3.50	5.00	17.50	42.00	125	275	—
1936	972,094	1.75	3.50	8.00	15.00	70.00	150	—
1936 dot	153,322	20.00	50.00	120	225	600	1,400	—

Note: David Akers John Jay Pittman sale Part Three, 10-99, nearly Choice Unc. realized $6,900; considered a possible specimen example

Maple Leaf

KM# 35　Weight: 5.8319 g. **Composition:** 0.8000 Silver 0.1500 oz. ASW

Date	Mintage	VG-8	F-12	VF-20	XF-40	MS-60	MS-63	Proof
1937	2,690,176	1.00	1.50	2.25	3.50	10.00	25.00	—
1938	3,149,245	1.00	1.50	3.25	5.00	40.00	85.00	—
1939	3,532,495	1.00	1.50	2.25	4.50	35.00	75.00	—
1940	9,583,650	BV	1.00	1.50	2.50	10.00	20.00	—
1941	6,654,672	BV	1.00	1.50	2.50	10.00	20.00	—
1942	6,935,871	BV	1.00	1.50	2.50	10.00	20.00	—
1943	13,559,575	BV	1.00	1.50	2.50	10.00	20.00	—
1944	7,216,237	BV	1.00	1.50	2.50	15.00	25.00	—
1945	5,296,495	BV	1.00	1.50	2.00	10.00	20.00	—
1946	2,210,810	BV	1.50	3.00	5.00	30.00	45.00	—

Date	Mintage	VG-8	F-12	VF-20	XF-40	MS-60	MS-63	Proof
1947	1,524,554	BV	1.50	4.00	8.00	30.00	55.00	—
1947 dot after 7	Inc. above	25.00	30.00	50.00	85.00	175	375	—
1947 maple leaf	4,393,938	BV	1.00	2.00	3.00	10.00	20.00	—

KM# 44 Obverse: Modified legend **Weight:** 5.8319 g. **Composition:** 0.8000 Silver 0.1500 oz. ASW

Date	Mintage	VG-8	F-12	VF-20	XF-40	MS-60	MS-63	Proof
1948	2,564,424	BV	1.50	3.00	5.00	35.00	70.00	—
1949	7,988,830	—	BV	1.25	2.00	5.00	11.00	—
1950	9,673,335	—	BV	1.25	1.50	4.00	9.00	—
1951	8,290,719	—	BV	1.25	1.50	3.00	8.00	—
1952	8,859,642	—	BV	1.25	1.50	3.00	7.00	—

KM# 52 Obv. Designer: Gillick **Obverse:** Elizabeth II effigy **Weight:** 5.8319 g. **Composition:** 0.8000 Silver 0.1500 oz. ASW

Date	Mintage	VG-8	F-12	VF-20	XF-40	MS-60	MS-63	Proof
1953 without strap	10,546,769	—	BV	1.25	1.50	3.00	7.00	—
1953 with strap	Inc. above	—	BV	1.25	1.50	4.00	12.00	—
1954	2,318,891	BV	1.25	2.00	4.00	15.00	25.00	—
1955	9,552,505	—	—	BV	1.25	2.50	5.00	—
1956	11,269,353	—	—	BV	1.25	2.00	4.00	—
1957	12,770,190	—	—	BV	1.00	1.50	3.00	—
1958	9,336,910	—	—	BV	1.00	1.50	3.00	—
1959	13,503,461	—	—	—	BV	1.25	2.25	—
1960	22,835,327	—	—	—	BV	1.00	1.50	—
1961	18,164,368	—	—	—	BV	1.00	1.50	—
1962	29,559,266	—	—	—	BV	1.00	1.25	—
1963	21,180,652	—	—	—	BV	1.00	1.25	—
1964	36,479,343	—	—	—	BV	1.00	1.25	—

KM# 62 Obv. Designer: Machin **Obverse:** Elizabeth II effigy **Weight:** 5.8319 g. **Composition:** 0.8000 Silver 0.1500 oz. ASW

Date	Mintage	VG-8	F-12	VF-20	XF-40	MS-60	MS-63	Proof
1965	44,708,869	—	—	—	BV	1.00	1.25	—
1966	25,626,315	—	—	—	BV	1.00	1.25	—

KM# 62a Obv. Designer: Machin **Obverse:** Elizabeth II effigy **Weight:** 5.8319 g. **Composition:** 0.5000 Silver 0.0937 oz. ASW

Date	Mintage	VG-8	F-12	VF-20	XF-40	MS-60	MS-63	Proof
1968	71,464,000	—	—	—	BV	0.75	1.25	—

KM# 62b Obv. Designer: Machin **Obverse:** Elizabeth II effigy **Composition:** Nickel

Date	Mintage	VG-8	F-12	VF-20	XF-40	MS-60	MS-63	Proof
1968	88,686,931	—	—	—	0.30	0.50	0.75	—
1969	133,037,929	—	—	—	0.30	0.50	0.75	—
1970	10,302,010	—	—	—	0.30	1.25	2.25	—
1971	48,170,428	—	—	—	0.30	0.50	0.75	—
1972	43,743,387	—	—	—	0.30	0.50	0.75	—
1974	192,360,598	—	—	—	0.30	0.50	0.75	—
1975	141,148,000	—	—	—	0.30	0.50	0.75	—
1976	86,898,261	—	—	—	0.30	0.50	0.75	—
1977	99,634,555	—	—	—	0.30	0.50	0.75	—
1978	176,475,408	—	—	—	0.30	0.50	0.75	—

KM# 74   Obv. Designer: Machin **Obverse:** Elizabeth II effigy, smaller bust **Composition:** Nickel

Date	Mintage	VG-8	F-12	VF-20	XF-40	MS-60	MS-63	Proof
1979	131,042,905	—	—	—	0.30	0.50	0.75	—
1980	76,178,000	—	—	—	0.30	0.50	0.75	—
1981	131,580,272	—	—	—	0.30	0.50	0.75	—
1981 Proof	199,000	—	—	—	—	—	—	2.00
1982	171,926,000	—	—	—	0.30	0.50	0.75	—
1982 Proof	180,908	—	—	—	—	—	—	2.00
1983	13,162,000	—	—	—	0.30	0.75	1.50	—
1983 Proof	168,000	—	—	—	—	—	—	3.00
1984	121,668,000	—	—	—	0.30	0.50	0.75	—
1984 Proof	161,602	—	—	—	—	—	—	2.00
1985	158,734,000	—	—	—	0.30	0.50	0.75	—
1985 Proof	157,037	—	—	—	—	—	—	2.00
1986	132,220,000	—	—	—	0.30	0.50	0.75	—
1986 Proof	175,745	—	—	—	—	—	—	2.00
1987	53,408,000	—	—	—	0.30	0.65	1.25	—
1987 Proof	179,004	—	—	—	—	—	—	2.00
1988	80,368,473	—	—	—	0.30	0.50	1.00	—
1988 Proof	175,259	—	—	—	—	—	—	2.00
1989	119,796,307	—	—	—	0.30	0.50	0.75	—
1989 Proof	170,928	—	—	—	—	—	—	2.00

KM# 184   Obv. Designer: dePedery-Hunt **Obverse:** Elizabeth II effigy **Composition:** Nickel

Date	Mintage	VG-8	F-12	VF-20	XF-40	MS-60	MS-63	Proof
1990	31,258,000	—	—	—	0.30	0.50	1.00	—
1990 Proof	140,649	—	—	—	—	—	—	2.50
1991	459,000	—	—	2.00	4.00	8.00	12.00	—
1991 Proof	131,888	—	—	—	—	—	—	20.00
1993	73,758,000	—	—	—	0.30	0.50	0.75	—
1993 Proof	143,065	—	—	—	—	—	—	2.00
1994	77,670,000	—	—	—	0.30	0.50	0.75	—
1994 Proof	146,424	—	—	—	—	—	—	3.00
1995	89,210,000	—	—	—	0.30	0.50	0.75	—
1995 Proof	50,000	—	—	—	—	—	—	3.00
1996 Proof	—	—	—	—	—	—	—	6.00
1996	28,106,000	—	—	—	—	—	1.50	—
1997	—	—	—	—	—	—	1.50	—
1997 Proof	—	—	—	—	—	—	—	6.00
1998W	—	—	—	—	—	—	5.00	—
1999	—	—	—	—	—	—	1.50	—
1999 Proof	—	—	—	—	—	—	—	6.00
2000 Proof	—	—	—	—	—	—	—	6.00
2000	—	—	—	—	—	—	1.50	—
2000W	—	—	—	—	—	—	5.00	—
2001 Proof	—	—	—	—	—	—	—	6.00
2001	8,409,000	—	—	—	—	—	1.75	—
2002	—	—	—	—	—	—	0.50	—
2003	—	—	—	—	—	—	0.50	—

KM# 184a   Weight: 5.9000 g. **Composition:** 0.9250 Silver 0.1754 oz. ASW

Date	Mintage	VG-8	F-12	VF-20	XF-40	MS-60	MS-63	Proof
1996 Proof	—	—	—	—	—	—	—	6.50
1997 Proof	—	—	—	—	—	—	—	6.50
1998 Proof	—	—	—	—	—	—	—	5.50
1998O Proof	—	—	—	—	—	—	—	5.50
1999 Proof	—	—	—	—	—	—	—	5.50
2001 Proof	—	—	—	—	—	—	—	6.50
2002 Proof	—	—	—	—	—	—	—	10.00
2003 Proof	—	—	—	—	—	—	—	6.50

KM# 184b   Composition: Nickel Plated Steel **Note:** No 2000 dated coins of this type were minted.

Date	Mintage	VG-8	F-12	VF-20	XF-40	MS-60	MS-63	Proof
1999 P	Est. 20,000	—	—	—	—	—	20.00	—
2000 P 3-5 Known	—	—	—	—	—	—	2,000	—
2001 P	52,153,000	—	—	—	—	0.60	1.00	—
2002 P	—	—	—	—	—	—	0.50	—

KM# 493   Obverse: New effigy by Susanna Blunt **Composition:** Nickel

Date	Mintage	VG-8	F-12	VF-20	XF-40	MS-60	MS-63	Proof
2003W	—	—	—	—	—	—	—	3.00

50 CENTS

KM# 6   Weight: 11.6200 g. **Composition:** 0.9250 Silver .3456 oz. ASW

Date	Mintage	VG-8	F-12	VF-20	XF-40	MS-60	MS-63	Proof
1870	450,000	475	800	1,600	3,100	13,500	24,500	—
1870 LCW	Inc. above	40.00	70.00	160	375	3,250	10,000	—
1871	200,000	45.00	100.00	220	500	4,000	10,500	—
1871H	45,000	80.00	175	350	800	6,500	11,000	—
1872H	80,000	40.00	70.00	170	400	3,600	10,250	—
1872H inverted A for V in Victoria	Inc. above	95.00	200	495	1,500	6,600	11,000	—
1881H	150,000	40.00	80.00	175	450	4,000	10,500	—
1888	60,000	150	220	475	950	5,400	11,000	—
1890H	20,000	600	1,200	1,800	3,200	11,000	20,000	—
1892	151,000	45.00	90.00	300	500	6,000	10,500	—
1894	29,036	225	425	920	2,000	8,100	15,000	—
1898	100,000	45.00	100.00	225	450	4,500	10,500	—
1899	50,000	90.00	190	425	1,100	7,100	12,000	—
1900	118,000	40.00	65.00	160	365	4,000	10,500	—
1901	80,000	42.00	70.00	165	400	4,200	10,500	—

Victorian Leaves

KM# 12   Weight: 11.6200 g. **Composition:** 0.9250 Silver .3456 oz. ASW

Date	Mintage	VG-8	F-12	VF-20	XF-40	MS-60	MS-63	Proof
1902	120,000	11.00	22.50	85.00	200	1,100	3,000	—
1903H	140,000	16.00	35.00	100.00	225	1,100	3,000	—
1904	60,000	85.00	160	285	625	2,050	7,000	—
1905	40,000	100.00	200	425	1,000	4,000	10,000	—
1906	350,000	10.00	25.00	70.00	190	1,000	3,000	—
1907	300,000	8.00	25.00	70.00	200	1,000	3,500	—
1908	128,119	14.75	45.00	125	275	800	1,650	—
1909	302,118	13.00	40.00	150	350	2,000	6,000	—
1910 Victorian leaves	649,521	8.00	25.00	75.00	225	1,100	3,500	—

Edwardian Leaves

KM# 12a   Weight: 11.6638 g. **Composition:** 0.9250 Silver .3461 oz. ASW

Date	Mintage	VG-8	F-12	VF-20	XF-40	MS-60	MS-63	Proof
1910 Edwardian leaves	Inc. above	8.00	22.00	65.00	200	1,000	3,150	—

KM# 19   **Weight:** 11.6638 g. **Composition:** 0.9250 Silver .3461 oz. ASW

Date	Mintage	VG-8	F-12	VF-20	XF-40	MS-60	MS-63	Proof
1911	209,972	6.00	55.00	200	425	1,100	2,900	—

KM# 25   **Obverse:** Modified legend **Weight:** 11.6638 g. **Composition:** 0.9250 Silver .3461 oz. ASW

Date	Mintage	VG-8	F-12	VF-20	XF-40	MS-60	MS-63	Proof
1912	285,867	4.00	16.00	65.00	175	850	2,200	—
1913	265,889	4.00	16.00	85.00	200	1,100	4,000	—
1914	160,128	8.00	40.00	120	375	2,000	6,000	—
1916	459,070	3.00	9.00	35.00	95.00	550	1,800	—
1917	752,213	3.00	7.00	25.00	70.00	350	950	—
1918	754,989	3.00	6.00	20.00	60.00	300	800	—
1919	1,113,429	3.00	6.00	20.00	60.00	300	1,100	—

KM# 25a   **Weight:** 11.6638 g. **Composition:** 0.8000 Silver .3000 oz. ASW

Date	Mintage	VG-8	F-12	VF-20	XF-40	MS-60	MS-63	Proof
1920	584,691	3.00	7.00	25.00	90.00	400	950	—
1921 75 to 100 known	—	12,000	17,000	20,750	21,000	35,000	45,000	—
Note: David Akers John Jay Pittman sale, Part Three, 10-99, Gem Unc. realized $63,250								
1929	228,328	3.00	7.00	25.00	75.00	375	900	—
1931	57,581	6.00	18.00	60.00	175	725	1,700	—
1932	19,213	90.00	125	300	600	2,800	7,000	—
1934	39,539	10.00	20.00	60.00	175	500	1,150	—
1936	38,550	10.00	18.00	50.00	135	400	900	—

KM# 36   **Weight:** 11.6638 g. **Composition:** 0.8000 Silver .3000 oz. ASW

Date	Mintage	VG-8	F-12	VF-20	XF-40	MS-60	MS-63	Proof
1937	192,016	2.00	3.00	4.50	7.00	20.00	50.00	—
1938	192,018	3.00	4.00	8.00	22.00	90.00	275	—
1939	287,976	2.50	3.50	5.50	13.00	60.00	170	—

Date	Mintage	VG-8	F-12	VF-20	XF-40	MS-60	MS-63	Proof
1940	1,996,566	BV	1.75	2.50	4.00	18.00	60.00	—
1941	1,714,874	BV	1.75	2.50	4.00	18.00	60.00	—
1942	1,974,164	BV	1.75	2.50	4.00	18.00	60.00	—
1943	3,109,583	BV	1.75	2.50	4.00	18.00	60.00	—
1944	2,460,205	BV	1.75	2.50	4.00	18.00	60.00	—
1945	1,959,528	BV	1.75	2.50	4.00	18.00	60.00	—
1946	950,235	BV	2.00	3.50	7.00	40.00	110	—
1946 hoof in 6	Inc. above	10.00	20.00	35.00	100.00	900	2,000	—
1947 straight 7	424,885	BV	2.50	3.50	9.00	50.00	160	—
1947 curved 7	Inc. above	BV	2.50	3.50	9.00	50.00	160	—
1947 maple leaf, straight 7	38,433	14.00	18.00	25.00	50.00	125	230	—
1947 maple leaf, curved 7	Inc. above	900	1,150	1,400	1,900	3,000	6,000	—

KM# 45   Obverse: Modified legend **Weight:** 11.6638 g. **Composition:** 0.8000 Silver .3000 oz. ASW

Date	Mintage	VG-8	F-12	VF-20	XF-40	MS-60	MS-63	Proof
1948	37,784	35.00	42.00	50.00	75.00	110	175	—
1949	858,991	BV	2.00	3.50	7.00	25.00	100.00	—
1949 hoof over 9	Inc. above	5.00	10.00	18.00	45.00	225	550	—
1950 no lines	2,384,179	2.50	4.00	7.00	15.00	110	175	—
1950 lines in 0	Inc. above	BV	1.75	2.75	3.50	8.00	20.00	—
1951	2,421,730	BV	1.50	2.50	3.00	6.00	17.00	—
1952	2,596,465	BV	1.50	2.50	3.00	6.00	11.00	—

KM# 53   Obv. Designer: Gillick **Obverse:** Elizabeth II Effigy **Weight:** 11.6638 g. **Composition:** 0.8000 Silver .3000 oz. ASW

Date	Mintage	VG-8	F-12	VF-20	XF-40	MS-60	MS-63	Proof
1953 small date	1,630,429	—	BV	2.00	2.50	4.50	10.00	—
1953 lg. date, straps	Inc. above	—	BV	2.50	3.00	10.00	22.00	—
1953 lg. date without straps	Inc. above	BV	2.00	3.50	9.00	50.00	90.00	—
1954	506,305	BV	2.00	3.50	7.00	18.00	30.00	—
1955	753,511	—	BV	2.50	3.50	10.00	20.00	—
1956	1,379,499	—	BV	2.00	2.50	4.50	9.00	—
1957	2,171,689	—	BV	—	1.75	3.50	6.00	—
1958	2,957,266	—	BV	—	1.75	3.00	5.50	—

KM# 56   Reverse: New shield **Weight:** 11.6638 g. **Composition:** 0.8000 Silver .3000 oz. ASW

Date	Mintage	VG-8	F-12	VF-20	XF-40	MS-60	MS-63	Proof
1959 horizontal shading	3,095,535	—	—	BV	1.75	2.50	4.50	—
1960	3,488,897	—	—	—	BV	2.25	3.25	—
1961	3,584,417	—	—	—	BV	2.00	3.00	—
1962	5,208,030	—	—	—	BV	1.75	3.00	—
1963	8,348,871	—	—	—	BV	1.75	3.00	—
1964	9,377,676	—	—	—	BV	1.75	3.00	—

KM# 63 Obv. Designer: Machin **Obverse:** Elizabeth II effigy **Weight:** 11.6638 g. **Composition:** 0.8000 Silver .3000 oz. ASW

Date	Mintage	VG-8	F-12	VF-20	XF-40	MS-60	MS-63	Proof
1965	12,629,974	—	—	—	BV	1.75	3.00	—
1966	7,920,496	—	—	—	BV	1.75	3.00	—

KM# 75.1   Composition: Nickel

Date	Mintage	VG-8	F-12	VF-20	XF-40	MS-60	MS-63	Proof
1968	3,966,932	—	—	—	0.50	0.65	1.00	—
1969	7,113,929	—	—	—	0.50	0.65	1.00	—
1970	2,429,526	—	—	—	0.50	0.65	1.00	—
1971	2,166,444	—	—	—	0.50	0.65	1.00	—
1972	2,515,632	—	—	—	0.50	0.65	1.00	—
1973	2,546,096	—	—	—	0.50	0.65	1.00	—
1974	3,436,650	—	—	—	0.50	0.65	1.00	—
1975	3,710,000	—	—	—	0.50	0.65	1.00	—
1976	2,940,719	—	—	—	0.50	0.65	1.00	—

KM# 75.2   Obverse: Smaller bust **Composition:** Nickel

Date	Mintage	VG-8	F-12	VF-20	XF-40	MS-60	MS-63	Proof
1977	709,839	—	—	0.50	0.75	1.35	2.00	—

KM# 75.3   Reverse: Redesigned arms **Composition:** Nickel

Date	Mintage	VG-8	F-12	VF-20	XF-40	MS-60	MS-63	Proof
1978 square jewels	3,341,892	—	—	—	0.50	0.65	1.00	—
1978 round jewels	Inc. above	—	—	0.50	2.50	3.00	4.00	—
1979	3,425,000	—	—	—	0.50	0.65	1.00	—
1980	1,574,000	—	—	—	0.50	0.65	1.00	—
1981	2,690,272	—	—	—	0.50	0.65	1.00	—
1981 Proof	199,000	—	—	—	—	—	—	3.00
1982 small beads	2,236,674	—	—	—	20.00	40.00	60.00	—
1982 small beads; Proof	180,908	—	—	—	—	—	—	3.00
1982 large beads	Inc. above	—	—	—	0.50	0.65	1.00	—
1983	1,177,000	—	—	—	0.50	0.65	1.00	—
1983 Proof	168,000	—	—	—	—	—	—	3.00
1984	1,502,989	—	—	—	0.50	0.65	1.00	—
1984 Proof	161,602	—	—	—	—	—	—	3.00
1985	2,188,374	—	—	—	0.50	0.65	1.00	—
1985 Proof	157,037	—	—	—	—	—	—	3.00
1986	781,400	—	—	—	0.50	1.00	1.25	—
1986 Proof	175,745	—	—	—	—	—	—	3.00
1987	373,000	—	—	—	0.50	1.00	1.50	—
1987 Proof	179,004	—	—	—	—	—	—	3.50
1988	220,000	—	—	—	0.50	1.00	1.50	—
1988 Proof	175,259	—	—	—	—	—	—	3.00

Date	Mintage	VG-8	F-12	VF-20	XF-40	MS-60	MS-63	Proof
1989	266,419	—	—	—	0.50	1.00	1.50	—
1989 Proof	170,928	—	—	—	—	—	—	3.00

KM# 185 Obv. Designer: dePedery-Hunt **Obverse:** Elizabeth II effigy **Composition:** Nickel

Date	Mintage	VG-8	F-12	VF-20	XF-40	MS-60	MS-63	Proof
1990	207,000	—	—	—	0.50	1.00	1.50	—
1990 Proof	140,649	—	—	—	—	—	—	5.00
1991	490,000	—	—	—	0.50	0.85	1.00	—
1991 Proof	131,888	—	—	—	—	—	—	7.00
1993	393,000	—	—	—	0.50	0.85	1.00	—
1993 Proof	143,065	—	—	—	—	—	—	3.00
1994	987,000	—	—	—	0.50	0.75	1.00	—
1994 Proof	146,424	—	—	—	—	—	—	4.00
1995	626,000	—	—	—	0.50	0.75	1.00	—
1995 Proof	50,000	—	—	—	—	—	—	4.00
1996	458,000	—	—	—	0.50	0.65	1.00	—
1996 Proof	—	—	—	—	—	—	—	—

KM# 185a Weight: 11.6380 g. **Composition:** 0.9250 Silver .3461 oz. ASW

Date	Mintage	VG-8	F-12	VF-20	XF-40	MS-60	MS-63	Proof
1996 Proof	—	—	—	—	—	—	—	9.00

KM# 290 Reverse: Redesigned arms **Composition:** Nickel

Date	Mintage	VG-8	F-12	VF-20	XF-40	MS-60	MS-63	Proof
1997 Proof	—	—	—	—	—	—	—	—
1997	387,000	—	—	—	0.50	0.65	1.00	—
1998	308,000	—	—	—	0.50	0.65	1.00	—
1998 Proof	—	—	—	—	—	—	—	—
1998W	—	—	—	—	—	—	2.00	—
1999	496,000	—	—	—	0.50	0.65	1.00	—
1999 Proof	—	—	—	—	—	—	—	—
2000 Proof	—	—	—	—	—	—	—	—
2000	559,000	—	—	—	0.50	0.65	1.00	—
2000W	—	—	—	—	—	—	1.50	—
2003	—	—	—	—	—	—	1.00	—

KM# 290a Weight: 11.6380 g. **Composition:** 0.9250 Silver .3461 oz. ASW

Date	Mintage	VG-8	F-12	VF-20	XF-40	MS-60	MS-63	Proof
1997 Proof	—	—	—	—	—	—	—	10.00
1998 Proof	—	—	—	—	—	—	—	10.00
1999 Proof	—	—	—	—	—	—	—	10.00
2000 Proof	—	—	—	—	—	—	—	10.00
2001 Proof	—	—	—	—	—	—	—	10.00
2002 Proof	—	—	—	—	—	—	—	10.00
2003 Proof	—	—	—	—	—	—	—	10.00

KM# 290b Reverse: Redesigned arms **Composition:** Nickel Plated Steel

Date	Mintage	VG-8	F-12	VF-20	XF-40	MS-60	MS-63	Proof
1999	Est. 20,000	—	—	—	—	—	15.00	—
2000P	Est. 50	—	—	—	—	1,500	2,000	—
Note: Available only in RCM presentation coin clocks								
2001	—	—	—	—	—	1.25	2.50	—
2002	—	—	—	—	—	1.25	2.50	—
2002P	—	—	—	—	—	—	1.00	—

KM# 494 Obverse: New effigy by Susanna Blunt **Composition:** Nickel

Date	Mintage	VG-8	F-12	VF-20	XF-40	MS-60	MS-63	Proof
2003W	—	—	—	—	—	—	1.50	—

DOLLAR

KM# 31   Reverse: Voyageur **Weight:** 23.3276 g. **Composition:** 0.8000 Silver 0.6000 oz. ASW

Date	Mintage	F-12	VF-20	XF-40	AU-50	MS-60	MS-63	Proof
1936	339,600	8.50	12.50	16.50	21.50	35.00	72.00	5,000

 Blunt 7

 Pointed 7

 Maple Leaf

KM# 37   Reverse: Voyageur **Weight:** 23.3276 g. **Composition:** 0.8000 Silver 0.6000 oz. ASW

Date	Mintage	F-12	VF-20	XF-40	AU-50	MS-60	MS-63	Proof
1937	207,406	9.00	9.50	11.00	13.00	25.00	65.00	—
1937 Mirror Proof	1,295	—	—	—	—	—	—	650
1937 Matte Proof	Inc. above	—	—	—	—	—	—	250
1938	90,304	23.50	32.00	40.00	50.00	65.00	175	6,000
1945	38,391	65.00	90.00	110	125	175	450	2,000
1946	93,055	12.50	22.50	31.00	37.50	65.00	225	1,800
1947 pointed 7		55.00	70.00	85.00	110	275	900	3,500
1947 blunt 7	65,595	35.00	50.00	70.00	90.00	110	225	4,500
1947 maple leaf	21,135	100.00	130	150	160	225	450	1,800

KM# 46   Obverse: Modified left legend **Reverse:** Voyageur **Weight:** 23.3276 g. **Composition:** 0.8000 Silver 0.6000 oz. ASW

Date	Mintage	F-12	VF-20	XF-40	AU-50	MS-60	MS-63	Proof
1948	18,780	300	350	400	500	600	900	3,000
1950 with 3 water lines	261,002	5.00	7.00	9.00	12.00	15.00	28.00	800
1950 with 4 water lines, 1 known, Matte Proof	—	—	—	—	—	—	—	—
1950 arnprior with 2-1/2 water lines	Inc. above	6.50	8.50	12.50	16.00	25.00	75.00	1,500
1951 with 3 water lines	416,395	4.00	5.00	6.50	7.50	9.00	22.50	650
1951 arnprior with 1-1/2 water lines	Inc. above	15.00	30.00	45.00	60.00	100.00	250	2,000
1952 with 3 water lines	406,148	4.00	5.00	6.50	7.50	10.00	22.50	1,000
1952 short water lines, arnprior type	Inc. above	8.00	12.00	15.00	18.00	25.00	60.00	1,250
1952 without water lines	Inc. above	5.00	6.00	8.00	10.00	16.50	30.00	—

KM# 54 Obv. Designer: Gillick **Obverse:** Elizabeth II effigy **Reverse:** Voyageur **Weight:** 23.3276 g.
Composition: 0.8000 Silver 0.6000 oz. ASW **Note:** All genuine circulation strike 1955 Arnprior dollars have a die break running along the top of TI in the word GRATIA on the obverse.

Date	Mintage	F-12	VF-20	XF-40	AU-50	MS-60	MS-63	Proof
1953 without strap, wire rim	1,074,578	BV	3.90	4.50	5.00	7.00	13.00	400
1953 with strap, flat rim	Inc. above	BV	3.90	4.50	5.00	7.00	13.00	—
1954	246,606	4.00	6.00	8.00	10.00	16.50	31.50	—
1955 with 3 water lines	268,105	4.50	6.00	8.00	10.00	15.00	25.00	—
1955 arnprior with 1-1/2 water lines* and die break	Inc. above	40.00	45.00	55.00	65.00	75.00	140	—
1956	209,092	7.00	9.00	12.50	15.50	19.00	30.00	—
1957 with 3 water lines	496,389	—	BV	4.75	5.50	7.50	11.00	—
1957 with 1 water line	Inc. above	4.50	5.50	7.50	8.50	10.00	20.00	—
1959	1,443,502	—	—	—	BV	5.00	6.50	—
1960	1,420,486	—	—	—	BV	5.00	6.50	—
1961	1,262,231	—	—	—	BV	5.00	6.50	—
1962	1,884,789	—	—	—	BV	5.00	6.50	—
1963	4,179,981	—	—	—	BV	5.00	6.50	—

Small Beads

Medium Beads

Large Beads

KM# 64.1 Obv. Designer: Machin **Obverse:** Elizabeth II effigy **Reverse:** Voyageur **Weight:** 23.3276 g.
Composition: 0.8000 Silver 0.6000 oz. ASW

Date	Mintage	F-12	VF-20	XF-40	AU-50	MS-60	MS-63	Proof
1965 small beads, pointed 5	10,768,569	—	—	—	BV	4.00	6.00	—
1965 small beads, blunt 5	Inc. above	—	—	—	BV	4.00	6.00	—
1965 large beads, blunt 5	Inc. above	—	—	—	BV	4.00	6.00	—
1965 large beads, pointed 5	Inc. above	—	—	—	BV	4.75	8.00	—
1965 medium beads, pointed 5	Inc. above	BV	5.00	7.00	9.00	12.00	25.00	—
1966 large beads	9,912,178	—	—	—	BV	4.00	6.00	—
1966 small beads	485	—	—	750	1,000	1,350	1,550	—

KM# 76.1 Obverse: Large bust **Reverse:** Voyageur **Composition:** Nickel **Size:** 32 mm.

Date	Mintage	MS-63	P/L	Proof
1968	5,579,714	1.25	—	—
1968	1,408,143	—	1.75	—
1968 Small island	—	5.00	—	—
1968 No island	—	—	4.00	—
1968 Doubled die	—	—	25.00	—

Date	Mintage	MS-63	P/L	Proof
Note: Exhibits extra water lines				
1969	4,809,313	1.25	—	—
1969	594,258	—	2.00	—
1972	2,676,041	1.50	—	—
1972	405,865	—	2.50	—

KM# 64.2a Obverse: Smaller bust **Reverse:** Voyageur **Weight:** 23.3276 g. **Composition:** 0.5000 Silver 0.3750 oz. ASW **Size:** 36 mm.

Date	Mintage	MS-63	P/L	Proof
1972 Proof	341,598	—	—	5.00

Note: Specimen $5.50.

KM# 76.2 Obverse: Smaller bust **Reverse:** Voyageur **Composition:** Nickel **Size:** 32 mm.

Date	Mintage	MS-63	P/L	Proof
1975	3,256,000	1.50	—	—
1975	322,325	—	2.50	—
1976	2,498,204	1.50	—	—
1976	274,106	—	2.50	—

KM# 76.3 Reverse: Voyageur **Composition:** Nickel **Size:** 32 mm. **Note:** Only known in prooflike sets with 1976 obverse slightly modified.

Date	Mintage	MS-63	P/L	Proof
1975 mule w/1976 obv.	Inc. above	—	3.00	—

KM# 117 Reverse: Voyageur modified **Composition:** Nickel **Size:** 32 mm.

Date	Mintage	MS-63	P/L	Proof
1977	1,393,745	2.25	—	—

KM# 120.1 Reverse: Voyageur **Composition:** Nickel **Size:** 32 mm. **Note:** Modified design.

Date	Mintage	MS-63	P/L	Proof
1978	2,948,488	1.50	—	—
1979	2,954,842	1.50	—	—
1980	3,291,221	1.50	—	—
1981	2,778,900	1.50	—	—
1981 Proof	—	—	—	—
1982	1,098,500	1.50	2.50	—
1982 Proof	180,908	—	—	5.25
1983	2,267,525	1.50	4.00	—
1983 Proof	166,779	—	—	5.25
1984	1,223,486	1.50	—	—
1984 Proof	161,602	—	—	6.00
1985	3,104,092	1.50	3.50	—
1985 Proof	153,950	—	—	7.00
1986	3,089,225	2.00	4.00	—
1986 Proof	176,224	—	—	7.50
1987	287,330	3.50	5.00	—
1987 Proof	175,686	—	—	7.50

KM# 120.2 Reverse: Voyageur **Composition:** Nickel **Size:** 32 mm. **Note:** Modified design.

Date	Mintage	MS-63	P/L	Spec.
1985 mule w/New Zealand 50 cent, KM-37 obverse	—	1,200	—	—

KM# 157 Obv. Designer: Machin **Obverse:** Elizabeth II effigy **Reverse:** Loon **Composition:** Aureate-Bronze Plated Nickel

Date	Mintage	MS-63	P/L	Proof
1987	205,405,000	2.25	—	—
1987 Proof	178,120	—	—	8.00
1988	138,893,539	2.25	4.00	—
1988 Proof	175,259	—	—	6.75
1989	184,773,902	3.00	4.00	—
1989 Proof	170,928	—	—	6.75

KM# 186 Obv. Designer: dePedery-Hunt **Obverse:** Elizabeth II effigy **Reverse:** Loon **Composition:** Nickel

Date	Mintage	MS-63	P/L	Proof
1990	68,402,000	1.75	4.00	—
1990 Proof	140,649	—	—	7.00
1991	23,156,000	1.75	6.50	—
1991 Proof	—	—	—	13.00
1993	33,662,000	2.00	3.00	—
1993 Proof	—	—	—	6.00
1994	36,237,000	2.00	3.50	—
1994 Proof	—	—	—	7.00
1995	41,813,000	3.00	4.50	—
1995 Proof	—	—	—	7.00
1996	17,101,000	2.00	6.00	—
1996 Proof	—	—	—	7.50
1997	—	5.00	6.00	—
1997 Proof	—	—	—	8.00

Date	Mintage	MS-63	P/L	Proof
1998	—	3.50	6.00	—
1998 Proof	—	—	—	10.00
1998W	—	—	4.50	—
1999	—	5.00	6.00	—
1999 Proof	—	—	—	8.00
2000	—	5.00	6.00	—
2000 Proof	—	—	—	8.00
2001	—	5.00	6.00	—
2001 Proof	—	—	—	8.00
2002	—	—	12.00	—
2002 Proof	—	—	12.00	—
2003	—	7.00	—	—
2003 Proof	100,000	—	—	12.00

KM# 186a Subject: Olympic Win **Composition:** Gold Plated

Date	Mintage	MS-63	P/L	Proof
2002 Proof	—	—	—	30.00

KM# 467 Subject: Elizabeth II Golden Jubilee **Composition:** Nickel **Note:** Double-dated 1952-2002.

Date	Mintage	VG-8	F-12	VF-20	XF-40	MS-60	MS-63	Proof
ND(2002)	—	—	—	—	—	—	2.50	—
ND(2002) In proof sets only	—	—	—	—	—	—	—	8.00

KM# 462 Reverse: Family of Loons **Composition:** Aureate-Bronze Plated Nickel **Note:** Double-dated 952-2002.

Date	Mintage	VG-8	F-12	VF-20	XF-40	MS-60	MS-63	Proof
ND(2002) In Specimen Sets only	75,000	—	—	—	—	—	8.00	—

KM# 495 Obverse: New effigy by Susanna Blunt **Composition:** Nickel

Date	Mintage	VG-8	F-12	VF-20	XF-40	MS-60	MS-63	Proof
2003W	—	—	—	—	—	—	6.00	—

2 DOLLARS

KM# 270 Reverse: Polar bear **Size:** 28 mm. **Note:** The Type III design has two lines outlining the star.

Date	Mintage	MS-63	P/L	Proof
1996	375,483,000	3.25	5.00	10.00
1997	16,942,000	3.25	—	—
1998	4,926,000	3.25	—	—
1998W	—	—	4.00	—
1999	—	3.25	—	—
2000	—	3.25	—	—
2000W	—	—	—	—
2001	11,910,000	3.25	—	—
2002	—	3.25	—	—
2003	—	3.25	—	—

KM# 270a Reverse: Polar bear **Size:** 32 mm.

Date	Mintage	MS-63	P/L	Proof
1996 Proof	5,000	—	—	175

KM# 270b Reverse: Polar bear

Date	Mintage	MS-63	P/L	Proof
1996 Proof	10,000	—	—	50.00
1998 Proof	—	—	—	—

KM# 270c Reverse: Polar bear

Date	Mintage	MS-63	P/L	Proof
1996	10,000	—	—	—
1997 Proof	—	—	—	10.00
1998O Proof	—	—	—	12.00
1999 Proof	—	—	—	12.00
2000 Proof	—	—	—	12.00
2001 Proof	—	—	—	12.00

KM# 496 Obverse: New effigy by Susanna Blunt **Composition:** Bi-Metallic

Date	Mintage	MS-60	MS-63	Proof
2003W	—	—	3.50	—

KM# 270d Subject: 100th Anniversary of the Cobalt Silver Strike **Composition:** Bi-Metallic

Date	Mintage	MS-60	MS-63	Proof
2003 In proof sets only	100,000	—	—	25.00

5 DOLLARS

KM# 26   Weight: 8.3592 g. **Composition:** 0.9000 Gold 0.2419 oz. AGW

Date	Mintage	F-12	VF-20	XF-40	AU-50	MS-60	MS-63
1912	165,680	110	125	150	175	225	550
1913	98,832	110	125	150	175	225	550
1914	31,122	150	250	300	400	625	1,750

10 DOLLARS

KM# 27   Weight: 16.7185 g. **Composition:** 0.9000 Gold 0.4838 oz. AGW

Date	Mintage	F-12	VF-20	XF-40	AU-50	MS-60	MS-63
1912	74,759	225	275	325	375	500	2,000
1913	149,232	225	275	325	375	525	2,650
1914	140,068	225	275	350	400	575	2,750

SOVEREIGN

KM# 14   Reverse: Mint mark below horse's rear hooves **Weight:** 7.9881 g. **Composition:** 0.9170 Gold .2354 oz. AGW

Date	Mintage	VG-8	F-12	VF-20	XF-40	MS-60	MS-63	Proof
1908C	636	—	1,000	1,750	2,000	2,700	3,000	—
1909C	16,273	—	110	170	200	475	1,600	—
1910C	28,012	—	100.00	150	180	475	2,000	—

KM# 20   Weight: 7.9881 g. **Composition:** 0.9170 Gold 0.2354 oz. AGW

Date	Mintage	VG-8	F-12	VF-20	XF-40	MS-60	MS-63	Proof
1911C	256,946	—	—	—	BV	90.00	150	—
1913C	3,715	—	350	450	550	1,000	2,000	—
1914C	14,871	—	150	200	275	325	600	—
1916C about 20 known	—	—	8,000	12,500	11,000	16,000	25,000	—

Note: Stacks' A.G. Carter Jr. Sale 12-89 Gem BU realized $82,500.

Date	Mintage	VG-8	F-12	VF-20	XF-40	MS-60	MS-63	Proof
1917C	58,845	—	—	BV	85.00	100.00	300	—
1918C	106,514	—	—	BV	85.00	110	450	—
1919C	135,889	—	—	BV	85.00	100.00	350	—

COMMEMORATIVE COINAGE

CENT

KM# 65 Subject: Confederation Centennial **Composition:** Bronze

Date	Mintage	VG-8	F-12	VF-20	XF-40	MS-60	MS-63	Proof
ND(1967)	345,140,645	—	—	—	—	0.10	0.25	1.00

KM# 204 Subject: Confederation 125 **Composition:** Bronze

Date	Mintage	VG-8	F-12	VF-20	XF-40	MS-60	MS-63	Proof
ND(1992)	673,512,000	—	—	—	—	0.10	0.15	—
ND(1902) Proof	147,061	—	—	—	—	—	—	2.50

KM# 309 Subject: 90th Anniversary Royal Canadian Mint - 1908-1998 **Weight:** 5.6700 g. **Composition:** 0.9250 Copper-Plated Silver 0.1677 oz.

Date	Mintage	VG-8	F-12	VF-20	XF-40	MS-60	MS-63	Proof
ND(1998)	25,000	—	—	—	—	—	16.00	—
Note: Antique finish								
ND(1998) Proof	—	—	—	—	—	—	—	—

KM# 332 Subject: 90th Anniversary Royal Canadian Mint - 1908-1998 **Obverse:** With "Canada" added to bust **Weight:** 5.6700 g. **Composition:** 0.9250 Silver .1677 oz. ASW

Date	Mintage	VG-8	F-12	VF-20	XF-40	MS-60	MS-63	Proof
ND(2000) Proof	25,000	—	—	—	—	—	—	16.00
Note: Mirror finish								

KM# 468 Subject: 50th Anniversary of the Coronation of Elizabeth II **Obverse:** 1953 effigy with dual dates 1953-2003 **Composition:** Copper

Date	Mintage	VG-8	F-12	VF-20	XF-40	MS-60	MS-63	Proof
ND(2003) In Coronation Proof sets only	—	—	—	—	—	—	2.50	—

3 CENTS

KM# 410 Subject: 1st Canadian Postage Stamp **Obverse:** Queen's head right. **Reverse:** Partial stamp design. **Edge:** Plain. **Weight:** 31.1035 g. **Composition:** 0.9250 Silver .1600 oz. ASW **Size:** 21.1 mm.

Date	Mintage	MS-63	Proof
2001 Proof	90,000	—	25.00

5 CENTS

KM# 40 Subject: Victory **Composition:** Tombac

Date	Mintage	VG-8	F-12	VF-20	XF-40	MS-60	MS-63	Proof
1943	24,760,256	0.20	0.30	0.40	0.85	2.00	6.00	—
1944 1 known	8,000	—	—	—	—	—	—	—

KM# 40a Composition: Chrome Plated Steel

Date	Mintage	VG-8	F-12	VF-20	XF-40	MS-60	MS-63	Proof
1944	11,532,784	0.15	0.25	0.45	1.00	2.00	4.00	—
1945	18,893,216	0.15	0.25	0.45	1.00	2.00	4.00	—

KM# 48 Subject: Nickel Bicentennial **Composition:** Nickel

Date	Mintage	VG-8	F-12	VF-20	XF-40	MS-60	MS-63	Proof
ND(1951)	9,028,507	0.15	0.20	0.25	0.50	1.75	3.50	—

KM# 66 Subject: Confederation Centennial **Composition:** Copper Nickel

Date	Mintage	VG-8	F-12	VF-20	XF-40	MS-60	MS-63	Proof
ND(1967)	36,876,574	—	—	—	—	0.25	0.40	1.00

KM# 205 Subject: Confederation 125 **Composition:** Copper-Nickel

Date	Mintage	VG-8	F-12	VF-20	XF-40	MS-60	MS-63	Proof
ND(1992)	53,732,000	—	—	—	—	0.10	0.20	—
ND(1992) Proof	147,061	—	—	—	—	—	—	4.00

KM# 310   Subject: 90th Anniversary Royal Canadian Mint **Weight:** 1.1670 g. **Composition:** 0.9250 Silver .0347 oz. ASW

Date	Mintage	VG-8	F-12	VF-20	XF-40	MS-60	MS-63	Proof
ND(1998)	25,000	—	—	—	—	—	12.00	—
ND(1998) Proof	25,000	—	—	—	—	—	—	12.00

KM# 400   Subject: First French-Canadian Regiment **Obverse:** Queen's portrait **Reverse:** Regimental drums, sash and baton **Edge:** Plain **Composition:** 0.9250 Silver **Size:** 21.2 mm.

Date	Mintage	VG-8	F-12	VF-20	XF-40	MS-60	MS-63	Proof
2000 Proof	—	—	—	—	—	—	—	11.50

KM# 413   Subject: Royal Military College **Obverse:** Queen's head right **Reverse:** Marching cadets and arch **Edge:** Plain **Weight:** 5.3500 g. **Composition:** 0.9250 Silver .1591 oz. ASW **Size:** 21.2 mm.

Date	Mintage	VG-8	F-12	VF-20	XF-40	MS-60	MS-63	Proof
2001 Proof	—	—	—	—	—	—	—	11.50

KM# 453   Subject: Vimy Ridge - WWI **Obverse:** Queen's head right **Reverse:** Vimy Ridge Memorial, allegorical figure and dates 1917-2003 **Composition:** 0.9250 Silver

Date	Mintage	MS-63	Proof
ND Proof	Est. 40,000	—	12.50

KM# 446a   Subject: Elizabeth II Golden Jubilee **Composition:** 0.9250 Silver **Note:** Double-dated 1952-2002.

Date	Mintage	VG-8	F-12	VF-20	XF-40	MS-60	MS-63	Proof
ND(2002) In proof sets only	100,000	—	—	—	—	—	—	11.50

KM# 469   Subject: 50th Anniversary of the Coronation of Elizabeth II **Obverse:** 1953 effigy with dual dates 1953-2003 **Composition:** 0.9250 Silver

Date	Mintage	VG-8	F-12	VF-20	XF-40	MS-60	MS-63	Proof
ND(2003) In Coronation Proof sets only	30,000	—	—	—	—	—	11.50	—

10 CENTS

KM# 67   Subject: Confederation Centennial **Weight:** 2.3328 g. **Composition:** 0.8000 Silver 0.0600 oz. ASW

Date	Mintage	VG-8	F-12	VF-20	XF-40	MS-60	MS-63	Proof
ND(1967)	62,998,215	—	—	—	BV	0.50	1.00	2.00

KM# 67a   Subject: Confederation Centennial **Weight:** 2.3328 g. **Composition:** 0.5000 Silver 0.0372 oz. ASW

Date	Mintage	VG-8	F-12	VF-20	XF-40	MS-60	MS-63	Proof
ND(1967)	Inc. above	—	—	—	BV	0.50	1.00	—

KM# 206 Subject: Confederation 125 **Composition:** Nickel

Date	Mintage	VG-8	F-12	VF-20	XF-40	MS-60	MS-63	Proof
ND(1992)	174,476,000	—	—	—	—	0.25	0.35	—
ND(1992) Proof	147,061	—	—	—	—	—	—	3.00

KM# 299 Subject: John Cabot **Weight:** 2.4000 g. **Composition:** 0.9250 Silver .0714 oz. ASW

Date	Mintage	VG-8	F-12	VF-20	XF-40	MS-60	MS-63	Proof
ND(1997) Proof	49,848	—	—	—	—	—	—	17.50

KM# 311 Subject: 90th Anniversary Royal Canadian Mint **Weight:** 2.3200 g. **Composition:** 0.9250 Silver .0690 oz. ASW

Date	Mintage	VG-8	F-12	VF-20	XF-40	MS-60	MS-63	Proof
ND(1998) Matte	25,000	—	—	—	—	—	—	10.00
ND(1998) Proof	25,000	—	—	—	—	—	—	10.00

KM# 409 Subject: First Canadian Credit Union **Obverse:** Queen's head right. **Reverse:** Alphonse Desjardins' house, (founder of the first credit union in Canada). **Edge:** Reeded. **Weight:** 2.4000 g. **Composition:** 0.9250 Silver .0714 oz. ASW **Size:** 18 mm.

Date	Mintage	VG-8	F-12	VF-20	XF-40	MS-60	MS-63	Proof
ND(2000) Proof	66,336	—	—	—	—	—	—	11.00

KM# 412 Subject: Year of the Volunteer **Obverse:** Queen's head right. **Reverse:** Three portraits and radiant sun. **Edge:** Reeded. **Weight:** 1.7700 g. **Composition:** Nickel Plated Steel **Size:** 18 mm.

Date	Mintage	VG-8	F-12	VF-20	XF-40	MS-60	MS-63	Proof
2001P Proof	—	—	—	—	—	—	—	—

KM# 412a Subject: Year of the Volunteer **Obverse:** Queen's head right. **Reverse:** 3 conjoined busts above banner, radiant sun below. **Edge:** Reeded. **Weight:** 2.4000 g. **Composition:** 0.9250 Silver .0714 oz. ASW **Size:** 18 mm.

Date	Mintage	MS-63	Proof
2001P Proof	50,000	—	12.50

KM# 447a Subject: Elizabeth II Golden Jubilee **Composition:** 0.9250 Silver **Note:** Double-dated 1952-2002.

Date	Mintage	VG-8	F-12	VF-20	XF-40	MS-60	MS-63	Proof
ND(2002) In proof sets only	100,000	—	—	—	—	—	—	12.50

KM# 470 Subject: 50th Anniversary of the Coronation of Elizabeth II **Composition:** 0.9250 Silver

Date	Mintage	VG-8	F-12	VF-20	XF-40	MS-60	MS-63	Proof
ND(2003) In Coronation Proof sets only	30,000	—	—	—	—	—	12.00	—

25 CENTS

KM# 68 Subject: Confederation Centennial **Weight:** 5.8319 g. **Composition:** 0.8000 Silver 0.1500 oz. ASW

Date	Mintage	VG-8	F-12	VF-20	XF-40	MS-60	MS-63	Proof
ND(1967)	48,855,500	—	—	—	BV	1.00	1.75	—

KM# 68a Subject: Confederation Centennial **Weight:** 5.8319 g. **Composition:** 0.5000 Silver 0.0937 oz. ASW

Date	Mintage	VG-8	F-12	VF-20	XF-40	MS-60	MS-63	Proof
ND(1967)	Inc. above	—	—	—	BV	1.00	1.75	—

KM# 81.1 Subject: RCMP Centennial **Composition:** Nickel **Note:** 120 beads.

Date	Mintage	VG-8	F-12	VF-20	XF-40	MS-60	MS-63	Proof
ND(1973)	134,958,587	—	—	—	0.30	0.50	0.80	—

KM# 81.2 Subject: RCMP Centennial **Composition:** Nickel **Note:** 132 beads.

Date	Mintage	VG-8	F-12	VF-20	XF-40	MS-60	MS-63	Proof
ND(1973)	Inc. above	30.00	50.00	60.00	70.00	85.00	110	—

KM# 207 Subject: Confederation 125 **Composition:** Nickel

Date	Mintage	VG-8	F-12	VF-20	XF-40	MS-60	MS-63	Proof
ND(1992)	442,986	—	—	—	—	—	12.50	—
ND(1992) Proof	147,061	—	—	—	—	—	—	20.00

KM# 203 Subject: 125th Anniversary of Confederation, New Brunswick **Composition:** Nickel

Date	Mintage	VG-8	F-12	VF-20	XF-40	MS-60	MS-63	Proof
ND(1992)	12,174,000	—	—	—	—	0.35	0.75	—

KM# 203a Subject: 125th Anniversary of Confederation, New Brunswick **Weight:** 5.8319 g. **Composition:** 0.9250 Silver 0.1734 oz. ASW

Date	Mintage	VG-8	F-12	VF-20	XF-40	MS-60	MS-63	Proof
ND(1992) Proof	149,579	—	—	—	—	—	—	7.50

KM# 212 Subject: 125th Anniversary of Confederation, North West Territories **Composition:** Nickel

Date	Mintage	VG-8	F-12	VF-20	XF-40	MS-60	MS-63	Proof
ND(1992)	12,582,000	—	—	—	—	0.35	0.75	—

KM# 212a Subject: 125th Anniversary of Confederation, North West Territories **Weight:** 5.8319 g. **Composition:** 0.9250 Silver 0.1734 oz. ASW

Date	Mintage	VG-8	F-12	VF-20	XF-40	MS-60	MS-63	Proof
ND(1992) Proof	149,579	—	—	—	—	—	—	7.50

KM# 213   Subject: 125th Anniversary of Confederation, Newfoundland **Composition:** Nickel

Date	Mintage	VG-8	F-12	VF-20	XF-40	MS-60	MS-63	Proof
ND(1992)	11,405,000	—	—	—	—	0.35	0.75	—

KM# 213a   Subject: 125th Anniversary of Confederation, Newfoundland **Weight:** 5.8319 g. **Composition:** 0.9250 Silver 0.1734 oz. ASW

Date	Mintage	VG-8	F-12	VF-20	XF-40	MS-60	MS-63	Proof
ND(1992) Proof	149,579	—	—	—	—	—	—	7.50

KM# 214   Subject: 125th Anniversary of Confederation, Manitoba **Composition:** Nickel

Date	Mintage	VG-8	F-12	VF-20	XF-40	MS-60	MS-63	Proof
ND(1992)	11,349,000	—	—	—	—	0.35	0.75	—

KM# 214a   Subject: 125th Anniversary of Confederation, Manitoba **Weight:** 5.8319 g. **Composition:** 0.9250 Silver 0.1734 oz. ASW

Date	Mintage	VG-8	F-12	VF-20	XF-40	MS-60	MS-63	Proof
ND(1992) Proof	149,579	—	—	—	—	—	—	7.50

KM# 220   Subject: 125th Anniversary of Confederation, Yukon **Composition:** Nickel

Date	Mintage	VG-8	F-12	VF-20	XF-40	MS-60	MS-63	Proof
ND(1992)	10,388,000	—	—	—	—	0.35	0.75	—

KM# 220a   Subject: 125th Anniversary of Confederation, Yukon **Weight:** 5.8319 g. **Composition:** 0.9250 Silver 0.1734 oz. ASW

Date	Mintage	VG-8	F-12	VF-20	XF-40	MS-60	MS-63	Proof
ND(1992) Proof	149,579	—	—	—	—	—	—	7.50

KM# 221   Subject: 125th Anniversary of Confederation, Alberta **Composition:** Nickel

Date	Mintage	VG-8	F-12	VF-20	XF-40	MS-60	MS-63	Proof
ND(1992)	12,133,000	—	—	—	—	0.35	0.75	—

KM# 221a   Subject: 125th Anniversary of Confederation, Alberta **Weight:** 5.8319 g. **Composition:** 0.9250 Silver 0.1734 oz. ASW

Date	Mintage	VG-8	F-12	VF-20	XF-40	MS-60	MS-63	Proof
ND(1992) Proof	—	—	—	—	—	—	—	7.50

KM# 222   Subject: 125th Anniversary of Confederation, Prince Edward Island **Composition:** Nickel

Date	Mintage	VG-8	F-12	VF-20	XF-40	MS-60	MS-63	Proof
ND(1992)	13,001,000	—	—	—	—	0.35	0.75	—

KM# 222a   Subject: 125th Anniversary of Confederation, Prince Edward Island **Weight:** 5.8319 g. **Composition:** 0.9250 Silver 0.1734 oz. ASW

Date	Mintage	VG-8	F-12	VF-20	XF-40	MS-60	MS-63	Proof
ND(1992) Proof	149,579	—	—	—	—	—	—	7.50

KM# 223   Subject: 125th Anniversary of Confederation, Ontario **Composition:** Nickel

Date	Mintage	VG-8	F-12	VF-20	XF-40	MS-60	MS-63	Proof
ND(1992)	14,263,000	—	—	—	—	0.35	0.75	—

KM# 223a   Subject: 125th Anniversary of Confederation, Ontario **Weight:** 5.8319 g. **Composition:** 0.9250 Silver 0.1734 oz. ASW

Date	Mintage	VG-8	F-12	VF-20	XF-40	MS-60	MS-63	Proof
ND(1992) Proof	149,579	—	—	—	—	—	—	7.50

KM# 231 Subject: 125th Anniversary of Confederation, Nova Scotia **Composition:** Nickel

Date	Mintage	VG-8	F-12	VF-20	XF-40	MS-60	MS-63	Proof
ND(1992)	13,600,000	—	—	—	—	0.35	0.75	

KM# 231a Subject: 125th Anniversary of Confederation, Nova Scotia **Weight:** 5.8319 g. **Composition:** 0.9250 Silver 0.1734 oz. ASW

Date	Mintage	VG-8	F-12	VF-20	XF-40	MS-60	MS-63	Proof
ND(1992) Proof	149,579	—	—	—	—	—	—	7.50

KM# 232 Subject: 125th Anniversary of Confederation, British Columbia **Composition:** Nickel

Date	Mintage	VG-8	F-12	VF-20	XF-40	MS-60	MS-63	Proof
ND(1992)	14,001,000	—	—	—	—	0.35	0.75	—

KM# 232a Subject: 125th Anniversary of Confederation, British Columbia **Weight:** 5.8319 g. **Composition:** 0.9250 Silver 0.1734 oz. ASW

Date	Mintage	VG-8	F-12	VF-20	XF-40	MS-60	MS-63	Proof
ND(1992) Proof	149,579	—	—	—	—	—	—	7.50

KM# 233 Subject: 125th Anniversary of Confederation, Saskatchewan **Composition:** Nickel

Date	Mintage	VG-8	F-12	VF-20	XF-40	MS-60	MS-63	Proof
ND(1992)	14,165,000	—	—	—	—	0.35	0.75	—

KM# 233a Subject: 125th Anniversary of Confederation, Saskatchewan **Weight:** 5.8319 g. **Composition:** 0.9250 Silver 0.1734 oz. ASW

Date	Mintage	VG-8	F-12	VF-20	XF-40	MS-60	MS-63	Proof
ND(1992) Proof	149,579	—	—	—	—	—	—	7.50

KM# 234 Subject: 125th Anniversary of Confederation, Quebec **Composition:** Nickel

Date	Mintage	VG-8	F-12	VF-20	XF-40	MS-60	MS-63	Proof
ND(1992)	13,607,000	—	—	—	—	0.35	0.75	

KM# 234a Subject: 125th Anniversary of Confederation, Quebec **Weight:** 5.8319 g. **Composition:** 0.9250 Silver 0.1734 oz. ASW

Date	Mintage	VG-8	F-12	VF-20	XF-40	MS-60	MS-63	Proof
ND(1992) Proof	149,579	—	—	—	—	—	—	7.50

KM# 342 Subject: Millennium, January **Reverse:** Totem pole, portraits **Composition:** Nickel

Date	Mintage	VG-8	F-12	VF-20	XF-40	MS-60	MS-63	Proof
1999	—	—	—	—	—	0.50	0.70	—

KM# 342a Subject: Millennium, January **Reverse:** Totem pole, portraits **Weight:** 5.8319 g. **Composition:** 0.9250 Silver 0.1734 oz. ASW

Date	Mintage	VG-8	F-12	VF-20	XF-40	MS-60	MS-63	Proof
1999 Proof	—	—	—	—	—	—	—	8.00

KM# 343 Subject: Millennium, February **Reverse:** Native petroglyphs **Composition:** Nickel

Date	Mintage	VG-8	F-12	VF-20	XF-40	MS-60	MS-63	Proof
1999	—	—	—	—	—	0.50	0.70	—

KM# 343a Subject: Millennium, February **Reverse:** Native petroglyphs **Weight:** 5.8319 g. **Composition:** 0.9250 Silver 0.1734 oz. ASW

Date	Mintage	VG-8	F-12	VF-20	XF-40	MS-60	MS-63	Proof
1999 Proof	—	—	—	—	—	—	—	8.00

KM# 344   Subject: Millennium, March **Reverse:** Lumberjack **Composition:** Nickel

Date	Mintage	VG-8	F-12	VF-20	XF-40	MS-60	MS-63	Proof
1999	—	—	—	—	—	0.50	0.70	—

KM# 344a   Subject: Millennium, March **Reverse:** Lumberjack **Weight:** 5.8319 g. **Composition:** 0.9250 Silver 0.1734 oz. ASW

Date	Mintage	VG-8	F-12	VF-20	XF-40	MS-60	MS-63	Proof
1999 Proof	—	—	—	—	—	—	—	8.00

KM# 345   Subject: Millennium, April **Reverse:** Owl, polar bear **Composition:** Nickel

Date	Mintage	VG-8	F-12	VF-20	XF-40	MS-60	MS-63	Proof
1999	—	—	—	—	—	0.50	0.70	—

KM# 345a   Subject: Millennium, April **Reverse:** Owl, polar bear **Weight:** 5.8319 g. **Composition:** 0.9250 Silver 0.1734 oz. ASW

Date	Mintage	VG-8	F-12	VF-20	XF-40	MS-60	MS-63	Proof
1999 Proof	—	—	—	—	—	—	—	8.00

KM# 346   Subject: Millennium, May **Reverse:** Voyageurs in canoe **Composition:** Nickel

Date	Mintage	VG-8	F-12	VF-20	XF-40	MS-60	MS-63	Proof
1999	—	—	—	—	—	0.50	0.70	—

KM# 346a   Subject: Millennium, May **Reverse:** Voyageurs in canoe **Weight:** 5.8319 g. **Composition:** 0.9250 Silver 0.1734 oz. ASW

Date	Mintage	VG-8	F-12	VF-20	XF-40	MS-60	MS-63	Proof
1999 Proof	—	—	—	—	—	—	—	8.00

KM# 347   Subject: Millennium, June **Reverse:** 19th-century locomotive **Composition:** Nickel

Date	Mintage	VG-8	F-12	VF-20	XF-40	MS-60	MS-63	Proof
1999	—	—	—	—	—	0.50	0.70	—

KM# 347a   Subject: Millennium, June **Reverse:** 19th-century locomotive **Weight:** 5.8319 g. **Composition:** 0.9250 Silver 0.1734 oz. ASW

Date	Mintage	VG-8	F-12	VF-20	XF-40	MS-60	MS-63	Proof
1999 Proof	—	—	—	—	—	—	—	8.00

KM# 348   Subject: Millennium, July **Reverse:** 6 stylized portraits **Composition:** Nickel

Date	Mintage	VG-8	F-12	VF-20	XF-40	MS-60	MS-63	Proof
1999	—	—	—	—	—	0.50	0.70	—

KM# 348a   Subject: Millennium, July **Reverse:** 6 stylized portraits **Weight:** 5.8319 g. **Composition:** 0.9250 Silver 0.1734 oz. ASW

Date	Mintage	VG-8	F-12	VF-20	XF-40	MS-60	MS-63	Proof
1999 Proof	—	—	—	—	—	—	—	8.00

KM# 349   Subject: Millennium, August **Reverse:** Hay harvesting **Composition:** Nickel

Date	Mintage	VG-8	F-12	VF-20	XF-40	MS-60	MS-63	Proof
1999	—	—	—	—	—	0.50	0.70	—

KM# 349a   Subject: Millennium, August **Reverse:** Hay harvesting **Weight:** 5.8319 g. **Composition:** 0.9250 Silver 0.1734 oz. ASW

Date	Mintage	VG-8	F-12	VF-20	XF-40	MS-60	MS-63	Proof
1999 Proof	—	—	—	—	—	—	—	8.00

KM# 350   Subject: Millennium, September **Reverse:** Childlike artwork **Composition:** Nickel

Date	Mintage	VG-8	F-12	VF-20	XF-40	MS-60	MS-63	Proof
1999	—	—	—	—	—	0.50	0.70	—

KM# 350a   Subject: Millennium, September **Reverse:** Childlike artwork **Weight:** 5.8319 g. **Composition:** 0.9250 Silver 0.1734 oz. ASW

Date	Mintage	VG-8	F-12	VF-20	XF-40	MS-60	MS-63	Proof
1999 Proof	—	—	—	—	—	—	—	8.00

KM# 351   Subject: Millennium, October **Reverse:** Aboriginal artwork **Composition:** Nickel

Date	Mintage	VG-8	F-12	VF-20	XF-40	MS-60	MS-63	Proof
1999	—	—	—	—	—	0.50	0.70	—

KM# 351a   Subject: Millennium, October **Reverse:** Aboriginal artwork **Weight:** 5.8319 g. **Composition:** 0.9250 Silver 0.1734 oz. ASW

Date	Mintage	VG-8	F-12	VF-20	XF-40	MS-60	MS-63	Proof
1999 Proof	—	—	—	—	—	—	—	8.00

KM# 352   Subject: Millennium, November **Reverse:** Bush plane with landing skis **Composition:** Nickel

Date	Mintage	VG-8	F-12	VF-20	XF-40	MS-60	MS-63	Proof
1999	—	—	—	—	—	0.50	0.70	—

KM# 352a   Subject: Millennium, November **Reverse:** Bush plane with landing skis **Weight:** 5.8319 g. **Composition:** 0.9250 Silver 0.1734 oz. ASW

Date	Mintage	VG-8	F-12	VF-20	XF-40	MS-60	MS-63	Proof
1999 Proof	—	—	—	—	—	—	—	8.00

KM# 353   Subject: Millennium, December **Reverse:** Eclectic geometric design **Composition:** Nickel

Date	Mintage	VG-8	F-12	VF-20	XF-40	MS-60	MS-63	Proof

KM# 353a   Subject: Millennium, December **Reverse:** Eclectic geometric design **Weight:** 5.8319 g. **Composition:** 0.9250 Silver 0.1734 oz. ASW

Date	Mintage	VG-8	F-12	VF-20	XF-40	MS-60	MS-63	Proof
1999 Proof	—	—	—	—	—	—	—	8.00

KM# 373   Subject: Health **Reverse:** Ribbon and caduceus **Composition:** Nickel

Date	Mintage	VG-8	F-12	VF-20	XF-40	MS-60	MS-63	Proof
2000	—	—	—	—	—	0.50	0.70	—

KM# 373a   Subject: Health **Reverse:** Ribbon and caduceus **Composition:** 0.9250 Silver

Date	Mintage	VG-8	F-12	VF-20	XF-40	MS-60	MS-63	Proof

KM# 374 Subject: Freedom **Reverse:** 2 children and rising sun **Composition:** Nickel

Date	Mintage	VG-8	F-12	VF-20	XF-40	MS-60	MS-63	Proof
2000	—	—	—	—	—	0.50	0.70	—

KM# 374a Subject: Freedom **Reverse:** 2 children and rising sun **Composition:** 0.9250 Silver

Date	Mintage	VG-8	F-12	VF-20	XF-40	MS-60	MS-63	Proof
2000 Proof	—	—	—	—	—	—	—	8.00

KM# 375a Subject: Family **Reverse:** Circular native carvings **Composition:** 0.9250 Silver

Date	Mintage	VG-8	F-12	VF-20	XF-40	MS-60	MS-63	Proof
2000 Proof	—	—	—	—	—	—	—	8.00

KM# 375 Subject: Family **Reverse:** Circular native carvings **Composition:** Nickel

Date	Mintage	VG-8	F-12	VF-20	XF-40	MS-60	MS-63	Proof
2000	—	—	—	—	—	0.50	0.70	—

KM# 376 Subject: Community **Reverse:** Map on globe **Composition:** Nickel

Date	Mintage	VG-8	F-12	VF-20	XF-40	MS-60	MS-63	Proof
2000	—	—	—	—	—	0.50	0.70	—

KM# 376a Subject: Community **Reverse:** Map on globe **Composition:** 0.9250 Silver

Date	Mintage	VG-8	F-12	VF-20	XF-40	MS-60	MS-63	Proof
2000 Proof	—	—	—	—	—	—	—	8.00

KM# 377 Subject: Harmony **Reverse:** Maple leaf **Composition:** Nickel

Date	Mintage	VG-8	F-12	VF-20	XF-40	MS-60	MS-63	Proof
2000	—	—	—	—	—	0.50	0.70	—

KM# 377a Subject: Harmony **Reverse:** Maple leaf **Composition:** 0.9250 Silver

Date	Mintage	VG-8	F-12	VF-20	XF-40	MS-60	MS-63	Proof
2000 Proof	—	—	—	—	—	—	—	8.00

KM# 378 Subject: Wisdom **Reverse:** Man with young child **Composition:** Nickel

Date	Mintage	VG-8	F-12	VF-20	XF-40	MS-60	MS-63	Proof
2000	—	—	—	—	—	0.50	0.70	—

KM# 378a Subject: Wisdom **Reverse:** Man with young child **Composition:** 0.9250 Silver

Date	Mintage	VG-8	F-12	VF-20	XF-40	MS-60	MS-63	Proof
2000 Proof	—	—	—	—	—	—	—	8.00

KM# 379 Subject: Creativity **Reverse:** Canoe full of children **Composition:** Nickel

Date	Mintage	VG-8	F-12	VF-20	XF-40	MS-60	MS-63	Proof
2000	—	—	—	—	—	0.50	0.70	—

KM# 379a Subject: Creativity **Reverse:** Canoe full of children **Composition:** 0.9250 Silver

Date	Mintage	VG-8	F-12	VF-20	XF-40	MS-60	MS-63	Proof
2000 Proof	—	—	—	—	—	—	—	8.00

KM# 380 Subject: Ingenuity **Reverse:** Crescent-shaped city views **Composition:** Nickel

Date	Mintage	VG-8	F-12	VF-20	XF-40	MS-60	MS-63	Proof
2000	—	—	—	—	—	0.50	0.70	—

KM# 380a Subject: Ingenuity **Reverse:** Crescent-shaped city view **Composition:** 0.9250 Silver

Date	Mintage	VG-8	F-12	VF-20	XF-40	MS-60	MS-63	Proof
2000 Proof	—	—	—	—	—	—	—	8.00

KM# 381 Subject: Achievement **Reverse:** Rocket above jagged design **Composition:** Nickel

Date	Mintage	VG-8	F-12	VF-20	XF-40	MS-60	MS-63	Proof
2000	—	—	—	—	—	0.50	0.70	—

KM# 381a Subject: Achievement **Reverse:** Rocket above jagged design **Composition:** 0.9250 Silver

Date	Mintage	VG-8	F-12	VF-20	XF-40	MS-60	MS-63	Proof
2000 Proof	—	—	—	—	—	—	—	8.00

KM# 382 Subject: Natural legacy **Reverse:** Environmental elements **Composition:** Nickel

Date	Mintage	VG-8	F-12	VF-20	XF-40	MS-60	MS-63	Proof
2000	—	—	—	—	—	0.50	0.70	—

KM# 382a Subject: Natural legacy **Reverse:** Environmental elements **Composition:** 0.9250 Silver

Date	Mintage	VG-8	F-12	VF-20	XF-40	MS-60	MS-63	Proof
2000 Proof	—	—	—	—	—	—	—	8.00

KM# 383 Subject: Celebration **Reverse:** Fireworks, children behind flag **Composition:** Nickel

Date	Mintage	VG-8	F-12	VF-20	XF-40	MS-60	MS-63	Proof
2000	—	—	—	—	—	0.50	0.70	—

KM# 383a Subject: Celebration **Reverse:** Fireworks, children behind flag **Composition:** 0.9250 Silver

Date	Mintage	VG-8	F-12	VF-20	XF-40	MS-60	MS-63	Proof
2000 Proof	—	—	—	—	—	—	—	8.00

KM# 384.1 Subject: Pride **Obverse:** Queen's portrait **Reverse:** Red with 3 small maple leaves on large maple leaf **Edge:** Reeded **Composition:** Nickel **Size:** 23.9 mm. **Note:** Colorized version.

Date	Mintage	VG-8	F-12	VF-20	XF-40	MS-60	MS-63	Proof
2000	—	—	—	—	—	—	6.50	—

KM# 384.2   Subject: Pride **Reverse:** 2 with three small maple leaves on large maple leaf **Composition:** Nickel

Date	Mintage	VG-8	F-12	VF-20	XF-40	MS-60	MS-63	Proof
2000	—	—	—	—	—	0.50	0.70	—

KM# 384.2a   Subject: Pride **Reverse:** 2 with 3 small maple leaves on large maple leaf **Composition:** 0.9250 Silver

Date	Mintage	VG-8	F-12	VF-20	XF-40	MS-60	MS-63	Proof
2000 Proof	—	—	—	—	—	—	—	8.00

KM# 419   Subject: Spirit of Canada **Obverse:** Queen's head right. **Reverse:** Maple leaf at center, children holding hands below. **Edge:** Reeded. **Weight:** 5.0600 g. **Composition:** Nickel Plated Steel **Size:** 23.9 mm.

Date	Mintage	VG-8	F-12	VF-20	XF-40	MS-60	MS-63	Proof
2001	—	—	—	—	—	—	—	—

KM# 448   Subject: Elizabeth II Golden Jubilee **Composition:** Nickel Plated Steel **Note:** Double-dated 1952-2002.

Date	Mintage	VG-8	F-12	VF-20	XF-40	MS-60	MS-63	Proof
ND(2002)	—	—	—	—	—	—	2.00	—

KM# 448a   Subject: Elizabeth II Golden Jubilee **Composition:** 0.9250 Silver **Note:** Double-dated 1952-2002.

Date	Mintage	VG-8	F-12	VF-20	XF-40	MS-60	MS-63	Proof
ND(2002) In proof sets only	100,000	—	—	—	—	—	—	12.50

KM# 474   Obverse: Queen's head right **Reverse:** Polar bear and red maple leaves **Composition:** 0.9250 Silver

Date	Mintage	MS-63	Proof
2003 Proof	—	—	7.50

KM# 471   Subject: 50th Anniversary of the Coronation of Elizabeth II **Obverse:** 1953 portrait dual-dated 1953-2003 **Composition:** 0.9250 Silver

Date	Mintage	VG-8	F-12	VF-20	XF-40	MS-60	MS-63	Proof
ND(2003) In coronation proof sets only	30,000	—	—	—	—	—	12.50	—

50 CENTS

KM# 69   Subject: Confederation centennial **Weight:** 11.6638 g. **Composition:** 0.8000 Silver .3000 oz. ASW

Date	Mintage	VG-8	F-12	VF-20	XF-40	MS-60	MS-63	Proof
ND(1967)	4,211,392	—	—	—	2.50	3.00	5.00	—

KM# 208   Subject: Confederation 125 **Composition:** Nickel

Date	Mintage	VG-8	F-12	VF-20	XF-40	MS-60	MS-63	Proof
ND(1992)	445,000	—	—	—	0.50	0.75	1.00	—
ND(1992) Proof	147,061	—	—	—	—	—	—	5.00

KM# 261 **Subject:** Atlantic puffin **Weight:** 11.6638 g. **Composition:** 0.9250 Silver .3461 oz. ASW

Date	Mintage	VG-8	F-12	VF-20	XF-40	MS-60	MS-63	Proof
1995 Proof	—	—	—	—	—	—	—	15.00

KM# 262 **Subject:** Whooping crane **Weight:** 11.6638 g. **Composition:** 0.9250 Silver .3461 oz. ASW

Date	Mintage	VG-8	F-12	VF-20	XF-40	MS-60	MS-63	Proof
1995 Proof	—	—	—	—	—	—	—	15.00

KM# 263 **Subject:** Gray jays **Weight:** 11.6638 g. **Composition:** 0.9250 Silver .3461 oz. ASW

Date	Mintage	VG-8	F-12	VF-20	XF-40	MS-60	MS-63	Proof
1995 Proof	—	—	—	—	—	—	—	20.00

KM# 264 **Subject:** White-tailed ptarmigans **Weight:** 11.6638 g. **Composition:** 0.9250 Silver .3461 oz. ASW

Date	Mintage	VG-8	F-12	VF-20	XF-40	MS-60	MS-63	Proof
1995 Proof	—	—	—	—	—	—	—	20.00

KM# 283 **Subject:** Moose calf **Weight:** 11.6638 g. **Composition:** 0.9250 Silver .3461 oz. ASW

Date	Mintage	VG-8	F-12	VF-20	XF-40	MS-60	MS-63	Proof
1996 Proof	—	—	—	—	—	—	—	14.00

KM# 284   Subject: Wood ducklings **Weight:** 11.6638 g. **Composition:** 0.9250 Silver .3461 oz. ASW

Date	Mintage	VG-8	F-12	VF-20	XF-40	MS-60	MS-63	Proof
1996 Proof	—	—	—	—	—	—	—	14.00

KM# 285   Subject: Cougar kittens **Weight:** 11.6638 g. **Composition:** 0.9250 Silver .3461 oz. ASW

Date	Mintage	VG-8	F-12	VF-20	XF-40	MS-60	MS-63	Proof
1996 Proof	—	—	—	—	—	—	—	14.00

KM# 286   Subject: Black bear cubs **Weight:** 11.6638 g. **Composition:** 0.9250 Silver .3461 oz. ASW

Date	Mintage	VG-8	F-12	VF-20	XF-40	MS-60	MS-63	Proof
1996 Proof	—	—	—	—	—	—	—	14.00

KM# 292   Subject: Duck tolling retriever **Weight:** 11.6638 g. **Composition:** 0.9250 Silver .3461 oz. ASW

Date	Mintage	VG-8	F-12	VF-20	XF-40	MS-60	MS-63	Proof
1997 Proof	—	—	—	—	—	—	—	14.00

KM# 293   Subject: Labrador retriever **Weight:** 11.6638 g. **Composition:** 0.9250 Silver .3461 oz. ASW

Date	Mintage	VG-8	F-12	VF-20	XF-40	MS-60	MS-63	Proof
1997 Proof	—	—	—	—	—	—	—	14.00

KM# 294   Subject: Newfoundland **Weight:** 11.6638 g. **Composition:** 0.9250 Silver .3461 oz. ASW

Date	Mintage	VG-8	F-12	VF-20	XF-40	MS-60	MS-63	Proof
1997 Proof	—	—	—	—	—	—	—	14.00

KM# 295   Subject: Eskimo dog **Weight:** 11.6638 g. **Composition:** 0.9250 Silver .3461 oz. ASW

Date	Mintage	VG-8	F-12	VF-20	XF-40	MS-60	MS-63	Proof
1997 Proof	—	—	—	—	—	—	—	14.00

KM# 313   Subject: 90th Anniversary Royal Canadian Mint **Weight:** 11.6638 g. **Composition:** 0.9250 Silver .3461 oz. ASW

Date	Mintage	VG-8	F-12	VF-20	XF-40	MS-60	MS-63	Proof
ND(1998) Matte	25,000	—	—	—	—	—	—	15.00
ND(1998) Proof	25,000	—	—	—	—	—	—	15.00

KM# 314   Subject: 110 years Canadian speed and figure skating **Weight:** 11.6638 g. **Composition:** 0.9250 Silver .3461 oz. ASW

Date	Mintage	VG-8	F-12	VF-20	XF-40	MS-60	MS-63	Proof
ND(1998) Proof	—	—	—	—	—	—	—	12.00

KM# 315   Subject: 100 years Canadian ski racing **Weight:** 11.6638 g. **Composition:** 0.9250 Silver .3461 oz. ASW

Date	Mintage	VG-8	F-12	VF-20	XF-40	MS-60	MS-63	Proof
ND(1998) Proof	—	—	—	—	—	—	—	12.00

KM# 318   Subject: Killer whales **Weight:** 11.6638 g. **Composition:** 0.9250 Silver .3461 oz. ASW

Date	Mintage	VG-8	F-12	VF-20	XF-40	MS-60	MS-63	Proof
1998 Proof	—	—	—	—	—	—	—	12.00

KM# 319   Subject: Humpback whale **Weight:** 11.6638 g. **Composition:** 0.9250 Silver .3461 oz. ASW

Date	Mintage	VG-8	F-12	VF-20	XF-40	MS-60	MS-63	Proof
1998 Proof	—	—	—	—	—	—	—	12.00

KM# 320   Subject: Beluga whale **Weight:** 11.6638 g. **Composition:** 0.9250 Silver .3461 oz. ASW

Date	Mintage	VG-8	F-12	VF-20	XF-40	MS-60	MS-63	Proof
1998 Proof	—	—	—	—	—	—	—	12.00

KM# 321   Subject: Blue whale **Weight:** 11.6638 g. **Composition:** 0.9250 Silver .3461 oz. ASW

Date	Mintage	VG-8	F-12	VF-20	XF-40	MS-60	MS-63	Proof
1998 Proof	—	—	—	—	—	—	—	12.00

KM# 327   Subject: 110 years Canadian soccer **Weight:** 11.6638 g. **Composition:** 0.9250 Silver .3461 oz. ASW

Date	Mintage	VG-8	F-12	VF-20	XF-40	MS-60	MS-63	Proof
ND(1998) Proof	—	—	—	—	—	—	—	12.00

KM# 328   Subject: 20 years Canadian auto racing **Weight:** 11.6638 g. **Composition:** 0.9250 Silver .3461 oz. ASW

Date	Mintage	VG-8	F-12	VF-20	XF-40	MS-60	MS-63	Proof
ND(1998) Proof	—	—	—	—	—	—	—	12.00

KM# 333 Subject: 1904 Canadian open **Weight:** 11.6638 g. **Composition:** 0.9250 Silver .3461 oz. ASW

Date	Mintage	VG-8	F-12	VF-20	XF-40	MS-60	MS-63	Proof
ND(1999) Proof	—	—	—	—	—	—	—	13.50

KM# 334 Subject: First U.S.-Canadian yacht race **Weight:** 11.6638 g. **Composition:** 0.9250 Silver .3461 oz. ASW

Date	Mintage	VG-8	F-12	VF-20	XF-40	MS-60	MS-63	Proof
ND(1999) Proof	—	—	—	—	—	—	—	12.00

KM# 335 Subject: Canadian cats, Cymric **Weight:** 11.6638 g. **Composition:** 0.9250 Silver .3461 oz. ASW

Date	Mintage	VG-8	F-12	VF-20	XF-40	MS-60	MS-63	Proof
1999 Proof	—	—	—	—	—	—	—	14.00

KM# 336 Subject: Canadian cats, Tonkinese **Weight:** 11.6638 g. **Composition:** 0.9250 Silver .3461 oz. ASW

Date	Mintage	VG-8	F-12	VF-20	XF-40	MS-60	MS-63	Proof
1999 Proof	—	—	—	—	—	—	—	14.00

KM# 337 Subject: Canadian cats, Cougar **Weight:** 11.6638 g. **Composition:** 0.9250 Silver .3461 oz. ASW

Date	Mintage	VG-8	F-12	VF-20	XF-40	MS-60	MS-63	Proof
1999 Proof	—	—	—	—	—	—	—	12.00

KM# 338   Subject: Canadian cats, Lynx **Weight:** 11.6638 g. **Composition:** 0.9250 Silver .3461 oz. ASW

Date	Mintage	VG-8	F-12	VF-20	XF-40	MS-60	MS-63	Proof
1999 Proof	—	—	—	—	—	—	—	12.00

KM# 371   Subject: Basketball **Obverse:** Queen's portrait **Reverse:** Basketball players **Edge:** Reeded **Weight:** 9.3600 g. **Composition:** 0.9250 Silver 0.2784 oz. ASW **Size:** 27.1 mm.

Date	Mintage	VG-8	F-12	VF-20	XF-40	MS-60	MS-63	Proof
1999 Proof	—	—	—	—	—	—	—	12.00

KM# 372   Subject: Football **Obverse:** Queen's portrait **Reverse:** Football players **Edge:** Reeded **Weight:** 9.3600 g. **Composition:** 0.9250 Silver 0.2784 oz. ASW **Size:** 27.1 mm.

Date	Mintage	VG-8	F-12	VF-20	XF-40	MS-60	MS-63	Proof
1999 Proof	—	—	—	—	—	—	—	12.00

KM# 385   Subject: Ice hockey **Reverse:** 4 hockey players **Composition:** 0.9250 Silver

Date	Mintage	VG-8	F-12	VF-20	XF-40	MS-60	MS-63	Proof
ND(2000) Proof	—	—	—	—	—	—	—	12.00

KM# 386   Subject: Curling **Reverse:** Motion study of a curler **Composition:** 0.9250 Silver

Date	Mintage	VG-8	F-12	VF-20	XF-40	MS-60	MS-63	Proof
ND(2000) Proof	—	—	—	—	—	—	—	12.00

KM# 389   Subject: Great horned owl **Composition:** 0.9250 Silver

Date	Mintage	VG-8	F-12	VF-20	XF-40	MS-60	MS-63	Proof
2000 Proof	—	—	—	—	—	—	—	12.00

KM# 390   Subject: Red-tail hawk **Composition:** 0.9250 Silver

Date	Mintage	VG-8	F-12	VF-20	XF-40	MS-60	MS-63	Proof
2000 Proof	—	—	—	—	—	—	—	12.00

KM# 391   Subject: Osprey **Composition:** 0.9250 Silver

Date	Mintage	VG-8	F-12	VF-20	XF-40	MS-60	MS-63	Proof
2000 Proof	—	—	—	—	—	—	—	12.00

KM# 392   Subject: Bald eagle **Composition:** 0.9250 Silver

Date	Mintage	VG-8	F-12	VF-20	XF-40	MS-60	MS-63	Proof
2000 Proof	—	—	—	—	—	—	—	12.00

KM# 393   Subject: Steeplechase **Composition:** 0.9250 Silver

Date	Mintage	VG-8	F-12	VF-20	XF-40	MS-60	MS-63	Proof
2000 Proof	—	—	—	—	—	—	—	12.00

KM# 394   Subject: Bowling **Composition:** 0.9250 Silver

Date	Mintage	VG-8	F-12	VF-20	XF-40	MS-60	MS-63	Proof
2000 Proof	—	—	—	—	—	—	—	12.00

KM# 444   Subject: Queen's Golden Jubilee **Obverse:** Bust of Queen Elizabeth II right and monogram. **Reverse:** Canadian arms. **Edge:** Reeded. **Weight:** 6.8300 g. **Composition:** Nickel Plated Steel **Size:** 27 mm.

Date	Mintage	VG-8	F-12	VF-20	XF-40	MS-60	MS-63	Proof
ND(2002)	—	—	—	—	—	2.00	—	—

KM# 420   Subject: Festivals - Quebec, **Obverse:** Queen's head right. **Reverse:** Snowman and Chateau Frontenac. **Edge:** Reeded. **Weight:** 9.3000 g. **Composition:** 0.9250 Silver .2766 oz. ASW **Size:** 27.13 mm.

Date	Mintage	VG-8	F-12	VF-20	XF-40	MS-60	MS-63	Proof
2001 Proof	—	—	—	—	—	—	—	15.00

KM# 421 Subject: Festivals - Nunavut, **Obverse:** Queen's head right. **Reverse:** Dancer, dog sled and snowmobiles. **Edge:** Reeded. **Weight:** 9.3000 g. **Composition:** 0.9250 Silver .2766 oz. ASW **Size:** 27.13 mm.

Date	Mintage	VG-8	F-12	VF-20	XF-40	MS-60	MS-63	Proof
2001 Proof	—	—	—	—	—	—	—	15.00

KM# 422 Subject: Festivals - Newfoundland, **Obverse:** Queen's head right. **Reverse:** Sailor and musical people. **Edge:** Reeded. **Weight:** 9.3000 g. **Composition:** 0.9250 Silver .2766 oz. ASW **Size:** 27.13 mm.

Date	Mintage	VG-8	F-12	VF-20	XF-40	MS-60	MS-63	Proof
2001 Proof	—	—	—	—	—	—	—	15.00

KM# 423 Subject: Festivals - Prince Edward Island, **Obverse:** Queen's head right. **Reverse:** Family, juggler and building. **Edge:** Reeded. **Weight:** 9.3000 g. **Composition:** 0.9250 Silver .2766 oz. ASW **Size:** 27.13 mm.

Date	Mintage	VG-8	F-12	VF-20	XF-40	MS-60	MS-63	Proof
2001 Proof	—	—	—	—	—	—	—	15.00

KM# 424 Subject: Folklore - The Sled, **Obverse:** Queen's head right. **Reverse:** Family scene. **Edge:** Reeded. **Weight:** 9.3000 g. **Composition:** 0.9250 Silver .2766 oz. ASW **Size:** 27.13 mm.

Date	Mintage	VG-8	F-12	VF-20	XF-40	MS-60	MS-63	Proof
2001 Proof	—	—	—	—	—	—	—	17.00

KM# 425 Subject: Folklore - The Maiden's Cave, **Obverse:** Queen's head right. **Reverse:** Woman shouting. **Edge:** Reeded. **Weight:** 9.3000 g. **Composition:** 0.9250 Silver .2766 oz. ASW **Size:** 27.13 mm.

Date	Mintage	VG-8	F-12	VF-20	XF-40	MS-60	MS-63	Proof
2001 Proof	—	—	—	—	—	—	—	17.00

KM# 426   Subject: Folklore - The Small Jumpers,   **Obverse:** Queen's head right. **Reverse:** Jumping children on seashore. **Edge:** Reeded. **Weight:** 9.3000 g. **Composition:** 0.9250 Silver .2766 oz. ASW **Size:** 27.13 mm.

Date	Mintage	VG-8	F-12	VF-20	XF-40	MS-60	MS-63	Proof
2001 Proof	—	—	—	—	—	—	—	17.00

KM# 461   Subject: Canadian Folklore and Legends, The Pig That Wouldn't Get Over the Stile **Composition:** 0.9250 Silver

Date	Mintage	MS-63	Proof
2002 Proof	—	—	18.50

KM# 458   Subject: Squamish Days Logger Sports **Composition:** 0.9250 Silver

Date	Mintage	MS-63	Proof
2002 Proof	—	—	16.50

KM# 456   Subject: Folklorama **Composition:** 0.9250 Silver

Date	Mintage	MS-63	Proof
2002 Proof	—	—	16.50

KM# 460   Subject: Canadian Folklore and Legends, The Ghost Ship **Composition:** 0.9250 Silver

Date	Mintage	MS-63	Proof
2002 Proof	—	—	18.50

KM# 457   Subject: Calgary Stampede **Composition:** 0.9250 Silver

Date	Mintage	MS-63	Proof
2002 Proof	—	—	16.50

KM# 454   Subject: Annapolis Valley Apple Blossom Festival **Composition:** 0.9250 Silver

Date	Mintage	MS-63	Proof
2002 Proof	—	—	16.50

KM# 459   Subject: Canadian Folklore and Legends, **Obverse:** Queen's head right **Reverse:** The Shoemaker in Heaven **Composition:** 0.9250 Silver

Date	Mintage	MS-63	Proof
2002 Proof	—	—	18.50

KM# 455   Subject: Stratford Festival **Obverse:** Queen's head right **Reverse:** Couple with building in background **Composition:** 0.9250 Silver

Date	Mintage	MS-63	Proof
2002 Proof	—	—	16.50

KM# 444a   Subject: Elizabeth II Golden Jubilee **Composition:** 0.9250 Silver **Note:** Double-dated 1952-2002.

Date	Mintage	MS-63	Proof
ND(2002) In proof sets only	100,000	—	17.50

KM# 479   Subject: Great Northern Arts Festival **Composition:** 0.9250 Silver

Date	Mintage	MS-63	Proof
2003 Proof	—	—	16.50

KM# 476   Subject: Yukon International Storytelling Festival **Composition:** 0.9250 Silver

Date	Mintage	MS-63	Proof
2003 Proof	—	—	16.50

KM# 477   Subject: Festival acadien de Caraquet **Obverse:** Queen's head right **Reverse:** Sailboat and couple **Composition:** 0.9250 Silver

Date	Mintage	MS-63	Proof
2003 Proof	—	—	16.50

KM# 478   Subject: Back to batoche **Composition:** 0.9250 Silver

Date	Mintage	MS-63	Proof
2003 Proof	—	—	16.50

KM# 475   Subject: Golden Daffodil **Composition:** 0.9250 Silver

Date	Mintage	MS-63	Proof
2003 Proof	55,000	—	27.50

KM# 472   Subject: 50th Anniversary of the Coronation of Elizabeth II **Obverse:** 1953 portrait dual-dated 1953-2003 **Composition:** 0.9250 Silver

Date	Mintage	MS-63	Proof
ND(2003) In coronation proof sets only	30,000	15.00	—

DOLLAR

KM# 30   Subject: Silver Jubilee **Weight:** 23.3276 g. **Composition:** 0.8000 Silver 0.6000 oz. ASW

Date	Mintage	F-12	VF-20	XF-40	AU-50	MS-60	MS-63	Proof
1935	428,707	11.50	17.50	28.00	32.00	36.50	60.00	4,500

KM# 38   Subject: Royal Visit **Weight:** 23.3276 g. **Composition:** 0.8000 Silver 0.6000 oz. ASW

Date	Mintage	F-12	VF-20	XF-40	AU-50	MS-60	MS-63	Proof
1939	1,363,816	5.00	6.00	7.00	8.50	11.50	20.00	—
1939 Matte specimen	—	—	—	—	—	—	—	475

KM# 47 Subject: Newfoundland **Weight:** 23.3276 g. **Composition:** 0.8000 Silver 0.6000 oz. ASW

Date	Mintage	F-12	VF-20	XF-40	AU-50	MS-60	MS-63	Proof
1949	672,218	9.00	11.00	16.50	21.50	25.00	30.00	—
1949 Specimen proof	—	—	—	—	—	—	—	1,200

KM# 55 Subject: British Columbia **Weight:** 23.3276 g. **Composition:** 0.8000 Silver 0.6000 oz. ASW

Date	Mintage	F-12	VF-20	XF-40	AU-50	MS-60	MS-63	Proof
ND(1958)	3,039,630	BV	3.50	4.50	5.00	6.50	10.00	—

KM# 58 Subject: Charlottetown **Weight:** 23.3276 g. **Composition:** 0.8000 Silver 0.6000 oz. ASW

Date	Mintage	F-12	VF-20	XF-40	AU-50	MS-60	MS-63	Proof
ND(1964)	7,296,832	—	—	—	BV	4.00	5.00	—
ND(1964) Specimen proof	Inc. above	—	—	—	—	—	—	250

KM# 70 Subject: Confederation Centennial **Reverse:** Goose **Weight:** 23.3276 g. **Comp.:** 0.8000 Silver 0.6000 oz. ASW

Date	Mintage	MS-63	P/L	Proof
ND(1967)	6,767,496	6.00	7.00	10.00

KM# 78   Subject: Manitoba **Composition:** Nickel **Size:** 32 mm.

Date	Mintage	MS-63	P/L	Proof
1970	4,140,058	2.00	—	—
1970	645,869	—	2.50	—

KM# 79   Subject: British Columbia **Composition:** Nickel **Size:** 32 mm.

Date	Mintage	MS-63	P/L	Proof
1971	4,260,781	2.00	—	—
1971	468,729	—	2.25	—

KM# 80   Subject: British Columbia **Weight:** 23.3276 g. **Composition:** 0.5000 Silver 0.3750 oz. ASW **Size:** 36 mm.

Date	Mintage	MS-63	P/L	Spec.
1971	585,674	—	—	5.50

KM# 82   Subject: Prince Edward Island **Composition:** Nickel **Size:** 32 mm.

Date	Mintage	MS-63	P/L	Proof
1973	3,196,452	2.00	—	—
1973 (c)	466,881	—	2.50	—

KM# 83   Subject: Mountie **Weight:** 23.3276 g. **Composition:** 0.5000 Silver 0.3750 oz. ASW **Size:** 36 mm.

Date	Mintage	MS-63	P/L	Spec.
1973	1,031,271	—	—	5.50

KM# 88   Subject: Winnipeg Centennial **Composition:** Nickel **Size:** 32 mm.

Date	Mintage	MS-63	P/L	Proof
1974	2,799,363	2.00	—	—
1974 (c)	363,786	—	2.50	—

KM# 88a Subject: Winnipeg Centennial
Composition: 0.5000 Silver **Size:** 36 mm.

Date	Mintage	MS-63	P/L	Spec.
1974	728,947	—		5.50

KM# 118 Subject: Silver Jubilee **Weight:**
23.3276 g. **Composition:** 0.5000 Silver 0.3750 oz.
ASW **Size:** 36 mm.

Date	Mintage	MS-63	P/L	Spec.
1977	744,848	—	—	5.00
1977 red case VIP	Inc. above	—	—	25.00

KM# 97 Subject: Calgary **Weight:** 23.3276 g.
Composition: 0.5000 Silver 0.3750 oz. ASW **Size:**
36 mm.

Date	Mintage	MS-63	P/L	Spec.
1975	930,956	—	—	5.50

KM# 121 Subject: XI Commonwealth Games
Weight: 23.3276 g. **Composition:** 0.5000 Silver
0.3750 oz. ASW **Size:** 36 mm.

Date	Mintage	MS-63	P/L	Spec.
1978	709,602	—	—	5.00

KM# 106 Subject: Parliament Library **Weight:**
23.3276 g. **Composition:** 0.5000 Silver 0.3750 oz.
ASW **Size:** 36 mm.

Date	Mintage	MS-63	P/L	Spec.
1976	578,708	—	—	6.00
1976 blue case VIP	Inc. above	—	—	15.00

KM# 124 Subject: Griffon **Weight:** 23.3276 g.
Composition: 0.5000 Silver 0.3750 oz. ASW **Size:**
36 mm.

Date	Mintage	MS-63	P/L	Spec.
1979	826,695	—	—	8.00

KM# 128 Subject: Arctic Territories **Weight:**
23.3276 g. **Composition:** 0.5000 Silver 0.3750 oz.
ASW **Size:** 36 mm.

Date	Mintage	MS-63	P/L	Spec.
1980	539,617	—	—	17.50

KM# 130 Subject: Transcontinental Railroad
Weight: 23.3276 g. **Composition:** 0.5000 Silver
0.3750 oz. ASW **Size:** 36 mm.

Date	Mintage	MS-63	P/L	Proof
1981	699,494	7.50	—	13.50
1981 Proof	—	—	—	—

KM# 133 Subject: Regina **Weight:** 23.3276 g.
Composition: 0.5000 Silver 0.3750 oz. ASW **Size:**
36 mm.

Date	Mintage	MS-63	P/L	Proof
1982	144,930	7.50	—	—
1982 Proof	758,958	—	—	5.00

KM# 134 Subject: Constitution **Composition:**
Nickel **Size:** 32 mm.

Date	Mintage	MS-63	P/L	Proof
1982	9,709,422	3.00	6.00	—

KM# 138 Subject: Edmonton University Games
Weight: 23.3276 g. **Composition:** 0.5000 Silver
0.3750 oz. ASW **Size:** 36 mm.

Date	Mintage	MS-63	P/L	Proof
1983	159,450	5.00	—	—
1983 Proof	506,847	—	—	6.00

KM# 140 Subject: Toronto Sesquicentennial
Weight: 23.3276 g. **Composition:** 0.5000 Silver
0.3750 oz. ASW **Size:** 36 mm.

Date	Mintage	MS-63	P/L	Proof
1984	133,610	7.50	—	—
1984 Proof	732,542	—	—	5.00

KM# 141 Subject: Jacques Cartier **Composition:**
Nickel **Size:** 32 mm.

Date	Mintage	MS-63	P/L	Proof
1984	7,009,323	2.25	—	—
1984 Proof	87,760	—	—	6.00

KM# 143 Subject: National Parks/Moose **Weight:** 23.3276 g. **Composition:** 0.5000 Silver 0.3750 oz. ASW **Size:** 36 mm.

Date	Mintage	MS-63	P/L	Proof
1985	163,314	7.50	—	—
1985 Proof	733,354	—	—	6.00

KM# 149 Subject: Vancouver **Weight:** 23.3276 g. **Composition:** 0.5000 Silver 0.3750 oz. ASW **Size:** 36 mm.

Date	Mintage	MS-63	P/L	Proof
1986	125,949	7.50	—	—
1986 Proof	680,004	—	—	7.00

KM# 154 Subject: John Davis **Weight:** 23.3276 g. **Composition:** 0.5000 Silver 0.3750 oz. ASW **Size:** 36 mm.

Date	Mintage	MS-63	P/L	Proof
1987	118,722	7.50	—	—
1987 Proof	602,374	—	—	9.00

KM# 161 Subject: Ironworks **Weight:** 23.3276 g. **Composition:** 0.5000 Silver 0.3750 oz. ASW **Size:** 36 mm.

Date	Mintage	MS-63	P/L	Proof
1988	106,872	7.50	—	—
1988 Proof	255,013	—	—	15.00

KM# 168 Subject: MacKenzie River **Weight:** 23.3276 g. **Composition:** 0.5000 Silver 0.3750 oz. ASW **Size:** 36 mm.

Date	Mintage	MS-63	P/L	Proof
1989	99,774	7.50	—	—
1989 Proof	244,062	—	—	15.00

KM# 170 Subject: Henry Kelsey **Weight:** 23.3276 g. **Composition:** 0.5000 Silver 0.3750 oz. ASW **Size:** 36 mm.

Date	Mintage	MS-63	P/L	Proof
1990	99,455	7.50	—	—
1990 Proof	254,959	—	—	12.50

KM# 179 Subject: S.S. Frontenac **Weight:**
23.3276 g. **Composition:** 0.5000 Silver 0.3750 oz.
ASW **Size:** 36 mm.

Date	Mintage	MS-63	P/L	Proof
1991	73,843	7.50	—	—
1991 Proof	195,424	—	—	18.00

KM# 210 Subject: Stagecoach service **Weight:**
25.1750 g. **Composition:** 0.9250 Silver 0.7487 oz.
ASW **Size:** 36 mm.

Date	Mintage	MS-63	P/L	Proof
1992	78,160	7.50	—	—
1992 Proof	187,612	—	—	12.50

KM# 209 Subject: Loon **Composition:** Aureate
Size: 32 mm.

Date	Mintage	MS-63	P/L	Proof
ND(1992)	4,242,085	2.00	4.00	8.00
ND(1992) Proof	—	—	—	—

KM# 218 Subject: Parliament **Composition:**
Aureate **Size:** 26 mm.

Date	Mintage	MS-63	P/L	Proof
ND(1992)	23,915,000	2.25	5.00	—
ND(1992) Proof	24,227	—	—	9.00

KM# 235 Subject: Stanley Cup hockey **Weight:**
25.1750 g. **Composition:** 0.9250 Silver 0.7487 oz.
ASW **Size:** 36 mm.

Date	Mintage	MS-63	P/L	Proof
1993	88,150	7.50	—	—
1993 Proof	294,314	—	—	12.50

Subject: Stanley Cup hockey **Composition:**
Aureate **Size:** 26 mm.

Date	Mintage	MS-63	P/L	Proof
1993 Proof	54,524	—	—	12.50

KM# 251 Subject: Last RCMP sled-dog patrol
Weight: 25.1750 g. **Composition:** 0.9250 Silver
0.7487 oz. ASW **Size:** 36 mm.

Date	Mintage	MS-63	P/L	Proof
1994	61,561	8.50	—	—
1994 Proof	170,374	—	—	24.50

KM# 248 Subject: War Memorial **Composition:**
Aureate **Size:** 26 mm.

Date	Mintage	MS-63	P/L	Proof
1994	15,000,000	2.25	—	—
1994 Proof	54,524	—	—	10.00

KM# 258 Subject: Peacekeeping Monument in Ottawa **Composition:** Aureate **Size:** 26 mm. **Note:** Mintage included with KM#186.

Date	Mintage	MS-63	P/L	Proof
1995	—	2.25	—	—
1995 Proof	43,293	—	—	10.00

KM# 259 Subject: Hudson Bay Co. **Weight:** 25.1750 g. **Composition:** 0.9250 Silver 0.7487 oz. ASW **Size:** 36 mm.

Date	Mintage	MS-63	P/L	Proof
1995	61,819	8.50	—	—
1995 Proof	166,259	—	—	17.00

KM# 274 Subject: McIntosh Apple **Weight:** 25.1750 g. **Composition:** 0.9250 Silver 0.7487 oz. ASW **Size:** 36 mm.

Date	Mintage	MS-63	P/L	Proof
1996	58,834	8.50	—	—
1996 Proof	133,779	—	—	17.00

KM# 282 Subject: 25th Anniversary Hockey Victory **Weight:** 25.1750 g. **Composition:** 0.9250 Silver 0.7487 oz. ASW **Size:** 36 mm.

Date	Mintage	MS-63	P/L	Proof
ND(1997)	155,252	8.50	—	—
ND(1997) Proof	184,965	—	—	24.00

KM# 291 Subject: Loon Dollar 10th Anniversary **Composition:** Aureate **Size:** 26 mm.

Date	Mintage	MS-63	P/L	Proof
1997	—	—	20.00	—

KM# 296 Subject: Loon Dollar 10th Anniversary **Weight:** 25.1750 g. **Composition:** 0.9250 Silver 0.7487 oz. ASW **Size:** 36 mm.

Date	Mintage	MS-63	P/L	Proof
1997 Proof	24,995	—	—	65.00

KM# 306 Subject: 120th Anniversary Royal Canadian Mounted Police **Weight:** 25.1750 g. **Composition:** 0.9250 Silver 0.7487 oz. ASW **Size:** 36 mm. **Note:** Individually cased prooflikes, proofs or specimens are from broken-up prooflike or specimen sets.

Date	Mintage	MS-63	P/L	Proof
1998	79,777	—	10.00	—
1998 Proof	120,172	—	—	18.00

KM# 355 Subject: International Year of Old Persons **Weight:** 25.1750 g. **Composition:** 0.9250 Silver 0.7487 oz. ASW **Size:** 36 mm.

Date	Mintage	MS-63	P/L	Proof
1999 Proof	24,976	—	—	32.50

KM# 356 Subject: Discovery of Queen Charlotte Isle **Weight:** 25.1750 g. **Composition:** 0.9250 Silver 0.7487 oz. ASW **Size:** 36 mm.

Date	Mintage	MS-63	P/L	Proof
ND(1999)	67,655	—	10.00	—
ND(1999) Proof	126,435	—	—	22.50

KM# 401 Subject: Voyage of Discovery **Obverse:** Queen's portrait **Reverse:** Human and space shuttle **Weight:** 25.1750 g. **Composition:** 0.9250 Silver 0.7487 oz. ASW **Size:** 36 mm.

Date	Mintage	MS-63	P/L	Proof
2000	60,100	—	10.00	—
2000 Proof	114,130	—	—	22.50

KM# 443 Subject: Queen's Royal Jubilee **Obverse:** Queen's portrait with anniversary date **Reverse:** Queen in her coach and a view of the coach **Edge:** Reeded **Weight:** 25.1750 g.

Composition: 0.9250 Silver 0.7487 oz. ASW **Size:** 36 mm.

Date	Mintage	MS-63	P/L	Proof
ND(2000) Proof	125,000	—	—	20.00
ND(2002)	—	—	12.00	—
ND(2002) Proof	—	—	—	21.50

KM# 414 Subject: National Ballet **Obverse:** Queen's head right. **Reverse:** Ballet dancers. **Edge:** Reeded. **Weight:** 25.1750 g. **Composition:** 0.9250 Silver 0.7487 oz. ASW **Size:** 36 mm.

Date	Mintage	MS-63	P/L	Proof
2001	65,000	—	12.00	—
2001 Proof	225,000	—	—	21.50

KM# 434 Obverse: Bust of Queen Elizabeth II right. **Reverse:** Recycled 1911 pattern dollar design: denomination, country name and dates in crowned wreath. **Edge:** Reeded. **Weight:** 25.1750 g. **Composition:** 0.9250 Silver 0.7487 oz. ASW **Size:** 36 mm.

Date	Mintage	MS-63	P/L	Proof
ND(2001) Proof	25,000	—	—	45.00

KM# 450 Subject: Cobalt Mining Centennial **Obverse:** Queen's portrait **Reverse:** Mine tower and fox **Edge:** Reeded **Weight:** 25.1750 g.

Composition: 0.9999 Silver 0.8093 oz. ASW **Size:** 36 mm.

Date	Mintage	MS-63	Proof
ND(2003)	75,000	—	—
ND(2003) Proof	125,000	—	25.00

KM# 480 Subject: Coronation of Queen Elizabeth II **Composition:** 0.9999 Silver

Date	Mintage	MS-63	Proof
2003 Proof	30,000	—	37.50

KM# 473 Subject: 50th Anniversary of the Coronation of Elizabeth II **Obverse:** 1953 effigy dual-dated 1953-2003 **Reverse:** Voyageur design similar to KM#54 **Composition:** 0.9999 Silver

Date	Mintage	MS-63	Proof
ND(2003) In coronation proof sets only	30,000	30.00	—

2 DOLLARS

KM# 357 Subject: Nunavut

Date	Mintage	MS-63	P/L	Proof
1999	—	3.50	—	—
1999	—	3.50	—	—

KM# 357a Subject: Nunavut **Obverse:** Queen's head right. **Reverse:** Drum dancer. **Edge:** Interrupted reeding. **Size:** 28 mm.

Date	Mintage	MS-63	P/L	Proof
1999 Proof	—	—	—	14.00
1999 Proof	—	—	—	14.00

KM# 357b Subject: Nunavut **Obverse:** Queen's head right. **Reverse:** Drum dancer.

Date	Mintage	MS-63	P/L	Proof
1999 Proof	10,000	—	—	175
1999 Proof	10,000	—	—	175

KM# 399 Subject: Knowledge **Reverse:** Polar bear and 2 cubs **Edge:** Reeded and plain sections. **Size:** 28 mm.

Date	Mintage	MS-63	P/L	Proof
2000	—	3.50	5.00	—
2000	—	3.50	5.00	—

KM# 399a Subject: Knowledge **Reverse:** Polar bear and 2 cubs **Note:** Gold plated.

Date	Mintage	MS-63	P/L	Proof
2000 Proof	40,000	—	—	12.00
2000 Proof	40,000	—	—	12.00

KM# 399b Subject: Knowledge **Reverse:** Polar bear and two cubs right.

Date	Mintage	MS-63	P/L	Proof
2000 Proof	—	—	—	175

KM# 449 Subject: Elizabeth II Golden Jubilee **Note:** Double-dated 1952-2002.

Date	Mintage	MS-63	Proof
ND(2002)	—	4.00	—

KM# 449a Subject: Elizabeth II Golden Jubilee **Composition:** Bi-Metallic **Note:** Double-dated 1952-2002.

Date	Mintage	MS-63	Proof
ND(2002) In proof sets only	100,000	—	12.00

5 DOLLARS

KM# 84 Subject: 1976 Montreal Olympics **Reverse:** Sailboat "Kingston" **Weight:** 24.3000 g. **Composition:** 0.9250 Silver 0.7227 oz. ASW **Size:** 38 mm. **Note:** Series I.

Date	Mintage	MS-63	Proof
1973	—	5.00	—
1973 Proof	165,203	—	6.25

KM# 85 Subject: 1976 Montreal Olympics **Reverse:** North American map **Composition:** 0.9250 Silver 0.7227 oz. ASW **Note:** Series I.

Date	Mintage	MS-63	Proof
1973	—	5.00	—
1973 Proof	165,203		6.25

KM# 89 Subject: 1976 Montreal Olympics
Reverse: Olympic rings **Weight:** 24.3000 g.
Composition: 0.9250 Silver 0.7227 oz. ASW **Size:**
38 mm. **Note:** Series II.

Date	Mintage	MS-63	Proof
1974	—	5.00	—
1974 Proof	97,431		6.25

KM# 91 Subject: 1976 Montreal Olympics
Reverse: Rowing **Weight:** 24.3000 g.
Composition: 0.9250 Silver 0.7227 oz. ASW **Size:**
38 mm. **Note:** Series III.

Date	Mintage	MS-63	Proof
1974	—	5.00	—
1974 Proof	104,684		6.25

KM# 90 Subject: 1976 Montreal Olympics
Reverse: Athlete with torch **Weight:** 24.3000 g.
Composition: 0.9250 Silver 0.7227 oz. ASW **Size:**
38 mm. **Note:** Series II.

Date	Mintage	MS-63	Proof
1974	—	5.00	—
1974 Proof	97,431		6.25

KM# 92 Subject: 1976 Montreal Olympics
Reverse: Canoeing **Weight:** 24.3000 g.
Composition: 0.9250 Silver 0.7227 oz. ASW **Size:**
38 mm. **Note:** Series III.

Date	Mintage	MS-63	Proof
1974	—	5.00	—
1974 Proof	104,684		6.25

KM# 98 Subject: 1976 Montreal Olympics
Reverse: Marathon **Weight:** 24.3000 g.
Composition: 0.9250 Silver 0.7227 oz. ASW **Size:**
38 mm. **Note:** Series IV.

Date	Mintage	MS-63	Proof
1975	—	5.00	—
1975 Proof	89,155	—	6.25

KM# 100 Subject: 1976 Montreal Olympics
Reverse: Swimmer **Weight:** 24.3000 g.
Composition: 0.9250 Silver 0.7227 oz. ASW **Size:**
38 mm. **Note:** Series V.

Date	Mintage	MS-63	Proof
1975	—	5.00	—
1975 Proof	89,155	—	6.25

KM# 99 Subject: 1976 Montreal Olympics
Reverse: Women's javelin **Weight:** 24.3000 g.
Composition: 0.9250 Silver 0.7227 oz. ASW **Size:**
38 mm. **Note:** Series IV.

Date	Mintage	MS-63	Proof
1975	—	5.00	—
1975 Proof	89,155	—	6.25

KM# 101 Subject: 1976 Montreal Olympics
Reverse: Diver **Weight:** 24.3000 g. **Composition:**
0.9250 Silver 0.7227 oz. ASW **Size:** 38 mm. **Note:**
Series V.

Date	Mintage	MS-63	Proof
1975	—	5.00	—
1975 Proof	89,155	—	6.25

KM# 107   Subject: 1976 Montreal Olympics
Reverse: Fencing **Weight:** 24.3000 g.
Composition: 0.9250 Silver 0.7227 oz. ASW **Size:**
38 mm. **Note:** Series VI.

Date	Mintage	MS-63	Proof
1976	—	5.00	—
1976 Proof	82,302	—	6.50

KM# 109   Subject: 1976 Montreal Olympics
Reverse: Olympic village **Weight:** 24.3000 g.
Composition: 0.9250 Silver 0.7227 oz. ASW **Size:**
38 mm. **Note:** Series VII.

Date	Mintage	MS-63	Proof
1976	—	5.00	—
1976 Proof	76,908	—	6.50

KM# 108   Subject: 1976 Montreal Olympics
Obv. Legend: Boxing **Weight:** 24.3000 g.
Composition: 0.9250 Silver 0.7227 oz. ASW **Size:**
38 mm. **Note:** Series VI.

Date	Mintage	MS-63	Proof
1976	—	5.00	—
1976 Proof	82,302	—	6.50

KM# 110   Subject: 1976 Montreal Olympics
Reverse: Olympic flame **Weight:** 24.3000 g.
Composition: 0.9250 Silver 0.7227 oz. ASW **Size:**
38 mm. **Note:** Series VII.

Date	Mintage	MS-63	Proof
1976	—	5.00	—
1976 Proof	79,102	—	6.50

KM# 316   Subject: Dr. Norman Bethune **Weight:** 31.3900 g. **Composition:** 0.9999 Silver 1.0091 oz. ASW

Date	Mintage	MS-63	Proof
1998 in proof sets only	61,000	—	35.00

KM# 398 Reverse: Viking ship under sail **Composition:** Copper-Zinc-Nickel **Note:** Sold in sets with Norway 20 kroner, KM#465.

Date	Mintage	MS-63	Proof
1999 Proof	—	—	16.50

KM# 435 Subject: Guglielmo Marconi **Obverse:** Bust of Queen Elizabeth II right. **Reverse:** Gold-plated cameo portrait of Marconi. **Edge:** Reeded. **Weight:** 16.8600 g. **Composition:** 0.9250 Silver 0.5014 oz. ASW **Size:** 28.4 mm. **Note:** Only issued in two coin set with British 2 pounds KM#1014a.

Date	Mintage	MS-60	MS-63
ND(2001) Proof	30,000	—	—

10 DOLLARS

KM# 86.1 Subject: 1976 Montreal Olympics **Reverse:** World map **Weight:** 48.6000 g. **Composition:** 0.9250 Silver 1.4454 oz. ASW **Size:** 45 mm. **Note:** Series I.

Date	Mintage	MS-63	Proof
1973	103,426	10.00	—
1973 Proof	165,203	—	11.50

KM# 87 Subject: 1976 Montreal Olympics **Reverse:** Montreal skyline **Weight:** 48.6000 g. **Composition:** 0.9250 Silver 1.4454 oz. ASW **Size:** 87 mm. **Note:** Series I.

Date	Mintage	MS-63	Proof
1973	—	10.00	—
1973 Proof	165,203	—	11.50

KM# 86.2 Subject: 1976 Montreal Olympics **Reverse:** World map **Weight:** 48.6000 g. **Composition:** 0.9250 Silver 1.4454 oz. ASW **Size:** 45 mm. **Note:** Series I.

Date	Mintage	MS-63	Proof
1974 Error: mule	320	275	—

KM# 93   Subject: 1976 Montreal Olympics **Reverse:** Head of Zeus **Weight:** 48.6000 g. **Composition:** 0.9250 Silver 1.4454 oz. ASW **Size:** 45 mm. **Note:** Series II.

Date	Mintage	MS-63	Proof
1974	—	10.00	—
1974 Proof	104,684	—	11.50

KM# 95   Subject: 1976 Montreal Olympics **Reverse:** Cycling **Weight:** 48.6000 g. **Composition:** 0.9250 Silver 1.4454 oz. ASW **Size:** 45 mm. **Note:** Series III.

Date	Mintage	MS-63	Proof
1974	—	10.00	—
1974 Proof	97,431	—	11.50

KM# 94   Subject: 1976 Montreal Olympics **Reverse:** Temple of Zeus **Weight:** 48.6000 g. **Composition:** 0.9250 Silver 1.4454 oz. ASW **Size:** 45 mm. **Note:** Series II.

Date	Mintage	MS-63	Proof
1974	—	10.00	—
1974 Proof	104,684	—	11.50

KM# 96   Subject: 1976 Montreal Olympics **Reverse:** Lacrosse **Weight:** 48.6000 g. **Composition:** 0.9250 Silver 1.4454 oz. ASW **Size:** 45 mm. **Note:** Series III.

Date	Mintage	MS-63	Proof
1974	—	10.00	—
1974 Proof	97,431	—	11.50

KM# 102 **Subject:** 1976 Montreal Olympics
Reverse: Men's hurdles **Weight:** 48.6000 g.
Composition: 0.9250 Silver 1.4454 oz. ASW **Size:**
45 mm. **Note:** Series IV.

Date	Mintage	MS-63	Proof
1975	—	10.00	—
1975 Proof	82,302	—	11.50

KM# 104 **Subject:** 1976 Montreal Olympics
Reverse: Sailing **Weight:** 48.6000 g.
Composition: 0.9250 Silver 1.4454 oz. ASW **Size:**
45 mm. **Note:** Series V.

Date	Mintage	MS-63	Proof
1975	—	10.00	—
1975 Proof	89,155	—	11.50

KM# 103 **Subject:** 1976 Montreal Olympics
Reverse: Women's shot put **Weight:** 48.6000 g.
Composition: 0.9250 Silver 1.4454 oz. ASW **Size:**
45 mm. **Note:** Series IV.

Date	Mintage	MS-63	Proof
1975	—	10.00	—
1975 Proof	82,302	—	11.50

KM# 105 **Subject:** 1976 Montreal Olympics
Reverse: Canoeing **Weight:** 48.6000 g.
Composition: 0.9250 Silver 1.4454 oz. ASW **Size:**
45 mm. **Note:** Series V.

Date	Mintage	MS-63	Proof
1975	—	10.00	—
1975 Proof	89,155	—	11.50

KM# 111   Subject: 1976 Montreal Olympics
Reverse: Football **Weight:** 48.6000 g.
Composition: 0.9250 Silver 1.4454 oz. ASW **Size:**
45 mm. **Note:** Series VI.

Date	Mintage	MS-63	Proof
1976	—	10.00	—
1976 Proof	76,908	—	12.00

KM# 112   Subject: 1976 Montreal Olympics
Reverse: Field hockey **Weight:** 48.6000 g.
Composition: 0.9250 Silver 1.4454 oz. ASW **Size:**
45 mm. **Note:** Series VI.

Date	Mintage	MS-63	Proof
1976	—	10.00	—
1976 Proof	76,908	—	12.00

KM# 113   Subject: 1976 Montreal Olympics
Reverse: Olympic Stadium **Weight:** 48.6000 g.
Composition: 0.9250 Silver 1.4454 oz. ASW **Size:**
45 mm. **Note:** Series VII.

Date	Mintage	MS-63	Proof
1976	—	10.00	—
1976 Proof	79,102	—	12.00

KM# 114   Subject: 1976 Montreal Olympics
Reverse: Olympic Velodrome **Weight:** 48.6000 g.
Composition: 0.9250 Silver 1.4454 oz. ASW **Size:**
45 mm. **Note:** Series VII.

Date	Mintage	MS-63	Proof
1976	—	10.00	—
1976 Proof	79,102	—	12.00

15 DOLLARS

KM# 215 Subject: 1992 Olympics **Reverse:** Coaching track **Weight:** 33.6300 g. **Composition:** 0.9250 Silver 1.0000 oz. ASW **Size:** 39 mm.

Date	Mintage	MS-63	Proof
1992 Proof	275,000	—	28.00

KM# 216 Subject: 1992 Olympics **Reverse:** High jump, rings, speed skating **Weight:** 33.6300 g. **Composition:** 0.9250 Silver 1.0000 oz. ASW

Date	Mintage	MS-63	Proof
1992 Proof	275,000	—	28.00

KM# 304 Subject: Year of the Tiger **Size:** 32 mm.

Date	Mintage	MS-63	Proof
1998 Proof	68,888	—	250

KM# 331 Subject: Year of the Rabbitt

Date	Mintage	MS-63	Proof
1999 Proof	—	—	40.00

KM# 387 Subject: Year of the Dragon

Date	Mintage	MS-63	Proof
2000 Proof	—	—	55.00

KM# 415 Subject: Year of the Snake **Obverse:** Queen's head right. **Reverse:** Snake within circle of lunar calendar signs. **Edge:** Reeded. **Weight:** 33.6300 g. **Composition:** 0.9250 Silver 1 oz. ASW **Size:** 40 mm.

Date	Mintage	MS-63	Proof
2001 Proof	—	—	50.00

KM# 463 Subject: Year of the Horse
Composition: 0.9250 Silver

Date	Mintage	MS-63	Proof
2002 Proof	68,888	—	60.00

KM# 481 Subject: Year of the Sheep
Composition: 0.9250 Silver **Size:** 32 mm.

Date	Mintage	MS-63	Proof
2003 Proof	68,888	—	60.00

20 DOLLARS

KM# 71 Subject: Centennial **Weight:** 18.2733 g.
Composition: 0.9000 Gold 0.5288 oz. AGW

Date	Mintage	MS-63	Proof
1967 Proof	337,688	—	185

KM# 145 Subject: 1988 Calgary Olympics
Reverse: Downhill skier **Edge:** Lettered **Weight:**
33.6300 g. **Composition:** 0.9250 Silver 1.0000 oz.
ASW **Size:** 40 mm.

Date	Mintage	MS-63	Proof
1985 Proof	406,360	—	21.50
1985 Plain edge; Proof	Inc. above	—	175

KM# 146 Subject: 1988 Calgary Olympics
Reverse: Speed skater **Edge:** Lettered **Weight:**

33.6300 g. **Composition:** 0.9250 Silver 1.0000 oz.
ASW **Size:** 40 mm.

Date	Mintage	MS-63	Proof
1985 Proof	354,222	—	21.50
1985 Plain edge; Proof	Inc. above	—	175

KM# 147 Subject: 1988 Calgary Olympics
Reverse: Biathlon **Edge:** Lettered **Weight:**
33.6300 g. **Composition:** 0.9250 Silver 1.0000 oz.
ASW **Size:** 40 mm.

Date	Mintage	MS-63	Proof
1986 Proof	308,086	—	21.50
1986 Plain edge; Proof	Inc. above	—	175

KM# 148 Subject: 1988 Calgary Olympics
Reverse: Hockey **Edge:** Lettered **Weight:**
33.6300 g. **Composition:** 0.9250 Silver 1.0000 oz.
ASW **Size:** 40 mm.

Date	Mintage	MS-63	Proof
1986 Proof	396,602	—	21.50
1986 Plain edge; Proof	Inc. above	—	175

KM# 150 Subject: 1988 Calgary Olympics
Reverse: Cross-country skier **Weight:** 33.6300 g.
Composition: 0.9250 Silver 1.0000 oz. ASW **Size:**
40 mm.

Date	Mintage	MS-63	Proof
1986 Proof	303,199	—	21.50

KM# 155 Subject: 1988 Calgary Olympics
Reverse: Figure skater **Weight:** 34.1070 g.
Composition: 0.9250 Silver 1.0000 oz. ASW **Size:**
40 mm.

Date	Mintage	MS-63	Proof
1987 Proof	334,875	—	21.50

KM# 151 Subject: 1988 Calgary Olympics
Reverse: Free-style skier **Edge:** Lettered **Weight:**
33.6300 g. **Composition:** 0.9250 Silver 1.0000 oz.
ASW **Size:** 40 mm.

Date	Mintage	MS-63	Proof
1986 Proof	294,322	—	21.50
1986 Plain edge; Proof	Inc. above	—	175

KM# 156 Subject: 1988 Calgary Olympics
Reverse: Curling **Weight:** 34.1070 g.
Composition: 0.9250 Silver 1.0000 oz. ASW **Size:**
40 mm.

Date	Mintage	MS-63	Proof
1987 Proof	286,457	—	21.50

KM# 159   Subject: 1988 Calgary Olympics
Reverse: Ski jumper **Weight:** 34.1070 g.
Composition: 0.9250 Silver 1.0000 oz. ASW **Size:**
40 mm.

Date	Mintage	MS-63	Proof
1987 Proof	290,954	—	21.50

KM# 172   Subject: Aviation **Reverse:** Lancaster/
Fauquier **Weight:** 31.1030 g. **Composition:**
0.9250 Silver 0.9743 oz. ASW **Size:** 38 mm.

Date	Mintage	MS-63	Proof
1990 Proof	43,596	—	100

KM#160   Subject: 1988 Calgary Olympics **Reverse:**
Bobsled **Weight:** 34.1070 g. **Composition:** 0.9250
Silver 1.0000 oz. ASW **Size:** 40 mm.

Date	Mintage	MS-63	Proof
1987 Proof	274,326	—	21.50

KM# 173   Subject: Aviation **Reverse:** Anson and
Harvard **Weight:** 31.1030 g. **Composition:** 0.9250
Silver 0.9743 oz. ASW **Size:** 38 mm.

Date	Mintage	MS-63	Proof
1990 Proof	41,844	—	35.00

KM# 196   Subject: Aviation **Reverse:** Silver Dart
Weight: 31.1030 g. **Composition:** 0.9250 Silver
0.9743 oz. ASW **Size:** 38 mm.

Date	Mintage	MS-63	Proof
1991 Proof	28,791	—	30.00

KM# 224   Subject: Aviation **Reverse:** Curtiss JN-
4 Canick ("Jenny") **Weight:** 31.1030 g.
Composition: 0.9250 Silver 0.9743 oz. ASW **Size:**
38 mm.

Date	Mintage	MS-63	Proof
1992 Proof	33,105	—	30.00

KM# 197   Subject: Aviation **Reverse:** de Haviland
Beaver **Weight:** 31.1030 g. **Composition:** 0.9250
Silver 0.9742 oz. ASW **Size:** 38 mm.

Date	Mintage	MS-63	Proof
1991 Proof	29,399	—	30.00

KM# 225   Subject: Aviation **Reverse:** de Haviland
Gypsy Moth **Weight:** 31.1030 g. **Composition:**
0.9250 Silver 0.9743 oz. ASW **Size:** 38 mm.

Date	Mintage	MS-63	Proof
1992 Proof	32,537	—	30.00

KM# 236 Subject: Aviation **Reverse:** Fairchild
71C float plane **Weight:** 31.1030 g. **Composition:**
0.9250 Silver 0.0257 oz. ASW **Size:** 38 mm.

Date	Mintage	MS-63	Proof
1993 Proof	32,199	—	30.00

KM# 246 Subject: Aviation **Reverse:** Curtiss HS-
2L seaplane **Weight:** 31.1030 g. **Composition:**
0.9250 Silver 0.9743 oz. ASW **Size:** 38 mm.

Date	Mintage	MS-63	Proof
1994 Proof	31,242	—	30.00

KM# 237 Subject: Aviation **Reverse:** Lockheed
14 **Weight:** 31.1030 g. **Composition:** 0.9250 Silver
0.9743 oz. ASW **Size:** 38 mm.

Date	Mintage	MS-63	Proof
1993 Proof	32,550	—	30.00

KM# 247 Subject: Aviation **Reverse:** Vickers
Vedette **Weight:** 31.1030 g. **Composition:** 0.9250
Silver 0.9743 oz. ASW **Size:** 38 mm.

Date	Mintage	MS-63	Proof
1994 Proof	30,880	—	30.00

KM# 271 Subject: Aviation **Reverse:** C-FEA1
Fleet Cannuck **Weight:** 31.1030 g. **Composition:**
0.9250 Silver 0.9743 oz. ASW **Size:** 38 mm.

Date	Mintage	MS-63	Proof
1995 Proof	17,438	—	30.00

KM# 276 Subject: Aviation **Reverse:** CF-100
Cannuck **Weight:** 31.1030 g. **Composition:**
0.9250 Silver 0.9743 oz. ASW **Size:** 38 mm.

Date	Mintage	MS-63	Proof
1996 Proof	18,508	—	30.00

KM# 272 Subject: Aviation **Reverse:** DHC-1
Chipmunk **Weight:** 31.1030 g. **Composition:**
0.9250 Silver 0.9743 oz. ASW **Size:** 38 mm.

Date	Mintage	MS-63	Proof
1995 Proof	17,722	—	30.00

KM#277 Subject: Aviation **Obv. Legend:** CF-105
Arrow **Weight:** 31.1030 g. **Composition:** 0.9250
Silver 0.9743 oz. ASW **Size:** 38 mm.

Date	Mintage	MS-63	Proof
1996 Proof	27,163	—	50.00

KM# 297   Subject: Aviation **Reverse:** Canadair F-86 Sabre **Weight:** 31.1030 g. **Composition:** 0.9250 Silver 0.9743 oz. ASW **Size:** 38 mm.

Date	Mintage	MS-63	Proof
1997 Proof	14,389	—	30.00

KM# 329   Subject: Aviation **Reverse:** CP-107 Argus **Weight:** 31.1030 g. **Composition:** 0.9250 Silver 0.9743 oz. ASW **Size:** 38 mm.

Date	Mintage	MS-63	Proof
1998 Proof	50,000,000	—	37.50

KM# 298   Subject: Aviation **Reverse:** Canadair CT-114 Tutor **Weight:** 31.1030 g. **Composition:** 0.9250 Silver 0.9743 oz. ASW **Size:** 38 mm.

Date	Mintage	MS-63	Proof
1997 Proof	15,669	—	30.00

KM# 330   Subject: Aviation **Reverse:** CP-215 Waterbomber **Weight:** 31.1030 g. **Composition:** 0.9250 Silver 0.9743 oz. ASW **Size:** 38 mm.

Date	Mintage	MS-63	Proof
1998 Proof	50,000,000	—	37.50

KM# 339
Subject: Aviation **Reverse:** DHC-6 Twin Otter **Weight:** 31.1030 g. **Composition:** 0.9250 Silver 0.9743 oz. ASW **Size:** 38 mm.

Date	Mintage	MS-63	Proof
1999 Proof	50,000,000	—	37.50

KM#340
Subject: Aviation **Reverse:** DHC-8 Dash 8 **Weight:** 31.1030 g. **Composition:** 0.9250 Silver 0.9743 oz. ASW **Size:** 38 mm.

Date	Mintage	MS-63	Proof
1999 Proof	50,000,000	—	37.50

KM# 395
Subject: First Canadian locomotive **Reverse:** Locomotive below multicolored cameo **Composition:** 0.9250 Silver **Size:** 38 mm.

Date	Mintage	MS-63	Proof
2000 Proof	—	—	40.00

KM# 396
Subject: First Canadian self-propelled car **Reverse:** Car below multicolored cameo **Composition:** 0.9250 Silver **Size:** 38 mm.

Date	Mintage	MS-63	Proof
2000 Proof	—	—	40.00

KM# 397
Subject: Bluenose sailboat **Reverse:** Boat below multicolored cameo **Composition:** 0.9250 Silver **Size:** 38 mm.

Date	Mintage	MS-63	Proof
2000 Proof	—	—	125

KM# 411
Subject: First Canadian Steel Boiler Steam Locomotive **Obverse:** Queen's head right. **Reverse:** Locomotive and cameo hologram. **Edge:** Reeded and plain sections. **Weight:** 31.1035 g. **Composition:** 0.9250 Silver .9250 oz. ASW **Size:** 38 mm.

Date	Mintage	MS-63	Proof
2001 Proof	15,000	—	40.00

KM# 427
Subject: Transportation - The Marco Polo, **Obverse:** Queen's head right. **Reverse:** Sailship with hologram cameo. **Edge:** Reeded and plain sections. **Weight:** 31.1030 g. **Composition:** 0.9250 Silver .9250 oz. ASW **Size:** 38 mm.

Date	Mintage	MS-63	Proof
2001 Proof	15,000	—	40.00

KM# 428
Subject: Transportation - Russell Touring Car, **Obverse:** Queen's head right. **Reverse:** Russell touring car with hologram cameo. **Edge:** Reeded and plain sections. **Weight:** 31.1030 g. **Composition:** 0.9250 Silver .9250 oz. ASW **Size:** 38 mm.

Date	Mintage	MS-63	Proof
2001 Proof	15,000	—	40.00

KM# 464   Obverse: Queen's head right **Reverse:** Gray-Dort Model 25-SM with cameo hologram **Composition:** 0.9250 Silver

Date	Mintage	MS-63	Proof
2002 Proof	Est. 15,000	—	45.00

KM# 465   Subject: Sailing Ship William D. Lawrence **Composition:** 0.9250 Silver

Date	Mintage	MS-63	Proof
2002 Proof	15,000	—	45.00

KM# 484   Subject: Canadian National FA-1 diesel-electric locomotive **Composition:** Sterling Silver

Date	Mintage	MS-63	Proof
2003 Proof	15,000	—	45.00

KM# 485   Obverse: Queens head right **Reverse:** The Bricklin SV-1 **Composition:** Silver With Partial Gold Plating

Date	Mintage	MS-63	Proof
2003 Proof	Est. 15,000	—	45.00

KM# 482   Obverse: Queens head right **Reverse:** Niagara Falls - hologram **Composition:** 0.9999 Silver

Date	Mintage	MS-63	Proof
2003 Proof	Est. 30,000	—	45.00

KM#483   Subject: The HMCS Bras d'or (FHE-400) **Composition:** 0.9250 Silver

Date	Mintage	MS-63	Proof
2003 Proof	15,000	—	45.00

100 DOLLARS

KM# 115   Subject: 1976 Montreal Olympics **Obverse:** Beaded borders **Weight:** 13.3375 g. **Composition:** 0.5830 Gold 0.2500 oz. AGW **Size:** 27 mm.

Date	Mintage	MS-63	Proof
1976	650,000	85.00	—

KM# 116   Subject: 1976 Montreal Olympics **Obverse:** Plain borders **Weight:** 16.9655 g. **Composition:** 0.9170 Gold 0.5000 oz. AGW **Size:** 25 mm.

Date	Mintage	MS-63	Proof
1976 Proof	337,342	—	180

KM# 119   Subject: Queen's silver jubilee **Weight:** 16.9655 g. **Composition:** 0.9170 Gold 0.5000 oz. AGW

Date	Mintage	MS-63	Proof
ND(1977) Proof	180,396	—	195

KM# 122   Subject: Canadian unification **Weight:** 16.9655 g. **Composition:** 0.9170 Gold 0.5000 oz. AGW

Date	Mintage	MS-63	Proof
1978 Proof	200,000	—	180

KM# 126   Subject: International Year of the Child **Weight:** 16.9655 g. **Composition:** 0.9170 Gold 0.5000 oz. AGW

Date	Mintage	MS-63	Proof
1979 Proof	250,000	—	180

KM# 129   Subject: Arctic Territories **Weight:** 16.9655 g. **Composition:** 0.9170 Gold 0.5000 oz. AGW

Date	Mintage	MS-63	Proof
1980 Proof	300,000	—	190

KM# 131   Subject: National anthem **Weight:** 16.9655 g. **Composition:** 0.9170 Gold 0.5000 oz. AGW

Date	Mintage	MS-63	Proof
1981 Proof	102,000	—	180

KM# 137 Subject: New Constitution **Weight:**
16.9655 g. **Composition:** 0.9170 Gold 0.5000 oz.
AGW

Date	Mintage	MS-63	Proof
1982 Proof	121,708	—	180

KM# 152 Subject: Peace **Weight:** 16.9655 g.
Composition: 0.9170 Gold 0.5000 oz. AGW

Date	Mintage	MS-63	Proof
1986 Proof	76,409	—	180

KM#139 Subject: 400th Anniversary of St. John's,
Newfoundland **Weight:** 16.9655 g. **Composition:**
0.9170 Gold 0.5000 oz. AGW

Date	Mintage	MS-63	Proof
ND(1983) Proof	83,128	—	190

KM# 158 Subject: 1988 Calgary Olympics
Reverse: Torch and logo **Weight:** 13.3375 g.
Composition: 0.5830 Gold 0.2500 oz. AGW

Date	Mintage	MS-63	Proof
1987 lettered edge; Proof	142,750	—	90.00
1987 plain edge; Proof	Inc. above	—	350

KM# 142 Subject: Jacques Cartier **Weight:**
16.9655 g. **Composition:** 0.9170 Gold 0.5000 oz.
AGW

Date	Mintage	MS-63	Proof
ND(1984) Proof	67,662	—	185

KM# 162 Subject: Whales **Weight:** 13.3375 g.
Composition: 0.5830 Gold 0.2500 oz. AGW

Date	Mintage	MS-63	Proof
1988 Proof	52,594	—	95.00

KM# 144 Subject: National Parks **Reverse:** Big-
horn sheep **Weight:** 16.9655 g. **Composition:**
0.9170 Gold 0.5000 oz. AGW

Date	Mintage	MS-63	Proof
ND(1985) Proof	61,332	—	190

KM# 169 Subject: Sainte-Marie **Weight:**
13.3375 g. **Composition:** 0.5830 Gold 0.2500 oz.
AGW

Date	Mintage	MS-63	Proof
ND(1989) Proof	59,657	—	95.00

KM# 171 Subject: International Literacy Year
Weight: 13.3375 g. **Composition:** 0.5830 Gold
0.2500 oz. AGW

Date	Mintage	MS-63	Proof
1990 Proof	49,940	—	95.00

KM# 180 Subject: S.S. Empress of India **Weight:**
13.3375 g. **Composition:** 0.5830 Gold 0.2500 oz.
AGW

Date	Mintage	MS-63	Proof
1991 Proof	33,966	—	95.00

KM# 211 Subject: Montreal **Weight:** 13.3375 g.
Composition: 0.5830 Gold 0.2500 oz. AGW

Date	Mintage	MS-63	Proof
1992 Proof	28,162	—	95.00

KM# 245 Subject: Antique Automobiles **Weight:**
13.3375 g. **Composition:** 0.5830 Gold 0.2500 oz.
AGW

Date	Mintage	MS-63	Proof
1993 Proof	25,971	—	100

KM# 249 Subject: World War II Home Front
Weight: 13.3375 g. **Composition:** 0.5830 Gold
0.2500 oz. AGW

Date	Mintage	MS-63	Proof
1994 Proof	16,201	—	125

KM# 260 Subject: Louisbourg **Weight:**
13.3375 g. **Composition:** 0.5830 Gold 0.2500 oz.
AGW

Date	Mintage	MS-63	Proof
1995 Proof	16,916	—	125

KM# 273 Subject: Klondike Gold Rush Centennial
Weight: 13.3375 g. **Composition:** 0.5830 Gold
0.2500 oz. AGW

Date	Mintage	MS-63	Proof
ND(1996) Proof	17,973	—	135

KM# 287 Subject: Alexander Graham Bell
Weight: 13.3375 g. **Composition:** 0.5830 Gold
0.2500 oz. AGW

Date	Mintage	MS-63	Proof
1997 Proof	14,775	—	155

KM# 307 Subject: Discovery of Insulin **Weight:** 13.3375 g. **Composition:** 0.5830 Gold 0.2500 oz. AGW

Date	Mintage	MS-63	Proof
1998 Proof	11,220	—	155

KM# 341 Subject: 50th Anniversary Newfoundland Unity With Canada **Weight:** 13.3375 g. **Composition:** 0.5830 Gold 0.2500 oz. AGW

Date	Mintage	MS-63	Proof
1999 Proof	10,242	—	170

KM# 402 Subject: McClure's Arctic expedition **Obverse:** Queen's portrait **Reverse:** Six men pulling supply sled to an icebound ship **Edge:** Reeded **Weight:** 13.3375 g. **Composition:** 0.5830 Gold 0.2500 oz. AGW **Size:** 27 mm.

Date	Mintage	MS-63	Proof
2000 Proof	9,767	—	185

KM# 416 Subject: Library of Parliament **Obverse:** Queen's head right. **Reverse:** Statue in domed building. **Edge:** Reeded. **Weight:** 13.3375 g. **Composition:** 0.5830 Gold 0.2500 oz. AGW **Size:** 27 mm.

Date	Mintage	MS-63	Proof
2001 Proof	10,000	—	185

KM# 486 Subject: 100th Anniversary of the Discovery of Marquis Wheat **Composition:** Gold

Date	Mintage	MS-63	Proof
2003 Proof	10,000	—	215

150 DOLLARS

KM# 388 Subject: Year of the Dragon **Weight:** 13.6100 g. **Composition:** 0.7500 Gold .3282 oz. AGW

Date	Mintage	MS-63	Proof
2000 Proof	8,851	—	475

KM# 417 Subject: Year of the Snake **Obverse:** Queen's head right. **Reverse:** Multicolor snake hologram. **Edge:** Reeded. **Weight:** 13.6100 g. **Composition:** 0.7500 Gold .3282 oz. AGW **Size:** 28 mm.

Date	Mintage	MS-63	Proof
2001 Proof	6,888	—	265

KM# 487 Subject: Year of the Sheep **Composition:** Gold

Date	Mintage	MS-63	Proof
2003 Proof	6,888	—	300

175 DOLLARS

KM# 217 Subject: 1992 Olympics **Reverse:** Passing the torch **Weight:** 16.9700 g. **Composition:** 0.9170 Gold 0.5000 oz. AGW

Date	Mintage	MS-63	Proof
1992 Proof	22,092	—	210

200 DOLLARS

KM# 178 Subject: Canadian flag silver jubilee **Weight:** 17.1060 g. **Composition:** 0.9170 Gold 0.5042 oz. AGW **Size:** 29 mm.

Date	Mintage	MS-63	Proof
1990 Proof	20,980	—	185

KM# 202   Subject: Hockey **Weight:** 17.1060 g.
Composition: 0.9170 Gold 0.5042 oz. AGW **Size:**
29 mm.

Date	Mintage	MS-63	Proof
1991 Proof	10,215	—	200

KM# 265   Subject: Maple-syrup production
Weight: 17.1350 g. **Composition:** 0.9170 Gold
0.5500 oz. AGW **Size:** 29 mm.

Date	Mintage	MS-63	Proof
1995 Proof	6,579	—	225

KM# 230   Subject: Niagara Falls **Weight:**
17.1060 g. **Composition:** 0.9170 Gold 0.5042 oz.
AGW **Size:** 29 mm.

Date	Mintage	MS-63	Proof
1992 Proof	9,465	—	250

KM# 275   Subject: Transcontinental Canadian
Railway **Weight:** 17.1350 g. **Composition:** 0.9170
Gold 0.5500 oz. AGW **Size:** 29 mm.

Date	Mintage	MS-63	Proof
1996 Proof	8,047	—	265

KM# 244   Subject: Mounted police **Weight:**
17.1350 g. **Composition:** 0.9170 Gold 0.5500 oz.
AGW **Size:** 29 mm.

Date	Mintage	MS-63	Proof
1993 Proof	10,807	—	190

KM# 288   Subject: Haida mask **Weight:**
17.1350 g. **Composition:** 0.9170 Gold 0.5500 oz.
AGW **Size:** 29 mm.

Date	Mintage	MS-63	Proof
1997 Proof	11,610	—	300

KM# 250   Subject: Novel: Anne of Green Gables
Weight: 17.1350 g. **Composition:** 0.9170 Gold
0.5500 oz. AGW **Size:** 29 mm.

Date	Mintage	MS-63	Proof
1994 Proof	10,655	—	210

KM# 317   Subject: Legendary white buffalo
Weight: 17.1350 g. **Composition:** 0.9170 Gold
0.5500 oz. AGW **Size:** 29 mm.

Date	Mintage	MS-63	Proof
1998 Proof	7,149	—	275

350 DOLLARS

KM# 358 Subject: Mikmaq butterfly **Weight:** 17.1350 g. **Composition:** 0.9170 Gold 0.5500 oz. AGW **Size:** 29 mm.

Date	Mintage	MS-63	Proof
1999 Proof	6,510	—	280

KM# 403 Subject: Motherhood **Reverse:** Inuit mother with infant **Edge:** Reeded **Weight:** 17.1350 g. **Composition:** 0.9170 Gold 0.5500 oz. AGW **Size:** 29 mm.

Date	Mintage	MS-63	Proof
2000 Proof	6,284	—	280

KM# 418 Subject: Cornelius David Krieghoff **Obverse:** Queen's head right. **Reverse:** Farm homestead circa 1856. **Edge:** Reeded. **Weight:** 17.1350 g. **Composition:** 0.9170 Gold 0.5500 oz. AGW **Size:** 29 mm.

Date	Mintage	MS-63	Proof
2001 Proof	10,000	—	275

KM# 466 Subject: The Jack Pine (1916-1917) **Composition:** Gold

Date	Mintage	MS-63	Proof
2002 Proof	10,000	—	315

KM# 488 Subject: Houses (1929) **Composition:** Gold

Date	Mintage	MS-63	Proof
2003 Proof	10,000	—	315

KM# 308 Subject: Flowers of Canada's Coat of Arms **Weight:** 38.0500 g. **Composition:** 0.9999 Gold 1.2233 oz. AGW

Date	Mintage	MS-63	Proof
1998 Proof	664	—	800

KM# 370 Subject: Lady's slipper **Weight:** 38.0500 g. **Composition:** 0.9999 Gold 1.2233 oz. AGW

Date	Mintage	MS-63	Proof
1999 Proof	1,990	—	665

KM# 404 Subject: Pacific Dogwood **Obverse:** Queen's portrait **Reverse:** Three flowers **Edge:** Reeded **Weight:** 38.0500 g. **Composition:** 0.9999 Gold 1.2233 oz. AGW **Size:** 34 mm.

Date	Mintage	MS-63	Proof
2000 Proof	1,506	—	665

KM# 433 Subject: The Mayflower Flower **Obverse:** Queen's head right. **Reverse:** Two flowers. **Edge:** Reeded. **Weight:** 38.0500 g. **Composition:** 0.9999 Gold 1.2233 oz. AGW **Size:** 34 mm.

Date	Mintage	MS-63	Proof
2001 Proof	—	—	676

SILVER BULLION COINAGE

5 DOLLARS

KM# 163 Obv. Designer: Machin **Obverse:**
Elizabeth II effigy **Reverse:** Maple leaf **Weight:**
31.1000 g. **Comp.:** 0.9999 Silver 1.0000 oz. ASW

Date	Mintage	MS-63	Proof
1988	1,155,931	8.00	—
1989	3,288,235	7.25	—
1989 Proof	43,965	—	28.50

KM# 187 Obv. Designer: de Pedery-Hunt
Obverse: New Elizabeth II effigy **Reverse:** Maple
leaf **Weight:** 31.1000 g. **Composition:** 0.9999
Silver 1.0000 oz. ASW

Date	Mintage	MS-63	Proof
1990	1,708,800	8.00	—
1991	644,300	10.00	—
1992	343,800	9.50	—
1993	889,946	7.50	—
1994	1,133,900	7.75	—
1995	326,244	8.50	—
1996	250,445	30.00	—
1997	100,970	12.00	—
1998 Tiger privy mark	25,000	13.50	—
1998 Proof; 20 Years ANS privy mark	—	—	35.00
1998 Titanic privy mark	26,000	100.00	—
1998 R.C.M.P. privy mark	25,000	15.00	—

Date	Mintage	MS-63	Proof
1998 90th Anniversary R.C.M. privy mark	13,025	16.50	—
1998	—	—	—
1999 Rabbit privy mark	25,000	13.50	—
1999 "Y2K" privy mark	9,999	18.00	—
2000 Expo Hanover privy mark	—	18.50	—
2000 Dragon privy mark	25,000	14.50	—
2001 Snake privy mark	25,000	13.50	—

KM# 363 Reverse: Maple leaf with fireworks privy
mark **Weight:** 31.1000 g. **Composition:** 0.9999
Silver 1 oz. ASW

Date	Mintage	MS-63	Proof
1999/2000	298,775	9.50	—

KM# 436 Subject: Maple Leaves **Obverse:**
Queen's portrait. **Reverse:** Three maple leaves in
multicolor. **Edge:** Reeded. **Weight:** 31.1035 g.
Composition: 0.9999 Silver 0.9999 oz. ASW **Size:**
38 mm.

Date	Mintage	MS-63	Proof
2001	50,000	22.50	—

KM# 437 Subject: Multicolor Holographic Maple
Leaf **Obverse:** Queen's portrait. **Reverse:** Radiant
maple leaf hologram ith date privy mark. **Edge:**
Reeded. **Weight:** 31.1035 g. **Composition:** 0.9999
Silver 0.9999 oz. ASW **Size:** 38 mm.

Date	Mintage	MS-63	Proof
2001	30,000	25.50	—

50 DOLLARS

KM# 326 Subject: 10th Anniversary Silver Maple Leaf **Weight:** 311.0350 g. **Composition:** 0.9999 Silver 10.0000 oz. ASW

Date	Mintage	MS-63	Proof
1998 Proof	25,000	—	125

GOLD BULLION COINAGE

DOLLAR

KM# 238 Weight: 1.5551 g. **Composition:** 0.9999 Gold 0.05 oz. AGW

Date	Mintage	MS-63	Proof
1993	37,080	BV+37%	—
1994	78,860	BV+37%	—
1995	85,920	BV+37%	—
1996	56,520	BV+37%	—
1997	59,720	BV+37%	—
1998	44,260	BV+37%	—
1999 Maple leaf with oval "20 Years ANS" privy mark	—	BV+46%	—
2000 Maple leaf with oval "2000" privy mark	—	—	—

KM# 365 Reverse: Maple leaf hologram **Weight:** 1.5551 g. **Composition:** 0.9999 Gold 0.05 oz. AGW

Date	Mintage	MS-63	Proof
1999	—	—	—

2 DOLLARS

KM# 256 Reverse: Maple leaf **Weight:** 2.0735 g. **Composition:** 0.9999 Gold 0.0666 oz. AGW

Date	Mintage	MS-63	Proof
1994	5,493	55.00	—

5 DOLLARS

KM# 135 Obv. Designer: Machin **Obverse:** Elizabeth II effigy **Reverse:** Maple leaf **Weight:** 3.1200 g. **Composition:** 0.9999 Gold .1000 oz. AGW

Date	Mintage	MS-63	Proof
1982	246,000	BV+14%	—
1983	304,000	BV+14%	—
1984	262,000	BV+14%	—
1985	398,000	BV+14%	—
1986	529,516	BV+14%	—
1987	459,000	BV+14%	—
1988	506,500	BV+14%	—
1989	539,000	BV+14%	—
1989 Proof	16,992	—	50.00

KM# 188 Obv. Designer: dePedery-Hunt **Obverse:** Elizabeth II effigy **Reverse:** Maple leaf **Weight:** 3.1200 g. **Composition:** 0.9999 Gold 0.1000 oz. AGW

Date	Mintage	MS-63	Proof
1990	476,000	BV+14%	—
1991	322,000	BV+14%	—
1992	384,000	BV+14%	—
1993	248,630	BV+14%	—
1994	313,150	BV+14%	—
1995	294,890	BV+14%	—
1996	179,220	BV+14%	—
1997	188,540	BV+14%	—
1998	301,940	BV+14%	—
1999 Maple leaf with oval "20 Years ANS" privy mark	—	BV+19%	—
2000	—	BV+19%	—

KM# 366 Reverse: Maple leaf hologram **Weight:** 3.1200 g. **Composition:** 0.9999 Gold 0.1000 oz. AGW

Date	Mintage	MS-63	Proof
1999	—	—	—

KM# 439 Subject: Holographic Maple Leaves **Obverse:** Queen's portrait. **Reverse:** Three maple leaves multicolor hologram. **Edge:** Reeded. **Weight:** 3.1310 g. **Composition:** 0.9999 Gold 0.1007 oz. AGW **Size:** 16 mm.

Date	Mintage	MS-63	Proof
2001 in sets only	600	—	—

10 DOLLARS

KM# 136   Obv. Designer: Machin **Obverse:** Elizabeth II effigy **Reverse:** Maple leaf **Weight:** 7.7850 g. **Composition:** 0.9999 Gold 0.2500 oz. AGW

Date	Mintage	MS-63	Proof
1982	184,000	BV+10%	—
1983	308,800	BV+10%	—
1984	242,400	BV+10%	—
1985	620,000	BV+10%	—
1986	915,200	BV+10%	—
1987	376,000	BV+10%	—
1988	436,000	BV+10%	—
1989	328,800	BV+10%	—
1989 Proof	6,998	—	125

KM# 189   Obv. Designer: dePedery-Hunt **Obverse:** Elizabeth II effigy **Reverse:** Maple leaf **Weight:** 7.7850 g. **Composition:** 0.9999 Gold 0.2500 oz. AGW

Date	Mintage	MS-63	Proof
1990	253,600	BV+10%	—
1991	166,400	BV+10%	—
1992	179,600	BV+10%	—
1993	158,452	BV+10%	—
1994	148,792	BV+10%	—
1995	127,596	BV+10%	—
1996	89,148	BV+10%	—
1997	98,104	BV+10%	—
1998	85,472	BV+10%	—
1999 Maple leaf with oval "20 Years ANS" privy mark	—	BV+15%	—
2000 Maple leaf with oval "2000" privy mark	—	BV+15%	—

KM# 367   Reverse: Maple leaf hologram **Weight:** 7.7850 g. **Composition:** 0.9999 Gold 0.2500 oz. AGW

Date	Mintage	MS-63	Proof
1999	—	—	—

KM# 440   Subject: Holographic Maples Leaves **Obverse:** Queen's portrait. **Reverse:** Three maple leaves multicolor hologram. **Edge:** Reeded. **Weight:** 7.7970 g. **Composition:** 0.9999 Gold 0.2507 oz. AGW **Size:** 20 mm.

Date	Mintage	MS-63	Proof
2001	15,000	196	—

20 DOLLARS

KM# 153   Obv. Designer: Machin **Obverse:** Elizabeth II effigy **Weight:** 15.5515 g. **Composition:** 0.9999 Gold 0.5000 oz. AGW **Size:** 32 mm.

Date	Mintage	MS-63	Proof
1986	529,200	BV+7%	—
1987	332,800	BV+7%	—
1988	538,400	BV+7%	—
1989	259,200	BV+7%	—
1989 Proof	6,998	—	225

KM# 190   Obv. Designer: dePedery-Hunt **Obverse:** Elizabeth II effigy **Reverse:** Maple leaf **Weight:** 15.5515 g. **Composition:** 0.9999 Gold 0.5000 oz. AGW

Date	Mintage	MS-63	Proof
1990	174,400	BV+7%	—
1991	96,200	BV+7%	—
1992	108,000	BV+7%	—
1993	99,492	BV+7%	—
1994	104,766	BV+7%	—
1995	103,162	BV+7%	—
1996	66,246	BV+7%	—
1997	63,354	BV+7%	—
1998	65,366	BV+7%	—
1999 Maple leaf with oval "20 Years ANS" privy mark	—	BV+12%	—
2000	—	BV+12%	—

KM# 368   Reverse: Maple leaf hologram **Weight:** 15.5515 g. **Composition:** 0.9999 Gold 0.5000 oz. AGW

Date	Mintage	MS-63	Proof
1999	—	—	—

KM# 441   Subject: Holographic Maples Leaves **Obverse:** Queen's portrait. **Reverse:** Three maple leaves multicolor hologram. **Edge:** Reeded. **Weight:** 15.5840 g. **Composition:** 0.9999 Gold 0.501 oz. AGW **Size:** 25 mm.

Date	Mintage	MS-63	Proof
2001 in set only	600	465	—

50 DOLLARS

KM# 125.1 Reverse: Maple leaf flanked by .9999
Weight: 31.1030 g. **Composition:** 0.9990 Gold
1.0000 oz. AGW

Date	Mintage	MS-63	Proof
1979	1,000,000	BV+4%	—
1980	1,251,500	BV+4%	—
1981	863,000	BV+4%	—
1982	883,000	BV+4%	—

KM# 125.2 Reverse: Maple leaf flanked by .9999
Weight: 31.1030 g. **Composition:** 0.9999 Gold
1.0000 oz. AGW

Date	Mintage	MS-63	Proof
1983	843,000	BV+4%	—
1984	1,067,500	BV+4%	—
1985	1,908,000	BV+4%	—
1986	779,115	BV+4%	—
1987	978,000	BV+4%	—
1988	826,500	BV+4%	—
1989	856,000	BV+4%	—
1989 Proof	17,781	—	375

KM# 191 Obv. Designer: dePedery-Hunt
Obverse: Elizabeth II effigy **Reverse:** Maple leaf
flanked by .9999 **Weight:** 31.1030 g. **Composition:**
0.9999 Gold 1.000 oz. AGW

Date	Mintage	MS-63	Proof
1990	815,000	BV+4%	—
1991	290,000	BV+4%	—

Date	Mintage	MS-63	Proof
1992	368,900	BV+4%	—
1993	321,413	BV+4%	—
1994	180,357	BV+4%	—
1995	208,729	BV+4%	—
1996	143,682	BV+4%	—
1997	478,211	BV+4%	—
1998	593,704	BV+4%	—
1999 Maple leaf with oval "20 Years ANS" privy mark	—	BV+7%	—
2000 Maple leaf with oval	—	BV+7%	—

KM# 305 Reverse: Mountie **Weight:** 31.1030 g.
Composition: 0.9999 Gold 1 oz. AGW

Date	Mintage	MS-63	Proof
1997	12,913	350	—

KM# 369 Reverse: Maple leaf hologram **Weight:**
31.1030 g. **Composition:** 0.9999 Gold 1.0000 oz.
AGW

Date	Mintage	MS-63	Proof
1999	—	—	—

KM# 364 Reverse: Maple leaf with fireworks privy
mark **Weight:** 31.1030 g. **Composition:** 0.9999
Gold 1.0000 oz. AGW

Date	Mintage	MS-63	Proof
1999/2000	—	—	—

KM# 442 Subject: Holographic Maples Leaves
Obverse: Queen's portrait. **Reverse:** Three maple
leaves multicolor hologram. **Edge:** Reeded.
Weight: 31.1500 g. **Composition:** 0.9999 Gold
1.0014 oz. AGW **Size:** 30 mm.

Date	Mintage	MS-63	Proof
2001 in set only	600	1,163	

PLATINUM BULLION COINAGE

DOLLAR

KM# 239   Reverse: Maple leaf **Weight:** 1.5552 g.
Composition: 0.9995 Platinum 0.0500 oz. APW

Date	Mintage	MS-63	Proof
1993	2,120	BV+35%	—
1994	4,260	BV+35%	—
1995	460	100.00+35%	—
1996	1,640	BV+35%	—
1997	1,340	BV+35%	—
1998	2,000	BV+35%	—
1999	2,000	BV+35%	—

2 DOLLARS

KM# 257   Reverse: Maple leaf **Weight:** 2.0735 g.
Composition: 0.9995 Platinum 0.0666 oz. APW

Date	Mintage	MS-63	Proof
1994	1,470	250	—

5 DOLLARS

KM# 164   Obv. Designer: Machin **Obverse:**
Elizabeth II effigy **Weight:** 3.1203 g. **Composition:**
0.9995 Platinum 0.1000 oz. APW

Date	Mintage	MS-63	Proof
1988	74,000	BV+18%	—
1989	18,000	BV+18%	—
1989 Proof	11,999	—	75.00

KM# 192   Obv. Designer: dePedery-Hunt
Obverse: Elizabeth II effigy **Weight:** 3.1203 g.
Composition: 0.9995 Platinum 0.1000 oz. APW

Date	Mintage	MS-63	Proof
1990	9,000	BV+18%	—
1991	13,000	BV+18%	—
1992	16,000	BV+18%	—
1993	14,020	BV+18%	—
1994	19,190	BV+18%	—
1995	8,940	BV+18%	—
1996	8,820	BV+18%	—
1997	7,050	BV+18%	—
1998	5,710	BV+18%	—
1999	2,000	BV+18%	—

10 DOLLARS

KM# 165   Obv. Designer: Machin **Obverse:**
Elizabeth II effigy **Reverse:** Maple leaf **Weight:**
7.7857 g. **Composition:** 0.9995 Platinum
0.2500 oz. APW

Date	Mintage	MS-63	Proof
1988	93,600	BV+13%	—
1989	3,200	BV+13%	—
1989 Proof	1,999	—	175

KM# 193   Obv. Designer: dePedery-Hunt
Obverse: Elizabeth II effigy **Reverse:** Maple leaf
Weight: 7.7857 g. **Composition:** 0.9995 Platinum
0.2500 oz. APW

Date	Mintage	MS-63	Proof
1990	1,600	BV+13%	—
1991	7,200	BV+13%	—
1992	11,600	BV+13%	—
1993	8,048	BV+13%	—
1994	9,456	BV+13%	—
1995	6,524	BV+13%	—
1996	6,160	BV+13%	—
1997	4,552	BV+13%	—
1998	3,816	BV+13%	—
1999	2,000	BV+13%	—

20 DOLLARS

KM# 166   Obv. Designer: Machin **Obverse:**
Elizabeth II effigy **Reverse:** Maple leaf **Weight:**
15.5519 g. **Composition:** 0.9995 Platinum
0.5000 oz. APW

Date	Mintage	MS-63	Proof
1988	23,600	BV+9%	—
1989	4,800	BV+9%	—
1989 Proof	1,999	—	400

KM# 194   Obv. Designer: dePedery-Hunt
Obverse: Elizabeth II effigy **Reverse:** Maple leaf
Weight: 15.5519 g. **Composition:** 0.9995
Platinum 0.5000 oz. APW

Date	Mintage	MS-63	Proof
1990	2,600	BV+9%	—
1991	5,600	BV+9%	—
1992	12,800	BV+9%	—
1993	6,022	BV+9%	—
1994	6,710	BV+9%	—
1995	6,308	BV+9%	—
1996	5,490	BV+9%	—
1997	3,990	BV+9%	—
1998	5,486	BV+9%	—
1999	500	BV+15%	—

30 DOLLARS

KM# 174 Reverse: Polar bear swimming **Weight:** 3.1100 g. **Composition:** 0.9990 Platinum 0.1000 oz. APW

Date	Mintage	MS-63	Proof
1990 Proof	2,629	—	85.00

KM# 198 Reverse: Snowy owl **Weight:** 3.1100 g. **Composition:** 0.9990 Platinum 0.1000 oz. APW

Date	Mintage	MS-63	Proof
1991 Proof	3,500	—	85.00

KM# 226 Reverse: Cougar head and shoulders **Weight:** 3.1100 g. **Composition:** 0.9990 Platinum 0.1000 oz. APW

Date	Mintage	MS-63	Proof
1992 Proof	3,500	—	85.00

KM# 240 Reverse: Arctic fox **Weight:** 3.1100 g. **Composition:** 0.9990 Platinum 0.1000 oz. APW

Date	Mintage	MS-63	Proof
1993 Proof	3,500	—	100

KM# 252 Reverse: Sea otter **Weight:** 3.1100 g. **Composition:** 0.9990 Platinum 0.1000 oz. APW **Note:** 1,500 sets only.

Date	Mintage	MS-63	Proof
1994 Proof	1,500	—	110

KM# 266 Reverse: Canadian lynx **Weight:** 3.1100 g. **Composition:** 0.9990 Platinum 0.1000 oz. APW

Date	Mintage	MS-63	Proof
1995 Proof	620	—	100

KM# 278 Reverse: Falcon portrait **Weight:** 3.1100 g. **Composition:** 0.9990 Platinum 0.1000 oz. APW

Date	Mintage	MS-63	Proof
1996 Proof	489		100

KM# 300 Reverse: Bison head **Weight:** 3.1320 g. **Composition:** 0.9995 Platinum 0.1006 oz. APW

Date	Mintage	MS-63	Proof
1997 Proof	5,000	—	100

KM# 322 Reverse: Grey wolf **Weight:** 3.1100 g. **Composition:** 0.9990 Platinum 0.1 oz. APW

Date	Mintage	MS-63	Proof
ND(1998) Proof	2,000	—	100

KM# 359 Reverse: Musk ox **Weight:** 3.1320 g. **Composition:** 0.9995 Platinum 0.1006 oz. APW

Date	Mintage	MS-63	Proof
1999 Proof	1,500	—	100

KM# 405 Obverse: Queen's portrait **Reverse:** Pronghorn antelope head **Edge:** Reeded **Weight:** 3.1320 g. **Composition:** 0.9995 Platinum .1006 oz. APW **Size:** 16 mm.

Date	Mintage	MS-63	Proof
2000 Proof	600	—	100

KM# 429 Subject: Platinum Collector Bullion **Obverse:** Queen's head right. **Reverse:** Harlequin duck's head. **Edge:** Reeded. **Weight:** 3.1320 g. **Composition:** 0.9995 Platinum .1006 oz. APW **Size:** 16 mm.

Date	Mintage	MS-63	Proof
2001 Proof	—	—	100

50 DOLLARS

KM# 167   Obv. Designer: Machin **Obverse:** Elizabeth II effigy **Reverse:** Maple leaf **Weight:** 31.1030 g. **Composition:** 0.9995 Platinum 1.0000 oz. APW

Date	Mintage	MS-63	Proof
1988	37,500	BV+4%	—
1989	10,000	BV+4%	—
1989 Proof	5,965	—	BV

KM# 195   Obv. Designer: dePedery-Hunt **Obverse:** Elizabeth II effigy **Reverse:** Maple leaf **Weight:** 31.1030 g. **Composition:** 0.9995 Platinum 1.0000 oz. APW

Date	Mintage	MS-63	Proof
1990	15,100	BV+4%	—
1991	31,900	BV+4%	—
1992	40,500	BV+4%	—
1993	17,666	BV+4%	—
1994	36,245	BV+4%	—
1995	25,829	BV+4%	—
1996	62,273	BV+4%	—
1997	25,480	BV+4%	—
1998	10,403	BV+4%	—
1999	1,300	BV+10%	—

75 DOLLARS

KM# 175   Reverse: Polar bear resting **Weight:** 7.7760 g. **Composition:** 0.9990 Platinum 0.2500 oz. APW

Date	Mintage	MS-63	Proof
1990 Proof	2,629	—	200

KM# 199   Reverse: Snowy owls perched on branch **Weight:** 7.7760 g. **Composition:** 0.9990 Platinum 0.2500 oz. APW

Date	Mintage	MS-63	Proof
1991 Proof	3,500	—	200

KM# 227   Reverse: Cougar prowling **Weight:** 7.7760 g. **Composition:** 0.9990 Platinum 0.2500 oz. APW

Date	Mintage	MS-63	Proof
1992 Proof	3,500	—	225

KM# 241   Reverse: Two Arctic foxes **Weight:** 7.7760 g. **Composition:** 0.9990 Platinum 0.2500 oz. APW

Date	Mintage	MS-63	Proof
1993 Proof	3,500	—	225

KM# 253   Reverse: Sea otter eating urchin **Weight:** 7.7760 g. **Composition:** 0.9990 Platinum 0.2500 oz. APW

Date	Mintage	MS-63	Proof
1994 Proof	1,500	—	250

KM# 267   Reverse: Two lynx kittens **Weight:** 7.7760 g. **Composition:** 0.9990 Platinum 0.2500 oz. APW

Date	Mintage	MS-63	Proof
1995 Proof	1,500	—	225

KM# 279   Reverse: Peregrine falcon, diving falcon **Weight:** 7.7760 g. **Composition:** 0.9990 Platinum 0.2500 oz. APW

Date	Mintage	MS-63	Proof
1996 Proof	1,500	—	225

KM# 301   Reverse: Two bison calves **Weight:** 7.7760 g. **Composition:** 0.9990 Platinum 0.2500 oz. APW

Date	Mintage	MS-63	Proof
1997 Proof	1,500	—	225

KM# 323   Reverse: Gray wolf **Weight:** 7.7760 g. **Composition:** 0.9990 Platinum 0.2500 oz. APW

Date	Mintage	MS-63	Proof
1998 Proof	1,000	—	225

KM# 360   Reverse: Musk ox **Weight:** 7.7760 g. **Composition:** 0.9990 Platinum 0.2500 oz. APW

Date	Mintage	MS-63	Proof
1999 Proof	500	—	250

KM# 406 **Obverse:** Queen's portrait **Reverse:**
Standing pronghorn antelope **Edge:** Reeded
Weight: 7.7760 g. **Composition:** 0.9990 Platinum
.25 oz. APW **Size:** 20 mm.

Date	Mintage	MS-63	Proof
2000 Proof	600	—	250

KM# 430 **Subject:** Platinum Collector Bullion
Obverse: Queen's head right. **Reverse:** Harlequin
duck in flight. **Edge:** Reeded. **Weight:** 7.8000 g.
Composition: 0.9995 Platinum .2506 oz. APW
Size: 20 mm.

Date	Mintage	MS-63	Proof
2001 Proof	—	—	250

150 DOLLARS

KM# 176 **Reverse:** Polar bear walking **Weight:**
15.5520 g. **Composition:** 0.9990 Platinum
0.5000 oz. APW

Date	Mintage	MS-63	Proof
1990 Proof	2,629	—	400

KM# 200 **Reverse:** Snowy owl flying **Weight:**
15.5520 g. **Composition:** 0.9990 Platinum
0.5000 oz. APW

Date	Mintage	MS-63	Proof
1991 Proof	3,500	—	400

KM# 228 **Reverse:** Cougar mother and cub
Weight: 15.5520 g. **Composition:** 0.9990
Platinum 0.5000 oz. APW

Date	Mintage	MS-63	Proof
1992 Proof	3,500	—	425

KM# 242 **Reverse:** Arctic fox by lake **Weight:**
15.5520 g. **Composition:** 0.9990 Platinum
0.5000 oz. APW

Date	Mintage	MS-63	Proof
1993 Proof	3,500	—	425

KM# 254 **Reverse:** Sea otter mother carrying pup
Weight: 15.5520 g. **Composition:** 0.9990
Platinum 0.5000 oz. APW

Date	Mintage	MS-63	Proof
1994 Proof	—	—	450

KM# 268 **Reverse:** Prowling lynx **Weight:**
15.5520 g. **Composition:** 0.9990 Platinum
0.5000 oz. APW

Date	Mintage	MS-63	Proof
1995 Proof	226	—	425

KM# 280 **Reverse:** Peregrine falcon - falcon on
branch **Weight:** 15.5520 g. **Composition:** 0.9990
Platinum 0.5000 oz. APW

Date	Mintage	MS-63	Proof
1996 Proof	100	—	425

KM# 302 **Reverse:** Bison bull **Weight:** 15.5520 g.
Composition: 0.9990 Platinum 0.5000 oz. APW

Date	Mintage	MS-63	Proof
1997 Proof	4,000	—	425

KM# 324 Reverse: Two gray wolf cubs **Weight:** 15.5520 g. **Composition:** 0.9990 Platinum 0.5000 oz. APW

Date	Mintage	MS-63	Proof
1998 Proof	2,000	—	425

KM# 361 Reverse: Musk ox **Weight:** 15.5520 g. **Composition:** 0.9990 Platinum 0.5000 oz. APW

Date	Mintage	MS-63	Proof
1999 Proof	500	—	450

KM# 407 Obverse: Queen's portrait **Reverse:** Two pronghorn antelope **Edge:** Reeded **Weight:** 15.5520 g. **Composition:** 0.9990 Platinum .5 oz. APW **Size:** 25 mm.

Date	Mintage	MS-63	Proof
2000 Proof	600	—	450

KM# 431 Subject: Platinum Collector Bullion **Obverse:** Queen's head right. **Reverse:** Two harlequin ducks. **Edge:** Reeded. **Weight:** 15.5900 g. **Composition:** 0.9995 Platinum .5010 oz. APW **Size:** 25 mm.

Date	Mintage	MS-63	Proof
2001 Proof	—	—	450

300 DOLLARS

KM# 177 Reverse: Polar bear mother and cub **Weight:** 31.1035 g. **Composition:** 0.9990 Platinum 1.0000 oz. APW

Date	Mintage	MS-63	Proof
1990 Proof	2,629	—	800

KM#201 Reverse: Snowy owl with chicks **Weight:** 31.1035 g. **Composition:** 0.9990 Platinum 1.0000 oz. APW

Date	Mintage	MS-63	Proof
1991 Proof	3,500	—	800

KM#229 Reverse: Cougar resting in tree **Weight:** 31.1035 g. **Composition:** 0.9990 Platinum 1.0000 oz. APW

Date	Mintage	MS-63	Proof
1992 Proof	3,500	—	800

KM# 243 Reverse: Mother fox and three kits **Weight:** 31.1035 g. **Composition:** 0.9990 Platinum 1.0000 oz. APW

Date	Mintage	MS-63	Proof
1993 Proof	3,500	—	800

KM# 255 Reverse: Two otters swimming **Weight:** 31.1035 g. **Composition:** 0.9990 Platinum 1.0000 oz. APW

Date	Mintage	MS-63	Proof
1994 Proof	—	—	900

KM# 269 Reverse: Female lynx and three kittens **Weight:** 31.1035 g. **Composition:** 0.9990 Platinum 1.0000 oz. APW

Date	Mintage	MS-63	Proof
1995 Proof	1,500	—	800

KM# 281 Reverse: Peregrine falcon feeding nestlings **Weight:** 31.1035 g. **Composition:** 0.9990 Platinum 1.0000 oz. APW

Date	Mintage	MS-63	Proof
1996 Proof	1,500	—	800

KM# 303 Reverse: Bison family **Weight:** 31.1035 g. **Composition:** 0.9990 Platinum 1.0000 oz. APW

Date	Mintage	MS-63	Proof
1997 Proof	1,500	—	800

KM# 325 Reverse: Gray wolf and two cubs **Weight:** 31.1035 g. **Composition:** 0.9990 Platinum 1.0000 oz. APW

Date	Mintage	MS-63	Proof
1998 Proof	—	—	850

KM# 362 Reverse: Musk ox **Weight:** 31.1035 g. **Composition:** 0.9990 Platinum 1.0000 oz. APW

Date	Mintage	MS-63	Proof
1999 Proof	500	—	900

KM# 408 Obverse: Queen's portrait **Reverse:** Four pronghorn antelope **Edge:** Reeded **Weight:** 31.1035 g. **Composition:** 0.9990 Platinum 1.0000 oz. APW **Size:** 30 mm.

Date	Mintage	MS-63	Proof
2000 Proof	600	—	900

KM# 432 Subject: Platinum Collector Bullion **Obverse:** Queen's head right. **Reverse:** Two standing harlequin ducks. **Edge:** Reeded. **Weight:** 31.1600 g. **Composition:** 0.9995 Platinum 1.0013 oz. APW **Size:** 30 mm.

Date	Mintage	MS-63	Proof
2001 Proof	—	—	900

SETS

CUSTOM PROOF-LIKE SETS (CPL)

KM#	Date	Mintage	Identification	Issue Price	Mkt. Value
CPL1	1971 (7)	33,517	KM59.1 (2 pcs.), 60.1, 62b-75.1, 77.1 ,79	6.50	5.00
CPL2	1971 (7)	38,198	KM59.1 (2 pcs.), 60.1, 62b, 75.1-77.1	6.50	5.00
CPL3	1973 (7)	35,676	KM59.1 (2 pcs.), 60.1, 75.1, 77.1, 81.1 obv. 120 beads, 82	6.50	5.00
CPL4	1973 (7)	Inc. above	KM59.1 (2 pcs.), 60.1, 75.1, 77.1, 81.1 obv. 132 beads, 82	6.50	140
CPL5	1974 (7)	44,296	KM59.1 (2 pcs.), 60.1, 62b-75.1, 88	8.00	5.00
CPL6	1975 (7)	36,851	KM59.1 (2 pcs.), 60.1, 62b-75.1, 76.2, 77.1	8.00	5.00
CPL7	1976 (7)	28,162	KM59.1 (2 pcs.), 60.1, 62b-75.1, 76.2, 77.1	8.00	5.50
CPL8	1977 (7)	44,198	KM59.1 (2 pcs.), 60.1, 62b-75.2, 77.1, 117	8.15	5.50
CPL9	1978 (7)	41,000	KM59.1 (2 pcs.), 60.1, 62b-75.3, 77.1, 120.1	—	5.50
CPL10	1979 (7)	31,174	KM59.2 (2 pcs.), 60.2, 74, 75.3, 77.2, 120.1	10.75	5.50
CPL11	1980 (7)	41,447	KM60.2, 74, 75.3, 77.2, 120.1, 127 (2 pcs.)	10.75	6.00

MINT SETS

KM#	Date	Mintage	Identification	Issue Price	Mkt. Value
MS1	1973 (4)	Inc. above	KM84-85, 86.1, 87; Olympic Commemoratives, Series I	45.00	30.00
MS2	1974 (4)	Inc. above	KM89-90, 93-94; Olympic Commemoratives, Series II	48.00	30.00
MS3	1974 (4)	Inc. above	KM91-92, 95-96; Olympic Commemoratives, Series III	48.00	30.00
MS4	1975 (4)	Inc. above	KM98-99, 102-103; Olympic Commemoratives, Series IV	48.00	30.00
MS5	1975 (4)	Inc. above	KM100-101, 104-105; Olympic Commemoratives, Series V	60.00	30.00
MS6	1976 (4)	Inc. above	KM107-108, 111-112; Olympic Commemoratives, Series VI	60.00	30.00
MS7	1976 (4)	Inc. above	KM109-110, 113-114; Olympic Commemoratives, Series VII	60.00	30.00
MS8	2001 (5)	600	KM438-442	1,996	2,000
MS10	2002 (7)	—	KM#444-449, 467	17.00	16.00
MS11	2002 (7)	—	KM#444-449, 467	17.00	16.00
MS9	2002 (7)	135,000	Double-dated 1952-2002, KM#444-449, 467	11.75	11.00
MS12	2003 (7)	135,000	KM#289, 182-184, 290, 186, 270	12.00	12.00
MS13	2003 (7)	75,000	KM#490-496	13.25	14.00
MS14	2003 (7)	—	KM#289, 182-184, 290, 186, 270	17.75	16.00
MS15	2003 (7)	—	KM#289, 182-184, 290, 186, 270	17.75	16.00

OLYMPIC COMMEMORATIVES (OCP)

KM#	Date	Mintage	Identification	Issue Price	Mkt. Value
OCP1	1973 (4)	Inc. above	KM84-87, Series I	78.50	37.50
OCP2	1974 (4)	Inc. above	KM89-90, 93-94, Series II	88.50	37.50
OCP3	1974 (4)	Inc. above	KM91-92, 95-96, Series III	88.50	37.50
OCP4	1975 (4)	Inc. above	KM98-99, 102-103, Series IV	88.50	37.50
OCP5	1975 (4)	Inc. above	KM100-101, 104-105, Series V	88.50	37.50
OCP6	1976 (4)	Inc. above	KM107-108, 111-112, Series VI	88.50	38.50
OCP7	1976 (4)	Inc. above	KM109-110, 113-114, Series VII	88.50	38.50

PROOF SETS

KM#	Date	Mintage	Identification	Issue Price	Mkt. Value
PS1	1981 (7)	199,000	KM60.2, 74, 75.3, 77.2, 120.1, 127, 130	36.00	17.50
PS2	1982 (7)	180,908	KM60.2a, 74, 75.3, 77.2, 120.1, 132-133	36.00	11.00
PS3	1983 (7)	166,779	KM60.2a, 74, 75.3, 77.2, 120.1, 132, 138	36.00	12.50
PS4	1984 (7)	161,602	KM60.2a, 74, 75.3, 77.2, 120.1, 132, 140	30.00	13.50
PS5	1985 (7)	157,037	KM60.2a, 74, 75.3, 77.2, 120.1, 132, 143	30.00	14.00
PS6	1986 (7)	175,745	KM60.2a, 74, 75.3, 77.2, 120.1, 132, 149	30.00	14.00
PS7	1987 (7)	179,004	KM60.2a, 74, 75.3, 77.2, 120.1, 132, 154	34.00	14.00
PS8	1988 (7)	175,259	KM60.2a, 74, 75.3, 77.2, 132, 157, 161	37.50	22.50
PS10	1989 (4)	6,823	KM125.2, 135-136, 153	1,190	800
PS11	1989 (4)	1,995	KM164-167	1,700	1,350
PS12	1989 (3)	2,550	KM125.2, 163, 167	1,530	1,200
PS13	1989 (3)	9,979	KM135, 163-164	165	155
PS9	1989 (7)	170,928	KM60.2a, 74, 75.3, 77.2, 132, 157, 168	40.00	22.50
PS14	1990 (7)	158,068	KM170, 181, 182, 183, 184, 185, 186	41.00	22.50
PS15	1990 (4)	2,629	KM174-177	1,720	1,250
PS16	1991 (7)	14,629	KM179, 181, 182, 183, 184, 185, 186	—	45.00
PS17	1991 (4)	873	KM198-201	1,760	1,250
PS18	1992 (13)	84,397	KM203a, 212a-214a, 218, 220a-223a, 231a-234a	—	60.00
PS19	1992 (7)	147,061	KM204-210	42.75	25.00
PS20	1992 (4)	3,500	KM226-229	1,680	1,250
PS21	1993 (7)	143,065	KM181, 182, 183, 184, 185, 186, 235	42.75	18.00
PS22	1993 (4)	3,500	KM240-243	1,329	1,250

KM#	Date	Mintage	Identification	Issue Price	Mkt. Value
PS23	1994 (7)	47,303	KM181-186, 248	47.50	28.00
PS24	1994 (7)	99,121	KM181, 182, 183, 184, 185, 186, 251	43.00	28.00
PS25	1994 (4)	1,500	KM252-255	915	1,450
PS26	1995 (7)	Inc. above	KM181, 182, 183, 184, 185, 186, 259	37.45	25.00
PS27	1995 (7)	50,000	KM181, 182, 183, 184, 185, 258-259	49.45	22.00
PS28	1995 (4)	Inc. above	KM261-264	42.00	60.00
PS29	1995 (4)	682	KM266-269	1,555	1,400
PS30	1995 (2)	Inc. above	KM261-262	22.00	21.00
PS31	1995 (2)	Inc. above	KM263-264	22.00	30.00
PS32	1996 (4)	423	KM278-281	1,555	1,400
PS33	1996 (7)	Inc. above	KM181a, 182a, 183a, 184a, 185a, 186, 274	49.00	35.00
PS34	1996 (4)	Inc. above	KM283-286	44.45	45.00
PS35	1997 (8)	Inc. above	KM182a, 183a, 184a, 209, 270c, 282, 289,	60.00	30.00
PS36	1997 (4)	Inc. above	KM292-295	44.45	35.00
PS37	1997 (4)	Inc. above	KM300-303	1,530	1,400
PS38	1998 (8)	Inc. above	KM182a, 183a, 184a, 186, 270b, 289, 290a, 306	59.45	50.00
PS39	1998 (5)	25,000	KM309-313	73.50	55.00
PS40	1998	61,000	KM316 w/China Y-727	72.50	30.00
PS41	1998 (4)	Inc. above	KM318-321	44.45	38.00
PS42	1998 (4)	1,000	KM322-325	1,552	1,400
PS43	1998 (5)	25,000	KM310-313, 332	73.50	30.00
PS44	1999 (8)	Inc. above	KM182a-184a, 186, 270c, 289, 290a,	59.45	60.00
PS45	1999 (4)	Inc. above	KM335-338	39.95	40.00
PS46	1999 (12)	Inc. above	KM342a-353a	99.45	75.00
PS47	1999 (4)	Inc. above	KM359-362	1,425	1,450
PS48	2000 (12)	—	KM373a, 374a, 375a, 376a, 377a, 378a, 379a, 380a, 381a, 382a, 383a, 384.2a	101	90.00
PS49	2000 (4)	—	KM389-392	44.00	40.00
PS50	2000 (4)	600	KM405-408	1,416	1,420
PS51	2001 (4)	—	KM429, 430, 431, 432	—	1,420
PS52	2002 (8)	100,000	KM#443, 444a,445,446a-449a, 467	60.00	65.00
PS53	2002 (3)	—	KM#459-461	57.50	55.00
PS54	2003 (8)	100,000	KM#182-184, 186, 270d, 289, 290a, 450	62.50	72.50
PS55	2003 (6)	30,000	KM#468-473	75.00	72.50

PROOF-LIKE DOLLARS

KM#	Date	Mintage	Identification	Issue Price	Mkt. Value
D1.1	1951	Inc. above	KM46, Canoe		175
D1.2	1951	Inc. above	KM46, Arnprior		700
D2.1	1952	Inc. above	KM46, water lines		1,200
D2.2	1952	Inc. above	KM46, without water lines		175
D3	1953 (1)	1,200	KM54, Canoe w/shoulder fold	—	300
D4	1954 (1)	5,300	KM54, Canoe	1.25	125
D5	1955 (1)	7,950	KM54, Canoe	1.25	100.00
D5a	1955 (1)	Inc. above	KM54, Arnprior	1.25	150
D6	1956	10,212	KM54, Canoe	1.25	50.00
D7	1957 (1)	16,241	KM54, Canoe	1.25	22.00
D8	1958 (1)	33,237	KM55, British Columbia	1.25	18.00
D9	1959 (1)	45,160	KM54, Canoe	1.25	10.00
D10	1960 (1)	82,728	KM54, Canoe	1.25	7.00
D11	1961 (1)	120,928	KM54, Canoe	1.25	7.00
D12	1962 (1)	248,901	KM54, Canoe	1.25	6.00
D13	1963 (1)	963,525	KM54, Canoe	1.25	4.50
D14	1964 (1)	2,862,441	KM58, Charlottetown	1.25	4.50
D15	1965 (1)	2,904,352	KM64.1, Canoe	—	4.50
D16	1966 (1)	672,514	KM64.1, Canoe	—	4.50
D17	1967 (1)	1,036,176	KM70, Confederation	—	6.50

PROOF-LIKE SETS (PL)

KM#	Date	Mintage	Identification	Issue Price	Mkt. Value
PL1	1953 (6)	1,200	KM49 w/o shoulder fold, 50-54	2.20	1,250
PL2	1953 (6)	Inc. above	KM49-54	2.20	760
PL3	1954 (6)	3,000	KM49-54	2.50	275
PL4	1954 (6)	Inc. above	KM49 w/o shoulder fold, 50-54	2.50	550
PL5	1955 (6)	6,300	KM49, 50a, 51-54	2.50	165
PL6	1955 (6)	Inc. above	KM49, 50a, 51-54, Arnprior	2.50	265
PL7	1956 (6)	6,500	KM49, 50a, 51-54	2.50	100.00
PL8	1957 (6)	11,862	KM49, 50a, 51-54	2.50	65.00
PL9	1958 (6)	18,259	KM49, 50a, 51-53, 55	2.50	45.00
PL10	1959 (6)	31,577	KM49, 50a, 51, 52, 54, 56	2.50	20.00
PL11	1960 (6)	64,097	KM49, 50a, 51, 52, 54, 56	3.00	14.00
PL12	1961 (6)	98,373	KM49, 50a, 51, 52, 54, 56	3.00	14.00
PL13	1962 (6)	200,950	KM49, 50a, 51, 52, 54, 56	3.00	10.00
PL14	1963 (6)	673,006	KM49, 51, 52, 54, 56, 57	3.00	7.00

KM#	Date	Mintage	Identification	Issue Price	Mkt. Value
PL15	1964 (6)	1,653,162	KM49, 51, 52, 56-58	3.00	7.00
PL16	1965 (6)	2,904,352	KM59.1-60.1, 61-63, 64.1	4.00	7.00
PL17	1966 (6)	672,514	KM59.1-60.1, 61-63, 64.1	4.00	7.00
PL18	1967 (6)	961,887	KM65-70 (pliofilm flat pack)	4.00	11.00
PL18A	1967 (6)	70,583	KM65-70 and Silver Medal (red box)	12.00	15.25
PL18B	1967 (7)	337,688	KM65-71 (black box)	40.00	200
PL19	1968 (6)	521,641	KM59.1-60.1, 62b, 72a, 75.1-76.1	4.00	2.25
PL20	1969 (6)	326,203	KM59.1-60.1, 62b, 75.1-77.1	4.00	2.75
PL21	1970 (6)	349,120	KM59.1-60.1, 62b, 75.1, 77.1, 78	4.00	3.25
PL22	1971 (6)	253,311	KM59.1-60.1, 62b, 75.1, 77.1, 79	4.00	2.75
PL23	1972 (6)	224,275	KM59.1-60.1, 62b-77.1	4.00	2.75
PL24	1973 (6)	243,695	KM59.1-60.1, 62b-75.1 obv. 120 beads, 77.1, 81.1, 82	4.00	4.00
PL25	1973 (6)	Inc. above	KM59.1-60.1, 62b-75.1 obv. 132 beads, 77.1, 81.2, 82	4.00	110
PL26	1974 (6)	213,589	KM59.1-60.1, 62b-75.1, 77.1, 88	5.00	3.00
PL27.1	1975 (6)	197,372	KM59.1, 60.1, 62b-75.1, 76.2, 77.1	5.00	2.50
PL27.2	1975 (6)	Inc. above	KM59.1, 60.1, 62b-75.1, 76.3, 77.1	5.00	5.00
PL28	1976 (6)	171,737	KM59.1, 60.1, 62b-75.1, 76.2, 77.1	5.15	2.75
PL29	1977 (6)	225,307	KM59.1, 60.1, 62b, 75.2, 77.1, 117.1	5.15	2.75
PL30	1978 (6)	260,000	KM59.1-60.1, 62b, 75.3, 77.1, 120.1	5.25	2.75
PL31	1979 (6)	187,624	KM59.2-60.2, 74, 75.3, 77.2, 120.1	6.25	2.75
PL32	1980 (6)	410,842	KM60.2, 74, 75.3, 77.2, 120.1, 127	6.50	4.50
PL33	1981 (6)	186,250	KM60.2, 74, 75.3, 77.2, 120.1, 123	5.00	3.25
PL34	1982 (6)	203,287	KM60.2, 74, 75.3, 77.2, 120.1, 123	6.00	2.50
PL36	1983 (6)	190,838	KM60.2a, 74, 75.3, 77.2, 120.1, 132	5.00	5.00
PL36.1	1983 (6)	Inc. above	KM60.2a, 74, 75.3, 77.2, 120.1, 132; set in folder packaged by British Royal Mint Coin Club	—	—
PL37	1984 (6)	181,249	KM60.2a, 74, 75.3, 77.2, 120.1, 132	5.25	5.00
PL38	1985 (6)	173,924	KM60.2a, 74, 75.3, 77.2, 120.1, 132	5.25	6.00
PL39	1986 (6)	167,338	KM60.2a, 74, 75.3, 77.2, 120.1, 132	5.25	6.50
PL40	1987 (6)	212,136	KM60.2a, 74, 75.3, 77.2, 120.1, 132	5.25	5.00
PL41	1988 (6)	182,048	KM60.2a, 74, 75.3, 77.2, 132, 157	6.05	5.00
PL42	1989 (6)	173,622	KM60.2a, 74, 75.3, 77.2, 132, 157	6.60	8.00
PL43	1990 (6)	170,791	KM181-186	7.40	8.00
PL44	1991 (6)	147,814	KM181-186	7.40	25.00
PL45	1992 (6)	217,597	KM204-209	8.25	11.00
PL46	1993 (6)	171,680	KM181-186	8.25	4.50
PL47	1994 (6)	141,676	KM181-185, 258	8.50	6.00
PL48	1994 (6)	18,794	KM181-185, 258 (Oh Canada holder)	—	10.00
PL49	1995 (6)	143,892	KM181-186	6.95	6.50
PL50	1995 (6)	50,927	KM181-186 (Oh Canada holder)	14.65	10.00
PL51	1995 (6)	36,443	KM181-186 (Baby Gift holder)	—	11.00
PL52	1996 (6)	116,736	KM181-186	—	13.00
PL53	1996 (6)	29,747	KM181-186 (Baby Gift holder)	—	15.00
PL54	1996 (6)	Inc. above	KM181a-185a, 186	8.95	15.00
PL55	1996 (6)	Inc. above	KM181a-185a, 186 (Oh Canada holder)	14.65	12.00
PL56	1996 (6)	Inc. above	KM181a-185a, 186 (Baby Gift holder)	—	12.00
PL57	1997 (7)	Inc. above	KM182a-184a, 209, 270, 289-290	10.45	8.00
PL58	1997 (7)	Inc. above	KM182a-184a, 270, 289-291 (Oh Canada holder)	16.45	20.00
PL59	1997 (7)	Inc. above	KM182a-184a, 209, 270, 289-290 (Baby Gift holder)	18.50	10.00
PL60	1998 (7)	Inc. above	KM182-184, 186, 270, 289-290	10.45	10.00
PL61	1998 (7)	Inc. above	KM182-184, 186, 270, 289-290 (Oh Canada holder)	16.45	12.00
PL62	1998 (7)	Inc. above	KM182-184, 186, 270, 289-290 (Tiny Treasures holder)	16.45	12.00
PL63	1999 (12)	Inc. above	KM342-353	16.95	10.00
PL64	2000 (12)	—	KM373-384	16.95	10.00

SPECIMEN SETS (SS)

KM#	Date	Mintage	Identification	Issue Price	Mkt. Value
SS1	1858 (4)	Inc. above	KM1-4, Reeded edge	—	9,000
SS2	1858 (4)	Inc. above	KM1-4, Plain edge	—	6,000
SS3	1858 (8)	Inc. above	KM1-4; Double Set	—	15,000
SS4	1858 (8)	Inc. above	KM1 (overdate), 2-4; Double Set	—	15,000
SS5	1870 (4)	100	KM2, 3, 5, 6 (reeded edges)	—	28,500
SS6	1870 (8)	Inc. above	KM2, 3, 5, 6; Double Set (plain edges)	—	55,000
SS7	1872 (4)	Inc. above	KM2, 3, 5, 6	—	12,500
SS8	1875 (3)	Inc. above	KM2 (Large date), 3, 5	—	65,000
SS9	1880 (3)	Inc. above	KM2, 3, 5 (Narrow 0)	—	35,000
SS10	1881 (5)	Inc. above	KM7, 2, 3, 5, 6	—	26,500
SS11	1892 (2)	Inc. above	KM3, 5	—	10,000
SS12	1902 (5)	100	KM8-12	—	25,000
SS13	1902 (3)	Inc. above	KM9 (Large H), 10, 11	—	6,500
SS14	1903 (3)	Inc. above	KM10, 12, 13	—	7,000
SS15	1908 (5)	1,000	KM8, 10-13	—	2,200
SS16	1911 (5)	1,000	KM15-19	—	5,500
SS17	1911/12	5	KM15-20, 26-27	—	52,250
SS18	1921 (5)	Inc. above	KM22-25, 28	—	120,000
SS19	1922 (2)	Inc. above	KM28, 29	—	2,500

KM#	Date	Mintage	Identification	Issue Price	Mkt. Value
SS20	1923 (2)	Inc. above	KM28, 29	—	5,000
SS21	1924 (2)	Inc. above	KM28, 29	—	4,000
SS22	1925 (2)	Inc. above	KM28, 29	—	7,000
SS23	1926 (2)	Inc. above	KM28, 29 (Near 6)	—	5,000
SS24	1927 (3)	Inc. above	KM24a, 28, 29	—	8,000
SS25	1928 (4)	Inc. above	KM23a, 24a, 28, 29	—	12,000
SS26	1929 (5)	Inc. above	KM23a,-25a, 28, 29	—	22,500
SS27	1930 (4)	Inc. above	KM23a, 24a. 28, 29	—	16,000
SS28	1931 (5)	Inc. above	KM23a-25a, 28, 29	—	26,500
SS29	1932 (5)	Inc. above	KM23a-25a, 28, 29	—	20,000
SS30	1934 (5)	Inc. above	KM23-25, 28, 29	—	23,000
SS31	1936 (5)	Inc. above	KM23-25, 28, 29	—	12,000
SS32	1936 (6)	Inc. above	KM23a(dot), 24a(dot), 25a, 28(dot), 29, 30	—	400,000
SS33	1937 (6)	1,025	KM32-37, Matte Finish	—	750
SS34	1937 (4)	Inc. above	KM32-35, Mirror Fields	—	1,350
SS35	1937 (6)	75	KM32-37, Mirror Fields	—	3,900
SS36	1938 (6)	Inc. above	KM32-37	—	18,250
SS-A36	1939 (6)	Inc. above	KM32-35, 38, Matte Finish	—	—
SS-B36	1939 (6)	Inc. above	KM32-35, 38, Mirror Fields	—	—
SS-C36	1942 (2)	Inc. above	KM32, 33	—	1,000
SS-D36	1943 (2)	Inc. above	KM32, 40	—	1,000
SS-A37	1944 (2)	Inc. above	KM32, 40a	—	1,000
SS37	1944 (5)	3	KM32, 34-37, 40a	—	11,300
SS-A38	1945 (2)	Inc. above	KM32, 40a	—	1,000
SS38	1945 (6)	6	KM32, 34-37, 40a	—	4,650
SS39	1946 (6)	15	KM32, 34-37, 39a	—	4,000
SS40	1947 (6)	Inc. above	KM32, 34-37(7 curved), 37(7 pointed),	—	8,500
SS41	1947 (6)	Inc. above	KM32, 34-36(7 curved), 37(blunt 7), 39a	—	6,200
SS42	1947 (6)	Inc. above	KM32, 34-36(7 curved right), 37, 39a	—	4,250
SS43	1948 (6)	30	KM41-46	—	6,000
SS44	1949 (6)	20	KM41-45, 47	—	6,400
SS44A	1949 (2)	Inc. above	KM47	—	1,550
SS45	1950 (6)	12	KM41-46	—	1,650
SS46	1950 (6)	Inc. above	KM41-45, 46 (Arnprior)	—	3,175
SS47	1951 (7)	12	KM41, 48, 42a, 43-46 (w/water lines)	—	2,725
SS48	1952 (6)	2,317	KM41, 42a, 43-46 (water lines)	—	3,175
SS48A	1952 (6)	Inc. above	KM41, 42a, 43-46 (w/o water lines)	—	3,175
SS49	1953 (6)	28	KM49 w/o straps, 50-54	—	1,850
SS50	1953 (6)	Inc. above	KM49 w/ straps, 50-54	—	875
SS51	1964 (6)	Inc. above	KM49, 51, 52, 56-58	—	850
SS52	1965 (6)	Inc. above	KM59.1-60.1, 61-63, 64.1	—	850
SS56	1971 (7)	66,860	KM59.1-60.1, 62b-75.1, 77.1, 79 (2 pcs.); Double Dollar Prestige Sets	12.00	9.50
SS57	1972 (7)	36,349	KM59.1,-60.1, 62b-75.1, 76.1 (2 pcs.), 77; Double Dollar Prestige Sets	12.00	18.00
SS58	1973 (7)	119,819	KM59.1-60.1, 75.1, 77.1, 81.1, 82, 83; Double Dollar Prestige Sets	12.00	10.00
SS59	1973 (7)	Inc. above	KM59.1-60.1, 75.1, 77.1, 81.2, 82, 83; Double Dollar Prestige Sets	—	125
SS60	1974 (7)	85,230	KM59.1-60.1, 62b-75.1, 77.1, 88, 88a; Double Dollar Prestige Sets	15.00	10.00
SS61	1975 (7)	97,263	KM59.1-60.1, 62b-75.1, 76.2, 77.1, 97; Double Dollar Prestige Sets	15.00	10.00
SS62	1976 (7)	87,744	KM59.1-60, 62b-75.1, 76.2, 77.1, 106; Double Dollar Prestige Sets	16.00	10.00
SS63	1977 (7)	142,577	KM59.1-60.1, 62b, 75.2, 77.1, 117.1, 118; Double Dollar Prestige Sets	16.50	10.00
SS64	1978 (7)	147,000	KM59.1-60.1, 62b, 75.3, 77.1, 120.1, 121; Double Dollar Prestige Sets	16.50	10.00
SS65	1979 (7)	155,698	KM59.2-60.2, 74, 75.3, 77.2, 120, 124; Double Dollar Prestige Sets	18.50	11.50
SS66	1980 (7)	162,875	KM60.2, 74-75.3, 77.2, 120, 127, 128; Double Dollar Prestige Sets	30.50	22.50
SS67	1981 (6)	71,300	KM60.2, 74, 75.3, 77.2, 120.1, 127; Regular Specimen Sets Resumed	10.00	6.00
SS68	1982 (6)	62,298	KM60.2a, 74, 75.3, 77.2, 120.1, 132; Regular Specimen Sets Resumed	11.50	6.00
SS69	1983 (6)	60,329	KM60.2a, 74, 75.3, 77.2, 120.1, 132; Regular Specimen Sets Resumed	12.75	6.00
SS70	1984 (6)	60,400	KM60.2a, 74, 75.3, 77.2, 120.1, 132; Regular Specimen Sets Resumed	10.00	6.00
SS71	1985 (6)	61,553	KM60.2a, 74, 75.3, 77.2, 120.1, 132; Regular Specimen Sets Resumed	10.00	6.50
SS72	1986 (6)	67,152	KM60.2a, 74, 75.3, 77.2, 120.1, 132; Regular Specimen Sets Resumed	10.00	6.50
SS72A	1987 (6)	75,194	KM60.2a, 74, 75.3, 77.2, 120.1, 132; Regular Specimen Sets Resumed	11.00	7.00
SS73	1988 (6)	70,205	KM60.2a, 74, 75.3, 77.2, 132, 157; Regular Specimen Sets Resumed	12.30	7.00
SS74	1989 (6)	75,306	KM60.2a, 74, 75.3, 77.2, 132, 157; Regular Specimen Sets Resumed	14.50	9.00
SS75	1990 (6)	76,611	KM181-186; Regular Specimen Sets Resumed	15.50	9.00
SS76	1991 (6)	68,552	KM181-186; Regular Specimen Sets Resumed	15.50	22.00
SS77	1992 (6)	78,328	KM204-209; Regular Specimen Sets Resumed	16.25	13.00
SS78	1993 (6)	77,351	KM181-186; Regular Specimen Sets Resumed	16.25	7.00
SS79	1994 (6)	77,349	KM181-186; Regular Specimen Sets Resumed	16.50	10.00
SS80	1995 (6)	Inc. above	KM181-186; Regular Specimen Sets Resumed	13.95	10.00
SS82	1996 (6)	Inc. above	KM181a-185a, 186; Regular Specimen Sets Resumed	18.95	12.00
SS83	1997 (7)	Inc. above	KM182a-184a, 270, 289-291; Regular Specimen Sets Resumed	19.95	25.00
SS84	1998 (7)	Inc. above	KM182-184, 186, 270, 289, 290; Regular Specimen Sets Resumed	19.95	12.00
SS85	1998 (7)	Inc. above	KM182-184, 186, 270, 289a, 290; Regular Specimen Sets Resumed	19.95	12.00
SS90	2002 (7)	75,000	KM#444-449,462	30.00	22.50
SS91	2003 (7)	75,000	KM#182-184, 186, 270, 289, 290	30.00	27.50

V.I.P. SPECIMEN SETS (VS)

KM#	Date	Mintage	Identification	Issue Price	Mkt. Value
VS I	1969	4	KM59.1-60.1, 74.1-75.1, 77.1, 78	—	2,000
VS2	1970	100	KM59.1-60.1, 74.1-75.1, 77.1, 78	—	525
VS3	1971	69	KM59.1-60.1, 74.1-75.1, 77.1, 79(2 pcs.)	—	525
VS4	1972	25	KM59.1-60.1, 74.1-75.1, 76.1, (2 pcs.), 77.1	—	650
VS5	1973	26	KM59.1-60.1, 75.1, 77.1, 81.1, 82, 83	—	650
VS6	1974	72	KM59.1-60.1, 74.1-75.1, 77.1, 88, 88a	—	525
VS7	1975	94	KM59.1-60.1, 74.1-75.1, 76.2, 77.1, 97	—	525
VS8	1976	Inc. above	KM59.1-60.1, 74.1-75.1, 76.2, 77.1, 106	—	525

NEW BRUNSWICK

DECIMAL COINAGE

HALF CENT

KM# 5   Composition: Bronze

Date	Mintage	VG-8	F-12	VF-20	XF-40	MS-60	MS-63	Proof
1861	222,800	60.00	90.00	150	200	375	800	—
1861 Proof	—	—	—	—	—	—	—	2,200

CENT

KM# 6   Composition: Bronze

Date	Mintage	VG-8	F-12	VF-20	XF-40	MS-60	MS-63	Proof
1861	1,000,000	2.25	4.00	8.00	13.00	100.00	250	—
1861 Proof	—	—	—	—	—	—	—	450
1864 short 6	1,000,000	2.25	4.00	8.00	13.00	110	245	—
1864 long 6	Inc. above	2.25	4.00	8.00	13.00	110	245	—

5 CENTS

KM# 7   Weight: 1.1620 g. **Composition:** 0.9250 Silver .0346 oz. ASW

Date	Mintage	VG-8	F-12	VF-20	XF-40	MS-60	MS-63	Proof
1862	100,000	35.00	65.00	150	300	1,500	3,200	—
1862 Proof	—	—	—	—	—	—	—	3,500
1864 small 6	100,000	35.00	65.00	150	300	1,500	3,200	—
1864 large 6	Inc. above	35.00	65.00	150	300	1,500	3,200	—

10 CENTS

KM# 8   Weight: 2.3240 g. **Composition:** 0.9250 Silver .0691 oz. ASW

Date	Mintage	VG-8	F-12	VF-20	XF-40	MS-60	MS-63	Proof
1862	150,000	35.00	65.00	150	300	975	2,450	—
1862 recut 2	Inc. above	42.50	85.00	250	500	2,000	3,250	—
1862 Proof	—	—	—	—	—	—	—	2,850
1864	100,000	35.00	65.00	150	300	1,500	2,750	—

20 CENTS

KM# 9   Weight: 4.6480 g. **Composition:** 0.9250 Silver .1382 oz. ASW

Date	Mintage	VG-8	F-12	VF-20	XF-40	MS-60	MS-63	Proof
1862	150,000	14.00	30.00	60.00	200	1,000	2,350	—
1862 Proof	—	—	—	—	—	—	—	2,850
1864	150,000	14.00	30.00	60.00	200	1,000	2,500	—

STERLING COINAGE

HALFPENNY TOKEN

KM# 1   Composition: Copper

Date	Mintage	VG-8	F-12	VF-20	XF-40	MS-60	MS-63	Proof
1843	480,000	3.00	6.00	11.50	30.00	110	265	—
1843 Proof	—	—	—	—	—	—	—	750

KM# 3   Composition: Copper

Date	Mintage	VG-8	F-12	VF-20	XF-40	MS-60	MS-63	Proof
1854	864,000	3.00	6.00	11.50	30.00	100.00	265	—

KM# 3a   Composition: Bronze

Date	Mintage	VG-8	F-12	VF-20	XF-40	MS-60	MS-63	Proof
1854 Proof	—	—	—	—	—	—	—	400

1 PENNY TOKEN

KM# 2 Composition: Copper

Date	Mintage	VG-8	F-12	VF-20	XF-40	MS-60	MS-63	Proof
1843	480,000	3.75	7.50	15.00	37.50	165	325	—
1843 Proof	—	—	—	—	—	—	—	800

KM# 4 Composition: Copper

Date	Mintage	VG-8	F-12	VF-20	XF-40	MS-60	MS-63	Proof
1854	432,000	3.75	7.50	15.00	40.00	175	350	—

NEWFOUNDLAND
PROVINCE
CIRCULATION COINAGE

CENT (LARGE)

KM# 1 Composition: Bronze

Date	Mintage	VG-8	F-12	VF-20	XF-40	MS-60	MS-63	Proof
1865	240,000	2.25	3.50	6.00	20.00	120	550	—
1872H	200,000	2.50	4.00	7.00	15.00	60.00	160	—
1872H Proof	—	—	—	—	—	—	—	800
1873	200,025	2.50	4.50	13.00	30.00	225	1,100	—
1873 Proof	—	—	—	—	—	—	—	3,000
1876H	200,000	2.50	4.00	7.00	25.00	160	450	—
1876H Proof, reported not confirmed	—	—	—	—	—	—	—	—
1880 round O, even date	400,000	2.00	3.00	6.00	20.00	90.00	300	—
1880 round O, low O	Inc. above	2.25	4.00	9.00	30.00	200	550	—
1880 oval 0	Inc. above	85.00	130	250	325	700	1,400	—
1880 oval O Proof	—	—	—	—	—	—	—	2,500
1885	40,000	16.50	27.00	55.00	125	400	1,250	—
1885 Proof	—	—	—	—	—	—	—	2,500
1888	50,000	15.00	25.00	40.00	125	450	1,970	—
1890	200,000	2.25	3.50	6.00	20.00	140	450	—
1894	200,000	2.25	3.50	6.00	20.00	140	475	—
1894 Proof	—	—	—	—	—	—	—	1,500
1896	200,000	2.25	3.50	5.50	18.00	120	350	—
1896 Proof	—	—	—	—	—	—	—	1,500

KM# 9 Composition: Bronze

Date	Mintage	VG-8	F-12	VF-20	XF-40	MS-60	MS-63	Proof
1904H	100,000	7.00	11.00	22.00	37.50	275	650	—
1904H Proof	—	—	—	—	—	—	—	4,000
1907	200,000	1.50	2.50	4.00	12.00	110	375	—
1909	200,000	1.50	2.50	4.00	10.50	90.00	150	—
1909 Proof	—	—	—	—	—	—	—	400

KM# 16 Obverse: George V bust facing left Reverse: Similar to KM#9 Composition: Bronze

Date	Mintage	VG-8	F-12	VF-20	XF-40	MS-60	MS-63	Proof
1913	400,000	0.75	1.50	2.00	4.00	40.00	75.00	—
1917C	702,350	0.75	1.50	2.00	4.00	65.00	185	—
1917C Proof	—	—	—	—	—	—	—	800
1919C	300,000	0.80	1.60	2.25	5.00	100.00	275	—
1919C Proof	—	—	—	—	—	—	—	1,000

Date	Mintage	VG-8	F-12	VF-20	XF-40	MS-60	MS-63	Proof
1920C	302,184	0.75	1.50	3.50	12.00	200	1,000	—
1929C	300,000	0.75	1.50	2.00	4.00	55.00	100.00	—
1929C Proof	—	—	—	—	—	—	—	1,000
1936	300,000	0.75	1.25	1.75	3.00	28.00	75.00	—

CENT (SMALL)

KM# 18   Composition: Bronze

Date	Mintage	VG-8	F-12	VF-20	XF-40	MS-60	MS-63	Proof
1938	500,000	0.50	0.75	1.50	2.50	16.00	40.00	—
1938 Proof	—	—	—	—	—	—	—	1,000
1940	300,000	1.25	2.00	3.00	7.00	35.00	175	—
1940 re-engraved date	—	16.00	27.50	40.00	70.00	185	500	—
1940 Proof	—	—	—	—	—	—	—	1,000
1941C	827,662	0.35	0.45	0.70	1.50	13.50	120	—
1941C re-engraved date	—	9.00	13.00	20.00	35.00	100.00	400	—
1942	1,996,889	0.35	0.45	0.70	1.50	13.50	70.00	—
1943C	1,239,732	0.35	0.45	0.70	1.50	13.50	70.00	—
1944C	1,328,776	1.00	2.00	3.00	7.00	90.00	335	—
1947C	313,772	0.90	1.65	2.50	6.00	35.00	200	—
1947C Proof	—	—	—	—	—	—	—	2,000

5 CENTS

KM# 2   Weight: 1.1782 g. **Composition:** 0.9250 Silver .0350 oz. ASW

Date	Mintage	VG-8	F-12	VF-20	XF-40	MS-60	MS-63	Proof
1865	80,000	20.00	32.50	60.00	125	775	1,500	—
1865 Proof	—	—	—	—	—	—	—	4,000
1870	40,000	35.00	50.00	90.00	175	1,100	2,000	—
1870 Proof	—	—	—	—	—	—	—	4,000
1872H	40,000	22.00	32.00	60.00	140	600	1,400	—
1873	44,260	45.00	75.00	145	300	1,750	2,850	—
1873H	Inc. above	650	1,000	1,875	3,300	8,200	12,500	—
1873 Proof	—	—	—	—	—	—	—	10,000
1876H	20,000	65.00	90.00	175	275	1,100	2,750	—
1880	40,000	22.00	40.00	80.00	150	1,000	1,850	—
1880 Proof	—	—	—	—	—	—	—	5,000
1881	40,000	15.00	30.00	45.00	120	900	1,850	—
1881 Proof	—	—	—	—	—	—	—	5,000
1882H	60,000	15.00	27.00	40.00	100.00	800	1,500	—
1882H Proof	—	—	—	—	—	—	—	2,000
1885	16,000	90.00	130	225	400	1,650	4,500	—
1885 Proof	—	—	—	—	—	—	—	7,500
1888	40,000	20.00	30.00	60.00	140	850	2,450	—
1888 Proof	—	—	—	—	—	—	—	7,500
1890	160,000	6.00	12.00	30.00	70.00	600	1,500	—
1890 Proof	—	—	—	—	—	—	—	5,000
1894	160,000	6.50	12.50	30.00	75.00	600	1,500	—
1894 Proof	—	—	—	—	—	—	—	5,000
1896	400,000	4.00	8.00	20.00	45.00	575	1,350	—
1896 Proof	—	—	—	—	—	—	—	5,000

KM# 7   Weight: 1.1782 g. **Composition:** 0.9250 Silver .0350 oz. ASW

Date	Mintage	VG-8	F-12	VF-20	XF-40	MS-60	MS-63	Proof
1903	100,000	3.00	6.00	18.00	45.00	425	1,200	—
1903 Proof	—	—	—	—	—	—	—	2,000
1904H	100,000	2.00	5.00	14.00	35.00	160	275	—
1904H Proof	—	—	—	—	—	—	—	1,200
1908	400,000	1.75	3.50	11.50	25.00	160	400	—

KM# 13   Obverse: George V bust facing left **Reverse:** Similar to KM#7 **Weight:** 1.1782 g. **Composition:** 0.9250 Silver .0350 oz. ASW

Date	Mintage	VG-8	F-12	VF-20	XF-40	MS-60	MS-63	Proof
1912	300,000	1.00	2.00	5.00	20.00	125	275	—
1912 Proof	—	—	—	—	—	—	—	2,000
1917C	300,319	1.00	2.00	4.00	14.00	200	450	—
1917C Proof	—	—	—	—	—	—	—	2,000
1919C	100,844	1.25	3.00	10.00	30.00	750	1,250	—
1919C Proof	—	—	—	—	—	—	—	2,000
1929	300,000	1.00	1.75	3.25	12.00	165	350	—

KM# 19   Weight: 1.1782 g. **Composition:** 0.9250 Silver .0350 oz. ASW

Date	Mintage	VG-8	F-12	VF-20	XF-40	MS-60	MS-63	Proof
1938	100,000	0.80	0.90	1.50	4.00	65.00	150	—
1938 Proof	—	—	—	—	—	—	—	1,000
1940C	200,000	0.80	0.90	1.50	4.00	60.00	200	—
1940C Proof	—	—	—	—	—	—	—	2,000
1941C	621,641	0.60	0.90	1.50	2.50	15.00	30.00	—
1942C	298,348	0.85	0.90	2.00	2.50	15.00	30.00	—
1943C	351,666	0.55	0.85	1.25	2.50	15.00	27.50	—

KM# 19a   Weight: 1.1664 g. **Composition:** 0.8000 Silver .0300 oz. ASW

Date	Mintage	VG-8	F-12	VF-20	XF-40	MS-60	MS-63	Proof
1944C	286,504	1.25	1.75	3.00	4.00	25.00	50.00	—
1945C	203,828	0.55	0.85	1.25	2.50	13.00	26.00	—
1946C	2,041	200	225	325	400	1,100	1,750	—
1946C Prooflike	—	—	—	—	—	—	2,500	—
1947C	38,400	2.00	3.00	5.00	10.00	60.00	100.00	—
1947C Prooflike	—	—	—	—	—	—	350	—

10 CENTS

KM# 3   Weight: 2.3564 g. **Composition:** 0.9250 Silver .0701 oz. ASW

Date	Mintage	VG-8	F-12	VF-20	XF-40	MS-60	MS-63	Proof
1865	80,000	13.50	22.00	55.00	160	1,100	2,250	—
1865 plain edge, Proof	—	—	—	—	—	—	—	5,500
1870	30,000	120	190	335	725	2,350	5,000	—
1870 Proof	—	—	—	—	—	—	—	10,000
1872H	40,000	13.50	20.00	50.00	135	800	1,700	—
1873 flat 3	23,614	15.00	35.00	90.00	345	1,675	2,900	—
1873 round 3	Inc. above	15.00	35.00	90.00	345	1,675	2,900	—
1873 Proof	—	—	—	—	—	—	—	12,000
1876H	10,000	20.00	35.00	80.00	225	1,400	2,500	—
1880/70	10,000	22.00	45.00	100.00	275	1,800	2,950	—
1880 Proof	—	—	—	—	—	—	—	7,500
1882H	20,000	15.00	30.00	80.00	310	2,185	3,410	—
1882H Proof	—	—	—	—	—	—	—	3,000
1885	8,000	60.00	110	200	475	2,100	4,250	—
1885 Proof	—	—	—	—	—	—	—	8,000
1888	30,000	11.50	27.50	70.00	345	2,185	2,500	—
1888 Proof	—	—	—	—	—	—	—	8,000
1890	100,000	5.50	11.50	20.00	75.00	700	1,550	—
1890 Proof	—	—	—	—	—	—	—	5,000
1894	100,000	5.50	11.50	20.00	75.00	700	1,550	—
1894 Proof	—	—	—	—	—	—	—	5,000
1896	230,000	5.00	10.00	20.00	75.00	600	1,500	—
1896 Proof	—	—	—	—	—	—	—	5,000

KM# 8   Weight: 2.3564 g. **Composition:** 0.9250 Silver .0701 oz. ASW

Date	Mintage	VG-8	F-12	VF-20	XF-40	MS-60	MS-63	Proof
1903	100,000	5.00	10.00	35.00	110	850	2,000	—
1903 Proof	—	—	—	—	—	—	—	2,500
1904H	100,000	2.50	6.50	20.00	55.00	175	250	—
1904H Proof	—	—	—	—	—	—	—	1,500

KM# 20   Weight: 2.3564 g. **Composition:** 0.9250 Silver .0701 oz. ASW

Date	Mintage	VG-8	F-12	VF-20	XF-40	MS-60	MS-63	Proof
1938	100,000	0.75	1.50	2.75	7.00	80.00	300	—
1938 Proof	—	—	—	—	—	—	—	2,000
1940	100,000	0.65	1.20	2.50	6.00	80.00	300	—
1940 Proof	—	—	—	—	—	—	—	2,500
1941C	483,630	0.60	1.40	2.20	3.50	27.00	125	—
1942C	293,736	0.60	1.50	2.20	3.50	30.00	130	—
1943C	104,706	0.60	1.50	2.40	3.50	60.00	200	—
1944C	151,471	2.50	3.50	5.00	7.50	90.00	250	—

KM# 20a   Weight: 2.3328 g. **Composition:** 0.8000 Silver .0600 oz. ASW

Date	Mintage	VG-8	F-12	VF-20	XF-40	MS-60	MS-63	Proof
1945C	175,833	0.65	1.25	2.00	4.00	27.00	185	—
1946C	38,400	2.00	4.00	7.00	15.00	60.00	250	—
1946C Proof	—	—	—	—	—	—	—	700
1947C	61,988	1.50	3.00	4.50	9.00	45.00	245	—

20 CENTS

KM# 4   Weight: 4.7127 g. **Composition:** 0.9250 Silver .1401 oz. ASW

Date	Mintage	VG-8	F-12	VF-20	XF-40	MS-60	MS-63	Proof
1865	100,000	11.00	16.00	45.00	125	950	2,000	—
1865 plain edge, Proof	—	—	—	—	—	—	—	6,500
1865 reeded edge, Proof	—	—	—	—	—	—	—	10,000
1870	50,000	12.00	20.00	60.00	140	1,250	2,500	—
1870 plain edge, Proof	—	—	—	—	—	—	—	6,500
1870 reeded edge, Proof	—	—	—	—	—	—	—	6,500
1872H	90,000	7.00	14.00	30.00	90.00	750	1,800	—
1873	45,797	9.00	18.00	60.00	160	1,500	3,000	—
1873 Proof	—	—	—	—	—	—	—	12,000
1876H	50,000	10.00	16.00	50.00	175	1,350	2,700	—
1880/70	30,000	15.00	25.00	65.00	160	1,350	3,000	—
1880 Proof	—	—	—	—	—	—	—	8,000
1881	60,000	5.00	12.00	35.00	90.00	900	1,900	—
1881 Proof	—	—	—	—	—	—	—	8,000
1882H	100,000	5.00	12.00	27.50	80.00	900	1,900	—
1882H Proof	—	—	—	—	—	—	—	3,500
1885	40,000	8.00	12.50	40.00	120	1,300	2,600	—
1885 Proof	—	—	—	—	—	—	—	10,000
1888	75,000	5.00	10.00	32.00	100.00	900	2,200	—
1888 Proof	—	—	—	—	—	—	—	10,000
1890	100,000	4.00	7.00	22.00	70.00	625	1,600	—
1890 Proof	—	—	—	—	—	—	—	6,500
1894	100,000	4.00	7.00	22.00	60.00	650	1,700	—
1894 Proof	—	—	—	—	—	—	—	6,500
1896 small 96	125,000	3.00	6.00	20.00	70.00	700	1,800	—
1896 large 96	Inc. above	4.00	10.00	22.00	90.00	725	1,900	—
1896 large 96, Proof	—	—	—	—	—	—	—	6,500

Date	Mintage	VG-8	F-12	VF-20	XF-40	MS-60	MS-63	Proof
1899 small 99	125,000	15.00	30.00	55.00	175	1,000	2,200	—
1899 large 99	Inc. above	3.25	6.50	18.00	65.00	700	1,900	—
1900	125,000	3.00	5.00	15.00	55.00	700	1,900	—
1900 Proof	—	—	—	—	—	—	—	6,500

KM# 10 Weight: 4.7127 g. **Composition:** 0.9250 Silver .1401 oz. ASW

Date	Mintage	VG-8	F-12	VF-20	XF-40	MS-60	MS-63	Proof
1904H	75,000	6.00	16.00	50.00	175	2,000	4,250	—
1904H Proof	—	—	—	—	—	—	—	1,750

KM# 15 Obverse: George V bust facing left **Reverse:** Similar to KM#10 **Weight:** 4.7127 g. **Composition:** 0.9250 Silver .1401 oz. ASW

Date	Mintage	VG-8	F-12	VF-20	XF-40	MS-60	MS-63	Proof
1912	350,000	2.00	3.00	8.00	30.00	275	650	—
1912 Proof	—	—	—	—	—	—	—	2,500

25 CENTS

KM# 17 Weight: 5.8319 g. **Composition:** 0.9250 Silver .1734 oz. ASW

Date	Mintage	VG-8	F-12	VF-20	XF-40	MS-60	MS-63	Proof
1917C	464,779	1.50	2.00	4.00	8.00	120	250	—
1917C Proof	—	—	—	—	—	—	—	2,500
1919C	163,939	1.50	2.25	4.25	12.00	220	700	—
1919C Proof	—	—	—	—	—	—	—	2,500

50 CENTS

KM# 6 Weight: 11.7818 g. **Composition:** 0.9250 Silver .3504 oz. ASW

Date	Mintage	VG-8	F-12	VF-20	XF-40	MS-60	MS-63	Proof
1870	50,000	12.00	15.00	55.00	300	1,400	3,600	—
1870 plain edge, Proof	—	—	—	—	—	—	—	25,000
1870 reeded edge, Proof	—	—	—	—	—	—	—	25,000
1872H	48,000	10.00	15.00	50.00	175	1,250	3,600	—
1873	37,675	40.00	70.00	225	700	4,350	6,000	—

Date	Mintage	VG-8	F-12	VF-20	XF-40	MS-60	MS-63	Proof
1873 Proof	—	—	—	—	—	—	—	40,000
1874	80,000	20.00	32.00	100.00	425	2,500	5,000	—
1874 Proof	—	—	—	—	—	—	—	40,000
1876H	28,000	30.00	40.00	125	400	2,250	5,250	—
1880	24,000	20.00	40.00	150	450	2,500	5,250	—
1880 Proof	—	—	—	—	—	—	—	40,000
1881	50,000	11.50	22.00	85.00	300	2,250	5,250	—
1881 Proof	—	—	—	—	—	—	—	40,000
1882H	100,000	9.00	14.00	55.00	175	1,600	3,600	—
1882H Proof	—	—	—	—	—	—	—	8,000
1885	40,000	14.00	25.00	80.00	325	2,250	5,500	—
1885 Proof	—	—	—	—	—	—	—	40,000
1888	20,000	23.00	45.00	130	450	2,500	5,500	—
1888 Proof	—	—	—	—	—	—	—	40,000
1894	40,000	5.00	13.00	50.00	200	2,000	3,800	—
1896	60,000	5.00	10.00	35.00	150	1,400	3,600	—
1896 Proof	—	—	—	—	—	—	—	25,000
1898	76,607	5.00	10.00	35.00	150	1,700	3,600	—
1899 wide 9's	150,000	5.00	10.00	30.00	125	1,500	3,600	—
1899 narrow 9's	Inc. above	5.00	10.00	30.00	125	1,500	3,600	—
1900	150,000	5.00	10.00	30.00	125	1,500	3,600	—

KM# 11   Weight: 11.7800 g. **Composition:** 0.9250 Silver .3504 oz. ASW

Date	Mintage	VG-8	F-12	VF-20	XF-40	MS-60	MS-63	Proof
1904H	140,000	3.25	5.00	13.00	35.00	225	650	—
1904H Proof	—	—	—	—	—	—	—	5,000
1907	100,000	3.00	5.00	13.00	45.00	250	800	—
1908	160,000	3.25	4.50	12.50	32.50	175	600	—
1909	200,000	3.25	4.50	12.50	35.00	200	600	—

KM# 12   Weight: 11.7800 g. **Composition:** 0.9250 Silver .3504 oz. ASW

Date	Mintage	VG-8	F-12	VF-20	XF-40	MS-60	MS-63	Proof
1911	200,000	2.75	3.25	6.00	20.00	175	450	—
1917C	375,560	2.75	3.25	6.00	16.50	125	285	—
1917C Proof	—	—	—	—	—	—	—	2,500
1918C	294,824	2.75	3.25	6.00	16.50	125	285	—
1919C	306,267	2.75	3.25	6.00	16.50	125	380	—
1919C Proof	—	—	—	—	—	—	—	2,500

2 DOLLARS

KM# 5   Weight: 3.3284 g. **Composition:** 0.9170 Gold .0981 oz. AGW

Date	Mintage	F-12	VF-20	XF-40	AU-50	MS-60	MS-63
1865	10,000	125	150	210	350	1,050	4,950
1865 plain edge, Specimen-63, $15,000.	Est. 10	—	—	—	—	—	—
1870	10,000	150	180	225	410	1,050	5,850

Date	Mintage	F-12	VF-20	XF-40	AU-50	MS-60	MS-63
1870 reeded edge, Specimen-63 $20,000.	Est. 5	—	—	—	—	—	—
1872	6,050	150	275	300	590	2,100	8,650
1872 Specimen-63 $12,500.	Est. 10	—	—	—	—	—	—
1880	2,500	775	950	1,150	2,300	4,650	14,250
1880/70	—	—	—	—	—	—	—
Note: Specimen. Bowers and Merena Norweb sale 11-96, specimen 64 realized $70,400.							
1881	10,000	110	145	180	300	1,100	4,750
1881 Specimen; Rare	—	—	—	—	—	—	—
1882H	25,000	105	140	175	200	375	1,300
1882H Specimen $4,250.	—	—	—	—	—	—	—
1885	10,000	110	145	180	300	475	1,900
1885 Specimen	—	—	—	—	—	—	—
Note: Bowers and Merena Norweb sale 11-96, specimen 66 realized $44,000							
1888	25,000	105	140	175	200	365	1,550
1888 Specimen; Rare	—	—	—	—	—	—	—

NOVA SCOTIA

STERLING COINAGE

HALFPENNY TOKEN

KM# 1a Composition: Copper

Date	Mintage	VG-8	F-12	VF-20	XF-40	MS-60	MS-63	Proof
1382 1382 (error)	—	500	700	1,650	—	—	—	—
1832/1382	—	6.00	15.00	50.00	100.00	—	—	—
1832 (imitation)	—	3.00	6.00	18.00	40.00	50.00	100.00	—

KM# 1 Composition: Copper

Date	Mintage	VG-8	F-12	VF-20	XF-40	MS-60	MS-63	Proof
1823	400,000	3.00	5.00	8.00	20.00	75.00	150	—
1823 without hyphen	Inc. above	5.00	10.00	20.00	35.00	170	350	—
1824	118,636	3.00	5.00	12.50	25.00	150	225	—
1832	800,000	3.00	5.00	7.50	15.00	60.00	150	—

KM# 3 Composition: Copper

Date	Mintage	VG-8	F-12	VF-20	XF-40	MS-60	MS-63	Proof
1840 small 0	300,000	3.50	5.00	10.00	22.00	115	165	—
1840 medium 0	Inc. above	2.50	4.00	7.50	15.00	95.00	125	—
1840 large 0	Inc. above	4.00	6.00	12.50	27.50	125	185	—
1843	300,000	3.00	5.00	12.00	25.00	85.00	160	—

KM# 5 Composition: Copper

Date	Mintage	VG-8	F-12	VF-20	XF-40	MS-60	MS-63	Proof
1856 without LCW	720,000	2.00	4.00	7.50	15.00	70.00	175	—
1856 without LCW, Proof	—	—	—	—	—	—	—	600
1856 without LCW, inverted A for V in PROVINCE, Proof	—	—	—	—	—	—	—	600

KM# 5a Composition: Bronze

Date	Mintage	VG-8	F-12	VF-20	XF-40	MS-60	MS-63	Proof
1856 with LCW, Proof	—	—	—	—	—	—	—	600

1 PENNY TOKEN

KM# 2 Composition: Copper

Date	Mintage	VG-8	F-12	VF-20	XF-40	MS-60	MS-63	Proof
1824	217,776	3.00	6.00	10.00	25.00	100.00	250	—
1832	200,000	3.00	6.00	10.00	22.50	80.00	230	—

KM# 2a Composition: Copper

Date	Mintage	VG-8	F-12	VF-20	XF-40	MS-60	MS-63	Proof
1832 (imitation)	—	3.75	7.50	22.50	42.50	—	—	—

KM# 4 Composition: Copper **Size:** 32 mm.

Date	Mintage	VG-8	F-12	VF-20	XF-40	MS-60	MS-63	Proof
1840	150,000	2.50	5.00	7.50	20.00	100.00	175	—
1843/0	150,000	12.00	20.00	40.00	80.00	150	—	—
1843	Inc. above	3.00	6.00	10.00	22.50	110	200	—

KM# 6 Composition: Copper

Date	Mintage	VG-8	F-12	VF-20	XF-40	MS-60	MS-63	Proof
1856 without LCW	360,000	2.50	5.00	8.50	19.00	110	135	—
1856 with LCW	Inc. above	2.50	5.00	7.00	15.00	85.00	115	—

KM# 6a Composition: Bronze

Date	Mintage	VG-8	F-12	VF-20	XF-40	MS-60	MS-63	Proof
1856 Proof	—	—	—	—	—	—	—	400

DECIMAL COINAGE

HALF CENT

KM# 7 Composition: Bronze

Date	Mintage	VG-8	F-12	VF-20	XF-40	MS-60	MS-63	Proof
1861	400,000	3.00	5.00	8.00	12.00	60.00	165	—
1864	400,000	3.00	5.00	8.00	12.00	55.00	165	—
1864 Proof	—	—	—	—	—	—	—	300

CENT

KM# 8 Composition: Bronze **Note:** The Royal Mint report records mintage of 1 million for 1862, which is considered incorrect.

Date	Mintage	VG-8	F-12	VF-20	XF-40	MS-60	MS-63	Proof
1861	800,000	2.00	3.00	5.00	10.00	90.00	215	—
1862	Est. 1,000,000	15.00	22.50	45.00	95.00	500	1,300	—
1864	800,000	2.00	3.00	5.00	10.00	100.00	225	—

PRINCE EDWARD ISLAND
DECIMAL COINAGE

CENT

KM# 4 Composition: Bronze

Date	Mintage	VG-8	F-12	VF-20	XF-40	MS-60	MS-63	Proof
1871	2,000,000	1.75	2.50	4.50	10.50	75.00	185	—
1871 Proof	—	—	—	—	—	—	—	2,000

CUT & COUNTERMARKED COINAGE
ca. 1813

SHILLING

KM# 1 Composition: Silver **Note:** Countermark on center plug of Spanish or Spanish Colonial 8 Reales.

Date	Mintage	VG-8	F-12	VF-20	XF-40	MS-60	MS-63	Proof
ND	1,000	2,000	3,000	5,000	—	—	—	—

5 SHILLING

KM# 2 Composition: Silver **Note:** Countermark on holed Mexico City 8 Reales, KM#109.

Date	Mintage	VG-8	F-12	VF-20	XF-40	MS-60	MS-63	Proof
1791-1808	—	800	1,350	2,250	—	—	—	—

KM# 3 Composition: Silver **Note:** Countermark on holed Lima 8 Reales, C#96.

Date	Mintage	VG-8	F-12	VF-20	XF-40	MS-60	MS-63	Proof
ND	1,000	1,000	1,750	3,000	—	—	—	—

MEXICO

The United States of Mexico, located immediately south of the United States has an area of 759,529 sq. mi. (1,967,183 sq. km.) and an estimated population of 88 million. Capital: Mexico City. The economy is based on agriculture, manufacturing and mining. Oil, cotton, silver, coffee, and shrimp are exported.

Mexico was the site of highly advanced Indian civilizations 1,500 years before conquistador Hernando Cortes conquered the wealthy Aztec empire of Montezuma, 1519-21, and founded a Spanish colony which lasted for nearly 300 years. During the Spanish period, Mexico, then called New Spain, stretched from Guatemala to the present states of Wyoming and California, its present northern boundary having been established by the secession of Texas during 1836 and the war of 1846-48 with the United States.

Independence from Spain was declared by Father Miguel Hidalgo on Sept. 16, 1810, (Mexican Independence Day) and was achieved by General Agustín de Iturbide in 1821. Iturbide became emperor in 1822 but was deposed when a republic was established a year later. For more than fifty years following the birth of the republic, the political scene of Mexico was characterized by turmoil which saw two emperors (including the unfortunate Maximilian), several dictators and an average of one new government every nine months passing swiftly from obscurity to oblivion. The land, social, economic and labor reforms promulgated by the Reform Constitution of Feb. 5, 1917 established the basis for sustained economic development and participative democracy that have made Mexico one of the most politically stable countries of modern Latin America.

COLONIAL
COB COINAGE

1/2 REAL   KM# 24   Weight: 1.6900 g. **Composition:** 0.9310 Silver **Ruler:** Philip V **Obverse:** Legend around crowned PHILIPVS monogram **Reverse:** Legend around cross, lions and castles **Note:** Struck at Mexico City Mint, mint mark M, Mo.

Date	Mintage	Good	VG	F	VF	XF
ND(1701-28)						
Date off flan	—	—	20.00	35.00	65.00	—
1701 L	—	—	100	125	225	—
1702 L	—	—	100	125	225	—
1703 L	—	—	100	125	225	—
1704 L	—	—	100	125	225	—
1705 L	—	—	100	125	225	—
1706 J	—	—	100	125	225	—
1707 J	—	—	100	125	225	—
1708 J	—	—	100	125	175	—
1709 J	—	—	100	125	175	—
1710 J	—	—	100	125	175	—
1711 J	—	—	100	125	175	—
1712 J	—	—	100	125	175	—
1714 J	—	—	100	125	175	—
1715 J	—	—	100	125	175	—
1716 J	—	—	100	125	175	—
1717 J	—	—	100	125	175	—
1718 J	—	—	100	125	175	—
1719 J	—	—	100	125	175	—
1720 J	—	—	100	125	175	—
1721 J	—	—	100	125	175	—
1722 J	—	—	100	125	175	—
1723 J	—	—	100	125	175	—
1724 J	—	—	100	125	175	—
1724 D	—	—	100	125	175	—
1725 D	—	—	100	125	175	—
1726 D	—	—	100	125	175	—
1727 D	—	—	100	125	175	—
1728 D	—	—	100	125	175	—

1/2 REAL   KM# 25   Weight: 1.6900 g. **Composition:** 0.9310 Silver **Ruler:** Luis I **Obverse:** Legend around crowned LVDOVICVS monogram **Reverse:** Legend around cross, lions and castles **Note:** Struck at Mexico City Mint, mint mark M, Mo.

Date	Mintage	Good	VG	F	VF	XF
ND(1724-25)						
Date off flan	—	—	125	200	250	—
1724 D	—	—	325	450	550	—
1725 D	—	—	325	450	550	—

1/2 REAL   KM# 24a   Weight: 1.6900 g. **Composition:** 0.9160 Silver **Ruler:** Philip V **Obverse:** Legend around crowned PHILIPVS monogram **Reverse:** Legend around cross, lions and castles **Note:** Struck at Mexico City Mint, mint mark M, Mo.

Date	Mintage	Good	VG	F	VF	XF
ND(1729-33)						
Date off flan	—	—	20.00	35.00	60.00	—
1729 R	—	—	90.00	120	150	—
1730 R	—	—	90.00	120	150	—
1731 F	—	—	90.00	120	150	—
1732/1 F	—	—	90.00	120	150	—
1732 F	—	—	90.00	120	150	—
1733/2 F	—	—	90.00	120	150	—
1733 F	—	—	90.00	120	150	—

REAL   KM# 30   Weight: 3.3800 g. **Composition:** 0.9310 Silver **Ruler:** Philip V **Obverse:** Legend and date around crowned arms **Obv. Legend:** PHILIPVS V DEI G **Note:** Struck at Mexico City Mint, mint mark M, Mo.

Date	Mintage	Good	VG	F	VF	XF
ND(1701-28)						
Date off flan	—	—	30.00	50.00	70.00	—
1701 L	—	—	125	175	275	—
1702 L	—	—	125	175	275	—
1703 L	—	—	125	175	275	—
1704 L	—	—	125	175	275	—
1705 L	—	—	125	175	275	—
1706 J	—	—	125	175	275	—
1707 J	—	—	125	175	275	—
1708 J	—	—	125	175	275	—
1709 J	—	—	125	175	275	—
1710 J	—	—	125	175	275	—
1711 J	—	—	125	175	275	—
1712 J	—	—	125	175	275	—
1713 J	—	—	125	175	275	—
1714 J	—	—	125	175	275	—
1715 J	—	—	100	175	275	—
1716 J	—	—	100	175	275	—
1717 J	—	—	100	175	275	—
1718 J	—	—	100	175	275	—
1719 J	—	—	100	175	275	—
1720/19 J	—	—	100	175	275	—

Date	Mintage	Good	VG	F	VF	XF
1720 J	—	—	100	175	275	—
1721 J	—	—	100	175	275	—
1722 J	—	—	100	175	275	—
1723 J	—	—	100	175	275	—
1726 D	—	—	100	175	275	—
1727 D	—	—	100	175	275	—
1728 D	—	—	100	175	275	—

REAL   KM# A31   Weight: 3.3834 g. **Composition:** 0.9310 Silver .1013 oz. ASW **Ruler:** Luis I **Note:** A significant portion of the legend must be visibile for proper attribution. Struck at Mexico City Mint, mint mark M, Mo.

Date	Mintage	Good	VG	F	VF	XF
1724 D Rare	—	—	—	—	—	—
1725 D Rare	—	—	—	—	—	—

REAL   KM# 30a   Weight: 3.3800 g. **Composition:** 0.9160 Silver **Ruler:** Philip V **Obverse:** Legend and date around crowned arms **Obv. Legend:** PHILIPVS V DEI G **Note:** Struck at Mexico City Mint, mint mark M, Mo.

Date	Mintage	Good	VG	F	VF	XF
ND(1729-32)						
Date off flan	—	—	25.00	40.00	65.00	—
1729 R	—	—	90.00	125	175	—
1730 R	—	—	90.00	125	175	—
1730 F	—	—	90.00	125	175	—
1730 G	—	—	90.00	125	175	—
1731 F	—	—	90.00	125	175	—
1732 F	—	—	90.00	125	175	—

2 REALES   KM# 35   Weight: 6.7700 g. **Composition:** 0.9310 Silver **Ruler:** Philip V **Obverse:** Legend and date around crowned arms **Obv. Legend:** PHILIPVS V DEI G **Note:** Struck at Mexico City Mint, mint mark M, Mo.

Date	Mintage	Good	VG	F	VF	XF
ND(1701-28)						
Date off flan	—	—	45.00	65.00	100	—
1701 L	—	—	125	150	250	—
1702 L	—	—	125	150	250	—
1703 L	—	—	125	150	250	—
1704 L	—	—	125	150	250	—
1705 L	—	—	125	150	250	—
1706 J	—	—	125	150	250	—
1707 J	—	—	125	150	250	—
1708 J	—	—	125	150	250	—
1710 J	—	—	125	150	250	—
1711 J	—	—	125	150	250	—
1712 J	—	—	125	150	250	—
1713 J	—	—	125	150	250	—
1714 J	—	—	150	185	300	—
1715 J	—	—	150	185	300	—
1716 J	—	—	150	185	300	—
1717 J	—	—	150	185	300	—
1718 J	—	—	150	185	300	—
1719 J	—	—	150	185	300	—
1720 J	—	—	150	185	300	—
1721 J	—	—	150	185	300	—
1722 J	—	—	150	185	300	—
1723 J	—	—	150	185	300	—
1724 J	—	—	150	185	300	—
1726 D	—	—	150	185	300	—
1727 D	—	—	150	185	300	—
1728 D	—	—	150	185	300	—

4 REALES   KM# 40   Weight: 13.5400 g. **Composition:** 0.9310 Silver **Ruler:** Philip V **Obverse:** Legend and date around crowned arms **Obv. Legend:** PHILIPVS V DEI G **Note:** Struck at Mexico City Mint, mint mark M, Mo.

Date	Mintage	Good	VG	F	VF	XF
1701 L	—	—	175	250	375	—
1702 L	—	—	175	250	375	—
1703 L	—	—	175	250	375	—
1704 L	—	—	175	250	375	—
1705 L	—	—	175	250	375	—
1706 J	—	—	175	250	375	—
1707 J	—	—	175	250	375	—
1708 J	—	—	175	250	375	—
1709 J	—	—	175	250	375	—
1710 J	—	—	175	250	375	—
1711 J	—	—	175	250	375	—
1712 J	—	—	175	250	375	—
1713 J	—	—	175	250	375	—
1714 J	—	—	175	250	375	—
1715 J	—	—	125	225	375	—
1716 J	—	—	200	300	500	—
1717 J	—	—	200	300	500	—
1718 J	—	—	200	300	500	—
1719 J	—	—	200	300	500	—
1720 J	—	—	200	300	500	—
1721 J	—	—	200	300	500	—
1722 J	—	—	200	300	500	—
1723 J	—	—	200	300	500	—
1726 D	—	—	200	300	500	—
1727 D	—	—	200	300	500	—
1728 D	—	—	200	300	500	—

4 REALES   KM# 42   Weight: 13.5400 g. **Composition:** 0.9310 Silver **Ruler:** Luis I **Obverse:** Legend around crowned arms **Obv. Legend:** LVDOVICUS I DEI G **Reverse:** Legend around cross, lions and castles **Note:** A significant portion of the legend must be visible for proper attribution. Struck at Mexico City Mint, mint mark M, Mo.

Date	Mintage	Good	VG	F	VF	XF
1724 D Rare	—	—	—	—	—	—
1725 D Rare	—	—	—	—	—	—

4 REALES   KM# 40a   Weight: 13.5400 g. **Composition:** 0.9160 Silver **Ruler:** Philip V **Obverse:** Legend and date around crowned arms **Obv. Legend:** PHILIPVS V DEI G **Note:** Struck at Mexico City Mint, mint mark M, Mo.

Date	Mintage	Good	VG	F	VF	XF
ND(1729-33)						
Date off flan	—	—	50.00	70.00	100	—
1729 D	—	—	125	200	275	—
1730 R	—	—	125	200	275	—
1730 G	—	—	125	200	275	—
1731 F	—	—	125	200	275	—

2 REALES   KM# 35a   Weight: 6.7700 g. **Composition:** 0.9160 Silver **Ruler:** Philip V **Obverse:** Legend and date around crowned arms **Obv. Legend:** PHILIPVS V DEI G **Note:** Struck at Mexico City Mint, mint mark M, Mo.

Date	Mintage	Good	VG	F	VF	XF
ND(1729-32)						
Date off flan	—	—	40.00	60.00	90.00	—
1729 R	—	—	100	125	150	—
1730 R	—	—	100	125	150	—
1731 F	—	—	100	125	150	—
1731/0 F	—	—	100	125	150	—
1732 F	—	—	100	125	150	—

Date	Mintage	Good	VG	F	VF	XF
1732/1 F	—	—	125	175	250	—
1732 F	—	—	125	175	250	—
1733/2 F	—	—	125	175	250	—

Date	Mintage	Good	VG	F	VF	XF
1707 J	—	—	200	350	500	—
1708 J	—	—	200	350	500	—
1709 J	—	—	200	350	500	—
1710 J	—	—	200	350	500	—
1711 J	—	—	175	300	475	—
1712 J	—	—	175	300	475	—
1713 J	—	—	175	300	475	—
1714 J	—	—	175	300	475	—
1715 J	—	—	175	300	475	—
1716 J	—	—	375	575	800	—
1717 J	—	—	375	575	800	—
1718/7 J	—	—	375	575	800	—
1718 J	—	—	350	500	800	—
1719 J	—	—	350	500	800	—
1720 J	—	—	350	500	800	—
1721 J	—	—	350	500	800	—
1722 J	—	—	350	500	800	—
1723 J	—	—	350	500	800	—
1724 D	—	—	350	500	800	—
1725 D	—	—	350	500	800	—
1726 D	—	—	350	500	800	—
1727 D	—	—	350	500	800	—
1728 D	—	—	400	600	1,000	—

4 REALES   KM# 41   Weight: 13.5400 g. **Composition:** 0.9160 Silver **Ruler:** Philip V **Obverse:** Legend and date around crowned arms **Obv. Legend:** PHILIPVS V DEI G **Reverse:** Legend around cross, lions and castles **Note:** Klippe. Similar to KM#40a. Struck at Mexico City Mint, mint mark M, Mo.

Date	Mintage	Good	VG	F	VF	XF
1733 F	—	—	450	600	750	—
1733 MF	—	—	450	600	750	—
1734/3 MF	—	—	450	600	750	—

8 REALES   KM# 46   Weight: 27.0700 g. **Composition:** 0.9310 Silver **Ruler:** Charles II **Obverse:** Legend and date around crowned arms **Obv. Legend:** CAROLVS II DEI G **Reverse:** Legend around cross, lions and castles **Note:** Struck at Mexico City Mint, mint mark M, Mo.

Date	Mintage	Good	VG	F	VF	XF
1701 L	—	—	700	1,000	1,700	—

8 REALES   KM# 49   Weight: 27.0700 g. **Composition:** 0.9310 Silver **Ruler:** Luis I **Obverse:** Legend and date around crowned arms **Obv. Legend:** LVDOVICVS I DEI G **Reverse:** Legend around cross, lions and castles **Note:** A significant portion of the legend must be visible for proper attribution. Struck at Mexico City Mint, mint mark M, Mo.

Date	Mintage	Good	VG	F	VF	XF
ND(1724-25) Date off flan; Rare	—	—	—	—	—	—
1724 D Rare	—	—	—	—	—	—
1725 D Rare	—	—	—	—	—	—

8 REALES   KM# 47a   Weight: 27.0700 g. **Composition:** 0.9160 Silver **Ruler:** Philip V **Obverse:** Legend and date around crowned arms **Obv. Legend:** PHILIPVS V DEI G **Reverse:** Legend around cross, lions and castles **Note:** Struck at Mexico City Mint, mint mark M, Mo.

Date	Mintage	Good	VG	F	VF	XF
ND(1729-33) Date off flan	—	—	70.00	90.00	110	—
1729 R	—	—	150	250	400	—
1730 G/R	—	—	150	250	400	—
1730 R	—	—	150	250	400	—
1730 G	—	—	150	250	400	—
1730 F	—	—	150	250	400	—
1731/0 F	—	—	150	250	400	—
1731 F	—	—	150	250	400	—
1732/1 F	—	—	150	250	400	—

8 REALES   KM# 47   Weight: 27.0700 g. **Composition:** 0.9310 Silver **Ruler:** Philip V **Obverse:** Legend and date around crowned arms **Obv. Legend:** PHILIPVS V DEI G **Reverse:** Legend around cross, lions and castles **Note:** Struck at Mexico City Mint, mint mark M, Mo.

Date	Mintage	Good	VG	F	VF	XF
ND(1702-28) Date off flan	—	—	70.00	90.00	120	—
1702 L	—	—	200	350	500	—
1703 L	—	—	200	350	500	—
1704 L Rare	—	—	—	—	—	—
1705 L	—	—	200	350	600	—
1706 J	—	—	200	350	600	—

Date	Mintage	Good	VG	F	VF	XF
1732 F	—	—	150	250	400	—
1733/2 F	—	—	150	250	400	—
1733 F	—	—	150	250	400	—

8 REALES KM# 48 **Weight:** 0.9160 g. **Composition:** Silver **Ruler:** Philip V **Note:** Klippe. Similar to KM#47a. Struck at Mexico City Mint, mint mark M, Mo.

Date	Mintage	Good	VG	F	VF	XF
ND(1733-34) Date off flan	—	—	150	200	300	—
1733 F	—	—	550	750	1,150	—
1733 MF	—	—	350	500	650	—
1734/3 MF	—	—	500	750	1,000	—
1734 MF	—	—	500	750	1,000	—

ESCUDO KM# 50 **Weight:** 3.3800 g. **Composition:** 0.9170 Gold **Ruler:** Charles II **Obverse:** Legend and date around crowned arms **Obv. Legend:** CAROLVS II DEI G **Reverse:** Legend around cross, lions and castles **Note:** Struck at Mexico City Mint, mint mark MXo.

Date	Mintage	VG	F	VF	XF	Unc
1701/0MXo L	—	—	3,000	4,000	5,000	—

ESCUDO KM# 51.1 **Weight:** 3.3800 g. **Composition:** 0.9170 Gold .0997 oz. AGW **Ruler:** Philip V **Obverse:** Legend and date around crowned arms **Obv. Legend:** PHILIPVS V DEI G **Reverse:** Legend around cross, lions and castles **Note:** Struck at Mexico City Mint, mint mark MXo.

Date	Mintage	VG	F	VF	XF	Unc
ND(1702-13) Date off flan	—	—	1,000	1,350	1,500	—
1702MXo L	—	—	1,500	2,500	3,500	—
1703/2MXo L	—	—	1,500	2,500	3,500	—
1704MXo L	—	—	1,500	2,500	3,500	—
1707MXo J	—	—	1,500	2,500	3,500	—
1708MXo J	—	—	1,500	2,500	3,500	—
1709MXo J	—	—	1,500	2,500	3,500	—
1710MXo J	—	—	1,500	2,500	3,500	—
1711MXo J	—	—	1,500	2,500	3,500	—

Date	Mintage	VG	F	VF	XF	Unc
1712MXo J	—	—	1,500	2,500	3,500	—
1713MXo J	—	—	1,500	2,500	3,500	—

ESCUDO KM# 51.2 **Weight:** 3.3800 g. **Composition:** 0.9170 Gold .0997 oz. AGW **Ruler:** Philip V **Obverse:** Legend and date around crowned arms **Obv. Legend:** PHILIPVS V DEI G **Reverse:** Legend around cross, lions and castles **Note:** Struck at Mexico City Mint, mint mark Mo.

Date	Mintage	VG	F	VF	XF	Unc
ND(1702-13) Date off flan	—	—	1,200	1,500	1,750	—
1712Mo J	—	—	2,000	3,000	4,000	—
1714Mo J	—	—	1,400	2,000	3,000	—
1714Mo J J's 1's (J7J4J)	—	—	2,000	3,000	4,000	—
1715Mo J	—	—	2,000	3,000	4,000	—
1727Mo J Rare	—	—	—	—	—	—
1728Mo J Rare	—	—	—	—	—	—

Note: Die-struck counterfiets of 1731 F exist

2 ESCUDOS KM# 52 **Weight:** 6.7700 g. **Composition:** 0.9170 Gold .1996 oz. AGW **Ruler:** Philip V **Obverse:** Legend and date around crowned arms **Obv. Legend:** CAROLVS II DEI G **Reverse:** Legend around cross **Note:** Struck at Mexico City Mint, mint mark MXo.

Date	Mintage	VG	F	VF	XF	Unc
1701MXo L	—	—	4,000	2,200	6,000	—

2 ESCUDOS KM# 53.1 **Weight:** 6.7700 g. **Composition:** 0.9170 Gold .1996 oz. AGW **Ruler:** Philip V **Obverse:** Legend and date around crowned arms **Obv. Legend:** PHILIPVS V DEI G **Reverse:** Legend around cross **Note:** Struck at Mexico City Mint, mint mark MXo.

Date	Mintage	VG	F	VF	XF	Unc
ND(1704-13) Date off flan	—	—	1,200	1,500	1,750	—
1704MXo L	—	—	2,750	3,750	4,750	—
1708MXo J	—	—	2,750	3,750	4,750	—
1710MXo J	—	—	2,750	3,750	4,750	—
1711MXo J	—	—	2,750	3,750	4,750	—
1712MXo J	—	—	2,750	3,750	4,750	—
1713MXo J	—	—	2,750	3,750	4,750	—

2 ESCUDOS KM# 53.2 **Weight:** 6.7700 g. **Composition:** 0.9170 Gold .1996 oz. AGW **Ruler:** Philip V

Obverse: Legend and date around crowned arms
Obv. Legend: PHILIPVS V DEI G **Reverse:** Legend around cross **Note:** Struck counterfeits exist for 1731. Struck at Mexico City Mint, mint mark Mo.

Date	Mintage	VG	F	VF	XF	Unc
ND(1714-31) Date off flan	—	—	1,500	1,750	2,500	—
1714Mo J	—	—	—	2,500	3,500	—
1717Mo J Rare	—	—	—	—	—	—
1722Mo J Rare	—	—	—	—	—	—
1729Mo R Rare	—	—	—	—	—	—
1731Mo F Rare	—	—	—	—	—	—

2 ESCUDOS   KM# A54   Weight: 6.7700 g. **Composition:** 0.9170 Gold .1996 oz. AGW **Ruler:** Luis I **Obverse:** Legend and date around crowned arms **Obv. Legend:** LVDOVICVS I DEI G. **Reverse:** Legend around cross **Note:** A significant portion of the legend must be visible for proper attribution. Struck at Mexico City Mint, mint mark MXo.

Date	Mintage	VG	F	VF	XF	Unc
NDMXo F Rare	—	—	—	—	—	—

4 ESCUDOS   KM# 55.1   Weight: 13.5400 g. **Composition:** 0.9170 Gold .3992 oz. AGW **Ruler:** Philip V **Obverse:** Legend and date around crowned arms **Obv. Legend:** PHILIPVS V DEI G **Reverse:** Legend around cross **Note:** Struck at Mexico City Mint, mint mark MXo.

Date	Mintage	VG	F	VF	XF	Unc
ND(1705-13) Date off flan	—	—	2,500	3,000	4,000	—
1705MXo J	—	—	4,000	5,750	6,750	—
1706MXo L	—	—	4,000	5,750	6,750	—
1711MXo J	—	—	4,000	5,750	6,750	—
1712MXo J	—	—	4,000	5,750	6,750	—
1713MXo J	—	—	4,000	5,750	6,750	—

4 ESCUDOS   KM# 55.2   Weight: 13.5400 g. **Composition:** 0.9170 Gold .3992 oz. AGW **Ruler:** Philip V **Obverse:** Legend and date around crowned arms **Obv. Legend:** PHILIPVS V DEI G **Reverse:** Legend around cross **Note:** Struck at Mexico City Mint, mint mark Mo.

Date	Mintage	VG	F	VF	XF	Unc
ND(1714-20) Date off flan	—	—	2,500	3,750	5,000	—
1714Mo J	—	—	—	5,750	7,500	—
1715Mo J	—	—	—	5,750	7,500	—
1720Mo J Rare	—	—	—	—	—	—

8 ESCUDOS   KM# 57.1   Weight: 27.0700 g. **Composition:** 0.9170 Gold .7980 oz. AGW **Ruler:** Philip V **Obverse:** Legend and date around crowned arms **Obv. Legend:** PHILIPVS V DEI G **Reverse:** Legend around cross **Note:** Struck at Mexico City Mint, mint mark MXo.

Date	Mintage	VG	F	VF	XF	Unc
ND(1701-13) Date off flan	—	—	2,000	3,000	4,000	—
1701MXo L	—	—	6,000	7,500	9,000	—
1703MXo L	—	—	6,000	7,500	9,000	—
1706MXo J	—	—	6,000	7,500	9,000	—
1708MXo J	—	—	6,000	7,500	9,000	—
1709MXo J	—	—	6,000	7,500	9,000	—
1710MXo J	—	—	6,000	7,500	9,000	—
1711MXo J	—	—	3,500	4,000	5,750	—
1712MXo J	—	—	3,500	4,000	5,750	—
1713MXo J	—	—	3,500	4,000	5,750	—

8 ESCUDOS   KM# 57.2   Weight: 27.0700 g. **Composition:** 0.9170 Gold .7980 oz. AGW **Ruler:** Philip V **Obverse:** Legend and date around crowned arms **Obv. Legend:** PHILIPVS V DEI G **Reverse:** Legend around cross **Note:** Struck at Mexico City Mint, mint mark Mo.

Date	Mintage	VG	F	VF	XF	Unc
ND(1714-32)Mo Date off flan	—	—	2,750	3,750	4,750	—
1714Mo J	—	—	5,000	6,000	7,500	—
1714Mo Date over GRAT on obverse	—	—	6,000	7,500	9,000	—
1715Mo J Rare	—	—	—	—	—	—
1717/6Mo J Rare	—	—	—	—	—	—
1720/19Mo J Rare	—	—	—	—	—	—
1723Mo J Rare	—	—	—	—	—	—
1727/6Mo D Rare	—	—	—	—	—	—
1728/7Mo D Rare	—	—	—	—	—	—
1729Mo R Rare	—	—	—	—	—	—
1730Mo R Rare	—	—	—	—	—	—
1730Mo F Rare	—	—	—	—	—	—
1731Mo F Rare	—	—	—	—	—	—
1732Mo F Rare	—	—	—	—	—	—

8 ESCUDOS KM# 57.3 Weight: 27.0700 g.
Composition: 0.9170 Gold .7980 oz. AGW **Obverse:** Date around crowned arms **Obv. Legend:** PHILIPVS V DEI G **Reverse:** Legend and date around cross **Note:** Struck at Mexico City Mint, mint mark Mo.

Date	Mintage	VG	F	VF	XF	Unc
1714Mo J Date on reverse	—	—	6,000	7,500	9,000	—

8 ESCUDOS KM# 58 Weight: 27.0700 g. **Composition:** 0.9170 Gold .7980 oz. AGW **Ruler:** Luis I **Obverse:** Legend and date around crowned arms **Obv. Legend:** LVDOVICVS I DEI G **Reverse:** Legend around cross **Note:** A significant portion of the legend must be visible for proper attribution. Struck at Mexico City Mint, mint mark Mo.

Date	Mintage	VG	F	VF	XF	Unc
ND(1724-25) Mo D Rare	—	—	—	—	—	—

ROYAL COINAGE

Struck on specially prepared round planchets using well centered dies in excellent condition to prove the quality of the minting to the Viceroy or even to the King.

1/2 REAL KM# R24 Weight: 1.6917 g. **Composition:** 0.9130 Silver .0506 oz. ASW **Ruler:** Philip V **Note:** Normally found holed. Struck at Mexico City Mint, mint mark Mo.

Date	Mintage	Good	VG	F	VF	XF
1715Mo J	—	—	250	500	750	—
1719Mo J	—	—	250	500	750	—
1721Mo J	—	—	250	500	750	—
1726Mo D	—	—	250	500	750	—
1727Mo D	—	—	250	500	750	—

1/2 REAL KM# R25 Weight: 1.6917 g. **Composition:** 0.9310 Silver .0506 oz. ASW **Ruler:** Luis I **Note:** Struck at Mexico City Mint, mint mark Mo.

Date	Mintage	Good	VG	F	VF	XF
1724Mo D Rare	—	—	—	—	—	—

1/2 REAL KM# R24a Weight: 1.6917 g. **Composition:** 0.9170 Silver .0498 oz. ASW **Ruler:** Philip V **Note:** Normally found holed. Struck at Mexico City Mint, mark mark Mo.

Date	Mintage	Good	VG	F	VF	XF
1730Mo D	—	—	250	500	750	—

REAL KM# R29 Weight: 3.3834 g. **Composition:** 0.9310 Silver .1013 oz. ASW **Ruler:** Charles II **Obv. Legend:** CAROLVS II DEI G **Note:** Struck at Mexico City Mint, mint mark Mo.

Date	Mintage	Good	VG	F	VF	XF
1699Mo L Rare	—	—	—	—	—	—

REAL KM# R30 Weight: 3.3834 g. **Composition:** 0.9310 Silver .1013 oz. ASW **Ruler:** Philip V **Obv. Legend:** PHILIPVS V DEI G **Note:** Struck at Mexico City Mint, mint mark Mo.

Date	Mintage	Good	VG	F	VF	XF
1715Mo J Rare	—	—	—	—	—	—
1716Mo J Rare	—	—	—	—	—	—
1718Mo J Rare	—	—	—	—	—	—

2 REALES KM# R35 Weight: 6.7668 g. **Composition:** 0.9310 Silver .2026 oz. ASW **Ruler:** Philip V **Obv. Legend:** PHILIPVS V DEI G **Note:** Struck at Mexico City Mint, mint mark Mo.

Date	Mintage	Good	VG	F	VF	XF
1715Mo J Rare	—	—	—	—	—	—

2 REALES KM# R35a Weight: 6.7668 g. **Composition:** 0.9170 Silver .1995 oz. ASW **Ruler:** Philip V **Note:** Struck at Mexico City Mint, mint mark Mo.

Date	Mintage	Good	VG	F	VF	XF
1730Mo R Rare	—	—	—	—	—	—

4 REALES KM# R40 Weight: 13.5337 g. **Composition:** 0.9310 Silver .4051 oz. ASW **Ruler:** Philip V **Obv. Legend:** PHILIPVS V DEI G **Note:** Struck at Mexico City Mint, mint mark Mo.

Date	Mintage	Good	VG	F	VF	XF
1716Mo J Rare	—	—	—	—	—	—
1719Mo J Rare	—	—	—	—	—	—
1721Mo J Rare	—	—	—	—	—	—

Date	Mintage	Good	VG	F	VF	XF
1722Mo J Rare	—	—	—	—	—	—
1723Mo J Rare	—	—	—	—	—	—

8 REALES KM# R47 Weight: 27.0674 g. **Composition:** 0.9310 Silver .8102 oz. ASW **Ruler:** Philip V **Obv. Legend:** PHILIPVS V DEI G **Note:** Struck at Mexico City Mint, mint mark Mo.

Date	Mintage	Good	VG	F	VF	XF
1702Mo L Rare	—	—	—	—	—	—
1703Mo L Rare	—	—	—	—	—	—
1705Mo J Rare	—	—	—	—	—	—
1706Mo J Rare	—	—	—	—	—	—
1709Mo J Rare	—	—	—	—	—	—
1711Mo J Rare	—	—	—	—	—	—
1714Mo J Rare	—	—	—	—	—	—
1715Mo J Rare	—	—	—	—	—	—
1716Mo J Rare	—	—	—	—	—	—
1717Mo J Rare	—	—	—	—	—	—
1719Mo J Rare	—	—	—	—	—	—
1721Mo J Rare	—	—	—	—	—	—
1722Mo J Rare	—	—	—	—	—	—
1723Mo J Rare	—	—	—	—	—	—
1724Mo D Rare	—	—	—	—	—	—
1725Mo D Rare	—	—	—	—	—	—
1726/5Mo D Rare	—	—	—	—	—	—
1726Mo D Rare	—	—	—	—	—	—
1727Mo D Rare	—	—	—	—	—	—

8 REALES KM# R49 Weight: 27.0674 g. **Composition:** 0.9310 Silver .8102 oz. ASW **Ruler:** Luis I **Note:** Struck at Mexico City Mint, mint mark Mo.

Date	Mintage	Good	VG	F	VF	XF
1724 D Rare	—	—	—	—	—	—
1725 D Rare	—	—	—	—	—	—

8 REALES KM# R47a Weight: 27.0674 g. **Composition:** 0.9170 Silver .7980 oz. ASW **Note:** Struck at Mexico City Mint, mint mark Mo.

Date	Mintage	Good	VG	F	VF	XF
1729 R Rare	—	—	—	—	—	—
1730 R/D Rare	—	—	—	—	—	—
1730 G Rare	—	—	—	—	—	—

ESCUDO KM# R51.2 Weight: 3.3834 g. **Composition:** 0.9170 Gold .0997 oz. AGW **Note:** Struck at Mexico City Mint, mint mark Mo.

Date	Mintage	Good	VG	F	VF	XF
1714Mo J Rare	—	—	—	—	—	—
1715Mo J Rare	—	—	—	—	—	—

2 ESCUDOS KM# R53.1 Weight: 6.7668 g. **Composition:** 0.9170 Gold .1995 oz. AGW **Note:** Struck at Mexico City Mint, mint mark MXo.

Date	Mintage	Good	VG	F	VF	XF
1711MXo J Rare	—	—	—	—	—	—
1712MXo J Rare	—	—	—	—	—	—

4 ESCUDOS KM# R55.1 Weight: 13.5337 g. **Composition:** 0.9170 Gold .3990 oz. AGW **Note:** Struck at Mexico City Mint, mint mark M, Mo.

Date	Mintage	Good	VG	F	VF	XF
1711 Rare	—	—	—	—	—	—

4 ESCUDOS KM# R55.2 Weight: 13.5337 g. **Composition:** 0.9170 Gold .3990 oz. AGW **Note:** Struck at Mexico City Mint, mint mark M, Mo.

Date	Mintage	Good	VG	F	VF	XF
1714 Rare	—	—	—	—	—	—

8 ESCUDOS KM# R56 Weight: 27.0674 g. **Composition:** 0.9170 Gold .7980 oz. AGW **Note:** Fully struck sample specimens referred to as "Royal" strikes are seldom encountered. Struck at Mexico City Mint, mint mark MXo.

Date	Mintage	Good	VG	F	VF	XF
1695MXo L Rare	—	—	—	—	—	—
1698MXo L Rare	—	—	—	—	—	—

8 ESCUDOS KM# R57.1 Weight: 27.0674 g. **Composition:** 0.9170 Gold .7980 oz. AGW **Ruler:** Philip V **Note:** Struck at Mexico City Mint, mint mark MXo.

Date	Mintage	Good	VG	F	VF	XF
1702MXo L Rare	—	—	—	—	—	—
1711MXo J Rare	—	—	—	—	—	—
1712MXo J Rare	—	—	—	—	—	—
1713MXo J Rare	—	—	—	—	—	—

8 ESCUDOS KM# R57.3 Weight: 27.0674 g. **Composition:** 0.9170 Gold .7980 oz. AGW **Note:** Struck at Mexico City Mint, mint mark Mo.

Date	Mintage	Good	VG	F	VF	XF
1714Mo J Rare	—	—	—	—	—	—
1715Mo J Rare	—	—	—	—	—	—
1717Mo J Rare	—	—	—	—	—	—

Date	Mintage	Good	VG	F	VF	XF
1718Mo J Rare	—	—	—	—	—	—
1723Mo J Rare	—	—	—	—	—	—

MILLED COINAGE

16 Pilones = 1 Real; 8 Tlaco = 1 Real,
16 Reales = 1 Escudo

1/16 REAL (1/8 Pilon)   KM# 59   Composition: Copper
Obverse: Crowned F VII monogram **Reverse:** Castles and
lions in wreath **Note:** Struck at Mexico City Mint, mint mark
M, Mo.

Date	Mintage	VG	F	VF	XF	Unc
1814	—	10.00	20.00	45.00	120	—
1815	—	10.00	20.00	45.00	120	—

1/8 REAL (1/4 Tlaco)   KM# 63   Composition: Copper
Obverse: Legend around crowned F. VII **Obv. Legend:**
FERDIN. VII... **Note:** Struck at Mexico City Mint, mint mark
M, Mo.

Date	Mintage	VG	F	VF	XF	Unc
1814	—	12.00	25.00	50.00	150	—
1815	—	12.00	25.00	50.00	150	—
1816	—	12.00	25.00	50.00	150	—

1/4 REAL   KM# 62   Weight: 0.8458 g. **Composition:**
0.8960 Silver .0244 oz. ASW **Obverse:** Castle **Reverse:**
Lion **Note:** Struck at Mexico City Mint, mint mark M, Mo.

Date	Mintage	VG	F	VF	XF	Unc
1796	—	15.00	30.00	55.00	90.00	—
1797	—	15.00	30.00	55.00	90.00	—
1798	—	12.50	22.00	50.00	75.00	—
1799/8	—	12.50	22.00	50.00	75.00	—
1799	—	10.00	20.00	40.00	70.00	—
1800	—	10.00	25.00	55.00	90.00	—
1801/0	—	10.00	20.00	40.00	70.00	—
1801	—	10.00	20.00	40.00	70.00	—
1802	—	10.00	20.00	40.00	70.00	—
1803	—	10.00	20.00	40.00	70.00	—
1804	—	10.00	20.00	40.00	75.00	—
1805/4	—	12.50	25.00	55.00	85.00	—
1805	—	10.00	22.00	50.00	75.00	—
1806	—	10.00	22.00	50.00	80.00	—
1807/797	—	15.00	30.00	55.00	85.00	—
1807	—	12.50	25.00	50.00	80.00	—
1808	—	12.50	25.00	50.00	80.00	—
1809/8	—	12.50	25.00	50.00	80.00	—
1809	—	12.50	25.00	50.00	80.00	—
1810	—	12.50	25.00	50.00	75.00	—
1811	—	12.50	25.00	50.00	75.00	—
1812	—	12.50	25.00	50.00	75.00	—
1813	—	10.00	20.00	40.00	70.00	—
1815	—	12.50	22.00	50.00	75.00	—
1816	—	10.00	20.00	40.00	70.00	—

1/4 REAL (2/4 2 Tlaco)   KM# 64   Composition: Copper
Obverse: Legend around crowned F. VII **Obv. Legend:**
FERDIN. VII... **Note:** Struck at Mexico City Mint, mint mark
M, Mo.

Date	Mintage	VG	F	VF	XF	Unc
1814	—	12.00	25.00	50.00	150	—
1815/4	—	15.00	30.00	60.00	165	—
1815	—	12.00	25.00	50.00	150	—
1816	—	12.00	25.00	50.00	150	—
1821	—	20.00	40.00	75.00	200	—

1/2 REAL   KM# 65   Weight: 1.6917 g. **Composition:**
0.9170 Silver .0498 oz. ASW **Obv. Legend:** PHILIP. V. D.
G. HISPAN. ET IND. REX **Note:** Struck at Mexico City
Mint, mint mark M, Mo.

Date	Mintage	VG	F	VF	XF	Unc
1732 Rare	—	—	—	—	—	—
1732 F	—	500	800	1,200	2,000	—
1733 MF (MX)	—	400	600	1,000	1,500	—
1733 F	—	200	325	550	800	—
1733/2 MF	—	300	400	600	800	—
1733 MF	—	300	400	600	800	—
1734/3 MF	—	12.00	25.00	45.00	85.00	—
1734 MF	—	12.00	25.00	45.00	85.00	—
1735/4 MF	—	10.00	20.00	45.00	85.00	—
1735 MF	—	10.00	20.00	45.00	85.00	—
1736/5 MF	—	10.00	20.00	45.00	85.00	—
1736 MF	—	10.00	20.00	45.00	85.00	—
1737/6 MF	—	10.00	20.00	45.00	85.00	—
1737 MF	—	10.00	20.00	45.00	85.00	—
1738/7 MF	—	10.00	20.00	45.00	85.00	—
1738 MF	—	10.00	20.00	45.00	85.00	—
1739 MF	—	10.00	20.00	45.00	85.00	—
1740/30 MF	—	8.00	18.00	40.00	75.00	—
1740 MF	—	8.00	18.00	40.00	75.00	—
1741 MF	—	8.00	18.00	40.00	75.00	—

1/2 REAL   KM# 66   Weight: 1.6900 g. **Composition:**
0.9170 Silver .0498 oz. ASW **Obv. Legend:** PHS. V. D. G.
HISP. ET IND. R **Note:** Struck at Mexico City Mint, mint
mark M, Mo.

Date	Mintage	VG	F	VF	XF	Unc
1742 M	—	8.00	18.00	40.00	75.00	—
1743 M	—	8.00	18.00	40.00	75.00	—
1744/3 M	—	8.00	18.00	40.00	75.00	—
1744 M	—	8.00	18.00	40.00	75.00	—
1745 M EST IND - Rare	—	—	—	—	—	—
1745 M	—	8.00	18.00	40.00	75.00	—
1746/5 M	—	8.00	18.00	40.00	75.00	—
1746 M	—	8.00	18.00	40.00	75.00	—
1747 M	—	8.00	18.00	40.00	75.00	—

1/2 REAL   KM# 67.1 (KM67)   Weight: 1.6900 g.
Composition: 0.9170 Silver .0498 oz. ASW **Obverse:**
Royal crown **Obv. Legend:** FRD. VI. D. G. HIPS. ET IND.
R **Note:** Struck at Mexico City Mint, mint mark M, Mo.

Date	Mintage	VG	F	VF	XF	Unc
1747/6 M	—	—	—	—	—	—
1747 M	—	8.00	18.00	40.00	75.00	—
1748/7 M	—	8.00	18.00	40.00	75.00	—
1748 M	—	8.00	18.00	40.00	75.00	—
1749 M	—	8.00	18.00	40.00	75.00	—
1750 M	—	8.00	18.00	40.00	75.00	—
1751 M	—	10.00	20.00	45.00	85.00	—
1752 M	—	8.00	18.00	40.00	75.00	—
1753 M	—	8.00	18.00	40.00	75.00	—
1754 M	—	12.00	25.00	55.00	100	—
1755/6 M	—	12.00	25.00	55.00	100	—
1755 M	—	8.00	18.00	40.00	75.00	—
1756/5 M	—	8.00	18.00	40.00	75.00	—
1756 M	—	8.00	18.00	40.00	75.00	—

Date	Mintage	VG	F	VF	XF	Unc
1757/6 M	—	8.00	18.00	40.00	75.00	—
1757 M	—	8.00	18.00	40.00	75.00	—

1/2 REAL   KM# 67.2   Weight: 1.6917 g. **Composition:** 0.9170 Silver .0498 oz. ASW **Obverse:** Different crown **Note:** Struck at Mexico City Mint, mint mark M, Mo.

Date	Mintage	VG	F	VF	XF	Unc
1757 M	—	8.00	18.00	40.00	75.00	—
1758/7 M	—	8.00	18.00	40.00	75.00	—
1758 M	—	8.00	18.00	40.00	75.00	—
1759 M	—	8.00	18.00	40.00	75.00	—
1760/59 M	—	8.00	18.00	40.00	75.00	—
1760 M	—	8.00	18.00	40.00	75.00	—

1/2 REAL   KM# 68   Weight: 1.6900 g. **Composition:** 0.9170 Silver .0498 oz. ASW **Obv. Legend:** CAR. III. D. G. HISP. ET IND. R **Note:** Struck at Mexico City Mint, mint mark M, Mo.

Date	Mintage	VG	F	VF	XF	Unc
1760/59 M	—	8.00	18.00	40.00	75.00	—
1760 M	—	8.00	18.00	40.00	75.00	—
1761 M	—	8.00	18.00	40.00	75.00	—
1762 M	—	8.00	18.00	40.00	75.00	—
1763/2 M	—	8.00	18.00	40.00	75.00	—
1763 M	—	8.00	18.00	40.00	75.00	—
1764 M	—	8.00	18.00	40.00	75.00	—
1765/4 M	—	10.00	20.00	42.00	80.00	—
1765 M	—	8.00	18.00	40.00	75.00	—
1766 M	—	8.00	18.00	40.00	75.00	—
1767 M	—	10.00	20.00	45.00	85.00	—
1768/6 M	—	10.00	20.00	42.00	80.00	—
1768 M	—	8.00	18.00	40.00	75.00	—
1769 M	—	10.00	20.00	42.00	80.00	—
1770 M	—	10.00	20.00	42.00	80.00	—
1770 F	—	15.00	30.00	60.00	100	—
1771 F	—	10.00	20.00	42.00	80.00	—

1/2 REAL   KM# 69.1   Weight: 1.6900 g. **Composition:** 0.9030 Silver .0490 oz. ASW **Obv. Legend:** CAROLUS. III. DEI. GRATIA **Reverse:** Inverted FM and mint mark **Note:** Struck at Mexico City Mint, mint mark Mo.

Date	Mintage	VG	F	VF	XF	Unc
1772Mo FM	—	5.00	12.00	27.00	65.00	—
1773Mo FM	—	4.50	10.00	25.00	55.00	—

1/2 REAL   KM# 69.2   Weight: 1.6917 g. **Composition:** 0.9030 Silver .0491 oz. ASW **Obv. Legend:** CAROLUS. III. DEI. GRATIA **Reverse:** Normal initials and mint mark **Note:** Struck at Mexico City Mint, mint mark Mo.

Date	Mintage	VG	F	VF	XF	Unc
1772Mo FF	—	9.00	18.00	35.00	80.00	—
1773Mo FM	—	4.50	10.00	25.00	60.00	—
1773Mo FM CAROLS (error)	—	75.00	150	250	400	—
1774Mo FM	—	4.50	10.00	25.00	55.00	—
1775Mo FM	—	4.50	10.00	25.00	55.00	—
1776Mo FM	—	4.50	10.00	25.00	55.00	—
1777/6Mo FM	—	10.00	18.00	35.00	75.00	—
1777Mo FM	—	7.00	15.00	30.00	65.00	—
1778Mo FF	—	4.50	10.00	25.00	55.00	—
1779Mo FF	—	4.50	10.00	25.00	55.00	—
1780/79Mo FF	—	6.00	12.50	30.00	75.00	—
1780Mo FF	—	4.50	10.00	25.00	55.00	—
1781Mo FF	—	4.50	10.00	25.00	55.00	—
1782/1Mo FF	—	6.00	12.50	30.00	75.00	—
1782Mo FF	—	4.50	10.00	25.00	55.00	—
1783Mo FF	—	4.50	10.00	25.00	55.00	—
1783Mo FM	—	125	300	450	—	—
1784Mo FF	—	4.50	10.00	25.00	55.00	—
1784Mo FM	—	7.00	15.00	35.00	80.00	—

1/2 REAL   KM# 69.2a   Weight: 1.6917 g. **Composition:** 0.8960 Silver .0487 oz. ASW **Reverse:** Normal initials and mint mark **Note:** Struck at Mexico City Mint, mint mark M, Mo.

Date	Mintage	VG	F	VF	XF	Unc
1785/4 FM	—	7.00	15.00	35.00	80.00	—
1785 FM	—	5.00	12.00	27.00	60.00	—
1786 FM	—	4.50	10.00	25.00	55.00	—
1787 FM	—	4.50	10.00	25.00	55.00	—
1788 FM	—	4.50	10.00	25.00	55.00	—
1789 FM	—	8.00	16.00	40.00	100	—

1/2 REAL   KM# 70   Weight: 1.6917 g. **Composition:** 0.8960 Silver .0487 oz. ASW **Obverse:** Armored bust of Charles III **Obv. Legend:** CAROLUS. IV... **Note:** Struck at Mexico City Mint, mint mark M, Mo.

Date	Mintage	VG	F	VF	XF	Unc
1789 FM	—	12.00	25.00	50.00	100	—
1790 FM	—	12.00	25.00	50.00	100	—

1/2 REAL   KM# 71   Weight: 1.6917 g. **Composition:** 0.8960 Silver .0487 oz. ASW **Obverse:** Armored bust of Charles III **Obv. Legend:** CAROLUS IIII... **Note:** Struck at Mexico City Mint, mint mark M, Mo.

Date	Mintage	VG	F	VF	XF	Unc
1790 FM	—	12.00	25.00	50.00	100	—

1/2 REAL   KM# 72   Weight: 1.6900 g. **Composition:** 0.9030 Silver .0490 oz. ASW **Obverse:** Armored bust of Charles IIII **Reverse:** Pillars and arms **Note:** Struck at Mexico City Mint, mint mark M, Mo.

Date	Mintage	VG	F	VF	XF	Unc
1792 FM	—	6.00	12.00	25.00	50.00	—
1793 FM	—	6.00	12.00	25.00	50.00	—
1794/3 FM	—	7.50	15.00	30.00	75.00	—
1794 FM	—	5.00	10.00	22.00	45.00	—
1795 FM	—	4.00	10.00	22.00	45.00	—
1796 FM	—	4.00	10.00	22.00	45.00	—
1797 FM	—	4.00	10.00	22.00	45.00	—
1798/7 FM	—	5.00	11.50	25.00	50.00	—
1798 FM	—	4.00	10.00	22.00	45.00	—
1799 FM	—	4.00	10.00	22.00	45.00	—
1800/799 FM	—	5.00	11.50	25.00	50.00	—
1800 FM	—	4.00	10.00	22.00	45.00	—
1801 FM	—	7.50	15.00	30.00	80.00	—
1801 FT	—	4.00	10.00	22.00	45.00	—
1802 FT	—	4.00	10.00	22.00	45.00	—
1803 FT	—	5.00	11.50	25.00	50.00	—
1804 TH	—	4.00	10.00	22.00	45.00	—
1805 TH	—	4.00	10.00	22.00	45.00	—
1806 TH	—	4.00	10.00	22.00	45.00	—
1807/6 TH	—	5.00	11.50	25.00	50.00	—
1807 TH	—	4.00	10.00	22.00	45.00	—
1808/7 TH	—	5.00	11.50	25.00	50.00	—
1808 TH	—	4.00	10.00	22.00	45.00	—

1/2 REAL   KM# 73   Weight: 1.6900 g. **Composition:** 0.9030 Silver .0490 oz. ASW **Obverse:** Armored bust of Ferdinand VII **Reverse:** Pillars and arms **Note:** Struck at Mexico City Mint, mint mark M, Mo.

Date	Mintage	VG	F	VF	XF	Unc
1808 TH	—	3.50	8.00	20.00	35.00	—
1809 TH	—	3.50	8.00	20.00	35.00	—
1810 TH	—	5.00	10.00	22.00	45.00	—
1810 HJ	—	3.50	8.00	20.00	35.00	—
1811 HJ	—	3.50	8.00	20.00	35.00	—
1812/1 HJ	—	7.50	15.00	35.00	80.00	—
1812 HJ	—	3.50	8.00	20.00	35.00	—
1812 JJ	—	12.00	25.00	45.00	100	—
1813/2 JJ	—	12.00	25.00	45.00	100	—
1813 TH	—	3.50	8.00	20.00	35.00	—
1813 JJ	—	6.00	12.00	25.00	75.00	—
1813 HJ	—	7.50	15.00	35.00	90.00	—
1814/3 JJ	—	7.50	15.00	35.00	90.00	—
1814 JJ	—	5.00	10.00	22.00	45.00	—

1/2 REAL   KM# 74   Weight: 1.6900 g. **Composition:** 0.9030 Silver .0490 oz. ASW **Ruler:** Ferdinand VII **Obverse:** Draped bust of Ferdinand VII **Reverse:** Pillars and arms **Note:** Struck at Mexico City Mint, mark mark M, Mo.

Date	Mintage	VG	F	VF	XF	Unc
1815 JJ	—	3.50	8.00	20.00	40.00	—
1816 JJ	—	3.50	8.00	20.00	40.00	—
1817/6 JJ	—	12.00	25.00	50.00	120	—
1817 JJ	—	3.50	8.00	28.00	45.00	—
1818/7 JJ	—	3.50	8.00	25.00	50.00	—
1818 JJ	—	3.50	8.00	25.00	50.00	—
1819/8 JJ	—	6.00	12.00	35.00	90.00	—
1819 JJ	—	3.50	8.00	20.00	40.00	—
1820 JJ	—	3.50	8.00	25.00	50.00	—
1821 JJ	—	3.50	8.00	20.00	40.00	—

REAL   KM# 75.1   Weight: 3.3834 g. **Composition:** 0.9170 Silver .0997 oz. ASW **Obv. Legend:** PHILIP. V. D. G. HISPAN. ET IND. REX **Reverse:** Pillars and arms **Note:** Struck at Mexico City Mint, mint mark M, Mo, (MX).

Date	Mintage	VG	F	VF	XF	Unc
1732 Rare	—	—	—	—	—	—
1732 F	—	—	—	—	—	—
1733 F (MX)	—	150	350	425	750	—
1733 MF (MX)	—	150	350	425	750	—
1733 F Rare	—	—	—	—	—	—
1733 MF	—	100	200	300	500	—
1734/3 MF	—	15.00	30.00	65.00	150	—
1734 MF	—	12.00	25.00	60.00	140	—
1735 MF	—	12.00	25.00	60.00	140	—
1736 MF	—	12.00	25.00	60.00	140	—
1737 MF	—	12.00	25.00	60.00	140	—
1738 MF	—	12.00	25.00	60.00	140	—
1739 MF	—	12.00	25.00	60.00	140	—
1740 MF	—	12.00	25.00	60.00	140	—
1741 MF	—	12.00	25.00	60.00	140	—

REAL   KM# 75.2   Weight: 3.3834 g. **Composition:** 0.9170 Silver .0997 oz. ASW **Obv. Legend:** PHS. V. D. G. HISP. ET. IND. R **Note:** Struck at Mexico City Mint, mint mark M, Mo.

Date	Mintage	VG	F	VF	XF	Unc
1742 M	—	10.00	20.00	50.00	120	—
1743 M	—	10.00	20.00	50.00	120	—
1744/3 M	—	10.00	20.00	50.00	120	—
1744 M	—	10.00	20.00	50.00	120	—
1745 M	—	8.00	18.00	50.00	120	—
1746/5 M	—	12.00	25.00	75.00	200	—
1746 M	—	10.00	20.00	55.00	125	—
1747 M	—	10.00	20.00	55.00	125	—

REAL   KM# 76.1 (KM76)   Weight: 3.3800 g. **Composition:** 0.9170 Silver .0996 oz. ASW **Obverse:** Royal crowns **Obv. Legend:** FRD. VI. D. G. HISP. ET IND. R **Note:** Struck at Mexico City Mint, mint mark M, Mo.

Date	Mintage	VG	F	VF	XF	Unc
1747 M	—	10.00	20.00	50.00	100	—
1748/7 M	—	10.00	20.00	50.00	100	—
1748 M	—	10.00	20.00	50.00	100	—
1749 M	—	10.00	20.00	50.00	100	—
1750/40 M	—	10.00	20.00	50.00	100	—
1750 M	—	10.00	20.00	50.00	100	—
1751 M	—	10.00	20.00	55.00	110	—
1752 M	—	10.00	20.00	50.00	100	—
1753 M	—	10.00	20.00	50.00	100	—
1754 M	—	10.00	20.00	55.00	110	—
1755/4 M	—	10.00	20.00	50.00	100	—
1755 M	—	10.00	20.00	50.00	100	—
1756 M	—	10.00	20.00	55.00	110	—
1757 M	—	10.00	20.00	55.00	110	—
1758/5 M	—	10.00	20.00	50.00	100	—
1758 M	—	10.00	20.00	50.00	100	—

REAL   KM# 76.2   Weight: 3.3834 g. **Composition:** 0.9170 Silver .0997 oz. ASW **Obverse:** Royal and Imperial crowns **Note:** Struck at Mexico City Mint, mint mark M, Mo.

Date	Mintage	VG	F	VF	XF	Unc
1757 M	—	10.00	20.00	50.00	100	—
1758/7 M	—	10.00	20.00	50.00	100	—
1758 M	—	10.00	20.00	50.00	100	—
1759 M	—	10.00	20.00	55.00	110	—
1760 M	—	15.00	30.00	70.00	140	—

REAL   KM# 77   Weight: 3.3800 g. **Composition:** 0.9170 Silver .0996 oz. ASW **Obv. Legend:** CAR. III. D. G. HISP. ET IND. R **Note:** Struck at Mexico City Mint, mint mark M, Mo.

Date	Mintage	VG	F	VF	XF	Unc
1760 M	—	10.00	20.00	50.00	100	—
1761/0 M	—	10.00	20.00	55.00	125	—
1761 M	—	10.00	20.00	50.00	100	—
1762 M	—	10.00	20.00	50.00	100	—
1763/2 M	—	12.00	25.00	60.00	120	—
1763 M	—	10.00	20.00	50.00	100	—
1764 M	—	10.00	20.00	55.00	110	—
1765 M	—	10.00	20.00	55.00	110	—
1766 M	—	10.00	20.00	50.00	100	—
1767 M	—	10.00	20.00	55.00	110	—
1768 M	—	10.00	20.00	50.00	100	—
1769 M	—	10.00	20.00	50.00	100	—
1769/70 M	—	10.00	20.00	50.00	125	—
1770 M	—	10.00	20.00	55.00	125	—
1770 F	—	20.00	40.00	90.00	250	—
1771 F	—	20.00	40.00	90.00	250	—

REAL   KM# 78.1   Weight: 3.3834 g. **Composition:** 0.9030 Silver .0982 oz. ASW **Obv. Legend:** CAROLUS. III. DEI. GRATIA **Reverse:** Inverted FM and mint mark **Note:** Struck at Mexico City Mint, mint mark M, Mo.

Date	Mintage	VG	F	VF	XF	Unc
1772 FM	—	5.00	10.00	25.00	60.00	—
1773 FM	—	5.00	10.00	25.00	60.00	—

REAL   KM# 78.2   Weight: 3.3800 g. **Composition:** 0.9030 Silver .0981 oz. ASW **Obverse:** Draped bust of Ferdinand VII **Obv. Legend:** CAROLUS. III. DEI. GRATIA **Rev. Legend:** Normal initials and mint mark **Note:** Struck at Mexico City Mint, mint mark M, Mo.

Date	Mintage	VG	F	VF	XF	Unc
1774 FM	—	5.00	10.00	25.00	60.00	—
1775/4 FM	—	6.00	12.00	28.00	75.00	—
1775 FM	—	5.00	10.00	25.00	60.00	—
1776 FM	—	5.00	10.00	25.00	60.00	—
1777 FM	—	5.00	10.00	25.00	60.00	—
1778 FF/M	—	6.00	12.00	28.00	75.00	—
1778 FF	—	5.00	10.00	25.00	60.00	—
1779 FF	—	5.00	10.00	25.00	60.00	—
1780 FF	—	5.00	10.00	25.00	60.00	—
1780 F F/M	—	5.00	10.00	25.00	60.00	—
1781 FF	—	5.00	10.00	25.00	60.00	—
1782 FF	—	5.00	10.00	25.00	60.00	—
1783 FF	—	5.00	10.00	25.00	60.00	—
1784 FF	—	5.00	10.00	25.00	60.00	—

REAL   KM# 78.2a   Weight: 3.3834 g. **Composition:** 0.8960 Silver .0975 oz. ASW **Reverse:** Normal initials and mint mark **Note:** Struck at Mexico City Mint, mint mark M, Mo.

Date	Mintage	VG	F	VF	XF	Unc
1785 FF	—	6.00	12.00	28.00	75.00	—
1785 FM	—	6.00	12.00	28.00	75.00	—
1786 FM	—	6.00	12.00	28.00	75.00	—
1787 FF	—	15.00	30.00	60.00	125	—
1787 FM	—	12.00	25.00	50.00	100	—
1788 FF	—	50.00	100	200	—	—
1788 FM	—	5.00	10.00	25.00	60.00	—
1789 FM	—	6.00	12.00	28.00	75.00	—

REAL   KM# 79   Weight: 3.3800 g. **Composition:** 0.9030 Silver .0981 oz. ASW **Obverse:** Armored bust of Charles III **Obv. Legend:** CAROLUS. IV... **Note:** Struck at Mexico City Mint, mint mark M, Mo.

Date	Mintage	VG	F	VF	XF	Unc
1789 FM	—	15.00	30.00	60.00	150	—
1790 FM	—	15.00	30.00	60.00	150	—

REAL   KM# 80   Weight: 3.3800 g. **Composition:** 0.9030 Silver .0981 oz. ASW **Obverse:** Armored bust of Charles III **Obv. Legend:** CAROLUS. IIII **Note:** Struck at Mexico City Mint, mint mark M, Mo.

Date	Mintage	VG	F	VF	XF	Unc
1790 FM	—	17.00	35.00	70.00	165	—

REAL   KM# 81   Weight: 3.3834 g. **Composition:** 0.8960 Silver .0975 oz. ASW **Obverse:** Armored bust of Charles IIII **Note:** Struck at Mexico City Mint, mint mark M, Mo.

Date	Mintage	VG	F	VF	XF	Unc
1792 FM	—	10.00	20.00	35.00	90.00	—
1793 FM	—	15.00	30.00	60.00	150	—
1794 FM	—	25.00	50.00	100	250	—
1795 FM	—	15.00	30.00	60.00	150	—
1796 FM	—	5.00	10.00	25.00	65.00	—
1797/6 FM	—	8.00	15.00	28.00	80.00	—
1797 FM	—	5.00	10.00	25.00	60.00	—
1798/7 FM	—	5.00	10.00	25.00	65.00	—
1798 FM	—	5.00	10.00	25.00	60.00	—
1799 FM	—	5.00	10.00	25.00	60.00	—
1800 FM	—	5.00	10.00	25.00	60.00	—
1801 FT/M	—	5.00	10.00	25.00	60.00	—
1801 FM	—	8.00	15.00	28.00	80.00	—
1801 FT	—	5.00	10.00	25.00	60.00	—
1802 FM	—	5.00	10.00	25.00	60.00	—
1802 FT	—	5.00	10.00	25.00	60.00	—
1802/1 FT	—	5.00	10.00	25.00	60.00	—
1802 FT/M	—	5.00	10.00	25.00	60.00	—
1803 FT	—	5.00	10.00	25.00	60.00	—
1804 TH	—	5.00	10.00	25.00	60.00	—
1805 TH	—	5.00	10.00	25.00	60.00	—
1806 TH	—	5.00	10.00	25.00	60.00	—
1807/6 TH	—	5.00	10.00	25.00	65.00	—
1807 TH	—	5.00	10.00	25.00	60.00	—
1808/7 TH	—	5.00	10.00	25.00	65.00	—
1808 FM	—	5.00	10.00	25.00	60.00	—

REAL   KM# 82   Weight: 3.3800 g. **Composition:** 0.9030 Silver .0981 oz. ASW **Obverse:** Armored bust of Ferdinand VII **Note:** Struck at Mexico City Mint, mint mark M, Mo.

Date	Mintage	VG	F	VF	XF	Unc
1809 TH	—	8.00	15.00	28.00	90.00	—
1810/09 TH	—	8.00	15.00	28.00	90.00	—
1810 TH	—	8.00	15.00	28.00	90.00	—
1811 TH	—	25.00	35.00	60.00	250	—
1811 HJ	—	8.00	15.00	28.00	90.00	—
1812 HJ	—	4.00	9.00	28.00	80.00	—
1812 JJ	—	10.00	20.00	40.00	120	—
1813 HJ	—	10.00	20.00	40.00	120	—
1813 JJ	—	50.00	100	150	250	—
1814 HJ	—	15.00	30.00	150	150	—
1814 JJ	—	50.00	100	175	300	—

REAL   KM# 83   Weight: 3.3800 g. **Composition:** 0.9030 Silver .0981 oz. ASW **Obverse:** Draped bust of Ferdinand VII **Note:** Struck at Mexico City Mint, mint mark M, Mo.

Date	Mintage	VG	F	VF	XF	Unc
1814 JJ	—	25.00	50.00	100	350	—
1815 HJ	—	15.00	30.00	60.00	150	—
1815 JJ	—	10.00	20.00	40.00	120	—
1816 JJ	—	5.00	10.00	25.00	70.00	—
1817 JJ	—	5.00	10.00	25.00	70.00	—

Date	Mintage	VG	F	VF	XF	Unc
1818 JJ	—	30.00	60.00	125	500	—
1819 JJ	—	5.00	10.00	25.00	70.00	—
1820 JJ	—	5.00	10.00	25.00	70.00	—
1821/0 JJ	—	8.00	15.00	30.00	110	—
1821 JJ	—	5.00	10.00	25.00	50.00	—

2 REALES   KM# 84   Weight: 6.7668 g. **Composition:**
0.9170 Silver .1995 oz. ASW **Obv. Legend:** PHILIP. V. D.
G. HISPAN. ET IND. REX **Note:** Struck at Mexico City Mint,
mint mark M, Mo, (MX).

Date	Mintage	VG	F	VF	XF	Unc
1732 Rare	—	—	—	—	—	—
1732 F	—	800	1,300	1,750	2,750	—
1733 F	—	600	800	1,350	2,250	—
1733 MF (MX)	—	350	600	1,000	1,650	—
1733 MF	—	600	900	1,500	2,500	—
1734/3 MF	—	20.00	40.00	85.00	170	—
1734 MF	—	20.00	40.00	85.00	170	—
1735/3 MF	—	15.00	30.00	75.00	150	—
1735/4 MF	—	15.00	30.00	75.00	150	—
1735 MF	—	15.00	30.00	75.00	150	—
1736/3 MF	—	18.00	35.00	80.00	160	—
1736/4 MF	—	18.00	35.00	80.00	160	—
1736/5 MF	—	18.00	35.00	80.00	160	—
1736 MF	—	18.00	35.00	80.00	160	—
1737/3 MF	—	18.00	35.00	80.00	160	—
1737 MF	—	18.00	35.00	80.00	160	—
1738/7 MF	—	18.00	35.00	80.00	160	—
1738 MF	—	18.00	35.00	80.00	160	—
1739 MF	—	18.00	35.00	80.00	160	—
1740/30 MF	—	18.00	35.00	80.00	160	—
1740 MF	—	18.00	35.00	80.00	160	—
1741 MF	—	18.00	35.00	80.00	160	—

2 REALES   KM# 85   Weight: 6.7700 g. **Composition:**
0.9170 Silver .1996 oz. ASW **Obv. Legend:** PHS. V. D. G.
HISP. ET IND. R **Note:** Struck at Mexico City Mint, mint
mark M, Mo.

Date	Mintage	F	VF	XF	Unc	BU
1742 M	—	30.00	75.00	125	—	—
1743/2 M	—	30.00	75.00	125	—	—
1743 M	—	30.00	75.00	125	—	—
1744/3 M	—	30.00	75.00	125	—	—
1744 M	—	30.00	75.00	125	—	—
1745/4 M	—	30.00	75.00	125	—	—
1745 M	—	30.00	75.00	125	—	—
1745 M HIP	—	400	—	—	—	—
1746/5 M	—	30.00	75.00	125	—	—
1746 M	—	30.00	75.00	125	—	—
1747 M	—	30.00	75.00	125	—	—
1750 M	—	450	650	1,000	—	—

2 REALES   KM# 86.1 (KM86)   Weight: 6.7668 g.
Composition: 0.9170 Silver .1995 oz. ASW **Obverse:**
Royal crowns **Obv. Legend:** FRD. VI. D. G. HISP. ET IND.
R **Note:** Struck at Mexico City Mint, mint mark M, Mo.

Date	Mintage	VG	F	VF	XF	Unc
1747 M	—	16.00	32.00	78.00	135	—
1748/7 M	—	16.00	32.00	78.00	135	—
1748 M	—	15.00	30.00	75.00	125	—

Date	Mintage	VG	F	VF	XF	Unc
1749 M	—	15.00	30.00	75.00	125	—
1750 M	—	15.00	30.00	75.00	125	—
1751/41 M	—	18.00	35.00	80.00	150	—
1751 M	—	15.00	30.00	75.00	125	—
1752 M	—	15.00	30.00	75.00	125	—
1753/2 M	—	18.00	35.00	80.00	150	—
1753 M	—	18.00	35.00	80.00	150	—
1754 M	—	18.00	35.00	80.00	150	—
1755/4 M	—	18.00	35.00	80.00	150	—
1755 M	—	18.00	35.00	80.00	150	—
1756/55 M	—	18.00	35.00	80.00	150	—
1756 M	—	18.00	35.00	80.00	140	—
1757/6 M	—	15.00	30.00	75.00	125	—
1757 M	—	18.00	35.00	80.00	150	—

2 REALES   KM# 86.2   Weight: 6.7668 g. **Composition:**
0.9170 Silver .1995 oz. ASW **Obverse:** Royal and Imperial
crowns **Note:** Struck at Mexico City Mint, mint mark M, Mo.

Date	Mintage	VG	F	VF	XF	Unc
1757 M	—	15.00	30.00	75.00	125	—
1758 M	—	15.00	30.00	75.00	125	—
1759/8 M	—	15.00	30.00	75.00	125	—
1759 M	—	20.00	40.00	90.00	175	—
1760 M	—	20.00	40.00	90.00	175	—

2 REALES   KM# 87   Weight: 6.7700 g. **Composition:**
0.9170 Silver .1996 oz. ASW **Obv. Legend:** CAR. III. D. G.
HISP. ET IND. R **Note:** Struck at Mexico City Mint, mint
mark M, Mo.

Date	Mintage	VG	F	VF	XF	Unc
1760 M	—	15.00	30.00	75.00	125	—
1761 M	—	15.00	30.00	75.00	125	—
1762/1 M	—	15.00	30.00	75.00	125	—
1762 M	—	15.00	30.00	75.00	125	—
1763/2 M	—	15.00	30.00	75.00	125	—
1763 M	—	15.00	30.00	75.00	125	—
1764 M	—	15.00	30.00	75.00	125	—
1765 M	—	15.00	30.00	75.00	125	—
1766 M	—	12.00	35.00	80.00	160	—
1767 M	—	15.00	30.00	75.00	125	—
1768/6 M	—	15.00	30.00	75.00	125	—
1768 M	—	15.00	30.00	75.00	125	—
1769 M	—	15.00	30.00	75.00	125	—
1770 M	—	350	550	—	—	—
1770 F Rare	—	—	—	—	—	—
1771 F	—	15.00	30.00	75.00	125	—

2 REALES   KM# 88.1   Weight: 6.7668 g. **Composition:**
0.9170 Silver .1964 oz. ASW **Obv. Legend:** CAROLUS. III.
DEI. GRATIA **Reverse:** Inverted FM and mint mark **Note:**
Struck at Mexico City Mint, mint mark M, Mo.

Date	Mintage	VG	F	VF	XF	Unc
1772 FM	—	7.00	15.00	30.00	100	—
1773 FM	—	7.00	15.00	30.00	100	—

2 REALES   KM# 88.2   Weight: 6.7700 g. **Composition:**
0.9030 Silver .1965 oz. ASW **Reverse:** Normal initials and
mint mark **Note:** Struck at Mexico City Mint, mint mark M, Mo.

Date	Mintage	VG	F	VF	XF	Unc
1773 FM	—	7.00	15.00	30.00	100	—
1774 FM	—	7.00	15.00	30.00	100	—
1775 FM	—	7.00	15.00	30.00	100	—
1776 FM	—	7.00	15.00	30.00	100	—
1777 FM	—	7.00	15.00	30.00	100	—
1778/7 FF	—	7.00	15.00	30.00	100	—
1778 FF	—	7.00	15.00	30.00	100	—
1779/8 FF	—	7.00	15.00	30.00	100	—
1779 FF	—	7.00	15.00	30.00	100	—
1780 FF	—	7.00	15.00	30.00	100	—
1781 FF	—	7.00	15.00	30.00	100	—
1782/1 FF	—	7.00	15.00	30.00	100	—
1782 FF	—	7.00	15.00	30.00	100	—
1783 FF	—	7.00	15.00	30.00	100	—
1784 FF	—	7.00	15.00	30.00	100	—
1784 FF DEI GRTIA (error)	—	100	150	250	600	—
1784 FM	—	70.00	120	225	575	—

2 REALES KM# 88.2a Weight: 6.7668 g. **Composition:** 0.8960 Silver .1949 oz. ASW **Note:** Struck at Mexico City Mint, mint mark Mo.

Date	Mintage	VG	F	VF	XF	Unc
1785Mo FM	—	7.00	15.00	30.00	100	—
1786Mo FF	—	200	350	550	950	—
1786Mo FM	—	7.00	15.00	30.00	100	—
1787Mo FM	—	7.00	15.00	30.00	100	—
1788/98Mo FM	—	7.00	15.00	30.00	100	—
1788Mo FM	—	7.00	15.00	30.00	100	—
1789Mo FM	—	12.00	25.00	50.00	150	—

2 REALES KM# 89 Weight: 6.7700 g. **Composition:** 0.9030 Silver .1965 oz. ASW **Obverse:** Armored bust of Charles III **Obv. Legend:** CAROLUS. IV... **Note:** Struck at Mexico City Mint, mint mark M, Mo.

Date	Mintage	VG	F	VF	XF	Unc
1789 FM	—	15.00	30.00	75.00	200	—
1790 FM	—	15.00	30.00	75.00	200	—

2 REALES KM# 90 Weight: 6.7700 g. **Composition:** 0.9030 Silver .1965 oz. ASW **Obverse:** Armored bust of Charles III **Obv. Legend:** CAROLUS. IIII... **Note:** Struck at Mexico City Mint, mint mark M, Mo.

Date	Mintage	VG	F	VF	XF	Unc
1790 FM	—	17.00	35.00	80.00	200	—

2 REALES KM# 91 Weight: 6.7668 g. **Composition:** 0.8960 Silver .1949 oz. ASW **Obverse:** Armored bust of Carolus IIII **Note:** Struck at Mexico City Mint, mint mark M, Mo.

Date	Mintage	VG	F	VF	XF	Unc
1792 FM	—	15.00	30.00	60.00	200	—
1793 FM	—	15.00	30.00	60.00	200	—
1794/3 FM	—	50.00	100	200	450	—
1794 FM	—	40.00	75.00	150	400	—
1795 FM	—	7.00	15.00	30.00	85.00	—
1796 FM	—	7.00	15.00	30.00	85.00	—
1797 FM	—	7.00	15.00	30.00	85.00	—
1798 FM	—	7.00	15.00	30.00	85.00	—
1799/8 FM	—	7.00	15.00	32.00	90.00	—
1799 FM	—	7.00	15.00	30.00	85.00	—
1800 FM	—	7.00	15.00	30.00	85.00	—
1801 FT/M	—	7.00	15.00	30.00	85.00	—
1801 FT	—	7.00	15.00	30.00	85.00	—
1801 FM	—	20.00	40.00	75.00	250	—
1802 FT	—	7.00	15.00	30.00	85.00	—
1803 FT	—	7.00	15.00	30.00	85.00	—
1804/3 TH	—	7.00	15.00	30.00	85.00	—
1804 TH	—	7.00	15.00	30.00	85.00	—
1805 TH	—	7.00	15.00	30.00	85.00	—
1806/5 TH	—	7.00	15.00	32.00	90.00	—
1806 TH	—	7.00	15.00	30.00	85.00	—
1807/5 TH	—	7.00	15.00	32.00	90.00	—
1807/6 TH	—	15.00	30.00	60.00	200	—
1807 TH	—	7.00	15.00	30.00	85.00	—
1808/7 TH	—	7.00	15.00	32.00	90.00	—
1808 TH	—	7.00	15.00	30.00	85.00	—

2 REALES KM# 92 Weight: 6.7700 g. **Composition:** 0.9030 Silver .1965 oz. ASW **Obverse:** Armored bust of Ferdinand VII **Note:** Struck at Mexico City Mint, mint mark M, Mo.

Date	Mintage	VG	F	VF	XF	Unc
1809 TH	—	15.00	30.00	75.00	200	—
181/00 TH	—	15.00	30.00	75.00	200	—
181/00 HJ/TH	—	15.00	30.00	75.00	200	—
181/00 HJ	—	15.00	30.00	75.00	200	—
1810 TH	—	15.00	30.00	75.00	200	—
1810 HJ	—	15.00	30.00	75.00	200	—
1811 TH	—	150	250	350	750	—
1811 HJ	—	15.00	30.00	75.00	200	—
1811 HJ/TH	—	40.00	80.00	150	300	—

2 REALES KM# 93 Weight: 6.7700 g. **Composition:** 0.9030 Silver .1965 oz. ASW **Obverse:** Draped bust of Ferdinand VII **Note:** Struck at Mexico City Mint, mint mark M, Mo.

Date	Mintage	VG	F	VF	XF	Unc
1812 TH	—	60.00	125	250	550	—
1812 HJ	—	40.00	100	200	500	—
1812 JJ	—	10.00	20.00	60.00	200	—
1813 TH	—	15.00	30.00	100	400	—
1813 JJ	—	20.00	60.00	125	350	—
1813 HJ	—	40.00	100	200	500	—
1814/2 JJ	—	15.00	30.00	100	400	—
1814 JJ	—	15.00	30.00	100	400	—

Date	Mintage	VG	F	VF	XF	Unc
1815 JJ	—	6.00	12.00	28.00	85.00	—
1816 JJ	—	6.00	12.00	28.00	85.00	—
1817 JJ	—	6.00	12.00	28.00	85.00	—
1818 JJ	—	6.00	12.00	28.00	85.00	—
1819/8 JJ	—	5.50	12.00	30.00	85.00	—
1819 JJ	—	6.00	12.00	28.00	85.00	—
1820 JJ	—	175	—	—	—	—
1821/0 JJ	—	7.00	15.00	30.00	90.00	—
1821 JJ	—	6.00	12.00	28.00	85.00	—

4 REALES   KM# 94   Weight: 13.5337 g. **Composition:** 0.9170 Silver .3990 oz. ASW **Obv. Legend:** PHILLIP. V. D. G. HISPAN. ET IND. REX **Note:** Struck at Mexico City Mint, mint mark M, Mo, (MX).

Date	Mintage	VG	F	VF	XF	Unc
1732 Rare; Specimen	—	—	—	—	—	—
1732 F	—	2,000	3,000	5,000	10,000	—
1733/2 F	—	1,500	2,000	4,000	6,500	—
1733 MF	—	1,100	1,650	2,250	4,250	—
1733 MF (MX)	—	1,500	2,200	3,250	5,500	—
1733 MX/XM	—	1,500	2,200	3,250	5,500	—
1734/3 MF	—	150	300	600	1,200	—
1734 MF	—	150	300	600	1,200	—
1735/4 MF	—	100	175	300	600	—
1735 MF	—	100	175	300	600	—
1736 MF	—	100	175	300	600	—
1737 MF	—	100	175	300	600	—
1738/7 MF	—	100	175	300	600	—
1738 MF	—	100	175	300	600	—
1739 MF	—	100	175	300	600	—
1740/30 MF	—	100	200	325	625	—
1740 MF	—	100	175	300	600	—
1741 MF	—	100	175	300	600	—
1742/1 MF	—	100	175	300	600	—
1742/32 MF	—	100	175	300	600	—
1742 MF	—	100	175	300	600	—
1743 MF	—	100	175	300	600	—
1744/3 MF	—	100	200	325	625	—
1744 MF	—	100	175	300	600	—
1745 MF	—	100	175	300	600	—
1746 MF	—	100	175	300	600	—
1747 MF	—	150	275	400	650	—

4 REALES   KM# 95   Weight: 13.5400 g. **Composition:** 0.9170 Silver .3992 oz. ASW **Obv. Legend:** FERDND. VI. D. G. HISPAN. ET IND. REX **Note:** Struck at Mexico City Mint, mint mark M, Mo.

Date	Mintage	VG	F	VF	XF	Unc
1747 MF	—	100	150	300	550	—
1748/7 MF	—	100	150	300	550	—
1748 MF	—	100	125	250	500	—
1749 MF	—	150	225	350	650	—
1750/40 MF	—	100	125	250	500	—
1751/41 MF	—	100	125	250	500	—
1751 MF	—	100	125	250	500	—
1752 MF	—	100	125	250	500	—
1753 MF	—	100	125	300	550	—
1754 MF	—	250	375	500	850	—
1755 MM	—	100	125	250	500	—
1756 MM	—	100	150	300	550	—
1757 MM	—	100	150	300	550	—
1758 MM	—	100	125	250	500	—
1759 MM	—	100	125	250	500	—
1760/59 MM	—	100	175	350	600	—
1760 MM	—	100	175	350	600	—

4 REALES   KM# 96   Weight: 13.5400 g. **Composition:** 0.9170 Silver .3992 oz. ASW **Obv. Legend:** CAROLVS. III. D. G. HISPAN. ET IND. REX **Note:** Struck at Mexico City Mint, mint mark M, Mo.

Date	Mintage	VG	F	VF	XF	Unc
1760 MM	—	100	150	250	900	—
1761 MM	—	100	150	250	900	—
1761 MM Cross between H and I	—	100	150	250	900	—
1762 MM	—	75.00	125	250	500	—
1763/1 MM	—	100	150	300	600	—
1763 MM	—	100	150	300	600	—
1764 MM	—	400	600	1,000	2,000	—
1764 MF	—	350	500	1,000	2,000	—
1765 MF	—	350	500	1,000	2,000	—
1766 MF	—	250	350	550	1,250	—
1767 MF	—	100	150	300	600	—
1768 MF	—	75.00	125	250	500	—
1769 MF	—	75.00	125	250	500	—
1770 MF	—	75.00	125	250	500	—
1771 MF	—	125	200	325	700	—

4 REALES KM# 97.1 Weight: 13.5337 g. **Composition:**
0.9030 Silver .3929 oz. ASW **Obv. Legend:** CAROLUS. III.
DEI. GRATIA **Reverse:** Inverted FM and mint mark **Note:**
Struck at Mexico City Mint, mint mark M, Mo.

Date	Mintage	VG	F	VF	XF	Unc
1772 FM	—	90.00	125	250	500	—
1773 FM	—	100	175	300	650	—

4 REALES KM# 97.2 Weight: 13.5400 g. **Composition:**
0.9030 Silver .3931 oz. ASW **Obv. Legend:** CAROLUS. III.
DEI. GRATIA **Reverse:** Normal initials and mint mark **Note:**
Struck at Mexico City Mint, mint mark M, Mo.

Date	Mintage	VG	F	VF	XF	Unc
1774 FM	—	50.00	100	200	500	—
1775 FM	—	50.00	100	200	500	—
1776 FM	—	50.00	100	200	500	—
1777 FM	—	50.00	100	200	500	—
1778 FF	—	50.00	100	200	500	—
1779 FF	—	50.00	100	200	500	—
1780 FF	—	50.00	100	200	500	—
1781 FF	—	50.00	100	200	500	—
1782 FF	—	50.00	100	200	500	—
1783 FF	—	50.00	100	200	500	—
1784 FF	—	50.00	100	200	500	—
1784 FM	—	100	200	350	600	—

4 REALES KM# 97.2a Weight: 13.5337 g.
Composition: 0.8960 Silver .3899 oz. ASW **Reverse:**
Normal initials and mint mark **Note:** Struck at Mexico City
Mint, mint mark M, Mo.

Date	Mintage	VG	F	VF	XF	Unc
1785 FM	—	100	200	350	600	—
1786 FM	—	50.00	100	200	500	—
1787 FM	—	50.00	100	200	500	—
1788 FM	—	50.00	100	200	500	—
1789 FM	—	50.00	100	200	500	—

4 REALES KM# 98 Weight: 13.5400 g. **Composition:**
0.9030 Silver .3931 oz. ASW **Obverse:** Armored bust of

Charles III **Obv. Legend:** CAROLUS. IV... **Note:** Struck at
Mexico City Mint, mint mark M, Mo.

Date	Mintage	VG	F	VF	XF	Unc
1789 FM	—	65.00	125	250	550	—
1790 FM	—	50.00	100	200	500	—

4 REALES KM# 99 Weight: 13.5400 g. **Composition:**
0.9030 Silver .3931 oz. ASW **Obverse:** Armored bust of
Charles III **Obv. Legend:** CAROLUS. IIII... **Note:** Struck at
Mexico City Mint, mint mark M, Mo.

Date	Mintage	VG	F	VF	XF	Unc
1790 FM	—	65.00	125	250	550	—

4 REALES KM# 100 Weight: 13.5337 g. **Composition:**
0.8960 Silver .3899 oz. ASW **Obverse:** Armored bust of
Charles IIII **Reverse:** Pillars, arms **Note:** Struck at Mexico
City Mint, mint mark M, Mo.

Date	Mintage	VG	F	VF	XF	Unc
1792 FM	—	35.00	65.00	150	400	—
1793 FM	—	75.00	125	200	500	—
1794/3 FM	—	35.00	65.00	150	400	—
1794 FM	—	35.00	65.00	150	400	—
1795 FM	—	35.00	65.00	150	400	—
1796 FM	—	150	250	400	800	—
1797 FM	—	60.00	120	200	500	—
1798/7 FM	—	35.00	65.00	150	400	—
1798 FM	—	35.00	65.00	150	400	—
1799 FM	—	35.00	65.00	150	400	—
1800 FM	—	35.00	65.00	150	400	—
1801 FM	—	35.00	65.00	150	400	—
1801 FT	—	60.00	120	200	500	—
1802 FT	—	200	300	500	1,000	—
1803 FT	—	75.00	135	225	550	—
1803 FM	—	200	300	500	1,000	—
1804 TH	—	40.00	75.00	175	450	—
1805 TH	—	35.00	65.00	150	400	—
1806 TH	—	35.00	65.00	150	400	—
1807 TH	—	35.00	65.00	150	400	—
1808/7 TH	—	40.00	75.00	175	450	—
1808 TH	—	40.00	75.00	175	450	—

4 REALES   KM# 101   Weight: 13.5400 g. **Composition:** 0.9030 Silver .3931 oz. ASW **Obverse:** Armored bust of Ferdinand VII **Note:** Struck at Mexico City Mint, mint mark M, Mo.

Date	Mintage	VG	F	VF	XF	Unc
1809 HJ	—	75.00	135	250	750	—
1810 HJ	—	75.00	135	250	750	—
1811 HJ	—	75.00	135	250	750	—
1812 HJ	—	400	650	900	1,850	—

4 REALES   KM# 102   Weight: 13.5400 g. **Composition:** 0.9030 Silver .3931 oz. ASW **Obverse:** Draped bust of Ferdinand VII **Note:** Struck at Mexico City Mint, mint mark M, Mo.

Date	Mintage	VG	F	VF	XF	Unc
1816 JJ	—	150	200	325	700	—
1817 JJ	—	250	400	500	1,000	—
1818/7 JJ	—	250	400	500	1,000	—
1819 JJ	—	175	250	325	700	—
1820 JJ	—	175	250	325	700	—
1821 JJ	—	75.00	135	250	650	—

8 REALES   KM# 103   Weight: 27.0674 g. **Composition:** 0.9170 Silver .7980 oz. ASW **Obv. Legend:** PHILIP. V. D. G. HISPAN. ET IND. REX **Note:** Struck at Mexico City Mint, mint mark M, Mo, (MX).

Date	Mintage	VG	F	VF	XF	Unc
1732 F	—	2,750	4,750	8,000	—	—
1733/2 F (MX)	—	3,000	5,250	9,000	—	—
1733 F	—	2,000	3,000	5,000	9,000	—
1733 F (MX) Rare	—	—	—	—	—	—

Note: Rare; Bonhams Patterson sale 7-96 VF 1733 F (MX) realized $11,710

Date	Mintage	VG	F	VF	XF	Unc
1733 MF Large crown; Rare	—	—	—	—	—	—
1733 MF (MX) Rare	—	—	—	—	—	—
1733 MF Small crown	—	700	1,500	2,500	4,250	—
1734/3 MF	—	100	150	275	575	—
1734 MF	—	100	150	250	450	—
1735 MF	—	100	150	250	450	—
1736/5 MF	—	100	150	275	575	—
1736 MF Small planchet	—	100	150	250	450	—
1736 MF	—	100	150	250	450	—
1737 MF	—	65.00	100	200	400	—
1738/6 MF	—	65.00	100	200	400	—
1738/7 MF	—	65.00	100	200	400	—
1738 MF	—	65.00	100	200	400	—
1739/6 MF 9 over inverted 6	—	65.00	100	200	400	—
1739 MF	—	65.00	100	200	400	—
1740/30 MF	—	100	150	275	500	—
1740/39 MF	—	100	150	275	500	—
1740 MF	—	65.00	100	200	400	—
1741/31 MF	—	65.00	100	200	400	—
1741 MF	—	65.00	100	200	400	—
1742/32 MF	—	75.00	125	220	500	—
1742/1 MF	—	65.00	100	200	400	—
1742 MF	—	65.00	100	200	400	—
1743/2 MF	—	65.00	100	200	400	—
1743 MF	—	65.00	100	200	400	—
1744/34 MF	—	65.00	100	200	400	—
1744/3 MF	—	65.00	100	200	400	—
1744 MF	—	65.00	100	200	400	—
1745/4 MF	—	65.00	100	200	425	—
1745 MF	—	65.00	100	200	400	—
1746/5 MF	—	100	150	275	575	—
1746 MF	—	65.00	100	200	400	—
1747 MF	—	65.00	100	200	400	—

Date	Mintage	VG	F	VF	XF	Unc
1754 MM	—	60.00	110	200	375	—
1754 MF	—	150	285	550	950	—
1755/4 MM	—	55.00	100	185	325	—
1755 MM	—	50.00	75.00	125	250	—
1756/5 MM	—	55.00	100	165	275	—
1756 MM	—	50.00	75.00	125	250	—
1757/6 MM	—	50.00	75.00	125	250	—
1757 MM	—	55.00	100	185	325	—
1758 MM	—	50.00	75.00	125	250	—
1759 MM	—	50.00	75.00	125	250	—
1760/59 MM	—	55.00	100	165	275	—
1760 MM	—	50.00	75.00	125	250	—

8 REALES   KM# 104.1   Weight: 27.0674 g.
Composition: 0.9170 Silver .7080 oz. ASW **Obv. Legend:**
FERDND. VI. D. G. HISPAN. ET IND. REX **Reverse:** With
Royal crown on left pillar **Note:** Struck at Mexico City Mint,
mint mark M, Mo.

Date	Mintage	VG	F	VF	XF	Unc
1747 MF	—	55.00	100	175	300	—
1748/7 MF	—	60.00	120	250	450	—
1748 MF	—	50.00	75.00	125	250	—
1749 MF	—	50.00	75.00	125	250	—
1749/8 MF	—	50.00	75.00	125	250	—
1750 MF	—	50.00	75.00	125	250	—
1751/0 MF	—	55.00	100	165	275	—
1751 MF	—	50.00	75.00	125	250	—
1752/1 MF	—	55.00	100	165	275	—
1752 MF	—	50.00	75.00	125	250	—
1753/2 MF	—	50.00	75.00	125	250	—
1753 MF	—	55.00	100	165	275	—
1754/3 MF	—	55.00	100	185	325	—
1754 MF	—	50.00	75.00	125	250	—
1754 MM/MF	—	300	700	1,500	3,500	—
1754 MM	—	300	700	1,500	3,500	—

8 REALES   KM# 104.2   Weight: 27.0674 g.
Composition: 0.9170 Silver .7980 oz. ASW **Obv. Legend:**
FERDND. VI. D. G. HISPAN. ET IND. REX **Reverse:**
Imperial crown on left pillar **Note:** Struck at Mexico City Mint,
mint mark M, Mo.

8 REALES   KM# 105   Weight: 27.0674 g. **Composition:**
0.9170 Silver .7980 oz. ASW **Obv. Legend:** CAROLUS. III.
D. G. HISPAN. ET IND. REX **Note:** Struck at Mexico City
Mint, mint mark M, Mo.

Date	Mintage	VG	F	VF	XF	Unc
1760/59 MM CAROLUS. III/ Ferdin. Vi	—	450	700	—	—	—
1760 MM CAROLUS. III/ FERDIN. VI. recut die	—	60.00	100	150	325	—
1760 MM	—	60.00	100	150	300	—
1761/50 MM Tip of cross between I and S in legend	—	65.00	110	165	325	—
1761/51 MM Tip of cross between I and S in legend	—	65.00	110	165	325	—
1761/0 MM Tip of cross between H and I in legend	—	65.00	110	165	325	—
1761 MM Cross under I in legend	—	60.00	100	150	275	—
1761 MM Tip of cross between H and I in legend	—	60.00	100	150	275	—
1761 MM Tip of cross between I and S in legend	—	65.00	110	165	325	—
1762/1 MM Tip of cross between H and I in legend	—	70.00	120	175	450	—
1762/1 MM	—	70.00	120	175	450	—
1762 MM Tip of cross between H and I in legend	—	60.00	100	150	275	—
1762 MM Tip of cross between I and S in legend	—	50.00	75.00	125	250	—
1762 MF	—	500	750	1,250	2,300	—
1763/2 MM	—	300	450	750	1,350	—
1763 MM	—	450	650	1,150	2,250	—
1763/1 MF	—	50.00	75.00	125	250	—
1763/2 MF	—	50.00	75.00	125	250	—
1763 MF	—	50.00	75.00	125	250	—
1764 MF CAR/CRA	—	50.00	75.00	125	250	—
1764 MF	—	50.00	75.00	125	250	—
1765 MF	—	50.00	75.00	125	250	—

Date	Mintage	VG	F	VF	XF	Unc
1766/5 MF	—	75.00	150	225	575	—
1766 MF	—	50.00	75.00	125	250	—
1767/6 MF	—	50.00	75.00	125	250	—
1767 MF	—	50.00	75.00	125	250	—
1768/7 MF	—	85.00	165	250	600	—
1768 MF	—	50.00	75.00	125	250	—
1769 MF	—	50.00	75.00	125	250	—
1770/60 MF	—	100	185	300	650	—
1770 MF	—	50.00	75.00	125	250	—
1770/60 FM	—	100	185	300	650	—
1770/69 FM	—	100	185	300	650	—
1770 FM/F	—	50.00	75.00	125	250	—
1770 FM	—	50.00	75.00	125	250	—
1771/0 FM	—	50.00	75.00	125	250	—
1771 FM	—	50.00	75.00	125	250	—

Date	Mintage	VG	F	VF	XF	Unc
1786 FM	—	25.00	45.00	75.00	150	—
1787/6 FM	—	100	250	450	1,200	—
1787 FM	—	25.00	45.00	75.00	150	—
1788 FM	—	25.00	45.00	75.00	150	—
1789 FM	—	50.00	100	150	225	—

8 REALES   KM# 106.1   Weight: 27.0674 g.
Composition: 0.9030 Silver .7858 oz. ASW **Obv. Legend:**
CAROLUS. III. DEI. GRATIA **Reverse:** Inverted initials and
mint mark **Note:** Two varieties exist, one with inverted initials
"F.M." (left), and one with normal presentation (right). Struck
at Mexico City Mint, mint mark M, Mo.

Date	Mintage	VG	F	VF	XF	Unc
1772 FM	—	25.00	50.00	120	250	—
1772 FM	—	150	350	750	1,250	—
1773 FM	—	25.00	50.00	100	175	—

8 REALES   KM# 106.2   Weight: 27.0674 g.
Composition: 0.9030 Silver .7858 oz. ASW **Obv. Legend:**
CAROLUS. III. DEI. GRATIA **Reverse:** Normal initials and
mint mark **Note:** Struck at Mexico City Mint, mint mark M, Mo.

Date	Mintage	VG	F	VF	XF	Unc
1773 FM	—	25.00	50.00	80.00	160	—
1774 FM	—	25.00	45.00	75.00	150	—
1775 FM	—	25.00	45.00	75.00	150	—
1776 FM	—	25.00	45.00	75.00	150	—
1777/6 FM	—	35.00	65.00	180	300	—
1777 FM	—	25.00	45.00	75.00	150	—
1777 FF	—	35.00	50.00	100	250	—
1778 FM	—	—	—	—	—	—

Note: Superior Casterline sale 5-89 VF realized $17,600

Date	Mintage	VG	F	VF	XF	Unc
1778/7 FF	—	25.00	45.00	75.00	150	—
1778 FF	—	25.00	45.00	75.00	150	—
1779 FF	—	25.00	45.00	75.00	150	—
1780 FF	—	25.00	45.00	75.00	150	—
1781 FF	—	25.00	45.00	75.00	150	—
1782 FF	—	25.00	45.00	75.00	150	—
1783 FF	—	25.00	45.00	75.00	150	—
1783 FM	—	4,000	6,000	9,000	—	—
1784 FF	—	150	300	500	1,250	—
1784 FM	—	25.00	45.00	75.00	150	—

8 REALES   KM# 106.2a   Weight: 27.0674 g.
Composition: 0.8960 Silver .7797 oz. ASW **Obv. Legend:**
CAROLUS.III.DEI.GRATIA **Reverse:** Normal initials and
mint mark **Note:** Struck at Mexico City Mint, mint mark M, Mo.

Date	Mintage	VG	F	VF	XF	Unc
1785 FM	—	25.00	45.00	75.00	150	—
1786/5 FM	—	50.00	100	200	400	—

8 REALES   KM# 107   Weight: 27.0674 g. **Composition:**
0.9030 Silver .7858 oz. ASW **Obverse:** Armored bust of
Charles III **Obv. Legend:** CAROLUS. IV... **Note:** Struck at
Mexico City Mint, mint mark M, Mo.

Date	Mintage	VG	F	VF	XF	Unc
1789 FM	—	40.00	65.00	120	250	—
1790 FM	—	30.00	50.00	100	200	—

8 REALES   KM# 108   Weight: 27.0674 g. **Composition:**
0.9030 Silver .7858 oz. ASW **Obverse:** Armored bust of
Charles III **Obv. Legend:** CAROLUS. IIII **Note:** Struck at
Mexico City Mint, mint mark M, Mo.

Date	Mintage	VG	F	VF	XF	Unc
1790 FM	—	30.00	50.00	100	200	—

8 REALES KM# 109 Weight: 27.0674 g. **Composition:** 0.8960 Silver .7797 oz. ASW **Obverse:** Armored bust of Charles IIII **Note:** Struck at Mexico City Mint, mint mark M, Mo.

Date	Mintage	VG	F	VF	XF	Unc
1791 FM	—	20.00	35.00	50.00	100	—
1792 FM	—	20.00	35.00	50.00	100	—
1793 FM	—	20.00	35.00	50.00	100	—
1794 FM	—	20.00	35.00	50.00	100	—
1795/4 FM	—	20.00	35.00	50.00	100	—
1795 FM	—	20.00	35.00	50.00	100	—
1796 FM	—	20.00	35.00	50.00	100	—
1797 FM	—	20.00	35.00	50.00	100	—
1798 FM	—	20.00	35.00	50.00	100	—
1799 FM	—	20.00	35.00	50.00	100	—
1800/700 FM	—	20.00	35.00	50.00	100	—
1800 FM	—	20.00	35.00	50.00	100	—
1801/0 FT/FM	—	20.00	35.00	50.00	100	—
1801/791 FM	—	35.00	60.00	100	250	—
1801/0 FM	—	35.00	60.00	100	£50	—
1801 FM	—	20.00	40.00	100	250	—
1001 FT/M	—	35.00	60.00	100	250	—
1801 FT	—	20.00	35.00	50.00	100	—
1802/1 FT	—	35.00	60.00	100	250	—
1802 FT	—	20.00	35.00	50.00	100	—
1802 FT/M	—	20.00	35.00	50.00	100	—
1803 FT	—	20.00	35.00	50.00	110	—
1803 FT/M	—	20.00	35.00	50.00	100	—
1803 TH	—	75.00	150	250	500	—
1804/3 TH	—	35.00	60.00	100	250	—
1804 TH CARLUS (error)	—	20.00	35.00	50.00	100	—
1805/4 TH	—	40.00	80.00	125	275	—
1805 TH Narrow date	—	20.00	35.00	50.00	100	—
1805 Wide date	—	20.00	35.00	50.00	100	—
1806 TH	—	20.00	35.00	50.00	100	—
1807/6 TH	—	150	250	350	700	—
1807 TH	—	20.00	35.00	50.00	100	—
1808/7 TH	—	20.00	35.00	50.00	100	—
1808 TH	—	20.00	35.00	50.00	100	—

8 REALES KM# 110 Weight: 27.0674 g. **Composition:** 0.8960 Silver .7797 oz. ASW **Obverse:** Armored bust of Ferdinand VII **Note:** Struck at Mexico City Mint, mint mark M, Mo.

Date	Mintage	VG	F	VF	XF	Unc
1808 TH	—	25.00	40.00	75.00	145	—
1809/8 TH	—	25.00	40.00	75.00	145	—
1809 TH	—	20.00	35.00	55.00	120	—
1809 HJ	—	25.00	40.00	75.00	145	—
1809 HJ/TH	—	20.00	35.00	55.00	120	—
1810/09 HJ	—	25.00	40.00	75.00	145	—
1810 TH	—	75.00	150	300	600	—
1810 HJ/TH	—	25.00	40.00	75.00	145	—
1810 HJ	—	25.00	40.00	75.00	145	—
1811/0 HJ	—	20.00	35.00	55.00	120	—
1811 HJ	—	20.00	35.00	55.00	120	—
1811 HJ/TH	—	20.00	35.00	50.00	100	—

8 REALES KM# 111 Weight: 27.0700 g. **Composition:** 0.9030 Silver .7859 oz. ASW **Obverse:** Draped bust of Ferdinand VII **Note:** Struck at Mexico City Mint, mint mark M, Mo.

Date	Mintage	VG	F	VF	XF	Unc
1811 HJ	—	20.00	40.00	60.00	125	—
1812 HJ	—	50.00	75.00	125	250	—
1812 JJ/HJ	—	20.00	35.00	50.00	100	—
1812 JJ	—	20.00	35.00	50.00	100	—
1813 HJ	—	50.00	75.00	125	250	—
1813 JJ	—	20.00	35.00	50.00	100	—
1814/3 HJ	—	1,200	2,500	5,000	—	—
1814/3 JJ	—	20.00	35.00	50.00	100	—
1814 JJ	—	20.00	35.00	50.00	100	—

Date	Mintage	VG	F	VF	XF	Unc
1815/4 JJ	—	20.00	35.00	50.00	100	—
1815 JJ	—	20.00	35.00	50.00	100	—
1816/5 JJ	—	20.00	35.00	50.00	90.00	—
1816 JJ	—	20.00	35.00	50.00	90.00	—
1817 JJ	—	20.00	35.00	50.00	90.00	—
1818 JJ	—	20.00	35.00	50.00	90.00	—
1819 JJ	—	20.00	35.00	50.00	90.00	—
1820 JJ	—	20.00	35.00	50.00	90.00	—
1821 JJ	—	20.00	35.00	50.00	90.00	—

1/2 ESCUDO   KM# 112   Weight: 1.6917 g. **Composition:** 0.8750 Gold .0476 oz. AGW **Obv. Legend:** FERD. VII. D. G. HISP. ET IND **Note:** Struck at Mexico City Mint, mint mark M, Mo.

Date	Mintage	VG	F	VF	XF	Unc
1814 JJ	—	100	150	225	375	—
1815/4 JJ	—	150	200	250	400	—
1815 JJ	—	150	200	250	400	—
1816 JJ	—	100	150	225	375	—
1817 JJ	—	150	200	250	400	—
1818 JJ	—	150	200	250	400	—
1819 JJ	—	150	200	250	400	—
1820 JJ	—	200	300	400	550	—

ESCUDO   KM# 113   Weight: 3.3834 g. **Composition:** 0.9170 Gold .0997 oz. AGW **Obv. Legend:** PHILIP. V. D. G. HISPAN. ET IND. REX **Note:** Struck at Mexico City Mint, mint mark M, Mo.

Date	Mintage	VG	F	VF	XF	Unc
1732 F	—	1,000	2,000	3,000	4,000	—
1733/2 F	—	1,000	2,000	3,000	4,000	—
1734/3 MF	—	150	250	400	850	—
1735/4 MF	—	150	250	400	850	—
1735 MF	—	150	250	400	850	—
1736/5 MF	—	150	250	400	850	—
1736 MF	—	150	250	400	850	—
1737 MF	—	200	300	600	1,200	—
1738/7 MF	—	200	300	600	1,200	—
1738 MF	—	200	300	600	1,200	—
1739 MF	—	200	300	600	1,200	—
1740/30 MF	—	200	300	600	1,200	—
1741 MF	—	200	300	600	1,200	—
1742 MF	—	200	300	600	1,200	—
1743/2 MF	—	150	275	450	800	—
1743 MF	—	150	250	400	700	—
1744/3 MF	—	150	250	400	700	—
1744 MF	—	150	250	400	700	—
1745 MF	—	150	250	400	700	—
1746/5 MF	—	150	250	400	700	—
1747 MF Rare	—	—	—	—	—	—

ESCUDO   KM# 114   Weight: 3.3834 g. **Composition:** 0.9170 Gold .0997 oz. AGW **Obverse:** Long bust **Obv. Legend:** FERD. VI. D. G. HISPAN. ET IND. REX **Note:** Struck at Mexico City Mint, mint mark M, Mo.

Date	Mintage	VG	F	VF	XF	Unc
1747 MF	—	1,650	3,000	5,000	7,500	—

ESCUDO   KM# 115.1   Weight: 3.3834 g. **Composition:** 0.9170 Gold .0997 oz. AGW **Obverse:** Short bust **Obv. Legend:** FERD. VI. D. G. HISPAN. ET IND. REX **Note:** Struck at Mexico City Mint, mint mark M, Mo.

Date	Mintage	VG	F	VF	XF	Unc
1748 MF	—	250	350	550	950	—
1749 MF	—	300	450	700	1,150	—
1750 MF	—	150	250	400	800	—
1751 MF	—	150	250	400	800	—

ESCUDO   KM# 115.2   Weight: 3.3834 g. **Composition:** 0.9170 Gold .0997 oz. AGW **Obverse:** Short bust **Obv. Legend:** FERD. VI. D. G. HISPAN. ET IND. REX **Reverse:** Without 1 S flanking arms **Note:** Struck at Mexico City Mint, mint mark M, Mo.

Date	Mintage	VG	F	VF	XF	Unc
1752 MF	—	125	225	375	750	—
1753/2 MF	—	150	250	400	800	—
1753 MF	—	150	250	400	800	—
1754 MF	—	150	250	400	800	—
1755 MM	—	150	250	400	800	—
1756 MM	—	150	250	400	800	—

ESCUDO   KM# A116   Weight: 3.3834 g. **Composition:** 0.9170 Gold .0997 oz. AGW **Obverse:** Armored bust **Note:** Struck at Mexico City Mint, mint mark M, Mo.

Date	Mintage	VG	F	VF	XF	Unc
1757 MM	—	150	250	400	800	—
1759 MM	—	150	250	400	800	—

ESCUDO   KM# 116   Weight: 3.3834 g. **Composition:** 0.9170 Gold .0997 oz. AGW **Obv. Legend:** CAROLVS. III. D. G. HISPAN. ET IND. REX **Rev. Legend:** NOMINA MAGNA SEQUOR **Note:** Struck at Mexico City Mint, mint mark M, Mo.

Date	Mintage	VG	F	VF	XF	Unc
1760 MM	—	400	800	1,500	2,500	—
1761/0 MM	—	400	800	1,500	2,500	—
1761 MM	—	400	800	1,500	2,500	—

ESCUDO   KM# 117   Weight: 3.3834 g. **Composition:**
0.9170 Gold .0997 oz. AGW **Obverse:** Large bust
Obv. Legend: CAR. III. D. G. HISP. ET IND. R
Rev. Legend: IN. UTROQ. FELIX **Note:** Struck at Mexico
City Mint, mint mark M, Mo.

Date	Mintage	VG	F	VF	XF	Unc
1762 MM	—	250	375	600	1,000	—
1763 MM	—	275	425	700	1,100	—
1764 MM	—	250	375	600	1,000	—
1765 MF	—	250	375	600	1,000	—
1766 MF	—	250	375	600	1,000	—
1767 MF	—	250	375	600	1,000	—
1768 MF	—	250	375	600	1,000	—
1769 MF	—	250	375	600	1,000	—
1770 MF	—	250	375	600	1,000	—
1771 MF	—	250	375	600	1,000	—

ESCUDO   KM# 118.1   Weight: 3.3834 g. **Composition:**
0.9010 Gold .0980 oz. AGW **Obverse:** Large bust
Obv. Legend: CAROL. III. D. G. HISPAN. ET IND. R
Reverse: Initials and mint mark upright **Rev. Legend:** FELIX.
A. D **Note:** Struck at Mexico City Mint, mint mark M, Mo.

Date	Mintage	VG	F	VF	XF	Unc
1772 MF	—	125	150	275	475	—
1772 FM	—	125	150	275	475	—
1773 FM	—	125	150	275	475	—

ESCUDO   KM# 118.2   Weight: 3.3834 g. **Composition:**
0.9010 Gold .0980 oz. AGW **Obverse:** Large bust
Obv. Legend: CAROL. III. D. G. HISPAN. ET IND. R
Reverse: Initials and mint mark inverted **Rev. Legend:**
FELIX. A. D **Note:** Struck at Mexico City Mint, mint mark M, Mo.

Date	Mintage	VG	F	VF	XF	Unc
1773 FM	—	125	150	275	475	—
1774 FM	—	125	150	275	475	—
1775 FM	—	125	150	275	475	—
1776 FM	—	125	150	275	475	—
1777 FM	—	125	150	275	475	—
1778 FF	—	125	150	275	475	—
1779 FF	—	125	150	275	475	—
1780 FF	—	125	150	275	475	—
1781 FF	—	125	150	275	475	—
1782 FF	—	125	150	275	475	—
1783/2 FF	—	125	150	275	475	—
1783 FF	—	125	150	275	475	—
1784/3 FF	—	125	150	275	475	—
1784/3 FM/F	—	125	150	275	475	—

ESCUDO   KM# 118.2a   Weight: 3.3800 g. **Composition:**
0.8750 Gold .0950 oz. AGW **Obverse:** Large bust
Obv. Legend: CAROL. III. D. G. HISPAN. ET IND. R.
Reverse: Initials and mint mark inverted **Rev. Legend:** FELIX.
A. D. **Note:** Struck at Mexico City Mint, mint mark M, Mo.

Date	Mintage	VG	F	VF	XF	Unc
1785 FM	—	125	150	275	475	—
1786 FM	—	125	150	275	475	—
1787 FM	—	125	150	275	475	—
1788 FM	—	125	150	275	475	—

ESCUDO   KM# 118.1a   Weight: 3.3834 g. **Composition:**
0.8750 Gold .0952 oz. AGW **Obverse:** Large bust
Obv. Legend: CAROL. III. D. G. HISPA3N. ET IND. R
Reverse: Initial letters and mint mark upright **Rev. Legend:**
FELIX. A. D **Note:** Struck at Mexico City Mint, mint mark M, Mo.

Date	Mintage	VG	F	VF	XF	Unc
1788 FM	—	125	150	275	475	—

ESCUDO   KM# 119   Weight: 3.3834 g. **Composition:**
0.8750 Gold .0952 oz. AGW **Obverse:** Bust of Charles III
Obv. Legend: CAROLUS. IV. D. G... **Reverse:** Initial letters
and mint mark upright **Rev. Legend:** FELIX. A. D **Note:**
Struck at Mexico City Mint, mint mark M, Mo.

Date	Mintage	VG	F	VF	XF	Unc
1789 FM	—	300	550	1,000	2,000	—
1790 FM	—	300	550	1,000	2,000	—

ESCUDO   KM# 120   Weight: 3.3834 g. **Composition:**
0.8750 Gold .0952 oz. AGW **Obverse:** Armored bust of
Charles IV **Obv. Legend:** CAROLUS. IV. D. G... **Reverse:**
Initial letters and mint mark upright **Rev. Legend:** FELIX. A.
D **Note:** Struck at Mexico City Mint, mint mark M, Mo.

Date	Mintage	VG	F	VF	XF	Unc
1792 MF	—	125	165	235	345	—
1793 FM	—	125	165	235	345	—
1794 FM	—	125	165	235	345	—
1795 FM	—	125	165	235	345	—
1796 FM	—	125	165	235	345	—
1797 FM	—	125	165	235	345	—
1798 FM	—	125	165	235	345	—
1799 FM	—	125	165	235	345	—
1800 FM	—	125	165	235	345	—
1801 FM	—	125	165	235	345	—
1801 FT	—	125	165	235	345	—
1802 FT	—	125	165	235	345	—
1803 FT	—	125	165	235	345	—
1804/3 TH	—	125	165	235	345	—
1804 TH	—	125	165	235	345	—
1805 TH	—	125	165	235	345	—
1806/5 TH	—	125	165	235	345	—
1806 TH	—	125	165	235	345	—
1807 TH	—	125	165	235	345	—
1808 TH	—	125	165	235	345	—

ESCUDO   KM# 121   Weight: 3.3834 g. **Composition:**
0.8750 Gold .0952 oz. AGW **Obverse:** Armored bust of
Ferdinand VII **Obv. Legend:** CAROLUS. IV. D. G... **Reverse:**
Initial letters and mint mark upright **Rev. Legend:** FELIX. A.
D **Note:** Struck at Mexico City Mint, mint mark M, Mo.

Date	Mintage	VG	F	VF	XF	Unc
1809 HJ/TH	—	125	165	235	400	—
1809 HJ	—	125	165	235	400	—
1811/0 HJ	—	125	165	235	400	—
1812 HJ	—	150	250	300	500	—

ESCUDO   KM# 122   Weight: 3.3834 g. **Composition:**
0.8750 Gold .0952 oz. AGW **Obverse:** Undraped bust of
Ferdinand VII **Obv. Legend:** CAROLUS. IV. D. G... **Reverse:**
Initial letters and mint mark upright **Rev. Legend:** FELIX. A.
D **Note:** Struck at Mexico City Mint, mint mark M, Mo.

Date	Mintage	VG	F	VF	XF	Unc
1814 HJ	—	150	250	300	500	—
1815 HJ	—	150	250	300	500	—
1815 JJ	—	150	250	300	500	—
1816 JJ	—	175	275	325	550	—
1817 JJ	—	150	250	300	500	—
1818 JJ	—	150	250	300	500	—
1819 JJ	—	150	250	300	500	—
1820 JJ	—	150	250	300	500	—

2 ESCUDOS   KM# 124   Weight: 6.7660 g. **Composition:**
0.9170 Gold .1995 oz. AGW **Obv. Legend:** PHILIP. V. D.
G. HISPAN. ET IND. REX **Rev. Legend:** INITIUM
SAPIENTIAE TIMOR DOMINI **Note:** Struck at Mexico City
Mint, mint mark M, Mo.

Date	Mintage	VG	F	VF	XF	Unc
1732 F	—	1,000	1,500	2,000	3,000	—
1733 F	—	750	1,000	1,500	2,500	—
1734/3 MF	—	400	500	900	1,400	—
1735 MF	—	400	500	900	1,400	—
1736/5 MF	—	400	500	900	1,400	—
1736 MF	—	400	500	900	1,400	—
1737 MF	—	400	500	900	1,400	—
1738/7 MF	—	400	500	900	1,400	—
1739 MF	—	400	500	900	1,400	—
1740/30 MF	—	400	500	900	1,400	—
1741 MF	—	400	500	900	1,400	—
1742 MF	—	400	500	900	1,400	—
1743 MF	—	400	500	900	1,400	—
1744/2 MF	—	400	500	900	1,400	—
1744 MF	—	400	500	900	1,400	—
1745 MF	—	400	500	900	1,400	—
1746/5 MF	—	400	500	900	1,400	—
1747 MF	—	400	500	900	1,400	—

2 ESCUDOS   KM# 125   Weight: 6.7660 g. **Composition:**
0.9170 Gold .1995 oz. AGW **Obv. Legend:** FERD. VI. D. G...
Rev. Legend: INITIUM... **Note:** Struck at Mexico City Mint, mint mark M, Mo.

Date	Mintage	VG	F	VF	XF	Unc
1747 MF	—	3,000	5,500	9,000	15,000	—

2 ESCUDOS   KM# 126.1   Weight: 6.7660 g.
Composition: 0.9170 Gold .1995 oz. AGW **Obverse:** Small
young bust **Obv. Legend:** FERD. VI. D. G... **Rev. Legend:**
NOMINA MAGNA SEQUOR **Note:** Struck at Mexico City
Mint, mint mark M, Mo.

Date	Mintage	VG	F	VF	XF	Unc
1748 MF	—	450	750	1,500	3,000	—
1749/8 MF	—	450	750	1,500	3,000	—
1750 MF	—	400	700	1,400	2,850	—
1751 MF	—	400	700	1,400	2,850	—

2 ESCUDOS   KM# 126.2   Weight: 6.7660 g.
Composition: 0.9170 Gold .1995 oz. AGW **Obverse:** Small
young bust **Obv. Legend:** FERD. VI. D. G... **Reverse:**
Without 2 S by arms **Rev. Legend:** NOMINA MAGNA
SEQUOR **Note:** Struck at Mexico City Mint, mint mark M, Mo.

Date	Mintage	VG	F	VF	XF	Unc
1752 MF	—	400	700	1,400	2,850	—
1753 MF	—	400	700	1,400	2,850	—
1754 MF	—	600	850	1,750	3,500	—
1755 MM	—	400	700	1,400	2,850	—
1756 MM	—	600	850	1,750	3,500	—

2 ESCUDOS   KM# 127   Weight: 6.7660 g. **Composition:**
0.9170 Gold .1995 oz. AGW **Obverse:** Armored bust
Obv. Legend: FERDND. VI. D. G... **Reverse:** Without 2 S
by arms **Rev. Legend:** NOMINA MAGNA SEQUOR **Note:**
Struck at Mexico City Mint, mint mark M, Mo.

Date	Mintage	VG	F	VF	XF	Unc
1757 MM	—	450	750	1,500	3,000	—
1759 MM	—	450	750	1,500	3,000	—

2 ESCUDOS   KM# 128   Weight: 6.7660 g. **Composition:**
0.9170 Gold .1995 oz. AGW **Obverse:** Young bust
Obv. Legend: CAROLVS. III. D. G... **Reverse:** Without 2 S
by arms **Rev. Legend:** NOMINA MAGNA SEQUOR **Note:**
Struck at Mexico City Mint, mint mark M, Mo.

Date	Mintage	VG	F	VF	XF	Unc
1760 MM	—	550	1,000	2,000	4,000	—
1761 MM	—	550	1,000	2,000	4,000	—

2 ESCUDOS   KM# 129   Weight: 6.7668 g. **Composition:**
0.9170 Gold .1995 oz. AGW **Obverse:** Large young bust

Obv. Legend: CAROLUS. III. D. G... **Reverse:** Without 2 S by arms **Rev. Legend:** IN. UTROQ. FELIX. AUSPICE. DEO **Note:** Struck at Mexico City Mint, mint mark M, Mo.

Date	Mintage	VG	F	VF	XF	Unc
1762 MF	—	500	900	1,850	3,750	—
1763 MF	—	500	900	1,850	3,750	—
1764/3 MF	—	500	900	1,850	3,750	—
1765 MF	—	500	900	1,850	3,750	—
1766 MF	—	500	900	1,850	3,750	—
1767 MF	—	500	900	1,850	3,750	—
1768 MF	—	500	900	1,850	3,750	—
1769 MF	—	500	900	1,850	3,750	—
1770 MF	—	500	900	1,850	3,750	—
1771 MF	—	500	900	1,850	3,750	—

2 ESCUDOS   KM# 130.1 Weight: 6.7668 g. **Composition:** 0.9010 Gold .1960 oz. AGW **Obverse:** Older bust **Obv. Legend:** CAROLUS. III. D. G... **Reverse:** Initials and mint mark upright **Rev. Legend:** IN. UTROQ. FELIX. AUSPICE. DEO **Note:** Struck at Mexico City Mint, mint mark M, Mo.

Date	Mintage	VG	F	VF	XF	Unc
1772 FM	—	200	375	550	1,000	—
1773 FM	—	200	375	550	1,000	—

2 ESCUDOS   KM# 130.2 Weight: 6.7668 g. **Composition:** 0.9010 Gold .1960 oz. AGW **Obverse:** Older bust **Obv. Legend:** CAROLUS. III. D. G... **Reverse:** Initials and mint mark inverted **Rev. Legend:** IN. UTROQ. FELIX. AUSPICE. DEO **Note:** Struck at Mexico City Mint, mint mark M, Mo.

Date	Mintage	VG	F	VF	XF	Unc
1773 FM	—	200	375	550	1,000	—
1774 FM	—	200	375	550	1,000	—
1775 FM	—	200	375	550	1,000	—
1776 FM	—	200	375	550	1,000	—
1777 FM	—	175	300	450	900	—
1778 FF	—	175	300	450	900	—
1779 FF	—	175	300	450	900	—
1780 FF	—	175	300	450	900	—
1781 FM/M	—	175	300	450	900	—
1781 FF	—	175	300	450	900	—
1782 FF	—	175	300	450	900	—
1783 FF	—	175	300	450	900	—
1784 FF	—	175	300	450	900	—
1784 FM/F	—	175	300	450	900	—

2 ESCUDOS   KM# 130.2a Weight: 6.7668 g. **Comp.:** 0.8750 Gold .1904 oz. AGW **Obv. Legend:** CAROLUS. III. D. G... **Reverse:** Initials and mint mark inverted **Rev. Legend:** IN. UTROQ. FELIX. AUSPICE. DEO **Note:** Struck at Mexico City Mint, mint mark M, Mo.

Date	Mintage	VG	F	VF	XF	Unc
1785 FM	—	175	300	450	900	—
1786 FM	—	175	300	450	900	—
1787 FM	—	175	300	450	900	—
1788 FM	—	175	300	450	900	—

2 ESCUDOS   KM# 130.1a Weight: 6.7668 g. **Comp.:** 0.8750 Gold .1904 oz. AGW **Obverse:** Older bust **Obv. Legend:** CAROLUS. III. D. G... **Reverse:** Initials and mint mark upright **Rev. Legend:** IN. UTROQ. FELIX. AUSPICE. DEO **Note:** Struck at Mexico City Mint, mint mark M, Mo.

Date	Mintage	VG	F	VF	XF	Unc
1788 FM	—	175	300	450	900	—

2 ESCUDOS   KM# 131 Weight: 6.7668 g. **Composition:** 0.8750 Gold .1904 oz. AGW **Obverse:** Bust of Charles III **Obv. Legend:** CAROL. IV. D. G... **Reverse:** Initials and mint mark upright **Rev. Legend:** IN. UTROQ. FELIX. AUSPICE. DEO **Note:** Struck at Mexico City Mint, mint mark M, Mo.

Date	Mintage	VG	F	VF	XF	Unc
1789 FM	—	650	1,200	2,000	3,500	—
1790 FM	—	650	1,200	2,000	3,500	—

2 ESCUDOS   KM# 132 Weight: 6.7668 g. **Composition:** 0.8750 Gold .1904 oz. AGW **Obverse:** Armored bust of Charles IV **Obv. Legend:** CAROL. IV. D. G... **Reverse:** Initials and mint mark upright **Rev. Legend:** IN. UTROQ. FELIX. AUSPICE. DEO **Note:** Struck at Mexico City Mint, mint mark M, Mo.

Date	Mintage	VG	F	VF	XF	Unc
1791 FM Mo over inverted Mo	—	300	375	600	950	—
1792 FM	—	125	225	350	575	—
1793 FM	—	125	225	350	575	—
1794 FM	—	125	225	350	575	—
1795 FM	—	125	225	350	575	—
1796 FM	—	125	225	350	575	—
1797 FM	—	125	225	350	575	—
1798 FM	—	125	225	350	575	—
1799 FM	—	125	225	350	575	—
1800 FM	—	125	225	350	575	—
1801 FT	—	125	225	350	575	—
1802 FT	—	125	225	350	575	—
1803 FT	—	125	225	350	575	—
1804 TH	—	125	225	350	575	—
1805 TH	—	125	225	350	575	—
1806/5 TH	—	125	225	350	575	—
1807 TH	—	125	225	350	575	—
1808 TH	—	125	225	350	575	—

2 ESCUDOS   KM# 134 Weight: 6.7668 g. **Composition:** 0.8750 Gold .1904 oz. AGW **Obverse:** Undraped bust of Ferdinand VII **Obv. Legend:** CAROL. IV. D. G... **Reverse:** Initials and mint mark upright **Rev. Legend:** IN. UTROQ. FELIX. AUSPICE. DEO **Note:** Struck at Mexico City Mint, mint mark M, Mo.

Date	Mintage	VG	F	VF	XF	Unc
1814 JJ	—	250	425	700	1,200	—
1815 JJ	—	250	425	700	1,200	—
1816 JJ	—	250	425	700	1,200	—
1817 JJ	—	250	425	700	1,200	—
1818 JJ	—	250	425	700	1,200	—
1819 JJ	—	250	425	700	1,200	—
1820 JJ	—	250	425	700	1,200	—
1821 JJ	—	250	425	700	1,200	—

4 ESCUDOS   KM# 135 Weight: 13.5337 g. **Composition:** 0.9170 Gold .3990 oz. AGW **Obv. Legend:** PHILIP. V. D. G. HISPAN. ET IND. REX **Rev. Legend:** INITIUM SAPIENTIAE TIMOR DOMINI **Note:** Struck at Mexico City Mint, mint mark M, Mo.

Date	Mintage	VG	F	VF	XF	Unc
1732 Rare	—	—	—	—	—	—
1732 F Rare	—	—	—	—	—	—
1733 F Rare	—	—	—	—	—	—
1734/3 F	—	1,000	1,500	2,800	4,500	—
1734 MF	—	850	1,350	2,500	4,250	—
1735 MF	—	850	1,350	2,500	4,500	—
1736 MF	—	850	1,350	2,500	4,500	—
1737 MF	—	750	1,250	2,400	4,000	—
1738/7 MF	—	750	1,250	2,400	4,000	—
1738 MF	—	750	1,250	2,400	4,000	—
1739 MF	—	750	1,250	2,400	4,000	—
1740/30 MF	—	750	1,250	2,400	4,000	—
1740 MF	—	750	1,250	2,400	4,000	—
1741 MF	—	750	1,250	2,400	4,000	—
1742/32 MF	—	750	1,250	2,400	4,000	—
1743 MF	—	750	1,250	2,400	4,000	—
1744 MD	—	750	1,250	2,400	4,000	—
1745 MF	—	750	1,250	2,400	4,000	—
1746 MF	—	750	1,250	2,400	4,000	—
1747 MF	—	750	1,250	2,400	4,000	—
1746/5 MF	—	750	1,250	2,400	4,000	—

4 ESCUDOS　KM# 136　Weight: 13.5337 g.
Composition: 0.9170 Gold .3990 oz. AGW **Obverse:** Large bust **Obv. Legend:** FERDND. VI. D. G... **Rev. Legend:** INITIUM SAPIENTIAE TIMOR DOMINI **Note:** Struck at Mexico City Mint, mint mark M, Mo.

Date	Mintage	VG	F	VF	XF	Unc
1747 MF	—	7,500	13,500	20,000	30,000	—

4 ESCUDOS　KM# 137　Weight: 13.5337 g.
Composition: 0.9170 Gold .3990 oz. AGW **Obverse:** Small bust **Obv. Legend:** FERDND. VI. D. G... **Reverse:** 4S divided by arms **Rev. Legend:** NOMINA MAGNA... **Note:** Struck at Mexico City Mint, mint mark M, Mo.

Date	Mintage	VG	F	VF	XF	Unc
1748 MF	—	1,500	3,000	5,000	8,000	—
1749 MF	—	1,500	3,000	5,000	8,000	—
1750/48 MF	—	1,500	3,000	5,000	8,000	—
1750 MF	—	1,500	3,000	5,000	8,000	—
1751 MF	—	1,500	3,000	5,000	8,000	—

4 ESCUDOS　KM# 138　Weight: 13.5337 g.
Composition: 0.9170 Gold .3990 oz. AGW **Obverse:** Small bust **Obv. Legend:** FERDND. VI. D. G... **Reverse:** Without

value **Rev. Legend:** NOMINA MAGNA... **Note:** Struck at Mexico City Mint, mint mark M, Mo.

Date	Mintage	VG	F	VF	XF	Unc
1752 MF	—	1,000	2,000	3,500	6,000	—
1753 MF	—	1,000	2,000	3,500	6,000	—
1754 MF	—	1,000	2,000	3,500	6,000	—
1755 MM	—	1,000	2,000	3,500	6,000	—
1756 MM	—	1,000	2,000	3,500	6,000	—

4 ESCUDOS　KM# 139　Weight: 13.5337 g.
Composition: 0.9170 Gold .3990 oz. AGW **Obverse:** Large full bust **Obv. Legend:** FERDND. VI. D. G... **Reverse:** Without value **Rev. Legend:** NOMINA MAGNA... **Note:** Struck at Mexico City Mint, mint mark M, Mo.

Date	Mintage	VG	F	VF	XF	Unc
1757 MM	—	1,250	2,500	4,000	6,500	—
1759 MM	—	1,250	2,500	4,000	6,500	—

4 ESCUDOS　KM# 140　Weight: 13.5337 g.
Composition: 0.9170 Gold .3990 oz. AGW **Obverse:** Young bust **Obv. Legend:** CAROLVS. III. D. G... **Reverse:** Without value **Rev. Legend:** NOMINA MAGNA SEQUOR **Note:** Struck at Mexico City Mint, mint mark M, Mo.

Date	Mintage	VG	F	VF	XF	Unc
1760 MM	—	3,500	6,500	10,000	20,000	—
1761 MM	—	3,500	6,500	10,000	20,000	—

4 ESCUDOS　KM# 141　Weight: 13.5337 g.
Composition: 0.9170 Gold .3990 oz. AGW **Obverse:** Large young bust **Obv. Legend:** CAROLUS. III. D. G... **Reverse:** Without value **Rev. Legend:** IN. UTROQ. FELIX. AUSPICE. DEO **Note:** Struck at Mexico City Mint, mint mark M, Mo.

Date	Mintage	VG	F	VF	XF	Unc
1762 MF	—	2,500	4,500	7,500	15,000	—
1763 MF	—	2,500	4,500	7,500	15,000	—
1764 MF	—	2,500	4,500	7,500	15,000	—
1765 MF	—	2,500	4,500	7,500	15,000	—
1766/5 MF	—	2,500	4,500	7,500	15,000	—
1767 MF	—	2,500	4,500	7,500	15,000	—
1768 MF	—	2,500	4,500	7,500	15,000	—
1769 MF	—	2,500	4,500	7,500	15,000	—
1770 MF	—	2,500	4,500	7,500	15,000	—
1771 MF	—	2,500	4,500	7,500	15,000	—

4 ESCUDOS　KM# 142.1　Weight: 13.5337 g.
Composition: 0.9010 Gold .3920 oz. AGW **Obverse:** Large young bust **Obv. Legend:** CAROL. III. D. G... **Reverse:**

Initials and mint mark upright **Rev. Legend:** IN. UTROQ.
FELIX. AUSPICE. DEO **Note:** Struck at Mexico City Mint,
mint mark M, Mo.

Date	Mintage	VG	F	VF	XF	Unc
1772 FM	—	400	650	1,000	2,000	—
1773 FM	—	400	650	1,000	2,000	—

4 ESCUDOS KM# 142.2 Weight: 13.5337 g.
Composition: 0.9010 Gold .3920 oz. AGW **Obverse:** Large
young bust **Obv. Legend:** CAROL. III. D. G... **Reverse:**
Initials and mint mark inverted **Rev. Legend:** IN. UTROQ.
FELIX. AUSPICE. DEO **Note:** Struck at Mexico City Mint,
mint mark M, Mo.

Date	Mintage	VG	F	VF	XF	Unc
1773 FM	—	400	600	900	1,850	—
1774 FM	—	400	600	900	1,850	—
1775 FM	—	400	600	900	1,850	—
1776 FM	—	400	600	900	1,850	—
1777 FM	—	400	600	900	1,850	—
1778 FF	—	400	600	900	1,850	—
1779 FF	—	400	600	900	1,850	—
1780 FF	—	400	600	900	1,850	—
1781 FF	—	400	600	900	1,850	—
1782 FF	—	400	600	900	1,850	—
1783 FF	—	400	600	900	1,850	—
1784 FF	—	400	600	900	1,850	—
1784/3 FM/F	—	400	600	900	1,850	—

4 ESCUDOS KM# 142.2a Weight: 13.5337 g.
Composition: 0.8750 Gold .3807 oz. AGW **Obverse:** Large
young bust **Obv. Legend:** CAROL. III. D. G... **Reverse:**
Initials and mint mark inverted **Rev. Legend:** IN. UTROQ.
FELIX. AUSPICE. DEO **Note:** Struck at Mexico City Mint,
mint mark M, Mo.

Date	Mintage	VG	F	VF	XF	Unc
1785 FM	—	400	600	900	1,850	—
1786 FM/F	—	400	600	900	1,850	—
1786 FM	—	400	600	900	1,850	—
1787 FM	—	400	600	900	1,850	—
1788 FM	—	400	600	900	1,850	—

4 ESCUDOS KM# 142.1a Weight: 13.5337 g.
Composition: 0.8750 Gold .3807 oz. AGW **Obverse:** Large
young bust **Obv. Legend:** CAROL. III. D. G... **Reverse:**
Initials and mint mark upright **Rev. Legend:** IN. UTROQ.
FELIX. AUSPICE. DEO **Note:** Struck at Mexico City Mint,
mint mark M, Mo.

Date	Mintage	VG	F	VF	XF	Unc
1788 FM	—	400	650	1,000	2,000	—

4 ESCUDOS KM# 143.1 Weight: 13.5337 g.
Composition: 0.8750 Gold .3807 oz. AGW **Obverse:** Bust
of Charles III **Obv. Legend:** CAROL. IV. D. G **Reverse:**
Initials and mint mark upright **Rev. Legend:** IN. UTROQ.
FELIX. AUSPICE. DEO **Note:** Struck at Mexico City Mint,
mint mark M, Mo.

Date	Mintage	VG	F	VF	XF	Unc
1789 FM	—	500	700	1,100	2,150	—
1790 FM	—	500	700	1,100	2,150	—

4 ESCUDOS KM# 143.2 Weight: 13.5337 g.
Composition: 0.8750 Gold .3807 oz. AGW **Obverse:** Bust
of Charles III **Obv. Legend:** CAROL. IIII D. G... **Reverse:**
Initials and mint mark upright **Rev. Legend:** IN. UTROQ.
FELIX. AUSPICE. DEO **Note:** Struck at Mexico City Mint,
mint mark M, Mo.

Date	Mintage	VG	F	VF	XF	Unc
1790 FM	—	600	1,000	1,800	3,000	—

4 ESCUDOS KM# 144 Weight: 13.5337 g.
Composition: 0.8750 Gold .3807 oz. AGW **Obverse:**
Armored bust of Charles IIII **Obv. Legend:** CAROL. IIII D.
G... **Reverse:** Initials and mint mark upright **Rev. Legend:**
IN. UTROQ. FELIX. AUSPICE. DEO **Note:** Struck at Mexico
City Mint, mint mark M, Mo.

Date	Mintage	VG	F	VF	XF	Unc
1792 FM	—	300	500	750	1,500	—
1793 FM	—	300	500	750	1,500	—
1794/3 FM	—	300	500	750	1,500	—
1795 FM	—	300	500	750	1,500	—
1796 FM	—	300	500	750	1,500	—
1797 FM	—	300	500	750	1,500	—
1798/7 FM	—	300	500	750	1,500	—
1798 FM	—	300	500	750	1,500	—
1799 FM	—	300	500	750	1,500	—
1800 FM	—	300	500	750	1,500	—
1801 FM	—	300	500	750	1,500	—
1801 FT	—	300	500	750	1,500	—
1802 FT	—	300	500	750	1,500	—
1803 FT	—	300	500	750	1,500	—
1804/3 TH	—	300	500	750	1,500	—
1804 TH	—	300	500	750	1,500	—
1805 TH	—	300	500	750	1,500	—
1806/5 TH	—	300	500	750	1,500	—
1807 TH	—	300	500	750	1,500	—
1808/0 TH	—	300	500	750	1,500	—
1808 TH	—	300	500	750	1,500	—

4 ESCUDOS KM# 145 Weight: 13.5337 g.
Composition: 0.8750 Gold .3807 oz. AGW **Obverse:**
Armored bust of Ferdinand VII **Obv. Legend:** CAROL. IIII
D. G... **Reverse:** Initials and mint mark upright **Rev. Legend:**
IN. UTROQ. FELIX. AUSPICE. DEO **Note:** Struck at Mexico
City Mint, mint mark M, Mo.

Date	Mintage	VG	F	VF	XF	Unc
1810 HJ	—	350	500	850	1,700	—
1811 HJ	—	350	500	850	1,700	—
1812 HJ	—	350	500	850	1,700	—

4 ESCUDOS KM# 146 Weight: 13.5337 g.
Composition: 0.8750 Gold .3807 oz. AGW **Obverse:**
Undraped bust of Ferdinand VII **Obv. Legend:** CAROL. IIII
D. G... **Reverse:** Initials and mint mark upright **Rev. Legend:**

IN. UTROQ. FELIX. AUSPICE. DEO **Note:** Struck at Mexico
City Mint, mint mark M, Mo.

Date	Mintage	VG	F	VF	XF	Unc
1814 HJ	—	400	700	1,200	2,700	—
1815 HJ	—	400	700	1,200	2,700	—
1815 JJ	—	400	700	1,200	2,700	—
1816 JJ	—	400	700	1,200	2,700	—
1817 JJ	—	400	700	1,200	2,700	—
1818 JJ	—	400	700	1,200	2,700	—
1819 JJ	—	400	700	1,200	2,700	—
1820 JJ	—	400	700	1,200	2,700	—

8 ESCUDOS   KM# 148   Weight: 27.0674 g.
Composition: 0.9170 Gold .7980 oz. AGW **Obv. Legend:**
PHILIP. V. D. G. HISPAN. ET IND. REX **Rev. Legend:**
INITIUM SAPIENTIAE TIMOR DOMINI **Note:** Struck at
Mexico City Mint, mint mark M, Mo.

Date	Mintage	VG	F	VF	XF	Unc
1732 Rare	—	—	—	—	—	—
1732 F Rare	—	—	—	—	—	—
1733 F Rare	—	—	—	—	—	—
1734 MF	—	1,000	1,650	2,750	4,850	—
1734 MF/F	—	1,000	1,650	2,750	4,850	—
1735 MF	—	1,000	1,500	2,500	4,500	—
1736 MF	—	1,000	1,500	2,500	4,500	—
1737 MF	—	1,000	1,500	2,500	4,500	—
1738/7 MF	—	1,000	1,500	2,500	4,500	—
1738 MF	—	1,000	1,500	2,500	4,500	—
1739 MF	—	1,000	1,500	2,500	4,500	—
1740 MF	—	1,000	1,500	2,500	4,500	—
1740/30 MF	—	1,000	1,500	2,500	4,500	—
1741 MF	—	1,000	1,500	2,500	4,500	—
1742 MF	—	1,000	1,500	2,500	4,500	—
1743 MF	—	1,000	1,500	2,500 .	4,500	—
1744 MF	—	1,000	1,500	2,500	4,500	—
1744/3 MF	—	1,000	1,500	2,500	4,500	—
1745/4 MF	—	1,000	1,500	2,500	4,500	—
1745 MF	—	1,000	1,500	2,500	4,500	—
1746 MF	—	1,000	1,500	2,500	4,500	—
1746/5 MF	—	1,000	1,500	2,500	4,500	—
1747 MF	—	1,100	1,750	2,850	5,000	—

8 ESCUDOS   KM# 149   Weight: 27.0674 g.
Composition: 0.9170 Gold .7980 oz. AGW **Obverse:**
Young bust **Obv. Legend:** FERDND. VI. D. G...
Rev. Legend: INITIUM SAPIENTIAE TIMOR DOMINI **Note:**
Struck at Mexico City Mint, mint mark M, Mo.

Date	Mintage	VG	F	VF	XF	Unc
1747 MF	—	9,000	15,000	22,000	35,000	—

8 ESCUDOS   KM# 150   Weight: 27.0674 g.
Composition: 0.9170 Gold .7980 oz. AGW **Obverse:** Small
bust **Obv. Legend:** FERDND. VI. D. G... **Rev. Legend:**
NOMINA MAGNA SEQUOR **Note:** Struck at Mexico City
Mint, mint mark M, Mo.

Date	Mintage	VG	F	VF	XF	Unc
1748 MF	—	1,200	2,000	3,500	6,000	—
1749/8 MF	—	1,200	2,000	3,500	6,000	—
1749 MF	—	1,200	2,000	3,500	6,000	—
1750 MF	—	1,200	2,000	3,500	6,000	—
1751/0 MF	—	1,500	2,000	3,500	6,000	—
1751 MF	—	1,200	2,000	3,500	6,000	—

8 ESCUDOS   KM# 151   Weight: 27.0674 g.
Composition: 0.9170 Gold .7980 oz. AGW **Obverse:** Large
bust **Obv. Legend:** FERDND. VI. D. G... **Reverse:** Without
8 S divided by arms **Rev. Legend:** NOMINA MAGNA
SEQUOR **Note:** Struck at Mexico City Mint, mint mark M, Mo.

Date	Mintage	VG	F	VF	XF	Unc
1752 MF	—	1,200	2,000	3,500	6,000	—
1753 MF	—	1,200	2,000	3,500	6,000	—
1754 MF	—	1,200	2,000	3,500	6,000	—
1755 MM	—	1,200	2,000	3,500	6,000	—
1756 MM	—	1,200	2,000	3,500	6,000	—

8 ESCUDOS   KM# 153   Weight: 27.0674 g.
Composition: 0.9170 Gold .7980 oz. AGW **Obverse:**
Young bust with Order of the Golden Fleece at date
Obv. Legend: CAROLVS. III. D. G... **Reverse:** Without 8 S
divided by arms **Rev. Legend:** NOMINA MAGNA SEQUOR
Note: Struck at Mexico City Mint, mint mark M, Mo.

Date	Mintage	VG	F	VF	XF	Unc
1760 MM	—	1,750	3,000	5,000	9,000	—
1761/0 MM	—	2,000	3,500	5,500	10,000	—
1761 MM	—	2,000	3,500	5,500	10,000	—

8 ESCUDOS   KM# 152   Weight: 27.0674 g.
Composition: 0.9170 Gold .7980 oz. AGW **Obverse:**
Medium, full bust **Obv. Legend:** FERDND. VI. D. G...
Reverse: Without 8 S divided by arms **Rev. Legend:**
NOMINA MAGNA SEQUOR **Note:** Struck at Mexico City
Mint, mint mark M, Mo.

Date	Mintage	VG	F	VF	XF	Unc
1757 MM	—	1,200	2,000	3,500	6,000	—
1758 MM	—	1,200	2,000	3,500	6,000	—
1759 MM	—	1,200	2,000	3,500	6,000	—

8 ESCUDOS   KM# 154   Weight: 27.0674 g.
Composition: 0.9170 Gold .7980 oz. AGW **Obverse:**
Young bust with Order of the Golden Fleece on chest
Obv. Legend: CAROLVS. III. D. G... **Reverse:** Without 8 S
divided by arms **Rev. Legend:** NOMINA MAGNA SEQUOR
Note: Struck at Mexico City Mint, mint mark M, Mo.

Date	Mintage	VG	F	VF	XF	Unc
1761 MM	—	1,750	3,000	5,250	9,500	—

8 ESCUDOS   KM# 155   Weight: 27.0674 g.
Composition: 0.9170 Gold .7980 oz. AGW **Obverse:** Large
bust **Obv. Legend:** CAROLUS. III. D. G... **Reverse:** Without
8 S divided by arms **Rev. Legend:** IN. UTROQ. FELIX.
AUSPICE **Note:** Struck at Mexico City Mint, mint mark M, Mo.

Date	Mintage	VG	F	VF	XF	Unc
1762 MM	—	1,600	2,750	4,500	8,500	—
1763 MM	—	1,600	2,750	4,500	8,500	—
1764 MF	—	1,750	3,000	5,000	9,000	—

Date	Mintage	VG	F	VF	XF	Unc
1764/2 MF	—	1,750	3,000	5,000	9,000	—
1764 MM	—	1,750	3,000	5,000	9,000	—
1765/4 MF	—	1,750	3,000	5,000	9,000	—
1765/4 MM	—	1,750	3,000	5,000	9,000	—
1765 MF	—	1,750	3,000	5,000	9,000	—
1765 MM	—	1,500	2,500	4,000	7,500	—
1766 MF	—	1,500	2,500	4,000	7,500	—
1767/6 MF	—	1,500	2,500	4,000	7,500	—
1767 MF	—	1,500	2,500	4,000	7,500	—
1768/7 MF	—	1,500	2,500	4,000	7,500	—
1768 MF	—	1,500	2,500	4,000	7,500	—
1769 MF	—	1,500	2,500	4,000	7,500	—
1770 MF	—	1,500	2,500	4,000	7,500	—
1771 MF	—	1,750	3,000	5,000	9,000	—

8 ESCUDOS   KM# 156.2a Weight: 27.0674 g.
Composition: 0.8750 Gold .7615 oz. AGW **Obverse:**
Mature bust **Obv. Legend:** CAROL. III. D. G... **Reverse:**
Initials and mint mark inverted **Rev. Legend:** ... AUSPICE.
DEO **Note:** Struck at Mexico City Mint, mint mark M, Mo.

Date	Mintage	VG	F	VF	XF	Unc
1786 FM	—	500	700	1,100	1,650	—
1787 FM	—	500	700	1,100	1,650	—
1788 FM	—	500	700	1,100	1,650	—

8 ESCUDOS   KM# 156.1a Weight: 27.0674 g.
Composition: 0.8750 Gold .7615 oz. AGW **Obverse:**
Mature bust **Obv. Legend:** CAROL. III. D. G... **Reverse:**
Initials and mint mark upright **Rev. Legend:** ... AUSPICE.
DEO **Note:** Struck at Mexico City Mint, mint mark M, Mo.

Date	Mintage	VG	F	VF	XF	Unc
1788 FM	—	500	700	1,100	1,650	—

8 ESCUDOS   KM# 156.1 Weight: 27.0674 g.
Composition: 0.9010 Gold .7840 oz. AGW **Obverse:**
Mature bust **Obv. Legend:** CAROL. III. D. G... **Reverse:**
Initials and mint mark upright **Rev. Legend:** ... AUSPICE.
DEO **Note:** Struck at Mexico City Mint, mint mark M, Mo.

Date	Mintage	VG	F	VF	XF	Unc
1772 FM	—	500	750	1,250	2,000	—
1773 FM	—	550	850	1,350	2,250	—

8 ESCUDOS   KM# 156.2 Weight: 27.0674 g.
Composition: 0.9010 Gold .7840 oz. AGW **Obverse:**
Mature bust **Obv. Legend:** CAROL. III. D. G... **Reverse:**
Initials and mint mark inverted **Rev. Legend:** ... AUSPICE.
DEO **Note:** Struck at Mexico City Mint, mint mark M, Mo.

Date	Mintage	VG	F	VF	XF	Unc
1773 FM	—	500	700	1,100	1,650	—
1774 FM	—	500	700	1,100	1,650	—
1775 FM	—	500	700	1,100	1,650	—
1776 FM	—	500	700	1,100	1,650	—
1777/6 FM	—	500	700	1,100	1,650	—
1777 FM	—	500	700	1,100	1,650	—
1778 FF	—	500	700	1,100	1,650	—
1779 FF	—	500	700	1,100	1,650	—
1780 FF	—	500	700	1,100	1,650	—
1781 FF	—	500	700	1,100	1,650	—
1782 FF	—	500	700	1,100	1,650	—
1783 FF	—	500	700	1,100	1,650	—
1784 FF	—	500	700	1,100	1,650	—
1784 FM/F	—	500	700	1,100	1,650	—
1784 FM	—	500	700	1,100	1,650	—
1785 FM	—	500	700	1,100	1,650	—

8 ESCUDOS   KM# 157 Weight: 27.0674 g.
Composition: 0.8750 Gold .7615 oz. AGW **Obverse:** Bust
of Charles III **Obv. Legend:** CAROL. IV. D. G... **Reverse:**
Arms, Order chain **Rev. Legend:** IN UTROQ... A. D **Note:**
Struck at Mexico City Mint, mint mark M, Mo.

Date	Mintage	VG	F	VF	XF	Unc
1789 FM	—	500	700	1,150	2,000	—
1790 FM	—	500	700	1,150	2,000	—

Date	Mintage	VG	F	VF	XF	Unc
1801 FM	—	350	450	625	1,000	—
1801 FT	—	350	450	625	1,000	—
1802 FT	—	350	450	625	1,000	—
1803 FT	—	350	450	625	1,000	—
1804/3 TH	—	400	500	700	1,150	—
1804 TH	—	350	450	625	1,000	—
1805 TH	—	350	450	625	1,000	—
1806 TH	—	350	450	625	1,000	—
1807/6 TH	—	400	500	700	1,150	—
1807 TH Mo over inverted Mo	—	400	500	700	1,150	—
1808/7 TH	—	450	600	800	1,250	—
1807 TH	—	350	450	625	1,000	—
1808 TH	—	450	600	800	1,250	—

8 ESCUDOS   KM# 158   Weight: 27.0674 g.
Composition: 0.8750 Gold .7615 oz. AGW **Obverse:** Bust of Charles III **Obv. Legend:** CAROL. IIII. D. G... **Reverse:** Arms, Order chain **Rev. Legend:** IN UTROQ... A. D **Note:** Struck at Mexico City Mint, mint mark M, Mo.

Date	Mintage	VG	F	VF	XF	Unc
1790 FM	—	500	700	1,150	2,000	—

8 ESCUDOS   KM# 160   Weight: 27.0674 g.
Composition: 0.8750 Gold .7615 oz. AGW **Obverse:** Armored bust of Ferdinand VII **Obv. Legend:** CAROL. IIII. D. G... **Reverse:** Arms, Order chain **Rev. Legend:** IN UTROQ. FELIX **Note:** Struck at Mexico City Mint, mint mark M, Mo.

Date	Mintage	VG	F	VF	XF	Unc
1808 TH	—	400	500	750	1,250	—
1809 HJ	—	400	500	750	1,350	—
1810 HJ	—	375	475	700	1,200	—
1811/0 HJ	—	425	525	800	1,350	—
1811 HJ H/T	—	425	525	800	1,350	—
1811 HJ	—	425	525	800	1,350	—
1811 JJ	—	375	475	700	1,200	—
1812 JJ	—	375	475	700	1,200	—

8 ESCUDOS   KM# 159   Weight: 27.0674 g.
Composition: 0.8750 Gold .7615 oz. AGW **Obverse:** Armored bust of Charles IIII **Obv. Legend:** CAROL. IIII. D. G... **Reverse:** Arms, Order chain **Rev. Legend:** IN UTROQ. FELIX **Note:** Struck at Mexico City Mint, mint mark M, Mo.

Date	Mintage	VG	F	VF	XF	Unc
1791 FM	—	350	450	625	1,000	—
1792 FM	—	350	450	625	1,000	—
1793 FM	—	350	450	625	1,000	—
1794 FM	—	350	450	625	1,000	—
1795 FM	—	350	450	625	1,000	—
1796/5 FM	—	400	500	700	1,150	—
1796 FM	—	350	450	625	1,000	—
1797 FM	—	350	450	625	1,000	—
1797 FM EPLIX	—	400	500	700	1,150	—
1798 FM	—	350	450	625	1,000	—
1799 FM	—	350	450	625	1,000	—
1800 FM	—	350	450	625	1,000	—
1801/0 FT	—	400	500	700	1,150	—

8 ESCUDOS   KM# 161   Weight: 27.0674 g.
Composition: 0.8750 Gold .7615 oz. AGW **Obverse:** Undraped bust of Ferdinand VII **Obv. Legend:** CAROL. IIII.

D. G... **Reverse:** Arms, Order chain **Rev. Legend:** IN UTROQ. FELIX **Note:** Struck at Mexico City Mint, mint mark M, Mo.

Date	Mintage	VG	F	VF	XF	Unc
1814 JJ	—	360	465	650	1,000	—
1815/4 JJ	—	400	500	700	1,150	—
1815/4 HJ	—	400	500	700	1,150	—
1815 JJ	—	360	465	650	1,000	—
1815 HJ	—	360	465	650	1,000	—
1816 JJ	—	360	465	650	1,000	—
1817 JJ	—	400	500	700	1,150	—
1818/7 JJ	—	360	465	675	1,100	—
1818 JJ	—	360	465	675	1,100	—
1819 JJ	—	360	465	675	1,100	—
1820 JJ	—	360	465	675	1,100	—
1821 JJ	—	400	500	750	1,300	—

PROCLAMATION MEDALLIC COINAGE

The Q used in the following listings refer to Standard Catalog of Mexican Coins, Paper Money, Stocks, Bonds, and Medals by Krause Publications, Inc., ©1981.

1/2 REAL   KM# Q22   Weight: 1.6000 g. **Composition:** Silver **Issuer:** Mexico City **Obv. Legend:** A CARLOS IV REY DE ESPANA Y DE LAS YNDIAS **Rev. Legend:** PROCLAMADO EN MEXICO ANO DE 1789

Date	Mintage	F	VF	XF	Unc	BU
1789	—	20.00	28.50	40.00	—	—

1/2 REAL   KM# Q22a   Composition: Bronze **Issuer:** Mexico City **Obv. Legend:** A CARLOS IV REY DE ESPANA Y DE LAS YNDIAS **Rev. Legend:** PROCLAMADO EN MEXICO ANO DE 1789

Date	Mintage	F	VF	XF	Unc	BU
1789	—	22.50	35.00	50.00	—	—

1/2 REAL   KM# Q23   Composition: Silver **Issuer:** Mexico City **Obverse:** Crowned arms in double-lined circle **Obv. Legend:** A CARLOS IV REY DE ESPANA Y DE LAS YNDIAS **Rev. Legend:** PROCLAMADO EN MEXICO ANO DE 1789

Date	Mintage	F	VF	XF	Unc	BU
1789	—	20.00	28.50	40.00	—	—

1/2 REAL   KM# Q23a   Composition: Bronze **Issuer:** Mexico City **Obverse:** Crowned arms in double-lined circle **Obv. Legend:** A CARLOS IV REY DE ESPANA Y DE LAS YNDIAS **Rev. Legend:** PROCLAMADO EN MEXICO ANO DE 1789

Date	Mintage	F	VF	XF	Unc	BU
1789	—	22.50	35.00	50.00	—	—

REAL   KM# Q24   Composition: Silver **Issuer:** Mexico City **Obv. Legend:** A CARLOS IV REY DE ESPANA Y DE LAS YNDIAS **Rev. Legend:** PROCLAMADO EN MEXICO ANO DE 1789

Date	Mintage	F	VF	XF	Unc	BU
1789	—	20.00	28.50	40.00	—	—

REAL   KM# Q24a   Composition: Bronze **Issuer:** Mexico City **Obv. Legend:** A CARLOS IV REY DE ESPANA Y DE LAS YNDIAS **Rev. Legend:** PROCLAMADO EN MEXICO ANO DE 1789

Date	Mintage	F	VF	XF	Unc	BU
1789	—	22.50	35.00	50.00	—	—

REAL   KM# Q-A24   Composition: Silver **Issuer:** Mexico City **Obverse:** Crowned arms in double-lined circle **Obv. Legend:** A CARLOS IV REY DE ESPANA Y DE LAS YNDIAS **Rev. Legend:** PROCLAMADO EN MEXICO ANO DE 1789

Date	Mintage	F	VF	XF	Unc	BU
1789	—	20.00	28.50	40.00	—	—

REAL   KM# Q-A24a   Composition: Copper **Issuer:** Mexico City **Obverse:** Crowned arms in double-lined circle **Obv. Legend:** A CARLOS IV REY DE ESPANA Y DE LAS YNDIAS **Rev. Legend:** PROCLAMADO EN MEXICO ANO DE 1789

Date	Mintage	F	VF	XF	Unc	BU
1789	—	22.50	35.00	50.00	—	—

REAL   KM# Q8   Composition: Silver **Issuer:** Chiapa **Obverse:** Crowned arms between pillars, IR below **Obv. Legend:** FERNANDO VII REY DE ESPANA Y DE SUS INDIAS **Reverse:** Legend in 5 lines within wreath **Rev. Legend:** PROCLA/MADO/ENCIUD/R. DECHIAPPA/1808

Date	Mintage	F	VF	XF	Unc	BU
1808	—	22.50	35.00	50.00	—	—

2 REALES   KM# Q25   Weight: 6.7000 g. **Composition:** Silver **Issuer:** Mexico City **Obv. Legend:** A CARLOS IV REY DE ESPANA Y DE LAS YNDIAS **Rev. Legend:** PROCLAMADO EN MEXICO ANO DE 1789

Date	Mintage	F	VF	XF	Unc	BU
1789	—	35.00	50.00	75.00	—	—

2 REALES   KM# Q25a   Weight: 6.7000 g. **Composition:** Bronze **Issuer:** Mexico City **Obv. Legend:** A CARLOS IV REY DE ESPANA Y DE LAS YNDIAS **Rev. Legend:** PROCLAMADO EN MEXICO ANO DE 1789

Date	Mintage	F	VF	XF	Unc	BU
1789	—	30.00	45.00	60.00	—	—

2 REALES   KM# Q64   Composition: Silver **Issuer:** Queretaro **Obv. Legend:** FERNANDO VII REY DE ESPANA

Date	Mintage	F	VF	XF	Unc	BU
1808	—	35.00	50.00	75.00	—	—

2 REALES   KM# Q10   Composition: Silver **Issuer:** Chiapa **Obv. Legend:** FERNANDO VII REY DE ESPANA Y DE SUS INDIAS

Date	Mintage	F	VF	XF	Unc	BU
1808	—	50.00	70.00	100	—	—

4 REALES   KM# Q27   Weight: 13.6000 g. **Composition:** Silver **Issuer:** Mexico City **Obv. Legend:** A CARLOS IV REY DE ESPANA Y DE LAS YNDIAS **Rev. Legend:** PROCLAMADO EN MEXICO ANO DE 1789

Date	Mintage	F	VF	XF	Unc	BU
1789	—	100	150	225	—	—

4 REALES   KM# Q27a   Weight: 13.6000 g. **Composition:** Bronze **Issuer:** Mexico City **Obv. Legend:** A CARLOS IV REY DE ESPANA Y DE LAS YNDIAS **Rev. Legend:** PROCLAMADO EN MEXICO ANO DE 1789

Date	Mintage	F	VF	XF	Unc	BU
1789	—	70.00	100	150	—	—

4 REALES   KM# Q-A66   Composition: Silver **Issuer:** Queretaro **Obv. Legend:** FERNANDO VII REY DE ESPANA

Date	Mintage	F	VF	XF	Unc	BU
1808	—	140	200	300	—	—

8 REALES   KM# Q28   Weight: 27.0000 g. **Composition:** Silver **Issuer:** Mexico City **Obv. Legend:** A CARLOS IV REY DE ESPANA Y DE LAS YNDIAS **Rev. Legend:** PROCLAMADO EN MEXICO ANO DE 1789

Date	Mintage	F	VF	XF	Unc	BU
1789	—	200	275	400	—	—

8 REALES   KM# Q28a   Weight: 27.0000 g. **Composition:** Bronze **Issuer:** Mexico City **Obv. Legend:** A CARLOS IV REY DE ESPANA Y DE LAS YNDIAS **Rev. Legend:** PROCLAMADO EN MEXICO ANO DE 1789

Date	Mintage	F	VF	XF	Unc	BU
1789	—	70.00	100	150	—	—

8 REALES   KM# Q68   Composition: Silver **Issuer:** Queretaro **Obv. Legend:** FERNANDO VII REY DE ESPANA

Date	Mintage	F	VF	XF	Unc	BU
1808	—	300	425	600	—	—

EMPIRE OF ITURBIDE

RULERS
Augustin I Iturbide, 1822-1823

MINT MARKS
Mo - Mexico City

ASSAYERS INITIALS
JA - Jose Garcia Ansaldo, 1812-1833
JM - Joaquin Davila Madrid, 1809-1833

MILLED COINAGE

16 Pilones = 1 Real; 8 Tlaco = 1 Real;
16 Reales = 1 Escudo

1/8 REAL   KM# 299   Composition: Copper **Ruler:** Augustin I Iturbide **Note:** Struck at Nuera Viscaya.

Date	Mintage	Good	VG	F	VF	XF
1821	—	22.50	50.00	85.00	150	—
1822	—	6.00	12.50	27.50	55.00	—
1823	—	6.00	12.50	25.00	45.00	—

1/4 REAL   KM# 300   Composition: Copper **Ruler:** Augustin I Iturbide **Note:** Struck at Nueva Viscaya.

Date	Mintage	Good	VG	F	VF	XF
1822	—	150	275	400	550	—

1/2 REAL   KM# 301   Composition: 0.9030 Silver **Ruler:** Augustin I Iturbide

Date	Mintage	F	VF	XF	Unc	BU
1822Mo JM	—	20.00	40.00	80.00	300	—
1823Mo JM	—	15.00	30.00	60.00	250	—

REAL   KM# 302   Composition: 0.9030 Silver **Ruler:** Augustin I Iturbide

Date	Mintage	F	VF	XF	Unc	BU
1822Mo JM	—	175	350	550	900	—

2 REALES   KM# 303   Composition: 0.9030 Silver **Ruler:** Augustin I Iturbide

Date	Mintage	F	VF	XF	Unc	BU
1822Mo JM	—	50.00	100	350	1,000	—
1823Mo JM	—	40.00	80.00	250	850	—

8 REALES   KM# 304   Composition: 0.9030 Silver **Ruler:** Augustin I Iturbide

Date	Mintage	F	VF	XF	Unc	BU
1822Mo JM	—	75.00	150	300	950	—

8 REALES   KM# 305   Composition: 0.9030 Silver **Ruler:** Augustin I Iturbide **Obverse:** Bust similar to 8 Escudos, KM#131 **Reverse:** Similar to KM#304

Date	Mintage	F	VF	XF	Unc	BU
1822Mo JM Rare	—	—	—	—	—	—

8 REALES   KM# 306.1   Composition: 0.9030 Silver **Ruler:** Augustin I Iturbide **Obverse:** Legend divided **Reverse:** 8 R.J.M. at upper left of eagle **Note:** Type I.

Date	Mintage	F	VF	XF	Unc	BU
1822Mo JM	—	90.00	170	450	1,300	—

8 REALES   KM# 306.2   Composition: 0.9030 Silver **Ruler:** Augustin I Iturbide **Obverse:** Legend divided **Reverse:** Cross on crown **Note:** Type I.

Date	Mintage	F	VF	XF	Unc	BU
1822Mo JM	—	650	1,000	—	—	—

8 REALES   KM# 307   Composition: 0.9030 Silver **Ruler:** Augustin I Iturbide **Obverse:** Similar to KM#306 **Reverse:** Similar to KM#310 **Note:** Type II.

Date	Mintage	F	VF	XF	Unc	BU
1822Mo JM	—	150	350	650	2,250	—

8 REALES   KM# 308   Composition: 0.9030 Silver **Ruler:** Augustin I Iturbide **Obverse:** Continous legend with long smooth truncation **Reverse:** Similar to KM#306 **Note:** Type III.

Date	Mintage	F	VF	XF	Unc	BU
1822Mo JM	—	175	500	950	2,250	—

Note: Variety with long, straight truncation is valued at $5,000 in uncirculated condition

8 REALES   KM# 309   Composition: 0.9030 Silver **Ruler:** Augustin I Iturbide **Obverse:** Similar to KM#308 **Reverse:** Similar to KM#310 **Note:** Type IV.

Date	Mintage	F	VF	XF	Unc	BU
1822Mo JM	—	50.00	120	250	850	—

8 REALES   KM# 310 Composition: 0.9030 Silver **Ruler:** Augustin I Iturbide **Obverse:** Continuous legend with short irregular truncation **Reverse:** 8 R.J.M. below eagle **Note:** Type V.

Date	Mintage	F	VF	XF	Unc	BU
1822Mo JM	—	50.00	120	225	900	—
1823Mo JM	—	50.00	120	225	900	—

8 REALES   KM# 311 Composition: 0.9030 Silver **Ruler:** Augustin I Iturbide **Obverse:** Bust with long truncation **Reverse:** Similar to KM#310 **Note:** Type VI.

Date	Mintage	F	VF	XF	Unc	BU
1822Mo JM Rare	—	—	—	—	—	—

4 SCUDOS   KM# 312 Composition: 0.8750 Gold **Ruler:** Augustin I Iturbide **Obverse:** Bust **Reverse:** Eagle in shield

Date	Mintage	F	VF	XF	Unc	BU
1823Mo JM	—	1,000	1,750	2,850	5,500	—

8 SCUDOS   KM# 313.1 Composition: 0.8750 Gold **Ruler:** Augustin I Iturbide **Obv. Legend:** AUGUSTINUS

Date	Mintage	F	VF	XF	Unc	BU
1822Mo JM	—	1,200	2,000	3,750	—	—

Note: Superior Casterline sale 5-89 choice AU realized $11,000

8 SCUDOS   KM# 313.2 Composition: 0.8750 Gold **Ruler:** Augustin I Iturbide **Obverse:** Error in legend **Obv. Legend:** AUGUSTNUS

Date	Mintage	F	VF	XF	Unc	BU
1822Mo JM	—	1,250	2,250	4,200	—	—

8 SCUDOS   KM# 314 Composition: 0.8750 Gold **Ruler:** Augustin I Iturbide **Obverse:** Large bust **Reverse:** Eagle in shield

Date	Mintage	F	VF	XF	Unc	BU
1823Mo JM	—	1,000	1,800	3,250	6,000	—

REPUBLIC
First

MINT MARKS
A, AS - Alamos
CE - Real de Catorce
CA,CH - Chihuahua
C, Cn, Gn(error) - Culiacan
D, Do - Durango
EoMo - Estado de Mexico
Ga - Guadalajara
GC - Guadalupe y Calvo
G, Go - Guanajuato
H, Ho - Hermosillo
M, Mo - Mexico City
O, OA - Oaxaca
SLP, PI, P, I/P - San Luis Potosi
Z, Zs – Zacatecas

ASSAYERS INITIALS

ALAMOS MINT

PG	1862-68	Pascual Gaxiola
DL, L	1866-79	Domingo Larraguibel
AM	1872-74	Antonio Moreno
ML, L	1878-95	Manuel Larraguibel

REAL DE CATORCE MINT

ML	1863	Mariano Cristobal Ramirez

CHIHUAHUA MINT

MR	1831-34	Mariano Cristobal Ramirez
AM	1833-39	Jose Antonio Mucharraz
MJ	1832	Jose Mariano Jimenez
RG	1839-56	Rodrigo Garcia
JC	1856-65	Joaquin Campa
BA	1858	Bruno Arriada
FP	1866	Francisco Potts
JC	1866-	Jose Maria Gomez del
	1868	Campo
MM, M	1868-95	Manuel Merino
AV	1873-80	Antonio Valero
EA	1877	Eduardo Avila
JM	1877	Jacobo Mucharraz
GR	1877	Guadalupe Rocha
MG	1880-82	Manuel Gameros

CULIACAN MINT

CE	1846-70	Clemente
		Espinosa de los Monteros
C	1870	???
PV	1860-61	Pablo Viruega
MP, P	1871-76	Manuel Onofre Parodi
GP	1876	Celso Gaxiola & Manuel
		Onofre Parodi
CG, G	1876-78	Celso Gaxiola
JD, D	1878-82	Juan Dominguez
AM, M	1882-1899	Antonio Moreno
F	1870	Fernando Ferrari
JQ, Q	1899-1903	Jesus S. Quiroz

DURANGO MINT

RL	1825-1832	???
RM	1830-48	Ramon Mascarenas
OMC	1840	Octavio Martinez de Castro
CM	1848-76	Clemente Moron
JMR	1849-52	Jose Maria Ramirez
CP, P	1853-64,	Carlos Leon de la Pena
	1867-73	
LT	1864-65	???
JMP, P	1877	Carlos Miguel de la Palma
PE, E	1878	Pedro Espejo
TB, B	1878-80	Trinidad Barrera
JP	1880-94	J. Miguel Palma
MC, C,	1882-90	Manuel M. Canseco or
		Melchor Calderon
JB	1885	Jocobo Blanco
ND, D	1892-95	Norberto Dominguez

ESTADO DE MEXICO MINT

L	1828-30	Luis Valazquez de la Cadena
F	1828-30	Francisco Parodi

GUADALAJARA MINT

FS	1818-35	Francisco Suarez
JM	1830-32	???
JG	1836-39,	Juan de Dios Guzman
	1842-67	
MC	1839-46	Manuel Cueras
JM	1867-69	Jesus P. Manzano
IC, C	1869-77	Ignacio Canizo y Soto
MC	1874-75	Manuel Contreras
JA, A	1877-81	Julio Arancivia
FS, S	1880-82	Fernando Sayago
TB, B	1883-84	Trinidad Barrera
AH, H	1884-85	Antonio Hernandez y Prado
JS, S	1885-95	Jose S. Schiafino

GUADALUPE Y CALVO MINT

MP	1844-52	Manuel Onofre Parodi

GUANAJUATO MINT

JJ	1825-26	Jose Mariano Jimenez
MJ, MR, JM,		???
PG, PJ, PF		
PM	1841-48,	Patrick Murphy
	1853-61	
YF	1862-68	Yldefonso Flores
YE	1862-63	Ynocencio Espinoza
FR	1870-78	Faustino Ramirez
SB, RR		???
RS	1891-1900	Rosendo Sandoval

HERMOSILLO MINT

PP	1835-36	Pedro Peimbert
FM	1871-76	Florencio Monteverde
MP	1866	Manuel Onofre Parodi
PR	1866-75	Pablo Rubio
R	1874-75	Pablo Rubio
GR	1877	Guadalupe Rocha
AF, F	1876-77	Alejandro Fourcade
JA, A	1877-83	Jesus Acosta
FM, M	1883-86	Fernando Mendez
FG, G	1886-95	Fausto Gaxiola

MEXICO CITY MINT

Because of the great number of assayers for this mint (Mexico City is a much larger mint than any of the others) there is much confusion as to which initial stands for which assayer at any one time. Therefore we feel that it would be of no value to list the assayers.

OAXACA MINT

AE	1859-91	Agustin Endner
E	1889-90	Agustin Endner
FR	1861-64	Francisco de la Rosa
EN	1890	Eduardo Navarro Luna
N	1890	Eduardo Navarro Luna

POTOSI MINT

JS	1827-42	Juan Sanabria
AM	1838, 1843-49	Jose Antonio Mucharraz
PS	1842-43,	Pompaso Sanabria
	1848-49,	
	1857-61,	
	1867-70	
S	1869-70	Pomposo Sanabria
MC	1849-59	Mariano Catano
RO	1859-65	Romualdo Obregon
MH, H	1870-85	Manuel Herrera Razo
O	1870-73	Juan R. Ochoa
CA, G	1867-70	Carlos Aguirre Gomez
BE, E	1879-81	Blas Escontria
LC, C	1885-86	Luis Cuevas
MR, R	1886-93	Mariano Reyes

ZACATECAS MINT

A	1825-29	Adalco
Z	1825-26	Mariano Zaldivar
V	1824-31	Jose Mariano Vela
O	1829-67	Manuel Ochoa
M	1831-67	Manuel Miner
VL	1860-66	Vicente Larranaga
JS	1867-68, 1876-86	J.S. de Santa Ana
YH	1868-74	Ygnacio Hierro
JA	1874-76	Juan H. Acuna
FZ	18861905	Francisco de P. Zarate

Die Varieties
Similar basic designs were utilized by all the Mexican mints, but many variations are noticeable, particularly in the eagle, cactus and sprays.

1835 Durango, 8 Escudos
Illustration enlarged.
A large winged eagle was portrayed on the earlier coinage of the new republic.

1844 Durango, 8 Escudos
Illustration enlarged.
The early renditions of the hand held Liberty cap over open book were massive in the gold escudo series.

1849 Mexico City, 8 Escudos
Illustration enlarged.
The later eagle featured undersized wings.

1864 Durango, 8 Escudos
Illustration enlarged.
A finer, more petite style was adopted later on in the gold escudo series.

PROFILE EAGLE COINAGE

The first coins of the Republic were of the distinctive Profile Eagle style, sometimes called the "Hooked Neck Eagle". They were struck first in Mexico City in 1823 in denominations of eight reales and eight escudos. In 1824, they were produced at the Durango and Guanajuato mints in addition to Mexico City. Denominations included the one half, one, two and eight reales. No gold escudos of this design were struck in 1824. In 1825, only the eight reales were struck briefly at the Guanajuato mint.

NOTE: For a more extensive examination of Profile Eagle Coinage, please refer to Hookneck - El Aguila de Perfil by Clyde Hubbard and David O Harrow.

1/2 REAL KM# 369 Weight: 1.6900 g. Composition:
0.9030 Silver .0490 oz. ASW **Obverse:** Full breast Profile eagle **Reverse:** Cap and rays **Note:** Die varieties exist. Struck at Mexico City Mint, mint mark Mo.

Date	Mintage	F	VF	XF	Unc	BU
1824Mo JM	—	45.00	75.00	150	600	—

REAL KM# 371.1 Weight: 3.3800 g. Composition:
0.9030 Silver .081 oz. ASW **Obverse:** Thin Profile eagle **Reverse:** Reversed S **Note:** Struck at Durango Mint, mint mark Do.

Date	Mintage	F	VF	XF	Unc	BU
1824Do RL	—	3,750	7,500	10,000	15,000	—

REAL KM#371.2 Weight:3.3800 g.Composition:0.9030
Silver .081 oz. ASW **Obverse:** Thin Profile eagle **Reverse:** Regular S **Note:** Struck at Durango Mint, mint mark Do.

Date	Mintage	F	VF	XF	Unc	BU
1824Do RL 3 known	—	—	—	—	—	—

2 REALES KM# 373.2 Weight: 6.7600 g. Composition:
0.9030 Silver .1962 oz. **Obverse:** Thin Profile eagle

Reverse: Type I, dot before 2R in legend **Note:** Struck at Durango Mint, mint mark D.

Date	Mintage	F	VF	XF	Unc	BU
1824D RL	—	100	200	1,000	3,000	—

2 REALES KM#373.3 Weight: 6.7600 g. Composition:
0.9030 Silver .1962 oz. ASW **Obverse:** Thin Profile eagle **Reverse:** Type II, no dot before 2R in legend **Note:** Struck at Durango Mint, mint mark D.

Date	Mintage	F	VF	XF	Unc	BU
1824D RL	—	100	200	1,000	3,000	—

2 REALES KM#373.1 Weight: 6.7600 g. Composition:
0.9030 Silver .1962 oz. ASW **Obverse:** Profile eagle **Reverse:** Cap and rays **Note:** Struck at Durango Mint, mint mark Do. Die varieties exist.

Date	Mintage	F	VF	XF	Unc	BU
1824Do RL	—	50.00	125	850	2,200	—

2 REALES KM# 373.4 Obverse: Profile eagle Note:
Struck at Mexico City Mint, mint mark Mo. Varieties exist.

Date	Mintage	F	VF	XF	Unc	BU
1824Mo JM	—	30.00	70.00	450	2,000	—

Note: No coins are known with visible feather details on the eagle's breast

Tight snake loop at eagle's beak.

The Standard or Republic Edge

Open snake loop at eagle's beak.

The Colonial or Circle & Rectangle

The standard Flat-Topped Three

Mint mark: Mo
Edge: Standard or Republic.

8 REALES   KM# A376.2 Weight: 27.0700 g.
Composition: 0.9030 Silver .7859 oz. ASW **Obverse:** Full
breast profile eagle **Edge:** Standard or Republic **Note:**
Struck at Mexico City Mint, mint mark Mo.

Date	Mintage	F	VF	XF	Unc	BU
1823Mo JM	—	150	300	800	4,500	—
1824Mo JM	—	125	250	700	4,000	—

8 REALES   KM# A376.3 Weight: 27.0700 g.
Composition: 0.9030 Silver .7859 oz. ASW **Obverse:** Full
breast profile eagle **Edge:** Colonial or circle and rectangle
Note: Struck at Mexico City Mint, mint mark Mo.

Date	Mintage	F	VF	XF	Unc	BU
1823Mo JM Rare	—	—	—	—	—	—

The Round-Topped Three

8 REALES   KM# A376.4 Weight: 27.0700 g.
Composition: 0.9030 Silver .7859 oz. ASW **Obverse:** Full
breast profile eagle **Reverse:** Round topped three **Edge:**
Standard or Republic **Note:** Struck at Mexico City Mint, mint
mark Mo.

Date	Mintage	F	VF	XF	Unc	BU
1823Mo JM	—	2,000	4,000	6,000	8,000	—

Note: Many die varieties exist. Illustrations of one of the die differences is the size of the snake loop at the eagle's beak. This
difference is not apparent except on the 1824 Mo 8 Reales

8 REALES   KM# A376.5 Weight: 27.0700 g.
Composition: 0.9030 Silver .7859 oz. ASW **Obverse:**
REPUBLICA (error) **Note:** Struck at Mexico City Mint, mint
mark Mo.

Date	Mintage	F	VF	XF	Unc	BU
1824Mo JM	—	6,000	9,000	11,000	—	—

Note: Legible Libertads on the cap are not as prevalent on the
Mexico City 8 Reales as on the Durango 8 Reales. They are
much more numerous than on the Guanajuato 8 Reales

8 REALES

Typical Defiant
Snake Obverse

Typical Submissive
Snake Obverse

**Typical Folded
Snake Obverse**

NOTE: Legible Libertads on the Cap are common on Durango eight reales.

Med. Libertad Cap Reverse	**Small Libertad Cap Reverse**	**Large Libertad Cap Reverse**

NOTE: The three styles of obverses and the three styles of reverses were combined in to make six distinct varieties of coins.

8 REALES   KM# 376.1 Weight: 27.0700 g.
Composition: 0.9030 Silver .7859 oz. ASW **Obverse:** Thin profile eagle, defiant snake **Reverse:** Medium Libertad **Note:** Struck at Durango Mint, mint mark Do.

Date	Mintage	F	VF	XF	Unc	BU
1824Do RL	—	500	1,200	4,500	7,000	—

Note: Five die varieties are known, all are rare

8 REALES   KM# 376.2 Weight: 27.0700 g.
Composition: 0.9030 Silver .7859 oz. ASW **Obverse:** Thin profile eagle, defiant snake **Reverse:** Small Libertad **Note:** Struck at Durango Mint, mint mark Do.

Date	Mintage	F	VF	XF	Unc	BU
1824Do RL	—	300	400	1,600	3,500	—

Note: Ten die varieties are known, some are rare

8 REALES   KM# 376.3 Weight: 27.0700 g.
Composition: 0.9030 Silver .7859 oz. ASW **Obverse:** Thin profile eagle, submissive snake **Reverse:** Small Libertad **Note:** Struck at Durango Mint, mint mark Do.

Date	Mintage	F	VF	XF	Unc	BU
1824Do RL	—	200	350	1,250	2,750	—

Note: Six die varieties are known, some are rare

8 REALES   KM# 376.4 Weight: 27.0700 g.
Composition: 0.9030 Silver .7859 oz. ASW **Obverse:** Thin profile eagle, submissive snake **Reverse:** Large Libertad **Note:** Struck at Durango Mint, mint mark Do.

Date	Mintage	F	VF	XF	Unc	BU
1824Do RL	—	200	350	1,250	2,750	—

Note: Eleven die varieties known, some are rare

8 REALES   KM# 376.5 Weight: 27.0700 g.
Composition: 0.9030 Silver .7859 oz. ASW **Obverse:** Thin profile eagle, folded snake **Reverse:** Small Libertad **Note:** Struck at Durango Mint, mint mark Do.

Date	Mintage	F	VF	XF	Unc	BU
1824Do RL	—	200	350	1,200	2,500	—

Note: Only one die variety is known

8 REALES   KM# 376.6 Weight: 27.0700 g.
Composition: 0.9030 Silver .7859 oz. ASW **Obverse:** Thin profile eagle, folded snake **Reverse:** Large Libertad **Note:** Struck at Durango Mint, mint mark Do.

Date	Mintage	F	VF	XF	Unc	BU
1824Do RL	—	200	400	1,500	3,000	—

Note: Eleven die varieties known, some are rare

8 REALES   KM# A376.1 (KM376.1) Weight: 27.0700 g.
Composition: 0.9030 Silver .7859 oz. ASW **Obverse:** Full breast profile eagle **Note:** Struck at Mexico City Mint, mint mark Mo.

Date	Mintage	F	VF	XF	Unc	BU
1824Go JM	—	250	400	1,100	3,500	—
1825/4Go JJ	—	600	1,200	2,750	7,000	—
1825Go JJ	—	500	750	1,400	5,500	—

Type I Obverse/Reverse

NOTE: The cap on the reverse of the curved tail Type I points to the "A" of LIBERTAD.

8 ESCUDOS   KM# 382.1 Weight: 27.0700 g.
Composition: 0.6750 Gold .7616 oz. AGW **Obverse:** Profile eagle, snakes tail curved **Reverse:** Cap points to "A" of LIBERTAD **Note:** Struck at Mexico City Mint, mint mark Mo.

Date	Mintage	F	VF	XF	Unc	BU
1823Mo JM	—	6,000	9,000	12,500	20,000	—

Type II Obverse/Reverse

8 ESCUDOS   KM# 382.2   Weight: 27.0700 g.
Composition: 0.6750 Gold .7616 oz. AGW **Obverse:** Profile
eagle, snakes tail looped **Reverse:** Cap points to "T" of
LIBERTAD **Note:** Struck at Mexico City Mint, mint mark Mo.

Date	Mintage	F	VF	XF	Unc	BU
1823Mo JM	—	5,000	8,000	12,000	18,000	—

Note: The quality of the strikes of Type I coins is almost always superior to that of the Type II. Details of the eagle feathers, cactus and lettering on the open book are better on most
Type I coins but the Type II coins are scarcer. Type I coins out-
number Type II coins by about two to one

STATE COINAGE

1/16 REAL (Medio Octavo)   KM# 315   Composition:
Copper **Obv. Legend:** REPUBLICA MEXICANA **Note:**
Struck at Mexico City Mint.

Date	Mintage	VG	F	VF	XF	Unc
1831	—	10.00	20.00	50.00	100	—
1832/1	—	12.00	22.00	55.00	125	—
1832	—	10.00	20.00	50.00	100	—
1833	—	10.00	20.00	50.00	100	—

1/16 REAL (Medio Octavo)   KM# 315a   Composition:
Brass **Obv. Legend:** REPUBLICA MEXICANA **Note:** Struck
at Mexico City Mint.

Date	Mintage	VG	F	VF	XF	Unc
1832	—	13.50	22.50	60.00	165	—
1833	—	10.00	17.50	50.00	135	—
1835	—	400	800	1,250	2,500	—

1/16 REAL (Medio Octavo)   KM# 316   Composition:
Copper **Obv. Legend:** DEPARTMENTO DE JALISCO
Note: Struck at Jalisco Mint.

Date	Mintage	Good	VG	F	VF	XF
1860	—	3.00	7.50	15.00	55.00	—

1/16 REAL (Medio Octavo)   KM# 317   Composition:
Copper **Obv. Legend:** ESTADO LIBRE DE JALISO **Note:**
Struck at Jalisco Mint.

Date	Mintage	Good	VG	F	VF	XF
1861	—	2.50	6.00	12.50	42.50	—

1/8 REAL (Octavo Real)   KM# 320   Composition:
Copper **Rev. Legend:** LIBERTAD **Note:** These pieces were
frequently struck over 1/8 Real, dated 1821-23 of Nueva
Vizcaya. All known examples with these host dates are
collectable contemporary counterfeits. Struck at Durango
Mint, mint mark D.

Date	Mintage	Good	VG	F	VF	XF
1824D	—	5.00	12.50	35.00	85.00	—
1828D	—	150	250	400	1,000	—

1/8 REAL (Octavo Real)   KM# 338   Composition: Brass
Obv. Legend: ESTo LIBe FEDo DE ZACATECAS **Note:**
Struck at Zacatecas Mint.

Date	Mintage	Good	VG	F	VF	XF
1825	—	3.00	5.50	12.00	25.00	—
1827	—	3.00	5.50	12.00	25.00	—
1827 Inverted A for V in OCTAVO	—	12.00	20.00	40.00	100	—
1827 OCTAVA (error)	—	15.00	25.00	50.00	120	—
1827 Inverted 1	—	12.00	20.00	40.00	100	—
1829 Rare	—	—	—	—	—	—
1830	—	2.75	5.00	8.00	20.00	—
1831	—	4.50	6.75	13.50	27.50	—
1832	—	2.75	5.00	8.00	20.00	—
1833	—	2.75	5.00	8.00	20.00	—
1835	—	3.50	6.00	10.00	25.00	—
1846	—	3.50	6.00	10.00	25.00	—
1851	—	45.00	65.00	125	250	—
1852	—	3.50	6.00	10.00	25.00	—
1858	—	2.75	5.00	8.00	20.00	—
1859	—	2.75	5.00	8.00	20.00	—
1862	—	2.75	5.00	8.00	20.00	—
1863 Reversed 6 in date	—	2.75	5.00	8.00	20.00	—

1/8 REAL (Octavo Real)   KM# 321   Composition:
Copper **Reverse:** Date **Rev. Legend:** OCTo. DE. R. DE DO
Note: Struck at Durango Mint, mint mark Do.

Date	Mintage	Good	VG	F	VF	XF
1828Do	—	7.50	17.50	40.00	115	—

1/8 REAL (Octavo Real) KM# 329 Composition:
Copper **Obv. Legend:** ESTADO LIBRE DE JALISCO **Note:**
Struck at Jalisco Mint.

Date	Mintage	Good	VG	F	VF	XF
1828	—	3.00	5.00	8.00	22.50	—
1831	—	75.00	150	250	350	—
1832/28	—	4.50	6.50	11.00	22.50	—
1832	—	4.50	6.00	10.00	20.00	—
1833	—	3.50	5.50	9.00	25.00	—
1834	—	37.50	80.00	150	235	—

1/8 REAL (Octavo Real) KM# 335 Composition:
Copper **Obv. Legend:** ESTADO DE OCCIDENTE **Note:**
Struck at Occidente Mint.

Date	Mintage	Good	VG	F	VF	XF
1828 Reverse S	—	15.00	32.50	57.50	140	—
1829	—	13.50	30.00	50.00	120	—

1/8 REAL (Octavo Real) KM# 336 Composition:
Copper **Obv. Legend:** ESTADO LIBRE DE SAN LUIS
POTOSI **Note:** Struck at San Luis Potosi Mint.

Date	Mintage	Good	VG	F	VF	XF
1829	—	6.00	9.00	15.00	50.00	—
1830	—	8.50	13.50	22.50	60.00	—
1831	—	5.00	8.00	12.00	40.00	—
1859	—	5.00	8.00	12.00	40.00	—
1865/1 Reported, not confirmed	—	—	—	—	—	—

1/8 REAL (Octavo Real) KM# 333 Composition:
Copper **Obv. Legend:** REPUBLICA MEXICANA **Size:**
21 mm. **Note:** Struck at Mexico City Mint.

Date	Mintage	Good	VG	F	VF	XF
1829	—	7.50	12.00	25.00	55.00	—
1830	—	1.00	2.00	6.00	20.00	—
1831	—	1.50	3.50	7.00	25.00	—
1832	—	1.50	3.50	7.00	25.00	—
1833/2	—	1.50	3.50	7.00	25.00	—
1833	—	1.50	2.75	6.00	20.00	—
1834	—	1.50	2.75	6.00	20.00	—
1835/4	—	1.75	3.50	7.00	25.00	—
1835	—	1.50	2.75	6.00	20.00	—

1/8 REAL (Octavo Real) KM# 326 Composition:
Copper **Obv. Legend:** ESTADO LIBRE DE GUANAJUATO
Note: Struck at Guanajuato Mint.

Date	Mintage	Good	VG	F	VF	XF
1829	—	3.00	5.00	10.00	25.00	—
1829 error w/ GUANJUATO	—	4.00	6.50	12.50	27.50	—
1830	—	8.00	13.50	25.00	75.00	—

1/8 REAL (Octavo Real) KM# 332 Composition:
Copper **Obv. Legend:** REPUBLICA MEXICANA **Size:**
27 mm. **Note:** Struck at Mexico City Mint.

Date	Mintage	VG	F	VF	XF	Unc
1829	—	450	900	1,500	2,500	—

1/8 REAL (Octavo Real) KM# 322 Composition:
Copper **Obv. Legend:** ESTADO DE DURANGO **Note:**
Struck at Durango Mint.

Date	Mintage	Good	VG	F	VF	XF
1833 Rare	—	—	—	—	—	—

1/8 REAL (Octavo Real) KM# 318 Composition:
Copper **Obv. Legend:** ESTADO SOBERANO DE
CHIHUAHUA **Note:** Struck at Chihuahua Mint.

Date	Mintage	Good	VG	F	VF	XF
1833	—	350	750	—	—	—
1834	—	350	750	—	—	—
1835/3	—	350	750	—	—	—

1/8 REAL (Octavo Real) KM# 339 Composition:
Copper **Obv. Legend:** DEPARTMENTO DE ZACATECAS
Note: Struck at Zacatecas Mint.

Date	Mintage	Good	VG	F	VF	XF
1836	—	5.00	8.50	17.50	40.00	—
1845	—	7.50	12.50	22.50	50.00	—
1846	—	8.50	10.00	20.00	45.00	—

1/8 REAL (Octavo Real) KM# 334 Composition:
Copper **Obv. Legend:** LIBERTAD **Note:** Struck at Mexico
City Mint.

Date	Mintage	Good	VG	F	VF	XF
1841	—	6.00	15.00	30.00	75.00	—
1842	—	2.50	5.00	10.00	30.00	—
1850	—	12.50	20.00	30.00	80.00	—
1861	—	5.00	12.00	25.00	70.00	—

1/8 REAL (Octavo Real)   KM# 323   Composition:
Copper **Obv. Legend:** REPUBLICA MEXICANA **Note:**
Struck at Durango Mint.

Date	Mintage	Good	VG	F	VF	XF
1842/33	—	12.50	22.50	42.50	115	—
1842	—	8.50	15.00	32.50	100	—

1/8 REAL (Octavo Real)   KM# 324   Composition:
Copper **Obv. Legend:** REPUBLICA MEXICANA
Rev. Legend: DEPARTAMENTO DE DURANGO **Note:**
Struck at Durango Mint.

Date	Mintage	Good	VG	F	VF	XF
1845	—	22.50	50.00	100	250	—
1846 Rare	—	—	—	—	—	—
1847	—	3.50	5.00	11.00	35.00	—

1/8 REAL (Octavo Real)   KM# 325   Composition:
Copper **Obv. Legend:** REPUBLICA MEXICANA
Rev. Legend: ESTADO DE DURANGO **Note:** Struck at
Durango Mint.

Date	Mintage	Good	VG	F	VF	XF
1851	—	3.50	6.50	10.00	32.50	—
1852/1	—	3.50	6.50	10.00	32.50	—
1852	—	3.00	5.00	8.00	30.00	—
1854	—	6.00	10.00	20.00	65.00	—

1/8 REAL (Octavo Real)   KM# 319   Composition:
Copper **Obv. Legend:** ESTADO DE CHIHUAHUA **Note:**
Struck at Chihuahua Mint.

Date	Mintage	Good	VG	F	VF	XF
1855	—	5.00	8.50	25.00	75.00	—

1/8 REAL (Octavo Real)   KM# 330   Composition:
Copper **Obv. Legend:** ESTADO LIBRE DE JALISCO **Note:**
Struck at Jalisco Mint.

Date	Mintage	Good	VG	F	VF	XF
1856	—	3.00	6.00	9.00	18.50	—
1857	—	3.00	6.00	9.00	18.50	—
1858	—	3.00	6.00	9.00	18.50	—
1861	—	75.00	135	200	300	—
1862/1	—	4.00	7.00	10.00	22.50	—
1862	—	4.00	7.00	10.00	22.50	—

1/8 REAL (Octavo Real)   KM# 327   Composition: Brass
Obv. Legend: ESTADO LIBRE DE GUANAJUATO **Size:**
29 mm. **Note:** Struck at Guanajuato Mint.

Date	Mintage	Good	VG	F	VF	XF
1856	—	7.50	12.00	20.00	75.00	—

1/8 REAL (Octavo Real)   KM# 328   Composition: Brass
Obv. Legend: ESTADO LIBRE DE GUANAJUATO **Size:**
25 mm. **Note:** Struck at Guanajuato Mint.

Date	Mintage	Good	VG	F	VF	XF
1856	—	4.00	7.50	12.50	35.00	—
1857	—	3.50	6.00	10.00	30.00	—

1/8 REAL (Octavo Real)   KM# 328a   Composition:
Copper **Obv. Legend:** ESTADO LIBRE DE GUANAJUATO
Note: Struck at Guanajuato Mint.

Date	Mintage	Good	VG	F	VF	XF
1857	—	7.00	16.50	32.50	55.00	—

1/8 REAL (Octavo Real)   KM# 331   Composition:
Copper **Obv. Legend:** DEPARTMENTO DE JALISCO
Note: Struck at Jalisco Mint.

Date	Mintage	Good	VG	F	VF	XF
1858	—	4.00	7.50	10.00	25.00	—
1859	—	2.75	5.50	8.00	20.00	—
1860/59	—	3.25	6.00	9.00	22.50	—
1860	—	3.25	6.00	9.00	22.50	—
1862	—	4.00	8.00	17.50	37.50	—

1/8 REAL (Octavo Real) KM# 337 Composition:
Copper **Obv. Legend:** ESTO LIBE Y SOBO DE SONORA
Size: 28 mm. **Note:** Struck at Sonora Mint.

Date	Mintage	Good	VG	F	VF	XF
1859 Rare	—	—	—	—	—	—

1/4 REAL (Un Quarto/Una Quartilla) KM# 366
Composition: Brass **Obv. Legend:** ESTO LIBE FEDO DE
ZACATECAS **Note:** Struck at Zacatecas Mint.

Date	Mintage	Good	VG	F	VF	XF
1824 Rare	—	—	—	—	—	—
1825	—	2.50	5.00	8.00	20.00	—
1826	—	100	150	200	300	—
1827/17	—	2.50	5.00	8.00	20.00	—
1829	—	2.50	5.00	8.00	20.00	—
1830	—	2.50	5.00	8.00	20.00	—
1831	—	50.00	100	125	250	—
1832	—	2.50	5.00	8.00	20.00	—
1833	—	2.50	5.00	8.00	20.00	—
1834 Rare	—	—	—	—	—	—
1835	—	2.50	5.00	8.00	20.00	—
1846	—	2.50	5.00	8.00	20.00	—
1847	—	2.50	5.00	8.00	20.00	—
1852	—	2.50	5.00	8.00	20.00	—
1853	—	2.50	5.00	8.00	20.00	—
1855	—	4.50	10.00	20.00	65.00	—
1858	—	2.50	5.00	8.00	20.00	—
1859	—	2.50	5.00	8.00	20.00	—
1860	—	100	150	200	300	—
1862/57	—	2.50	5.00	8.00	20.00	—
1862/59/7	—	10.00	20.00	40.00	80.00	—
1862	—	2.50	5.00	8.00	20.00	—
1863/2	—	2.50	5.00	8.00	20.00	—
1863	—	2.50	5.00	8.00	20.00	—
1864	—	4.00	10.00	25.00	60.00	—

1/4 REAL (Un Quarto/Una Quartilla) KM# 351
Composition: Copper **Obv. Legend:** ESTADO LIBRE DE
GUANAJUATO **Note:** Struck at Guanajuato Mint.

Date	Mintage	Good	VG	F	VF	XF
1828	—	3.75	8.50	15.00	37.50	—
1828 Error with GUANJUATO	—	4.00	10.00	16.50	42.50	—
1829	—	5.00	12.50	18.50	45.00	—

1/4 REAL (Un Quarto/Una Quartilla) KM# 353
Composition: Copper **Obv. Legend:** ESTADO LIBRE DE
JALISCO **Note:** Struck at Jalisco Mint.

Date	Mintage	Good	VG	F	VF	XF
1828	—	3.25	6.00	12.00	37.50	—
1829/8	—	2.50	5.50	11.00	33.00	—
1829	—	2.50	5.50	11.00	33.00	—
1830/20	—	2.50	5.00	10.00	27.50	—
1830/29	—	2.50	5.00	10.00	27.50	—
1830	—	2.50	5.00	10.00	27.50	—
1831 Rare	—	—	—	—	—	—
1832/20	—	2.50	5.00	10.00	27.50	—
1832/28	—	2.50	5.00	10.00	27.50	—
1832	—	2.50	5.00	9.00	27.50	—
1833/2	—	2.50	5.00	9.00	27.50	—
1834	—	2.50	5.00	9.00	27.50	—
1835/3	—	2.50	5.00	9.00	27.50	—
1835	—	2.50	5.00	9.00	27.50	—
1836 Rare	—	—	—	—	—	—

1/4 REAL (Un Quarto/Una Quartilla) KM# 359
Composition: Copper **Obv. Legend:** ESTADO LIBRE DE
SAN LUIS POTOSI **Rev. Legend:** MEXICO LIBRE **Note:**
Struck at San Luis Potosi Mint.

Date	Mintage	Good	VG	F	VF	XF
1828	—	2.00	3.50	6.00	15.00	—
1829	—	2.50	4.00	7.00	16.50	—
1830	—	2.00	3.50	5.50	14.00	—
1832	—	2.50	4.00	7.00	16.50	—
1859 Large LIBRE	—	2.50	4.00	7.00	16.50	—
1859 Small LIBRE	—	2.50	4.00	7.00	16.50	—
1860	—	2.50	4.00	7.00	16.50	—

1/4 REAL (Un Quarto/Una Quartilla) KM# 358
Composition: Copper **Obv. Legend:** REPUBLICA
MEXICANA **Note:** Reduced size. Struck at Mexico City Mint.

Date	Mintage	VG	F	VF	XF	Unc
1829	—	12.00	25.00	50.00	150	—
1830	—	1.50	2.75	5.00	10.00	—
1831	—	1.50	2.75	5.00	10.00	—
1832	—	5.50	10.00	20.00	35.00	—
1833	—	1.50	2.75	5.00	10.00	—
1834/3	—	1.75	3.00	6.00	12.00	—
1834	—	1.50	2.75	5.00	10.00	—
1835	—	1.50	2.75	5.00	10.00	—
1836	—	1.50	2.75	5.00	10.00	—
1837	—	6.50	13.50	22.50	45.00	—

1/4 REAL (Un Quarto/Una Quartilla)   KM# 357
Composition: Copper **Obv. Legend:** REPUBLICA
MEXICANA **Note:** Struck at Mexico City Mint.

Date	Mintage	VG	F	VF	XF	Unc
1829	—	8.00	30.00	75.00	250	—

1/4 REAL (Un Quarto/Una Quartilla)   KM# 364
Composition: Copper **Obv. Legend:** EST. D. SONORA
UNA CUART **Note:** Struck at Hermosillo Mint (Sonora).

Date	Mintage	Good	VG	F	VF	XF
1831 L.S. Rare	—	—	—	—	—	—
1832 L.S.	—	3.00	5.00	15.00	50.00	—
1833/2 L.S.	—	2.00	4.00	12.50	37.50	—
1833 L.S.	—	2.00	4.00	12.50	37.50	—
1834 L.S.	—	2.00	4.00	12.50	37.50	—
1835/3 L.S.	—	2.00	4.00	12.50	37.50	—
1835 L.S.	—	2.00	4.00	12.50	37.50	—
1836 L.S.	—	2.00	4.00	12.50	37.50	—

1/4 REAL (Un Quarto/Una Quartilla)   KM# 358a.2
Composition: Brass **Obv. Legend:** REPUBLICA
MEXICANA **Note:** Without countermark. Struck at Mexico
City Mint.

Date	Mintage	VG	F	VF	XF	Unc
1831	—	—	—	—	—	—

1/4 REAL (Un Quarto/Una Quartilla)   KM# 358a.1
Composition: Brass **Countermark:** JM **Obv. Legend:**
REPUBLICA MEXICANA **Note:** Reduced size. Struck at
Mexico City Mint.

Date	Mintage	VG	F	VF	XF	Unc
1831	—	8.00	13.50	27.50	50.00	—

1/4 REAL (Un Quarto/Una Quartilla)   KM# 340
Composition: Copper **Obv. Legend:** ESTADO SOBERANO
DE CHIHUAHUA **Note:** Struck at Chihuahua Mint.

Date	Mintage	Good	VG	F	VF	XF
1833	—	7.50	13.50	37.50	85.00	—
1834	—	6.50	12.50	27.50	60.00	—
1835	—	5.00	9.00	16.50	50.00	—

1/4 REAL (Un Quarto/Una Quartilla)   KM# 354
Composition: Copper **Obv. Legend:** DEPARTMENTO DE
JALISCO **Note:** Struck at Jalisco Mint.

Date	Mintage	Good	VG	F	VF	XF
1836 Rare	—	—	—	—	—	—

1/4 REAL (Un Quarto/Una Quartilla)   KM# 367
Composition: Brass **Obv. Legend:** DEPARTMENTO DE
ZACATECAS **Note:** Struck at Zacatecas Mint.

Date	Mintage	Good	VG	F	VF	XF
1836	—	4.00	8.50	13.50	25.00	—
1845 Rare	—	—	—	—	—	—
1846	—	3.50	6.75	9.00	20.00	—

1/4 REAL (Un Quarto/Una Quartilla)   KM# 368   Weight:
0.8450 g. **Composition:** 0.9030 Silver .0245 oz. ASW **Note:**
Struck at Chihuahua Mint, mint mark CA.

Date	Mintage	VG	F	VF	XF	Unc
1843CA RG	—	75.00	125	300	500	—

1/4 REAL (Un Quarto/Una Quartilla)   KM# 368.1
Weight: 0.8450 g. **Composition:** 0.9030 Silver .0245 oz.
ASW **Note:** Struck at Culiacan Mint, mint mark C.

Date	Mintage	VG	F	VF	XF	Unc
1855C LR	—	50.00	100	200	400	—

1/4 REAL (Un Quarto/Una Quartilla)   KM# 368.2
Weight: 0.8450 g. **Composition:** 0.9030 Silver .0245 oz.
ASW **Note:** Struck at Durango Mint, mint mark Do.

Date	Mintage	VG	F	VF	XF	Unc
1842Do LR	—	12.00	20.00	40.00	125	—
1843Do	—	20.00	25.00	60.00	150	—

1/4 REAL (Un Quarto/Una Quartilla)   KM# 368.3
Weight: 0.8450 g. **Composition:** 0.9030 Silver .0245 oz.
ASW **Note:** Struck at Guadalajara Mint, mint mark Ga.

Date	Mintage	VG	F	VF	XF	Unc
1842Ga JG	—	2.50	5.50	8.00	20.00	—
1843/2Ga JG	—	—	—	—	—	—
1843Ga JG	—	6.00	9.00	12.50	30.00	—
1843Ga MC	—	4.00	6.50	9.00	25.00	—
1844Ga MC	—	4.00	6.50	9.00	25.00	—
1844Ga LR	—	2.50	5.00	7.50	15.00	—
1845Ga LR	—	2.50	4.50	7.50	15.00	—
1846Ga LR	—	5.00	8.00	10.00	25.00	—
1847Ga LR	—	4.00	6.50	9.00	25.00	—
1848Ga LR Rare	—	—	—	—	—	—
1850Ga LR Rare	—	—	—	—	—	—
1851Ga LR	—	6.00	10.00	20.00	50.00	—

Date	Mintage	VG	F	VF	XF	Unc
1852Ga LR	—	50.00	100	135	200	—
1854/3Ga LR	—	50.00	100	135	200	—
1854Ga LR	—	5.00	10.00	12.50	30.00	—
1855Ga LR	—	5.00	8.00	10.00	30.00	—
1857Ga LR	—	6.50	10.00	15.00	27.50	—
1862Ga LR	—	5.50	10.00	15.00	30.00	—

1/4 REAL (Un Quarto/Una Quartilla) KM# 368.4
Weight: 0.8450 g. **Composition:** 0.9030 Silver .0245 oz.
ASW **Note:** Struck at Guadalupe y Calvo Mint, mint mark GC.

Date	Mintage	VG	F	VF	XF	Unc
1844GC LR	—	50.00	75.00	125	300	—

1/4 REAL (Un Quarto/Una Quartilla) KM# 368.5
Weight: 0.8450 g. **Composition:** 0.9030 Silver .0245 oz.
ASW **Note:** Struck at Guanajuato Mint, mint mark Go.

Date	Mintage	VG	F	VF	XF	Unc
1842Go PM	—	4.00	6.00	10.00	20.00	—
1842Go LR	—	2.00	4.00	8.00	15.00	—
1843/2Go LR	—	4.00	6.00	10.00	20.00	—
1843Go LR	—	2.00	4.00	8.00	15.00	—
1844/3Go LR	—	—	—	—	—	—
1844Go LR	—	2.00	4.00	8.00	15.00	—
1845Go LR	—	8.00	15.00	30.00	60.00	—
1846/5Go LR	—	—	—	—	—	—
1846Go LR	—	4.00	6.00	10.00	20.00	—
1847Go LR	—	2.00	4.00	8.00	15.00	—
1848/7Go LR	—	2.00	4.00	8.00	15.00	—
1848Go LR	—	2.00	4.00	8.00	15.00	—
1849/7Go LR	—	8.00	15.00	30.00	60.00	—
1849Go LR	—	2.00	4.00	8.00	15.00	—
1850Go LR	—	2.00	4.00	8.00	15.00	—
1851Go LR	—	2.00	4.00	8.00	15.00	—
1852Go LR	—	2.00	4.00	8.00	15.00	—
1853Go LR	—	2.00	4.00	8.00	15.00	—
1855Go LR	—	4.00	8.00	15.00	30.00	—
1856/4Go LR	—	—	—	—	—	—
1856Go LR	—	5.00	10.00	20.00	35.00	—
1862/1Go LR	—	3.00	5.00	10.00	20.00	—
1862Go LR	—	2.00	4.00	8.00	15.00	—
1863Go	—	2.00	4.00	8.00	15.00	—

1/4 REAL (Un Quarto/Una Quartilla) KM# 368.6
Weight: 0.8450 g. **Composition:** 0.9030 Silver .0245 oz.
ASW **Note:** Struck at Mexico City Mint, mint mark Mo.

Date	Mintage	VG	F	VF	XF	Unc
1842Mo LR	—	2.00	4.00	8.00	15.00	—
1843Mo LR	—	2.00	4.00	8.00	15.00	—
1844/3Mo LR	—	8.00	12.00	20.00	40.00	—
1844Mo LR	—	4.00	6.00	10.00	20.00	—
1845Mo LR	—	4.00	6.00	10.00	20.00	—
1846Mo LR	—	2.00	4.00	8.00	15.00	—
1850Mo LR	—	5.00	10.00	20.00	35.00	—
1858Mo LR	—	4.00	8.00	15.00	30.00	—
1859Mo LR	—	4.00	6.00	10.00	20.00	—
1860Mo LR	—	4.00	6.00	10.00	20.00	—
1861Mo LR	—	4.00	6.00	10.00	20.00	—
1862Mo LR	—	4.00	6.00	10.00	20.00	—
1863/53Mo LR	—	—	—	—	—	—
1863Mo LR	—	4.00	6.00	10.00	20.00	—

1/4 REAL (Un Quarto/Una Quartilla) KM# 368.7 Weight:
0.8450 g. **Composition:** 0.9030 Silver .0245 oz. ASW **Note:**
Struck at San Luis Potosi Mint, mint mark SLP, PI, P, I/P.

Date	Mintage	VG	F	VF	XF	Unc
1842S.L.Pi	—	2.00	4.00	8.00	15.00	—
1843/2S.L.Pi	—	4.00	6.00	10.00	20.00	—
1843S.L.Pi	—	4.00	6.00	8.00	15.00	—
1844S.L.Pi	—	2.00	4.00	8.00	15.00	—
1845/3S.L.Pi	—	4.00	6.00	10.00	25.00	—
1845/4S.L.Pi	—	4.00	6.00	10.00	25.00	—
1845S.L.Pi	—	2.00	4.00	8.00	15.00	—
1847/5S.L.Pi	—	4.00	6.00	10.00	20.00	—
1847S.L.Pi	—	2.00	4.00	8.00	15.00	—
1851/47S.L.Pi	—	4.00	8.00	15.00	30.00	—
1854S.L.Pi	—	125	200	275	400	—
1856S.L.Pi	—	4.00	8.00	15.00	30.00	—
1857S.L.Pi	—	5.00	10.00	20.00	35.00	—
1862/57S.L.Pi	—	10.00	20.00	40.00	85.00	—

1/4 REAL (Un Quarto/Una Quartilla) KM# 368.8
Weight: 0.8450 g. **Composition:** 0.9030 Silver .0245 oz.
ASW **Note:** Struck at Zacatecas Mint, mint mark Zs.

Date	Mintage	VG	F	VF	XF	Unc
1842/1Zs LR	—	4.00	8.00	15.00	30.00	—
1842Zs LR	—	4.00	6.00	10.00	20.00	—

1/4 REAL (Un Quarto/Una Quartilla) KM# 345
Composition: Copper **Obv. Legend:** REPUBLICA
MEXICANA **Note:** Struck at Durango Mint.

Date	Mintage	Good	VG	F	VF	XF
1845 Rare	—	—	—	—	—	—

1/4 REAL (Un Quarto/Una Quartilla) KM# 341
Composition: Copper **Obv. Legend:** ESTADO LIBRE DE
CHIHUAHUA **Note:** Struck at Chihuahua Mint.

Date	Mintage	Good	VG	F	VF	XF
1846 With fraction bar	—	3.50	6.00	12.00	37.50	—
1846 Without fraction bar	—	5.00	8.50	15.00	45.00	—

1/4 REAL (Un Quarto/Una Quartilla) KM# 363
Composition: Copper **Obv. Legend:** ESTADO LIBRE Y
SOBERANO DE SINALOA **Note:** Struck at Sinaloa Mint.

Date	Mintage	Good	VG	F	VF	XF
1847	—	3.50	5.50	9.00	20.00	—
1848	—	3.50	5.50	9.00	20.00	—
1859	—	3.00	4.50	6.00	13.50	—
1861	—	1.50	3.00	4.00	9.00	—
1862	—	1.50	3.00	4.00	9.00	—
1863	—	2.50	4.00	5.00	10.00	—
1864/3	—	2.50	4.00	5.00	10.00	—
1864	—	1.50	3.00	4.00	9.00	—
1865	—	3.00	5.50	7.00	15.00	—
1866/5	7,401,000	2.50	3.50	5.00	10.00	—
1866	Inc. above	1.50	3.00	4.00	9.00	—

1/4 REAL (Un Quarto/Una Quartilla) KM# 363a
Composition: Brass **Obv. Legend:** ESTADO LIBRE Y
SOBERANO DE SINALOA **Note:** Struck at Sinaloa Mint.

Date	Mintage	Good	VG	F	VF	XF
1847	—	5.00	9.00	18.50	42.50	—

1/4 REAL (Un Quarto/Una Quartilla)   KM# 342
Composition: Copper **Obv. Legend:** ESTADO DE
CHIHUAHUA **Note:** Struck at Chihuahua Mint.

Date	Mintage	Good	VG	F	VF	XF
1855	—	2.50	5.00	13.50	40.00	—
1856	—	2.50	5.00	13.50	40.00	—

Date	Mintage	Good	VG	F	VF	XF
1858	—	3.00	5.50	10.00	22.50	—
1861	—	3.50	5.50	12.50	28.50	—
1862	—	3.00	5.50	10.00	22.50	—

1/4 REAL (Un Quarto/Una Quartilla)   KM# 356
Composition: Copper **Obv. Legend:** DEPARTMENTO DE
JALISCO **Size:** 28 mm. **Note:** Struck at Jalisco Mint.

Date	Mintage	Good	VG	F	VF	XF
1858	—	2.75	5.00	8.50	18.50	—
1859/8	—	2.75	5.00	8.50	18.50	—
1859	—	2.75	5.00	8.50	18.50	—
1860	—	2.75	5.00	8.50	18.50	—

1/4 REAL (Un Quarto/Una Quartilla)   KM# 343
Composition: Copper **Obv. Legend:** DEPARTMENTO DE
CHIHUAHUA **Note:** Struck at Chihuahua Mint.

Date	Mintage	Good	VG	F	VF	XF
1855	—	3.00	5.00	10.00	45.00	—
1855 DE (reversed D)	—	4.50	7.00	13.50	50.00	—

1/4 REAL (Un Quarto/Una Quartilla)   KM# 346
Composition: Copper **Obv. Legend:** REPUBLICA
MEXICANA **Reverse:** Date, value **Rev. Legend:**
DURANGO **Note:** Struck at Durango Mint.

Date	Mintage	Good	VG	F	VF	XF
1858 Rare	—	—	—	—	—	—

1/4 REAL (Un Quarto/Una Quartilla)   KM# 352
Composition: Copper **Obv. Legend:** EST. LIB. DE
GUANAXUATO **Rev. Legend:** OMNIA VINCIT LABOR
Note: Struck at Guanajuato Mint.

Date	Mintage	Good	VG	F	VF	XF
1856	—	9.00	20.00	37.50	62.50	—
1857	—	7.50	15.00	25.00	42.50	—

1/4 REAL (Un Quarto/Una Quartilla)   KM# 352a
Composition: Brass **Obv. Legend:** EST. LIB. DE
GUANAXUATO **Rev. Legend:** OMNIA VINCIT LABOR
Note: Struck at Guanajuato Mint.

Date	Mintage	Good	VG	F	VF	XF
1856	—	3.25	6.75	12.50	27.50	—
1857	—	3.25	6.75	12.50	27.50	—

1/4 REAL (Un Quarto/Una Quartilla)   KM# 347
Composition: Copper **Obv. Legend:** ESTADO DE
DURANGO **Rev. Legend:** CONSTITUCION **Note:** Struck
at Durango Mint.

Date	Mintage	Good	VG	F	VF	XF
1858	—	3.50	8.50	20.00	47.50	—

1/4 REAL (Un Quarto/Una Quartilla)   KM# 347a
Composition: Brass **Obv. Legend:** ESTADO DE
DURANGO **Rev. Legend:** CONSTITUCION

Date	Mintage	Good	VG	F	VF	XF
1858	—	—	—	—	—	—

1/4 REAL (Un Quarto/Una Quartilla)   KM# 355
Composition: Copper **Obv. Legend:** ESTADO LIBRE DE
JALISCO **Size:** 31 mm. **Note:** Struck at Jalisco Mint.

1/4 REAL (Un Quarto/Una Quartilla)   KM# 360
Composition: Copper **Obv. Legend:** ESTADO LIBRE DE SAN LUIS POTOSI **Rev. Legend:** REPUBLICA MEXICANA **Note:** Struck at San Luis Potosi Mint.

Date	Mintage	Good	VG	F	VF	XF
1862	1,367	2.50	4.00	6.75	13.50	—
1862 LIBR	Inc. above	3.25	5.00	7.50	15.00	—

1/4 REAL (Un Quarto/Una Quartilla)   KM# 365
Composition: Copper **Obv. Legend:** ESTO. LIBE. Y SOBO. DE SONORA **Note:** Struck at Hermosilla Mint (Sonora).

Date	Mintage	Good	VG	F	VF	XF
1859	—	2.00	5.00	8.00	20.00	—
1861/59	—	3.00	6.50	11.00	25.00	—
1861	—	2.00	5.00	8.00	20.00	—
1862	—	2.00	5.00	8.00	20.00	—
1863/2	—	5.00	12.50	25.00	40.00	—

1/4 REAL (Un Quarto/Una Quartilla)   KM# 349
Composition: Copper **Obv. Legend:** ESTADO DE DURANGO **Rev. Legend:** INDEPENDENCIA Y LIBERTAD **Note:** Struck at Durango Mint.

Date	Mintage	Good	VG	F	VF	XF
1866	—	4.50	9.50	20.00	50.00	—

1/4 REAL (Un Quarto/Una Quartilla)   KM# 348
Composition: Copper **Obv. Legend:** DEPARTMENTO DE DURANGO **Rev. Legend:** LIBERTAD EN EL ORDEN **Note:** Struck at Durango Mint.

Date	Mintage	Good	VG	F	VF	XF
1860	—	2.00	5.00	15.00	37.50	—
1866	—	2.50	6.50	15.00	40.00	—

1/4 REAL (Un Quarto/Una Quartilla)   KM# 361
Composition: Copper **Obv. Legend:** ESTADO LIBRE Y SOBERANO DE S.L. POTOSI **Rev. Legend:** LIBERTAD Y REFORMA **Edge:** Milled **Note:** Struck at San Luis Potosi Mint.

Date	Mintage	Good	VG	F	VF	XF
1867	3,177,000	2.50	3.75	7.00	18.50	—
1867 AFG	Inc. above	2.50	3.75	7.00	18.50	—

Note: AFG are the coin designer/engraver initials

1/4 REAL (Un Quarto/Una Quartilla)   KM# 344
Composition: Copper **Obv. Legend:** E. CHIHA LIBERTAD **Note:** Struck at Chihuahua Mint.

Date	Mintage	Good	VG	F	VF	XF
1860	—	2.00	4.00	8.00	25.00	—
1861	—	2.00	4.00	8.00	25.00	—
1865/1	—	2.50	5.50	10.00	30.00	—
1865	—	7.50	16.50	28.50	65.00	—
1866/5	—	5.00	9.50	25.00	60.00	—
1866 Coin rotation	—	2.00	4.00	8.00	25.00	—
1866 Medal rotation	—	2.00	4.00	8.00	25.00	—

1/4 REAL (Un Quarto/Una Quartilla)   KM# 362
Composition: Copper **Obv. Legend:** ESTADO LIBRE Y SOBERANO DE S.L. POTOSI **Rev. Legend:** LIBERTAD Y REFORMA **Edge:** Plain **Note:** Struck at San Luis Potosi Mint.

Date	Mintage	Good	VG	F	VF	XF
1867	—	2.50	3.75	7.00	18.50	—
1867 AFG	Inc. above	2.50	3.75	7.00	18.50	—

Note: AFG are the coin designer/engraver initials

1/4 REAL (Un Quarto/Una Quartilla)   KM# 350a
Composition: Brass **Obv. Legend:** ESTADO DE DURANGO **Rev. Legend:** SUFRAGIO LIBRE

Date	Mintage	Good	VG	F	VF	XF
1872	—	—	—	—	—	—

1/4 REAL (Un Quarto/Una Quartilla) KM# 350
Composition: Copper **Obv. Legend:** ESTADO DE DURANGO **Rev. Legend:** SUFRAGIO LIBRE **Note:** Struck at San Luis Potosi Mint.

Date	Mintage	Good	VG	F	VF	XF
1872	—	2.00	3.75	8.00	18.50	—

1/2 REAL KM# 370 Weight: 1.6900 g. Composition:
0.9030 Silver .0490 oz. ASW **Obverse:** Hook-necked eagle **Note:** Struck at Alamos Mint, mint mark A.

Date	Mintage	F	VF	XF	Unc	BU
1862A PG Rare	—	—	—	—	—	—

1/2 REAL KM# 370.1 Weight: 1.6900 g. Composition:
0.9030 Silver .0490 oz. ASW **Obverse:** Facing eagle **Note:** Struck at Chihuahua Mint, mint mark Ca.

Date	Mintage	F	VF	XF	Unc	BU
1844 Ca RG	—	75.00	125	175	275	—
1845 Ca RG	—	75.00	125	150	250	—

1/2 REAL KM# 370.2 Weight: 1.6900 g. Composition:
0.9030 Silver .0490 oz. ASW **Obverse:** Facing eagle **Note:** Struck at Culiacan Mint, mint mark C, Co.

Date	Mintage	F	VF	XF	Unc	BU
1846 CE	—	30.00	50.00	75.00	150	—
1848/7 CE	—	15.00	25.00	45.00	90.00	—
1849/8 CE	—	15.00	25.00	45.00	90.00	—
1849 CE	—	—	—	—	—	—
1852 CE	—	12.50	20.00	40.00	80.00	—
1853/1 CE	—	12.50	20.00	40.00	80.00	—
1854 CE	—	20.00	35.00	50.00	100	—
1856 CE	—	12.50	20.00	40.00	80.00	—
1857/6 CE	—	20.00	35.00	50.00	100	—
1857 CE	—	15.00	25.00	45.00	90.00	—
1858 CE Error 1 for 1/2	—	12.50	20.00	40.00	80.00	—
1860/59 PV	—	20.00	35.00	50.00	100	—
1860 PV	—	12.50	20.00	40.00	80.00	—
1861 PV	—	12.50	20.00	40.00	80.00	—
1863 CE Error 1 for 1/2	—	15.00	25.00	45.00	90.00	—
1867 CE	—	12.50	20.00	40.00	80.00	—
1869 6/5 CE Error 1 for 1/2	—	12.50	20.00	40.00	80.00	—

1/2 REAL KM# 370.3 Weight: 1.6900 g. Composition:
0.9030 Silver .0490 oz. ASW **Obverse:** Facing eagle **Note:** Struck at Durango Mint, mint mark D, Do.

Date	Mintage	F	VF	XF	Unc	BU
1832 RM	—	125	225	350	600	—
1832 RM/L	—	—	—	—	—	—
1833/2 RM/L	—	75.00	100	150	225	—
1833/1 RM/L	—	12.50	20.00	40.00	80.00	—
1833 RM	—	25.00	40.00	75.00	150	—
1834/1 RM	—	25.00	40.00	75.00	150	—
1834 RM	—	12.50	20.00	40.00	80.00	—
1837/1 RM	—	12.50	30.00	60.00	200	—
1837/4 RM	—	12.50	30.00	60.00	200	—
1837/6 RM	—	12.50	30.00	60.00	200	—
1841/33 RM	—	15.00	30.00	60.00	250	—
1842/32 RM	—	12.50	20.00	40.00	80.00	—
1842 RM	—	12.50	20.00	40.00	80.00	—

Date	Mintage	F	VF	XF	Unc	BU
1842 8R RM Error	—	12.50	20.00	40.00	80.00	—
1842 1/2/8R RM	—	12.50	20.00	40.00	80.00	—
1843/33 RM	—	15.00	25.00	50.00	100	—
1843 RM	—	15.00	25.00	50.00	100	—
1845/31 RM	—	12.50	20.00	40.00	80.00	—
1845/34 RM	—	12.50	20.00	40.00	80.00	—
1845/35 RM	—	12.50	20.00	40.00	80.00	—
1845 RM	—	15.00	25.00	50.00	100	—
1846 RM	—	30.00	50.00	80.00	200	—
1848/5 RM	—	35.00	55.00	110	250	—
1848/36 RM	—	25.00	40.00	75.00	200	—
1849 JMR	—	25.00	40.00	75.00	200	—
1850 RM Rare	—	—	—	—	—	—
1850 JMR	—	25.00	40.00	75.00	200	—
1851 JMR	—	20.00	35.00	50.00	100	—
1852/1 JMR	—	65.00	125	250	600	—
1852 JMR	—	30.00	50.00	80.00	200	—
1853 CP	—	12.50	20.00	40.00	80.00	—
1854 CP	—	25.00	40.00	75.00	200	—
1855 CP	—	25.00	40.00	60.00	150	—
1856/5 CP	—	20.00	35.00	50.00	100	—
1857 CP	—	20.00	35.00	50.00	100	—
1858/7 CP	—	20.00	35.00	50.00	100	—
1859 CP	—	20.00	35.00	50.00	100	—
1860/59 CP	—	40.00	65.00	135	300	—
1861 CP	—	125	250	400	700	—
1862 CP	—	25.00	40.00	60.00	125	—
1864 LT	—	50.00	100	200	450	—
1869 CP	—	40.00	65.00	125	275	—

1/2 REAL KM# 370.4 Weight: 1.6900 g. Composition:
0.9030 Silver .0490 oz. ASW **Obverse:** Facing eagle **Note:** Struck at Estado de Mexico, mint mark EoMo.

Date	Mintage	F	VF	XF	Unc	BU
1829EoMo LF	—	175	300	500	1,400	—

1/2 REAL KM# 370.5 Weight: 1.6900 g. Composition:
0.9030 Silver .0490 oz. ASW **Obverse:** Facing eagle **Note:** Struck at Guadalajara Mint, mint mark Ga.

Date	Mintage	F	VF	XF	Unc	BU
1825Ga FS	—	25.00	40.00	75.00	200	—
1826Ga FS	—	10.00	15.00	35.00	80.00	—
1828/7Ga FS	—	12.50	20.00	40.00	90.00	—
1829Ga FS	—	7.50	15.00	30.00	70.00	—
1830/29Ga FS	—	40.00	60.00	100	200	—
1831Ga LP Rare	—	—	—	—	—	—
1832Ga FS	—	10.00	20.00	35.00	80.00	—
1834/3Ga FS	—	65.00	100	175	250	—
1834Ga FS	—	10.00	20.00	35.00	80.00	—
1835/4/3Ga FS/LP	—	15.00	25.00	40.00	90.00	—
1837/6Ga JG	—	50.00	100	150	250	—
1838/7Ga JG	—	15.00	25.00	40.00	90.00	—
1839/8Ga JG/FS	—	35.00	75.00	150	250	—
1839Ga MC	—	10.00	20.00	35.00	80.00	—
1840/39Ga MC/JG	—	—	—	—	—	—
1840Ga MC	—	15.00	20.00	40.00	90.00	—
1841Ga MC	—	20.00	35.00	50.00	100	—
1842/1Ga JG	—	15.00	25.00	40.00	90.00	—
1842Ga JG	—	10.00	20.00	35.00	80.00	—
1843/2Ga JG	—	15.00	30.00	50.00	100	—
1843Ga JG	—	10.00	20.00	35.00	80.00	—
1843Ga MC/JG	—	10.00	20.00	35.00	80.00	—
1843Ga MC	—	10.00	20.00	35.00	80.00	—
1844Ga MC	—	10.00	20.00	35.00	80.00	—
1845Ga MC	—	10.00	20.00	35.00	80.00	—
1845Ga JG	—	10.00	20.00	35.00	80.00	—
1846Ga MC	—	10.00	20.00	35.00	80.00	—
1846Ga JG	—	10.00	20.00	35.00	80.00	—
1847Ga JG	—	10.00	20.00	35.00	80.00	—
1848/7Ga JG	—	10.00	20.00	35.00	80.00	—
1849Ga JG	—	10.00	20.00	35.00	80.00	—
1850/49Ga JG	—	—	—	—	—	—
1850Ga JG	—	10.00	20.00	35.00	80.00	—
1851/0Ga JG	—	10.00	20.00	35.00	80.00	—
1852Ga JG	—	10.00	20.00	35.00	80.00	—
1853Ga JG	—	10.00	20.00	35.00	80.00	—
1854Ga JG	—	10.00	20.00	35.00	80.00	—
1855/4Ga JG	—	10.00	20.00	35.00	80.00	—
1855Ga JG	—	10.00	20.00	35.00	80.00	—
1856Ga JG	—	10.00	20.00	35.00	80.00	—

Date	Mintage	F	VF	XF	Unc	BU
1857Ga JG	—	10.00	20.00	35.00	80.00	—
1858/7Ga JG	—	10.00	20.00	35.00	80.00	—
1858Ga JG	—	10.00	20.00	35.00	80.00	—
1859/7Ga JG	—	10.00	20.00	35.00	80.00	—
1860/59Ga JG	—	10.00	20.00	35.00	80.00	—
1861Ga JG	—	5.00	12.50	25.00	60.00	—
1862/1Ga JG	—	15.00	25.00	40.00	90.00	—

1/2 REAL KM# 370.6 Weight: 1.6900 g. **Composition:** 0.9030 Silver .0490 oz. ASW **Obverse:** Facing eagle **Note:** Struck at Guadalupe Y Calvo Mint, mint mark GC.

Date	Mintage	F	VF	XF	Unc	BU
1844GC MP	—	50.00	100	150	350	—
1845GC MP	—	25.00	50.00	100	200	—
1846GC MP	—	25.00	50.00	100	200	—
1847GC MP	—	25.00	50.00	100	300	—
1848GC MP	—	20.00	40.00	75.00	150	—
1849GC MP	—	25.00	50.00	100	200	—
1850GC MP	—	30.00	60.00	125	250	—
1851GC MP	—	25.00	50.00	100	200	—

1/2 REAL KM# 370.7 Weight: 1.6900 g. **Composition:** 0.9030 Silver .0490 oz. ASW **Obverse:** Facing eagle **Note:** Struck at Guanajuato Mint, mint mark Go. Varieties exist.

Date	Mintage	F	VF	XF	Unc	BU
1826Go MJ	—	125	250	400	1,000	—
1827/6Go MJ	—	7.50	15.00	30.00	75.00	—
1828/7Go MJ	—	7.50	15.00	30.00	75.00	—
1828Go MJ Denomination 2/1	—	—	—	—	—	—
1828Go JG	—	—	—	—	—	—
1828Go MR	—	50.00	100	150	250	—
1829/8Go MJ	—	5.00	10.00	25.00	50.00	—
1829Go MJ	—	5.00	10.00	25.00	50.00	—
1829Go MJ Reversed N in MEXICANA	—	5.00	10.00	25.00	50.00	—
1830Go MJ	—	5.00	10.00	25.00	50.00	—
1831/29Go MJ	—	15.00	30.00	60.00	150	—
1831Go MJ	—	10.00	20.00	40.00	80.00	—
1832/1Go MJ	—	7.50	15.00	30.00	75.00	—
1832Go MJ	—	7.50	15.00	30.00	75.00	—
1833Go MJ Round top 3	—	10.00	20.00	40.00	80.00	—
1833Go MJ Flat top 3	—	10.00	20.00	40.00	80.00	—
1834Go PJ	—	5.00	10.00	25.00	50.00	—
1835Go PJ	—	5.00	10.00	25.00	50.00	—
1836/5Go PJ	—	7.50	15.00	30.00	75.00	—
1836Go PJ	—	5.00	10.00	25.00	50.00	—
1837Go PJ	—	5.00	10.00	25.00	50.00	—
1838/7Go PJ	—	5.00	10.00	25.00	50.00	—
1839Go PJ	—	5.00	10.00	25.00	50.00	—
1839Go PJ Error: REPUBLIGA	—	5.00	10.00	25.00	50.00	—
1840/39Go PJ	—	7.50	10.00	25.00	75.00	—
1840Go PJ Straight J	—	5.00	10.00	25.00	50.00	—
1840Go PJ Curved J	—	5.00	10.00	25.00	50.00	—
1841/31Go PJ	—	5.00	10.00	25.00	50.00	—
1841Go PJ	—	5.00	10.00	25.00	50.00	—
1842/1Go PJ	—	5.00	10.00	25.00	50.00	—
1842/1Go PM	—	5.00	10.00	25.00	50.00	—
1842Go PM/J	—	5.00	10.00	25.00	50.00	—
1842Go PJ	—	5.00	10.00	25.00	50.00	—
1842Go PM	—	5.00	10.00	25.00	50.00	—
1843/33Go PM 1/2 over 8	—	5.00	10.00	25.00	50.00	—
1843Go PM Convex wings	—	5.00	10.00	25.00	50.00	—
1843Go PM Concave wings	—	5.00	10.00	25.00	50.00	—
1844/3Go PM	—	5.00	10.00	25.00	50.00	—
1844Go PM	—	10.00	20.00	40.00	90.00	—
1845/4Go PM	—	5.00	10.00	25.00	50.00	—
1845Go PM	—	5.00	10.00	25.00	50.00	—
1846/4Go PM	—	5.00	10.00	25.00	50.00	—
1846/5Go PM	—	5.00	10.00	25.00	50.00	—
1846Go PM	—	5.00	10.00	25.00	50.00	—
1847/6Go PM	—	7.50	15.00	30.00	60.00	—
1847Go PM	—	7.50	15.00	30.00	60.00	—
1848/35Go PM	—	5.00	10.00	25.00	50.00	—
1848Go PM	—	5.00	10.00	25.00	50.00	—

Date	Mintage	F	VF	XF	Unc	BU
1848Go PF/M	—	5.00	10.00	25.00	50.00	—
1849/39Go PF	—	5.00	10.00	25.00	50.00	—
1849Go PF	—	5.00	10.00	25.00	50.00	—
1849Go PF Error: MEXCANA	—	5.00	10.00	25.00	50.00	—
1850Go PF	—	5.00	10.00	25.00	50.00	—
1851Go PF	—	5.00	10.00	25.00	50.00	—
1852/1Go PF	—	5.00	10.00	25.00	50.00	—
1852Go PF	—	2.50	7.50	17.50	40.00	—
1853Go PF/R	—	5.00	10.00	25.00	50.00	—
1853Go PF	—	5.00	10.00	25.00	50.00	—
1854Go PF	—	5.00	10.00	25.00	50.00	—
1855Go PF	—	5.00	10.00	25.00	50.00	—
1856/4Go PF	—	5.00	10.00	25.00	50.00	—
1856/5Go PF	—	5.00	10.00	25.00	50.00	—
1856Go PF	—	5.00	10.00	25.00	50.00	—
1857/6Go PF	—	5.00	10.00	25.00	50.00	—
1857Go PF	—	5.00	10.00	25.00	50.00	—
1858/7Go PF	—	7.50	15.00	30.00	60.00	—
1858Go PF	—	5.00	10.00	25.00	50.00	—
1859Go PF	—	5.00	10.00	25.00	50.00	—
1860Go PF Small 1/2	—	5.00	10.00	25.00	50.00	—
1860Go PF Large 1/2	—	5.00	10.00	25.00	50.00	—
1860/59Go PF	—	5.00	10.00	25.00	50.00	—
1861Go PF Small 1/2	—	5.00	10.00	25.00	50.00	—
1861Go PF Large 1/2	—	5.00	10.00	25.00	50.00	—
1862/1Go YE	—	5.00	10.00	25.00	50.00	—
1862Go YE	—	2.50	7.50	17.50	40.00	—
1862Go YF	—	5.00	10.00	25.00	50.00	—
1867Go YF	—	2.50	7.50	17.50	40.00	—
1868Go YF	—	2.50	7.50	17.50	40.00	—

1/2 REAL KM# 370.8 Weight: 1.6900 g. **Composition:** 0.9030 Silver .0490 oz. ASW **Obverse:** Facing eagle **Note:** Struck at Hermosillo Mint, mint mark Ho.

Date	Mintage	F	VF	XF	Unc	BU
1839Ho PP Unique	—	—	—	—	—	—
1862Ho FM	—	500	650	1,000	—	—
1867Ho PR/FM Inverted 6, and 7/1	—	100	175	250	500	—

1/2 REAL KM# 370.9 Weight: 1.6900 g. **Composition:** 0.9030 Silver .0490 oz. ASW **Obverse:** Facing eagle **Note:** Struck at Mexico City Mint, mint mark Mo.

Date	Mintage	F	VF	XF	Unc	BU
1825Mo JM Short top 5	—	10.00	20.00	40.00	80.00	—
1825Mo JM Long top 5	—	10.00	20.00	40.00	80.00	—
1826/5Mo JM	—	10.00	20.00	40.00	80.00	—
1826Mo JM	—	5.00	10.00	20.00	60.00	—
1827/6Mo JM	—	5.00	10.00	20.00	60.00	—
1827Mo JM	—	5.00	10.00	20.00	60.00	—
1828/7Mo JM	—	7.50	15.00	25.00	85.00	—
1828Mo JM	—	10.00	20.00	40.00	90.00	—
1829Mo JM	—	7.50	15.00	25.00	75.00	—
1830Mo JM	—	5.00	10.00	20.00	60.00	—
1831Mo JM	—	5.00	10.00	20.00	60.00	—
1832Mo JM	—	7.50	12.50	27.50	60.00	—
1833Mo MJ	—	7.50	12.50	27.50	60.00	—
1834Mo ML	—	5.00	10.00	20.00	60.00	—
1835Mo ML	—	5.00	10.00	20.00	60.00	—
1836/5Mo ML/MF	—	7.50	15.00	25.00	65.00	—
1836Mo ML	—	7.50	15.00	25.00	65.00	—
1838Mo ML	—	5.00	10.00	20.00	60.00	—
1839Mo ML	—	5.00	10.00	20.00	65.00	—
1839/8Mo ML	—	5.00	10.00	20.00	65.00	—
1840Mo ML	—	5.00	10.00	20.00	50.00	—
1841Mo ML	—	5.00	10.00	20.00	50.00	—
1842Mo ML	—	5.00	10.00	20.00	50.00	—
1842Mo MM	—	5.00	10.00	20.00	50.00	—
1843Mo MM	—	10.00	20.00	40.00	80.00	—
1844Mo MF	—	5.00	10.00	20.00	50.00	—
1845/4Mo MF	—	5.00	10.00	25.00	60.00	—
1845Mo MF	—	5.00	10.00	20.00	50.00	—
1846Mo MF	—	5.00	10.00	20.00	50.00	—
1847Mo RC	—	10.00	20.00	40.00	80.00	—

Date	Mintage	F	VF	XF	Unc	BU
1847Mo RC R/M	—	10.00	20.00	40.00	80.00	—
1848/7Mo GC/RC	—	5.00	10.00	20.00	50.00	—
1849Mo GC	—	5.00	10.00	20.00	50.00	—
1850Mo GC	—	5.00	10.00	20.00	50.00	—
1851Mo GC	—	5.00	10.00	20.00	50.00	—
1852Mo GC	—	5.00	10.00	20.00	50.00	—
1853Mo GC	—	5.00	10.00	20.00	50.00	—
1854Mo GC	—	5.00	10.00	20.00	50.00	—
1855Mo GC	—	5.00	10.00	20.00	50.00	—
1855Mo GF/GC	—	7.50	12.50	25.00	65.00	—
1856/5Mo GF	—	7.50	12.50	25.00	65.00	—
1857Mo GF	—	5.00	10.00	20.00	50.00	—
1858Mo FH	—	3.00	5.00	12.50	40.00	—
1858Mo FH F/G	—	5.00	10.00	20.00	50.00	—
1858/9Mo FH	—	5.00	10.00	20.00	50.00	—
1859Mo FH	—	3.00	6.00	15.00	50.00	—
1860Mo FH/GC	—	5.00	10.00	20.00	50.00	—
1860Mo FH	—	3.00	6.00	15.00	50.00	—
1860Mo TH	—	5.00	10.00	20.00	50.00	—
1860/59Mo FH	—	7.50	12.50	25.00	65.00	—
1861Mo CH	—	3.00	6.00	15.00	45.00	—
1862/52Mo CH	—	5.00	10.00	20.00	50.00	—
1862Mo CH	—	3.00	6.00	15.00	45.00	—
1863/55Mo TH/GC	—	5.00	10.00	20.00	50.00	—
1863Mo CH/GC	—	5.00	10.00	20.00	50.00	—
1863Mo CH	—	3.00	6.00	15.00	45.00	—

1/2 REAL   KM# 370.10   Weight: 1.6900 g. **Composition:** 0.9030 Silver .0490 oz. ASW **Obverse:** Facing eagle **Note:** Struck at San Luis Potosi Mint, mint mark Pi.

Date	Mintage	F	VF	XF	Unc	BU
1831 Pi JS	—	7.50	12.50	25.00	65.00	—
1841/36 Pi JS	—	20.00	40.00	75.00	125	—
1842/1 Pi PS	—	20.00	40.00	75.00	125	—
1842/1 Pi PS P/J	—	60.00	80.00	150	300	—
1842 Pi PS/PJ	—	50.00	75.00	125	250	—
1842 PS	—	60.00	80.00	150	300	—
1842 Pi JS	—	20.00	40.00	75.00	125	—
1843/2 Pi PS	—	17.50	25.00	40.00	80.00	—
1843 Pi PS	—	15.00	25.00	35.00	70.00	—
1843 Pi AM	—	10.00	15.00	25.00	60.00	—
1844 Pi AM	—	10.00	15.00	30.00	65.00	—
1845 Pi AM	—	250	375	500	1,500	—
1846/5 Pi AM	—	40.00	75.00	125	200	—
1847/6 Pi AM	—	15.00	25.00	40.00	80.00	—
1848 Pi AM	—	15.00	25.00	40.00	80.00	—
1849 Pi MC/AM	—	15.00	25.00	40.00	80.00	—
1849 Pi MC	—	12.50	20.00	35.00	70.00	—
1850/49 Pi MC	—	—	—	—	—	—
1850 Pi MC	—	10.00	15.00	25.00	60.00	—
1850P MC	—	—	—	—	—	—
1851 Pi MC	—	10.00	15.00	25.00	60.00	—
1852 Pi MC	—	10.00	20.00	30.00	65.00	—
1853 Pi MC	—	7.50	12.50	20.00	60.00	—
1854 Pi MC	—	7.50	12.50	20.00	60.00	—
1855 Pi MC	—	15.00	20.00	35.00	70.00	—
1856 Pi MC	—	15.00	25.00	50.00	100	—
1856PI (no I)	—	—	—	—	—	—
1857 Pi MC	—	7.50	12.50	20.00	60.00	—
1857 Pi PS	—	10.00	15.00	30.00	65.00	—
1858 Pi MC	—	12.50	20.00	35.00	70.00	—
1858 Pi PS	—	12.50	20.00	35.00	70.00	—
1859 Pi MC Rare	—	—	—	—	—	—
1860/59 Pi PS	—	12.50	20.00	35.00	70.00	—
1861 Pi RO	—	10.00	15.00	30.00	60.00	—
1862/1 Pi RO	—	15.00	25.00	50.00	125	—
1862 Pi RO	—	15.00	25.00	50.00	125	—
1863/2 Pi RO	—	15.00	25.00	45.00	100	—

1/2 REAL   KM# 370.11   Weight: 1.6900 g. **Composition:** 0.9030 Silver .0490 oz. ASW **Obverse:** Facing eagle **Note:** Struck at Zacatecas Mint, mint mark Z, Zs.

Date	Mintage	F	VF	XF	Unc	BU
1826 AZ	—	5.00	10.00	20.00	60.00	—
1826 AO	—	5.00	10.00	20.00	60.00	—
1827 AO	—	5.00	10.00	20.00	60.00	—
1828/7 AO	—	5.00	10.00	20.00	60.00	—
1829 AO	—	5.00	10.00	20.00	60.00	—
1830 OV	—	5.00	10.00	20.00	60.00	—
1831 OV	—	25.00	50.00	75.00	150	—
1831 OM	—	5.00	10.00	20.00	60.00	—
1832 OM	—	5.00	10.00	20.00	60.00	—
1833 OM	—	5.00	10.00	20.00	60.00	—
1834 OM	—	5.00	10.00	20.00	60.00	—
1835/4 OM	—	5.00	10.00	20.00	60.00	—
1835 OM	—	5.00	10.00	20.00	60.00	—
1836 OM	—	5.00	10.00	20.00	60.00	—
1837 OM	—	10.00	20.00	40.00	80.00	—
1838 OM	—	5.00	10.00	20.00	60.00	—
1839 OM	—	7.50	15.00	30.00	65.00	—
1840 OM	—	10.00	25.00	45.00	90.00	—
1841 OM	—	10.00	25.00	45.00	90.00	—
1842/1 OM	—	5.00	10.00	20.00	60.00	—
1842 OM	—	5.00	10.00	20.00	60.00	—
1843 OM	—	40.00	75.00	115	250	—
1844 OM	—	5.00	10.00	20.00	60.00	—
1845 OM	—	5.00	10.00	20.00	60.00	—
1846 OM	—	7.50	15.00	30.00	65.00	—
1847 OM	—	5.00	10.00	20.00	50.00	—
1848 OM	—	5.00	10.00	20.00	50.00	—
1849 OM	—	5.00	10.00	20.00	50.00	—
1850 OM	—	5.00	10.00	20.00	50.00	—
1851 OM	—	5.00	10.00	20.00	50.00	—
1852 OM	—	5.00	10.00	20.00	50.00	—
1853 OM	—	5.00	10.00	20.00	50.00	—
1854/3 OM	—	5.00	10.00	20.00	50.00	—
1854 OM	—	5.00	10.00	20.00	50.00	—
1855/3 OM	—	7.50	15.00	30.00	65.00	—
1855 OM	—	5.00	10.00	20.00	50.00	—
1856 OM	—	5.00	10.00	20.00	50.00	—
1857 MO	—	5.00	10.00	20.00	50.00	—
1858 MO	—	5.00	10.00	20.00	50.00	—
1859 MO	—	6.00	8.50	17.50	35.00	—
1859 VL	—	6.00	8.50	17.50	40.00	—
1860/50 VL Inverted A for V	—	5.00	10.00	20.00	50.00	—
1860/59 VL Inverted A for V	—	5.00	10.00	20.00	50.00	—
1860 MO	—	5.00	10.00	20.00	50.00	—
1860 VL	—	5.00	10.00	20.00	50.00	—
1861/0 VL Inverted A for V	—	7.50	15.00	30.00	65.00	—
1861 VL Inverted A for V	—	5.00	10.00	20.00	50.00	—
1862 VL Inverted A for V	—	5.00	10.00	20.00	50.00	—
1863/1 VL Inverted A for V	—	7.50	15.00	30.00	65.00	—
1863 VL Inverted A for V	—	5.00	10.00	20.00	50.00	—
1869 YH	—	5.00	10.00	20.00	50.00	—

REAL   KM# 372   Weight: 3.3800 g. **Composition:** 0.9030 Silver .0981 oz. ASW **Note:** Struck at Chihuahua Mint, mint mark Ca.

Date	Mintage	F	VF	XF	Unc	BU
1844 Ca RG	—	500	1,000	1,500	2,750	—
1845 Ca RG	—	500	1,000	1,500	2,750	—
1855 Ca RG	—	100	150	225	450	—

REAL   KM# 372.1   Weight: 3.3800 g. **Composition:** 0.9030 Silver .0981 oz. ASW **Note:** Struck at Culiacan Mint, mint mark C.

Date	Mintage	F	VF	XF	Unc	BU
1846C CE	—	12.50	25.00	40.00	110	—
1848C CE	—	12.50	25.00	40.00	110	—
1850C CE	—	12.50	25.00	40.00	110	—
1851/0C CE	—	12.50	25.00	40.00	110	—
1852/1C CE	—	7.50	15.00	30.00	100	—
1853/2C CE	—	7.50	15.00	30.00	100	—
1854C CE	—	7.50	15.00	30.00	100	—
1856C CE	—	40.00	65.00	100	225	—
1857/4C CE	—	10.00	20.00	35.00	100	—
1857/6C CE	—	10.00	20.00	35.00	100	—

Date	Mintage	F	VF	XF	Unc	BU
1858C CE	—	5.00	7.50	15.00	100	—
1859C CE	—	—	—	—	—	—
1860C PV	—	5.00	7.50	15.00	100	—
1861C PV	—	5.00	7.50	15.00	100	—
1863C CE 3 known	—	—	1,650	2,250	—	—
1869C CE	—	—	7.50	15.00	100	—

REAL KM# 372.2 Weight: 3.3800 g. **Composition:** 0.9030 Silver .0981 oz. ASW **Note:** Struck at Durango Mint, mint mark Do.

Date	Mintage	F	VF	XF	Unc	BU
1832/1Do RM	—	5.00	10.00	20.00	90.00	—
1832Do RM/RL	—	10.00	15.00	30.00	100	—
1832Do RM	—	5.00	10.00	20.00	100	—
1834/24Do RM/RL	—	15.00	25.00	50.00	150	—
1834/3Do RM/RL	—	15.00	25.00	50.00	150	—
1834Do RM	—	10.00	20.00	40.00	110	—
1836/4Do RM	—	5.00	7.50	15.00	100	—
1836Do RM	—	5.00	7.50	15.00	100	—
1837Do RM 3/2	—	12.50	20.00	40.00	110	—
1837Do RM	—	12.50	20.00	40.00	110	—
1841Do RM	—	7.50	15.00	30.00	100	—
1842/32Do RM	—	10.00	20.00	40.00	110	—
1842Do RM	—	7.50	15.00	30.00	100	—
1843Do RM	—	5.00	7.50	15.00	100	—
1844/34Do RM	—	15.00	25.00	45.00	125	—
1845Do RM	—	5.00	7.50	15.00	100	—
1846Do RM	—	7.50	15.00	30.00	100	—
1847Do RM	—	10.00	15.00	35.00	100	—
1848/31Do RM	—	10.00	15.00	35.00	100	—
1848/33Do RM	—	10.00	15.00	35.00	100	—
1848/5Do RM	—	10.00	15.00	35.00	100	—
1848Do RM	—	7.50	12.50	20.00	100	—
1849/8Do CM	—	10.00	15.00	30.00	100	—
1850Do JMR	—	20.00	40.00	75.00	175	—
1851Do JMR	—	20.00	40.00	75.00	175	—
1852Do JMR	—	20.00	40.00	75.00	175	—
1853Do CP	—	12.50	20.00	35.00	100	—
1854/1Do CP	—	10.00	15.00	25.00	100	—
1854Do CP	—	7.50	12.50	30.00	100	—
1855Do CP	—	10.00	15.00	25.00	100	—
1856Do CP	—	12.50	20.00	35.00	100	—
1857Do CP	—	12.50	20.00	35.00	100	—
1858Do CP	—	12.50	20.00	35.00	100	—
1859Do CP	—	7.50	12.50	20.00	100	—
1800/59Do CP	—	10.00	15.00	25.00	100	—
1861Do CP	—	15.00	25.00	40.00	110	—
1862/1Do CP	—	225	300	450	1,250	—
1864Do LT	—	15.00	25.00	40.00	110	—

REAL KM# 372.3 Weight: 3.3800 g. **Composition:** 0.9030 Silver .0981 oz. ASW **Note:** Struck at Estado de Mexico Mint, mint mark EoMo.

Date	Mintage	F	VF	XF	Unc	BU
1828EoMo LF	—	200	300	450	1,500	—

REAL KM# 372.4 Weight: 3.3800 g. **Composition:** 0.9030 Silver .0981 oz. ASW **Note:** Struck at Guadalajara Mint, mint mark Ga.

Date	Mintage	F	VF	XF	Unc	BU
1826Ga FS	—	15.00	30.00	50.00	125	—
1828/7Ga FS	—	15.00	30.00	50.00	125	—
1829/8/7Ga FS	—	—	—	—	—	—
1829Ga FS	—	15.00	30.00	50.00	125	—
1830Ga FS	—	250	425	600	—	—
1831Ga LP	—	15.00	30.00	50.00	125	—
1831Ga LP/FS	—	300	450	600	—	—
1832Ga FS	—	250	350	500	—	—
1833/2Ga G FS	—	100	150	275	550	—
1833Ga FS	—	75.00	125	225	500	—
1834/3Ga FS	—	75.00	125	225	500	—
1835Ga FS	—	—	—	—	—	—
1837/6Ga JG/FS	—	12.50	20.00	35.00	100	—
1838/7Ga JG/FS	—	12.50	20.00	35.00	100	—

Date	Mintage	F	VF	XF	Unc	BU
1839Ga JG	—	250	350	500	—	—
1840Ga JG	—	12.50	20.00	35.00	100	—
1840Ga MC	—	7.50	12.50	25.00	70.00	—
1841Ga MC	—	50.00	75.00	125	250	—
1842/0Ga JG/MC	—	10.00	15.00	30.00	100	—
1842Ga JG	—	7.50	12.50	20.00	100	—
1843Ga JG	—	150	200	300	750	—
1843Ga MC	—	5.00	7.50	15.00	100	—
1844Ga MC	—	7.50	12.50	20.00	100	—
1845Ga MC	—	10.00	15.00	25.00	100	—
1845Ga JG	—	5.00	7.50	20.00	100	—
1846Ga JG	—	12.50	20.00	35.00	100	—
1847/6Ga JG	—	10.00	15.00	25.00	100	—
1847Ga JG	—	10.00	15.00	25.00	100	—
1848Ga JG	—	400	550	700	—	—
1849Ga JG	—	7.50	12.50	20.00	100	—
1850Ga JG	—	175	275	400	—	—
1851Ga JG	—	10.00	15.00	25.00	100	—
1852Ga JG	—	10.00	15.00	25.00	100	—
1853/2Ga JG	—	10.00	15.00	25.00	100	—
1854Ga JG	—	10.00	15.00	25.00	100	—
1855Ga JG	—	15.00	25.00	40.00	100	—
1856Ga JG	—	7.50	12.50	20.00	100	—
1857/6Ga JG	—	12.50	20.00	35.00	100	—
1858/7Ga JG	—	15.00	25.00	40.00	110	—
1859/8Ga JG	—	25.00	50.00	75.00	150	—
1860/59Ga JG	—	30.00	60.00	90.00	225	—
1861/0Ga JG	—	20.00	30.00	50.00	125	—
1861Ga JG	—	25.00	50.00	100	250	—
1862Ga JG	—	7.50	12.50	20.00	100	—

REAL KM# 372.5 Weight: 3.3800 g. **Composition:** 0.9030 Silver .0981 oz. ASW **Note:** Struck at Guadalupe y Calvo Mint, mint mark GC.

Date	Mintage	F	VF	XF	Unc	BU
1844GC MP	—	40.00	60.00	100	250	—
1845GC MP	—	40.00	60.00	100	250	—
1846GC MP	—	40.00	60.00	100	250	—
1847GC MP	—	40.00	60.00	100	250	—
1848GC MP	—	40.00	60.00	100	250	—
1849/7GC MP	—	40.00	60.00	100	250	—
1849/8GC MP	—	40.00	60.00	100	250	—
1849GC MP	—	40.00	60.00	100	250	—
1850GC MP	—	40.00	60.00	100	250	—
1851GC MP	—	40.00	60.00	100	250	—

REAL KM# 372.6 Weight: 3.3800 g. **Composition:** 0.9030 Silver .0981 oz. ASW **Note:** Struck at Guanajuato Mint, mint mark Go.

Date	Mintage	F	VF	XF	Unc	BU
1826/5Go JJ	—	5.00	7.50	15.00	85.00	—
1826Go MJ	—	4.00	6.00	15.00	85.00	—
1827Go MJ	—	4.00	6.00	15.00	65.00	—
1827Go JM	—	10.00	15.00	25.00	75.00	—
1828/7Go MR	—	4.00	6.00	15.00	85.00	—
1828Go MJ Straight J, small 8	—	4.00	6.00	15.00	85.00	—
1828Go MJ Full J, large 8	—	4.00	6.00	15.00	85.00	—
1828G MR/JJ	—	4.00	6.00	15.00	85.00	—
1828Go MR	—	4.00	6.00	15.00	85.00	—
1829/8Go MG Small eagle	—	4.00	6.00	15.00	85.00	—
1829Go MJ Small eagle	—	4.00	6.00	15.00	85.00	—
1829Go MJ Large eagle	—	4.00	6.00	15.00	85.00	—
1830Go MJ Small initials	—	4.00	6.00	15.00	85.00	—
1830Go MJ Medium initials	—	4.00	6.00	15.00	85.00	—

Date	Mintage	F	VF	XF	Unc	BU
1830Go MJ Large initials	—	4.00	6.00	15.00	85.00	—
1830Go MJ Reversed N in MEXICANA	—	4.00	6.00	15.00	85.00	—
1830GC MJ 3/2	—	4.00	6.00	15.00	85.00	—
1831/0Go MJ Reversed N in MEXICANA	—	4.00	6.00	15.00	85.00	—
1831Go MJ	—	4.00	6.00	15.00	85.00	—
1832/1Go MJ	—	15.00	30.00	50.00	125	—
1832Go MJ	—	15.00	30.00	50.00	125	—
1833Go MJ Top of 3 round	—	4.00	6.00	15.00	85.00	—
1833Go MJ Top of 3 flat	—	4.00	6.00	15.00	85.00	—
1834Go PJ	—	4.00	6.00	15.00	85.00	—
1835Go PJ	—	7.50	12.50	20.00	85.00	—
1836Go PJ	—	4.00	6.00	15.00	85.00	—
1837Go PJ	—	15.00	30.00	50.00	125	—
1838/7Go PJ	—	10.00	20.00	35.00	85.00	—
1839Go PJ	—	4.00	6.00	15.00	85.00	—
1840/39Go PJ	—	4.00	6.00	15.00	85.00	—
1840Go PJ	—	4.00	6.00	15.00	85.00	—
1841/31Go PJ	—	10.00	20.00	35.00	85.00	—
1841Go PJ	—	4.00	6.00	15.00	85.00	—
1842Go PJ	—	4.00	6.00	15.00	85.00	—
1842Go PM	—	4.00	6.00	15.00	85.00	—
1843Go PM Convex wings	—	4.00	6.00	15.00	85.00	—
1843Go PM Concave wings	—	4.00	6.00	15.00	85.00	—
1844Go PM	—	4.00	6.00	15.00	85.00	—
1845/4Go PM	—	4.00	6.00	15.00	85.00	—
1845Go PM	—	4.00	6.00	15.00	85.00	—
1846/5Go PM	—	7.50	12.50	20.00	85.00	—
1846Go PM	—	4.00	6.00	15.00	85.00	—
1847/6Go PM	—	4.00	6.00	15.00	85.00	—
1847Go PM	—	4.00	6.00	15.00	85.00	—
1848Go PM	—	4.00	6.00	15.00	85.00	—
1849Go PF	—	10.00	20.00	35.00	85.00	—
1850Go PF	—	4.00	6.00	15.00	85.00	—
1851Go PF	—	10.00	20.00	35.00	100	—
1853/2Go PF	—	7.50	12.50	20.00	75.00	—
1853Go PF	—	4.00	6.00	15.00	75.00	—
1853Go PF/M 5/4	—	7.50	12.50	20.00	75.00	—
1854/3Go PF	—	4.00	6.00	15.00	75.00	—
1854Go PF Large eagle	—	4.00	6.00	15.00	75.00	—
1854Go PF Small eagle	—	4.00	6.00	15.00	75.00	—
1855/3Go PF	—	4.00	6.00	15.00	75.00	—
1855/4Go PF	—	4.00	6.00	15.00	75.00	—
1855Go PF	—	4.00	6.00	15.00	75.00	—
1856/5Go PF	—	4.00	6.00	15.00	75.00	—
1856Go PF	—	4.00	6.00	15.00	75.00	—
1857/6Go PF	—	4.00	6.00	15.00	75.00	—
1857Go PF	—	4.00	6.00	15.00	75.00	—
1858Go PF	—	4.00	6.00	15.00	75.00	—
1859Go PF	—	4.00	6.00	15.00	75.00	—
1860/50Go PF	—	4.00	6.00	15.00	75.00	—
1860Go PF	—	4.00	6.00	15.00	75.00	—
1861Go PF	—	4.00	6.00	15.00	75.00	—
1862Go YE	—	4.00	6.00	15.00	75.00	—
1862/1Go YF	—	7.50	12.50	20.00	75.00	—
1862Go YF	—	4.00	6.00	15.00	75.00	—
1867Go YF	—	4.00	6.00	15.00	75.00	—
1868/7Go YF	—	4.00	6.00	15.00	75.00	—

REAL KM# 372.7 Weight: 3.3800 g. Composition: 0.9030 Silver .0981 oz. ASW **Note:** Struck at Hermosillo Mint, mint mark Ho.

Date	Mintage	F	VF	XF	Unc	BU
1867Ho PR Small 7/1	—	50.00	65.00	100	250	—
1867Ho PR Large 7/ small 7	—	50.00	65.00	100	250	—
1868Ho PR	—	50.00	65.00	100	250	—

REAL KM# 372.8 Weight: 3.3800 g. Composition: 0.9030 Silver .0981 oz. ASW **Note:** Struck at Mexico City Mint, mint mark Mo.

Date	Mintage	F	VF	XF	Unc	BU
1825Mo JM	—	10.00	20.00	40.00	110	—
1826Mo JM	—	7.50	15.00	30.00	100	—
1827/6Mo JM	—	7.50	15.00	30.00	75.00	—
1827Mo JM	—	5.00	10.00	20.00	70.00	—
1828Mo JM	—	7.50	15.00	30.00	100	—
1830/29Mo JM	—	5.00	10.00	20.00	100	—
1830Mo JM	—	5.00	12.50	25.00	100	—
1831Mo JM	—	100	200	300	750	—
1832Mo JM	—	5.00	10.00	20.00	100	—
1833/2Mo MJ	—	5.00	10.00	20.00	100	—
1850Mo GC	—	5.00	10.00	20.00	100	—
1852Mo GC	—	275	425	575	—	—
1854Mo GC	—	10.00	20.00	40.00	100	—
1855Mo GF	—	5.00	10.00	20.00	80.00	—
1856Mo GF	—	5.00	10.00	20.00	80.00	—
1857Mo GF	—	5.00	10.00	20.00	80.00	—
1858Mo FH	—	5.00	10.00	20.00	80.00	—
1859Mo FH	—	5.00	10.00	20.00	80.00	—
1861Mo CH	—	5.00	10.00	20.00	80.00	—
1862Mo CH	—	5.00	10.00	20.00	80.00	—
1863/2Mo CH	—	7.50	12.50	25.00	80.00	—

REAL KM# 372.9 Weight: 3.3800 g. Composition: 0.9030 Silver .0981 oz. ASW **Note:** Struck at San Luis Potosi Mint, mint mark Pi.

Date	Mintage	F	VF	XF	Unc	BU
1831 Pi JS	—	5.00	10.00	20.00	125	—
1837 Pi JS	—	600	750	1,000	—	—
1838/7 Pi JS	—	250	300	375	—	—
1838 Pi JS	—	20.00	35.00	60.00	125	—
1840/39 Pi JS	—	7.50	15.00	30.00	125	—
1840 Pi JS	—	7.50	15.00	30.00	125	—
1841 Pi JS	—	7.50	15.00	30.00	125	—
1842 Pi JS	—	15.00	30.00	55.00	150	—
1842 Pi PS	—	5.00	10.00	20.00	125	—
1843 Pi PS	—	12.50	20.00	35.00	125	—
1843 Pi AM	—	40.00	60.00	80.00	150	—
1844 Pi AM	—	40.00	60.00	80.00	150	—
1845 Pi AM	—	7.50	15.00	30.00	125	—
1846/5 Pi AM	—	7.50	15.00	30.00	125	—
1847/6 Pi AM	—	7.50	15.00	30.00	125	—
1847 Pi AM	—	7.50	15.00	30.00	125	—
1848/7 Pi AM	—	7.50	15.00	30.00	125	—
1849 Pi PS	—	7.50	15.00	30.00	125	—
1849/8 Pi SP	—	60.00	100	150	—	—
1849 Pi SP	—	15.00	25.00	40.00	125	—
1850 Pi MC	—	5.00	10.00	20.00	125	—
1851/0 Pi MC	—	7.50	15.00	30.00	125	—
1851 Pi MC	—	7.50	15.00	30.00	125	—
1852/1/0 Pi MC	—	10.00	20.00	35.00	125	—
1852 Pi MC	—	7.50	15.00	30.00	125	—
1853/1 Pi MC	—	12.50	20.00	35.00	125	—
1853 Pi MC	—	10.00	20.00	35.00	125	—
1854/2 Pi MO	—	30.00	60.00	100	—	—
1854/3 Pi MC	—	20.00	40.00	60.00	150	—
1855/4 Pi MC	—	20.00	40.00	60.00	150	—
1855 Pi MC	—	15.00	25.00	45.00	125	—
1856 Pi MC	—	15.00	25.00	45.00	125	—
1857 Pi PS	—	20.00	35.00	55.00	135	—
1857 Pi MC	—	20.00	40.00	60.00	150	—
1858 Pi MC	—	12.50	20.00	35.00	125	—
1859 Pi PS	—	10.00	15.00	30.00	125	—
1860/59 Pi PS	—	10.00	15.00	30.00	125	—
1861 Pi PS	—	7.50	12.50	20.00	125	—
1861 Pi RO	—	12.50	20.00	35.00	125	—
1862/1 Pi RO	—	12.50	20.00	35.00	90.00	—
1862 Pi RO	—	7.50	12.50	20.00	125	—

REAL KM# 372.10 Weight: 3.3800 g. Composition: 0.9030 Silver .0981 oz. ASW **Note:** Struck at Zacatecas Mint, mint mark Zs.

Date	Mintage	F	VF	XF	Unc	BU
1826Zs AZ	—	5.00	12.50	35.00	120	—
1826Zs AO	—	5.00	12.50	35.00	120	—
1827Zs AO	—	5.00	12.50	35.00	120	—
1828/7Zs AO	—	5.00	12.50	35.00	120	—
1828Zs AO	—	5.00	12.50	35.00	120	—
1828Zs AO Inverted V for A	—	5.00	12.50	35.00	120	—
1829Zs AO	—	5.00	12.50	35.00	120	—

Date	Mintage	F	VF	XF	Unc	BU
1830Zs ZsOV	—	5.00	12.50	35.00	120	—
1830Zs ZOV	—	5.00	12.50	35.00	120	—
1831Zs OV	—	5.00	12.50	35.00	120	—
1831Zs OM	—	5.00	12.50	30.00	120	—
1832Zs OM	—	5.00	12.50	30.00	120	—
1833/2Zs OM	—	5.00	12.50	30.00	120	—
1833/2Zs OM/V	—	5.00	12.50	30.00	120	—
1833Zs OM	—	5.00	12.50	30.00	120	—
1834/3Zs OM	—	5.00	12.50	30.00	120	—
1834Zs OM	—	5.00	12.50	30.00	120	—
1835/4Zs OM	—	20.00	35.00	60.00	150	—
1835Zs OM	—	4.00	8.00	20.00	65.00	—
1836/5Zs OM	—	4.00	8.00	20.00	85.00	—
1836Zs OM	—	4.00	8.00	20.00	85.00	—
1837Zs OM	—	4.00	8.00	20.00	85.00	—
1838Zs OM	—	4.00	8.00	20.00	85.00	—
1839Zs OM	—	4.00	8.00	20.00	85.00	—
1840Zs OM	—	4.00	8.00	20.00	85.00	—
1841Zs OM	—	20.00	40.00	60.00	150	—
1842/1Zs OM	—	4.00	8.00	20.00	85.00	—
1842Zs OM	—	4.00	8.00	20.00	85.00	—
1843Zs OM	—	4.00	8.00	20.00	85.00	—
1844Zs OM	—	4.00	8.00	20.00	85.00	—
1845/4Zs OM	—	5.00	12.50	30.00	100	—
1845Zs OM	—	4.00	8.00	20.00	85.00	—
1846Zs OM Old font and obverse	—	4.00	8.00	20.00	85.00	—
1846Zs OM New font and obverse	—	4.00	8.00	20.00	85.00	—
1847Zs OM	—	4.00	8.00	20.00	85.00	—
1848Zs OM	—	4.00	8.00	20.00	85.00	—
1849Zs OM	—	10.00	25.00	50.00	125	—
1850Zs OM	—	4.00	6.00	15.00	85.00	—
1851Zs OM	—	4.00	6.00	15.00	85.00	—
1852Zs OM	—	4.00	6.00	15.00	85.00	—
1853Zs OM	—	4.00	6.00	15.00	85.00	—
1854/2Zs OM	—	4.00	6.00	15.00	85.00	—
1854/3Zs OM	—	4.00	6.00	15.00	85.00	—
1854Zs OM	—	4.00	6.00	15.00	85.00	—
1855/4Zs OM	—	4.00	6.00	15.00	85.00	—
1855Zs OM	—	4.00	6.00	15.00	85.00	—
1855Zs MO	—	4.00	6.00	15.00	85.00	—
1856Zs MO	—	4.00	6.00	15.00	85.00	—
1856Zs MO/OM	—	4.00	6.00	15.00	85.00	—
1857Zs MO	—	4.00	6.00	15.00	85.00	—
1858Zs MO	—	4.00	6.00	15.00	85.00	—
1859Zs MO	—	4.00	6.00	15.00	75.00	—
1860 MO	—	250	—	—	—	—
1860Zs VL	—	4.00	6.00	15.00	75.00	—
1860Zs VL Inverted A for V	—	4.00	6.00	15.00	75.00	—
1861Zs VL	—	4.00	6.00	15.00	75.00	—
1861Zs VL Inverted A for V	—	4.00	6.00	15.00	75.00	—
1862Zs VL	—	5.00	12.50	30.00	100	—
1868Zs JS	—	25.00	45.00	90.00	175	—
1869Zs YH	—	4.00	8.00	20.00	75.00	—

2 REALES KM# 374 Weight: 6.7600 g. **Composition:** 0.9030 Silver .1962 oz. ASW **Obverse:** Facing eagle **Edge:** Reeded **Note:** Struck at Alamos Mint, mint mark A.

Date	Mintage	F	VF	XF	Unc	BU
1872A AM	15,000	40.00	100	200	500	—

2 REALES KM# 374.1 Weight: 6.7600 g. **Composition:** 0.9030 Silver .1962 oz. ASW **Obverse:** Facing eagle **Edge:** Reeded **Note:** Struck at Real de Catorce Mint, mint mark Ce.

Date	Mintage	F	VF	XF	Unc	BU
1863 Ce ML	—	125	200	325	675	—

2 REALES KM# 374.2 Weight: 6.7600 g. **Composition:** 0.9030 Silver .1962 oz. ASW **Obverse:** Facing eagle **Edge:** Reeded **Note:** Struck at Chihuahua Mint, mint mark Ca.

Date	Mintage	F	VF	XF	Unc	BU
1832 Ca MR	—	30.00	60.00	100	200	—
1833 Ca MR	—	30.00	60.00	125	500	—
1834 Ca MR	—	35.00	75.00	125	500	—
1834 Ca AM	—	35.00	75.00	125	500	—
1835 Ca AM	—	35.00	75.00	125	500	—
1836 Ca AM	—	20.00	40.00	80.00	200	—
1844 Ca AM Rare	—	—	—	—	—	—
1844 Ca RG Unique	—	—	—	—	—	—
1845 Ca RG	—	20.00	40.00	80.00	200	—
1855 Ca RG	—	20.00	40.00	80.00	200	—

2 REALES KM# 374.3 Weight: 6.7600 g. **Composition:** 0.9030 Silver .1962 oz. ASW **Obverse:** Facing eagle **Edge:** Reeded **Note:** Struck at Culiacan Mint, mint mark C.

Date	Mintage	F	VF	XF	Unc	BU
1846/1146C CE	—	25.00	50.00	100	225	—
1847C CE	—	12.50	20.00	40.00	200	—
1848C CE	—	12.50	20.00	40.00	200	—
1850C CE	—	25.00	50.00	75.00	200	—
1851C CE	—	12.50	20.00	40.00	200	—
1852/1C CE	—	12.50	20.00	40.00	200	—
1853/2C CE	—	12.50	20.00	40.00	200	—
1854C CE	—	15.00	30.00	50.00	200	—
1856C CE	—	20.00	35.00	70.00	200	—
1857C CE	—	12.50	20.00	40.00	200	—
1860C PV	—	12.50	20.00	40.00	200	—
1861C PV	—	12.50	20.00	40.00	200	—
1869C CE	—	12.50	20.00	40.00	200	—

2 REALES KM# 374.4 Weight: 6.7600 g. **Composition:** 0.9030 Silver .1962 oz. ASW **Obverse:** Facing eagle **Edge:** Reeded **Note:** Struck at Durango Mint, mint mark Do.

Date	Mintage	F	VF	XF	Unc	BU
1826Do RL	—	20.00	40.00	60.00	200	—
1832Do RM Style of pre-1832	—	20.00	40.00	60.00	200	—
1832Do RM Style of post-1832	—	20.00	40.00	60.00	200	—
1834/2Do RM	—	20.00	40.00	60.00	200	—
1834/3Do RM	—	20.00	40.00	60.00	200	—
1835/4Do RM/RL	—	200	300	500	—	—
1841/31Do RM	—	50.00	75.00	125	250	—
1841Do RM	—	50.00	75.00	125	250	—
1842/32Do RM	—	12.50	20.00	40.00	200	—
1843Do RM/RL	—	12.50	20.00	40.00	200	—
1844Do RM	—	35.00	50.00	80.00	200	—
1845/34Do RM/RL	—	12.50	20.00	40.00	200	—
1846/36Do RM	—	100	150	200	350	—
1848/36Do RM	—	12.50	20.00	40.00	200	—
1848/37Do RM	—	12.50	20.00	40.00	200	—
1848/7Do RM	—	12.50	20.00	40.00	200	—
1848Do RM	—	12.50	20.00	40.00	200	—
1849Do CM/RM	—	12.50	20.00	40.00	200	—
1849Do CM	—	12.50	20.00	40.00	200	—
1851Do JMR/RL	—	12.50	20.00	40.00	200	—
1852Do JMR	—	12.50	20.00	40.00	200	—
1854Do CP/CR	—	30.00	50.00	80.00	200	—
1855Do CP	—	250	350	500	—	—
1856Do CP	—	100	150	250	500	—
1858Do CP	—	12.50	20.00	40.00	200	—
1859/8Do CP	—	12.50	20.00	40.00	200	—
1861Do CP	—	12.50	20.00	40.00	200	—

2 REALES KM# 374.5 Weight: 6.7600 g. **Composition:** 0.9030 Silver .1962 oz. ASW **Obverse:** Facing eagle **Edge:** Reeded **Note:** Struck at Estado de Mexico Mint, mint mark EoMo.

Date	Mintage	F	VF	XF	Unc	BU
1828EoMo LF	—	325	525	900	2,500	—

2 REALES KM# 374.6 Weight: 6.7600 g. **Composition:** 0.9030 Silver .1962 oz. ASW **Obverse:** Facing eagle **Edge:** Reeded **Note:** Struck at Guadalajara Mint, mint mark Ga.

Date	Mintage	F	VF	XF	Unc	BU
1825Ga FS	—	20.00	40.00	80.00	200	—
1826Ga FS	—	20.00	40.00	80.00	200	—
1828/7Ga FS	—	100	150	225	400	—
1829Ga FS Rare	—	—	—	—	—	—
1832/0Ga FS/LP	—	100	150	225	350	—
1832Ga FS	—	12.50	20.00	40.00	200	—
1833/2Ga FS/LP	—	12.50	20.00	40.00	200	—
1834/27Ga FS Rare	—	—	—	—	—	—
1834Ga FS	—	12.50	20.00	40.00	200	—
1835Ga FS	—	2,100	—	—	—	—
1837Ga JG	—	12.50	20.00	40.00	200	—
1838Ga JG	—	12.50	20.00	40.00	200	—
1840/30Ga MC	—	12.50	20.00	40.00	200	—
1841Ga MC	—	30.00	50.00	200	500	—

Date	Mintage	F	VF	XF	Unc	BU
1842/32Ga JG/MC	—	35.00	50.00	100	200	—
1842Ga JG	—	20.00	40.00	80.00	200	—
1843Ga JG	—	12.50	20.00	40.00	200	—
1843Ga MC/JG	—	12.50	20.00	40.00	200	—
1844Ga MC	—	12.50	20.00	40.00	200	—
1845/3Ga MC/JG	—	12.50	20.00	40.00	200	—
1845/4Ga MC/JG	—	12.50	20.00	40.00	200	—
1845Ga JG	—	12.50	20.00	40.00	200	—
1846Ga JG	—	12.50	20.00	40.00	200	—
1847/6Ga JG	—	25.00	40.00	80.00	200	—
1848/7Ga JG	—	12.50	20.00	40.00	200	—
1849Ga JG	—	12.50	20.00	40.00	200	—
1850/40Ga JG	—	12.50	20.00	40.00	200	—
1851Ga JG	—	250	350	500	—	—
1852Ga JG	—	12.50	20.00	40.00	200	—
1853/1Ga JG	—	12.50	20.00	40.00	200	—
1854/3Ga JG	—	250	350	500	—	—
1855Ga JG	—	35.00	50.00	80.00	200	—
1856Ga JG	—	12.50	20.00	40.00	200	—
1857Ga JG	—	250	350	500	—	—
1859/8Ga JG	—	12.50	20.00	40.00	200	—
1859Ga JG	—	12.50	20.00	40.00	200	—
1862/1Ga JG	—	12.50	20.00	40.00	200	—

2 REALES   KM# 374.7 Weight: 6.7600 g.
Composition: 0.9030 Silver .1962 oz. ASW **Obverse:**
Facing eagle **Edge:** Reeded **Note:** Struck at Guadalupe y
Calvo Mint, mint mark GC.

Date	Mintage	F	VF	XF	Unc	BU
1844GC MP	—	40.00	60.00	125	275	—
1845GC MP	—	40.00	60.00	125	275	—
1846GC MP	—	50.00	100	150	300	—
1847GC MP	—	35.00	50.00	100	250	—
1848GC MP	—	50.00	100	150	300	—
1849GC MP	—	50.00	100	150	300	—
1850GC MP	—	125	250	—	—	—
1851/0GC MP	—	50.00	100	150	300	—
1851GC MP	—	50.00	100	150	300	—

2 REALES   KM# 374.8 Weight: 6.7600 g. **Composition:**
0.9030 Silver .1962 oz. ASW **Obverse:** Facing eagle **Edge:**
Reeded **Note:** Struck at Guanajuato Mint, mint mark Go.
Varieties exist.

Date	Mintage	F	VF	XF	Unc	BU
1825Go JJ	—	7.50	15.00	30.00	150	—
1826/5Go JJ	—	7.50	15.00	30.00	150	—
1826Go JJ	—	7.50	10.00	25.00	150	—
1826Go MJ	—	7.50	10.00	25.00	150	—
1827/6Go MJ	—	7.50	10.00	25.00	150	—
1827Go MJ	—	7.50	10.00	25.00	150	—
1828/7Go MR	—	7.50	15.00	30.00	150	—
1828Go MJ	—	7.50	10.00	20.00	150	—
1828Go JM	—	7.50	10.00	20.00	150	—
1829Go MJ	—	7.50	10.00	20.00	150	—
1831Go MJ	—	7.50	10.00	20.00	150	—
1832Go MJ	—	7.50	10.00	20.00	150	—
1833Go MJ	—	7.50	10.00	20.00	150	—
1834Go PJ	—	7.50	10.00	20.00	150	—
1835/4Go PJ	—	7.50	15.00	30.00	150	—
1835Go PJ	—	7.50	10.00	20.00	150	—
1836Go PJ	—	7.50	10.00	20.00	150	—
1837/6Go PJ	—	7.50	10.00	20.00	150	—
1837Go PJ	—	7.50	10.00	20.00	150	—
1838/7Go PJ	—	7.50	10.00	20.00	150	—
1838Go PJ	—	7.50	10.00	20.00	150	—
1839/8Go PJ	—	7.50	15.00	30.00	150	—
1839Go PJ	—	7.50	10.00	20.00	150	—
1840Go PJ	—	7.50	10.00	20.00	150	—
1841Go PJ	—	7.50	10.00	20.00	150	—
1842Go PJ	—	7.50	10.00	20.00	150	—
1842Go PM/PJ	—	7.50	10.00	20.00	150	—
1842Go PM	—	7.50	10.00	20.00	150	—
1843/2Go PM Concave wings, thin rays, small letters	—	7.50	10.00	20.00	150	—
1843Go PM Convex wings, thick rays, large letters	—	7.50	10.00	20.00	150	—
1844Go PM	—	7.50	10.00	20.00	150	—
1845/4Go PM	—	7.50	10.00	20.00	150	—
1845Go PM	—	7.50	10.00	20.00	150	—
1846/5Go PM	—	10.00	15.00	35.00	150	—
1846Go PM	—	7.50	10.00	20.00	150	—
1847Go PM	—	7.50	10.00	20.00	150	—
1848/7Go PM	—	7.50	15.00	30.00	150	—
1848Go PM	—	7.50	15.00	30.00	150	—
1848Go PF	—	100	150	250	500	—
1849/8Go PF/PM	—	7.50	10.00	20.00	150	—
1849Go PF	—	7.50	10.00	20.00	150	—
1850/40Go PF	—	7.50	10.00	20.00	150	—
1850Go PF	—	7.50	10.00	20.00	150	—
1851Go PF	—	7.50	10.00	20.00	150	—
1852/1Go PF	—	7.50	10.00	20.00	150	—
1852Go PF	—	7.50	10.00	20.00	150	—
1853Go PF	—	7.50	10.00	20.00	150	—
1854/3Go PF	—	7.50	10.00	20.00	150	—
1854Go PF Old font and obverse	—	7.50	10.00	20.00	150	—
1854Go PF New font and obverse	—	7.50	10.00	20.00	150	—
1855Go PF	—	7.50	10.00	20.00	150	—
1855Go PF Star in G of mint mark	—	7.50	10.00	20.00	150	—
1856/5Go PF	—	10.00	15.00	35.00	150	—
1856Go PF	—	10.00	15.00	25.00	150	—
1857/6Go PF	—	7.50	10.00	20.00	150	—
1857Go PF	—	7.50	10.00	20.00	150	—
1858/7Go PF	—	7.50	10.00	20.00	150	—
1858Go PF	—	7.50	10.00	20.00	150	—
1859/7Go PF	—	7.50	10.00	20.00	150	—
1859Go PF	—	7.50	10.00	20.00	150	—
1860/7Go PF	—	7.50	10.00	20.00	150	—
1860/50Go PF	—	7.50	10.00	20.00	150	—
1860/59Go PF	—	7.50	10.00	20.00	150	—
1860Go PF	—	7.50	10.00	20.00	150	—
1861/51Go PF	—	7.50	10.00	20.00	150	—
1861/57Go PF	—	7.50	10.00	20.00	150	—
1861/0Go PF	—	7.50	10.00	20.00	150	—
1861Go PF	—	7.50	10.00	20.00	150	—
1862/1Go YE	—	7.50	10.00	20.00	125	—
1862Go YE	—	7.50	10.00	20.00	125	—
1862/57Go YE	—	7.50	10.00	20.00	125	—
1862Go YE/PF	—	7.50	10.00	20.00	125	—
1862Go YF	—	7.50	10.00	20.00	125	—
1863/52Go YF	—	7.50	10.00	20.00	125	—
1863Go YF	—	7.50	10.00	20.00	125	—
1867/57Go YF	—	7.50	10.00	20.00	125	—
1868/57Go YF	—	10.00	15.00	25.00	125	—

2 REALES   KM# 374.9 Weight: 6.7600 g. **Composition:**
0.9030 Silver .1962 oz. ASW **Obverse:** Facing eagle **Edge:**
Reeded **Note:** Struck at Hermosillo Mint, mint mark Ho.

Date	Mintage	F	VF	XF	Unc	BU
1861Ho FM	—	200	300	400	650	—
1862/52Ho FM/C.CE	—	250	350	500	—	—
1867/1Ho PR/FM	—	75.00	150	250	500	—

2 REALES   KM# 374.10 Weight: 6.7600 g.
Composition: 0.9030 Silver .1962 oz. ASW **Obverse:**
Facing eagle **Edge:** Reeded **Note:** Struck at Mexico City
Mint, mint mark Mo. Varieties exist.

Date	Mintage	F	VF	XF	Unc	BU
1825Mo JM	—	10.00	15.00	30.00	175	—
1826Mo JM	—	10.00	15.00	30.00	175	—

Date	Mintage	F	VF	XF	Unc	BU
1827Mo JM	—	10.00	15.00	30.00	175	—
1828Mo JM	—	10.00	15.00	30.00	175	—
1829/8Mo JM	—	10.00	15.00	30.00	175	—
1829Mo JM	—	10.00	15.00	30.00	175	—
1830Mo JM	—	40.00	60.00	125	250	—
1831Mo JM	—	10.00	15.00	30.00	175	—
1832Mo JM	—	100	200	400	—	—
1833/2Mo MJ/JM	—	10.00	15.00	30.00	175	—
1834Mo ML	—	50.00	100	200	400	—
1836Mo MF	—	10.00	15.00	30.00	175	—
1837Mo ML	—	10.00	15.00	30.00	175	—
1840/7Mo ML	—	150	225	350	—	—
1840Mo ML	—	150	225	350	—	—
1841Mo ML	—	15.00	40.00	100	250	—
1842 ML Rare	—	—	—	—	—	—
1847Mo RC Narrow date	—	10.00	15.00	30.00	175	—
1847Mo RC Wide date	—	10.00	15.00	30.00	175	—
1848Mo GC	—	10.00	15.00	30.00	175	—
1849Mo GC	—	10.00	15.00	30.00	175	—
1850Mo GC	—	10.00	15.00	30.00	175	—
1851Mo GC	—	40.00	60.00	125	250	—
1852Mo GC	—	10.00	15.00	30.00	175	—
1853Mo GC	—	10.00	15.00	30.00	175	—
1854/44Mo GC	—	10.00	15.00	30.00	175	—
1855Mo GC	—	10.00	15.00	30.00	175	—
1855Mo GF/GC	—	10.00	15.00	30.00	175	—
1855Mo GF	—	10.00	15.00	30.00	175	—
1856/5Mo GF/GC	—	10.00	15.00	30.00	175	—
1857Mo GF	—	10.00	15.00	30.00	175	—
1858Mo FH	—	7.50	12.50	25.00	150	—
1858Mo FH/GF	—	7.50	12.50	25.00	150	—
1859Mo FH	—	7.50	12.50	25.00	150	—
1860Mo FH	—	7.50	12.50	25.00	150	—
1860Mo TH	—	7.50	12.50	25.00	150	—
1861Mo CH	—	7.50	12.50	25.00	150	—
1862Mo CH	—	7.50	12.50	25.00	150	—
1863Mo CH	—	7.50	12.50	25.00	150	—
1863Mo TH	—	7.50	12.50	25.00	150	—
1867Mo CH	—	7.50	12.50	25.00	150	—
1868Mo CH	—	10.00	15.00	25.00	150	—
1868Mo PH	—	7.50	12.50	25.00	150	—

2 REALES KM# 374.11 Weight: 6.7600 g.
Composition: 0.9030 Silver .1962 oz. ASW **Obverse:**
Facing eagle **Edge:** Reeded **Note:** Struck at San Luis Potosi Mint, mint mark Pi.

Date	Mintage	F	VF	XF	Unc	BU
1829 Pi JS	—	10.00	15.00	30.00	200	—
1830/20 Pi JS	—	20.00	30.00	60.00	200	—
1837 Pi JS	—	10.00	15.00	30.00	200	—
1841 Pi JS	—	10.00	15.00	30.00	200	—
1842/1 Pi JS	—	10.00	15.00	30.00	200	—
1842 Pi JS	—	10.00	15.00	30.00	200	—
1842 Pi PS	—	20.00	35.00	60.00	200	—
1843 Pi PS	—	12.50	20.00	40.00	200	—
1843 Pi AM	—	10.00	15.00	30.00	200	—
1844 Pi AM	—	10.00	15.00	30.00	200	—
1845 Pi AM	—	10.00	15.00	30.00	200	—
1846 Pi AM	—	10.00	15.00	30.00	200	—
1849 Pi MC	—	10.00	15.00	30.00	200	—
1850 Pi MC	—	10.00	15.00	30.00	200	—
1856 Pi MC	—	40.00	60.00	125	250	—
1857 Pi MC	—	—	—	—	—	—
1858 Pi MC	—	12.50	20.00	40.00	200	—
1859 Pi MC	—	50.00	70.00	100	200	—
1861 Pi PS	—	10.00	15.00	30.00	200	—
1862 Pi RO	—	12.50	20.00	40.00	200	—
1863 Pi RO	—	100	250	350	500	—
1868 Pi PS	—	10.00	15.00	30.00	200	—
1869/8 Pi PS	—	10.00	15.00	30.00	200	—
1869 Pi PS	—	10.00	15.00	30.00	200	—

2 REALES KM# 374.12 Weight: 6.7600 g.
Composition: 0.9030 Silver .1962 oz. ASW **Obverse:**
Facing eagle **Edge:** Reeded **Note:** Struck at Zacatecas Mint, mint mark Zs. Varieties exist.

Date	Mintage	F	VF	XF	Unc	BU
1825Zs AZ	—	10.00	15.00	30.00	150	—
1826Zs AV A is inverted V	—	7.50	10.00	25.00	150	—
1826Zs AZ A is inverted V	—	7.50	10.00	25.00	150	—
1826Zs AO	—	10.00	15.00	30.00	150	—
1827Zs AO A is inverted V	—	6.00	8.00	12.00	150	—
1827Zs AO	—	6.00	8.00	12.00	150	—
1828/7Zs AO	—	15.00	30.00	60.00	175	—
1828Zs AO	—	7.50	10.00	25.00	100	—
1828Zs AO A is inverted V	—	7.50	10.00	25.00	150	—
1829Zs AO	—	7.50	10.00	25.00	150	—
1829Zs OV	—	7.50	10.00	25.00	150	—
1830Zs OV	—	7.50	10.00	25.00	150	—
1831Zs OV	—	7.50	10.00	25.00	150	—
1831Zs O M/OV	—	7.50	10.00	25.00	150	—
1831Zs OM	—	7.50	10.00	25.00	150	—
1832/1Zs OM	—	15.00	30.00	60.00	150	—
1832Zs OM	—	7.50	10.00	25.00	150	—
1833/27Zs OM	—	7.50	10.00	25.00	150	—
1833/2Zs OM	—	7.50	10.00	25.00	150	—
1833Zs OM	—	7.50	10.00	25.00	150	—
1834Zs OM	—	40.00	60.00	125	200	—
1835Zs OM	—	7.50	10.00	25.00	150	—
1836Zs OM	—	7.50	10.00	25.00	150	—
1837Zs OM	—	7.50	10.00	25.00	150	—
1838Zs OM	—	15.00	30.00	60.00	150	—
1839Zs OM	—	7.50	10.00	20.00	150	—
1840Zs OM	—	7.50	10.00	20.00	150	—
1841/0Zs OM	—	7.50	10.00	20.00	150	—
1841Zs OM	—	7.50	10.00	20.00	150	—
1842Zs OM Narrow date	—	7.50	10.00	20.00	150	—
1842Zs OM Wide date	—	7.50	10.00	20.00	150	—
1843Zs OM	—	7.50	10.00	20.00	150	—
1844Zs OM	—	7.50	10.00	20.00	150	—
1845Zs OM Smalll letters with leaves	—	7.50	10.00	20.00	150	—
1845Zs OM Large letters with leaves	—	7.50	10.00	20.00	150	—
1846Zs OM	—	7.50	10.00	20.00	150	—
1847Zs OM	—	7.50	10.00	20.00	150	—
1848Zs OM	—	7.50	10.00	20.00	150	—
1849Zs OM	—	7.50	10.00	20.00	150	—
1850Zs OM	—	7.50	10.00	20.00	150	—
1851Zs OM	—	7.50	10.00	20.00	150	—
1852Zs OM	—	7.50	10.00	20.00	150	—
1853Zs OM	—	7.50	10.00	20.00	150	—
1854/3Zs OM	—	7.50	10.00	20.00	150	—
1854Zs OM	—	7.50	10.00	20.00	150	—
1855/4Zs OM	—	7.50	10.00	20.00	150	—
1855Zs OM	—	7.50	10.00	20.00	150	—
1855Zs MO	—	7.50	10.00	20.00	150	—
1856/5Zs MO	—	7.50	10.00	20.00	150	—
1856Zs MO	—	7.50	10.00	20.00	150	—
1857Zs MO	—	7.50	10.00	20.00	150	—
1858Zs MO	—	7.50	10.00	20.00	150	—
1859Zs MO	—	7.50	10.00	20.00	150	—
1860/59Zs MO	—	7.50	10.00	20.00	150	—
1860Zs MO	—	7.50	10.00	20.00	100	—
1860Zs VL	—	7.50	10.00	20.00	150	—
1861Zs VL	—	7.50	10.00	20.00	150	—
1862Zs VL	—	7.50	10.00	20.00	100	—
1863Zs MO	—	12.50	20.00	40.00	150	—
1863Zs VL	—	7.50	10.00	20.00	150	—
1864Zs MO	—	7.50	10.00	20.00	150	—
1864Zs VL	—	7.50	10.00	20.00	150	—
1865Zs MO	—	7.50	10.00	20.00	150	—
1867Zs JS	—	7.50	10.00	20.00	150	—
1868Zs JS	—	10.00	15.00	35.00	150	—
1868Zs YH	—	7.50	10.00	20.00	150	—
1869Zs YH	—	7.50	10.00	20.00	150	—
1870Zs YH	—	7.50	10.00	20.00	150	—

4 REALES   KM# 375   Weight: 13.5400 g. **Composition:** 0.9030 Silver .3925 oz. ASW **Obverse:** Facing eagle **Note:** Struck at Real de Catorce Mint, mint mark Ce.

Date	Mintage	F	VF	XF	Unc	BU
1863 Ce ML Large C	—	200	500	850	4,000	—
1863 Ce ML Small C	—	225	650	1,500	6,000	—

4 REALES   KM# 375.1   Weight: 13.5400 g. **Composition:** 0.9030 Silver .3925 oz. ASW **Obverse:** Facing eagle **Note:** Struck at Culiacan, mint mark C.

Date	Mintage	F	VF	XF	Unc	BU
1846C CE	—	400	550	900	—	—
1850C CE	—	75.00	125	250	700	—
1852C CE	—	200	300	500	1,250	—
1857C CE Rare	—	—	—	—	—	—
1858C CE	—	100	200	350	1,000	—
1860C PV	—	25.00	50.00	125	650	—

4 REALES   KM# 375.2   Weight: 13.5400 g. **Composition:** 0.9030 Silver .3925 oz. ASW **Obverse:** Facing eagle **Note:** Struck at Guadalajara Mint, mint mark Ga.

Date	Mintage	F	VF	XF	Unc	BU
1843Ga MC	—	20.00	40.00	80.00	600	—
1844/3Ga MC	—	30.00	60.00	125	600	—
1844Ga MC	—	20.00	40.00	80.00	600	—
1845Ga MC	—	20.00	40.00	80.00	600	—
1845Ga JG	—	20.00	40.00	80.00	600	—
1846Ga JG	—	20.00	40.00	80.00	600	—
1847Ga JG	—	40.00	80.00	150	600	—
1848/7Ga JG	—	40.00	80.00	150	600	—
1849Ga JG	—	40.00	80.00	150	600	—
1850Ga JG	—	65.00	125	250	650	—
1852Ga JG Rare	—	—	—	—	—	—
1854Ga JG Rare	—	—	—	—	—	—
1855Ga JG	—	100	200	400	1,250	—
1856Ga JG Rare	—	—	—	—	—	—
1857/6Ga JG	—	65.00	125	250	700	—
1858Ga JG	—	125	250	450	1,250	—
1859/8Ga JG	—	125	250	450	1,250	—
1860Ga JG	—	850	1,450			—
1863/2Ga JG	—	150	300	1,250	7,500	—
1863Ga JG	—	150	300	1,250	7,500	—

4 REALES   KM# 375.3   Weight: 13.5400 g. **Composition:** 0.9030 Silver .3925 oz. ASW **Obverse:** Facing eagle **Note:** Struck at Guadalupe y Calvo Mint, mint mark GC.

Date	Mintage	F	VF	XF	Unc	BU
1844GC MP	—	2,000	4,000	3,000	—	—
1845GC MP	—	3,000	4,000	5,000	9,000	—
1846GC MP	—	1,700	2,800	—	—	—
1847GC MP	—	1,500	2,500	—	—	—
1849GC MP	—	2,000	3,000	—	—	—
1850GC MP	—	500	1,000	—	—	—

4 REALES   KM# 375.4   Weight: 13.5400 g. **Composition:** 0.9030 Silver .3925 oz. ASW **Obverse:** Facing eagle **Note:** Struck at Guanajuato Mint, mint mark Go. Varieties exist. Some 1862 dates appear to be 1869 because of weak dies.

Date	Mintage	F	VF	XF	Unc	BU
1835Go PJ	—	12.50	25.00	60.00	600	—
1836/5Go PJ	—	15.00	30.00	75.00	600	—
1836Go PJ	—	15.00	30.00	75.00	600	—
1837Go PJ	—	12.50	25.00	60.00	600	—
1838/7Go PJ	—	15.00	30.00	75.00	600	—
1838Go PJ	—	12.50	30.00	75.00	600	—

Date	Mintage	F	VF	XF	Unc	BU
1839Go PJ	—	12.50	25.00	60.00	600	—
1840/30Go PJ	—	20.00	50.00	100	600	—
1840 PJ	—	20.00	50.00	100	600	—
1841/30 PJ	—	200	325	600	1,500	—
1841/31Go PJ	—	150	250	450	1,250	—
1842Go PJ Rare	—	—	—	—	—	—
1842Go PM	—	15.00	30.00	75.00	400	—
1843/2Go PM Eagle with convex wings, thick rays	—	12.50	25.00	60.00	400	—
1843Go PM Eagle with concave wings, thin rays	—	12.50	25.00	60.00	400	—
1844/3Go PM	—	15.00	30.00	75.00	600	—
1844Go PM	—	20.00	50.00	100	600	—
1845/4Go PM	—	20.00	50.00	100	600	—
1845Go PM	—	20.00	50.00	100	600	—
1846/5Go PM	—	15.00	30.00	75.00	600	—
1846Go PM	—	15.00	30.00	75.00	600	—
1847/6Go PM	—	15.00	30.00	75.00	600	—
1847Go PM	—	15.00	30.00	75.00	600	—
1848/7Go PM	—	20.00	50.00	100	600	—
1848Go PM	—	20.00	50.00	100	600	—
1849Go PF	—	20.00	50.00	100	600	—
1850Go PF	—	12.50	25.00	60.00	600	—
1851Go PF	—	12.50	25.00	60.00	600	—
1852Go PF	—	15.00	30.00	75.00	600	—
1852Go PF 5/4	—	20.00	50.00	100	600	—
1853Go PF	—	15.00	30.00	75.00	600	—
1854Go PF Large eagle	—	15.00	30.00	75.00	600	—
1854Go PF Small eagle	—	15.00	30.00	75.00	600	—
1855/4Go PF	—	15.00	30.00	75.00	600	—
1855Go PF	—	12.50	25.00	60.00	600	—
1856Go PF	—	12.50	25.00	60.00	600	—
1857Go PF	—	20.00	50.00	100	600	—
1858Go PF	—	20.00	50.00	100	600	—
1859Go PF	—	20.00	50.00	100	600	—
1860/59Go PF	—	15.00	30.00	75.00	600	—
1860Go PF	—	15.00	30.00	75.00	600	—
1861/51Go PF	—	15.00	30.00	75.00	600	—
1861Go PF	—	20.00	50.00	100	600	—
1862/1Go YE	—	15.00	30.00	75.00	600	—
1862/1Go YF	—	15.00	30.00	75.00	600	—
1862Go YE/PF	—	15.00	30.00	75.00	600	—
1862Go YE	—	15.00	30.00	75.00	600	—
1862Go YF	—	15.00	30.00	75.00	600	—
1863/53Go YF	—	15.00	30.00	75.00	600	—
1863Go YF/PF	—	15.00	30.00	75.00	600	—
1863Go YF	—	15.00	30.00	75.00	600	—
1867/57Go YF/PF	—	15.00	30.00	75.00	600	—
1868/58Go Y F/PF	—	15.00	30.00	75.00	600	—
1870Go FR	—	15.00	30.00	75.00	600	—

4 REALES   KM# 375.5   Weight: 13.5400 g. **Composition:** 0.9030 Silver .3925 oz. ASW **Obverse:** Facing eagle **Note:** Struck at Hermosillo Mint, mint mark Ho.

Date	Mintage	F	VF	XF	Unc	BU
1861Ho FM	—	200	350	500	2,500	—
1867/1Ho PR/FM	—	150	275	400	2,500	—

4 REALES   KM# 375.6   Weight: 13.5400 g. **Composition:** 0.9030 Silver .3925 oz. ASW **Obverse:** Facing eagle **Note:** Struck at Mexico City Mint, mint mark Mo.

Date	Mintage	F	VF	XF	Unc	BU
1827/6Mo JM	—	200	400			—
1850Mo GC Rare	—	—	—	—	—	—
1852Mo GC Rare	—	—	—	—	—	—
1854Mo GC Rare	—	—	—	—	—	—
1855Mo GF/GC	—	50.00	100	200	1,250	—
1855Mo GF	—	100	200	350	1,500	—
1856Mo GF/GC	—	50.00	125	400	1,200	—
1856Mo GF Rare	—	—	—	—	—	—
1859Mo FH	—	20.00	50.00	150	1,000	—
1861Mo CH	—	15.00	35.00	125	1,000	—
1862Mo CH	—	20.00	50.00	150	1,000	—
1863/2Mo CH	—	20.00	50.00	150	1,000	—
1863Mo CH	—	75.00	150	300	1,500	—

Date	Mintage	F	VF	XF	Unc	BU
1867Mo CH	—	20.00	50.00	150	1,000	—
1868Mo CH/PH	—	30.00	75.00	150	1,000	—
1868Mo CH	—	20.00	50.00	150	1,000	—
1868Mo PH	—	30.00	75.00	200	1,250	—

4 REALES   KM# 375.7   Weight: 13.5400 g.
Composition: 0.9030 Silver .3925 oz. ASW **Obverse:**
Facing eagle **Note:** Struck at Oaxaca Mint, mint mark O.

Date	Mintage	F	VF	XF	Unc	BU
1861O FR Ornamental edge	—	225	450	750	2,750	—
1861O FR Herringbone edge	—	300	550	850	2,850	—
1861O FR Obliquely reeded edge	—	200	400	700	—	—

4 REALES   KM# 375.8   Weight: 13.5400 g. **Composition:**
0.9030 Silver .3925 oz. ASW **Obverse:** Facing eagle **Note:**
Struck at San Luis Potosi Mint, mint mark Pi.

Date	Mintage	F	VF	XF	Unc	BU
1837 Pi JS	—	200	350	—	—	—
1838 Pi JS	—	150	250	400	650	—
1842 Pi PS	—	50.00	100	200	650	—
1843/2 Pi PS	—	50.00	100	200	650	—
1843/2 Pi PS 3 cut from 8 punch	—	50.00	100	200	650	—
1843 Pi AM	—	30.00	75.00	150	650	—
1843 Pi PS	—	50.00	100	200	650	—
1844 Pi AM	—	30.00	75.00	150	650	—
1845/4 Pi AM	—	20.00	50.00	100	650	—
1845 Pi AM	—	20.00	50.00	100	650	—
1846 Pi AM	—	20.00	50.00	100	650	—
1847 Pi AM	—	75.00	150	250	700	—
1848 Pi AM Rare	—	—	—	—	—	—
1849 Pi MC/AM	—	20.00	50.00	100	650	—
1849 Pi MC	—	20.00	50.00	100	650	—
1849 Pi PS	—	20.00	50.00	100	650	—
1850 Pi MC	—	20.00	50.00	100	650	—
1851 Pi MC	—	20.00	50.00	100	650	—
1852 Pi MC	—	20.00	50.00	100	650	—
1853 Pi MC	—	20.00	50.00	100	650	—
1854 Pi MC	—	100	200	400	1,100	—
1855 Pi MC	—	175	300	750	2,000	—
1856 Pi MC	—	250	400	700	—	—
1857 Pi MC Rare	—	—	—	—	—	—
1857 Pi PS Rare	—	—	—	—	—	—
1858 Pi MC	—	100	200	400	1,000	—
1859 Pi MC	—	2,000	3,000	—	—	—
1860 Pi PS	—	300	450	700	—	—
1861 Pi PS	—	30.00	75.00	150	650	—
1861 Pi RO/PS	—	30.00	75.00	150	650	—
1861 Pi RO	—	50.00	100	200	650	—
1862 Pi RO	—	30.00	75.00	150	650	—
1863 Pi RO	—	30.00	75.00	150	650	—
1864 Pi RO	—	1,600	2,600	—	—	—
1868 Pi PS	—	30.00	75.00	150	650	—
1869/8 Pi PS	—	30.00	75.00	150	650	—
1869 Pi PS	—	30.00	75.00	150	650	—

4 REALES   KM# 375.9   Weight: 13.5400 g.
Composition: 0.9030 Silver .3925 oz. ASW **Obverse:**
Facing eagle **Note:** Struck at Zacatecas Mint, mint mark Zs.

Date	Mintage	F	VF	XF	Unc	BU
1830Zs OM	—	20.00	50.00	100	600	—
1831Zs OM	—	15.00	30.00	75.00	600	—
1832/1Zs OM	—	20.00	50.00	100	600	—
1832Zs OM	—	20.00	50.00	100	600	—
1833/2Zs OM	—	20.00	50.00	100	600	—
1833/27Zs OM	—	15.00	30.00	75.00	600	—
1833Zs OM	—	15.00	30.00	75.00	600	—
1834/3Zs OM	—	20.00	50.00	100	600	—
1834Zs OM	—	15.00	30.00	75.00	600	—
1835Zs OM	—	15.00	30.00	75.00	600	—
1836Zs OM	—	15.00	30.00	75.00	600	—
1837/5Zs OM	—	20.00	50.00	100	600	—
1837/6Zs OM	—	20.00	50.00	100	600	—
1837Zs OM	—	20.00	50.00	100	600	—
1838/7Zs OM	—	15.00	30.00	75.00	600	—
1839Zs OM	—	250	375	500	—	—
1840Zs OM	—	500	1,300	—	—	—
1841Zs OM	—	15.00	30.00	75.00	600	—

Date	Mintage	F	VF	XF	Unc	BU
1842Zs OM Small letters	—	15.00	40.00	85.00	600	—
1842Zs OM Large letters	—	15.00	30.00	75.00	600	—
1843Zs OM	—	15.00	30.00	75.00	600	—
1844Zs OM	—	20.00	50.00	100	600	—
1845Zs OM	—	20.00	50.00	100	600	—
1846/5Zs OM	—	25.00	60.00	125	600	—
1846Zs OM	—	20.00	50.00	100	600	—
1847Zs OM	—	15.00	30.00	75.00	600	—
1848/6Zs OM	—	50.00	75.00	125	600	—
1848Zs OM	—	20.00	50.00	100	600	—
1849Zs OM	—	20.00	50.00	100	600	—
1850Zs OM	—	20.00	50.00	100	600	—
1851Zs OM	—	15.00	30.00	75.00	600	—
1852Zs OM	—	15.00	30.00	75.00	600	—
1853Zs OM	—	20.00	50.00	100	600	—
1854/3Zs OM	—	30.00	75.00	150	600	—
1855/4Zs OM	—	20.00	50.00	100	600	—
1855Zs OM	—	15.00	30.00	75.00	600	—
1856Zs OM	—	15.00	30.00	75.00	600	—
1856Zs MO	—	20.00	50.00	100	600	—
1857/5Zs MO	—	20.00	50.00	100	600	—
1857Zs O/M	—	20.00	50.00	100	600	—
1857Zs MO	—	15.00	30.00	75.00	600	—
1858Zs MO	—	20.00	50.00	100	600	—
1859Zs MO	—	15.00	30.00	75.00	600	—
1860/59Zs MO	—	20.00	50.00	100	600	—
1860Zs MO	—	15.00	30.00	75.00	600	—
1860Zs VL	—	20.00	50.00	100	600	—
1861/0Zs VL	—	20.00	50.00	100	600	—
1861Zs VL	—	15.00	30.00	75.00	600	—
1861Zs VL 6/5	—	20.00	50.00	100	600	—
1862/1Zs VL	—	20.00	50.00	100	600	—
1862Zs VL	—	20.00	50.00	100	600	—
1863Zs VL	—	20.00	50.00	100	600	—
1863Zs MO	—	20.00	50.00	100	600	—
1864Zs VL	—	15.00	30.00	75.00	600	—
1868Zs JS	—	20.00	50.00	100	600	—
1868Zs YH	—	15.00	30.00	75.00	600	—
1869Zs YH	—	15.00	30.00	75.00	600	—
1870Zs YH	—	15.00	30.00	75.00	600	—

8 REALES   KM# 377   Weight: 27.0700 g. **Composition:**
0.9030 Silver .7859 oz. ASW **Obverse:** Facing eagle **Note:**
Struck at Alamos Mint, mint mark A, As. Varieties exist.

Date	Mintage	F	VF	XF	Unc	BU
1864 PG	—	750	1,250	2,000	—	—
1865/4 PG Rare	—	—	—	—	—	—
1865 PG	—	500	750	1,000	—	—
1866/5 PG Rare	—	—	—	—	—	—
1866 PG	—	1,250	2,250	—	—	—
1866 DL Rare	—	—	—	—	—	—
1867 DL	—	1,150	2,150	—	—	—
1868 DL	—	50.00	90.00	150	300	—

Date	Mintage	F	VF	XF	Unc	BU
1869/8 DL	—	50.00	90.00	150	—	—
1869 DL	—	50.00	80.00	120	300	—
1870 DL	—	30.00	60.00	120	300	—
1871 DL	—	20.00	35.00	75.00	200	—
1872 AM/DL	—	25.00	50.00	100	300	—
1872 AM	—	25.00	50.00	100	250	—
1873 AM	509,000	15.00	25.00	50.00	150	—
1874/3 As DL	—	25.00	50.00	100	250	—
1874 DL	—	15.00	25.00	50.00	150	—
1875A DL 7/7	—	40.00	80.00	120	300	—
1875A DL	—	15.00	25.00	50.00	150	—
1875 As DL	—	30.00	60.00	110	250	—
1876 DL	—	15.00	25.00	50.00	150	—
1877 DL	515,000	15.00	25.00	50.00	150	—
1878 DL	513,000	15.00	25.00	50.00	150	—
1879 DL	—	20.00	35.00	75.00	175	—
1879 ML	—	30.00	60.00	125	350	—
1880 ML	—	12.00	15.00	30.00	140	—
1881 ML	966,000	12.00	15.00	30.00	140	—
1882 ML	480,000	12.00	15.00	30.00	140	—
1883 ML	464,000	12.00	15.00	30.00	140	—
1884 ML	—	12.00	15.00	30.00	140	—
1885 ML	280,000	12.00	15.00	30.00	140	—
1886 ML	857,000	12.00	15.00	25.00	110	—
1886/0As/Cn ML/JD	Inc. above	15.00	20.00	35.00	160	—
1887 ML	650,000	12.00	15.00	25.00	110	—
1888/7 ML	508,000	30.00	60.00	100	400	—
1888 ML	Inc. above	12.00	15.00	25.00	110	—
1889 ML	427,000	12.00	15.00	25.00	110	—
1890 ML	450,000	12.00	15.00	25.00	110	—
1891 ML	533,000	12.00	15.00	25.00	110	—
1892/0	—	20.00	30.00	60.00	160	—
1892 ML	465,000	12.00	15.00	25.00	110	—
1893 ML	734,000	10.00	12.00	22.00	85.00	—
1894 ML	725,000	10.00	12.00	22.00	85.00	—
1895 ML	477,000	10.00	12.00	22.00	85.00	—

8 REALES   KM# 377.1 Weight: 27.0700 g. **Composition:** 0.9030 Silver .7859 oz. ASW **Obverse:** Facing eagle **Note:** Struck at Real de Catorce Mint, mint mark Ce.

Date	Mintage	F	VF	XF	Unc	BU
1863 Ce ME	—	425	700	1,350	3,000	—
1863 Ce /Pl ML/MC	—	425	750	1,500	3,250	—

8 REALES   KM# 377.2 Weight: 27.0700 g. **Composition:** 0.9030 Silver .7859 oz. ASW **Obverse:** Facing eagle **Note:** Struck at Chihuahua Mint, mint mark Ca. Varieties exist.

Date	Mintage	F	VF	XF	Unc	BU
1831 Ca MR	—	1,000	1,750	2,250	3,250	—
1832 Ca MR	—	125	200	300	600	—
1833 Ca MR	—	250	550	1,000	—	—
1834 Ca MR	—	300	600	1,150	—	—
1834 Ca AM	—	350	500	700	—	—
1835 Ca AM	—	150	250	475	900	—
1836 Ca AM	—	100	200	300	600	—
1837 Ca AM	—	550	1,150	—	—	—
1838 Ca AM	—	100	200	300	600	—
1839 Ca RG	—	750	1,250	2,500	—	—

Date	Mintage	F	VF	XF	Unc	BU
1840 Ca RG 1 dot after date	—	300	500	800	1,500	—
1840 Ca RG 3 dots after date	—	300	500	800	1,500	—
1841 Ca RG	—	50.00	100	150	300	—
1842 Ca RG	—	25.00	40.00	75.00	150	—
1843 Ca RG	—	40.00	80.00	125	250	—
1844/1 Ca RG	—	35.00	70.00	100	200	—
1844 Ca RG	—	25.00	40.00	75.00	160	—
1845 Ca RG	—	25.00	40.00	75.00	160	—
1846 Ca RG	—	30.00	60.00	100	250	—
1847 Ca RG	—	40.00	80.00	125	250	—
1848 Ca RG	—	35.00	70.00	125	250	—
1849 Ca RG	—	30.00	60.00	100	200	—
1850/40 Ca RG	—	40.00	80.00	125	250	—
1850 Ca RG	—	30.00	60.00	100	200	—
1851/41 Ca RG	—	100	200	300	500	—
1851 Ca RG	—	150	250	400	750	—
1852/42 Ca RG	—	150	250	400	750	—
1852 Ca RG	—	150	250	400	750	—
1853/43 Ca RG	—	150	250	400	750	—
1853 Ca RG	—	150	250	350	700	—
1854/44 Ca RG	—	100	200	300	500	—
1854 Ca RG	—	50.00	100	150	300	—
1855/45 Ca RG	—	100	200	350	650	—
1855 Ca RG	—	50.00	100	150	300	—
1856/45 Ca RG	—	275	450	750	1,250	—
1856/5 Ca RG	—	400	700	1,500	3,500	—
1857 Ca JC/RG	—	40.00	80.00	125	250	—
1857 Ca JC	—	50.00	100	150	250	—
1858 Ca JC	—	35.00	70.00	125	250	—
1858 Ca BA	—	2,000	3,500	—	—	—
1859 Ca JC	—	40.00	80.00	125	250	—
1860 Ca JC	—	20.00	40.00	90.00	175	—
1861 Ca JC	—	15.00	25.00	55.00	125	—
1862 Ca JC	—	15.00	25.00	55.00	125	—
1863 Ca JC	—	20.00	35.00	75.00	150	—
1864 Ca JC	—	20.00	35.00	75.00	150	—
1865 Ca JC	—	100	200	350	600	—
1865 Ca FP	—	1,350	2,150	3,250	—	—
1866 Ca JC	—	750	1,150	2,250	—	—
1866 Ca FP	—	1,000	2,000	3,250	5,000	—
1866 Ca JG	—	850	1,650	2,750	4,250	—
1867 Ca JG	—	100	200	350	600	—
1868 Ca JG	—	75.00	150	250	400	—
1868 Ca MM	—	65.00	125	200	350	—
1869 Ca MM	—	20.00	35.00	65.00	135	—
1870 Ca MM	—	20.00	35.00	65.00	135	—
1871/0 Ca MM	—	15.00	25.00	55.00	125	—
1871 Ca MM	—	15.00	25.00	55.00	125	—
1871 Ca MM First M/ inverted M	—	20.00	35.00	65.00	135	—
1873 Ca MM	—	20.00	35.00	65.00	135	—
1873 Ca MM/T	—	15.00	25.00	55.00	125	—
1874 Ca MM	—	12.00	15.00	30.00	100	—
1875 Ca MM	—	12.00	15.00	30.00	100	—
1876 Ca MM	—	12.00	15.00	30.00	100	—
1877 Ca EA	472,000	20.00	40.00	85.00	200	—
1877 Ca GR	Inc. above	25.00	45.00	65.00	150	—
1877 Ca JM	Inc. above	12.00	15.00	30.00	100	—
1877 Ca AV	Inc. above	100	200	350	750	—
1878 Ca AV	439,000	12.00	15.00	25.00	80.00	—
1879 Ca AV	—	12.00	15.00	25.00	80.00	—
1880 Ca AV	—	200	350	600	1,250	—
1880 Ca PM	—	500	800	1,250	2,500	—
1880 Ca MG Normal initials	—	12.00	15.00	25.00	100	—
1880 Ca MG Tall initials	—	12.00	15.00	25.00	100	—
1880 Ca MM	—	12.00	15.00	25.00	100	—
1881 Ca MG	1,085,000	10.00	12.00	20.00	65.00	—
1882 Ca MG	779,000	10.00	12.00	20.00	65.00	—
1882 Ca MM	Inc. above	10.00	12.00	20.00	65.00	—

Date	Mintage	F	VF	XF	Unc	BU
1882 Ca MM M sideways	Inc. above	20.00	45.00	100	175	—
1883 Ca MM Sideways M	818,000	—	—	—	—	—
1883/2 Ca MM/G	—	12.00	15.00	30.00	80.00	—
1883 Ca MM	Inc. above	10.00	12.00	20.00	65.00	—
1884/3 Ca MM	—	12.00	15.00	30.00	90.00	—
1884 Ca MM	—	10.00	12.00	20.00	65.00	—
1885/4 Ca MM	1,345,000	15.00	25.00	55.00	125	—
1885/6 Ca MM	Inc. above	15.00	25.00	55.00	125	—
1885 Ca MM	Inc. above	10.00	12.00	20.00	65.00	—
1886 Ca MM	2,483,000	10.00	12.00	20.00	65.00	—
1887 Ca MM	2,625,000	10.00	12.00	20.00	65.00	—
1888/7 Ca MM	2,434,000	15.00	25.00	65.00	135	—
1888 Ca MM	Inc. above	10.00	12.00	20.00	65.00	—
1889 Ca MM	2,681,000	10.00	12.00	20.00	65.00	—
1890/89 Ca MM	—	15.00	25.00	55.00	125	—
1890 Ca MM	2,137,000	10.00	12.00	20.00	65.00	—
1891/0 Ca MM	2,268,000	15.00	25.00	55.00	135	—
1891 Ca MM	Inc. above	10.00	12.00	20.00	80.00	—
1892 Ca MM	2,527,000	10.00	12.00	20.00	65.00	—
1893 Ca MM	2,632,000	10.00	12.00	20.00	65.00	—
1894 Ca MM	2,642,000	10.00	12.00	20.00	65.00	—
1895 Ca MM	1,112,000	10.00	12.00	20.00	65.00	—

8 REALES   KM# 377.3   Weight: 27.0700 g.
Composition: 0.9030 Silver .7859 oz. ASW **Obverse:**
Facing eagle **Note:** Struck at Culiacan Mint, mint mark C, Cn. Varieties exist.

Date	Mintage	F	VF	XF	Unc	BU
1846 CE	—	150	300	800	1,500	—
1846 CE Dot after G	—	175	385	900	1,650	—
1846 CE No dot after G	—	125	265	750	1,450	—
1847 CE	—	400	700	1,500	—	—
1848 CE	—	125	250	450	1,000	—
1849 CE	—	75.00	125	200	400	—
1850 CE	—	75.00	125	200	400	—
1851 CE	—	125	250	450	1,000	—
1852/1 CE	—	100	150	250	500	—
1852 CE	—	100	200	300	600	—
1853/0 CE	—	200	350	700	1,300	—
1853/2/0	—	200	400	750	1,400	—
1853 CE T hick rays	—	100	175	300	600	—
1853 CE Error: MEXIGANA	—	200	350	650	—	—
1854 CE	—	750	1,250	—	—	—
1854 CE Large eagle and hat	—	175	350	750	1,200	—
1855/6 CE	—	40.00	60.00	100	200	—
1855 CE	—	25.00	40.00	75.00	150	—
1856 CE	—	50.00	100	175	350	—
1857 CE	—	20.00	35.00	75.00	150	—
1858 CE	—	30.00	40.00	75.00	150	—
1859 CE	—	20.00	35.00	75.00	150	—
1860/9 PV/CV	—	50.00	70.00	100	200	—
1860/9 PV/E	—	50.00	70.00	100	200	—
1860 CE	—	25.00	40.00	75.00	150	—
1860 PV	—	40.00	60.00	90.00	175	—
1861/0 CE	—	50.00	80.00	120	250	—
1861 PV/CE	—	75.00	125	200	350	—
1861 CE	—	20.00	35.00	60.00	150	—
1862 CE	—	20.00	35.00	60.00	150	—
1863/2 CE	—	30.00	50.00	75.00	200	—
1863 CE	—	20.00	30.00	60.00	150	—
1864 CE	—	30.00	60.00	100	300	—
1865 CE	—	125	200	325	650	—
1866 CE	—	400	750	1,250	2,250	—
1867 CE	—	125	200	350	700	—
1868/7 CE	—	30.00	40.00	75.00	150	—
1868/8	—	50.00	100	150	300	—
1868 CE	—	30.00	40.00	75.00	150	—
1869 CE	—	30.00	40.00	75.00	175	—
1870 CE	—	50.00	100	150	350	—
1873 MP	—	50.00	100	150	300	—
1874/3 MP	—	30.00	40.00	75.00	150	—
1874C MP	—	20.00	30.00	45.00	100	—
1874 CN MP	—	125	200	300	600	—
1875 MP	—	12.00	15.00	22.00	80.00	—

Date	Mintage	F	VF	XF	Unc	BU
1876 GP	—	12.00	15.00	30.00	90.00	—
1876 CG	—	12.00	15.00	22.00	80.00	—
1877 CG	339,000	12.00	15.00	22.00	80.00	—
1877Gn CG Error	—	65.00	125	200	400	—
1877 JA	Inc. above	35.00	75.00	125	250	—
1878/7 CG	483,000	35.00	75.00	125	250	—
1878 CG	Inc. above	15.00	25.00	35.00	125	—
1878 JD/CG	—	25.00	35.00	50.00	150	—
1878 JD	Inc. above	15.00	20.00	30.00	125	—
1878 JD D/ retrograde D	Inc. above	20.00	30.00	40.00	150	—
1879 JD	—	12.00	15.00	30.00	135	—
1880/70 JD	—	15.00	20.00	30.00	90.00	—
1880 JD	—	12.00	15.00	22.00	120	—
1881/0 JD	1,032,000	15.00	20.00	30.00	90.00	—
1881C JD	Inc. above	12.00	15.00	22.00	80.00	—
1881Cn JD	Inc. above	40.00	60.00	90.00	150	—
1882 JD	397,000	12.00	15.00	22.00	80.00	—
1882 AM	Inc. above	12.00	15.00	22.00	80.00	—
1883 AM	333,000	12.00	15.00	22.00	125	—
1884 AM	—	12.00	15.00	22.00	80.00	—
1885/6 AM	227,000	20.00	30.00	45.00	110	—
1885C AM	Inc. above	35.00	70.00	150	350	—
1885Cn AM	Inc. above	12.00	15.00	22.00	80.00	—
1885Gn AM Error	Inc. above	25.00	50.00	100	275	—
1886 AM	571,000	12.00	15.00	22.00	80.00	—
1887 AM	732,000	12.00	15.00	22.00	80.00	—
1888 AM	768,000	12.00	15.00	22.00	80.00	—
1889 AM	1,075,000	12.00	15.00	22.00	80.00	—
1890 AM	874,000	10.00	12.00	20.00	65.00	—
1891 AM	777,000	10.00	12.00	20.00	65.00	—
1892 AM	681,000	10.00	12.00	20.00	65.00	—
1893 AM	1,144,000	10.00	12.00	20.00	65.00	—
1894 AM	2,118,000	10.00	12.00	20.00	65.00	—
1895 AM	1,834,000	10.00	12.00	20.00	65.00	—
1896 AM	2,134,000	10.00	12.00	20.00	65.00	—
1897 AM	1,580,000	10.00	12.00	20.00	65.00	—

8 REALES   KM# 377.4   Weight: 27.0700 g.
Composition: 0.9030 Silver .7859 oz. ASW **Obverse:**
Facing eagle **Note:** Struck at Durango Mint, mint mark Do. Varieties exist.

Date	Mintage	F	VF	XF	Unc	BU
1825Do RL	—	30.00	65.00	150	375	—
1826Do RL	—	40.00	85.00	200	475	—
1827/6Do RL	—	35.00	60.00	85.00	200	—
1827/8Do RL	—	150	275	500	—	—
1827Do RL	—	30.00	50.00	90.00	200	—
1828/7Do RL	—	35.00	60.00	90.00	200	—
1828Do RL	—	25.00	50.00	80.00	175	—
1829Do RL	—	25.00	50.00	80.00	175	—
1830Do RM B on eagle's claw	—	25.00	50.00	90.00	200	—
1831Do RM B on eagle's claw	—	20.00	30.00	60.00	150	—
1832Do RM Mexican dies, B on eagle's claw	—	35.00	60.00	120	300	—
1832/1Do RM/ RL French dies	—	25.00	35.00	75.00	165	—
1833/2Do RM/RL	—	20.00	35.00	75.00	165	—

Date	Mintage	F	VF	XF	Unc	BU
1833Do RM	—	15.00	30.00	60.00	150	—
1834/3/2Do RM/RL	—	20.00	35.00	75.00	165	—
1834Do RM	—	15.00	25.00	50.00	150	—
1835/4Do RM/RI	—	20.00	35.00	65.00	150	—
1835Do RM	—	20.00	35.00	65.00	150	—
1836/1Do RM	—	20.00	35.00	65.00	150	—
1836/4Do RM	—	20.00	35.00	65.00	150	—
1836/5/4Do RM/RL	—	75.00	150	250	500	—
1836Do RM	—	20.00	30.00	55.00	150	—
1836Do RM M on snake	—	20.00	30.00	55.00	150	—
1837/1Do RM	—	20.00	30.00	55.00	150	—
1837Do RM	—	20.00	30.00	55.00	150	—
1838/1Do RM	—	20.00	30.00	60.00	165	—
1838/7Do RM	—	20.00	30.00	60.00	165	—
1838Do RM	—	20.00	30.00	55.00	150	—
1839/1Do RM/RL	—	20.00	30.00	55.00	150	—
1839/1Do RM	—	20.00	30.00	55.00	150	—
1839Do RM	—	20.00	30.00	55.00	150	—
1840/38/31 Do RM	—	20.00	30.00	55.00	150	—
1840/39Do RM	—	20.00	30.00	55.00	150	—
1840Do RM	—	20.00	30.00	55.00	150	—
1841/31Do RM	—	65.00	125	275	450	—
1841/39Do RM/L	—	25.00	50.00	85.00	200	—
1841/39Do RM	—	25.00	50.00	85.00	200	—
1842/31Do RM B below cactus	—	125	250	400	750	—
1842/31Do RM	—	40.00	80.00	125	250	—
1842/32Do RM	—	40.00	80.00	125	250	—
1842Do RM Eagle of 1832-41	—	20.00	30.00	55.00	150	—
1842Do RM Pre-1832 eagle resumed	—	20.00	30.00	55.00	150	—
1842Do RM	—	40.00	80.00	125	250	—
1843/33Do RM	—	50.00	90.00	150	250	—
1843Do RM	—	50.00	90.00	150	250	—
1844/34Do RM	—	100	200	300	500	—
1844/35Do RM	—	100	200	300	500	—
1844/43Do RM	—	60.00	120	220	425	—
1845/31Do RM	—	100	200	300	500	—
1845/34Do RM	—	35.00	75.00	125	250	—
1845/35Do RM	—	35.00	75.00	125	250	—
1845Do RM	—	20.00	30.00	55.00	150	—
1846/31Do RM	—	20.00	30.00	55.00	150	—
1846/36Do RM	—	20.00	30.00	55.00	150	—
1846Do RM	—	20.00	30.00	55.00	150	—
1847Do RM	—	25.00	50.00	80.00	185	—
1848/7Do RM	—	125	250	400	750	—
1848/7Do CM/RM	—	100	200	350	700	—
1848Do CM/RM	—	100	200	350	700	—
1848Do RM	—	100	200	300	600	—
1848Do CM	—	50.00	100	200	400	—
1849/39Do CM	—	100	200	350	700	—
1849Do CM	—	65.00	125	250	550	—
1849Do JMR/CM Oval 0	—	200	400	450	800	—
1849Do JMR Oval 0	—	200	325	450	800	—
1849Do JMR Round 0	—	200	400	600	1,000	—
1850Do JMR	—	100	150	250	500	—
1851/0Do JMR	—	65.00	125	225	475	—
1851Do JMR	—	100	150	250	500	—
1852Do CP/JMR	—	450	800	1,500	—	—
1852Do CP	—	750	1,200	2,250	—	—
1852Do JMR	—	175	250	375	650	—
1853Do CP/JMR	—	125	235	350	600	—
1853Do CP	—	200	350	600	1,200	—
1854Do CP	—	25.00	35.00	65.00	300	—
1855Do CP Eagle type of 1854	—	50.00	100	175	350	—
1855Do CP Eagle type of 1856	—	50.00	100	175	350	—
1856Do CP	—	50.00	100	175	350	—
1857Do CP	—	35.00	65.00	125	250	—
1858/7Do CP	—	25.00	35.00	70.00	165	—
1858Do CP	—	20.00	30.00	60.00	165	—
1859Do CP	—	20.00	30.00	60.00	165	—
1860/59Do CP	—	30.00	50.00	100	200	—
1860Do CP	—	20.00	30.00	60.00	165	—
1861/0Do CP	—	20.00	30.00	60.00	165	—
1861Do CP	—	20.00	30.00	60.00	125	—
1862/1Do CP	—	25.00	35.00	60.00	125	—
1862Do CP	—	20.00	30.00	60.00	175	—
1863/1Do CP	—	30.00	60.00	90.00	200	—
1863/2Do CP	—	25.00	50.00	75.00	175	—
1863/53Do CP	—	30.00	60.00	90.00	200	—
1863Do CP	—	25.00	50.00	75.00	175	—
1864Do CP	—	100	150	250	500	—
1864Do LT	—	25.00	40.00	80.00	175	—
1864Do LT/T	—	25.00	40.00	80.00	175	—
1864Do LT/CP	—	50.00	100	175	350	—
1865Do LT Rare	—	—	—	—	—	—
1866/4Do CM	—	2,750	5,500	—	—	—
1866Do CM	—	1,750	3,250	5,500	8,000	—
1867Do CM	—	3,500	—	—	—	—
1867/6Do CP	—	200	400	600	1,200	—
1867Do CP	—	175	300	500	1,000	—
1867Do CP/CM	—	125	250	400	900	—
1867Do CP/LT	—	200	400	650	1,250	—
1868Do CP	—	25.00	40.00	80.00	175	—
1869Do CP	—	20.00	30.00	50.00	135	—
1870/69Do CP	—	20.00	30.00	50.00	125	—
1870/9Do CP	—	20.00	30.00	50.00	125	—
1870Do CP	—	20.00	30.00	50.00	125	—
1873Do CP	—	125	225	325	600	—
1873Do CM	—	30.00	50.00	100	200	—
1874/3Do CM	—	12.00	15.00	22.00	100	—
1874Do CM	—	10.00	15.00	22.00	80.00	—
1874Do JH	—	1,150	1,750	2,750	—	—
1875Do CM	—	10.00	15.00	22.00	80.00	—
1875Do JH	—	80.00	150	250	450	—
1876Do CM	—	10.00	15.00	22.00	80.00	—
1877Do CM	431,000	1,450	2,500	—	—	—
1877Do CP	Inc. above	10.00	15.00	22.00	80.00	—
1877Do JMP	Inc. above	750	1,250	2,000	—	—
1878Do PE	409,000	15.00	25.00	40.00	100	—
1878Do TB	Inc. above	10.00	15.00	25.00	90.00	—
1879Do TB	—	10.00	15.00	22.00	80.00	—
1880/70Do TB	—	60.00	100	175	350	—
1880/70Do TB/JP	—	150	250	375	650	—
1880/70Do JP	—	15.00	25.00	40.00	100	—
1880Do TB	—	150	250	375	650	—
1880Do JP	—	10.00	15.00	22.00	80.00	—
1881Do JP	928,000	10.00	15.00	25.00	90.00	—
1882Do JP	414,000	10.00	15.00	22.00	80.00	—
1882Do MC/JP	Inc. above	30.00	60.00	100	200	—
1882Do MC	Inc. above	25.00	50.00	75.00	150	—
1883/73Do MC	452,000	15.00	25.00	40.00	90.00	—
1883Do MC	Inc. above	10.00	15.00	22.00	80.00	—
1884/3Do MC	—	15.00	25.00	40.00	90.00	—
1884Do MC	—	10.00	15.00	22.00	80.00	—
1885Do MC	547,000	10.00	12.00	20.00	70.00	—
1885Do JB	Inc. above	25.00	35.00	50.00	125	—
1886/5Do MC	—	15.00	25.00	40.00	100	—
1886/3Do MC	955,000	15.00	25.00	40.00	100	—
1886Do MC	Inc. above	10.00	12.00	20.00	70.00	—
1887Do MC	1,004,000	10.00	12.00	20.00	70.00	—
1888/7Do MC	—	65.00	125	250	450	—
1888Do MC	996,000	10.00	12.00	20.00	70.00	—
1889Do MC	874,000	10.00	12.00	20.00	70.00	—
1890Do MC	1,119,000	10.00	12.00	20.00	70.00	—
1890Do JP	—	10.00	12.00	20.00	70.00	—
1891Do JP	1,487,000	10.00	12.00	20.00	70.00	—
1892Do JP	1,597,000	10.00	12.00	20.00	70.00	—
1892Do ND	Inc. above	25.00	50.00	100	200	—
1893Do ND	1,617,000	10.00	12.00	20.00	70.00	—
1894Do ND	1,537,000	10.00	12.00	20.00	70.00	—
1895/3Do ND	761,000	15.00	25.00	40.00	100	—

Date	Mintage	F	VF	XF	Unc	BU
1895Do ND	Inc. above	10.00	12.00	20.00	70.00	—
1895Do ND/P	—	15.00	25.00	40.00	100	—

8 REALES KM# 377.5 Weight: 27.0700 g.
Composition: 0.9030 Silver .7859 oz. ASW **Obverse:** Facing eagle **Note:** Struck at Estado de Mexico Mint, mark mark EoMo.

Date	Mintage	F	VF	XF	Unc	BU
1828EoMo LF/LP	—	350	850	2,150	—	—
1828EoMo LF	—	350	850	2,150	5,500	—
1829EoMo LF	—	300	750	1,850	4,500	—
1830/20EoMo LF	—	1,250	2,750	4,250	—	—
1830EoMo LF	—	1,000	2,000	3,250	6,000	—

8 REALES KM# 377.6 Weight: 27.0700 g.
Composition: 0.9030 Silver .7859 oz. ASW **Obverse:** Facing eagle **Note:** Struck at Guadalajara Mint, mint mark Ga. Varieties exist.

Date	Mintage	F	VF	XF	Unc	BU
1825Ga FS	—	150	275	475	1,000	—
1826/5Ga FS	—	125	250	450	1,000	—
1826Ga FS	—	125	250	450	1,000	—
1827/87Ga FS	—	125	250	450	1,000	—
1827Ga FS	—	125	250	450	1,000	—
1287Ga FS Error	—	8,500	9,500	—	—	—
1828Ga FS	—	200	375	550	1,200	—
1829/8Ga FS	—	200	375	550	1,200	—
1829Ga FS	—	175	325	475	950	—
1830/29Ga FS	—	100	175	300	600	—
1830Ga FS	—	100	175	300	600	—
1830Ga LP/FS	—	800	1,450	—	—	—

Note: The 1830 LP/FS is currently only known with a Philippine countermark.

Date	Mintage	F	VF	XF	Unc	BU
1831Ga LP	—	200	400	600	1,200	—
1831Ga FS/LP	—	300	500	750	1,500	—
1831Ga FS	—	125	275	400	—	—
1832/1Ga FS	—	50.00	100	175	300	—
1832/1Ga FS/LP	—	50.00	100	175	300	—
1832Ga FS/LP	—	75.00	150	285	550	—
1832Ga FS	—	25.00	50.00	100	225	—

Date	Mintage	F	VF	XF	Unc	BU
1833/2/1Ga FS/LP	—	45.00	75.00	125	250	—
1833/2Ga FS	—	25.00	50.00	100	225	—
1834/2Ga FS	—	60.00	125	200	350	—
1834/3Ga FS	—	60.00	125	200	350	—
1834/0Ga FS	—	50.00	100	150	300	—
1834Ga FS	—	50.00	100	150	300	—
1835Ga FS	—	25.00	50.00	100	225	—
1836/5Ga FS	—	175	350	—	—	—
1836/1Ga JG/FS	—	40.00	80.00	125	250	—
1836Ga FS	—	275	450	750	—	—
1836Ga JG/FS	—	25.00	50.00	100	225	—
1836Ga JG	—	25.00	50.00	100	225	—
1837/6Ga JG/FS	—	50.00	100	175	300	—
1837/6Ga JG	—	45.00	90.00	160	285	—
1837Ga JG	—	40.00	80.00	125	250	—
1838/7Ga JG	—	100	175	300	550	—
1838Ga JG	—	100	150	275	500	—
1839Ga MC	—	100	200	350	600	—
1839Ga MC/JG	—	100	200	300	550	—
1839Ga JG	—	60.00	125	200	350	—
1840/30Ga MC	—	50.00	75.00	150	275	—
1840Ga MC	—	30.00	60.00	125	250	—
1841Ga MC	—	30.00	60.00	125	250	—
1842/1Ga JG/MG	—	100	150	250	450	—
1842/1Ga JG/MC	—	100	150	250	450	—
1842Ga JG	—	25.00	50.00	100	225	—
1842Ga JG/MG	—	25.00	50.00	100	225	—
1843/2Ga MC/JG	—	25.00	50.00	100	225	—
1843Ga MC/JG	—	25.00	50.00	100	225	—
1843Ga JG	—	400	600	900	1,650	—
1843Ga MC	—	50.00	100	150	300	—
1844Ga MC	—	50.00	100	150	300	—
1845Ga MC	—	75.00	150	300	700	—
1845Ga JG	—	500	850	1,250	1,850	—
1846Ga JG	—	40.00	80.00	150	300	—
1847Ga JG	—	100	150	225	400	—
1848/7Ga JG	—	55.00	85.00	125	250	—
1848Ga JG	—	50.00	75.00	100	225	—
1849Ga JG	—	90.00	125	175	325	—
1849/39Ga JG	—	250	500	—	—	—
1850Ga JG	—	50.00	100	150	300	—
1851Ga JG	—	125	200	350	650	—
1852Ga JG	—	100	150	250	450	—
1853/2Ga JG	—	125	175	250	475	—
1853Ga JG	—	90.00	125	175	300	—
1854/3Ga JG	—	65.00	90.00	125	250	—
1854Ga JG	—	50.00	75.00	110	225	—
1855/4Ga JG	—	50.00	100	150	275	—
1855Ga JG	—	25.00	50.00	100	225	—
1856/4Ga JG	—	60.00	125	175	300	—
1856/5Ga 56	—	60.00	125	175	300	—
1856Ga JG	—	50.00	100	150	275	—
1857Ga JG	—	50.00	100	225	450	—
1858Ga JG	—	100	150	300	500	—
1859/7Ga JG	—	25.00	50.00	110	225	—
1859/8Ga JG	—	25.00	50.00	100	200	—
1859Ga JG	—	20.00	40.00	80.00	175	—
1860Ga JG Without dot	—	350	750	1,200	2,250	—
1860Ga JG Dot in loop of snake's tail, base alloy	—	2,000	3,250	4,500	—	—
1861Ga JG	—	2,200	5,750	—	—	—
1862Ga JG	—	850	1,350	2,750	4,500	—
1863/52Ga JG	—	—	—	—	—	—
1863/59Ga JG	—	45.00	50.00	85.00	145	—
1863/2Ga JG	—	30.00	50.00	90.00	175	—
1863/4Ga JG	—	40.00	75.00	150	250	—
1863Ga JG	—	25.00	45.00	75.00	150	—
1863Ga FV Rare	—	—	—	—	—	—
1867Ga JM Rare	—	—	—	—	—	—
1868/7Ga JM	—	50.00	75.00	125	200	—
1868Ga JM	—	50.00	75.00	125	200	—
1869Ga JM	—	50.00	75.00	125	200	—
1869Ga IC	—	75.00	125	200	375	—
1870/60Ga IC	—	60.00	90.00	150	275	—
1870Ga IC	—	60.00	90.00	150	275	—
1873Ga IC	—	15.00	25.00	50.00	125	—

Date	Mintage	F	VF	XF	Unc	BU
1874Ga IC	—	10.00	15.00	22.00	90.00	—
1874Ga MC	—	25.00	50.00	100	200	—
1875Ga IC	—	15.00	30.00	60.00	125	—
1875Ga MC	—	10.00	15.00	22.00	90.00	—
1876Ga IC	559,000	15.00	30.00	50.00	100	—
1876Ga MC	Inc. above	125	175	250	375	—
1877Ga IC	928,000	10.00	15.00	22.00	90.00	—
1877/6Ga JA	—	10.00	15.00	22.00	90.00	—
1877Ga JA	Inc. above	10.00	15.00	22.00	90.00	—
1878Ga JA	764,000	10.00	15.00	22.00	90.00	—
1879Ga JA	—	10.00	15.00	22.00	90.00	—
1880/70Ga FS	—	15.00	25.00	50.00	125	—
1880Ga JA	—	10.00	15.00	22.00	90.00	—
1880Ga FS	—	10.00	15.00	22.00	90.00	—
1881Ga FS	1,300,000	10.00	15.00	22.00	90.00	—
1882/1Ga FS	537,000	15.00	25.00	50.00	125	—
1882Ga FS	Inc. above	10.00	15.00	22.00	90.00	—
1882Ga TB/FS	Inc. above	50.00	100	175	300	—
1882Ga TB	Inc. above	50.00	100	175	300	—
1883Ga TB	561,000	15.00	25.00	40.00	125	—
1884Ga TB	—	10.00	12.00	20.00	85.00	—
1884Ga AH	—	10.00	12.00	20.00	85.00	—
1885Ga AH	443,000	10.00	12.00	20.00	90.00	—
1885Ga JS	Inc. above	30.00	60.00	100	200	—
1886Ga JS/H	—	10.00	12.00	20.00	85.00	—
1886Ga JS	1,038,999	10.00	12.00	20.00	85.00	—
1887Ga JS	878,000	10.00	12.00	20.00	85.00	—
1888Ga JS	1,159,000	10.00	12.00	20.00	85.00	—
1889Ga JS	1,583,000	10.00	12.00	20.00	85.00	—
1890Ga JS	1,658,000	10.00	12.00	20.00	85.00	—
1891Ga JS	1,507,000	10.00	12.00	20.00	85.00	—
1892/1Ga JS	1,627,000	15.00	25.00	50.00	125	—
1892Ga JS	Inc. above	10.00	12.00	20.00	80.00	—
1893Ga JS	1,952,000	10.00	12.00	20.00	80.00	—
1894Ga JS	2,045,999	10.00	12.00	20.00	80.00	—
1895/3Ga JS	—	12.00	20.00	35.00	100	—
1895Ga JS	1,146,000	10.00	12.00	20.00	65.00	—

8 REALES KM#377.7 **Weight:** 27.0700 g. **Composition:** 0.9030 Silver .7859 oz. ASW **Obverse:** Facing eagle **Note:** Struck at Guadalupe y Calvo Mint, mint mark GC.

Date	Mintage	F	VF	XF	Unc	BU
1844GC MP	—	350	500	1,000	2,000	—
1844GC MP Error, reversed S in Ds, Gs	—	400	600	1,200	2,250	—
1845GC MP Eagle's tail square	—	125	200	325	700	—
1845GC MP Eagle's tail round	—	175	350	650	1,200	—
1846GC MP Eagle's tail square	—	175	350	750	1,650	—
1846GC MP Eagle's tail round	—	125	200	350	750	—
1847GC MP	—	150	250	400	800	—

Date	Mintage	F	VF	XF	Unc	BU
1848GC MP	—	175	300	500	900	—
1849GC MP	—	175	300	525	1,000	—
1850GC MP	—	175	300	575	1,100	—
1851GC MP	—	300	500	900	1,600	—
1852GC MP	—	350	600	1,250	2,500	—

8 REALES KM# 377.8 **Weight:** 27.0700 g. **Composition:** 0.9030 Silver .7859 oz. ASW **Obverse:** Facing eagle **Note:** Struck at Guanajuato Mint, mint mark Go. Varieties exist.

Date	Mintage	F	VF	XF	Unc	BU
1825Go JJ	—	40.00	70.00	150	300	—
1825G JJ Error mint mark G	—	1,250	1,650	—	—	—
1826Go JJ Straight J's	—	40.00	80.00	175	350	—
1826Go JJ Full J's	—	30.00	60.00	125	250	—
1826Go MJ	—	250	450	850	—	—
1827Go MJ	—	40.00	75.00	125	250	—
1827Go MJ/JJ	—	40.00	75.00	125	250	—
1827Go MR	—	100	200	350	600	—
1828Go MJ Error mint mark Goo	—	—	—	—	—	—
1828Go MJ	—	30.00	60.00	125	250	—
1828/7Go MR	—	150	300	600	1,200	—
1828Go MR	—	150	300	600	1,200	—
1829Go MJ	—	20.00	35.00	55.00	165	—
1830Go MJ Oblong beading and narrow J	—	20.00	30.00	55.00	165	—
1830Go MJ Regular beading and wide J	—	20.00	30.00	55.00	165	—
1831Go MJ Colon after date	—	12.00	20.00	40.00	150	—
1831Go MJ 2 stars after date	—	12.00	20.00	40.00	150	—
1832Go MJ	—	12.00	20.00	40.00	150	—
1832Go MJ 1 of date over inverted 1	—	20.00	35.00	65.00	175	—
1833Go MJ/1	—	20.00	35.00	65.00	175	—
1833Go MJ	—	12.00	20.00	40.00	150	—
1833Go JM	—	400	750	1,250	2,500	—
1834Go PJ	—	12.00	20.00	40.00	150	—
1835Go PJ Star on cap	—	12.00	20.00	40.00	150	—
1835Go PJ Dot on cap	—	12.00	20.00	40.00	150	—
1836Go PJ	—	12.00	20.00	40.00	150	—
1837Go PJ	—	12.00	20.00	40.00	150	—
1838Go PJ	—	12.00	20.00	40.00	150	—
1839Go PJ/JJ	—	12.00	20.00	40.00	150	—
1839Go PJ	—	12.00	20.00	40.00	150	—
1840/30Go PJ	—	20.00	30.00	50.00	150	—
1840Go PJ	—	12.00	20.00	35.00	125	—
1841/31Go PJ	—	12.00	20.00	35.00	125	—
1841Go PJ	—	12.00	20.00	35.00	125	—
1842/1Go PM	—	20.00	30.00	50.00	125	—
1842/31Go PM/PJ	—	25.00	35.00	60.00	150	—
1842Go PJ	—	20.00	30.00	50.00	125	—
1842Go PM/PJ	—	12.00	20.00	35.00	125	—
1842Go PM	—	12.00	20.00	35.00	125	—
1843Go PM Dot after date	—	12.00	20.00	35.00	125	—

Date	Mintage	F	VF	XF	Unc	BU
1843Go PM Triangle of dots after date	—	12.00	20.00	35.00	125	—
1844Go PM	—	12.00	20.00	35.00	125	—
1845Go PM	—	12.00	20.00	35.00	125	—
1846/5Go PM Eagle type of 1845	—	20.00	30.00	50.00	150	—
1846Go PM Early type of 1847	—	15.00	25.00	40.00	135	—
1847Go PM Narrow date	—	12.00	20.00	35.00	125	—
1847Go PM Wide date	—	12.00	20.00	35.00	125	—
1848/7Go PM	—	20.00	35.00	65.00	150	—
1848Go PM	—	20.00	35.00	65.00	150	—
1848Go PF	—	12.00	20.00	35.00	125	—
1849Go PF	—	12.00	20.00	35.00	125	—
1850Go PF	—	12.00	20.00	35.00	125	—
1851/0Go PF	—	20.00	30.00	50.00	150	—
1851Go PF	—	12.00	20.00	35.00	125	—
1852/1Go PF	—	20.00	30.00	50.00	150	—
1852Go PF	—	12.00	20.00	35.00	125	—
1853/2Go PF	—	20.00	30.00	50.00	150	—
1854Go PF	—	12.00	20.00	35.00	125	—
1855Go PF Large letters	—	12.00	20.00	35.00	125	—
1855Go PF Small letters	—	12.00	20.00	35.00	125	—
1856/5Go PF	—	20.00	30.00	50.00	150	—
1856Go PF	—	12.00	20.00	35.00	125	—
1857/5Go PF	—	20.00	30.00	50.00	150	—
1857/6Go PF	—	20.00	35.00	70.00	200	—
1857Go PF	—	12.00	15.00	20.00	75.00	—
1858/7Go PI	—	12.00	20.00	35.00	125	—
1858Go PF	—	12.00	20.00	35.00	125	—
1859/7Go PF	—	12.00	20.00	35.00	125	—
1859/8Go PF	—	20.00	30.00	50.00	150	—
1859Go PF	—	12.00	20.00	35.00	125	—
1860/50Go PF	—	20.00	30.00	50.00	150	—
1860/59Go PF	—	12.00	18.00	25.00	85.00	—
1860Go PF	—	12.00	15.00	20.00	75.00	—
1861/51Go PF	—	15.00	20.00	30.00	100	—
1861/0Go PF	—	12.00	15.00	20.00	75.00	—
1861Go PF	—	12.00	15.00	20.00	75.00	—
186/52Go YE	—	—	—	—	—	—
1862Go YE/PF	—	12.00	15.00	20.00	75.00	—
1862Go YE	—	12.00	15.00	20.00	75.00	—
1862Go YF	—	12.00	15.00	20.00	75.00	—
1862Go YF/PF	—	12.00	15.00	20.00	75.00	—
1863/53Go YF	—	12.00	18.00	25.00	75.00	—
1863/54Go YF	—	15.00	20.00	30.00	100	—
1863Go YE Rare	—	—	—	—	—	—
1863Go YF	—	12.00	15.00	20.00	75.00	—
1867/57Go YF	—	15.00	20.00	30.00	100	—
1867Go YF	—	12.00	15.00	20.00	75.00	—
1868/58Go YF	—	15.00	20.00	30.00	100	—
1868/7Go YF	—	15.00	20.00	30.00	100	—
1868Go YF	—	12.00	15.00	20.00	75.00	—
1870/60Go YF	—	20.00	30.00	50.00	150	—
1870Go YF	—	1,800	3,000	5,000	7,500	—
1870Go FR/YF	—	20.00	35.00	70.00	200	—
1870Go FR	—	12.00	15.00	20.00	75.00	—
1873Go FR	—	12.00	15.00	20.00	75.00	—
1874/3Go FR	—	15.00	20.00	30.00	85.00	—
1874Go FR	—	15.00	25.00	35.00	100	—
1875/3Go FR	—	15.00	20.00	30.00	85.00	—
1875/6Go FR	—	15.00	20.00	30.00	85.00	—
1875Go FR Small circle with dot on eagle	—	12.00	15.00	20.00	75.00	—
1876/5Go FR	—	15.00	20.00	30.00	85.00	—
1876Go FR	—	12.00	15.00	20.00	60.00	—
1877Go FR	2,477,000	12.00	15.00	20.00	60.00	—
1878/7Go FR	2,273,000	15.00	20.00	30.00	75.00	—
1878/7Go SM	—	15.00	20.00	30.00	75.00	—
1878Go FR	Inc. above	12.00	15.00	20.00	65.00	—
1878Go SM, S/F	—	15.00	20.00	25.00	70.00	—
1878Go SM	—	12.00	15.00	20.00	65.00	—
1879/7Go SM	—	15.00	20.00	30.00	75.00	—
1879/8Go SM	—	15.00	20.00	30.00	75.00	—

Date	Mintage	F	VF	XF	Unc	BU
1879/8Go SM/FR	—	15.00	20.00	30.00	75.00	—
1879Go SM	—	12.00	15.00	20.00	65.00	—
1879Go SM/FR	—	15.00	20.00	30.00	75.00	—
1880/70Go SB	—	15.00	20.00	30.00	75.00	—
1880Go SB/SM	—	12.00	15.00	20.00	65.00	—
1880Go SB	—	12.00	15.00	20.00	65.00	—
1881/71Go SB	3,974,000	15.00	20.00	30.00	75.00	—
1881/0Go SB	Inc. above	15.00	20.00	30.00	75.00	—
1881Go SB	Inc. above	12.00	15.00	20.00	65.00	—
1882Go SB	2,015,000	12.00	15.00	20.00	75.00	—
1883Go SB	2,100,000	35.00	75.00	125	250	—
1883Go BR	Inc. above	12.00	15.00	20.00	65.00	—
1883Go BR/SR	—	12.00	15.00	20.00	65.00	—
1883Go BR/SB	Inc. above	12.00	15.00	20.00	65.00	—
1884/73Go BR	—	20.00	30.00	40.00	100	—
1884/74Go BR	—	20.00	30.00	40.00	100	—
1884/3Go BR	—	20.00	30.00	60.00	150	—
1884Go BR	—	12.00	15.00	20.00	65.00	—
1884/74Go RR	—	50.00	100	175	350	—
1884Go RR	—	25.00	50.00	100	250	—
1885/75Go RR	2,363,000	15.00	20.00	30.00	75.00	—
1885Go RR	Inc. above	12.00	15.00	20.00	65.00	—
1886/75Go RR	4,127,000	15.00	20.00	25.00	70.00	—
1886/76Go RR	Inc. above	12.00	15.00	20.00	65.00	—
1886/5Go RR/BR	Inc. above	12.00	15.00	20.00	65.00	—
1886Go RR	Inc. above	12.00	15.00	20.00	65.00	—
1887Go RR	4,205,000	10.00	15.00	20.00	65.00	—
1888Go RR	3,985,000	10.00	15.00	20.00	65.00	—
1889Go RR	3,646,000	10.00	15.00	20.00	65.00	—
1890Go RR	3,615,000	10.00	15.00	20.00	65.00	—
1891Go RS/R	—	10.00	15.00	20.00	65.00	—
1891Go RS	3,197,000	10.00	15.00	20.00	65.00	—
1892/0Go RS	—	10.00	15.00	20.00	65.00	—
1892Go RS	3,672,000	10.00	15.00	20.00	65.00	—
1893Go RS	3,854,000	10.00	15.00	20.00	65.00	—
1894Go RS	4,127,000	10.00	15.00	20.00	65.00	—
1895/1Go RS	3,768,000	15.00	20.00	25.00	75.00	—
1895/3Go RS	Inc. above	15.00	20.00	25.00	75.00	—
1895Go RS	Inc. above	10.00	15.00	20.00	65.00	—
1896/1Go/As RS/ML	5,229,000	15.00	20.00	25.00	75.00	—
1896/1Go RS	Inc. above	12.00	15.00	20.00	65.00	—
1896Go/Ga RS	Inc. above	—	—	—	—	—
1896Go RS	Inc. above	10.00	12.00	18.00	60.00	—
1897Go RS	4,344,000	10.00	12.00	18.00	60.00	—

8 REALES   KM# 377.9   Weight: 27.0700 g.
Composition: 0.9030 Silver .7859 oz. ASW **Obverse:**
Facing eagle **Note:** Struck at Hermosillo Mint, mint mark Ho.
Varieties exist.

Date	Mintage	F	VF	XF	Unc	BU
1835Ho PP Rare	—	—	—	—	—	—
1836Ho PP Rare	—	—	—	—	—	—
1839Ho PR Unique	—	—	—	—	—	—
1861Ho FM Reeded edge	—	4,500	7,500	—	—	—
1862Ho FM Plain edge, snakes tail left, long ray over *8R; Rare	—	—	—	—	—	—
1862Ho FM Plain edge, snake's tail left	—	1,550	2,700	—	—	—

Date	Mintage	F	VF	XF	Unc	BU
1862Ho FM						
Reeded edge, snakes tail right	—	1,650	2,750	—	—	—
1863Ho FM	—	150	300	800	—	—
1864Ho FM	—	850	1,650	2,750	—	—
1864Ho PR/FM	—	1,200	2,200			—
1864Ho PR	—	650	1,250	2,150	3,350	—
1865Ho FM	—	250	500	950	1,850	—
1866Ho FM	—	1,150	2,150	3,500	5,500	—
1866Ho MP	—	950	1,750	3,000	4,650	—
1867Ho PR	—	100	175	275	500	—
1868Ho PR	—	20.00	35.00	65.00	175	—
1869Ho PR	—	40.00	60.00	125	250	—
1870Ho PR	—	100	175	275	550	—
1871/0Ho PR	—	50.00	75.00	125	250	—
1871Ho PR	—	30.00	50.00	90.00	200	—
1872/1Ho PR	—	35.00	60.00	90.00	200	—
1872Ho PR	—	30.00	50.00	75.00	175	—
1873Ho PR	351,000	30.00	50.00	85.00	150	—
1874Ho PR	—	15.00	20.00	40.00	125	—
1875Ho PR	—	15.00	20.00	40.00	125	—
1876Ho AF	—	15.00	20.00	40.00	125	—
1877Ho AF	410,000	20.00	30.00	50.00	150	—
1877Ho GR	Inc. above	100	150	225	400	—
1877Ho JA	Inc. above	25.00	50.00	85.00	175	—
1878Ho JA	451,000	15.00	20.00	40.00	120	—
1879Ho JA	—	15.00	20.00	40.00	120	—
1880Ho JA	—	15.00	20.00	40.00	120	—
1881Ho JA	586,000	15.00	20.00	40.00	120	—
1882Ho JA O above H	240,000	25.00	40.00	65.00	125	—
1882Ho JA O after H	Inc. above	25.00	40.00	65.00	125	—
1883/2Ho JA	204,000	200	350	500	1,000	—
1883/2Ho FM/JA	Inc. above	25.00	40.00	75.00	150	—
1883Ho FM/JA	—	27.00	45.00	85.00	165	—
1883Ho FM	Inc. above	20.00	30.00	60.00	125	—
1883Ho JA	Inc. above	275	450	800	1,500	—
1884/3Ho FM	—	20.00	25.00	50.00	125	—
1884Ho FM	—	15.00	20.00	40.00	120	—
1885Ho FM	132,000	15.00	20.00	40.00	120	—
1886Ho FM	225,000	20.00	30.00	45.00	125	—
1886Ho FG	Inc. above	20.00	30.00	45.00	125	—
1887/6Ho FG	—	20.00	35.00	65.00	150	—
1887Ho FG	150,000	20.00	35.00	65.00	150	—
1888Ho FG	364,000	12.00	18.00	25.00	100	—
1889Ho FG	490,000	12.00	18.00	25.00	100	—
1890Ho FG	565,000	12.00	18.00	25.00	100	—
1891Ho FG	738,000	12.00	18.00	25.00	100	—
1892Ho FG	643,000	12.00	18.00	25.00	100	—
1893Ho FG	518,000	12.00	18.00	25.00	100	—
1894Ho FG	504,000	12.00	18.00	25.00	100	—
1895Ho FG	320,000	12.00	18.00	25.00	100	—

8 REALES   KM# 377.10   Weight: 27.0700 g.
Composition: 0.9030 Silver .7859 oz. ASW **Obverse:**
Facing eagle **Note:** Struck at Mexico City Mint, mint mark
Mo. Varieties exist. 1874 CP is a die struck counterfeit.

Date	Mintage	F	VF	XF	Unc	BU
1824Mo JM Round tail	—	75.00	125	250	500	—
1824Mo JM Square tail	—	75.00	125	250	500	—

Date	Mintage	F	VF	XF	Unc	BU
1825Mo JM	—	25.00	40.00	75.00	200	—
1826/5Mo JM	—	25.00	40.00	75.00	200	—
1826Mo JM	—	20.00	30.00	55.00	165	—
1827Mo JM Medal alignment	—	25.00	35.00	60.00	175	—
1827Mo JM Coin alignment	—	25.00	35.00	60.00	175	—
1828Mo JM	—	30.00	60.00	100	250	—
1829Mo JM	—	20.00	30.00	90.00	220	—
1830/20Mo JM	—	35.00	5.00	150	300	—
1830Mo JM	—	30.00	50.00	90.00	220	—
1831Mo JM	—	30.00	50.00	100	240	—
1832/1Mo JM	—	25.00	40.00	65.00	180	—
1832Mo JM	—	20.00	30.00	55.00	165	—
1833Mo MJ	—	25.00	40.00	80.00	200	—
1833Mo ML	—	450	650	950	2,000	—
1834/3Mo ML	—	25.00	35.00	60.00	175	—
1834Mo ML	—	20.00	30.00	55.00	165	—
1835Mo ML Narrow date	—	20.00	30.00	55.00	165	—
1835Mo ML Wide date	—	20.00	30.00	55.00	165	—
1836Mo ML	—	50.00	100	150	325	—
1836Mo ML/MF	—	50.00	100	150	325	—
1836Mo MF	—	30.00	50.00	90.00	220	—
1836Mo MF/ML	—	35.00	60.00	100	240	—
1837/6Mo ML	—	30.00	50.00	80.00	200	—
1837/6Mo MM	—	30.00	50.00	80.00	200	—
1837/6Mo MM/ML	—	30.00	50.00	80.00	200	—
1837/6Mo MM/MF	—	30.00	50.00	80.00	200	—
1837Mo ML	—	30.00	50.00	80.00	200	—
1837Mo MM	—	75.00	125	175	325	—
1838Mo MM	—	30.00	50.00	80.00	200	—
1838Mo ML	—	20.00	35.00	60.00	180	—
1838Mo ML/MM	—	20.00	35.00	60.00	180	—
1839Mo ML Narow date	—	15.00	25.00	50.00	165	—
1839Mo ML Wide date	—	15.00	25.00	50.00	165	—
1840Mo ML	—	15.00	25.00	50.00	165	—
1841Mo ML	—	15.00	25.00	45.00	150	—
1842Mo ML	—	15.00	25.00	45.00	150	—
1842Mo MM	—	15.00	25.00	45.00	150	—
1843Mo MM	—	15.00	25.00	45.00	150	—
1844Mo MF/MM	—	—	—	—	—	—
1844Mo MF	—	15.00	25.00	45.00	150	—
1845/4Mo MF	—	15.00	25.00	45.00	150	—
1845Mo MF	—	15.00	25.00	45.00	150	—
1846/5Mo MF	—	15.00	25.00	50.00	165	—
1846Mo MF	—	15.00	25.00	50.00	165	—
1847/6Mo MF	—	2,000	3,550	—		—
1847Mo MF	—	1,650	3,000	5,000	7,500	—
1847Mo RC	—	20.00	30.00	55.00	165	—
1847Mo RC/MF	—	15.00	25.00	45.00	150	—
1848Mo GC	—	15.00	25.00	45.00	150	—
1849/8Mo GC	—	20.00	35.00	60.00	180	—
1849Mo GC	—	15.00	25.00	45.00	150	—
1850/40Mo GC	—	25.00	50.00	100	240	—
1850/49Mo GC	—	25.00	50.00	100	240	—
1850Mo GC	—	20.00	40.00	75.00	200	—
1851Mo GC	—	20.00	40.00	60.00	175	—
1852Mo GC	—	20.00	40.00	75.00	200	—
1853Mo GC	—	15.00	25.00	50.00	160	—
1854Mo GC	—	12.00	15.00	30.00	125	—
1855Mo GC	—	20.00	35.00	65.00	180	—
1855Mo GF	—	12.00	15.00	30.00	125	—
1855Mo GF/GC	—	12.00	15.00	30.00	125	—
1856/4Mo GF	—	15.00	25.00	45.00	145	—
1856/5Mo GF	—	15.00	25.00	45.00	145	—
1856Mo GF	—	12.00	15.00	30.00	125	—
1857Mo GF	—	10.00	15.00	30.00	125	—
1858/7Mo FH/GF	—	10.00	15.00	30.00	125	—
1858Mo FH Narrow date	—	10.00	15.00	30.00	125	—
1858Mo FH Wide date	—	10.00	15.00	30.00	125	—
1859Mo FH	—	10.00	15.00	30.00	125	—
1859/8Mo FH	—	25.00	50.00	100	240	—
1860/59Mo FH	—	15.00	20.00	30.00	125	—

Date	Mintage	F	VF	XF	Unc	BU
1860Mo FH	—	10.00	15.00	30.00	125	—
1860Mo TH	—	12.00	18.00	40.00	145	—
1861Mo TH	—	12.00	18.00	40.00	145	—
1861Mo CH	—	10.00	15.00	20.00	75.00	—
1862Mo CH	—	10.00	15.00	20.00	75.00	—
1863Mo CH	—	10.00	15.00	20.00	75.00	—
1863Mo CH/TH	—	10.00	15.00	20.00	75.00	—
1863Mo TH	—	10.00	15.00	20.00	75.00	—
1867Mo CH	—	10.00	15.00	20.00	65.00	—
1867Mo CH/TH	—	20.00	45.00	70.00	185	—
1868Mo PH	—	10.00	15.00	20.00	65.00	—
1868Mo CH	—	10.00	15.00	20.00	65.00	—
1868Mo CH/PH	—	10.00	15.00	20.00	65.00	—
1868Mo PH Narrow date	—	10.00	15.00	20.00	65.00	—
1868Mo PH Wide date	—	10.00	15.00	20.00	65.00	—
1869Mo CH	—	10.00	15.00	20.00	65.00	—
1873Mo MH	—	10.00	15.00	20.00	65.00	—
1873Mo MH/HH	—	12.00	18.00	25.00	75.00	—
1874/69Mo MH	—	20.00	45.00	70.00	185	—
1874Mo MH	—	12.00	18.00	25.00	75.00	—
1874Mo BH/MH	—	12.00	18.00	25.00	75.00	—
1874Mo BH	—	12.00	18.00	25.00	85.00	—
1875Mo BH	—	10.00	15.00	20.00	65.00	—
1876/4Mo BH	—	12.00	18.00	25.00	75.00	—
1876/5Mo BH	—	12.00	18.00	25.00	75.00	—
1876Mo BH	—	10.00	15.00	20.00	65.00	—
1877Mo MH	898,000	10.00	15.00	20.00	65.00	—
1877Mo MH/BH	Inc. above	12.00	18.00	25.00	75.00	—
1878Mo MH	2,154,000	10.00	15.00	20.00	65.00	—
1879/8Mo MH	—	10.00	15.00	20.00	75.00	—
1879Mo MH	—	10.00	15.00	20.00	65.00	—
1880/79Mo MH	—	15.00	20.00	30.00	75.00	—
1880Mo MH	—	10.00	15.00	20.00	75.00	—
1881Mo MH	5,712,000	10.00	15.00	20.00	65.00	—
1882/1Mo MH	2,746,000	12.00	15.00	20.00	75.00	—
1882Mo MH	Inc. above	10.00	15.00	20.00	65.00	—
1883/2Mo MH	2,726,000	12.00	18.00	25.00	85.00	—
1883Mo MH Narrow date	Inc. above	10.00	15.00	20.00	65.00	—
1883Mo MH Wide date	—	10.00	15.00	20.00	65.00	—
1884/3Mo MH	—	15.00	20.00	30.00	75.00	—
1884Mo MH	—	10.00	15.00	20.00	65.00	—
1885Mo MH	3,649,000	10.00	15.00	20.00	65.00	—
1886Mo MH	7,558,000	10.00	12.00	18.00	60.00	—
1887Mo MH	7,681,000	10.00	12.00	18.00	60.00	—
1888Mo MH Narrow date	7,179,000	10.00	12.00	18.00	60.00	—
1888Mo MH Wide date	—	10.00	12.00	18.00	60.00	—
1889Mo MH	7,332,000	10.00	15.00	20.00	65.00	—
1890Mo MH Narrow date	7,412,000	10.00	12.00	18.00	60.00	—
1890Mo AM Wide date	—	10.00	12.00	18.00	60.00	—
1890Mo AM	Inc. above	10.00	12.00	18.00	60.00	—
1891Mo AM	8,076,000	10.00	12.00	18.00	60.00	—
1892Mo AM	9,392,000	10.00	12.00	18.00	60.00	—
1893Mo AM	10,773,000	10.00	12.00	18.00	55.00	—
1894Mo AM	12,394,000	10.00	12.00	18.00	45.00	—
1895Mo AM	10,474,000	10.00	12.00	18.00	45.00	—
1895Mo AB	Inc. above	10.00	12.00	18.00	60.00	—
1896Mo AB	9,327,000	10.00	12.00	18.00	60.00	—
1896Mo AM	Inc. above	10.00	12.00	18.00	60.00	—
1897Mo AM	8,621,000	10.00	12.00	18.00	60.00	—

8 REALES   KM# 377.11   Weight: 27.0700 g.
Composition: 0.9030 Silver .7859 oz. ASW **Obverse:**
Facing eagle **Note:** Struck at Oaxaca Mint, mint mark O, Oa.
Varieties exist.

Date	Mintage	F	VF	XF	Unc	BU
1858O AE	—	2,500	4,000	—	—	—
1858 Oa AE Unique	—	—	—	—	—	—
1859 AE A in O of mint mark	—	500	900	1,750	—	—
1860 AE A in O of mint mark	—	200	450	800	—	—
1861O FR	—	125	250	550	1,350	—
1861 Oa FR	—	150	350	700	—	—
1862O FR	—	40.00	80.00	200	375	—
1862 Oa FR	—	65.00	125	250	450	—
1863O FR	—	30.00	60.00	100	250	—
1863O AE	—	30.00	60.00	100	250	—
1863 Oa AE A in O of mint mark	—	100	150	250	450	—
1863 Oa AE A above O in mint mark	—	1,000	1,750	2,750	—	—
1864 FR	—	25.00	50.00	75.00	200	—
1865 AE	—	1,850	3,000	—	—	—
1867 AE	—	40.00	80.00	150	400	—
1868 AE	—	40.00	80.00	150	400	—
1869 AE	—	30.00	60.00	100	250	—
1873 AE	—	200	300	550	1,350	—
1874 AE	142,000	15.00	30.00	50.00	200	—
1875/4 AE	131,000	25.00	50.00	75.00	200	—
1875 AE	Inc. above	15.00	30.00	40.00	135	—
1876 AE	140,000	20.00	35.00	55.00	200	—
1877 AE	139,000	20.00	30.00	50.00	200	—
1878 AE	125,000	20.00	30.00	50.00	200	—
1879 AE	153,000	20.00	30.00	50.00	200	—
1880 AE	143,000	15.00	30.00	45.00	150	—
1881 AE	134,000	20.00	35.00	60.00	150	—
1882 AE	100,000	20.00	35.00	60.00	150	—
1883 AE	122,000	15.00	30.00	45.00	150	—
1884 AE	142,000	15.00	30.00	50.00	150	—
1885 AE	158,000	15.00	25.00	40.00	135	—
1886 AE	120,000	15.00	30.00	45.00	150	—
1887/6 AE	115,000	25.00	50.00	80.00	200	—
1887 AE	Inc. above	15.00	25.00	40.00	135	—
1888 AE	145,000	15.00	25.00	40.00	135	—
1889 AE	150,000	20.00	30.00	60.00	175	—
1890 AE	181,000	20.00	30.00	60.00	175	—
1891 EN	160,000	15.00	25.00	40.00	135	—
1892 EN	120,000	15.00	25.00	40.00	135	—
1893 EN	66,000	45.00	75.00	115	300	—

8 REALES   KM# 377.12 Weight: 27.0700 g.
Composition: 0.9030 Silver .7859 oz. ASW **Obverse:**
Facing eagle **Note:** Struck at San Luis Potosi Mint, mark
mark Pi. Varieties exist.

Date	Mintage	F	VF	XF	Unc	BU
1827 Pi JS	—	3,800	—	—	—	—
1827 Pi SA	—	6,000	9,000	—	—	—
1828/7 Pi JS	—	275	425	650	1,250	—
1828 Pi JS	—	225	375	550	1,100	—
1829 Pi JS	—	35.00	65.00	125	250	—
1830 Pi JS	—	30.00	50.00	100	200	—
1831/0 Pi JS	—	35.00	75.00	200	350	—
1831 Pi JS	—	25.00	35.00	75.00	200	—
1832/22 Pi JS	—	25.00	35.00	65.00	165	—
18/032 Pi JS	—	40.00	80.00	175	300	—
1832 Pi JS	—	25.00	35.00	65.00	165	—
1833/2 Pi JS	—	30.00	45.00	80.00	250	—
1833 Pi JS Narrow date	—	20.00	30.00	50.00	150	—
1833 Pi JS Wide date	—	20.00	30.00	50.00	150	—
1834/3 Pi JS	—	35.00	65.00	125	300	—
1834 Pi JS	—	15.00	25.00	50.00	150	—
1835/4 Pi JS	—	60.00	125	250	500	—
1835 Pi JS Denomination 8R	—	20.00	30.00	65.00	175	—
1835 Pi JS Denomination 8Rs	—	15.00	25.00	50.00	150	—
1836 Pi JS	—	20.00	30.00	55.00	150	—
1837 Pi JS	—	30.00	50.00	85.00	200	—
1838 Pi JS	—	20.00	30.00	55.00	150	—
1839 Pi JS	—	20.00	40.00	70.00	150	—
1840 Pi JS	—	20.00	30.00	60.00	150	—
1841 Pi JS	—	25.00	40.00	85.00	200	—
1841iP JS Error	—	200	350	550	—	—
1842/1 Pi JS	—	40.00	65.00	125	300	—
1842/1 Pi JS/PS	—	35.00	55.00	90.00	200	—
1842 Pi JS Eagle type of 1843	—	30.00	50.00	80.00	175	—
1842 Pi PS	—	30.00	50.00	80.00	175	—
1842 Pi PS/JS Eagle type of 1841	—	30.00	50.00	80.00	175	—
1843/2 Pi PS Round top 3	—	50.00	75.00	150	300	—
1843 Pi PS Flat top 3	—	60.00	100	200	475	—
1843 Pi AM Round top 3	—	20.00	30.00	55.00	150	—
1843 Pi AM Flat top 3	—	20.00	30.00	55.00	150	—
1844 Pi AM	—	20.00	30.00	55.00	150	—
1845/4 Pi AM	—	35.00	55.00	120	250	—
1845 Pi AM	—	25.00	50.00	100	225	—
1846/5 Pi AM	—	40.00	65.00	125	300	—
1846 Pi AM	—	15.00	25.00	50.00	150	—
1847 Pi AM	—	30.00	50.00	85.00	175	—
1848/7 Pi AM	—	30.00	60.00	100	200	—
1848 Pi AM	—	30.00	50.00	85.00	175	—
1849/8 Pi PS/AM	—	950	1,750	—	—	—
1849 Pi PS	—	950	1,750	—	—	—
1849 Pi MC/PS	—	60.00	125	250	500	—
1849 Pi AM	—	1,850	3,250	5,000	—	—

Date	Mintage	F	VF	XF	Unc	BU
1849 Pi MC	—	60.00	125	250	500	—
1850 Pi MC	—	40.00	80.00	150	300	—
1851 Pi MC	—	75.00	150	275	550	—
1852 Pi MC	—	75.00	125	200	400	—
1853 Pi MC	—	150	275	400	850	—
1854 Pi MC	—	100	150	250	500	—
1855 Pi MC	—	100	150	250	500	—
1856 Pi MC	—	65.00	100	200	400	—
1857 Pi MC	—	400	700	1,250	—	—
1857 Pi PS/MC	—	150	250	450	1,000	—
1857 Pi PS	—	125	200	350	650	—
1858 Pi MC/PS	—	250	400	650	1,200	—
1858 Pi MC	—	250	400	650	1,200	—
1858 Pi PS	—	650	1,150	1,750	—	—
1859/8 Pi MC/PS	—	3,650	5,750	—	—	—
1859 Pi MC/PS	—	900	1,750	—	—	—
1859 Pi MC	—	2,000	3,500	5,000	—	—
1859 Pi PS/MC	—	800	1,500	2,500	—	—
1860 Pi FC Rare	—	—	—	—	—	—
1860 Pi FE Rare	—	—	—	—	—	—
1860 Pi MC	—	1,750	2,750	6,000	—	—
1860 Pi PS/FE	—	500	1,000	—	—	—
1860 Pi RO Rare	—	—	—	—	—	—

Note: Spink America Gerber sale 6-96 cleaned VF or better
realized $33,000

Date	Mintage	F	VF	XF	Unc	BU
1860 Pi PS	—	400	600	900	1,750	—
1861 Pi PS	—	30.00	60.00	90.00	175	—
1861 Pi RO	—	25.00	35.00	55.00	125	—
1862/1 Pi RO	—	20.00	25.00	50.00	125	—
1862 Pi RO	—	15.00	20.00	40.00	100	—
1862 Pi RO Oval O in RO	—	15.00	20.00	40.00	100	—
1862 Pi RO Round O in RO, 6 is inverted 9	—	20.00	30.00	50.00	125	—
1863/2 Pi RO	—	25.00	35.00	65.00	150	—
1863 Pi RO	—	15.00	20.00	40.00	125	—
1863 6/inverted 6	—	25.00	35.00	55.00	125	—
1863 Pi FC	—	2,750	4,750	—	—	—
1864 Pi RO Rare	—	—	—	—	—	—
1867 Pi CA	—	300	500	—	—	—
1867 Pi LR	—	250	400	650	—	—
1867 Pi PS/CA	—	850	—	—	—	—
1867 Pi PS	—	30.00	60.00	125	275	—
1868/7 Pi PS	—	30.00	60.00	125	250	—
1868 Pi PS	—	20.00	30.00	50.00	125	—
1869/8 Pi PS	—	20.00	25.00	45.00	125	—
1869 Pi PS	—	15.00	20.00	40.00	125	—
1870/69 Pi PS	—	750	1,450	3,500	—	—
1870 Pi PS	—	650	1,250	2,500	—	—
1873 Pi MH	—	18.00	25.00	45.00	150	—
1874/3 Pi MH	—	25.00	50.00	120	250	—
1874 Pi MH	—	10.00	12.00	22.00	120	—
1875 Pi MH	—	10.00	12.00	22.00	100	—
1876/5 Pi MH	—	18.00	25.00	45.00	150	—
1876 Pi MH	—	10.00	12.00	22.00	100	—
1877/6 Pi MH	—	165	325	550	—	—
1877 Pi MH	1,018,000	10.00	12.00	22.00	120	—
1878 Pi MH	1,046,000	15.00	30.00	100	225	—
1879/8 Pi MH	—	15.00	20.00	30.00	125	—
1879 Pi MH	—	10.00	12.00	22.00	100	—
1879 Pi BE	—	25.00	50.00	75.00	150	—
1879 Pi MR	—	30.00	50.00	100	200	—
1880 Pi MR	—	250	375	750	—	—
1880 Pi MH/R	—	10.00	12.00	22.00	100	—
1880 Pi MH	—	10.00	12.00	22.00	100	—
1881 Pi MH/R	—	10.00	12.00	22.00	100	—
1881 Pi MH	2,100,000	10.00	12.00	22.00	100	—
1882/1 Pi MH	1,602,000	15.00	20.00	30.00	125	—
1882 Pi MH	Inc. above	10.00	12.00	22.00	100	—
1883/2 Pi MH	—	15.00	20.00	30.00	125	—
1883 Pi MH	1,545,000	10.00	12.00	22.00	100	—
1884/3 Pi MH	—	15.00	20.00	30.00	125	—
1884 Pi MH/MM	—	12.00	15.00	22.00	90.00	—
1884 Pi MH	—	10.00	12.00	20.00	80.00	—
1885/4 Pi MH	1,736,000	15.00	20.00	30.00	125	—

Date	Mintage	F	VF	XF	Unc	BU
1885/8 Pi MH	Inc. above	15.00	20.00	30.00	125	—
1885 Pi MH	Inc. above	10.00	12.00	20.00	80.00	—
1885 Pi LC	Inc. above	12.00	18.00	25.00	100	—
1886 Pi LC	3,347,000	10.00	12.00	20.00	80.00	—
1886 Pi MR	Inc. above	10.00	12.00	20.00	80.00	—
1887 Pi MR	2,922,000	10.00	12.00	20.00	80.00	—
1888/7 Pi MR	—	15.00	20.00	30.00	125	—
1888 Pi MR	2,438,000	10.00	12.00	20.00	70.00	—
1889 Pi MR	2,103,000	10.00	12.00	20.00	80.00	—
1890 Pi MR	1,562,000	10.00	12.00	20.00	70.00	—
1891 Pi MR	1,184,000	10.00	12.00	20.00	70.00	—
1892 Pi MR	1,336,000	10.00	12.00	20.00	70.00	—
1893 Pi MR	530,000	10.00	12.00	20.00	80.00	—

8 REALES   KM# 377.13   Weight: 27.0700 g.
Composition: 0.9030 Silver .7859 oz. ASW **Obverse:**
Facing eagle **Note:** Struck at Zacatecas Mint, mint mark Zs.
Varieties exist.

Date	Mintage	F	VF	XF	Unc	BU
1825Zs AZ	—	25.00	35.00	65.00	175	—
1826/5Zs AZ	—	25.00	45.00	85.00	200	—
1826Zs AZ	—	100	200	400	800	—
1826Zs AV	—	175	350	600	1,500	—
1826/5Zs AO/AZ	—	300	600	1,000	2,000	—
1826Zs AO	—	200	350	750	2,000	—
1827Zs AO/AZ	—	35.00	50.00	125	250	—
1827Zs AO	—	25.00	45.00	85.00	200	—
1828Zs AO	—	15.00	20.00	45.00	165	—
1829Zs AO	—	15.00	20.00	45.00	165	—
1829Zs OV	—	50.00	90.00	150	300	—
1830Zs OV	—	15.00	20.00	45.00	165	—
1831Zs OV	—	25.00	50.00	90.00	200	—
1831Zs OM	—	15.00	25.00	55.00	165	—
1832/1Zs OM	—	20.00	25.00	45.00	165	—
1832Zs OM	—	15.00	20.00	40.00	150	—
1833/2Zs OM	—	20.00	30.00	45.00	165	—
1833Zs OM/MM	—	15.00	25.00	40.00	150	—
1834Zs OM	—	15.00	20.00	35.00	150	—
1835Zs OM	—	15.00	20.00	40.00	150	—
1836/4Zs OM	—	20.00	30.00	50.00	165	—
1836/5Zs OM	—	20.00	30.00	50.00	165	—
1836Zs OM	—	15.00	20.00	35.00	150	—
1837Zs OM	—	15.00	20.00	35.00	150	—
1838/7Zs OM	—	20.00	30.00	45.00	165	—
1838Zs OM	—	15.00	20.00	35.00	150	—
1839Zs OM	—	15.00	20.00	35.00	150	—
1840Zs OM	—	15.00	20.00	35.00	150	—
1841Zs OM	—	15.00	20.00	35.00	150	—
1842Zs OM Eagle type of 1841	—	15.00	20.00	35.00	150	—
1842Zs OM Eagle type of 1843	—	15.00	20.00	35.00	150	—
1843Zs OM	—	15.00	20.00	35.00	150	—
1844Zs OM	—	15.00	20.00	35.00	150	—
1845Zs OM	—	15.00	20.00	35.00	150	—
1846Zs OM	—	15.00	20.00	35.00	150	—
1847Zs OM	—	15.00	20.00	35.00	150	—
1848/7Zs OM	—	20.00	30.00	45.00	165	—
1848Zs OM	—	15.00	20.00	35.00	150	—
1849Zs OM	—	15.00	20.00	35.00	150	—
1850Zs OM	—	15.00	20.00	35.00	150	—
1851Zs OM	—	15.00	20.00	35.00	150	—
1852Zs OM	—	15.00	20.00	35.00	150	—
1853Zs OM	—	30.00	45.00	75.00	200	—
1854/3Zs OM	—	20.00	30.00	60.00	175	—
1854Zs OM	—	15.00	25.00	45.00	165	—
1855Zs OM	—	20.00	30.00	60.00	175	—
1855Zs MO	—	30.00	60.00	90.00	200	—
1856/5Zs MO	—	20.00	30.00	45.00	165	—
1856Zs MO	—	15.00	20.00	35.00	150	—
1857/5Zs MO	—	20.00	30.00	45.00	165	—
1857Zs MO	—	15.00	20.00	35.00	150	—
1858/7Zs MO	—	15.00	20.00	35.00	150	—
1858Zs MO	—	15.00	20.00	35.00	150	—
1859/8Zs MO	—	15.00	20.00	35.00	150	—
1859Zs MO	—	15.00	20.00	35.00	150	—
1859Zs VL/MO	—	25.00	50.00	75.00	175	—
1859Zs VL	—	20.00	40.00	60.00	165	—

Date	Mintage	F	VF	XF	Unc	BU
1860/50Zs MO	—	10.00	12.00	20.00	80.00	—
1860/59Zs MO	—	10.00	12.00	20.00	80.00	—
1860Zs MO	—	10.00	12.00	20.00	80.00	—
1860Zs VL/MO	—	10.00	12.00	20.00	80.00	—
1860Zs VL	—	10.00	12.00	20.00	80.00	—
1861/0Zs VL/MO	—	10.00	12.00	20.00	80.00	—
1861Zs VL	—	10.00	12.00	20.00	80.00	—
1861/0Zs VL	—	10.00	12.00	20.00	80.00	—
1862/1Zs VL	—	15.00	20.00	35.00	100	—
1862Zs VL	—	10.00	12.00	20.00	80.00	—
1863Zs VL	—	10.00	12.00	20.00	80.00	—
1863Zs MO	—	10.00	12.00	20.00	80.00	—
1864/3Zs VL	—	15.00	20.00	35.00	100	—
1864Zs VL	—	10.00	12.00	20.00	80.00	—
1864Zs MO	—	15.00	20.00	35.00	100	—
1865/4Zs MO	—	200	450	800	1,550	—
1865Zs MO	—	150	300	600	1,250	—
1866Zs VL Contemporary counterfeit	—	—	—	—	—	—
1867Zs JS Rare	—	—	—	—	—	—
1868Zs JS	—	10.00	12.00	20.00	80.00	—
1868Zs YH	—	10.00	12.00	20.00	80.00	—
1869Zs YH	—	10.00	12.00	20.00	80.00	—
1870Zs YH Rare	—	—	—	—	—	—
1873Zs YH	—	10.00	12.00	20.00	80.00	—
1874Zs YH	—	10.00	12.00	20.00	80.00	—
1874Zs JA/YA	—	10.00	12.00	20.00	80.00	—
1874Zs JA	—	10.00	12.00	20.00	80.00	—
1875Zs JA	—	10.00	12.00	20.00	80.00	—
1876Zs JA	—	10.00	12.00	20.00	80.00	—
1876Zs JS	—	10.00	12.00	20.00	80.00	—
1877Zs JS	2,700,000	10.00	12.00	20.00	80.00	—
1878Zs JS	2,310,000	10.00	12.00	20.00	80.00	—
1879/8Zs JS	—	15.00	20.00	35.00	100	—
1879Zs JS	—	10.00	12.00	20.00	80.00	—
1880Zs JS	—	10.00	12.00	20.00	80.00	—
1881Zs JS	5,592,000	10.00	12.00	20.00	80.00	—
1882/1Zs JS	2,485,000	15.00	20.00	35.00	100	—
1882Zs JS Straight J	Inc. above	10.00	12.00	20.00	65.00	—
1882Zs JS Full J	Inc. above	10.00	12.00	20.00	65.00	—
1883/2Zs JS	2,563,000	15.00	20.00	35.00	100	—
1883Zs JS	Inc. above	10.00	12.00	20.00	80.00	—
1884Zs JS	—	10.00	12.00	20.00	80.00	—
1885Zs JS	2,252,000	10.00	12.00	20.00	65.00	—
1886/5Zs JS	5,303,000	15.00	20.00	35.00	100	—
1886/8Zs JS	Inc. above	15.00	20.00	35.00	100	—
1886Zs JS	Inc. above	10.00	12.00	20.00	65.00	—
1886Zs FZ	Inc. above	10.00	12.00	20.00	65.00	—
1887Zs FZ	4,733,000	10.00	12.00	20.00	65.00	—
1887Z FZ	Inc. above	20.00	30.00	50.00	100	—
1888/7Zs FZ	5,132,000	12.00	15.00	25.00	80.00	—
1888Zs FZ	Inc. above	10.00	12.00	20.00	65.00	—
1889Ze FZ	4,344,000	10.00	12.00	20.00	65.00	—
1890Zs FZ	3,887,000	10.00	12.00	20.00	65.00	—
1891Zs FZ	4,114,000	10.00	12.00	20.00	65.00	—
1892/1Zs FZ	4,238,000	12.00	15.00	25.00	80.00	—
1892Zs FZ Narrow date	Inc. above	10.00	12.00	20.00	65.00	—
1892Zs FZ Wide date	—	10.00	12.00	20.00	65.00	—
1893Zs FZ	3,872,000	10.00	12.00	20.00	65.00	—
1894Zs FZ	3,081,000	10.00	12.00	20.00	65.00	—
1895Zs FZ	4,718,000	10.00	12.00	20.00	65.00	—
1896Zs FZ	4,226,000	10.00	12.00	20.00	55.00	—
1897Zs FZ	4,877,000	10.00	12.00	20.00	55.00	—

1/2 ESCUDO   KM# 378   Weight: 1.6900 g. **Composition:**
0.8750 Gold .0475 oz. AGW **Obverse:** Facing eagle **Note:**
Struck at Culiacan Mint, mint mark C.

Date	Mintage	VG	F	VF	XF	Unc
1848C CE	—	35.00	50.00	75.00	150	—
1853C CE	—	35.00	50.00	75.00	150	—
1854C CE	—	35.00	50.00	75.00	150	—
1856C CE	—	50.00	100	150	250	—
1857C CE	—	35.00	50.00	75.00	150	—
1859C CE	—	35.00	50.00	75.00	150	—
1860C CE	—	35.00	50.00	75.00	150	—
1862C CE	—	35.00	50.00	75.00	125	—
1863C CE	—	35.00	50.00	75.00	125	—
1866C CE	—	35.00	50.00	75.00	125	—

Date	Mintage	VG	F	VF	XF	Unc
1867C CE	—	35.00	50.00	75.00	125	—
1870C CE	—	75.00	150	275	450	—

1/2 ESCUDO KM# 378.1 Weight: 1.6900 g.
Composition: 0.8750 Gold .0475 oz. AGW **Obverse:** Facing eagle **Note:** Struck at Durango Mint, mint mark Do.

Date	Mintage	VG	F	VF	XF	Unc
1833Do RM/RL	—	35.00	50.00	75.00	150	—
1834/1Do RM	—	35.00	50.00	75.00	150	—
1834/3Do RM	—	35.00	50.00	75.00	150	—
1835/2Do RM	—	35.00	50.00	75.00	150	—
1835/3Do RM	—	35.00	50.00	75.00	150	—
1835/4Do RM	—	35.00	50.00	75.00	150	—
1836/4Do RM	—	35.00	50.00	75.00	150	—
1837Do RM	—	35.00	50.00	75.00	150	—
1838Do RM	—	40.00	60.00	100	175	—
1843Do RM	—	40.00	60.00	100	175	—
1844/33Do RM	—	40.00	60.00	100	175	—
1844/33Do R/RL	—	65.00	125	275	450	—
1845Do CM	—	40.00	60.00	100	175	—
1846Do RM	—	40.00	60.00	100	175	—
1848Do RM	—	40.00	60.00	100	175	—
1850/33Do JMR	—	40.00	60.00	100	175	—
1851Do JMR	—	40.00	60.00	100	200	—
1852Do JMR	—	40.00	60.00	100	175	—
1853/33Do CP	—	75.00	150	300	500	—
1853Do CP	—	35.00	50.00	75.00	150	—
1854Do CP	—	35.00	50.00	75.00	150	—
1855Do CP	—	35.00	50.00	75.00	150	—
1859Do CP	—	35.00	50.00	75.00	150	—
1861Do CP	—	35.00	50.00	75.00	150	—
1862Do CP	—	35.00	50.00	75.00	150	—
1864Do LT	—	75.00	125	250	400	—

1/2 ESCUDO KM# 378.2 Weight: 1.6900 g.
Composition: 0.8750 Gold .0475 oz. AGW **Obverse:** Facing eagle **Note:** Struck at Guadalajara Mint, mint mark Ga.

Date	Mintage	VG	F	VF	XF	Unc
1825Ga FS	—	40.00	60.00	100	175	—
1829Ga FS	—	40.00	60.00	100	175	—
1831Ga FS	—	40.00	60.00	100	175	—
1834Ga FS	—	40.00	60.00	100	175	—
1835Ga FS	—	40.00	60.00	100	175	—
1837Ga JG	—	40.00	60.00	100	175	—
1838Ga JG	—	40.00	60.00	100	175	—
1839Ga JG	—	—	—	—	—	—
1842Ga JG	—	—	—	—	—	—
1847Ga JG	—	40.00	60.00	100	175	—
1850Ga JG	—	35.00	50.00	75.00	150	—
1852Ga JG	—	35.00	50.00	75.00	150	—
1859Ga JG	—	40.00	60.00	100	175	—
1861Ga JG	—	35.00	50.00	75.00	150	—

1/2 ESCUDO KM# 378.3 Weight: 1.6900 g.
Composition: 0.8750 Gold .0475 oz. AGW **Obverse:** Facing eagle **Note:** Struck at Guadalupe y Calvo Mint, mint mark GC.

Date	Mintage	VG	F	VF	XF	Unc
1846GC MP	—	50.00	75.00	100	175	—
1847GC MP	—	50.00	75.00	100	175	—
1848/7GC MP	—	50.00	75.00	100	200	—
1850GC MP	—	50.00	75.00	100	175	—
1851GC	—	50.00	75.00	100	175	—

1/2 ESCUDO KM# 378.4 Weight: 1.6900 g.
Composition: 0.8750 Gold .0475 oz. AGW **Obverse:** Facing eagle **Note:** Struck at Guanajuato Mint, mint mark Go.

Date	Mintage	VG	F	VF	XF	Unc
1845Go PM	—	30.00	40.00	65.00	125	—
1849Go PF	—	30.00	40.00	65.00	125	—
1851/41Go PF	—	30.00	40.00	65.00	125	—
1851Go PF	—	30.00	40.00	65.00	125	—
1852Go PF	—	30.00	40.00	65.00	125	—
1853Go PF	—	30.00	40.00	65.00	125	—
1855Go PF	—	30.00	50.00	80.00	150	—
1857Go PF	—	30.00	40.00	65.00	125	—

Date	Mintage	VG	F	VF	XF	Unc
1858/7Go PF	—	30.00	40.00	65.00	125	—
1859Go PF	—	30.00	40.00	65.00	125	—
1860Go PF	—	30.00	40.00	65.00	125	—
1861Go PF	—	30.00	40.00	65.00	125	—
1862/1Go YE	—	30.00	40.00	65.00	125	—
1863Go PF	—	30.00	50.00	80.00	150	—
1863Go YF	—	30.00	40.00	65.00	125	—

1/2 ESCUDO KM# 378.5 Weight: 1.6900 g.
Composition: 0.8750 Gold .0475 oz. AGW **Obverse:** Facing eagle **Note:** Struck at Mexico City Mint, mint mark Mo.

Date	Mintage	VG	F	VF	XF	Unc
1825/1Mo JM	—	50.00	75.00	125	200	—
1825/4Mo JM	—	50.00	75.00	125	200	—
1825Mo JM	—	30.00	40.00	80.00	150	—
1827/6Mo JM	—	30.00	40.00	80.00	150	—
1827Mo JM	—	30.00	40.00	80.00	150	—
1829Mo JM	—	30.00	40.00	80.00	150	—
1831/0Mo JM	—	30.00	40.00	80.00	150	—
1831Mo JM	—	30.00	40.00	60.00	125	—
1832Mo	—	30.00	40.00	60.00	125	—
1833Mo MJ Olive and oak branches reversed	—	30.00	50.00	90.00	175	—
1834Mo ML	—	30.00	40.00	60.00	125	—
1835Mo ML	—	30.00	40.00	80.00	150	—
1838Mo ML	—	30.00	50.00	90.00	175	—
1839Mo ML	—	30.00	50.00	90.00	175	—
1840Mo ML	—	30.00	40.00	60.00	125	—
1841Mo ML	—	30.00	40.00	60.00	125	—
1842Mo ML	—	30.00	40.00	80.00	150	—
1842Mo MM	—	30.00	40.00	80.00	150	—
1843Mo MM	—	30.00	40.00	60.00	125	—
1844Mo MF	—	30.00	40.00	60.00	125	—
1845Mo MF	—	30.00	40.00	60.00	125	—
1846/5Mo MF	—	30.00	40.00	60.00	125	—
1846Mo MF	—	30.00	40.00	60.00	125	—
1848Mo GC	—	30.00	40.00	60.00	125	—
1850Mo GC	—	30.00	40.00	60.00	125	—
1851Mo GC	—	30.00	40.00	60.00	125	—
1852Mo GC	—	30.00	40.00	60.00	125	—
1853Mo GC	—	30.00	40.00	60.00	125	—
1854Mo GC	—	30.00	40.00	60.00	125	—
1855Mo GF	—	30.00	40.00	60.00	125	—
1856/4Mo GF	—	30.00	40.00	60.00	125	—
1857Mo GF	—	30.00	40.00	60.00	125	—
1858/7Mo FH/GF	—	35.00	50.00	75.00	150	—
1858Mo FH	—	30.00	40.00	60.00	125	—
1859Mo FH	—	30.00	40.00	60.00	125	—
1860/59Mo FH	—	30.00	40.00	60.00	125	—
1861Mo CH/FH	—	30.00	40.00	80.00	150	—
1862Mo CH	—	30.00	40.00	60.00	125	—
1863/57Mo CH/GF	—	30.00	40.00	60.00	125	—
1868/58Mo PH	—	30.00	40.00	80.00	150	—
1869/59Mo CH	—	30.00	40.00	80.00	150	—

1/2 ESCUDO KM# 378.6 Weight: 1.6900 g.
Composition: 0.8750 Gold .0475 oz. AGW **Obverse:** Facing eagle **Note:** Struck at Zacatecas Mint, mint mark Zs.

Date	Mintage	VG	F	VF	XF	Unc
1860Zs VL	—	35.00	50.00	75.00	150	—
1862/1Zs VL	—	35.00	50.00	75.00	150	—
1862Zs VL	—	30.00	40.00	65.00	125	—

ESCUDO KM# 379 Weight: 3.3800 g. **Composition:** 0.8750 Gold .0950 oz. AGW **Obverse:** Facing eagle **Note:** Struck at Culiacan Mint, mint mark C.

Date	Mintage	VG	F	VF	XF	Unc
1846C CE	—	75.00	100	200	350	—
1847C CE	—	50.00	75.00	125	175	—
1848C CE	—	50.00	75.00	125	175	—
1849/8C CE	—	60.00	100	150	225	—
1850C CE	—	50.00	75.00	125	175	—
1851C CE	—	60.00	100	150	225	—
1853/1C CE	—	60.00	100	150	225	—
1854C CE	—	50.00	75.00	125	175	—
1856/5/4C CE	—	60.00	100	150	225	—
1856C CE	—	50.00	75.00	125	175	—
1857/1C CE	—	60.00	100	150	225	—

Date	Mintage	VG	F	VF	XF	Unc
1857C CE	—	50.00	75.00	125	175	—
1861C PV	—	50.00	75.00	125	175	—
1862C CE	—	50.00	75.00	125	175	—
1863C CE	—	50.00	75.00	125	175	—
1866C CE	—	50.00	75.00	125	175	—
1870C CE	—	50.00	75.00	125	175	—

ESCUDO KM# 379.1 Weight: 3.3800 g. **Composition:** 0.8750 Gold .0950 oz. AGW **Obverse:** Facing eagle **Note:** Struck at Durango Mint, mint mark Do.

Date	Mintage	VG	F	VF	XF	Unc
1833/2Do RM/RL	—	75.00	125	200	300	—
1834Do RM	—	60.00	100	150	200	—
1835Do RM	—	—	—	—	—	—
1836Do RM/RL	—	60.00	100	150	200	—
1838Do RM	—	60.00	100	150	200	—
1846/38Do RM	—	75.00	125	200	300	—
1850Do JMR	—	75.00	125	175	225	—
1851/31Do JMR	—	75.00	125	200	300	—
1851Do JMR	—	75.00	125	175	225	—
1853Do CP	—	75.00	125	175	225	—
1854/34Do CP	—	75.00	125	175	225	—
1854/44Do CP/RP	—	75.00	125	175	225	—
1855Do CP	—	75.00	125	175	225	—
1859Do CP	—	75.00	125	175	225	—
1861Do CP	—	75.00	125	175	225	—
1864Do LT/CP	—	75.00	125	175	225	—

ESCUDO KM# 379.2 Weight: 3.3800 g. **Composition:** 0.8750 Gold .0950 oz. AGW **Obverse:** Facing eagle **Note:** Struck at Guadalajara Mint, mint mark Ga.

Date	Mintage	VG	F	VF	XF	Unc
1825Ga FS	—	60.00	90.00	125	200	—
1826Ga FS	—	60.00	90.00	125	200	—
1829Ga FS	—	—	—	—	—	—
1831Ga FS	—	60.00	90.00	125	200	—
1834Ga FS	—	60.00	90.00	125	200	—
1835Ga JG	—	60.00	90.00	125	200	—
1842Ga JG/MC	—	60.00	90.00	125	200	—
1843Ga MC	—	60.00	90.00	125	200	—
1847Ga JG	—	60.00	90.00	125	200	—
1848/7Ga JG	—	60.00	90.00	125	200	—
1849Ga JG	—	60.00	90.00	125	200	—
1850/40Ga JG	—	65.00	125	225	325	—
1850Ga JG	—	60.00	90.00	125	200	—
1852/1Ga JG	—	60.00	90.00	125	200	—
1856Ga JG	—	60.00	90.00	125	200	—
1857Ga JG	—	60.00	90.00	125	200	—
1859/7Ga JG	—	60.00	90.00	125	200	—
1860/59Ga JG	—	65.00	100	175	275	—
1860Ga	—	60.00	90.00	125	200	—

ESCUDO KM# 379.3 Weight: 3.3800 g. **Composition:** 0.8750 Gold .0950 oz. AGW **Obverse:** Facing eagle **Note:** Struck at Guadalupe y Calvo Mint, mint mark GC.

Date	Mintage	VG	F	VF	XF	Unc
1844GC MP	—	75.00	100	175	250	—
1845GC MP	—	75.00	100	175	250	—
1846GC MP	—	75.00	100	175	250	—
1847GC MP	—	75.00	100	175	250	—
1848GC MP	—	75.00	100	175	250	—
1849GC MP	—	75.00	100	175	250	—
1850GC MP	—	75.00	100	175	250	—
1851GC MP	—	75.00	100	175	250	—

ESCUDO KM# 379.4 Weight: 3.3800 g. **Composition:** 0.8750 Gold .0950 oz. AGW **Obverse:** Facing eagle **Note:** Struck at Guanajuato Mint, mint mark Go.

Date	Mintage	VG	F	VF	XF	Unc
1845Go PM	—	60.00	75.00	125	200	—
1849Go PF	—	60.00	75.00	125	200	—
1851Go PF	—	60.00	75.00	125	200	—
1853Go PF	—	60.00	75.00	125	200	—
1860Go PF	—	75.00	125	200	300	—
1862Go PE	—	60.00	75.00	125	200	—

ESCUDO KM# 379.5 Weight: 3.3800 g. **Composition:** 0.8750 Gold .0950 oz. AGW **Obverse:** Facing eagle **Note:** Struck at Mexico City Mint, mint mark Mo.

Date	Mintage	VG	F	VF	XF	Unc
1825Mo JM	—	50.00	70.00	100	150	—
1827/6Mo JM	—	50.00	70.00	100	150	—
1827Mo JM	—	50.00	70.00	100	150	—
1830/29Mo JM	—	50.00	70.00	100	150	—
1831Mo JM	—	50.00	70.00	100	150	—
1832Mo JM	—	50.00	70.00	125	175	—
1833Mo MJ	—	50.00	70.00	100	150	—
1834Mo ML	—	50.00	70.00	125	175	—
1841Mo ML	—	50.00	70.00	125	175	—
1843Mo MM	—	50.00	70.00	100	150	—
1845Mo MF	—	50.00	70.00	100	150	—
1846/5Mo MF	—	50.00	70.00	100	150	—
1848Mo GC	—	50.00	70.00	125	175	—
1850Mo GC	—	50.00	70.00	125	175	—
1856/4Mo GF	—	50.00	70.00	100	150	—
1856/5Mo GF	—	50.00	70.00	100	150	—
1856Mo GF	—	50.00	70.00	100	150	—
1858Mo FH	—	50.00	70.00	125	175	—
1859Mo FH	—	50.00	70.00	100	150	—
1860Mo TH	—	50.00	70.00	125	175	—
1861Mo CH	—	50.00	70.00	100	150	—
1862Mo CH	—	50.00	70.00	125	175	—
1863Mo TH	—	50.00	70.00	100	150	—
1869Mo CH	—	50.00	70.00	100	150	—

ESCUDO KM# 379.6 Weight: 3.3800 g. **Composition:** 0.8750 Gold .0950 oz. AGW **Obverse:** Facing eagle **Note:** Struck at Zacatecas Mint, mint mark Zs.

Date	Mintage	VG	F	VF	XF	Unc
1853Zs OM	—	100	125	200	300	—
1860/59Zs VL V is inverted A	—	75.00	100	200	350	—
1860Zs VL	—	75.00	100	150	200	—
1862Zs VL	—	75.00	100	150	200	—

2 ESCUDOS KM# 380.3 Weight: 6.7700 g. **Composition:** 0.8750 Gold .1904 oz. AGW **Obverse:** Facing eagle **Note:** Struck at Guadalajara Mint, mint mark Ga.

Date	Mintage	VG	F	VF	XF	Unc
1835Ga FS	—	100	150	225	325	—
1836/5Ga JG	—	125	200	400	500	—
1839/5Ga JG	—	—	—	—	—	—
1839Ga JG	—	100	150	200	285	—
1840Ga MC	—	100	150	200	285	—
1841Ga MC	—	100	150	250	400	—
1847/6Ga JG	—	100	150	225	300	—
1848/7Ga JG	—	100	150	225	300	—
1850/40Ga JG	—	100	150	200	285	—
1851Ga JG	—	100	150	200	285	—
1852Ga JG	—	100	150	225	325	—
1853Ga JG	—	100	150	200	285	—
1854/2Ga JG	—	—	—	—	—	—
1858Ga JG	—	100	150	200	285	—
1859/8Ga JG	—	100	150	225	300	—
1859Ga JG	—	100	150	200	285	—
1860/50Ga JG	—	100	150	225	300	—
1860Ga JG	—	100	150	225	300	—
1861/59Ga JG	—	100	150	200	285	—
1861/0Ga JG	—	100	150	200	285	—
1863/1Ga JG	—	100	150	200	285	—
1870Ga IC	—	100	150	200	285	—

2 ESCUDOS KM# 380.4 Weight: 6.7700 g. **Composition:** 0.8750 Gold .1904 oz. AGW **Obverse:** Facing eagle **Note:** Struck at Guadalupe y Calvo Mint, mint mark GC.

Date	Mintage	VG	F	VF	XF	Unc
1844GC MP	—	150	200	275	400	—
1845GC MP	—	750	1,250	2,000	3,000	—
1846GC MP	—	750	1,250	2,000	3,000	—

Date	Mintage	VG	F	VF	XF	Unc
1847GC MP	—	125	175	350	500	—
1848GC MP	—	150	200	350	450	—
1849GC MP	—	150	200	300	400	—
1850GC MP	—	150	200	300	400	—

2 ESCUDOS   KM# 380.5 Weight: 6.7700 g.
Composition: 0.8750 Gold .1904 oz. AGW **Obverse:**
Facing eagle **Note:** Struck at Guanajuato Mint, mint mark Go.

Date	Mintage	VG	F	VF	XF	Unc
1845Go PM	—	100	150	250	400	—
1849Go PF	—	100	150	250	400	—
1853Go PF	—	100	150	250	400	—
1856Go PF	—	100	150	250	400	—
1859Go PF	—	100	150	250	400	—
1860/59Go PF	—	100	150	250	400	—
1860Go PF	—	100	150	250	400	—
1862Go YE	—	100	150	250	400	—

2 ESCUDOS   KM# 380 Weight: 6.7700 g. **Composition:**
0.8750 Gold .1904 oz. AGW **Obverse:** Facing eagle **Note:**
Struck at Culiacan Mint, mint mark C.

Date	Mintage	VG	F	VF	XF	Unc
1846C CE	—	100	150	225	325	—
1847C CE	—	100	150	225	325	—
1848C CE	—	100	150	225	325	—
1852C CE	—	100	150	225	325	—
1854C CE	—	100	175	250	375	—
1856/4C CE	—	100	175	250	375	—
1857C CE	—	100	150	225	325	—

2 ESCUDOS   KM# 380.1 Weight: 6.7700 g.
Composition: 0.8750 Gold .1904 oz. AGW **Obverse:**
Facing eagle **Note:** Struck at Durango Mint, mint mark Do.

Date	Mintage	VG	F	VF	XF	Unc
1833Do RM	—	300	450	700	1,200	—
1837/4Do RM	—	—	—	—	—	—
1837Do RM	—	—	—	—	—	—
1844Do RM	—	275	400	600	1,000	—

2 ESCUDOS   KM# 380.7 Weight: 6.7700 g.
Composition: 0.8750 Gold .1904 oz. AGW **Obverse:**
Facing eagle **Note:** Struck at Mexico City Mint, mint mark Mo.

Date	Mintage	VG	F	VF	XF	Unc
1825Mo JM	—	100	150	200	285	—
1827/6Mo JM	—	100	150	200	285	—
1827Mo JM	—	100	150	200	285	—
1830/29Mo JM	—	100	150	200	285	—
1831Mo JM	—	100	150	200	285	—
1833Mo ML	—	100	150	200	285	—
1841Mo ML	—	100	150	200	285	—
1844Mo MF	—	100	150	200	285	—
1845Mo MF	—	100	150	200	285	—
1846Mo MF	—	125	200	400	600	—
1848Mo GC	—	100	150	200	285	—
1850Mo GC	—	100	150	200	285	—
1856/5Mo GF	—	100	150	200	285	—
1856Mo GF	—	100	150	200	285	—
1858Mo FH	—	100	150	200	285	—
1859Mo FH	—	100	150	200	285	—
1861Mo TH	—	100	150	200	285	—
1861Mo CH	—	100	150	200	300	—
1862Mo CH	—	100	150	200	300	—
1863Mo TH	—	100	150	200	300	—
1868Mo PH	—	100	150	200	300	—
1869Mo CH	—	100	150	200	300	—

2 ESCUDOS   KM# 380.8 Weight: 6.7700 g.
Composition: 0.8750 Gold .1904 oz. AGW **Obverse:**
Facing eagle **Note:** Struck at Zacatecas Mint, mint mark Zs.

Date	Mintage	VG	F	VF	XF	Unc
1860Zs VL	—	150	300	600	1,200	—
1862Zs VL	—	250	500	800	1,200	—
1864Zs MO	—	150	300	600	1,200	—

2 ESCUDOS   KM# 380.2 Weight: 6.7700 g.
Composition: 0.8750 Gold .1904 oz. AGW **Obverse:**
Facing eagle **Note:** Struck at Estado de Mexico Mint, mint
mark EoMo.

Date	Mintage	VG	F	VF	XF	Unc
1828EoMo LF	—	700	1,000	1,750	2,500	—

2 ESCUDOS   KM# 380.6 Weight: 6.7700 g.
Composition: 0.8750 Gold .1904 oz. AGW **Obverse:**
Facing eagle **Note:** Struck at Hermosillo Mint, mint mark Ho.

Date	Mintage	VG	F	VF	XF	Unc
1861Ho FM	—	500	1,000	1,500	2,000	—

4 ESCUDOS   KM# 381 Weight: 13.5400 g.
Composition: 0.8750 Gold .3809 oz. AGW **Obverse:**
Facing eagle **Note:** Struck at Culiacan Mint, mint mark C.

Date	Mintage	VG	F	VF	XF	Unc
1846C CE	—	1,200	1,700	—	—	—
1847C CE	—	400	650	850	1,350	—
1848C CE	—	600	900	1,250	1,850	—

4 ESCUDOS   KM# 381.1 Weight: 13.5400 g.
Composition: 0.8750 Gold .3809 oz. AGW **Obverse:**
Facing eagle **Note:** Struck at Durango Mint, mint mark Do.

Date	Mintage	VG	F	VF	XF	Unc
1832Do RM/LR Rare	—	—	—	—	—	—
1832Do RM	—	600	900	1,250	1,850	—
1833Do RM/RL Rare	—	—	—	—	—	—
1852Do JMR Rare	—	—	—	—	—	—

4 ESCUDOS   KM# 381.3 Weight: 13.5400 g.
Composition: 0.8750 Gold .3809 oz. AGW **Obverse:** Facing
eagle **Note:** Struck at Guadalupe y Calvo Mint, mint mark GC.

Date	Mintage	VG	F	VF	XF	Unc
1844GC MP	—	400	650	850	1,350	—
1845GC MP	—	350	500	700	1,000	—
1846GC MP	—	400	650	850	1,350	—
1848GC MP	—	400	650	850	1,350	—
1850GC MP	—	500	750	1,000	1,600	—

4 ESCUDOS   KM# 381.4 Weight: 13.5400 g.
Composition: 0.8750 Gold .3809 oz. AGW **Obverse:**
Facing eagle **Note:** Struck at Guanajuato Mint, mint mark Go.

Date	Mintage	VG	F	VF	XF	Unc
1829/8Go MJ	—	200	300	450	850	—
1829Go JM	—	200	300	450	850	—
1829Go MJ	—	200	300	450	850	—
1831Go MJ	—	200	300	450	850	—
1832Go MJ	—	200	300	450	850	—
1833Go MJ	—	200	300	500	900	—
1834Go PJ	—	250	450	650	1,000	—
1835Go PJ	—	250	450	650	1,000	—
1836Go PJ	—	200	300	500	900	—
1837Go PJ	—	200	300	500	900	—
1838Go PJ	—	200	300	500	900	—
1839Go PJ	—	250	450	650	1,000	—
1840Go PJ	—	200	300	500	900	—
1841Go PJ	—	250	450	650	1,000	—
1845Go PM	—	200	300	500	900	—
1847/5Go YE	—	250	450	650	1,000	—
1847Go PM	—	250	450	650	1,000	—
1849Go PF	—	250	450	650	1,000	—
1851Go PF	—	250	450	650	1,000	—
1852Go PF	—	200	300	500	900	—
1855Go PF	—	200	300	500	900	—
1857/5Go PF	—	200	300	500	900	—
1858/7Go PF	—	200	300	500	900	—
1858Go PF	—	200	300	500	900	—
1859/7Go PF	—	250	450	650	1,000	—
1860Go PF	—	275	475	750	1,200	—
1862Go YE	—	200	300	500	900	—
1863Go YF	—	200	300	500	900	—

4 ESCUDOS KM# 381.6 Weight: 13.5400 g.
Composition: 0.8750 Gold .3809 oz. AGW **Obverse:**
Facing eagle **Note:** Struck at Mexico City Mint, mint mark Mo.

Date	Mintage	VG	F	VF	XF	Unc
1825Mo JM	—	200	300	525	950	—
1827/6Mo JM	—	200	300	500	900	—
1829Mo JM	—	200	350	650	1,000	—
1831Mo JM	—	200	350	650	1,000	—
1832Mo JM	—	275	475	750	1,200	—
1844Mo MF	—	200	350	650	1,000	—
1850Mo GC	—	200	350	650	1,000	—
1856Mo GF	—	200	300	500	900	—
1857/6Mo GF	—	200	300	500	900	—
1857Mo GF	—	200	300	500	900	—
1858Mo FH	—	200	350	650	1,000	—
1859/8Mo FH	—	200	350	650	1,000	—
1861Mo CH	—	400	800	1,200	1,750	—
1863Mo CH	—	200	350	650	1,000	—
1868Mo PH	—	200	300	500	900	—
1869Mo CH	—	200	300	500	900	—

4 ESCUDOS KM# 381.8 Weight: 13.5400 g.
Composition: 0.8750 Gold .3809 oz. AGW **Obverse:**
Facing eagle **Note:** Struck at Zacatecas Mint, mint mark Zs.

Date	Mintage	VG	F	VF	XF	Unc
1860 VL Rare	—	—	—	—	—	—
1862Zs VL	—	750	1,250	2,250	3,750	—

4 ESCUDOS KM# 381.2 Weight: 13.5400 g.
Composition: 0.8750 Gold .3809 oz. AGW **Obverse:**
Facing eagle **Note:** Struck at Guadalajara Mint, mint mark Ga.

Date	Mintage	VG	F	VF	XF	Unc
1844Ga MC	—	500	750	1,000	1,600	—
1844Ga JG	—	400	650	850	1,350	—

4 ESCUDOS KM# 381.5 Weight: 13.5400 g.
Composition: 0.8750 Gold .3809 oz. AGW **Obverse:**
Facing eagle **Note:** Struck at Hermosillo Mint, mint mark Ho.

Date	Mintage	VG	F	VF	XF	Unc
1861Ho FM	—	1,000	1,500	2,500	3,750	—

4 ESCUDOS KM# 381.7 Weight: 13.5400 g.
Composition: 0.8750 Gold .3809 oz. AGW **Obverse:**
Facing eagle **Note:** Struck at Oaxaca Mint, mint mark O, Oa.

Date	Mintage	VG	F	VF	XF	Unc
1861 FR	—	1,500	2,500	4,000	6,500	—

8 ESCUDOS KM# 383 Weight: 27.0700 g.
Composition: 0.8750 Gold .7616 oz. AGW **Obverse:**
Facing eagle **Note:** Struck at Alamos Mint, mint mark A.

Date	Mintage	F	VF	XF	Unc	BU
1864A PG	—	650	1,250	2,250	—	—
1866A DL	—	—	—	7,500	—	—
1868/7A DL	—	1,500	2,250	3,250	—	—
1869A DL	—	650	1,250	2,250	—	—
1870A DL	—	1,500	2,250	3,250	—	—
1872A AM Rare	—	—	—	—	—	—

8 ESCUDOS KM# 383.1 Weight: 27.0700 g.
Composition: 0.8750 Gold .7616 oz. AGW **Obverse:**
Facing eagle **Note:** Struck at Chihuahua Mint, mint mark Ca.

Date	Mintage	F	VF	XF	Unc	BU
1841 Ca RG	—	400	750	1,250	1,750	—
1842 Ca RG	—	350	500	1,000	1,500	—
1843 Ca RG	—	350	500	1,000	1,500	—
1844 Ca RG	—	350	500	1,000	1,500	—
1845 Ca RG	—	350	500	1,000	1,500	—
1846 Ca RG	—	500	1,250	1,500	2,000	—
1847 Ca RG	—	1,000	2,500	—	—	—

Date	Mintage	F	VF	XF	Unc	BU
1848 Ca RG	—	350	500	1,000	1,500	—
1849 Ca RG	—	350	500	1,000	1,500	—
1850/40 Ca RG	—	350	500	1,000	1,500	—
1851/41 Ca RG	—	50.00	500	1,000	1,500	—
1852/42 Ca RG	—	350	500	1,000	1,500	—
1853/43 Ca RG	—	350	500	1,000	1,500	—
1854/44 Ca RG	—	350	500	1,000	1,500	—
1855/43 Ca RG	—	350	500	1,000	1,500	—
1856/46 Ca RG	—	400	650	1,250	1,750	—
1857 Ca JC/RG	—	325	475	750	1,250	—
1858 Ca JC	—	325	475	750	1,250	—
1858 Ca BA/RG	—	325	475	750	1,250	—
1859 Ca JC/RG	—	325	475	750	1,250	—
1860 Ca JC/RG	—	350	500	1,000	1,500	—
1861 Ca JC	—	350	475	750	1,250	—
1862 Ca JC	—	350	475	750	1,250	—
1863 Ca JC	—	500	1,000	1,750	2,250	—
1864 Ca JC	—	400	750	1,250	1,750	—
1865 Ca JC	—	750	1,500	2,500	3,500	—
1866 Ca JC	—	350	500	1,000	1,500	—
1866 Ca FP	—	600	1,250	2,000	2,500	—
1866 Ca JG	—	350	500	1,000	1,500	—
1867 Ca JG	—	350	475	750	1,250	—
1868 Ca JG Concave wings	—	350	475	750	1,250	—
1869 Ca MM Regular eagle	—	350	475	750	1,250	—
1870/60 Ca MM	—	350	475	750	1,250	—
1871/61 Ca MM	—	350	475	750	1,250	—

8 ESCUDOS KM# 383.2 Weight: 27.0700 g.
Composition: 0.8750 Gold .7616 oz. AGW **Obverse:**
Facing eagle **Note:** Struck at Culiacan Mint, mint mark C.

Date	Mintage	F	VF	XF	Unc	BU
1846C CE	—	350	500	1,000	1,750	—
1847C CE	—	350	500	800	1,250	—
1848C CE	—	350	500	1,000	1,750	—
1849C CE	—	325	450	700	1,250	—
1850C CE	—	325	450	700	1,250	—
1851C CE	—	350	500	800	1,250	—
1852C CE	—	350	500	800	1,250	—
1853/1C CE	—	325	450	700	1,250	—
1854C CE	—	325	450	700	1,250	—
1855/4C CE	—	350	500	1,000	1,750	—
1855C CE	—	350	500	800	1,250	—
1856C CE	—	325	450	700	1,250	—
1857C CE	—	325	450	700	1,250	—
1857C CE Without periods after C's	—	—	—	—	—	—
1858C CE	—	325	450	700	1,250	—
1859C CE	—	325	450	700	1,250	—
1860/58C CE	—	350	500	800	1,250	—
1860C CE	—	350	500	800	1,250	—
1860C PV	—	325	450	700	1,250	—
1861C PV	—	350	500	800	1,250	—
1861C CE	—	350	500	800	1,250	—
1862C CE	—	350	500	800	1,250	—
1863C CE	—	350	500	800	1,250	—
1864C CE	—	325	450	700	1,250	—
1865C CE	—	350	500	800	1,250	—
1866/5C CE	—	325	450	700	1,250	—
1866C CE	—	325	450	700	1,250	—

Date	Mintage	F	VF	XF	Unc	BU
1867C CB Error	—	325	450	700	1,250	—
1867C CE/CB	—	325	450	700	1,250	—
1868C CB Error	—	350	500	800	1,250	—
1869C CE	—	350	500	800	1,250	—
1870C CE	—	350	500	800	1,250	—

8 ESCUDOS   KM# 383.3 Weight: 27.0700 g.
Composition: 0.8750 Gold .7616 oz. AGW **Obverse:**
Facing eagle **Note:** Struck at Durango Mint, mint mark Do.

Date	Mintage	F	VF	XF	Unc	BU
1832Do RM	—	850	1,750	2,000	3,000	—
1833Do RM/RL	—	350	500	800	1,250	—
1834Do RM	—	350	500	800	1,250	—
1835Do RM	—	350	500	800	1,250	—
1836Do RM/RL	—	350	500	800	1,250	—
1836Do RM M on snake	—	350	500	800	1,250	—
1837Do RM	—	350	500	800	1,250	—
1838/6Do RM	—	350	500	800	1,250	—
1838Do RM	—	350	500	800	1,250	—
1839Do RM	—	325	450	700	1,250	—
1840/30Do RM/RL	—	400	600	1,000	1,750	—
1841/30Do RM	—	550	750	1,250	2,000	—
1841/31Do RM	—	350	500	800	1,250	—
1841/34Do RM	—	350	500	800	1,250	—
1841Do RM/RL	—	350	500	800	1,250	—
1842/32Do RM	—	350	500	800	1,250	—
1843/33Do RM	—	550	750	1,250	2,000	—
1843/1Do RM	—	350	500	800	1,250	—
1843Do RM	—	350	500	800	1,250	—
1844/34Do RM/RL	—	500	1,000	1,500	2,500	—
1844Do RM	—	450	800	1,250	2,000	—
1845/36Do RM	—	400	600	1,000	1,750	—
1845Do RM	—	400	600	1,000	1,750	—
1846Do RM	—	350	500	800	1,250	—
1847/37Do RM	—	350	500	800	1,250	—
1848/38Do CM	—	350	500	800	1,250	—
1849/39Do CM	—	350	500	800	1,250	—
1849Do JMR	—	400	750	1,250	2,000	—
1850Do JMR	—	400	750	1,250	2,000	—
1851Do JMR	—	400	750	1,250	2,000	—
1852/1Do JMR	—	450	800	1,250	2,000	—
1852Do CP	—	450	800	1,250	2,000	—
1853Do CP	—	450	800	1,250	2,000	—
1854Do CP	—	400	600	1,000	1,750	—
1855/4Do CP	—	350	500	800	1,250	—
1855Do CP	—	350	500	800	1,250	—
1856Do CP	—	400	600	1,000	1,750	—
1857Do CP French style eagle, 1832-57	—	350	500	800	1,250	—
1857Do CP Mexican style eagle	—	350	500	800	1,250	—
1858Do CP	—	350	500	800	1,250	—
1859Do CP	—	350	500	800	1,250	—
1860/59Do CP	—	450	700	1,250	2,200	—
1861/0Do CP	—	400	600	1,000	1,750	—
1862/52Do CP	—	350	500	800	1,250	—
1862/1Do CP	—	350	500	800	1,250	—
1862Do CP	—	350	500	800	1,250	—
1863/53Do CP	—	350	500	800	1,250	—

Date	Mintage	F	VF	XF	Unc	BU
1864Do LT	—	350	500	800	1,250	—
1865/4Do LT	—	500	1,000	1,650	2,750	—
1866/4Do CM	—	1,250	2,000	2,500	—	—
1866Do CM	—	400	600	1,000	1,750	—
1867/56Do CP	—	400	600	1,000	1,750	—
1867/4Do CP	—	350	500	800	1,250	—
1868/4Do CP/LT	—	—	—	—	—	—
1869Do CP	—	500	1,250	1,750	2,750	—
1870Do CP	—	400	600	1,000	1,750	—

8 ESCUDOS   KM# 383.4 Weight: 27.0700 g.
Composition: 0.8750 Gold .7616 oz. AGW **Obverse:** Facing
eagle **Note:** Struck at Estado de Mexico Mint, mint mark EoMo.

Date	Mintage	F	VF	XF	Unc	BU
1828EoMo LF	—	3,500	5,500	8,500	—	—
1829EoMo LF	—	3,500	5,500	8,500	—	—

8 ESCUDOS   KM# 383.5 Weight: 27.0700 g.
Composition: 0.8750 Gold .7616 oz. AGW **Obverse:**
Facing eagle **Note:** Struck at Guadalajara Mint, mint mark Ga.

Date	Mintage	F	VF	XF	Unc	BU
1825Ga FS	—	500	1,000	1,250	1,750	—
1826Ga FS	—	500	1,000	1,250	1,750	—
1830Ga FS	—	500	1,000	1,250	1,750	—
1836Ga FS	—	750	1,500	2,000	3,000	—
1836Ga JG	—	1,000	2,500	3,500	—	—
1837Ga JG	—	1,000	2,500	3,500	—	—
1840Ga MC	—	750	1,500	2,000	3,000	—
1841/31Ga MC	—	1,000	2,500	—	—	—
1841Ga MC	—	850	1,650	2,250	—	—
1842Ga JG	—	—	—	—	—	—
1843Ga MC	—	—	—	—	—	—
1845Ga MC	—	400	850	1,100	1,650	—
1847Ga JG	—	2,250	—	—	—	—
1849Ga JG	—	500	1,000	1,250	1,750	—
1850Ga JG	—	400	850	1,100	1,650	—
1851Ga JG	—	400	850	1,100	1,650	—
1852/1Ga JG	—	500	1,000	1,250	1,750	—
1855Ga JG	—	1,000	2,500	3,500	—	—
1856Ga JG	—	400	850	1,100	1,650	—
1857Ga JG	—	400	850	1,100	1,650	—
1861/0Ga JG	—	500	1,000	1,250	1,750	—
1861Ga JG	—	400	700	1,200	1,750	—
1863/1Ga JG	—	500	1,000	1,250	1,750	—
1866Ga JG	—	400	850	1,100	1,650	—

8 ESCUDOS   KM# 383.6 Weight: 27.0700 g.
Composition: 0.8750 Gold .7616 oz. AGW **Obverse:**
Facing eagle **Note:** Struck at Guadalupe y Calvo Mint, mint
mark GC.

Date	Mintage	F	VF	XF	Unc	BU
1844GC MP	—	550	750	1,250	2,000	—
1845GC MP Eagles' tail square	—	550	750	1,250	2,000	—
1845GC MP Eagle's tail round	—	550	750	1,250	2,000	—
1846GC MP Eagle's tail square	—	450	650	1,000	1,750	—
1846GC MP Eagle's tail round	—	450	650	1,000	1,750	—
1847GC MP	—	450	650	1,000	1,750	—
1848GC MP	—	550	750	1,250	2,000	—
1849GC MP	—	550	750	1,250	2,000	—
1850GC MP	—	450	650	1,000	1,750	—

Date	Mintage	F	VF	XF	Unc	BU
1851GC MP	—	450	650	1,000	1,750	—
1852GC MP	—	550	750	1,250	2,000	—

8 ESCUDOS KM# 383.7 Weight: 27.0700 g.
Composition: 0.8750 Gold .7616 oz. AGW Obverse:
Facing eagle **Note:** Struck at Guanajuato Mint, mint mark Go.

Date	Mintage	F	VF	XF	Unc	BU
1828Go MJ	—	700	1,750	2,250	3,000	—
1829Go MJ	—	600	1,500	2,000	2,750	—
1830Go MJ	—	350	500	750	1,000	—
1831Go MJ	—	600	1,500	2,000	2,750	—
1832Go MJ	—	500	1,250	1,750	2,500	—
1833Go MJ	—	350	500	700	1,000	—
1834Go PJ	—	350	500	700	1,000	—
1835Go PJ	—	350	500	700	1,000	—
1836Go PJ	—	400	650	900	1,250	—
1837Go PJ	—	400	650	900	1,250	—
1838/7Go PJ	—	350	500	700	1,000	—
1838Go PJ	—	350	500	800	1,200	—
1839/8Go PJ	—	350	500	700	1,000	—
1839Go PJ Regular eagle	—	350	500	800	1,200	—
1840Go PJ Concave wings	—	350	500	700	1,000	—
1841Go PJ	—	350	500	700	1,000	—
1842Go P.I	—	325	400	500	900	—
1842Go PM	—	350	500	700	1,000	—
1843Go PM Small eagle	—	350	500	700	1,000	—
1844/3Go PM	—	400	650	900	1,250	—
1844Go PM	—	350	500	700	1,000	—
1845Go PM	—	350	500	700	1,000	—
1846/5Go PM	—	350	500	800	1,200	—
1846Go PM	—	350	500	700	1,000	—
1847Go PM	—	400	650	900	1,250	—
1848/7Go PM	—	350	500	700	1,000	—
1848Go PM	—	350	500	700	1,000	—
1848Go PF	—	350	500	700	1,000	—
1849Go PF	—	325	400	500	900	—
1850Go PF	—	325	400	500	900	—
1851Go PF	—	375	500	700	1,000	—
1852Go PF	—	375	500	700	1,000	—
1853Go PF	—	325	400	500	900	—
1854Go PF Eagle of 1853	—	350	500	700	1,000	—
1854Go PF Eagle of 1855	—	350	500	700	1,000	—
1855/4Go PF	—	400	650	900	1,250	—
1855Go PF	—	350	500	700	1,000	—
1856Go PF	—	350	500	700	1,000	—
1857Go PF	—	350	500	700	1,000	—
1858Go PF	—	350	500	700	1,000	—
1859Go PF	—	325	400	500	800	—
1860/50Go PF	—	325	400	500	900	—
1860/59Go PF	—	400	650	900	1,250	—
1860Go PF	—	375	500	700	1,100	—
1861/0Go PF	—	325	400	500	800	—
1861Go PF	—	325	400	500	800	—
1862/1Go YE	—	350	500	700	1,000	—
1862Go YE	—	350	500	700	1,000	—
1862Go YF	—	—	—	—	—	—
1863/53Go YF	—	350	500	700	1,000	—
1863Go PF	—	350	500	700	1,000	—
1867/57Go YF/PF	—	350	500	700	1,000	—

Date	Mintage	F	VF	XF	Unc	BU
1867Go YF	—	350	500	700	1,000	—
1868/58Go YF	—	350	500	700	1,000	—
1870Go FR	—	325	400	500	900	—

8 ESCUDOS KM# 383.8 Weight: 27.0700 g.
Composition: 0.8750 Gold .7616 oz. AGW Obverse:
Facing eagle **Note:** Struck at Hermosillo Mint, mint mark Ho.

Date	Mintage	F	VF	XF	Unc	BU
1863Ho FM	—	400	650	1,000	2,000	—
1864Ho FM	—	600	1,250	1,750	2,750	—
1864Ho PR/FM	—	400	650	1,000	2,000	—
1865Ho FM/PR	—	500	800	1,250	2,500	—
1867/57Ho PR	—	400	650	1,000	2,000	—
1868Ho PR	—	500	800	1,250	2,500	—
1868Ho PR/FM	—	500	800	1,250	2,500	—
1869Ho PR/FM	—	400	650	1,000	2,000	—
1869Ho PR	—	400	650	1,000	2,000	—
1870Ho PR	—	400	650	1,000	2,000	—
1871/0Ho PR	—	500	800	1,250	2,500	—
1871Ho PR	—	500	800	1,250	2,500	—
1872/1Ho PR	—	600	1,250	1,750	2,750	—
1873Ho PR	—	400	650	1,000	2,000	—

8 ESCUDOS KM# 383.9 Weight: 27.0700 g.
Composition: 0.8750 Gold .7616 oz. AGW Obverse:
Facing eagle **Note:** Struck at Mexico City Mint, mint mark Mo. Formerly reported 1825/3 JM is merely a reworked 5.

Date	Mintage	F	VF	XF	Unc	BU
1824Mo JM Large book reverse	—	500	1,000	1,250	2,000	—
1825Mo JM Small book reverse	—	325	400	500	1,000	—
1826/5Mo JM	—	700	1,750	2,250	3,000	—
1827Mo JM	—	350	500	700	1,000	—
1828Mo JM	—	350	500	700	1,000	—
1829Mo JM	—	350	500	700	1,000	—
1830Mo JM	—	350	500	700	1,000	—
1831Mo JM	—	350	500	700	1,000	—
1832/1Mo JM	—	350	500	700	1,000	—
1832Mo JM	—	350	500	700	1,000	—
1833Mo MJ	—	400	750	1,000	1,500	—
1833Mo ML	—	325	400	500	900	—
1834Mo ML	—	400	750	1,000	1,500	—
1835/4Mo ML	—	500	1,000	1,250	2,000	—
1836Mo ML	—	325	400	500	900	—
1836Mo MF	—	500	700	1,200	2,000	—
1837/6Mo ML	—	325	400	500	900	—
1838Mo ML	—	325	400	500	900	—
1839Mo ML	—	325	400	500	900	—
1840Mo ML	—	325	400	500	900	—
1841Mo ML	—	325	400	500	900	—
1842/1Mo ML	—	—	—	—	—	—
1842Mo ML	—	325	400	500	900	—
1842Mo MM	—	—	—	—	—	—
1843Mo MM	—	325	400	500	900	—
1844Mo MF	—	325	400	500	900	—
1845Mo MF	—	325	400	500	900	—
1846Mo MF	—	500	1,000	1,250	2,000	—
1847Mo MF	—	950	2,250	—	—	—
1847Mo RC	—	325	500	800	1,250	—
1848Mo GC	—	325	400	500	900	—
1849Mo GC	—	325	400	500	900	—
1850Mo GC	—	325	400	500	900	—
1851Mo GC	—	325	400	500	900	—
1852Mo GC	—	325	400	500	900	—
1853Mo GC	—	325	400	500	900	—
1854/44Mo GC	—	325	400	500	900	—
1854/3Mo GC	—	325	400	500	900	—
1855Mo GF	—	325	400	500	900	—
1856/5Mo GF	—	325	400	500	900	—
1856Mo GF	—	325	400	500	900	—
1857Mo GF	—	325	400	500	900	—
1858Mo FH	—	325	400	500	900	—
1859Mo FH	—	400	750	1,000	1,500	—
1860Mo FH	—	325	400	500	900	—
1860Mo TH	—	325	400	500	900	—
1861/51Mo CH	—	325	400	500	900	—
1862Mo CH	—	325	400	500	900	—
1863/53Mo CH	—	325	400	500	900	—
1863/53Mo TH	—	325	400	500	900	—
1867Mo CH	—	325	400	500	900	—
1868Mo CH	—	325	400	500	900	—

Date	Mintage	F	VF	XF	Unc	BU
1868Mo PH	—	325	400	500	900	—
1869Mo CH	—	325	400	500	900	—

CENTAVO   KM# 384   Composition: Copper **Ruler:**
Maximilian **Note:** Struck at Mexico City Mint, mint mark M.

Date	Mintage	F	VF	XF	Unc	BU
1864M	—	40.00	75.00	225	1,100	—

8 ESCUDOS   KM# 383.10   Weight: 27.0700 g.
Composition: 0.8750 Gold .7616 oz. AGW **Obverse:**
Facing eagle **Note:** Struck at Oaxaca Mint, mint mark O.

Date	Mintage	F	VF	XF	Unc	BU
1858O AE	—	2,000	3,000	4,000	6,000	—
1859O AE	—	1,000	2,500	3,750	5,500	—
1860O AE	—	1,000	2,500	3,750	5,500	—
1861O FR	—	450	850	1,250	2,750	—
1862O FR	—	450	850	1,250	2,750	—
1863O FR	—	450	850	1,250	2,750	—
1864O FR	—	450	850	1,250	2,750	—
1867O AE	—	450	850	1,250	2,750	—
1868O AE	—	450	850	1,250	2,750	—
1869O AE	—	450	850	1,250	2,750	—

8 ESCUDOS   KM# 383.11   Weight: 27.0700 g.
Composition: 0.8750 Gold .7616 oz. AGW **Obverse:**
Facing eagle **Note:** Struck at Zacatecas Mint, mint mark Zs.

Date	Mintage	F	VF	XF	Unc	BU
1858Zs MO	—	400	750	1,000	2,000	—
1859Zs MO	—	325	400	500	900	—
1860/59Zs VL/MO	—	2,000	3,000	4,000	—	—
1860/9Zs MO	—	400	750	1,000	2,000	—
1860Zs MO	—	375	500	700	1,000	—
1861/0Zs VL	—	375	500	700	1,000	—
1861Zs VL	—	375	500	700	1,000	—
1862Zs VL	—	375	500	700	1,100	—
1863Zs VL	—	375	525	750	1,150	—
1863Zs MO	—	375	500	700	1,000	—
1864Zs MO	—	750	1,000	1,500	3,000	—
1865Zs MO	—	375	500	700	1,000	—
1865Zs MP Contemporary counterfeit	—	—	—	—	—	—
1868Zs JS	—	400	600	800	1,250	—
1868Zs YH	—	400	600	800	1,250	—
1869Zs YH	—	400	600	800	1,250	—
1870Zs YH	—	400	600	800	1,250	—
1871Zs YH	—	400	600	800	1,250	—

PATTERNS
Including off metal strikes

8 ESCUDOS   Composition: Silver

Date	Mintage	F	VF	XF	Unc	BU
1823Mo JM Rare	—	—	—	—	—	—

EMPIRE OF MAXIMILIAN

RULER
Maximilian, Emperor, 1864-1867

MINT MARKS
Refer To Republic Coinage

MONETARY SYSTEM
100 Centavos = 1 Peso (8 Reales)

MILLED COINAGE

16 Pilones = 1 Real; 8 Tlaco = 1 Real;
16 Reales = 1 Escudo

5 CENTAVOS   KM# 385   Weight: 1.3537 g.
Composition: 0.9030 Silver .0393 oz. ASW **Ruler:**
Maximilian **Note:** Struck at Guanajuato Mint, mint mark G.

Date	Mintage	F	VF	XF	Unc	BU
1864G	90,000	17.50	35.00	75.00	320	—
1865G	—	20.00	30.00	55.00	285	—
1866G	—	75.00	150	300	1,800	—

5 CENTAVOS   KM# 385.1   Weight: 1.3537 g.
Composition: 0.9030 Silver .0393 oz. ASW **Ruler:**
Maximilian **Note:** Struck at Mexico City Mint, mint mark M.

Date	Mintage	F	VF	XF	Unc	BU
1864M	—	12.50	20.00	55.00	285	—
1866/4M	—	25.00	40.00	75.00	385	—
1866M	—	20.00	35.00	65.00	375	—

5 CENTAVOS   KM# 385.2   Weight: 1.3537 g.
Composition: 0.9030 Silver .0393 oz. ASW **Ruler:**
Maximilian **Note:** Struck at San Luis Potosi Mint, mint mark P.

Date	Mintage	F	VF	XF	Unc	BU
1864P	—	100	215	950	2,300	—

5 CENTAVOS   KM# 385.3   Weight: 1.3537 g.
Composition: 0.9030 Silver .0393 oz. ASW **Ruler:**
Maximilian **Note:** Struck at Zacatecas Mint, mint mark Z.

Date	Mintage	F	VF	XF	Unc	BU
1865	—	25.00	45.00	150	425	—

10 CENTAVOS   KM# 386   Weight: 2.7073 g.
Composition: 0.9030 Silver .0786 oz. ASW **Ruler:**
Maximilian **Note:** Struck at Guanajuato Mint, mint mark G.

Date	Mintage	F	VF	XF	Unc	BU
1864G	45,000	20.00	45.00	90.00	325	—
1865G	—	30.00	60.00	110	375	—

10 CENTAVOS   KM# 386.2   Weight: 2.7073 g.
Composition: 0.9030 Silver .0786 oz. ASW **Ruler:**
Maximilian **Note:** Struck at San Luis Potosi Mint, mint mark P.

Date	Mintage	F	VF	XF	Unc	BU
1864P	—	70.00	150	300	600	—

10 CENTAVOS   KM# 386.1   Weight: 2.7073 g.
Composition: 0.9030 Silver .0786 oz. ASW **Ruler:**
Maximilian **Note:** Struck at Mexico City Mint, mint mark M.

Date	Mintage	F	VF	XF	Unc	BU
1864M	—	15.00	25.00	55.00	285	—
1866/4M	—	25.00	35.00	70.00	320	—
1866/5M	—	25.00	40.00	85.00	375	—
1866M	—	25.00	35.00	75.00	375	—

10 CENTAVOS   KM# 386.3   Weight: 2.7073 g.
Composition: 0.9030 Silver .0786 oz. ASW **Ruler:**
Maximilian **Note:** Struck at Zacatecas Mint, mint mark Z.

Date	Mintage	F	VF	XF	Unc	BU
1865Z	—	25.00	55.00	165	475	—

50 CENTAVOS   KM# 387   Weight: 13.5365 g.
Composition: 0.9030 Silver .3929 oz. ASW **Ruler:**
Maximilian **Note:** Struck at Mexico City Mint, mint mark Mo.

Date	Mintage	F	VF	XF	Unc	BU
1866Mo	31,000	40.00	95.00	200	600	—

PESO   KM# 388   Weight: 27.0700 g. **Composition:**
0.9030 Silver .7857 oz. ASW **Ruler:** Maximilian **Note:** Struck
at Guanajuato Mint, mint mark Go.

Date	Mintage	F	VF	XF	Unc	BU
1866Go	—	300	500	800	2,150	—

PESO   KM# 388.1   Weight: 27.0700 g. **Composition:**
0.9030 Silver .7857 oz. ASW **Ruler:** Maximilian **Note:** Struck
at Mexico City Mint, mint mark Mo.

Date	Mintage	F	VF	XF	Unc	BU
1866Mo	2,148,000	30.00	45.00	125	375	—
1867Mo	1,238,000	40.00	65.00	175	425	—

PESO   KM# 388.2   Weight: 27.0700 g. **Composition:**
0.9030 Silver .7857 oz. ASW **Ruler:** Maximilian **Note:** Struck
at San Luis Potosi Mint, mint mark Pi.

Date	Mintage	F	VF	XF	Unc	BU
1866 Pi	—	45.00	90.00	275	725	—

20 PESOS   KM# 389   Weight: 33.8400 g. **Composition:**
0.8750 Gold .9520 oz. AGW **Ruler:** Maximilian **Note:** Struck
at Mexico City Mint, mint mark Mo.

Date	Mintage	F	VF	XF	Unc	BU
1866Mo	8,274	500	900	1,350	2,500	—

REPUBLIC
Second

MINT MARKS
A, AS - Alamos
CE - Real de Catorce
CA,CH - Chihuahua
C, Cn, Gn(error) - Culiacan
D, Do - Durango
EoMo - Estado de Mexico
Ga - Guadalajara
GC - Guadalupe y Calvo
G, Go - Guanajuato
H, Ho - Hermosillo
M, Mo - Mexico City
O, OA - Oaxaca
SLP, PI, P, I/P - San Luis Potosi
Z, Zs – Zacatecas

ZACATECAS MINT

Initials	Years	Mint Officials
FZ	1886-1905	Francisco de P. Zarate
FM	1904-05	Francisco Mateos

DECIMAL COINAGE
100 Centavos = 1 Peso

CENTAVO   KM# 390   Composition: Copper **Obverse:**
Seated Liberty **Reverse:** Thick wreath. **Size:** 25 mm. **Note:**
Struck at Mexico City Mint, mint mark Mo.

Date	Mintage	F	VF	XF	Unc	BU
1863Mo Round top 3, reeded edge	—	15.00	30.00	75.00	500	—
1863Mo Round top 3, plain edge	—	15.00	30.00	75.00	500	—
1863Mo Flat top 3, reeded edge	—	12.00	28.00	70.00	500	—

CENTAVO   KM# 390.1   Composition: Copper **Obverse:**
Seated Liberty **Reverse:** Thin wreath **Size:** 26.5 mm. **Note:**
Struck at San Luis Potosi Mint, mint mark SLP.

Date	Mintage	F	VF	XF	Unc	BU
1863SLP	1,024,999	15.00	30.00	60.00	400	—

CENTAVO   KM# 391   Composition: Copper **Obverse:**
Standing eagle **Edge:** Reeded. **Note:** Struck at Alamos Mint,
mint mark As.

Date	Mintage	F	VF	XF	Unc	BU
1875 As Rare	—	—	—	—	—	—
1876 As	50,000	100	200	300	650	—
1880 As	—	25.00	50.00	125	400	—
1881 As	—	30.00	60.00	125	350	—

CENTAVO   KM# 391.1   Composition: Copper **Obverse:**
Standing eagle **Edge:** Plain **Note:** Struck at Culiacan Mint,
mint mark Cn.

Date	Mintage	F	VF	XF	Unc	BU
1874Cn	266,000	12.50	17.50	35.00	250	—
1875/4Cn	153,000	15.00	20.00	45.00	250	—
1875Cn	Inc. above	10.00	15.00	25.00	250	—
1876Cn	154,000	5.00	8.00	15.00	200	—
1877/6Cn	993,000	7.50	11.50	17.50	200	—
1877Cn	Inc. above	6.00	9.00	15.00	200	—
1880Cn	142,000	7.50	10.00	12.50	200	—
1881Cn	167,000	7.50	10.00	25.00	200	—
1897Cn Large N in mint mark	300,000	2.50	5.00	12.00	50.00	—
1897Cn Small N in mint mark	Inc. above	2.50	5.00	9.00	45.00	—

CENTAVO   KM# 391.2   Composition: Copper **Obverse:**
Standing eagle **Note:** Struck at Durango Mint, mint mark Do.

Date	Mintage	F	VF	XF	Unc	BU
1879Do	110,000	10.00	17.50	35.00	150	—
1880Do	69,000	40.00	90.00	175	500	—

Date	Mintage	F	VF	XF	Unc	BU
1891Do	—	8.00	11.00	30.00	150	—
1891Do/Mo	—	8.00	11.00	30.00	150	—

CENTAVO   KM# 391.3   Composition: Copper **Obverse:** Standing eagle **Note:** Struck at Guadalajara Mint, mint mark Ga.

Date	Mintage	F	VF	XF	Unc	BU
1872Ga	263,000	15.00	30.00	60.00	200	—
1873Ga	333,000	6.00	9.00	25.00	150	—
1874Ga	76,000	15.00	25.00	50.00	175	—
1875Ga	—	10.00	15.00	30.00	150	—
1876Ga	303,000	3.00	6.00	17.50	150	—
1877Ga	108,000	4.00	6.00	20.00	150	—
1878Ga	543,000	4.00	6.00	15.00	150	—
1881/71Ga	975,000	7.00	9.00	20.00	175	—
1881Ga	Inc. above	7.00	9.00	20.00	175	—
1889Ga/Mo	—	3.50	5.00	25.00	125	—
1890Ga	—	4.00	7.50	20.00	100	—

CENTAVO   KM# 391.4   Composition: Copper **Obverse:** Standing eagle **Note:** Struck at Guanajuato Mint, mint mark Go.

Date	Mintage	F	VF	XF	Unc	BU
1874Go	—	20.00	40.00	80.00	250	—
1875Go	190,000	11.50	20.00	60.00	200	—
1876Go	—	125	200	350	750	—
1877Go Rare	—	—	—	—	—	—
1878Go	576,000	8.00	11.00	30.00	175	—
1880Go	890,000	6.00	10.00	25.00	175	—

CENTAVO   KM# 391.5   Composition: Copper **Obverse:** Standing eagle **Note:** Struck at Hermosillo Mint, mint mark Ho.

Date	Mintage	F	VF	XF	Unc	BU
1875Ho	3,500	450	—	—	—	—
1876Ho	8,508	50.00	100	225	500	—
1880Ho Short H, round O	102,000	7.50	15.00	35.00	150	—
1880Ho Tall H, oval O	Inc. above	7.50	15.00	35.00	150	—
1881Ho	459,000	5.00	10.00	25.00	150	—

CENTAVO   KM# 391.6   Composition: Copper **Obverse:** Standing eagle **Note:** Struck at Mexico City Mint, mint mark Mo. Varieties exist.

Date	Mintage	F	VF	XF	Unc	BU
1869Mo	1,874,000	7.50	25.00	60.00	200	—
1870/69Mo	1,200,000	10.00	25.00	60.00	225	—
1870Mo	Inc. above	8.00	20.00	50.00	200	—
1871Mo	918,000	8.00	15.00	40.00	200	—
1872/1Mo	1,625,000	6.50	10.00	30.00	200	—
1872Mo	Inc. above	6.00	9.00	25.00	200	—
1873Mo	1,605,000	4.00	7.50	20.00	200	—
1874/3Mo	1,700,000	5.00	7.00	15.00	100	—
1874Mo	Inc. above	3.00	5.50	15.00	100	—
1874Mo	Inc. above	5.00	10.00	25.00	200	—
1875Mo	1,495,000	6.00	8.00	30.00	100	—
1876Mo	1,600,000	3.00	5.50	12.50	100	—
1877Mo	1,270,000	3.00	5.50	13.50	100	—
1878/5Mo	1,900,000	7.50	11.00	22.50	125	—
1878/6Mo	Inc. above	7.50	11.00	22.50	125	—
1878/7Mo	Inc. above	7.50	11.00	20.00	125	—
1878Mo	Inc. above	6.00	9.00	13.50	100	—
1879/8Mo	1,505,000	4.50	6.50	13.50	100	—
1879Mo	Inc. above	3.00	5.50	12.50	75.00	—
1880/70Mo	1,130,000	5.50	7.50	15.00	100	—
1880/72Mo	Inc. above	20.00	50.00	100	250	—
1880/79Mo	Inc. above	15.00	35.00	75.00	175	—
1880Mo	Inc. above	4.25	6.00	12.50	75.00	—
1881Mo	1,060,000	4.50	7.00	15.00	75.00	—
1886Mo	12,687,000	1.50	2.00	10.00	40.00	—
1887Mo	7,292,000	1.50	2.00	10.00	35.00	—
1888/78Mo	9,984,000	2.50	3.00	10.00	30.00	—
1888/7Mo	Inc. above	2.50	3.00	10.00	30.00	—

Date	Mintage	F	VF	XF	Unc	BU
1888Mo	Inc. above	1.50	2.00	10.00	30.00	—
1889Mo	19,970,000	2.00	3.00	10.00	30.00	—
1890/89Mo	18,726,000	2.50	3.00	12.00	40.00	—
1890/990Mo	Inc. above	2.50	3.00	12.00	40.00	—
1890Mo	Inc. above	1.50	2.00	10.00	30.00	—
1891Mo	14,544,000	1.50	2.00	10.00	30.00	—
1892Mo	12,908,000	1.50	2.00	10.00	30.00	—
1893/2Mo	5,078,000	2.50	3.00	12.00	35.00	—
1893Mo	Inc. above	1.50	2.00	10.00	30.00	—
1894/3Mo	1,896,000	3.00	6.00	15.00	50.00	—
1894Mo	Inc. above	2.00	3.00	12.00	35.00	—
1895/3Mo	3,453,000	3.00	4.50	12.50	35.00	—
1895/85Mo	Inc. above	3.00	6.00	15.00	50.00	—
1895Mo	Inc. above	2.00	3.00	10.00	30.00	—
1896Mo	3,075,000	2.00	3.00	10.00	30.00	—
1897Mo	4,150,000	1.50	2.00	10.00	30.00	—

CENTAVO   KM# 391.7   Composition: Copper **Obverse:** Standing eagle **Note:** Struck at Oaxaca Mint, mint mark Oa.

Date	Mintage	F	VF	XF	Unc	BU
1872 Oa	16,000	300	500	1,200	—	—
1873 Oa	11,000	350	600	—	—	—
1874 Oa	4,835	450	—	—	—	—
1875 Oa	2,860	500	—	—	—	—

CENTAVO   KM# 391.8   Composition: Copper **Obverse:** Standing eagle **Note:** Struck at San Luis Potosi Mint, mint mark Pi.

Date	Mintage	F	VF	XF	Unc	BU
1871 Pi Rare	—	—	—	—	—	—
1877 Pi	249,000	15.00	50.00	200	—	—
1878 Pi	751,000	12.50	25.00	50.00	200	—
1878 Pp error mintmark - rare	—	—	—	—	—	—
1891Pi/Mo	—	10.00	17.50	35.00	150	—
1891 Pi	—	8.00	15.00	30.00	150	—

CENTAVO   KM# 391.9   Composition: Copper **Obverse:** Standing eagle **Note:** Struck at Zacatecas Mint, mint mark Zs.

Date	Mintage	F	VF	XF	Unc	BU
1872Zs	55,000	22.50	30.00	100	300	—
1873Zs	1,460,000	4.00	8.00	25.00	150	—
1874/3Zs	685,000	5.50	11.00	30.00	250	—
1874Zs	Inc. above	4.00	8.00	25.00	200	—
1875/4Zs	200,000	8.50	17.00	45.00	250	—
1875Zs	Inc. above	7.00	14.00	35.00	200	—
1876Zs	—	5.00	10.00	25.00	200	—
1877Zs	—	50.00	125	300	750	—
1878Zs	—	4.50	9.00	25.00	200	—
1880Zs	100,000	5.00	10.00	30.00	200	—
1881Zs	1,200,000	4.25	8.00	25.00	150	—

CENTAVO   KM# 392   Composition: Copper-Nickel **Note:** Struck at Mexico City Mint, mint mark Mo.

Date	Mintage	F	VF	XF	Unc	BU
1882Mo	99,955,000	7.50	12.50	17.50	35.00	—
1883Mo	Inc. above	0.50	0.75	1.00	1.50	—

CENTAVO   KM# 393   Composition: Copper **Obverse:** Restyled eagle **Note:** Struck at Mexico City Mint, mint mark Mo. Varieties exist.

Date	Mintage	F	VF	XF	Unc	BU
1898Mo	1,529,000	4.00	6.00	15.00	50.00	—

CENTAVO KM# 394.1 Composition: Copper Note: Struck at Mexico City Mint, mint mark M, Mo. Reduced size. Varieties exist.

Date	Mintage	F	VF	XF	Unc	BU
1899	51,000	150	175	300	800	—
1900 Wide date	4,010,000	2.50	4.00	8.00	28.00	—
1900 Narrow date	Inc. above	2.50	4.00	8.00	28.00	—
1901	1,494,000	3.00	8.00	17.50	50.00	—
1901	1,494,000	3.00	8.00	17.50	50.00	—
1902/899	2,090,000	30.00	60.00	100	175	—
1902	Inc. above	2.25	4.00	10.00	40.00	—
1903	8,400,000	1.50	3.00	7.00	20.00	—
1904/3	10,250,000	1.50	10.00	20.00	55.00	—
1904	Inc. above	1.50	3.00	7.00	25.00	—
1905	3,643,000	2.25	4.00	10.00	40.00	—

CENTAVO KM# 394 Composition: Copper Note: Struck at Culiacan Mint, mint mark C, Cn. Reduced size. Varieties exist.

Date	Mintage	F	VF	XF	Unc	BU
1901	220,000	15.00	22.50	35.00	65.00	—
1902	320,000	15.00	22.50	50.00	90.00	—
1903	536,000	7.50	12.50	20.00	50.00	—
1904/3	148,000	35.00	50.00	75.00	125	—
1905	110,000	100	150	250	550	—

2 CENTAVOS KM# 395 Composition: Copper-Nickel Note: Struck at Mexico City Mint.

Date	Mintage	F	VF	XF	Unc	BU
1882	50,023,000	2.00	3.00	7.50	15.00	—
1883/2	Inc. above	2.00	3.00	7.50	15.00	—
1883	Inc. above	0.50	0.75	1.00	2.50	—

5 CENTAVOS KM# 396 Weight: 1.3530 g. Composition: 0.9030 Silver .0392 oz. ASW Obverse: Facing eagle Reverse: Deonomination in wreath Note: Struck at Chihuahua Mint, mint mark Ca.

Date	Mintage	F	VF	XF	Unc	BU
1868 Ca	—	40.00	65.00	125	450	—
1869 Ca	30,000	25.00	40.00	100	400	—
1870/69 Ca	—	35.00	55.00	120	425	—
1870 Ca	35,000	30.00	50.00	100	400	—

5 CENTAVOS KM# 396.1 Weight: 1.3530 g. Composition: 0.9030 Silver .0392 oz. ASW Obverse: Facing eagle Reverse: Deonomination in wreath Note: Struck at San Luis Potosi Mint, mint mark SLP.

Date	Mintage	F	VF	XF	Unc	BU
1863SLP	—	75.00	125	350	1,200	—

5 CENTAVOS KM# 397 Weight: 1.3530 g. Composition: 0.9030 Silver .0392 oz. ASW Obverse: Facing eagle Reverse: Cap and rays Note: Struck at Mexico City Mint, mint mark Mo. Varieties exist.

Date	Mintage	F	VF	XF	Unc	BU
1867/3Mo	—	25.00	50.00	125	425	—
1867Mo	—	20.00	40.00	100	400	—
1868/7Mo	—	25.00	50.00	150	500	—
1868Mo	—	20.00	40.00	100	400	—

5 CENTAVOS KM# 397.1 Weight: 1.3530 g. Composition: 0.9030 Silver .0392 oz. ASW Obverse: Facing eagle Reverse: Cap and rays Note: Struck at San Luis Potosi Mint, mint mark P.

Date	Mintage	F	VF	XF	Unc	BU
1868/7P	34,000	25.00	50.00	125	450	—
1868P	Inc. above	20.00	45.00	100	400	—
1869P	14,000	200	300	600	—	—

5 CENTAVOS KM# 398.2 Weight: 1.3530 g. Composition: 0.9030 Silver .0392 oz. ASW Obverse: Standing eagle Reverse: Cap and rays Note: Struck at Culiacan Mint, mint mark Cn.

Date	Mintage	F	VF	XF	Unc	BU
1871Cn P	—	125	200	350	—	—
1873Cn P	4,992	50.00	100	200	400	—
1874Cn P	—	25.00	50.00	100	200	—
1875Cn P Rare	—	—	—	—	—	—
1876Cn P	—	25.00	50.00	100	200	—
1886Cn M	10,000	25.00	50.00	100	200	—
1887Cn M	10,000	25.00	50.00	100	200	—
1888Cn M	119,000	1.50	3.00	6.00	30.00	—
1889Cn M	66,000	4.00	7.50	15.00	50.00	—
1890Cn M	180,000	1.50	3.00	6.00	25.00	—
1890/9Cn M	—	2.00	4.00	8.00	40.00	—
1890Cn D Error	Inc. above	125	175	250	—	—
1891Cn M	87,000	2.00	4.00	7.50	25.00	—
1894Cn M	24,000	4.00	7.50	15.00	40.00	—
1896Cn M	16,000	7.50	12.50	25.00	75.00	—
1897Cn M	223,000	1.50	2.50	5.00	20.00	—

5 CENTAVOS KM# 398 Weight: 1.3530 g. Composition: 0.9030 Silver .0392 oz. ASW Obverse: Standing eagle Reverse: Cap and rays Note: Struck at Alamos Mint, mint mark As.

Date	Mintage	F	VF	XF	Unc	BU
1874 As DL	—	10.00	20.00	40.00	150	—
1875 As DL	—	10.00	20.00	40.00	150	—
1876 As L	—	22.00	45.00	70.00	160	—
1878 As L Mule, gold peso reverse	—	250	350	650	—	—
1879 As L Mule, gold peso obverse	—	40.00	65.00	120	275	—
1880 As L Mule, gold peso obverse	12,000	55.00	85.00	165	325	—
1886 As L	43,000	12.00	25.00	50.00	165	—
1886 As L Mule, gold peso obverse	Inc. above	55.00	85.00	165	300	—
1887 As L	20,000	25.00	50.00	75.00	165	—
1888 As L	32,000	12.00	25.00	50.00	125	—
1889 As L	16,000	25.00	50.00	100	200	—
1890 As L	30,000	25.00	50.00	85.00	175	—
1891 As L	8,000	65.00	125	200	400	—
1892 As L	13,000	20.00	40.00	60.00	125	—
1893 As L	24,000	10.00	20.00	45.00	90.00	—
1895 As L	20,000	10.00	20.00	45.00	90.00	—

5 CENTAVOS   KM# 398.1   Weight: 1.3530 g.
Composition: 0.9030 Silver .0392 oz. ASW **Obverse:**
Standing eagle **Reverse:** Cap and rays **Note:** Struck at
Chihuahua Mint, mint mark Ca, Ch.

Date	Mintage	F	VF	XF	Unc	BU
1871 M	14,000	20.00	40.00	100	250	—
1873 M Crude date	—	100	150	250	500	—
1874 M Crude date	—	25.00	50.00	75.00	150	—
1886 M	25,000	7.50	15.00	30.00	100	—
1887 M	37,000	7.50	15.00	30.00	100	—
1887 Ca/MoM	Inc. above	10.00	20.00	40.00	125	—
1888 M	145,000	1.50	3.00	6.00	25.00	—
1889 M	44,000	5.00	10.00	20.00	50.00	—
1890 M	102,000	1.50	3.00	6.00	25.00	—
1891 M	164,000	1.50	3.00	6.00	25.00	—
1892 M	85,000	1.50	3.00	6.00	25.00	—
1892 M 9/ inverted 9	Inc. above	2.00	4.00	7.50	30.00	—
1893 M	133,000	1.50	3.00	6.00	25.00	—
1894 M	108,000	1.50	3.00	6.00	25.00	—
1895 M	74,000	2.00	4.00	7.50	30.00	—

5 CENTAVOS   KM# 398.3   Weight: 1.3530 g.
Composition: 0.9030 Silver .0392 oz. ASW **Obverse:**
Standing eagle **Reverse:** Cap and rays **Note:** Struck at
Durango Mint, mint mark Do.

Date	Mintage	F	VF	XF	Unc	BU
1874Do M	—	100	150	225	500	—
1877Do P	4,795	75.00	125	225	450	—
1878/7Do E/P	4,300	200	300	450	—	—
1879Do B	—	125	200	350	—	—
1880Do B Rare	—	—	—	—	—	—
1881Do P	3,020	300	500	800	—	—
1887Do C	42,000	5.00	8.00	17.50	60.00	—
1888/9Do C	91,000	6.00	10.00	20.00	70.00	—
1888Do C	Inc. above	4.00	7.50	15.00	55.00	—
1889Do C	49,000	3.50	6.00	12.50	50.00	—
1890Do C	136,000	4.00	7.50	15.00	55.00	—
1890Do P	Inc. above	5.00	8.00	17.50	60.00	—
1891/0Do P	48,000	3.50	6.00	12.50	50.00	—
1891Do P	Inc. above	3.00	5.00	10.00	45.00	—
1894Do D	38,000	3.50	6.00	12.50	50.00	—

5 CENTAVOS   KM# 398.4   Weight: 1.3530 g.
Composition: 0.9030 Silver .0392 oz. ASW **Obverse:**
Standing eagle **Reverse:** Cap and rays **Note:** Struck at
Guadalajara Mint, mint mark Ga.

Date	Mintage	F	VF	XF	Unc	BU
1877Ga A	—	15.00	30.00	60.00	150	—
1881Ga S	156,000	4.00	7.50	15.00	60.00	—
1886Ga S	87,000	2.00	4.00	7.50	25.00	—
1888Ga S Large G	262,000	2.00	4.00	10.00	30.00	—
1888Ga S Small G	Inc. above	2.00	4.00	10.00	30.00	—
1889Ga S	178,000	1.50	3.00	7.50	25.00	—
1890Ga S	68,000	4.00	7.50	12.50	35.00	—
1891Ga S	50,000	4.00	6.50	10.00	35.00	—
1892Ga S	78,000	2.00	4.00	7.50	25.00	—
1893Ga S	44,000	4.00	7.50	15.00	45.00	—

5 CENTAVOS   KM# 398.5   Weight: 1.3530 g.
Composition: 0.9030 Silver .0392 oz. ASW **Obverse:**
Standing eagle **Reverse:** Cap and rays **Note:** Struck at
Guanajuato Mint, mint mark Go.

Date	Mintage	F	VF	XF	Unc	BU
1869Go S	80,000	15.00	30.00	75.00	175	—
1871Go S	100,000	5.00	10.00	25.00	75.00	—
1872Go S	30,000	30.00	60.00	125	250	—
1873Go S	40,000	30.00	60.00	125	250	—
1874Go S	—	7.00	12.00	25.00	75.00	—
1875Go S	—	8.00	15.00	30.00	75.00	—
1876Go S	—	8.00	15.00	30.00	75.00	—
1877Go S	—	7.00	12.00	20.00	75.00	—
1878/7Go S	20,000	8.00	15.00	25.00	75.00	—
1879Go S	—	8.00	15.00	25.00	75.00	—
1880Go S	55,000	15.00	30.00	60.00	200	—
1881/0Go S	160,000	5.00	8.00	17.50	60.00	—
1881Go S	Inc. above	4.00	6.00	12.00	45.00	—
1886Go R	230,000	1.50	3.00	6.00	30.00	—
1887Go R/S	—	1.50	3.00	6.00	30.00	—
1887Go R	230,000	1.50	2.50	5.00	30.00	—
1888Go R	320,000	1.50	2.50	5.00	20.00	—
1889Go R	60,000	4.00	6.00	12.00	45.00	—
1890/5Go R/S	—	1.50	3.00	6.00	30.00	—

Date	Mintage	F	VF	XF	Unc	BU
1890Go R	250,000	1.50	2.50	5.00	20.00	—
1891/0Go R	168,000	1.80	3.00	6.00	30.00	—
1891Go R	Inc. above	1.50	2.50	5.00	20.00	—
1892Go R	138,000	1.50	3.00	6.00	25.00	—
1893Go R	200,000	1.25	2.50	5.00	20.00	—
1894Go R	200,000	1.25	2.50	5.00	20.00	—
1896Go R	525,000	1.25	2.00	4.00	15.00	—
1896Go R/S	—	1.50	3.00	6.00	25.00	—
1897Go R	596,000	1.50	2.00	4.00	15.00	—
1898Go R	—	—	—	—	—	—

5 CENTAVOS   KM# 398.9   Weight: 1.3530 g.
Composition: 0.9030 Silver .0392 oz. ASW **Obverse:**
Standing eagle **Reverse:** Cap and rays **Note:** Struck at San
Luis Potosi Mint, mint mark Pi. Varieties exist.

Date	Mintage	F	VF	XF	Unc	BU
1869 Pi S	—	300	400	500	—	—
1870 Pi G/MoC Rare	20,000	—	—	—	—	—
1870 Pi O	Inc. above	200	300	400	—	—
1871 Pi O Rare	5,400	—	—	—	—	—
1872 Pi O	—	75.00	100	175	400	—
1873 Pi Rare	5,000	—	—	—	—	—
1874 Pi H	—	30.00	50.00	100	225	—
1875 Pi H	—	7.50	12.50	30.00	75.00	—
1876 Pi H	—	10.00	20.00	45.00	100	—
1877 Pi H	—	7.50	12.50	20.00	60.00	—
1878/7 Pi H Rare	—	—	—	—	—	—
1878 Pi H	—	60.00	90.00	150	300	—
1879 H	—	200	400	—	—	—
1880 Pi H Rare	6,200	—	—	—	—	—
1881 Pi H Rare	4,500	—	—	—	—	—
1886 Pi R	33,000	12.50	25.00	50.00	125	—
1887/0 Pi R	169,000	4.00	7.50	15.00	45.00	—
1887 Pi R	Inc. above	3.00	5.00	10.00	32.00	—
1888 Pi R	210,000	2.00	4.00	9.00	30.00	—
1889/7 Pi R	197,000	2.50	5.00	10.00	32.00	—
1889 Pi R	Inc. above	2.00	4.00	9.00	30.00	—
1890 Pi R	221,000	2.00	4.00	6.00	25.00	—
1891/89 Pi R/B	176,000	2.00	4.00	8.00	25.00	—
1891 Pi R	Inc. above	2.00	3.00	6.00	20.00	—
1892/89 Pi R	182,000	2.00	4.00	8.00	25.00	—
1892/0 Pi R	Inc. above	2.00	4.00	8.00	25.00	—
1892 Pi R	Inc. above	2.00	3.00	6.00	20.00	—
1893 Pi R	41,000	5.00	10.00	20.00	60.00	—

5 CENTAVOS   KM# 398.7   Weight: 1.3530 g.
Composition: 0.9030 Silver .0392 oz. ASW **Obverse:**
Standing eagle **Reverse:** Cap and rays **Note:** Struck at
Mexico City Mint, mint mark Mo. Varieties exist.

Date	Mintage	F	VF	XF	Unc	BU
1869/8Mo C	40,000	8.00	15.00	40.00	120	—
1870Mo C	140,000	4.00	7.00	20.00	60.00	—
1871Mo C	103,000	9.00	20.00	40.00	100	—
1871Mo M	Inc. above	7.50	12.50	25.00	60.00	—
1872Mo M	266,000	5.00	8.00	20.00	55.00	—
1873Mo M	20,000	40.00	60.00	100	225	—
1874/69Mo M	—	7.50	15.00	30.00	75.00	—
1874Mo M	—	4.00	7.00	17.50	50.00	—
1874/3Mo B	—	5.00	8.00	22.50	55.00	—
1874Mo B	—	5.00	8.00	22.50	55.00	—
1875Mo B	—	4.00	7.00	15.00	50.00	—
1875Mo B/M	—	6.00	9.00	17.50	60.00	—
1876/5Mo B	—	4.00	7.00	15.00	50.00	—
1876Mo B	—	4.00	7.00	12.50	50.00	—
1877/6Mo M	80,000	4.00	7.00	15.00	60.00	—
1877Mo M	Inc. above	4.00	7.00	12.50	60.00	—
1878/7Mo M	100,000	4.00	7.00	15.00	55.00	—
1878Mo M	Inc. above	2.50	5.00	12.50	45.00	—
1879/8Mo M	—	8.00	12.50	22.50	55.00	—
1879Mo M	—	4.50	7.00	15.00	50.00	—
1879Mo M 9/ inverted 9	—	10.00	15.00	25.00	75.00	—

Date	Mintage	F	VF	XF	Unc	BU
1880/76Mo M/B	—	5.00	7.50	15.00	50.00	—
1880/76Mo M	—	5.00	7.50	15.00	50.00	—
1880Mo M	—	4.00	6.00	12.00	40.00	—
1881/0Mo M	180,000	4.00	6.00	10.00	35.00	—
1881Mo M	Inc. above	3.00	4.50	9.00	35.00	—
1886/0Mo M	398,000	2.00	2.75	7.50	25.00	—
1886/1Mo M	Inc. above	2.00	2.75	7.50	25.00	—
1886Mo M	Inc. above	1.75	2.25	6.00	20.00	—
1887Mo m	720,000	1.75	2.00	5.00	20.00	—
1887Mo M/m	Inc. above	1.75	2.00	6.00	20.00	—
1888/7Mo M	1,360,000	2.25	2.50	6.00	20.00	—
1888Mo M	Inc. above	1.75	2.00	5.00	20.00	—
1889/8Mo M	1,242,000	2.25	2.50	6.00	20.00	—
1889Mo M	Inc. above	1.75	2.00	5.00	20.00	—
1890/00Mo M	1,694,000	1.75	2.75	6.00	20.00	—
1890Mo M	Inc. above	1.50	2.00	5.00	20.00	—
1891Mo M	1,030,000	1.75	2.00	5.00	20.00	—
1892Mo M	1,400,000	1.75	2.00	5.00	20.00	—
1892Mo M 9/inverted 9	Inc. above	2.00	2.75	7.50	20.00	—
1893Mo M	220,000	1.75	2.00	5.00	15.00	—
1894Mo M	320,000	1.75	2.00	5.00	15.00	—
1895Mo M	78,000	3.00	5.00	8.00	25.00	—
1896Mo B	80,000	1.75	2.00	5.00	20.00	—
1897Mo B	160,000	1.75	2.00	5.00	15.00	—

5 CENTAVOS   KM# 398.6   Weight: 1.3530 g.
Composition: 0.9030 Silver .0392 oz. ASW **Obverse:**
Standing eagle **Reverse:** Cap and rays **Note:** Struck at
Hermosillo Mint, mint mark Ho.

Date	Mintage	F	VF	XF	Unc	BU
1874/69Ho R	—	125	225	350	—	—
1874Ho R	—	100	200	325	—	—
1878/7Ho A Rare	22,000	—	—	—	—	—
1878Ho A	Inc. above	20.00	40.00	80.00	175	—
1878Ho A Mule, gold peso obverse	Inc. above	40.00	80.00	150	300	—
1880Ho A	43,000	7.50	15.00	30.00	75.00	—
1886Ho G	44,000	5.00	10.00	20.00	75.00	—
1887Ho G	20,000	5.00	10.00	20.00	75.00	—
1888Ho G	12,000	7.50	15.00	30.00	85.00	—
1889Ho G	67,000	3.00	6.00	12.50	40.00	—
1890Ho G	50,000	3.00	6.00	12.50	40.00	—
1891Ho G	46,000	3.00	6.00	12.50	40.00	—
1893Ho G	84,000	2.50	5.00	10.00	30.00	—
1894Ho G	68,000	2.00	4.00	10.00	30.00	—

5 CENTAVOS   KM# 398.8   Weight: 1.3530 g.
Composition: 0.9030 Silver .0392 oz. ASW **Obverse:**
Standing eagle **Reverse:** Cap and rays **Note:** Struck at
Oaxaca Mint, mint mark Oa.

Date	Mintage	F	VF	XF	Unc	BU
1890 Oa E Rare	48,000	—	—	—	—	—
1890 Oa N	Inc. above	65.00	125	200	350	—

5 CENTAVOS   KM# 398.10   Weight: 1.3530 g.
Composition: 0.9030 Silver .0392 oz. ASW **Obverse:**
Standing eagle **Reverse:** Cap and rays **Note:** Struck at
Zacatecas Mint, mint mark Zs.

Date	Mintage	F	VF	XF	Unc	BU
1871Zs H	40,000	12.50	25.00	50.00	125	—
1872Zs H	40,000	12.50	25.00	50.00	125	—
1873/2Zs H	20,000	35.00	65.00	125	275	—
1873Zs H	Inc. above	25.00	50.00	100	250	—
1874Zs H	—	7.50	12.50	25.00	75.00	—
1874Zs A	—	40.00	75.00	150	300	—
1875Zs A	—	7.50	12.50	25.00	75.00	—
1876Zs A	—	50.00	75.00	150	500	—
1876/5Zs S	—	15.00	30.00	60.00	150	—
1876Zs S	—	12.50	25.00	50.00	125	—
1877Zs S	—	3.00	6.00	12.00	40.00	—
1878Zs S	60,000	3.00	6.00	12.00	40.00	—
1879/8Zs S	—	3.00	6.00	15.00	50.00	—
1879Zs S	—	3.00	6.00	12.00	40.00	—
1880/79Zs S	130,000	6.00	10.00	20.00	60.00	—
1880Zs S	Inc. above	5.00	8.00	16.00	45.00	—
1881Zs S	210,000	2.50	5.00	10.00	35.00	—
1886/4Zs S	360,000	6.00	10.00	20.00	60.00	—

Date	Mintage	F	VF	XF	Unc	BU
1886Zs S	Inc. above	2.00	3.00	6.00	20.00	—
1886Zs Z	Inc. above	5.00	10.00	25.00	65.00	—
1887Zs Z	400,000	2.00	3.00	6.00	25.00	—
1888/7Zs Z	500,000	2.00	3.00	6.00	25.00	—
1888Zs Z	Inc. above	2.00	3.00	6.00	25.00	—
1889Zs Z	520,000	2.00	3.00	6.00	25.00	—
1889Zs Z 9/ inverted 9	Inc. above	2.00	3.00	6.00	25.00	—
1889Zs Z/MoM	Inc. above	2.00	3.00	6.00	25.00	—
1890Zs Z	580,000	1.75	2.50	5.00	20.00	—
1890Zs Z/MoM	Inc. above	2.00	3.00	6.00	20.00	—
1890Zs ZsZ 9/8	—	2.00	3.00	6.00	25.00	—
1890Zs ZsZ 0/9 Z/M	—	2.00	3.00	6.00	25.00	—
1891Zs Z	420,000	1.75	2.50	5.00	20.00	—
1892Zs Z	346,000	1.75	2.50	5.00	20.00	—
1893Zs Z	258,000	1.75	2.50	5.00	20.00	—
1894Zs Z	228,000	1.75	2.50	5.00	20.00	—
1894Zs ZoZ Error	Inc. above	2.00	4.00	8.00	30.00	—
1895Zs Z	260,000	1.75	2.50	5.00	20.00	—
1895Zs Z	260,000	1.75	2.50	5.00	20.00	—
1895/4Zs ZsZ	—	2.00	3.00	6.00	25.00	—
1896Zs Z	200,000	1.75	2.50	5.00	20.00	—
1896Zs 6/ inverted 6	Inc. above	2.00	3.00	6.00	25.00	—
1897/6Zs Z	200,000	2.00	3.00	6.00	25.00	—
1897Zs Z	Inc. above	1.75	2.50	5.00	20.00	—
1870Zs H	40,000	12.50	25.00	50.00	125	—

5 CENTAVOS   KM# 399   Composition: Copper-Nickel
Note: Struck at Mexico City Mint.

Date	Mintage	F	VF	XF	Unc	BU
1882	Inc. above	0.50	1.00	2.50	7.50	—
1883	Inc. above	25.00	50.00	80.00	250	—

5 CENTAVOS   KM# 400.2   Composition: 0.9030 Silver
Obverse: Restyled eagle **Note:** Struck at Mexico City Mint,
mint mark Mo.

Date	Mintage	F	VF	XF	Unc	BU
1898Mo M	80,000	2.00	4.00	7.00	25.00	—
1899Mo M	168,000	1.75	2.50	4.50	15.00	—
1900/800Mo M	300,000	4.50	6.50	10.00	30.00	—
1900Mo M	Inc. above	1.75	2.50	4.50	15.00	—
1901Mo M	100,000	1.75	2.50	4.50	15.00	—
1902Mo M	144,000	1.25	2.00	3.75	12.00	—
1902/1Mo MoM	—	1.75	3.00	6.00	16.50	—
1903Mo M	500,000	1.25	2.00	3.75	12.00	—
1904/804Mo M	1,090,000	1.75	3.00	6.00	16.50	—
1904/94Mo M	Inc. above	1.75	3.00	6.00	16.50	—
1904Mo M	Inc. above	1.75	3.00	6.00	15.00	—
1905Mo M	344,000	1.75	3.00	7.50	18.50	—

5 CENTAVOS   KM# 400.3   Composition: 0.9030 Silver
Obverse: Restyled eagle **Note:** Struck at Zacatecas Mint,
mint mark Zs.

Date	Mintage	F	VF	XF	Unc	BU
1898Zs Z	100,000	1.75	2.25	4.50	12.50	—
1899Zs Z	50,000	2.00	3.00	7.00	20.00	—
1900Zs Z	55,000	1.75	2.50	5.00	16.50	—
1901Zs Z	40,000	1.75	2.50	5.00	16.50	—
1902/1Zs Z	34,000	2.00	4.50	9.00	22.50	—
1902Zs Z	Inc. above	1.75	3.75	7.50	18.50	—
1903Zs Z	217,000	1.25	2.00	5.00	12.50	—
1904Zs Z	191,000	1.75	2.50	5.00	12.50	—
1904Zs M	Inc. above	1.75	2.50	6.00	16.50	—
1905Zs M	46,000	2.00	4.50	9.00	22.50	—
1905Zs M Repullica - Rare	Inc. above	—	—	—	—	—

5 CENTAVOS   KM# 400.1   Composition: 0.9030 Silver
Obverse: Restyled eagle **Note:** Struck at Guanajuato Mint, mint mark Go. Varieties exist.

Date	Mintage	F	VF	XF	Unc	BU
1898Go R Mule, gold peso obverse	180,000	7.50	15.00	30.00	75.00	—
1899Go R	260,000	1.75	2.50	4.50	15.00	—
1900Go R	200,000	1.75	2.50	4.50	15.00	—

5 CENTAVOS   KM# 400   Composition: 0.9030 Silver
Obverse: Restyled eagle **Note:** Struck at Culiacan Mint, mint mark Cn. Varieties exist.

Date	Mintage	F	VF	XF	Unc	BU
1898Cn M	44,000	1.75	4.00	8.00	20.00	—
1899Cn M	111,000	5.50	8.50	20.00	50.00	—
1899Cn Q	Inc. above	1.75	2.50	4.50	15.00	—
1900/800Cn Q	239,000	3.50	5.00	12.50	30.00	—
1900Cn Q Round Q, single tail	Inc. above	1.75	3.00	6.00	16.50	—
1900Cn Q Narrow C, oval Q	Inc. above	1.75	3.00	6.00	16.50	—
1900Cn Q Wide C, oval Q	Inc. above	1.75	3.00	6.00	16.50	—
1901Cn Q	148,000	1.75	2.50	4.50	15.00	—
1902Cn Q Narrow C, heavy serifs	262,000	1.75	3.00	6.00	16.50	—
1902Cn Q Wide C, light serifs	Inc. above	1.75	3.00	6.00	16.50	—
1903/1Cn Q	331,000	2.00	3.00	6.00	16.50	—
1903Cn Q	Inc. above	1.75	2.50	4.50	15.00	—
1903/1898Cn V	Inc. above	3.50	4.50	9.00	22.50	—
1903Cn V	Inc. above	1.75	2.50	4.50	15.00	—
1904Cn H	352,000	1.75	2.25	5.00	16.50	—
1904Cn H 0/9	—	1.75	2.50	5.00	16.50	—
1904Cn H/C	—	1.75	2.50	5.00	16.50	—

10 CENTAVOS   KM# 401.2   Weight: 2.7070 g.
Composition: 0.9030 Silver .0785 oz. ASW **Obverse:**
Eagle **Reverse:** Value within wreath **Note:** Struck at San Luis Potosi Mint, mint mark SLP.

Date	Mintage	F	VF	XF	Unc	BU
1863SLP	—	75.00	150	275	900	—

10 CENTAVOS   KM# 402   Weight: 2.7070 g.
Composition: 0.9030 Silver .0785 oz. ASW **Obverse:**
Eagle **Reverse:** Value within wreath **Note:** Struck at Mexico City Mint, mint mark Mo.

Date	Mintage	F	VF	XF	Unc	BU
1867/3Mo	—	50.00	100	200	550	—
1867Mo	—	20.00	50.00	150	450	—
1868/7Mo	—	20.00	50.00	175	500	—
1868Mo	—	20.00	55.00	175	500	—

10 CENTAVOS   KM# 402.1   Weight: 2.7070 g.
Composition: 0.9030 Silver .0785 oz. ASW **Obverse:**
Eagle **Reverse:** Value within wreath **Note:** Struck at San Luis Potosi Mint, mint mark P.

Date	Mintage	F	VF	XF	Unc	BU
1868/7 P	38,000	45.00	90.00	175	650	—
1868 P	Inc. above	20.00	40.00	100	550	—
1869/7 P	4,900	55.00	125	250	800	—

10 CENTAVOS   KM# 401   Weight: 2.7070 g.
Composition: 0.9030 Silver .0785 oz. ASW **Obverse:**
Eagle **Reverse:** Value within wreath **Note:** Struck at Chihuahua Mint, mint mark Ca.

Date	Mintage	F	VF	XF	Unc	BU
1868/7 Ca	—	30.00	60.00	150	550	—
1868 Ca	—	30.00	60.00	150	550	—
1869 Ca	15,000	25.00	50.00	125	600	—
1870 Ca	17,000	22.50	45.00	100	550	—

10 CENTAVOS   KM# 403.2   Weight: 2.7070 g.
Composition: 0.9030 Silver .0785 oz. ASW **Obverse:**
Eagle **Reverse:** Value within wreath **Note:** Struck at Culiacan Mint, mint mark Cn.

Date	Mintage	F	VF	XF	Unc	BU
1871Cn P Rare	—	—	—	—	—	—
1873Cn P	8,732	20.00	50.00	100	225	—
1881Cn D	9,440	75.00	175	325	500	—
1882Cn D	12,000	75.00	125	200	400	—
1885Cn M Mule, gold 2-1/2 peso obverse	18,000	25.00	50.00	100	200	—
1886Cn M Mule, gold 2-1/2 peso obverse	13,000	50.00	100	150	300	—
1887Cn M	11,000	20.00	40.00	75.00	175	—
1888Cn M	56,000	5.00	10.00	25.00	125	—
1889Cn M	42,000	5.00	10.00	20.00	75.00	—
1890Cn M	132,000	2.00	4.00	7.50	75.00	—
1891Cn M	84,000	5.00	10.00	20.00	75.00	—
1892/1Cn M	37,000	4.00	8.00	15.00	75.00	—
1892Cn M	Inc. above	2.50	5.00	10.00	75.00	—
1894Cn M	43,000	2.50	5.00	10.00	75.00	—
1895Cn M	23,000	2.50	5.00	10.00	60.00	—
1896Cn M	121,000	1.50	2.50	5.00	50.00	—

10 CENTAVOS   KM# 403.3   Weight: 2.7070 g.
Composition: 0.9030 Silver .0785 oz. ASW **Obverse:**
Eagle **Reverse:** Value within wreath **Note:** Struck at Durango Mint, mint mark Do.

Date	Mintage	F	VF	XF	Unc	BU
1878Do E	2,500	100	175	300	600	—
1879Do B Rare	—	—	—	—	—	—
1880/70Do B Rare	—	—	—	—	—	—
1880/79Do B Rare	—	—	—	—	—	—
1884Do C	—	30.00	60.00	100	225	—
1886Do C	13,000	75.00	150	300	500	—
1887Do C	81,000	4.00	8.00	15.00	100	—
1888Do C	31,000	6.00	12.00	30.00	100	—
1889Do C	55,000	4.00	8.00	15.00	100	—
1890Do C	50,000	4.00	8.00	15.00	100	—
1891Do P	139,000	2.00	4.00	8.00	80.00	—
1892Do P	212,000	2.00	4.00	8.00	80.00	—
1892Do D	Inc. above	2.00	4.00	8.00	80.00	—
1893Do D	258,000	2.00	4.00	8.00	80.00	—
1893Do D/C	Inc. above	2.50	5.00	10.00	80.00	—
1894Do D	184,000	1.50	3.00	6.00	80.00	—
1894Do D/C	Inc. above	2.00	4.00	8.00	80.00	—
1895Do D	142,000	1.50	3.00	6.00	80.00	—

10 CENTAVOS   KM# 403.4   Weight: 2.7070 g.
Composition: 0.9030 Silver .0785 oz. ASW **Obverse:**
Eagle **Reverse:** Value within wreath **Note:** Struck at Guadalajara Mint, mint mark Ga. Varieties exist.

Date	Mintage	F	VF	XF	Unc	BU
1871Ga C	4,734	75.00	125	200	500	—
1873/1Ga C	25,000	10.00	15.00	35.00	150	—
1873Ga C	Inc. above	10.00	15.00	35.00	150	—
1874Ga C	—	10.00	15.00	35.00	150	—
1877Ga A	—	10.00	15.00	30.00	150	—
1881Ga S	115,000	5.00	10.00	25.00	150	—
1883Ga B	90,000	4.00	8.00	15.00	90.00	—
1884Ga B	—	5.00	10.00	20.00	90.00	—
1884Ga B/S	—	6.00	12.50	25.00	90.00	—
1884Ga H	—	3.00	5.00	10.00	90.00	—
1885Ga H	93,000	3.00	5.00	10.00	90.00	—
1886Ga S	151,000	2.50	4.00	9.00	90.00	—
1887Ga S	162,000	1.50	3.00	6.00	90.00	—
1888Ga S	225,000	1.50	3.00	6.00	90.00	—

Date	Mintage	F	VF	XF	Unc	BU
1888Ga GaS/HoG	Inc. above	1.50	3.00	6.00	90.00	—
1889Ga S	310,000	1.50	3.00	6.00	40.00	—
1890Ga S	303,000	1.50	3.00	6.00	40.00	—
1891Ga S	199,000	5.00	10.00	20.00	45.00	—
1892Ga S	329,000	1.50	3.00	6.00	40.00	—
1893Ga S	225,000	1.50	3.00	6.00	40.00	—
1894Ga S	243,000	3.00	6.00	12.00	40.00	—
1895Ga S	80,000	1.50	3.00	6.00	40.00	—

10 CENTAVOS   KM# 403.5 Weight: 2.7070 g.
Composition: 0.9030 Silver .0785 oz. ASW **Obverse:**
Eagle **Reverse:** Value within wreath **Note:** Struck at
Guanajuato Mint, mint mark Go. Varieties exist.

Date	Mintage	F	VF	XF	Unc	BU
1869Go S	7,000	20.00	40.00	80.00	200	—
1871/0Go S	60,000	15.00	25.00	50.00	125	—
1872Go S	60,000	15.00	25.00	50.00	125	—
1873Go S	50,000	15.00	25.00	50.00	125	—
1874Go S	—	15.00	25.00	50.00	125	—
1875Go S	—	250	350	500	800	—
1876Go S	—	10.00	20.00	40.00	100	—
1877Go S	—	80.00	120	200	400	—
1878/7Go S	10,000	10.00	20.00	45.00	110	—
1878Go S	Inc. above	7.50	12.00	20.00	75.00	—
1879Go S	—	7.50	12.00	20.00	75.00	—
1880Go S	—	100	200	300	450	—
1881/71Go S	100,000	3.00	5.00	10.00	75.00	—
1881/0Go S	Inc. above	3.50	5.00	10.00	75.00	—
1881Go S	Inc. above	3.00	5.00	10.00	75.00	—
1882/1Go S	40,000	3.00	6.00	12.00	75.00	—
1883Go B	—	3.00	5.00	10.00	75.00	—
1884Go B	—	1.50	3.00	6.00	75.00	—
1884Go S	—	6.00	12.50	25.00	90.00	—
1885Go R	100,000	1.50	3.00	6.00	75.00	—
1886Go R	95,000	3.00	5.00	10.00	75.00	—
1887Go R	330,000	2.50	5.00	10.00	75.00	—
1888Go R	270,000	1.50	3.00	6.00	75.00	—
1889Go R	205,000	2.00	4.00	8.00	75.00	—
1889Go Go R/HoG	Inc. above	3.00	5.00	10.00	75.00	—
1890Go R	270,000	1.50	3.00	6.00	35.00	—
1890Go Go R/Cn M	Inc. above	1.50	3.00	6.00	35.00	—
1891Go R	523,000	1.50	3.00	6.00	35.00	—
1891Go R/G	—	1.50	3.00	6.00	35.00	—
1891Go Go R/HoG	Inc. above	1.50	3.00	6.00	35.00	—
1892Go R	440,000	1.50	3.00	6.00	35.00	—
1893/1Go R	389,000	3.00	5.00	10.00	35.00	—
1893Go R	Inc. above	1.50	3.00	6.00	35.00	—
1894Go R	400,000	1.50	2.50	5.00	35.00	—
1895Go R	355,000	1.50	2.50	5.00	35.00	—
1896Go R	190,000	1.50	2.50	5.00	35.00	—
1897Go R	205,000	1.50	2.50	5.00	35.00	—

10 CENTAVOS   KM# 403.6 Weight: 2.7070 g.
Composition: 0.9030 Silver .0785 oz. ASW **Obverse:**
Eagle **Reverse:** Value within wreath **Note:** Struck at
Hermosillo Mint, mint mark Ho.

Date	Mintage	F	VF	XF	Unc	BU
1874Ho R	—	30.00	60.00	100	200	—
1876Ho F	3,140	200	300	450	750	—
1878Ho A	—	5.00	10.00	15.00	85.00	—
1879Ho A	—	25.00	50.00	90.00	175	—
1880Ho A	—	3.00	6.00	12.50	85.00	—
1881Ho A	28,000	4.00	7.00	15.00	85.00	—
1882/1Ho A	25,000	5.00	10.00	20.00	85.00	—
1882/1Ho a	Inc. above	6.00	12.50	25.00	85.00	—
1882Ho A	Inc. above	4.00	7.00	15.00	85.00	—
1883Ho	7,000	65.00	100	200	400	—
1884Ho A	—	35.00	75.00	150	300	—
1884/3Ho M	—	10.00	20.00	40.00	90.00	—
1884Ho M	—	7.50	15.00	30.00	85.00	—
1885Ho M	21,000	12.50	25.00	50.00	100	—
1886Ho M Rare	10,000	—	—	—	—	—
1886Ho G	Inc. above	7.50	12.50	25.00	85.00	—
1887Ho G	—	25.00	50.00	75.00	150	—
1888Ho G	25,000	6.00	12.50	25.00	85.00	—
1889Ho G	42,000	3.00	6.00	10.00	85.00	—
1890Ho G	48,000	3.00	6.00	10.00	85.00	—
1891/80Ho G	136,000	3.00	6.00	10.00	85.00	—
1891/0Ho G	Inc. above	3.00	6.00	10.00	85.00	—
1891Ho G	Inc. above	3.00	6.00	10.00	85.00	—
1892Ho G	67,000	3.00	6.00	10.00	85.00	—
1893Ho G	67,000	3.00	6.00	10.00	85.00	—

10 CENTAVOS   KM# 403.9 Weight: 2.7070 g.
Composition: 0.9030 Silver .0785 oz. ASW **Obverse:**
Eagle **Reverse:** Value within wreath **Note:** Struck at San
Luis Potosi Mint, mint mark Pi. Varieties exist.

Date	Mintage	F	VF	XF	Unc	BU
1869/8 Pi S Rare	4,000	—	—	—	—	—
1870/69 Pi O Rare	18,000	—	—	—	—	—
1870 Pi G	Inc. above	125	200	325	600	—
1871 Pi O	21,000	50.00	100	150	300	—
1872 Pi O	16,000	150	225	350	650	—
1873 Pi O Rare	4,750	—	—	—	—	—
1874 Pi H	—	25.00	50.00	100	200	—
1875 Pi H	—	75.00	125	200	400	—
1876 Pi H	—	75.00	125	200	400	—
1877 Pi H	—	75.00	125	200	400	—
1878 Pi H	—	250	500	750	—	—
1879 Pi H	—	—	—	—	—	—
1880 Pi H	—	150	250	350	—	—
1881 Pi H	7,600	250	350	500	—	—
1882 Pi H Rare	4,000	—	—	—	—	—
1883 Pi H	—	125	200	300	500	—
1884 Pi H	—	25.00	50.00	100	200	—
1885 Pi H	51,000	25.00	50.00	100	200	—
1885 Pi C Rare	Inc. above	—	—	—	—	—
1886 Pi C	52,000	15.00	30.00	60.00	150	—
1886 Pi R	Inc. above	5.00	10.00	20.00	65.00	—
1887 Pi R	118,000	2.50	5.00	10.00	50.00	—
1888 Pi R	136,000	2.50	5.00	10.00	50.00	—
1889/8 Pi R/G	—	7.50	12.50	20.00	60.00	—
1889/7 Pi R	131,000	7.50	12.50	20.00	60.00	—
1890 Pi R	204,000	1.50	3.00	7.50	40.00	—
1891/89 Pi R	163,000	2.50	5.00	10.00	40.00	—
1891 Pi R	Inc. above	1.50	3.50	6.00	30.00	—
1892/0 Pi R	200,000	2.00	4.00	8.00	40.00	—
1892 Pi R	Inc. above	1.50	2.50	5.00	40.00	—
1892 Pi R/G	—	2.00	4.00	8.00	40.00	—
1893 Pi R/G	—	1.50	10.00	17.50	60.00	—
1893 Pi R	48,000	7.50	10.00	17.50	60.00	—

10 CENTAVOS   KM# 403.7 Weight: 2.7070 g.
Composition: 0.9030 Silver .0785 oz. ASW **Obverse:**
Eagle **Reverse:** Value within wreath **Note:** Struck at Mexico
City Mint, mint mark Mo. Varieties exist.

Date	Mintage	F	VF	XF	Unc	BU
1869/8Mo C	30,000	10.00	20.00	40.00	100	—
1869Mo C	Inc. above	8.00	17.50	35.00	90.00	—
1870Mo C	110,000	3.00	7.50	15.00	50.00	—
1871Mo C	84,000	50.00	75.00	125	250	—
1871Mo M	Inc. above	12.00	17.50	45.00	125	—
1872/69Mo M	198,000	10.00	20.00	35.00	100	—
1872Mo M	Inc. above	3.00	7.50	15.00	65.00	—
1873Mo M	40,000	10.00	15.00	30.00	75.00	—
1874Mo M	—	5.00	10.00	20.00	65.00	—
1874Mo M/C	—	5.00	10.00	20.00	65.00	—
1874/64Mo B	—	5.00	10.00	20.00	65.00	—
1874Mo B/M	—	20.00	40.00	60.00	125	—
1874Mo B	—	5.00	10.00	15.00	65.00	—
1875Mo B	—	20.00	40.00	60.00	125	—
1876/5Mo B	—	3.00	5.00	9.00	65.00	—
1876/5Mo B/M	—	3.00	5.00	9.00	65.00	—
1877/6Mo M	—	3.00	5.00	9.00	65.00	—
1877/6Mo M/B	—	3.00	5.00	9.00	65.00	—
1877Mo M	—	3.00	5.00	9.00	65.00	—
1878/7Mo M	100,000	3.00	5.00	9.00	65.00	—
1878Mo M	Inc. above	3.00	5.00	9.00	65.00	—
1879/69Mo M	—	3.00	5.00	9.00	65.00	—

Date	Mintage	F	VF	XF	Unc	BU
1879Mo M/C	—	3.00	5.00	9.00	65.00	—
1880/79Mo M	—	3.00	5.00	9.00	65.00	—
1881/0Mo M	510,000	3.00	5.00	9.00	35.00	—
1881Mo M	Inc. above	3.00	5.00	9.00	35.00	—
1882/1Mo M	550,000	3.00	5.00	9.00	35.00	—
1882Mo M	Inc. above	3.00	5.00	9.00	35.00	—
1883/2Mo M	250,000	3.00	5.00	9.00	35.00	—
1884Mo M	—	3.00	5.00	9.00	35.00	—
1885Mo M	470,000	3.00	5.00	9.00	35.00	—
1886Mo M	603,000	3.00	5.00	9.00	35.00	—
1887Mo M	580,000	3.00	5.00	9.00	35.00	—
1888/7Mo MoM	710,000	3.00	5.00	9.00	35.00	—
1888Mo MoM	Inc. above	3.00	5.00	9.00	35.00	—
1888Mo MOM	Inc. above	3.00	5.00	9.00	35.00	—
1889/8Mo M	622,000	3.00	5.00	9.00	35.00	—
1889Mo M	Inc. above	3.00	5.00	9.00	35.00	—
1890/89Mo M	815,000	3.00	5.00	9.00	35.00	—
1890Mo M	Inc. above	3.00	5.00	9.00	35.00	—
1891Mo M	859,000	1.50	2.50	7.00	25.00	—
1892Mo M	1,030,000	1.50	2.50	7.00	25.00	—
1893Mo M	310,000	1.50	2.50	7.00	25.00	—
1893Mo M/C	Inc. above	1.50	2.50	7.00	25.00	—
1893Mo Mo/Ho M/G	—	1.50	2.50	7.00	25.00	—
1894/3Mo M	—	5.00	10.00	20.00	60.00	—
1894Mo M	350,000	5.00	10.00	20.00	60.00	—
1895Mo M	320,000	1.50	2.50	7.00	25.00	—
1896Mo B/G	340,000	1.50	2.50	7.00	25.00	—
1896Mo M	Inc. above	35.00	70.00	100	150	—
1897Mo M	170,000	1.50	2.50	5.00	20.00	—

10 CENTAVOS   KM# 403.8   Weight: 2.7070 g.
Composition: 0.9030 Silver .0785 oz. ASW **Obverse:** Eagle **Reverse:** Value within wreath **Note:** Struck at Oaxaca Mint, mint mark Oa.

Date	Mintage	F	VF	XF	Unc	BU
1889 Oa E	21,000	200	400	600	—	—
1890 Oa E	31,000	100	150	250	500	—
1890 Oa N Rare	Inc. above	—	—	—	—	—

10 CENTAVOS   KM# 403   Weight: 2.7070 g.
Composition: 0.9030 Silver .0785 oz. ASW **Obverse:** Eagle **Reverse:** Value within wreath **Note:** Struck as Alamos Mint, mint mark As. Varieties exist.

Date	Mintage	F	VF	XF	Unc	BU
1874 As DL	—	20.00	40.00	80.00	175	—
1875 As L	—	5.00	10.00	25.00	90.00	—
1876 As L	—	10.00	18.00	45.00	110	—
1878/7 As L	—	10.00	18.00	45.00	120	—
1878 As L	—	5.00	10.00	30.00	100	—
1879 As L	—	10.00	18.00	40.00	110	—
1880 As L	13,000	10.00	18.00	40.00	110	—
1882 As L	22,000	10.00	18.00	40.00	110	—
1883 As L	8,520	25.00	50.00	100	225	—
1884 As L	—	7.50	12.50	35.00	100	—
1885 As L	15,000	7.50	12.50	35.00	100	—
1886 As L	45,000	7.50	12.50	35.00	100	—
1887 As L	15,000	7.50	12.50	35.00	100	—
1888 As L	38,000	7.50	12.50	35.00	100	—
1889 As L	20,000	7.50	12.50	35.00	100	—
1890 As L	40,000	7.50	12.50	35.00	100	—
1891 As L	38,000	7.50	12.50	35.00	100	—
1892 As L	57,000	5.00	10.00	25.00	90.00	—
1893 As L	70,000	10.00	18.00	40.00	110	—

Note: An 1891 As L over 1889 HoG exists which was evidently produced at the Alamos Mint using dies sent from the Hermosillo Mint

10 CENTAVOS   KM# 403.10   Weight: 2.7070 g.
Composition: 0.9030 Silver .0785 oz. ASW **Obverse:** Eagle **Reverse:** Value within wreath **Note:** Struck at Zacatecas Mint, mint mark Zs. Varieties exist.

Date	Mintage	F	VF	XF	Unc	BU
1871/0Zs H	10,000	—	—	—	—	—
1871Zs H	Inc. above	—	—	—	—	—
1872Zs H	10,000	150	200	275	500	—
1873Zs H	10,000	250	350	600	—	—
1874/3Zs H	—	50.00	75.00	150	300	—
1874Zs A	—	200	300	500	—	—
1875Zs A	—	5.00	10.00	25.00	100	—
1876Zs A	—	5.00	10.00	25.00	100	—
1876Zs S	—	100	200	300	500	—

Date	Mintage	F	VF	XF	Unc	BU
1877Zs S Small S	—	7.50	12.50	25.00	100	—
1877Zs S Regular S	—	7.50	12.50	25.00	100	—
1878/7Zs S	30,000	5.00	10.00	20.00	80.00	—
1878Zs S	Inc. above	5.00	10.00	20.00	80.00	—
1879Zs S	—	5.00	10.00	20.00	80.00	—
1880Zs S	—	5.00	10.00	20.00	80.00	—
1881/0Zs S	120,000	3.00	6.00	12.50	50.00	—
1881Zs S	Inc. above	3.00	6.00	12.50	50.00	—
1882/1Zs S	64,000	12.50	25.00	50.00	125	—
1882Zs S	Inc. above	12.50	25.00	50.00	125	—
1883/73Zs S	102,000	2.00	4.00	8.00	50.00	—
1883Zs S	Inc. above	2.00	4.00	8.00	50.00	—
1884/3Zs S	—	2.00	4.00	8.00	50.00	—
1884Zs S	—	2.00	4.00	8.00	50.00	—
1885Zs S	297,000	1.50	2.50	5.00	50.00	—
1885Zs S Small S in mint mark	Inc. above	2.50	4.00	8.00	50.00	—
1885Zs Z Without assayers initials (error)	Inc. above	3.50	7.50	15.00	65.00	—
1886Zs S	274,000	1.50	2.50	5.00	30.00	—
1886Zs Z	Inc. above	12.50	25.00	50.00	125	—
1887Zs ZsZ	233,000	1.50	2.50	5.00	30.00	—
1887Zs Z Z (Error)	Inc. above	3.50	10.00	25.00	100	—
1888Zs ZsZ	270,000	1.50	2.50	5.00	30.00	—
1888Zs Z Z (Error)	Inc. above	3.50	10.00	25.00	100	—
1889/7Zs Z/S	240,000	4.00	8.00	12.50	40.00	—
1889Zs ZS	Inc. above	1.50	4.00	8.00	30.00	—
1889Zs Z/G	—	1.50	4.00	8.00	30.00	—
1889Zs Z	Inc. above	1.50	2.50	5.00	30.00	—
1890Zs ZsZ	410,000	1.50	2.50	5.00	30.00	—
1890Zs Z Z (Error)	Inc. above	3.75	10.00	25.00	100	—
1891Zs Z	1,105,000	1.50	2.50	5.00	30.00	—
1891Zs ZsZ Double s	Inc. above	2.00	4.00	7.00	30.00	—
1892Zs Z	1,102,000	1.50	2.50	5.00	30.00	—
1892Zs Z/G	—	2.00	4.00	7.00	30.00	—
1893/2Zs Z	—	2.00	4.00	8.00	40.00	—
1893Zs Z	1,010,999	1.50	2.50	5.00	25.00	—
1894Zs Z	892,000	1.50	2.50	5.00	30.00	—
1895Zs Z	920,000	1.50	2.50	5.00	30.00	—
1895Zs Z 9/5	—	2.00	4.00	7.00	30.00	—
1896/5Zs Z/G	—	1.50	2.50	5.00	30.00	—
1896Zs Z/G	—	1.50	2.50	5.00	30.00	—
1896/5Zs ZsZ	700,000	1.50	2.50	5.00	30.00	—
1896Zs ZsZ	Inc. above	1.50	2.50	5.00	30.00	—
1896Zs Z Z (Error)	Inc. above	3.75	10.00	25.00	100	—
1897/6Zs ZsZ	900,000	2.00	5.00	10.00	30.00	—
1897/6Zs Z Z (Error)	Inc. above	3.75	10.00	25.00	100	—
1897Zs Z	Inc. above	1.50	2.50	5.00	30.00	—
1870Zs H	20,000	100	150	200	400	—

10 CENTAVOS   KM# 403.1   Weight: 2.7070 g.
Composition: 0.9030 Silver .0785 oz. ASW **Obverse:** Eagle **Reverse:** Value within wreath **Note:** Struck at Chihuahua, mint mark CH, Ca. Varieties exist.

Date	Mintage	F	VF	XF	Unc	BU
1871 M	8,150	15.00	30.00	60.00	150	—
1873 M Crude date	—	35.00	75.00	125	175	—
1874 M	—	10.00	17.50	35.00	100	—
1880/70 G	7,620	20.00	40.00	80.00	175	—
1880 G/g	Inc. above	15.00	25.00	50.00	125	—
1881 Rare	340	—	—	—	—	—
1883 M	9,000	10.00	20.00	40.00	125	—
1884/73	—	5.00	30.00	60.00	150	—
1884 M	—	10.00	20.00	40.00	125	—
1886 M	45,000	7.50	12.50	30.00	100	—
1887/3 M/G	96,000	5.00	10.00	20.00	75.00	—
1887 M/G	—	2.00	4.00	8.00	75.00	—
1887 M	Inc. above	2.00	4.00	8.00	75.00	—
1888 M/G	—	2.00	4.00	8.00	75.00	—
1888 M	299,000	1.50	2.50	5.00	75.00	—
1888 Ca/Mo	Inc. above	1.50	2.50	5.00	75.00	—
1889/8 M	115,000	2.00	4.00	8.00	75.00	—

Date	Mintage	F	VF	XF	Unc	BU
1889 M Small 89 (5 Centavo font)	Inc. above	2.00	4.00	8.00	75.00	—
1890/80 M	140,000	2.00	4.00	8.00	75.00	—
1890/89 M	Inc. above	2.00	4.00	8.00	75.00	—
1890 M	Inc. above	1.50	3.00	7.00	75.00	—
1891 M	163,000	1.50	3.00	7.00	75.00	—
1892 M	169,000	1.50	3.00	7.00	75.00	—
1892 M 9/inverted 9	Inc. above	2.00	4.00	8.00	75.00	—
1893 M	246,000	1.50	3.00	7.00	75.00	—
1894 M	163,000	1.50	3.00	7.00	75.00	—
1895 M	127,000	1.50	3.00	7.00	75.00	—

10 CENTAVOS   KM# 404   Weight: 2.7070 g.
Composition: 0.9030 Silver .0785 oz. ASW **Obverse:** Restyled eagle **Note:** Struck at Culiacan Mint, mint mark Cn. Varieties exist.

Date	Mintage	F	VF	XF	Unc	BU
1898Cn M	9,870	50.00	100	200	500	—
1899Cn Q Round Q, single tail	80,000	5.00	7.50	25.00	100	—
1899Cn Q Oval Q, double tail	Inc. above	5.00	7.50	25.00	100	—
1900Cn Q	160,000	1.50	2.50	5.00	20.00	—
1901Cn Q	235,000	1.50	2.50	5.00	20.00	—
1902Cn Q	186,000	1.50	2.50	5.00	20.00	—
1903Cn Q	256,000	1.50	2.50	6.00	20.00	—
1903Cn V	Inc. above	1.50	2.50	5.00	15.00	—
1904Cn H	307,000	1.50	2.50	5.00	15.00	—

10 CENTAVOS   KM# 404.1   Weight: 2.7070 g.
Composition: 0.9030 Silver .0785 oz. ASW **Obverse:** Restyled eagle **Note:** Struck at Guanajuato Mint, mint mark Go.

Date	Mintage	F	VF	XF	Unc	BU
1898Go R	435,000	1.50	2.50	5.00	20.00	—
1899Go R	270,000	1.50	2.50	5.00	25.00	—
1900Go R	130,000	7.50	12.50	25.00	60.00	—

10 CENTAVOS   KM# 404.2   Weight: 2.7070 g.
Composition: 0.9030 Silver .0785 oz. ASW **Obverse:** Restyled eagle **Note:** Struck at Mexico City Mint, mint mark Mo.

Date	Mintage	F	VF	XF	Unc	BU
1898Mo M	130,000	1.50	2.50	5.00	20.00	—
1899Mo M	190,000	1.50	2.50	5.00	20.00	—
1900Mo M	311,000	1.50	2.50	5.00	20.00	—
1901Mo M	80,000	2.50	3.50	7.00	22.50	—
1902Mo M	181,000	1.50	2.50	5.00	20.00	—
1903Mo M	581,000	1.50	2.50	5.00	20.00	—
1904Mo M	1,266,000	1.25	2.00	4.50	18.00	—
1904Mo MM (Error)	Inc. above	2.50	5.00	10.00	25.00	—
1905Mo M	266,000	2.00	3.75	7.50	20.00	—

10 CENTAVOS   KM# 404.3   Weight: 2.7070 g.
Composition: 0.9030 Silver .0785 oz. ASW **Obverse:** Restyled eagle **Note:** Struck at Zacatecas Mint, mint mark Zs.

Date	Mintage	F	VF	XF	Unc	BU
1898Zs Z	240,000	1.50	2.50	7.50	20.00	—
1899Zs Z	105,000	1.50	3.00	10.00	22.00	—
1900Zs Z	219,000	7.50	10.00	20.00	45.00	—
1901Zs Z	70,000	2.50	5.00	10.00	25.00	—
1902Zs Z	120,000	2.50	5.00	10.00	25.00	—
1903Zs Z	228,000	1.50	3.00	10.00	25.00	—
1904Zs Z	368,000	1.50	3.00	10.00	20.00	—
1904Zs M	Inc. above	1.50	3.00	10.00	25.00	—
1905Zs M	66,000	7.50	20.00	50.00	200	—

20 CENTAVOS   KM# 405   Weight: 5.4150 g.
Composition: 0.9030 Silver .1572 oz. ASW **Obverse:** Restyled eagle **Note:** Struck at Culiacan Mint, mint mark Cn.

Date	Mintage	F	VF	XF	Unc	BU
1898Cn Q	114,000	5.00	12.50	35.00	140	—
1899Cn M	44,000	12.00	20.00	45.00	225	—
1899Cn Q	Inc. above	20.00	35.00	100	250	—
1900Cn Q	68,000	6.50	12.50	35.00	140	—
1901Cn Q	185,000	5.00	10.00	30.00	120	—
1902/802Cn Q	98,000	6.00	10.00	30.00	120	—
1902Cn Q	Inc. above	4.00	9.00	30.00	120	—
1903Cn Q	93,000	4.00	9.00	30.00	120	—
1904/3Cn H	258,000	—	—	—	—	—
1904Cn H	Inc. above	5.00	10.00	30.00	120	—

20 CENTAVOS   KM# 405.1   Weight: 5.4150 g.
Composition: 0.9030 Silver .1572 oz. ASW **Obverse:** Restyled eagle **Note:** Struck at Guanajuato Mint, mint mark Go.

Date	Mintage	F	VF	XF	Unc	BU
1898Go R	135,000	4.00	8.00	20.00	100	—
1899Go R	215,000	4.00	8.00	20.00	100	—
1900/800Go R	38,000	10.00	20.00	60.00	250	—

20 CENTAVOS   KM# 405.2   Weight: 5.4150 g.
Composition: 0.9030 Silver .1572 oz. ASW **Obverse:** Restyled eagle **Note:** Struck at Mexico City Mint, mint mark Mo. Varieties exist.

Date	Mintage	F	VF	XF	Unc	BU
1898Mo M	150,000	4.00	8.00	20.00	90.00	—
1899Mo M	425,000	4.00	8.00	20.00	90.00	—
1900/800Mo M	295,000	4.00	8.00	20.00	90.00	—
1901Mo M	110,000	4.00	8.00	20.00	90.00	—
1902Mo M	120,000	4.00	8.00	20.00	90.00	—
1903Mo M	213,000	4.00	8.00	20.00	90.00	—
1904Mo M	276,000	4.00	8.00	20.00	90.00	—
1905Mo M	117,000	6.50	20.00	50.00	150	—

20 CENTAVOS   KM# 405.3   Weight: 5.4150 g.
Composition: 0.9030 Silver .1572 oz. ASW **Obverse:** Restyled eagle **Note:** Struck at Zacatecas Mint, mint mark Zs.

Date	Mintage	F	VF	XF	Unc	BU
1898Zs Z	195,000	5.00	10.00	20.00	100	—
1899Zs Z	210,000	5.00	10.00	20.00	100	—
1900/800Zs Z	97,000	5.00	10.00	20.00	100	—
1901Zs Z	Inc. above	5.00	10.00	20.00	100	—
1901/0Zs Z	130,000	25.00	50.00	100	250	—
1902Zs Z	105,000	5.00	10.00	20.00	100	—
1903Zs Z	143,000	5.00	10.00	20.00	100	—
1904Zs Z	246,000	5.00	10.00	20.00	100	—
1904Zs M	Inc. above	5.00	10.00	50.00	300	—
1905Zs M	59,000	10.00	70.00	50.00	400	—

25 CENTAVOS   KM# 406   Weight: 6.7680 g.
Composition: 0.9030 Silver .1965 oz. ASW **Note:** Struck at Alamos Mint, mint mark A, As.

Date	Mintage	F	VF	XF	Unc	BU
1874 L	—	20.00	40.00	90.00	200	—
1875 L	—	15.00	30.00	70.00	200	—
1876 L	—	30.00	50.00	100	200	—
1877 L	11,000	200	300	500	—	—
1877.	Inc. above	10.00	25.00	60.00	200	—
1878 L	25,000	10.00	25.00	60.00	200	—
1879 L	—	10.00	25.00	60.00	200	—
1880 L	—	10.00	25.00	60.00	200	—
1880. L	—	10.00	25.00	60.00	200	—
1881 L	8,800	500	700	—	—	—
1882 L	7,777	15.00	35.00	80.00	200	—
1883 L	28,000	10.00	25.00	60.00	200	—
1884 L	—	10.00	25.00	60.00	200	—
1885 L	—	20.00	40.00	90.00	200	—
1886 L	46,000	15.00	30.00	70.00	200	—
1887 L	12,000	12.50	27.50	65.00	200	—
1888 L	20,000	12.50	27.50	65.00	200	—
1889 L	14,000	12.50	27.50	65.00	200	—
1890 L	23,000	10.00	25.00	60.00	200	—

25 CENTAVOS   KM# 406.1   Weight: 6.7680 g.
Composition: 0.9030 Silver .1965 oz. ASW **Note:** Struck at Chihuahua Mint, mint mark CA, CH, Ca.

Date	Mintage	F	VF	XF	Unc	BU
1871 M	18,000	25.00	50.00	100	200	—
1872 M Very crude date	24,000	50.00	100	150	300	—
1883 M	12,000	10.00	25.00	50.00	175	—
1885/3 M	35,000	10.00	25.00	50.00	175	—
1885 M	Inc. above	10.00	25.00	50.00	175	—
1886 M	22,000	10.00	25.00	50.00	175	—
1887/6 M	26,000	10.00	15.00	30.00	175	—
1887 M	Inc. above	10.00	15.00	30.00	175	—

Date	Mintage	F	VF	XF	Unc	BU
1888 M	14,000	10.00	25.00	50.00	175	—
1889 M	50,000	10.00	15.00	30.00	175	—

25 CENTAVOS   KM# 406.2   Weight: 6.7680 g.
Composition: 0.9030 Silver .1965 oz. ASW **Note:** Struck at Culiacan Mint, mint mark Cn.

Date	Mintage	F	VF	XF	Unc	BU
1871Cn P	—	250	500	750	—	—
1872Cn P	2,780	300	550	800	—	—
1873Cn P	20,000	100	150	250	500	—
1874Cn P	—	20.00	50.00	125	250	—
1875Cn P	—	250	500	750	—	—
1876Cn P Rare	—	—	—	—	—	—
1878/7Cn D/S	—	100	150	250	500	—
1878Cn Cn/Go D/S	—	100	150	250	500	—
1878Cn D	—	100	150	250	500	—
1879Cn D	—	15.00	35.00	70.00	175	—
1880Cn D	—	250	500	750	—	—
1881/0Cn D	18,000	15.00	30.00	60.00	175	—
1882Cn D	—	200	350	600	—	—
1882Cn M Rare	—	—	—	—	—	—
1883Cn M	15,000	50.00	100	150	300	—
1884Cn M	—	20.00	40.00	80.00	175	—
1885/4Cn M	19,000	20.00	40.00	80.00	175	—
1886Cn M	22,000	12.50	20.00	50.00	175	—
1887Cn M	32,000	12.50	20.00	50.00	175	—
1888Cn M	86,000	7.50	15.00	30.00	175	—
1888Cn M Cn/Mo	—	—	—	—	—	—
1889Cn M	50,000	10.00	25.00	50.00	175	—
1890Cn M 9/8	—	7.50	17.50	40.00	175	—
1890Cn M	91,000	7.50	17.50	40.00	175	—
1892/0Cn M	16,000	20.00	40.00	80.00	200	—
1892Cn M	Inc. above	20.00	40.00	80.00	200	—

25 CENTAVOS   KM# 406.3   Weight: 6.7680 g.
Composition: 0.9030 Silver .1965 oz. ASW **Note:** Struck at Durango Mint, mint mark Do.

Date	Mintage	F	VF	XF	Unc	BU
1873Do P Rare	892	—	—	—	—	—
1877Do P	—	25.00	50.00	100	200	—
1878/7Do E	—	250	500	750	—	—
1878Do B Rare	—	—	—	—	—	—
1879Do B	—	50.00	75.00	125	250	—
1880Do B Rare	—	—	—	—	—	—
1882Do C	17,000	25.00	50.00	100	225	—
1884/3Do C	—	25.00	50.00	100	200	—
1885Do C	15,000	20.00	40.00	80.00	200	—
1885Do C/S	—	20.00	40.00	80.00	200	—
1886Do C	33,000	15.00	30.00	60.00	200	—
1887Do C	27,000	10.00	20.00	50.00	200	—
1888Do C	25,000	10.00	20.00	50.00	200	—
1889Do C	29,000	10.00	20.00	50.00	200	—
1890Do C	68,000	7.50	15.00	40.00	200	—

25 CENTAVOS   KM# 406.4   Weight: 6.7680 g.
Composition: 0.9030 Silver .1965 oz. ASW **Note:** Struck at Guadalajara Mint, mint mark Ga.

Date	Mintage	F	VF	XF	Unc	BU
1880Ga A	38,000	25.00	50.00	100	200	—
1881/0Ga S	39,000	25.00	50.00	100	200	—
1881Ga S	Inc. above	25.00	50.00	100	200	—
1882Ga S	18,000	25.00	50.00	100	200	—
1883/2Ga B/S	—	50.00	100	150	300	—
1884Ga B	—	20.00	40.00	80.00	150	—
1889Ga S	30,000	20.00	40.00	80.00	150	—

25 CENTAVOS   KM# 406.5   Weight: 6.7680 g.
Composition: 0.9030 Silver .1965 oz. ASW **Note:** Struck at Guanajuato Mint, mint mark Go. Varieties exist.

Date	Mintage	F	VF	XF	Unc	BU
1870Go S	128,000	10.00	20.00	50.00	125	—
1871Go S	172,000	10.00	20.00	50.00	125	—
1872/1Go S	178,000	10.00	20.00	50.00	125	—
1872Go S	Inc. above	10.00	20.00	50.00	125	—
1873Go S	120,000	10.00	20.00	50.00	125	—
1874Go S	—	15.00	30.00	60.00	150	—
1875/4Go S	—	15.00	30.00	60.00	150	—
1875Go S	—	10.00	20.00	50.00	125	—
1876Go S	—	20.00	40.00	80.00	175	—
1877Go S	124,000	10.00	20.00	50.00	125	—
1878Go S	146,000	10.00	20.00	50.00	125	—

Date	Mintage	F	VF	XF	Unc	BU
1879Go S	—	10.00	20.00	50.00	125	—
1880Go S	—	20.00	40.00	80.00	175	—
1881Go S	408,000	7.50	17.50	45.00	125	—
1882Go S	204,000	7.50	17.50	45.00	125	—
1883Go B	168,000	7.50	17.50	45.00	125	—
1884/69Go B	—	7.50	17.50	45.00	125	—
1884/3Go B	—	7.50	17.50	45.00	125	—
1884/3Go B/R	—	7.50	17.50	45.00	125	—
1884Go B	—	7.50	17.50	45.00	125	—
1885/65Go R	300,000	7.50	17.50	45.00	125	—
1885/69Go R	Inc. above	7.50	17.50	45.00	125	—
1885Go R	Inc. above	7.50	17.50	45.00	125	—
1886/66Go R	322,000	7.50	17.50	45.00	125	—
1886/69Go R/S	Inc. above	7.50	17.50	45.00	125	—
1886/5/69Go R	Inc. above	7.50	15.00	45.00	125	—
1886Go R	Inc. above	7.50	15.00	45.00	125	—
1887Go R	254,000	7.50	15.00	45.00	125	—
1887Go/Cn R/D	Inc. above	7.50	15.00	45.00	125	—
1888Go R	312,000	7.50	15.00	45.00	125	—
1889/8Go R	304,000	7.50	15.00	45.00	125	—
1889/8Go/Cn R/D	Inc. above	7.50	15.00	45.00	125	—
1889Go R	Inc. above	7.50	15.00	45.00	125	—
1890Go R	236,000	7.50	15.00	45.00	125	—

25 CENTAVOS   KM# 406.6   Weight: 6.7680 g.
Composition: 0.9030 Silver .1965 oz. ASW **Note:** Struck at Hermosillo Mint, mint mark Ho. Varieties exist.

Date	Mintage	F	VF	XF	Unc	BU
1874/64Ho R	Inc. above	10.00	20.00	40.00	125	—
1874/69Ho R	—	10.00	20.00	40.00	125	—
1874Ho R	23,000	10.00	20.00	40.00	125	—
1875Ho R Rare	—	—	—	—	—	—
1876/4Ho F/R	34,000	10.00	20.00	50.00	150	—
1876Ho F/R	Inc. above	10.00	25.00	60.00	150	—
1876Ho F	Inc. above	10.00	25.00	55.00	135	—
1877Ho F	—	10.00	20.00	50.00	125	—
1878Ho A	23,000	10.00	20.00	50.00	125	—
1879Ho A	—	10.00	20.00	50.00	125	—
1880Ho A	—	15.00	30.00	60.00	125	—
1881Ho A	19,000	15.00	30.00	60.00	125	—
1882Ho A	8,120	20.00	40.00	80.00	150	—
1883Ho M	2,000	100	200	300	600	—
1884Ho M	—	12.50	25.00	50.00	150	—
1885Ho M	—	10.00	20.00	50.00	125	—
1886Ho G	6,400	30.00	60.00	125	250	—
1887Ho G	12,000	10.00	20.00	40.00	125	—
1888Ho G	20,000	10.00	20.00	40.00	125	—
1889Ho G	28,000	10.00	20.00	40.00	125	—
1890/80Ho G	18,000	25.00	50.00	100	125	—
1890Ho G	Inc. above	25.00	50.00	100	125	—

25 CENTAVOS   KM# 406.7   Weight: 6.7680 g.
Composition: 0.9030 Silver .1965 oz. ASW **Note:** Struck at Mexico City Mint, mint mark Mo. Varieties exist.

Date	Mintage	F	VF	XF	Unc	BU
1869Mo C	76,000	10.00	25.00	50.00	125	—
1870/69Mo C	—	6.00	12.00	30.00	125	—
1870/9Mo C	136,000	6.00	12.00	30.00	125	—
1870Mo C	Inc. above	6.00	12.00	30.00	125	—
1871Mo M	138,000	6.00	12.00	30.00	125	—
1872Mo M	220,000	6.00	12.00	30.00	125	—
1873/1Mo M	48,000	10.00	25.00	50.00	125	—
1873Mo M	Inc. above	10.00	25.00	50.00	125	—
1874/69Mo B/M	—	10.00	25.00	50.00	125	—
1874/3Mo M	—	10.00	25.00	50.00	125	—
1874/3Mo B	—	10.00	25.00	50.00	125	—
1874/3Mo B/M	—	10.00	25.00	50.00	125	—

Date	Mintage	F	VF	XF	Unc	BU
1874Mo M	—	6.00	12.00	30.00	125	—
1874Mo B/M	—	10.00	25.00	50.00	125	—
1875Mo B	—	6.00	12.00	30.00	125	—
1876/5Mo B	—	7.50	15.00	40.00	125	—
1876Mo B	—	6.00	12.00	30.00	125	—
1877Mo M	56,000	10.00	25.00	50.00	125	—
1878/1Mo M	120,000	10.00	25.00	50.00	125	—
1878/7Mo M	Inc. above	10.00	25.00	50.00	125	—
1878Mo M	Inc. above	6.00	12.00	30.00	125	—
1879Mo M	—	10.00	20.00	40.00	125	—
1880Mo M	—	7.50	15.00	35.00	125	—
1881/0Mo M	300,000	10.00	25.00	50.00	125	—
1881Mo M	Inc. above	10.00	25.00	50.00	125	—
1882Mo M	212,000	7.50	15.00	35.00	125	—
1883Mo M	108,000	7.50	15.00	35.00	125	—
1884/3Mo M	—	10.00	25.00	50.00	125	—
1884Mo M	—	10.00	20.00	40.00	125	—
1885Mo M	216,000	10.00	25.00	50.00	125	—
1886/5Mo M	436,000	7.50	15.00	35.00	125	—
1886Mo M	Inc. above	7.50	15.00	35.00	125	—
1887Mo M	376,000	7.50	15.00	35.00	125	—
1888Mo M	192,000	7.50	15.00	35.00	125	—
1889Mo M	132,000	7.50	15.00	35.00	125	—
1890Mo M	60,000	10.00	20.00	40.00	125	—

25 CENTAVOS KM# 406.8 Weight: 6.7680 g.
Composition: 0.9030 Silver .1965 oz. ASW **Note:** Struck at San Luis Potosi Mint, mint mark Pi. Varieties exist.

Date	Mintage	F	VF	XF	Unc	BU
1869 Pi S	—	25.00	75.00	150	300	—
1870 Pi G	50,000	10.00	30.00	75.00	150	—
1870 Pi O	Inc. above	15.00	35.00	85.00	175	—
1871 Pi O	30,000	10.00	30.00	75.00	150	—
1872 Pi O	46,000	10.00	30.00	75.00	150	—
1873 Pi O	13,000	15.00	40.00	90.00	175	—
1874 Pi H	—	15.00	40.00	90.00	200	—
1875 Pi H	—	10.00	20.00	60.00	150	—
1876/5 Pi H	—	15.00	30.00	80.00	175	—
1876 Pi H	—	10.00	25.00	65.00	150	—
1877 Pi H	19,000	10.00	25.00	65.00	150	—
1878 Pi H	—	15.00	30.00	60.00	150	—
1879/8 Pi H	—	10.00	25.00	60.00	150	—
1879 Pi H	—	10.00	25.00	60.00	150	—
1879 Pi E	—	100	200	300	600	—
1880 Pi H	—	20.00	40.00	100	200	—
1880 Pi H/M	—	20.00	40.00	100	200	—
1881 Pi H	50,000	20.00	40.00	80.00	175	—
1881 Pi E Rare	Inc. above	—	—	—	—	—
1882 Pi H	20,000	10.00	25.00	60.00	150	—
1883 Pi H	17,000	10.00	25.00	65.00	150	—
1884 Pi H	—	10.00	25.00	65.00	150	—
1885/4 Pi H	—	10.00	20.00	60.00	150	—
1885 Pi H	43,000	10.00	20.00	60.00	150	—
1886 Pi C	78,000	10.00	25.00	65.00	150	—
1886 Pi R	Inc. above	7.50	20.00	50.00	150	—
1886 Pi R 6/inverted 6	Inc. above	7.50	20.00	50.00	150	—
1887Pi/ZsR	92,000	7.50	20.00	50.00	150	—
1887Pi/ZsB	Inc. above	100	150	300	500	—
1887 Pi R	—	7.50	20.00	50.00	150	—
1888 Pi R	106,000	7.50	20.00	50.00	150	—
1888Pi/ZsR	Inc. above	10.00	20.00	50.00	150	—
1888 Pi R/B	Inc. above	10.00	20.00	50.00	150	—
1889 Pi R	115,000	7.50	15.00	40.00	150	—
1889Pi/ZsR	Inc. above	10.00	20.00	50.00	150	—
1889 Pi R/B	Inc. above	10.00	20.00	50.00	150	—
1890 Pi R	64,000	10.00	20.00	50.00	150	—
1890Pi/ZsR/B	Inc. above	7.50	15.00	40.00	150	—
1890 Pi R/B	Inc. above	10.00	20.00	50.00	150	—

25 CENTAVOS KM# 406.9 Weight: 6.7680 g.
Composition: 0.9030 Silver .1965 oz. ASW **Note:** Struck at Zacatecas Mint, mint mark Zs. Varieties exist.

Date	Mintage	F	VF	XF	Unc	BU
1870Zs H	152,000	6.00	15.00	50.00	125	—
1871Zs H	250,000	6.00	15.00	50.00	125	—

Date	Mintage	F	VF	XF	Unc	BU
1872Zs H	260,000	6.00	15.00	50.00	125	—
1872Zs H	—	—	—	—	—	—
1873Zs H	132,000	6.00	15.00	50.00	125	—
1874Zs H	—	10.00	20.00	60.00	125	—
1874Zs A	—	10.00	20.00	60.00	125	—
1875Zs A	—	7.00	20.00	60.00	125	—
1876Zs A	—	6.00	15.00	50.00	125	—
1876Zs S	—	6.00	15.00	50.00	125	—
1877Zs S	350,000	6.00	15.00	50.00	125	—
1878Zs S	252,000	6.00	15.00	50.00	125	—
1878/1Zs S	—	7.00	20.00	60.00	125	—
1878/7Zs S	—	7.00	20.00	60.00	125	—
1879Zs S	—	6.00	15.00	50.00	125	—
1880Zs S	—	6.00	15.00	50.00	125	—
1881/0Zs S	570,000	6.00	15.00	50.00	125	—
1881Zs S	Inc. above	6.00	15.00	50.00	125	—
1882/1Zs S	300,000	10.00	17.50	55.00	125	—
1882Zs S	Inc. above	6.00	15.00	50.00	125	—
1883/2Zs S	193,000	10.00	17.50	55.00	125	—
1883Zs S	Inc. above	6.00	15.00	50.00	125	—
1884/3Zs S	—	10.00	17.50	55.00	125	—
1884Zs S	—	6.00	15.00	50.00	125	—
1885Zs S	309,000	6.00	15.00	50.00	125	—
1886/2Zs S	—	10.00	17.50	55.00	125	—
1886/5Zs S	613,000	6.00	15.00	50.00	125	—
1886Zs S	Inc. above	6.00	15.00	50.00	125	—
1886Zs Z	Inc. above	6.00	15.00	55.00	125	—
1887Zs Z	389,000	6.00	15.00	50.00	125	—
1888Zs Z	408,000	6.00	15.00	50.00	125	—
1889Zs Z	400,000	6.00	15.00	50.00	125	—
1890Zs Z	269,000	6.00	15.00	50.00	125	—

50 CENTAVOS KM# 407.7 Weight: 13.5360 g.
Composition: 0.9030 Silver .3930 oz. ASW **Reverse:** Balance scale **Note:** Struck at San Luis Potosi Mint, mint mark Pi.

Date	Mintage	F	VF	XF	Unc	BU
1870 Pi G	Inc. above	20.00	40.00	100	450	—
1870/780 Pi G	50,000	25.00	45.00	110	500	—
1870 Pi O	Inc. above	20.00	40.00	100	450	—
1871 Pi O	—	15.00	30.00	80.00	400	—
1871 Pi O/G	64,000	15.00	30.00	80.00	400	—
1872 Pi O	52,000	15.00	30.00	80.00	400	—
1872 Pi O/G	Inc. above	15.00	30.00	80.00	400	—
1873 Pi O	32,000	20.00	40.00	100	450	—
1873 Pi H	Inc. above	25.00	50.00	125	550	—
1874 Pi H/O	—	15.00	30.00	80.00	400	—
1875/3 Pi H	—	15.00	30.00	80.00	400	—
1875 Pi H	—	15.00	30.00	80.00	400	—
1876 Pi H	—	30.00	60.00	150	700	—
1877 Pi H	34,000	20.00	40.00	100	450	—
1878 Pi H	9,70?	20.00	40.00	100	450	—
1879/7 Pi H	—	15.00	35.00	90.00	450	—
1879 Pi H	—	15.00	35.00	90.00	400	—
1880 Pi H	—	20.00	40.00	100	450	—
1881 Pi H	28,000	20.00	40.00	100	450	—
1882 Pi H	22,000	15.00	30.00	80.00	400	—
1883 Pi H 8/8	29,000	50.00	100	200	750	—
1883 Pi H	Inc. above	15.00	30.00	80.00	400	—
1884 Pi H	—	50.00	100	175	600	—
1885/3 Pi H	—	20.00	40.00	100	450	—
1885/0 Pi H	45,000	20.00	40.00	100	450	—
1885/4 Pi H	Inc. above	20.00	40.00	100	450	—
1885 Pi H	Inc. above	25.00	50.00	125	450	—
1885 Pi C	Inc. above	15.00	30.00	80.00	400	—
1886/1 Pi R	92,000	50.00	100	175	600	—
1886/1 Pi C	—	25.00	40.00	100	450	—
1886 Pi C	Inc. above	15.00	30.00	80.00	400	—
1886 Pi R	Inc. above	15.00	30.00	80.00	400	—
1887 Pi R	32,000	15.00	30.00	90.00	450	—

50 CENTAVOS   KM# 407.8   Weight: 13.5360 g.
Composition: 0.9030 Silver .3930 oz. ASW **Reverse:**
Balance scale **Note:** Struck at Zacatecas Mint, mint mark
Zs. Varieties exist.

Date	Mintage	F	VF	XF	Unc	BU
1870Zs H	86,000	12.00	25.00	60.00	450	—
1871Zs H	146,000	12.00	25.00	50.00	400	—
1872Zs H	132,000	12.00	25.00	50.00	400	—
1873Zs H	56,000	12.00	25.00	50.00	400	—
1874Zs H	—	12.00	25.00	50.00	400	—
1874Zs A Rare	—	—	—	—	—	—
1875Zs A	—	12.00	25.00	50.00	400	—
1876/5Zs A	—	15.00	30.00	60.00	450	—
1876Zs A	—	12.00	25.00	50.00	400	—
1876Zs S	—	100	200	350	750	—
1877Zs S	100,000	12.00	25.00	50.00	400	—
1878/7Zs S	254,000	15.00	30.00	60.00	450	—
1878Zs S	Inc. above	15.00	30.00	60.00	450	—
1879Zs S	—	12.00	25.00	50.00	400	—
1880Zs S	—	12.00	25.00	50.00	400	—
1881Zs S	201,000	12.00	25.00	50.00	400	—
1882/1Zs S	2,000	50.00	100	250	650	—
1882Zs S	Inc. above	50.00	100	250	650	—
1883Zs/Za S	31,000	30.00	60.00	100	450	—
1883Zs S	Inc. above	25.00	50.00	100	450	—
1884/3Zs S	—	15.00	30.00	60.00	450	—
1884Zs S	—	12.00	25.00	50.00	400	—
1885/4Zs S	2,000	25.00	50.00	125	450	—
1885Zs S	Inc. above	25.00	50.00	125	450	—
1886Zs Z	2,000	150	275	400	1,000	—
1887Zs Z	63,000	30.00	60.00	125	450	—

50 CENTAVOS   KM# 407   Weight: 13.5360 g.
Composition: 0.9030 Silver .3930 oz. ASW **Reverse:**
Balance scale **Note:** Struck at Alamos Mint, mint mark A, As.

Date	Mintage	F	VF	XF	Unc	BU
1875 L	—	12.00	25.00	70.00	400	—
1876/5 L	—	25.00	50.00	120	450	—
1876 L	—	12.00	25.00	70.00	400	—
1876 L	—	—	—	—	—	—
1877 L	26,000	15.00	30.00	85.00	450	—
1878 L	—	12.00	25.00	70.00	400	—
1879 L	—	25.00	50.00	120	450	—
1880 L	57,000	12.00	25.00	70.00	400	—
1881 L	18,000	15.00	30.00	80.00	450	—
1884 L	6,286	65.00	120	250	650	—
1885As/HoL	21,000	15.00	35.00	90.00	450	—
1888 L	—	4,000	5,000	7,000	—	—

50 CENTAVOS   KM# 407.1   Weight: 13.5360 g.
Composition: 0.9030 Silver .3930 oz. ASW **Reverse:**
Balance scale **Note:** Struck at Chihuahua Mint, mint mark
Ca, CHa.

Date	Mintage	F	VF	XF	Unc	BU
1883/9 M	—	30.00	60.00	125	500	—
1883 M	12,000	30.00	60.00	125	500	—
1884 M	—	25.00	50.00	125	500	—
1885 M	13,000	15.00	35.00	90.00	400	—
1886 M	18,000	20.00	40.00	100	450	—
1887 M	26,000	25.00	65.00	150	500	—

50 CENTAVOS   KM# 407.2   Weight: 13.5360 g.
Composition: 0.9030 Silver .3930 oz. ASW **Reverse:**
Balance scale **Note:** Struck at Culiacan Mint, mint mark Cn.

Date	Mintage	F	VF	XF	Unc	BU
1871Cn P	—	400	550	750	1,500	—
1873Cn P	—	400	550	750	1,500	—
1874Cn P	—	200	300	500	1,000	—
1875/4Cn P	—	20.00	40.00	75.00	450	—
1875Cn P	—	12.00	25.00	50.00	450	—
1876Cn P	—	15.00	30.00	60.00	450	—
1877/6Cn G	—	15.00	30.00	60.00	450	—
1877Cn G	—	12.00	25.00	50.00	450	—
1878Cn G	18,000	20.00	40.00	75.00	450	—
1878Cn/Mo D	Inc. above	30.00	60.00	100	450	—
1878Cn D	Inc. above	15.00	35.00	75.00	450	—
1879Cn D	—	12.00	25.00	50.00	450	—
1879Cn D/G	—	12.00	25.00	50.00	450	—
1880/8Cn D	—	15.00	30.00	60.00	450	—
1880Cn D	—	15.00	30.00	60.00	450	—
1881/0Cn D	188,000	15.00	30.00	60.00	450	—
1881Cn D	Inc. above	15.00	30.00	60.00	450	—
1881Cn G	Inc. above	125	175	275	550	—
1882Cn D	—	175	300	500	2,000	—

Date	Mintage	F	VF	XF	Unc	BU
1882Gn G	—	100	250	300	1,000	—
1883 D	19,000	25.00	50.00	100	500	—
1885/3CN/Pi M/H	9,254	30.00	60.00	100	500	—
1885Cn	—	30.00	60.00	100	500	—
1886Cn M/G	7,030	50.00	100	300	1,500	—
1886Cn M	Inc. above	40.00	80.00	150	800	—
1887Cn M	76,000	20.00	40.00	100	450	—
1888Cn M	—	4,000	6,000	—	—	—
1892Cn M	8,200	40.00	80.00	150	650	—

50 CENTAVOS   KM# 407.3   Weight: 13.5360 g.
Composition: 0.9030 Silver .3930 oz. ASW **Reverse:**
Balance scale **Note:** Struck at Durango Mint, mint mark Do.

Date	Mintage	F	VF	XF	Unc	BU
1871Do P Rare	591	—	—	—	—	—
1873Do P	4,010	150	250	500	1,250	—
1873Do M/P	Inc. above	150	250	500	1,250	—
1874Do M	—	20.00	40.00	175	750	—
1875Do M	—	20.00	40.00	80.00	350	—
1875Do H	—	150	250	450	1,000	—
1876/5Do M	—	35.00	70.00	150	500	—
1876Do M	—	35.00	70.00	150	500	—
1877Do P	2,000	30.00	45.00	150	1,250	—
1878Do B Rare	—	—	—	—	—	—
1879Do B Rare	—	—	—	—	—	—
1880Do P	—	30.00	60.00	125	500	—
1881Do P	10,000	40.00	80.00	150	550	—
1882Do C	8,957	30.00	75.00	200	800	—
1884/2Do C	—	20.00	50.00	125	600	—
1884Do C	—	—	—	—	—	—
1885Do B	—	15.00	40.00	100	500	—
1885Do B/P	—	15.00	40.00	100	500	—
1886Do C	16,000	15.00	40.00	100	500	—
1887Do/Mo C	28,000	15.00	40.00	100	500	—
1887Do C	—	15.00	40.00	100	500	—

50 CENTAVOS   KM# 407.4   Weight: 13.5360 g.
Composition: 0.9030 Silver .3930 oz. ASW **Reverse:**
Balance scale **Note:** Struck at Guanajuato Mint, mitn mark
Go. Varieties exist.

Date	Mintage	F	VF	XF	Unc	BU
1869Go S	—	15.00	35.00	75.00	550	—
1870Go S	166,000	12.00	25.00	50.00	450	—
1871Go S	148,000	12.00	25.00	50.00	450	—
1872/1Go S	144,000	15.00	30.00	60.00	500	—
1872Go S	Inc. above	12.00	25.00	50.00	450	—
1873Go S	50,000	12.00	25.00	50.00	450	—
1874Go S	—	12.00	25.00	50.00	450	—
1875Go S	—	15.00	35.00	75.00	450	—
1876/5Go S	—	12.00	25.00	50.00	450	—
1877Go S	76,000	12.00	25.00	60.00	450	—
1878Go S	37,000	15.00	30.00	75.00	550	—
1879/8Go S	—	15.00	30.00	60.00	500	—
1879Go S	—	12.00	25.00	50.00	450	—
1880Go S	—	12.00	25.00	50.00	450	—
1881/79Go S	32,000	15.00	30.00	60.00	500	—
1881Go S	Inc. above	12.00	25.00	50.00	450	—
1882Go S	18,000	12.00	25.00	50.00	450	—
1883/2Go B/S	—	15.00	30.00	60.00	500	—
1883Go S	—	12.00	25.00	50.00	450	—
1883Go S Rare	—	—	—	—	—	—
1884Go B/S	—	15.00	30.00	60.00	500	—
1885/4Go R/B	—	15.00	30.00	60.00	500	—
1885Go R	53,000	12.00	25.00	50.00	450	—
1886/5Go R/B	59,000	15.00	30.00	60.00	500	—
1886/5Go R/S	Inc. above	20.00	40.00	75.00	500	—
1886Go R	Inc. above	20.00	40.00	75.00	450	—
1887Go R	18,000	20.00	40.00	75.00	550	—
1888Go R 1 known; Rare	—	—	—	—	—	—

50 CENTAVOS   KM# 407.5   Weight: 13.5360 g.
Composition: 0.9030 Silver .3930 oz. ASW **Reverse:**
Balance scale **Note:** Struck at Hermosillo Mint, mint mark
Ho. Varieties exist.

Date	Mintage	F	VF	XF	Unc	BU
1874Ho R	—	20.00	40.00	100	600	—
1875/4Ho R	—	20.00	50.00	125	600	—
1875Ho R	—	20.00	50.00	125	600	—
1876/5Ho F/R	—	15.00	35.00	100	550	—

Date	Mintage	F	VF	XF	Unc	BU
1876Ho F	—	15.00	35.00	100	550	—
1877Ho F	—	50.00	75.00	150	650	—
1880/70Ho A	—	15.00	35.00	100	550	—
1880Ho A	—	15.00	35.00	100	550	—
1881Ho A	13,000	15.00	35.00	100	550	—
1882Ho A	—	75.00	150	250	750	—
1888Ho G	—	2,000	3,000	6,000	—	—
1894Ho G	59,000	15.00	30.00	100	450	—
1895Ho G	8,000	250	350	700	1,500	—

50 CENTAVOS KM# 407.6 Weight: 13.5360 g.
Composition: 0.9030 Silver .3930 oz. ASW **Reverse:**
Balance scale **Note:** Struck at Mexico City Mint, mint mark
Mo.

Date	Mintage	F	VF	XF	Unc	BU
1869Mo C	46,000	15.00	35.00	95.00	600	—
1870Mo C	52,000	15.00	30.00	90.00	550	—
1871Mo C	14,000	40.00	75.00	150	650	—
1871Mo M/C	Inc. above	35.00	75.00	150	600	—
1872/1Mo M	60,000	35.00	75.00	150	550	—
1872Mo M	Inc. above	35.00	75.00	150	550	—
1873Mo M	6,000	35.00	75.00	150	600	—
1874/3Mo M	—	200	400	600	1,250	—
1874/2Mo B	—	15.00	30.00	75.00	500	—
1874/2Mo B/M	—	15.00	30.00	75.00	500	—
1874/3Mo B/M	—	15.00	30.00	75.00	500	—
1874Mo B	—	15.00	30.00	75.00	500	—
1875Mo B	—	15.00	30.00	75.00	500	—
1876/5Mo B	—	15.00	30.00	75.00	500	—
1876Mo B	—	12.00	25.00	75.00	500	—
1877/2Mo M	—	20.00	40.00	100	550	—
1877Mo M	—	15.00	30.00	90.00	500	—
1878/7Mo M	8,000	25.00	50.00	125	600	—
1878Mo M	Inc. above	15.00	35.00	100	550	—
1879Mo M	—	25.00	50.00	125	550	—
1880Mo M	—	100	150	250	750	—
1881Mo M	16,000	25.00	50.00	125	600	—
1881/0Mo M	—	30.00	50.00	125	600	—
1882/1Mo M	2,000	30.00	60.00	150	750	—
1883/2Mo M	4,000	150	225	350	1,000	—
1884Mo M	—	150	225	350	1,000	—
1885Mo M	12,000	30.00	60.00	150	600	—
1886/5Mo M	66,000	15.00	35.00	90.00	475	—
1886Mo M	Inc. above	12.00	25.00	75.00	450	—
1887/6Mo M	88,000	15.00	35.00	90.00	475	—
1887Mo M	Inc. above	15.00	30.00	75.00	475	—
1888Mo M	—	3,000	4,000	6,000	—	—

PESO KM# 408 Weight: 27.0730 g. **Composition:**
0.9030 Silver .7860 oz. ASW **Reverse:** Balance scale **Note:**
Struck at Chihuahua Mint, mint mark CH.

Date	Mintage	F	VF	XF	Unc	BU
1872CH M	Inc. above	17.50	25.00	50.00	250	—
1872CH P/M	747,000	750	1,500	3,500	—	—
1872CH P	—	350	700	1,500	—	—
1872/1CH M	Inc. above	25.00	40.00	75.00	400	—
1873CH M	320,000	20.00	30.00	60.00	265	—
1873CH M/P	Inc. above	25.00	40.00	75.00	350	—

PESO KM# 408.1 Weight: 27.0730 g. **Composition:**
0.9030 Silver .7860 oz. ASW **Reverse:** Balance scale **Note:**
Struck at Culiacan Mint, mint mark Cn.

Date	Mintage	F	VF	XF	Unc	BU
1870Cn E	—	40.00	80.00	150	500	—
1871/11Cn P	478,000	25.00	45.00	100	450	—
1871Cn P	Inc. above	20.00	40.00	75.00	300	—
1872/1Cn P	—	20.00	40.00	75.00	300	—
1872Cn P	209,000	20.00	40.00	75.00	300	—
1873Cn P narrow date	527,000	20.00	40.00	75.00	300	—
1873Cn P wide date	Inc. above	20.00	40.00	75.00	300	—

PESO KM# 408.2 Weight: 27.0730 g. **Composition:**
0.9030 Silver .7860 oz. ASW **Reverse:** Balance scale **Note:**
Struck at Durango Mint, mint mark Do.

Date	Mintage	F	VF	XF	Unc	BU
1870Do P	—	50.00	100	175	450	—
1871Do P	427,000	25.00	50.00	75.00	300	—
1872Do P	296,000	20.00	40.00	75.00	350	—
1872Do PT	Inc. above	100	175	250	850	—
1873Do P	203,000	25.00	45.00	85.00	350	—

PESO KM# 408.3 Weight: 27.0730 g. **Composition:**
0.9030 Silver .7860 oz. ASW **Reverse:** Balance scale **Note:**
Struck at Guadalajara Mint, mint mark Ga.

Date	Mintage	F	VF	XF	Unc	BU
1870Ga C	—	650	850	—	—	—
1871Ga C	829,000	25.00	65.00	135	600	—
1872Ga C	485,000	40.00	90.00	175	650	—
1873/2Ga C	277,000	40.00	90.00	175	700	—
1873Ga C	Inc. above	25.00	65.00	135	600	—

PESO KM# 408.4 Weight: 27.0730 g. **Composition:**
0.9030 Silver .7860 oz. ASW **Reverse:** Balance scale **Note:**
Struck at Guanajuato Mint, mint mark Go.

Date	Mintage	F	VF	XF	Unc	BU
1871/0Go S	3,946,000	30.00	50.00	90.00	350	—
1871/3Go S	Inc. above	20.00	35.00	70.00	275	—
1871Go S	Inc. above	12.00	20.00	40.00	220	—
1872Go S	4,067,000	12.00	20.00	40.00	250	—
1873/2Go S	1,560,000	15.00	25.00	50.00	250	—
1873Go S	Inc. above	12.00	20.00	45.00	250	—
1873Go/Mo/S/M	Inc. above	12.00	20.00	45.00	250	—

PESO KM# 408.5 Weight: 27.0730 g. **Composition:**
0.9030 Silver .7860 oz. ASW **Reverse:** Balance scale **Note:**
Struck at Mexico City Mint, mark mark Mo.

Date	Mintage	F	VF	XF	Unc	BU
1869Mo C	—	35.00	65.00	135	600	—
1870/69Mo C	5,115,000	15.00	25.00	55.00	275	—
1870Mo C	Inc. above	12.00	20.00	40.00	250	—
1870Mo M/C	Inc. above	18.00	30.00	60.00	275	—
1870Mo M	Inc. above	18.00	30.00	60.00	275	—
1871/0Mo M	6,974,000	15.00	25.00	55.00	275	—
1871Mo M	Inc. above	12.00	20.00	40.00	250	—
1872/1Mo M	—	15.00	25.00	50.00	275	—
1872/1Mo M/C	4,801,000	15.00	25.00	50.00	275	—
1872Mo M	Inc. above	12.00	20.00	40.00	250	—
1873Mo M	1,765,000	12.00	20.00	40.00	250	—

Note: The 1869 C with large LEY on the scroll is a pattern

PESO KM# 408.6 Weight: 27.0730 g. **Composition:**
0.9030 Silver .7860 oz. ASW **Reverse:** Balance scale **Note:**
Struck at Oaxaca Mint, mint mark Oa.

Date	Mintage	F	VF	XF	Unc	BU
1869 Oa E	—	275	400	600	2,000	—
1870 Oa E Small A	Inc. above	15.00	30.00	75.00	400	—
1870OA E Large A	Inc. above	100	150	300	900	—
1871/69 Oa E	140,000	30.00	50.00	125	550	—
1871 Oa E Small A	Inc. above	15.00	30.00	60.00	300	—
1871OA E Large A	Inc. above	15.00	30.00	75.00	400	—
1872 Oa E Small A	180,000	15.00	30.00	75.00	400	—
1872OA E Large A	Inc. above	50.00	100	200	450	—
1873 Oa E	105,000	15.00	30.00	75.00	350	—

PESO KM# 408.7 Weight: 27.0730 g. **Composition:**
0.9030 Silver .7860 oz. ASW **Reverse:** Balance scale **Note:**
Struck at San Luis Potosi Mint, mint mark Pi. Varieties exist.

Date	Mintage	F	VF	XF	Unc	BU
1870 Pi S	1,967,000	200	350	500	1,000	—
1870 Pi S/A	Inc. above	200	350	500	1,000	—
1870 Pi G	Inc. above	25.00	50.00	125	450	—

Date	Mintage	F	VF	XF	Unc	BU
1870 Pi H Contemporarary counterfeits	Inc. above	—	—	—	—	—
1870 Pi O/G	Inc. above	25.00	35.00	125	450	—
1870 Pi O	Inc. above	20.00	30.00	100	350	—
1871/69 Pi O	2,103,000	75.00	150	250	500	—
1871 Pi O/G	Inc. above	15.00	30.00	60.00	300	—
1871 Pi O	—	15.00	30.00	60.00	300	—
1872 Pi O	1,873,000	15.00	30.00	60.00	300	—
1873 Pi O	893,000	15.00	30.00	60.00	300	—
1873 Pi H	Inc. above	15.00	30.00	60.00	300	—

PESO   KM# 408.8   Weight: 27.0730 g. **Composition:** 0.9030 Silver .7860 oz. ASW **Reverse:** Balance scale **Note:** Struck at Zacatecas Mint, mint mark Zs. Varieties exist.

Date	Mintage	F	VF	XF	Unc	BU
1870Zs H	4,519,000	12.00	30.00	40.00	220	—
1871Zs H	4,459,000	12.00	20.00	40.00	220	—
1872Zs H	4,039,000	12.00	20.00	40.00	220	—
1873/1Zs H	Inc. above	12.00	20.00	40.00	220	—
1873Zs H	1,782,000	12.00	20.00	40.00	220	—

PESO   KM# 409   Weight: 27.0730 g. **Composition:** 0.9030 Silver .7860 oz. ASW **Reverse:** Liberty cap **Note:** Struck at Culiacan Mint, mint mark Cn.

Date	Mintage	F	VF	XF	Unc	BU
1898Cn AM	1,720,000	10.00	15.00	25.00	65.00	—
1898Cn/ MoAM	Inc. above	15.00	30.00	90.00	150	—
1899Cn AM	1,722,000	25.00	50.00	90.00	175	—
1899Cn JQ	Inc. above	10.00	15.00	50.00	125	—
1900Cn JQ	1,804,000	10.00	15.00	25.00	75.00	—
1901Cn JQ	1,473,000	10.00	15.00	25.00	75.00	—
1902Cn JQ	1,194,000	10.00	15.00	45.00	125	—
1903Cn JQ	1,514,000	10.00	15.00	30.00	85.00	—
1903Cn FV	Inc. above	25.00	50.00	100	225	—
1904Cn MH	1,554,000	10.00	15.00	25.00	75.00	—
1904Cn RP	Inc. above	50.00	100	150	350	—
1905Cn RP	598,000	25.00	50.00	100	250	—

PESO   KM# 409.1   Weight: 27.0730 g. **Composition:** 0.9030 Silver .7860 oz. ASW **Reverse:** Liberty cap **Note:** Struck at Guanajuato Mint, mint mark Go. Varieties exist.

Date	Mintage	F	VF	XF	Unc	BU
1898Go RS	4,256,000	10.00	15.00	35.00	75.00	—
1898Go/MoRS	Inc. above	20.00	30.00	60.00	125	—
1899Go RS	3,207,000	10.00	15.00	30.00	75.00	—
1900Go RS	1,489,000	25.00	50.00	100	250	—

PESO   KM# 409.2   Weight: 27.0730 g. **Composition:** 0.9030 Silver .7860 oz. ASW **Reverse:** Liberty cap **Note:** Struck at Mexico City Mint, mint mark Mo. Varieties exist.

Date	Mintage	F	VF	XF	Unc	BU
1898Mo AM Original strike - reverse with 139 beads	10,156,000	9.00	11.50	18.50	60.00	—
1898Mo AM Restrike (1949) - reverse with 134 beads	10,250,000	9.00	11.50	16.50	40.00	—
1899Mo AM	7,930,000	10.00	12.50	20.00	70.00	—
1900Mo AM	8,226,000	10.00	12.50	20.00	70.00	—
1901Mo AM	14,505,000	9.00	11.50	20.00	70.00	—
1902/1Mo AM	16,224,000	150	300	500	950	—
1902Mo AM	Inc. above	9.00	11.50	20.00	70.00	—
1903Mo AM	22,396,000	9.00	11.50	20.00	70.00	—

Date	Mintage	F	VF	XF	Unc	BU
1903Mo AM (Error)	Inc. above	1,500	2,500	3,500	7,500	—
1904Mo AM	14,935,000	9.00	11.50	20.00	70.00	—
1905Mo AM	3,557,000	15.00	25.00	55.00	125	—
1908Mo AM	7,575,000	10.00	12.50	20.00	60.00	—
1908Mo GV	Inc. above	10.00	12.50	18.50	40.00	—
1909Mo GV	2,924,000	10.00	12.50	18.50	40.00	—

PESO   KM# 409.3   Weight: 27.0730 g. **Composition:** 0.9030 Silver .7860 oz. ASW **Reverse:** Liberty cap **Note:** Struck at Zacatecas Mint, mint mark Zs. Varieties exist.

Date	Mintage	F	VF	XF	Unc	BU
1898Zs FZ	5,714,000	10.00	12.50	20.00	60.00	—
1899Zs FZ	5,618,000	10.00	12.50	20.00	65.00	—
1900Zs FZ	5,357,000	10.00	12.50	20.00	65.00	—
1901Zs FZ	Inc. above	10.00	12.50	20.00	55.00	—
1901Zs AZ	5,706,000	4,000	6,500	10,000	—	—
1902Zs FZ	7,134,000	10.00	12.50	20.00	55.00	—
1903/2Zs FZ	3,080,000	12.50	15.00	50.00	125	—
1903Zs FZ	Inc. above	10.00	12.50	20.00	65.00	—
1904Zs FZ	2,423,000	10.00	15.00	25.00	85.00	—
1904Zs FM	Inc. above	10.00	15.00	25.00	75.00	—
1905Zs FM	995,000	20.00	40.00	60.00	150	—

PESO   KM# 410   Weight: 1.6920 g. **Composition:** 0.8750 Gold .0476 oz. AGW **Note:** Struck at Alamos Mint, mint mark As.

Date	Mintage	F	VF	XF	Unc	BU
1888AsL/MoM Rare	—	—	—	—	—	—
1888 As L Rare	—	—	—	—	—	—

PESO   KM# 410.1   Weight: 1.6920 g. **Composition:** 0.8750 Gold .0476 oz. AGW **Note:** Struck at Chihuahua Mint, mint mark Ca/MoM.

Date	Mintage	F	VF	XF	Unc	BU
1888Ca/MoM Rare	104	—	—	—	—	—

PESO   KM# 410.2   Weight: 1.6920 g. **Composition:** 0.8750 Gold .0476 oz. AGW **Note:** Struck at Culiacan Mint, mint mark Cn.

Date	Mintage	F	VF	XF	Unc	BU
1873Cn P	1,221	75.00	100	150	250	—
1875Cn P	—	85.00	125	150	250	—
1878Cn G	248	100	175	225	475	—
1879Cn D	—	100	150	175	285	—
1881/0Cn D	338	100	150	175	285	—
1882Cn D	340	100	150	175	285	—
1883Cn D	—	100	150	175	285	—
1884Cn M	—	100	150	175	285	—
1886/4Cn M	277	100	150	225	450	—
1888/7Cn M	2,586	100	175	225	450	—
1888Cn M	Inc. above	65.00	100	150	265	—
1889Cn M Rare						
1891/89Cn M	969	75.00	100	150	265	—
1892Cn M	780	75.00	100	150	265	—
1893Cn M	498	85.00	125	150	265	—
1894Cn M	493	80.00	125	150	265	—
1895Cn M	1,143	65.00	100	150	250	—
1896/5Cn M	1,028	65.00	100	150	250	—
1897Cn M	785	65.00	100	150	250	—
1898Cn M	3,521	65.00	100	150	225	—
1898Cn/MoM	Inc. above	65.00	100	150	250	—
1899Cn Q	2,000	65.00	100	150	225	—
1901/0Cn Q	2,350	65.00	100	150	225	—
1902Cn Q	2,480	65.00	100	150	225	—
1902Cn/MoQ/C	Inc. above	65.00	100	150	225	—
1904Cn H	3,614	65.00	100	150	225	—
1904Cn/Mo/ H	Inc. above	65.00	100	150	250	—
1905Cn P	1,000	—	—	—	—	—

Note: Reported, not confirmed

PESO   KM# 410.3   Weight: 1.6920 g. **Composition:** 0.8750 Gold .0476 oz. AGW **Note:** Struck at Guanajuato Mint, mint mark Go.

Date	Mintage	F	VF	XF	Unc	BU
1870Go S	—	100	125	150	265	—
1871Go S	500	100	175	225	475	—
1888Go R	210	125	200	250	550	—
1890Go R	1,916	75.00	100	150	265	—
1892Go R	533	100	150	175	350	—
1894Go R	180	150	200	250	550	—
1895Go R	676	100	150	175	325	—
1896/5Go R	4,671	65.00	100	150	250	—
1897/6Go R	4,280	65.00	100	150	250	—
1897Go R	Inc. above	65.00	100	150	250	—

Date	Mintage	F	VF	XF	Unc	BU
1898Go R Regular obverse	5,193	65.00	100	150	250	—
1898Go R Mule, 5 Centavos obverse, normal reverse	Inc. above	75.00	100	150	250	—
1899Go R	2,748	65.00	100	150	250	—
1900/800Go R	864	75.00	125	150	285	—

PESO   KM# 410.4   Weight: 1.6920 g. **Composition:** 0.8750 Gold .0476 oz. AGW **Note:** Struck at Hermosillo Mint, mint mark Ho.

Date	Mintage	F	VF	XF	Unc	BU
1875Ho R Rare	310	—	—	—	—	—
1876Ho F Rare	—	—	—	—	—	—
1888Ho G/MoM Rare	—	—	—	—	—	—

PESO   KM# 410.5   Weight: 1.6920 g. **Composition:** 0.8750 Gold .0476 oz. AGW **Note:** Struck at Mexico City Mint, mint mark Mo.

Date	Mintage	F	VF	XF	Unc	BU
1870Mo C	2,540	40.00	60.00	90.00	185	—
1871Mo M/C	1,000	50.00	100	150	250	—
1872Mo M/C	3,000	40.00	60.00	90.00	185	—
1873/1Mo M	2,900	40.00	60.00	90.00	185	—
1873Mo M	Inc. above	40.00	60.00	90.00	185	—
1874Mo M	—	40.00	60.00	90.00	185	—
1875Mo B/M	—	40.00	60.00	90.00	185	—
1876/5Mo B/M	—	40.00	60.00	90.00	185	—
1877Mo M	—	40.00	60.00	90.00	185	—
1878Mo M	2,000	40.00	60.00	90.00	185	—
1879Mo M	—	40.00	60.00	90.00	185	—
1880/70Mo M	—	40.00	60.00	90.00	185	—
1881/71Mo M	1,000	40.00	60.00	90.00	185	—
1882/72Mo M	—	40.00	60.00	90.00	185	—
1883/72Mo M	1,000	40.00	60.00	90.00	185	—
1884Mo M	—	40.00	60.00	90.00	185	—
1885/71Mo M	—	40.00	60.00	90.00	185	—
1885Mo M	—	40.00	60.00	90.00	185	—
1886Mo M	1,700	40.00	60.00	90.00	185	—
1887Mo M	2,200	40.00	60.00	90.00	185	—
1888Mo M	1,000	40.00	60.00	90.00	185	—
1889Mo M	500	100	150	200	285	—
1890Mo M	570	100	150	200	285	—
1891Mo M	746	100	150	200	285	—
1892/0Mo M	2,895	40.00	60.00	90.00	185	—
1893Mo M	5,917	40.00	60.00	90.00	185	—
1894/3MMo	—	40.00	60.00	90.00	185	—
1894Mo M	6,244	40.00	60.00	90.00	185	—
1895Mo M	8,994	40.00	60.00	90.00	185	—
1895Mo B	Inc. above	40.00	60.00	90.00	185	—
1896Mo B	7,166	40.00	60.00	90.00	185	—
1896Mo M	Inc. above	40.00	60.00	90.00	185	—
1897Mo M	5,131	40.00	60.00	90.00	185	—
1898/7Mo M	5,368	40.00	60.00	90.00	185	—
1899Mo M	9,515	40.00	60.00	90.00	185	—
1900/800Mo M	9,301	40.00	60.00	90.00	185	—
1900/880Mo M	Inc. above	40.00	60.00	90.00	185	—
1900/890Mo M	Inc. above	40.00	60.00	90.00	185	—
1900Mo M	Inc. above	40.00	60.00	90.00	185	—
1901Mo M Small date	Inc. above	40.00	60.00	90.00	185	—
1901/801Mo M Large date	8,293	40.00	60.00	90.00	185	—
1902Mo M Large date	11,000	40.00	60.00	90.00	185	—
1902Mo M Small date	Inc. above	40.00	60.00	90.00	185	—
1903Mo M Large date	10,000	40.00	60.00	90.00	185	—
1903Mo M Small date	Inc. above	50.00	80.00	120	200	—
1904Mo M	9,845	40.00	60.00	90.00	185	—
1905Mo M	3,429	40.00	60.00	90.00	185	—

PESO   KM# 410.6   Weight: 1.6920 g. **Composition:** 0.8750 Gold .0476 oz. AGW **Note:** Struck at Zacatecas Mint, mint mark Zs.

Date	Mintage	F	VF	XF	Unc	BU
1872Zs H	2,024	125	150	175	275	—
1875/3Zs A	—	125	150	200	325	—
1878Zs S	—	125	150	175	275	—
1888Zs Z	280	175	225	325	700	—
1889Zs Z	492	150	175	225	450	—
1890Zs Z	738	150	175	225	450	—

2-1/2 PESOS   KM# 411   Weight: 4.2300 g. **Composition:** 0.8750 Gold .1190 oz. AGW **Note:** Struck at Alamos Mint, mint mark As.

Date	Mintage	F	VF	XF	Unc	BU
1888As/MoL Rare	—	—	—	—	—	—

2-1/2 PESOS   KM# 411.1   Weight: 4.2300 g. **Composition:** 0.8750 Gold .1190 oz. AGW **Note:** Struck at Culiacan Mint, mint mark Cn.

Date	Mintage	F	VF	XF	Unc	BU
1893Cn M	141	1,500	2,000	2,500	3,500	—

2-1/2 PESOS   KM# 411.2   Weight: 4.2300 g. **Composition:** 0.8750 Gold .1190 oz. AGW **Note:** Struck at Durango Mint, mint mark Do.

Date	Mintage	F	VF	XF	Unc	BU
1888Do C Rare	—	—	—	—	—	—

2-1/2 PESOS   KM# 411.3   Weight: 4.2300 g. **Composition:** 0.8750 Gold .1190 oz. AGW **Note:** Struck at Guanajuato Mint, mint mark Go.

Date	Mintage	F	VF	XF	Unc	BU
1871Go S	600	1,250	2,000	2,500	3,250	—
1888Go/MoR	110	1,750	2,250	2,750	3,500	—

2-1/2 PESOS   KM# 411.4   Weight: 4.2300 g. **Composition:** 0.8750 Gold .1190 oz. AGW **Note:** Struck at Hermosillo Mint, mint mark Ho.

Date	Mintage	F	VF	XF	Unc	BU
1874Ho R Rare	—	—	—	—	—	—
1888Ho G Rare	—	—	—	—	—	—

2-1/2 PESOS   KM# 411.5   Weight: 4.2300 g. **Composition:** 0.8750 Gold .1190 oz. AGW **Note:** Struck at Mexico City Mint, mint mark Mo.

Date	Mintage	F	VF	XF	Unc	BU
1870Mo C	820	150	250	350	750	—
1872Mo M/C	800	150	250	350	750	—
1873/2Mo M	—	200	350	750	1,350	—
1874Mo M	—	200	350	750	1,350	—
1874Mo B/M	—	200	350	750	1,350	—
1875Mo B	—	200	350	750	1,350	—
1876Mo B	—	250	500	1,000	1,600	—
1877Mo M	—	200	350	750	1,350	—
1878Mo M	400	200	350	750	1,350	—
1879Mo M	—	200	350	750	1,350	—
1880/79Mo M	—	200	350	750	1,350	—
1881Mo M	400	200	350	750	1,350	—
1882Mo M	—	200	350	750	1,350	—
1883/73Mo M	400	200	350	750	1,350	—
1884Mo M	—	250	500	1,000	1,600	—
1885Mo M	—	200	350	750	1,350	—
1886Mo M	400	200	350	750	1,350	—
1887Mo M	400	200	350	750	1,350	—
1888Mo M	540	200	350	750	1,350	—
1889Mo M	240	150	300	525	950	—
1890Mo M	420	200	350	750	1,350	—
1891Mo M	188	200	350	750	1,350	—
1892Mo M	240	200	350	750	1,350	—

2-1/2 PESOS   KM# 411.6   Weight: 4.2300 g. **Composition:** 0.8750 Gold .1190 oz. AGW **Note:** Struck at Zacatecas Mint, mint mark Zs.

Date	Mintage	F	VF	XF	Unc	BU
1872Zs H	1,300	200	350	500	1,200	—
1873Zs H	—	175	325	450	850	—
1875/3Zs A	—	200	350	750	1,350	—
1877Zs S	—	200	350	750	1,350	—
1878Zs S	300	200	350	750	1,350	—
1888Zs/MoS	80	300	500	1,000	1,800	—
1889Zs/Mo Z	184	250	450	950	1,350	—
1890Zs Z	326	200	350	750	1,350	—

5 PESOS   KM# 412.1   Weight: 8.4600 g. **Composition:** 0.8750 Gold .2380 oz. AGW **Note:** Struck at Chihuahua Mint, mint mark Ca.

Date	Mintage	F	VF	XF	Unc	BU
1888 Ca M Rare	120	—	—	—	—	—

5 PESOS KM# 412.2 **Weight:** 8.4600 g. **Composition:** 0.8750 Gold .2380 oz. AGW **Note:** Struck at Culiacan Mint, mint mark Cn.

Date	Mintage	F	VF	XF	Unc	BU
1873Cn P	—	300	600	1,000	1,500	—
1874Cn P	—	—	—	—	—	—
1875Cn P	—	300	500	700	1,250	—
1876Cn P	—	300	500	700	1,250	—
1877Cn G	—	300	500	700	1,250	—
1882Cn Rare	174	—	—	—	—	—
1888Cn M	—	500	1,000	1,350	2,000	—
1890Cn M	435	250	500	750	1,250	—
1891Cn M	1,390	250	400	500	1,000	—
1894Cn M	484	250	500	750	1,600	—
1895Cn M	142	500	750	1,500	2,500	—
1900Cn Q	1,536	150	300	400	900	—
1903Cn Q	1,000	150	300	400	750	—

5 PESOS KM# 412 **Weight:** 8.4600 g. **Composition:** 0.8750 Gold .2380 oz. AGW **Note:** Struck at Alamos Mint, mint mark As.

Date	Mintage	F	VF	XF	Unc	BU
1875 As L	—	—	—	—	—	—
1878 As L	383	900	1,700	3,000	4,500	—

5 PESOS KM# 412.3 **Weight:** 8.4600 g. **Composition:** 0.8750 Gold .2380 oz. AGW **Note:** Struck at Durango Mint, mint mark Do.

Date	Mintage	F	VF	XF	Unc	BU
1873/2Do P	—	700	1,250	1,800	3,000	—
1877Do P	—	700	1,250	1,800	3,000	—
1878Do E	—	700	1,250	1,800	3,000	—
1879/7Do B	—	700	1,250	1,800	3,000	—
1879Do B	—	700	1,250	1,800	3,000	—

5 PESOS KM# 412.4 **Weight:** 8.4600 g. **Composition:** 0.8750 Gold .2380 oz. AGW **Note:** Struck at Guanajuato Mint, mint mark Go.

Date	Mintage	F	VF	XF	Unc	BU
1871Go S	1,600	400	800	1,250	2,500	—
1887Go R	140	600	1,200	1,500	2,750	—
1888Go R Rare	65	—	—	—	—	—
1893Go R Rare	16	—	—	—	—	—

5 PESOS KM# 412.5 **Weight:** 8.4600 g. **Composition:** 0.8750 Gold .2380 oz. AGW **Note:** Struck at Hermosillo Mint, mint mark Ho.

Date	Mintage	F	VF	XF	Unc	BU
1877Ho R	990	750	1,250	2,000	3,000	—
1877Ho A	Inc. above	650	1,100	1,750	2,750	—
1888Ho G Rare	—	—	—	—	—	—
1874Ho R	—	1,750	2,500	3,000	4,500	—

5 PESOS KM# 412.6 **Weight:** 8.4600 g. **Composition:** 0.8750 Gold .2380 oz. AGW **Note:** Struck at Mexico City Mint, mint mark Mo.

Date	Mintage	F	VF	XF	Unc	BU
1870Mo C	550	200	400	550	900	—
1871/69Mo M	1,600	150	300	400	650	—
1871Mo M	Inc. above	150	300	400	650	—
1872Mo M	1,600	150	300	400	650	—
1873/2Mo M	—	200	400	550	850	—
1874Mo M	—	200	400	550	850	—
1875/3Mo B/M	—	200	400	550	950	—
1875Mo B	—	200	400	550	950	—
1876/5Mo B/M	—	200	400	550	1,000	—
1877Mo M	—	250	450	750	1,250	—
1878/7Mo M	400	200	400	550	1,250	—
1878Mo M	Inc. above	200	400	550	1,250	—
1879/8Mo M	—	200	400	550	1,250	—
1880Mo M	—	200	400	550	1,250	—
1881Mo M	—	200	400	550	1,250	—
1882Mo M	200	250	450	750	1,250	—
1883Mo M	200	250	450	750	1,250	—
1884Mo M	—	250	450	750	1,250	—

Date	Mintage	F	VF	XF	Unc	BU
1886Mo M	200	250	450	750	1,250	—
1887Mo M	200	250	450	750	1,250	—
1888Mo M	250	200	400	550	1,250	—
1889Mo M	190	250	450	750	1,250	—
1890Mo M	149	250	450	750	1,250	—
1891Mo M	156	250	450	750	1,250	—
1892Mo M	214	250	450	750	1,250	—
1893Mo M	1,058	200	400	500	800	—
1897Mo M	370	200	400	550	1,000	—
1898Mo M	376	200	400	550	1,000	—
1900Mo M	1,014	150	300	400	650	—
1901Mo M	1,071	150	300	400	650	—
1902Mo M	1,478	150	300	400	650	—
1903Mo M	1,162	150	300	400	650	—
1904Mo M	1,415	150	300	400	650	—
1905Mo M	563	200	400	550	1,500	—

5 PESOS KM# 412.7 **Weight:** 8.4600 g. **Composition:** 0.8750 Gold .2380 oz. AGW **Note:** Struck at Zacatecas Mint, mint mark Zs.

Date	Mintage	F	VF	XF	Unc	BU
1874Zs A	—	250	500	750	1,500	—
1875Zs A	—	200	400	500	1,000	—
1877Zs S/A	—	200	400	550	1,000	—
1878/7Zs S/A	—	200	400	550	1,000	—
1883Zs S	—	150	300	450	700	—
1888Zs Z	70	1,000	1,500	2,000	3,000	—
1889Zs Z	373	200	300	500	850	—
1892Zs Z	1,229	150	300	450	700	—

10 PESOS KM# 413 **Weight:** 16.9200 g. **Composition:** 0.8750 Gold .4760 oz. AGW **Reverse:** Balance scale **Note:** Struck at Alamos Mint, mint mark As.

Date	Mintage	F	VF	XF	Unc	BU
1874 As DL Rare	—	—	—	—	—	—
1875 As L	642	600	1,250	2,500	3,500	—
1878 As L	977	500	1,000	2,000	3,000	—
1879 As L	1,078	500	1,000	2,000	3,000	—
1880 As L	2,629	500	1,000	2,000	3,000	—
1881 As L	2,574	500	1,000	2,000	3,000	—
1882 As L	3,403	500	1,000	2,000	3,000	—
1883 As L	3,597	500	1,000	2,000	3,000	—
1884 As L Rare	—	—	—	—	—	—
1885 As L	4,562	500	1,000	2,000	3,000	—
1886 As L	4,643	500	1,000	2,000	3,000	—
1887 As L	3,667	500	1,000	2,000	3,000	—
1888 As L	4,521	500	1,000	2,000	3,000	—
1889 As L	5,615	500	1,000	2,000	3,000	—
1890 As L	4,920	500	1,000	2,000	3,000	—
1891 As L	568	500	1,000	2,000	3,000	—
1892 As L	—	—	—	—	—	—
1893 As L	817	500	1,000	2,000	3,000	—
1894/3 As L	1,658	—	—	—	—	—
1894 As L	Inc. above	500	1,000	2,000	3,000	—
1895 As L	1,237	500	1,000	2,000	3,000	—

10 PESOS KM# 413.1 **Weight:** 16.9200 g. **Composition:** 0.8750 Gold .4760 oz. AGW **Reverse:** Balance scale **Note:** Struck at Chihuahua Mint, mint mark Ca.

Date	Mintage	F	VF	XF	Unc	BU
1888 Ca M	175	—	7,500	—	—	—

10 PESOS KM# 413.2 **Weight:** 16.9200 g. **Composition:** 0.8750 Gold .4760 oz. AGW **Reverse:** Balance scale **Note:** Struck at Culiacan Mint, mint mark Cn.

Date	Mintage	F	VF	XF	Unc	BU
1881Cn D	—	400	600	1,000	1,750	—
1882Cn D	874	400	600	1,000	1,750	—
1882Cn E	Inc. above	400	600	1,000	1,750	—
1883Cn D	221	—	—	—	—	—
1883Cn M	Inc. above	400	600	1,000	1,750	—
1884Cn D	—	400	600	1,000	1,750	—
1884Cn M	—	400	600	1,000	1,750	—
1885Cn M	1,235	400	600	1,000	1,750	—
1886Cn M	981	400	600	1,000	1,750	—
1887Cn M	2,289	400	600	1,000	1,750	—
1888Cn M	767	400	600	1,000	1,750	—
1889Cn M	859	400	600	1,000	1,750	—
1890Cn M	1,427	400	600	1,000	1,750	—
1891Cn M	670	400	600	1,000	1,750	—
1892Cn M	379	400	600	1,000	1,750	—
1893Cn M	1,806	400	600	1,000	1,750	—
1895Cn M	179	500	1,000	1,500	2,500	—
1903Cn Q	774	400	600	1,000	1,750	—

10 PESOS KM# 413.3 Weight: 16.9200 g.
Composition: 0.8750 Gold .4760 oz. AGW **Reverse:**
Balance scale **Note:** Struck at Durango Mint, mint mark Do.

Date	Mintage	F	VF	XF	Unc	BU
1872Do P	1,755	350	500	800	1,250	—
1873/2Do P	1,091	350	550	900	1,450	—
1873/2Do M/P	Inc. above	350	550	900	1,450	—
1874Do M	—	350	550	900	1,450	—
1875Do M	—	350	550	900	1,450	—
1876Do M	—	450	750	1,250	2,000	—
1877Do P	—	350	550	900	1,450	—
1878Do E	582	350	550	900	1,450	—
1879/8Do B	—	350	550	900	1,450	—
1879Do B	—	350	550	900	1,450	—
1880Do P	2,030	350	550	900	1,450	—
1881/79Do P	2,617	350	550	900	1,450	—
1882Do P Rare	1,528	—	—	—	—	—
1882Do C	Inc. above	350	550	900	1,450	—
1883Do C	793	450	750	1,250	2,000	—
1884Do C	108	450	750	1,250	2,000	—

10 PESOS KM# 413.4 Weight: 16.9200 g. **Composition:**
0.8750 Gold .4760 oz. AGW **Reverse:** Balance scale **Note:**
Struck at Guadalajara Mint, mint mark Ga.

Date	Mintage	F	VF	XF	Unc	BU
1870Ga C	490	500	800	1,000	1,550	—
1871Ga C	1,910	400	800	1,500	2,250	—
1872Ga C	780	500	1,000	2,000	2,500	—
1873Ga C	422	500	1,000	2,000	3,000	—
1874/3Ga C	477	500	1,000	2,000	3,000	—
1875Ga C	710	500	1,000	2,000	3,000	—
1878Ga A	183	600	1,200	2,500	3,500	—
1879Ga A	200	600	1,200	2,500	3,500	—
1880Ga S	404	500	1,000	2,000	3,000	—
1881Ga S	239	600	1,200	2,500	3,500	—
1891Ga S	196	600	1,200	2,500	3,500	—

10 PESOS KM# 413.5 Weight: 16.9200 g. **Composition:**
0.8750 Gold .4760 oz. AGW **Reverse:** Balance scale **Note:**
Struck at Guanajuato Mint, mint mark Go.

Date	Mintage	F	VF	XF	Unc	BU
1872Go S	1,400	2,000	4,000	6,500	10,000	—
1887Go R Rare	80	—	—	—	—	—

Note: Stack's Rio Grande Sale 6-93, P/L AU realized,
$12,650

1888Go R Rare	68	—	—	—	—	—

10 PESOS KM# 413.6 Weight: 16.9200 g.
Composition: 0.8750 Gold .4760 oz. AGW **Reverse:**
Balance scale **Note:** Struck at Hermosillo Mint, mint mark Ho.

Date	Mintage	F	VF	XF	Unc	BU
1874Ho R Rare	—	—	—	—	—	—
1876Ho F Rare	357	—	—	—	—	—
1878Ho A	814	1,750	3,000	3,500	5,500	—
1879Ho A	—	1,000	2,000	2,500	4,000	—
1880Ho A	—	1,000	2,000	2,500	4,000	—
1881Ho A Rare	—	—	—	—	—	—

10 PESOS KM# 413.7 Weight: 16.9200 g. **Composition:**
0.8750 Gold .4760 oz. AGW **Reverse:** Balance scale **Note:**
Struck at Mexico City Mint, mint mark Mo.

Date	Mintage	F	VF	XF	Unc	BU
1870Mo C	480	500	900	1,200	2,000	—
1872/1Mo M/C	2,100	350	550	900	1,350	—
1873Mo M	—	400	600	950	1,450	—
1874/3Mo M	—	400	600	950	1,450	—
1875Mo B/M	—	400	600	950	1,450	—
1876Mo B Rare	—	—	—	—	—	—
1878Mo M	300	400	600	950	1,450	—
1879Mo M	—	—	—	—	—	—
1881Mo M	100	500	1,000	1,600	2,500	—
1882Mo M	—	400	600	950	1,450	—
1883Mo M	100	600	1,000	1,600	2,500	—
1884Mo M	—	600	1,000	1,600	2,500	—
1885Mo M	—	400	600	950	1,450	—
1886Mo M	100	600	1,000	1,600	2,500	—
1887Mo M	100	600	1,000	1,625	2,750	—
1888Mo M	144	450	750	1,200	2,000	—
1889Mo M	88	600	1,000	1,600	2,500	—
1890Mo M	137	600	1,000	1,600	2,500	—
1891Mo M	133	600	1,000	1,600	2,500	—
1892Mo M	45	600	1,000	1,600	2,500	—
1893Mo M	1,361	350	550	900	1,350	—
1897Mo M	239	400	600	950	1,450	—
1898/7Mo M	244	425	625	1,000	1,750	—

Date	Mintage	F	VF	XF	Unc	BU
1900Mo M	733	400	600	950	1,450	—
1901Mo M	562	350	500	800	1,250	—
1902Mo M	719	350	500	800	1,250	—
1903Mo M	713	350	500	800	1,250	—
1904Mo M	694	350	500	800	1,250	—
1905Mo M	401	400	600	950	1,500	—

10 PESOS KM# 413.8 Weight: 16.9200 g.
Composition: 0.8750 Gold .4760 oz. AGW **Reverse:**
Balance scale **Note:** Struck at Oaxaca Mint, mint mark Oa.

Date	Mintage	F	VF	XF	Unc	BU
1870 Oa E	4,614	400	600	900	1,350	—
1871 Oa E	2,705	400	600	900	1,350	—
1872 Oa E	5,897	400	600	900	1,350	—
1873 Oa E	3,537	400	600	950	1,500	—
1874 Oa E	2,205	400	600	1,200	1,800	—
1875 Oa E	312	450	750	1,400	2,250	—
1876 Oa E	766	450	750	1,400	2,250	—
1877 Oa E	463	450	750	1,400	2,250	—
1878 Oa E	229	450	750	1,400	2,250	—
1879 Oa E	210	450	750	1,400	2,250	—
1880 Oa E	238	450	750	1,400	2,250	—
1881 Oa E	961	400	600	1,200	2,000	—
1882 Oa E	170	600	1,000	1,500	2,500	—
1883 Oa E	111	600	1,000	1,500	2,500	—
1884 Oa E	325	450	750	1,400	2,250	—
1885 Oa E	370	450	750	1,400	2,250	—
1886 Oa E	400	450	750	1,400	2,250	—
1887 Oa E	—	700	1,250	2,250	4,000	—
1888 Oa E	—	—	—	—	—	—

10 PESOS KM# 413.9 Weight: 16.9200 g.
Composition: 0.8750 Gold .4760 oz. AGW **Reverse:**
Balance scale **Note:** Struck at Zacatecas Mint, mint mark Zs.

Date	Mintage	F	VF	XF	Unc	BU
1871Zs H	2,000	350	500	800	1,250	—
1872Zs H	3,092	300	500	750	1,150	—
1873Zs H	936	400	600	950	1,450	—
1874Zs H	—	400	600	950	1,450	—
1875/3Zs A	—	400	600	1,000	1,750	—
1876/5Zs S	—	400	600	1,000	1,750	—
1877Zs S/H	506	400	600	1,000	1,750	—
1878Zs S	711	400	600	1,000	1,750	—
1879/8Zs S	—	450	750	1,400	2,250	—
1879Zs S	—	450	750	1,400	2,250	—
1880Zs S	2,089	350	550	950	1,450	—
1881Zs S	736	400	600	1,000	1,750	—
1882Zs S	1,599	350	550	950	1,450	—
1883/2Zs S	256	400	600	1,000	1,750	—
1884/3Zs S	—	350	550	950	1,600	—
1884Zs S	—	350	550	950	1,600	—
1885Zs S	1,588	350	550	950	1,450	—
1886Zs S	5,364	350	550	950	1,450	—
1887Zs Z	2,330	350	550	950	1,450	—
1888Zs Z	4,810	350	550	950	1,450	—
1889Zs Z	6,154	300	500	750	1,250	—
1890Zs Z	1,321	350	550	950	1,450	—
1891Zs Z	1,930	350	550	950	1,450	—
1892Zs Z	1,882	350	550	950	1,450	—
1893Zs Z	2,899	350	550	950	1,450	—
1894Zs Z	2,501	350	550	950	1,450	—
1895Zs Z	1,217	350	550	950	1,450	—

20 PESOS   KM # 414   Weight: 33.8400 g. **Composition:** 0.8750 Gold .9520 oz. AGW **Reverse:** Balance scale **Note:** Struck at Alamos Mint, mint mark As.

Date	Mintage	F	VF	XF	Unc	BU
1876 As L Rare	276	—	—	—	—	—
1877 As L Rare	166	—	—	—	—	—
1878 As L	—	—	—	—	—	—
1888 As L Rare	—	—	—	—	—	—

20 PESOS   KM # 414.1   Weight: 33.8400 g. **Composition:** 0.8750 Gold .9520 oz. AGW **Reverse:** Balance scale **Note:** Struck at Chihuahua Mint, mint mark CH, Ca.

Date	Mintage	F	VF	XF	Unc	BU
1872 M	995	500	700	1,000	2,500	—
1873 M	950	500	700	1,000	2,500	—
1874 M	1,116	450	675	950	2,500	—
1875 M	750	500	700	1,000	2,500	—
1876 M	600	500	800	1,250	2,750	—
1877 Rare	55	—	—	—	—	—
1882 M	1,758	450	675	950	2,500	—
1883 M	161	600	1,000	1,500	3,000	—
1884 M	496	500	700	1,000	2,500	—
1885 M	122	600	1,000	1,500	3,000	—
1887 M	550	500	700	1,000	2,500	—
1888 M	351	500	700	1,000	2,500	—
1889 M	464	500	700	1,000	2,500	—
1890 M	1,209	450	675	950	2,500	—
1891 M	2,004	425	650	900	2,250	—
1893 M	418	500	700	950	2,500	—
1895 M	133	600	1,000	1,500	3,000	—

20 PESOS   KM # 414.2   Weight: 33.8400 g. **Composition:** 0.8750 Gold .9520 oz. AGW **Reverse:** Balance scale **Note:** Struck at Culiacan Mint, mint mark Cn.

Date	Mintage	F	VF	XF	Unc	BU
1870Cn E	3,749	450	675	950	2,000	—
1871Cn P	3,046	450	675	950	2,000	—
1872Cn P	972	450	675	950	2,000	—
1873Cn P	1,317	450	675	950	2,000	—
1874Cn P	—	450	675	950	2,000	—
1875Cn P	—	600	1,200	1,800	2,500	—
1876Cn P	—	450	675	950	2,000	—
1876Cn G	—	450	675	950	2,000	—
1877Cn G	167	600	1,000	1,500	3,000	—
1878Cn Rare	842	—	—	—	—	—
1881/0Cn D	2,039	—	—	—	—	—
1881Cn D	Inc. above	450	675	950	2,000	—
1882/1Cn D	736	450	675	950	2,000	—
1883Cn M	1,836	450	675	950	2,000	—
1884Cn M	—	450	675	950	2,000	—
1885Cn M	544	450	675	950	2,000	—
1886Cn M	882	450	675	950	2,000	—
1887Cn M	837	450	675	950	2,000	—
1888Cn M	473	450	675	950	2,000	—
1889Cn M	1,376	450	675	950	2,000	—
1890Cn M	—	450	675	950	2,000	—
1891Cn M	237	500	900	1,200	2,250	—
1892Cn M	526	450	675	950	2,000	—
1893Cn M	2,062	450	675	950	2,000	—
1894Cn M	4,516	450	675	950	2,000	—
1895Cn M	3,193	450	675	950	2,000	—
1896Cn M	4,072	450	675	950	2,000	—
1897/6Cn M	959	450	675	950	2,000	—
1897Cn M	Inc. above	450	675	950	2,000	—
1898Cn M	1,660	450	675	950	2,000	—
1899Cn M	1,243	450	675	950	2,000	—
1899Cn Q	Inc. above	500	900	1,200	2,250	—
1900Cn Q	1,558	450	675	950	2,000	—
1901Cn Q	Inc. above	450	675	950	2,000	—
1901/0Cn Q	1,496	—	—	—	—	—
1902Cn Q	1,059	450	675	950	2,000	—
1903Cn Q	1,121	450	675	950	2,000	—
1904Cn H	4,646	450	675	950	2,000	—
1905Cn P	1,738	500	900	1,200	2,250	—

20 PESOS   KM # 414.3   Weight: 33.8400 g. **Composition:** 0.8750 Gold .9520 oz. AGW **Reverse:** Balance scale **Note:** Struck at Durango Mint, mint mark Do.

Date	Mintage	F	VF	XF	Unc	BU
1870Do P	416	1,000	1,500	2,000	2,500	—
1871/0Do P	1,073	1,000	1,750	2,250	2,750	—
1871Do P	Inc. above	1,000	1,500	2,000	2,500	—
1872/1Do PT	—	1,500	3,000	4,500	7,000	—
1876Do M	—	1,000	1,500	2,000	2,500	—

Date	Mintage	F	VF	XF	Unc	BU
1877Do P	94	1,500	2,250	2,750	3,250	—
1878Do Rare	258	—	—	—	—	—

20 PESOS   KM # 414.4   Weight: 33.8400 g. **Composition:** 0.8750 Gold .9520 oz. AGW **Reverse:** Balance scale **Note:** Struck at Guanajuato Mint, mint mark Go.

Date	Mintage	F	VF	XF	Unc	BU
1870Go S	3,250	425	650	900	1,500	—
1871Go S	20,000	425	650	900	1,500	—
1872Go S	18,000	425	650	900	1,500	—
1873Go S	7,000	425	650	900	1,500	—
1874Go S	—	425	650	900	1,500	—
1875Go S	—	425	650	900	1,500	—
1876Go S	—	425	650	900	1,500	—
1876Go M/S						
1877Go M/S Rare	15,000	—	—	—	—	—
1877Go R	Inc. above	425	650	900	1,500	—
1877Go S Rare	Inc. above					
1878/7Go M/S	13,000	650	1,250	2,000	2,800	—
1878Go M	Inc. above	650	1,250	2,000	2,800	—
1878Go S	Inc. above	425	650	900	1,500	—
1879Go S	8,202	500	800	1,200	2,300	—
1880Go S	7,375	425	650	900	1,500	—
1881Go S	4,909	425	650	900	1,500	—
1882Go S	4,020	425	650	900	1,500	—
1883/2Go B	3,705	500	750	1,150	2,250	—
1883Go B	Inc. above	425	650	900	1,500	—
1884Go B	1,798	425	650	900	1,500	—
1885Go R	2,660	425	650	900	1,500	—
1886Go R	1,090	550	800	1,250	2,500	—
1887Go R	1,009	550	800	1,250	2,500	—
1888Go R	1,011	550	800	1,250	2,500	—
1889Go R	956	550	800	1,250	2,500	—
1890Go R	879	550	800	1,250	2,500	—
1891Go R	818	550	800	1,250	2,500	—
1892Go R	730	550	800	1,250	2,500	—
1893Go R	3,343	425	650	1,000	2,000	—
1894/3Go R	6,734	425	650	900	1,500	—
1894Go R	Inc. above	425	650	900	1,500	—
1895/3Go R	7,118	425	650	900	1,500	—
1895Go R	Inc. above	425	650	900	1,500	—
1896Go R	9,219	425	650	900	1,500	—
1897/6Go R	6,781	425	650	900	1,500	—
1897Go R	Inc. above	425	650	900	1,500	—
1898Go R	7,710	425	650	900	1,500	—
1899Go R	8,527	425	650	900	1,500	—
1900Go R	4,512	550	800	1,250	2,350	—

20 PESOS   KM # 414.5   Weight: 33.8400 g. **Composition:** 0.8750 Gold .9520 oz. AGW **Reverse:** Balance scale **Note:** Struck at Hermosillo Mint, mint mark Ho.

Date	Mintage	F	VF	XF	Unc	BU
1874Ho R Rare	—	—	—	—	—	—
1875Ho R Rare	—	—	—	—	—	—
1876Ho F Rare	—	—	—	—	—	—
1888Ho g Rare	—	—	—	—	—	—

20 PESOS   KM # 414.6   Weight: 33.8400 g. **Composition:** 0.8750 Gold .9520 oz. AGW **Reverse:** Balance scale **Note:** Struck at Mexico City Mint, mint mark Mo.

Date	Mintage	F	VF	XF	Unc	BU
1870Mo C	14,000	400	600	850	1,450	—
1871Mo M	21,000	400	600	850	1,450	—
1872/1Mo M	11,000	400	600	850	1,600	—
1872Mo M	Inc. above	400	600	850	1,450	—
1873Mo M	5,600	400	600	850	1,450	—
1874/2Mo M	—	400	600	850	1,450	—

Date	Mintage	F	VF	XF	Unc	BU
1874/2Mo B	—	450	700	1,000	1,600	—
1875Mo B	—	425	650	900	1,500	—
1876Mo B	—	425	650	900	1,500	—
1876Mo M Reported, not confirmed	—	—	—	—	—	—
1877Mo M	2,000	450	700	1,100	2,000	—
1878Mo M	7,000	425	650	900	1,500	—
1879Mo M	—	425	650	900	1,750	—
1880Mo M	—	425	650	900	1,750	—
1881/0Mo M	11,000	425	600	850	1,450	—
1881Mo M	Inc. above	425	600	850	1,450	—
1882/1Mo M	5,800	425	600	850	1,450	—
1882Mo M	Inc. above	425	600	850	1,450	—
1883/1Mo M	4,000	425	600	850	1,450	—
1883Mo M	Inc. above	425	600	850	1,450	—
1884/3Mo M	—	425	650	900	1,500	—
1884Mo M	—	425	650	900	1,500	—
1885Mo M	6,000	425	650	900	1,750	—
1886Mo M	10,000	400	600	850	1,450	—
1887Mo M	12,000	600	800	1,500	2,500	—
1888Mo M	7,300	400	600	850	1,450	—
1889Mo M	6,477	400	600	900	1,650	—
1890Mo M	7,852	400	600	850	1,500	—
1891/0Mo M	8,725	400	600	850	1,500	—
1891Mo M	Inc. above	400	600	850	1,500	—
1892Mo M	11,000	400	600	850	1,450	—
1893Mo M	15,000	400	600	850	1,450	—
1894Mo M	14,000	400	600	850	1,450	—
1895Mo M	13,000	400	600	850	1,450	—
1896Mo B	14,000	400	600	850	1,450	—
1897/6Mo M	12,000	400	600	850	1,450	—
1897Mo M	Inc. above	400	600	850	1,450	—
1898Mo M	20,000	400	600	850	1,450	—
1899Mo M	23,000	400	600	850	1,450	—
1900Mo M	21,000	400	600	850	1,450	—
1901Mo M	29,000	400	600	850	1,450	—
1902Mo M	38,000	400	600	850	1,450	—
1903/2Mo M	31,000	400	600	850	1,450	—
1903Mo M	Inc. above	400	600	850	1,450	—
1904Mo M	52,000	400	600	850	1,450	—
1905Mo M	9,757	400	600	850	1,450	—

20 PESOS KM# 414.7 Weight: 33.8400 g.
Composition: 0.8750 Gold .9520 oz. AGW **Reverse:** Balance scale **Note:** Struck at Oaxaca Mint, mint mark Oa.

Date	Mintage	F	VF	XF	Unc	BU
1870 Oa E	1,131	750	1,500	2,500	5,000	—
1871 Oa E	1,591	750	1,500	2,500	5,000	—
1872 Oa E	255	1,000	1,750	3,000	7,000	—
1888 Oa E	170	2,000	3,000	5,000	—	—

20 PESOS KM# 414.8 Weight: 33.8400 g.
Composition: 0.8750 Gold .9520 oz. AGW **Reverse:** Balance scale **Note:** Struck at Zacatecas Mint, mint mark Zs.

Date	Mintage	F	VF	XF	Unc	BU
1871Zs H	1,000	3,500	6,500	7,000	9,000	—
1875Zs A	—	4,000	6,000	7,500	9,500	—
1878Zs S	441	4,000	6,000	7,500	9,500	—
1888Zs Z Rare	50	—	—	—	—	—
1889Zs Z	640	3,500	5,500	7,000	9,000	—

UNITED STATES

MINT MARK
o
M - Mexico City

DECIMAL COINAGE
100 Centavos = 1 Peso

CENTAVO KM# 415 Composition: Bronze **Size:** 20 mm. **Note:** Struck at Mexico City Mint, mint mark Mo.

Date	Mintage	F	VF	XF	Unc	BU
1905 Narrow date	6,040,000	3.25	5.75	12.50	95.00	—
1905 Wide date	—	3.25	5.75	12.50	95.00	—
1906 Narrow date	Est. 67,505,000	0.50	0.75	1.25	14.00	—

Note: 50,000,000 pcs. were struck at the Birmingham Mint

Date	Mintage	F	VF	XF	Unc	BU
1906 Wide date	Inc. above	0.65	1.25	2.25	22.00	—
1910 Narrow date	8,700,000	1.50	2.50	6.50	90.00	—
1910 Wide date	—	1.50	2.50	6.50	90.00	—
1911 Narrow date	16,450,000	0.60	1.00	2.75	22.50	—
1911 Wide date	Inc. above	0.75	1.25	5.00	32.00	—
1912	12,650,000	0.75	1.25	3.00	32.00	—
1913	12,850,000	0.65	1.00	2.75	33.00	—
1914 Narrow date	17,350,000	0.60	0.85	2.50	14.50	—
1914 Wide date	Inc. above	0.60	0.85	2.50	14.50	—
1915	2,277,000	9.00	21.50	65.00	250	—
1916	500,000	30.00	65.00	165	1,200	—
1920	1,433,000	15.00	30.00	65.00	400	—
1921	3,470,000	4.25	13.50	42.50	275	—
1922	1,880,000	8.00	15.00	45.00	300	—
1923	4,800,000	0.50	0.75	1.75	11.50	—
1924/3	2,000,000	50.00	140	250	500	—
1924	Inc. above	4.00	10.00	20.00	220	—
1925	1,550,000	3.75	9.25	20.00	210	—
1926	5,000,000	0.90	1.75	3.50	26.00	—
1927/6	6,000,000	25.00	40.00	60.00	140	—
1927	Inc. above	0.60	1.25	4.50	36.00	—
1928	5,000,000	0.60	0.80	3.25	16.50	—
1929	4,500,000	0.60	0.80	1.75	18.00	—
1930	7,000,000	0.75	1.00	2.25	19.00	—
1933	10,000,000	0.25	0.35	1.75	16.50	—
1934	7,500,000	0.40	0.95	3.25	35.00	—
1935	12,400,000	0.15	0.25	0.40	11.50	—
1936	20,100,000	0.15	0.20	0.30	8.00	—
1937	20,000,000	0.15	0.25	0.35	3.50	—
1938	10,000,000	0.10	0.15	0.30	2.25	—
1939	30,000,000	0.10	0.20	0.30	1.25	—
1940	10,000,000	0.20	0.30	0.60	6.50	—
1941	15,800,000	0.15	0.25	0.35	2.25	—
1942	30,400,000	0.15	0.20	0.30	1.25	—
1943	4,310,000	0.30	0.50	0.75	9.00	—
1944	5,645,000	0.15	0.25	0.50	7.00	—
1945	26,375,000	0.10	0.15	0.25	1.00	—
1946	42,135,000	—	0.15	0.20	0.60	—
1947	13,445,000	—	0.10	0.15	0.80	—
1948	20,040,000	—	0.15	0.30	1.10	—
1949	6,235,000	0.10	0.15	0.30	1.75	—

Note: Varieties exist.

CENTAVO KM# 416 Composition: Bronze **Size:** 16 mm. **Note:** Zapata issue. Struck at Mexico City Mint, mint mark Mo. Reduced size.

Date	Mintage	F	VF	XF	Unc	BU
1915	179,000	16.00	27.50	50.00	75.50	—

CENTAVO KM# 417 Composition: Brass **Size:** 16 mm. **Note:** Struck at Mexico City Mint, mint mark Mo.

Date	Mintage	F	VF	XF	Unc	BU
1950	12,815,000	—	0.15	0.30	1.75	2.00
1951	25,740,000	—	0.15	0.25	0.65	1.10
1952	24,610,000	—	0.10	0.25	0.40	0.75
1953	21,160,000	—	0.10	0.25	0.40	0.85
1954	25,675,000	—	0.10	0.15	0.85	1.20
1955	9,820,000	—	0.15	0.25	0.85	1.50
1956	11,285,000	—	0.15	0.25	0.80	1.45
1957	9,805,000	—	0.15	0.25	0.85	1.35
1958	12,155,000	—	0.10	0.25	0.45	0.80
1959	11,875,000	—	0.10	0.25	0.75	1.25
1960	10,360,000	—	0.10	0.15	0.40	0.65

Date	Mintage	F	VF	XF	Unc	BU
1961	6,385,000	—	0.10	0.15	0.45	0.85
1962	4,850,000	—	0.10	0.15	0.55	0.90
1963	7,775,000	—	0.10	0.15	0.25	0.45
1964	4,280,000	—	0.10	0.15	0.20	0.35
1965	2,255,000	—	0.10	0.15	0.25	0.40
1966	1,760,000	—	0.10	0.25	0.60	0.75
1967	1,290,000	—	0.10	0.15	0.40	0.70
1968	1,000,000	—	0.10	0.20	0.85	1.25
1969	1,000,000	—	0.10	0.15	0.75	1.25

CENTAVO   KM# 418 Composition: Brass **Size:** 13 mm.
Note: Reduced size.

Date	Mintage	F	VF	XF	Unc	BU
1970	1,000,000	—	0.20	0.40	1.30	1.80
1972	1,000,000	—	0.20	0.45	2.50	3.25
1972/2	—	—	0.50	1.25	3.25	5.00
1973	1,000,000	—	1.65	2.75	8.00	9.75

2 CENTAVOS   KM# 419 Composition: Bronze **Size:**
25 mm. **Note:** Struck at Mexico City Mint, mint mark Mo.

Date	Mintage	F	VF	XF	Unc	BU
1905	50,000	125	275	425	1,200	—
1906 Inverted 6	9,998,000	25.00	50.00	110	375	—
1906 Wide date	Inc. above	4.00	10.00	21.50	80.00	—
1906 Narrow date	Inc. above	6.50	12.50	25.00	85.00	—

Note: 5,000,000 pieces were struck at the Birmingham Mint

1920	1,325,000	6.50	21.50	60.00	350	—
1921	4,275,000	2.50	4.75	10.00	90.00	—
1922	—	225	550	1,350	4,000	—
1924	750,000	8.50	20.00	50.00	450	—
1925	3,650,000	2.50	3.50	9.00	40.00	—
1926	4,750,000	1.00	2.25	5.50	35.00	—
1927	7,250,000	0.60	1.00	4.50	22.75	—
1928	3,250,000	0.75	1.50	3.75	25.00	—
1929	250,000	45.00	120	500	1,000	—
1935	1,250,000	4.25	9.25	22.50	200	—
1939	5,000,000	0.60	0.90	2.25	20.00	—
1941	3,550,000	0.45	0.60	1.25	18.00	—

2 CENTAVOS   KM# 420 Composition: Bronze **Size:**
20 mm. **Note:** Zapata issue. Struck at Mexico City Mint, mint
mark Mo. Reduced size.

Date	Mintage	F	VF	XF	Unc	BU
1915	487,000	6.50	9.00	13.50	65.00	—

5 CENTAVOS   KM# 421 Composition: Nickel **Note:**
Struck at Mexico City Mint, mint mark Mo. Varieties exist.

Date	Mintage	F	VF	XF	Unc	BU
1905	1,420,000	6.00	9.50	22.50	290	—
1906/5	10,615,000	12.00	23.50	60.00	375	—
1906	Inc. above	0.75	1.20	3.25	50.00	—
1907	4,000,000	1.25	3.50	10.00	350	—
1909	2,052,000	3.25	9.50	42.50	360	—
1910	6,181,000	1.15	3.20	5.50	77.00	115
1911 Narrow date	4,487,000	0.75	3.00	5.00	85.00	125
1911 Wide date	Inc. above	2.50	4.25	9.00	110	160
1912 Small mint mark	420,000	97.50	120	210	725	—
1912 Large mint mark	Inc. above	60.00	85.00	160	575	—
1913	2,035,000	1.65	3.75	9.00	100	150

Note: Wide and narrow dates exist for 1913

1914	2,000,000	0.75	1.75	3.50	60.00	90.00

Note: 5,000,000 pieces appear to have been struck at the Birmingham Mint in 1914 and all of 1909-1911. The Mexican Mint
report does not mention receiving the 1914 dated coins

5 CENTAVOS   KM# 422 Composition: Bronze **Note:**
Struck at Mexico City Mint, mint mark Mo.

Date	Mintage	F	VF	XF	Unc	BU
1914	2,500,000	10.00	21.50	45.00	225	—
1915	11,424,000	2.50	4.50	14.50	125	—
1916	2,860,000	13.50	32.00	150	690	—
1917	800,000	60.00	150	320	820	—
1918	1,332,000	28.00	70.00	175	625	—
1919	400,000	100	190	335	925	—
1920	5,920,000	3.00	7.50	40.00	285	—
1921	2,080,000	9.00	21.50	70.00	275	—
1924	780,000	35.00	80.00	235	625	—
1925	4,040,000	4.75	10.00	42.50	225	—
1926	3,160,000	5.50	11.00	43.50	300	—
1927	3,600,000	3.25	6.75	27.50	220	—
1928 Large date	1,740,000	10.00	17.50	68.00	250	—
1928 Small date	Inc. above	25.00	45.00	90.00	385	—
1929	2,400,000	4.75	10.00	40.00	180	—
1930 Large oval O in date	2,600,000	4.00	7.50	27.50	210	—
1930 Small square O in date	Inc. above	50.00	115	220	565	—
1931	—	475	675	1,000	3,250	—
1933	8,000,000	1.25	2.00	3.25	25.00	—
1934	10,000,000	1.00	1.50	2.50	22.50	—
1935	21,980,000	0.75	1.20	2.25	20.00	—

5 CENTAVOS KM# 423 Composition: Copper-Nickel
Note: Struck at Mexico City Mint, mint mark Mo.

Date	Mintage	F	VF	XF	Unc	BU
1936	46,700,000	—	0.65	1.25	6.50	9.00
1937	49,060,000	—	0.50	1.00	6.00	9.00
1938	3,340,000	—	5.00	12.50	65.00	250
1940	22,800,000	—	0.75	1.50	8.00	12.00
1942	7,100,000	—	1.50	3.20	35.00	45.00

5 CENTAVOS KM# 424 Ring Composition: Bronze
Reverse: "Josefa" Ortiz de Dominguez **Note:** Struck at
Mexico City Mint, mint mark Mo.

Date	Mintage	F	VF	XF	Unc	BU
1942	900,000	—	20.00	60.00	350	500
1943	54,660,000	—	0.40	0.65	3.00	4.00
1944	53,463,000	—	0.25	0.35	0.75	1.00
1945	44,262,000	—	0.25	0.35	0.90	1.65
1946	49,054,000	—	0.50	0.75	2.00	2.75
1951	50,758,000	—	0.60	0.85	3.00	4.75
1952	17,674,000	—	1.25	2.25	9.25	11.50
1953	31,568,000	—	1.10	1.75	7.00	10.00
1954	58,680,000	—	0.40	0.75	2.75	4.00
1955	31,114,000	—	1.85	2.50	10.00	14.00

5 CENTAVOS KM# 425 Composition: Copper-Nickel
Reverse: White Josefa **Note:** Struck at Mexico City Mint,
mint mark Mo.

Date	Mintage	F	VF	XF	Unc	BU
1950	5,700,000	—	0.75	1.50	6.25	8.00

Note: 5,600,000 pieces struck at Connecticut melted

5 CENTAVOS KM# 426 Composition: Brass **Reverse:**
White Josefa **Note:** Struck at Mexico City Mint, mint mark Mo.

Date	Mintage	F	VF	XF	Unc	BU
1954 Dot	—	—	9.00	32.00	325	375
1954 Without dot	—	—	12.00	25.00	250	290
1955	12,136,000	—	0.75	1.50	9.00	12.50
1956	60,216,000	—	0.20	0.30	0.90	1.50
1957	55,288,000	—	0.15	0.20	0.90	1.50
1958	104,624,000	—	0.15	0.20	0.60	1.00
1959	106,000,000	—	0.15	0.25	0.90	1.50

Date	Mintage	F	VF	XF	Unc	BU
1960	99,144,000	—	0.10	0.15	0.50	0.75
1961	61,136,000	—	0.10	0.15	0.40	0.70
1962	47,232,000	—	0.10	0.15	0.30	0.55
1963	156,680,000	—	—	0.15	0.20	0.35
1964	71,168,000	—	—	0.15	0.20	0.40
1965	155,720,000	—	—	0.15	0.25	0.35
1966	124,944,000	—	—	0.15	0.40	0.65
1967	118,816,000	—	—	0.15	0.25	0.40
1968	189,588,000	—	—	0.15	0.50	0.75
1969	210,492,000	—	—	0.15	0.55	0.80

5 CENTAVOS KM# 426a Composition: Copper-Nickel
Reverse: White Josefa **Note:** Struck at Mexico City Mint,
mint mark Mo.

Date	Mintage	F	VF	XF	Unc	BU
1960	—	—	300	450	—	—
1962	19	—	300	450	—	—
1965	—	—	300	450	—	—

5 CENTAVOS KM# 427 Composition: Brass **Reverse:**
White Josefa **Size:** 18 mm. **Note:** Due to some minor alloy
variations this type is often encountered with a bronze color
toning. Reduced size.

Date	Mintage	F	VF	XF	Unc	BU
1970	163,368,000	—	0.10	0.15	0.35	0.45
1971	198,844,000	—	0.10	0.15	0.25	0.30
1972	225,000,000	—	0.10	0.15	0.25	0.30
1973 Flat top 3	595,070,000	—	0.10	0.15	0.25	0.40
1973 Round top 3	Inc. above	—	0.10	0.15	0.20	0.30
1974	401,584,000	—	0.10	0.15	0.30	0.40
1975	342,308,000	—	0.10	0.15	0.25	0.35
1976	367,524,000	—	0.10	0.15	0.40	0.60

10 CENTAVOS KM# 428 Weight: 2.5000 g.
Composition: 0.8000 Silver .0643 oz. ASW **Note:** Struck at
Mexico City Mint, mint mark Mo.

Date	Mintage	F	VF	XF	Unc	BU
1905	3,920,000	—	5.25	7.00	35.00	50.00
1906	8,410,000	—	4.75	6.25	25.00	35.00
1907/6	5,950,000	—	45.00	115	275	350
1907	Inc. above	—	5.50	7.75	35.00	42.50
1909	2,620,000	—	8.00	12.50	70.00	85.00
1910/00	3,450,000	—	10.00	32.00	75.00	100
1910	Inc. above	—	8.00	12.50	25.00	30.00
1911 Narrow date	2,550,000	—	10.00	15.00	88.00	125
1911 Wide date	Inc. above	—	6.00	8.50	42.50	60.00
1912	1,350,000	—	9.00	16.00	120	135
1912 Low 2	Inc. above	—	8.00	15.00	110	130
1913/2	1,990,000	—	7.50	14.00	35.00	65.00
1913	Inc. above	—	6.00	8.50	30.00	40.00
1914	3,110,000	—	4.50	5.75	13.50	20.00

Note: Wide and narrow dates exist for 1914

10 CENTAVOS KM# 429 Weight: 1.8125 g.
Composition: 0.8000 Silver .0466 oz. ASW **Size:** 15 mm.
Note: Struck at Mexico City Mint, mint mark Mo. Reduced size.

Date	Mintage	F	VF	XF	Unc	BU
1919	8,360,000	—	6.00	12.00	70.00	100

10 CENTAVOS KM# 430 Composition: Bronze Note:
Struck at Mexico City Mint, mint mark Mo.

Date	Mintage	F	VF	XF	Unc	BU
1919	1,232,000	—	20.00	60.00	450	525
1920	6,612,000	—	12.50	40.00	400	475
1921	2,255,000	—	30.00	75.00	650	800
1935	5,970,000	—	12.00	25.00	125	175

10 CENTAVOS KM# 431 Weight: 1.6600 g.
Composition: 0.7200 Silver .0384 oz. ASW Note: Struck at Mexico City Mint, mint mark Mo.

Date	Mintage	F	VF	XF	Unc	BU
1925/15	5,350,000	—	18.00	35.00	110	125
1925/3	Inc. above	—	18.00	35.00	115	130
1925	Inc. above	—	2.00	4.00	35.00	47.50
1926/16	2,650,000	—	25.00	55.00	160	175
1926	Inc. above	—	3.50	6.00	62.50	80.00
1927	2,810,000	—	2.25	3.00	17.50	21.50
1928	5,270,000	—	1.75	2.25	12.00	14.25
1930	2,000,000	—	3.75	5.00	18.75	22.50
1933	5,000,000	—	1.50	3.00	10.00	12.50
1934	8,000,000	—	1.75	2.25	8.00	9.50
1935	3,500,000	—	2.75	4.00	11.00	13.50

10 CENTAVOS KM# 432 Composition: Copper-Nickel
Note: Struck at Mexico City Mint, mint mark Mo.

Date	Mintage	F	VF	XF	Unc	BU
1936	33,030,000	—	0.65	2.25	8.25	10.00
1937	3,000,000	—	2.75	42.50	200	250
1938	3,650,000	—	1.75	5.50	60.00	75.00
1939	6,920,000	—	1.00	3.50	30.00	40.00
1940	12,300,000	—	0.40	1.00	5.00	6.50
1942	14,380,000	—	0.60	1.50	7.00	8.50
1945	9,558,000	—	0.40	0.70	3.50	4.00
1946	46,230,000	—	0.25	0.45	2.25	3.10

10 CENTAVOS KM# 433 Composition: Bronze
Reverse: Benito Juarez Note: Struck at Mexico City Mint, mint mark Mo.

Date	Mintage	F	VF	XF	Unc	BU
1955	1,818,000	—	0.60	3.00	22.00	30.00
1956	5,255,000	—	0.50	3.00	22.00	35.00
1957	11,925,000	—	0.20	0.40	5.50	8.00
1959	26,140,000	—	0.20	0.35	0.65	1.25

Date	Mintage	F	VF	XF	Unc	BU
1966	5,873,000	—	0.15	0.25	0.65	1.50
1967	32,318,000	—	0.10	0.15	0.30	0.40

10 CENTAVOS KM# 434.1 Composition: Copper-Nickel Reverse: Five full rows of kernels, sharp stem, wide date Note: Variety I

Date	Mintage	F	VF	XF	Unc	BU
1974	6,000,000	—	—	0.35	0.85	1.00
1975	5,550,000	—	0.10	0.35	0.85	1.75
1976	7,680,000	—	0.10	0.20	0.30	0.40
1977	144,650,000	—	1.25	2.25	3.50	4.50
1978	271,870,000	—	—	1.00	1.50	2.25
1979	375,660,000	—	—	0.50	1.00	1.75
1980/79	21,290,000	—	2.45	3.75	6.00	7.00
1980	Inc. above	—	1.50	2.00	4.50	5.00

10 CENTAVOS KM# 434.2 Composition: Copper-Nickel Reverse: Five full, plus one partial row at left, blunt stem, narrow date Note: Variety II

Date	Mintage	F	VF	XF	Unc	BU
1974	Inc. above	—	—	0.10	0.25	0.35
1977	Inc. above	—	—	0.10	0.30	0.35
1978	Inc. above	—	—	0.10	0.30	0.40
1979	Inc. above	—	0.15	0.50	1.00	2.00
1980	Inc. above	—	—	0.10	0.30	0.35

10 CENTAVOS KM# 434.4 Composition: Copper-Nickel Reverse: Five full, plus one partial row, sharp stem and narrow date Note: Variety IV

Date	Mintage	F	VF	XF	Unc	BU
1974	—	—	—	—	1.50	2.50
1979	—	—	—	—	1.50	2.50

10 CENTAVOS KM# 434.3 Composition: Copper-Nickel Reverse: Five full, plus one partial row, blunt stem and wide date Note: Variety III

Date	Mintage	F	VF	XF	Unc	BU
1980/79	—	—	—	—	—	—

20 CENTAVOS KM# 435 Weight: 5.0000 g.
Composition: 0.8000 Silver .1286 oz. ASW Note: Struck at Mexico City Mint, mint mark Mo.

Date	Mintage	F	VF	XF	Unc	BU
1905	2,565,000	—	9.00	15.00	145	175
1906	6,860,000	—	7.25	14.50	60.00	80.00
1907 Straight 7	4,000,000	—	8.50	17.50	65.00	95.00
1907 Curved 7	5,435,000	—	7.50	13.50	70.00	90.00
1908	350,000	—	85.00	200	1,500	—
1910	1,135,000	—	9.50	15.00	80.00	95.00
1911	1,150,000	—	14.00	32.00	125	150
1912	625,000	—	25.00	70.00	335	375
1913	1,000,000	—	14.50	30.00	95.00	115
1914	1,500,000	—	10.00	21.50	62.50	75.00

20 CENTAVOS KM# 436 Weight: 3.6250 g.
Composition: 0.8000 Silver .0932 oz. ASW **Size:** 19 mm.
Note: Struck at Mexico City Mint, mint mark Mo. Reduced size.

Date	Mintage	F	VF	XF	Unc	BU
1919	4,155,000	—	25.00	50.00	190	245

20 CENTAVOS KM# 437 Composition: Bronze **Note:** Struck at Mexico City Mint, mint mark Mo.

Date	Mintage	F	VF	XF	Unc	BU
1920	4,835,000	—	40.00	110	575	700
1935	20,000,000	—	5.50	8.50	85.00	125

20 CENTAVOS KM# 438 Weight: 3.3333 g.
Composition: 0.7200 Silver .0772 oz. ASW **Note:** Struck at Mexico City Mint, mint mark Mo.

Date	Mintage	F	VF	XF	Unc	BU
1920	3,710,000	—	4.75	10.00	165	215
1921	6,160,000	—	4.50	10.00	100	145
1925	1,450,000	—	8.00	17.00	125	150
1926/5	1,465,000	—	18.00	45.00	325	375
1926	Inc. above	—	4.50	6.25	80.00	110
1927	1,405,000	—	3.75	6.25	80.00	115
1928	3,630,000	—	2.50	4.50	14.50	19.50
1930	1,000,000	—	3.50	6.25	22.00	30.00
1933	2,500,000	—	2.25	2.75	10.00	11.50
1934	2,500,000	—	2.25	3.00	11.00	12.50
1935	2,460,000	—	2.25	2.75	10.00	11.50
1937	10,000,000	—	2.25	2.50	4.75	5.50
1939	8,800,000	—	1.75	2.00	4.00	5.00
1940	3,000,000	—	1.75	2.00	3.50	5.00
1941	5,740,000	—	1.50	2.00	3.00	3.50
1942	12,460,000	—	1.50	2.00	3.25	3.80
1943	3,955,000	—	2.00	2.50	3.50	4.25

20 CENTAVOS KM# 439 Composition: Bronze **Note:** Struck at Mexico City Mint, mint mark Mo.

Date	Mintage	F	VF	XF	Unc	BU
1943	46,350,000	—	0.75	2.75	18.00	25.00
1944	83,650,000	—	0.40	0.65	8.00	10.00
1945	26,801,000	—	1.10	3.50	9.50	12.00
1946	25,695,000	—	0.90	2.00	6.00	8.25
1951	11,385,000	—	2.50	5.50	80.00	100
1952	6,560,000	—	2.50	4.50	25.00	32.50
1953	26,948,000	—	0.35	0.75	7.25	11.00
1954	40,108,000	—	0.35	0.80	8.00	11.50
1955	16,950,000	—	2.50	6.00	60.00	75.00

20 CENTAVOS KM# 440 Composition: Bronze **Note:** Struck at Mexico City Mint, mint mark Mo.

Date	Mintage	F	VF	XF	Unc	BU
1955 Inc. KM#439	Inc. above	—	0.65	1.50	13.50	18.50
1966	22,431,000	—	0.30	0.35	3.00	5.00
1957	13,455,000	—	0.45	1.25	9.00	12.00
1959	6,017,000	—	4.00	7.50	65.00	95.00
1960	39,756,000	—	0.15	0.25	0.85	1.25
1963	14,869,000	—	0.25	0.35	0.90	1.25
1964	28,654,000	—	0.25	0.40	0.90	1.25
1965	74,162,000	—	0.20	0.40	0.85	1.20
1966	43,745,000	—	0.15	0.25	0.90	1.30
1967	46,487,000	—	0.20	0.55	1.20	1.50
1968	15,477,000	—	0.30	0.55	1.35	1.65
1969	63,647,000	—	0.20	0.40	1.00	1.50
1970	76,287,000	—	0.15	0.20	0.90	1.30
1971	49,892,000	—	0.30	0.50	1.40	1.75

20 CENTAVOS KM# 441 Composition: Bronze

Date	Mintage	F	VF	XF	Unc	BU
1971 Inc. KM#440	Inc. above	—	0.20	0.35	1.75	2.35
1973	78,398,000	—	0.25	0.35	0.95	1.50
1974	34,200,000	—	0.20	0.35	1.25	1.75

20 CENTAVOS   KM# 442   Composition: Copper-Nickel
Reverse: Francisco Madero

Date	Mintage	F	VF	XF	Unc	BU
1974	112,000,000	—	0.10	0.15	0.25	0.30
1975	611,000,000	—	0.10	0.15	0.30	0.35
1976	394,000,000	—	0.10	0.15	0.35	0.45
1977	394,350,000	—	0.10	0.15	0.40	0.45
1978	527,950,000	—	0.10	0.15	0.25	0.30
1979	524,615,000	—	0.10	0.15	0.30	0.40
1979 Doubled die obv. large/ small letters	—	—	1.25	2.00	4.00	8.00
1980	326,500,000	—	0.15	0.25	0.40	0.60
1981 Open 8	106,205,000	—	0.30	0.50	1.00	2.00
1981 Closed 8, high date	248,500,000	—	0.30	0.50	1.00	2.00
1981 Closed 8, low date	—	—	1.00	1.50	3.50	4.25
1981/1982	—	—	30.00	75.00	160	190

Note: The 1981/1982 overdate is often mistaken as 1982/ 1981

Date	Mintage	F	VF	XF	Unc	BU
1982	286,855,000	—	0.40	0.60	0.90	1.10
1983 Round top 3	100,930,000	—	0.25	0.40	1.75	2.25
1983 Flat top 3	Inc. above	—	0.25	0.50	1.25	1.75
1983 Proof	998	Value: 15.00				

20 CENTAVOS   KM# 491   Composition: Bronze
Subject: Olmec Culture

Date	Mintage	F	VF	XF	Unc	BU
1983	260,000,000	—	0.20	0.25	0.90	1.10
1983 Proof	53	Value: 165				
1984	180,320,000	—	0.20	0.25	1.50	1.70

25 CENTAVOS   KM# 443   Weight: 3.3330 g.
Composition: 0.3000 Silver .0321 oz. ASW **Note:** Struck at Mexico City Mint, mint mark Mo.

Date	Mintage	F	VF	XF	Unc	BU
1950	77,060,000	—	0.50	0.75	1.75	2.25
1951	41,172,000	—	0.50	0.75	1.60	2.00
1952	29,264,000	—	0.75	1.10	1.80	2.50
1953	38,144,000	—	0.60	0.70	1.50	2.00

25 CENTAVOS   KM# 444   Composition: Copper-Nickel
Reverse: Francisco Madero

Date	Mintage	F	VF	XF	Unc	BU
1964	20,686,000	—	—	0.15	0.25	0.40
1966 Closed beak	180,000	—	0.65	1.00	2.50	3.00
1966 Open beak	Inc. above	—	1.75	3.50	10.00	14.00

50 CENTAVOS   KM# 445   Weight: 12.5000 g.
Composition: 0.8000 Silver .3215 oz. ASW **Note:** Struck at Mexico City Mint, mint mark Mo.

Date	Mintage	F	VF	XF	Unc	BU
1905	2,446,000	—	12.50	20.00	150	225
1906 Open 9	16,966,000	—	5.00	10.00	30.00	50.00
1906 Closed 9	Inc. above	—	4.50	8.50	27.50	40.00
1907 Straight 7	18,920,000	—	4.50	7.25	25.00	28.50
1907 Curved 7	14,841,000	—	5.25	8.00	25.00	28.50
1908	488,000	—	65.00	150	525	625
1912	3,736,000	—	10.00	12.50	45.00	60.00
1913/07	10,510,000	—	30.00	70.00	225	275
1913/2	Inc. above	—	18.00	22.50	65.00	85.00
1913	Inc. above	—	5.50	8.50	25.00	30.00
1914	7,710,000	—	6.75	13.50	30.00	40.00
1916 Narrow date	480,000	—	50.00	75.00	200	290
1916 Wide date	Inc. above	—	50.00	75.00	200	290
1917	37,112,000	—	5.50	8.50	20.00	22.50
1918	1,320,000	—	60.00	110	250	335

50 CENTAVOS   KM# 446   Weight: 9.0625 g.
Composition: 0.8000 Silver .2331 oz. ASW **Size:** 27 mm.
Note: Struck at Mexico City Mint, mint mark Mo. Reduced size.

Date	Mintage	F	VF	XF	Unc	BU
1918/7	2,760,000	—	525	625	1,250	—
1918	Inc. above	—	15.00	50.00	300	385
1919	29,670,000	—	7.00	16.50	85.00	110

50 CENTAVOS   KM# 447   Weight: 8.3333 g.
Composition: 0.7200 Silver .1929 oz. ASW **Note:** Struck at Mexico City Mint, mint mark Mo.

Date	Mintage	F	VF	XF	Unc	BU
1919	10,200,000	—	8.00	18.50	87.50	110
1920	27,166,000	—	6.00	8.50	65.00	80.00
1921	21,864,000	—	6.50	9.00	80.00	95.00
1925	3,280,000	—	14.00	30.00	120	160
1937	20,000,000	—	3.75	5.00	7.50	8.50
1938	100,000	—	40.00	75.00	225	300
1939	10,440,000	—	5.25	7.25	14.00	16.50

Date	Mintage	F	VF	XF	Unc	BU
1942	800,000	—	5.50	7.50	15.00	17.00
1943	41,512,000	—	2.75	4.00	5.50	6.50
1944	55,806,000	—	3.00	3.75	5.50	6.50
1945	56,766,000	—	3.00	3.75	6.00	6.50

50 CENTAVOS   KM# 448 Weight: 7.9730 g.
Composition: 0.4200 Silver .1076 oz. ASW **Note:** Struck at Mexico City Mint, mint mark Mo.

Date	Mintage	F	VF	XF	Unc	BU
1935	70,800,000	—	2.20	2.75	5.00	6.00

50 CENTAVOS   KM# 449 Weight: 6.6600 g.
Composition: 0.3000 Silver .0642 oz. ASW **Reverse:** Cuauhtemoc **Note:** Struck at Mexico City Mint, mint mark Mo.

Date	Mintage	F	VF	XF	Unc	BU
1950	13,570,000	—	1.50	1.80	3.00	4.00
1951	3,650,000	—	2.00	2.50	3.75	5.00

50 CENTAVOS   KM# 450 Composition: Bronze **Note:** Struck at Mexico City Mint, mint mark Mo.

Date	Mintage	F	VF	XF	Unc	BU
1955	3,502,000	—	1.20	2.20	27.50	35.00
1956	34,643,000	—	0.65	1.00	3.25	4.50
1957	9,675,000	—	1.00	2.00	6.50	7.50
1959	4,540,000	—	0.35	0.50	1.50	2.00

50 CENTAVOS   KM# 451 Composition: Copper-Nickel

Date	Mintage	F	VF	XF	Unc	BU
1964	43,806,000	—	0.15	0.20	0.45	0.65
1965	14,326,000	—	0.20	0.25	0.45	0.65
1966	1,726,000	—	0.20	0.40	1.30	1.75
1967	55,144,000	—	0.20	0.30	0.65	1.00
1968	80,438,000	—	0.15	0.30	0.65	0.80
1969	87,640,000	—	0.20	0.35	0.80	1.15

50 CENTAVOS   KM# 452 Composition: Copper-Nickel
Obverse: Stylized eagle **Note:** Coins dated 1975 and 1976 exist with and without dots in centers of three circles on plumage on reverse. Edge varieties exist.

Date	Mintage	F	VF	XF	Unc	BU
1970	76,236,000	—	0.15	0.20	0.90	1.25
1971	125,288,000	—	0.15	0.20	0.90	1.30
1972	16,000,000	—	1.25	2.00	3.00	4.75
1975 Dots	177,958,000	—	0.60	1.25	3.50	6.00
1975 No dots	Inc. above	—	0.15	0.20	0.50	0.75
1976 Dots	37,480,000	—	0.75	1.25	5.00	6.00
1976 No dots	Inc. above	—	0.15	0.20	0.50	0.75
1977	12,410,000	—	6.50	10.00	32.50	42.50
1978	85,400,000	—	0.15	0.25	0.50	0.75
1979 Round 2nd 9 in date	229,000,000	—	0.15	0.25	0.50	0.65
1979 Square 9's in date	Inc. above	—	0.20	0.40	1.60	2.10
1980 Narrow date, square 9	89,978,000	—	0.45	0.75	1.00	2.00
1980 Wide date, round 9	178,188,000	—	0.20	0.25	1.00	1.15
1981 Rectangular 9, narrow date	142,212,000	—	0.50	0.75	1.75	2.50
1981 Round 9, wide date	Inc. above	—	0.30	0.50	1.25	1.75
1982	45,474,000	—	0.20	0.40	1.50	2.40
1983	90,318,000	—	0.50	0.75	2.25	2.85
1983 Proof	998	Value: 16.00				

50 CENTAVOS   KM# 492 Composition: Stainless Steel
Subject: Palenque Culture **Obverse:** Stylized eagle
Reverse: Cuauhtemoc

Date	Mintage	F	VF	XF	Unc	BU
1983	99,540,000	—	—	0.30	1.50	2.50
1983 Proof	53	Value: 165				

PESO KM# 453 Weight: 27.0700 g. **Composition:**
0.9030 Silver .7859 oz. ASW **Subject:** Caballito **Note:**
Struck at Mexico City Mint, mint mark Mo.

Date	Mintage	F	VF	XF	Unc	BU
1910	3,814,000	—	30.00	45.00	155	250
1911 Long lower left ray on reverse	1,227,000	—	45.00	75.00	200	275
1911 Short lower left ray on reverse	Inc. above	—	135	225	600	800
1912	322,000	—	95.00	200	350	500
1913/2	2,880,000	—	45.00	75.00	265	400
1913	Inc. above	—	45.00	70.00	160	250

Note: 1913 coins exist with even and unevenly spaced date

Date	Mintage	F	VF	XF	Unc	BU
1914	120,000	—	600	950	3,000	—

PESO KM# 455 Weight: 16.6600 g. **Composition:**
0.7200 Silver .3856 oz. ASW **Note:** Struck at Mexico City
Mint, mint mark Mo.

Date	Mintage	F	VF	XF	Unc	BU
1920/10	8,830,000	—	50.00	90.00	320	—
1920	Inc. above	—	6.50	18.00	150	200
1921	5,480,000	—	8.00	20.00	160	200
1922	33,620,000	—	3.25	5.00	20.00	26.00
1923	35,280,000	—	3.25	5.00	20.00	28.00
1924	33,060,000	—	3.25	5.00	20.00	26.00
1925	9,160,000	—	4.50	9.50	60.00	75.00
1926	28,840,000	—	3.25	5.00	20.00	25.00
1927	5,060,000	—	5.00	10.00	55.00	75.00
1932 Open 9	50,770,000	—	2.75	4.00	5.00	7.00
1932 Closed 9	Inc. above	—	2.75	4.00	5.00	7.00
1933/2	43,920,000	—	15.00	25.00	80.00	—
1933	Inc. above	—	2.75	4.00	5.00	7.00
1934	22,070,000	—	3.25	4.50	9.00	10.50
1935	8,050,000	—	4.50	6.00	11.50	13.50
1938	30,000,000	—	2.75	4.00	6.00	7.50
1940	20,000,000	—	2.75	3.50	5.00	6.50
1943	47,662,000	—	2.75	3.25	4.50	6.00
1944	39,522,000	—	2.75	3.50	4.50	6.00
1945	37,300,000	—	2.75	3.50	4.50	6.00

PESO KM# 454 Weight: 18.1300 g. **Composition:**
0.8000 Silver .4663 oz. ASW **Subject:** Caballito **Note:**
Struck at Mexico City Mint, mint mark Mo.

Date	Mintage	F	VF	XF	Unc	BU
1918	3,050,000	—	30.00	100	1,350	2,100
1919	6,151,000	—	18.00	45.00	900	1,600

PESO KM# 456 Weight: 14.0000 g. **Composition:**
0.5000 Silver .2250 oz. ASW **Reverse:** Jose Morelos y
Pavon **Note:** Struck at Mexico City Mint, mint mark Mo.

Date	Mintage	F	VF	XF	Unc	BU
1947	61,460,000	—	1.75	2.50	4.50	5.50
1948	22,915,000	—	2.25	3.50	5.50	6.50
1949	4,000,000	—	—	1,200	1,600	2,500

Note: Not released for circulation

Date	Mintage	F				
1949 Proof		—	Value: 5,000			

PESO   KM# 457   Weight: 13.3300 g. **Composition:**
0.3000 Silver .1285 oz. ASW **Reverse:** Jose Morelos y
Pavon **Note:** Struck at Mexico City Mint, mint mark Mo.

Date	Mintage	F	VF	XF	Unc	BU
1950	3,287,000	—	2.50	4.00	7.00	8.50

PESO   KM# 458   Weight: 16.0000 g. **Composition:**
0.1000 Silver .0514 oz. ASW **Subject:** 100th Anniversary of
Constitution **Note:** Struck at Mexico City Mint, mint mark Mo.

Date	Mintage	F	VF	XF	Unc	BU
1957	500,000	—	3.50	5.00	13.50	18.00

PESO   KM# 459   Weight: 16.0000 g. **Composition:**
0.1000 Silver .0514 oz. ASW **Subject:** 100th Anniversary of
Constitution **Reverse:** Jose Morelos y Pavon **Note:** Struck
at Mexico City Mint, mint mark Mo.

Date	Mintage	F	VF	XF	Unc	BU
1957	28,273,000	—	0.65	1.00	2.25	3.00
1958	41,899,000	—	0.65	0.85	1.85	2.50
1959	27,369,000	—	1.25	2.00	5.50	7.00
1960	26,259,000	—	0.65	1.10	3.25	3.50
1961	52,601,000	—	0.50	0.90	2.25	3.00
1962	61,094,000	—	0.50	0.90	2.10	2.75
1963	26,394,000	—	BV	0.80	2.00	2.40
1964	15,615,000	—	BV	0.75	2.00	2.40
1965	5,004,000	—	BV	0.60	1.85	2.00
1966	30,998,000	—	BV	0.60	1.85	2.00
1967	9,308,000	—	BV	0.60	2.75	3.50

Tall Narrow Date   **Short Wide Date**

PESO   KM# 460   Composition: Copper-Nickel **Reverse:**
Jose Morelos y Pavon

Date	Mintage	F	VF	XF	Unc	BU
1970 Narrow date	102,715,000	—	0.25	0.35	0.75	0.90
1970 Wide date	Inc. above	—	1.25	2.50	8.00	10.00
1971	426,222,000	—	0.20	0.25	0.50	0.65
1972	120,000,000	—	0.20	0.25	0.40	0.65
1974	63,700,000	—	0.20	0.25	0.65	0.90
1975 Tall narrow date	205,979,000	—	0.25	0.45	1.00	1.35
1975 Short wide date	Inc. above	—	0.30	0.40	0.75	1.00
1976	94,489,000	—	0.15	0.20	0.50	0.75
1977 Thick date	94,364,000	—	0.25	0.45	1.00	1.25
1977 Thin date	Inc. above	—	1.00	2.00	6.50	13.50
1978 Closed 8	208,300,000	—	0.20	0.30	0.65	1.15
1978 Open 8	55,140,000	—	0.75	1.50	11.00	16.50
1979 Thin date	117,884,000	—	0.20	0.30	1.00	1.50
1979 Thick date	Inc. above	—	0.40	0.60	1.25	1.75
1980 Closed 8	318,800,000	—	0.25	0.35	1.00	1.20
1980 Open 8	23,865,000	—	0.75	1.50	9.00	12.75
1981 Closed 8	413,349,000	—	0.20	0.30	0.85	1.00
1981 Open 8	58,616,000	—	0.50	1.25	7.00	8.50
1982	235,000,000	—	0.25	0.75	2.25	2.50
1983 Wide date	100,000,000	—	0.50	1.10	3.00	3.50
1983 Narrow date	Inc. above	—	0.30	0.45	3.25	3.75
1983 Proof	1,051,000	Value: 15.00				

PESO   KM# 496   Composition: Stainless Steel **Reverse:**
Jose Morelos y Pavon

Date	Mintage	F	VF	XF	Unc	BU
1984	722,802,000	—	0.10	0.25	0.65	0.85
1985	985,000,000	—	0.10	0.25	0.50	0.75
1986	740,000,000	—	0.10	0.25	0.50	0.75
1987	250,000,000	—	—	0.25	0.50	0.80
1987 Proof; 2 known	—	Value: 1,250				

2 PESOS   KM# 461   Weight: 1.6666 g. **Composition:**
0.9000 Gold .0482 oz. AGW **Note:** Struck at Mexico City
Mint, mint mark Mo.

Date	Mintage	F	VF	XF	Unc	BU
1919	1,670,000	—	BV	25.00	32.00	—
1920	4,282,000	—	BV	25.00	32.00	—
1944	10,000	27.50	35.00	50.00	80.00	—
1945	Est. 140,000	—	—	—BV+20%		—
1946	168,000	30.00	45.00	55.00	80.00	—
1947	25,000	27.50	35.00	50.00	65.00	—
1948 No specimens known	45,000	—	—	—	—	—

Note: During 1951-1972 a total of 4,590,493 pieces were re-struck, most likely dated 1945. In 1996 matte restrikes were produced

Date	Mintage	F	VF	XF	Unc	BU
1907	1,088,000	—	BV	50.00	70.00	—
1910	100,000	BV	55.00	70.00	120	—
1918/7	609,000	BV	55.00	70.00	120	—
1918	Inc. above	—	BV	50.00	70.00	—
1919	506,000	—	BV	50.00	70.00	—
1920	2,385,000	—	BV	50.00	70.00	—
1955	Est. 48,000	—	—	—BV+11%		—

Note: During 1955-1972 a total of 1,767,645 pieces were re-struck, most likely dated 1955. In 1996 matte restrikes were produced

2 PESOS   KM# 462   Weight: 26.6667 g. **Composition:** 0.9000 Silver .7717 oz. ASW **Subject:** Centennial of Independence **Note:** Struck at Mexico City Mint, mint mark Mo.

Date	Mintage	F	VF	XF	Unc	BU
1921	1,278,000	—	30.00	55.00	265	400

5 PESOS   KM# 465   Weight: 30.0000 g. **Composition:** 0.9000 Silver .8681 oz. ASW **Reverse:** Head of Cuauhtemoc left **Note:** Struck at Mexico City Mint, mint mark Mo.

Date	Mintage	F	VF	XF	Unc	BU
1947	5,110,000	—	BV	6.25	8.75	10.00
1948	26,740,000	—	BV	6.00	8.00	9.00

2-1/2 PESOS   KM# 463   Weight: 2.0833 g. **Composition:** 0.9000 Gold .0602 oz. AGW **Note:** Struck at Mexico City Mint, mint mark Mo.

Date	Mintage	F	VF	XF	Unc	BU
1918	1,704,000	—	BV	28.00	45.00	—
1919	984,000	—	BV	28.00	45.00	—
1920/10	607,000	—	BV	55.00	100	—
1920	Inc. above	—	BV	28.00	45.00	—
1944	20,000	—	BV	28.00	45.00	—
1945	Est. 180,000	—	—	—BV+18%		—
1946	163,000	—	BV	28.00	45.00	—
1947	24,000	200	265	325	400	—
1948	63,000	BV	35.00	40.00	65.00	—

Note: During 1951-1972 a total of 5,025,087 pieces were re-struck, most likely dated 1945. In 1996 matte restrikes were produced

5 PESOS   KM# 464   Weight: 4.1666 g. **Composition:** 0.9000 Gold .1205 oz. AGW **Note:** Struck at Mexico City Mint, mint mark Mo.

Date	Mintage	F	VF	XF	Unc	BU
1905	18,000	100	150	200	400	—
1906	4,638,000	—	BV	50.00	70.00	—

5 PESOS   KM# 466   Weight: 27.7800 g. **Composition:** 0.7200 Silver .06431 oz. ASW **Subject:** Opening of Southern Railroad **Note:** Struck at Mexico City Mint, mint mark Mo.

Date	Mintage	F	VF	XF	Unc	BU
1950	200,000	—	22.50	27.50	35.00	45.00

Note: It is recorded that 100,000 pieces were melted to be used for the 1968 Mexican Olympic 25 Pesos

5 PESOS   KM# 467   Weight: 27.7800 g. **Composition:** 0.7200 Silver .6431 oz. ASW **Reverse:** Miguel Hidalgo y Costilla **Note:** Struck at Mexico City Mint, mint mark Mo.

Date	Mintage	F	VF	XF	Unc	BU
1951	4,958,000	—	BV	5.75	7.00	10.00
1952	9,595,000	—	BV	5.50	6.75	9.00
1953	20,376,000	—	BV	5.25	6.75	9.00
1954	30,000	—	27.50	45.00	65.00	80.00

5 PESOS   KM# 468   Weight: 27.7800 g. **Composition:** 0.7200 Silver .6431 oz. ASW **Subject:** Bicentennial of Hidalgo's Birth **Note:** Struck at Mexico City Mint, mint mark Mo.

Date	Mintage	F	VF	XF	Unc	BU
1953	1,000,000	—	BV	5.50	7.50	10.00

5 PESOS   KM# 469   Weight: 18.0500 g. **Composition:** 0.7200 Silver .4170 oz. ASW **Note:** Struck at Mexico City Mint, mint mark Mo.

Date	Mintage	F	VF	XF	Unc	BU
1955	4,271,000	—	3.25	4.00	4.75	7.00
1956	4,596,000	—	3.25	4.00	4.75	7.00
1957	3,464,000	—	3.25	4.00	4.75	7.00

5 PESOS   KM# 470   Weight: 18.0500 g. **Composition:** 0.7200 Silver .4170 oz. ASW **Subject:** 100th Anniversary of Constitution **Note:** Struck at Mexico City Mint, mint mark Mo.

Date	Mintage	F	VF	XF	Unc	BU
1957	200,000	—	5.50	7.50	13.50	15.50

5 PESOS   KM# 471   Weight: 27.7800 g. **Composition:** 0.7200 Silver .6431 oz. ASW **Subject:** Centennial of Carranza's Birth **Note:** Struck at Mexico City Mint, mint mark Mo.

Date	Mintage	F	VF	XF	Unc	BU
1959	1,000,000	—	BV	4.50	6.50	9.50

Small Date   Large Date

5 PESOS   KM# 472   Composition: Copper-Nickel **Reverse:** Vicente Guerrero **Note:** Small date, large date varieties.

Date	Mintage	F	VF	XF	Unc	BU
1971	28,457,000	—	0.50	0.95	2.50	3.25
1972	75,000,000	—	0.60	1.25	2.00	2.50
1973	19,405,000	—	1.25	2.10	5.00	7.50
1974	34,500,000	—	0.50	0.80	1.75	2.25
1976 Small date	26,121,000	—	0.75	1.45	3.50	4.25
1976 Large date	121,550,000	—	0.35	0.50	1.50	1.75
1977	102,000,000	—	0.50	0.75	1.50	2.00
1978	25,700,000	—	1.00	1.50	5.25	6.75

5 PESOS   KM# 485   Composition: Copper-Nickel
Subject: Quetzalcoatl

Date	Mintage	F	VF	XF	Unc	BU
1980	266,899,999	—	0.25	0.50	1.75	2.25
1981	30,500,000	—	0.45	0.65	2.75	3.25
1982	20,000,000	—	1.50	2.35	4.25	5.25
1982 Proof	1,051	Value: 18.00				
1983 Proof; 7 known		Value: 1,150				
1984	16,300,000	—	1.25	2.00	4.75	6.00
1985	76,900,000	—	2.25	4.00	4.50	5.25

5 PESOS   KM# 502   Composition: Brass **Subject:**
Quetzalcoatl **Note:** Circulation coinage.

Date	Mintage	F	VF	XF	Unc	BU
1985	30,000,000	—	—	0.15	0.35	0.50
1987	81,900,000	—	8.00	9.50	12.50	15.00
1988	76,600,000	—	—	0.10	0.25	0.35
1988 Proof; 2 known	—	Value: 600				

10 PESOS   KM# 473   Weight: 8.3333 g. **Composition:**
0.9000 Gold .2411 oz. AGW **Reverse:** Miguel Hidalgo **Note:**
Struck at Mexico City Mint, mint mark Mo.

Date	Mintage	F	VF	XF	Unc	BU
1905	39,000	110	125	155	200	—
1906	2,949,000	—	BV	100	150	—
1907	1,589,000	—	BV	100	150	—
1908	890,000	—	BV	100	150	—
1910	451,000	—	BV	100	150	—
1916	26,000	110	120	150	275	—
1917	1,967,000	—	BV	100	150	—
1919	266,000	—	BV	100	150	—
1920	12,000	150	250	400	650	—
1959	Est. 50,000	—	—	—	BV+7%	—

Note: *During 1961-1972 a total of 954,983 pieces were re-struck, most likely dated 1959. In 1996 matte restrikes were produced

10 PESOS   KM# 474   Weight: 28.8800 g. **Composition:**
0.9000 Silver .8357 oz. ASW **Reverse:** Miguel Hidalgo
Note: Struck at Mexico City Mint, mint mark Mo.

Date	Mintage	F	VF	XF	Unc	BU
1955	585,000	—	BV	6.00	8.75	12.00
1956	3,535,000	—	BV	5.50	8.50	12.50

10 PESOS   KM# 475   Weight: 28.8800 g. **Composition:**
0.9000 Silver .8357 oz. ASW **Subject:** 100th Anniversary of
Constutution **Note:** Struck at Mexico City Mint, mint mark Mo.

Date	Mintage	F	VF	XF	Unc	BU
1957	100,000	—	12.50	22.50	37.50	45.00

10 PESOS   KM# 476   Weight: 28.8800 g. **Composition:**
0.9000 Silver .8357 oz. ASW **Subject:** 150th Anniversary -
War of Independence **Note:** Struck at Mexico City Mint, mint
mark Mo.

Date	Mintage	F	VF	XF	Unc	BU
1960	1,000,000	—	BV	6.00	9.00	13.50

10 PESOS **KM# 477.1** **Composition:** Copper-Nickel **Reverse:** Miguel Hidalgo **Shape:** 7-sided **Note:** Thin flan - 1.6mm

Date	Mintage	F	VF	XF	Unc	BU
1974	3,900,000	—	0.50	1.00	3.50	4.25
1974 Proof	—	Value: 625				
1975	1,000,000	—	2.25	3.25	7.75	15.00
1976	74,500,000	—	0.25	0.75	1.75	2.25
1977	79,620,000	—	0.50	1.00	2.00	3.00

10 PESOS **KM# 477.2** **Composition:** Copper-Nickel **Reverse:** Miguel Hidalgo **Note:** Thick flan - 2.3mm

Date	Mintage	F	VF	XF	Unc	BU
1978	124,850,000	—	0.50	0.75	2.50	2.75
1979	57,200,000	—	0.50	0.75	2.25	2.50
1980	55,200,000	—	0.50	0.75	2.50	3.75
1981	222,768,000	—	0.40	0.60	2.25	2.60
1982	151,770,000	—	0.50	0.80	2.50	3.50
1982 Proof	1,051	Value: 18.00				
1983 Proof; 3 known	—	Value: 1,600				
1985	58,000,000	—	1.25	1.75	5.75	7.50

10 PESOS **KM# 512** **Composition:** Stainless Steel **Reverse:** Miguel Hidalgo **Note:** Date varieties exist.

Date	Mintage	F	VF	XF	Unc	BU
1985	257,000,000	—	—	0.15	0.50	0.75
1986	392,000,000	—	—	0.15	0.50	1.50
1987	305,000,000	—	—	0.15	0.35	0.50
1988	500,300,000	—	—	0.15	0.25	0.35
1989	—	—	0.20	0.25	0.75	1.50
1990	—	—	—	0.25	0.75	1.25
1990 Proof; 2 known	—	Value: 500				

20 PESOS **KM# 478** **Weight:** 16.6666 g. **Composition:** 0.9000 Gold .4823 oz. AGW **Note:** Struck at Mexico City Mint, mint mark Mo.

Date	Mintage	F	VF	XF	Unc	BU
1917	852,000	—	BV	155	185	—
1918	2,831,000	—	BV	155	185	—
1919	1,094,000	—	BV	155	185	—
1920/10	462,000	—	BV	160	195	—
1920	Inc. above	—	BV	155	185	—
1921/11	922,000	—	BV	160	195	—
1921/10	—	—	—	—	—	—
1921	Inc. above	—	BV	155	185	—
1959	Est. 13,000	—	—	—	—	—

Note: During 1960-1971 a total of 1,158,414 pieces were restruck, most likely dated 1959. In 1996 matte restrikes were produced

20 PESOS **KM# 486** **Composition:** Copper-Nickel

Date	Mintage	F	VF	XF	Unc	BU
1980	84,900,000	—	0.50	0.85	2.50	3.40
1981	250,573,000	—	0.60	0.80	2.50	3.50
1982	236,892,000	—	1.00	1.75	2.75	3.85
1982 Proof	1,051	Value: 18.00				
1983 Proof; 3 known	—	—	—	—	—	—
1984	55,000,000	—	1.00	1.50	3.75	7.50

20 PESOS **KM# 508** **Composition:** Brass **Reverse:** Guadalupe Victoria, First President

Date	Mintage	F	VF	XF	Unc	BU
1985 Wide date	25,000,000	—	0.10	0.20	1.00	1.25
1985 Narrow date	Inc. above	—	0.10	0.25	1.50	2.00
1986	10,000,000	—	1.00	1.75	5.00	6.00
1988	355,200,000	—	0.10	0.20	0.50	1.00
1989	—	—	0.15	0.30	1.50	2.00
1990	—	—	0.15	0.30	1.50	2.50
1990 Proof; 3 known	—	Value: 475				

Normal Tongue

25 PESOS   KM# 479.1   Weight: 22.5000 g.
Composition: 0.7200 Silver .5209 oz. ASW **Note:** Type I,
Rings aligned.

Date	Mintage	F	VF	XF	Unc	BU
1968	27,182,000	—	BV	4.00	4.75	6.00

25 PESOS   KM# 479.2   Weight: 22.5000 g. **Composition:**
0.7200 Silver .5209 oz. ASW **Subject:** Summer Olympics -
Mexico City **Note:** Type II, center ring low.

Date	Mintage	F	VF	XF	Unc	BU
1968	Inc. above	—	4.00	5.00	9.00	10.50

**Long Curved
Tongue**

25 PESOS   KM# 479.3   Weight: 22.5000 g.
Composition: 0.7200 Silver .5209 oz. ASW **Subject:**
Summer Olympics - Mexico City **Note:** Normal tongue and
long curved tongue Type III, center rings low. Snake with
long curved tongue.

Date	Mintage	F	VF	XF	Unc	BU
1968	Inc. above	—	4.25	5.25	9.50	11.00

25 PESOS   KM# 480   Weight: 22.5000 g. **Composition:**
0.7200 Silver .5209 oz. ASW **Reverse:** Benito Juarez

Date	Mintage	F	VF	XF	Unc	BU
1972	2,000,000	—	—	4.00	6.00	9.00

25 PESOS   KM# 497   Weight: 7.7760 g. **Composition:**
0.7200 Silver .1800 oz. ASW **Subject:** 1986 World Cup
Soccer Games

Date	Mintage	F	VF	XF	Unc	BU
1985	354,000	—	—	—	—	6.50

25 PESOS   KM# 503   Weight: 8.4060 g. **Composition:**
0.9250 Silver .2450 oz. ASW **Subject:** 1986 World Cup
Soccer Games

Date	Mintage	F	VF	XF	Unc	BU
1985 Proof	277,000	Value: 9.00				

25 PESOS   KM# 514   Weight: 8.4060 g. **Composition:**
0.9250 Silver .2450 oz. ASW **Subject:** 1986 World Cup
Soccer Games

Date	Mintage	F	VF	XF	Unc	BU
1985 Proof	234,000	Value: 9.00				

Date	Mintage	F	VF	XF	Unc	BU
1946	1,588,000	—	—	BV	450	—
1947	309,000	—	—	—BV+3%	—	
1947 Specimen	—	—	—	—	—	—

Note: Value, $6,500

50 PESOS KM# 482 Weight: 41.6666 g. **Composition:** 0.9000 Gold 1.2057 oz. AGW

Date	Mintage	F	VF	XF	Unc	BU
1943	89,000	—	—	—	BV	525

25 PESOS KM# 519 Weight: 8.4060 g. **Composition:** 0.9250 Silver .2450 oz. ASW **Subject:** 1986 World Cup Soccer Games

Date	Mintage	F	VF	XF	Unc	BU
1986 Proof	— Value: 9.00					

25 PESOS KM# 497a Weight: 8.4060 g. **Composition:** 0.9250 Silver .2450 oz. ASW **Subject:** 1986 World Cup Soccer Games **Reverse:** Without fineness statement

Date	Mintage	F	VF	XF	Unc	BU
1986 Proof	— Value: 9.00					

25 PESOS KM# 554 Weight: 7.7758 g. **Composition:** 0.9990 Silver .2500 oz. ASW **Reverse:** Eagle warrior

Date	Mintage	F	VF	XF	Unc	BU
1992	50,000	—	—	—	6.50	—
1992 Proof	3,000 Value: 10.50					

50 PESOS KM# 490 Composition: Copper-Nickel **Subject:** Coyolxauhqui **Note:** Doubled die examples of 1982 and 1983 dates exist.

Date	Mintage	F	VF	XF	Unc	BU
1982	222,890,000	—	1.00	2.50	5.00	6.25
1983	45,000,000	—	1.50	3.00	6.00	6.50
1983 Proof	1,051	Value: 22.00				
1984	73,537,000	—	1.00	1.35	3.50	4.00
1984 Proof; 4 known	—	Value: 750				

50 PESOS KM# 495 Composition: Copper-Nickel **Subject:** Benito Juarez

Date	Mintage	F	VF	XF	Unc	BU
1984	94,216,000	—	0.65	1.25	2.75	3.50
1985	296,000,000	—	0.25	0.45	1.50	2.25
1986	50,000,000	—	5.00	7.00	11.00	12.50
1987	210,000,000	—	0.25	0.45	1.00	1.25
1988	80,200,000	—	6.25	9.00	12.50	14.50

50 PESOS KM# 495a Composition: Stainless Steel **Subject:** Benito Juarez **Edge:** Plain.

Date	Mintage	F	VF	XF	Unc	BU
1988	353,300,000	—	—	0.20	0.75	1.50
1989	—	—	—	—	—	—
1990	—	—	—	0.30	1.00	2.00
1991	—	—	—	—	—	—
1992	—	—	—	0.25	1.00	2.75

50 PESOS KM# 481 Weight: 41.6666 g. **Composition:** 0.9000 Gold 1.2057 oz. AGW **Subject:** Centennial of Independence **Note:** During 1949-1972 a total of 3,975,654 pieces were restruck, most likely dated 1947. In 1996 matte restrikes were produced. Struck at Mexico City Mint, mint mark Mo.

Date	Mintage	F	VF	XF	Unc	BU
1921	180,000	—	—	BV	525	—
1922	463,000	—	—	BV	460	—
1923	432,000	—	—	BV	460	—
1924	439,000	—	—	BV	460	—
1925	716,000	—	—	BV	460	—
1926	600,000	—	—	BV	460	—
1927	606,000	—	—	BV	460	—
1928	538,000	—	—	BV	460	—
1929	458,000	—	—	BV	460	—
1930	372,000	—	—	BV	460	—
1931	137,000	—	—	BV	475	—
1944	593,000	—	—	BV	450	—
1945	1,012,000	—	—	BV	450	—

50 PESOS KM# 498 Weight: 15.5520 g. **Composition:** 0.7200 Silver .3601 oz. ASW **Subject:** 1986 World Cup Soccer Games

Date	Mintage	F	VF	XF	Unc	BU
1985	347,000	—	—	—	—	7.50

50 PESOS   KM# 504   Weight: 16.8310 g. **Composition:**
0.9250 Silver .5000 oz. ASW **Subject:** 1986 World Cup
Soccer Games **Reverse:** Without fineness statement

Date	Mintage	F	VF	XF	Unc	BU
1985 Proof	347,000	Value: 13.50				

50 PESOS   KM# 515   Weight: 16.8310 g. **Composition:**
0.9250 Silver .5000 oz. ASW **Subject:** 1986 World Cup
Soccer Games

Date	Mintage	F	VF	XF	Unc	BU
1985 Proof	234,000	Value: 13.50				

50 PESOS   KM# 523   Weight: 16.8310 g. **Composition:**
0.9250 Silver .5000 oz. ASW **Subject:** 1986 World Cup
Soccer Games

Date	Mintage	F	VF	XF	Unc	BU
1986 Proof	190,000	Value: 13.50				

50 PESOS   KM# 498a   Weight: 16.8310 g. **Composition:**
0.9250 Silver .5000 oz. ASW **Subject:** 1986 World Cup
Soccer Games **Reverse:** Without fineness statement

Date	Mintage	F	VF	XF	Unc	BU
1986 Proof	10,000	Value: 13.50				

50 PESOS   KM# 532   Weight: 15.5500 g. **Composition:**
0.9990 Silver .5000 oz. ASW **Subject:** 50th Anniversary -
Nationalization of Oil Industry

Date	Mintage	F	VF	XF	Unc	BU
ND(1988)	30,000	—	—	—	12.00	15.00

50 PESOS   KM# 555   Weight: 15.5517 g. **Composition:**
0.9990 Silver .5000 oz. ASW **Subject:** 50th Anniversary -
Nationalization of Oil Industry **Reverse:** Eagle warrior

Date	Mintage	F	VF	XF	Unc	BU
1992	50,000	—	—	—	8.50	—
1992 Proof	3,000	Value: 18.50				

Low 7's

100 PESOS   KM# 483.1   Weight: 27.7700 g.
Composition: 0.7200 Silver .6429 oz. ASW **Reverse:** Jose
Morelos y Pavon **Note:** Low 7's and high 7's.

Date	Mintage	F	VF	XF	Unc	BU
1977 Low 7's, sloping shoulder	5,225,000	—	BV	4.00	6.00	10.00
1977 High 7's, sloping shoulder	Inc. above	—	BV	4.00	6.00	10.50

High 7's

100 PESOS KM# 483.2 Weight: 27.7700 g.
Composition: 0.7200 Silver .6429 oz. ASW **Reverse:** Jose
Morelos y Pavon **Note:** Low 7's and high 7's.

Date	Mintage	F	VF	XF	Unc	BU
1977 Date in line, higher right shoulder. Inc. KM#483.1	—	—	BV	4.00	5.00	6.50
1978	9,879,000	—	BV	4.00	6.50	8.50
1979	784,000	—	BV	4.00	6.50	8.50
1979 Proof	—	Value: 550				

100 PESOS KM# 493 Composition: Aluminum-Bronze
Reverse: Venustiano Carranza

Date	Mintage	F	VF	XF	Unc	BU
1984	227,809,000	—	0.45	0.60	2.75	4.00
1985	377,423,000	—	0.30	0.50	2.00	3.00
1986	43,000,000	—	1.00	2.50	4.75	7.50
1987	165,000,000	—	0.60	1.25	2.50	3.50
1988	433,100,000	—	0.30	0.50	2.00	2.75
1989	—	—	0.35	0.65	2.00	2.75
1990	—	—	0.15	0.40	1.50	2.50
1990 Proof; 1 known	—	Value: 650				
1991	—	—	0.15	0.25	1.00	2.50
1992	—	—	0.30	0.75	1.75	3.00

100 PESOS KM# 499 Weight: 31.1030 g. **Composition:**
0.7200 Silver .7201 oz. ASW **Subject:** 1986 World Cup
Soccer Games

Date	Mintage	F	VF	XF	Unc	BU
1985	302,000	—	—	—	—	11.50

100 PESOS KM# 499a Weight: 32.6250 g. **Composition:**
0.9250 Silver 1.0000 oz. ASW **Subject:** 1986 World Cup
Soccer Games **Reverse:** Without fineness statement

Date	Mintage	F	VF	XF	Unc	BU
1985 Proof	9,006	Value: 18.50				

100 PESOS KM# 505 Weight: 32.6250 g. **Composition:**
0.9250 Silver 1.0000 oz. ASW **Subject:** 1986 World Cup
Soccer Games **Reverse:** Without fineness statement

Date	Mintage	F	VF	XF	Unc	BU
1985 Proof	9,006	Value: 18.50				

100 PESOS KM#521 Weight: 32.6250 g. **Composition:** 0.9250 Silver 1.0000 oz. ASW **Subject:** 1986 World Cup Soccer Games **Reverse:** Without fineness statement

Date	Mintage	F	VF	XF	Unc	BU
1986 Proof	208,000	Value: 18.50				

100 PESOS KM#533 Weight: 31.1030 g. **Composition:** 0.9990 Silver 1.0000 oz. ASW **Subject:** 50th Anniversary - Nationalization of Oil Industry

Date	Mintage	F	VF	XF	Unc	BU
1988	10,000	—	—	—	28.00	35.00

100 PESOS KM#524 Weight: 32.6250 g. **Composition:** 0.9250 Silver 1.0000 oz. ASW **Subject:** 1986 World Cup Soccer Games **Reverse:** Without fineness statement

Date	Mintage	F	VF	XF	Unc	BU
1986 Proof	190,000	Value: 18.50				

100 PESOS KM#539 Weight: 33.6250 g. **Composition:** 0.9250 Silver 1.0000 oz. ASW **Subject:** Save the Children

Date	Mintage	F	VF	XF	Unc	BU
1991 Proof	30,000	Value: 35.00				

100 PESOS KM#537 Weight: 32.6250 g. **Composition:** 0.9250 Silver 1.0000 oz. ASW **Subject:** World Wildlife Fund **Reverse:** Monarch butterflies

Date	Mintage	F	VF	XF	Unc	BU
1987 Proof	Est. 30,000	Value: 40.00				

100 PESOS KM#540 Weight: 27.0000 g. **Composition:** 0.9250 Silver .8029 oz. ASW **Subject:** Ibero - American Series **Reverse:** Pillars

Date	Mintage	F	VF	XF	Unc	BU
1991 Proof	50,000	Value: 47.50				
1992 Proof	75,000	Value: 42.50				

100 PESOS KM#566 Weight: 31.1035 g. **Composition:** 0.9990 Silver 1.0000 oz. ASW **Subject:** Save the Vaquita Porpoise

Date	Mintage	F	VF	XF	Unc	BU
1992 Proof	—	Value: 40.00				

100 PESOS KM#563 Weight: 31.1035 g. **Composition:** 0.9990 Silver 1.0000 oz. ASW **Reverse:** Brasero Efigie - The God of Rain

Date	Mintage	F	VF	XF	Unc	BU
1992 Proof	4,000	Value: 37.50				

100 PESOS KM#556 Weight: 31.1035 g. **Composition:** 0.9990 Silver 1.0000 oz. ASW **Reverse:** Eagle warrior

Date	Mintage	F	VF	XF	Unc	BU
1992	205,000	—	—	—	11.50	—
1992	4,000	Value: 37.50				

100 PESOS KM#564 Weight: 31.1035 g. **Composition:** 0.9990 Silver 1.0000 oz. ASW **Reverse:** Huehueteotl - The God of Fire

Date	Mintage	F	VF	XF	Unc	BU
1992 Proof	4,000	Value: 37.50				

100 PESOS KM#562 Weight: 31.1035 g. **Composition:** 0.9990 Silver 1.0000 oz. ASW **Reverse:** Xochipilli - The God of Joy, Music and Dance

Date	Mintage	F	VF	XF	Unc	BU
1992 Proof	4,000	Value: 37.50				

200 PESOS KM#509 Composition: Copper-Nickel **Subject:** 175th Anniversary of Independence

Date	Mintage	F	VF	XF	Unc	BU
1985	75,000,000	—	—	0.25	3.25	4.75

200 PESOS   KM# 510   Composition: Copper-Nickel
Subject: 175th Anniversary of 1910 Revolution

Date	Mintage	F	VF	XF	Unc	BU
1985	98,590,000	—	—	0.25	3.25	4.25

200 PESOS   KM# 525   Composition: Copper-Nickel
Subject: 1986 World Cup Soccer Games

Date	Mintage	F	VF	XF	Unc	BU
1986	50,000,000	—	—	1.00	3.50	4.50

200 PESOS   KM#526   Weight: 62.2060 g. **Composition:**
0.9990 Silver 2.0000 oz. ASW **Subject:** 1986 World Cup
Soccer Games

Date	Mintage	F	VF	XF	Unc	BU
1986	50,000	—	—	—	40.00	50.00

250 PESOS   KM# 500.1   Weight: 8.6400 g.
Composition: 0.9000 Gold .2500 oz. AGW **Subject:** 1986
World Cup Soccer Games

Date	Mintage	F	VF	XF	Unc	BU
1985	100,000	—	—	—	—	100
1986	—	—	—	—	—	100

250 PESOS   KM#500.2   Weight: 8.6400 g. **Composition:**
0.9000 Gold .2500 oz. AGW **Subject:** 1986 World Cup Soccer
Games **Reverse:** Without fineness statement

Date	Mintage	F	VF	XF	Unc	BU
1985 Proof	4,506	Value: 110				
1986 Proof	—	Value: 135				

250 PESOS   KM# 506.1   Weight: 8.6400 g.
Composition: 0.9000 Gold .2500 oz. AGW **Subject:** 1986
World Cup Soccer Games

Date	Mintage	F	VF	XF	Unc	BU
1985	88,000	—	—	—	—	110

250 PESOS   KM# 506.2   Weight: 8.6400 g. **Composition:**
0.9000 Gold .2500 oz. AGW **Subject:** 1986 World Cup Soccer
Games **Reverse:** Without fineness statement

Date	Mintage	F	VF	XF	Unc	BU
1985 Proof	Est. 80,000	Value: 115				

250 PESOS   KM# 558   Weight: 7.7758 g. **Composition:**
0.9990 Gold .2500 oz. AGW **Subject:** Native Culture
Reverse: Sculpture of jaguar head

Date	Mintage	F	VF	XF	Unc	BU
1992	10,000	—	—	—	145	—
1992 Proof	2,000	Value: 250				

500 PESOS   KM# 501.1   Weight: 17.2800 g.
Composition: 0.9000 Gold .5000 oz. AGW **Subject:** 1986
World Cup Soccer Games **Obverse:** Eagle facing left with
snake in beak

Date	Mintage	F	VF	XF	Unc	BU
1985	102,000	—	—	—	—	210
1986	—	—	—	—	—	210

500 PESOS   KM# 501.2   Weight: 17.2800 g.
Composition: 0.9000 Gold .5000 oz. AGW **Subject:** 1986
World Cup Soccer Games **Obverse:** Eagle facing left with
snake in beak **Reverse:** Without fineness statement

Date	Mintage	F	VF	XF	Unc	BU
1985 Proof	5,506	Value: 225				
1986 Proof	—	Value: 225				

500 PESOS   KM#507.1   Weight: 17.2800 g. **Composition:**
0.9000 Gold .5000 oz. AGW **Subject:** 1986 World Cup Soccer
Games **Obverse:** Eagle facing left with snake in beak

Date	Mintage	F	VF	XF	Unc	BU
1985	—	—	—	—	—	225

500 PESOS   KM# 507.2   Weight: 17.2800 g.
Composition: 0.9000 Gold .5000 oz. AGW **Subject:** 1986
World Cup Soccer Games **Obverse:** Eagle facing left with
snake in beak **Reverse:** Without fineness statement

Date	Mintage	F	VF	XF	Unc	BU
1985 Proof	—	Value: 225				

500 PESOS   KM# 511   Weight: 3334500.0000 g.
Composition: 0.9250 Silver 1.0000 oz. ASW **Subject:** 17th
Anniversary of 1910 Revolution **Obverse:** Eagle facing left
with snake in beak

Date	Mintage	F	VF	XF	Unc	BU
1985 Proof	40,000	Value: 30.00				

500 PESOS   KM# 529   Composition: Copper-Nickel
Reverse: Francisco Madero

Date	Mintage	F	VF	XF	Unc	BU
1986	20,000,000	—	—	1.00	2.50	3.00
1987	180,000,000	—	—	0.75	2.00	2.50
1988	230,000,000	—	—	0.50	2.00	2.50
1988 Proof; 2 known	—	Value: 650				
1989	—	—	—	0.75	2.00	3.00
1992	—	—	—	1.00	2.25	3.50

500 PESOS   KM# 534   Weight: 17.2800 g. **Composition:**
0.9000 Gold .5000 oz. AGW **Subject:** 50th Anniversary -
Nationalization of Oil Industry **Reverse:** Monument **Note:**
Similar to 5000 Pesos, KM#531.

Date	Mintage	F	VF	XF	Unc	BU
1988	—	—	—	—	—	225

500 PESOS   KM# 559   Weight: 15.5517 g. **Composition:**
0.9990 Gold .5000 oz. AGW **Subject:** Native Culture -
Sculpture of Jaguar Head

Date	Mintage	F	VF	XF	Unc	BU
1992	10,000	—	—	—	200	—
1992 Proof	2,000	Value: 400				

1000 PESOS   KM# 513   Weight: 17.2800 g.
Composition: 0.9000 Gold .5000 oz. AGW **Subject:** 175th
Anniversary of Independence

Date	Mintage	F	VF	XF	Unc	BU
1985 Proof	—	Value: 325				

1000 PESOS   KM# 527   Weight: 31.1030 g.
Composition: 0.9990 Gold 1.0000 oz. AGW **Subject:** 1986
World Cup Soccer Games

Date	Mintage	F	VF	XF	Unc	BU
1986	—	—	—	—	—	550

1000 PESOS   KM# 536   Composition: Aluminum-Bronze
Note: Juana de Asbaje

Date	Mintage	F	VF	XF	Unc	BU
1988	229,300,000	—	0.85	1.25	3.75	4.25
1989	—	—	0.85	1.25	3.45	4.25
1990	—	—	0.85	1.25	2.25	4.25
1990 Proof; 2 known	—	Value: 550				
1991	—	—	1.00	1.50	2.50	4.25
1992	—	—	1.00	1.50	2.25	3.50

1000 PESOS   KM# 535   Weight: 34.5590 g.
Composition: 0.9000 Gold 1.0000 oz. AGW **Subject:** 50th
Anniversary - Nationalization of Oil Industry **Reverse:**
Portrait of Cardenas **Note:** Similar to 5000 Pesos, KM#531.

Date	Mintage	F	VF	XF	Unc	BU
1988 Proof	—	Value: 440				

1000 PESOS   KM# 560   Weight: 31.1035 g.
Composition: 0.9990 Gold 1.0000 oz. AGW **Subject:**
Native Culture **Reverse:** Sculpture of jaguar head

Date	Mintage	F	VF	XF	Unc	BU
1992	18,000	—	—	—	400	—
1992 Proof	2,000	Value: 600				

2000 PESOS   KM# 528 Weight: 62.2000 g.
Composition: 0.9990 Gold 2.0000 oz. AGW **Subject:** 1986
World Cup Soccer Games

Date	Mintage	F	VF	XF	Unc	BU
1986	—	—	—	—	—	900

5000 PESOS   KM# 531 Composition: Copper-Nickel
Subject: 50th Anniversary - Nationalization of Oil Industry

Date	Mintage	F	VF	XF	Unc	BU
ND(1988)	50,000,000	—	—	4.75	7.75	10.00

10000 PESOS   KM# 557 Weight: 155.5175 g.
Composition: 0.9990 Silver 5.0000 oz. ASW **Subject:**
Pieora De Tizoc **Reverse:** Native warriors taking female
captive **Size:** 64 mm. **Note:** Illustration reduced.

Date	Mintage	F	VF	XF	Unc	BU
1992	52,000	—	—	—	46.00	—
1992 Proof	3,005	Value: 80.00				

REFORM COINAGE
1 New Peso = 1000 Old Pesos

5 CENTAVOS   KM# 546 Composition: Stainless Steel
Note: Illustration reduced.

Date	Mintage	F	VF	XF	Unc	BU
1992	—	—	—	0.15	0.25	—
1993	—	—	—	0.15	0.25	—
1994	—	—	—	0.15	0.25	—
1995	—	—	—	0.15	0.25	—
1995 Proof	—	Value: 0.50				
1996	—	—	—	0.15	0.25	—
1997	—	—	—	0.15	0.25	—
1998	—	—	—	0.15	0.25	—
1999	—	—	—	0.15	0.25	—
2000Mo	—	—	—	0.15	0.25	—

10 CENTAVOS   KM# 547 Composition: Stainless Steel

Date	Mintage	F	VF	XF	Unc	BU
1992	—	—	—	0.20	0.30	—
1993	—	—	—	0.20	0.30	—
1994	—	—	—	0.20	0.30	—
1995	—	—	—	0.20	0.30	—
1995 Proof	—	Value: 0.60				
1996	—	—	—	0.20	0.30	—
1997	—	—	—	0.20	0.30	—
1998	—	—	—	0.20	0.30	—
1999	—	—	—	0.20	0.30	—
2000	—	—	—	0.20	0.30	—
2001Mo	—	—	—	0.20	0.30	—

20 CENTAVOS   KM# 548 Composition: Aluminum-
Bronze

Date	Mintage	F	VF	XF	Unc	BU
1992	—	—	—	0.25	0.35	—
1993	—	—	—	0.25	0.35	—
1994	—	—	—	0.25	0.35	—
1995	—	—	—	0.25	0.35	—
1995 Proof	—	Value: 0.75				
1996	—	—	—	0.25	0.35	—
1997	—	—	—	0.25	0.35	—
1998	—	—	—	0.25	0.35	—
1999	—	—	—	0.25	0.35	—
2000	—	—	—	0.25	0.35	—

50 CENTAVOS   KM# 549 Composition: Aluminum-
Bronze

Date	Mintage	F	VF	XF	Unc	BU
1992	—	—	—	0.45	0.85	—
1993	—	—	—	0.45	0.75	—
1994	—	—	—	0.45	0.75	—
1995	—	—	—	0.45	0.75	—
1995 Proof	—	Value: 0.90				
1996	—	—	—	0.45	0.75	—
1997	—	—	—	0.45	0.75	—
1998	—	—	—	0.45	0.75	—
1999	—	—	—	0.45	0.75	—
2000	—	—	—	0.45	0.75	—
2001	—	—	—	0.45	0.75	—
2002	—	—	—	0.45	0.75	—

NUEVO PESO KM# 550 Ring Composition: Stainless Steel **Center Composition:** Aluminum-Bronze

Date	Mintage	F	VF	XF	Unc	BU
1992	—	—	—	0.60	1.25	—
1992	—	—	—	0.60	1.25	—
1993	—	—	—	0.60	1.25	—
1993	—	—	—	0.60	1.25	—
1994	—	—	—	0.60	1.25	—
1994	—	—	—	0.60	1.25	—
1995	—	—	—	0.60	1.25	—
1995	—	—	—	0.60	1.25	—
1995 Proof	—	Value: 2.50				
1995 Proof	—	Value: 2.50				

NUEVO PESO KM# 644 Weight: 7.7700 g.
Composition: 0.9990 Silver .2496 oz. ASW **Subject:** Eagle Warrior **Obverse:** National arms **Reverse:** Costumed warrior **Edge:** Reeded **Size:** 26.8 mm.

Date	Mintage	F	VF	XF	Unc	BU
1993 Proof	—	—	—	—	11.50	—

NUEVO PESO KM# 567 Weight: 7.7601 g.
Composition: 0.9990 Silver .2498 oz. ASW **Subject:** Bajorrelieve Del El Tajin

Date	Mintage	F	VF	XF	Unc	BU
1993	100,000	—	—	—	6.50	—
1993 Proof	3,000	Value: 10.50				

NUEVO PESO KM# 572 Weight: 7.7601 g.
Composition: 0.9990 Silver .2498 oz. ASW **Subject:** Chaac Mool

Date	Mintage	F	VF	XF	Unc	BU
1994 Matte	30,000	—	—	—	6.50	—
1994 Proof	2,500	Value: 10.50				

PESO KM# 593 Weight: 7.7750 g. **Composition:** 0.9990 Silver .2500 oz. ASW **Subject:** Senor De Las Limas **Note:** Similar to 5 Pesos, KM#595.

Date	Mintage	F	VF	XF	Unc	BU
1996	4,000	—	—	—	4.00	—
1996 Proof	2,200	Value: 25.00				
1998 Matte	2,400	—	—	—	3.25	—

PESO KM# 603 Ring Composition: Stainless Steel **Center Composition:** Aluminum-Bronze **Note:** Similar to KM#550 but without N.

Date	Mintage	F	VF	XF	Unc	BU
1996Mo	—	—	—	—	1.25	—
1996Mo	—	—	—	—	1.25	—
1997Mo	—	—	—	—	1.25	—
1997Mo	—	—	—	—	1.25	—
1998Mo	—	—	—	—	1.25	—
1998Mo	—	—	—	—	1.25	—
1999Mo	—	—	—	—	1.25	—
1999Mo	—	—	—	—	1.25	—
2000Mo	—	—	—	—	1.25	—
2000Mo	—	—	—	—	1.25	—
2001Mo	—	—	—	—	1.25	—
2001Mo	—	—	—	—	1.25	—
2002Mo	—	—	—	—	1.25	—
2002Mo	—	—	—	—	1.25	—

PESO KM# 617 Weight: 7.7759 g. **Composition:** 0.9990 Silver .2500 oz. ASW **Subject:** Disco De La Muerte **Obverse:** Mexican eagle

Date	Mintage	F	VF	XF	Unc	BU
1997	3,000	—	—	—	4.00	—
1997 Proof	1,600	Value: 10.50				
1998 Proof	500	Value: 15.00				
1998 Matte	2,400	—	—	—	10.50	—

PESO KM# 661 Weight: 7.7759 g. **Composition:** 0.9990 Silver .2500 oz. ASW **Subject:** Jaguar **Obverse:** National emblem **Reverse:** Jaguar carving **Edge:** Reeded **Size:** 27 mm.

Date	Mintage	F	VF	XF	Unc	BU
1998	6,000	—	—	—	4.00	—
1998 Proof	4,800	Value: 8.00				

2 NUEVO PESOS KM# 551 Ring Composition: Stainless Steel **Center Composition:** Aluminum-Bronze

Date	Mintage	F	VF	XF	Unc	BU
1992	—	—	—	1.50	2.50	—
1992	—	—	—	1.50	2.50	—
1993	—	—	—	1.00	2.35	—
1993	—	—	—	1.00	2.35	—
1994	—	—	—	1.00	2.35	—
1994	—	—	—	1.00	2.35	—
1995	—	—	—	1.00	2.35	—
1995	—	—	—	1.00	2.35	—
1995 Proof	—	Value: 4.50				
1995 Proof	—	Value: 4.50				

2 NUEVO PESOS KM# 568 Weight: 15.5516 g. **Composition:** 0.9990 Silver .4995 oz. ASW **Subject:** Bajorrelieve Del El Tajin

Date	Mintage	F	VF	XF	Unc	BU
1993	100,000	—	—	—	6.50	—
1993 Proof	3,000	Value: 10.50				

2 NUEVO PESOS KM# 573 Weight: 15.5516 g. **Composition:** 0.9990 Silver .4995 oz. ASW **Subject:** Chaac Mool

Date	Mintage	F	VF	XF	Unc	BU
1994 Matte	30,000	—	—	—	6.50	—
1994 Proof	2,500	Value: 10.50				

2 PESOS KM# 594 Weight: 15.5517 g. **Composition:** 0.9990 Silver .5000 oz. ASW **Subject:** Senor De Las Limasl **Note:** Similar to 5 Pesos, KM#595.

Date	Mintage	F	VF	XF	Unc	BU
1996	4,000	—	—	—	6.00	—
1996 Proof	2,200	Value: 18.50				
1998 Matte	2,400	—	—	—	8.50	—

2 PESOS KM# 604 Ring Composition: Stainless Steel **Center Composition:** Aluminum-Bronze **Note:** Similar to KM#551, but denomination without N.

Date	Mintage	F	VF	XF	Unc	BU
1996Mo	—	—	—	—	2.50	—
1996Mo	—	—	—	—	2.50	—
1997Mo	—	—	—	—	2.50	—
1997Mo	—	—	—	—	2.50	—
1998Mo	—	—	—	—	2.50	—
1998Mo	—	—	—	—	2.50	—
1999Mo	—	—	—	—	2.50	—
1999Mo	—	—	—	—	2.50	—
2000Mo	—	—	—	—	2.50	—
2000Mo	—	—	—	—	2.50	—
2001Mo	—	—	—	—	2.50	—
2001Mo	—	—	—	—	2.50	—
2002Mo	—	—	—	—	2.50	—
2002Mo	—	—	—	—	2.50	—

2 PESOS KM# 618 Weight: 15.5517 g. **Composition:** 0.9990 Silver .5000 oz. ASW **Subject:** Disco De La Muerte **Obverse:** Mexican eagle

Date	Mintage	F	VF	XF	Unc	BU
1997	3,000	—	—	—	6.00	—
1997 Proof	1,600	Value: 10.50				
1998	2,400	—	—	—	6.50	—
1998 Proof	500	Value: 15.00				

2 PESOS KM# 662 Weight: 15.5517 g. **Composition:** 0.9990 Silver .5000 oz. ASW **Subject:** Jaguar **Obverse:** National emblem **Reverse:** Jaguar carving **Edge:** Reeded **Size:** 33 mm.

Date	Mintage	F	VF	XF	Unc	BU
1998	6,000	—	—	—	8.00	—
1998 Proof	4,800	Value: 16.00				

5 NUEVO PESOS   KM# 552   Ring Composition:
Stainless Steel **Center Composition:** Aluminum-Bronze

Date	Mintage	F	VF	XF	Unc	BU
1992	—	—	—	2.00	4.00	—
1992	—	—	—	2.00	4.00	—
1993	—	—	—	2.00	4.00	—
1993	—	—	—	2.00	4.00	—
1994	—	—	—	2.00	4.00	—
1994	—	—	—	2.00	4.00	—
1995 Proof	—	Value: 25.00				
1995 Proof	—	Value: 25.00				

5 NUEVO PESOS   KM# 647   Weight: 31.0000 g.
Composition: 0.9990 Silver .9957 oz. ASW **Subject:**
Xochipilli **Obverse:** National arms **Reverse:** Seated figure
sculpture **Edge:** Reeded **Size:** 40 mm.

Date	Mintage	F	VF	XF	Unc	BU
1993 Proof	—	Value: 45.00				

5 NUEVO PESOS   KM# 583   Weight: 31.1035 g.
Composition: 0.9990 Silver .9991 oz. ASW **Subject:**
Anciano Con Brasero **Reverse:** Kneeling figure sculpture

Date	Mintage	F	VF	XF	Unc	BU
1993	2,650	—	—	—	12.00	—
1993 Proof	1,500	Value: 37.50				

5 NUEVO PESOS   KM# 648   Weight: 31.0000 g.
Composition: 0.9990 Silver .9957 oz. ASW **Subject:**
Brasco Efigie **Obverse:** National arms **Reverse:** Sculpture
Edge: Reeded **Size:** 40 mm.

Date	Mintage	F	VF	XF	Unc	BU
1993 Proof	—	Value: 45.00				

5 NUEVO PESOS   KM# 646   Weight: 31.0500 g.
Composition: 0.9990 Silver .9973 oz. ASW **Subject:** Eagle
Warrior **Obverse:** National arms **Reverse:** Costumed
warrior **Edge:** Reeded **Size:** 40 mm.

Date	Mintage	F	VF	XF	Unc	BU
1993 Proof	—	Value: 46.00				

5 NUEVO PESOS   KM# 649   Weight: 31.0000 g.
Composition: 0.9990 Silver .9957 oz. ASW **Subject:**
Huchucteotl **Obverse:** National arms **Reverse:** Aztec
sculpture **Edge:** Reeded **Size:** 40 mm.

Date	Mintage	F	VF	XF	Unc	BU
1993 Proof	—	Value: 45.00				

5 NUEVO PESOS   KM# 574   Weight: 31.1035 g.
Composition: 0.9990 Silver .9991 oz. ASW **Subject:**
Chaac Mool **Reverse:** Sculptured head

Date	Mintage	F	VF	XF	Unc	BU
1994 Matte	50,000	—	—	—	12.00	—
1994 Proof	3,000	Value: 37.50				

5 NUEVO PESOS   KM# 569   Weight: 31.1035 g.
Composition: 0.9990 Silver .9991 oz. ASW **Subject:**
Bajorrelieve Del El Tajin **Obverse:** Mexican eagle

Date	Mintage	F	VF	XF	Unc	BU
1993	100,000	—	—	—	12.00	—
1993 Proof	3,000	Value: 37.50				

5 NUEVO PESOS   KM# 575   Weight: 31.1035 g.
Composition: 0.9990 Silver .9991 oz. ASW **Subject:**
Chaac Mool **Reverse:** Tomb of Palenque Memorial Stone

Date	Mintage	F	VF	XF	Unc	BU
1994	4,500	—	—	—	12.00	—
1994 Proof	2,500	Value: 37.50				

5 NUEVO PESOS   KM# 582   Weight: 31.1035 g.
Composition: 0.9990 Silver .9991 oz. ASW **Subject:** Palma
Con Cecodrilo **Obverse:** National emblem **Reverse:** Aerial
view of crocodile

Date	Mintage	F	VF	XF	Unc	BU
1993	4,500	—	—	—	12.00	—
1993 Proof	2,650	Value: 37.50				

5 NUEVO PESOS   KM# 584   Weight: 31.1035 g.
Composition: 0.9990 Silver .9991 oz. ASW **Subject:** Carita
Sonriente **Reverse:** Sculptured head

Date	Mintage	F	VF	XF	Unc	BU
1993	4,500	—	—	—	12.00	—
1993 Proof	3,300	Value: 36.00				

5 NUEVO PESOS   KM# 577   Weight: 31.1035 g.
Composition: 0.9990 Silver .9991 oz. ASW **Subject:**
Mascaron Del Dios Chaac **Reverse:** Elaborately carved wall
segment

Date	Mintage	F	VF	XF	Unc	BU
1994	4,500	—	—	—	12.00	—
1994 Proof	2,500	Value: 37.50				

Date	Mintage	F	VF	XF	Unc	BU
1996 Proof	1,800	Value: 36.00				
1998 Matte	2,000	—	—	—	10.00	—

5 NUEVO PESOS **KM# 578** **Weight:** 31.1035 g.
Composition: 0.9990 Silver .9991 oz. ASW **Subject:** Dintel
26 **Reverse:** Two seated figures wall carving

Date	Mintage	F	VF	XF	Unc	BU
1994	4,500	—	—	—	12.00	—
1994 Proof	2,600	Value: 37.50				

5 PESOS **KM# 595** **Weight:** 31.1035 g. **Composition:**
0.9990 Silver 1.0000 oz. ASW **Subject:** Senor De Las Limas

Date	Mintage	F	VF	XF	Unc	BU
1996	4,000	—	—	—	12.00	—
1996 Proof	3,000	Value: 36.00				
1998 Matte	3,400	—	—	—	16.25	—

5 NUEVO PESOS **KM# 588** **Weight:** 27.0000 g.
Composition: 0.9250 Silver .8030 oz. ASW **Subject:**
Environmental Protection **Reverse:** Pacific Ridley Sea Turtle

Date	Mintage	F	VF	XF	Unc	BU
1994 Proof	20,000	Value: 37.50				

5 PESOS **KM# 597** **Weight:** 31.1035 g. **Composition:**
0.9990 Silver 1.0000 oz. ASW **Subject:** El Luchador

Date	Mintage	F	VF	XF	Unc	BU
1996	4,500	—	—	—	13.50	—
1996 Proof	2,700	Value: 36.00				
1998 Matte	2,000	—	—	—	10.00	—

5 PESOS **KM# 596** **Weight:** 31.1035 g. **Composition:**
0.9990 Silver 1.0000 oz. ASW **Subject:** Hombre Jaguar

Date	Mintage	F	VF	XF	Unc	BU
1996	3,500	—	—	—	13.50	—

5 PESOS **KM# 598** **Weight:** 31.1035 g. **Composition:**
0.9990 Silver 1.0000 oz. ASW **Subject:** Hacha Ceremonial

Date	Mintage	F	VF	XF	Unc	BU
1996	4,500	—	—	—	10.00	—
1996 Proof	2,700	Value: 36.00				
1998 Matte	2,000	—	—	—	10.00	—

5 PESOS   KM# 605   Ring Composition: Stainless Steel
Center Composition: Aluminum-Bronze **Note:** Similar to
KM#552 but deonomination without N.

Date	Mintage	F	VF	XF	Unc	BU
1997Mo	—	—	—	—	5.50	—
1998Mo	—	—	—	—	5.50	—
1999Mo	—	—	—	—	5.50	—
2000Mo	—	—	—	—	5.50	—
2001Mo	—	—	—	—	5.50	—
2002Mo	—	—	—	—	5.50	—

5 PESOS   KM# 629   Weight: 27.0000 g. **Composition:**
0.9250 Silver .8030 oz. ASW **Subject:** Jarabe Tapatio
Obverse: Mexican emblem within circle of arms **Reverse:**
Two dancers

Date	Mintage	F	VF	XF	Unc	BU
1997 Proof	20,000	Value: 30.00				

5 PESOS   KM# 619   Weight: 31.1035 g. **Composition:**
0.9990 Silver 1.0000 oz. ASW **Subject:** Teohituacan - Disco
de la Muerte **Obverse:** Eagle and snake

Date	Mintage	F	VF	XF	Unc	BU
1997	3,500	—	—	—	13.50	—
1997 Proof	Est. 1,800	Value: 36.00				
1998	3,400	—	—	—	13.50	—
1998 Proof	500	Value: 40.00				

5 PESOS   KM# 621   Weight: 31.1035 g. **Composition:**
0.9990 Silver 1.0000 oz. ASW **Subject:** Teohituacan - Vasija
Obverse: Eagle and snake

Date	Mintage	F	VF	XF	Unc	BU
1997	4,500	—	—	—	9.00	—
1997 Proof	Est. 1,800	Value: 36.00				
1998 Matte	2,000	—	—	—	13.50	—
1998 Proof	500	Value: 40.00				

5 PESOS   KM# 622   Weight: 31.1035 g. **Composition:**
0.9990 Silver 1.0000 oz. ASW **Subject:** Teohituacan -
Jugador of Pelota **Obverse:** Eagle and snake

Date	Mintage	F	VF	XF	Unc	BU
1997	4,500	—	—	—	9.00	—
1997 Proof	Est. 1,800	Value: 36.50				
1998 Matte	2,000	—	—	—	10.00	—

5 PESOS   KM# 620   Weight: 31.1035 g. **Composition:**
0.9990 Silver 1.0000 oz. ASW **Subject:** Teohituacan -
Mascara **Obverse:** Eagle and snake

Date	Mintage	F	VF	XF	Unc	BU
1997	4,500	—	—	—	13.50	—
1997 Proof	Est. 1,800	Value: 36.00				

Date	Mintage	F	VF	XF	Unc	BU
1998	2,000	—	—	—	13.50	—
1998 Proof	500	Value: 40.00				

5 PESOS   KM# 627   Weight: 31.1035 g. **Composition:**
0.9990 Silver 1.0000 oz. ASW **Subject:** World Wildlife Fund
Obverse: Mexican eagle

Date	Mintage	F	VF	XF	Unc	BU
1998 Proof	Est. 15,000	Value: 42.50				

5 PESOS   KM# 663   Weight: 31.1035 g. **Composition:**
0.9990 Silver 1.0000 oz. ASW **Subject:** Jaguar **Obverse:**
National emblem **Reverse:** Jaguar carving **Edge:** Reeded
Size: 40 mm.

Date	Mintage	F	VF	XF	Unc	BU
1998	6,000	—	—	—	18.00	—
1998 Proof	4,800	Value: 40.00				

5 PESOS   KM# 664   Weight: 31.1035 g. **Composition:**
0.9990 Silver 1.0000 oz. ASW **Obverse:** National emblem
Reverse: Sacerdote sculpture **Edge:** Reeded **Size:** 40 mm.

Date	Mintage	F	VF	XF	Unc	BU
1998	5,000	—	—	—	18.00	—
1998 Proof	4,800	Value: 40.00				

5 PESOS   KM# 666   Weight: 31.1035 g. **Composition:**
0.9990 Silver 1.0000 oz. ASW **Subject:** Serpiente con
Craneo **Obverse:** National emblem **Reverse:** Large
sculpture **Edge:** Reeded **Size:** 40 mm.

Date	Mintage	F	VF	XF	Unc	BU
1998	5,000	—	—	—	18.00	—
1998 Proof	4,800	Value: 40.00				

5 PESOS   KM# 665   Weight: 31.1035 g. **Composition:**
0.9990 Silver 1.0000 oz. ASW **Subject:** Quetzalcoatle
Obverse: National emblem **Reverse:** Quetzalcoatle
sculpture **Edge:** Reeded **Size:** 40 mm.

Date	Mintage	F	VF	XF	Unc	BU
1998	5,000	—	—	—	18.00	—
1998 Proof	4,800	Value: 40.00				

5 PESOS   KM# 630   Weight: 31.1800 g. **Composition:**
0.9990 Silver 1.0025 oz. ASW **Subject:** Millennium Series
Obverse: Current national eagle within circle of obsolete
versions **Reverse:** Butterfly, dates

Date	Mintage	F	VF	XF	Unc	BU
1999-2000 Proof	75,000	Value: 30.00				

5 PESOS   KM# 631 Weight: 31.1800 g. **Composition:**
0.9990 Silver 1.0025 oz. ASW **Subject:** Millennium Series
Obverse: Current national eagle within circle of obsolete
versions **Reverse:** Stylized dove/hand of peace

Date	Mintage	F	VF	XF	Unc	BU
1999-2000 Proof	75,000	Value: 30.00				

5 PESOS   KM# 632 Weight: 31.1800 g. **Composition:**
0.9990 Silver 1.0025 oz. ASW **Subject:** Millennium Series
Obverse: Current national eagle within circle of obsolete
versions **Reverse:** Aztec bird design, denomination

Date	Mintage	F	VF	XF	Unc	BU
1999-2000 Proof	75,000	Value: 30.00				

5 PESOS   KM# 635 Weight: 19.6000 g. **Composition:**
0.9250 Silver .6411 oz. ASW **Subject:** Millennium Series
Obverse: Current national eagle within circle of obsolete
versions **Reverse:** Naval training ship Cuauhtemoc

Date	Mintage	F	VF	XF	Unc	BU
1999	—	Value: 35.00				

5 PESOS   KM# 640 Weight: 31.1030 g. **Composition:**
0.9990 Silver .9990 oz. ASW **Subject:** UNICEF **Obverse:**
National arms **Reverse:** Two children flying kite **Edge:**
Reeded **Size:** 40 mm.

Date	Mintage	F	VF	XF	Unc	BU
1999	—	Value: 37.50				

5 NUEVO PESOS   KM# 657 Weight: 31.1710 g.
Composition: 0.9990 Silver 1.0012 oz. ASW **Series:**
Endangered Wildlife - Berrendo **Obverse:** National arms
past and present **Reverse:** Peninsula antelope, giant cardon
cactus in back **Size:** 40 mm.

Date	Mintage	F	VF	XF	Unc	BU
2000	50,000	—	—	—	27.50	—

5 NUEVO PESOS   KM# 652 Weight: 31.1710 g.
Composition: 0.9990 Silver 1.0012 oz. ASW **Series:**
Endangered Wildlife **Subject:** Aguila Real **Obverse:**
National arms past and present **Reverse:** Eagle on branch
Size: 40 mm.

Date	Mintage	F	VF	XF	Unc	BU
2000	50,000	—	—	—	27.50	—

5 NUEVO PESOS   KM# 654   Weight: 31.1710 g.
Composition: 0.9990 Silver 1.0012 oz. ASW **Series:**
Endangered Wildlife **Subject:** Oso Negro **Obverse:** National
arms past and present **Reverse:** Black bear **Size:** 40 mm.

Date	Mintage	F	VF	XF	Unc	BU
2001	50,000	—	—	—	27.50	—

5 NUEVO PESOS   KM# 655   Weight: 31.1710 g.
Composition: 0.9990 Silver 1.0012 oz. ASW **Series:**
Endangered Wildlife **Subject:** Cocodrilo de Rio **Obverse:**
National arms past and present **Reverse:** Crocodile **Size:**
40 mm.

Date	Mintage	F	VF	XF	Unc	BU
2000	50,000	—	—	—	27.50	—

5 NUEVO PESOS   KM# 651   Weight: 31.1710 g.
Composition: 0.9990 Silver 1.0012 oz. ASW **Series:**
Endangered Wildlife **Obverse:** National arms past and
present **Reverse:** West Indian Manati **Edge:** Reeded **Size:**
40 mm.

Date	Mintage	F	VF	XF	Unc	BU
2001	50,000	—	—	—	27.50	—

5 NUEVO PESOS   KM# 656   Weight: 31.1710 g.
Composition: 0.9990 Silver 1.0012 oz. ASW **Series:**
Endangered Wildlife **Subject:** Nutria de Rio **Obverse:**
National arms past and present **Reverse:** Nutria **Size:**
40 mm.

Date	Mintage	F	VF	XF	Unc	BU
2000	50,000	—	—	—	27.50	—

5 NUEVO PESOS   KM# 658   Weight: 31.1710 g.
Composition: 0.9990 Silver 1.0012 oz. ASW **Series:**
Endangered Wildlife **Obverse:** National arms past and
present **Reverse:** Jaguar resting **Size:** 40 mm.

Date	Mintage	F	VF	XF	Unc	BU
2001	50,000	—	—	—	27.50	—

5 NUEVO PESOS   KM# 653   Weight: 31.1710 g.
Composition: 0.9990 Silver 1.0012 oz. ASW **Subject:**
Aguila Arpia **Obverse:** National arms past and present
Reverse: Harpie Eagle **Size:** 40 mm.

Date	Mintage	F	VF	XF	Unc	BU
2001	50,000	—	—	—	27.50	—

5 NUEVO PESOS   **KM# 659**   **Weight:** 31.1710 g.
Composition: 0.9990 Silver 1.0012 oz. ASW **Series:**
Endangered Wildlife **Obverse:** National arms past and
present **Reverse:** Black-tailed Prairie dog **Size:** 40 mm.

Date	Mintage	F	VF	XF	Unc	BU
2001	50,000	—	—	—	27.50	—

5 NUEVO PESOS   **KM# 660**   **Weight:** 31.1710 g.
Composition: 0.9990 Silver 1.0012 oz. ASW **Series:**
Endangered Wildlife **Obverse:** National arms past and
present **Reverse:** Volcano Rabbit **Size:** 40 mm.

Date	Mintage	F	VF	XF	Unc	BU
2001	50,000	—	—	—	27.50	—

10 NUEVO PESOS   **KM# 650**   **Weight:** 155.3100 g.
Composition: 0.9990 Silver 4.9883 oz. ASW **Subject:**
Piedra de Tizoc **Obverse:** National arms **Reverse:** Warrior
capturing woman **Edge:** Reeded **Size:** 64 mm. **Note:**
Illustration reduced.

Date	Mintage	F	VF	XF	Unc	BU
1992 Proof	—	Value: 85.00				
1993	—	—	—	—	55.00	—

10 NUEVO PESOS   **KM# 553**   **Ring Composition:**
Aluminum-Bronze **Center Weight:** 11.1400 g. **Center
Composition:** 0.9250 Silver .1666 oz. ASW

Date	Mintage	F	VF	XF	Unc	BU
1992	—	—	—	—	7.50	—
1993	—	—	—	—	7.50	—
1994	—	—	—	—	7.50	—
1995	—	—	—	—	7.50	—

10 NUEVO PESOS   **KM# 570**   **Center Weight:**
115.5175 g. **Center Composition:** 0.9990 Silver 4.9956 oz.
ASW **Subject:** Piramide Del El Tajin **Size:** 64 mm. **Note:**
Illustration reduced.

Date	Mintage	F	VF	XF	Unc	BU
1993	50,000	—	—	—	46.00	—
1993 Proof	3,100	Value: 78.00				

10 NUEVO PESOS   **KM# 576**   **Center Weight:**
115.5175 g. **Center Composition:** 0.9990 Silver 4.9956 oz.
ASW **Subject:** Piramide del Castillo **Size:** 64 mm. **Note:**
Illustration reduced.

Date	Mintage	F	VF	XF	Unc	BU
1994	20,000	—	—	—	46.50	—
1994 Proof	2,100	Value: 80.00				

Date	Mintage	F	VF	XF	Unc	BU
1997	1,500	—	—	—	50.00	—
1997 Proof	2,100	Value: 95.00				
1998 Matte	2,150	—	—	—	46.00	—

10 PESOS   KM# 616   Ring Composition: Brass **Center Composition:** Copper-Nickel-Zinc **Subject:** Cabeza Olmeca **Obverse:** National emblem **Reverse:** Aztec design

Date	Mintage	F	VF	XF	Unc	BU
1997	—	—	—	—	7.50	—
1998	—	—	—	—	7.50	—

Note: Small date, date on brass ring

1998	—	—	—	—	7.50	—

Note: Large date, date partially on copper-nickel center

1999	—	—	—	—	7.50	—

10 PESOS   KM# 634   Weight: 155.7300 g. **Composition:** 0.9990 Silver 5.0018 oz. ASW **Subject:** Atlantes **Obverse:** National arms **Reverse:** Three curved statues

Date	Mintage	F	VF	XF	Unc	BU
1998	3,500	—	—	—	50.00	—
1998 Proof	4,200	Value: 95.00				

10 PESOS   KM# 633   Weight: 62.0300 g. **Composition:** 0.9990 Silver 1.9923 oz. ASW **Subject:** Millennium Series **Obverse:** Current national eagle within circle of obsolete versions **Reverse:** Old and modern buildings, dates

Date	Mintage	F	VF	XF	Unc	BU
1999-2000 Proof	75,000	Value: 55.00				

10 PESOS   KM# 599   Center Weight: 1555.5175 g. **Center Composition:** 0.9990 Silver 5.0000 oz. ASW **Subject:** Cabeza Olmeca **Size:** 64 mm. **Note:** Illustration reduced.

Date	Mintage	F	VF	XF	Unc	BU
1996	2,000	—	—	—	46.00	—
1996 Proof	2,750	Value: 80.00				
1998 Matte	2,150	—	—	—	46.00	—

10 PESOS   KM# 606   Center Weight: 11.1400 g. **Center Composition:** 0.9250 Silver .1666 oz. ASW **Note:** Similar to KM#553, but denomination without N.

Date	Mintage	F	VF	XF	Unc	BU
1996	—	—	—	—	7.50	—

10 PESOS   KM# 636   Ring Composition: Brass **Center Composition:** Copper-Nickel **Subject:** Millennium Series **Reverse:** Aztec carving

Date	Mintage	F	VF	XF	Unc	BU
2000Mo	—	—	—	—	7.00	—
2001Mo	—	—	—	—	7.00	—

20 NUEVO PESOS   KM# 561   Ring Composition: Aluminum-Bronze .2499 oz. **Center Composition:** Silver

Date	Mintage	F	VF	XF	Unc	BU
1993	—	—	—	—	12.00	—
1994	—	—	—	—	12.00	—
1995	—	—	—	—	12.00	—

10 PESOS   KM# 623   Weight: 1555.5175 g. **Composition:** 0.9990 Silver 5.0000 oz. ASW **Subject:** Piramide Del Sol **Obverse:** Mexican eagle **Size:** 64 mm. **Note:** Illustration reduced.

20 PESOS   KM# 641   Weight: 6.2210 g. **Composition:** 0.9990 Gold .1998 oz. AGW **Subject:** UNICEF **Obverse:** National arms **Reverse:** Child playing with lasso **Edge:** Reeded **Size:** 21.9 mm.

Date	Mintage	F	VF	XF	Unc	BU
1999	—	—	—	—	170	—

20 PESOS   KM# 637   Ring Composition: Brass **Center Composition:** Copper-Nickel **Subject:** Xiutecuhtli **Reverse:** Aztec with torch

Date	Mintage	F	VF	XF	Unc	BU
2000	—	—	—	—	15.00	—

20 PESOS   KM# 638   Ring Composition: Brass **Center Composition:** Copper-Nickel **Subject:** Octavio Paz **Reverse:** Portrait facing

Date	Mintage	F	VF	XF	Unc	BU
2000	—	—	—	—	15.00	—

25 NUEVO PESOS   KM# 585   Weight: 7.7758 g. **Composition:** 0.9990 Gold .2500 oz. AGW **Subject:** Hacha Ceremonial **Note:** Similar to 100 New Pesos, KM#587.

Date	Mintage	F	VF	XF	Unc	BU
1993	15,500	—	—	—	145	—
1993 Proof	500	Value: 250				

25 NUEVO PESOS   KM# 579   Weight: 7.7758 g. **Composition:** 0.9990 Gold .2500 oz. AGW **Subject:** Personaje de Jaina **Reverse:** Seated figure

Date	Mintage	F	VF	XF	Unc	BU
1994	2,000	—	—	—	165	—
1994 Proof	500	Value: 300				

25 PESOS   KM# 600   Weight: 7.7758 g. **Composition:** 0.9990 Gold .2500 oz. AGW **Subject:** Sacerdote **Note:** Similar to 100 Pesos, KM#602.

Date	Mintage	F	VF	XF	Unc	BU
1996	500	—	—	—	200	—
1996 Proof	600	Value: 250				

25 PESOS   KM# 624   Weight: 7.7758 g. **Composition:** 0.9990 Gold .2500 oz. AGW **Subject:** Serpiente Emplumada **Obverse:** Mexican eagle **Note:** Similar to 100 Pesos, KM#626.

Date	Mintage	F	VF	XF	Unc	BU
1997	500	—	—	—	200	—
1997 Proof	200	Value: 250				

50 NUEVO PESOS   KM# 586   Weight: 15.5517 g. **Composition:** 0.9990 Gold .5000 oz. AGW **Subject:** Hacha Ceremonial **Note:** Similar to 100 New Pesos, KM#587.

Date	Mintage	F	VF	XF	Unc	BU
1993	15,500	—	—	—	275	—
1993 Proof	500	Value: 425				

50 NUEVO PESOS   KM# 571   Ring Composition: Brass **Center Weight:** 34.0000 g. **Center Composition:** 0.9250 Silver .5051 oz. ASW **Subject:** Nino Heroes

Date	Mintage	F	VF	XF	Unc	BU
1993	—	—	—	—	28.00	—
1993	—	—	—	—	28.00	—
1994	—	—	—	—	28.00	—
1994	—	—	—	—	28.00	—
1995	—	—	—	—	28.00	—
1995	—	—	—	—	28.00	—

50 NUEVO PESOS   KM# 580   Weight: 15.5517 g. **Composition:** 0.9990 Gold .5000 oz. AGW **Subject:** Personaje de Jaina **Reverse:** Seated figure

Date	Mintage	F	VF	XF	Unc	BU
1994	1,000	—	—	—	300	—
1994 Proof	500	Value: 475				

50 PESOS   KM# 601   Weight: 15.5517 g. **Composition:** 0.9990 Gold .5000 oz. AGW **Subject:** Sacerdote **Note:** Similar to 100 Pesos, KM#602.

Date	Mintage	F	VF	XF	Unc	BU
1996	500	—	—	—	375	—
1996 Proof	500	Value: 425				

50 PESOS   KM# 608   Weight: 15.5517 g. **Composition:** 0.9990 Silver .5000 oz. ASW **Note:** Similar to 50 New Pesos, KM#571 without "N" before denomination.

Date	Mintage	F	VF	XF	Unc	BU
1996	—	—	—	—	22.00	—

50 PESOS   KM# 625   Weight: 15.5517 g. **Composition:** 0.9990 Gold .5000 oz. AGW **Subject:** Serpiente Emplumada **Obverse:** Mexican eagle **Note:** Similar to 100 Pesos, KM#626.

Date	Mintage	F	VF	XF	Unc	BU
1997	500	—	—	—	350	—
1997 Proof	200	Value: 450				

100 NUEVO PESOS   KM# 587   Weight: 31.1035 g. **Composition:** 0.9990 Gold 1.0000 oz. AGW **Subject:** Hacha Ceremonial

Date	Mintage	F	VF	XF	Unc	BU
1993	7,150	—	—	—	525	—
1993 Proof	500	Value: 650				

100 NUEVO PESOS   KM# 581   Weight: 31.1035 g.
Composition: 0.9990 Gold 1.0000 oz. AGW **Subject:**
Personaje de Jaina

Date	Mintage	F	VF	XF	Unc	BU
1994	1,000	—	—	—	575	—
1994 Proof	500	Value: 700				

100 PESOS   KM# 602   Weight: 31.1035 g. **Composition:**
0.9990 Gold 1.0000 oz. AGW **Subject:** Sacerdote

Date	Mintage	F	VF	XF	Unc	BU
1996	500	—	—	—	575	—
1996 Proof	500	Value: 600				

100 PESOS   KM# 626   Weight: 31.1035 g. **Composition:**
0.9990 Gold 1.0000 oz. AGW **Subject:** Teohituacan -
Serpiente Emplumada **Obverse:** Eagle and snake

Date	Mintage	F	VF	XF	Unc	BU
1997	500	—	—	—	600	—
1997 Proof	Est. 200	Value: 650				

SILVER BULLION COINAGE

1/20 ONZA (1/20 Troy Ounce of Silver)   KM# 542   Weight:
1.5551 g. **Composition:** 0.9990 Silver .0500 oz. ASW

Date	Mintage	F	VF	XF	Unc	BU
1991	50,017	—	—	—	—	3.50
1992	295,783	—	—	—	—	3.50
1992 Proof	5,000	Value: 10.00				
1993	100,000	—	—	—	—	3.50
1993 Proof	—	Value: 10.00				
1994	90,100	—	—	—	—	3.50
1994 Proof	10,000	Value: 10.00				

Date	Mintage	F	VF	XF	Unc	BU
1995	50,000	—	—	—	—	3.50
1995 Proof	2,000	Value: 10.00				

1/20 ONZA (1/20 Troy Ounce of Silver)   KM# 609
Weight: 1.5551 g. **Composition:** 0.9990 Silver .0500 oz.
ASW **Obverse:** Mexican eagle **Reverse:** Winged Victory

Date	Mintage	F	VF	XF	Unc	BU
1996	50,000	—	—	—	—	3.50
1996 Proof	1,000	Value: 10.00				
1997	20,000	—	—	—	—	3.50
1997 Proof	800	Value: 10.00				
1998	6,400	—	—	—	—	3.50
1998 Proof	300	Value: 12.00				
1999	8,001	—	—	—	—	3.50
1999 Proof	600	Value: 10.00				
2000	57,500	—	—	—	—	3.50
2000 Proof	900	Value: 10.00				
2001	—	—	—	—	—	3.50
2001 Proof	—	Value: 10.00				
2002	—	—	—	—	—	3.50
2002 Proof	—	Value: 10.00				

1/10 ONZA (1/10 Troy Ounce of Silver)   KM# 543
Weight: 3.1103 g. **Composition:** 0.9990 Silver .1000 oz.
ASW **Obverse:** Mexican eagle **Reverse:** Winged Victory

Date	Mintage	F	VF	XF	Unc	BU
1991	50,017	—	—	—	—	4.00
1992	299,983	—	—	—	—	4.00
1992 Proof	5,000	Value: 12.00				
1993	100,000	—	—	—	—	4.00
1993 Proof	—	Value: 12.00				
1994	90,100	—	—	—	—	4.00
1994 Proof	10,000	Value: 12.00				
1995	50,000	—	—	—	—	4.00
1995 Proof	2,000	Value: 12.00				

1/10 ONZA (1/10 Troy Ounce of Silver)   KM# 610
Weight: 3.1103 g. **Composition:** 0.9990 Silver .1000 oz.
ASW **Obverse:** Mexican eagle **Reverse:** Winged Victory

Date	Mintage	F	VF	XF	Unc	BU
1996	50,000	—	—	—	—	4.00
1996 Proof	1,000	Value: 12.00				
1997	20,000	—	—	—	—	4.00
1997 Proof	800	Value: 12.00				
1998	6,400	—	—	—	—	4.00
1998 Proof	300	Value: 15.00				
1999	8,000	—	—	—	—	4.00
1999 Proof	600	Value: 12.00				
2000	27,500	—	—	—	—	4.00
2000 Proof	1,000	Value: 12.00				
2001	—	—	—	—	—	4.00
2001 Proof	—	Value: 12.00				
2002	—	—	—	—	—	4.00
2002 Proof	—	Value: 12.00				

1/4 ONZA (1/4 Troy Ounce of Silver)   KM# 544   Weight:
7.7758 g. **Composition:** 0.9990 Silver .2500 oz. ASW
Obverse: Mexican eagle **Reverse:** Winged Victory

Date	Mintage	F	VF	XF	Unc	BU
1991	50,017	—	—	—	—	5.50
1992	104,000	—	—	—	—	5.50
1992 Proof	5,000	Value: 15.00				
1993	86,500	—	—	—	—	5.50
1993 Proof	—	Value: 15.00				
1994	90,100	—	—	—	—	5.50
1994 Proof	15,000	Value: 15.00				
1995	50,000	—	—	—	—	5.50
1995 Proof	2,000	Value: 15.00				

1/4 ONZA (1/4 Troy Ounce of Silver)   KM# 611   Weight:
7.7758 g. **Composition:** 0.9990 Silver .2500 oz. ASW
Obverse: Mexican eagle **Reverse:** Winged Victory

Date	Mintage	F	VF	XF	Unc	BU
1996	50,000	—	—	—	—	5.50
1996 Proof	1,000	Value: 15.00				
1997	20,000	—	—	—	—	5.50
1997 Proof	800	Value: 15.00				
1998	6,400	—	—	—	—	5.50
1998 Proof	300	Value: 20.00				
1999	7,000	—	—	—	—	5.50
1999 Proof	600	Value: 15.00				
2000	21,000	—	—	—	—	5.50
2000 Proof	700	Value: 15.00				
2001	—	—	—	—	—	5.50
2001 Proof	—	Value: 15.00				
2002	—	—	—	—	—	5.50
2002 Proof	—	Value: 15.00				

1/2 ONZA (1/2 Troy Ounce of Silver)   KM# 545   Weight:
15.5517 g. **Composition:** 0.9990 Silver .5000 oz. ASW
Obverse: Mexican eagle **Reverse:** Winged Victory

Date	Mintage	F	VF	XF	Unc	BU
1991	50,618	—	—	—	—	7.50
1992	119,000	—	—	—	—	7.50

Date	Mintage	F	VF	XF	Unc	BU
1992 Proof	5,000	Value: 17.50				
1993	71,500	—	—	—	—	7.50
1993 Proof	—	Value: 17.50				
1994	90,100	—	—	—	—	7.50
1994 Proof	15,000	Value: 17.50				
1995	50,000	—	—	—	—	7.50
1995 Proof	2,000	Value: 17.50				

1/2 ONZA (1/2 Troy Ounce of Silver)   KM# 612   Weight:
15.5517 g. **Composition:** 0.9990 Silver .5000 oz. ASW
Obverse: Mexican eagle **Reverse:** Winged Victory

Date	Mintage	F	VF	XF	Unc	BU
1996	50,000	—	—	—	—	7.50
1996 Proof	1,000	Value: 17.50				
1997	20,000	—	—	—	—	7.50
1997 Proof	800	Value: 17.50				
1998	6,400	—	—	—	—	7.50
1998 Proof	300	Value: 25.00				
1999	7,000	—	—	—	—	7.50
1999 Proof	600	Value: 17.50				
2000	20,000	—	—	—	—	7.50
2000 Proof	700	Value: 17.50				
2001	—	—	—	—	—	7.50
2001 Proof	—	Value: 17.50				
2002	—	—	—	—	—	7.50
2002 Proof	—	Value: 17.50				

ONZA (Troy Ounce of Silver)   KM# 494.1   Weight:
31.1000 g. **Composition:** 0.9990 Silver 1.0000 oz. ASW
Subject: Libertad

Date	Mintage	F	VF	XF	Unc	BU
1982	1,050,000	—	—	—	BV	12.00
1983	1,002,000	—	—	—	BV	12.00
1983 Proof	998	Value: 185				
1984	1,014,000	—	—	—	BV	12.00
1985	2,017,000	—	—	—	BV	12.00
1986	1,699,426	—	—	—	BV	12.50
1986 Proof	30,006	Value: 22.00				
1987	500,000	—	—	—	BV	35.00
1987 Proof	12,000	Value: 40.00				
1988	1,500,500	—	—	—	BV	30.00
1989	1,396,500	—	—	—	BV	22.00
1989 Proof	10,000	Value: 35.00				

ONZA (Troy Ounce of Silver)   KM# 494.2   Weight:
31.1000 g. **Composition:** 0.9990 Silver 1.0000 oz. ASW
Edge: Reeded

Date	Mintage	F	VF	XF	Unc	BU
1988 Proof	10,000	Value: 42.50				
1990	1,200,000	—	—	—	BV	12.50

Date	Mintage	F	VF	XF	Unc	BU
1990 Proof	10,000	Value: 35.00				
1991	1,650,518	—	—	—	BV	14.50

ONZA (Troy Ounce of Silver) KM# 494.5 Weight:
31.1000 g. **Composition:** 0.9990 Silver 1.0000 oz. ASW
Subject: Libertad **Obverse:** KM#494.3 **Reverse:** KM#494.2
Edge: Reeded edge **Note:** Mule

Date	Mintage	F	VF	XF	Unc	BU
1991 Proof	10,000	Value: 32.00				

ONZA (Troy Ounce of Silver) KM# 494.3 Weight:
31.1000 g. **Composition:** 0.9990 Silver 1.0000 oz. ASW
Subject: Libertad **Obverse:** Eight dots below eagle's left talons **Reverse:** Revised design and lettering **Edge:** Reeded edge **Note:** Mule

Date	Mintage	F	VF	XF	Unc	BU
1991	Inc. above	—	—	—	BV	20.00
1992	2,458,000	—	—	—	BV	11.50
1992 Proof	10,000	Value: 32.00				

ONZA (Troy Ounce of Silver) KM# 494.4 Weight:
31.1000 g. **Composition:** 0.9990 Silver 1.0000 oz. ASW
Subject: Libertad **Obverse:** Seven dots below eagle's left talons, dull claws on right talon, thick letters **Reverse:** Revised design and lettering **Edge:** Reeded edge **Note:** Mule

Date	Mintage	F	VF	XF	Unc	BU
1993	1,000,000	—	—	—	BV	11.50
1993 Proof	—	Value: 34.00				
1994	400,000	—	—	—	BV	14.00
1994 Proof	10,000	Value: 34.00				
1995	500,000	—	—	—	BV	12.50
1995 Proof	2,000	Value: 35.00				

ONZA (Troy Ounce of Silver) KM# 613 Weight:
33.6250 g. **Composition:** 0.9250 Silver 1.0000 oz. ASW
Obverse: Mexican eagle **Reverse:** Winged Victory

Date	Mintage	F	VF	XF	Unc	BU
1996	300,000	—	—	—	—	12.00
1996 Proof	2,000	Value: 35.00				
1997	100,000	—	—	—	—	14.00
1997 Proof	1,500	Value: 35.00				
1998	67,000	—	—	—	—	17.50
1998 Proof	500	Value: 40.00				
1999	95,000	—	—	—	—	14.50
1999 Proof	600	Value: 40.00				
2000	340,000	—	—	—	—	14.00
2000 Proof	1,600	Value: 35.00				
2001	—	—	—	—	—	12.00
2001 Proof	—	Value: 32.50				
2002	—	—	—	—	—	12.00
2002 Proof	—	Value: 32.50				

ONZA (Troy Ounce of Silver) KM# 639 Weight:
31.1000 g. **Composition:** 0.9990 Silver 1.0000 oz. ASW
Subject: Libertad **Obverse:** Modern Mexican eagle within circle of obsolete versions **Edge:** Reeded edge **Note:** Mule

Date	Mintage	F	VF	XF	Unc	BU
2000	—	—	—	—	—	10.00
2000	—	Value: 35.00				

2 ONZAS (2 Troy Ounces of Silver) KM# 614 Weight:
62.2070 g. **Composition:** 0.9990 Silver 2.0000 oz. ASW
Subject: Libertad **Obverse:** Mexican eagle **Reverse:** Winged Victory

Date	Mintage	F	VF	XF	Unc	BU
1996	50,000	—	—	—	—	22.00
1996 Proof	1,200	Value: 45.00				
1997	15,000	—	—	—	—	20.00
1997 Proof	1,300	Value: 45.00				
1998	7,000	—	—	—	—	28.50
1998 Proof	400	Value: 50.00				
1999	5,000	—	—	—	—	32.50
1999 Proof	280	Value: 70.00				

Date	Mintage	F	VF	XF	Unc	BU
2000	7,500	—	—	—	—	30.00
2000 Proof	500	Value: 47.50				
2001	—	—	—	—	—	22.50
2001 Proof	—	Value: 45.00				
2002	—	—	—	—	—	22.50
2002 Proof	—	Value: 45.00				

5 ONZAS (5 Troy Ounces of Silver)   KM# 615   Weight: 155.5175 g. **Composition:** 0.9990 Silver 5.0000 oz. ASW **Subject:** Libertad **Obverse:** Mexican eagle **Reverse:** Winged Victory

Date	Mintage	F	VF	XF	Unc	BU
1996	20,000	—	—	—	—	50.00
1996 Proof	1,200	Value: 85.00				
1997	10,000	—	—	—	—	50.00
1997 Proof	1,300	Value: 85.00				
1998	3,500	—	—	—	—	60.00
1998 Proof	400	Value: 100				
1999	2,800	—	—	—	—	60.00
1999 Proof	100	Value: 150				
2000	4,000	—	—	—	—	48.50
2000 Proof	500	Value: 80.00				
2001	—	—	—	—	—	48.50
2001 Proof	—	Value: 80.00				
2002	—	—	—	—	—	48.50
2002 Proof	—	Value: 80.00				

GOLD BULLION COINAGE

1/20 ONZA (1/20 Ounce of Pure Gold)   KM# 530 Weight: 1.7500 g. **Composition:** 0.9000 Gold .0500 oz. AGW **Obverse:** Winged Victory **Reverse:** Calendar stone

Date	Mintage	F	VF	XF	Unc	BU
1987	—	—	—	—	—	BV+ 30%
1988	—	—	—	—	—	BV+30%

1/20 ONZA (1/20 Ounce of Pure Gold)   KM# 589 Weight: 1.5551 g. **Composition:** 0.9990 Gold .500 oz. AGW **Obverse:** Winged Victory **Reverse:** Eagle and snake

Date	Mintage	F	VF	XF	Unc	BU
1991	10,000	—	—	—	—	BV+30%
1992	65,225	—	—	—	—	BV+30%
1993	10,000	—	—	—	—	BV+30%
1994	10,000	—	—	—	—	BV+30%

1/20 ONZA (1/20 Ounce of Pure Gold)   KM# 642 Weight: 1.5551 g. **Composition:** 0.9990 Gold .500 oz. AGW **Obverse:** Winged Victory **Reverse:** Teocuitlatl and an indian working

Date	Mintage	F	VF	XF	Unc	BU
2000 Proof	—	Value: 50.00				

1/15 ONZA (1/15 Ounce of Pure Gold)   KM# 628 Composition: 0.9990 Gold **Obverse:** Winged Victory above legend

Date	Mintage	F	VF	XF	Unc	BU
1987	—	—	—	—	—	BV+25%

1/10 ONZA (1/10 Ounce of Pure Gold)   KM# 541   Weight: 3.1103 g. **Composition:** 0.9990 Gold .1000 oz. AGW

Date	Mintage	F	VF	XF	Unc	BU
1991	10,000	—	—	—	—	BV+20%
1992	50,777	—	—	—	—	BV+20%
1993	10,000	—	—	—	—	BV+20%
1994	10,000	—	—	—	—	BV+20%

1/4 ONZA (1/4 Ounce of Pure Gold)   KM# 487   Weight: 8.6396 g. **Composition:** 0.9000 Gold .2500 oz. AGW **Note:** Similar to KM#488.

Date	Mintage	F	VF	XF	Unc	BU
1981	313,000	—	—	—	—	BV+11%

1/4 ONZA (1/4 Ounce of Pure Gold)   KM# 590   Weight: 7.7758 g. **Composition:** 0.9990 Gold .2500 oz. AGW **Obverse:** Winged Victory above legend **Reverse:** Eagle and snake

Date	Mintage	F	VF	XF	Unc	BU
1991	10,000	—	—	—	—	BV+11%
1992	28,106	—	—	—	—	BV+11%
1993	2,500	—	—	—	—	BV+11%
1994	2,500	—	—	—	—	BV+11%

1/2 ONZA (1/2 Ounce of Pure Gold)   KM# 488   Weight: 17.2792 g. **Composition:** 0.9000 Gold .5000 oz. AGW

Date	Mintage	F	VF	XF	Unc	BU
1981	193,000	—	—	—	—	BV+8%
1989 Proof	704	Value: 500				

1/2 ONZA (1/2 Ounce of Pure Gold)   KM# 591   Weight: 15.5517 g. **Composition:** 0.9990 Gold .5000 oz. AGW **Obverse:** Winged Victory above legend **Reverse:** Eagle and snake

Date	Mintage	F	VF	XF	Unc	BU
1991	10,000	—	—	—	—	BV+8%
1992	25,220	—	—	—	—	BV+8%
1993	2,500	—	—	—	—	BV+8%
1994	2,500	—	—	—	—	BV+8%

ONZA (Ounce of Pure Gold)   KM# 489   Weight: 34.5585 g. **Composition:** 0.9000 Gold 1.0000 oz. AGW **Note:** Similar to KM#488.

Date	Mintage	F	VF	XF	Unc	BU
1981	596,000	—	—	—	—	BV+3%
1985	—	—	—	—	—	BV+3%
1988	—	—	—	—	—	BV+3%

ONZA (Ounce of Pure Gold)   KM# 592   Weight: 31.1035 g. **Composition:** 0.9990 Gold 1.0000 oz. AGW **Obverse:** Winged Victory above legend **Reverse:** Eagle and snake

Date	Mintage	F	VF	XF	Unc	BU
1991	109,193	—	—	—	—	BV+3%
1992	46,281	—	—	—	—	BV+3%
1993	10,000	—	—	—	—	BV+3%
1994	1,000	—	—	—	—	BV+3%

PLATINUM BULLION COINAGE

1/4 ONZA (1/4 Ounce) **KM# 538** **Weight:** 7.7775 g.
Composition: 0.9990 Platinum .2500 oz. APW

Date	Mintage	F	VF	XF	Unc	BU
1989	704	Value: 300				

MEDALLIC COINAGE

10 PESOS **KM# M91a** **Weight:** 8.3333 g. **Composition:**
0.9000 Gold .2411 oz. AGW **Subject:** 200th Anniversary -
Birth of Hidalgo

Date	Mintage	F	VF	XF	Unc	BU
1953	—	—	—	—	BV	110

10 PESOS **KM# M123a** **Weight:** 8.3333 g.
Composition: 0.9000 Gold .2411 oz. AGW **Subject:**
Centennial of Constitution

Date	Mintage	F	VF	XF	Unc	BU
1957	Est. 73,000	—	—	—	BV	110

Note: Mintage includes #M122a

20 PESOS **KM# M92a** **Weight:** 16.6666 g.
Composition: 0.9000 Gold .4823 oz. AGW **Subject:** 200th
Anniversary - Birth of Hidalgo

Date	Mintage	F	VF	XF	Unc	BU
1953	—	—	—	—	BV	200

50 PESOS **KM# M122a** **Weight:** 41.6666 g.
Composition: 0.9000 Gold 1.2057 oz. AGW **Subject:**
Centennial of Constitution

Date	Mintage	F	VF	XF	Unc	BU
1957 Inc. M123a	—	—	—	—	BV	520

ONZA (Troy Ounce of Silver) **KM# M49a** **Weight:**
33.6250 g. **Composition:** 0.9250 Silver 1.0000 oz. ASW
Obverse: Mint mark above coin press

Date	Mintage	F	VF	XF	Unc	BU
1949	1,000,000	—	10.00	12.50	17.50	27.50

ONZA (Troy Ounce of Silver)   KM# M49b.1   Weight:
33.6250 g. **Composition:** 0.9250 Silver 1.0000 oz. ASW
Obverse: Wide spacing between DE MONEDA **Reverse:**
Mint mark below balance scale **Note:** Type I

Date	Mintage	F	VF	XF	Unc	BU
1978	280,000	—	—	BV	7.50	16.50

ONZA (Troy Ounce of Silver)   KM# M49b.2   Weight:
33.6250 g. **Composition:** 0.9250 Silver 1.0000 oz. ASW
Obverse: Close spacing between DE MONEDA **Reverse:**
Mint mark below balance scale **Note:** Type II

Date	Mintage	F	VF	XF	Unc	BU
1978	Inc. above	—	—	BV	7.50	15.00

ONZA (Troy Ounce of Silver)   KM# M49b.3   Weight:
33.6250 g. **Composition:** 0.9250 Silver 1.0000 oz. ASW
Obverse: Close spacing between DE MONEDA **Reverse:**
Left scale pan points to U in UNA **Note:** Type III

Date	Mintage	F	VF	XF	Unc	BU
1979	4,508,000	—	—	BV	6.75	13.50

ONZA (Troy Ounce of Silver)   KM# M49b.4   Weight:
33.6250 g. **Composition:** 0.9250 Silver 1.0000 oz. ASW
Obverse: Close spacing between DE MONEDA **Reverse:**
Left scale pan points between U and N of UNA **Note:** Type IV

Date	Mintage	F	VF	XF	Unc	BU
1979	Inc. above	—	—	BV	6.75	13.50

ONZA (Troy Ounce of Silver)   KM# M49b.5   Weight:
33.6250 g. **Composition:** 0.9250 Silver 1.0000 oz. ASW
Obverse: Close spacing between DE MONEDA **Reverse:**
Left scale pan points between U and N of UNA **Note:** Type V

Date	Mintage	F	VF	XF	Unc	BU
1980	6,104,000	—	—	BV	6.75	11.00
1980/70	Inc. above	—	—	BV	6.75	14.50

MINT SETS

KM#	Date	Mintage	Identification	Issue Price	Mkt Val
MSA2	1977 (9)	—	434.1, 434.2, 442, 452, 460 thick date, 460 thin date, 472, 477.1, 483.2, Type II for 3-ring binder	—	85.00
MS2	1978 (9)	500	434.1, 434.2, 442, 452, 460 open 8, 460 closed 8, 472, 477.2, 483.2, Type I flat pack	—	150
MS3	1978 (9)	—	KM434.1, 434.2, 442, 452, 460 open 8, 460 closed 8, 472, 477.2, 483.2, Type II for 3-ring binder	—	65.00
MS4	1979 (8)	—	KM434.2, 442, 452 square 9, 452 round 9, 460 (2), 477.2, 483.2, Type I flat pack	11.00	8.00
MS5	1979 (8)	—	KM434.1, 434.2, 442, 452 square 9, 452 round 9, 460, 477.2, 483.2, Type II for 3-ring binder	11.00	9.00
MS6	1980 (9)	—	KM434.2, 442, 452 square 9, 452 round 9, 460 open 8, 460 closed 8, 477.2, 485-486	4.20	11.00
MS7	1981 (9)	—	KM442 open 8, 442 closed 8, 452 rectangular 9, 452 round 9, 460 open 8, 460 closed 8, 477.2, 485, 486	4.20	11.00
MS8	1982 (7)	—	KM442, 452, 460, 477.2, 485, 486, 490	—	15.00
MS10	1983 (11)	—	KM442 (2), 452 (2), 460 (2), 490 (1), 491 (2), 492 (2) for 3-ring plastic set	—	12.50
MS9	1983 (11)	—	KM442 (2), 452 (2), 460 (2), 490 (1), 491 (2), 492 (2), hard case set	—	12.50
MS11	1984 (8)	—	KM485, 486, 490, 491, 493, 495 (2), 496	—	17.50
MS12	1985 (12)	—	KM477.2, 485, 493 (2), 495 (2), 496, 502, 508, 509, 510, 512	—	16.00
MS14	1985/1986 (7)	—	KM493, 495, 496, 502, 508, 509, 512	—	18.50
MS13	1986 (7)	—	KM493, 495, 496, 508, 512, 525, 529	—	18.00
MS15	1987 (9)	—	KM493, 495 (2), 496, 502 (2), 512, 529 (2)	—	35.00
MS16	1988 (8)	—	KM493, 495a, 502, 508, 512, 529, 531, 536	—	20.00
MS17	1996 (6)	—	KM546-549, 603-604	12.00	15.00

PROOF SETS

KM#	Date	Mintage	Identification	Issue Price	Mkt Val
PS1	1982/1983 (8)	998	KM442, 452, 460, 485, 477.2, 486, 490, 494.1	495	275
PS2	1982/1983 (8)	—	KM460, 477.2, 485, 486, 490, 491, 492, PnB169 (in white box with Mo. in gold)	—	—
PS3	1982/1983 (7)	23	KM460, 477.2, 485, 486, 490, 491, 492 (in white box with Mo in gold)	—	500
PS4	1982/1983 (7)	17	KM460, 477.2, 485, 486, 490, 491, 492 (in white box)	—	500
PS5	1982/1983 (7)	8	KM460, 477.2, 485, 486, 490, 491, 492 (in white box)	—	500
PS6	1983 (7)	3	KM460, 477.2, 485, 486, 490, 491, 492	—	—
PS10	1985 (3)	—	KM503-505 (in blue box)	—	60.00
PS11	1985 (2)	—	KM511, 513	—	350
PS7	1985/1986 (12)	—	KM497a-499a, 503-505, 514-515, 519, 521, 523-524	—	250
PS8	1985 (4)	—	KM500.2-501.2, 506.2, 507.2	—	700
PS9	1985 (3)	—	KM499a, 514, 515 (in blue box)	—	60.00
PS12	1989 (3)	704	KM488, 494.1, 538, Rainbow	730	850
PS13	1992 (5)	5,000	KM494.3, 542-545	—	87.50
PS14	1993 (5)	5,000	KM494.4, 542-545	—	87.50
PS15	1994 (5)	5,000	KM494.4, 542-545	—	85.00
PS16	1995 (7)	—	KM546-550, 552, 553, 555	45.00	45.00

CHIHUAHUA
WAR OF INDEPENDENCE
ROYALIST COINAGE

The Chihuahua Mint was established by a decree of October 8, 1810 as a temporary mint. Their first coins were cast 8 Reales using Mexico City coins as patterns and obliterating/changing the mint mark and moneyer initials. Two c/m were placed on the obverse - on the left, a T designating receipt by the Royal Treasurer, crowned pillars of Hercules on the right with pomegranate beneath, the comptrollers symbol.

In 1814, standard dies were made available, thus machine struck 8 Reales were produced until 1822. Only the one denomination was made at Chihuahua.

Mint mark: CA.

8 REALES   KM# 123   Composition: Cast Silver **Ruler:**
Ferdinand VII **Countermark:** T at left, pillars at right,
pomegranate below **Obverse:** Imaginary bust of Ferdinand
VII **Obv. Legend:** FERDIN. VII. DEI. GRATIA

Date	Mintage	Good	VG	F	VF	XF
1810CA RP Rare	—	—	—	—	—	—
1811CA RP	—	45.00	60.00	100	150	—
1812CA RP	—	30.00	40.00	60.00	90.00	—
1813CA RP	—	30.00	40.00	60.00	90.00	—

8 REALES   KM# 111.1   Weight: 27.0700 g.
Composition: 0.9030 Silver .7860 oz. ASW **Ruler:**
Ferdinand VII **Obverse:** Draped bust of Ferdinand VII

Obv. Legend: FERDIN. VII. DEI. GRATIA **Reverse:** Similar
to KM#123

Date	Mintage	VG	F	VF	XF	Unc
1815CA RP	—	200	275	350	500	—
1816CA RP	—	80.00	125	150	275	—
1817CA RP	—	100	150	185	275	—
1818CA RP	—	100	150	185	275	—
1819/8 RP	—	125	175	250	350	—
1819CA RP	—	125	175	250	350	—
1820CA RP	—	200	275	350	500	—
1821CA RP	—	200	275	350	500	—
1822CA RP	—	400	600	800	1,100	—

Note: KM#111.1 is normally found struck over earlier cast 8
Reales, KM#123 and Monclova (MVA) 1812 cast countermark 8 Reales, KM#202 and Zacatecas 8 Reales, KM#190

DURANGO
WAR OF INDEPENDENCE
ROYALIST COINAGE

The Durango mint was authorized as a temporary mint on the same day as the Chihuahua Mint, October 8, 1810. The mint opened in 1811 and made coins of 6 denominations between 1811 and 1822.

Mint mark: D.

1/8 REAL   KM# 60   Composition: Copper **Ruler:**
Ferdinand VII **Obverse:** Crown above double F7 monogram
Reverse: EN DURANGO, value, date

Date	Mintage	VG	F	VF	XF	Unc
1812D	—	32.50	75.00	125	250	—
1813D Rare	—	—	—	—	—	—
1814D Rare	—	—	—	—	—	—

1/8 REAL   KM# 61   Composition: Copper **Ruler:**
Ferdinand VII **Obverse:** Crown above double F7 monogram
Reverse: Spray added above date

Date	Mintage	VG	F	VF	XF	Unc
1814D	—	15.00	30.00	50.00	90.00	—
1815D	—	18.00	35.00	60.00	100	—
1816D	—	18.00	35.00	60.00	100	—
1817D	—	15.00	30.00	50.00	90.00	—
1818D	—	15.00	30.00	50.00	90.00	—
1818D OCTAVO DD REAL (error)	—	45.00	80.00	125	225	—

1/2 REAL   KM# 74.1   Weight: 1.6900 g. **Composition:**
0.9030 Silver .0491 oz. ASW **Ruler:** Ferdinand VII **Obverse:**
Draped bust of Ferdinand VII

Date	Mintage	VG	F	VF	XF	Unc
1813D RM	—	250	450	750	1,800	—
1814D MZ	—	250	450	750	1,850	—
1816D MZ	—	250	450	750	1,850	—

REAL   KM# 83.1   Weight: 3.3800 g. Composition:
0.9030 Silver .0981 oz. ASW **Ruler:** Ferdinand VII **Obverse:**
Draped bust of Ferdinand VII

Date	Mintage	VG	F	VF	XF	Unc
1813D RM	—	250	450	650	1,650	—
1814D MZ	—	250	450	650	1,650	—
1815D MZ	—	250	450	650	1,650	—

2 REALES   KM# 92.2   Weight: 6.7700 g. Composition:
0.9030 Silver .1966 oz. ASW **Ruler:** Ferdinand VII **Obverse:**
Armored bust of Ferdinand VII **Rev. Legend:** MON PROV
DE DURANGO...

Date	Mintage	VG	F	VF	XF	Unc
1811D RM	—	375	450	850	1,750	—

2 REALES   KM# 92.3   Weight: 6.7700 g. Composition:
0.9030 Silver .1966 oz. ASW **Ruler:** Ferdinand VII **Obverse:**
Armored bust of Ferdinand VII **Rev. Legend:** HISPAN ET
IND REX...

Date	Mintage	VG	F	VF	XF	Unc
1812 RM	—	250	400	750	1,650	—

8 REALES   KM# 110.1   Weight: 27.0700 g.
Composition: 0.9030 Silver .7860 oz. ASW **Ruler:**
Ferdinand VII **Obverse:** Armored bust of Ferdinand VII

Date	Mintage	VG	F	VF	XF	Unc
1811D RM	—	600	1,000	1,750	5,000	—
1812D RM	—	350	650	1,000	3,500	—
1814D MZ	—	350	650	1,000	3,500	—

2 REALES   KM# 93.1   Weight: 6.7700 g. Composition:
0.9030 Silver .1966 oz. ASW **Ruler:** Ferdinand VII **Obverse:**
Draped bust of Ferdinand VII

Date	Mintage	VG	F	VF	XF	Unc
1812D RM	—	250	400	750	1,650	—
1813D RM	—	300	600	1,000	2,750	—
1813D MZ	—	300	600	1,000	2,750	—
1814D MZ	—	300	600	1,000	2,750	—
1815D MZ	—	300	600	1,000	2,750	—
1816D MZ	—	300	600	1,000	2,750	—
1817D MZ	—	300	600	1,000	2,750	—

4 REALES   KM# 102.1   Weight: 13.5400 g.
Composition: 0.9030 Silver .3931 oz. ASW **Ruler:**
Ferdinand VII **Obverse:** Draped bust of Ferdinand VII

Date	Mintage	VG	F	VF	XF	Unc
1814D MZ	—	550	1,000	1,650	4,500	—
1816D MZ	—	450	900	1,400	4,000	—
1817D MZ	—	450	900	1,400	4,000	—

8 REALES   KM# 111.2   Weight: 27.0700 g.
Composition: 0.9030 Silver .7860 oz. ASW **Ruler:**
Ferdinand VII **Obverse:** Draped bust of Ferdinand VII

Date	Mintage	VG	F	VF	XF	Unc
1812D RM	—	125	175	275	800	—
1813D RM	—	150	200	325	850	—
1813D MZ	—	125	175	275	750	—
1814/2D MZ	—	150	200	300	750	—
1814D MZ	—	150	200	300	750	—
1815D MZ	—	75.00	125	225	600	—
1816D MZ	—	50.00	75.00	125	325	—
1817D MZ	—	30.00	50.00	90.00	250	—
1818D MZ	—	50.00	75.00	125	350	—
1818D RM	—	50.00	75.00	125	325	—
1818D CG/RM	—	100	125	150	350	—
1818D CG	—	50.00	75.00	125	325	—
1819D CG/RM	—	50.00	100	150	300	—
1819D CG	—	30.00	60.00	100	250	—
1820D CG	—	30.00	60.00	100	250	—
1821D CG	—	30.00	40.00	80.00	200	—
1822D CG	—	30.00	50.00	90.00	240	—

Note: Occasionally these are found struck over cast Chihuahua 8 reales and are very rare in general, specimens dated
prior to 1816 are rather crudely struck

GUADALAJARA
WAR OF INDEPENDENCE
ROYALIST COINAGE

The Guadalajara Mint made its first coins in 1812 and the mint operated until April 30, 1815. It was to reopen in 1818 and continue operations until 1822. It was the only Royalist mint to strike gold coins, both 4 and 8 Escudos. In addition to these it struck the standard 5 denominations in silver.

Mint mark: GA.

1/2 REAL KM# 74.2 Weight: 1.6900 g. **Composition:** 0.9030 Silver .0491 oz. ASW **Ruler:** Ferdinand VII **Obverse:** Draped bust of Ferdinand VII

Date	Mintage	VG	F	VF	XF	Unc
1812GA MR Rare	—	—	—	—	—	—
1814GA MR	—	40.00	100	200	300	—
1815GA MR	—	200	350	500	1,000	—

REAL KM# 83.2 Weight: 3.3800 g. **Composition:** 0.9030 Silver .0981 oz. ASW **Ruler:** Ferdinand VII **Obverse:** Draped bust of Ferdinand VII

Date	Mintage	VG	F	VF	XF	Unc
1813GA MR	—	300	500	800	—	—
1814GA MR	—	150	200	350	650	—
1815GA MR	—	300	500	800	—	—

2 REALES KM# 93.2 Weight: 6.7700 g. **Composition:** 0.9030 Silver .1966 oz. ASW **Ruler:** Ferdinand VII **Obverse:** Draped bust of Ferdinand VII

Date	Mintage	VG	F	VF	XF	Unc
1812GA MR	—	300	500	800	2,500	—
1814/2GA MR	—	75.00	125	250	600	—
1814GA MR	—	75.00	125	250	600	—
1815/4GA MR	—	425	725	1,100	3,600	—
1815GA MR	—	400	700	1,000	3,500	—
1821GA FS	—	200	250	350	900	—

4 REALES KM# 102.2 Weight: 13.5400 g. **Composition:** 0.9030 Silver .3931 oz. ASW **Ruler:** Ferdinand VII **Obverse:** Draped small bust of Ferdinand VII

Date	Mintage	VG	F	VF	XF	Unc
1814GA MR	—	40.00	65.00	150	250	—
1815GA MR	—	80.00	150	300	500	—

4 REALES KM# 102.3 Weight: 13.5400 g. **Composition:** 0.9030 Silver .3931 oz. ASW **Ruler:** Ferdinand VII **Obverse:** Large bust

Date	Mintage	VG	F	VF	XF	Unc
1814GA MR	—	50.00	100	200	400	—

4 REALES KM# 102.4 Weight: 13.5400 g. **Composition:** 0.9030 Silver .3931 oz. ASW **Ruler:** Ferdinand VII **Obverse:** Large bust with berries in laurel

Date	Mintage	VG	F	VF	XF	Unc
1814GA MR	—	60.00	120	250	450	—

8 REALES KM# 111.3 Weight: 27.0700 g.
Composition: 0.9030 Silver .7860 oz. ASW **Ruler:**
Ferdinand VII **Obverse:** Draped bust of Ferdinand VII

Date	Mintage	VG	F	VF	XF	Unc
1812GA MR	—	2,000	3,500	5,000	7,000	—
1813/2GA MR	—	60.00	100	150	400	—
1813GA MR	—	60.00	100	150	400	—
1814GA MR	—	20.00	35.00	60.00	180	—

Note: Several bust varieties exist for the 1814 issue

Date	Mintage	VG	F	VF	XF	Unc
1815GA MR	—	150	200	350	750	—
1818GA FS	—	30.00	50.00	75.00	200	—
1821/18GA FS	—	30.00	50.00	75.00	200	—
1821GA FS	—	25.00	35.00	60.00	165	—
1821/2GA FS	—	30.00	50.00	75.00	200	—
1822/1GA FS	—	30.00	50.00	75.00	200	—
1822GA FS	—	30.00	50.00	75.00	200	—

Note: Die varieties exist. Early dates are also encountered struck over other types

4 ESCUDOS KM# 147 Weight: 13.5400 g.
Composition: 0.8750 Gold .3809 oz. AGW **Ruler:**
Ferdinand VII **Obverse:** Uniformed bust of Ferdinand VII

Date	Mintage	VG	F	VF	XF	Unc
1812GA MR Rare	—	—	—	—	—	—

8 ESCUDOS KM# 162 Weight: 27.0700 g. **Composition:**
0.8750 Gold .7616 oz. AGW **Ruler:** Ferdinand VII **Obverse:**
Large uniformed bust of Ferdinand VII

Date	Mintage	VG	F	VF	XF	Unc
1812GA MR Rare	—	—	—	—	—	—
1813GA MR	—	5,250	8,250	12,500	21,000	—

8 ESCUDOS KM# 163 Weight: 27.0700 g.
Composition: 0.8750 Gold .7616 oz. AGW **Ruler:**
Ferdinand VII **Obverse:** Small uniformed bust of Ferdinand VII

Date	Mintage	VG	F	VF	XF	Unc
1813GA MR	—	10,000	16,000	30,000	45,000	—

Note: Spink America Gerber sale 6-96 VF or better realized $46,200

8 ESCUDOS KM# 161.1 Weight: 27.0700 g.
Composition: 0.8750 Gold .7616 oz. AGW **Ruler:**
Ferdinand VII **Obverse:** Undraped bust of Ferdinand VII

Date	Mintage	VG	F	VF	XF	Unc
1821GA FS	—	1,200	2,000	4,000	6,500	—

8 ESCUDOS KM# 164 Weight: 27.0700 g.
Composition: 0.8750 Gold .7616 oz. AGW **Ruler:**
Ferdinand VII **Obverse:** Draped bust of Ferdinand VII

Date	Mintage	VG	F	VF	XF	Unc
1821GA FS	—	5,000	7,500	14,000	23,000	—

GUANAJUATO
WAR OF INDEPENDENCE
ROYALIST COINAGE

The Guanajuato Mint was authorized December 24, 1812 and started production shortly thereafter; closing for unknown reasons on May 15, 1813. The mint was reopened in April, 1821 by the insurgents, who struck coins of the old royal Spanish design to pay their army, even after independence, well into 1822.

Only the 2 and 8 Reales coins were made.

Mint mark: Go.

2 REALES KM# 93.3 Weight: 6.7700 g. **Composition:**
0.9030 Silver .1966 oz. ASW **Ruler:** Ferdinand VII **Obverse:**
Draped bust of Ferdinand VII

Date	Mintage	VG	F	VF	XF	Unc
1821Go JM	—	35.00	65.00	100	185	—
1822Go JM	—	30.00	50.00	75.00	145	—

8 REALES KM# 111.4 Weight: 27.0700 g.
Composition: 0.9030 Silver .7860 oz. ASW **Ruler:**
Ferdinand VII **Obverse:** Draped bust of Ferdinand VII

Date	Mintage	VG	F	VF	XF	Unc
1812Go JJ	—	1,250	2,500	—	—	—
1813Go JJ	—	125	175	275	600	—
1821Go JM	—	25.00	50.00	75.00	200	—
1822Go JM	—	20.00	35.00	60.00	185	—

NUEVA GALICIA
WAR OF INDEPENDENCE
INSURGENT COINAGE

(Later became Jalisco State)

In early colonial times, Nueva Galicia was an extensive province which substantially combined later provinces of Zacatecas and Jalisco. These are states of Mexico today although the name was revived during the War of Independence. The only issue was 2 Reales of rather enigmatic origin. No decrees or other authorization to strike this coin has yet been located or reported.

2 REALES   KM# 218   Composition: 0.9030 Silver **Obverse:** N. G. in center, date **Obv. Legend:** PROVYCIONAL... **Reverse:** 2R in center **Rev. Legend:** ... A. JUNIANA...

Date	Mintage	Good	VG	F	VF	XF
1813	—	1,000	2,500	4,500	—	—

Note: Excellent struck counterfeits exist.

NUEVA VISCAYA
WAR OF INDEPENDENCE
ROYALIST COINAGE

(Later became Durango State)

This 8 Reales, intended for the province of Nueva Viscaya, was minted in the newly-opened Durango Mint during February and March of 1811, before the regular coinage of Durango was started.

8 REALES   KM# 181   Weight: 27.0700 g. **Composition:** 0.9030 Silver .7860 oz. ASW **Ruler:** Ferdinand VII **Obverse:** Arms of Durango **Obv. Legend:** MON. PROV. DE NUEV. VIZCAYA **Reverse:** Royal arms

Date	Mintage	Good	VG	F	VF	XF
1811 RM	—	1,000	2,250	2,850	5,500	—

Note: Several varieties exist.

OAXACA
WAR OF INDEPENDENCE
ROYALIST COINAGE

The city of Oaxaca was in the midst of a coin shortage when it became apparent the city would be taken by the Insurgents. Royalist forces under Lt. Gen. Saravia had coins made. They were cast in a blacksmith shop. 1/2, 1, and 8 Reales were made only briefly in 1812 before the Royalists surrendered the city.

1/2 REAL   KM# 166   Composition: 0.9030 Silver **Ruler:** Ferdinand VII **Obverse:** Cross separating castle, lion, Fo, 7o **Reverse:** Legend around shield **Rev. Legend:** PROV. D. OAXACA

Date	Mintage	Good	VG	F	VF	XF
1812	—	1,000	1,500	2,500	3,500	—

REAL   KM# 167   Composition: 0.9030 Silver **Ruler:** Ferdinand VII **Obverse:** Cross separating castle, lion, Fo, 7o **Reverse:** Legend around shield **Rev. Legend:** PROV. D. OAXACA

Date	Mintage	Good	VG	F	VF	XF
1812	—	350	650	1,200	2,500	—

8 REALES   KM# 168   Composition: 0.9030 Silver **Obverse:** Cross seperating castle, lion, Fo, 7o **Reverse:** Shield, authorization mark above **Note:** These issues usually display a second mark 'O' between the crowned pillars on the obverse. Varieties of large and small lion in shield also exist.

Date	Mintage	Good	VG	F	VF	XF
1812 "A"	—	1,300	1,900	3,300	5,000	—
1812 "B"	—	1,300	1,900	3,300	5,000	—
1812 "C"	—	1,300	1,900	3,300	5,000	—
1812 "D"	—	1,300	1,900	3,300	5,000	—
1812 "K"	—	1,300	1,900	3,300	5,000	—
1812 "L"	—	1,300	1,900	3,300	5,000	—
1812 "Mo"	—	1,300	1,900	3,300	5,000	—
1812 "N"	—	1,300	1,900	3,300	5,000	—
1812 "O"	—	1,300	1,900	3,300	5,000	—
1812 "R"	—	1,300	1,900	3,300	5,000	—
1812 "V"	—	1,300	1,900	3,300	5,000	—
1812 "Z"	—	1,300	1,900	3,300	5,000	—

INSURGENT COINAGE

Oaxaca was the hub of Insurgent activity in the south where coinage started in July 1811 and continued until October 1814. The Oaxaca issues represent episodic strikings, usually under dire circumstances by various individuals. Coins were commonly made of copper due to urgency and were intended to be redeemed at face value in gold or silver once silver was available to the Insurgents. Some were later made in silver, but most appear to be of more recent origin, to satisfy collectors.

1/2 REAL KM# 219 Composition: Struck Copper **Issuer:** SUD, Under General Morelos **Obverse:** Bow, arrow, SUD **Reverse:** Morelos monogram Mo, date

Date	Mintage	Good	VG	F	VF	XF
1811	—	6.75	11.50	20.00	35.00	—
1812	—	6.75	11.50	20.00	35.00	—
1813	—	5.50	9.00	17.50	30.00	—
1814	—	9.00	16.50	25.00	40.00	—

Note: Uniface strikes exist of #219

1/2 REAL KM# 220.1 Composition: Struck Silver **Issuer:** SUD, Under General Morelos **Obverse:** Bow, arrow, SUD **Reverse:** Morelos monogram Mo, date

Date	Mintage	Good	VG	F	VF	XF
1811	—	—	—	—	—	—
1812	—	—	—	—	—	—
1813	—	—	—	—	—	—

1/2 REAL KM# 220.2 Composition: Struck Silver **Issuer:** SUD, Under General Morelos **Obverse:** Bow, arrow, SUD **Reverse:** Morelos monogram Mo, date

Date	Mintage	Good	VG	F	VF	XF
1811	—	—	—	—	—	—
1812	—	—	—	—	—	—
1813	—	25.00	50.00	100	150	—

Note: Use caution as silver specimens appear questionable and may be considered spurious

1/2 REAL KM# 221 Composition: Struck Silver **Issuer:** SUD, Under General Morelos **Obverse:** Bow, arrow **Obv. Legend:** PROVICIONAL DE OAXACA **Reverse:** Lion **Rev. Legend:** AMERICA MORELOS

Date	Mintage	Good	VG	F	VF	XF
1812	—	35.00	60.00	100	150	—
1813	—	35.00	60.00	100	150	—

1/2 REAL KM# 221a Composition: Struck Copper **Issuer:** SUD, Under General Morelos **Obverse:** Bow, arrow **Obv. Legend:** PROVICIONAL DE OAXACA **Reverse:** Lion **Rev. Legend:** AMERICA MORELOS

Date	Mintage	Good	VG	F	VF	XF
1812	—	27.50	42.50	70.00	100	—
1813	—	20.00	35.00	60.00	85.00	—

1/2 REAL KM# A222 Composition: Struck Copper **Issuer:** SUD, Under General Morelos **Obverse:** Similar to KM#220 **Reverse:** Similar to KM#221 but with 1/2 at left of lion **Rev. Legend:** AMERICA MORELOS

Date	Mintage	Good	VG	F	VF	XF
1813	—	27.50	42.50	70.00	100	—

1/2 REAL KM# 243 Composition: Struck Copper **Issuer:** Tierra Caliente (Hot Country), Under General Morelos **Obverse:** Bow, T.C., SUD **Reverse:** Morelos monogram, value, date

Date	Mintage	Good	VG	F	VF	XF
1813	—	37.50	70.00	125	200	—

REAL KM# 222 Composition: Struck Copper **Issuer:** SUD, Under General Morelos **Obverse:** Bow, arrow, SUD **Reverse:** Morelos monogram, 1 R., date

Date	Mintage	Good	VG	F	VF	XF
1811	—	4.75	9.00	18.00	38.00	—
1812	—	3.75	7.00	14.00	30.00	—
1813	—	3.75	7.00	14.00	30.00	—

REAL KM# 222a Composition: Struck Silver **Issuer:** SUD, Under General Morelos **Obverse:** Bow, arrow, SUD **Reverse:** Morelos monogram, 1 R., date

Date	Mintage	Good	VG	F	VF	XF
1812	—	—	—	—	—	—
1813	—	—	—	—	—	—

REAL KM# 223 Composition: Cast Silver **Issuer:** SUD, Under General Morelos **Obverse:** Bow, arrow, SUD with floral ornaments **Reverse:** Morelos monogram, 1 R., date

Date	Mintage	Good	VG	F	VF	XF
1812	—	—	—	—	—	—
1813	—	27.50	60.00	115	160	—

Note: Use caution as many silver specimens appear questionable and may be considered spurious

REAL KM# 224 Composition: Struck Copper **Issuer:** SUD, Under General Morelos **Obverse:** Bow, arrow/SUD **Reverse:** Lion **Rev. Legend:** AMERICA MORELOS

Date	Mintage	Good	VG	F	VF	XF
1813	—	27.50	42.50	75.00	110	—

REAL KM# 225 Composition: Silver **Issuer:** SUD, Under General Morelos **Obverse:** Bow, arrow/SUD **Reverse:** Lion **Rev. Legend:** AMERICA MORELOS

Date	Mintage	Good	VG	F	VF	XF
1813 Rare	—	—	—	—	—	—

REAL KM# 244 Composition: Struck Copper **Issuer:** Tierra Caliente (Hot Country), Under General Morelos **Obverse:** Bow, T.C., SUD **Reverse:** Morelos monogram, value, date

Date	Mintage	Good	VG	F	VF	XF
1813	—	13.50	25.00	50.00	80.00	—

2 REALES   KM# 226.1   Composition: Struck Copper
Issuer: SUD, Under General Morelos **Obverse:** Bow, arrow/
SUD **Reverse:** Morelos monogram, .2.R., date

Date	Mintage	Good	VG	F	VF	XF
1811	—	12.50	25.00	55.00	100	—
1811 inverted 2	—	15.00	30.00	60.00	120	—
1812	—	2.50	4.00	6.50	12.00	—
1813	—	3.00	5.00	8.00	15.00	—
1814	—	13.50	28.00	65.00	120	—

2 REALES   KM# 226.1a   Composition: Struck Silver
Issuer: SUD, Under General Morelos **Obverse:** Bow, arrow/
SUD **Reverse:** Morelos monogram, .2.R., date

Date	Mintage	Good	VG	F	VF	XF
1812	—	175	300	500	750	—

2 REALES   KM# 229   Composition: Cast Silver **Issuer:**
SUD, Under General Morelos **Obverse:** Bow, arrow, SUD
Reverse: Morelos monogram, value, date in center with
ornamentation around

Date	Mintage	Good	VG	F	VF	XF
1812	—	60.00	100	150	225	—
1812 Filled in D in SUD	—	60.00	100	150	225	—

Note: Use caution as many silver specimens appear questionable and may be considered spurious

2 REALES   KM# 245   Composition: Struck Copper
Issuer: Tierra Caliente (Hot Country), Under General
Morelos **Obverse:** Bow, T.C., SUD **Reverse:** Morelos
monogram, value, date

Date	Mintage	Good	VG	F	VF	XF
1813	—	9.00	22.50	35.00	50.00	—

2 REALES   KM# 227   Composition: Struck Silver **Issuer:**
SUD, Under General Morelos **Obverse:** Bow, arrow
Obv. Legend: SUD-OXA **Reverse:** Morelos monogram,
value, date

Date	Mintage	Good	VG	F	VF	XF
1813	—	60.00	100	200	300	—
1814	—	60.00	100	200	300	—

2 REALES   KM# 228   Composition: Struck Silver **Issuer:**
SUD, Under General Morelos **Obverse:** Bow, arrow
Obv. Legend: SUD. OAXACA **Reverse:** Morelos
monogram, value, date

Date	Mintage	Good	VG	F	VF	XF
1814	—	60.00	100	200	325	—

2 REALES   KM# 226.2   Composition: Struck Silver
Issuer: SUD, Under General Morelos **Obverse:** Three large
stars added **Reverse:** Morelos monogram, .2.R., date

Date	Mintage	Good	VG	F	VF	XF
1814	—	10.00	20.00	40.00	60.00	—

2 REALES   KM# 246   Composition: Struck Copper
Issuer: Tierra Caliente (Hot Country), Under General
Morelos **Obverse:** Bow, T.C., SUD **Reverse:** Morelos
monogram, value, date

Date	Mintage	Good	VG	F	VF	XF
1814	—	22.50	50.00	100	175	—

8 REALES   KM# 234   Composition: Copper **Issuer:**
SUD, Under General Morelos **Obverse:** Bow, arrow, SUD
in floral ornamentation **Obv. Legend:** SUD-OXA **Reverse:**
Morelos monogram, .8.R., date surrounded by ornate
flowery fields

Date	Mintage	Good	VG	F	VF	XF
1811	—	75.00	125	150	225	—
1812	—	4.00	6.00	10.00	20.00	—
1813	—	4.00	6.00	10.00	20.00	—
1814	—	10.00	15.00	25.00	50.00	—

8 REALES   KM# 235   Composition: Cast Silver **Issuer:**
SUD, Under General Morelos **Obverse:** Bow, arrow, SUD
in floral ornamentation **Reverse:** Morelos monogram, value,
date surrounded by ornate flowery fields

Date	Mintage	Good	VG	F	VF	XF
1811	—	—	—	—	—	—
1812	—	75.00	125	200	350	—
1813	—	60.00	100	175	300	—

Date	Mintage	Good	VG	F	VF	XF
1814						

Note: Most silver specimens available in today's market are considered spurious

8 REALES   KM# 234a   Composition: Struck Silver **Issuer:** SUD, under General Morelos **Obverse:** Bow, arrow, SUD in floral ornamentation **Reverse:** Morelos monogram, .8.R., date surrounded by ornate flowery fields

Date	Mintage	Good	VG	F	VF	XF
1811	—	—	—	2500	4000	—
1812	—	—	—	1200	2000	—

8 REALES   KM# 233.1   Composition: Copper **Issuer:** SUD, Under General Morelos **Obverse:** Bow, arrow, SUD **Reverse:** Morelos monogram, 8.R., date, plain fields

Date	Mintage	Good	VG	F	VF	XF
1812	—	15.00	30.00	60.00	90.00	—

8 REALES   KM# 233.1a   Composition: Struck Silver **Issuer:** SUD, Under General Morelos **Obverse:** Bow, arrow, SUD **Reverse:** Morelos monogram, 8.R., date, plain fields

Date	Mintage	Good	VG	F	VF	XF
1812	—	100	150	250	450	—

8 REALES   KM# 233.2   Composition: Copper **Issuer:** SUD, Under General Morelos **Obverse:** Bow, arrow, SUD **Reverse:** Morelos monogram, 8 R, date, plain fields

Date	Mintage	Good	VG	F	VF	XF
1812	—	6.00	8.00	12.00	15.00	—
1813	—	6.00	8.00	12.00	15.00	—
1814	—	10.00	12.00	15.00	20.00	—

Note: Similar to KM#233.4 but lines below bow slant left

8 REALES   KM# 233.5a   Composition: Silver **Issuer:** SUD, Under General Morelos **Obverse:** 8 dots below bow, SUD, plain fields **Reverse:** Morelos monogram, 8.R., date

Date	Mintage	Good	VG	F	VF	XF
1812	—	—	—	1,200	2,000	—

8 REALES   KM# 242   Composition: Copper **Issuer:** Huautla, Under General Morelos **Obverse:** Legend around bow, arrow/SUD **Obv. Legend:** MONEDA PROVI. CIONAL PS. ES. **Rev. Legend:** FABRICADO EN HUAUTLA

Date	Mintage	Good	VG	F	VF	XF
1812	—	1,000	1,500	2,000	—	—

8 REALES   KM# 236   Composition: 0.9030 Struck Silver **Issuer:** SUD, Under General Morelos **Obverse:** M monogram **Obv. Legend:** PROV. D. OAXACA **Reverse:** Lion shield with or without bow above

Date	Mintage	Good	VG	F	VF	XF
1812 Rare	—	—	—	—	—	—

8 REALES   KM# 237   Composition: 0.9030 Sterling Silver **Issuer:** SUD, Under General Morelos **Obverse:** M monogram, without legend **Reverse:** Lion shield with or without bow above

Date	Mintage	Good	VG	F	VF	XF
1813 Rare	—	—	—	—	—	—

8 REALES   KM# 238   Composition: 0.9030 Struck Silver **Issuer:** SUD, Under General Morelos **Obverse:** Bow/M/ SUD **Reverse:** PROV. DE. ... arms

Date	Mintage	Good	VG	F	VF	XF
1813 Rare	—	—	—	—	—	—

8 REALES   KM# 248   Composition: Struck Copper **Issuer:** Tierra Caliente (Hot Country), Under General Morelos **Obverse:** Bow, T.C., SUD **Reverse:** Morelos monogram, value, date

Date	Mintage	Good	VG	F	VF	XF
1813	—	9.00	20.00	40.00	75.00	—

8 REALES   KM# 249   Composition: Cast Silver **Issuer:** Tierra Caliente (Hot Country), Under General Morelos **Obverse:** Bow, T.C., SUD **Reverse:** Morelos monogram, value, date

Date	Mintage	Good	VG	F	VF	XF
1813	—	—	—	—	—	—

Note: Use caution as many silver specimens appear questionable and may be considered spurious

8 REALES   KM# 233.2a   Composition: Silver **Issuer:** SUD, Under General Morelos **Obverse:** bow, arrow, SUD **Reverse:** Morelos monogram, 8R, date, plain fields

Date	Mintage	Good	VG	F	VF	XF
1813	—	—	—	1,200	2,000	—

8 REALES   KM# 233.3   Composition: Struck Copper **Issuer:** SUD, Under General Morelos **Obverse:** Bow, arrow, SUD, with left slant lines below bow **Reverse:** Morelos monogram, 8.R., date, plain fields

Date	Mintage	Good	VG	F	VF	XF
1813	—	10.00	17.50	30.00	50.00	—

8 REALES   KM# 233.4   Composition: Struck Copper **Issuer:** SUD, Under General Morelos **Obverse:** Bow, arrow, SUD, with right slant lines below bow **Reverse:** Morelos monogram, 8.R., date, plain fields

Date	Mintage	Good	VG	F	VF	XF
1813	—	10.00	17.50	30.00	50.00	—

8 REALES   KM# 239   Composition: Cast Silver **Issuer:** SUD, Under General Morelos **Obverse:** Bow, arrow **Obv. Legend:** SUD-OXA **Reverse:** Morelos monogram

Date	Mintage	Good	VG	F	VF	XF
1814 Rare	—	—	—	—	—	—

8 REALES   KM# 240   Composition: Copper **Issuer:** SUD, Under General Morelos **Obverse:** Bow, arrow **Obv. Legend:** SUD-OXA **Reverse:** Morelos monogram, 8.R., date

Date	Mintage	Good	VG	F	VF	XF
1814	—	35.00	70.00	150	250	—

8 REALES   KM# 241   Composition: Copper **Issuer:** SUD, Under General Morelos **Obverse:** Bow, arrow **Obv. Legend:** SUD-OAXACA **Reverse:** Morelos monogram, 8.R., date

Date	Mintage	Good	VG	F	VF	XF
1814	—	100	200	350	550	—

PUEBLA
WAR OF INDEPENDENCE
INSURGENT COINAGE

The coins of Puebla emanated from Zacatlan, the headquarters of the hit-and-run Insurgent leader Osorno. The mint opened in April 1812 and operated through 1813.

1/2 REAL   KM# 250   Composition: Copper **Issuer:** Zacatlan, struck by General Osorno **Obverse:** Osorno monogram, ZACATLAN, date **Reverse:** Crossed arrows, wreath, value

Date	Mintage	Good	VG	F	VF	XF
1813 Rare	—	—	—	—	—	—

REAL   KM# 251   Composition: Copper **Issuer:** Zacatlan, struck by General Osorno **Obverse:** Osorno monogram, ZACATLAN, date **Reverse:** Crossed arrows, wreath, value

Date	Mintage	Good	VG	F	VF	XF
1813	—	100	150	225	450	—

2 REALES   KM# 252   Composition: Copper **Issuer:** Zacatlan, struck by General Osorno **Obverse:** Osorno monogram, ZACATLAN, date **Reverse:** Crossed arrows, wreath, value

Date	Mintage	Good	VG	F	VF	XF
1813	—	125	175	275	500	—

REAL DEL CATORCE
WAR OF INDEPENDENCE
ROYALIST COINAGE

(City in San Luis Potosi)

Real del Catorce is an important mining center in the Province of San Luis Potosi. In 1811 an 8 Reales coin was issued under very primitive conditions while the city was still in Royalist hands. Few survive.

8 REALES   KM# 169   Composition: 0.9030 Silver **Ruler:** Ferdinand VII **Obv. Legend:** EL R. D. CATORC. POR FERNA. VII **Rev. Legend:** MONEDA. PROVISIONAL. VALE. 8R

Date	Mintage	VG	F	VF	XF	Unc
1811	—	7,000	15,000	35,000	65,000	—

Note: Spink America Gerber Sale 6-96 VF or XF realized $63,800

SAN FERNANDO DE BEXAR
WAR OF INDEPENDENCE
ROYALIST COINAGE

San Fernando de Bexar, known today as San Antonio, was a military center and capital of the Province of Texas in New Spain. In the early part of the 19th century it experienced a shortage of small denomination coinage, which caused problems with the flow of local trade.

In 1817, Manual Barrera, a local merchant was granted the right by the Governor of the Province to issue small denomination pieces to relieve this problem. No examples of the Barrera tokens resulting from March 20, 1817 decree are known to exist.

Later that year a new Governor was appointed and in 1818 Jose Antonio de la Garza, the city's Postmaster applied for and was granted, by Governor Martinez decree of November 30, 1818, permission to strike and circulate small copper pieces of 1/2 Real denomination. De la Garza was required to redeem any Barrera pieces still in circulation within 12 days, exchanging them for his new copper jolas, to be bonded and to redeem his own pieces on command. The Governor's proclamation of December 6, 1818 made these details known to the public.

It is presumed that all Barrera pieces were destroyed upon redemption. Similarly the tokens of Jose Antonio de la Garza were mostly destroyed after redemption, with most of the few remaining examples being discovered along the banks of the San Antonio River, where de la Garza owned property.

1/2 REAL (Jola) KM# Tn1 (KM170) Composition: Copper **Ruler:** Ferdinand VII

Date	Mintage	Good	VG	F	VF	XF
1818	8,000	350	650	1,250	2,500	—

1/2 REAL (Jola) KM# Tn2 (KM171) Composition: Copper **Ruler:** Ferdinand VII

Date	Mintage	Good	VG	F	VF	XF
1818	Inc. above	500	750	1,500	3,000	—

Note: Bowers and Merena ANA Millennium sale 8-00, EF-40 realized $12,650

SAN LUIS POTOSI
WAR OF INDEPENDENCE
ROYALIST COINAGE

1/4 REAL KM# A172 Composition: Copper **Ruler:** Ferdinand VII **Issuer:** Sierra de Pinos, Villa

Date	Mintage	Good	VG	F	VF	XF
1814	—	75.00	125	200	350	

1/4 REAL KM# A172a Composition: Silver **Ruler:** Ferdinand VII

Date	Mintage	Good	VG	F	VF	XF
1814 Rare	—	—	—	—	—	—

SOMBRERETE
WAR OF INDEPENDENCE
ROYALIST COINAGE

(Under Royalist Vargas)

The Sombrerete Mint opened on October 8, 1810 in an area that boasted some of the richest mines in Mexico. The mint operated only until July 16, 1811, only to reopen in 1812 and finally close for good at the end of the year. Mines Administrator Fernando Vargas, was also in charge of the coining, all coins bear his name.

1/2 REAL KM# 172 Composition: 0.9030 Silver **Ruler:** Ferdinand VII **Obverse:** Legend around crowned globes **Obv. Legend:** FERDIN. VII. SOMBRERETE... **Reverse:** Legend above lys in oval, sprays, date below **Rev. Legend:** VARGAS

Date	Mintage	Good	VG	F	VF	XF
1811	—	45.00	70.00	150	250	—
1812	—	50.00	90.00	175	275	—

REAL KM# 173 Composition: 0.9030 Silver **Ruler:** Ferdinand VII **Obverse:** Legend around crowned globes **Obv. Legend:** FERDIN. VII. SOMBRERETE... **Reverse:** Legend above lys in oval with denomination flanking, sprays, date below **Rev. Legend:** VARGAS

Date	Mintage	Good	VG	F	VF	XF
1811	—	45.00	70.00	150	250	—

Note: For 1811, denomination reads as '1R' or 'R1'

Date	Mintage	Good	VG	F	VF	XF
1812	—	50.00	90.00	175	275	

4 REALES KM# 175 (KM175.2) Composition: 0.9030 Silver **Ruler:** Ferdinand VII **Obverse:** Crowned Royal arms **Obv. Legend:** R. CAXA. DE. SOMBRERETE **Reverse:** Large legend **Rev. Legend:** VARGAS/1811

Date	Mintage	Good	VG	F	VF	XF
1812	—	50.00	100	200	450	—

8 REALES KM# 176 Composition: 0.9030 Silver **Ruler:** Ferdinand VII **Countermark:** VARGAS, date, S **Obverse:** Royal arms **Obv. Legend:** R. CAXA. DE SOMBRERETE **Reverse:** Several countermarks between crowned pillars

Date	Mintage	Good	VG	F	VF	XF
1810	—	1,000	1,750	2,750	4,000	—
1811	—	225	325	450	600	—

they intended to mint coins of 1/2, 1, 2, 4, and 8 Reales, but specimens are extant of only the three higher denominations.

2 REALES   KM# 253   Composition: 0.9030 Silver **Issuer:** Zongolica **Obverse:** Bow and arrow **Obv. Legend:** VIVA FERNANDO VII Y AMERICA **Reverse:** Value, crossed palm branch, sword, date **Rev. Legend:** ZONGOLICA

Date	Mintage	Good	VG	F	VF	XF
1812	—	85.00	175	300	500	—

8 REALES   KM# 177   Composition: 0.9030 Silver **Ruler:** Ferdinand VII **Obverse:** Crowned Royal arms **Obv. Legend:** R. CAXA. DE SOMBRETE **Rev. Legend:** VARGAS/date/3, S between crowned pillars

Date	Mintage	Good	VG	F	VF	XF
1811	—	125	185	245	500	—
1812	—	125	175	225	475	—

VALLADOLID MICHOACAN

WAR OF INDEPENDENCE
ROYALIST COINAGE

(Now Morelia)

Valladolid, capitol of Michoacan province, was a strategically important center for military thrusts into the adjoining provinces. The Royalists made every effort to retain the position. In 1813, with the advance of the insurgent forces, it became apparent that to maintain the position would be very difficult. During 1813 it was necessary to make coins in the city due to lack of traffic with other areas. These were made only briefly before the city fell and were also used by the insurgents with appropriate countermarks.

8 REALES   KM# 178   Composition: 0.9030 Silver **Ruler:** Ferdinand VII **Obverse:** Royal arms in wreath, value at sides **Reverse:** PROVISIONAL/DE VALLADOLID/1813

Date	Mintage	Good	VG	F	VF	XF
1813 Rare	—	—	—	—	—	—

8 REALES   KM# 179   Composition: 0.9030 Silver **Ruler:** Ferdinand VII **Obverse:** Bust **Obv. Legend:** FERDIN. VII. **Reverse:** Arms, pillars, P. D. V. in legend

Date	Mintage	Good	VG	F	VF	XF
1813 Rare	—	—	—	—	—	—

Note: Spink America Gerber sale 6-96 good realized $23,100

VERACRUZ

WAR OF INDEPENDENCE
INSURGENT COINAGE

In Zongolica, in the province of Veracruz, 2 priests and a lawyer decided to raise an army to fight for independence. Due to isolation from other Insurgent forces, they decided to make their own coins. Records show that

8 REALES   KM# 255   Composition: 0.9030 Silver **Issuer:** Zongolica **Obverse:** Bow and arrow **Obv. Legend:** VIVA FERNANDO VII Y AMERICA **Reverse:** Value, crossed palm branch, sword, date **Rev. Legend:** ZONGOLICA **Note:** Similar to 2 Reales, KM#253.

Date	Mintage	Good	VG	F	VF	XF
1812 Rare	—	—	—	—	—	—

Note: Spink America Gerber sale 6-96 VF to XF realized $57,200

INSURGENT COUNTERMARKED COINAGE
Congress of Chilpanzingo

Type A: Hand holding bow and arrow between quiver with arrows, sword and bow.

Type B: Crowned eagle on bridge.

1/2 REAL   KM# 256.1   Composition: Silver **Issuer:** Congress of Chilpanzingo **Countermark:** Type A hand holding bow and arrow between quiver with arrows, sword and bow **Note:** Countermark on cast Mexico City KM#72.

Date	Mintage	Good	VG	F	VF	XF
1812(1812)	—	42.50	70.00	90.00	120	—

1/2 REAL   KM# 256.2 Composition: Silver **Issuer:** Congress of Chilpanzingo **Countermark:** Type A hand holding bow and arrow between quiver with arrows, sword and bow **Note:** Countermark on Zacatecas KM#181.

Date	Mintage	Good	VG	F	VF	XF
1811(1812)	—	50.00	75.00	100	125	—

REAL   KM# A257 Composition: Cast Silver **Issuer:** Congress of Chilpanzingo **Countermark:** Type A hand holding bow and arrow between quiver with arrows, sword and bow **Note:** Countermark on cast Mexico City KM#81.

Date	Mintage	Good	VG	F	VF	XF
1803(1812)	—	18.50	30.00	50.00	80.00	—

2 REALES   KM# 257.1 Composition: Silver **Issuer:** Congress of Chilpanzingo **Countermark:** Type B crowned eagle on bridge **Note:** Countermark on 1/4 cut of 8 Reales.

Date	Mintage	Good	VG	F	VF	XF
ND(1812) Unique	—	—	—	—	—	—

2 REALES   KM# 257.2 Composition: Silver **Issuer:** Congress of Chilpanzingo **Countermark:** Type B crowned eagle on bridge **Note:** Countermark on Zacatecas KM#186.

Date	Mintage	Good	VG	F	VF	XF
1811(1812) Unique	—	—	—	—	—	—

8 REALES   KM# 258.1 Composition: Silver **Issuer:** Congress of Chilpanzingo **Countermark:** Type A hand holding bow and arrow between quiver with arrows, sword and bow **Note:** Countermark on cast Mexico City KM#109.

Date	Mintage	Good	VG	F	VF	XF
1805(1813)	—	45.00	65.00	85.00	125	—

Note: A countermark appears on coins dated 1805 TH

8 REALES   KM# 258.2 Composition: Silver **Issuer:** Congress of Chilpanzingo **Countermark:** Type A hand holding bow and arrow between quiver with arrows, sword and bow **Note:** Countermark on cast Mexico City KM#110.

Date	Mintage	Good	VG	F	VF	XF
1810(1813) HJ	—	50.00	75.00	100	150	—

8 REALES   KM# 258.3 Composition: Silver **Issuer:** Congress of Chilpanzingo **Countermark:** Type A hand holding bow and arrow between quiver with arrows, sword and bow **Note:** Countermark on cast Mexico City KM#111.

Date	Mintage	Good	VG	F	VF	XF
1811(1813) HJ	—	45.00	65.00	85.00	125	—
1812(1813) HJ	—	100	125	175	275	—

8 REALES   KM# 259.1 Composition: Silver **Issuer:** Congress of Chilpanzingo **Countermark:** Type B crowned

eagle on bridge **Note:** Countermark on Chihuahua KM#111.1.

Date	Mintage	Good	VG	F	VF	XF
1816(1813) RP	—	200	250	300	350	—

8 REALES   KM# 259.2 Composition: Silver **Issuer:** Congress of Chilpanzingo **Countermark:** Type B crowned eagle on bridge **Note:** Countermark on cast Mexico City KM#111.

Date	Mintage	Good	VG	F	VF	XF
1811(1813) HJ	—	130	140	150	175	—

8 REALES   KM# 259.3 Composition: Silver **Issuer:** Congress of Chilpanzingo **Countermark:** Type B crowned eagle on bridge **Note:** Countermark on Valladolid KM#178.

Date	Mintage	Good	VG	F	VF	XF
1813(1813)	—	1,000	2,000	3,000	5,000	—

8 REALES   KM# 259.4 Composition: Silver **Issuer:** Congress of Chilpanzingo **Countermark:** Type B crowned eagle on bridge **Note:** Countermark on Zacatecas KM#190.

Date	Mintage	Good	VG	F	VF	XF
1810(1813)	—	400	500	600	750	—

INSURGENT
COUNTERMARKED COINAGE
Don Jose Maria De Linares

8 REALES   KM# 263.1 Composition: Silver **Issuer:** Don Jose Maria De Linares **Countermark:** LINA/RES* **Note:** Countermark on Mexico City KM#110.

Date	Mintage	Good	VG	F	VF	XF
1808(1813) TH	—	250	300	375	500	—

8 REALES   KM# 263.2 Composition: Silver **Issuer:** Don Jose Maria De Linares **Countermark:** LINA/RES * **Note:** Countermark on Zacatecas KM#190.

Date	Mintage	Good	VG	F	VF	XF
1811(1813)	—	300	375	450	575	—

8 REALES   KM# 263.3 Composition: Silver **Issuer:** Don Jose Maria De Linares **Countermark:** LINA/RES* **Note:** Countermark on Zacatecas KM#191.

Date	Mintage	Good	VG	F	VF	XF
1812(1813)	—	250	300	375	500	—

INSURGENT COUNTERMARKED COINAGE
Ensaie

8 REALES KM# 260.3 Composition: Silver **Issuer:** Ensaie **Countermark:** Eagle over ENSAIE, crude sling below **Note:** Countermark on Zacatecas KM#190.

Date	Mintage	Good	VG	F	VF	XF
1810(1810)	—	—	—	—	—	—
1811(1812)	—	100	150	200	300	—

8 REALES KM# 260.4 Composition: Silver **Issuer:** Ensaie **Countermark:** Eagle over ENSAIE, crude sling below **Note:** Countermark on Zacatecas KM#191.

Date	Mintage	Good	VG	F	VF	XF
1810(1810)	—	500	700	900	1,200	—
1811(1812)	—	250	300	375	500	—
1812(1812)	—	200	250	285	400	—

8 REALES KM# 260.1 Composition: Silver **Issuer:** Ensaie **Countermark:** Eagle over ENSAIE, crude sling below **Note:** Countermark on Mexico City KM#110.

Date	Mintage	Good	VG	F	VF	XF
1811(1812) HJ	—	150	200	275	350	—

8 REALES KM# 260.2 Composition: Silver **Issuer:** Ensaie **Countermark:** Eagle over ENSAIE, crude sling below **Note:** Countermark on Zacatecas KM#189.

Date	Mintage	Good	VG	F	VF	XF
1811(1812)	—	200	400	600	800	—

INSURGENT COUNTERMARKED COINAGE
Jose Maria Liceaga

J.M.L. with banner on cross, crossed olive branches.

(J.M.L./V., D.s, S.M., S.Y.S.L., Ve, A.P., s.r.a., Sea, P.G., S., S.M., El)

1/2 REAL KM# A260 Composition: Silver **Issuer:** Jose Maria Liceaga **Countermark:** JML/SM with banner on cross, crossed olive branches **Note:** Countermark on cast Mexico City 1/2 Real.

Date	Mintage	Good	VG	F	VF	XF
ND(1812)	—	100	150	200	275	—

2 REALES KM# 261.6 Composition: Silver **Issuer:** Jose Maria Liceaga **Countermark:** J.M.L./V. with banner on cross, crossed olive branches **Note:** Countermark on Zacatecas KM#187.

Date	Mintage	Good	VG	F	VF	XF
1811(1812)	—	200	225	250	300	—

2 REALES KM# 261.7 Composition: Silver **Issuer:** Jose Maria Liceaga **Countermark:** J.M.L./DS with banner on cross, crossed olive branches **Note:** Countermark on Zacatecas KM#187.

Date	Mintage	Good	VG	F	VF	XF
1811(1812)	—	200	235	275	325	—

2 REALES KM# 261.8 Composition: Silver **Issuer:** Jose Maria Liceaga **Countermark:** J.M.L./S.M. with banner on cross, crossed olive branches **Note:** Countermark on Zacatecas KM#187.

Date	Mintage	Good	VG	F	VF	XF
1811(1812)	—	200	235	275	325	—

2 REALES KM# 261.9 Composition: Silver **Issuer:** Jose Maria Liceaga **Countermark:** J.M.L./S.Y. with banner on cross, crossed olive branches **Note:** Countermark on Zacatecas KM#187.

Date	Mintage	Good	VG	F	VF	XF
1811(1812)	—	200	235	275	325	—

2 REALES KM# 261.1 Composition: Silver **Issuer:** Jose Maria Liceaga **Countermark:** J.M.L./Ve with banner on cross, crossed olive branches **Note:** Countermark on 1/4 cut of 8 Reales.

Date	Mintage	Good	VG	F	VF	XF
ND(1812)	—	175	225	300	—	—

2 REALES   KM#261.2 Composition: Silver **Issuer:** Jose Maria Liceaga **Countermark:** J.M.L./V with banner on cross, crossed olive branchs **Note:** Countermark on Zacatecas KM#186.

Date	Mintage	Good	VG	F	VF	XF
1811(1812)	—	200	225	250	300	—

2 REALES   KM#261.3 Composition: Silver **Issuer:** Jose Maria Liceaga **Countermark:** J.M.L./DS with banner on cross, crossed olive branches **Note:** Countermark on Zacatecas KM#186.

Date	Mintage	Good	VG	F	VF	XF
1811(1812)	—	200	235	275	325	—

2 REALES   KM#261.4 Composition: Silver **Issuer:** Jose Maria Liceaga **Countermark:** J.M.L./S.M. with banner on cross, crossed olive branches **Note:** Countermark on Zacatecas KM#186.

Date	Mintage	Good	VG	F	VF	XF
1811(1812)	—	200	235	275	325	—

2 REALES   KM#261.5 Composition: Silver **Issuer:** Jose Maria Liceaga **Countermark:** J.M.L./S.Y. with banner on cross, crossed olive branches **Note:** Countermark on Zacatecas KM#186.

Date	Mintage	Good	VG	F	VF	XF
1811(1812)	—	200	235	275	325	—

8 REALES   KM#262.2 Composition: Silver **Issuer:** Jose Maria Liceaga **Countermark:** J.M.L./E with banner on cross, crossed olive branches **Note:** Countermark on Zacatecas KM#190.

Date	Mintage	Good	VG	F	VF	XF
1811(1812)	—	225	300	400	550	—

8 REALES   KM#262.3 Composition: Silver **Issuer:** Jose Maria Liceaga **Countermark:** J.M.L./P.G. with banner on cross, crossed olive branches **Note:** Countermark on Durango KM#111.2.

Date	Mintage	Good	VG	F	VF	XF
1813(1812) RM	—	200	275	375	525	—

8 REALES   KM#262.1 Composition: Silver **Issuer:** Jose Maria Liceaga **Countermark:** J.M.L./D.S. with banner on cross, crossed olive branches **Note:** Countermark on Zacatecas KM#190.

Date	Mintage	Good	VG	F	VF	XF
1811(1812)	—	250	325	425	550	—

8 REALES   KM#262.4 Composition: Silver **Issuer:** Jose Maria Liceaga **Countermark:** J.M.L./S.F. with banner on cross, crossed olive branches **Note:** Countermark on Zacatecas KM#190.

Date	Mintage	Good	VG	F	VF	XF
1811(1812)	—	200	275	375	525	—

8 REALES   KM#262.5 Composition: Silver **Issuer:** Jose Maria Liceaga **Countermark:** J.M.L./S.M. with banner on cross, crossed olive branches **Note:** Countermark on Zacatecas KM#190.

Date	Mintage	Good	VG	F	VF	XF
1811(1812)	—	200	275	375	525	—

8 REALES   KM#262.6 Composition: Silver **Issuer:** Jose Maria Liceaga **Countermark:** J.M.L./V.E. with banner on cross, cross olive branches **Note:** Countermark on Zacatecas KM#190.

Date	Mintage	Good	VG	F	VF	XF
1811(1812)	—	200	275	375	525	—

INSURGENT
COUNTERMARKED COINAGE
L.V.S. - Labor Vincit Semper

Some authorities believe L.V.S. is for La Villa de Sombrerete.

8 REALES   KM# 264.1   Composition: Cast Silver **Issuer:** Labor Vincit Semper, Some authorities believe L.V.S. is for "La Villa de Sombrerete" **Countermark:** L.V.S. **Note:** Countermark on Chihuahua KM#123.

Date	Mintage	Good	VG	F	VF	XF
1811(1811) RP	—	275	350	450	550	—
1812(1820) RP	—	200	250	300	375	—

8 REALES   KM# 264.2   Composition: Silver **Issuer:** Labor Vincit Semper, Some authorities believe L.V.S. is for "La Villa de Sombrerete" **Countermark:** L.V.S. **Note:** Countermark on Chihuahua KM#111.1 overstruck on KM#123.

Date	Mintage	Good	VG	F	VF	XF
1816(1820) RP	—	250	300	325	375	—
1817(1820) RP	—	250	300	325	375	—
1818(1820) RP	—	250	300	325	375	—
1819(1820) RP	—	400	450	500	600	—
1820(1820) RP	—	450	500	550	650	—

8 REALES   KM# 264.3   Composition: Silver **Issuer:** Labor Vincit Semper, Some authorities believe L.V.S. is for "La Villa de Sombrerete" **Countermark:** L.V.S. **Note:** Countermark on Guadalajara KM#111.3.

Date	Mintage	Good	VG	F	VF	XF
1817(1820)	—	185	220	250	310	—

8 REALES   KM# 264.4   Composition: Silver **Issuer:** Labor Vincit Semper, Some authorities believe L.V.S. is for "La Villa de Sombrerete" **Countermark:** L.V.S. **Note:** Countermark on Nueva Vizcaya KM#165.

Date	Mintage	Good	VG	F	VF	XF
1811(1820) RM	—	1,150	3,150	5,250	8,250	—

8 REALES   KM# 264.5   Composition: Silver **Issuer:** Labor Vincit Semper, Some authorities believe L.V.S. is for "La Villa de Sombrerete" **Countermark:** L.V.S. **Note:** Countermark on Sombrerete KM#177.

Date	Mintage	Good	VG	F	VF	XF
1811(1820)	—	300	350	450	550	—
1812(1820)	—	300	350	450	550	—

8 REALES   KM# 264.6   Composition: Silver **Issuer:** Labor Vincit Semper, Some authorities believe L.V.S. is for "La Villa de Sombrerete" **Countermark:** L.V.S. **Note:** Countermark on Zacatecas KM#190.

Date	Mintage	Good	VG	F	VF	XF
1811(1820)	—	350	400	450	550	—

8 REALES   KM# 264.7   Composition: Silver **Issuer:** Labor Vincit Semper, Some authorities believe L.V.S. is for "La Villa de Sombrerete" **Countermark:** L.V.S. **Note:** Countermark on Zacatecas KM#192.

Date	Mintage	Good	VG	F	VF	XF
1813(1820)	—	350	400	450	550	—

INSURGENT
COUNTERMARKED COINAGE
Morelos

Morelos monogram

Type A: Stars above and below monogram in circle.

Type B: Dots above and below monogram in oval.

Type C: Monogram in rectangle.

Note: Many specimens of Type C available in todays market are considered spurious.

2 REALES   KM# A265   Composition: Copper **Issuer:** Morelos **Countermark:** Type A stars above and below monogram in circle **Note:** Countermark on Oaxaca Sud, KM#226.1.

Date	Mintage	Good	VG	F	VF	XF
1812(1815)	—	—	—	—	—	—

8 REALES   KM# 265.1   Composition: Silver **Issuer:**
Morelos **Countermark:** Type A star above and below
monogram in circle **Note:** Countermark on Mexico City
KM#109.

Date	Mintage	Good	VG	F	VF	XF
1797(1815) FM	—	45.00	50.00	60.00	85.00	—
1798(1815) FM	—	45.00	50.00	60.00	85.00	—
1800(1815) FM	—	45.00	50.00	60.00	85.00	—
1807(1815) TH	—	45.00	50.00	60.00	85.00	—

8 REALES   KM# 265.2   Composition: Silver **Issuer:**
Morelos **Countermark:** Type A stars above and below
monogram in circle **Note:** Countermark on Mexico City
KM#110.

Date	Mintage	Good	VG	F	VF	XF
1809(1815) TH	—	55.00	65.00	85.00	120	—
1811(1815) HJ	—	55.00	65.00	85.00	120	—

8 REALES   KM# 265.3   Composition: Silver **Issuer:**
Morelos **Countermark:** Type A stars above and below
monogram in circle **Note:** Countermark on Mexico City
KM#111.

Date	Mintage	Good	VG	F	VF	XF
1812(1815) JJ	—	50.00	60.00	75.00	110	—

8 REALES   KM# 265.5   Composition: Cast Silver **Issuer:**
Morelos **Countermark:** Type A stars above and below
monogram in circle **Note:** Countermark on Supreme
National Congress KM#206.

Date	Mintage	Good	VG	F	VF	XF
1811(1815)	—	200	250	375	600	—

8 REALES   KM# 266.1   Composition: Silver **Issuer:**
Morelos **Countermark:** Type B dots above and below
monogram in oval **Note:** Countermark on Guatamala 8
Reales, C#67.

Date	Mintage	Good	VG	F	VF	XF
1810(1815) M Rare	—	—	—	—	—	—

8 REALES   KM# 266.2   Composition: Silver **Issuer:**
Morelos **Countermark:** Type B dots above and below
monogram in oval **Note:** Countermark on Mexico City
KM#110.

Date	Mintage	Good	VG	F	VF	XF
1809(1815) TH	—	45.00	55.00	65.00	90.00	—

8 REALES   KM# 267.1   Composition: Silver **Issuer:**
Morelos **Countermark:** Type C monogram in rectangle
Note: Countermark on Zacatecas KM#189. Many
specimens of Type C available in today's market are
considered spurious.

Date	Mintage	Good	VG	F	VF	XF
1811(1815)	—	300	350	425	650	—

8 REALES   KM# 265.4   Composition: Silver **Issuer:**
Morelos **Countermark:** Type A stars above and below
monogram in circle **Note:** Countermark on Oaxaca Sud
KM#233.2.

Date	Mintage	Good	VG	F	VF	XF
1812(1815)	—	12.50	17.50	25.00	40.00	—
1813(1815)	—	12.50	17.50	25.00	40.00	—
1814(1815)	—	12.50	17.50	25.00	40.00	—

8 REALES   KM# 265.6   Composition: Silver **Issuer:**
Morelos **Countermark:** Type A stars above and below
monogram in circle **Note:** Countermark on Zacatecas
KM#190.

Date	Mintage	Good	VG	F	VF	XF
1811(1815)	—	200	250	375	600	—

8 REALES   KM# 265.7   Composition: Silver **Issuer:**
Morelos **Countermark:** Type A stars above and below
monogram in circle **Note:** Countermark on Zacatecas
KM#191.

Date	Mintage	Good	VG	F	VF	XF
1811(1815)	—	200	250	375	600	—

8 REALES   KM# 267.2   Composition: Copper **Issuer:**
Morelos **Countermark:** Type C: monogram in rectangle
Note: Countermark Type C on Zacatecas KM#190. Many
specimens of Type C available in today's market are
considered spurious.

Date	Mintage	Good	VG	F	VF	XF
1811(1815)	—	300	350	425	650	—

INSURGENT
COUNTERMARKED COINAGE
Norte

Issued by the Supreme National Congress and the
Army of the North.

Countermark: Eagle on cactus; star to left; NORTE
below.

1/2 REAL   KM# 268   Composition: Silver **Issuer:**
Supreme National Congress and the Army of the North
Countermark: Eagle on cactus; star to left; NORTE below
Note: Countermark on Zacatecas KM#180.

Date	Mintage	Good	VG	F	VF	XF
1811(1814)	—	250	300	375	450	—

2 REALES   KM# 269   Composition: Silver **Issuer:**
Supreme National Congress and the Army of the North
Countermark: Eagle on cactus; star to left; NORTE below
Note: Countermark on Zacatecas KM#187.

Date	Mintage	Good	VG	F	VF	XF
1811(1814)	—	225	275	325	400	—

2 REALES   KM# A269   Composition: Silver **Issuer:**
Supreme National Congress and the Army of the North
Countermark: Eagle on cactus; star to left; NORTE below
Note: Countermark on Zacatecas KM#188.

Date	Mintage	Good	VG	F	VF	XF
1812(1814)	—	—	—	—	—	—

4 REALES   KM# B269   Composition: Silver **Issuer:**
Supreme National Congress and the Army of the North
Countermark: Eagle on cactus; star to left; NORTE below
Note: Countermark on Sombrerete KM#175.

Date	Mintage	Good	VG	F	VF	XF
1812(1814)	—	100	150	200	275	—

8 REALES   KM# 270.4   Composition: Silver **Issuer:**
Supreme National Congress and the Army of the North
Countermark: Eagle on cactus; star to left; NORTE below
Note: Countermark on Zacatecas KM#191.

Date	Mintage	Good	VG	F	VF	XF
1811(1811)	—	200	300	400	550	—
1811(1814)	—	200	300	400	550	—
1812(1814)	—	200	300	400	550	—

8 REALES   KM# 270.1   Composition: Silver **Issuer:**
Supreme National Congress and the Army of the North
Countermark: Eagle on cactus; star to left; NORTE below
Note: Countermark on Chihuahua KM#111.1.

Date	Mintage	Good	VG	F	VF	XF
1813(1814) RP	—	250	350	450	550	—

8 REALES   KM# 270.2   Composition: Silver **Issuer:**
Supreme National Congress and the Army of the North
Countermark: Eagle on cactus; star to left; NORTE below
Note: Countermark on Guanajuato KM#111.4.

Date	Mintage	Good	VG	F	VF	XF
1813(1814) JM	—	400	550	700	800	—

8 REALES   KM# 270.3   Composition: Silver **Issuer:**
Supreme National Congress and the Army of the North
Countermark: Eagle on cactus; star to left; NORTE below
Note: Countermark on Zacatecas KM#190.

Date	Mintage	Good	VG	F	VF	XF
1811(1814)	—	300	400	500	650	—

INSURGENT
COUNTERMARKED COINAGE
Osorno

Countermark: Osorno monogram. (Jose Francisco
Osorno)

1/2 REAL   KM# 271.1   Composition: Silver **Issuer:** Jose
Francisco Osorno **Countermark:** Osorno monogram **Note:**
Countermark on Mexico City KM#72.

Date	Mintage	Good	VG	F	VF	XF
1798(1814) FM	—	65.00	100	150	200	—
1802(1814) FT	—	65.00	100	150	200	—
1806(1814)	—	65.00	100	150	200	—

1/2 REAL   KM# 271.2 Composition: Silver **Issuer:** Jose Francisco Osomo **Countermark:** Osomo monogram **Note:** Countermark on Mexico City KM#73.

Date	Mintage	Good	VG	F	VF	XF
1809(1814) TH	—	65.00	100	150	200	—

REAL   KM# 272.1 Composition: Silver **Issuer:** Jose Francisco Osomo **Countermark:** Osomo monogram **Note:** Countermark on Mexico City KM#81.

Date	Mintage	Good	VG	F	VF	XF
1803(1814) FT	—	65.00	100	150	200	—

REAL   KM# 272.2 Composition: Silver **Issuer:** Jose Francisco Osomo **Countermark:** Osomo monogram **Note:** Countermark on Potosi KM#70.

Date	Mintage	Good	VG	F	VF	XF
ND(1814)	—	75.00	115	175	250	—

REAL   KM# 272.3 Composition: Silver **Issuer:** Jose Francisco Osomo **Countermark:** Osomo monogram **Note:** Countermark on Guatemala KM#54.

Date	Mintage	Good	VG	F	VF	XF
1804(1814)	—	75.00	115	175	250	—

2 REALES   KM# A272.1 Composition: Silver **Issuer:** Jose Francisco Osomo **Countermark:** Osomo monogram **Note:** Countermark on Mexico City KM#88.2.

Date	Mintage	Good	VG	F	VF	XF
1788(1814) FM	—	75.00	125	175	250	—

2 REALES   KM# A272.2 Composition: Silver **Issuer:** Jose Francisco Osomo **Countermark:** Osomo monogram **Note:** Countermark on Mexico City KM#91.

Date	Mintage	Good	VG	F	VF	XF
1808(1814) TH	—	75.00	125	175	250	—

2 REALES   KM# A272.3 Composition: Silver **Issuer:** Jose Francisco Osomo **Countermark:** Osomo monogram **Note:** Countermark on Mexico City KM#92.

Date	Mintage	Good	VG	F	VF	XF
1809(1814) TH	—	75.00	125	175	250	—

2 REALES   KM# A272.4 Composition: Silver **Issuer:** Jose Francisco Osomo **Countermark:** Osomo monogram **Note:** Countermark on Zacatlian KM#252.

Date	Mintage	Good	VG	F	VF	XF
1813(1814)	—	150	200	300	400	—

4 REALES   KM# 273.1 Composition: Silver **Issuer:** Jose Francisco Osomo **Countermark:** Osomo monogram **Note:** Countermark on Mexico City KM#97.2.

Date	Mintage	Good	VG	F	VF	XF
1782(1814) FF	—	85.00	150	200	275	—

4 REALES   KM# 273.2 Composition: Silver **Issuer:** Jose Francisco Osomo **Countermark:** Osomo monogram **Note:** Countermark on Mexico City KM#100.

Date	Mintage	Good	VG	F	VF	XF
1799(1814) FM	—	85.00	150	200	275	—

8 REALES   KM# 274.1 Composition: Silver **Issuer:** Jose Francisco Osomo **Countermark:** Osomo monogram **Note:** Countermark on Lima 8 Reales, C#101.

Date	Mintage	Good	VG	F	VF	XF
1811(1814) JP	—	200	225	250	300	—

8 REALES KM# 275 Composition: Cast Silver **Issuer:** Julian Villagran **Countermark:** VILLA/GRAN **Note:** Countermark on cast Mexico City KM#109.

Date	Mintage	Good	VG	F	VF	XF
1796(1796) FM	—	200	250	300	400	—
1806(1811) TH	—	200	250	300	400	—

INSURGENT COUNTERMARKED COINAGE
General Vicente Guerrero

The countermark of an eagle facing left within a pearled oval has been attributed by some authors as that of General Vicente Guerrero, a leader of the insurgents in the south, 1816-1821.

1/2 REAL KM# 276 Composition: Silver **Issuer:** General Vicente Guerrero **Countermark:** Eagle **Note:** Countermark on Mexico City KM#72.

Date	Mintage	Good	VG	F	VF	XF
ND(1816)	—	40.00	60.00	80.00	175	—

8 REALES KM#274.2 Composition: Silver **Issuer:** Jose Francisco Osorno **Countermark:** Osorno monogram **Note:** Countermark on Mexico City KM#110.

Date	Mintage	Good	VG	F	VF	XF
1809(1814) TH	—	125	150	225	300	—
1810(1814) HJ	—	125	150	225	300	—
1811(1814) HJ	—	125	150	225	300	—

INSURGENT COUNTERMARKED COINAGE
VILLA / GRAN

REAL KM# 277 Composition: Silver **Issuer:** General Vicente Guerrero **Countermark:** Eagle **Note:** Countermark on Mexico City KM#78.

Date	Mintage	Good	VG	F	VF	XF
1772(1816) FM	—	35.00	50.00	75.00	165	—

2 REALES KM# 278.1 Composition: Silver **Issuer:** General Vicente Guerrero **Countermark:** Eagle **Note:** Countermark on Mexico City KM#88.

Date	Mintage	Good	VG	F	VF	XF
1784(1784) FM	—	40.00	60.00	100	225	—
1798(1798)	—	40.00	60.00	100	225	—

(Julian Villagran)

2 REALES KM# 298 Composition: Cast Silver, Julian Villagran **Countermark:** VILLA/GRAN **Note:** Countermark on cast Mexico City KM#91.

Date	Mintage	Good	VG	F	VF	XF
1799(1799) FM	—	150	200	250	350	—
1802(1802) FT	—	150	200	250	350	—

2 REALES KM# 278.2 Composition: Silver **Issuer:** General Vicente Guerrero **Countermark:** Eagle **Note:** Countermark on Mexico City KM#91.

Date	Mintage	Good	VG	F	VF	XF
1807(1816) PJ	—	30.00	50.00	80.00	200	—

8 REALES   KM# 279   Composition: Silver **Issuer:**
General Vicente Guerrero **Countermark:** Eagle **Note:**
Countermark on Zacatecas KM#191.

Date	Mintage	Good	VG	F	VF	XF
1811(1816)	—	100	150	200	350	—

INSURGENT
COUNTERMARKED COINAGE
ZMY

8 REALES   KM# 286   Composition: Silver **Issuer:**
Unknown, presumed insurgent **Countermark:** ZMY **Note:**
Countermark on Zacatecas KM#191.

Date	Mintage	Good	VG	F	VF	XF
1812(1809)	—	100	150	200	350	—

COUNTERMARKED COINAGE
Multiple Countermarks

Many combinations of Royalist and Insurgent countermarks are usually found on the cast copies produced
by Chihuahua and Mexico City and on the other crude
provisional issues of this period. Struck Mexico City
coins were used to make molds for casting necessity issues and countermarked afterwards to show issuing authority. Some were marked again by either both or separate opposing friendly forces to authorize circulation in
their areas of occupation. Some countermarks are only
obtainable with companion markings.

2 REALES   KM# 289   Composition: Silver **Issuer:**
C.M.S. and S.C.M. **Countermark:** C.M.S. (Comandancia
Militar Suriana) and eagle with S.C.M. (Soberano Congreso
Mexicano) **Note:** Countermark on Mexico City KM#91.

CM Date	Host Date	Good	VG	F	VF	XF
ND	ND	—	—	—	—	—

2 REALES   KM# 295   Composition: Silver **Issuer:** Militar
del Sur and Soberano Congreso Mexicano
Countermark: M.d.S. and eagle with S.C.M **Note:**
Countermark on Mexico City KM#91.

CM Date	Host Date	Good	VG	F	VF	XF
ND	ND	150	250	450	—	—

2 REALES   KM# 296   Composition: Silver **Issuer:** Jose
Francisco Osorno and Julian Villagran
Countermark: Osorno monogram and VILLA/GRAN **Note:**
Countermark on cast Mexico City KM#110.

CM Date	Host Date	Good	VG	F	VF	XF
ND	1809 TH	—	—	—	—	—

2 REALES   KM# A286   Composition: Silver **Issuer:** Jose
Maria Liceaga and VTIL **Countermark:** J.M.L./D.S. AND
VTIL **Note:** Countermark on Zacatecas KM#186.

CM Date	Host Date	Good	VG	F	VF	XF
ND	1811	75.00	125	175	250	—

2 REALES   KM# B286   Composition: Silver **Issuer:** Jose
Maria Liceaga and VTIL **Countermark:** J.M.L./V.E. and
VTIL **Note:** Countermark on Zacatecas KM#186.

CM Date	Host Date	Good	VG	F	VF	XF
ND	1810	75.00	125	175	250	—
ND	1811	75.00	125	175	250	—

8 REALES   KM# 285.2   Composition: Silver **Issuer:**
Chilpanzingo and Morelos **Countermark:** Chilpanzingo

Type A and Morelos monogram Type A **Note:** Countermark on cast Mexico City KM#110.

CM Date	Host Date	Good	VG	F	VF	XF
ND	1810 HJ	35.00	45.00	60.00	140	—
ND	1811 HJ	35.00	45.00	60.00	140	—

8 REALES   KM# C286   Composition: Silver **Issuer:** Chilpanzingo and Morelos and LVS **Countermark:** Chilpanzingo Type A, Morelos Type A and LVS monogram on cast Mexico City KM#110

CM Date	Host Date	Good	VG	F	VF	XF
ND	1809 HJ	50.00	75.00	125	275	—

8 REALES   KM# A298   Composition: Silver **Issuer:** S.J.N.G. and VTIL **Countermark:** S.J.N.G and VTIL on Zacatecas KM#191

CM Date	Host Date	Good	VG	F	VF	XF
ND	ND	35.00	50.00	75.00	200	—

8 REALES   KM# A297   Composition: Silver **Issuer:** Chilpanzingo and ENSAIE **Countermark:** Chilpanzingo Type B and ENSAIE **Note:** Countermark on Zacatecas KM#189.

CM Date	Host Date	Good	VG	F	VF	XF
ND	ND	175	250	350	—	—

8 REALES   KM# 297   Composition: Silver **Issuer:** Chilpanzingo and LVA **Countermark:** Chilpanzingo Type A and LVA **Note:** Countermark on Mexico City KM#109.

CM Date	Host Date	Good	VG	F	VF	XF
ND	1805 TH	45.00	75.00	145	250	—

8 REALES   KM# 281   Composition: Silver **Issuer:** Chilpanzingo and LVS **Countermark:** Chilpanzingo Type A and script LVS **Note:** Countermark on cast Mexico City KM#110.

CM Date	Host Date	Good	VG	F	VF	XF
ND	1809 HJ	45.00	65.00	135	250	—

8 REALES   KM# 288.2 (KM288)   Composition: Silver **Issuer:** Chilpanzingo and Suprema Junta Nacional Gubernativa **Countermark:** Chilpanzingo Type B **Note:** Countermark on Zacatecas KM#190.

CM Date	Host Date	Good	VG	F	VF	XF
ND	1811	—	—	—	—	—

8 REALES   KM# 290.2 (KM290)   Composition: Silver **Issuer:** ENSAIE and VTIL **Countermark:** ENSAIE and VTIL **Note:** Countermark on Zacatecas KM#190.

CM Date	Host Date	Good	VG	F	VF	XF
ND	1811	100	175	275	350	—

8 REALES   KM# 291 Composition: Silver **Issuer:** Jose Maria Liceaga and VTIL **Countermark:** J.M.L./D.S. and VTIL **Note:** Countermark on Mexico City KM#110.

CM Date	Host Date	Good	VG	F	VF	XF
ND	1810 HJ	85.00	150	250	400	—

8 REALES   KM# 282 Composition: Silver **Issuer:** La Comandancia Militar and Morelos **Countermark:** L.C.M and Morelos monogram Type A **Note:** Countermark on cast Mexico City KM#109.

CM Date	Host Date	Good	VG	F	VF	XF
ND	1792 FM	—	—	—	—	—

8 REALES   KM# 283 Composition: Silver **Issuer:** Morelos and Morelos **Countermark:** Morelos Type A and C **Note:** Countermark on cast Mexico City KM#109.

CM Date	Host Date	Good	VG	F	VF	XF
ND	1806 TH	—	—	—	—	—

8 REALES   KM# 284 Composition: Silver **Issuer:** Chilpanzingo and Morelos **Countermark:** Chilpanzingo Type A and Morelos monogram Type A **Note:** Countermark on cast Mexico City KM#109.

CM Date	Host Date	Good	VG	F	VF	XF
ND	1806 TH	35.00	50.00	100	200	—
ND	1807 TH	35.00	50.00	100	200	—

8 REALES   KM# 285.1 Composition: Silver **Issuer:** Chilpanzingo and Morelos **Countermark:** Chilpanzingo Type A and Morelos monogram Type A **Note:** Countermark on struck Mexico City KM#110.

CM Date	Host Date	Good	VG	F	VF	XF
ND	1809 TH	45.00	65.00	135	250	—

8 REALES   KM# 285.3 Composition: Silver **Issuer:** Chilpanzingo and Morelos **Countermark:** Chilpanzingo Type A and Morelos monogram Type A **Note:** Countermark on cast Mexico City KM#111.

CM Date	Host Date	Good	VG	F	VF	XF
ND	1811 HJ	75.00	120	175	275	—

8 REALES   KM# A290 Composition: Silver **Issuer:** ENSAIE and Jose Maria Liceaga **Countermark:** ENSAIE and J.M.L. **Note:** Countermark on Zacatecas KM#190.

CM Date	Host Date	Good	VG	F	VF	XF
ND	1811	100	175	275	350	—

8 REALES   KM# 294 Composition: Silver **Issuer:** L.V.A. and Morelos **Countermark:** Script LVA and Morelos monogram Type A **Note:** Countermark on cast Mexico City KM#110.

CM Date	Host Date	Good	VG	F	VF	XF
ND	ND HJ	45.00	75.00	135	250	—

8 REALES   KM# 288.1 Composition: Silver **Issuer:** Chilpanzingo and Suprema Junta Nacional Gubernativa **Countermark:** Chilpanzingo Type B and S.J.N.G **Note:** Countermark on Zacatecas KM#189.

CM Date	Host Date	Good	VG	F	VF	XF
ND	1811	—	—	—	—	—

8 REALES   KM# 290.1 Composition: Silver **Issuer:** ENSAIE and VTIL **Countermark:** ENSAIE and VTIL **Note:** Countermark on Zacatecas KM#189.

CM Date	Host Date	Good	VG	F	VF	XF
ND	1811	100	175	275	350	—

8 REALES   KM# 280.1 Composition: Silver **Issuer:** Chilpanzingo and Crown and flag **Countermark:** Chilpanzingo Type B and Crown and flag **Note:** Countermark on Zacatecas KM#189.

CM Date	Host Date	Good	VG	F	VF	XF
ND	1811	—	—	—	—	—

8 REALES   KM# 280.2 Composition: Silver **Issuer:** Chilpanzingo and crown and flag **Countermark:** Chilpanzingo Type B and crown and flag **Note:** Countermark on Zacatecas KM#190.

CM Date	Host Date	Good	VG	F	VF	XF
ND	1811	—	—	—	—	—

8 REALES   KM# 287   Composition: Silver **Issuer:** Chilpanzingo - Provisional De Valladolid **Countermark:** Chilpanzingo Type B and P.D.V **Note:** Countermark on Valladolid KM#178.

CM Date	Host Date	Good	VG	F	VF	XF
ND	1813	—	—	—	—	—

ZACATECAS

WAR OF INDEPENDENCE

ROYALIST COINAGE

The city of Zacatecas, in a rich mining region has provided silver for the world since mid-1500. On November 14, 1810 a mint began production for the Royalist cause. Zacatecas was the most prolific during the War of Independence. Four of the 5 standard silver denominations were made here, 4 Reales were not. The first, a local type showing mountains of silver on the coins were made only in 1810 and 1811. Some 1811 coins were made by the Insurgents who took the city on April 15, 1811, later retaken by the Royalists on May 21, 1811. Zacatecas struck the standard Ferdinand VII bust type until 1922.

Mint marks: Z, ZS, Zs.

1/2 REAL   KM# 180   Composition: 0.9030 Silver **Ruler:** Ferdinand VII **Obverse:** Local arms with flowers and castles **Reverse:** Mountain **Note:** Mint marks: Z, ZS, Zs.

Date	Mintage	Good	VG	F	VF	XF
1810	—	75.00	125	200	400	—
1811	—	30.00	50.00	90.00	175	—

Note: Date aligned with legend

1/2 REAL   KM# 181   Composition: 0.9030 Silver **Ruler:** Ferdinand VII **Obverse:** Royal arms **Reverse:** Mountain **Rev. Legend:** MONEDA PROVISIONAL DE ZACATECAS **Note:** Mint marks: Z, ZS, Zs.

Date	Mintage	Good	VG	F	VF	XF
1811	—	30.00	50.00	90.00	175	—

1/2 REAL   KM# 182   Composition: 0.9030 Silver **Ruler:** Ferdinand VII **Obverse:** Provincial bust **Obv. Legend:** FERDIN. VII **Reverse:** Mountain **Rev. Legend:** MONEDA PROVISIONAL DE ZACATECAS **Note:** Mint marks: Z, ZS, Zs.

Date	Mintage	Good	VG	F	VF	XF
1811	—	30.00	40.00	65.00	135	—
1812	—	25.00	35.00	60.00	120	—

1/2 REAL   KM# 73.1   Weight: 1.6900 g. **Composition:** 0.9030 Silver .0491 oz. ASW **Ruler:** Ferdinand VII **Obverse:** Armored bust of Ferdinand VII **Reverse:** Crowned arms, pillars **Note:** Mint marks: Z, ZS, Zs.

Date	Mintage	Good	VG	F	VF	XF
1813 AG	—	20.00	40.00	60.00	100	—
1813 FP	—	25.00	45.00	85.00	175	—
1814 AG	—	15.00	30.00	60.00	100	—
1815 AG	—	12.50	25.00	40.00	60.00	—
1816 AG	—	10.00	15.00	25.00	50.00	—
1817 AG	—	10.00	15.00	25.00	50.00	—
1818 AG	—	10.00	15.00	25.00	50.00	—
1819 AG	—	10.00	15.00	25.00	50.00	—

1/2 REAL   KM# 74.3   Weight: 1.6900 g. **Composition:** 0.9030 Silver .0491 oz. ASW **Ruler:** Ferdinand VII **Obverse:** Draped bust Ferdinand VII **Reverse:** Crowned arms, pillars **Note:** Mint marks: Z, ZS, Zs.

Date	Mintage	VG	F	VF	XF	Unc
1819 AG	—	8.00	12.00	25.00	50.00	—
1820 AG	—	8.00	12.00	25.00	50.00	—
1820 RG	—	5.00	10.00	20.00	45.00	—
1821 AG	—	150	250	450	850	—
1821 RG	—	5.00	10.00	20.00	45.00	—

REAL   KM# 183   Composition: 0.9030 Silver **Ruler:** Ferdinand VII **Obverse:** Local arms with flowers and castles **Reverse:** Mountain **Note:** Mint marks: Z, ZS, Zs.

Date	Mintage	Good	VG	F	VF	XF
1810	—	100	150	300	500	—
1811	—	20.00	40.00	75.00	150	—

Note: Date aligned with legend

REAL   KM# 184   Composition: 0.9030 Silver **Ruler:** Ferdinand VII **Obverse:** Royal arms **Reverse:** Mountain **Rev. Legend:** MONEDA PROVISIONAL DE ZACATECAS **Note:** Mint marks: Z, ZS, Zs.

Date	Mintage	Good	VG	F	VF	XF
1811	—	15.00	30.00	60.00	135	—

REAL   KM# 185   Composition: 0.9030 Silver **Ruler:** Ferdinand VII **Obverse:** Provincial bust **Obv. Legend:** FERDIN. VII. **Reverse:** Crowned arms, pillars **Rev. Legend:** MONEDA PROVISIONAL DE ZACATECAS **Note:** Mint marks: Z, ZS, Zs.

Date	Mintage	Good	VG	F	VF	XF
1811	—	50.00	85.00	120	200	—
1812	—	40.00	70.00	100	175	—

REAL KM# 82.1 Weight: 3.3800 g. **Composition:**
0.9030 Silver .0981 oz. ASW **Ruler:** Ferdinand VII **Obverse:**
Armored bust of Ferdinand VII **Obv. Legend:** FERDIN. VII.
Reverse: Crowned arms, pillars **Note:** Mint marks: Z, ZS, Zs.

Date	Mintage	Good	VG	F	VF	XF
1813 FP	—	50.00	100	150	250	—
1814 FP	—	20.00	35.00	50.00	85.00	—
1814 AG	—	20.00	35.00	50.00	85.00	—
1815 AG	—	20.00	35.00	50.00	85.00	—
1816 AG	—	10.00	20.00	30.00	65.00	—
1817 AG	—	6.50	12.50	20.00	45.00	—
1818 AG	—	6.50	12.50	20.00	45.00	—
1819 AG	—	5.00	9.00	15.00	35.00	—

REAL KM# 83.3 Weight: 3.3800 g. **Composition:**
0.9030 Silver .0981 oz. ASW **Ruler:** Ferdinand VII **Obverse:**
Draped bust of Ferdinand VII **Obv. Legend:** FERDIN. VII.
Reverse: Crowned arms, pillars **Note:** Mint marks: Z, ZS, Zs.

Date	Mintage	VG	F	VF	XF	Unc
1820 AG	—	5.00	10.00	20.00	60.00	—
1820 RG	—	5.00	10.00	20.00	60.00	—
1821 AG	—	15.00	30.00	45.00	90.00	—
1821 AZ	—	10.00	20.00	40.00	85.00	—
1821 RG	—	6.00	12.00	25.00	65.00	—
1822 AZ	—	6.00	12.00	25.00	65.00	—
1822 RG	—	15.00	30.00	45.00	90.00	—

2 REALES KM# 186 Composition: 0.9030 Silver **Ruler:**
Ferdinand VII **Obverse:** Local arms with flowers and castles
Reverse: Mountain **Note:** Mint marks: Z, ZS, Zs.

Date	Mintage	Good	VG	F	VF	XF
1810 Rare	—	—	—	—	—	—
1811	—	25.00	40.00	70.00	120	—

Note: Date aligned with legend

2 REALES KM# 187 Composition: 0.9030 Silver **Ruler:**
Ferdinand VII **Obverse:** Royal arms **Reverse:** Mountain
above L. V. O **Rev. Legend:** MONEDA PROVISIONAL DE
ZACATECAS **Note:** Mint marks: Z, ZS, Zs.

Date	Mintage	Good	VG	F	VF	XF
1811	—	15.00	30.00	60.00	100	—

2 REALES KM# 188 Composition: 0.9030 Silver **Ruler:**
Ferdinand VII **Obverse:** Armored bust **Obv. Legend:**
FERDIN. VII **Reverse:** Crowned arms, pillars **Rev. Legend:**
MONEDA PROVISIONAL DE ZACATECAS **Note:** Mint
marks: Z, ZS, Zs.

Date	Mintage	Good	VG	F	VF	XF
1811	—	35.00	65.00	135	225	—
1812	—	30.00	60.00	125	200	—

2 REALES KM# 92.1 Weight: 6.7700 g. **Composition:**
0.9030 Silver .1966 oz. ASW **Ruler:** Ferdinand VII **Obverse:**
Large armored bust of Ferdinand VII **Obv. Legend:**
FERDIN. VII **Reverse:** Crowned arms, pillars **Note:** Mint
marks: Z, ZS, Zs.

Date	Mintage	Good	VG	F	VF	XF
1813 FP	—	35.00	50.00	75.00	125	—
1814 FP	—	35.00	50.00	75.00	125	—
1814 AG	—	35.00	50.00	75.00	125	—
1815 AG	—	6.50	12.50	25.00	55.00	—
1816 AG	—	6.50	12.50	25.00	55.00	—
1817 AG	—	6.50	12.50	25.00	55.00	—
1818 AG	—	6.50	12.50	25.00	55.00	—

2 REALES KM# 93.4 Weight: 6.7700 g. **Composition:**
0.9030 Silver .1966 oz. ASW **Ruler:** Ferdinand VII **Obverse:**
Draped bust of Ferdinand VII **Obv. Legend:** FERDIN. VII
Reverse: Crowned arms, pillars **Note:** Mint marks: Z, ZS, Zs.

Date	Mintage	VG	F	VF	XF	Unc
1818 AG	—	6.50	12.50	25.00	50.00	—
1819 AG	—	10.00	20.00	40.00	85.00	—
1819 AG Reversed 'S' In HISPAN	—	10.00	20.00	40.00	85.00	—
1820 AG	—	10.00	20.00	40.00	85.00	—
1820 RG	—	10.00	20.00	40.00	85.00	—
1821 AG	—	10.00	20.00	40.00	85.00	—
1821 AZ/RG	—	10.00	20.00	40.00	85.00	—
1821 AZ	—	10.00	20.00	40.00	85.00	—
1821 RG	—	10.00	20.00	40.00	85.00	—
1822 AG	—	10.00	20.00	40.00	85.00	—
1822 RG	—	10.00	20.00	40.00	85.00	—

2 REALES KM# A92 Weight: 6.7700 g. **Composition:**
0.9030 Silver .1966 oz. ASW **Ruler:** Ferdinand VII **Obverse:**
Small armored bust of Ferdinand VII **Obv. Legend:**

FERDIN. VII **Reverse:** Crowned arms, pillars **Note:** Mint marks: Z, ZS, Zs.

Date	Mintage	Good	VG	F	VF	XF
1819 AG	—	45.00	100	200	400	—

8 REALES   KM# 189   Composition: 0.9030 Silver **Ruler:** Ferdinand VII **Obverse:** Local arm with flowers and castles **Reverse:** Mountain above L.V.O. **Note:** Mint Zacatecas.

Date	Mintage	Good	VG	F	VF	XF
1810	—	300	500	750	1,250	—
1811	—	100	150	225	350	—

Note: Date aligned with legend. Also exists with incomplete date

8 REALES   KM# 190   Composition: 0.9030 Silver **Ruler:** Ferdinand VII **Obverse:** Royal arms **Obv. Legend:** FERDIN. VII. DEI... **Reverse:** Mountain above L. V. O **Rev. Legend:** MONEDA PROVISIONAL DE ZACATECAS **Note:** Mint Zacatecas.

Date	Mintage	Good	VG	F	VF	XF
1811	—	65.00	100	135	220	—

Note: Date aligned with legend

8 REALES   KM# 191   Composition: 0.9030 Silver **Ruler:** Ferdinand VII **Obverse:** Armored bust of Ferdinand VII **Obv. Legend:** FERDIN. VII. 8.R. DEI... **Reverse:** Crowned arms, pillars **Rev. Legend:** MONEDA PROVISIONAL DE ZACATECAS **Note:** Mint Zacatecas.

Date	Mintage	Good	VG	F	VF	XF
1811	—	45.00	75.00	145	275	—
1812	—	50.00	85.00	160	300	—

8 REALES   KM# 192   Composition: 0.9030 Silver **Ruler:** Ferdinand VII **Obverse:** Draped bust of Ferdinand VII **Obv. Legend:** FERDIN. VII. DEI... **Reverse:** Crowned arms, pillars **Rev. Legend:** MONEDA PROVISIONAL DE ZACATECAS **Note:** Mint Zacatecas.

Date	Mintage	Good	VG	F	VF	XF
1812	—	75.00	150	275	450	—

8 REALES   KM# 111.5   Weight: 27.0700 g. **Composition:** 0.9030 Silver .7860 oz. ASW **Ruler:** Ferdinand VII **Obverse:** Draped bust of Ferdinand VII **Obv. Legend:** FERDIN. VII. DEI. GRATIA **Reverse:** Crowned arms, pillars **Rev. Legend:** HISPAN. ET IND. REX **Note:** Mint mark: Zs. Several bust types exist for the 1821 issues.

Date	Mintage	VG	F	VF	XF	Unc
1813 FP	—	75.00	125	175	275	—
1814 FP	—	150	250	350	450	—
1814 AG	—	100	150	200	300	—
1814 AG D over horizontal D in IND	—	125	175	225	325	—
1814 AG/FP	—	100	150	200	300	—
1815 AG	—	50.00	100	150	250	—
1816 AG	—	35.00	50.00	65.00	125	—
1817 AG	—	35.00	50.00	65.00	125	—
1818 AG	—	30.00	40.00	50.00	100	—
1819 AG	—	30.00	40.00	50.00	100	—
1819 AG 'GRATIA' error	—	100	200	300	400	—
1820 AG 18/11 error	—	100	200	300	400	—
1820 AG	—	30.00	40.00	50.00	100	—
1820 RG	—	30.00	40.00	50.00	100	—
1821/81 RG	—	75.00	150	225	300	—
1821 RG	—	15.00	25.00	35.00	65.00	—
1821 AZ/RG	—	50.00	100	150	200	—
1821 AZ	—	50.00	100	150	200	—
1822 RG	—	40.00	60.00	100	175	—

8 REALES   KM# 111.6   Weight: 27.0700 g. **Composition:** 0.9030 Silver .7860 oz. ASW **Ruler:** Ferdinand VII **Obverse:** Draped bust of Ferdinand VII **Obv. Legend:** FERDIN. VII. DEI. GRATIA **Reverse:** Crown with lower rear arc **Rev. Legend:** HISAV. ET IND. REX

Date	Mintage	VG	F	VF	XF	Unc
1821 Zs	—	160	320	550	750	—

ROYALIST COUNTERMARKED COINAGE
LCM - La Comandancia Militar

Crown and Flag

This countermark exists in 15 various sizes.

2 REALES   KM# 193.1   Composition: 0.9030 Silver **Issuer:** La Comandancia Militar **Countermark:** LCM **Note:** Countermark on Mexico KM#92.

Date	Mintage	Good	VG	F	VF	XF
1809(1820) TH	—	85.00	165	250	400	—

2 REALES   KM# 193.2   Composition: 0.9030 Silver
Issuer: La Comandancia Militar, (The LCM countermark
exists in 15 various sizes) **Countermark:** LCM **Note:**
Countermark on Mexico KM#186.

Date	Mintage	Good	VG	F	VF	XF
1811(1820)	—	85.00	165	250	400	—

8 REALES   KM# 194.1   Composition: Cast Silver **Issuer:**
La Comandancia Militar, (The LCM countermark exists in
15 various sizes) **Countermark:** LCM **Note:** Countermark
on Chihuahua KM#123.

Date	Mintage	Good	VG	F	VF	XF
1811(1820) RP	—	100	200	300	450	—
1812(1820) RP	—	100	200	300	450	—

8 REALES   KM# 194.2   Composition: 0.9030 Silver
Issuer: La Comandancia Militar, The LCM countermark
exists in 15 different sizes **Countermark:** LCM **Note:**
Countermark on Chihuahua KM#111.1 struck over KM#123.

Date	Mintage	Good	VG	F	VF	XF
1815 RP(1820)	—	200	275	400	550	—
1817 RP(1820)	—	125	175	225	300	—
1820 RP(1820)	—	125	175	225	300	—
1821 RP(1820)	—	125	175	225	300	—

8 REALES   KM# 194.3   Composition: 0.9030 Silver
Issuer: La Comandancia Militar, The LCM countermark
exists in 15 different sizes **Countermark:** LCM **Note:**
Countermark on Durango KM#111.2.

Date	Mintage	Good	VG	F	VF	XF
1812 RM(1820)	—	70.00	125	190	250	—
1821 CG(1820)	—	70.00	125	190	250	—

8 REALES   KM# 194.4   Composition: 0.9030 Silver
Issuer: La Comandancia Militar, The LCM countermark
exists in 15 different sizes **Countermark:** LCM **Note:**
Countermark on Guadalajara KM#111.3.

Date	Mintage	Good	VG	F	VF	XF
1813(1820) MR	—	150	225	300	475	—

8 REALES   KM# 194.5   Composition: 0.9030 Silver
Issuer: La Comandancia Militar, The LCM countermark
exists in 15 different sizes **Countermark:** LCM **Note:**
Countermark on Guanajuato KM#111.4.

Date	Mintage	Good	VG	F	VF	XF
1813(1820) JJ	—	225	350	475	650	—

8 REALES   KM# 194.6   Composition: 0.9030 Silver
Issuer: La Comandancia Militar, The LCM countermark
exists in 15 different sizes **Countermark:** LCM **Note:**
Countermark on Nueva Vizcaya KM#165.

Date	Mintage	Good	VG	F	VF	XF
1811(1820) RM Rare	—	—	—	—	—	—

8 REALES   KM# 194.7   Composition: 0.9030 Silver
Issuer: La Comandancia Militar, The LCM countermark
exists in 15 different sizes **Countermark:** LCM **Note:**
Countermark on Mexico KM#111.

Date	Mintage	Good	VG	F	VF	XF
1811(1820) HJ	—	125	225	350	600	—
1812(1820) JJ	—	110	135	190	325	—
1817(1820) JJ	—	50.00	65.00	85.00	125	—
1818(1820) JJ	—	50.00	65.00	85.00	125	—
1820(1820) JJ	—	—	—	—	—	—

8 REALES   KM# 194.8   Composition: 0.9030 Silver
Issuer: La Comandancia Militar, The LCM countermark
exists in 15 different sizes **Countermark:** LCM **Note:**
Countermark on Sombrerete KM#176.

Date	Mintage	Good	VG	F	VF	XF
1811(1820) Rare	—	—	—	—	—	—
1812(1820) Rare	—	—	—	—	—	—

8 REALES   KM# 194.9 Composition: 0.9030 Silver **Issuer:** La Comandancia Militar, The LCM countermark exists in 15 different sizes **Countermark:** LCM **Note:** Countermark on Zacatecas KM#190.

Date	Mintage	Good	VG	F	VF	XF
1811(1820)	—	225	350	450	—	—

8 REALES   KM# 194.10 Composition: 0.9030 Silver **Issuer:** La Comandancia Militar, The LCM countermark exists in 15 different sizes **Countermark:** LCM **Note:** Countermark on Zacatecas KM#111.5.

Date	Mintage	Good	VG	F	VF	XF
1813(1820) FP	—	—	—	—	—	—
1814(1820) AG	—	—	—	—	—	—
1822(1820) RG	—	—	—	—	—	—

ROYALIST
COUNTERMARKED COINAGE
LCV - Las Cajas de Veracruz

The Royal Treasury of the City of Veracruz

7 REALES   KM# 195 Composition: Silver **Issuer:** Las Cajas de Veracruz, The Royal Treasury of the City of Veracruz **Countermark:** LCV **Note:** Countermark and 7 on underweight 8 Reales.

Date	Mintage	Good	VG	F	VF	XF
ND(1813) Rare	—	—	—	—	—	—

Note: Most examples are counterfeit

7-1/4 REALES   KM# 196 Composition: Silver **Issuer:** Las Cajas de Veracruz, The Royal Treasury of the City of Veracruz **Countermark:** LCV **Note:** Countermark and 7-1/4 on underweight 8 Reales.

Date	Mintage	Good	VG	F	VF	XF
ND(1813) Rare	—	—	—	—	—	—

Note: Most examples are counterfeit

7-1/2 REALES   KM# 197 Composition: Silver **Issuer:** Las Cajas de Veracruz, The Royal Treasury of the City of Veracruz **Countermark:** LCV **Note:** Countermark and 7-1/2 on underweight 8 Reales.

Date	Mintage	Good	VG	F	VF	XF
ND(1813) Rare	—	—	—	—	—	—

Note: Most examples are counterfeit

7-3/4 REALES   KM# 198 Composition: Silver **Issuer:** Las Cajas de Veracruz, The Royal Treasury of the City of Veracruz **Countermark:** LCV **Note:** Countermark and 7-3/4 on underweight 8 Reales.

Date	Mintage	Good	VG	F	VF	XF
ND(1813)	—	300	375	450	600	—

Note: Many examples are counterfeit

8 REALES   KM# A198 Composition: Cast Silver **Issuer:** Las Cajas de Veracruz, The Royal Treasury of the City of Veracruz **Countermark:** LCV **Note:** Countermark on Chihuahua KM#123.

Date	Mintage	Good	VG	F	VF	XF
1811(1813) RP	—	150	250	400	500	—

8 REALES   KM# 199 Composition: Silver **Issuer:** Las Cajas de Veracruz, The Royal Treasury of the City of Veracruz **Countermark:** LCV **Note:** Countermark on Zacatecas KM#191.

Date	Mintage	Good	VG	F	VF	XF
1811(1813)	—	175	225	275	350	—
1812(1813)	—	175	225	275	350	—

ROYALIST
COUNTERMARKED COINAGE
MS (Monogram) - Manuel Salcedo

8 REALES   KM# 200 Composition: Silver **Issuer:** Manuel Salcedo **Countermark:** MS monogram **Note:** Countermark on Mexico KM#110.

Date	Mintage	Good	VG	F	VF	XF
1809(1812) TH	—	150	250	400	500	—
1810(1812) HJ	—	150	250	400	500	—
1811(1812) HJ	—	150	250	400	500	—

ROYALIST COUNTERMARKED COINAGE
MVA - Monclova

8 REALES   KM# 202.3 Composition: Silver **Issuer:** Monclova, MVA **Countermark:** MVA/1812 **Note:** Countermark on cast Mexico KM#110.

Date	Mintage	Good	VG	F	VF	XF
1809(1809) HJ	—	100	150	250	350	—
1809(1812) TH	—	100	150	250	350	—
1810(1812) HJ	—	100	150	250	350	—

8 REALES   KM# 201 Composition: Silver **Issuer:** Monclova, MVA **Countermark:** MVA/1812 **Note:** Countermark on Chihuahua KM#111.1; struck over cast Mexico KM#110.

Date	Mintage	Good	VG	F	VF	XF
1809(1811)	—	250	450	700	1,000	—
1816 RP(1817)	—	250	450	700	1,000	—
1821 RP(1822)	—	250	450	700	1,000	—

8 REALES   KM# 202.5 Composition: Silver **Issuer:** Monclova, MVA **Countermark:** MVA/1812 **Note:** Countermark on Zacatecas KM#189.

Date	Mintage	Good	VG	F	VF	XF
1813(1812)	—	300	350	450	550	—

8 REALES   KM# 202.1 Composition: Silver **Issuer:** Monclova, MVA **Countermark:** MVA/1812 **Note:** Countermark on Chihuahua KM#111.1; struck over cast Mexico KM#109.

Date	Mintage	Good	VG	F	VF	XF
1810(1812)	—	125	175	250	350	—

8 REALES   KM# 202.2 Composition: Silver **Issuer:** Monclova, MVA **Countermark:** MVA/1812 **Note:** Countermark on cast Mexico KM#109.

Date	Mintage	Good	VG	F	VF	XF
1798(1812) FM	—	100	150	250	350	—
1802(1812) FT	—	100	150	250	350	—

INSURGENT COINAGE
American Congress

REAL   KM# 216 Composition: 0.9030 Silver **Issuer:** American Congress **Obv. Legend:** CONGRESO AMERICANO **Reverse:** F. 7 on spread mantle **Rev. Legend:** DEPOSIT D.L. AUCTORI J

Date	Mintage	Good	VG	F	VF	XF
ND(1813)	—	35.00	75.00	120	200	—

REAL   KM# 217 Composition: 0.9030 Silver **Issuer:** American Congress **Obverse:** Eagle on cactus **Obv. Legend:** CONGR. AMER. **Reverse:** F. 7 on spread mantle **Rev. Legend:** DEPOS. D. L. AUT. D.

Date	Mintage	Good	VG	F	VF	XF
ND(1813)	—	35.00	75.00	120	200	—

INSURGENT COINAGE
National Congress

1/2 REAL   KM# 209   Composition: Struck Copper **Issuer:** National Congress **Obverse:** Eagle on bridge **Obv. Legend:** VICE FERD. VII DEI GRATIA ET **Reverse:** Value, bow quiver, etc **Rev. Legend:** S. P. CONG. NAT. IND.

Date	Mintage	Good	VG	F	VF	XF
1811	—	45.00	85.00	150	200	—
1812	—	27.50	60.00	100	150	—
1813	—	27.50	60.00	100	150	—
1814	—	45.00	85.00	150	200	—

1/2 REAL   KM# 210   Composition: 0.9030 Silver **Issuer:** National Congress **Obverse:** Eagle on bridge **Obv. Legend:** VICE FERD. VII DEI GRATIA ET **Reverse:** Value, bow quiver, etc **Rev. Legend:** S. P. CONG. NAT. IND.

Date	Mintage	Good	VG	F	VF	XF
1812	—	27.50	60.00	100	150	—
1813	—	45.00	90.00	175	275	—

Note: 1812 exists with the date reading inwards and outwards

REAL   KM# 211   Composition: 0.9030 Silver **Issuer:** National Congress **Obverse:** Eagle on bridge **Obv. Legend:** VICE FERD. VII DEI GRATIA ET **Reverse:** Value, bow quiver, etc **Rev. Legend:** S. P. CONG. NAT. IND.

Date	Mintage	Good	VG	F	VF	XF
1812	—	22.50	45.00	80.00	125	—
1813	—	22.50	45.00	80.00	125	—

Note: 1812 exists with the date reading either inward or outward

2 REALES   KM#212   Composition: Struck Copper **Issuer:** National Congress **Obverse:** Eagle on bridge **Obv. Legend:** VICE FERD. VII DEI GRATIA ET **Reverse:** Value, bow quiver, etc **Rev. Legend:** S. P. CONG. NAT. IND.

Date	Mintage	Good	VG	F	VF	XF
1812	—	100	150	200	275	—
1813	—	23.50	50.00	75.00	120	—
1814	—	32.50	75.00	110	165	—

2 REALES   KM# A213   Composition: Struck Silver **Issuer:** National Congress **Obverse:** Eagle on bridge **Obv. Legend:** VICE FERD. VII DEI GRATIA ET **Reverse:** Value, bow quiver, etc **Rev. Legend:** S. P. CONG. NAT. IND.

Date	Mintage	Good	VG	F	VF	XF
1813	—	950	1,750	3,000	4,850	—

2 REALES   KM# 213   Composition: 0.9030 Silver **Issuer:** National Congress **Obverse:** Eagle on bridge in shield, denomination at sides **Obv. Legend:** VICE FERD. VII DEI GRATIA ET **Reverse:** Canon, quiver, arm, etc

Date	Mintage	Good	VG	F	VF	XF
1813	—	75.00	155	265	375	—

Note: These dies were believed to be intended for the striking of 2 Escudos

4 REALES   KM# 214   Composition: 0.9030 Silver **Issuer:** National Congress **Obverse:** Eagle on bridge **Obv. Legend:** VICE FERD. VII DEI GRATIA ET **Reverse:** Value, bow, quiver, etc **Rev. Legend:** S. P. CONG. NAT. IND.

Date	Mintage	Good	VG	F	VF	XF
1813	—	600	1,200	2,450	4,400	—

8 REALES   KM# 215.1   Composition: 0.9030 Silver **Issuer:** National Congress **Obverse:** Small crowned eagle **Obv. Legend:** VICE FERD. VII DEI GRATIA ET **Reverse:** Value, bow, quiver, etc **Rev. Legend:** S. P. CONG. NAT. IND.

Date	Mintage	Good	VG	F	VF	XF
1812Mo	—	600	1,150	2,350	4,250	—

8 REALES   KM# 215.2   Composition: 0.9030 Silver
Issuer: National Congress **Obverse:** Large crowned eagle
Obv. Legend: VICE FERD. VII DEI GRATIA ET **Reverse:**
Value, bow, quiver, etc **Rev. Legend:** S. P. CONG. NAT. IND.

Date	Mintage	Good	VG	F	VF	XF
1813Mo	—	600	1,150	2,350	4,250	—

INSURGENT COINAGE
Supreme National Congress of America

PDV - Provisional de Valladolid

VTIL - Util = useful

(Refer to Multiple countermarks)

1/2 REAL   KM# 203   Composition: Struck Copper
Issuer: Supreme National Congress of America **Obverse:**
Eagle on bridge **Obv. Legend:** FERDIN. VII DEI GRATIA
Reverse: Value, bow, quiver, etc **Rev. Legend:** S. P.
CONG. NAT. IND. GUV.T.

Date	Mintage	Good	VG	F	VF	XF
1811	—	27.50	45.00	60.00	100	—
1812	—	27.50	45.00	60.00	100	—
1813	—	27.50	45.00	60.00	100	—
1814	—	27.50	45.00	60.00	100	—

REAL   KM# 204   Composition: Struck Copper **Issuer:**
Supreme National Congress of America **Obverse:** Eagle on
bridge **Obv. Legend:** FERDIN. VII DEI GRATIA **Reverse:**
Value, bow, quiver, etc **Rev. Legend:** S. P. CONG. NAT.
IND. GUV.T.

Date	Mintage	Good	VG	F	VF	XF
1811	—	45.00	75.00	125	200	—

2 REALES   KM# 205   Composition: Struck Copper
Issuer: Supreme National Congress of America **Obverse:**
Eagle on bridge **Obv. Legend:** FERDIN. VII DEI GRATIA
Reverse: Value, bow, quiver, etc

Date	Mintage	Good	VG	F	VF	XF
1812	—	225	325	475	750	—

8 REALES   KM# 206   Composition: Cast Silver **Issuer:**
Supreme National Congress of America **Obverse:** Eagle on
bridge **Obv. Legend:** FERDIN. VII DEI GRATIA **Reverse:**
Value, bow, quiver, etc

Date	Mintage	Good	VG	F	VF	XF
1811	—	150	250	350	500	—
1812	—	150	250	350	500	—

8 REALES   KM# 207   Composition: Struck Silver **Issuer:**
Supreme National Congress of America **Obverse:** Eagle on
bridge **Obv. Legend:** FERDIN. VII DEI GRATIA **Reverse:**
Value, bow, quiver, etc

Date	Mintage	Good	VG	F	VF	XF
1811	—	—	—	—	—	—
1812	—	300	600	1,000	1,500	—

8 REALES   KM# 208   Composition: Struck Copper
Issuer: Supreme National Congress of America **Obverse:**
Eagle on bridge **Obv. Legend:** FERDIN. VII... **Reverse:**
Bow, sword and quiver **Rev. Legend:** PROVICIONAL POR
LA SUPREMA JUNTA DE AMERICA

Date	Mintage	Good	VG	F	VF	XF
1811	—	100	150	225	450	—
1812	—	100	150	225	450	—

Bibliography

Boyd, Julian P. (Editor). *The Papers of Thomas Jefferson*. Vol. 7. New Jersey: Princeton University Press, 1953.

Bowers, Q. David. *The History of United States Coinage as Illustrated by the Garrett Collection*. Los Angeles: Bowers & Ruddy Galleries, 1979.

Breen, Walter. *Walter Breen's Complete Encyclopedia of U.S. and Colonial Coins*. New York: F.C.I. Press, Doubleday, 1988.

Bressett, Ken, and Kosoff, A. *Official A.N.A. Grading Standard for United States Coins*. Fourth Edition. Colorado Springs, Colo.: American Numismatic Association, 1991.

Brown, Martin R., and Dunn, John W. *A Guide to the Grading of United States Coins*. Fourth and Fifth Editions. Racine, Wis.: Whitman Publishing Co., 1964 and 1969.

Bullowa, David M. *Numismatic Notes and Monographs No. 83: The Commemorative Coinage of the United States 1892-1938*. New York, N.Y.: American Numismatic Society, 1938.

Evans, George G. *Illustrated History of the United States Mint*. Revised Edition. Philadelphia: George G. Evans, 1892.

Fitzpatrick, John E. (Editor). *The Writings of George Washington*. Vol. 28. Washington: U.S. Government Printing Office, 1938.

Heath, Dr. George. *The Numismatist*, September 1888 and February 1892.

Hepburn, A. Barton. *A History of Currency in the United States*. Revised Edition. New York: Sentry Press, 1967.

Krause, Chester L., and Mishler, Clifford. Colin R. Bruce II (Senior Editor). *The Standard Catalog of World Gold Coins*. Fourth Edition. Iola, Wis.: Krause Publications, 2000.

Krueger, Kurt R. "Grading: Bestial Pandemonium Unleashed." *The Numismatist*, January 1976. Colorado Springs, Colo.: American Numismatic Association, 1975.

Ruddy, James F. *Photograde*. Wolfeboro, N.H.: Bowers and Merena Galleries In., 1983.

Sheldon, William H. *Early American Cents*. New York: Harper & Row. 1949.

Syrett, Harold C. *The Papers of Alexander Hamilton*. Vol. 7. New York: Columbia University Press, 1963.

Taxay, Don. *The U.S. Mint and Coinage: An Illustrated History From 1776 to the Present*. Second Edition. New York: Arco Publishing Co., 1969.

U.S. Congress. Senate. *International Monetary Conference*. 1878. Senate Ex. Doc. 58. 45th Congress, Third Session. Washington, 1879.

U.S. Congress. Senate. *Coinage Laws of the United States 1792 to 1894 with an Appendix of Statistics Relating to Coins and Currency*. Fourth Edition. Washington, D.C.: Government Printing Office, 1894.

Van Allen, Leroy C., and Mallis, A. George. *Comprehensive Catalog and Encyclopedia of U.S. Morgan and Peace Silver Dollars*. New York: F.C.I. Press, 1976.

Willem, John M. *The United States Trade Dollar: America's Only Unwanted, Unhonored Coin*. New York: By the author, 1959; reprint edition, Racine, Wis.: Western Publishing Co., 1965.

Yeoman, R.S. *A Guidebook of United States Coins*. 45th Edition. Racine, Wis.: Western Publishing Co., 1991.